SEAGULLS!

SEAGULLS!

The Story of

BRIGHTON & HOVE ALBION F.C.

Tim Carder & Roger Harris

**GOLDSTONE
BOOKS**

First published in Great Britain by Goldstone Books, 1993.

ISBN 0 9521337 0 9

British Library Cataloguing-in-Publication Data:
A catalogue record for this book is available from the British Library.

Printed by FotoDirect Ltd
Unit A2, Enterprise Estate
Crowhurst Road
Brighton BN1 8AF

Goldstone Books
c/o Goldstone Ground
Newtown Road
Hove
East Sussex
BN3 7DE

CONTENTS

Introduction 7

Acknowledgements 8

Explanatory notes on statistics 9

Season-by-season history 11

Club honours 259

Other first-team matches 260

    Mini-tournaments 260   Non-Sussex charity cups 266
    Miscellaneous competitive matches 260   Other miscellaneous matches played
    Other tour matches 261   by the first team 266
    Friendly and benefit matches 262

Reserves, 'A' team, youth team and local competitions 267

    Reserve team history 267   Youth team league and cup summary 278
    Reserve team league summary 267   F.A. Youth Cup 279
    South Eastern League 269   Sussex Professional Cup 280
    Southern League 270   Sussex Senior Cup 281
    London Combination and Cup 271   Roy Haydon Memorial Trophy 281
    Football Combination and Cup 272   Sussex Floodlight Cup 282
    Midweek League and Cup 274   Sussex (R.U.R.) Charity Cup 282
    'A' team history 275   Local charity cups 283
    'A' team league summary 275   Albion juniors history 284
    Metropolitan League and Cups 276   Sussex wartime competitions 284
    Youth team history 277   Baldwin Cup 284

Records and reference 285

    Complete competitive record 285   Directors and chairmen 299
    Record against other clubs 286   Albion players 1901–93 300
    Sequences 291   Albion wartime players 1939–46 312
    Seasonal records 292   Appearance records 314
    Most frequent opponents 292   Goalscoring records 315
    Team scoring records 293   Players' age records 318
    Record victories and defeats 293   Players of the Season 318
    Attendance records 294   Captains 319
    Admission prices 296   Transfer records 319
    Giant-killing 297   International and other representative
    Club colours 297   appearances 320
    Managerial records 298   Beneficiaries 323

Notes on some opponents and competitions 325

Index 327

INTRODUCTION

SEAGULLS! The name has become synonymous in recent years with Brighton & Hove Albion Football Club, so much so that even those with little interest in the game know who 'The Seagulls' are. It was a nickname born amid the burgeoning crowds of the mid 1970s at the start of the club's golden years, helping to cement the growing bond between the team and its supporters.

Since that time many of those fans have drifted away and the club has, at times, struggled to survive. It is a familiar story: Brighton & Hove Albion was formed in 1901 following the failure of two previous attempts to establish top-class football in the twin towns. Both of these early clubs, Brighton United and Brighton & Hove Rangers, failed to attract sufficient numbers of spectators, and the Albion, following their early successes, also complained of the lack of support.

But the early pioneers persevered, and it is thanks to their efforts, and to those of many other dedicated men over the last 92 years, that the club has thrilled generations of supporters. Memories of men such as Edgar Everest, William Avenell, John Jackson, Noah Clark and George Broadbridge have faded, but their legacy lives on. May it ever continue to do so.

We have both been supporters of the club since our respective childhoods and have grown up hearing of such legendary names as Bert Longstaff and Tommy Cook, Charlie Webb and Tug Wilson, Jimmy Langley and Joe Wilson. It was a desire to discover more about these men and their contemporaries that led to to the writing of what, we hope, is the definitive history of the club. Fuelled by compelling interests in cigarette-cards, postcards and statistics, we set out to chronicle and illustrate their exploits, and those of the club, in a permanent record that will invite older supporters to reminisce and introduce younger fans to the noble history of their club.

We have tried to record accurately the famous, not-so-famous and, indeed, infamous names and events in Albion's history by way of a seasonal narrative, from the formation of Brighton United in 1897 to the present day. We have also published, for the first time, full details of all the club's matches, a total of over 4,100 games. There are also comprehensive sections on friendly and benefit matches, all the reserves' and 'A' team's competitive results, and details of the youth team and the local Sussex competitions. In addition there are 40 pages of records and reference material.

The use of anecdotal material has been deliberately avoided. Memories do fade with time and facts do get distorted; the classic example is, we believe, the very formation of the club in June 1901. We have therefore limited our research, as much as possible, to contemporary written material, be it from newspapers, programmes or other documents.

This has been a massive project for both of us, immensely time-consuming but hugely enjoyable, and we have learnt much along the way. The research has taken us to a variety of unlikely places – from the Office of Population Censuses & Surveys to the Brighton & Preston Cemetery (where we identified the now-unmarked resting place of the club's founder, John Jackson) – and introduced us to many helpful people.

This project really started around 1980 when, unknown to each other, we both started to amass data on the Albion, principally by reading each edition of the *Sussex Daily News* (from the turn of the century onwards) and *Evening Argus* on the microfilm readers of Brighton Reference Library. A chance meeting led to a collaboration and a determination to see the results of our hard work in print. Ten years or so after that first encounter we are exultant to see the fruits of our labour, and hope that readers will be as pleased with the result as we are.

It is not our intention to stop here. We hope to follow up this initial publication with a 'Who's Who' of the Albion (and Brighton United), a volume containing biographies and as many photographs as possible of the 1,000 or so players (and their managers) who have appeared for the club since 1901. There may be other publications to follow.

Brighton & Hove Albion is unique: it is the only senior club named after two towns, and is undeniably a credit to both. But it is more than that: it is a major attraction for many supporters from Worthing, Crawley, Eastbourne and, indeed, from all over the county. Interest in it is passed on from generation to generation, and it is a way of life for a substantial number of people. Sussex without Brighton & Hove Albion is unthinkable!.

The 1992–93 season just passed has probably been the most traumatic ever witnessed by supporters. At times the very existence of the club, now only eight years from its centenary, was severely threatened and it appeared that this book might well have been a loving epitaph. But the club survived, the board's plans for the future redevelopment of the Goldstone as a retail site have finally been approved, a scheme for a new ground is taking shape, and enthusiasm was renewed, principally due to the intervention of Des Lynam.

We hope this book will play its part in helping to regenerate that enthusiasm; that everyone who reads it will be inspired to visit the Goldstone Ground to support **their** club. The 1993–94 season could well see the renaissance of the Albion, a movement that will see the Seagulls flying higher and higher. We look forward to chronicling many more glorious chapters in the story.

Tim Carder and Roger Harris
June 1993

ACKNOWLEDGEMENTS

NIGEL BISHOP: the authors are deeply indebted to Nigel for his tremendous help in obtaining photographic material, and especially for his contribution to the compilation of the club's history over the period 1960–70. A renowned contributor to the old Supporters' Club handbooks and other publications, he is now domiciled in Scotland but maintains an undying interest in the Albion. Thanks are also due to Nigel and his wife Diana for their meticulous and expert perusal of the text which resulted in numerous helpful suggestions and corrections.

The greater part of this history has been researched from a myriad of contemporary newspapers, and the authors would like to record their appreciation of the reporters, photographers, editors and proprietors of the journals involved. This project would have been impossible without the publications of the Southern Publishing Company, in particular the *Sussex Daily News*, the *Evening Argus* and the *Brighton & Hove Gazette*. The *Brighton & Hove Herald*, the *Hove Echo*, the *Brighton & Hove Guardian*, *The Sportsman* and the *Mid Sussex Times* – many thanks to the latter for their co-operation – have also proved invaluable. Most of the research has been undertaken at Brighton and Hove Reference Libraries, and at the British Library's Newspaper Division at Colindale; the authors would like to express their gratitude to staff involved.

Other major sources of information include the offices of the Football League and the Football Association; Companies House; the Public Record Office; the Office of Population Censuses and Surveys (St Catherine's House); and the Association of Football Statisticians. The help of all those involved at these establishments is most gratefully acknowledged.

Thanks are due to the following libraries for answering queries by post: Aldershot, Alicante (Spain), Croydon, Dartford, Folkestone, Fürth (Germany), Gillingham, Grays, Hastings, High Wycombe, Leicester, Liège (Belgium), Newport (Isle of Wight), Norwich, Nottingham, Palma de Mallorca (Spain), Plymouth, Redruth, Southampton, Swansea, Swindon, Tonbridge, Torquay, Tunbridge Wells and Watford. Over 25 other libraries and the East Sussex Record Office have been visited in the course of research.

The following organisations have also given valuable information: Brighton, Hove, Worthing & District F.A. (Ron Beal); Sussex County F.A.; Football Association of Ireland; Football Association of Wales; Southern Youth League; South East Counties League; Arsenal F.C.; Dagenham F.C. (Fred Hawthorn); East Grinstead F.C.; Newbury Town F.C. (Charlie Rogers and Neville Whiting); and Portsmouth F.C.

The following individuals, many of them members of the Association of Football Statisticians, have provided data for which the authors are deeply grateful: Richard Lindsay, John Treleven, Gerry Desmond (*Irish Football Handbook*), Andy Porter, John Wells, Tony Ambrosen, Derek Blow, Paul Clayton, Sean Creedon, Philip Donaldson, David Downs, Stewart Fell, Frank Grande, Trefor Jones, Fred Lee, Lawrence Magnanie, Mike Purkiss, David Salmon, Roger Triggs, Paul Voller, Roger Wash, Richard Wells; and three ex-Albion players, Stan Hickman, Stan Willemse and the late Ernie Marriott.

Many thanks also to Cooke Technology Limited of Portslade for the use of equipment, and to Maurice Rewers and Judith Bateman for translations.

Illustrations

EVENING ARGUS: the authors are deeply indebted to the *Evening Argus* for permission to use of many of their excellent photographs. It would have been impossible to illustrate the post-war era without the considerable help and generous co-operation of the county's daily newspaper.
EAST SUSSEX COUNTY LIBRARY: many thanks are due to the East Sussex County Library, especially for permission to use a number of photographs from their *Brighton & Hove Herald* collection. The authors are immensely grateful for their co-operation and for the help of the staff involved.
BRIGHTON & HOVE ALBION F.C.: thanks also, of course, are due to the club for permission to use the seagull logo and other illustrations to which they may hold rights.
Picture acknowledgements (with sincere thanks): Brighton Borough Council (jacket, p3); Hove Borough Council (jacket, p3); *Brighton & Hove Gazette*/East Sussex County Library (pp13, 123); Gary Chalk (p14); Alan Golds (p24); East Sussex County Library (p29); Companies House (p35); *Sussex Daily News* (pp36, 98, 118, 119, 150, 152); Dave Ticehurst (p66); Aerofilms/East Sussex County Library (p94); *The Illustrated London News* (p99); *Brighton & Hove Herald*/East Sussex County Library (pp104, 108, 115, 131, 136, 137, 139, 143, 154, 158, 168, 170, 177); *Pike's Directory of Brighton & Hove*/East Sussex County Library (p117); Alec Whitcher, *The Voice of Soccer* (p125); Alec Whitcher, *Ace of Games* (p127); Stadtarchiv Fürth (p147); *Brighton & Hove Gazette* (p159, 191, 208, 212); *Brighton & Hove Herald* (pp166, 171, 179, 184); *Sussex Express* (p194); *Evening Argus* (pp148, 156, 158, 159, 160, 163, 164, 175, 180, 182, 185, 187, 196, 197, 202, 204, 204, 204, 211, 214, 215, 217, 219, 220, 224, 225, 226, 228, 229, 230, 231, 233, 234, 236, 241, 243, 245, 247, 250, 251, 252, 253, 258); Tudor Press (p158); Kevin Hampson (p199); Tony Hagon/*Evening Argus* (p216).

The remaining illustrations (and many mentioned above) come from the private collections of supporters of the Albion, including a number from the old Supporters' Club handbooks.

The publishers have been unable to trace the copyright holders of many of the illustrations used and offer sincere apologies to anyone whose rights may have been infringed. Any photographer or other copyright holder is cordially invited to contact the publishers in writing, providing proof of copyright.

EXPLANATORY NOTES ON STATISTICS

ALBION MATCHES covered by the statistics in this volume, unless otherwise stated, are those played in the following competitions only (which are deemed to be first-team competitions because the first eleven would normally be fielded). They are referred to throughout by the abbreviations given in brackets:

Football League, including all its sponsored titles, 1920–39 and 1946–93 (**FL**), and the Second Division play-offs 1990–91 (**FL D2 PO**). (Two abandoned matches, 16.9.1968 and 1.1.1977, and three matches of the cancelled 1939–40 season are not included in any statistics. The section contested in 1920–21 was known as Division Three (*South*) according to the League's official history.)

Football Association Challenge Cup 1901–39 and 1945–93 including all qualifying ties (**FAC**). (The match on 16.1.1908, abandoned in extra-time, was deemed by the F.A. to be a 1–1 draw, the full-time score, and is so treated here.)

Football League Cup, including all its sponsored titles, 1960–93 (**FLC**).

Football League **Full Members Cup**, including all its sponsored titles, 1985–87 & 1988–92 (**FMC**).

Football League **Associate Members Cup** 1987–88 and its continuation in 1992–93, including all its sponsored titles (**AMC**).

Football League Division Three Southern Section Challenge Cup, commonly known as the 'Southern Section Cup', 1933–39 (**SSC**). Note that the 1938–39 tournament is included although it was never completed.

Southern League 1901–15 & 1919–20 (**SL**) (not including the reserves in Division Two in 1904–05 and 1907–08), and the test match 1903 (**SL Test**). (The abandoned match on 18.1.1908 is not included in any statistics.)

Football Association Charity Shield 1910 (**FA Ch. Shield**).

United League 1905–07 (**Utd League**). (The abandoned match on 2.10.1905 is not included in any statistics.)

Western League 1907–09 (**WL**), and the championship match and replay 1909 (**WL Champ.** & **WL Ch. Rep.**). (The abandoned match on 11.11.1907 is not included in any statistics.)

Southern Football Alliance 1912–14 (**S Alliance**).

Southern Professional Charity Cup 1907–15 (**SCC**), including those matches in 1912–13 and 1913–14 played by the reserves.

South Eastern League 1902–03 only (**SE League**), regarded as a first-team competition that season but contested mainly by the reserves thereafter.

Matches during the Second World War which allowed unregistered players are also included and are grouped under the label **Wartime** for record purposes:

Football League south regional competitions 1939–41 & 1942–45 (**FL (South)**). (The abandoned matches on 18.9.1940 and 12.10.1940 were counted in the table and are included in all statistics. The abandoned match on 21.9.1940 did not count and is not included in any statistics.)

Football League South 1940–41. (This league used the results from the Football League south regional competition, but there was a separate challenge match on 31.5.1941 which is included separately in statistics (**FLS Chall.**).)

Football League War Cup 1939–41 (**FLWC**).

London War League 1941–42 (**London WL**).

London War Cup 1941–42 (**London WC**).

Football League (South) Cup 1942–45 (**FL (S'th) Cup**).

Football League Division Three (South) South 1945–46 (**FL D3(S)S**).

Football League Division Three (South) Cup 1945–46 (**FL D3(S)Cup**).

In the case of minor and non-competitive matches, which are not included in statistics, a game has been designated 'first-team' when a large number of those participating were current first-team members, or the first-team played part of the match.

ABBREVIATIONS include:

First round, second round, …	**R1, R2, …**	First leg, second leg	**Lg1, Lg2**	Penalty goal	**pen**
First qualifying round, …	**Q1, …**	Replay, second replay, …	**Rep, 2Rep, …**	Thames & Medway Combination .	**T & M Comb.**
Intermediate round	**Int.**	Division One, Division Two, …	**D1, D2, …**	Brighton Charity Cup	**BCC**
Preliminary round	**Prelim.**	Southern, South	**S**	Brighton Challenge Shield	**BCS**
Quarter-final, semi-final, final	**QF, SF, F**	After extra time	**aet**	Sussex Senior Challenge Cup	**Susx SC**

SCORES and **RESULTS** (W, D or L) given in all statistical charts and tables include the Albion score first and relate only to the match concerned at full time (or extra time where played). Penalty shoot-outs are not included (but are noted) and the result given is not necessarily that of the whole tie in cup competitions.

VICTORIES & DEFEATS are graded firstly by the number of goals scored, and then by the margin. Thus a 4–2 win is 'bigger' than a 3–0 victory and a 4–3 win.

OPPONENTS are described by the name in use at the time of the match. (See page 325 for further information.)

VENUE is the usual ground of the home club at the time unless otherwise noted. Neutral venues are regarded as away venues for record purposes.

SCORERS are named in the order in which they scored during the match wherever possible.

ATTENDANCES in the period until 1925, and also during the Second World War, are usually reporter's estimates, which may be recognised by the 'rounded' figures. Rather vague estimates were common and such comments have been interpreted. Thus a gate of, say, 'over 5,000' has been quantified as 5,200. In the period from 1925 until 1957 (for home games) and 1951 (away), the Football League's records have been used where possible and exact figures are given. After these dates the attendances are generally those published in the Press (which have now corresponded to the League's figures for several years). Averages refer to league games only.

LEAGUE POSITION is that at the end of the day of the match, as would have appeared in the Press at the time. Equal positions are denoted by =.

PLAYERS wore no numbers on their shirts until 1939; the numbers given until that time relate as nearly as possible to the positions of the players in the traditional 2–3–5 formation. After 1939 players are numbered 1–11 as nearly as possible with the actual shirt numbers they wore. Goalkeepers are always given the number 1. From 1965, players marked † were substituted by the player numbered 12, and players marked ‡ were substituted by no.14. Players marked N were non-playing substitutes. Note that a few line-ups – four in the South Eastern League in 1902–03, one in the Southern Alliance in 1913–14 and eleven in the London War League and Cup of 1941–42 – have not yet been confirmed; the players recorded were expected to play and are included in all statistics.

APPEARANCE and **GOAL TOTALS** of individual players in the Southern League, Western League and Football League include the 1902–03 Southern League test match, the 1908–09 Western League championship match and replay, and the 1990–91 Football League play-offs unless otherwise stated.

TRANSFER FEES are confidential and all fees quoted are generally those that appeared in the Press. Some early fees are from Football League records.

NOTES are generally marked by an asterisk (*). The reader should refer to the bottom of the table or chart.

Can you help add to the knowledge of the history of the club and its players? Do you have information that would fill any gaps in the story? Have you any memorabilia – photographs, old documents, programmes, handbooks, etc. – which may be of interest? If you have any such items or interesting information relating to the Albion or its players, please write to:

Goldstone Books
c/o Goldstone Ground
Newtown Road
Hove
East Sussex
BN3 7DE

SEASON-BY-SEASON HISTORY

November 1897: Queen Victoria reigned over a Great Britain at the height of its power and influence. The Empire stretched to all parts of the globe, while at home the Industrial Revolution had made the country the centre of world manufacturing and trade. It was an era of scientific and technological advance: Madame Curie was about to discover radium, while Marconi was developing his radio transmitter, now two years old. Electricity was the wonder of the age and a permanent supply had been generated in Brighton for fifteen years.

It was against this background of industry and empire that football evolved rapidly in the last two decades of the nineteenth century. Until then the organised game had been largely the pursuit of the middle classes. The Football Association, the governing body of the sport, was formed in London in 1863 and was dominated by the public-school, university and Army networks. In the Midlands, northern England and Scotland, however, football was seen as an opportunity for the urban working-class to escape the drudgery of their everyday lives and indulge in healthy recreation. Clubs sprang up in industrial towns and cities, often in connection with churches or factories, and the game began to develop as a spectator sport. The better players saw football as a means of earning a living, but any payment had to be made covertly as professionalism was strictly forbidden by the English and Scottish hierarchies.

The northern clubs affiliated to the Football Association and took part in the F.A. Cup (or English Cup as it was usually called until Cardiff City annexed the trophy in 1927), but the final was the sole preserve of the gentlemen amateurs until Blackburn Rovers reached the last stage in 1882. Blackburn Olympic lifted the trophy the following year, and then Rovers themselves, playing in the shadows of the cotton mills, secured a hat-trick of triumphs in 1884, '85 and '86, paving the way for other provincial sides. The clamour of the North could no longer be denied and the payment of players was finally sanctioned by the F.A. in 1885. Professionalism subsequently spread throughout the North and Midlands, and the need for regular fixtures led to the formation of the Football League in 1888.

By November 1897, therefore, the legitimate professional game was twelve years old and well established. The South had lagged behind the North, but professional clubs had been formed in many of the larger southern towns since the early 1890s. Throughout Sussex, though, the game followed a strictly amateur format. The Sussex County Football Association was formed in September 1882. The founder members included the public schools of Ardingly, Brighton and Lancing Colleges, and their old-boy teams dominated the Sussex Senior Cup in its infant years along with clubs such as Burgess Hill and Eastbourne whose line-ups were dotted with 'Honourables' and 'Reverends'. Eastbourne, for many years the bastion of the amateur ideal, regularly included members of the famed Corinthians, players such as Arthur Topham and Morris Stanbrough, both full England caps. The club comprised schoolmasters and other professional men, and it was not until the formation of the East and West Sussex Leagues in 1896 that the influence of the upper- and middle-class teams diminished with the emergence of club sides like Southwick, Shoreham, Hastings & St Leonards, Worthing and Hove. But Brighton, by far the largest town in Sussex, had no single side to represent it.

While long established as the country's most popular resort, Brighton was also as densely populated as any northern city and had a considerable industrial economy centred on the railway workshops. The population of around 120,000 was concentrated in the central area and on the steep slopes to the east. The spacious, middle-class suburb of Preston had developed rapidly over the last 20 years or so, while neighbouring Hove was also growing and its population had risen to around 29,000. Horse-buses still dominated the streets, but an electric tram system was to be in place within four years and the age of the motor car was dawning fast. Entertainment was provided chiefly by the many theatres, music halls and taverns, although local 'kinematic' pioneers were giving moving-picture shows at Hove Town Hall and other venues.

The highest grade of football in the town was played on council pitches in Preston Park by teams such as Brighton Hornets, Brighton Athletic and North End Rangers. Regular

Edgar Everest, the father of professional football in Brighton
Born in the town in 1865, 'Chippie' Everest was a Western Road tobacconist and lived at 9 West Hill Road. He was secretary of the County F.A. for 56 years from 1889 until 1945, and was also an F.A. councillor for 20 years.

competition was provided by the East Sussex League and the two main knock-out trophies: the Sussex Senior Cup and the Brighton Challenge Shield.

It was with a view to forming a strong, amateur combination to represent the town that Edgar Everest, the secretary of the Sussex County F.A., had advocated the amalgamation of the leading teams under one name – 'Brighton United' – as early as 1893. A former Sussex representative at inside-right and player-secretary of the Brighton Hornets club for five years, Everest strove to improve the standard of local football, and was instrumental in bringing Preston North End and Nottingham Forest to the county to play representative teams labelled 'Sussex Martlets': North End won 4–1 at Preston Park Cricket Ground in 1892 and Forest won 8–2 at Sheffield Park in 1894.

The enthusiasm surrounding these and other prestige fixtures convinced Everest that Sussex wanted – and needed – a higher grade of football than the local amateurs could provide. As the '90s wore on, the formation of a professional club in Brighton was mooted on a number of occasions. In November 1897, Everest, together with Sussex F.A. councillor Charles Meaden (another well-known local ex-player who had won Senior Cup honours at right-half with the Hornets in 1892), decided that the time was right to bring the idea to fruition.

On 17 March 1897, West Bromwich Albion and Stoke played a match in aid of the Brighton Children's Free Dinner Fund, a charity that fed 1,200 poor children daily. Stoke won the game, which was played at the Preston Park Cricket Ground, 4–2. Eight days later English Cup holders Sheffield Wednesday played a match with East Sussex League club Brighton Athletic at the County Ground, Hove, in aid of the Mayor of Brighton's Indian Famine Fund. Strengthened by the inclusion of several leading local amateurs, Athletic put up a splendid show but the First Division side ran out 2–0 winners. The illustrious, Newhaven-born cricketer W. G. 'Billy' Quaife, of Warwickshire and England, guested on Athletic's right wing.

PROFESSIONALISM COMES TO BRIGHTON

After some preliminary discussions, the pair convened a meeting of interested persons at the Imperial Hotel, 43–44 Queen's Road, on Friday, 26 November 1897. (The hotel was the usual meeting place of both the Sussex County F.A. and the Brighton & Hove Association.) The *Sussex Daily News* takes up the story:

PROFESSIONAL CLUB FOR BRIGHTON

A meeting of those interested in the formation of a Professional Club for Brighton was held at the Imperial Hotel, Queen's Road, last evening, when there were present Messrs C. F. Butcher, A. P. Cleather, George Cole, F. W. Cushman, T. A. Chinn, Elliott, C. T. Emary, E. W. Everest, T. M. Gilder, T. Harrington, C. Meaden, W. E. Nash, G. H. Rose, A. M. Sleight, and T. Sweetman. The meeting was convened by Messrs E. W. Everest and C. Meaden, and the latter was voted to the chair.

The Chairman said that for many years suggestions had been made that Brighton should have a professional Club, and it was now thought that the time had arrived when serious steps should be taken to form such a Club. He thought there might be two objections to the movement. Many regarded a professional footballer with horror, but he held that an expert player was entitled to benefit himself by his superior play. Professionalism was, however, fully recognised and ought to be encouraged. Many might also urge that the professional team would injure local Clubs, but he held that the amateur Clubs should endeavour, as in years past, to exist without the assistance of gate money. In the North professional teams had not interfered with local Clubs, but, on the contrary, amateur football had been improved, and the professionals had been recruited from the local Clubs.

A Limited Company Suggested

A professional team in Brighton would act as tutors to the amateur footballers and tend to improve their play. He thought that the Club, if started, had a fair chance of being included in the Southern League. An enormous liability would be incurred and it was suggested a Limited Company should be formed. At present it would be impossible to have their own ground, and the Sussex County Cricket Club had been approached for the use of the County Ground, Hove. If the terms proved satisfactory the suggested Company might then be formed. Referring to the Southampton Club he said the receipts of that Club amounted last season to £3,300, and it was expected they would exceed £4,000 this season. Up to the present time he thought their expenditure had exceeded income. He believed a professional Club would provide better sport than they had experienced, and would prove such an attraction that the movement would be heartily taken up by the townspeople.

In response to Mr Chinn, the Chairman said the Southampton Club, on taking over the goodwill of the Southampton St Mary's Club, incurred a liability of £250, and paid, last season, £1,800 for the expenses of trainer and players. In reply to Mr Gilder, he said the Brighton Club would require a capital of £5,000.

Mr E. W. Everest gave particulars of the success of the Sussex County Association during the past seven years. There had been a steady improvement in the gate, and last season one attendance numbered 7,000. He held that if amateur football was so successful professional would do even better. Southampton, last season, played 66 matches, and those not League matches were guarantee games. He believed a good professional team would command greater support than all the local amateur clubs put together.

In Every Way Desirable

In answer to Mr Emary, the Chairman said the expenses of the first year would amount to over £2,000.

Mr Everest said they had some 60 supporters, and would, doubtless, secure more when the negotiations with the Sussex

County Club had been concluded. In reply to Mr Sweetman, he said a good team would at once enable them to enter the Southern League, and, in answer to Mr Rose, said they had friends on the Southern League Committee, but everything depended on the excellence of the team.

Mr A. M. Sleight thought the movement was a step in the right direction for at present Brighton had no team that entered for the English Cup or the Amateur Cup.

Mr T. Harrington said there could not be two opinions about the improvement the club would effect in local sport, but thought the great difficulty was in making a start.

The Chairman said a sum of £50 would be needed for preliminary expense, and ultimately the sum of £40 was guaranteed by those present.

Mr G. H. Rose proposed and Mr T. A. Chinn seconded, 'That this meeting is of the opinion that a professional team in Brighton is necessary, and request Mr Everest and Mr Meaden to continue their negotiations with that object, and report at a future meeting.'

The proposition was unanimously carried, and the meeting terminated with a vote of thanks to the Chairman.

Not all parties in the town were convinced that the venture would succeed. The *Brighton Guardian* warned that

> The promoters of a professional team for Brighton will find that the public require very high-class fare, which is expensive … [and that] football enthusiasts are always wanting when there is anything to pay.

Nevertheless, Everest and Meaden continued with their task. Negotiations were pursued with the Sussex County Club and the County Ground was secured for home matches. By March 1898 everything was ready for the launch of the company and an advertisement for supporters – potential shareholders – appeared in the *Evening Argus* of 5 March:

BRIGHTON UNITED F.C. LIMITED

Those interested in the proposed formation of Brighton United Football Club, Limited, and desirous of supporting the same, are invited to communicate with Mr Everest, 144, Western-road.

The chosen name, 'Brighton United', was the title coined by Everest in 1893, but was now to be realised in a professional, rather than amateur, form.

The embryo club was affiliated to the County F.A. a week later and registered as a limited company on 21 March. The authorised capital of £2,000 was issued as £1 shares purchasable in four 5-shilling instalments which were advertised from the beginning of April. The first board of directors of Brighton United comprised Councillor Edward Butt-Thompson of Brighton (chairman); George Cole, chairman of the Sussex County F.A. and president of the Brighton and Hove F.A. (vice-chairman); Frank Allen, a plumber and decorator, a member of the North End Rangers club and donor of the Brighton Challenge Shield in 1895–96; Alderman John Clark, owner of a bread factory in Fonthill Road, Hove; Robert Gill, barrister; William Hollis, auctioneer; William Nash, proprietor of the *Brighton and Hove Times* and the *Sussex Evening Times*; Arthur Nye, a Hove coal merchant; and Charles Meaden himself, a solicitor's clerk. Edgar Everest was appointed club secretary and his shop at 144 Western Road was registered as the company's first office.

There was a good deal of enthusiasm for the venture which was seen as a great boost to the town's civic pride and a potential attraction for visitors, but getting supporters to part with their money proved difficult and by July only 892 of the 2,000 shares had been taken up. Nevertheless, there were some impressive names on the list of shareholders. Among them were Alfred Bunting, landlord of the Imperial Hotel; Councillor Herbert Carden, one of the greatest figures in Brighton's civic

Edward Butt-Thompson, the first chairman of Brighton United F.C.
A member of the Brighton County Borough Council, Butt-Thompson lived at 13 Richmond Place.

history; Councillor John Stafford, Mayor of Brighton 1899–1902; Bruce Vernon-Wentworth, M.P. for Brighton 1893–1906 and donor of the Vernon-Wentworth Cup in 1894–95, still played for by local intermediate teams; Thomas Gilder, the secretary of the Brighton and Hove F.A.; Billy Newham, player-secretary of the Sussex County Cricket Club; George Wisden, athletic outfitter of Duke Street; and Tamplins Brewery, the largest of the local brewing concerns.

During May, Everest and Meaden travelled widely in search of suitable players and, in line with the majority of professional clubs of the era, turned to Scotland as a rich source of talent. No fewer than seven of the Dundee side were signed; not surprisingly, Dundee were to finish bottom of the Scottish First Division in the ensuing season. Leicester Fosse's trainer John Jackson was recruited as trainer-manager. Previously on the training staffs at Wolverhampton Wanderers, Loughborough and Liverpool, Jackson was seen as the ideal man to organise and run the team.

In the meantime an application was made to join the Southern League. In 1898 the Football League consisted of two divisions, both of eighteen teams of which only two were from the South: Luton Town and Woolwich Arsenal. The majority of the leading southern clubs were members of the Southern League. Formed four years earlier in 1894, it also comprised two sections, the First Division containing teams such as Southampton, Tottenham Hotspur, Millwall, Reading, New Brompton (later Gillingham), Bristol City and Swindon Town. The strength of the competition can be judged by results in the English Cup: Southampton were losing finalists in 1900 and 1902, and had just lost to Nottingham Forest in a semi-final replay; Spurs became the only club outside the Football League (or Premier League) since its formation to win the trophy in 1901; Millwall reached the semi-final stage in 1900 and 1903; and there were numerous victories over Football League sides in the earlier rounds. The standard was extremely high.

The Southern League committee welcomed an application from a club representing a town the size of Brighton, and, with the team judged to be of a high standard, United were elected directly into the First Division for the coming season. Entry was also gained to the United League, primarily a midweek competition formed in 1896, in the hope of harvesting extra revenue. Playing in two competitions was common practice for the majority of southern professional sides up to the Great War.

> It appears that the founders of Brighton United had far-reaching ambitions of developing the club as a general sporting concern. The company's aims are recorded as including 'the promotion of the businesses of football, cricket, tennis, athletics, bicycling and gymnastics'.

BRIGHTON UNITED 1898–99

The club's first training session was held at 'a private venue' on 16 August with the following professionals present: Davie Willocks, William Longair, John Low, Jock Malloch, Willie McArthur, Willie Hendry and Joe Clark, all from the Dundee club; Jock Caldwell, Frank McAvoy and Paddy Farrell from Woolwich Arsenal; John Carter and Peter McWhirter from the Bristol club Warmley; Jimmy Davidson from Spurs; Roddy McLeod from Leicester Fosse; and goalkeeper Leo Bullimer from Reading. It was a fair collection of experienced players for a newly formed club. Longair was a Scottish international and McLeod had gained an English Cup winner's medal with West Bromwich Albion in 1892. These fifteen professionals were to be augmented by the pick of the local amateurs, and that evening the players were presented to the

directors at a social gathering held at the Imperial Hotel. The adopted colours were green shirts with white knickers, resulting in the nickname 'Greenbacks'.

Two weeks later, on Thursday, 1 September, United made their début in a friendly against West Sussex Senior League side Southwick on the latter's Croft Meadow ground (part of a farm situated at the western end of the present Southwick Recreation Ground). The Brighton side scored a crushing 8–1 victory, and subsequent heavy wins over most of the leading Sussex teams were to emphasise the gulf between local amateur football and the professional game.

The following Saturday saw the initial competitive fixture, a Southern League match with the reigning champions Southampton which coincided with the opening of the Saints' excellent new ground, The Dell. United's line-up for this historic encounter was

> Bullimer; Hendry and
> Caldwell; Farrell, Longair
> (captain) and McAvoy;
> Clark, McLeod, McArthur,
> Malloch and Willocks.

Nine Scots, one Irishman and an Englishman! Some 8,000 spectators – including many Brighton fans who had travelled by special train – saw the Mayor of Southampton start the game. United lost Willie McArthur after only 20 minutes as the result of a kick on the jaw and he was taken to the Southampton Infirmary for stitches. The Saints, with three internationals, dominated the match, but brave goalkeeping by Bullimer kept them at bay. Although losing 4–1, general opinion was that the new team had performed well against the South's most powerful combination.

Brighton United's first Southern League match, at Southampton on 8 September 1898
This picture, of the first-ever match to be played at The Dell, shows the Saints, in stripes, attacking the Archers Road End. Note the old pitch markings. Penalty kicks were introduced in 1891 and for ten years or so the penalty areas extended across the pitch twelve yards from the goal line. The kicks could be taken from anywhere on the line.

BRIGHTON UNITED SEASON 1898–99

Date	Comp.	Ven.	Opponents	Result	HT	Pos.	Scorers	Atten.	Bullimer L	Caldwell J	Carter J	Clark J	Collins A	Davidson J	Farrell P	Freeman S	Halman C	Hendry W	Longair W	Low J	McArthur W	McAvoy F	McLeod R	McWhirter P	Malloch J	Paige J	Sharp A	Spicer T	Willocks D
Sep 3	SL D1	(a)	Southampton	L 1–4	0–2	6	McLeod	8,000	1	3		7			4			2	5		9	6	8		10				11
10	SL D1	(a)	New Brompton	L 0–3	0–0	10		3,000	1	3		7		8	4			2	5			6	9		10				11
14	SL D1	(a)	Bedminster	W 2–1	1–0	7	McArthur, Longair	1,000	1	3				7				2	5	6	9		8	4	11				10
17	FAC Prelim.	(h)	Romford	W 8–0	4–0	–	Malloch 3, Willocks, McLeod 3, McArthur	3,000	1	3				7				2	5	6	9		8	4	11				10
21	Utd League	(a)	Bristol City	L 0–4	0–2	9		2,000	1	3				7				2	6	4	9		8	5	11				10
24	SL D1	(h)	R.A. Portsmouth	W 8–0	3–0	5	McLeod 3, Willocks, McArthur 4	3,500	1	3				7				2	5	6	9		8	4	10				11
Oct 1	FAC Q1	(h)	Ashford United	W 5–0	0–0	–	Willocks, McLeod, McArthur 2, Longair	2,659	1	3				7	5			2	6	4	9		8		11				10
5	Utd League	(h)	Tottenham H'spur	L 1–2	1–0	9	Willocks	3,000	1	3				7	5			2	6	4	9		8		11				10
8	SL D1	(a)	Gravesend	L 2–5	0–3	8	Own goal, McArthur	1,800	1	3				7				2	5	6	9		8	4	11				10
15	FAC Q2	(h)	Thames Ironworks	D 0–0	0–0	–		2,600	1	3	2			7	5				6	4	9		8		11				10
17	Utd League	(h)	Luton Town	W 5–3	2–0	8	McArthur 3, Own goal, Willocks	500	1	3	2			7	5				6	4	9		8		11				10
19	FAC Q2 Rep	(a)	Thames Ironworks	W 4–1	2–0	–	McArthur, Own goal, Willocks 2	500	1	3				7	5			2	6	4	9		8		11				10
22	SL D1	(a)	R.A. Portsmouth	L 0–2	0–2	9		4,000	1	3				7	5			2	6	4	9		8		11				10
26	Utd League	(h)	Bristol City	W 2–1	1–0	5	McWhirter, McLeod	2,000	1	3					5		11	2	6	4	9		8	7					10
29	FAC Q3	(a)	Millwall	L 0–3	0–0	–		5,000	1	3					5			2	6	4	9		8	7	11				10
31	Utd League	(a)	Woolwich Arsenal	L 2–5	0–2	7	Collins 2	2,000	1	3		7	9					2		4	5	6	8		11				10
Nov 5	SL D1	(h)	Millwall	D 2–2	2–1	10	McLeod 2	3,300	1	3		7		8				2	6	4		5	9		11				10
9	Utd League	(h)	Southampton	W 5–3	3–2	6	McLeod 3, McAvoy, Willocks	1,900	1	3	6	7		8				2		4		5	9		11				10
12	SL D1	(a)	Swindon Town	L 1–3	1–1	10	McLeod	3,500	1	3	2	7		8	6					4		5	9		11				10
30	SL D1	(h)	Bedminster	L 0–2	0–1	11		1,560	1	3	2	7		8				4		6		5	9		11				10
Dec 1	Utd League	(a)	Millwall	L 1–4	0–1	9	McLeod	900	1	3		7		8				2	6	4		5	9		11				10
10	SL D1	(a)	Chatham	L 1–3	1–1	11	Hendry	1,500	1	3	4	7		8				2	6		9	5			11				10
17	SL D1	(h)	Reading	D 1–1	0–1	11	Willocks	1,500	1	3				7	4			2	6		9	5	8		11				10
24	Utd League	(h)	Kettering Town	W 2–0	1–0	8	Willocks, McArthur	1,600	1	3					4			2	6		9	5	8	7	11				10
31	SL D1	(a)	Millwall	L 1–8	1–4	12	McLeod	2,000	1	3					4			2	6		9	5	8	7	11				10
Jan 4	Utd League	(h)	Woolwich Arsenal	D 1–1	1–0	8	Willocks	1,500	1	3		8			4			2	6		9	5		7	11				10
11	SL D1	(h)	Bristol City	W 2–1	2–0	11	Malloch, McArthur	800	1	3	8				4			2	6		9	5		7	11				10
14	SL D1*	(h)	Warmley*	W 3–2	1–0	11	Malloch 2, Willocks	2,000	1	3		8			4			2	6		9	5		7	11				10
18	Utd League	(a)	Southampton	L 0–3	0–2	8		2,000		3					4			2	6	8	9	5		7	11			1	10
21	SL D1	(h)	Tottenham H'spur	L 0–1	0–1	11		3,000	1	3					4			2	6		9	5	8	7	11				10
23	Utd League	(a)	Wellingborough T.	W 2–1	0–1	8	McArthur, McLeod		1	3	2	8			4					6	10	5	9	7					11
28	SL D1	(h)	Swindon Town	W 2–0	2–0	11	McLeod 2	2,700	1	3	2				4				6		11	5	9	7		8			10
Feb 1	Utd League	(a)	Reading	L 1–3	0–3	8	Paige	2,000	1	3	2				4				6		10	5	9	7		8			11
4	SL D1	(h)	New Brompton	W 2–1	1–0	10	Willocks, McLeod	2,700		3					4			2	6		10	5	9	7		8		1	11
11	Utd League	(a)	Rushden	L 2–3	2–1	8	Paige, Willocks	1,200	1	3					4			2	6		10	5	9	7		8			11
15	Utd League	(h)	Luton Town	W 5–0	1–0	7	McLeod 2, McWhirter 2, Paige	1,100		3	2								6	4	11	5	9	7		8		1	10
18	Utd League	(a)	Kettering Town	L 0–2	0–1	7		2,000		3	2								6	4		5	9	7		8	10	1	11
22	Utd League	(h)	Reading	W 2–1	2–1	6	Willocks, Caldwell	1,200		3	2			8					6	4	10	5	9	7				1	11
Mar 1	SL D1	(h)	Sheppey United	W 4–1	3–1	10	McArthur 2, McLeod 2	1,000			2				4	3			6		10	5	9	7			8	1	11
4	SL D1	(a)	Reading	L 0–1	0–1	11		3,000						8	4			2	3	6	10	5	9	7				1	11
6	Utd League	(a)	Wellingborough T.	W 2–0	0–0	5	Willocks, McLeod	1,000	1		3				4			2	6		10	5	9	7			8		11
11	SL D1	(h)	Gravesend	W 2–1	1–1	10	McWhirter, Willocks	2,500		3				8	4			2	6		10	5	9	7				1	11
18	Utd League	(h)	Rushden	W 4–1	2–1	4	Own goal, McLeod 2, McArthur	1,600		3				10	4			2	6		5		9	7		8		1	11
23	Utd League	(h)	Millwall	W 4–2	1–0	4	Willocks 2, McWhirter, Davidson	1,000		3				8	4			2	6		9	5		7	11			1	10
25	SL D1	(a)	Tottenham H'spur	W 3–1	2–1	9	Willocks, Longair, McArthur	4,000		3				8	4			2	6		9	5		7	11			1	10
27	SL D1	(h)	Southampton	L 0–2	0–0	9		2,000		3				8	4			2	6		9	5		7	11			1	10
31	SL D1	(a)	Sheppey United	W 2–1	1–1	7	McLeod, Willocks	1,900		3								2	6	4	9	5	8	7	11			1	10
Apr 1	SL D1	(h)	Chatham	L 0–1	0–0	9		3,800		3					4			2	6		9	5	8	7	11			1	10
4	Utd League	(a)	Tottenham H'spur	L 0–3	0–2	4		3,000		3				10				2	6	4	9	5	8	7	11			1	
8	SL D1	(a)	Bristol City	L 1–3	1–1	10	Willocks	5,000			2			8				3	6	4	9	5		7	11			1	10
							Southern League appearances		15	21	7	6	0	15	16	1	0	21	22	10	20	20	19	16	19	2	1	9	24
							Southern League goals	OG – 1										1	2		10		14	1	1				7
							United League appearances		13	19	8	5	1	9	12	0	1	14	17	13	17	15	17	15	11	5	2	7	19
							United League goals	OG – 2		1			2	1							6	1	11	4		3			10

Notes: Home matches played at the County Ground, Hove.
Jan 14 – Warmley withdrew from the Southern League around Jan 20 and their matches were deleted from the record. This match is not included in the end-of-season Southern League statistics.

The club's initial matches were all away games because the Sussex County Cricket Club required the use of the County Ground for the first and last few weeks of the season. (The football pitch was marked out at the Cromwell Road end.) This was to be a big factor in the ultimate demise of United.

Gates of 3,000 to 4,000 were anticipated, but severe weather during November and December had a devastating effect on attendances, there being no covered accommodation on the ground, and the average turned out to be around 2,300 in the Southern League and 1,600 for the United League fixtures.

The club's Southern League fortunes fluctuated throughout the season. Home form was good, Tottenham Hotspur, Bedminster, Chatham and eventual champions Southampton being the only victors at the County Ground, but in the 'out' matches only six points were gathered, including two from a splendid 3–1 win at

When Leo Bullimer and Frank McAvoy pulled a drowning man from the sea at Portslade, the United goalkeeper ruined his pocket-watch and the pivot lost a ring. Brighton United supporters opened a fund for the pair, and at a smoking-concert the Mayor of Hove presented Bullimer with a handsome silver watch and McAvoy with a gold signet-ring, both engraved with their respective initials.

Southern League Division 1 1898–99

		P	W	D	L	F	A	W	D	L	F	A	Pts
1.	Southampton	24	9	2	1	34	9	6	3	3	20	15	35
2.	Bristol City	24	11	0	1	39	16	4	3	5	16	17	33
3.	Millwall	24	7	2	3	34	17	5	4	3	25	18	30
4.	Chatham	24	6	4	2	19	8	4	4	4	13	15	28
5.	Reading	24	9	2	1	24	4	0	6	6	7	20	26
6.	New Brompton	24	7	3	2	24	9	3	2	7	14	21	25
7.	Tottenham Hotspur	24	8	2	2	24	11	2	2	8	16	25	24
8.	Bedminster	24	7	1	4	19	13	3	3	6	16	26	24
9.	Swindon Town	24	7	4	1	33	21	2	1	9	10	28	23
10.	**BRIGHTON UNITED**	24	6	2	4	23	13	3	0	9	14	35	20
11.	Gravesend	24	6	3	3	31	20	1	2	9	11	32	19
12.	Sheppey United	24	5	2	5	16	18	0	1	11	7	35	13
13.	R.A. Portsmouth	24	3	4	5	11	16	1	0	11	6	44	12

Note: Warmley withdrew from the League in January.

United League 1898–99

		P	W	D	L	F	A	Pts
1.	Millwall	20	14	3	3	42	19	31
2.	Southampton	20	12	1	7	53	32	25
3.	Woolwich Arsenal	20	10	4	6	30	30	24
4.	Tottenham Hotspur	20	11	2	7	35	25	24
5.	Bristol City	20	11	0	9	43	31	22
6.	Reading	20	8	5	7	36	25	21
7.	**BRIGHTON UNITED**	20	10	1	9	41	40	21
8.	Wellingborough Town	20	7	1	12	32	40	15
9.	Kettering Town	20	8	1	11	20	33	15
10.	Rushden	20	6	1	13	26	46	13
11.	Luton Town	20	2	3	5	24	71	7

Note: Kettering Town had two points deducted on 12.10.1898 for fielding an ineligible player.

Brighton United 1898–99

Standing left to right: John Jackson (trainer-manager), John Carter, Willie Hendry, Leo Bullimer, Paddy Farrell, Frank McAvoy, Bill Longair (captain).
Seated left to right: Peter McWhirter, Jock Caldwell, Willie McArthur, Davie Willocks, Jock Malloch.
On ground left to right: Jimmy Davidson, Roddy McLeod, Joe Clark, John Low.

John Jackson enjoyed a benefit match on 20 March when United beat a crack Army team, the 2nd Scots Guards, 5–2 at the County Ground. Prior to the game, United's half-back Paddy Farrell and the Hove goal-keeper William Gorsuch met for a prize of £5 in a challenge sprint race over 300 yards. Farrell led all the way but won only narrowly, by just half a yard.

Tottenham. Nevertheless, a creditable tenth position was achieved which, together with a mid-table spot in the United League, represented a good return for a club in its first season.

United reached the third qualifying round of the English Cup with home wins over Romford (8–2 in the first match staged at the County Ground, watched by 3,000 spectators) and Ashford (5–0), followed by a 4–1 victory at Thames Ironworks (forerunners of West Ham United) after a goal-less home draw. The Greenbacks eventually went out at Millwall, losing 3–0.

Financially, however, the story was not so rosy. In fact, until Christmas many local critics of professionalism were gleefully forecasting the imminent closure of the club. Attractive friendlies were arranged with opposition from the Football League to boost revenue: John Jackson's old team, Leicester Fosse, sent a reserve side which was beaten 2–0, while First Division giants Notts County triumphed 2–1 at Hove in February. In the New Year the bad weather relented, attendances rose, and increased gate receipts and monies raised from fund-raising smoking-concerts organised by an enthusiastic committee saw the club through to the end of the campaign with high hopes for the future. Nevertheless, United had incurred a loss of over £1,000 in their first season, with an expenditure of £3,472 (£2,044 on wages) and an income of £2,460. At the a.g.m. held during the close season, doubts were raised regarding the financial situation, but Charles Meaden assured shareholders that everything possible was being done to bring about an improvement. A fund had been opened to which the mayors of both Brighton and Hove had promised contributions. At the same meeting Mr William Avenell was thanked for securing a covered stand for the northern side of the pitch.

Brighton United
First-team friendly matches 1898–99

Date	Opponents			Scorers
Sep 1	Southwick	(a)	8–1	Malloch 2, Willocks 3, Clark 2, McLeod
Sep 7	Worthing	(a)	9–1	Willocks 3, McLeod 5, Davidson
Sep 28	Hastings & St Leonards	(a)	9–0	Willocks, McArthur 2, Malloch, ?
Nov 19	Leicester Fosse (res.)	(h)	2–0	Willocks, Clark
Nov 26	Burton Wanderers	(h)	2–1	Willocks 2
Dec 3	Grays United	(h)	4–0	Willocks 4
Dec 14	Southern Suburban Lge. XI	(h)	8–0	Willocks, McAvoy, McArthur 2, Caldwell, Davidson 2, Farrell
Dec 26	Brighton Athletic	(h)	3–1	McLeod 2, Willocks
Dec 27	Eastbourne Swifts	(h)	6–0	McWhirter 3, Clark, Malloch, Willocks
Jan 7	Clapton	(a)	4–2	Willocks, McWhirter, McArthur 2 (1 pen.)
Feb 8	West Sussex League XI	(a)	4–0	Willocks, Paige, McArthur, Davidson
Above match played at Littlehampton				
Feb 14	Leicester Fosse	(a)	4–6	McLeod, McWhirter, Willocks 2
Feb 25	Notts County	(h)	1–2	Farrell
John Jackson benefit match:				
Mar 20	2nd Scots Guards	(h)	5–2	McArthur 2, Willocks, Malloch 2
Apr 3	Scottish Amateur XI	(h)	6–0	McLeod 3, Longair, McAvoy, McArthur
Apr 5	Eastbourne	(a)	4–2	McLeod, McArthur, Willocks, Baker
Apr 15	Sussex County F.A. XI	(a)	3–0	McWhirter, Hendry, Davidson
Above match played at Worthing				

BRIGHTON UNITED 1899–1900

The management were far from idle during the summer. They scoured the 'not retained' lists for suitable players and brought some considerable talent to the town: Welshman Maurice Parry from Second Division Loughborough; goalkeeper Arthur Howes from Leicester Fosse; Bob Turner from Newton Heath (later to become Manchester United); Johnny Mercer, an Irish international from Belfast Distillery; Harry Ashby from Burton Swifts, who was the new captain; Harry Oakden from Swindon Town; and Bob Hill from Millwall. With most of the previous season's staff retained, the team looked a formidable one. The club left the United League along with most Southern League sides, but failed to gain admission to the Southern District Combination and instead joined the Thames & Medway Combination, a three-year-old alliance of Southern League clubs in north Kent and south-west Essex. A regular programme of friendlies was introduced for a reserve side, mainly against Sussex teams and the second elevens of other Southern Leaguers. A new strip of green-and-white stripes was adopted.

The campaign opened with a trip to Queen's Park Rangers' Kensal Rise ground, but a 6–0 thrashing heralded a disastrous run of eight consecutive Southern League defeats which sent the Greenbacks to the bottom of the table. December saw United unbeaten and rising above Cowes, the only team they had been able to defeat in the first three months (5–1 at the County Ground), but ironically this victory was wiped from the record when the Isle of Wight club folded just before Christmas to leave the Brighton side bottom once more. Inexplicably, in the Thames and Medway Combination, United won six of their first seven fixtures and vied for the leadership with Chatham into March. In the English Cup, victories over Eastbourne (6–1) and Brighton Athletic (9–0) preceded defeat at Chatham by two goals to nil in the third qualifying round.

The abysmal Southern League form continued in January and February with just three League points won. Attendances dwindled, dropping on occasion below four figures when a gate of 3,000 was required to ensure a successful company. Again the weather was unkind and a friendly with Wellingborough Town had to be postponed; the fixture was eventually played at the end of February, but United were unable to pay the Northamptonshire side the £17 10s. guaranteed. By this time the club was living from week to week, relying on home games for money to pay the players' wages: clubs were obliged to meet

A preview in the *Sussex Daily News* of 17 March 1900 for a fund-raising concert makes interesting reading.

What promises to be a very successful and enjoyable concert will be given at Hove Town Hall this evening in aid of the funds of the Brighton United. Today being St Patrick's Day, advantage will naturally be taken of the occasion to give an Irish programme, and several talented local artistes are announced to appear. Miss Edith Welling will sing, and Miss Muriel Woodman will give Irish dances. That the humorous element will be well-sustained, the names of Messrs Arthur, Collins and A. J. Marks will be sufficient guarantee. Those clever banjoists, Messrs W. M. Tebbe and H. Woodriff, will give selections, and the programme will also be contributed to by Miss Augusta Fielder, Mr Arthur Blackman, Mr J. M. F. Cohen, Mr A. J. Clark, and Mr J. Lambert Payne.

In November 1899, with New Brompton having to call off their friendly at Hove because of Cup commitments, United staged a match at the County Ground between their English players and a team comprising their Scottish, Irish and Welsh members. The game ended in a 1–1 draw.

only their visitors' expenses and these were often slow in arriving. A donation was sought from Tamplins Brewery, a firm which had shares in the club, but was refused.

On Saturday, 17 March, with the cricket season approaching, the final home Southern League match was due to be played, a very attractive fixture with Southampton, and the directors were hoping for a bumper gate to see the club through the remainder of the season. Six away games remained from which little could be expected in the way of cash. Unfortunately for United, Southampton had reached the semi-finals of the English Cup and the tie was scheduled for 17 March, so the Southern League match was rearranged for the following Monday. Tragically, Saints and Millwall drew their semi-final and the replay was fixed for the Wednesday. Southampton understandably called off the League match and it was postponed to an unspecified date. This was the death-knell for United, and a meeting of shareholders on the Monday evening decided that a motion to dissolve the company must be put to an extraordinary general meeting ten days later.

Two more matches were played at the County Ground during the following week, against New Brompton and Chatham in the Thames and Medway Combination; both ended in defeat and the attendances were poor. On the evening of Thursday, 29 March, the extraordinary general meeting was held at the Imperial Hotel. Chairman Charles Meaden opened by stating that the meeting was called for the consideration of a resolution to wind up the company. He added that the club was being pressed by one of the players for his wages, while another [Harry Oakden, owed £23] had reported his situation to the F.A.; if the club continued, it must pay him or be suspended by the Association [the same also applied to the money owing to Wellingborough Town].

He went on to provide figures proving the club's insolvency, adding that receipts this season were down by £1,000 on the previous term and were £300 less than the wage-bill. The first home match had realised £85 but the last only £15. Six more 'out' matches remained and these would entail further liabilities of £180. The club was also in debt to the Sussex County Cricket Club to the tune of £125 for rent; the cricket club had been very reasonable in letting them carry on thus far. In reply to questions, Meaden said that letters had been received from three players stating that they were not available and therefore a team could not be fielded at Millwall the following day.

The directors had done their best to make the company successful and courted every inquiry into their accounts which had been admirably kept by Mr Everest. Liabilities amounted to £989 6s. 4d. and assets to just £60, the latter comprising money owed by other clubs. United's bank-balance was a sorry £1 0s. 9d. The resolution was carried unanimously and Edgar Everest was appointed as liquidator. Meaden closed by saying that he still hoped a professional football club would one day be

BRIGHTON UNITED — SEASON 1899–1900

Date	Comp.	Ven.	Opponents	Result	HT	Pos.	Scorers	Atten.
Sep 2	SL D1	(a)	Queen's Park R.	L 0–6	0–4	13=		5,500
5	T & M Comb.	(a)	Sheppey United	W 2–1	1–0	1	McArthur 2	500
9	SL D1	(a)	Bedminster	L 1–3	1–1	15	Malloch	3,000
16	SL D1	(h)	Bristol Rovers	L 1–2	1–1	16	Willocks	3,000
20	T & M Comb.	(h)	Sheppey United	W 1–0	1–0	1	Malloch	'fairly well patronised'
23	SL D1	(a)	Portsmouth	L 1–3	0–2	17	Oakden	6,000
30	FAC Q1	(h)	Eastbourne	W 6–1	2–1	–	Hill 2, Malloch, Williams, Willocks, Parry	1,000
Oct 4	SL D1	(h)	Thames Ironworks	L 0–1	0–0	17		700
7	SL D1	(a)	Tottenham H'spur	L 1–6	0–2	17	Oakden	6,500
14	FAC Q2	(h)	Brighton Athletic	W 9–0	7–0	–	Malloch, Sharp 3, Hill 3, Oakden, Mercer	1,400
21	SL D1	(a)	Gravesend	L 1–3	0–2	17	Oakden	'moderate'
23	T & M Comb.	(a)	New Brompton	W 2–1	1–1	2	Willocks, Malloch	'small'
28	FAC Q3	(a)	Chatham	L 0–2	0–0	–		2,500
Nov 1	T & M Comb.	(h)	Gravesend	W 3–0	1–0	1	Mercer, Sharp, Hill	950
4	SL D1	(a)	Bristol City	L 2–3	1–2	17	Hill 2	2,000
11	SL D1*	(h)	Cowes*	W 5–1	3–1	17	Davidson 2, Malloch, Hill, Mercer	2,000
18	SL D1	(a)	Southampton	L 1–4	1–3	17	Farrell	4,000
22	T & M Comb.	(a)	Chatham	L 1–2	0–1		Mills	'small'
25	SL D1	(h)	Millwall	L 0–2	0–0	17		3,000
29	T & M Comb.	(h)	Thames Ironworks	W 5–3	3–2	1	Davidson 2, McArthur, Mercer 2	'limited'
Dec 9	SL D1	(h)	Chatham	D 1–1	0–0	17	Baker	2,000
16	SL D1	(h)	Reading	W 4–2	2–1	16	Baker, Davidson, Malloch, Hill	2,000
23	SL D1	(h)	Sheppey United	W 3–2	3–0	16	Davidson 2, Hill	1,200
25	SL D1	(a)	Reading	D 1–1	1–1	16	Malloch	6,000
Jan 6	SL D1	(h)	Bedminster	L 1–4	1–1	16	Malloch	2,500
10	SL D1	(h)	Queen's Park R.	W 2–1	1–1	16	Oakden, Malloch	1,000
13	SL D1	(a)	Bristol Rovers	L 0–2	0–0	15		2,000
20	SL D1	(h)	Portsmouth	L 1–2	1–2	16	Hill	600
27	SL D1	(a)	New Brompton	L 0–2	0–0	15		1,200
Feb 3	SL D1	(a)	Thames Ironworks	L 1–2	1–1	15	Hill	'very few'
7	SL D1	(h)	Swindon Town	D 2–2	0–1	15	Hill, Davidson	800
10	SL D1	(h)	Tottenham H'spur	L 0–3	0–0	15		1,800
17	SL D1	(a)	New Brompton	L 0–1	0–1	16		1,000
24	SL D1	(h)	Gravesend	L 0–2	0–1	16		1,000
Mar 3	SL D1	(a)	Swindon Town	L 0–4	0–2	16		2,000
7	T & M Comb.	(h)	Grays United	W 1–0	0–0	2	Hill	'poor'
10	SL D1	(h)	Bristol City	D 1–1	0–0	16	Hill	'moderate'
21	T & M Comb.	(h)	New Brompton	L 0–4	0–1	3		'moderate'
24	T & M Comb.	(h)	Chatham	L 0–1	0–1	3		500

Player columns (left to right): Ashby H, Baker H, Collins E, Davidson J, Farrell P, Hadden S, Harland A, Harrison J, Hill R, Howes A, Low J, McArthur W, McAvoy F, Malloch J, Mercer J, Mills A, Norman W, Oakden H, Parry M, Sharp A, Spicer T, Sutherland J, Turner R, Williams C, Willocks D.

End-of-season summary:

	Ashby H	Baker H	Collins E	Davidson J	Farrell P	Hadden S	Harland A	Harrison J	Hill R	Howes A	Low J	McArthur W	McAvoy F	Malloch J	Mercer J	Mills A	Norman W	Oakden H	Parry M	Sharp A	Spicer T	Sutherland J	Turner R	Williams C	Willocks D
Southern League appearances	8	7	1	16	20	3	3	1	23	10	19	16	23	21	20	25	0	13	26	5	16	1	1	3	5
Southern League goals		2		4	1				8					5				4							1
Thames & Medway Combination appearances	3	1	3	5	5	3	2	1	4	1	6	8	8	7	6	5	1	3	8	4	8	1	1	0	5
Thames & Medway Combination goals				2					2			3		2	3	1				1					1

Notes: Home matches played at the County Ground.

Nov 11 – Cowes withdrew from the Southern League around Dec 21 and their matches were deleted from the record. This match is not included in the end-of-season Southern League statistics.

Brighton United were wound up on Mar 29; the four outstanding Southern League fixtures and three outstanding Thames & Medway Combination fixtures were never played.

Southern League Division 1 1899–1900 (at 29.3.1900)

		P	W	D	L	F	A	W	D	L	F	A	Pts
1.	Tottenham Hotspur	24	11	1	0	40	9	6	3	3	20	12	38
2.	Portsmouth	24	13	0	0	38	6	4	1	6	11	18	35
3.	Southampton	20	9	0	2	48	9	5	1	3	14	9	29
4.	Reading	26	9	2	2	24	7	4	0	9	15	23	28
5.	Swindon Town	24	11	0	1	26	9	2	2	8	16	25	28
6.	Bedminster	23	8	1	2	23	15	5	0	7	18	23	27
7.	Millwall	22	8	0	4	23	16	4	2	4	11	11	26
8.	New Brompton	26	7	3	2	25	14	3	2	9	14	31	25
9.	Bristol City	24	8	0	5	30	25	0	7	4	10	18	23
10.	Bristol Rovers	24	7	2	2	27	12	3	1	9	16	36	23
11.	Queen's Park R.	22	6	2	2	24	9	4	0	8	21	31	22
12.	Gravesend	24	7	4	2	27	19	2	0	9	8	27	22
13.	Thames Ironworks	25	5	3	3	11	7	2	1	11	11	32	18
14.	Chatham	25	7	1	4	22	14	0	2	11	12	43	17
15.	Sheppey United	23	1	3	7	8	22	2	2	8	14	35	11
16.	**BRIGHTON UNITED**	26	3	3	8	16	27	0	1	11	9	38	10

Note: Cowes withdrew from the League in December.

Southern League Division 1 1899–1900

		P	W	D	L	F	A	W	D	L	F	A	Pts
1.	Tottenham Hotspur	28	13	1	0	42	8	7	3	4	25	18	44
2.	Portsmouth	28	14	0	0	39	5	6	1	7	20	24	41
3.	Southampton	28	11	0	3	53	14	6	1	7	18	19	35
4.	Reading	28	10	2	2	25	6	5	0	9	16	22	32
5.	Swindon Town	28	12	1	1	30	11	3	1	10	20	31	32
6.	Bedminster	28	9	1	4	27	18	4	1	9	17	27	28
7.	Millwall	28	9	0	5	25	17	3	3	8	11	20	27
8.	Queen's Park R.	28	8	2	4	28	19	4	0	10	21	38	26
9.	Bristol City	28	9	0	5	33	23	0	7	7	10	23	25
10.	Bristol Rovers	28	9	2	3	31	16	2	1	11	15	39	25
11.	New Brompton	28	7	3	4	26	17	2	3	9	13	32	24
12.	Gravesend	28	7	4	3	28	25	3	0	11	10	34	24
13.	Chatham	28	9	1	4	26	16	1	2	11	12	42	23
14.	Thames Ironworks	28	6	4	4	13	9	2	1	11	11	32	21
15.	Sheppey United	28	1	5	8	10	25	2	2	10	14	41	13

Note: Cowes withdrew from the League in December, and Brighton United withdrew on 29.3.1900.

Thames & Medway Combination 1899–1900 (at 29.3.1900)

		P	W	D	L	F	A	W	D	L	F	A	Pts
1.	New Brompton	11	4	0	1	12	3	4	1	1	12	5	17
2.	Chatham	10	3	2	1	13	8	3	1	0	7	3	15
3.	**BRIGHTON UNITED**	9	4	0	2	10	8	2	0	1	5	4	12
4.	Thames Ironworks	10	4	2	0	19	5	0	3	2	7	11	10
5.	Gravesend	8	3	0	0	9	3	1	2	2	4	8	10
6.	Sheppey United	9	0	1	3	4	7	0	0	5	4	15	1
7.	Grays United	9	0	1	3	2	8	0	0	5	3	23	1

Thames & Medway Combination 1899–1900

		P	W	D	L	F	A	W	D	L	F	A	Pts
1.	New Brompton	10	5	0	0	12	1	3	1	1	8	5	17
2.	Chatham	10	2	2	1	11	7	3	1	1	9	5	13
3.	Thames Ironworks	10	4	2	0	19	5	0	4	1	5	7	11
4.	Gravesend	10	3	1	1	11	7	1	2	2	5	7	11
5.	Sheppey United	10	1	2	2	6	7	0	1	4	5	15	5
6.	Grays United	10	0	2	3	3	9	0	1	4	4	23	3

Note: Brighton United withdrew from the Combination on 29.3.1900.

In January 1900 an F.A. Emergency Committee censured United for an illegal approach to North End Rangers' Jim Sutherland, who went on to play for United, Brighton and Hove Rangers, and the Albion. The committee found that

the spirit of Rule 37 had been violated, or rather neglected, by Brighton United; and that it would be sufficient if this were pointed out to both clubs, and a caution administered to Brighton United Football Club.

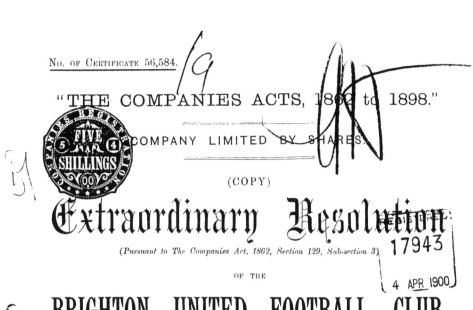

No. of Certificate 56,584.

"THE COMPANIES ACTS, 1862 to 1898."

COMPANY LIMITED BY SHARES.

(COPY)

Extraordinary Resolution

(Pursuant to The Companies Act, 1862, Section 129, Sub-section 3)

17943

4 APR 1900

OF THE

BRIGHTON UNITED FOOTBALL CLUB,
LIMITED.

Passed 29th March, 1900.

At an EXTRAORDINARY GENERAL MEETING of the Members of the above-named Company, duly convened, and held at the Imperial Hotel, Brighton, in the County of Sussex, on the 29th day of March, 1900, the following EXTRAORDINARY RESOLUTION was duly passed :—

> "That it has been proved to the satisfaction of the Company that it cannot, by reason of its liabilities, continue its business, and that it is advisable to wind up the same, and accordingly that the Company be wound up voluntarily; and that EDGAR WILLIAM EVEREST, of 9 Westhill Road, Brighton, be appointed Liquidator for the purpose of winding up the affairs of the Company."

Witness to the Signature of

Chas. Meaden
Chairman.

John _____
Solicitor,
BRIGHTON.

Filed with the Registrar of Joint Stock Companies on the 4th day of April, 1900.

JORDAN & SONS, LIMITED,
COMPANY REGISTRATION AGENTS, PRINTERS, PUBLISHERS, AND STATIONERS,
120 CHANCERY LANE, AND BELL YARD, LONDON, W.C.

Death certificate of a football club
This document confirms the failure of the first attempt to establish a professional football club in Brighton and Hove.

established in Brighton. (His hopes were to be realised, but if Southampton hadn't reached the English Cup semi-final in 1900 we might well have been supporting Brighton United at the Goldstone today!)

In May 1900 a Football Association commission was appointed to inquire into the affairs of United, and in August reported that

> there was no reckless trading and Brighton United had been managed with due care up to the date of liquidation.

The suspension of the now-defunct club and its officials was lifted. A general meeting of the company on 16 January 1901 discharged Mr Everest from his duties and Brighton United was officially laid to rest two days later.

United entertained a touring team of black South Africans known as 'The Kaffirs' at the County Ground on Boxing Day. In a light-hearted game United won 10–5, Bob Hill cracking a beauty past his own goalkeeper much to the merriment of the crowd. The tourists played some 40 matches in Britain but failed to win a single game, being beaten by some huge scores.

Brighton United First-team friendly matches 1899–1900

Date	Opponents			Scorers
Sep 27	Notts County	(h)	3–1	Williams 2, McArthur
Oct 11	Richmond Association	(h)	5–0	Mercer 2, Hill, H. Oakden, McAvoy
Oct 18	Queen's Park Rangers	(h)	3–0	Malloch 2, McAvoy
Nov 9	Ryde	(a)	1–1	Mercer
Nov 15	Hastings & St Leonards	(a)	6–1	Malloch 2, Davidson, Hill, Farrell, Mercer
For the Transvaal War Fund:				
Dec 2	Dolphins	(h)	1–1	McArthur
Dec 26	The Kaffirs	(h)	10–5	Hill 3, Baker 2, Sutherland, Mercer 2, Malloch 2
Dec 27	Brighton Athletic	(h)	7–0	Davidson 2, Sharp, Parry 4
Feb 28	Wellingborough Town	(h)	0–0	
Mar 14	Eastbourne	(a)	0–2	

Brighton United players 1898–1900

Players marked with an asterisk (*) also played for the Albion. Statistics include all matches played by Brighton United except 14.1.1899 v. Warmley and 11.11.1899 v. Cowes which were deleted from the record because of the withdrawal of those clubs from the Southern League.

Player	SL		FAC		Utd League		T & M Comb.	
ASHBY, Harry	8	–	3	–	–	–	3	–
BAKER, Bert *	7	2 gls	–	–	–	–	1	–
BULLIMER, Leo	15	–	5	–	13	–	–	–
CALDWELL, Jock *	21	–	5	–	19	1 gl	–	–
CARTER, John	7	–	1	–	8	–	–	–
CLARK, Joe	6	–	–	–	5	–	–	–
COLLINS, Ned *	1	–	–	–	–	–	3	–
DAVIDSON, Jimmy	31	4 gls	4	–	9	1 gl	5	2 gls
FARRELL, Paddy *	36	1 gl	4	–	12	–	5	–
FREEMAN, Stan	1	–	–	–	–	–	–	–
HADDEN, Sid	3	–	–	–	–	–	3	–
HALMAN, Charles	–	–	–	–	1	–	–	–
HARLAND, Alf *	3	–	–	–	–	–	2	–
HARRISON, John	1	–	–	–	–	–	1	–
HENDRY, Willie	21	1 gl	4	–	14	–	–	–
HILL, Bob	23	8 gls	3	5 gls	–	–	4	2 gls
HOWES, Arthur *	10	–	–	–	–	–	1	–
LONGAIR, Bill	22	2 gls	5	1 gl	17	–	–	–
LOW, John	29	–	6	–	13	–	6	–
McARTHUR, Willie	36	10 gls	8	4 gls	17	6 gls	8	3 gls
McAVOY, Frank *	43	–	3	–	15	1 gl	8	–
McLEOD, Roddy	19	14 gls	5	4 gls	17	11 gls	–	–
McWHIRTER, Peter	16	1 gl	2	–	15	4 gls	–	–
MALLOCH, Jock	40	6 gls	8	5 gls	11	–	7	2 gls
MERCER, Toby	20	–	2	1 gl	–	–	6	3 gls
MILLS, Andy	25	–	3	–	–	–	5	1 gl
NORMAN, Walter	–	–	–	–	–	–	1	–
OAKDEN, Harry	13	4 gls	2	1 gl	–	–	–	–
PAIGE, Jimmy	2	–	–	–	5	3 gls	–	–
PARRY, Maurice	26	–	3	1 gl	–	–	8	–
SHARP, Alf *	6	–	1	3 gls	2	–	4	1 gl
SPICER, Tom	25	–	3	–	7	–	8	–
SUTHERLAND, Jim *	1	–	–	–	–	–	1	–
TURNER, Bob	1	–	–	–	–	–	1	–
WILLIAMS, Conde	3	–	1	1 gl	–	–	–	–
WILLOCKS, Davie	29	8 gls	7	5 gls	19	10 gls	5	1 gl

OUT OF THE ASHES — BRIGHTON & HOVE RANGERS 1900–01

On the collapse of Brighton United the professional players dispersed and went their separate ways: Maurice Parry to Liverpool, to win fame as a Welsh internationalist; Paddy Farrell to Belfast Distillery, to win Irish caps against Wales and Scotland during the coming season; Andy Mills to Leicester Fosse; Jock Malloch to Sheffield Wednesday, to win League championship medals in 1903 and 1904; Tom Spicer to Woolwich Arsenal; and Jimmy Davidson to Burnley.

Having tasted the big time, several influential United supporters led by shareholder William Avenell, a West Street photographer, decided to continue the struggle to raise the standard of football in the area, this time with an amateur side which could attract the best of local players – most of them having appeared for Brighton United – to play against some first-class opposition. It was seen by the Press as 'consolation after the disbandment of the Brighton United professionals'. With these aims in mind, an approach was made to one of the leading clubs in Brighton.

North End Rangers, members of the Brighton and Hove F.A., were formed in 1891 and had progressed rapidly with some success. They lost the Sussex Junior Cup final to Hastings Amateur Athletic in 1893 but won the trophy in 1895, defeating Shoreham 5–0 at the County Ground. In 1894 they triumphed in the Brighton Challenge Cup and became founder members of the East Sussex League in 1896, winning the championship in its first season. The champions of the East and West Sussex

Leagues competed for the Royal Irish Rifles Charity Cup at the end of the season, and Rangers lost 3–2 to Southwick at Beach House Park, Worthing. In 1898–99, however, the club hit hard times and, unable to complete its fixtures, resigned from the League, continuing to play friendly matches and cup-ties only. From its inception North End Rangers had played in Preston Park along with the other leading clubs, but in May 1900 Brighton Council gave notice that the turf in part of the park was to be relaid in October and that some pitches would be unavailable until further notice.

Faced with the possibility of losing their pitch, North End Rangers accepted the overtures from Avenell and his colleagues in what amounted to a virtual takeover, and, with the permission of the F.A., the name of the reorganised club was changed to 'Brighton and Hove Rangers' in order to demonstrate its wider scope. A committee of eight was formed with Avenell as chairman and treasurer, and Harry Rose of North End Rangers as secretary. A great servant of the game locally for many years, Rose was the leading figure in the formation of the Brighton, Hove and District League in 1903 and was assistant secretary of the local Schools F.A. The other members of the committee were W. Barbour, W. Marks, H. W. Stringer, W. Sandifer, G. Kelly and G. Drury.

An arrangement was made with a local farmer, David Hampton, for a private ground at Home Farm, Withdean, at a cost of £30 per season for two years. Admission charges were fixed at 3*d.*, although the more prestigious fixtures would be charged at 6*d.* (2·5p), while season tickets could be obtained for 5 shillings (25p). Membership of the club cost 1 guinea (£1.05). Rangers decided to compete for the English Cup, the Sussex Senior Cup and the Brighton Challenge Shield, but, because of the great expense and the stringent rules involved, declined to enter the Amateur Cup.

On Friday, 20 July 1900, a public meeting was held at the Black Lion Shades in Black Lion Street to inform supporters of

On 22 January 1901, Queen Victoria died in her 64th year as sovereign. Her funeral was held on Saturday, 2 February, and the first round of the English Cup and all Football League and Southern League matches were postponed. Brighton and Hove Rangers were due to play F.C. Français, a representative team of French international players, in Paris the following day, but the trip was called off.

the progress thus far. Among those present were ex-United trainer-manager John Jackson, now landlord of the Farm Tavern in Farm Road, Hove, and two of his former players, Jim Sutherland and Bert Baker.

Having explained the arrangements, William Avenell made an appeal to the audience, and to the public in general, to subscribe to the club. Thus far £19 had been raised, but £50 would be required if the Rangers were to open their programme on 1 September. John Jackson was optimistic about the club's chances, as this extract from the *Brighton and Hove Times* confirms:

Mr Jackson thought the team would be able to hold its own and give any team a good game, and said never was there a club started with better prospects. They had a good ground capable of holding, with comfort, 10,000 people [!]. It was close to the railway and as easy of access as the County Ground. There was no heavy wage-bill, and all that was wanted was a few pounds to put the club on a good footing. It was sure to pay for itself.

(John Jackson's involvement with Brighton and Hove Rangers appears to be fleeting. Although present at this inaugural meeting, he was not a committee member and was not mentioned again by the local Press until the following June. He was probably a passive supporter. Indeed, he could well have been one of the United officials suspended by the F.A.)

Home Farmhouse, Withdean
Brighton and Hove Rangers played their home games behind this nineteenth-century flint cottage, which can still be seen at the junction of London Road and Peacock Lane. Their pitch is still an open space, now known as Surrenden Field, at the bottom of Surrenden Crescent.

The meeting concluded with the passing of a resolution to carry on with the club. The *Brighton Gazette* enthused about the calibre of the men in charge, adding that Rangers 'enjoy the support of many influential gentlemen'. The *Gazette* concluded: 'The club is doing everything possible to ensure its popularity, and its outlook is certainly most promising.'

A covered stand, with dressing-rooms, refreshment bar and accommodation for the Press, was erected on the Withdean ground at a cost of £60, and by September everything was ready for the opening fixture. Described as a 'fine, level field', the pitch was situated on the eastern side of the London Road in the parish of Patcham, opposite Tongdean Lane and less than half a mile from the terminus of the horse-bus routes at Clermont Road (which was also the limit of the county borough of Brighton until 1928). The area was completely rural apart from a number of large villa residences that lined the London Road as far as the new ground.

The nucleus of the club's playing staff was the rump of the North End Rangers side – Alfred Crunden, Frank Crunden, John Harrison, William Kerry, F. Mitchell and Herbert Mott – together with a number of players who had made appearances in the Brighton United first team: Bert Baker, Stan Freeman, Alf Sharp and Jim Sutherland, the latter pair former professionals reinstated as amateurs. The long-serving North End Rangers skipper, Alfred Crunden, was also appointed captain of Brighton and Hove Rangers. Some leading amateurs from the Midlands and elsewhere were brought in to bolster the side, and in addition the following advertisement appeared in the local Press throughout August:

> Brighton and Hove Rangers are prepared to receive applications from good amateur players – small subscriptions – apply H. E. Rose, 16 Viaduct-road.

The club's inaugural match was played at Home Farm on 1 September 1900 against a strong Clapton side, and around 400 spectators paid a 6*d.* entrance fee to be entertained prior to the game by the Hove Brass Band. Rangers were represented by the following team:

Squire Whitehurst; John Harrison and Alfred Crunden (captain); William Kerry, Jim Sutherland and F. Mitchell; Bert Baker, Albert Smith, Frank Dollman, Alf Sharp and Herbert Mott.

The Mayor of Brighton, Alderman John Stafford, ceremoniously kicked off at a quarter past four with Rangers defending the north goal. The match ended in a goal-less draw, a very encouraging result against a club which had been established for more than 20 years, and the crowd was well behaved,

March 4th, 1901: Aston Villa arrived at the County Ground to play a match with Sussex for the benefit of Edgar Everest, the County F.A. secretary and founder of Brighton United. The reigning League champions travelled down from London where they had beaten the Corinthians 1–0 in the Sheriff of London's Charity Shield match (forerunner of the F.A. Charity Shield) at The Crystal Palace two days earlier. The star-studded First Division side cantered to a 4–0 victory in front of 2,500 spectators. Brighton and Hove Rangers' Jim Sutherland turned out at centre-half for Sussex.

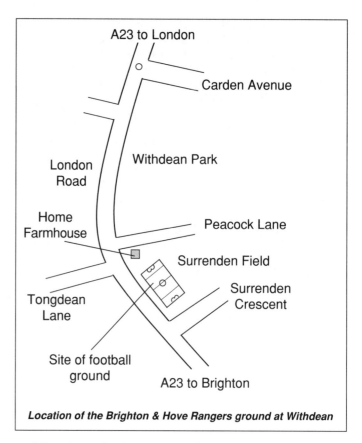

Location of the Brighton & Hove Rangers ground at Withdean

enabling the authorities to grant the club an occasional licence for the sale of liquor. The first win came a week later with a 3–0 victory over Southampton reserves, and a club dinner was held with satisfaction on 13 September. Right-back John Harrison told the assembly that there was a 'jolly good feeling among all the players', and he was sure the team would prove itself the best in Sussex. It was hoped that the early success would lead to a large increase in subscribers. The evening's entertainment was provided by the players.

As the season wore on, some excellent opposition was brought in from outside Sussex as had been promised and results continued to give cause for optimism. There were good wins over Portsmouth 'A' (2–1), Fulham reserves (7–1) and the Irish Corinthians (4–0), coupled with creditable draws with Queen's Park Rangers reserves, Leicester Fosse and West Ham United, the latter two sides fielding their first elevens. There was also a narrow defeat (1–2) at the hands of New Brompton's Southern League side.

The ground, which must have been second only to the County Ground in the area, also staged other prestigious matches. Sussex drew two-all with Surrey at Withdean on 12 December with Rangers' Squire Whitehurst, John Harrison, Jim Sutherland and Bert Baker in the side; and Brighton Boys played Portsmouth Boys (2–2) before giving way to their senior counterparts on 1 December.

In the English Cup the team proved its superiority over Sussex sides, defeating Eastbourne 3–0 and Brighton Athletic 4–0 before losing 5–1 to the professionals of Chatham in the third qualifying round, all staged at Home Farm. With the exception of cup matches played on neutral grounds, Rangers played only four away games all season. One of these was at the Oxen Field, home of Shoreham F.C., on 15 December, a third-round Sussex Senior Cup tie. The Brighton side won 2–0, but there was trouble after the match, as reported by the *Brighton and Hove Times*:

BRIGHTON & HOVE RANGERS SEASON 1900–01

Date	Comp.	Ven.	Opponents	Result	HT	Pos.	Scorers	Atten.	Baker H	Breeds B	Clayton T	Crunden A	Crunden F	Curling J	Dollman F	Freeman S	Frew S	Harrison J	Horsnall A	Jupp R	Kerry W	Mansfield W	Mitchell F	Mott H	Petty G	Sharp A	Smith Albert	Standen A	Steel A	Sutherland J	Whitehurst S
Oct 6	FAC Q1	(h)	Eastbourne	W 3–0	2–0	–	Curling, Baker 2	1,000	7		3		11	10	6		2				4					9	8			5	1
20	FAC Q2	(h*)	Brighton Athletic	W 4–0	1–0	–	Smith, Sharp 3	1,000	7		2			10		3					4		6	11		9	8			5	1
Nov 3	FAC Q3	(h)	Chatham	L 1–5	1–2	–	Baker	2,000	7		2			10	4	3							6		11	9	8			5	1
10	BCC R1	(h)	Preston Wanderers	W 5–0	1–0	–	Sharp, F Crunden, Petty, Dollman, Own goal	'small'			2	7		10	6	3							4		11	9	8			5	1
17	BCS R1	(h)	Brighton Havelock	W 4–1	3–0	–	A Crunden 2, Smith (pen.), Mott	'meagre'				9	7	10	2	3				4			6	11			8			5	1
24	Susx SC R2	(h)	Brighton Athletic	W 2–1	0–0	–	Smith, Baker	'not large'	7		2			10		3				4			6	11		9	8			5	1
Dec 15	Susx SC R3	(a)	Shoreham	W 2–0	0–0	–	Dollman, Sharp	'good'	7		2		11	10		3		4					6			9	8			5	1
Feb 16	Susx SC SF	(n*)	Hove	W 2–1	0–1	–	Curling, Sharp	1,000			3	10	11	6		2							4			9	8			5	1
20	BCS SF	(n*)	Glengall Rovers	D 2–2	0–1	–	F Crunden, Sharp		7	11	3		10			2							6			9	8	4		5	1
Mar 9	BCS SF Rep	(n*)	Glengall Rovers	W 2–1	2–0	–	Baker 2	700	7		3	8	10			6										11	9		4	5	1
16	Susx SC F	(n*)	Eastbourne	L 1–3	1–2	–	Clayton	2,600			2	8	11	9	3								6		4	10	7			5	1
23	BCS F	(n*)	Brighton Athletic	D 2–2	2–1	–	Clayton, Sharp	800				8			6	3						10	2	4	11	9	7			5	1
27	BCS F Rep	(n*)	Brighton Athletic	L 2–3	2–2	–	Dollman, Sharp	400					8		5					6	11	10	3			9	4	7	2		1
30	BCC SF*	(n*)	Brighton Athletic	– –	–	–	–	–																							

Notes: Home matches played at Home Farm, Withdean.

Oct 20 – tie drawn away but switched to Home Farm.

Feb 16, Feb 20, Mar 9, Mar 16, Mar 23, and Mar 27 – matches played at the County Ground, Hove.

Mar 30 – Rangers withdrew from the match, due to be played at Preston Park, because they were unable to raise a team.

Good Friday, 1901: a charity match was played at Withdean between Rangers and a Harry Rose XI dressed in comic costumes. (Such matches were not uncommon at the turn of the century and attracted good crowds.) Play was of the 'go-as-you-please order', and the Pierrot, the Boer and two players in feminine garb were particularly impressive for the Costume XI. In the second half the Costume XI adopted normal playing-strip as their apparel became too hot. Final score was 3–3.

As usual, there was a disorderly scene subsequently to the match in the lane leading to the station [now Buckingham Road], the Shoreham supporters taking their defeat in a very unsportsmanlike manner.

Rangers beat Hove in the semi-final to reach the final at the County Ground, but lost 3–1 to Eastbourne who thereby registered a hat-trick of triumphs in the competition and gained ample revenge for their English Cup defeat. Skippered by England international Arthur Topham, the Eastbourne side faced a good deal of hostility from the near-3,000 crowd which was largely behind the local men, but took the honours comfortably. Rangers started the game with only ten men when their left-wing 'flyer', Joseph Curling, failed to arrive on time. A second lieutenant with the Royal Field Artillery stationed at Preston Barracks, Curling turned up some minutes after his place had been taken by Frank Crunden, but, to the consternation of the Rangers' supporters, the referee – quite correctly – refused to allow the pair to swap.

Rangers were also beaten in the final of the Brighton Challenge Shield, Brighton Athletic triumphing 3–2 in a replay to register their third win in the six years of the trophy; they had also been runners-up on two occasions. Feelings between the two clubs ran high for a time. Athletic had been the leading team in the town before the advent of Brighton and Hove Rangers, and they had lost Frank Dollman and Stan Freeman to the newcomers. Rangers had also, by mistake, appropriated and altered two Athletic crossbars, a matter which was settled by the County F.A. On the Saturday following the Shield final, Rangers were due to meet Brighton Athletic again in the Brighton Charity Cup semi-final in Preston Park, but withdrew from the match stating that they were unable to raise a team. Relations improved by the end of the season, though, with several of the Rangers players invited to the Athletic's annual dinner.

Brighton & Hove Rangers First-team friendly matches

Date	Opponents		Scorers
Sep 1	Clapton	(h) 0–0	
Sep 8	Southampton (res.)	(h) 3–0	Petty, Sharp, Dollman
Sep 15	Royal Field Artillery (Preston Barracks)	(h) 5–1	Sharp 4, Dollman
Sep 22	Crouch End Vampires	(h) 0–2	
Sep 29	Eastleigh	(h) 2–3	Sharp, Baker
Oct 13	Borough Polytechnic	(h) 2–3	Dollman, Smith
Oct 27	Romford	(h) 3–2	Smith, Petty, Dollman
Dec 1	Portsmouth ('A')	(h) 2–1	Sutherland, Dollman
Dec 8	Worthing	(a) 2–0	Sutherland, Smith
Dec 22	Fulham (res.)	(h) 7–1	Baker 4 (1 pen.), Smith, F. Crunden, Sharp
Dec 26	Queen's Park Rangers (res.)	(h) 2–2	?
Dec 29	Portsmouth (res.)	(a) 0–3	
Jan 5	Willesden Town	(h) 6–2	Gibson 3, Own goal, Sharp, Baker (pen.)
Jan 12	Clapton (res.)	(h) 2–0	Baker, Own goal
Jan 19	Royal Horse Artillery (Woolwich)	(h) 5–0	Dollman, Smith 2, Sharp 2
Feb 9	Burgess Hill	(h) 3–0	Sharp, Mansfield 2
Feb 23	Eastbourne Old Town	(a) 2–4	Sharp, Sutherland
Apr 5	Harry Rose's Costume XI	(h) 3–3	?
Apr 6	Crouch End Vampires	(h) 3–2	Sutherland, Smith (pen.), Own goal
Apr 8	New Brompton	(h) 1–2	Sharp
Apr 10	Irish Corinthians	(h) 4–0	Smith, Lewis, Barge 2
Apr 13	Leicester Fosse	(h) 0–0	
Above match had 30-minute first half, 40-minute second half because of weather conditions			
Apr 20	HMS Pembroke (Chatham)	(h) 0–3	
Apr 27	West Ham United	(h) 1–1	Barge

Nearly 50 players wore the club's black-and-white striped shirts, yet, from a playing viewpoint, it was a highly successful initial campaign. Some first-class professional opposition had been attracted to Withdean, previously almost unknown amongst local amateur clubs, and had been well matched; and two finals had been reached, including that of the county's premier competition. The achievements of the season did not go unnoticed in other quarters and in the last week of April, following a meeting of the Southern League management committee in London, Rangers were invited to join the Second Division for the 1901–02 season. (It is an interesting point that the secretary of the Southern League, Nat Whittaker, had refereed the recent Sussex Senior Cup final with Eastbourne.)

THE BIRTH OF THE ALBION

(The events of the 1901 close season gave life to the Brighton and Hove Albion club we know today, but, over 90 years later, they are shrouded in mystery and confusion. Popular history has it that Brighton and Hove Rangers simply turned professional and changed their name to Albion. Unfortunately, all relevant documents of the main parties involved have been lost; the only contemporary written sources remaining are the records of the Football Association and the newspapers of the period. Extensive research into these sources has revealed a different story.)

Brighton and Hove Rangers responded to the Southern League's invitation and, on 1 May, were provisionally accepted into the Second Division at a management committee meeting. Three days later the *Southern Weekly News* informed its readers that the club was to drop the 'Rangers' suffix. The League's a.g.m. was held on 1 June in Fleet Street, London, and *The Sportsman*, a daily sporting newspaper published in the capital, records that 'Brighton and Hove Rangers' were formally elected. So Rangers were still operating at the beginning of June and circulars were distributed to the local Press under the new name of 'Brighton and Hove Club':

BRIGHTON AND HOVE CLUB

Mr John Jackson, who has been actively promoting next season's arrangements for the Brighton and Hove Club, has received a letter from Mr W. Newham, Secretary of the Sussex County Cricket Club, stating that the Committee has decided to grant the Club the use of the County Ground next season for matches in the Second Division of the Southern League. On Saturday, Mr Jackson attended a meeting of the Southern League when the Club's application for admission to the League was granted.

John Jackson was, of course, the former trainer-manager of Brighton United. Since the collapse of that club he had been landlord of the Farm Tavern and, apart from his appearance at the inaugural meeting of Brighton and Hove Rangers in July 1900, this appears to have been his first active involvement in football since that time. Rangers probably intended turning professional under their new title of 'Brighton and Hove' and engaged the most experienced football professional in the town to assist them.

However, despite its playing successes and the prospect of Southern League football, the club's plans went awry. The local Press (see below) reports that Rangers were a failure and disbanded, becoming the subject of an F.A. investigation. The inquiry dragged on for some months, for, on 8 January 1902, the former Rangers chairman and treasurer William Avenell was prompted to ask a meeting of the Sussex County F.A. when the matter would be resolved. He was informed that the following telegram had been received from Mr Frederick Wall, the F.A. secretary, that very day:

After our discussion we agreed to take no further action re Brighton and Hove Rangers.

The specific reason for the club's demise and the F.A. inquiry remains unknown and can only be guessed at; the Football Association's minutes make no mention of the matter and the local newspapers are almost as unhelpful. One possibility is that Rangers were accused of professional activities during the season just passed, a heinous crime that led to the downfall of several other clubs. They had, after all, brought in amateurs from other parts of the country in order to establish themselves as the leading club in the area; arrangements presumably had to be made for the welfare of these outside players. Such an accusation would would certainly have been a matter for an inquiry by the Association.

Perhaps the club was also insolvent, or heading for insolvency with the prospect of greatly increased expenses in the Southern League and a private ground to maintain, the inaccessibility of which restricted gates. A hint of financial trouble had been reported in the *Brighton Gazette* of 2 May 1901:

Although a new club, it has shown an enterprising spirit in arranging matches with big London and other important teams, previously almost unknown among local amateur clubs; but it is feared their financial reward is not commensurate therewith.

Like Brighton United, the club may not have been able to pay guarantees to opponents in friendly matches, another situation which would have provoked scrutiny from the F.A.

There is also the notion that the club, which had 'poached' a number of local players, did not meet with general approval in the town and may therefore have lacked adequate support; note the phrase '… toward a new Club provided that it meets with the approbation of Brightonians in general' in the circular of 14 June below. If the intention had been to turn professional, financial and political problems could have made the move impossible and led to disbandment. There also appeared to be some difficulty in getting players to turn out: the club had had to scratch from the Brighton Charity Cup, and had drafted soldiers from Preston Barracks on other occasions. Whatever the specific reason, Avenell put the general failure down to a lack of clear leadership from the rather large committee.

John Jackson, founder of
Brighton and Hove Albion Football Club
The former manager of Brighton United was the driving-force behind the movement that led to the formation of the Albion in June 1901.

Brighton and Hove Rangers, the phoenix risen from the ashes of Brighton United, was itself dead.

Jackson, no doubt dismayed at a second soccer failure in the town, then took centre-stage and pressed ahead with the Brighton and Hove Club, now presumably just a name with a place in the Southern League's Second Division and a pitch at the County Ground. The Rangers' collapse probably came in early June as a second circular, issued on 14 June, solicited support for a 'new' club to be run on semi-professional lines:

BRIGHTON AND HOVE FOOTBALL CLUB

It having been the wish of many people of Brighton and Hove that our towns should be properly represented in the football world, many influential supporters have promised assistance toward a new Club provided that it meets with the approbation of Brightonians in general. One of the hardest matters has been successfully dealt with, and the County Ground has been secured on very reasonable terms. The Club have been elected to the Southern League (Division II), and have fair hopes of ultimately getting into Division I, a position which Brighton and Hove ought to occupy. The idea is to run the Club on semi-professional lines. Support has been received from many of Brighton's best footballers, some of whom may be remembered as belonging to the previous professional organisation. According to the support others will be engaged, and at the moment many men whose names are household ones in Brighton and the South are eager to come. The efforts in securing the ground and the admittance to the League, the fixtures of which are nearly complete, are due to the energy displayed by Mr J. Jackson, whose previous experience in football should be of great service to the new Club. A meeting of supporters will be held in due course, notice of which will be given. All communication should be addressed to Mr John Jackson, 13, Farm-road, Hove.

The *Sussex Evening Times*, whose proprietor was William Nash, an ex-director of Brighton United, was not confident about the new venture:

PROFESSIONALISM IN BRIGHTON

CAN IT SUCCEED?

There is a proposal to establish yet another football club. It is to be called the Brighton and Hove Club, and is to be run on semi-professional lines. Whether or not it is likely to succeed is a matter of opinion, but studying the events of the past few years, not only in Brighton but throughout the South of England, this seems extremely doubtful. We are influenced in our opinion by the experience of the Brighton United Club, which, although able to command during its brief career players of considerable repute and a place in the First Division of the Southern League, came to an inglorious end after an existence of but two seasons. How then can a club hope to succeed if it is unable to present the public with the same attractions as possessed by the Brighton United, for we understand that it is the Second and not the First Division of the Southern League that the club has been invited to enter. As in other parts of the South of England, so in Brighton, there is not the number of people who take a real and lasting interest in the game, and would be likely to stick to a professional club, or even a semi-professional club, in its period of adversity, as well as when it is on the high road of success.

Despite the pessimism in some quarters, the meeting of supporters proposed in the circular went ahead on 24 June at the Seven Stars public house in Ship Street. The only surviving record of this historic gathering is reproduced below from the *Brighton and Hove Guardian*, 26 June 1901:

BRIGHTON AND HOVE FOOTBALL CLUB

The initial meeting of the club, when its formation was confirmed, took place at the Seven Stars, Ship Street, on Monday evening, a large number of enthusiasts of this winter pastime being present. The chair was taken *pro tem.* by Mr D. Butt [sic — Bott], whose election to that position was afterwards confirmed by a unanimous vote of the meeting.

Before the business of the meeting began, Mr Jackson gave a few facts as to the prospects of the new club. He said there were no great initial expenses to be met as in a professional club, and in fact the club started under very favourable circumstances. He had received a reply to his communication to Mr W. Newham, the secretary of the Sussex County Cricket Club, stating the terms on which the club would grant the use of the ground to the club. The conditions would be that the Sussex County Club should receive a third of the gate receipts and a half of the receipts of the stands. This ground, Mr Jackson said, was the finest that could be obtained in the district, and the terms were, he considered, equitable.

After the name of the club had been settled as 'Brighton and Hove United', some discussion ensued on the terms offered by the Sussex County Cricket Club. Several technicalities were touched upon, and on the proposition of the chairman it was decided to communicate with Mr Newham on certain points regarding season-ticket holders and leave the discussion of the terms to a further meeting.

Mr Avenell, before the election of the officers took place, gave some details with regard to the working of the late Brighton and Hove Rangers Club. He said that he was practically a prisoner at the bar but he wished to help forward the interests of the club, which was then under formation. He strongly advised them to have 'a clear-headed lot of men as the committee'. The downfall of the Rangers was due principally to the large committee and to the predominance of 'working men' on the committee. He did not wish to disparage the working men, but it was diversity of opinion among them that was responsible for the lack of success of the Rangers. In conclusion, he strongly urged them to have only a limited committee and to keep it select.

Mr J. Harrison, as a member of the Brighton and Hove Rangers, also expressed views in concurrence with these remarks.

Mr W. Newham kindly offered to officiate as treasurer, and his appointment was agreed to with enthusiasm. Mr Hannan was unanimously elected secretary on the proposition of Mr J. Harrison, and Mr J. Jackson was appointed team manager. A working committee was elected as follows: Messrs Butt [sic] (chairman), Stevens, I. de Costa, Clark and Allen.

Mr J. Clark and I. de Costa both subscribed a guinea towards the funds of the club.

Votes of thanks to Mr de Costa for his kindness in placing the room at the disposal of the meeting, and also to the chairman for presiding were passed. This terminated the meeting.

Birthplace of the Albion
The Seven Stars public house in Ship Street, Brighton, now known as the Helsinki. The building, which has an extraordinary, late-Victorian façade, was the scene of the club's formation meeting on Monday, 24 June 1901. In the years to come the team would acknowledge the cheers of its supporters from the balcony.

It is interesting to note the choice of name, made perhaps because of the numerous links with the old Brighton United club. It was rather curiously stated later that the original circulars headed simply 'Brighton and Hove Football Club' had been incorrect all along because of a printer's error which had omitted the suffix 'United', but this explanation may have been a move by the committee to distance itself from the failed Rangers club – now probably coming under F.A. scrutiny – and its proposed change of name to 'Brighton and Hove'. There had been a number of unsettling rumours linking the two clubs. The *Hove Echo* reported that

> certain people allege that many of the officers who were involved in the failure of the now-defunct Rangers are holding official positions in connection with the new club.

Secretary George Hannan quickly quashed the damaging and baseless allegations, confident that United would be a revelation to those who predicted another unsuccessful venture.

The chosen committee was the small, select band William Avenell had hoped for. Daniel Bott was the manager of Allsopps Brewery in West Street. George Hannan was manager of The Hove Typewriting Bureau, 101 Church Road, Hove, which was registered as the club office. Billy Newham, the secretary of Sussex C.C.C., offered his services as treasurer no doubt with an eye to ensuring that the cricket club received its dues. Frederick Stevens was a jeweller who later became a director of the Albion. Noah Clark, a fish merchant and shareholder of Brighton United, would also serve the Albion for many years as a director. Isaac de Costa, known as 'Ike', was a bookmaker and had been the proprietor of the Seven Stars since 1897. Frank Allen, a plumber and decorator, was an ex-director of Brighton United.

Optimism for the new United was high. The *Sussex Daily News* carried the following commentary on 9 July 1901:

BRIGHTON AND HOVE UNITED CLUB

The inaugurators of the football club which has recently been formed under the above title to provide amusement for local enthusiasts during the winter months are making headway towards turning out a team which shall be worthy of the two towns. Already some of the best talent has been procured, and negotiations are going on from day to day for the signing of smart professionals, and by the beginning of September, at the present rate of progress, there is little doubt that a good combination will have been got together under the scrutiny of Mr J. Jackson.

However, when the confusion over the name eventually cleared, the members of Hove F.C. were furious and formally complained that they found it 'obnoxious'. It was feared that the suffix 'United' would be construed as an amalgamation between themselves and the professionals which could seriously affect their gates. They were appeased by a change from 'United' to 'Albion' in July, but a certain amount of ill feeling remained and the amateurs continued to watch their professional neighbours with a critical eye.

Quite why 'Albion' – 'an ancient and literary name for England' (*New World Encyclopaedia*) – was chosen as the alternative title is not clear. Popular theory has it that John Jackson came up with the name because of his former links with West Bromwich Albion and that the blue-and-white striped shirts were adopted for the same reason, but this story is unsubstantiated under research: despite every effort by the authors, no connection has been discovered between Jackson and the Midlands club, and the striped shirts were not introduced until 1904. Nearly 40 years later, Bert Baker, the club's outside-right, said that he had suggested the name (again influenced by West Bromwich Albion), but certain other of his reminiscences cast doubt on this story.

West Bromwich established a good precedent for an 'Albion' football club, but the term had many uses in the local area, both sporting and commercial, long before the appearance of Brighton and Hove Albion or, indeed, West Brom. The Royal Albion Hotel, for example, had been welcoming guests in the Old Steine since 1826; the Albion Brewery (and adjacent Albion Inn) in Brighton's Albion Street was a well-established concern by 1892 when it was purchased by Tamplins Brewery, a company which had held 20 shares in the Brighton United club (and would buy 200 Brighton and Hove Albion shares) and which owned Jackson's pub, the Farm Tavern; and there was a cricket and football club called Hove Albion before the turn of the century, but the football section disbanded at the end of the 1896–97 season after failing to complete its fixtures.

It is worthy of note that, among the various commercial concerns bearing the 'Albion' title, at least two had definite links with the club. Tom Gadd was involved from the very earliest days of the Albion, while his brother, Harry, became a director when the club formed a limited company in 1904. The pair ran a temperance establishment at 35 Queen's Road, otherwise known as — the Albion Hotel. The Gadds had become proprietors in 1890, before which it was the Albion Coffee House. Albert Grinyer was also among the first members of the board in 1904 and was licensee of a Tamplins pub at 110 Church Road, Hove — the Albion Inn. Grinyer was well-known in local football circles and was also involved with the Hove and Hove Park clubs at various times.

Could any of these connections have influenced the choice of name? Whatever the reason, which will probably never be known for sure, Brighton and Hove Albion were now up and running.

> Billy Newham, Albion's first treasurer, was a great servant of the Sussex County Cricket Club for 63 years. An attractive, middle-order batsman from 1881 until 1905, he played one test match for England on the 1887–88 tour of Australia and was county captain in 1889 and 1891. Billy also performed the duties of secretary from 1889 until 1908, and then assistant secretary until his death in 1944 at the age of 83. Also a stalwart enthusiast of the winter game, Newham was one of the eight founders of the Sussex County F.A. in 1882, and appeared in the Sussex Senior Cup final with Ardingly College in 1884 in addition to representing the county at full-back on many occasions.

THE OPENING SEASON 1901–02

By the end of August the management had assembled a useful collection of professionals to form the nucleus of the team. Former Brighton United players Jock Caldwell, Frank McAvoy and Paddy Farrell were signed up; Ephraim Colclough came from Watford; Hove's Clem Barker was registered as a professional, along with C. J. Mendham and Brighton & Hove Rangers' Squire Whitehurst. Another ex-Ranger, Jim Sutherland, and Blackburn Rovers' Jock Russell were both registered as professionals in September. The team was to be augmented from a pool of twelve useful amateurs including Bert Baker and F. Mitchell (both ex-Rangers), Donald Coles, Ned Collins and Edgar Ffennell (a former Brighton United shareholder). The players trained at Dyke Road Field at the top of Convent Hill (now called The Upper Drive).

A meeting of the club at the Seven Stars on 29 August revealed that the committee had been enlarged. Ike de Costa and Locke Lancaster were now vice-presidents, and Messrs Baxter, W. Green, Thomas Harrington, R. Major, Poole and Price had been appointed to the committee. Frederick Stevens, it appears, was no longer involved. There was general optimism that the team would occupy a good position in the League.

Because of the unavailability of the County Ground – Prince Ranjitsinhji and C. B. Fry were still occupying the crease, as indeed they had for most of the summer – the Albion's opening fixture was played at Dyke Road Field on 7 September 1901, a friendly with a strengthened Shoreham side from the West Sussex Senior League. The pitch was of small dimensions rather restrictive to the play, but a large crowd assembled to see

Albion 1901–02
Standing left to right: Alf Sharp, C. J. Mendham, Squire Whitehurst, Marley, Ned Collins, Jock Caldwell, Albert Smith.
Seated left to right: Paddy Farrell, Jim Sutherland, F. Mitchell, John Jackson (trainer-manager),
*   George Hannan (secretary).*
On ground left to right: Bert Baker, Frank McAvoy (captain), Clem Barker, Ephraim Colclough, Jock Russell.

> Although it hardly affected the newborn Albion yet, a maximum wage – £4 per week with no bonuses – was imposed throughout English professional football by the F.A. for the first time this season. Seen as a means of preventing wealthy clubs from 'snapping up' the best players – and thereby maintaining a degree of equality and competitiveness – the move was bitterly opposed by the Players' Union and remained a contentious issue for 60 years.

BRIGHTON & HOVE ALBION — SEASON 1901–02

Date	Comp.	Ven.	Opponents	Result	HT	Pos.	Scorers	Atten.	Baker H	Barker C	Blunden B	Caldwell J	Callow J	Colclough E	Coles D	Collins E	Dollman F	Farrell P	Gardiner J	Hill W	King E	King P	McAvoy F	Mansfield W	Mendham C	Mitchell F	Russell J	Sear	Sharp A	Smith Albert	Sutherland J	Telford J	Thair S	Whitehurst S	Woodhams W
Sep 21	FAC Prelim.	(h*)	Brighton Athletic	W 6–2	2–1	–	Baker 3, Barker 2, Mendham	1,200	7	9		3			2			4					10		8	6	11				5			1	
28	SL D2	(a)	Shepherd's Bush	W 2–0	1–0	2=	McAvoy, Barker	1,200		9		3			2			4					10	7	8	6	11				5			1	
Oct 5	FAC Q1	(h)	Eastbourne	W 3–1	1–1	–	McAvoy, Russell, Barker	2,000	7	9		3			2			4					10		8	6	11				5			1	
19	FAC Q2	(h)	Hastings & St L.	W 5–0	3–0	–	Colclough 2, McAvoy, Mendham 2	2,000	7			3		10	2			4					9		8	6	11				5			1	
26	SL D2	(h)	West Hampstead	W 4–0	1–0	3	McAvoy 2, Russell, Smith	1,500	7			3		9	2			4					10			6	11			8	5			1	
Nov 2	FAC Q3	(h)	Clapton	L 2–3	1–0	–	Barker, McAvoy (pen)	2,500	7	8		3			2			4					9			6	11			10	5			1	
30	SL D2	(h)	Fulham	W 2–0	2–0	2	Barker, McAvoy	1,900	7	9		3			2			4					10			6	11			8	5			1	
Dec 7	SL D2	(h)	Grays United	W 2–1	0–0	1	Barker, Baker	2,000	7	9		3			2			4					10			6	11			8	5			1	
14	SL D2	(a)	Chesham Town	W 7–2	4–1	1	Mendham 2, Russell 2, Coles 2, Smith, Caldwell (pen)	'very poor'				3		10	2			4					9		7	6	11			8	5			1	
21	SL D2*	(a)	Maidenhead	W 3–2	2–2	1	Barker, Mendham 2			8		3						4					9		7	6	11			10	5			1	
Jan 4	SL D2	(a)	Grays United	L 0–1	0–1	1		800	7			3		10	2			4					9			6	11			8	5		1		
25	SL D2	(h)	Shepherd's Bush	W 3–1	0–1	1	Colclough, Baker, Caldwell (pen)	1,700	7			3		9	2			4					10			6	11			8	5			1	
Feb 1	SL D2	(a)	Maidenhead	W 2–1	2–0	1	Blunden, McAvoy	'meagre'			9	3		7	2			4					10			6	11			8	5		1		
8	SL D2	(h)	Southall	W 2–1	1–1	1	McAvoy, Caldwell	2,000	7		9	3			2			4					10			6	11			8	5		1		
15	SL D2	(a)	Southall	L 0–1	0–0	1		'good'	7	8	9	3			2			4					10			6	11				5		1		
Mar 1	SL D2	(h*)	Chesham Town	W 4–0	1–0	1	Mitchell, Sear, Own goal, Sutherland	'encouraging'				3			2			4	7	8	10					6	11	9			5		1		
8	SL D2	(h)	Wycombe Wand.	W 1–0	0–0	1	Caldwell (pen)	1,500				3			2			4	7	8	10					6	11	9			5		1		
22	SL D2	(a)	Fulham	L 1–2	1–2	1	Caldwell (pen)	'several thousand'				3			2			4	7	8	9	10				6	11				5		1		
Apr 1	SL D2	(a)	Wycombe Wand.	L 0–2	0–1	2			7			3		10	2			4	9	8						6	11				5		1		
5	SL D2	(a)	West Hampstead	L 1–3	1–1	2	Blunden	'big'	7		9	3			2			4		8						6	11				5		1		10
League appearances									9	5	7	16	3	3	13	4	2	16	4	4	3	1	11	1	3	15	13	2	1	5	15	1	9	7	2
League goals							OG – 1		2	4	2	5		1	2								6		4	1	2	1		2	1				

Notes: Home matches played at the County Ground, Hove, except: Mar 1 – played at the Goldstone Ground, Hove FC.

Sep 21 – tie drawn away but switched to the County Ground.

Dec 21 – Albion played only ten men because E. Collins did not arrive.

Brighton and Hove Albion, in their fisherman's-blue shirts and white knickers, win 2–0. That first-ever Albion line-up was

Squire Whitehurst; Donald Coles and Jock Caldwell;
Paddy Farrell, Jim Sutherland and F. Mitchell;
C. J. Mendham, Clem Barker, Frank McAvoy (capt.),
W. Smith and Edgar Ffennell.

Southern League Division 2 1901–02							
	P	W	D	L	F	A	Pts
1. Fulham	16	13	0	3	51	19	26
2. Grays United	16	12	1	3	49	14	25
3. **ALBION**	16	11	0	5	34	17	22
4. Wycombe Wanderers	16	7	3	6	36	30	17
5. West Hampstead	16	6	4	6	39	29	16
6. Shepherd's Bush	16	6	1	9	31	31	13
7. Southall	16	5	2	9	28	52	12
8. Maidenhead	16	3	1	12	23	59	7
9. Chesham Town	16	2	2	12	24	64	6

Barker and McAvoy scored the club's first goals. One more match was played at Dyke Road, a 4–2 friendly win over Woolwich Polytechnic, before Albion moved in at the County Ground. The club made its competitive début there on 21 September, a preliminary-round English Cup tie against Brighton Athletic, and a crowd of around 1,200 witnessed a 6–2 victory for the professionals. Another week saw the first Southern League match, away to Shepherd's Bush, resulting in a 2–0 win. Against mainly amateur opposition, Albion won their first six League games, an excellent start. In the English Cup, further wins over Eastbourne (3–1) and Hastings & St Leonards (5–0) preceded a 3–2 defeat at the hands of Clapton in the third qualifying round at the County Ground.

After the home defeat of Grays United on 7 December, Albion sat on top of the division and remained there until the end of March, despite losing at lowly Southall in mid February. This setback prompted the committee to 'engage some good-class forwards, owing to the continued weakness of the present set' in order to maintain the challenge for the title. In came Eddie King, the Eastbourne county player, W. Hill and Sear, and Chesham Town were sent packing 4–0 in the next fixture.

The lack of scoring-power was not the only problem within the team, though. It emerged that John Jackson had a blazing row with his captain, Frank McAvoy, at Christmas, and the situation simmered until late February when McAvoy set upon Jackson and knocked him to the ground. Needless to say, the Scot never played for the club again, but the feud continued. With Jackson apparently going in fear of permanent injury from the ex-captain and his pal Clem Barker, things came to a head in August 1902 when the two former players went looking for the manager at his Farm Tavern beer-house. Fortunately Jackson was in Lewes at the time, but McAvoy allegedly warned Mrs Jackson that 'We are going to the station to meet your husband, and you must consider yourself lucky if he is brought home alive!' Enough was enough. A couple of weeks later the pair were convicted of threatening behaviour at Hove Police Court and were bound over to keep the peace for six months in the sum of £10.

Back on the pitch, Albion, having dropped only four points all season, defeated Wycombe Wanderers 1–0 on 8 March to maintain a single-point lead over Grays United, but the final three games were all away from home and all ended in defeat. Grays, who had tracked Albion all the way, moved ahead on 29 March but lost their final game at Southall to finish three points ahead. This allowed Fulham, who won their last eight matches, to clinch the title by one point with victory at West Hampstead on 19 April. Albion thus finished in a disappointing third place, four points behind the champions.

On Boxing Day, Second Division Blackpool came to the County Ground to play an attractive friendly match and a 3,500 crowd, the biggest thus far, saw the northerners triumph 3–1.

The average League attendance at the County Ground was only around 1,700, but the lessons learned from the Brighton United episode kept the club afloat. Only nine professionals were employed during the season compared with the fourteen on the United pay-roll at the time of liquidation. It cost just over £18 a week to run the club and extra cash from various fund-raising schemes helped to provide a firmer footing for the future.

The first season had been a reasonably successful one for the Albion, but throughout the term events had been taking place less than a mile from the County Ground that were to have a huge impact on the fledgling club.

THE GOLDSTONE GROUND

On the conclusion of the 1900–01 season the amateurs of Hove F.C. decided to look for a site that would be suitable for an enclosed ground. The club had been in existence for seventeen years, competing in the East and West Sussex Leagues at various times. Up to this point they had played in Hove Park (now Hove Recreation Ground) and the committee felt that it would enhance the club's standing to be able to 'take a gate', noting that new rulings insisted that cup matches should henceforth be played on enclosed grounds.

Their requirements came to the notice of Alderman John Clark whose home, Goldstone House, was situated in Fonthill Road close to his bread factory. Clark was a keen football supporter and had served as a director on the Brighton United board. He also owned the adjoining Goldstone Farm on a lease from the Stanford Estate.

(The name 'Goldstone' derives from a famous stone, reputed to be of druidic origin, which stood in the area for many years. The largest of several such stones and said to weigh 20 tons, it became a great attraction in the early nineteenth century and was a favourite haunt of sightseers and picnickers. Around 1830 the man who farmed the area, William Rigden, exasperated with the intrusions onto his land, had the rock buried in a sixteen-foot pit, but some 70 years later in 1900 local historian William Hollamby set out to locate the hidden relic and unearthed it in what was by then John Clark's orchard. The stone was eventually mounted in the new Hove Park when it opened in 1906 and can still be seen there, less than a goal kick away from the football ground to which it gave its name.)

Part of Clark's farm was a large meadow at the southern end of Goldstone Bottom, which in the eighteenth century had on occasion been used for the execution of convicted criminals and mutineers. It was flat, and the turf was of a quality to enable the Brighton Hockey Club to play on it during the previous year. In June 1901, Clark offered the field to the Hove club on a three-year lease at a rental of £100 per annum, a great deal of money in those days. They would have the use of the field on an average of two days a week throughout the football season; the rest of the week it would be used to graze sheep and cattle.

Clark also offered £600 for the erection of a substantial fence to surround the ground, with gates and a turnstile, and for a covered stand with room for 400 spectators, dressing-rooms, lavatories and shower-baths. In return he would require 50 per cent of the total gate receipts in excess of £200 each season.

At a meeting held at Hove Town Hall on 25 June 1901 (the day after Albion's formation meeting), the Hove club decided to accept the offer, although grave doubts were voiced by some members as to the ability to attract a sufficient number of paying customers to meet the rent. The advent of a professional rival added weight to those fears.

Hove christened their 'magnificent' new ground with an attractive match against Clapton (how often they figured in these early days) on 7 September 1901, the same day and only a mile distant from the Albion's début at Dyke Road; it was not recorded which game attracted the larger audience. Prior to the kick-off the assembly was entertained by the obligatory Hove Brass Band and an athletics meeting for local footballers. A telegram arrived from Edinburgh:

> Good luck today and success to the new venture. Coleman. Mayor.

Clapton proceeded to cast a cloud over the occasion, winning comfortably 3–0.

Until 1904 it was customary to stage important local cup-ties at the County Ground, including the semi-finals and final of the Sussex Senior Cup. On 22 February 1902, Albion were scheduled to play a home friendly with Southampton Wanderers, but on the same day the first semi-final of the Senior Cup was due to take place between Eastbourne and Shoreham so the Albion were forced to seek an alternative venue. It was noted that the Hove club had no fixture at the Goldstone Ground and the committee approached the amateurs for permission to transfer the match to the new arena. Hove agreed, and Albion went on to play their first game on the ground which was destined to become their home. For the record, the match

Recovery of the Goldstone
The 20-ton megalith was unearthed on 29 September 1900 from its pit on land now occupied by the Sackville Trading Estate, at the instigation of Councillor William Hollamby. The stone was laid in its present position when Hove Park opened in 1906.

was won 7–1. A similar situation arose the following Saturday when the other semi-final was played between Hailsham and Hove. Albion switched the Southern League game with Chesham Town to the Goldstone and again won, this time by four goals to nil. Albion played three more friendlies at the Goldstone in 1901–02, including an excellent 1–0 win over Northampton Town and a 5–1 drubbing of Hove themselves.

During the summer of 1902 it became apparent to the Hove committee that attendances were not sufficient to enable the club to meet the rent for the Goldstone Ground without resorting to fund-raising activities. The obvious solution to their problem was to share the tenancy with another club – ground-sharing is nothing new! – and the idea was put to the Albion officials, proposing that the professionals could have the use of the Goldstone on weeks when it was not required by themselves. Albion accepted the offer, which was to lead to the occasional ludicrous situation of Albion being forced to postpone important Southern League games because of a cup replay or even a rearranged friendly being played by the Hove side. The clubs were to share the ground for two seasons until 1904 when Hove, at the end of their three-year lease, returned to Hove Park leaving Albion as the sole occupants.

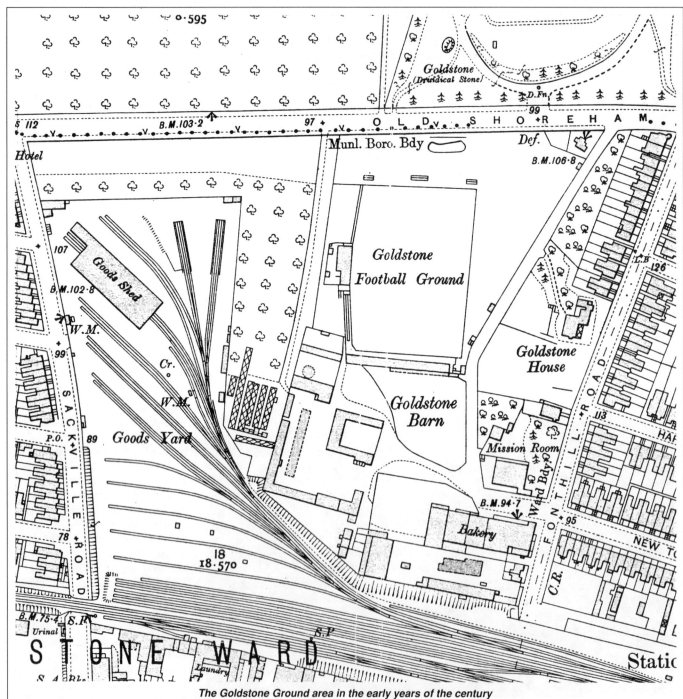

The Goldstone Ground area in the early years of the century
This 1:2,500 (25" to 1 mile) plan, reproduced from the 1911 Ordnance Survey map, shows the Goldstone Ground with a small West Stand and a South Stand extending to the width of the pitch; the pond to the north of the ground by the Old Shoreham Road; the buildings of Goldstone Farm; the residence (Goldstone House), bakery and orchard (to the west of the football ground) of Alderman John Clark; and the recently opened (1906) Hove Park with the Goldstone itself in its present position. The railway goods yard had been extended since 1901, cutting off Newtown Road which would itself eventually be extended around the football ground to its present junction with Old Shoreham Road.

SEASON 1902–03

During the close season Albion moved lock, stock and barrel to the Goldstone. The ground was far more Spartan than it is today. There was no terracing; the spectators on the east side stood on a natural bank which rose in elevation from south to north. A small, wooden stand seating 400 spectators straddled the halfway line on the western side with dressing-rooms at the rear. Admission to the stand was from inside the ground, which was enclosed by an eight-foot wooden fence with entrances at the north-west and south-east corners. The playing area was surrounded by a single-bar fence. When large crowds were anticipated, farm wagons and carts were placed behind the standing spectators to enable more people to view the proceedings. From the south-east the ground was approached via Newtown Road, which carried on past John Clark's bread factory and the Goldstone Farm buildings behind the south goal directly to Sackville Road in the west. A cart-track, now Goldstone Lane, branched off to give access to the ground entrance in that corner. Behind the north goal was a small pond which provided drainage for the Old Shoreham Road until sewers were laid in the early 1920s; during hot, dry spells it was not unknown for the lively ball to be deliberately punted into the pond to soften the leather. Overlooking the ground from the east was John Clark's residence, Goldstone House; its extensive garden became a popular venue for football-afternoon tea-parties hosted by Alderman Clark. To the north was open country, criss-crossed by tracks, stretching away to the Downs. The only building in that area was the Goldstone pumping station of the Brighton Corporation Waterworks, now the British Engineerium museum off Nevill Road.

Only six clubs were to contest the Second Division this season, so to augment their regular fixtures Albion gained entry to the South Eastern League, a mixed bag of amateur sides from the Home Counties and the reserve sides of Southern League First Division clubs which had been formed the previous year. Albion fielded a first eleven on all but two occasions, often using the matches to blood promising reserves and trialists. A few friendly matches were also arranged for a reserve team. George Hannan had departed and John Jackson was now secretary-manager with his Farm Tavern registered as the club office. Jackson's role as trainer had passed to W. Maslen.

Two important signings were made during the summer: Arthur Hulme from Bristol Rovers and Ben Garfield from West Bromwich Albion. Garfield had been tremendously popular at West Brom. and had gained an England cap against Ireland in 1898, but he had suffered greatly from injury problems; nevertheless, at 30 years of age he was a remarkable capture for the infant club. Hulme began an association with the Albion that

Good Friday, 1903: the famous music-hall comedian George Robey – 'The Prime Minister of Mirth' – guested for Albion in a friendly match with West Norwood at the Goldstone Ground and scored the first goal in a 3–0 victory. He also played against the Birmingham Works F.A. on Easter Tuesday 1907 and scored once in a 5–0 win. George took his football very seriously but the spectators were always expecting him to do something funny; he did not, but they laughed all the same. Robey also played cricket for the M.C.C.

was to last for seven seasons. He quickly became a great favourite with the Goldstone crowd and was the club's first long-serving professional.

After a 13–0 thrashing of Hove, their co-tenants at the Goldstone, Albion's Southern League campaign opened with a 4–2 victory over Southall, followed by crushing English Cup wins over Brighton Amateurs (14–2) and Shoreham (12–0). (The Amateurs were an amalgamation of Brighton Athletic and Brighton Hornets, much as Edgar Everest had advocated nine years earlier.) Grays United were beaten 3–0 in a third-qualifying-round replay after a thrilling, five-all encounter at the Goldstone in which Albion were 4–1 down at half time, but Ilford ended hopes of reaching the competition proper, winning the fourth qualifier by a goal to nil.

By November, Albion were lying third in the Southern League behind Fulham and Grays United, the two clubs that had pipped them the previous season, but they then embarked on a run of five wins and a draw in the last six matches to set a target of fifteen points at the top of the table. Grays were beaten 4–2 and Fulham 3–1 at the Goldstone, the latter match attracting a record crowd of around 4,200. Both rivals, seven points behind Albion with five games to play, closed in during March and April. The Cottagers' victory over Grays on 11 April assured Albion of a top-two position, but when the Essex club gained a 2–1 win in the return fixture Albion and Fulham were left on the same points tally at the head of the table. Goal-average did not count and it was expected that the Southern League would order a play-off to decide the championship, but, as there was no opportunity for such a match before the end of the season, it was decreed that the two clubs would share the honour.

Promotion was not automatic. The Southern League required that 'test matches' be played between the last two teams in Division One and the top two in the Second Division, neither a very popular nor satisfactory method of resolving the issue; indeed, this was the last occasion on which the system was employed. The matches were played on 27 April. Fulham were defeated 7–2 by Brentford at Shepherd's Bush while Albion met Watford at West Ham United's Canning Town Memorial Ground. Within fifteen minutes of the kick-off Albion built up a three-goal lead courtesy of Ben Garfield and Sid Thair, but Watford brought the score back to 3–3 in the second half. With both sides striving for supremacy it was the redoubtable Garfield who became the hero of the hour with two more goals to add to his first-half brace, and Albion won a splendid, hard-fought game 5–3. When the team arrived back at Brighton Central Station that evening, a large crowd was on hand to escort them to their headquarters, the Seven Stars. The players and officials made an appearance on the balcony to the accompaniment of loud cheering, with a special greeting reserved for four-goal Ben Garfield.

A few days prior to the test match the club had announced that, whatever the result, the committee had decided to remain in Division Two. It was felt that the club's finances could not support a team in the senior section, but after the euphoria of the Watford game the supporters brought such pressure to bear to reconsider that a meeting was convened for the evening of 8 May at the Athenaeum Hall in North Street.

SEASON 1902–03

Date	Comp.	Ven.	Opponents	Result	HT	Pos.	Scorers	Atten.	Allen	Baker H	Broughton F	Caldwell J	Coles D	Farrell P	Gardiner J	Garfield B	Gooch A	Grayer S	Hammond H	Hardman J	Harland A	Hill W	Howes A	Hulme A	Lamb W	Lee B	Millard A	Mitchell F	Owen F	Payne	Scott F	Smith Albert	Sweetman T	Taylor A	Thair S	Ward W	West C	Whitehurst S
Sep 13	SL D2	(h)	Southall	W 4–2	3–1	1	Baker, Scott, Thair, Caldwell (pen)	2,200	7	5	3	4		1		11					6		2		8						9				10			
17	SE League	(h)	Luton Town (res.)	L 1–2	0–0	7=	Scott	850	8		3	4		1		11					6		2		5	7					9				10			
20	SE League	(h)	Grays United	W 2–1	0–1	6	Garfield, Scott	2,100	7		3	4		1		11					6		2		5	8					9				10			
24	SE League	(h)	Tottenham H. (res.)	L 1–3	1–1	6	Hill	2,000	4		3					11					6	8	1	2	5						9				10		7	
27	SE League	(a)	Bedford Queen's	D 2–2	0–2	6	West, Hulme (pen)		4							11	3				5		1	2		7	6				9				10		8	
Oct 1	SE League	(h)	West Ham U. (res.)	L 2–3	0–1	7	Farrell, Garfield	700		5	3	4		1		11	8						1	2	10	6					9						7	
4	FAC Q1	(h)	Brighton Amateurs	W 14–2	4–0	–	Caldwell 2 (2 pens), West 3, Lee 3, Harland, Scott 2, Garfield 3	1,600			3	4				11				8	6		1	2	5	10					9						7	
11	SL D2	(a)	Fulham	L 0–1	0–0	3		1,200			3	4				11					6	8	1	2	5	10					9						7	
18	FAC Q2	(a)	Shoreham	W 12–0	8–0	–	Garfield, Lee 2, Thair 3, Scott 4, Own goal, Harland	'large'			3	4				11					6		1	2	5	8					9				10		7	
also	SE League*	(a)	St Albans Amat'rs	W 1–0	0–0	6	Gooch	1,500		6					2		5															8						1
25	SL D2	(h)	Chesham Town	W 5–0	2–0	2	Hardman, Lee, Garfield 2, Lamb	1,500	7		3	6				11				4				2	5	8					9				10			1
27	SE League*	(a)	Tottenham H.	L 0–3	0–1	6		2,000			3	4				11				4	6		1	2	5	10					9						7	1
Nov 1	FAC Q3	(h)	Grays United	D 5–5	1–4	–	Garfield, Lee 2, Scott, Caldwell	2,900	7		3	4				11					6		1	2	5	8					9				10			
5	FAC Q3 Rep	(a)	Grays United	W 3–0	0–0	–	Scott 2, Thair		7		3	4				11				8	6			2	5						9				10			1
8	SL D2	(a)	Grays United	L 0–3	0–2	3		'good'	7		3	4				11				8	6		1	2	5						9				10			
15	FAC Q4	(a)	Ilford	L 0–1	0–1	–		2,500	7		3	4				11				8	6			2	5						9				10			1
22	SE League*	(a)	Queen's P.R. (res.)	L 2–3	0–1	7	Scott, Thair	'very small'			3	4*				11					6*			2	5*			8			9				10		7	1
Dec 6	SE League*	(a)	Luton Town (res.)	L 0–3	0–1	9					3	4				11					6			2	5			8			9		7				1
20	SL D2	(h)	Grays United	W 2–0	2–0	3	Scott 2, Thair, Caldwell (pen)	2,000			3	4				11					6			2	5	8					9			7	10			1
27	SL D2	(h)	Wycombe Wand.	W 5–0	3–0	2	Taylor 2, Smith 2, Scott	3,000			3	2									6				4	5			11		9	8		7	10			1
Jan 3	SE League	(a)	Chesham Gen'rals	W 3–0	1–0	8	Scott, Caldwell (pen), Thair	1,500			3	2									6				4	5	10				9	8		7	11			1
17	SE League	(h)	Queen's P.R. (res.)	D 1–1	1–1	9	Scott	2,250			3	2				11					6				4	5	8				9			7	10			1
24	SL D2	(a)	Chesham Town	W 4–1	2–0	1	Thair 2, Scott, Garfield	'not many'			3	2				11					6				4	5					9	8		7	10			1
31	SL D2	(a)	Fulham	W 3–1	1–1	1	Lee, Caldwell 2 (2 pens)	4,200	7		3	2									6				4	5	8				9			11	10			1
Feb 7	SL D2	(a)	Wycombe Wand.	D 1–1	1–0	1	Scott				3	2	4								6			8	5	7					9			11	10			1
14	SE League	(h)	Watford (res.)	W 5–1	2–0	8	Lamb, Taylor, Scott 2, Thair	2,200			3	2				11					6				4	5	8				9			7	10			1
21	SE League*	(a)	West Ham U. (res.)	L 0–5	0–2	9					3*	2*	4			11*			6*					5			8				9*			7*	10*			1*
28	SL D2	(a)	Southall	W 8–0	3–0	1	Caldwell (pen), Scott 5, Thair, Garfield	'few hundred'			3	2	4			11			5		6				8						9			7	10			1
Mar 9	SE League	(a)	Chesham Gen'rals	W 2–0	2–0	7	Caldwell (pen), Taylor				3	4				11				2	6	1			5			8			9	10			7			
14	SE League	(h)	St Albans Amat'rs	W 3–0	1–0	7	Lamb, Smith	1,000			3	4				11				2	6	1			5						9	8		7	10			
21	SE League*	(a)	Brentford (res.)	W 3–0	1–0	7	Scott, Thair 2				6	3*			4*	11			8		2				1	5					9				7*	10			
25	SE League	(h)	Hitchin Town	W 9–1	4–0	5	Garfield 3, Ward 2, Taylor, Scott 2, Thair	'poor'			3	4				11					6	1	2		5						9			7	10	8		
Apr 4	SE League	(a)	Watford (res.)	L 1–6	0–1	7	Garfield	1,000		6	3					11				2					1	4	5				9	7				10	8	
11	SE League	(h)	Bedford Queen's	W 4–0	1–0	6	Ward 3, Garfield	2,000			3	4			7	11			5				2		6						9					10	8	1
14	SE League	(h)	Brentford (res.)	W 3–0	1–0	6	Thair 2, Scott	1,800			3	2	4			11			5		6				8						9	7				10		1
18	SE League*	(h)	Hitchin Town	W 1–0	0–0	5	Smith				6	3	2				5			1	10	8									9	7						
25	SE League	(a)	Grays United	L 0–5	?	5		200	3*								4*	5*					2*					9*		6*			10*	11*		7*	8*	1*
27	SL Test	(n*)	Watford	W 5–3	3–1	–	Garfield 4, Thair	200			3	4				11					6				2	5					9	8		7	10			1
Southern League appearances									0	4	1	11	5	8	1	8	0	0	0	4	9	1	2	10	9	8	0	0	0	0	11	3	0	7	10	0	1	8
Southern League goals										1		5				8									1	2					11	2		2	6			
South Eastern League appearances									1	0	8	18	7	13	2	18	3	2	1	11	14	1	10	17	17	8	1	2	4	1	20	8	1	9	15	3	7	10
South Eastern League goals												2		1		7	1							1	1	2				11	2		3	8	5	1	

Notes: Nov 22, Feb 21, Mar 21 and Apr 25 – the full line-ups are not confirmed; those players asterisked were expected to play and are included in the end-of-season South Eastern League statistics.

Apr 27 – Southern League test match played at the Canning Town Memorial Ground, West Ham United FC, and included in the end-of-season Southern League statistics.

The following additional players each made one appearance in the South Eastern League:
- Oct 18: Craven, W. (no.10), Mansfield, W. (no.11), Reed, W. (no.3), Starks, T. (no.9), Sutherland, J. (no.4) and Wickham, A. (no.7).
- Oct 27: Lanham, C. (no.8).
- Dec 6: Goulding (no.10).
- Apr 18: Ffennell, E. (no.11) and Smith, W. (no.4).

Treasurer Tom Cooter opened the proceedings by stating that it would cost £25 per week to maintain a team in the First Division, compared with the £18 3s. that it had cost during the recently completed season. Manager John Jackson was of the opinion that the extra expense would be offset by increased attendances and intimated that the club would struggle to break even anyway if it remained in Division Two. Several prominent committee members, Noah Clark and Ike De Costa among them, re-stated their view that the club should stay in the Second Division, but promises by 26 of those present to take one-guinea (£1.05) season tickets and a further 87 to take half-guinea tickets carried the evening. The closing vote was overwhelmingly in favour of accepting promotion and the meeting broke up amid scenes of great enthusiasm.

To round off a capital season, Albion met First Division opposition from the Football League for the first time on 29 April when Everton won a closely contested friendly match at the Goldstone Ground 2–1. The team also finished in a respectable fifth place in the South Eastern League, winning seven of the last nine fixtures. Centre-forward Frank Scott scored

Southern League Division 2 1902–03

		P	W	D	L	F	A	Pts
1.	ALBION	10	7	1	2	34	11	15
1.	Fulham	10	7	1	2	27	7	15
3.	Grays United	10	7	0	3	28	12	14
4.	Wycombe Wanderers	10	3	3	4	13	19	9
5.	Chesham Town	10	2	1	7	9	37	5
6.	Southall	10	1	0	9	10	35	2

Note: Albion and Fulham were deemed to have finished level in first place but a proposed championship play-off never materialised.

South Eastern League 1902–03

		P	W	D	L	F	A	Pts
1.	Tottenham H. (res.)	22	17	2	3	79	16	36
2.	Queen's Park R. (res.)	22	14	5	3	47	20	33
3.	Grays United	22	12	4	6	50	24	28
4.	Luton Town (res.)	22	10	6	6	40	44	26
5.	ALBION	22	11	2	9	45	39	24
6.	West Ham Utd (res.)	22	10	4	8	41	39	24
7.	Watford (res.)	22	9	3	10	40	42	21
8.	Brentford (res.)	22	7	5	10	50	42	18
9.	Bedford Queen's E.W.	22	6	4	12	33	64	16
10.	Chesham Generals	22	7	1	14	29	58	15
11.	St Albans Amateurs	22	5	1	16	31	60	11
12.	Hitchin Town	22	3	5	14	26	63	11

Albion's popular trainer, W. Maslen, was presented with a handsome timepiece and barometer during the interval of the South Eastern League match with Chesham Generals on 3 January. The presentation was made by treasurer Tom Cooter on behalf of the players. The clock was inscribed: 'Presented to W. Maslen, trainer, by the players and a few friends of the Brighton and Hove Albion F.C., as token of esteem and good fellowship.'

31 goals in all competitive matches, and added 12 more in an extensive series of friendlies.

The Second Division championship trophy, a silver cup, was presented to club chairman Harry Callaghan at a smoking-concert staged at The Dome on Friday, 24 July 1903, by the Southern League chairman, Colin Gordon, and eleven players – Whitehurst, Coles, Caldwell, Farrell, Lamb, Harland, Taylor, Hulme, Scott, Thair and Garfield – received Southern League gold medals from the Mayor of Brighton, Alderman John Buckwell. On a red-letter day for the club, however, the attendance at the function was most disappointing. Now that the Albion had shown their mettle, both Gordon and Callaghan appealed to the public of Brighton and Hove to rally round the club and to give it the support it deserved.

Season-ticket rates for 1902–03:	£	s.	d.
Covered stand	1	1	0
Stand and enclosure	0	10	6
Ground	0	7	6
Ladies tickets at reduced rate.			

SEASON 1903–04

To compete with the higher-class professional sides of the First Division, the management strengthened the team by bringing in seven new players including George Rushton from Burslem Port Vale; Billy Roberts, a tremendously skilful ball-player from Grays United who had starred in the previous season's cup-ties; Ted Parsons from Stoke; and Jack Pryce from Queen's Park Rangers.

As far as results were concerned it was to prove a disappointing campaign. The team struggled throughout the season, rarely climbing out of the bottom four, and finished one place above the basement in seventeenth position. Of the 34 matches, 12 were drawn and only 6 won, but there were some bright

Southern League Division 1 1903–04

		P	W	D	L	F	A	W	D	L	F	A	Pts
1.	Southampton	34	12	3	2	43	15	10	3	4	32	15	50
2.	Tottenham Hotspur	34	10	5	2	34	19	6	6	5	20	18	43
3.	Bristol Rovers	34	11	4	2	40	12	6	4	7	26	30	42
4.	Portsmouth	34	11	4	2	24	11	6	4	7	17	27	42
5.	Queen's Park R.	34	13	3	1	34	12	2	8	7	19	25	41
6.	Reading	34	8	6	3	27	15	6	7	4	21	20	41
7.	Millwall	34	10	2	5	42	20	6	6	5	23	22	40
8.	Luton Town	34	12	4	1	23	9	2	8	7	15	24	40
9.	Plymouth Argyle	34	8	5	4	27	16	5	5	7	17	18	36
10.	Swindon Town	34	7	7	3	18	14	3	4	10	12	28	31
11.	Fulham	34	7	6	4	23	14	2	6	9	11	22	30
12.	West Ham United	34	8	4	5	26	14	2	3	12	13	30	27
13.	Brentford	34	8	4	5	25	18	1	5	11	9	30	27
14.	Wellingborough Town	34	7	4	6	34	25	4	1	12	10	38	27
15.	Northampton Town	34	8	4	5	22	20	2	3	12	14	40	27
16.	New Brompton	34	4	10	3	18	15	2	3	12	8	28	25
17.	**ALBION**	34	5	6	6	27	29	1	6	10	18	40	24
18.	Kettering Town	34	6	4	7	23	23	0	3	14	16	55	19

SEASON 1903–04

Date	Comp.	Ven.	Opponents	Result	HT	Pos.	Scorers	Atten.	Boulton W	Caldwell J	Cameron	Dennett J	Farrell P	Garfield B	Haig-Brown A	Hardman J	Howes A	Hulme A	Hyde L	Lamb W	McAteer T	McCairns T	Paddington A	Parsons E	Pryce J	Roberts W	Rushton G	Scott F	Thair S	Whitehurst S
Sep 5	SL D1	(a)	Wellingborough T.	L 1–3	0–0	14	Roberts	2,000	3					11				2	7	5	4		6			8		9	10	1
12	SL D1	(h)	Bristol Rovers	D 2–2	0–2	14	Scott, Garfield	4,500	3					11			1	2	7	5	4		6			8		9	10	
19	SL D1	(h)	Swindon Town	L 0–1	0–1	16		5,000	3					11			1	2	7	4	5		6			8	10	9		
26	SL D1	(a)	Portsmouth	W 3–0	3–0	14=	Rushton, Garfield, Own goal	7,000		3				11			1	2	7	5	4		6			8	9		10	
Oct 3	SL D1	(h)	Northampton T.	L 0–4	0–3	16		5,000		3				11			1	2	7	5	4		6			8	9		10	
10	SL D1	(a)	Brentford	L 0–1	0–1	17		7,000		2							1	3	11	4	5		6			8	7	9	10	
17	SL D1	(h)	West Ham United	W 3–2	0–1	15	Scott 2, Garfield	3,000		2		4		11			1	3	7		5		6			8		9	10	
24	SL D1	(a)	Tottenham H'spur	D 2–2	0–1	13=	Thair, Garfield	10,000		3		4		11			1	2	7		5		6			8		9	10	
31	FAC Q3	(a)	West Ham United	L 0–4	0–1	–		5,000		3		4		11	7		1	2			5		6			8	9		10	
Nov 7	SL D1	(a)	New Brompton	L 1–2	1–1	15	Garfield	3,000		3		4		10			1	2	11		5		6			8	7	9		
14	SL D1	(h*)	Kettering Town	W 3–1	0–0	12	McAteer (pen), Roberts, Hyde	4,000		2	3			11			1	4	7		5		6			8		9	10	
21	SL D1	(a)	Southampton	L 1–5	0–3	14	Roberts	'small'		2	3			11			1	4	7		5		6			8		9	10	
Dec 12	SL D1	(h)	Queen's Park R.	L 1–3	1–1	15	Roberts	3,000	3		2			11			1		8		5		4	6		7		9	10	
19	SL D1	(a)	Plymouth Argyle	L 2–4	1–1	15	McAteer (pen), Rushton	3,000	2		3						1		7		5		6	4	10	8	9	11		
28	SL D1	(h)	Reading	D 2–2	0–2	18	Roberts 2	7,000			3						1	2	11		5	9	6	4	8	10	7			
Jan 2	SL D1	(h)	Wellingborough T.	W 5–1	3–0	15	Roberts 2, Hyde, Pryce, McCairns	4,000			2						1	3	10		5	9	4	6	7	11	8			
9	SL D1	(a)	Bristol Rovers	L 0–2	0–1	17		4,000			2						1	3	11		5	9	6	4	7	10	8			
16	SL D1	(a)	Swindon Town	L 1–1	1–0	16	Rushton	3,000	3								1	2	11		5	9	6	4	8	10	7			
23	SL D1	(h)	Portsmouth	D 1–1	0–1	16	Rushton	8,500		3							1	2	11		5	9	6	4	8	10	7			
30	SL D1	(a)	Northampton T.	D 2–2	1–2	17	Pryce, McCairns	1,000		3			11				1	2			5	9	6	4	8	10	7			
Feb 6	SL D1	(h)	Brentford	W 3–1	0–0	15	Hyde, Pryce, McCairns	3,000		2					4	1	3	11		5	9		6	8	10	7				
13	SL D1	(a)	West Ham United	L 0–5	0–3	16		3,000		3							1	2	11		5	9	6	4	8	10	7			
20	SL D1	(h)	Plymouth Argyle	D 0–0	0–0	15		4,200		3							1	2	11		5	9	6	4	8	10	7			
24	SL D1	(h)	Fulham	W 2–1	1–1	12	Garfield, McAteer (pen)	4,000		3			11				1	2	7		5	9	4	6	8	10				
27	SL D1	(a)	Luton Town	L 0–2	0–1	13		4,000		3				11			1	2	7		5	9	6	4	8	10				
Mar 5	SL D1	(h)	New Brompton	L 1–3	0–1	14	McAteer (pen)	4,800		3				11			1	2	7		5		6	4	8	10	9			
12	SL D1	(a)	Kettering Town	D 1–1	1–1	13	McCairns	1,500	3						6	1	2	11		5	9		4	8	10	7				
19	SL D1	(h)	Southampton	L 1–3	1–1	16	Garfield	8,200	3				11		6	1	2	7		5	9		4	8	10					
26	SL D1	(a)	Fulham	L 0–3	0–2	16		8,000	3				11			1	2		8	5	9	6	4		10	7				
Apr 1	SL D1	(a)	Millwall	D 3–3	2–2	16	McAteer 2 (1 pen), McCairns	7,000	3				11			1	2			5	9	6	4	8	10	7			
2	SL D1	(h)	Millwall	D 0–0	0–0	16		6,000	3				11			1	2	5			9	6	4	8	10	7				
5	SL D1	(h)	Luton Town	D 2–2	1–2	16	Pryce 2	3,000	3				11			1	2	7		5		6	4	8	10		9			
9	SL D1	(a)	Queen's Park R.	D 1–1	1–0	15	Hyde	6,000	3				11			1	2	7		5		6	4	8	10		9			
13	SL D1	(h)	Tottenham H'spur	L 1–2	1–0	15	Roberts	8,000	3				4	11		1	2	7		5	9		6	4	8	10				
23	SL D1	(a)	Reading	L 0–3	0–1	17		3,000	3				11			1	2			5	9	6	4	8	10	7			
League appearances									6	11	19	2	4	23	0	3	33	32	29	8	33	17	31	22	21	34	21	14	10	1
League goals				OG – 1							7			4				6	5			5	9	4	3	1			

Note: Nov 14 – played at the County Ground, Hove.

moments, a 3–0 victory at Portsmouth (the season's only away win) and a 2–2 draw at Tottenham being the highlights. The Southern League game with Kettering Town on 14 November had to be moved to the County Ground because Hove required the use of the Goldstone for their East Sussex League fixture with St Leonards. In the English Cup, Albion were exempted to the third qualifying round where they were swiftly eliminated at West Ham by four goals to nil. Inside-forward Billy Roberts, the only ever-present, was also top scorer with nine goals.

With the increased number of matches, and in line with the other First Division sides, Albion entered a reserve team in the South Eastern League (although the first team did play four of the fixtures largely for practice). Thus regular, competitive reserve matches were seen at the Goldstone for the first time, the team finishing fifth of the thirteen clubs.

The most pleasing aspect of the season was the marked increase in attendances, fully justifying the crucial decision made the previous May. The average at the Goldstone nearly doubled to just over 5,000, and in January some 8,500 spectators filled the ground for the visit of Portsmouth, by far the largest gate to date. Around 600 extra seats were installed, as they were again in March when champions-elect Southampton provided the opposition. Ground entry for this latter match was doubled on the day to one shilling (5p), much to the anger of the fans, but over 8,000 still witnessed the Saints' 3–1 victory.

Albion 1903–04

Standing left to right: John Jackson (secretary-manager), George Rushton, Arthur Howes, Cameron, Bert Baker, Billy Lamb, Squire Whitehurst, A. J. Taylor, Tom Sweetman, C. Brown (trainer).
Seated left to right: Donald Coles, Tom McAteer (captain), Bill Boulton, Ben Garfield, Arthur Hulme.
On ground left to right: Len Hyde, Billy Roberts, Frank Scott, Sid Thair, Albert Paddington.

At the end of the season bottom-placed Kettering Town withdrew from the Southern League and Watford were promoted to replace them. Portsmouth's reserve team had finished runners-up to Watford but could not be granted promotion, and Albion were fortunate to be re-elected to the First Division for the coming season.

ALBION LIMITED

An important milestone in Albion's history was reached on 11 April 1904. A packed meeting of supporters at the Royal Pavilion's Music Room was informed of the intention to incorporate the club as a limited liability company, with capital of £4,000 to be issued in 16,000 five-shilling (25p) shares. George Broadbridge, a member of the club committee, took the chair and informed the gathering that a flotation was seen as the best means of continuing the considerable progress that had been made in the last three years, and, in particular, of raising the funds required to attract and keep quality players. There was an immediate need for £400 to £500; the committee, which had been the target of some criticism and innuendo, had, in fact, already advanced considerable sums from their own pockets to keep the club going. The Millwall directors, with ten years experience of running a company behind them, urged their Brighton counterparts forward with a telegram: 'Go on at all costs.'

After a lively debate, the motion to form a limited company was proposed by Charles Bunker and carried unanimously. The sanction of the Football Association was obtained in May, and The Brighton and Hove Albion Football Club, Limited, was registered on 27 May 1904. The company's office was listed initially as 129 Church Road (Bunker's fish shop), Hove, and then at 94 Queen's Road, Brighton.

The first board of directors comprised George Broadbridge as chairman, Reg Alderton, Charles Bunker, Tom Cooter, Frederick Stevens, Albert Grinyer and Ben Parker; they were soon joined by Noah Clark, Harry Gadd, William Baker and Richard Merriman, with Bunker and Grinyer stepping down. Expressly forbidden from receiving remuneration by the company's Articles of Association, these dedicated men oversaw the flotation and published a prospectus for potential shareholders in May. Below are some of the aims and hopes set out in the company's prospectus.

This Company is formed for the purpose of carrying on the Professional Football Club for the Boroughs of Brighton and Hove, called "THE BRIGHTON AND HOVE ALBION FOOT-BALL CLUB," and ... to encourage and promote Professional Football in Brighton and Hove by the playing of matches ....

Judging from the increasing popularity of Professional Football and the increased support given to it during the present season, the Directors believe that in addition to keeping up the efficiency of the Company as an Athletic Undertaking, the Shareholders may reasonably expect to receive a fair interest on their Capital. [In fact, a dividend has been an exceptionally rare event, the first not being paid until 1923.]

DUPLICATE FOR THE FILE.

No. 81077

Certificate of Incorporation

I hereby Certify, That the

Brighton and Hove Albion Football Club, Limited

is this day Incorporated under the Companies' Acts, 1862 to 1900, and that the Company is **Limited**.

Given under my hand at London this *Twenty-seventh* day of *May* One Thousand Nine Hundred and *four*.

Fees and Deed Stamps £ *6 - 10 - 0*

Stamp Duty on Capital £ *10 " 0 " 0*

H. V. Bartlett

Registrar of Joint Stock Companies.

Certificate received by *Wm. Smith,*

For Jordan & Sons, Ld.,
12 Chancery Lane, W.C.

Date *30th May 1904.*

Albion Limited
A copy of the certificate held by Companies House which confirms the establishment of the Brighton and Hove Albion Football Club as a limited liability company in 1904.

During the present season the Club has held a fairly good position [finishing one off the bottom!] in the First Division of the Southern League, and in some of the matches in which they were successful shewed such excellent form, that it is confidently believed that if the present team is strengthened by the addition of some first-class men, who it is hoped the Company will be able to engage, there is every reason to believe that the Club will next season hold a still higher place in the First Division of the Southern League.

The Club has been greatly handicapped this season owing to their inability to have the use of the Goldstone Ground at all times, which compelled the Second Eleven to remain idle, at a great loss to the Club; but now the Directors have been enabled to secure the Goldstone Ground at Hove, which can be used for all home matches, the Public will have an opportunity of witnessing more games by both Elevens than hitherto, and this will prove a source of additional profit.

The minimum subscription on which the Directors will proceed to allotment is £1,000.

George Broadbridge, Albion's first chairman of directors
The initial board was composed mainly of publicans and shopkeepers. The notable exception was 35-year-old George Broadbridge, a chartered company secretary who, as Sir George, was Lord Mayor of London at the time of the coronation in 1937 and became Lord Broadbridge of Brighton in 1945. He was still involved with Albion as president after the Second World War.

The flotation was not a great success and it was something of a struggle to reach the vital £1,000 (4,000 shares) mark. Indeed, it was only the late purchase of 560 shares by the directors, bringing the board's total to 1,460 out of an allotment of 4,078, that enabled the company to begin trading at the end of July. There was disappointment that the shareholders – mostly shopkeepers, small businessmen and white-collar workers throughout Brighton, Hove and Portslade – numbered only 350. The largest shareholder was director Ben Parker, landlord of the Cliftonville Hotel, who held 480 (£120). William Baker, another director and publican (Standard Hotel), had 210 shares, while Tamplins Brewery purchased 200.

Nevertheless, 'Albion Limited' was now up and running, and the statutory meeting of the company was held at the Goldstone Ground on 26 August for the election of directors by members. After a long and animated discussion, eight of the ten current directors were returned with Richard Merriman and the recently appointed Meyer Cohen stepping down.

SEASON 1904–05

The dynamic decision to form a company, together with the increased gate money from the first season in Division One, eased the financial situation considerably and enabled the club to make great improvements to the accommodation at the Goldstone. There had been a proposal in April to purchase a new ground for £3,000 in the Preston district, but when the Hove club announced its return to Hove Park, leaving Albion as sole tenants of the Goldstone Ground, the plan was dropped and the decision was made to improve the existing facilities. In May the club secured a seven-year lease on the ground from John Clark, and during the summer Noah Clark and Ben Parker, through their own finances, obtained a wooden stand from an agricultural show being held in Preston Park; the generous pair were reimbursed when the club's status had improved some

years later. The stand, which was erected behind the south goal in time for the new season, seated 1,800 people and served for many years. In 1949 it was modernised and re-erected behind the newly constructed south terracing, and continued in use until 1954. There was now covered accommodation in the ground for 2,800 supporters, with several hundred more open-air seats to the north of the West Stand. The east banking was also improved, new turnstiles and entrances were built, better accommodation was provided for the players and the Press, and a telephone was installed.

With a ground of their own for the first time, Albion could practise on their home pitch from the beginning of August under the watchful eye of new trainer Mr Ryder, formerly of Stockport County. An application to join the Western League

SEASON 1904–05

Date	Comp.	Ven.	Opponents	Result	HT	Pos.	Scorers	Atten.
Sep 3	SL D1	(a)	New Brompton	D 2–2	1–1	10=	Good (pen), Gardner	3,800
10	SL D1	(h)	Northampton T.	L 1–2	0–1	13	Hulse	6,000
17	SL D1	(a)	Wellingborough T.	W 5–0	2–0	10	Good 2 (1 pen), Hulse, Roberts, Gardner	2,000
24	SL D1	(h)	Portsmouth	L 0–1	0–1	14		9,000
Oct 1	SL D1	(a)	Southampton	D 1–1	1–0	11	Roberts	6,000
8	SL D1	(h)	Brentford	L 0–1	0–0	13		5,000
15	SL D1	(a)	Fulham	L 0–1	0–0	14		12,000
22	SL D1	(h)	Queen's Park R.	W 3–0	1–0	13	Robertson, Roberts, Gardner	6,000
29	FAC Q3	(h*)	Shoreham	W 7–1	3–0	–	Hulse 2, Millar, Gardner, Ward 3	3,000
Nov 5	SL D1	(h)	Millwall	W 2–0	1–0	11	Good, Gardner	5,000
12	FAC Q4	(a)	New Brompton	W 1–0	0–0	–	Gardner	6,500
19	SL D1	(h)	Tottenham H'spur	D 1–1	0–1	13	Gardner	6,000
26	FAC Q5	(h)	Ilford	W 5–1	2–0	–	Livingstone, Good, White, Hulse, Roberts	3,316
Dec 3	SL D1	(h)	Luton Town	D 1–1	1–0	13	Gardner	3,752
10	FAC Q6	(a)	West Ham United	W 2–1	1–0	–	White, Gardner	7,000
17	SL D1	(a)	Swindon Town	L 0–1	0–0	15		2,800
24	SL D1	(h)	Bristol Rovers	L 1–2	1–2	16	Roberts	4,000
27	SL D1	(a)	West Ham United	W 1–0	0–0	14	Garfield	10,000
31	SL D1	(h)	New Brompton	W 3–1	2–0	12	Hulse 2, Garfield	4,000
Jan 7	SL D1	(a)	Northampton T.	L 0–3	0–0	13		3,000
14	FAC Int.	(h)	Bristol Rovers	L 1–2	0–1	–	Roberts	8,000
21	SL D1	(a)	Portsmouth	W 2–0	2–0	11	Lyon 2	5,000
28	SL D1	(h)	Southampton	W 1–0	0–0	10	Hulse	6,000
Feb 1	SL D1	(h)	Wellingborough T.	W 3–0	2–0	9	Good, Gardner, White	2,000
4	SL D1	(a)	Brentford	L 0–1	0–1	9		2,800
11	SL D1	(h)	Fulham	L 1–4	1–2	10	Roberts	5,000
18	SL D1	(a)	Queen's Park R.	W 2–1	1–0	8	Roberts, Gilhooly	6,000
22	SL D1	(a)	Reading	D 2–2	2–1	6	Hulse, Gilhooly	2,000
25	SL D1	(h)	Watford	W 1–0	1–0	6	Hulse	4,000
Mar 4	SL D1	(a)	Millwall	L 0–3	0–2	6		3,000
11	SL D1	(h)	Plymouth Argyle	W 2–0	0–0	6	Gilhooly 2	2,000
18	SL D1	(a)	Tottenham H'spur	D 1–1	0–1	6	Gilhooly	8,000
25	SL D1	(h)	West Ham United	W 3–1	1–1	5	Lyon 2 (1 pen), Gardner	4,067
Apr 1	SL D1	(a)	Luton Town	L 0–2	0–1	7		4,000
8	SL D1	(h)	Reading	L 0–1	0–0	9		4,414
15	SL D1	(h)	Swindon Town	W 2–0	1–0	8	Gardner, Lyon (pen)	5,000
21	SL D1	(a)	Plymouth Argyle	L 1–3	0–2	8	Parsons	12,000
22	SL D1	(a)	Bristol Rovers	L 1–4	0–1	8	Gardner	10,000
29	SL D1	(a)	Watford	L 1–5	1–0	12	Own goal	4,000

Note: Oct 29 – tie drawn away but switched to the Goldstone Ground.

Player appearances (shirt numbers)

Player	League appearances	League goals
Aspden T	7	
Gardner A	23	10
Garfield B	8	2
Gilhooly P	15	5
Good M	25	5
Hulme A	11	
Hulse B	26	7
Kelly W	3	
Leach G	2	
Livingstone A	26	
Lyon H	29	5
Mellors M	32	
Millar A	31	
O'Brien J	28	
Parsons E	15	1
Pryce J	2	
Roberts W	33	6
Robertson T	26	1
Robinson G	2	
Ward A	3	
White T	27	1
Own goals		OG – 1

Albion faced foreign opposition for the first time on Boxing Day 1904 when Athletique Parisien, a combination representing the French Association, were defeated 9–1 in a friendly match at the Goldstone. A return match in France, scheduled for March, was cancelled.

was turned down, but the reserve team was entered in both the Southern League's Second Division and the South Eastern League, although once again the first team would play a few fixtures in the latter competition for practice. The second eleven's programme had been greatly disrupted in 1903–04 by the requirements of the Hove club, with a consequent loss of gate receipts.

The club adopted a new strip for this season which was first seen in a public practice match on 27 August between the 'Blue shirts' and the 'Stripe shirts'; the blue-and-white stripes would become a traditional feature of the club for many years to come. Around 4,000 supporters attended the match to see the new players, with the proceeds going to the Brighton and Hove Dispensary in Sackville Road. Pre-season public practice matches continued as a regular event until 1960.

There were plenty of newcomers on show at the practice match. Having been given a lifeline by the Southern League at the end of the previous season, only half the first team was retained and thirteen new professionals were taken on. Among them were goalkeeper Mark Mellors from Notts County, Joe O'Brien and Mickey Good from Reading, Tom Robertson from Southampton, Archie Livingstone from Burton United, Andy

Southern League Division 1 1904–05

		P	W	D	L	F	A	W	D	L	F	A	Pts
1.	Bristol Rovers	34	13	4	0	51	11	7	4	6	23	25	48
2.	Reading	34	13	3	1	36	12	5	4	8	21	26	43
3.	Southampton	34	9	4	4	29	21	9	3	5	25	19	43
4.	Plymouth Argyle	34	14	3	0	38	11	4	2	11	19	28	41
5.	Tottenham Hotspur	34	10	3	4	34	15	5	5	7	19	19	38
6.	Fulham	34	10	5	2	32	9	4	5	8	14	25	38
7.	Queen's Park R.	34	10	2	5	36	19	4	6	7	15	27	36
8.	Portsmouth	34	12	1	4	39	19	4	3	10	22	37	36
9.	New Brompton	34	8	7	2	25	13	3	4	10	15	27	33
10.	Watford	34	12	0	5	30	19	3	3	11	14	26	33
11.	West Ham United	34	9	3	5	30	15	3	5	9	18	27	32
12.	**ALBION**	34	9	2	6	25	15	4	4	9	19	30	32
13.	Northampton Town	34	8	4	5	26	17	4	4	9	17	37	32
14.	Brentford	34	5	7	5	17	14	5	2	10	16	24	29
15.	Millwall	34	7	6	4	26	17	4	1	12	12	30	29
16.	Swindon Town	34	11	2	4	30	17	1	3	13	11	42	29
17.	Luton Town	34	11	1	5	35	18	1	2	14	10	36	27
18.	Wellingborough Town	34	4	3	10	16	37	1	0	16	9	70	13

Because of an English Cup replay with Reading two days later, Fulham unilaterally postponed their Second Division fixture with Albion reserves at Craven Cottage on 11 February and sent their own reserve team down to the Goldstone for the First Division match on the same day. Despite there being a completely different team on the printed match-cards, the Fulham officials refused to reveal the real names of their players to either the Brighton directorate or the Press. Having turned down the suggestion of making the match a friendly, the furious Albion officials reported the matter to the Southern League authorities. The Cottagers were fined £20 for postponing the reserve match and £20 for fielding their second eleven at Hove, but there was no financial compensation for the Albion. Nor was there to be a replay of the First Division match which, ironically, the Fulham reserves had won 4–1.

Albion 1904–05

Standing left to right: Charles Campbell (secretary), J. Ryder (trainer), Arthur Hulme, Bertie Lyon, Tom Robertson (captain), Mark Mellors, Joe O'Brien, Arthur Millar, Andy Gardner, John Jackson (manager), F. Shelly (assistant trainer).
Seated left to right: Tommy Aspden, Alf Ward, Ben Hulse, Tom White, Archie Livingstone, Billy Kelly.
On ground left to right: Ted Parsons, Paddy Gilhooly, Micky Good, Billy Roberts, Jack Pryce.

Gardner from Bolton Wanderers, Arthur Millar and Ben Hulse from Millwall, Bertie Lyon from West Ham United and Paddy Gilhooly from Spurs. Twenty-two professionals on the books indicated the board's confidence in the financial position.

(At this time players recruited from Football League clubs were signed without the payment of a transfer fee; the Southern League had no agreement with the Football League over registrations until 1910. A great many fine players, internationals among them, switched their allegiances to the Southern League when dissatisfied with the terms offered at the end of their contracts. The leading Southern League clubs could often pay better wages to star players and there were many cases of poaching which were almost impossible to prove.)

The League season saw a marked improvement in results, with Albion occupying a comfortable, mid-table spot for the second half of the campaign after a run of five wins in six games at the New Year. Rising to fifth spot in March, five defeats in the last six games saw the team finish in twelfth place, but taking three points from championship contenders Southampton and drawing home and away with Tottenham Hotspur had been excellent achievements. The team also did well in the English Cup, beating Shoreham, New Brompton and Ilford to set up a tie with West Ham United. A week at Leigh-on-Sea did the trick for Albion who triumphed 2–1 at Upton Park, but they went out at home to the eventual Southern League champions, Bristol

March 25th, 1905: in the 65th minute of an exceptionally rough and ill-tempered match with West Ham United at the Goldstone, centre-forward Bertie Lyon scored a beauty with a diving header to put Albion 2–1 ahead. As Lyon picked himself up, the Hammers' England international goalkeeper, Matt Kingsley, aimed a kick at him. The crowd, already incensed by the visitors' vigorous methods, spilled on to the pitch and swarmed around the West Ham players. Ugly scenes developed, and when order was restored Kingsley was dismissed from the field of play and Lyon was carried to the dressing-room to receive treatment. Albion eventually won the game 3–1.

At a 'smoker' after the monthly meeting of the South Eastern League committee at the George Hotel in the Strand, London, on 30 December 1904,

old friend John Jackson from Brighton astonished the gathering with his vocal talent.

Rovers, in the intermediate round. The West Country side returned home with a set of gold medals offered to the winning team by a 'zealous Brightonian' who was, no doubt, rather disappointed.

Amid widespread gossip concerning the club's financial position and rumours as to trouble with the F.A., an extraordinary general meeting of shareholders was called on 16 March at the Presbyterian Lecture Hall in North Road, Brighton. Those present heard chairman George Broadbridge defend the board with such aplomb that they took up around 750 shares to help with the payment of summer wages! He also announced that John Jackson was about to be replaced. The manager himself then took the floor to deny certain allegations that had been made about him, stating that 'no one has worked harder to establish first-class football in the town'. He had, after all, been manager of Brighton United and the driving-force behind the formation of the Albion.

There were no complaints regarding Jackson's performance as team manager – Albion were currently sixth in the Southern League – but it emerged that the club's books and administrative affairs in general were in a terrible state: there had, for instance, been no entries of receipts or outgoings since January. A few days later Frank Scott-Walford was brought in as secretary-manager to sort out the mess left by his predecessors, Jackson and secretary Charles Campbell. A well-known football administrator from the Middlesex area, Walford had formed the Enfield and District League some years earlier and had been a Football League linesman and a Southern League referee. Jackson was paid £75 in lieu of notice and was granted a testimonial, an Easter-holiday friendly against Spurs, thus becoming Albion's first beneficiary.

However, the problems would not go away. In April a Football Association commission began an investigation into the books and other affairs of the club, and reported at the end of May. The three-man inquiry decreed that the accounts were 'in a most unsatisfactory state' and that the affairs of the club were 'in a state of chaos'. The commission also found that an amateur goalkeeper, G. L. Robinson, was paid money 'considerably in excess of his expenses' for playing in two reserve matches in January a few days before he was registered as a professional; the club had, in fact, falsified receipts and other documents in connection with Robinson. It was also revealed that the players had received a present of ten shillings (50p) each from a supporter of the club after a Southern League match with Southampton.

As a result of these findings, George Broadbridge and fellow board members Noah Clark, Harry Gadd, Ben Parker and Frederick Stevens were suspended for three months, with Clark, Stevens and two ex-directors, Reg Alderton and Tom Cooter, receiving an additional three months for arranging the illegal payments. Goalkeeper Robinson also received a three-month suspension, while the recently departed Jackson and Campbell were severely censured for their part in the affairs. Broadbridge publicly denied all knowledge of the incidents.

As if that wasn't trouble enough, the board also had to announce the perennial 'serious financial position'. On 14 April, Broadbridge presided over a meeting at The Dome attended by 2,000 of the club's supporters, and informed the gathering that between £800 and £1,000 was needed to secure a first-class team for the coming season. With gates averaging 5,000, the chairman called upon every regular supporter to purchase one share in order to put the club on a sound footing. The new manager added his voice to the appeal. Further information on the grave situation was given in the company's first financial report, released in October 1905. The first ten months' trading had resulted in a net loss of nearly £1,500, as reported by the *Sussex Daily News*:

BRIGHTON AND HOVE ALBION

SERIOUS FINANCIAL POSITION

The Report and Statement of Accounts to be presented at the approaching meeting of the shareholders of the Brighton and Hove Albion Football Club have just been issued, and show that at the end of April last there was a deficit of about £1,500. The terms of the Report are as follows:

'The Directors herewith submit to the shareholders their Report and audited accounts for the ten months ended 30 April 1905.

'It will be seen from the accompanying accounts that, after making provision for depreciation of stands, plant, and office furniture, and the writing-off of the preliminary expenses in connection with the formation of the Company, the net loss is:

	£	s.	d.
	1,456	19	11

'To this must be added the liabilities taken over and paid by the Company £126 2 6
'Making an adverse balance to be carried forward of £1,583 2 5

'The Directors regret having to announce such a result, and at the same time desire to point out that owing to the recent decision of the Football Association in suspending several of the late Directors, the majority of the present Directors have only been in office a short time, and they trust the shareholders will continue their loyal support by attending and inducing their friends to attend the Club's matches during the present season. The Directors, in view of the financial position of the Club as shewn by the accompanying accounts, are considering the advisability of making a further public issue of shares, to enable them to maintain a first-class football team in Brighton. The following Directors retire in accordance with the Company's articles of association, and offer themselves for re-election: C. F. Butcher, H. J. Miles, and P. T. Vey.

'The Balance Sheet shows that the receipts for the ten months were as follows:

	£	s.	d.
Match Receipts	3,786	19	10
Season Tickets	136	0	6
Position and Fixture Cards	54	9	6
Sundry Receipts	9	17	9
Total	£3,987	7	7

'The expenditure is set forth as follows:

	£	s.	d.
Rent & Royalty of Ground & Office	208	2	0
Wages and Salaries	3,212	4	2
Signing-on Fees	66	10	0
General Expenses	306	2	10
Travelling Expenses	523	11	2
Match Expenses	425	7	4
Printing, Advertising, etc.	271	2	10
Outfit [kit, balls, etc.]	57	11	5
Donation re Hospital Match	31	10	0
Subscriptions to Leagues, etc.	31	8	6
Reserves for Audit Fee	16	16	0
Total	£5,150	6	3

'To this is added £57 19s. 2d. for depreciation on stands, ground plant, furniture, etc., making a total of £5,208 5s. 5d., and leaving a deficiency of £1,220 17s. 10d. To this deficiency have to be added £75 as compensation to late Manager in lieu of notice, and £161 2s. 1d. for preliminary expenses in connection with the formation of the Company, making the net loss £1,456 19s. 11d. The authorised capital of the Company is £4,000 in 16,000 shares of 5s. each, but the issued capital on 30 April was 4,951 shares, amounting to £1,217 15s. (allowing for £20 on unpaid calls). The liabilities at the same date comprised £250 8s. 9d. sundry creditors; £500 loans; and £43 4s. 11d. bank overdraft, making a total liability £2,011 8s. 8d. The assets were £8 7s. 3d. cash in hand, £417 16s. 3d. grand stand, plant, and furniture (after allowing for depreciation), £2 2s. 9d. sundry accounts paid in advance; total £428 6s. 3d. The Auditors' certificate states that all their requirements have been complied with as far as possible by the present Directors, and "we report that we have examined the Books, accounts, and vouchers of the Company, and find the same substantially correct, considering the lax manner in which they have been kept, and in our opinion the balance sheet is drawn up so as to exhibit a true and correct view of the state of the Company's affairs, as shewn by the books and papers which have been produced to us." '

SEASON 1905–06

Once again, sweeping changes were made to the team during the summer. At this time players signed a contract for one season and, if not retained, were free to peddle their wares elsewhere. The turnover of players at most clubs was enormous; indeed, many played for a different club each season throughout their careers. The new faces included the Buckley brothers, Frank (Aston Villa) and Chris (Manchester City); Dick Joynes and Harry Kent (Newark); Albert Fisher (Bristol City); Tom Allsopp (Leicester Fosse); Walter Anthony (Nottingham Forest); Proctor Hall (Manchester United); and Tom Turner (Blantyre).

After the troubles of last season a new board of directors was appointed under the chairmanship of William Goodwin, a local fishmonger and former full-back who had represented a number of counties. The other new directors were Frank Smith (vice-chairman), Henry Miles, Peter Vey, Reynolds Blogg, Charles Cardwell, and the former Sussex cricketer Cecil Butcher. Smith, Blogg and Cardwell soon faded from the scene to be replaced by Charles Brown, Thomas Banfield and Noah Clark. Six of these fine men were to render exceptional service to the club. Clark, one of the founders, remained on the board until his death in November 1930; Goodwin served until 1940; Brown resigned through ill health in August 1930, but returned to the board in August 1931 when Peter Vey also had to resign because of failing health; Butcher served until 1929; and Miles was still on the board when the Second World War broke out — in all, some 174 years of loyalty and service.

Three wise men
From left to right, Charles Brown, Noah Clark and William Goodwin, pictured in the 1920s; all three joined the reconstructed board of directors in the 1905–06 season. Brown, a Brighton tailor, served on the board for 29 years and was chairman from 1919 until 1930. Clark, a Brighton fish merchant, was one of the directors suspended in 1905 but returned to the board in 1906; in 1925 he was referred to as 'The Father of the Club' and, in all, was a director for 25 years. Goodwin, also a Brighton fishmonger, was a director from 1905 until 1940, and was chairman twice, from 1905 until 1909 and from 1930 until 1940; he was also president of the club from 1909 until the 1940s.

For the first time since being promoted, the first team was entered in a midweek competition, the United League which had reformed after folding some years earlier. This gave Albion an additional eighteen fixtures. With the company's deficit on the first year of trading standing at nearly £1,500, the extra income from these matches was vital. Former chairman George Broadbridge became president of the United League and in August 1905 presented a magnificent cup, valued at 50 guineas (£52.50), to be awarded annually to the competition winners. Frank Walford was elected vice-chairman of the new competition. Albion were also admitted as full members of the Football Association.

The team struggled for results in the Southern League, especially away from the Goldstone with only four points and just six goals registered in the seventeen 'out' matches, but good home form in the latter part of the season lifted Albion clear of the relegation zone after being bottom at the New Year. In fact, from Boxing Day the team remained unbeaten at home for the rest of the term in both the Southern and United Leagues. In the latter competition they finished seventh of the ten clubs, having been bottom in January.

In contrast, English Cup performances were good, the competition proper being reached for the first time. Albion were exempted to the fourth qualifying round in which they travelled north to account for Second Division Glossop by a goal to nil. This was the first occasion that Albion met Football League opposition in the English Cup and it was a match that was to have serious repercussions. Swindon Town were defeated 3–0 at the Goldstone in the first round, opening up the opportunity of a plum home tie with First Division big-spenders Middlesbrough.

Alf Shrubb, the world-famous long-distance runner, played outside-right for the reserves against Willesden Town at the Goldstone Ground on 9 December. Alf was an above-average footballer and regularly turned out for Horsham around this period, but following his appearance in Albion colours rumour spread throughout the Southern League that he had signed for the club and was to play on a regular basis. When approached by the Press, Shrubb quickly scotched the gossip.

SEASON 1905–06

Date	Comp.	Ven.	Opponents	Result	HT	Pos.	Scorers	Atten.	Allsopp T	Anthony W	Beale R	Buckley C	Buckley F	Clare E	Edwards W	Fisher A	Foster	Graham J	Haig-Brown A	Hall P	Harding F	Hulme A	Innes R	Joynes R	Kennedy J	Kennedy W	Kent H	Kitto R	Langley E	Lumley J	Mellors M	Mochan C	Rule A	Turner T	White T	Wragg W	Yates W
Sep 2	SL D1	(h)	Millwall	L 0–2	0–1	11=		5,500	11				5	2		8							4		6	9					1	3			7		10
6	Utd League	(h)	Leyton	L 0–2	0–0	6=		'not large'	11					6						8			4	7			5			9	1	3		2			10
9	SL D1	(a)	Luton Town	L 1–4	0–3	16	Innes	5,000	11				5	6		8							4	7		9					1	3		2			10
16	SL D1	(h)	Tottenham H'spur	W 2–0	2–0	13	Yates, F Buckley	6,000	11				5	2						8		3	4	7		9	6				1						10
20	Utd League	(a)	Swindon Town	L 0–3	0–0	8=		600	11	10			5	2		8						3	4	7		9					1					6	
23	SL D1	(a)	Brentford	L 0–2	0–1	15		8,000	11	10			5	2						8		3	4	7		9	6				1						
27	Utd League	(h)	Luton Town	W 2–1	1–1	7	Allsopp 2	'capital'	11				5	2		10				8			4	7			6			9	1					3	
30	SL D1	(h)	Norwich City	W 2–1	1–0	13	F Buckley, Hall	5,000	11				5	2						8			4	7			6				1		9			3	10
Oct 2	Utd League*	(a)	New Brompton	– –	1–0	7	W Kennedy			11			5	2		8						3	4	7		10	6			9	1						
7	SL D1	(a)	Plymouth Argyle	L 0–1	0–1	14		9,000	11				5	2						8			4	7		9	6				1					3	10
11	Utd League	(h)	Crystal Palace	L 2–3	0–0	7	C Buckley, Yates	1,200	11		1	9	5	2		8						3	4	7			6										10
14	SL D1	(h)	Southampton	L 1–3	0–1	14	Kent (pen)	6,000	11		1		5	2				9		8			4	7			6									3	10
21	SL D1	(a)	Reading	L 1–2	1–2	16	Hall	5,000	11		1			2						8			4	7	5	9	6									3	10
25	Utd League	(h)	New Brompton	W 2–0	1–0	6	Own goal, Kent (pen)	1,500	11		1			2		8			7			3	4		5		6			9							10
28	Utd League	(h)	Watford	L 0–2	0–1	6		3,000	11		1	6		2		8			7			3	4		5				9								10
Nov 2	Utd League	(a)	Southern United	L 1–4	0–1	7	Hulme (pen)	500	11			6		2						8		3	4	7	5	9					1						10
4	SL D1	(a)	Northampton T.	D 0–0	0–0	17		5,000	11	7			5	2		8							4	9			6				1			3			10
11	SL D1	(a)	West Ham United	L 0–2	0–2	18		8,000	11	7			5	2		8							4	9			6				1			3			10
18	SL D1	(h)	Fulham	L 1–2	1–1	18	Hall	6,000	11	7	1		5	2						8			4	9			6							3			10
22	Utd League	(a)	Crystal Palace	W 2–0	0–0	7	Yates, Anthony	600	11	7	1			2						8		3	4	9			5									6	10
25	SL D1	(a)	Queen's Park R.	D 0–0	0–0	18		10,000	11	7				2						8		3	4	9	6		5				1						10
Dec 2	SL D1	(h)	Bristol Rovers	W 2–1	1–0	17=	Hall, Allsopp	5,000	11	7				2						8		3	4	9	6		5				1						10
9	FAC Q4	(a)	Glossop	W 1–0	0–0	–	Yates	1,200	11	7				2						8		3	4	9	6		5				1						10
16	SL D1	(h)	Portsmouth	L 0–5	0–1	18		7,000	11	7				2						8		3	4	9	6		5				1						10
23	SL D1	(a)	Swindon Town	L 0–2	0–1	18		5,000	11	7				2								3	4	9	6		5			8	1						10
25	SL D1	(a)	New Brompton	L 0–1	0–0	18		4,000	11	7		4	6			8						3					5			9	1			2			10
26	SL D1	(h)	Watford	W 2–0	1–0	18	Allsopp, Anthony	8,500	11	7		4	6							8		3		9			5				1			2			10
30	SL D1	(a)	Millwall	L 1–2	0–1	18	Joynes	4,000	11	7		4	6							8		3		9			5				1			2			10
Jan 4	Utd League	(a)	Leyton	L 1–2	1–2	9	Fisher			7		4		2		9				8			6							11	1	3				5	10
6	SL D1	(h)	Luton Town	W 2–1	1–1	17	Kent, Joynes	3,000	11	7		4	6							8		3		9			5				1			2			10
13	FAC R1	(h)	Swindon Town	W 3–0	2–0	–	Yates 2, Hall	6,500	11	7		4	6							8		3		9			5				1			2			10
20	SL D1	(a)	Tottenham H'spur	L 1–3	1–0	17	Anthony	10,000	11	7		4	6							8		3		9			5				1			2			10
24	Utd League	(a)	Grays United	D 1–1	0–1	10	Joynes	'small'	11	7	1	4	6	3		8								9			5							2			10
27	SL D1	(h)	Brentford	W 3–2	1–2	15	Yates, Kent, Hall	4,000	11	7		4	6							8		3		9			5				1			2			10
31	Utd League	(h)	Clapton Orient	D 0–0	0–0	8					1			2	8						5		4			9		10		11		3			7	6	
Feb 3	FAC R2	(h)	Middlesbrough	D 1–1	0–1	–	J Kennedy	7,462	11	7		4								8		3		9	6		5				1			2			10
7	FAC R2 Rep	(a)	Middlesbrough	D 1–1*	0–0	–	Joynes	15,000	11	7		4								8		3		9	6		5				1			2			10
10	SL D1	(h)	Plymouth Argyle	D 0–0	0–0	16		3,000	11	7		4								8		3		9	6		5				1			2			10
12	FAC R2 2Rep	(n*)	Middlesbrough	L 1–3	1–1	–	Hulme (pen)	11,528	11	7		4								8		3		9	6		5				1			2			10
17	SL D1	(a)	Southampton	L 0–1	0–0	16		1,000	11	7		4								8		3		9	6		5				1			2			10
24	SL D1	(h)	Reading	W 3–2	2–2	15	Joynes, Yates, C Buckley	3,500	11	7		4	6							8		3		9			5				1			2			10
Mar 3	Utd League	(a)	Watford	L 1–2	0–2	8	Fisher			7		4	6			10				8		3		9			5				1			2			11
7	Utd League	(h)	Southern United	W 3–1	3–0	8	Fisher 2, J Kennedy	'very small'	11							9				8		3	4		5	10				6	1			2	7		
10	SL D1	(h)	Northampton T.	D 2–2	2–1	16	Allsopp, Hall	3,000	11			4	6							8		3		9			5				1			2	7		10
12	Utd League	(a)	Luton Town	D 3–3	3–1	8	Lumley, Fisher, Kent		11			4	6			9						3		7			5			8	1	2					10
17	SL D1	(h)	West Ham United	D 0–0	0–0	15		4,000	11			4	6			9				8		3		7			5				1			2			10
24	SL D1	(a)	Fulham	L 0–2	0–2	16		7,000	11			4	6			9				8		3		7			5				1			2			10
31	SL D1	(h)	Queen's Park R.	W 3–2	2–2	14	Joynes, Yates, Hall	4,000	11	7		4	6							8		3		9			5				1			2			10
Apr 2	Utd League	(a)	New Brompton	L 0–2	0–1	8		500	11			4	6				8								9		5			7	1	2				3	10
5	SL D1	(a)	Norwich City	L 0–2	0–0	14		5,000	11	7		4	6							8		3		9			5				1			2			10
7	SL D1	(a)	Bristol Rovers	L 1–2	0–0	14	J Kennedy	5,000	11	7		4	6							8		3			9		5				1			2			10
13	Utd League	(h)	Swindon Town	W 1–0	0–0	8	C Buckley	4,000	11			4	6	3						8					9		5				1			2	7		10
14	SL D1	(h)	New Brompton	D 0–0	0–0	14		4,000	11	7		4	6							8		3		9			5				1			2			10
16	SL D1	(a)	Watford	W 1–0	1–0	14	Anthony	6,000	11	7		4								8		3		9	6		5				1			2			10
21	SL D1	(a)	Portsmouth	L 0–5	0–1	14		7,000	11	7		4								8		3		9	6		5				1			2			10
23	Utd League	(a)	Clapton Orient	D 0–0	0–0	8					1					8							4	9	6	10	5			11		3		2	7		
28	SL D1	(h)	Swindon Town	D 1–1	0–1	16	Allsopp	3,000	11	7		4	6			8						3		9			5				1			2			10
30	Utd League	(h)	Grays United	W 9–2	3–2	7	Fisher 3, Joynes 3, Kent 2, Allsopp		11	7	1					8						3	4	9			5			6				2			10
Southern League appearances									34	24	3	19	25	15	0	8	0	1	0	27	0	25	15	31	11	6	32	0	0	2	31	2	1	23	2	4	33
Southern League goals									4	3		1	2							7			1	4	1		3										4
United League appearances									14	6	8	9	8	12	1	12	1	0	2	8	1	10	13	11	7	5	12	1	1	10	10	6	0	7	4	6	13
United League goals								OG – 1	3	1		2				8						1		4	1		4			1							2

Notes: Oct 2 – abandoned after 80 minutes because of darkness with score 1–0. Match not included in end-of-season statistics.

Feb 7 – after extra time (90-minute score 1–1).

Feb 12 – played at Bramall Lane, Sheffield United FC.

Southern League Division 1 1905–06

		P	W	D	L	F	A	W	D	L	F	A	Pts
1.	Fulham	34	10	7	0	22	6	9	5	3	22	9	50
2.	Southampton	34	13	2	2	32	11	6	5	6	26	28	45
3.	Portsmouth	34	13	3	1	39	11	4	6	7	22	24	43
4.	Luton Town	34	13	2	2	45	13	4	5	8	19	27	41
5.	Tottenham Hotspur	34	13	2	2	36	11	3	5	9	10	18	39
6.	Plymouth Argyle	34	11	3	3	32	13	5	4	8	20	20	39
7.	Norwich City	34	8	8	1	30	12	5	2	10	16	26	36
8.	Bristol Rovers	34	11	1	5	37	23	4	4	9	19	33	35
9.	Brentford	34	11	3	3	28	19	3	4	10	15	33	35
10.	Reading	34	9	7	1	34	15	3	2	12	19	31	33
11.	West Ham United	34	12	2	3	30	9	2	3	12	12	30	33
12.	Millwall	34	9	4	4	26	16	2	7	8	12	25	33
13.	Queen's Park R.	34	9	3	5	39	14	3	4	10	19	30	31
14.	Watford	34	7	6	4	28	20	1	4	12	10	37	26
15.	Swindon Town	34	6	4	7	21	23	2	5	10	10	29	25
16.	**ALBION**	34	8	5	4	24	24	1	2	14	6	31	25
17.	New Brompton	34	5	5	7	10	20	2	3	12	10	42	22
18.	Northampton Town	34	5	4	8	17	22	3	1	13	15	57	21

United League 1905–06

		P	W	D	L	F	A	W	D	L	F	A	Pts
1.	Watford	18	7	2	0	28	5	6	2	1	21	10	30
2.	Crystal Palace	18	6	1	2	27	13	7	0	2	24	8	27
3.	Leyton	18	6	2	1	23	15	2	2	5	10	16	20
4.	Luton Town	18	5	3	1	31	12	2	1	6	16	15	18
5.	Clapton Orient	18	5	3	1	16	11	0	5	4	8	16	18
6.	Swindon Town	18	5	1	3	24	15	2	2	5	9	14	17
7.	**ALBION**	18	5	1	3	19	11	1	3	5	9	17	16
8.	New Brompton	18	6	1	2	13	5	1	1	7	13	22	16
9.	Grays United	18	2	2	5	9	21	2	0	7	12	43	10
10.	Southern United	18	3	1	5	14	21	0	1	8	7	43	8

Albion 1905–06

*Back row left to right: unknown, Henry Miles (director), Cecil Butcher (director), unknown, unknown, Bob Beale, unknown, unknown,
    William Goodwin (chairman).*
*Third row left to right: Arthur Hulme (captain), Harry Kent, Harding, Powell, unknown, Bill Kennedy, Edwin Clare, Frank Buckley, Chris Buckley,
    Tom Turner, unknown, Frank Scott-Walford (secretary-manager), Joe Clayton (trainer).*
Seated left to right: Mark Mellors, Dick Joynes, Albert Fisher, Bob Innes, Billy Yates, Proctor Hall, Tom Allsopp, Walter Anthony.
On ground left to right: Tom White, Joe Lumley, Charlie Mochan, Jimmy Kennedy.
(Note: unidentified players in white – Herbert Schooley, F. A. Bowles, Frank Harker.)

The United League fixture with Clapton Orient on 6 January kicked off fifteen minutes late because of the late arrival of the Orient side. Even then, only five of the visitors' players took the field, the remaining half-dozen turning up ten minutes later still. Surely a field day for Albion? No, the final score was 0–0!

Owing to the serious illness of Alderman Clark, the Albion's landlord whose house overlooked the ground, a circular was handed to the Goldstone crowd at the match with Queen's Park Rangers on 31 March requesting that no unnecessary noise be made. The appeal was observed for most of the match, but when Proctor Hall scored the winner in a 3–2 victory the 4,000 spectators could no longer contain themselves.

For financial reasons the Yorkshire side offered to stage the match at Ayresome Park, but Albion refused. A record gate was anticipated at the Goldstone, but amid public outcry the ground admission was doubled to one shilling (5p) and in the event only 7,462 attended. The game ended in a 1–1 draw, Jimmy Kennedy scoring Albion's equaliser with only five minutes remaining. In the replay four days later, Dick Joynes put Albion in front on 70 minutes, but 'Boro levelled the scores eight minutes later and the game went into extra time with neither side able to break the deadlock. A second replay was staged at Bramall Lane, Sheffield, the following Monday. Middlesbrough took an early lead, but when Arthur Hulme equalised from the penalty spot on the stroke of half time Albion hopes were high. In the second half Alf Common, the first footballer to be transferred for £1,000, completed a hat-trick and so 'Boro went through to the third round where they were thrashed 6–1 at Southampton.

The following comment by Charles Alcock, secretary of the Football Association, appeared in the *Daily Mail* after he had attended Albion's first-round English Cup tie with Swindon Town at the Goldstone Ground on 13 January:

Presumably rule 40 of the Football Association has not reached Swindon yet. At all events the knickerbockers of the majority, if not all, of the visiting team certainly did not reach the knee. In this respect the captain was the most conspicuous offender.

In January, Albion were reported to the Football Association for illegally approaching opposition players at the time of the Glossop cup-tie. As a result of exhaustive investigations, an F.A. Commission decided that

1. Albion's secretary-manager Frank Walford be suspended from 16 April until 1 August 1906 for being mainly responsible for the irregularities;
2. The club be fined £10 towards the costs of the inquiry;
3. The players involved – Mellors, Innes and Clare, and Ross of the Glossop club – be fined £2 each for being parties to the irregularities;
4. The match referee, A. Colyer of Newark-on-Trent, be suspended for nine months for having acted as a football agent and seeking payment for his services in introducing players.

Controversy seemed to dog the club around this period, and locally it was felt that there was something of a 'witch-hunt' against the Albion as the following letter to the *Sussex Daily News*, written just after the illegal payments affair in June 1905, would suggest:

Sir,—I am surprised to notice that the extraordinary decision of the Southern League [sic] to suspend the old directors of the Brighton and Hove Albion has not elicited any local comment. Here are five gentlemen who have worked hard, spent money, and given a lot of time, for the love of football. All these gentlemen are suspended (without right of appeal) from carrying out their duties to the public and shareholders, for what after all appears to be a mere technical breach of the rules, as the player in question had promised to, and did, sign as a professional soon after the alleged offence.

Might I suggest to the directors that they should call the annual meeting at as early a date as possible, and lay the whole matter before the shareholders; and might I suggest to the shareholders that if they are satisfied with what their directors have done, and are doing, that they should pass a vote of confidence in them and select some gentlemen to carry on the affairs of the club until the old directors are able to resume their duties.

In conclusion I appeal to all true sportsmen and lovers of football to buck up, sink all minor differences, and determine that the Brighton and Hove Albion shall succeed in spite of jealous opposition, and thus show the football world what a southern team can do when the public, directors, and manager, are all pulling together.—Yours, etc.

Alfred W. Turner,
50 Preston Street,
Brighton.

Brighton and Hove Football Ground.

The Goldstone Ground in the 1900s
This view, from behind the South Stand, shows the small but attractive West Stand, the open benches to the north of it, and a packed northern end. In the distance is the Goldstone waterworks, now the British Engineerium. Note the predominant form of private transport in those days; bicycles had their own undercover parking area at the rear of the South Stand!

SEASON 1906–07

There was a vast improvement in the club's playing fortunes this season. Only seven new signings were made during the summer, compared with eighteen the previous year, and with seven players retained a greater understanding developed. The new men were Hugh MacDonald, a massively-built goalkeeper from Woolwich Arsenal; Jack Hall, a goalscoring centre-forward from Stoke; Wally and Alec Smith from Newark; Julius Gregory from Manchester City; Willie McDonald from Kilmarnock; and Jack Lewis from Bristol Rovers, signed only two months after representing Wales against England in Cardiff. Another significant first appearance was that in November of Bertie Longstaff, a young amateur from Shoreham who went on to make nearly 450 competitive first-team appearances for the club, overlapping into the Football League era.

Though never threatening to take the title, an excellent third place was achieved behind Fulham, who finished as champions, and second-placed Portsmouth. The main reason behind the best League standing so far was a great improvement in away performances: six wins and seventeen points provided by far the biggest haul away from the Goldstone since the club won promotion. As usual home form was good, with big wins over Plymouth Argyle and New Brompton, and in March 11,000 spectators (£300), a new ground record, witnessed a hard-fought, goal-less draw with League-leaders Fulham.

SEASON 1906–07

Player columns (left to right): Allsopp T, Anthony W, Gregory J, Hall JH, Harker F, Hulme A, Joynes R, Kent H, Lewis J, Longstaff A, Lumley J, MacDonald H, McDonald W, Schooley H, Smith Alec, Smith Wally, Turner T, Woolven H

Date	Comp.	Ven.	Opponents	Result	HT	Pos.	Scorers	Atten.
Sep 1	SL D1	(a)	Leyton	W 1–0	0–0	1=	Hall	5,000
5	Utd League	(h)	Luton Town	W 7–2	5–1	1	Anthony, Hall 3, Joynes 3	1,500
8	SL D1	(h)	Portsmouth	D 1–1	1–1	3=	Joynes	10,500
15	SL D1	(a)	New Brompton	L 3–4	0–2	11=	Lewis 2 (1 pen), W Smith	5,000
22	SL D1	(h)	Plymouth Argyle	W 4–1	2–0	6	W Smith 2, Hall, Anthony	8,000
24	Utd League	(h)	Luton Town	D 0–0	0–0	3		
29	SL D1	(h)	Bristol Rovers	D 1–1	1–0	8	Kent	7,370
Oct 4	Utd League	(a)	Leyton	W 2–1	1–1	3	Joynes, Hulme (pen)	
6	SL D1	(a)	Reading	W 1–0	0–0	6	Hall	5,000
11	Utd League	(a)	Norwich City	D 1–1	1–0	3	Lewis	4,000
13	SL D1	(h)	Watford	L 0–3	0–1	8		6,000
17	Utd League	(h)	Norwich City	W 4–3	2–3	2	Allsopp, W Smith, Woolven 2	2,000
20	SL D1	(a)	Northampton T.	D 1–1	0–1	9	Hall	6,000
22	Utd League	(a)	New Brompton	L 2–4	0–2	3	Joynes, W Smith	800
27	SL D1	(h)	Queen's Park R.	W 2–0	1–0	7	Kent, Hall	7,000
31	Utd League	(h)	Hastings & St L. U.	W 1–0	0–0	2	W Smith (pen)	1,000
Nov 3	SL D1	(a)	Fulham	L 0–2	0–0	9		16,000
7	Utd League	(a)	Crystal Palace	D 2–2	2–0	2	Hall, McDonald	
10	SL D1	(h)	Southampton	W 2–0	2–0	8	Allsopp, Lewis	6,000
14	Utd League	(h)	Watford	W 4–1	2–0	1	A Smith, Lumley, Lewis 2	1,500
17	SL D1	(a)	West Ham United	D 0–0	0–0	7		5,000
21	Utd League	(h)	New Brompton	D 1–1	1–1	1	Kent	1,000
24	SL D1	(h)	Tottenham H'spur	W 2–0	1–0	6	Hall, Lewis	8,000
Dec 1	SL D1	(a)	Swindon Town	D 0–0	0–0	6		5,000
5	SL D1	(h)	Millwall	W 3–1	2–1	4	W Smith, Hall, Anthony	3,500
8	SL D1	(h)	Norwich City	L 0–2	0–2	4		5,000
12	Utd League	(h)	Leyton	D 1–1	0–0	1	Longstaff	1,000
15	SL D1	(a)	Luton Town	L 1–3	0–1	6	Hall	5,000
22	SL D1	(h)	Crystal Palace	W 2–1	0–1	6	Hall, Kent (pen)	5,000
25	SL D1	(a)	Brentford	L 1–3	1–2	8	Hall	11,000
26	SL D1	(h)	Swindon Town	W 1–0	0–0	5	Joynes	8,250
29	SL D1	(h)	Leyton	D 1–1	1–0	6	Joynes	4,000
Jan 5	SL D1	(a)	Portsmouth	L 0–3	0–2	7		9,000
12	FAC R1	(a)	Bolton Wanderers	L 1–3	1–0	–	W Smith	19,330
19	SL D1	(h)	New Brompton	W 4–1	2–1	6	Anthony, Hall, Kent 2	5,000
26	SL D1	(a)	Plymouth Argyle	D 0–0	0–0	6		5,000
Feb 9	SL D1	(h)	Reading	W 1–0	0–0	5	Kent	3,000
13	Utd League	(a)	Hastings & St L.U.	L 1–6	1–4	2	Anthony	
16	SL D1	(a)	Watford	L 0–1	0–0	5		5,000
23	SL D1	(h)	Northampton T.	W 3–0	0–0	4	Lewis, Hall 2	5,000
Mar 2	SL D1	(a)	Queen's Park R.	W 2–0	2–0	5	Lewis, Allsopp	5,000
9	SL D1	(a)	Fulham	D 0–0	0–0	5		11,000
16	SL D1	(a)	Southampton	W 1–0	0–0	3	Lewis	4,000
18	SL D1	(a)	Millwall	L 1–4	0–3	3	Hall	1,500
23	SL D1	(h)	West Ham United	W 2–0	2–0	3	Hall 2	6,000
29	SL D1	(h)	Brentford	W 3–1	1–0	3	Hall 2, Joynes	10,000
30	SL D1	(a)	Tottenham H'spur	L 0–3	0–1	4		16,000
Apr 3	SL D1	(a)	Bristol Rovers	W 4–0	3–0	3	Hall 2, Kent, Lewis	
10	Utd League	(a)	Watford	W 4–1	2–1	2	Lewis, Anthony, Joynes, Gregory (pen)	1,500
13	Utd League	(a)	Norwich City	W 2–1	1–0	3	Allsopp, Hall	2,500
20	SL D1	(h)	Luton Town	L 1–3	0–2	3	Anthony	6,000
27	SL D1	(a)	Crystal Palace	D 2–2	1–2	3	Hall, W Smith	4,000
30	Utd League	(h)	Crystal Palace	D 3–3	1–1	2	Hall 2, Gregory (pen)	'very few'

Appearance / goal totals:

	Allsopp T	Anthony W	Gregory J	Hall JH	Harker F	Hulme A	Joynes R	Kent H	Lewis J	Longstaff A	Lumley J	MacDonald H	McDonald W	Schooley H	Smith Alec	Smith Wally	Turner T	Woolven H
Southern League appearances	38	35	36	37	0	21	11	37	32	1	18	38	32	0	12	36	34	0
Southern League goals	3	4		22			4	7	8							5		
United League appearances	11	12	11	9	1	11	11	10	10	4	9	14	12	1	8	5	12	3
United League goals	1	3	2	6		1	6	1	4	1	1		1		1	3		2

As reward for the Cup exploits of the previous season, Albion were exempted until the first round proper and were drawn away to First Division Bolton Wanderers, but interest was short-lived. Albion took the lead through Wally Smith in the thirteenth minute – much to the delight of the club mascot, a powdered clown – but Wanderers, fielding two current internationals – goalkeeper Dai Davies (Wales) and centre-forward Albert Shepherd (England) – equalised sixteen minutes into the second half and ran out comfortable 3–1 winners.

With only two defeats from fourteen games, Albion finished as runners-up to Crystal Palace in the United League. The reserves had an unhappy time, though, finishing bottom of the South Eastern League Division One, and in June the club withdrew from the competition after failing to gain re-election to the top section despite an increase in the number of teams.

Southern League Division 1 1906–07

		P	W	D	L	F	A	W	D	L	F	A	Pts
1.	Fulham	38	13	5	1	34	12	7	8	4	24	20	53
2.	Portsmouth	38	15	3	1	45	11	7	4	8	19	25	51
3.	ALBION	38	12	4	3	33	16	6	5	8	20	27	45
4.	Luton Town	38	12	4	3	38	22	6	5	8	15	30	45
5.	West Ham United	38	12	5	2	39	12	3	9	7	21	29	44
6.	Tottenham Hotspur	38	13	4	2	46	12	4	5	10	17	33	43
7.	Millwall	38	14	3	2	53	12	4	3	12	18	38	42
8.	Norwich City	38	9	6	4	34	21	6	6	7	23	27	42
9.	Watford	38	9	7	3	31	18	4	9	6	15	25	42
10.	Brentford	38	14	3	2	39	16	3	5	11	18	40	42
11.	Southampton	38	9	6	4	31	18	4	3	12	18	38	35
12.	Reading	38	12	3	4	42	11	2	3	14	15	36	34
13.	Leyton	38	9	6	4	26	23	2	6	11	12	37	34
14.	Bristol Rovers	38	10	4	5	41	21	2	5	12	14	33	33
15.	Plymouth Argyle	38	7	9	3	26	14	3	4	12	17	36	33
16.	New Brompton	38	9	4	6	30	21	3	5	11	17	38	33
17.	Swindon Town	38	11	7	1	28	8	0	4	15	15	46	33
18.	Queen's Park R.	38	9	5	5	32	16	2	5	12	15	39	32
19.	Crystal Palace	38	7	4	8	29	28	1	5	13	17	38	25
20.	Northampton Town	38	5	8	6	22	25	0	1	18	7	64	19

United League 1906–07

		P	W	D	L	F	A	Pts
1.	Crystal Palace	14	8	5	1	39	20	21
2.	ALBION	14	6	6	2	33	26	18
3.	Luton Town	14	8	1	5	23	27	17
4.	Norwich City	14	6	4	4	34	22	16
5.	Hastings & St L. Utd	14	6	2	6	27	24	14
6.	Leyton	14	3	4	7	24	27	10
7.	New Brompton	14	3	3	8	24	35	9
8.	Watford	14	3	1	10	15	38	7

Quite the most remarkable match of the campaign, if not of the whole pre-Football League period, was the 6–1 United League reverse at the Central Ground headquarters of Hastings and St Leonards United in February, a defeat that effectively ended Albion hopes of winning the competition. Hastings scored twice within two minutes of the kick-off and Brighton, fielding a full-strength side, simply fell apart, unable to find any answer to the onslaught. With the score at 4–1 midway through the second half, full-back Julius Gregory was injured and left the field. Astonishingly, Albion brought Hugh MacDonald out of goal to make up the deficiency, playing the rest of the match without a custodian ice-hockey-style.

Only fifteen players were employed in the Southern League games and Jack Hall took the scoring honours, registering 22 of the 53 Southern League goals and totalling 28 in all competitions. In line with results, the attendances at the Goldstone took an upward trend, the average of over 6,500 showing a marked increase over the previous season, and the directors announced a profit of £659 on the year.

Albion 1906–07

Standing left to right: Joe Clayton (trainer), Arthur Hulme, Tom Turner, Hugh MacDonald, Bob Beale, Julius Gregory, Dick Kitto (assistant trainer).
Third row left to right: unknown, unknown, Henry Miles (director), Tom Banfield (director), Noah Clark (director), Charles Brown (director), Frank Scott-Walford (secretary-manager).
Seated left to right: Peter Vey (director), Joe Lumley, Harry Kent (captain), William Goodwin (chairman), Willie McDonald, Alec Smith, Cecil Butcher (director).
On ground left to right: Dick Joynes, Walter Anthony, Jack Lewis, Jack Hall, Wally Smith, Tom Allsopp, Bertie Longstaff.

In the early days, the payment of summer wages to players involved a fair number of special fund-raising events. In the summer of 1906, for example, there was a Quarter-Million Penny Fund opened under the presidency of director Noah Clark, designed to bring in up to £1,000 with supporters marking off their contributions on special cards. (One old penny in 1906 was the cost of a daily newspaper; ground admission was 6d.) In 1906–07 the Summer Wage Fund was augmented by a friendly with First Division giants Sheffield United on 6 April (Albion lost 2–1), and by the second annual sports day, for both public and players, which was held at the Goldstone on the Bank Holiday Monday, 5 August 1907. Among the races were: dribbling the football (open), won by Teddy Elliott ahead of Jack Hall; 100-yard handicap (Albion), won by Hugh MacDonald from Joe Lumley; half-mile handicap (Albion), won by Tom Turner with Jimmy Burnett second; the 60-yard sack race, in which Teddy Elliott scored his second triumph of the day ahead of trainer Joe Clayton; and the quarter-mile obstacle race (Albion), in which Willie McDonald came home in front of Bob Beale. There were also wrestling and tug-of-war contests, and the winner of the ladies' 60-yard handicap went home with a valuable prize-bulldog puppy.

An Agreement made this 24 — day of *October*

1907, Between *Frank Scott Walford g Lancaster Villas*

of Brighton, in the County of Sussex, *Secretary & Manager*

for and on behalf of the BRIGHTON & HOVE ALBION FOOTBALL CLUB of the one part

and *Albert Edward Longstaff*

of *Myrtle House Shoreham Sussex*

Professional Football Player, of the other part, **Whereby** it is agreed by and between the parties as follows :—

1. The said *Albert Edward Longstaff* shall become a playing member of the " Brighton and Hove Albion " Football Club, from *the 24th day of October 1907* until the 30th day of April, *1908*, and shall be paid by the Club for his services the weekly salary or remuneration of £ *2 – 10 –* during such time as he shall play for the Club, but a weekly remuneration of £ ____ only shall be payable between the 1st day of May and the 1st day of September, 1

It is also agreed That the said Albert Edward Longstaff shall be allowed £3-3 — — for signing on fee allowed by the Football Association

The said Albert Edward Longstaff shall be allowed to do the necessary training at Shoreham if he so desires & also follow his usual occupation during such times as his services are not required by the club. "Match days excepted"

2. The said *Albert Edward Longstaff* shall conform to the Rules and Regulations now or hereafter in force in relation to the duties of a playing member of the Club, and shall subject himself to the control of the Officials of the Club or any person having lawful or deputed authority.

3. If the said *Albert Edward Longstaff* shall at any time be guilty of insubordination to any person in authority or shall neglect to keep himself sober and in good playing condition or render himself unfit to play by his own misconduct, the Directors may forthwith, after the commission of such offence, either fine or suspend the said *Albert Edward Longstaff* for such time as they think fit, during which time the payment of salary shall cease, or may discharge him without notice or payment whatsoever.

As **Witness** the hands of the parties.

Signed by the said *F Scott Walford* and *AE Longstaff* in presence of

Frank Scott Walford

Albert Edward Longstaff

Bert Longstaff signs pro.

Albert Longstaff's name first appeared on an Albion team-sheet in 1906, and it was rarely missing until he retired from professional football in 1922. He was the most successful local-born player ever to wear an Albion strip, and made 443 appearances – scoring 86 goals – in all first-team competitions in his sixteen-year Goldstone career (which included a four-year hiatus during the Great War). Born and bred in Shoreham, Longstaff nearly became a Tottenham player but his mother did not want him to leave the area. After nearly a year as an amateur, Bert signed a professional contract with the Albion, a copy of which is shown above, in October 1907, a few days after his 22nd birthday. He negotiated a 3 guinea (£3.15) signing-on fee, and also a special condition which allowed him to train at Shoreham and pursue his usual occupation – he was a tinsmith by trade – at such times when his services were not required by the club, match days excepted. On leaving the Goldstone, Bert reverted to amateur status with his home-town club, Shoreham.

SEASON 1907–08

After a most successful 1906–07 season, the club struggled throughout this term. The old problem of poor away form returned, a meagre eight points being harvested on the road, yet only four defeats were recorded at the Goldstone.

In contrast, Albion enhanced their growing reputation in the English Cup against two First Division sides from the Football League. In the first round, after a 1–1 draw at the Goldstone and a replay which was abandoned during extra time with Albion leading 2–1, Preston North End were beaten 1–0 at Stamford Bridge. In the second round Albion were drawn away to Liverpool and were given no chance by all but the faithful few, yet came away from Anfield with a magnificent 1–1 draw. The 36,000 crowd saw Jack Hall give Albion a half-time lead from the penalty spot, only for England international Jack Cox to level the scores with fifteen minutes remaining. Albion's two-day stop at nearby Birkdale had worked wonders.

A huge assembly awaited the team's return at Brighton Central Station later that night, but, having been swamped by jubilant fans after the Preston victory, the players left the train at Preston Park and completed the journey into town by hansom-cab. With the replay scheduled for the Wednesday, Walford did not want any unnecessary risks to his team.

The replay was witnessed by a record 12,000 spectators (£570) and the result was in doubt until late in the game. Jimmy Bradley gave Liverpool the lead in the 27th minute. Albion fought gamely for an equaliser but were outclassed by their more illustrious opponents. Although there was no further score until the 82nd minute, Liverpool dominated the play, and when Bradley and Cox scored late goals there were no complaints from the home supporters. Playing for Liverpool was former Brighton United favourite Maurice Parry, now the owner of eleven Welsh caps and a championship medal.

After the excitement of the Cup escapades, the season petered out into anti-climax, Albion finishing the term in a disappointing seventeenth position. Jack Hall was again the leading marksman with sixteen in the Southern League and a total of 26 in all competitions. In fact, he had so impressed the Middlesbrough scouts during the cup-run that he was transferred to the Yorkshire club, together with Harry Kent as a makeweight, for £700 before the end of the season. (There was a maximum transfer fee of £350 imposed by the Football

---

The following match report appeared in the *Sussex Daily News* of 12 November.

NEARLY LOST IN THE FOG

ALBION'S EXPERIENCE AT PARK ROYAL

SPECTATORS 'TOLD' OF A GOAL

A Western League match between Queen's Park Rangers and Brighton and Hove Albion was commenced at Park Royal yesterday afternoon in a dense fog. The players were absolutely out of sight, even the wing men being only just discernible from the ropes. The Referee thought it was good enough to play, and the kick-off took place fifteen minutes after the advertised time. The proceedings were quite a farce, and bursts of laughter came from the few spectators whenever the ball came into view, which was rarely. Craig, the Surrey poet, volunteered to tell everybody whenever a goal was scored! It is supposed that both sides had an even share of the game, judging by the varying excitement in different parts of the ground. Twenty minutes after the start it transpired that a goal had been scored by Brighton. Subsequently, it was ascertained that Hulme had netted from a penalty. Five minutes later the game was abandoned, Brighton then leading by one goal to none.

Albion 1907–08
Standing left to right: Joe Clayton (trainer), Tom Turner, Arthur Archer, Hugh MacDonald, Bob Beale, Julius Gregory, Dick Kitto (assistant trainer).
Seated left to right: Joe Lumley, Arthur Hulme, Harry Kent (captain), Frank Scott-Walford (secretary-manager), Tom Morris, Willie McDonald.
On ground left to right: Dick Joynes, Walter Anthony, Jimmy Burnett, Jack Hall, Duncan Ronaldson, Dick Wombwell.

A novel way of travelling to an away game was used on 21 September when 1,300 Albion fans made the trip for the Southern League fixture at Southampton on the *s.s. Brighton Queen*, a paddle-steamer. Sadly, a number of the intrepid supporters were reported by the referee for misbehaviour during the game which Albion lost by three goals to two.

SEASON 1907–08

Date	Comp.	Ven.	Opponents	Result	HT	Pos.	Scorers	Atten.	Anthony W	Archer A	Beale R	Burnett J	Dougal D	Fitchie T	Gregory J	Hall JH	Higham T	Hulme A	Joynes R	Kent H	Longstaff A	Lumley J	MacDonald H	MacDonald W	Morris T	Porter W	Rodger T	Ronaldson D	Townshend A	Turner T	Wombwell R
Sep 7	SL D1	(a)	Norwich City	W 2–1	1–1	8	Hall, Ronaldson	9,000	7	2		8			3	9				4			1	6	5			10			11
9	SCC R1	(h)	Queen's Park R.	W 3–1	1–0	–	Hall, Ronaldson, Burnett	2,500	7	2		8			3	9				4			1	6	5			10			11
14	SL D1	(h)	Northampton T.	D 2–2	0–1	10	Wombwell 2	8,000		2	1	8			3	9			7	4				6	5			10			11
18	WL D1 'A'	(a)	Portsmouth	L 1–3	0–1	6=	Longstaff	4,000			1	9			3				6	7	4	8			5			10		2	11
21	SL D1	(a)	Southampton	L 2–3	0–2	15	Hall, Ronaldson	8,000	7	2	1	8			3	9				4				6	5			10			11
28	SL D1	(h)	Plymouth Argyle	L 1–2	1–2	17	Hall	8,000	7	2	1	8			3	9				4				6	5			10			11
Oct 2	WL D1 'A'	(h)	Brentford	D 0–0	0–0	7		2,000		2	1		10		3					7	4	8		6	5			9		3	11
5	SL D1	(a)	West Ham United	D 0–0	0–0	15		6,000	7	2		8			3					9	4		1	6	5			10			11
9	WL D1 'A'	(h)	Plymouth Argyle	D 0–0	0–0	7		4,000	7			8			3					9	4		1	6	5			10			11
12	SL D1	(h)	Queen's Park R.	L 2–3	1–1	18	Hall, Ronaldson	8,500	7	2		8			3	9				4			1	6	5			10			
16	WL D1 'A'	(a)	Brentford	L 1–2	1–0	7	Burnett	2,000	7	2		8				9			10	4			1	6	5	11				3	
19	SL D1	(a)	Tottenham H'spur	D 1–1	1–1	18	Hall	12,000	7	2		10				9				4	8		1	6	5					3	11
23	WL D1 'A'	(h)	Portsmouth	W 3–1	2–0	6	Burnett, Longstaff, Hall	2,000	7			10				9		2		4	8		1	6	5					3	11
26	SL D1	(h)	Swindon Town	D 2–2	1–0	18	Hall, Morris	6,500	7	2		10				9				4	8		1	6	5					3	11
28	WL D1 'A'	(a)	Southampton	L 1–2	1–1	6	Anthony	1,500	7							9		2		8	4		1	6	5			10		3	11
30	SCC R2	(h)	West Ham United	D 0–0	0–0	–		2,250	7	2						9				10	4	8	1	6	5					3	11
Nov 2	SL D1	(a)	Crystal Palace	L 1–2	1–1	18	Hall	7,000	7	2		10				9				4	8		1	6	5					3	11
9	SL D1	(h)	Luton Town	W 1–0	1–0	17	Burnett	6,000	7	2		9								10	4	8	1	6	5					3	11
11	WL D1 'A'*	(a)	Queen's Park R.	–	–	6	Hulme (pen)	'several hundred'	7	2		9						4		10		8	1	6	5					3	11
16	SL D1	(h)	New Brompton	W 3–0	3–0	16	Longstaff, Wombwell, Hall	5,000	7	2		10				9				4	8		1	6	5					3	11
23	SL D1	(a)	Portsmouth	L 0–3	0–2	17		7,000	7	2		10				9				4	8		1	6	5					3	11
27	WL D1 'A'	(h)	Southampton	W 3–0	1–0	6	Hall, Wombwell, Longstaff	1,500	7			10			3	9		2		4	8		1	6	5						11
30	SL D1	(h)	Bradford (P.A.)	D 1–1	0–1	16	Hall	6,000	7	2		10			3	9				4	8		1	6	5						11
Dec 4	WL D1 'A'	(a)	Queen's Park R.	W 1–0	1–0	5	Morris	'disappointing'				10			3	9			7	4			1	6	5		8			2	11
7	SL D1	(a)	Millwall	L 2–3	0–2	17	Longstaff 2	5,000	11	2					3	9			7	4	10		1	6	5		8				
11	WL D1 'A'	(a)	Plymouth Argyle	W 3–2	1–1	4	Wombwell, Hall, Own goal	1,500	11						3	9			6	7	4		1		5		8	10		2	
14	SL D1	(h)	Brentford	W 1–0	0–0	15	Ronaldson	4,000	11	2						9			7	4			1	6	5		8	10		3	
18	WL D1 'A'	(h)	Leyton	W 2–1	2–0	3	Hulme (pen), Longstaff	1,000	11		1	9			3			2	7	4	10	6			5		8				
21	SL D1	(a)	Bristol Rovers	L 1–2	1–2	17	Hall	6,000	11	2						9			7	4			1	6	5		8	10		3	
25	SL D1	(h)	Reading	L 1–4	1–1	18	Kent	6,500	11	2					3	9			7	4	8		1	6	5			10			
26	SL D1	(h)	Watford	L 0–1	0–1	18		8,500	11	2					3	9			7	4	10		1	6	5		8				
28	SL D1	(h)	Leyton	W 3–2	0–1	17	Joynes, Anthony, Longstaff	3,000	11						3	9			7	4	8		1	6	5			10		2	
30	WL D1 'A'	(a)	Queen's Park R.	W 3–2	1–1	3	Hall 2, Wombwell	1,000	11						3	9			6	7	4	8	1		5			10		2	
Jan 4	SL D1	(h)	Norwich City	W 1–0	0–0	16	Ronaldson	5,000	11	2						9				5	7		1	6	4		8	10		3	
6	WL D1 'A'	(a)	Leyton	L 1–6	0–3	3	Ronaldson	500	11			8			3					5	6	7	4	1			9	10		2	
11	FAC R1	(a)	Preston North End	D 1–1	0–0	–	Hall	7,500	11	2		8				9				7	4		1	6	5			10		3	
16	FAC R1 Rep*	(a)	Preston North End	D 1–1*	1–0	–	Joynes	7,000	11	2		8				9			7	4			1	6	5					3	11
18	SL D1*	(h)	Southampton	–	–	17		3,000	11			8			3			2	7	5	10	4	1	6			9				
20	FAC R1 2Rep(n*)		Preston North End	W 1–0	1–0	–	Wombwell	20,000	11	2		8				9				7	4		1	6	5			10		3	
25	SL D1	(a)	Plymouth Argyle	W 3–2	2–0	14	Ronaldson, Longstaff 2	9,000	11	2		8								4	7	10	1	6	5		9			3	
Feb 1	FAC R2	(h)	Liverpool	D 1–1	1–1	–	Hall (pen)	36,000	11	2		8				9				4			1	6	5		7	10		3	
5	FAC R2 Rep	(h)	Liverpool	L 0–3	0–1	–		12,000	11	2		8				9				4			1	6	5		7	10		3	
8	SL D1	(a)	Queen's Park R.	L 0–1	0–1	15		8,000	11						3	9			7	4	8		1	6	5			10		2	
15	SL D1	(h)	Tottenham H'spur	W 2–0	1–0	14	Hall, Burnett	3,000	11			8			3	9				4	10		1	6	5		7			2	
27	SCC R2 Rep	(h)	West Ham United	D 2–2	1–1	–	Ronaldson, Hall	3,000		2					3	9			7	4			1	6	5		8	10			11
29	SL D1	(h)	Crystal Palace	L 0–1	0–0	16		4,000	11				7		3	9				4	8		1	6	5			10		2	
Mar 7	SL D1	(a)	Luton Town	L 0–1	0–0	18		4,000		2			7		3	9		4	11	5			1	6			8	10			
14	SL D1	(a)	New Brompton	L 1–2	1–0	19	Longstaff	4,000		2	1		7		3	9			11	5	8			6				10		4	
18	SL D1	(h)	Southampton	W 3–2	3–0	17	Hall, Longstaff, Hulme	2,000			1		7		3	9		4	11	5	8			6				10		2	
21	SL D1	(h)	Portsmouth	D 0–0	0–0	18		5,000		2			7		3	9		4	11	5	8		1	6				10			
25	SL D1	(h)	West Ham United	W 3–1	2–1	16	Longstaff 2, Dougal	1,500		2			7		3			4	11	5	8		1	6			9	10			
28	SL D1	(a)	Bradford (P.A.)	W 2–0	2–0	15	Rodger, Hall	10,000		2			7		3	9		4	11	5	8		1	6				10			
30	SCC R2 2Rep(n*)		West Ham United	L 1–2	0–0	–		3,000		2		10			3	9		4	11	5	8		1	6			7				
Apr 4	SL D1	(h)	Millwall	W 2–0	1–0	12	Hulme (pen), Hall	5,000		2			7		3	9		4	11	5	8		1	6				10			
8	SL D1	(a)	Swindon Town	L 1–5	1–3	13	Hall	4,000		2			7		3	9		4	11	5	8		1	6				10			
11	SL D1	(a)	Brentford	L 0–2	0–1	15		5,000		2					3	9		4	11	5	8		1	6			7	10			
17	SL D1	(h)	Reading	D 1–1	1–1	15	Hall	8,000		2			7		3	9		4	11	5	8	6	1					10			
18	SL D1	(h)	Bristol Rovers	D 1–1	0–1	14	Joynes	4,000		2			7		3	9		4	11	5	8	6	1					10			
20	SL D1	(a)	Watford	L 0–3	0–2	15		5,000		2	1		7		3				11	5	8			6			9	10			
21	SL D1	(a)	Northampton T.	L 0–1	0–1	15		8,000		2	1		7		3			4	11		8			6	5		9	10			
25	SL D1	(a)	Leyton	L 0–3	0–0	17		2,000		2			7		3			4	11		8		1	6	5		9	10			

Notes: Nov 11 – match abandoned after 25 minutes because of fog with score 1–0. Not included in end-of-season statistics.

Jan 16 – match abandoned after 22 minutes of extra time because of poor light with score 2–1, Hall scoring Albion's second goal. The match was deemed to be a 1–1 draw, the score at 90 minutes.

Jan 18 – match abandoned after 9 minutes because of fog with score 0–0. Not included in end-of-season statistics.

Jan 20 – played at Stamford Bridge, Chelsea FC.

Mar 30 – played at Stamford Bridge, Chelsea FC.

	Anthony W	Archer A	Beale R	Burnett J	Dougal D	Fitchie T	Gregory J	Hall JH	Higham T	Hulme A	Joynes R	Kent H	Longstaff A	Lumley J	MacDonald H	MacDonald W	Morris T	Porter W	Rodger T	Ronaldson D	Townshend A	Turner T	Wombwell R
Southern League appearances	21	28	7	16	14	0	28	30	5	13	28	35	28	0	31	36	24	0	15	19	0	21	19
Southern League goals	1			2	1			16		2	2	1	10				1		1	6			3
Western League appearances	8	2	3	8	0	1	8	7	1	8	9	10	7	4	9	9	8	1	0	9	1	10	9
Western League goals	OG – 1 / 1			2				5		1		4				1							3

Association at this time, but the wealthier clubs cleverly turned the situation to their advantage by paying £700 for two players, the one they really wanted plus another they did not, and the rule lasted only three months.)

Secretary-manager Frank Walford was released in April to take up a similar position with Leeds City, and he was presented with an 18-carat gold stop-watch by the Mayor of Hove, Major A. B. S. Fraser, an avid Albion fan. The directors were reluctant to release Walford when the Yorkshire club made its initial approach – there were two years of his contract remaining – but eventually agreed to the move and appointed Jack Robson as the new manager. Robson had been in charge of Crystal Palace from 1905 to 1907 and had led them to the Southern League Second Division championship at their first attempt; he was previously manager at Middlesbrough for six years. Walford returned to Hove during the close season to sign

Southern League Division 1 1907–08												
	P	W	D	L	F	A	W	D	L	F	A	Pts
1. Queen's Park R.	38	12	4	3	46	26	9	5	5	36	31	51
2. Plymouth Argyle	38	13	5	1	33	13	6	6	7	17	18	49
3. Millwall	38	11	5	3	25	9	8	3	8	24	23	46
4. Crystal Palace	38	10	4	5	35	28	7	6	6	19	23	44
5. Swindon Town	38	12	6	1	41	12	4	4	11	14	28	42
6. Bristol Rovers	38	11	5	3	36	19	5	5	9	23	37	42
7. Tottenham Hotspur	38	11	2	6	33	18	6	5	8	26	30	41
8. Northampton Town	38	9	5	5	30	17	6	6	7	20	24	41
9. Portsmouth	38	14	1	4	43	19	3	5	11	21	33	40
10. West Ham United	38	9	6	4	27	16	6	4	9	20	32	40
11. Southampton	38	11	5	3	32	21	5	1	13	19	39	38
12. Reading	38	12	1	6	38	18	3	5	11	17	32	36
13. Bradford (P.A.)	38	6	7	6	30	27	6	5	8	23	27	36
14. Watford	38	9	4	6	31	22	3	6	10	16	37	34
15. Brentford	38	13	3	3	38	15	1	2	16	11	37	33
16. Norwich City	38	10	4	5	31	16	2	5	12	15	33	33
17. **ALBION**	38	9	6	4	29	19	3	2	14	17	40	32
18. Luton Town	38	9	4	6	21	17	3	2	14	12	39	30
19. Leyton	38	6	6	7	29	31	2	5	12	22	43	27
20. New Brompton	38	7	3	9	24	29	2	4	13	20	46	25

Western League Division 1 Section 'A' 1907–08												
	P	W	D	L	F	A	W	D	L	F	A	Pts
1. Southampton	12	5	0	1	17	3	3	1	2	13	9	17
2. Portsmouth	12	3	1	2	12	10	4	0	2	13	8	15
3. **ALBION**	12	5	1	0	12	4	1	1	4	7	15	14
4. Plymouth Argyle	12	4	1	1	8	3	1	1	4	6	9	12
5. Queen's Park R.	12	2	0	4	12	14	3	1	2	8	9	11
6. Brentford	12	2	3	1	10	9	0	2	4	3	12	9
7. Leyton	12	2	1	3	9	9	0	1	5	2	18	6

Dick Joynes, Tom Rodger, Dave Dougal and Jimmy Burnett for his new club; they were soon followed by Tom Morris.

The United League was forsaken this season in favour of the Western League, the First Division of which was played in two sections, the sectional winners playing-off for the championship. Albion finished third in the 'A' section. The club also made its début in the Southern Professional Charity Cup, a competition now in its seventh season, but bowed out to West Ham United in the second round.

Thanks to the cup-run and the big fees received for Jack Hall, Walter Anthony and Dick Wombwell (the latter pair signed for Blackburn Rovers in February), the board announced a profit of around £1,300, allowing the club to pay off its debts and look forward to a more healthy future.

> The well-known Scottish international Tom Fitchie guested for the Albion in the Western League match with Brentford at the Goldstone Ground on 2 October. Tom won fame with Queen's Park (Glasgow), Woolwich Arsenal and Fulham.

SEASON 1908–09

The new manager immediately set about making changes in an attempt to improve performances. Sixteen newcomers joined the staff, including Bob Whiting (Chelsea), Joe Leeming (Bury), Billy Booth (Sheffield United), Joe Jee (Bolton Wanderers) and Tom Stewart (Clapton Orient). Worthing amateur Charles Webb made his début in January, thus beginning an association with the club that was to last for almost 40 years as player and later manager. Shortly after his first appearance, Webb was chosen for the full Ireland team against Scotland and Wales, thus becoming the first Albion player to win international honours while wearing the club's colours; he had previously won an amateur cap while serving with the Army in Ireland.

Despite the new faces it was to prove another disappointing season. Away form was yet again the major problem, only 9 of a possible 40 points being gained. Results at the Goldstone were encouraging with big wins over Brentford (4–0), Bristol Rovers (5–0), Coventry City (5–1) and Reading (6–2), but the outstanding performance was undoubtedly the 3–0 defeat of Swindon Town who had challenged for the championship all season, finishing as runners-up behind Northampton Town. Albion ended the campaign only one point ahead of the relegation zone.

There was little solace in the English Cup, Albion being beaten but far from disgraced in the first round by the ultimate winners and reigning Football League champions, Manchester United. Heavy rain prior to the kick-off, which turned the

> Alderman Clark was persuaded not to make a hay crop on the ground in the summer of 1908 as it was believed the playing surface would be improved for this season.

Albion 1908–09
Back row left to right: Joe Clayton (trainer), Bob Whiting, Bill Tustin, Jack Robson (manager).
Third row left to right: Arthur Hulme, Arthur Lloyd, Joe Leeming, Tom Stewart (captain), Tom Morris, Joe Wilson, Jimmy Atkinson, Tom Turner.
Seated left to right: John Hall, Fred Crump, Tom Grierson, Bert Longstaff, Jack Martin, Jim Robertson, Joe Jee, Bob Isherwood.
On ground left to right: Jimmy Brennan, Billy Booth.

SEASON 1908–09

Date	Comp.	Ven.	Opponents	Result	HT	Pos.	Scorers	Atten.	Atkinson J	Booth W	Brennan J	Crump F	Dalton E	Elliott E	Grierson T	Hall JE	Higham T	Hulme A	Isherwood R	Jee J	Leach G	Leeming J	Lloyd A	Longstaff A	Martin J	Morris T	Robertson J	Stewart T	Townshend A	Turner T	Tustin W	Webb C	Whiting R	Wilson J
Sep 2	SL D1	(h)	Southampton	L 1–3	0–2	14	Robertson	6,000	6	4						7				11		3		8	9		10	2			1			5
5	SL D1	(h)	West Ham United	W 3–2	2–2	11	Hall, Morris (pen), Longstaff	7,000	6	4		10				7				11				8	9	5		2		3	1			
7	SL D1	(a)	Southampton	L 1–4	1–2	13	Martin	5,000	6	4					10	7				11				8	9	5		2		3	1			
12	SL D1	(a)	Plymouth Argyle	W 1–0	0–0	9	Martin	9,000		4						7				11		3	6	8	9		10	2					1	5
16	WL D1 'A'	(h)	Croydon Common	W 5–0	2–0	3	Longstaff, Wilson, Robertson, Jee, Brennan	1,500		4	7	9								11		3	6	8			10	2					1	5
19	SL D1	(a)	Crystal Palace	L 0–4	0–2	13		10,000		4	7									11		3	6	8	9		10	2					1	5
26	SL D1	(h)	Brentford	W 4–0	4–0	10	Martin, Longstaff 2, Crump	6,000		4	7	10								11		3	6	8	9			2					1	5
30	WL D1 'A'	(h)	Reading	W 2–1	2–0	1	Crump, Brennan	1,500	6	4	7	10						3		11				8	9	5				2			1	
Oct 3	SL D1	(a)	Luton Town	L 1–3	1–2	14	Martin	5,000		4	7	10								11		3	6	8	9			2					1	5
7	WL D1 'A'	(a)	Reading	W 2–1	1–1	2	Martin, Robertson	1,000	6	5	7	10	2				4			11					9		8	3					1	
10	SL D1	(h)	Swindon Town	W 3–0	1–0	9	Martin, Jee 2	6,000	6	4	7	10								11				8	9			3		2			1	5
14	WL D1 'A'	(h)	Leyton	W 2–0	1–0	1	Crump, Martin	1,000	6			10	2			7	4		11			3			9		8						1	5
17	SL D1	(a)	Portsmouth	L 1–2	0–2	12	Longstaff	9,000	6	4	7	10				11						5		8	9			3		2			1	
21	WL D1 'A'	(a)	Croydon Common	D 1–1	1–0	1	Longstaff	1,500	4		7		2				6		11			5		8	9		10	3					1	
24	SL D1	(h)	Exeter City	L 1–2	0–2	16	Martin	6,000	6		7	10								11		4		8	9	5		3		2			1	
28	WL D1 'A'	(h)	Luton Town	W 2–0	2–0	1	Booth, Longstaff	1,000		4	7	10	2							11			6	8	9			3					1	5
31	SL D1	(a)	Northampton T.	L 1–2	1–1	17	Crump	8,000		4	7	9	2			11							6	8			10	3					1	5
Nov 2	WL D1 'A'	(a)	Leyton	L 1–2	1–2	1	Crump	500		4		9	2			7						6		8			10	3	11				1	5
7	SL D1	(h)	New Brompton	D 1–1	0–0	16	Longstaff	5,000		4	7		2							11			6	8	9		10	3					1	5
11	SL D1	(h)	Queen's Park R.	D 1–1	0–0	17	Brennan	5,000		4	7	10	2							11			6	8	9			3					1	5
14	SL D1	(a)	Millwall	L 0–2	0–1	17		5,000		4		9	2			7		3		11		10	6	8				5					1	
18	WL D1 'A'	(a)	Luton Town	D 1–1	1–1	1	Longstaff			4	7	8								11				10	9		6	3		2			1	5
25	WL D1 'A'	(h)	Crystal Palace	W 2–0	1–0	1	Stewart (pen), Martin	1,500	6	4	7	8	2							11				10	9			3					1	5
28	SL D1	(a)	Coventry City	L 1–2	1–1	19	Martin	5,000	6	4	7									11				10	9		8	3		2			1	5
Dec 2	WL D1 'A'	(a)	Crystal Palace	L 1–3	1–2	1	Robertson	2,000	6	4				7						11		5		8	9		10	3		2			1	
5	SL D1	(h)	Bristol Rovers	W 5–0	0–0	16	Martin, Elliott 2, Longstaff 2	4,000	6	4				7						11		5		8	9		10	3		2			1	
7	WL D1 'A'	(a)	Queen's Park R.	W 1–0	1–0	1	Robertson	1,000	6	4	7									11		5		8	9		10	3		2			1	
12	SL D1	(a)	Watford	D 1–1	1–0	17	Longstaff	3,000	6	4				7						11		5		8	9		10	3		2			1	
19	SL D1	(h)	Norwich City	W 3–0	3–0	14	Longstaff 2, Martin	3,000	6	4				7						11		5		8	9		10	3		2			1	
25	SL D1	(a)	Reading	L 0–4	0–0	18		7,500	6	4				7						11		5		8	9		10	3		2			1	
28	SL D1	(h)	Leyton	W 2–0	1–0	16	Atkinson, Martin	5,000	6	4				7						11		5		8	9		10	3		2			1	
Jan 2	SL D1	(a)	West Ham United	D 1–1	0–0	16	Webb	6,000	6	4						7						5		8	9		10	3		2		11	1	
9	SL D1	(h)	Plymouth Argyle	L 1–2	1–2	17	Robertson	5,000	6	4						7				11		5		8	9		10	3		2			1	
16	FAC R1	(a)	Manchester United	L 0–1	0–1	–		8,072	6	4						7				11		2		8	9	5	10	3					1	
23	SL D1	(h)	Crystal Palace	W 3–0	0–0	16	Grierson, Morris, Longstaff	5,000	6	4					7					11		2		8	9	5	10	3					1	
30	SL D1	(a)	Brentford	L 0–4	0–2	17		5,000	11	4			2		7							3		8	9	5	10						1	6
Feb 6	SL D1	(h)	Luton Town	D 0–0	0–0	16		5,000	5	4		10			7					11		2	6	8	9			3					1	
10	SCC R1	(a)	Reading	W 1–0	1–0	–	Booth	1,500	5	4		9			7					11		2	6	8			10	3					1	
13	SL D1	(a)	Swindon Town	L 0–2	0–2	17		4,000	5	4		9			7					11		2	6	8				3				10	1	
20	SL D1	(h)	Portsmouth	D 0–0	0–0	18		7,000	6	4						7				11		2		8	9			3				10	1	5
24	SL D1	(h)	Southend United	W 2–0	1–0	14	Jee 2	1,500	6	4						7				10		2		8	9			3				11	1	5
27	SL D1	(a)	Exeter City	L 0–1	0–0	14		4,500	6	4			2			7				10				8	9			3				11	1	5
Mar 3	WL D1 'A'	(h)	Queen's Park R.	L 3–4	0–2	1	Robertson, Jee, Martin	1,000	6	4			2		8	7				11					9		5	3			1	10		
6	SL D1	(h)	Northampton T.	L 2–4	1–1	17	Longstaff, Webb	3,500	6	4						7				10		2		8	9			3				11	1	5
13	SL D1	(a)	New Brompton	L 0–2	0–1	19		5,000	6	4						7				11		2		8	9			3				10	1	5
20	SL D1	(h)	Millwall	W 2–0	2–0	20	Hall, Longstaff	5,000	6	4						7				11	9	2		8	10			3					1	5
22	SL D1	(a)	Queen's Park R.	W 2–1	0–0	15	Martin 2	3,000	6	4										7		2		8	9		10	3				11	1	5
27	SL D1	(a)	Southend United	W 2–0	1–0	14	Martin, Robertson	4,000	6	4										7		2		8	9		10	3				11	1	5
31	SCC SF	(a)	Portsmouth	W 2–1	1–0	–	Leach, Martin	3,000	6	4			2			7					8				9		10	3				11	1	5
Apr 3	SL D1	(h)	Coventry City	W 5–1	2–0	13	Martin 2, Robertson, Jee, Webb	5,000	6	4										7		2		8	9		10	3				11	1	5
5	WL Champ.	(n*)	Millwall	D 1–1	0–0	–	Martin	2,500	6	4										7		2		8	9		10	3				11	1	5
9	SL D1	(h)	Reading	W 6–2	4–2	10	Martin 3 (1 pen), Hall, Longstaff, Webb	9,000	6	4						7						2		8	9		10	3				11	1	5
10	SL D1	(a)	Bristol Rovers	L 0–3	0–2	12		4,000	6	4						7						2		8	9		10	3				11	1	5
12	SL D1	(a)	Leyton	L 1–2	1–2	15	Webb	5,000	6	4						7					8	2			9		10	3				11	1	5
17	SL D1	(h)	Watford	L 1–2	0–2	18	Longstaff	4,000	6	4						7						2		8	9		10	3				11	1	5
22	WL Ch. Rep	(n*)	Millwall	L 1–2	1–1	–	Martin	2,000	6	4						7						2		8	9		10	3				11	1	5
24	SL D1	(a)	Norwich City	D 1–1	0–1	18	Robertson	5,000	6	4						7						2		8	9		10	3				11	1	5
29	SCC F	(h)	Brentford	L 0–2	0–1	–		2,000	6	4			2			7				11		3		8	9							10	1	5
							Southern League appearances		32	39	10	11	6	5	5	20	0	1	0	31	2	32	10	39	37	5	23	39	0	13	3	15	37	25
							Southern League goals		1		1	2		2	1	3				5				15	18	2	5					5		
							Western League appearances		10	12	8	8	7	1	1	4	3	1	2	10	0	8	2	11	12	1	11	12	1	4	1	3	13	8
							Western League goals			1	2	3								2				4	6		5	1						1

Notes: Apr 5 – played at Upton Park, West Ham United FC.
Apr 22 – played at Upton Park, West Ham United FC.
End-of-season statistics for the Western League include the two championship matches.

Southern League Division 1 1908–09

		P	W	D	L	F	A	W	D	L	F	A	Pts
1.	Northampton Town	40	15	3	2	55	14	10	2	8	35	31	55
2.	Swindon Town	40	18	0	2	68	15	4	5	11	28	40	49
3.	Southampton	40	13	4	3	44	26	6	6	8	23	32	48
4.	Portsmouth	40	13	5	2	42	17	5	5	10	26	43	46
5.	Bristol Rovers	40	13	5	2	39	20	4	4	12	21	43	43
6.	Exeter City	40	13	2	5	37	28	5	4	11	19	37	42
7.	New Brompton	40	12	2	6	30	22	5	5	10	18	37	41
8.	Reading	40	7	9	4	33	19	4	9	7	27	38	40
9.	Luton Town	40	16	1	3	45	15	1	5	14	14	45	40
10.	Plymouth Argyle	40	9	6	5	28	16	6	4	10	18	31	40
11.	Millwall	40	14	3	3	38	17	2	3	15	21	44	38
12.	Southend United	40	12	6	2	33	14	2	4	14	19	40	38
13.	Leyton	40	13	3	4	35	12	2	5	13	17	43	38
14.	Watford	40	12	7	1	37	16	2	2	16	14	48	37
15.	Queen's Park R.	40	10	6	4	41	24	2	6	12	11	26	36
16.	Crystal Palace	40	10	4	6	42	23	2	8	10	20	39	36
17.	West Ham United	40	16	1	3	43	13	0	3	17	13	37	36
18.	**ALBION**	40	11	4	5	46	20	3	3	14	14	41	35
19.	Norwich City	40	11	8	1	44	18	1	3	16	15	57	35
20.	Coventry City	40	10	4	6	44	37	5	0	15	20	54	34

Western League Division 1 Section 'A' 1908–09

		P	W	D	L	F	A	W	D	L	F	A	Pts
1.	**ALBION**	12	5	0	1	16	5	2	2	2	7	8	16
2.	Queen's Park R.	12	5	0	1	18	4	1	1	4	10	20	13
3.	Crystal Palace	12	4	1	1	17	6	1	1	4	6	16	12
4.	Luton Town	12	4	2	0	20	6	1	0	5	4	18	12
5.	Croydon Common	12	3	1	2	9	11	2	1	3	7	13	12
6.	Reading	12	2	1	3	8	8	2	1	3	11	13	10
7.	Leyton	12	2	1	3	9	12	2	0	4	7	9	9

Clayton Road pitch into a quagmire, and the questionable tactics employed by certain of the United players reduced the match as a spectacle for the 300 or so Albion fans who had travelled north. Harold Halse scored the only goal of the game after 28 minutes following a miskick by Albion's left-half Jimmy Atkinson, but the team continued to frustrate the First Division side and with five minutes remaining the great Welsh international Billy Meredith, robbed yet again by Albion skipper Tom Stewart, lashed out at the full-back and was ordered from the field of play. From the resultant free kick Stewart was crudely challenged by United's Jimmy Turnbull which resulted in Tom being carried to the dressing-room. The players surged around the referee, but Turnbull escaped with a caution.

Some consolation was gained by winning the Western League's First Division Section 'A', having led the competition since October, but Millwall won the championship play-off, defeating the Albion 2–1 after a 1–1 draw, both matches played at Upton Park. The team also experienced disappointment in the Southern Charity Cup, losing the final 2–0 at home to Brentford.

In an overall poor campaign, and in the absence of a run in the English Cup, a huge loss of £1,055 was announced at the end-of-season meeting of shareholders.

SEASON 1909–10

From the playing point of view 1908–09 had been unsuccessful, but the nucleus of a good side had been assembled. Robson shopped wisely during the summer and added Bill Hastings (West Hartlepool), Bill Jones (Birmingham), Joe McGhie (Sheffield United) and Fred Blackman (Hastings and St Leonards United) to the staff. Along with the retained players – Whiting, Booth, Webb, Longstaff and Leeming – they were to form the foundation of the team for several seasons to come. Jones, while only 5' 5" in height, packed a tremendous shot which earned him the nickname 'Bullet'.

The season opened with goal-less draws at Portsmouth and Brentford. Four successive wins, including 4–1 Goldstone victories over Pompey and Coventry City, moved Albion into second place behind New Brompton, the early leaders. A temporary lapse in November and early December brought consecutive away defeats at New Brompton, Queen's Park Rangers and Swindon Town, causing Albion hearts to flutter. The only home defeat of the season, at the hands of Crystal Palace on 18 December, dropped the club to eighth place.

Five points from the three Christmas-holiday games kept Albion in contention, but in January Bullet Jones was suspended for two months after being sent off during the home match with Norwich City on 1 December; former Albion goalie Bob Beale and his replacement, left-back Charlie Craig, both had to leave the field injured after clashes with Jones who also 'sauced' the referee before his dismissal. Not surprisingly Albion won 5–0, but the suspension of the club's leading scorer was a tremendous blow at a crucial time. To counter the loss of his star centre-forward, Robson called upon reserve left-half Jack Haworth and shuffled the team to accommodate him. In the event, four of the six Southern League matches played during Jones's absence ended in victory and two were drawn.

In fact, from mid December, Brighton's colours were lowered only once – by Southampton at The Dell – in a tremendous run of 23 League games which included fourteen wins. Albion went top in early February and were to stay there for the remainder of the campaign. Seven points out of eight were won over Easter, but still Albion could not shake off their closest rivals,

Albion 1909–10
Back row left to right: Alf Nelmes (trainer), Bob Whiting, Jack Robson (manager), Bill Crinson, J. Butt (assistant trainer).
Third row left to right: Joe McGhie, Dick Whittington, Joe Lumley, Ralph Routledge, Fred Blackman, Harry Middleton, Billy Booth, Teddy Elliott.
Seated left to right: Arthur Armstrong, George Featherstone, Bill Connor, Bert Longstaff, Joe Leeming (captain), Charlie Webb, Bill Jones, Bill Hastings, Harvey Longstaff.
On ground left to right: Jack Eacock, Jimmy Coleman, R. Craig, Jack Haworth.

On 10 November, Albion played a Sussex representative team at the Goldstone Ground for the benefit of Edgar Everest, the long-serving secretary of the Sussex County F.A. and founder of Brighton United, to mark the 21st anniversary of his appointment. Albion won 4–1, the Sussex reply coming from Charlie Webb who, as an amateur, was eligible for the County XI.

SEASON 1909–10

Date	Comp.	Ven.	Opponents	Result	HT	Pos.	Scorers	Atten.	Armstrong A	Blackman F	Booth W	Coleman J	Connor W	Eacock J	Featherstone G	Hastings W	Haworth J	Jones W	Leeming J	Longstaff A	McGhie J	Middleton H	Webb C	Whiting R
Sep 1	SL D1	(a)	Portsmouth	D 0–0	0–0	8=		8,000	3	4	2				8	11		9	6		7	5	10	1
4	SL D1	(a)	Brentford	D 0–0	0–0	9=		8,000	3	4	2				8	11		9	6		7	5	10	1
8	SL D1	(h)	Portsmouth	W 4–1	2–1	6	Jones 2 (1 pen), Hastings, Webb	6,000	2	4					8	11		9	6	3	7	5	10	1
11	SL D1	(h)	Coventry City	W 4–1	1–0	3	Featherstone 3, Jones	7,000	2	4					8	11		9	6	3	7	5	10	1
18	SL D1	(a)	Watford	W 2–1	1–1	4	Connor, Featherstone	5,000	2	4			9		8	11			6	3	7	5	10	1
25	SL D1	(h)	Reading	W 1–0	0–0	2	Jones	7,000	2	4					8	11		9	6	3	7	5	10	1
Oct 2	SL D1	(a)	Southend United	L 0–2	0–1	7		4,000	2	4					8	11		9	6	3	7	5	10	1
7	SL D1	(a)	Norwich City	D 1–1	0–1	7	Connor	3,554	2	4			9		8	11	6			3	7	5	10	1
9	SL D1	(h)	Leyton	W 2–0	1–0	6	Jones, Featherstone	7,000	2	4					8	11		9	6	3	7	5	10	1
16	SL D1	(a)	Plymouth Argyle	D 2–2	1–1	5=	Longstaff, Jones	3,800	7	2	4					11		9		3	8	5	6	10	1
20	SCC R1	(h)	Reading	W 3–1	3–0	–	Longstaff 2, Jones	1,500	7	2	4		10			11	5	9	3	8			6		1
23	SL D1	(h)	Southampton	D 2–2	2–1	6	Webb, Middleton	7,000	7	2	4					11		9	3	8	5	6	10	1
30	SL D1	(a)	Croydon Common	W 4–0	2–0	6	Webb, Longstaff, Jones, Hastings	5,000	2	4			8			11		9	3	7	5	6	10	1
Nov 6	SL D1	(h)	Millwall	W 2–0	2–0	4	Longstaff, Connor	7,000	2	4			8			11		9	3	7	5	6	10	1
13	SL D1	(a)	New Brompton	L 0–1	0–0	6		7,000	2	4			8			11		9	3	7	5	6	10	1
20	SL D1	(h)	Northampton T.	W 1–0	1–0	5	Webb	8,000	2	4					8	10		9	3	7	5	6	11	1
24	SCC R2	(h)	Southampton	W 1–0	1–0	–	Featherstone	1,500	2	4					8	11	5	9	3		6	10	1	
27	SL D1	(a)	Queen's Park R.	L 0–1	0–1	7		8,000	2	4					8	11		9	3	7	5	6	10	1
Dec 1	SL D1	(h)	Norwich City	W 5–0	2–0	4=	Featherstone 2, Longstaff 2, Hastings	2,000	2	4					8	11		9	3	7	5	6	10	1
11	SL D1	(a)	Swindon Town	L 0–1	0–1	7		3,000	2	4					8	11		9	3	7	5	6	10	1
18	SL D1	(h)	Crystal Palace	L 1–2	0–1	8	McGhie	6,000	2	4					8	11		9	3	7	5	6	10	1
25	SL D1	(a)	West Ham United	D 1–1	1–1	8	Jones	12,000	2	4		10			8	7		9	3			5	6	11	1
27	SL D1	(h)	West Ham United	W 3–0	2–0	7	Featherstone, Connor, Jones (pen)	10,000	2	4		10			8	7		9	3			5	6	11	1
28	SL D1	(h)	Bristol Rovers	W 1–0	0–0	5	Jones	6,000	2	4		10			8	7		9	3			5	6	11	1
Jan 1	SL D1	(h)	Luton Town	W 3–0	3–0	5	Jones 2, Longstaff	7,000	2	4					8	7		9	3	10	5	6	11	1
8	SL D1	(h)	Brentford	W 3–0	1–0	3	Longstaff 3	6,000	2	4		8				7	9		3	10	5	6	11	1
15	FAC R1	(h)	Southampton	L 0–1	0–1	–		10,000	2	4		8				7	9		3	10	5	6	11	1
22	SL D1	(a)	Coventry City	D 1–1	1–0	2	Haworth	7,000	2	4	10				8		6		3	7	5	9	11	1
29	SL D1	(h)	Watford	W 3–1	2–0	2	Middleton 2, Longstaff	4,000	2	4	8						6		3	7	5	9	10	1
Feb 5	SL D1	(a)	Reading	W 2–1	1–0	1	Own goal, Webb	2,000	2	4					8	11	6		3	7	5	9	10	1
12	SL D1	(h)	Southend United	D 1–1	0–0	1	Webb	5,000	2	4					8	11	6		3	7	5	9	10	1
21	SCC SF	(n*)	Swindon Town	W 3–0	1–0	–	Hastings, Haworth, Coleman	7,000	2	4	8						11	6		3	7	5	9	10	1
26	SL D1	(h)	Plymouth Argyle	W 1–0	0–0	1	Middleton	6,000	2	4	8						11	6		3	7	5	9	10	1
Mar 5	SL D1	(a)	Southampton	L 1–2	1–1	1	Webb	7,000	2	4							11	6	9	3	7	5	8	10	1
7	SL D1	(a)	Leyton	D 1–1	0–0	1	Hastings	3,000	2	4	8						11	6	9	3	7	5		10	1
12	SL D1	(h)	Croydon Common	W 1–0	0–0	1	Haworth (pen)	5,000	2	4							11	6	9	3	7	5	8	10	1
19	SL D1	(h)	Millwall	W 1–0	0–0	1	Middleton	3,000	2	4							11	6	9	3	7	5	8	10	1
25	SL D1	(h)	Exeter City	W 2–1	1–1	1	Longstaff, Jones	10,000	2	4							11	6	9	3	7	5	8	10	1
26	SL D1	(h)	New Brompton	W 5–1	1–0	1	Webb, Longstaff 2, Jones, Coleman	6,000	2	4	8						11	6	9	3	7	5		10	1
28	SL D1	(h)	Exeter City	W 1–0	0–0	1	Jones	7,000	2	4	8						11	6	9	3	7	5		10	1
29	SL D1	(a)	Bristol Rovers	D 0–0	0–0	1		8,000	2	4	8						11	5	9	3	7		6	10	1
Apr 2	SL D1	(a)	Northampton T.	D 1–1	1–1	1	Jones	6,000	2	4				8			11	6	9	3	7	5		10	1
4	SCC F	(n*)	Watford	D 1–0*	0–0	–	Jones	3,000	2	4							11	6	9	3	7	5	8	10	1
9	SL D1	(h)	Queen's Park R.	W 2–0	1–0	1	Jones 2 (1 pen)	10,500	2	4							11	6	9	3	7	5	8	10	1
16	SL D1	(a)	Luton Town	D 1–1	1–0	1	Webb	6,100	2	4	8						11	6	9	3	7	5		10	1
23	SL D1	(h)	Swindon Town	W 3–1	2–1	1	Jones 2, Longstaff	11,000	2	4	8						11	6	9	3	7	5		10	1
30	SL D1	(h)	Crystal Palace	D 0–0	0–0	1		10,000	2	4	8						11	6	9	3	7	5		10	1
League appearances									2	42	42	11	9	1	21	41	20	34	42	39	41	33	42	42
League goals								OG – 1				1	4		8	4	2	20		14	1	5	9	

Notes: Feb 21 – played at Stamford Bridge, Chelsea FC.
Apr 4 – played at Stamford Bridge, Chelsea FC.
– after extra time.

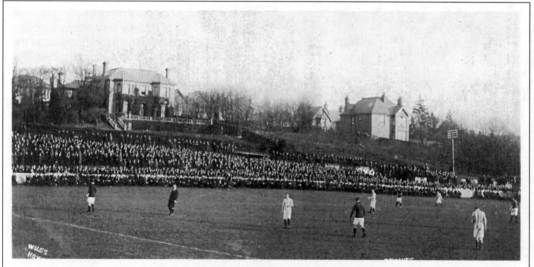

Albion 1 Plymouth Argyle 0, 26 February 1910
Harry Middleton scored the winner in the second half of this game which kept Albion on top of the Southern League. The attendance was around 6,000. The large house overlooking the popular east banking was Goldstone House, the residence of the club's landlord, Alderman John Clark.

In August, Bob Whiting and Bill Jones represented the Albion staff at a meeting convened in Birmingham to discuss the dispute with the F.A. over recognition of the Players' Union and the threatened strike. The maximum wage at this time was £4 per week, but agreement between all the parties was eventually reached in April 1910 with provision made for win-bonuses and for talent money for clubs finishing in the top five.

Southern League Division 1 1909–10

		P	W	D	L	F	A	W	D	L	F	A	Pts
1.	**ALBION**	42	18	2	1	50	11	5	11	5	19	17	59
2.	Swindon Town	42	15	3	3	63	20	7	7	7	29	26	54
3.	Queen's Park R.	42	12	5	4	41	28	7	8	6	15	19	51
4.	Northampton Town	42	16	3	2	66	11	6	1	14	24	33	48
5.	Southampton	42	11	7	3	39	25	5	9	7	25	30	48
6.	Portsmouth	42	13	5	3	43	17	7	2	12	27	46	47
7.	Crystal Palace	42	13	3	5	48	20	7	3	11	21	30	46
8.	Coventry City	42	11	6	4	50	24	8	2	11	21	36	46
9.	West Ham United	42	10	7	4	43	23	5	8	8	26	33	45
10.	Leyton	42	11	4	6	45	22	5	7	9	15	24	43
11.	Plymouth Argyle	42	14	5	2	40	8	2	6	13	21	46	43
12.	New Brompton	42	16	2	3	52	21	3	3	15	24	53	43
13.	Bristol Rovers	42	13	5	3	25	8	3	5	13	12	40	42
14.	Brentford	42	13	5	3	33	13	3	4	14	17	45	41
15.	Luton Town	42	10	7	4	45	34	5	4	12	27	58	41
16.	Millwall	42	9	6	6	24	17	6	1	14	21	42	37
17.	Norwich City	42	11	5	5	42	26	2	4	15	17	52	35
18.	Exeter City	42	12	4	5	45	22	2	2	17	15	47	34
19.	Watford	42	8	8	5	32	24	2	5	14	19	52	33
20.	Southend United	42	10	4	7	26	17	2	5	14	25	73	33
21.	Croydon Common	42	8	2	11	29	38	5	3	13	23	58	31
22.	Reading	42	7	6	8	27	25	0	4	17	11	48	24

Swindon Town. On 23 April, Swindon arrived at the Goldstone with Albion requiring one point from their two remaining fixtures to clinch the championship. Eleven thousand fans packed into the ground, creating an atmosphere of great excitement and anticipation. Albion got off to a cracking start when Jones opened the scoring in the first minute and added a second eight minutes later. Swindon bounced back through left-winger Freddie Fenton but never looked likely to take both points, and when Bertie Longstaff scored Albion's third with ten minutes remaining the outcome was beyond doubt. At the final whistle the crowd poured onto the pitch and the players were carried from the field amid scenes of wild jubilation.

Albion finished five points clear of Swindon Town. Bullet Jones led the marksmen with 22 in League and Cup, followed by Bertie Longstaff with 16. Fred Blackman, Billy Booth, Joe Leeming, Charlie Webb and Bob Whiting never missed a Southern League match, while Bill Hastings and Joe McGhie missed only one apiece, and, as a result, only 28 goals were conceded in the 42 League matches. Just sixteen players were used in League and Cup games, an all-time club record.

The following article, reminiscent of more recent times, appeared in the *Sussex Daily News* on New Year's Day, 1910.

ALBION AND A NEW GROUND

For some little time past, negotiations have been proceeding with the object of securing another ground as Brighton and Hove Albion's headquarters, and within the last day or so they have reached such a stage that there is now every probability of terms being arranged. The Directors have the offer of a central site, served by one of the tram routes, and are making the necessary financial arrangements with a view to its acquisition at the earliest possible date. Owing to the restrictions of the existing lease of the Goldstone Ground, which expires at the end of next season, they have felt it impossible to provide the accommodation they would like to for the supporters of the club. It is considered that one result of this has been to retard its progress and to keep many people away from the matches who would patronise them if the accommodation were more adequate. The Directors have, therefore, felt it absolutely imperative to secure a fresh ground, where larger crowds can be dealt with and more comfortably provided for.

By June, the negotiations for the site, which was off Dyke Road, were complete and the owners had accepted an offer from the Albion board. Plans for laying out the new ground had been prepared by Archibald Leitch, and a general meeting of supporters was proposed with a view to enlisting the necessary financial aid. (Leitch was the foremost architect of football grounds in the history of the British game, and was responsible for the design of most of the great stadia in England and Scotland in the first 40 years of this century.) However, at the last moment, the board dropped the scheme because of a possible lawsuit and turned instead to obtaining an improved arrangement with Alderman Clark for the Goldstone Ground.

The South Stand in 1910
This quaint structure occupied the southern end of the ground for 50 years from 1904 when it was purchased by directors Noah Clark and Ben Parker from an agricultural show in Preston Park. In 1949 it was raised and rebuilt behind new terracing, and was finally replaced by the present South Stand in 1954.

On 16 April the Goldstone Ground was honoured with its first representative match, an amateur international between England and France. A crowd of around 3,500 saw the English annihilate their Continental opponents 10–1, but the French party won many friends and the two teams spent a convivial evening at the Royal York Hotel.

Albion took a side to Hastings in February to play the financially embarrassed Hastings and St Leonards United club in a fund-raising friendly. Brighton played only for their 'train fares and their teas' and won 3–2. The sum of £17 was raised, but Hastings folded as a professional club at the end of the season.

Albion also won the Southern Professional Charity Cup – which was put on display in the Sussex Goldsmiths shop in Castle Square, Brighton – by defeating Watford in the final at Stamford Bridge, the only goal being scored by Bullet Jones during extra time. The competition was open to all professional teams in the South and was contested by the majority of the Southern League clubs, so Albion, in effect, completed the 'double'. The only disappointment in an otherwise marvellous season was the 1–0 home defeat at the hands of bogey-side Southampton in the English Cup first round. Skipper Joe Leeming was selected for the F.A.'s summer tour of South Africa and full-back Fred Blackman represented the Southern League against the Football League at Stamford Bridge in April. The reserve team, known as the Lambs, also had a fine season, finishing runners-up to Chelsea in the South Eastern

League. The average attendance at the Goldstone was 6,833, the highest thus far, and a most successful season brought a net profit of £780 6s. 3d. The club paid income tax, to the tune of £27 17s. 8d., for the first time.

It was a marvellous achievement for the club to win the championship of the Southern League just nine years after its formation. Brighton and Hove Albion were now well and truly on the footballing map, with still greater things to come.

February 5th, 1910: shortly before half time in the Lambs' South Eastern League match with Norwich City at Hove, 27-year-old amateur centre-half Henrie Reid, playing only his fourth game for City's reserves, left the pitch almost unnoticed. When the second half commenced, a director approached the referee and informed him that the player had died. The game was abandoned and the crowd left the ground in silence. After officials from both clubs had attended Reid's funeral in Romford, it was agreed to replay the match on Saturday, 19 February, with the two first teams. Both sides met their own expenses and a 3,000 crowd raised around £89 for Reid's widow. The coroner's report cited heart failure as the cause of death.

SEASON 1910–11

The profit from the previous season's success enabled large-scale ground improvements to be made during the summer months. The single-bar fence which surrounded the pitch was replaced with a sunken, wooden-paling fence (which was not modernised until the late 1950s) and the north banking was terraced over with sixteen steps. The east banking was also partially terraced.

The season opened with a Southern League fixture against Leyton at the Goldstone. There were few new faces among the professionals and the line-up for the match was the same as that for the closing game of the championship season. Albion won narrowly by a Bullet Jones penalty to nil, but most thoughts were focused on the following Monday and the F.A. Charity Shield match.

THE F.A. CHARITY SHIELD

In recent times the Charity Shield has become a 'curtain-raiser' to the new season with the F.A. Cup holders meeting the reigning League champions, but this has not always been the case. Over the years various formats have been employed, and for the five years from 1908, when the Southern League was in its heyday, the Shield was contested by the champions of the Southern League and the Football League. Albion thus qualified to meet the most famous club in the land, Aston Villa, on Monday, 5 September, at Stamford Bridge, Chelsea.

The meeting was anticipated with great relish by the Sussex public, and even non-football folk were caught up in the atmosphere. Throughout the summer, cricket took a back seat as talk in the pubs of Brighton and Hove inevitably turned to the Albion's chances against the might of Villa. As the summer drew to a close, excitement rose to fever pitch.

On the morning of the match the team left Brighton on a special train along with hundreds of supporters decked out in all manner of blue-and-white favours. On the journey to London little thought was given to the possibility of defeat. Some years later Charlie Webb reflected:

We drove in style to Stamford Bridge in a four-horse brake. The match had created a good deal of interest in the Metropolis and I have the feeling the majority of those non-partisan thousands who flocked in were secretly hoping it would be another David and Goliath story.

In the dressing-room the team was reported as being very nervous, but on taking the field their anxiety rapidly evaporated. The two sides lined up as follows:

Brighton and Hove Albion: Bob Whiting;
Fred Blackman and Joe Leeming (captain);
Billy Booth, Joe McGhie and Jack Haworth;
Bertie Longstaff, Jimmy Coleman, Bullet Jones,
Charlie Webb and Bill Hastings.

Aston Villa: Arthur Cartlidge; Tommy Lyons and
Freddie Miles; George Tranter, Chris Buckley and
George Hunter; Charlie Wallace, Joe Walters,
Walter Gerrish, Joe Bache and Albert Hall.

The following report is an edited version of the match report that appeared in the *Sussex Daily News*.

HOW THE ALBION BEAT ASTON VILLA

The season is only a few days old, but already Brighton and Hove Albion have added a much-coveted trophy to their collection and they have annexed it by defeating Aston Villa at Stamford Bridge. It was of course a great triumph for the Albion, and although a solitary goal decided the issue, the 'Hope of the South', as the Southern League representatives were not inaptly called, won thoroughly on merit and can now be dubbed as Champions of England. They did more pressing than the Villa and their forwards were certainly the more dangerous set in front of goal. Some of their movements may not have been so pretty to watch as those of the First Leaguers in that they did not keep the ball on the floor quite so skilfully as their rivals, but they had more dash and consistency.

The winners' defensive brigade played a great game as everyone who knows anything about last season's record was confident they would. Time after time the Villa forwards swept down the field only to be bottled up by the Albion halves, and with Leeming and Blackman giving of their best Whiting had so few really dangerous shots to stop that they could be counted on the fingers of one hand. The Villa have a great name and are one of the most polished combinations of the First League, but on their display at Chelsea's headquarters yesterday the Albion have nothing to learn from them, either in defence or attack.

The Villa had the benefit of a light wind in the first half, but the Albion forwards went off with rare sparkle, a thrilling incident in the early stages being when Hastings wheeled round Lyons and finished with a scorching drive. It was a fine effort, but the ball rose a trifle too high and went over the bar. Another near thing came when Jones followed up a good return by McGhie and, shaking off the attentions of the backs, hit the upright with a pile-driver. It was some little time before the Villa got into their stride and when they did nearly all the sting came from their England left-wing pair, Bache and Hall. They had an excellent understanding and led Booth a lively dance, but the Brighton half-back never knew when he was beaten and often got back in time to help Blackman save the situation.

Whiting was not often called upon, but he fisted away a splendid screw shot by Wallace. Midway through the first half a very unusual happening occurred when Hall took a corner and planted the ball straight into the net from the flag kick. The point, of course, did not count as no other player had touched the ball, but Whiting made a desperate effort to do so as the leather swerved into the net and it was just as well from the Brighton standpoint that he did not succeed. [Note: goals direct from corners were not allowed until 1924.] After this there was a spirited rally by the Albion and two splendid efforts came from Webb and Jones, the former hitting the side net with a beauty and the wily little Albion centre bringing Cartlidge to his knees with a rasping grounder. At the expiry of a fairly fast first half, the score sheet was still blank and the honours deserved to be even.

The second half, however, was distinctly Brighton's. The Villa forwards were so well held by the opposition that Whiting had very little to do. There were, it is true, several exciting mêlées in front of Whiting, but in each case the defence got the better of the argument, and with the exception of holding a few long shots the Albion custodian held a watching brief. Brighton owed a great deal to their half-backs who were not only resourceful in defence but a great help to their forwards. Jones frequently got his line travelling in business-like fashion and there were several near things, Hastings, Booth and Webb all shooting with power and precision. Longstaff was very nippy on the extreme right and his centres were a source of anxiety to the Villa backs, but nothing tangible was obtained until there were only eighteen minutes left for play. Then Albion forced a corner and Longstaff placed it splendidly. Cartlidge threw up his arms as the ball came across the mouth of goal and brought it down in a ruck of players a few yards out. Hastings fastened onto it and passed to Webb who cleverly evaded a couple of Villa defenders and found the net with a rising cross-shot.

The cheering that greeted Brighton's success was something to remember. The Villa tried desperately hard to save the game but their forwards could make little headway against the Albion's vigilant halves. On the other hand, Webb and Hastings beat the backs in turn and each came near to increasing the Albion's score with good cross-shots. Towards the end the Villa rearranged their forward line, but Webb promptly dropped back to make a fourth Albion half. The leaders meant to hold what they had won and they succeeded, the Villa being outpointed to the end.

The crowd included a large contingent of excursionists from Brighton and the Albion's victory was hailed with prolonged cheering. Thousands of people surged up in front of the stand, from the centre of which Mr Crump, vice-president of the Football Association, presented the shield on which the name of Albion will shortly be engraved with those of the two previous winners, Manchester United and Newcastle United. When Leeming came forward to receive it, the cheers were deafening. Afterwards the Mayoress of Fulham, Mrs Norris, distributed gold medals to both teams and, having cheered her for her kindness, the crowd melted away.

THE RETURN OF THE VICTORS

There were enthusiastic scenes when the team reached Brighton at half past eleven. The station square was packed with people and the players came down one of the central platforms amid a positive fusillade of cheering and waving of hats. To avoid what threatened to be an embarrassing welcome, they crossed within the barrier to the west side and left for Hove to the accompaniment of more cheers. The president of the club, Mr Goodwin, was one of the first to meet the players on the arrival platform and tender there his congratulations. There is nothing like letting the general celebration take a practical form and it is suggested that this can most fittingly be done by swelling the Players' Fund. They deserve handsome recognition and the committee should have no difficulty in securing the amount they have aimed at.

The Players' Fund realised £98 to which William Goodwin contributed an additional £25. On the evening of 22 September a smoking-concert was held at The Dome, and on display were the three trophies won by the club: the F.A. Charity Shield, the Southern League Championship Shield and the Southern Professional Charity Cup. The medals were presented to the players by the Mayor of Brighton, Alderman Edward Geere, and the testimonial fund was distributed among the professionals by the Mayor of Hove, Captain Fraser. As an amateur, match-winner Charlie Webb was presented with a gold tie-pin. The Charity Shield itself was put on display in the window of Mr Horton-Stephens's hosiery shop at no. 42 Western Road, Brighton. Mr Horton-Stephens was the official agent for the club's colours.

The Albion's triumph was the only time the Southern League champions beat the Football League champions. The capture of the Football Association's Charity Shield, to rank alongside such great clubs such as Manchester United and Newcastle United, remains one of the club's greatest-ever achievements, matched only by reaching the F.A. Cup final and the gaining of First Division status.

BRIGHTON & HOVE ALBION v. ASTON VILLA (First League Champions, 1909).

Played at Chelsea, Sept. 5th, 1910.   Result—Brighton (Webb), 1; Aston Villa, 0.

Season 1909.

Brighton Won Southern League Championship.

Southern Charity Cup.

Football Association Shield.

The Second Eleven were runners up in the South-Eastern League.

The first cartoon appeared on Chelsea Programme, and is published by permission. The other cartoon was drawn by F. GROVER (an employee of the Brighton Tramways). The profits from the sale to be devoted to the Players' Testimonial Fund.

Messrs. R. ALDERTON, Blacksmiths' Arms, and F. J. SHARPE, Hon. Secs.

"Want to take the famous Midland Champion on, do you? Very well, sir, step inside!"

"I only gave him one, sir!"

Produced by the direction and expenses guaranteed by Messrs. EDLIN BROS., Northern, King and Queen, Great Globe and Western Hotels.

G.M.F. Ltd., 112, Gloster Road, Brighton.

Champions of England
One of several mementoes issued to commemorate the Albion's magnificent and historic triumph in September 1910.

NORMAL FARE RESUMED — SEASON 1910–11

The team and its supporters returned to earth with a bump, going down 2–1 at Watford on the Saturday after the Villa match. After such momentous events it would be understandable if a reaction had set in, but in fact the opposite occurred and after the Watford defeat the team won seven successive League matches to head the table at the beginning of November. Added to this sequence were victories over Portsmouth and Reading in the Southern Charity Cup.

On 22 October, Albion were the visitors on the occasion of the opening of Millwall's new ground, The Den, and some 25,000 spectators thronged into the excellent arena hoping to see their favourites win. Visits to Millwall usually ended in heavy defeat for the Albion, but this time they came out on top thanks to a Jack Haworth goal eight minutes from time. The win saw Albion go top and remain there for three weeks, but the loss of a point in the 3–3 home draw with Luton Town enabled Swindon Town to take pole position, proving what a cracking pace was being set by the leading teams.

Home and away defeats against Swindon ended any hopes of winning the championship for a second time. The Wiltshire club had retained the leadership for most of the season and clinched the title when they defeated Albion 3–0 at the County Ground on 22 April. They also accounted for Albion in the final of the Southern Charity Cup, winning 1–0 at Craven Cottage

after a goal-less draw at the same venue. The Swindon side were a very strong combination around this period with the legendary Harold Fleming a regular in the England team. Albion had maintained a top-four position for all but a brief spell in December and eventually finished in third place, level on points with runners-up Northampton Town.

Albion were once again drawn against Football League opposition in the English Cup. Second Division Leeds City, still managed by Frank Walford, hosted the first-round tie, and in front of an 18,270 crowd (£610) Albion covered themselves in glory, winning comfortably by three goals to one. A stay at the

		P	W	D	L	F	A	W	D	L	F	A	Pts
	Southern League Division 1 1910–11												
1.	Swindon Town	38	16	2	1	54	9	8	3	8	26	22	53
2.	Northampton Town	38	14	3	2	39	7	4	9	6	15	20	48
3.	**ALBION**	38	15	2	2	41	12	5	6	8	17	24	48
4.	Crystal Palace	38	11	5	3	35	23	6	8	5	20	25	47
5.	West Ham United	38	12	6	1	44	17	5	5	9	19	29	45
6.	Queen's Park R.	38	11	6	2	37	16	2	8	9	15	25	40
7.	Leyton	38	13	3	3	37	15	3	5	11	20	37	40
8.	Plymouth Argyle	38	10	6	3	37	14	5	3	11	17	41	39
9.	Luton Town	38	13	4	2	42	18	2	4	13	25	45	38
10.	Norwich City	38	12	5	2	31	13	3	3	13	15	35	38
11.	Coventry City	38	12	4	3	47	21	4	2	13	18	47	38
12.	Brentford	38	12	5	2	32	13	2	4	13	9	29	37
13.	Exeter City	38	8	5	6	31	28	6	4	9	20	25	37
14.	Watford	38	10	5	4	32	23	3	4	12	17	42	35
15.	Millwall	38	8	3	8	21	20	3	6	10	21	34	31
16.	Bristol Rovers	38	6	6	7	24	23	4	4	11	18	32	30
17.	Southampton	38	8	3	8	25	28	3	5	11	17	39	30
18.	New Brompton	38	10	5	4	19	15	1	3	15	15	50	30
19.	Southend United	38	7	4	8	28	26	3	5	11	19	38	29
20.	Portsmouth	38	6	10	3	21	15	2	1	16	13	38	27

SEASON 1910–11

Date	Comp.	Ven.	Opponents	Result	HT	Pos.	Scorers	Atten.	Blackman F	Booth W	Coleman J	Crinson W	Ford G	Hastings W	Haworth J	Jones W	Leeming J	Longstaff A	Lumley J	McGhie J	Miller W	Perkins W	Routledge R	Sharpe I	Smart F	Smith J	Stott T	Thomas J	Wake T	Webb C	Whiting R
Sep 3	SL D1	(h)	Leyton	W 1–0	1–0	1=	Jones (pen)	8,000	2	4	8			11	6	9	3	7		5										10	1
5	FA Ch. Shield	(n*)	Aston Villa	W 1–0	0–0	–	Webb	13,000	2	4	8			11	6	9	3	7		5										10	1
10	SL D1	(a)	Watford	L 1–2	0–0	9=	Jones	6,000	2	4				11	6	9	3	7		5	8									10	1
14	SCC R1	(a)	Portsmouth	W 1–0	1–0	–	Hastings	2,000	2	4				11	6	9	3	7										8	5	10	1
17	SL D1	(h)	Plymouth Argyle	W 2–1	2–0	9	Jones 2 (1 pen)	7,000	2	4	8			11	6	9	3	7		5										10	1
24	SL D1	(a)	Southampton	W 2–1	1–1	6	Longstaff, Hastings	8,000	2	4	8			11	6	9	3	7		5										10	1
Oct 1	SL D1	(h)	Southend United	W 4–0	1–0	4	Jones 2, Webb 2	7,000	2	4	7			11	6	9	3	8		5										10	1
8	SL D1	(a)	Coventry City	W 2–0	0–0	3	Jones, Hastings	10,000	2	4	8			11	6	9	3	7		5										10	1
15	SL D1	(h)	New Brompton	W 2–0	1–0	2	Webb 2	7,000	2	4	8			11	6	9	3	7		5										10	1
19	SCC R2	(h)	Reading	W 2–0	1–0	–	Thomas, Hastings	1,000	2	4				11	6	9	3	7										8	5	10	1
22	SL D1	(a)	Millwall	W 1–0	0–0	1	Haworth	25,000	2	4	8			11	6	9	3	7		5										10	1
29	SL D1	(h)	Queen's Park R.	W 2–1	2–1	1	Webb, Coleman	8,000		4	8			11	6	9	3	7	2										5	10	1
Nov 5	SL D1	(a)	West Ham United	L 1–3	0–1	1	Webb	16,000	2	4	8			11	6	9	3	7											5	10	1
12	SL D1	(h)	Luton Town	D 3–3	3–1	2	Webb, Jones 2	7,000	2	4	8			11	6	9	3	7		5										10	1
19	SL D1	(a)	Portsmouth	L 0–1	0–1	3		11,000	2	4	8			11	6	9	3	7		5										10	1
26	SL D1	(h)	Northampton T.	W 5–0	1–0	3	Coleman 2, Hastings, Longstaff, Jones (pen)	7,000	2	4	8			11	6	9		7					3						5	10	1
28	SCC SF	(n*)	Watford	W 2–1	1–1	–	Webb, Longstaff	1,000	2	4	8			11	6	9		7					3						5	10	1
Dec 3	SL D1	(a)	Norwich City	D 1–1	1–1	3	Coleman	4,737	2	4	8			11	6	9		7					3						5	10	1
10	SL D1	(a)	Exeter City	L 1–2	0–1	3	Booth	5,000	2	4	8			11	6	9		7					3						5	10	1
17	SL D1	(h)	Swindon Town	L 0–1	0–0	5		8,000	2	4	8			11	6	9	3	7		5										10	1
24	SL D1	(a)	Bristol Rovers	W 2–1	2–1	5	Jones, Webb	5,000	2	4				11	6	9	3	7		5								8		10	1
26	SL D1	(h)	Crystal Palace	W 2–0	1–0	4	Jones, Coleman	12,000	2	4	8			11	6	9	3	7		5										10	1
27	SL D1	(a)	Crystal Palace	D 1–1	1–0	3	Hastings	20,000	2	4	8			11	6	9	3	7		5										10	1
31	SL D1	(a)	Leyton	D 1–1	1–1	4	Webb	5,000	2	4	8			11	6	9	3	7		5										10	1
Jan 7	SL D1	(h)	Watford	W 5–0	2–0	2	Webb 2, Smith 2, Jones	6,000	2	4				11	6	8	3	7								9			5	10	1
14	FAC R1	(a)	Leeds City	W 3–1	1–1	–	Jones 2, Smith	18,270		4				11	6	8	3	7		5						9				10	1
21	SL D1	(a)	Plymouth Argyle	D 2–2	1–1	3	Jones (pen), Smith	8,000		4				11	6	8	3	7	2	5						9				10	1
28	SL D1	(h)	Southampton	W 2–0	1–0	2	Webb, Jones (pen)	7,000	2	4				11	6	8	3	7		5						9				10	1
Feb 4	FAC R2	(h)	Coventry City	D 0–0	0–0	–		13,000	2	4					6	8	3	7		5			11			9				10	1
9	FAC R2 Rep	(a)	Coventry City	L 0–2	0–2	–		17,000	2	4				11	6	9	3	8		5			7							10	1
11	SL D1	(h)	Coventry City	W 2–1	2–0	3	Haworth, Webb	4,000		4	8			11	6		3	7	2	5						9				10	1
18	SL D1	(a)	New Brompton	L 0–1	0–1	4		5,000	2	4	8			11	6	9	3	7		5										10	1
22	SL D1	(a)	Southend United	W 1–0	0–0	2	Haworth	1,400	2	4	8			11	6	9	3			5	10		7								1
25	SL D1	(h)	Millwall	W 3–2	2–2	2	Haworth 2, Hastings	5,000	2	4	8			7	10		3			5	11					9			6		1
Mar 4	SL D1	(a)	Queen's Park R.	D 0–0	0–0	2		12,000	2	4	7		8	11	10		3			5						9			6		1
18	SL D1	(a)	Luton Town	L 0–1	0–1	3			2	4				11	10	9	3	7		5						8			6		1
25	SL D1	(h)	Portsmouth	W 2–1	1–0	2	Jones 2	5,000	2	4	8			11	6	9	3	7		5										10	1
Apr 1	SL D1	(a)	Northampton T.	L 0–3	0–3	4		6,000	2	4				11	6	9	3	7		5						8				10	1
8	SL D1	(h)	Norwich City	W 2–0	1–0	4	Smith, Longstaff	5,000	2	4				7	6	10	3	8		5						9				11	1
14	SL D1	(h)	Brentford	W 1–0	1–0	2	Smith	9,500	2	4				7	6	10	3	8		5						9				11	1
15	SL D1	(h)	Exeter City	L 0–2	0–2	3		8,000	2	4				7	6	10	3	8		5						9				11	1
17	SL D1	(a)	Brentford	D 1–1	0–1	3	Miller	11,000		4				11		10		7	2	5	8		3			9			6		1
22	SL D1	(a)	Swindon Town	L 0–3	0–2	4		7,000	2	4					6	10	3	7		5	8					9				11	1
24	SCC F	(n*)	Swindon Town	D 0–0*	0–0	–		3,000		4		1		11	6	8		7		3			2			9			5	10	
26	SCC F	(h)	West Ham United	W 3–0	1–0	3	Hastings, Webb, Scott	3,000	2	4		1		11	6	8		7		5			3			9				10	
27	SCC F Rep	(n*)	Swindon Town	L 0–1	0–1	–		1,500		4		1		11	6	8		7	2				3			9			5	10	
29	SL D1	(h)	Bristol Rovers	D 0–0	0–0	3		5,000	2	4				11	6	8		7		5			3			9				10	1
			League appearances						34	38	24	1	1	37	37	35	33	35	3	32	4	1	6	0	1	14	1	1	10	33	37
			League goals							1	5			6	5	17		3			1					5	1			14	

Notes: Sep 5 – played at Stamford Bridge, Chelsea FC.
Nov 28 – played at The Den, Millwall FC.
Apr 24 – played at Craven Cottage, Fulham FC.
– after extra time.
Apr 27 – played at Craven Cottage, Fulham FC.

Albion 1910–11

Standing left to right: J. Butt (assistant trainer), Gunner Higham, J. F. Franklin, Ralph Routledge, Fred Blackman, Bill Crinson, Jack Robson (manager), Joe Leeming (captain), Bob Whiting, Joe Lumley, Dick Whittington, Steve Weller, Alf Nelmes (trainer).
Seated left to right: Joe McGhie, Billy Booth, Bert Longstaff, Jimmy Coleman, Bill Jones, Charlie Webb, Bill Hastings, Jack Haworth, Harry Middleton.
On ground left to right: Teddy Elliott, Jack Thomas, Billy Miller, Tom Wake.
Trophies left to right: Southern Professional Charity Cup, Southern League Championship Shield, Football Association Charity Shield.

The old West Stand
Albion, in their change strip, take the field on 29 April 1911 in the last match of the season against Bristol Rovers. Clearly seen is the old West Stand, erected in 1901 by Alderman Clark for Hove F.C. The wooden structure stood, with additions, for 57 years until it was finally replaced by the present West Stand in 1958.

Adelphi Hotel, Harrogate, before the match had obviously done the trick, and around 300 fans had a happy journey back to Brighton – return fare twelve shillings (60p) – in their 'steam-heated corridor-train'. In the second round Coventry City were drawn at the Goldstone. Albion had already beaten the Warwickshire side in the away Southern League fixture and were expected to cruise through to the next stage, but, much to the disgust of the fans, City held out for a goal-less draw and won the replay 2–0. Irate letters were penned to the Press complaining of a lack of commitment in both matches. The teams met again the following Saturday in the return League match at the Goldstone; Albion won 2–1 and left the field to the accompaniment of ironic cheers. Ivan Sharpe, the noted England amateur international, guested for the Albion in the two Cup games with Coventry. He was to win great renown as a sports journalist and became president of the Football Writers' Association.

Bullet Jones led the goalscorers with seventeen, followed by Charlie Webb on fourteen. Fred Blackman gained further honours when he was selected to play in the England trial match at Tottenham in January.

After a notable Cup triumph away from home, it was traditional for large crowds to greet the team upon their arrival back at Brighton Central Station, but the scenes which met the victors on 14 January following the defeat of Leeds City were quite extraordinary. Supporters began to gather around 9 p.m., and by midnight there were about 1,500 people in the terminus. Impromptu 'concerts' were given and popular songs of the era were adapted much as they are today. The chief chorus ran:

Shoot for the goal, Brighton, shoot for the goal.
Fear not the City backs, for they're up the pole.
Get past the half-backs; keep the ball on the roll.
Let the forwards have it, and shoot for the goal.

There was also 'The Death of Poor Leeds City' to the tune of 'Cock Robin', and, presumably to the tune of 'Sussex by the Sea':

Good old Brighton by the Sea
Good old Brighton by the Sea
You can tell them they can play football
At good old Brighton by the Sea

At 1.45 a.m. the special train carrying the team and 300 supporters finally arrived. The 2,000-strong crowd broke through the ranks of police, charged down the platform to greet the players, and then singled out two-goal hero Bullet Jones. The *Sussex Daily News* takes up the story:

As he emerged from the carriage Jones was surrounded by hundreds of ardent – too ardent, in fact – admirers, who clapped him on the shoulder, shook him by both hands, and shouted till they were hoarse. Down the platform they came, through the gates and on to no.1 platform, where Jones, noting an empty train on the left, dashed into a carriage and, shutting the door, rushed out the other side in his endeavour to escape. Not to be denied, the crowd opened other carriage doors and also hurried through, while poor Jones, like an exhausted hare with hounds close on his track, 'ran to earth' in the porters' quarters on the western side of the station. Eventually he emerged apparently surrendered, but the crowd, intoxicated with excitement, still endeavoured to hoist him shoulder-high, and, growing desperate, Jones rushed through the carriages of two trains and gained at last a quiet quarter in the compartment of the Hove train. Even then his 'attendants' would not be satisfied, for they dashed after him, some through carriages and some across lines, and as the train moved off they frantically waved their hats, handkerchiefs and sticks, and cheered lustily.

Peace returned to the station at around half past two.

SEASON 1911–12

When compared with the previous two seasons, this was a quiet campaign. Three new players joined the professional ranks: Archie Needham (Wolverhampton Wanderers), Crosby Henderson (Birmingham) and Fred Goodwin (Leek United). Needham was a remarkably versatile footballer: during his time at the Goldstone he was to fill every outfield position in the Southern League team. He had played for Jack Robson at Crystal Palace and proved a great asset to the Albion.

This season saw the emergence of young Jimmy Smith as a prolific goalscorer. Having joined the club from Hanley in January 1911, he scored five goals in fourteen Southern League matches towards the end of the previous campaign. This term he did not gain a regular place until late October when an injury to Bullet Jones gave him the chance, but Jimmy grabbed the opportunity with both hands, scoring the first of four hat-tricks in only his third game (at Watford) and notching all four in a win over Stoke. The directors were so impressed with Smith's form that when Birmingham made an offer for Jones in January they did not hesitate in releasing the ever-popular little man, and he returned to the scene of his former glories for a £300 fee, a large sum in 1912.

Albion maintained a mid-table position in the Southern League, but inconsistency was a problem. There were some spectacular performances at the Goldstone with big wins over Bristol Rovers (5–1), Southampton (5–0), New Brompton (7–0) and Watford (7–1, with another Smith hat-trick). Queen's Park Rangers and Swindon Town were both beaten while leading the League. Bad results against lowly opposition nullified these achievements until February when a superb run of fifteen matches brought just one defeat, at the hands of Luton Town. If this form had been sustained throughout the season Albion would have undoubtedly taken the title for a second time, but

Southern League Division 1 1911–12

		P	W	D	L	F	A	W	D	L	F	A	Pts
1.	Queen's Park R.	38	12	5	2	36	14	9	6	4	23	21	53
2.	Plymouth Argyle	38	16	2	1	42	7	7	4	8	21	24	52
3.	Northampton Town	38	16	2	1	57	15	6	5	8	25	26	51
4.	Swindon Town	38	14	3	2	52	19	7	3	9	30	31	48
5.	**ALBION**	38	15	2	2	54	12	4	7	8	19	23	47
6.	Coventry City	38	14	3	2	46	15	3	5	11	20	39	42
7.	Crystal Palace	38	11	5	3	43	14	4	5	10	27	32	40
8.	Millwall	38	11	6	2	43	19	4	4	11	17	38	40
9.	Watford	38	10	5	4	35	20	3	5	11	21	48	36
10.	Stoke	38	11	4	4	35	25	2	6	11	16	38	36
11.	Reading	38	10	7	2	35	14	1	7	11	8	45	36
12.	Norwich City	38	8	10	1	27	17	2	4	13	13	43	34
13.	West Ham United	38	10	3	6	40	27	3	4	12	24	42	33
14.	Brentford	38	10	5	4	43	18	2	4	13	17	47	33
15.	Exeter City	38	8	6	5	30	22	3	5	11	18	40	33
16.	Southampton	38	9	3	7	29	27	1	8	10	17	36	31
17.	Bristol Rovers	38	7	8	4	24	18	2	5	12	17	44	31
18.	New Brompton	38	7	6	6	23	23	4	3	12	12	49	31
19.	Luton Town	38	7	5	7	33	28	2	5	12	16	33	28
20.	Leyton	38	6	8	5	15	19	1	3	15	12	43	25

SEASON 1911–12

Date	Comp.	Ven.	Opponents	Result	HT	Pos.	Scorers	Atten.	Booth W	Coleman J	Goodwin F	Hastings W	Haworth J	Henderson C	Higham T	Jones W	Leeming J	Longstaff A	Lumley J	McGhie J	Matthews C	Miller W	Needham A	Parker J	Parlett F	Piggin L	Routledge R	Smith J	Sulston C	Wake T	Webb C	Whiting R
Sep 2	SL D1	(a)	Stoke	L	1–2	0–1	16=	Jones	18,000	4		11	6			9	3	7		5			8			2			10	1			
6	SL D1	(h)	Brentford	L	0–2	0–1	18		4,500	4		11	6	3		9	7			5			8			2			5	10	1		
9	SL D1	(h)	Coventry City	W	3–1	2–1	12	Jones, Webb, Needham	7,000	4		11	7	6		9			2	5			8			3				10	1		
13	SCC R1	(a)	Southampton	D	1–1	0–1	–	Hastings	2,500	4		11	7	6		9			2	5			8			3				10	1		
16	SL D1	(a)	Leyton	D	1–1	0–0	10	Webb	5,000	4		11	7	6		9				5			2			3	8			10	1		
23	SL D1	(h)	Norwich City	D	1–1	0–1	13	Webb	8,000	4		11	7	6	2	9				5			8			3				10	1		
30	SL D1	(a)	Crystal Palace	D	1–1	0–1	11	Hastings	10,000			11	7	6	2	9				5			8			3		4		10	1		
Oct 7	SL D1	(h)	Southampton	W	5–0	5–0	5	Needham 2, Booth, Webb 2	4,000	4		11	7	6	2	9				5			8			3				10	1		
14	SL D1	(a)	Plymouth Argyle	L	0–1	0–1	9		9,000	4		11		6	2	9		7		5			8			3				10	1		
21	SL D1	(h)	Reading	D	1–1	1–1	10	Webb	6,000	4		11		6	2			7		5			8			3	9			10	1		
28	SL D1	(a)	Watford	D	3–3	1–0	11	Smith 3	6,000	4		11		6	2		3	7		5			8				9			10	1		
Nov 4	SL D1	(h)	New Brompton	W	7–0	5–0	6	Needham 3, Webb, Smith 2, Goodwin	5,000	4		11		6	2		3	7		5			8				9			10	1		
11	SL D1	(a)	Exeter City	W	3–1	3–1	6	Smith 2, Webb	2,500	4		11		6	2		3	7		5			8				9			10	1		
15	SCC R1 Rep	(h)	Southampton	W	6–2	1–0	–	Smith 2, Needham 3, Webb	3,000	4		11		6	2		3	7		5			8				9			10	1		
25	SL D1	(a)	Queen's Park R.	L	0–2	0–0	9		9,000	4		11		6	2		3	7		5			8				9			10	1		
Dec 2	SL D1	(h)	Millwall	L	0–1	0–1	10		5,000	4		11		6	2	4	3	7		5			8				9			10	1		
9	SL D1	(a)	West Ham United	L	0–1	0–0	13		8,000	4		11		6			3	7		5						2	9			10	1		
16	SL D1	(h)	Bristol Rovers	W	5–1	2–1	11	Webb, Jones, Smith, Booth, Goodwin	4,000	4		11		6		8	3	7		5						2	9			10	1		
23	SL D1	(a)	Swindon Town	W	3–1	1–0	9	Jones, Smith (pen), Longstaff	8,000	4		11		6		8	3	7		5						2	9			10	1		
25	SL D1	(h)	Northampton T.	W	2–1	1–1	7	Goodwin, Smith (pen)	11,500	4		11		6		8	3	7		5						2	9			10	1		
26	SL D1	(a)	Northampton T.	L	0–1	0–1	7		11,000	4		11		6		8	3	7		5						2	9			10	1		
30	SL D1	(h)	Stoke	W	4–0	3–0	7	Smith 4	6,000	4		11		6		8	3	7								2	9		5	10	1		
Jan 6	SL D1	(a)	Coventry City	L	0–2	0–1	9		4,000	4		11		6		8	3	7								2	9		5	10	1		
13	FAC R1	(a)	Darlington	L	1–2	0–1	–	Haworth	9,400	4		11		6		8	3	7								2	9		5	10	1		
20	SL D1	(a)	Leyton	W	4–0	3–0	7	Webb, Jones, Goodwin 2	5,000	4		11		6		8	3	7		5						2	9			10	1		
24	SCC R2	(h)	Reading	L	0–2	0–0	–		2,000	4			11	6		8	3	7		5						2	9			10	1		
27	SL D1	(a)	Norwich City	L	0–2	0–1	9		5,000	4		11		6			3	7		5			8			2	9			10	1		
Feb 10	SL D1	(h)	Southampton	W	3–1	3–1	8	Webb, Smith, Needham	5,000	4		11		6			3	7		5			8			2	9			10	1		
17	SL D1	(h)	Plymouth Argyle	W	1–0	1–0	6	Webb	6,000	4		11				6			8	5			7		3	2	9			10	1		
Mar 2	SL D1	(h)	Watford	W	7–1	5–1	7	Smith 3, Webb 2, McGhie, Needham	5,000	4		11				6		3	8	5			7			2	9			10	1		
9	SL D1	(a)	New Brompton	D	0–0	0–0	7		5,000	4		11				6		3	8	5			7			2	9			10	1		
16	SL D1	(h)	Exeter City	W	2–1	2–1	7	Goodwin, Webb (pen)	5,000	4		11				6		3	8	5			7			2	9			10	1		
23	SL D1	(a)	Brentford	D	1–1	1–1	7	Smith	2,500	4		11				6		3	8	5			7			2	9			10	1		
30	SL D1	(h)	Queen's Park R.	W	3–1	2–1	7	Smith 3	7,000	4		11				6		3	8	5			7			2	9			10	1		
Apr 5	SL D1	(a)	Luton Town	L	0–1	0–1	7		10,000	4	8	11				6		3		5			7			2	9			10	1		
6	SL D1	(a)	Millwall	W	2–1	1–0	7	Booth, Goodwin	19,000	4	8	11				6		3		5			7			2	9			10	1		
8	SL D1	(h)	Luton Town	W	1–0	1–0	5	Smith	10,000	4	8	11				6				5			7	3		2	9			10	1		
9	SL D1	(h)	Crystal Palace	W	4–1	3–0	5	Goodwin 2, Webb 2	2,500	4		11				6			8	5		10	7			3	2			9	1		
13	SL D1	(h)	West Ham United	W	2–0	1–0	5	Goodwin, Smith	5,000	4		11				6		5	8						3	2	9	7		10	1		
17	SL D1	(a)	Reading	D	0–0	0–0	5		1,000	4		11				6		3	8	2		10	7						5	9	1		
20	SL D1	(a)	Bristol Rovers	D	1–1	0–0	5	Longstaff	3,000	5		11				2	6	3	8				4				7			9	1		
27	SL D1	(h)	Swindon Town	W	2–0	0–0	5	McGhie, Smith	7,000	4		11				6		3	7	5			8			2	9			10	1		
			League appearances						36	3	36	7	24	12	15	16	27	30	2	32	1	2	29	1	1	2	31	29	1	5	38	38	
			League goals						3		10	1				5		2		2			8					25			17		

they had to settle for fifth place, six points behind champions Queen's Park Rangers who had vied with Swindon Town for top spot for almost the entire season.

A tragic event occurred in the Easter Monday fixture at the Goldstone when Luton Town's young full-back, Sammy Wightman, was hurt in a collision while challenging for the ball. He continued after treatment only to leave the field of play shortly afterwards complaining of feeling ill. Having recovered sufficiently to return home with the rest of the Luton team, Wightman collapsed and died two days later from the effects of a ruptured bowel.

On a happier note: on 4 March it was announced that a Supporters' Club was to be formed. The advice of the secretary of the well-established and flourishing Watford S.C. was sought at the meeting between the two sides on the previous Saturday (presumably before the match – it will be remembered that Albion had won 7–1!). Such clubs were springing up throughout the Southern League around this period and it was generally felt that the pioneering Watford set-up was the ideal to be followed. The leading light was Harry Edwards, a well-known fan, and the club was launched officially on Wednesday, 27 March 1912.

There were to be no F.A. Cup heroics this season. Darlington, of the North Eastern League, reversed the roles on Albion and performed the giant-killing act, winning 2–1 on their own ground in the first round.

Jimmy Smith topped the goalscoring list with 25 from only 29 League games; Charlie Webb weighed in with 17 and Fred Goodwin also reached double figures with 10. The average attendance showed a drop on the last two years, down to just under 6,000.

Albion 1911–12

Back row left to right: Alf Nelmes (trainer), Tom Wake, Jack Robson (manager), Joe Lumley, J. Butt (assistant trainer).
Third row left to right: Billy Booth, Crosby Henderson, Bill Crinson, Ralph Routledge, Joe Leeming (captain), Bob Whiting, Jack Haworth, Dick Whittington.
Seated left to right: Archie Needham, Joe McGhie, Bert Longstaff, Bill Jones, Charlie Webb, Bill Hastings, Fred Goodwin, Gunner Higham.
On ground left to right: Jimmy Coleman, Jimmy Smith, T. Stott, Billy Miller.

SEASON 1912–13

This was to be something of a transitional period for the club. Bill Hastings had been transferred to Birmingham for a £100 fee. Jack Haworth had left for Middlesbrough, Crosby Henderson for Luton Town and Jimmy Coleman for Swansea Town. These were difficult men to replace. The only significant recruits were Jack Woodhouse, a play-anywhere character who was to render long service stretching into the Football League era, and Frank Spencer, a full-back from the Parkside club of South Shields.

Since 1909, when the Southern League clubs had deserted the Western League *en bloc* owing to the excessive travelling costs involved, Albion had not participated in a midweek league. Club chairman Peter Vey advocated the formation of such a competition and during the summer of 1912 canvassed other Southern League clubs with the outline of his plan. The proposition met with great enthusiasm and the outcome was the Southern Football Alliance, a combination which required clubs to play at least seven first-team men in their side. Although Albion were to be very successful in the competition, it did not prove a great attraction for the public.

Considering the loss of so many experienced players, the season was reasonably successful. It opened with home wins over Portsmouth and Stoke, which raised hopes locally, but yet again away form was dismal: only one goal was scored away from the Goldstone before Christmas, and only one away win was achieved, at Norwich in March. The loss of full-back Ralph Routledge after four matches did

	Southern League Division 1 1912–13	P	W	D	L	F	A	W	D	L	F	A	Pts
1.	Plymouth Argyle	38	15	2	2	47	9	7	4	8	30	27	50
2.	Swindon Town	38	13	5	1	44	16	7	3	9	22	25	48
3.	West Ham United	38	11	6	2	39	15	7	6	6	27	31	48
4.	Queen's Park R.	38	14	4	1	33	10	4	6	9	13	26	46
5.	Crystal Palace	38	13	3	3	38	13	4	8	7	17	23	45
6.	Millwall	38	14	0	5	36	17	5	7	7	26	26	45
7.	Exeter City	38	13	3	3	29	16	5	5	9	19	28	44
8.	Reading	38	12	3	4	34	20	5	5	9	25	35	42
9.	**ALBION**	38	12	5	2	39	19	1	7	11	9	28	38
10.	Northampton Town	38	11	4	4	42	17	1	8	10	19	31	36
11.	Portsmouth	38	11	5	3	28	15	3	3	13	13	34	36
12.	Merthyr Town	38	9	8	2	27	17	3	4	12	16	43	36
13.	Coventry City	38	9	4	6	42	27	4	4	11	11	32	34
14.	Watford	38	8	5	6	28	24	4	5	10	15	26	34
15.	Gillingham	38	7	7	5	19	21	5	3	11	17	32	34
16.	Bristol Rovers	38	9	6	4	37	23	3	3	13	18	41	33
17.	Southampton	38	7	7	5	28	25	3	4	12	12	47	31
18.	Norwich City	38	8	7	4	26	17	2	2	15	13	33	29
19.	Brentford	38	10	3	6	27	17	1	2	16	15	38	27
20.	Stoke	38	8	3	8	21	17	2	1	16	18	58	24

	Southern Alliance 1912–13	P	W	D	L	F	A	W	D	L	F	A	Pts
1.	Croydon Common	16	7	1	0	21	5	2	5	1	10	11	24
2.	**ALBION**	16	4	4	0	18	7	4	1	3	10	12	21
3.	Luton Town	16	7	1	0	21	4	0	3	5	9	25	18
4.	Millwall	16	5	2	1	22	8	2	1	5	14	18	17
5.	Portsmouth	16	5	1	2	16	7	2	1	5	8	13	16
6.	Southend United	16	5	1	2	16	8	0	3	5	3	23	14
7.	Southampton	16	3	2	3	16	16	2	1	5	7	14	13
8.	Brentford	16	4	1	3	18	13	1	0	7	12	26	11
9.	Cardiff City	16	3	2	3	16	13	1	0	7	8	22	10

SEASON 1912–13

Date	Comp.	Ven.	Opponents	Result	HT	Pos.	Scorers	Atten.	Ault A	Birdsall G	Booth W	Brown W	Crinson W	Flannery T	Goodwin F	Higham T	Hodge W	Kitchen S	Leeming J	Longhurst G	Longstaff A	Longstaff H	McGhie J	Matthews C	Middleton W	Miller W	Needham A	Parkes D	Parlett F	Routledge R	Simpson R	Smart F	Smith J	Spencer F	Tyler A	Webb C	Whiting R	Whittington G	Williams DH	Williamson	Woodhouse J
Sep 4	SL D1	(h)	Portsmouth	W 2–0	1–0	1=	Smith 2 (1 pen)	6,000			4				11	6			3		7		5			8				2			9			10	1				
7	SL D1	(h)	Stoke	W 3–1	3–0	1	Needham, Webb 2	6,500			4				11	6			3		7		5				8			2			9			10	1				
11	SL D1	(a)	Portsmouth	L 0–1	0–1	2		8,000			4				11	6			3		7		5				8			2			9			10	1				
14	SL D1	(a)	Coventry City	D 1–1	1–1	3	Smith	8,000			4					6			3				5			8	7			2		11	9			10	1				
21	SL D1	(h)	Watford	W 3–0	1–0	2	Miller 2, Smith	7,000			4					6			3				5			8	7					11	9	2		10	1				
28	SL D1	(a)	Merthyr Town	L 0–1	0–1	6		10,000			4					6			3		7		5			8	2					11	9			10	1				
Oct 2	S Alliance	(a)	Southampton	L 1–3	0–2	7	Woodhouse	'small'			4			8		6			3		7		5			10	2					11					1				9
5	SL D1	(h)	Crystal Palace	L 1–2	0–1	8	Smith	6,000			4					6			3		7		5			8	2					11	9			10	1				
9	S Alliance	(h)	Croydon Common	D 0–0	0–0	7		1,000			4				11	6	2		3		8				7		5						9			10	1				
12	SL D1	(a)	Plymouth Argyle	L 0–1	0–0	12		10,000			4					6	2		3		8		5		7								11	9			10	1				
16	S Alliance	(a)	Luton Town	L 0–6	0–1	8										6			3		8	10	5	4	7								11		2		9	1				
19	SL D1	(h)	Southampton	W 5–2	4–1	9	Webb 4, Smart	5,500			4		1			5	2		3		7					8							11	9			10		6			
23	S Alliance*	(h)	Cardiff City	W 4–1	0–0	5	Booth, Webb (pen), Goodwin 2	3,000			4		1		11	5	2		3		7													9			10		6			
26	SL D1	(a)	Reading	L 0–1	0–1	13		3,000			4		1			6			3		7		5			8	2					11	9			10					
Nov 2	SL D1	(h)	Norwich City	D 2–2	1–0	14	Miller 2	5,000			4		1			6			3		7		5			8	2					11	9			10					
9	SL D1	(a)	Gillingham	D 0–0	0–0	14		5,000			4					6	2		3		8		5			10	7						9			11	1				
13	S Alliance*	(a)	Croydon Common	L 1–2	0–1	7	Woodhouse	1,000							11	6	2		3				5	4			7									10	1				9
16	SL D1	(h)	Northampton T.	W 2–1	1–0	12	Webb, Smith	5,000			4					6	2		3		8		5				7					11	9			10	1				
20	S Alliance	(h)	Luton Town	D 1–1	1–0	7	Smith	750								5	2		3		8			4			7					11	9			10	1	6			
23	SL D1	(a)	Queen's Park R.	D 0–0	0–0	13		11,000			4					6	2		3		8		5			10	7					11				9	1				
27	S Alliance*	(h)	Southampton	D 1–1	0–0	6	Miller	'meagre'			4				11	9	2		3		7					8	6									10	1				
Dec 4	S Alliance*	(h)	Southend United	W 4–0	2–0	6	Miller 2, Goodwin, A Longstaff	'small'			4				11	6	2		3		7					8	9										1	5			
7	SL D1	(a)	Millwall	L 0–2	0–1	13		16,000			4				11	6	2		3		7		5			8	9									10	1				
9	SCC R1	(a)	Southampton	D 1–1	0–0	–	Goodwin	1,000						10	11		2				7	6	5	4		8			3								1				9
14	SL D1	(h)	Bristol Rovers	W 3–1	0–1	10	Miller 2 (1 pen), Simpson	3,000			4				11	6	2		3		7		5			9					8					10	1				
21	SL D1	(a)	Swindon Town	L 0–4	0–2	10		6,000			4				11	6	2		3		7		5			9					8					10	1				
25	SL D1	(h)	Exeter City	W 1–0	1–0	10	Webb	3,000			4				11	5	2		3		7					9	6				8					10	1				
26	SL D1	(a)	Exeter City	L 1–2	0–2	13	Goodwin	5,000			4				11	5	2		3		7					9	6				8					10	1				
28	SL D1	(a)	Stoke	L 1–4	1–2	15	Goodwin	8,000			4				11	6	2		3		7		5			9					8					10	1				
Jan 4	SL D1	(h)	Coventry City	D 0–0	0–0	14		5,000			4				11	6	2				7		5				10				8			3		9	1				
15	FAC R1	(a)	Portsmouth	W 2–1	0–1	–	Webb, Higham	15,556			4				11	6			3		7		5				9				8			2		10	1				
18	SL D1	(a)	Watford	L 1–3	1–1	15	Simpson	4,000			4				11	6			3		7		5				9				8			2		10	1				
25	SL D1	(h)	Merthyr Town	W 2–0	0–0	14	Miller (pen), Needham	5,000			4					6			3		7		5			11	9				8			2		10	1				
29	SCC R1 Rep	(h)	Southampton	W 4–1	2–1	–	Flannery, Matthews, H Longstaff 2	800					1	10			2			7		9		8	11			5	3									6			4
Feb 1	FAC R2	(h)	Everton	D 0–0	0–0	–		11,000			4					6			3		7		5		11	9					8			2		10	1				
5	FAC R2 Rep	(a)	Everton	L 0–1*	0–0	–		30,000			4				11	6			3		7		5				9				8			2		10	1				
8	SL D1	(a)	Crystal Palace	D 1–1	1–0	13	H Longstaff	9,000			4					6			3		7	9	5				11				8			2		10	1				
15	SL D1	(h)	Plymouth Argyle	L 1–4	1–2	13	H Longstaff	5,000								5	6		3		7	9					11				8			2		10	1				4
19	S Alliance	(h)	Brentford	W 3–2	3–1	6	Flannery, Ault, Kitchen	600	9		4			8			3	10			7						11	5						2			1				6
22	SL D1	(a)	Southampton	D 1–1	0–1	13	Flannery	7,000			4			10		6			3		7	9					11	5			8			2			1				
26	S Alliance	(a)	Cardiff City	W 1–0	0–0	6	Williamson	4,000				9				6					7						2	5			10			3		11	1			8	4
Mar 1	SL D1	(h)	Reading	W 2–0	1–0	13	Simpson (pen), A Longstaff	5,000			4					6			3		7	9					11	5			8			2		10	1				
5	SL D1	(h)	Brentford	D 2–2	1–2	12	Simpson 2	1,500			4					6			3		7	9					11	5			8			2		10	1				
8	SL D1	(a)	Norwich City	W 1–0	1–0	10	Flannery	4,000			4			10		6			2		7						3	5			8					11	1				9
12	S Alliance	(a)	Portsmouth	W 4–1	3–1	4	Miller, Williams, Flannery, A Longstaff							8		6	3				7		5			10	2									11	1		9		4
15	SL D1	(h)	Gillingham	W 1–0	1–0	10	Webb	3,500								6			3		7		5			10	2				8					11	1		9		4
21	SL D1	(a)	West Ham United	D 1–1	0–1	10	A Longstaff	15,000			4	9		10		6			3		7						2	5			8					11	1				
22	SL D1	(a)	Northampton T.	L 0–1	0–0	10		6,000			4	9		10		6			3		7						2	5			8					11	1				
24	SL D1	(h)	West Ham United	D 0–0	0–0	9		10,000			4	9				6			3		7		5			10	2				8					11	1				
26	SCC R2	(a)	Reading	D 0–0	0–0	–		1,000					1	10	11		3					9			7			5						2				6		8	4
29	SL D1	(h)	Queen's Park R.	W 4–1	1–1	9	Woodhouse, Booth, Needham, Simpson	5,000			4					6			3		7		5				11				9			2		10	1				8
31	S Alliance	(a)	Millwall	D 0–0	0–0	4		'small'			4		1		11	6					7		5			9	2							3		10					8
Apr 5	SL D1	(a)	Brentford	L 1–4	0–2	9	Webb	5,000			4		1		11	6			3		7		5				2				9					10					8
9	S Alliance	(a)	Brentford	W 2–0	1–0	2	Brown 2	200			4	9	1		11	6					7		5				2							3		10				8	
10	SCC R2 Rep	(h)	Reading	W 3–1*	0–1	–	Flannery 3	'small'		9				8			2							4	7	10		5	3			11					1	6			
12	SL D1	(h)	Millwall	D 3–3	0–2	9	Woodhouse 2, Simpson	4,000			4				11	6					7		5				3				9			2		10	1				8
16	S Alliance	(h)	Portsmouth	W 3–0	1–0	2	Miller, Woodhouse, A Longstaff	2,000			4										7		5			10	3				9			2	11	6	1				8
17	SCC SF	(a)	Watford	W 2–1	2–1	–	Williamson, Flannery	500				9	1	8			2							4	7			5	3			11						6		10	
19	SL D1	(a)	Bristol Rovers	D 0–0	0–0	10		4,000			4	9		10							7		5				3					11		2		6	1				8
23	S Alliance*	(a)	Southend United	W 1–0	1–0	2	Webb				4					6							5				3							2	11	10	1				8
26	SL D1	(h)	Swindon Town	W 2–0	2–0	9	Woodhouse, Simpson	5,000			4	9				6					7		5				3				10			2		11	1				8
28	SCC F	(n*)	Queen's Park R.	L 1–4*	1–1	–	Brown	3,000				9		8			2							4	7	10		5	3			11					1	6			
30	S Alliance	(h)	Millwall	D 2–2	1–1	2	Middleton, Woodhouse	1,000			4	9				6					7		5		11		3							2		10	1				8
Southern League appearances									0	0	36	5	4	5	13	37	13	0	34	0	36	5	28	0	1	19	32	6	0	4	22	11	13	13	0	37	34	1	1	0	8
Southern League goals											1			2	2						2	2				7	3				8	1	6			10					4
Southern Alliance appearances									1	0	11	3	3	3	7	14	8	1	8	0	14	1	9	3	3	6	14	2	0	0	2	3	3	8	2	13	13	3	1	2	9
Southern Alliance goals									1		1	2		2	3			1			3				1	5							1			2			1	1	4

Notes: Feb 5 – after extra time.
Apr 10 – after extra time.
Apr 28 – played at The Den, Millwall FC.
– after extra time.

The following additional players each made one appearance in the Southern Alliance:

- Oct 23: Taylor, H. (no.8).
- Nov 13: Houghton, F. (no.8).
- Nov 27: Wake, T. (no.5).
- Dec 4: Nash, H. (no.10).
- Apr 23: Pinder, W. (no.7) and Turner (no.9).

Albion 1912–13

Back row left to right: Bill Crinson, Harvey Longstaff, Frank Parlett, Joe Leeming (captain), Gunner Higham, Bill Hodge.
Third row left to right: Alf Nelmes (trainer), Ralph Routledge, Billy Booth, Frank Spencer, Jack Robson (manager), Bob Whiting, S. G. Akehurst, Dick Whittington, Fred Coles (assistant trainer).
Seated left to right: Bert Longstaff, Joe McGhie, Tom Wake, Jack Woodhouse, Charlie Webb, Fred Goodwin, Billy Miller.
On ground left to right: Billy Middleton, Jimmy Smith, Tom Flannery, Archie Needham, Fred Bates (groundsman) with mascot Rose.

not help the situation. He received a serious leg injury against Coventry City and was forced into retirement on the doctor's advice.

In November, Bradford (P.A.) came up with an offer for Jimmy Smith that hard-up Albion could not ignore, and he departed to the Second Division club for a £735 fee plus the Bradford inside-forward Bobby Simpson. Simpson was to perform his task well, but Smith was a great loss to the club.

Albion were defeated only twice at the Goldstone, by Crystal Palace and subsequent champions Plymouth Argyle. In fact, Brighton played a prominent role in the destination of the championship shield. On 26 April, Swindon Town arrived in Hove for their final fixture, level on points with Plymouth at the top of the table. Argyle had two matches remaining, but if Swindon took both points they stood a good chance of taking the title. Albion turned in a first-rate performance, beating the Wiltshire side 2–0 while Plymouth were defeating Northampton Town by the same score. Argyle then lost their game in hand and thus won the championship by two points.

A visit to Fratton Park for the first round of the English Cup saw Albion belie their League form with an excellent 2–1 win over Portsmouth before a 15,556 crowd. In the second round Everton were drawn at home and their offer to transfer the tie to Goodison Park was declined by the board.

Heavy rain restricted the attendance to 11,000 and the game was played on a 'glue-pot'. A brilliant display by the Albion defence saw the Merseysiders held to a goal-less draw; in fact, Albion enjoyed the lion's share of the play. A crowd of over 30,000 witnessed the replay the following Wednesday afternoon when Albion again performed heroically. Bob Whiting and Joe McGhie were outstanding in defence, and after 90 minutes of endeavour the famed Everton forwards had still failed to score. Six minutes into extra time England international Frank Jefferis beat Whiting, but Albion had the consolation of coming away with a sizeable share of the £920 receipts.

The opening match in the Southern Charity Cup with Southampton was drawn, but, because of the forthcoming clash with Everton, the reserve team was fielded in the replay. The Lambs performed so well in beating Saints 4–1 that they were retained for the rest of the competition and went on to defeat strong Reading and Watford teams before losing 4–1 after extra time to a formidable Queen's Park Rangers side in the final at The Den. Albion also finished runners-up in the Southern Alliance behind Croydon Common, but the home games averaged fewer than 1,500 spectators.

Billy Booth was rewarded for his tremendous form when he was chosen as England's reserve for the match with Ireland in Belfast on 15 February, and was then selected for the Southern League against the Irish League at The Den on 15 March. But for these honours, Billy would have been ever-present.

Raising the flag

The Supporters' Club, founded in March 1912, presents the parent club with a new flag prior to the match on 5 October. The man holding the rope is the programme seller.

SEASON 1913–14

Around this time Albion were virtually invincible at the Goldstone Ground and, as in the previous season, only two home games were lost. The strength of the side was a very sound defence which was so consistent that it practically selected itself. The main cause for concern was the forward line: only 43 goals were scored in the 38 Southern League matches.

Before the start of the campaign one player was added to the professional staff, Jasper Batey from Portsmouth. Two youngsters were signed as amateurs: George Coomber, a lanky half-back from Tufnell Park, and Zacky March, a nippy little winger from Bosham. In October, Alfie Tyler from East Grinstead signed professional forms.

Albion opened the season confidently with a home win over Southampton and lost just three of the first sixteen games to reach third place. Swindon Town set the pace with eleven straight wins and, together with Crystal Palace, dominated the League from start to finish. Albion performed well against the two leading sides, taking three points off Swindon and drawing home and away with Palace, both games attracting large Easter-holiday crowds, but poor away form in the second half of the season meant a finish in seventh place, eight points behind champions Swindon.

In October, Bobby Simpson broke a leg in the Southern Alliance match at Newport and the management brought Bullet Jones back from Birmingham to replace him. George Dodd, a veteran utility forward from Millwall, was signed in December in an effort to add some punch to the attack.

In the English Cup it proved to be a record-breaking season for the club. Oldham Athletic were drawn away in the first round. To put things in perspective, it should be said that this was the golden era in Athletic's history. They finished fourth in the First Division this term, and in 1914–15 were runners-up,

one point behind Everton after losing their final two matches, both at home; they also reached the semi-final stage of the Cup in 1913. Their team contained several internationals including centre-half Charlie Roberts (England), left-half David Wilson (Scotland), inside-left George Woodger (England) and left-winger Joe Donnachie (Scotland) — an impressive line-up by any standard.

The Boundary Park match ended in a 1–1 draw, Bill Miller scoring Albion's equaliser with twelve minutes remaining, and the scene shifted to the Goldstone Ground for the Wednesday-afternoon replay. In a game dominated by both defences, Albion more than held their own in the strong wind with skipper Joe Leeming outstanding at left-back, and the outcome was stalemate. The game went into extra time with neither side looking likely to score, but, with only seven minutes remaining, Bert Longstaff flighted over a corner which brushed the crossbar and fell beyond the far post. David Parkes prevented the ball from going out of play and screwed it back into the crowded goalmouth. The Oldham defenders tried frantically to clear, but Billy Booth got a foot in first and steered the ball into the net. At the final whistle the players had to sprint for safety as the delighted crowd poured over the barriers.

Once again the town was gripped by cup-fever. The draw for the second round had already taken place and Albion qualified to meet Clapton Orient at the Goldstone three weeks later. A record crowd of 15,727 packed into the ground, paying record receipts of £990 18*s.* 6*d.* for the privilege. Only Hull City had conceded fewer goals than Orient in the Second Division and it was felt that Albion lacked the thrust to penetrate their powerful defence. In the first half, honours were even until the 33rd minute when a speculative long shot cannoned off Gunner Higham and flew into the corner of the net with Whiting

Albion take the field against Clapton Orient
Numerous mementoes, usually in the form of a postcard, were always issued when Albion enjoyed one of their many excellent English Cup runs in the period up until the mid 1930s. This one celebrates the 3–1 victory over Second Division Clapton Orient at the Goldstone before a record 15,727 crowd. Lending considerable support to Joe Leeming and his team is the club mascot, Rose.

On 8 October 1913, Joe Leeming and Charlie Webb played for a Southern Alliance representative team against the reigning champions, Croydon Common, at their Selhurst ground, The Nest. The select XI won 2–1. Webb's left-wing partner was Patsy Hendren, the legendary Middlesex and England batsman, who played for Brentford and became a vice-president of the Albion Supporters' Club after the Second World War.

SEASON 1913–14

Date	Comp.	Ven.	Opponents	Result	HT	Pos.	Scorers	Atten.
Sep 3	SL D1	(h)	Southampton	W 1–0	0–0	1=	Longstaff	4,500
6	SL D1	(a)	Coventry City	L 1–2	1–1	10=	Simpson	8,000
10	SL D1	(a)	Southampton	D 0–0	0–0	7=		5,000
13	SL D1	(h)	Watford	D 0–0	0–0	9=		5,000
20	SL D1	(a)	Norwich City	D 1–1	1–0	8=	Simpson	7,000
27	SL D1	(h)	Gillingham	W 2–0	1–0	4	Miller 2	5,000
Oct 2	S Alliance	(h)	Newport County	L 0–1	0–1	9		1,000
4	SL D1	(a)	Northampton T.	L 0–2	0–1	9=		6,000
8	S Alliance	(a)	Luton Town	L 0–2	0–2	9		1,200
11	S Alliance	(h)	Southend United	D 1–1	0–0	9=	Simpson	2,500
16	S Alliance	(a)	Newport County	W 2–1	0–0	7	Simpson, Longstaff	5,000
18	SL D1	(h)	Queen's Park R.	W 1–0	0–0	6	Miller (pen)	6,000
22	S Alliance	(h)	Luton Town	W 2–1	1–1	6	Batey 2	1,500
25	SL D1	(a)	Portsmouth	W 1–0	1–0	4	Booth	13,000
Nov 1	SL D1	(h)	Millwall	W 2–0	1–0	4	Miller 2 (1 pen)	6,000
5	S Alliance	(h)	Southampton	W 2–1	1–0	5=	Longstaff 2	'moderate'
8	SL D1	(a)	Exeter City	L 1–4	0–2	5	Webb	4,000
12	S Alliance	(a)	Southampton	D 2–2	1–1	4	Batey, Longstaff	1,000
15	SL D1	(h)	Cardiff City	W 2–1	1–1	4	Jones, Miller (pen)	6,000
19	S Alliance	(h)	Croydon Common	W 5–0	2–0	3	Brown 3, Woodhouse, Webb	2,000
22	SL D1	(a)	Swindon Town	D 1–1	0–0	5	Miller	7,000
26	S Alliance	(a)	Portsmouth	W 1–0	0–0	3	Miller	1,000
29	SL D1	(h)	Bristol Rovers	W 2–1	1–0	3	Woodhouse, Miller	5,500
Dec 3	SCC R1	(a)	Croydon Common	L 0–3	0–2	–		2,000
6	SL D1	(a)	Merthyr Town	L 0–1	0–0	3	Miller	3,000
13	SL D1	(h)	West Ham United	L 0–1	0–0	3		6,000
20	SL D1	(a)	Plymouth Argyle	D 2–2	2–2	3	Tyler, Miller	10,000
25	SL D1	(h)	Reading	L 0–2	0–1	5		9,000
26	SL D1	(a)	Reading	L 1–2	0–0	5	Miller	10,500
27	SL D1	(h)	Coventry City	D 2–2	2–2	5	Jones 2	6,000
Jan 3	SL D1	(a)	Watford	L 1–3	1–1	7	Webb	3,000
10	FAC R1	(h)	Oldham Athletic	D 1–1	0–1	–	Miller	14,500
14	FAC R1 Rep	(h)	Oldham Athletic	W 1–0*	0–0	–	Booth	10,700
17	SL D1	(h)	Norwich City	W 4–1	1–0	6	Miller 2, Dodd, Woodhouse	5,000
24	SL D1	(a)	Gillingham	L 0–4	0–2	7		6,000
31	FAC R2	(h)	Clapton Orient	W 3–1	1–0	–	Webb 2, Jones	15,727
Feb 4	S Alliance	(a)	Cardiff City	W 2–1	0–0	3	Webb 2	2,500
7	SL D1	(h)	Northampton T.	D 1–1	1–1	8	Webb	2,800
9	S Alliance	(a)	Brentford	D 1–1	1–1	3	Brown	
14	SL D1	(a)	Southend United	W 1–0	0–0	7	Webb	5,000
18	S Alliance	(h)	Brentford	W 7–0	2–0	3	Woodhouse (pen), Brown 3, Lowe 2, Spooner	750
21	FAC R3	(a)	Sheffield Wed.	L 0–3	0–0	–		38,997
25	S Alliance	(a)	Croydon Common	L 0–2	0–1	3		3,000
28	SL D1	(h)	Portsmouth	W 3–2	1–0	7	Longstaff 2, Dodd	6,000
Mar 7	SL D1	(a)	Millwall	L 1–3	0–2	7	Longstaff	14,000
14	SL D1	(h)	Exeter City	W 2–1	2–1	7	Jones, Webb	3,000
18	SL D1	(h)	Portsmouth	W 4–0	3–0	3	Longstaff 2, Webb 2	1,000
21	SL D1	(a)	Cardiff City	D 0–0	0–0	7		12,000
28	SL D1	(h)	Swindon Town	W 2–0	2–0	7	Longstaff, Webb	7,000
Apr 1	S Alliance	(h)	Cardiff City	W 4–0	2–0	3	Lowe 2, Miller, Webb (pen)	1,000
4	SL D1	(a)	Bristol Rovers	L 0–1	0–0	7		8,000
10	SL D1	(h)	Crystal Palace	D 0–0	0–0	7		12,300
11	SL D1	(h)	Merthyr Town	W 4–2	3–1	7	Jones, Lowe, Webb 2 (2 pens)	4,000
13	SL D1	(a)	Crystal Palace	D 0–0	0–0	7		20,000
18	SL D1	(a)	West Ham United	D 1–1	0–1	7	Webb	10,000
22	S Alliance*	(a)	Southend United	W 4–2	2–2	2	Miller 3, Webb	2,000
23	SL D1	(a)	Queen's Park R.	L 0–3	0–2	7		7,000
25	SL D1	(h)	Plymouth Argyle	W 1–0	0–0	7	Booth	4,000
29	S Alliance	(h)	Southend United	W 3–1	0–0	1	March, Miller, Longstaff	1,000

Season totals (player columns):

	Batey J	Booth W	Bridge M	Brown W	Carter W	Coomber G	Dodd G	Higham T	Hodge W	Jones W	Leeming J	Longstaff A	Lowe H	March Z	Matthews C	Miller W	Needham A	Parkes D	Parlett F	Paterson H	Regan J	Roberts J	Simpson R	Spencer F	Spooner W	Tyler A	Webb C	Whitehouse W	Whiting R	Whittington G	Wilcock G	Woodhouse J
Southern League appearances	10	38	0	1	0	7	17	35	1	23	25	37	2	2	0	21	22	27	3	0	0	0	8	25	1	24	36	0	34	0	4	15
Southern League goals	2			2			2			5		5	1			13							3			1	9					2
Southern Alliance appearances	9	8	2	7	1	9	0	9	5	0	4	12	5	4	3	6	11	3	1	1	1	1	3	11	4	11	13	1	11	4	5	11
Southern Alliance goals	3			7									7	4	1	6							1		1		7					2

Notes: Jan 14 – after extra time.

Apr 22 – the full line-up is not confirmed; those players asterisked were expected to play and are included in the end-of-season Southern Alliance statistics.

stranded on the opposite post. It was a soft goal, and Albion were unfortunate to be adrift at the interval. Brighton tore into their opponents in the second half, and when Charlie Webb equalised in the 57th minute it became a matter of how many they would score. Webb added a second six minutes later and Bullet Jones completed the scoring with a quarter of an hour left on the clock. The club had reached the last sixteen for the first time.

The third-round draw was eagerly awaited, but when Albion were tied with Sheffield Wednesday, away, there was some disappointment. The Owls had previously won the trophy on two occasions and were among the most famous clubs in the land. This season, however, they were struggling in the First Division and narrowly avoided relegation. With this in mind, the Albion and their supporters were quietly confident. A crowd of 38,997 turned up at Hillsborough, and the 400 travelling fans from Sussex were impressed by the recently opened 'swagger' stand that was said to have cost £15,000 to build. The match was played on a heavy pitch, and in the first half Albion put on a splendid display with Longstaff and Webb troubling the home defence on several occasions. There was no score at the interval, but on the resumption things began to go wrong, and when

Southern League Division 1 1913–14												
	P	W	D	L	F	A	W	D	L	F	A	Pts
1. Swindon Town	38	14	3	2	57	11	7	5	7	24	30	50
2. Crystal Palace	38	12	5	2	41	13	5	11	3	19	19	50
3. Northampton Town	38	11	8	0	31	11	3	11	5	19	26	47
4. Reading	38	14	4	1	32	12	3	6	10	11	24	44
5. Plymouth Argyle	38	11	6	2	25	12	4	7	8	21	30	43
6. West Ham United	38	9	7	3	39	22	6	5	8	22	38	42
7. **ALBION**	38	12	5	2	30	16	3	7	9	13	29	42
8. Queen's Park R.	38	10	6	3	28	14	6	3	10	17	29	41
9. Portsmouth	38	10	7	2	31	13	4	5	10	26	35	40
10. Cardiff City	38	10	6	3	27	11	3	6	10	19	31	38
11. Southampton	38	11	2	6	36	23	4	5	10	19	31	37
12. Exeter City	38	7	8	4	21	11	3	8	8	18	27	36
13. Gillingham	38	10	6	3	35	15	3	3	13	13	34	35
14. Norwich City	38	7	10	2	34	19	2	7	10	15	32	35
15. Millwall	38	10	6	3	34	20	1	6	12	17	36	34
16. Southend United	38	7	7	5	29	28	3	5	11	12	38	32
17. Bristol Rovers	38	10	5	4	32	25	0	6	13	14	42	31
18. Watford	38	9	4	6	37	20	1	5	13	13	36	29
19. Merthyr Town	38	7	7	5	23	18	2	3	14	15	43	28

Southern Alliance 1913–14												
	P	W	D	L	F	A	W	D	L	F	A	Pts
1. **ALBION**	16	7	0	1	27	4	4	2	2	12	11	24
2. Luton Town	16	7	0	1	21	7	4	1	3	15	13	23
3. Croydon Common	16	7	1	0	15	2	3	1	4	9	14	22
4. Cardiff City	16	5	1	2	21	9	0	3	5	5	16	14
5. Newport County	16	4	1	3	15	11	2	1	5	5	12	14
6. Southampton	16	5	1	2	21	12	0	1	7	6	20	12
7. Portsmouth	16	5	0	3	14	8	1	0	7	8	20	12
8. Brentford	16	3	3	2	11	9	1	1	6	7	24	12
9. Southend United	16	4	3	1	12	8	0	0	8	3	27	11

Dave McLean gave Wednesday the lead it soon became one-way traffic. Jimmy Gill and Jack Burkinshaw added further goals to complete a 3–0 scoreline, and by the end of the game Albion's Cup dreams were in tatters. Once again, though, they had the considerable consolation of a half-share of the £1,560 9s. receipts and the knowledge that the club's reputation as cup-fighters had been enhanced. The bank account had been swelled to the tune of £1,700 from the four ties, a welcome amount to a hard-up club.

Soon after the Hillsborough match, in which David Parkes had performed brilliantly, Wednesday offered a fee of £1,500 plus their reserve centre-forward George Beech in exchange for the 21-year-old centre-half and he joined them in March.

Albion had an excellent season in the Southern Alliance, winning their last four games to clinch the championship by a single point from Luton Town, but the competition was a financial disaster and the club withdrew from it at the end of the campaign.

Billy Booth, in his benefit season, was again ever-present and made a seventh appearance in the Southern League representative side. Bill Miller was the top marksman with thirteen goals from only 21 Southern League appearances.

Albion 1913–14

Back row left to right: F. C. Sparkes, Frank Parlett, Billy Miller, Jack Robson (manager), Charlie Webb, Bill Hodge, Bob Whiting.
Third row left to right: Alf Nelmes (trainer), Archie Needham, Jack Woodhouse, David Parkes, Joe Leeming (captain), Dick Whittington, Mick Bridge, Gunner Higham, Fred Coles (assistant trainer).
Seated left to right: Bert Longstaff, Bobby Simpson, Bill Brown, Billy Booth, Frank Spencer, Charlie Matthews, Harry Lowe.
On ground left to right: Ernie Townsend, Billy Spooner, Jasper Batey, Alfie Tyler, G. H. Moore.

SEASON 1914–15

Throughout the summer of 1914 there was growing anxiety over the political situation in Europe. On 28 June the Archduke and Duchess of Austria-Hungary were assassinated by a Serbian nationalist during a visit to the Bosnian city of Sarajevo; Austria-Hungary thus declared war on Serbia whose ally, Russia, was forced to mobilise. Germany subsequently declared war on Russia and also moved troops on to Belgian soil. Threatened by the presence of the Germans in Belgium, France in turn mobilised her forces. The United Kingdom sought assurance from the German Government that the neutrality of Belgium would be respected. No such assurance was forthcoming, and on 5 August His Majesty's Government declared war on Germany. The call to arms was made, and recruitment offices the length and breadth of the country were besieged by volunteers eager to join the fray.

Amid this intensely patriotic atmosphere, the opening of the football season went almost unnoticed. Sparse crowds turned out for the initial matches on 2 September and a general sense of outrage soon became apparent. Many people felt that well-conditioned sportsmen such as professional footballers should be assisting the war effort, not taking part in what was, after all, only a game. After much debate the authorities decided to carry on for the time being with a review at the end of the season.

Special training at the Goldstone
Albion players practise gun-drill on the pitch in the early days of the First World War. Initially the men had to make do with wooden replicas of rifles, but the reality of the conflict began to hit home in November 1914 when groundsman Fred Bates was killed in action.

The Albion management decided that something positive should be done to support the war effort and had a rifle-range built on the ground. Regular drills were held on the pitch under the supervision of ex-soldier Charlie Webb, but there were not enough rifles to go round and wooden replicas were used; in September the club advertised for donations of the real thing. As an Army reservist Gunner Higham was recalled on the outbreak of hostilities and within weeks was serving in France. He regularly wrote letters to the club which were often published in the local Press.

In early November the Albion's groundsman, Fred Bates, was killed in action while serving with the Royal Scots Fusiliers, and a collection was made on behalf of his widow at the Southern League match with Croydon Common which realised £3 2s. 9d.

Albion kicked off with a long trip to Plymouth and defeat at the hands of the Argyle by two goals to nil. Two signings had been made in the summer: Charlie Dexter, a left-back from

SEASON 1914–15

Date	Comp.	Ven.	Opponents	Result	HT	Pos.	Scorers	Atten.	Batey J	Beech G	Booth W	Coleman J	Coomber G	Dexter C	Jones W	Longstaff A	March Z	Miller W	Needham A	Reed WF	Routledge R	Spencer F	Tyler A	Webb C	Whiting R	Wilcock G	Woodhouse J
Sep 2	SL D1	(a)	Plymouth Argyle	L 0–2	0–1	14		3,000		8	4		5	3	9	7						2	11	10	1		6
5	SL D1	(h)	Gillingham	W 2–1	2–1	11	Batey, Longstaff	3,000	4	8			5	3	9	7						2	11	10	1		6
9	SL D1	(h)	Plymouth Argyle	D 2–2	2–0	8	Jones 2	2,000	6	8			5	3	9	7						2	11	10	1		4
12	SL D1	(a)	Crystal Palace	W 2–0	0–0	3	Jones, Miller	3,000	6		4		5	3	9	7		8				2	11	10	1		
16	SL D1	(a)	Watford	D 0–0	0–0	3		1,500	6		4		5	3	9	7		8				2	11	10	1		
19	SL D1	(a)	Cardiff City	W 1–0	1–0	2	Jones	7,000	6		4		5	3	9	7		8				2	11	10	1		
26	SL D1	(h)	Exeter City	W 2–1	1–1	1	Jones, Miller (pen)	3,500	6		4		5	3	9	7		8				2	11	10	1		
Oct 3	SL D1	(a)	Luton Town	W 1–0	0–0	1	Jones	6,000	6		4		5	3	9	7		8				2	11	10	1		
10	SL D1	(h)	Portsmouth	W 1–0	1–0	1	Miller	5,000	6		4		5	3	9	7		8				2	11	10	1		
17	SL D1	(a)	Swindon Town	L 1–2	0–1	3	Miller (pen)		6		4		5	3	9	7		8				2	11	10	1		
24	SL D1	(h)	Southend United	W 1–0	1–0	2	Longstaff	4,000	6		4		5	3	8	7		9				2	11	10	1		
31	SL D1	(a)	Queen's Park R.	W 1–0	0–0	2	Miller	5,000	6		4		5	3	9	7		8				2	11	10	1		
Nov 7	SL D1	(h)	Millwall	D 2–2	1–2	1	Own goal, Jones	5,000	6		4		5	3	9	7		8				2	11	10	1		
14	SL D1	(a)	Bristol Rovers	L 0–4	0–1	2		7,000	6		4		5	3	9	7		8		10		2	11		1		
21	SL D1	(h)	Croydon Common	W 4–1	2–0	2	Miller 3 (1 pen), Reed	3,000	6		4		5	3	9	7		8		10		2	11		1		
28	SL D1	(a)	Reading	L 1–3	0–0	3	Reed	3,500			4		5	3	9	7		8		10		2	11		1		6
Dec 5	SL D1	(h)	Southampton	W 4–0	4–0	3	Coomber, Reed 2, Miller	2,000	6		4		5	3		7		8		9		2	11		1	10	
12	SL D1	(a)	Northampton T.	L 1–2	0–1	4	Jones	5,000	6		4		5	3	9	7		8				2	11		1	10	
19	SCC R1	(a)	Reading	L 0–5	0–3	–		1,500	6		4		5	3	9	7		8				2	11		1	10	
25	SL D1	(h)	West Ham United	D 0–0	0–0	3		6,000	6		4		5	3	9	7		8				2	11		1	10	
26	SL D1	(a)	West Ham United	L 1–2	1–1	4	Longstaff	6,000	6		4		5	3	9	7		10				2	11		1	8	
Jan 2	SL D1	(a)	Gillingham	W 3–1	0–0	4	Reed 2, Miller	3,000			4		5	3	9	7		8		10		2	11		1		6
9	FAC R1	(h)	Lincoln City	W 2–1	0–0	–	Jones, Longstaff	7,000			4		5	3	9	7		8		10		2	11		1		6
23	SL D1	(h)	Cardiff City	W 2–1	2–1	3	Reed, Woodhouse (pen)	3,000	6		4		5	3	9	7		8				2	11		1	10	
30	FAC R2	(a)	Birmingham	D 0–0*	0–0	–		12,530	10		4		5	3	9	7		8				2	11		1		6
Feb 6	FAC R2 Rep	(a)	Birmingham	L 0–3	0–2	–		23,000			4		5	3	9	7		8		10		2	11		1		6
13	SL D1	(a)	Portsmouth	L 0–2	0–1	6		3,000			4	10	5	3	9	7		8				2	11		1		
20	SL D1	(h)	Swindon Town	L 1–3	1–1	10	Coomber	4,000			4	10	5	3	9	7		8				2	11		1		6
24	SL D1	(a)	Exeter City	L 0–1	0–1	11		1,500			4	10	5	3	9	7		8				2	11		1		6
27	SL D1	(a)	Southend United	D 2–2	1–1	8	Jones, Longstaff	3,000			4	10	5	3	9	7		8				2	11		1		6
Mar 6	SL D1	(h)	Queen's Park R.	W 1–0	1–0	6	Woodhouse	4,000			4	8	5	3	9	7						2	11	10	1		6
13	SL D1	(a)	Millwall	L 0–3	0–2	11		7,000			4	8	5	3	9	7						2	11	10	1		6
17	SL D1	(h)	Luton Town	L 0–1	0–1	11		1,000	9		4	8	5	3		7						2	11	10	1		6
20	SL D1	(h)	Bristol Rovers	D 0–0	0–0	11		2,000			4	8	5	3	9	7						2	11	10	1		6
27	SL D1	(a)	Croydon Common	L 0–1	0–1	11		5,000			4		5	3	9	8			7	10		2	11		1		6
Apr 2	SL D1	(h)	Norwich City	D 2–2	1–1	11	Jones, Woodhouse (pen)	5,000			4		5	3	9	8			7	10		2	11		1		6
3	SL D1	(h)	Reading	W 2–0	1–0	10	Reed, Jones	1,000			4		5		9	8			7	10	3	2	11		1		6
5	SL D1	(a)	Norwich City	L 1–2	1–1	11	March	5,800			4		5			8	9		7		3	2	11	10	1		6
10	SL D1	(a)	Southampton	L 2–4	1–1	11	Booth, Reed	5,000			4	8	5		9				7	10	3	2	11		1		6
17	SL D1	(h)	Northampton T.	W 1–0	0–0	11	Jones	2,500			4		5		9	8			7	10	3	2	11		1		6
24	SL D1	(a)	Watford	L 1–2	1–1	12	Longstaff	2,000			4		5		9	8			7	10	3	2	11		1		6
May 1	SL D1	(h)	Crystal Palace	W 1–0	0–0	10	March	2,200			4		5	3	9	8			7	10		2	11		1		6
League appearances									19	4	36	9	35	33	35	31	15	17	15	18	9	34	26	18	31	7	26
League goals								OG – 1	1		1		2		12	5	2	10		9							3

Note: Jan 30 – after extra time.

Portsmouth, and Billy Reed, a forward from the Northern League champions Willington. In addition Ralph Routledge made a welcome come-back after a two-year lay-off. After the defeat at Plymouth, a run of twelve games brought just one loss and by November Albion led the division. Good home form kept them among the leaders with a chance of winning the championship until February when a decline set in: of the final sixteen games only four were won and the team slid down the table to finish tenth. Watford clinched the title when they won 2–1 at the Goldstone on 24 April with former Albion stalwarts Jimmy Kennedy and Bill Hastings in their side. Because of the abnormal situation, the football season, which had always been strictly September to April (except for charity matches), was extended into May for the first time: Albion beat Crystal Palace at Hove on 1 May before just over 2,000 spectators.

By the New Year most of the players had enlisted in the newly formed 17th Battalion of the Duke of Cambridge's Own Middlesex Regiment, otherwise known as the 'Footballers' Battalion'. Second-in-command of the unit, which was composed entirely of professional footballers, was former Albion half-back Frank Buckley; currently a lieutenant, he was later promoted to major and given full charge. The players had to report for training to the White City in London and were

On 31 October an international rugby match was staged at the Goldstone Ground in aid of the Prince of Wales's Fund and the Belgian Refugee Fund: an English military team beat a Welsh military side 24–0 in front of 5,000 spectators. The two teams comprised leading first-class players, including many full internationals. On 19 December a second representative rugby match was played in support of the North Sea Fleet Fund, with an armed forces' Barbarian XV defeating Shoreham Camp 16–3 in an entertaining game. Again, many fine players took part including several internationals. In the evening both teams dined at the Royal York Hotel.

released at weekends to play for their clubs. On 10 March a match was staged at the Goldstone against the Footballers' Battalion, with the proceeds going to battalion funds. The 2,000 spectators witnessed a stirring ceremonial entrance into the ground by 700 soldiers of the 13th Battalion, accompanied by a drum-and-fife band. At half time, recruitment lectures were given by Mr Joynson-Hicks M.P. and the Regiment's commanding officer, Colonel Grantham. Though heavily outranked, Albion won 2–0.

The English Cup brought further success over Football League opposition when Second Division strugglers Lincoln City were beaten 2–1 at the Goldstone in the first round. The reward was a home tie with another Second Division outfit, Birmingham, but Albion were soundly beaten 3–0 in a replay at St Andrews after a goal-less draw at Hove.

Jack Robson was released in December to take over as manager at Manchester United, and he was presented with a silver rose-bowl in appreciation of his seven years at the helm and a job well done. The club saw out the rest of the season without a replacement, trainer Alf Nelmes looking after the playing affairs.

Attendances were understandably poor. In fact, they were down by almost half on 1913–14 at just over 3,000. During the early part of the campaign football clubs were ordered to cut wages by up to 15 per cent, and in some cases payment was suspended altogether. The players who returned to the Goldstone after the war were fully reimbursed with the money that was due to them.

After the 'Khaki' Cup Final of 1915, so called because of the large number of soldiers present, the F.A., with the backing of the Government, announced that it was desirable for purposes of morale to continue playing football. However, in order to reduce the amount of travelling involved, it was decided to reorganise the fixtures on a regional basis. Although most clubs carried on throughout the four-year closure, the Albion board decided to close down for the duration with the view that 'it was not a time for games, but for a far more serious business, the winning of the world war.'

Southern League Division 1 1914–15											
	P	W	D	L	F	A	W	D	L	F	A	Pts
1. Watford	38	12	4	3	37	15	10	4	5	31	31	52
2. Reading	38	12	4	3	37	16	9	3	7	31	27	49
3. Cardiff City	38	16	1	2	51	12	6	3	10	21	26	48
4. West Ham United	38	14	4	1	42	18	4	5	10	16	29	45
5. Northampton Town	38	11	5	3	37	22	5	6	8	19	29	43
6. Southampton	38	14	3	2	56	28	5	2	12	22	46	43
7. Portsmouth	38	10	5	4	26	14	6	5	8	28	28	42
8. Millwall	38	9	4	6	28	23	7	6	6	22	28	42
9. Swindon Town	38	11	5	3	55	21	4	6	9	22	38	41
10. **ALBION**	38	11	5	3	29	16	5	2	12	17	31	39
11. Exeter City	38	10	3	6	32	16	5	5	9	18	25	38
12. Queen's Park R.	38	8	4	7	30	28	5	8	6	25	28	38
13. Norwich City	38	10	6	3	33	16	1	8	10	20	40	36
14. Luton Town	38	6	3	10	27	34	7	5	7	34	39	34
15. Crystal Palace	38	8	4	7	24	25	5	4	10	23	36	34
16. Bristol Rovers	38	12	2	5	42	28	2	1	16	11	47	31
17. Plymouth Argyle	38	8	7	4	34	25	0	7	12	17	36	30
18. Southend United	38	8	5	6	27	20	2	3	14	17	44	28
19. Croydon Common	38	7	6	6	28	18	2	3	14	19	45	27
20. Gillingham	38	6	7	6	32	29	0	1	18	11	54	20

Albion side v. Birmingham, F.A. Cup second round at the Goldstone, 30 January 1915
In doorway left to right: Charlie Webb, Alf Nelmes (trainer).
Standing left to right: Charlie Dexter, Archie Needham, George Wilcock, Noah Clark (director), Billy Booth (captain), Jack Woodhouse, Jasper Batey.
Seated left to right: Bert Longstaff, Bill Jones, Billy Reed, Frank Spencer, Alfie Tyler.

THE WAR YEARS

Throughout the Great War the Goldstone lay neglected. The stands became dilapidated and the terraces overgrown with grass and weeds. The playing area returned to its former role as a grazing meadow for John Clark's livestock.

There was no competitive football in Sussex during the conflict. Friendly matches were organised between the numerous military units which sprang up all over the county, and various works' teams remained active. On the closure of the Albion, club secretary Albert Underwood and a local football official named Arthur Pauly, who had been associated with the Hove club for many years, formed a new team in an effort to keep the best players in the district together. It was called Brighton and Hove F.C., and usually played its home games at Wish Park (Aldrington Recreation Ground). The team became very strong and dominated the local scene throughout the war years. A number of Albion players assisted the club when on leave, the most prominent member of the side being George Coomber who, together with Bill Miller and Fred Eacock, served locally with the Sussex Volunteer Regiment in the latter part of the war. A name that was to become familiar in the coming years appeared on the team sheet for the first time in 1917: sixteen-year-old naval rating Tommy Cook, who was to star for both the Albion and Sussex C.C.C. during the next two decades.

On the morning of 11 November 1918, after more than four years of fighting, Germany signed an armistice agreement and the war was at an end. The whole country stopped work to celebrate, and as the war-weary servicemen began to drift home there was a prevailing sense of relief and jubilation. Inevitably, after the bloodiest conflict in history, many did not return, among them Albion players Bob Whiting, Jasper Batey, Charlie Matthews, Charlie Dexter and groundsman Fred Bates. Former players Arthur Hulme, Jimmy Smith, Alan Haig-Brown, Ernie Townsend (a reserve-team player) and Tom Morris also made the ultimate sacrifice. In October 1923 a memorial to Albion's war dead was unveiled in the Goldstone boardroom.

As things began to return to normal in 1919, the old Hove club, which had disbanded in 1914, was re-formed and took over the name of Brighton and Hove, adding the suffix 'Amateurs' to distinguish themselves from the Albion. They won the West Sussex Senior League and the Royal Irish Rifles Cup, beating Eastbourne 2–1 at The Saffrons, and in 1920 were founder members of the Sussex County League; they were also runners-up to Worthing in the R.U.R. Cup in 1921. At the end of the 1921–22 season there was a mass exodus of players which forced the club to fold, and a new outfit was formed in its wake under the name of Hove F.C.

SEASON 1919–20

Charlie Webb saw out the last months of the war as a prisoner of the Germans in the Rhineland town of Mainz, and it was while awaiting repatriation that he was appointed the new Albion manager. Club chairman Henry Miles wrote to Charlie offering him the vacant post, which he readily accepted, and on his release from the Army in June 1919 he returned to the Goldstone to restore the club to its pre-war status. It was hoped that Webb would continue to play, but the leg injury suffered during a match with Millwall in November 1914 would not allow it.

In April 1919 the club held a meeting of supporters at Hove Town Hall to invite financial support to 'renovate the ground and to assemble a first-class team'. The civic leaders of the twin towns endorsed the board's intentions, and a resolution of support was, as the *Brighton Herald* put it, 'carried with an enthusiasm that defies description in cold print.' In practical terms the club asked for the unallotted share capital of £2,600 to be taken up. Other donations were gratefully received and a Shilling Fund (5p) was established for those who could not afford the five-shilling shares. Only around 4,000 shares (£1,000) were taken up, but, altogether, the club spent £1,974 on the rebuilding programme.

By the summer of 1919 a number of the old team had returned, men such as Bullet Jones, Billy Booth, Bill Miller, Jack Woodhouse, George Coomber, Gunner Higham, Bert Longstaff, Zacky March and Frank Spencer. Under the supervision of hired contractors they set about the enormous task of renovating the Goldstone Ground. It was in a deplorable state: the stands were leaking, windows broken, turnstiles rusted solid, fences fallen down, and the whole place needed a lick of paint. Fortunately the pitch was in reasonable condition, and by the end of August all was ready for the kick-off.

In July a series of 'victory matches' were played up and down the country in aid of war charities. Albion travelled to Fratton Park to play their first match for over four years and, with a team containing several trialists, gained a 1–1 draw with Pompey in front of 3,000 spectators. Webb made some interesting new signings before the season opened – goalkeeper Billy Hayes from Preston North End, Jack Best from Birmingham and Wally Little from Army football – but undoubtedly the biggest capture was that of George Holley. George had played for Sunderland before the war, winning a League championship medal and ten England caps which may well have been

		P	W	D	L	F	A	W	D	L	F	A	Pts
1.	Portsmouth	42	13	6	2	48	14	10	6	5	25	13	58
2.	Watford	42	15	3	3	39	12	11	3	7	30	30	58
3.	Crystal Palace	42	15	5	1	44	15	7	7	7	25	28	56
4.	Cardiff City	42	15	3	3	44	14	3	14	4	26	29	53
5.	Plymouth Argyle	42	13	5	3	35	8	7	5	9	22	21	50
6.	Queen's Park R.	42	12	7	2	39	13	6	3	12	23	37	46
7.	Reading	42	11	5	5	30	14	5	8	8	21	29	45
8.	Southampton	42	13	4	4	51	22	5	4	12	21	41	44
9.	Swansea Town	42	11	4	6	28	14	5	7	9	25	31	43
10.	Exeter City	42	14	3	4	44	22	3	6	12	13	30	43
11.	Southend United	42	10	8	3	32	18	3	9	9	14	30	43
12.	Norwich City	42	12	7	2	46	17	3	4	14	18	40	41
13.	Swindon Town	42	13	4	4	45	26	4	3	14	20	42	41
14.	Millwall	42	10	7	4	32	14	4	5	12	20	35	40
15.	Brentford	42	11	5	5	35	21	4	5	12	18	38	40
16.	**ALBION**	42	11	5	5	43	28	3	3	15	17	44	36
17.	Bristol Rovers	42	10	7	4	43	29	1	6	14	19	49	35
18.	Newport County	42	11	5	5	32	18	2	2	17	13	52	33
19.	Northampton Town	42	8	4	9	35	40	4	5	12	29	63	33
20.	Luton Town	42	7	7	7	29	28	3	3	15	22	48	30
21.	Merthyr Town	42	7	6	8	30	32	2	5	14	17	47	29
22.	Gillingham	42	7	5	9	24	23	3	2	16	10	51	27

Southern League Division 1 1919–20

Albion's record signing
Former England international George Holley cost the club £200 but was injured before he could justify the fee.

Albion 1919–20
Back row left to right: Frank Spencer, Billy Hayes, Wally Little.
Third row left to right: Fred Coles (trainer), Jack Burnham, Billy Henderson, Charlie Webb (manager), Dick Whittington, Fred Osborne, Dickie Meades (assistant trainer).
Seated left to right: Bill Jones, Jack Woodhouse, George Coomber, Billy Booth (captain), Gunner Higham, Jimmy Pugh, Billy Miller.
On ground left to right: Bert Longstaff, Dave Williams, Jack Doran, George Ritchie, Tom Brown.

SEASON 1919–20

Date	Comp.	Ven.	Opponents	Result	HT	Pos.	Scorers	Atten.	Beech G	Best J	Booth W	Brand W	Brown T	Coomber G	Doran J	Eacock F	Groves H	Hayes W	Henderson W	Higham T	Holley G	Jones W	Little W	Longstaff A	March Z	Miller W	Moorhouse B	Osborne F	Pugh J	Ritchie G	Spencer F	Williams D	Woodhouse J
Aug 30	SL D1	(a)	Brentford	L 1–2	0–1	16	Jones	10,813		11	4						8	1		6		10	9	7						3	2		5
Sep 3	SL D1	(h)	Norwich City	D 2–2	1–1	15=	Jones, Holley	5,341		11	4						8	1		6		10	9	7						3	2		5
6	SL D1	(h)	Merthyr Town	D 1–1	0–0	17	Coomber (pen)	8,544		11	4			5		10		1		6		9	8	7						3	2		
13	SL D1	(a)	Plymouth Argyle	L 0–1	0–0	21		12,000		11	4			5		10		1		6		9	8	7						3	2		
20	SL D1	(h)	Bristol Rovers	W 3–1	2–0	17	Eacock, Holley 2	9,000		11	4			5		10		1		6	9		8	7						3	2		
24	SL D1	(h)	Portsmouth	L 0–3	0–2	17		7,250		11	4			5		10		1		6	9		8	7						3	2		
27	SL D1	(a)	Reading	L 0–2		21		8,000		11	4			5		10		1		6			9	7				8	3		2		
Oct 4	SL D1	(h)	Southampton	W 1–0	0–0	16	Jones	9,000			4			5		10		1		6		8	9	7	11				3			2	
8	SL D1	(a)	Portsmouth	D 0–0		16		7,000			4			5		10		1		6			9	7	11			8	3			2	
11	SL D1	(a)	Luton Town	L 0–2	0–1	20		7,000			4			5		10		1		6			9	7	11			8	3			2	
16	SL D1	(a)	Norwich City	L 0–2	0–2	20		4,500	9	11	4			5				1		6	8			7	10				3			2	
18	SL D1	(h)	Gillingham	W 3–0	0–0	16	Holley 2, Jones	8,000			4			5		10		1		6	8	9		7	11				3			2	
25	SL D1	(a)	Swansea Town	D 1–1	1–1	17	Best	10,000		11	4			5		10	7	1		6	8		9						3			2	
Nov 1	SL D1	(a)	Exeter City	D 0–0	0–0	16		8,000		11	4			5		10	7	1		6	8		9						3			2	
8	SL D1	(a)	Cardiff City	L 0–2	0–1	19		14,000	8	11	4			5		10		1		6			9	7					3			2	
15	SL D1	(h)	Queen's Park R.	L 2–3	1–1	19	Eacock 2	8,000		11	4			5		10	8	1		6			9	7					3			2	
22	SL D1	(a)	Swindon Town	L 1–2	0–1	20	March	8,000			4			5		10	8	1		6			9	7	11				3			2	
29	SL D1	(a)	Millwall	L 0–1	0–0	20		8,000			4			5		10	8	1		6			9	7	11				3			2	
Dec 6	SL D1	(h)	Watford	W 3–2	3–0	19	March 3	8,000			4			5		10		1		6		9	8	7	11				3			2	
13	SL D1	(a)	Newport County	L 0–1	0–1	19		7,000			4			5		10		1		6			8	7	11				3			2	9
20	FAC Q6	(h)	Luton Town	L 0–1	0–0			9,250			4			5		10		1		6	8	9		7	11				3			2	
25	SL D1	(h)	Crystal Palace	L 2–3	1–2	20	Miller, Best	9,200		11	4			5				1		6			8	7		9			3	10		2	
26	SL D1	(a)	Crystal Palace	L 0–4	0–1	21		16,000		11	4			5				1		6			8	7		9			3	10		2	
27	SL D1	(a)	Northampton T.	W 5–1	3–0	19	Own goal, Miller 2, Ritchie 2	7,000		11	4			5				1		6				7		9			3	10		2	8
Jan 3	SL D1	(h)	Brentford	W 4–0	1–0	18	Miller, Ritchie 2, Woodhouse	8,000		11	4			5				1		6				7		9			3	10		2	8
17	SL D1	(h)	Merthyr Town	L 1–2	0–0	19	Ritchie	6,000		11	4			5				1	6	6				7		9			3	10		2	8
24	SL D1	(h)	Plymouth Argyle	W 1–0	0–0	18	Woodhouse	9,000			4		11	5				1		6				7		9			3	10		2	8
31	SL D1	(a)	Bristol Rovers	W 3–2	1–1	17	Woodhouse, Miller 2	3,000			4		11	5				1		6				7		9			3	10		2	8
Feb 7	SL D1	(a)	Reading	D 2–2	1–1	17	Miller, Longstaff	11,000			4		11	5				1		6				7		9			3	10		2	8
14	SL D1	(a)	Southampton	L 0–3	0–1	17		10,500			4	6	11	5		10		1						7		9			3			2	8
21	SL D1	(h)	Luton Town	W 4–3	3–1	17	Longstaff 2, Miller, Coomber	8,000			4	6	11	5		10		1						7		9			3			2	8
28	SL D1	(a)	Gillingham	W 3–2	0–1	16	Brown, Williams, Miller	10,000			4		11	5				1		6				7		9			3	10		2	8
Mar 6	SL D1	(h)	Swansea Town	W 4–2	3–1	15	Woodhouse 2, Ritchie, Doran	10,000			4		11	5	9			1		6				7					3	10		2	8
13	SL D1	(a)	Exeter City	L 1–4	1–2	16	Woodhouse	5,000			4		11	5	9			1		6				7					3	10		2	8
20	SL D1	(h)	Cardiff City	D 1–1	0–1	16	Woodhouse	13,000			4		11	5	9			1		6				7					3	10		2	8
27	SL D1	(a)	Queen's Park R.	L 1–3	0–0	16	Doran (pen)	7,000			4		11	5	9			1		6				7					3	10		2	8
Apr 2	SL D1	(h)	Southend United	W 3–0	0–0	16	Doran 3	14,000			4		11	5	9			1		6				7					3	10		2	8
3	SL D1	(h)	Swindon Town	W 2–0	2–0	14	Doran 2 (1 pen)	12,500			4		11	5	9			1		6				7					3	10		2	8
5	SL D1	(a)	Southend United	D 0–0	0–0	14		6,500			4		11	5	9			1		6				7					3	10		2	8
10	SL D1	(a)	Millwall	L 0–5	0–3	16		18,000			4		11	5	9			1		6				7					3	10		2	8
17	SL D1	(a)	Watford	L 1–3		16		6,000			4		11	5	9			1	4	6				7					3	10		2	8
24	SL D1	(h)	Newport County	W 3–1	2–0	16	Williams 2, Doran	10,500			4			5	9			1		6				7	11				3	10		2	8
May 1	SL D1	(h)	Northampton T.	L 2–3	1–2	16	Doran 2	9,000			4		11	5	9			1		6				7					3	10		2	8
League appearances									2	17	38	2	16	33	10	13	5	42	2	32	12	13	23	39	12	21	4	22	18	37	10	36	
League goals	OG – 1									2			1	2	10	3						5	4		3	4	9				6		3	7

added to but for the four-year break. He cost Albion a club-record £200 fee and, though in the autumn of his career, was a huge attraction. Unfortunately for both club and player, George received a leg injury early in the season which forced his retirement in March.

From the playing viewpoint it was an undistinguished season. In the Southern League the early pace-setters were Watford and Reading, but in November Portsmouth took over at the top and, with the exception of the Easter weekend, remained there for the rest of the season. Even so it was a close finish, with Pompey taking the title on goal-average from Watford. Albion managed only three away wins, the best of which was the 5–1 drubbing of Northampton Town, but also gained an excellent 0–0 draw at Fratton Park. The highlights at the Goldstone were the 3–2 defeat of Watford and the 1–1 draw with Cardiff City, who finished fourth.

When it became evident that Holley's career was at an end, Webb signed Jack Doran from Norwich City to fill the gap. Doran, who had impressed when scoring both goals in Albion's 2–0 defeat in October, had scored eighteen goals for City and then hit ten in ten games for the Albion, including three against Southend United. As a result, he had the unusual distinction of finishing as top scorer for two clubs in the same season.

Albion ended up in sixteenth position in the Southern League and were eliminated at the first hurdle in the English Cup, losing 1–0 to Luton Town at the Goldstone. Goalkeeper Billy Hayes played in all 42 League games, while the evergreen Bert Longstaff and Billy Booth played in 39 and 38 respectively.

With post-war Britain thirsty for entertainment, attendances soared and the average home gate of around 9,200 was nearly 2,500 more than the previous highest in the championship season of 1909–10. The result was a net profit on the season of £1,254 2s. 4d., also the highest thus far, but the club was still in debt to the tune of £370. At the annual shareholders' meeting, held at the Oddfellows' Hall in Queen's Road, the board made special mention of the services rendered to the club – both moral and financial – by Lord Leconfield, the Lord Lieutenant of Sussex; Sir William Gentle; Alderman Charles Thomas-Stanford M.P.; Alderman John Clark; Alderman Herbert Carden; Alderman Alfred Sargeant, Mayor of Hove; Mr Bernard Oppenheimer; Mr David Sassoon; and Mr Harry Preston. These very prominent gentleman all held shares in the club. Indeed, by 1933 Lord Leconfield owned 500, a higher number than the majority of the directors.

THE FOOTBALL LEAGUE

Little did the Goldstone regulars realise that they were witnessing the end of an era: 1919–20 was to be the final season of the Southern League in its original form. Three times previously, in 1907, 1909 and January 1919, the Southern League clubs had approached the Football League with the proposal that the two should amalgamate, but the Football League had thrown the suggestion out on each occasion.

At a meeting between representatives of the two Leagues in Sheffield on 18 May 1920, it was proposed by Watford and seconded by Norwich City that the Southern League clubs were of the opinion that the time was opportune to form a Football League Third Division consisting of northern and southern sections.

At the Football League's a.g.m. on 29 May it was announced

that subject to the consent of the Football Association, a Third Division of the Football League be formed, and that the clubs at present forming the First Division of the Southern League shall comprise the Third Division for season 1920–21.

The Northern Section was to be formed the following season.

The departing clubs were ordered to pay £25 each to the Southern League secretary to safeguard the interests of that competition, and had to pay an entrance fee of £100 to the Football League, as associate members only without full voting rights.

Just before the historic decision was taken by the Football League, Cardiff City, who had finished fourth in the Southern League, were actually elected to the Second Division, with Grimsby Town, the re-election losers with the highest number of votes, taking their place in the new Third Division. The Welsh side went on to gain runner's-up spot behind Birmingham in 1920–21 and thus made the incredible step from Southern League to the First Division in just eighteen months. It was to take Albion 59 years to achieve the same!

SEASON 1920–21

In an effort to improve the Goldstone facilities, £720 was spent in the summer on a northward extension to the West Stand to accommodate an additional 300 fans; new dressing-rooms, more office space and a directors' room were also included in the project. Extra banking was provided on the popular east side of the ground to accommodate over 3,000 more spectators.

Webb brought seven new players to the club, the most notable being Harry Bentley, an experienced defender who had played for Sheffield Wednesday since 1910. The others included Jack Rutherford, a centre-half from Luton Town who was made team captain, and his brother Jim from Ashington of the Northern Alliance. Some old faithfuls had made their exits during the summer: Billy Booth, Gunner Higham, Bullet Jones and Frank Spencer would never appear in the Albion ranks again. For them the exciting new era had come too late, although Jones became assistant trainer and made occasional appearances for the Lambs.

In 1921 the club donated the 'Albion Shield', to be played for annually by Boys' Brigade and Boy Scout teams. The final was to be staged at the Goldstone Ground.

Albion 1920–21

Back row left to right: Dave Williams, Wally Little, Ossie Randall, Billy Hayes, Tom Brown, unknown.
Middle row left to right: Alf Nelmes (trainer), George Coomber, unknown, Jack Woodhouse, Charlie Webb (manager), Zacky March, Harry Bentley, Jack Burnham, Dickie Meades (assistant trainer).
Front row left to right: Bert Longstaff, Fretwell Hall, George Ritchie, Jack Rutherford (captain), Jack Doran, Ted Rodgerson, Billy Miller.

The first Football League match was played on 28 August 1920, an away fixture with Southend United which resulted in a 2–0 defeat. Albion's line-up for that initial Third Division match at Southend's Kursaal ground was

Billy Hayes; Jack Woodhouse (captain) and
Wally Little; Fretwell Hall, George Coomber and
Harry Bentley; Bert Longstaff, George Ritchie,
Jack Doran, Ted Rodgerson and Zacky March.

Jack Rutherford had been injured in the pre-season trial match and Jack Woodhouse took over as skipper for this game.

As in the Southern League days, home form was generally good with only four defeats, but away from the Goldstone it was a very different story. Albion gathered only eight points on their travels, including a fine 4–0 win over fellow strugglers Newport County, and in a disappointing campaign the team scrambled into eighteenth place. The lack of forward strength frequently let the side down, Jack Doran ploughing a lone furrow up front with 21 goals, exactly half the team's total. Champions Crystal Palace completed the double over Albion in the Yuletide fixtures which saw the biggest Goldstone League gate of the season, 14,000, at the 2–0 defeat on Christmas Day. Public response to the new league was encouraging and the average attendance, over 9,300, was the best to date.

In the English Cup, Albion thrashed First Division Oldham Athletic 4–1 in the first round. The tie attracted a new record crowd to the Goldstone, 16,972 spectators paying £1,443 18s. to see Albion dominate throughout the match after Zacky March had given them the lead in the very first minute. Only Bert Longstaff and Oldham's David Wilson remained from the line-ups of the same tie seven years earlier.

In the second round Albion were drawn at Hove against high-flying Cardiff City and the ground attendance record was again eclipsed, a crowd of 20,260 (£1,724 15s. 6d.) witnessing a goal-less draw. In the first half Albion's centre-half, Jack Bollington, broke a leg, the sickening crack being heard all over the ground;

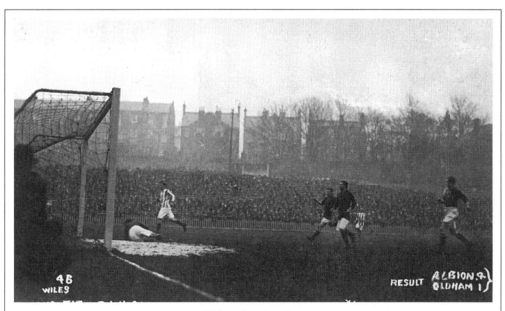

Albion slay the giants
Centre-forward Jack Doran scores the second goal of a one-sided match which saw Albion triumph 4–1 over Oldham Athletic. This first-round English Cup victory was a repeat of the giant-killing act of seven years earlier over the First Division side, and attracted a record crowd of 16,972.

SEASON 1920–21

Date	Comp.	Ven.	Opponents	Result	HT	Pos.	Scorers	Atten.	Bentley H	Bollington J	Broadhead A	Brown T	Burnham J	Coomber G	Doran J	Hall F	Hayes W	Little W	Longstaff A	March Z	Miller W	Neil A	Randall O	Ritchie G	Rodgerson E	Rutherford Jack	Rutherford Jim	Williams D	Wisden A	Woodhouse J
Aug 28	FL D3(S)	(a)	Southend United	L 0–2	0–1	17=		8,000	6					5	9	4	1	3	7	11				8	10					2
Sep 1	FL D3(S)	(h)	Merthyr Town	D 0–0	0–0	18		9,000	6			11		5	9	4	1	3	7					8	10					2
4	FL D3(S)	(a)	Southend United	W 1–0	1–0	12=	Doran	11,000	6			11		4	9		1	3	7						10	5		8		2
6	FL D3(S)	(h)	Merthyr Town	L 1–4	1–2	19	Rodgerson	15,000	6	4		11			9		1	3						10	7	5		8		2
11	FL D3(S)	(a)	Brentford	L 0–2	0–1	20		10,000	6	4		11			9		1	3	7						10	5		8		2
18	FL D3(S)	(h)	Brentford	W 4–0	2–0	18	Rodgerson, Doran, Jack Rutherford, Longstaff	5,500	6	4		11			9		1	3	7						10	5		8		2
25	FL D3(S)	(a)	Bristol Rovers	L 1–3	1–0	19	Rodgerson	8,000	6	4		11			9		1	3	7						10	5		8		2
29	FL D3(S)	(h)	Grimsby Town	L 1–3	1–1	19	Rodgerson	8,000	6	4		11			9			3	7				1		10	5		8		2
Oct 2	FL D3(S)	(h)	Bristol Rovers	W 2–0	0–0	15	Doran 2	7,000	3	4		11			9		1	6			10				8	5		7		2
9	FL D3(S)	(a)	Reading	W 1–0	1–0	13	Doran	10,000		4		11	3		9		1	6			10				8	5		7		2
16	FL D3(S)	(h)	Reading	D 2–2	1–1	12	Longstaff, Doran	11,000		4		11		6	9		1	3	7		10				8	5				2
23	FL D3(S)	(a)	Luton Town	L 2–3	2–2	15	Rodgerson 2	10,000	2	4				6			1	3	7						10	5		11	9	8
30	FL D3(S)	(h)	Luton Town	D 1–1	1–0	13	Doran	11,000	2	4				6	9		1	3	7	11					10	5				8
Nov 6	FL D3(S)	(a)	Plymouth Argyle	L 0–5	0–3	16		18,000	2	4				6	9		1	3		11					10	5		7		8
13	FL D3(S)	(h)	Plymouth Argyle	W 1–0	1–0	16	Williams	7,000	2					6	8		1	3	7	11	9					5		10		4
20	FL D3(S)	(a)	Swansea Town	D 0–0	0–0	15		17,000	2					6	8		1	3	7	11	9					5		10		4
27	FL D3(S)	(h)	Swansea Town	D 1–1	0–1	15	Williams	8,500	2					5	8	4	1		7	11	9						3	10		6
Dec 4	FL D3(S)	(h)	Queen's Park R.	W 2–1	1–0	10	Doran 2	9,000	2					4	9		1		7	11					8	5	3	10		6
11	FL D3(S)	(a)	Queen's Park R.	L 0–4	0–1	15		10,000	2					5	9	4	1		7	11					8		3	10		6
25	FL D3(S)	(h)	Crystal Palace	L 0–2	0–0	17		14,000	2							4	1		7	11		8			10	5	3	9		6
27	FL D3(S)	(a)	Crystal Palace	L 2–3	1–1	18=	Neil, Doran (pen)	18,000	2						9	4	1		7	11		8			10	5	3			6
Jan 1	FL D3(S)	(a)	Grimsby Town	D 2–2	1–2	18	Doran, Rodgerson	8,000	2	5				4	9		1		7	11		8			10		3			6
8	FAC R1	(h)	Oldham Athletic	W 4–1	3–0	–	March 2, Doran, Coomber	16,972	2	5				4	9		1		7	11		8			10		3			6
15	FL D3(S)	(a)	Exeter City	L 0–1	0–1	19		5,000	2	5				4	9		1		7	11		8			10		3			6
22	FL D3(S)	(h)	Exeter City	D 1–1	0–0	19	Doran (pen)	8,000	2	5				4	9		1		7	11		8			10		3			6
29	FAC R2	(h)	Cardiff City	D 0–0	0–0	–		20,260	2	5				4	9		1		7	11		8			10		3			6
Feb 2	FAC R2 Rep	(a)	Cardiff City	L 0–1	0–1	–		30,563	2					4			1	5	7	11		8			10		3	9		6
5	FL D3(S)	(h)	Southampton	D 1–1	0–1	18	Doran	9,000	2					5	9	4	1		7	11		8			10		3			6
12	FL D3(S)	(a)	Millwall	W 1–0	0–0	17	Longstaff	20,000	2					5	9	4	1		7	11		8			10		3			6
19	FL D3(S)	(h)	Millwall	W 1–0	1–0	16	Doran	9,000	2					5	9	4	1		7	11		8			10		3			6
23	FL D3(S)	(h)	Southampton	L 0–1	0–0	17		8,000	2					5	9	4	1		7	11					10		3	8		6
26	FL D3(S)	(a)	Newport County	W 4–0	1–0	14	Broadhead, Doran 2, Longstaff	9,000	2		8			5	9	4	1		7	11					10		3			6
Mar 5	FL D3(S)	(h)	Newport County	W 1–0	0–0	13	Broadhead	9,000	2		8			5	9	4	1		7	11					10		3			6
12	FL D3(S)	(a)	Gillingham	L 0–1	0–0	14		7,000	2		8			4	9		1		7	11					10	5	3			6
19	FL D3(S)	(h)	Gillingham	W 1–0	1–0	13	Doran	9,000	2		8			4	9		1		7	11					10	5	3			6
25	FL D3(S)	(h)	Norwich City	W 2–0	1–0	13	Rodgerson, Neil	14,000	2			11		4	9		1		7			8			10	5	3			6
26	FL D3(S)	(a)	Swindon Town	L 0–3	0–2	13		10,000	2			11		4	9		1		7			8			10	5	3			6
28	FL D3(S)	(a)	Norwich City	L 0–3	0–3	13		14,000	2			11		4	9		1		7			8			10	5	3			6
Apr 2	FL D3(S)	(a)	Swindon Town	L 0–2	0–1	14		8,000	2					4	9		1		7			8			10	5	3	11		6
9	FL D3(S)	(h)	Portsmouth	W 3–0	1–0	13	Rodgerson, Doran 2	9,000	2					4	9		1		7			8			10	5	3	11		6
16	FL D3(S)	(a)	Portsmouth	L 0–3	0–2	15		13,599	2					4	9		1		7			8			10	5	3	11		6
23	FL D3(S)	(h)	Watford	L 0–3	0–1	17		10,000	2					4	9		1		7	11		8			10	5	3			6
30	FL D3(S)	(a)	Watford	L 0–1	0–1	18		6,000	2					4	9		1		7	11		8			10	5	3			6
May 2	FL D3(S)	(a)	Northampton T.	L 0–1	0–0	18		6,000	2					4	9		1		7			10	8			5	3			6
7	FL D3(S)	(h)	Northampton T.	W 3–2	2–2	18	Doran 2, Jack Rutherford	8,000	2		10			4	9		1		7	11		8				5	3			6
							League appearances		40	14	5	14	1	33	40	12	41	16	38	24	7	18	1	3	37	29	26	20	1	42
							League goals			2					21				4			2			9	2		2		

An Albion legend

Charlie Webb was associated with the club as player and manager from 1908 until 1948. For 28 of those years he was team manager, by far the longest tenure in Albion history. This season Webb enjoyed a benefit match, the Third Division game against Watford on 23 April, and profited to the tune of £495 15s. 11d. (In those days beneficiaries received the gate of a scheduled fixture rather than a separate testimonial.) He was granted a second benefit in 1949 and received a long-service award from the Football League.

Football League Division 3 (South) 1920–21

		P	W	D	L	F	A	W	D	L	F	A	Pts
1.	Crystal Palace	42	15	4	2	45	17	9	7	5	25	17	59
2.	Southampton	42	14	5	2	46	10	5	11	5	18	18	54
3.	Queen's Park R.	42	14	4	3	38	11	8	5	8	23	21	53
4.	Swindon Town	42	14	5	2	51	17	7	5	9	22	32	52
5.	Swansea Town	42	9	10	2	32	19	9	5	7	24	26	51
6.	Watford	42	14	4	3	40	15	6	4	11	19	29	48
7.	Millwall	42	11	5	5	25	8	7	6	8	17	22	47
8.	Merthyr Town	42	13	5	3	46	20	2	10	9	14	29	45
9.	Luton Town	42	14	6	1	51	15	2	6	13	10	41	44
10.	Bristol Rovers	42	15	3	3	51	22	3	4	14	17	35	43
11.	Plymouth Argyle	42	10	7	4	25	13	1	14	6	10	21	43
12.	Portsmouth	42	10	8	3	28	14	2	7	12	18	34	39
13.	Grimsby Town	42	12	5	4	32	16	3	4	14	17	43	39
14.	Northampton Town	42	11	4	6	32	23	4	4	13	27	52	38
15.	Newport County	42	8	5	8	20	23	6	4	11	23	41	37
16.	Norwich City	42	9	10	2	31	14	1	6	14	13	39	36
17.	Southend United	42	13	2	6	32	20	1	6	14	12	41	36
18.	**ALBION**	42	11	6	4	28	20	3	2	16	14	41	36
19.	Exeter City	42	9	7	5	27	15	1	8	12	12	39	35
20.	Reading	42	8	4	9	26	22	4	3	14	16	37	31
21.	Brentford	42	7	9	5	27	23	2	3	16	15	44	30
22.	Gillingham	42	6	9	6	19	24	2	3	16	15	50	28

it was a dreadful injury that ended Jack's career. In the replay at Ninian Park, Albion again finished the match with ten men, Andy Neil, signed only six weeks earlier, being sent off for kicking an opponent. After a tremendous tussle the Welsh club scraped through by the only goal of the game scored by Arthur Cashmore in the thirteenth minute.

Jack Doran's goalscoring deeds were recognised by the Irish selectors when they chose him for the match with England at Roker Park in October. The Lambs had a magnificent season, finishing runners-up in the South Eastern League and winning the English Section of the Southern League, now a mixed bag of reserve sides and the smaller professional clubs. The Southern League championship match against the Welsh Section winners was held over to the following September, when Albion defeated Barry 2–1 at Ninian Park, after a 1–1 extra-time draw at The Den, to clinch the title.

The Goldstone fixture with Luton Town on 30 October was marred by crowd trouble after the referee, Mr Head of West Bromwich, allowed the Hatters' 85th-minute equaliser to stand despite having already blown for offside. At the final whistle hundreds of supporters swarmed onto the pitch with the intention of gaining access to the referee's room in the West Stand, and a corner flag was thrown, striking a policeman on the head. It was also alleged that a bottle was thrown at the official before the game ended. Ultimately the embittered crowd was quelled by an appeal from Jack Doran, and the misguided supporters dispersed. The incident was the worst of its kind at the Goldstone Ground until the mindless fighting between spectators which began in the late 1960s. The club was instructed to post notices with respect to the crowd misbehaviour, and was warned that the ground would be closed if there was any repetition.

SEASON 1921–22

With a number of new signings to strengthen the team, the feeling was one of optimism at the outset of the season. Early results boosted hopes when, after four games, Albion sat on top of the section, but the state of affairs did not prevail and seven of the next eight matches ended in defeat. The team plummeted into the lower half of the table where they stayed for the remainder of the campaign, eventually finishing nineteenth in one of the most disappointing seasons to date.

The team's in-and-out form was a constant source of bewilderment to management and supporters alike. Tremendous wins, such as the 7–0 annihilation of Northampton Town and a 3–0 win over championship challengers Portsmouth, paled into insignificance against defeat after defeat in matches that should have been won with ease. The defence was a highly capable unit, with left-back Jack Feebery, signed from Exeter City, and goalkeeper Billy Hayes ever-present, and George Coomber missing only two games at centre-half, but once again the lack of support for Jack Doran in the goalscoring department cost the club dear.

Doran began the season in startling fashion. In the opening matches he registered home and away hat-tricks against Exeter City, and by the beginning of November had netted seventeen goals in thirteen games, including five against Northampton Town. Indeed, no other player scored a goal until Andy Neil notched one against Charlton Athletic in the thirteenth match of the term. Jack was the Football League's top scorer at this stage and he was rewarded with further Irish caps against England and Wales. However, he was injured during the Christmas period and missed ten games; inevitably his form suffered and he scored only six more goals. There was no lack of skill up front with Andy Neil outstanding, but he scored only three times, and with Fred Groves and Ted Rodgerson out for long periods with injuries, left-half Wally Little was next to Doran on the scoring list with five.

The highlight of the season was another lucrative cup-run. In the opening round at the Goldstone, Albion turned the form book upside down and beat First Division Sheffield United by a goal to nil. The team was hit by a flu epidemic and the line-up had a strange look about it with full-back Jack Thompson at centre-forward. Nevertheless, Albion lived up to their Cup reputation, Wally Little giving them the lead before many of the crowd had taken their places, and, with the defence effectively soaking up the Blades' efforts, they never looked likely to concede an equaliser.

The second-round draw favoured Albion with another home tie against First Division opposition in the shape of Huddersfield Town. The great Herbert Chapman had recently taken the reins at Leeds Road and the club was at the beginning of its halcyon years. In

Albion's scoring machine
Centre-forward Jack Doran enjoyed an incredible start to the season, scoring the club's first twelve goals. His form brought him two more Irish international caps.

SEASON 1921–22

Date	Comp.	Ven.	Opponents	Result	HT	Pos.	Scorers	Atten.	Bentley H	Broadhead A	Channon V	Coomber G	Doran J	Evans T	Feebery J	Fuller E	Groves F	Hayes W	Little W	Longstaff A	McAllister W	March Z	Neil A	Nightingale J	Phillips R	Rodgerson E	Salt H	Thompson J	Woodhouse J
Aug 27	FL D3(S)	(h)	Southend United	D 0–0	0–0	7=		13,500	4				9	3	7	1						11	8			10	5	2	6
31	FL D3(S)	(a)	Exeter City	W 3–0	1–0	2=	Doran 3	6,000					9	3	10	1	6					11	8	7			5	2	4
Sep 3	FL D3(S)	(a)	Southend United	W 2–1	1–0	3	Doran 2	7,500				5	9	3	7	1	6						8		11	10		2	4
7	FL D3(S)	(h)	Exeter City	W 3–1	2–0	1	Doran 3	10,000				5	9	3	7	1	6						8		11	10		2	4
10	FL D3(S)	(a)	Aberdare Athletic	L 0–2	0–0	5=		12,000				5	9	3	7	1	6						8		11	10		2	4
12	FL D3(S)	(a)	Swansea Town	L 1–2	0–0	7	Doran	12,000				5	9	3		1	6		7			11	8			10		2	4
17	FL D3(S)	(h)	Aberdare Athletic	L 1–2	0–2	9	Doran (pen)	12,000				5	9	3		1	6		7			11	8			10		2	4
24	FL D3(S)	(a)	Southampton	L 0–3	0–3	12		13,000				5	9	3	7	1	6	10				11	8					2	4
Oct 1	FL D3(S)	(h)	Southampton	L 0–1	0–1	13=		10,500				5	9	3	7	1	6					11	8			10		2	4
8	FL D3(S)	(a)	Watford	L 0–1	0–1	17		6,000				5	9	3	7	1	6					11	8			10		2	4
15	FL D3(S)	(h)	Watford	D 1–1	1–0	17	Doran	9,000	2			5	9	3	7	1	6					11	8			10			4
22	FL D3(S)	(a)	Charlton Athletic	L 0–1	0–0	19		12,000	2			5		3		1	9	6	8		7	11	10						4
29	FL D3(S)	(h)	Charlton Athletic	W 2–0	2–0	16	Doran, Neil	9,000				5	9	3	7	1	6				10	11	8					2	4
Nov 5	FL D3(S)	(h)	Northampton T.	W 7–0	2–0	14	Doran 5, McAllister 2	8,000				5	9	3	7	1	6				10	11	8					2	4
12	FL D3(S)	(a)	Northampton T.	L 0–2	0–1	15		7,000				5	9	3	7	1	6				10		8			11		2	4
19	FL D3(S)	(h)	Queen's Park R.	W 2–1	2–0	14	Little, McAllister	9,000				5	9	3	7	1	6				10	11	8					2	4
26	FL D3(S)	(a)	Queen's Park R.	L 0–3	0–1	15		9,000				5	9	3	7	1	6				10	11	8					2	4
Dec 10	FL D3(S)	(h)	Swansea Town	D 0–0	0–0	15		7,500				5	9	3	7	1	6				10	11	8					2	4
24	FL D3(S)	(h)	Norwich City	L 0–2	0–0	16		6,000				5	9	3	7	1	6					11	8			10		2	4
26	FL D3(S)	(a)	Bristol Rovers	W 2–1	1–0	14	Little, Doran	20,000				5	9	3	7	1	6		8			11				10		2	4
27	FL D3(S)	(a)	Bristol Rovers	W 3–1	1–0	14	Groves, Rodgerson 2	12,000				5		3	7	1	6		8			11	9			10		2	4
31	FL D3(S)	(a)	Reading	D 0–0	0–0	12		9,000	2			5		3		1	9	6			10	11	8	7					4
Jan 7	FAC R1	(h)	Sheffield United	W 1–0	1–0	–	Little	15,238	2			5		3		1	6		9			11	8	7		10			4
14	FL D3(S)	(h)	Reading	D 1–1	0–1	14	Feebery (pen)	4,500	2			5		3	8	1	6				9	11	10	7					4
21	FL D3(S)	(a)	Portsmouth	W 3–0	1–0	12	Doran (pen), Little 2	3,000				5	9	3	7	1		10	6			11	8					2	4
28	FAC R2	(h)	Huddersfield Town	D 0–0	0–0	–		22,241	6			5	9	3	7	1					10	11	8					2	4
Feb 1	FAC R2 Rep	(a)	Huddersfield Town	L 0–2	0–0	–		28,086	6			5	9	3	7	1					10	11	8					2	4
4	FL D3(S)	(h)	Merthyr Town	L 1–3	1–2	13	Little	4,500	6			5		3	7	1	9		11		10		8					2	4
8	FL D3(S)	(a)	Portsmouth	D 0–0	0–0	13		6,000	2			5	9	3		1	6					11	8	7		10			4
11	FL D3(S)	(a)	Merthyr Town	L 1–2	1–2	13	Neil	6,000	2			5	9	3		1	6					11	8	7		10			4
18	FL D3(S)	(h)	Plymouth Argyle	D 1–1	0–1	13	Fuller	7,500	6			5		3		1	9		8		10	11		7				2	4
25	FL D3(S)	(a)	Plymouth Argyle	L 1–3	1–1	15	Nightingale	12,000	6			5		3		1	9		8		10	11		7				2	4
Mar 4	FL D3(S)	(h)	Newport County	W 3–0	1–0	13	Nightingale 2, Neil	6,000	2			5		3		1	9	6			10	11	8	7					4
11	FL D3(S)	(a)	Newport County	W 1–0	1–0	13	Own goal	7,000	2			5		3		1	9	6			10	11	8	7					4
18	FL D3(S)	(h)	Luton Town	D 1–1	1–1	13	Doran (pen)	7,500	6			5	9	3	8	1					10	11		7				2	4
25	FL D3(S)	(a)	Luton Town	L 0–2	0–0	13		7,000	6			5	9	3	8	1					10	11		7				2	4
Apr 1	FL D3(S)	(a)	Swindon Town	L 0–1	0–1	14		4,500	6	8		5		3		1	4		9			11		7		10		2	
6	FL D3(S)	(a)	Norwich City	D 1–1	1–0	13	Salt	8,000	6	8		5		3		1	4		9			11		7		10		2	
8	FL D3(S)	(h)	Swindon Town	W 2–1	1–0	11	Salt, Doran	7,500	6			5	9	4		1	3					11	8	7			10	2	
14	FL D3(S)	(a)	Brentford	L 0–4	0–1	14		14,000	6	11		5	9	4		1	3						8	7			10	2	
15	FL D3(S)	(a)	Gillingham	L 0–1	0–0	15		6,000	6	11		5	9	4		1	3						8	7			10	2	
17	FL D3(S)	(h)	Brentford	W 2–1	1–1	13	Doran 2	10,000	6			5	9	3		1					10	11	8	7				2	4
22	FL D3(S)	(h)	Gillingham	L 0–1	0–0	15		6,000	6			5	9	3		1			8		10	11		7				2	4
29	FL D3(S)	(a)	Millwall	L 0–2	0–1	17		15,000	6			5	9	3	8	1					10	11		7				2	4
May 6	FL D3(S)	(h)	Millwall	L 0–1	0–0	19		7,000	6	8		5	9	3		1					10	11		7				2	4
League appearances									24	3	2	40	31	5	42	9	23	42	28	3	21	32	40	20	3	16	6	35	37
League goals								OG – 1					23		1	1	1		5		3		3	3		2	2		

Albion 1921–22

Back row left to right: Jack Thompson, Reg Phillips, Ossie Randall, Charlie Webb (manager), Billy Hayes, Jack Feebery (captain), Harry Bentley.
Middle row left to right: Dickie Meades (assistant trainer), Tom Evans, Harold Salt, Jack Woodhouse, George Coomber, Wally Little, Billy Miller, Jim Rutherford, Ted Rodgerson, Alf Nelmes (trainer).
Front row left to right: Jack Nightingale, Arnold Broadhead, Andy Neil, Jack Doran, Tommy Cook, Fred Groves, Zacky March.

May 3rd, 1922: goalkeeper Sid Townsend was injured during the reserve-team match against a Sussex XI and Wally Little took over between the posts without first obtaining the referee's permission. The first time that Little handled the ball the official awarded a penalty kick which Wally duly saved. Ironically, Little became the Albion's penalty expert for several seasons, scoring 26 in League and Cup.

Football League Division 3 (South) 1921–22													
	P	W	D	L	F	A	W	D	L	F	A	Pts
1. Southampton	42	14	7	0	50	8	9	8	4	18	13	61
2. Plymouth Argyle	42	17	4	0	43	4	8	7	6	20	20	61
3. Portsmouth	42	13	5	3	38	18	5	12	4	24	21	53
4. Luton Town	42	16	2	3	47	9	6	6	9	17	26	52
5. Queen's Park R.	42	13	7	1	36	12	5	6	10	17	32	49
6. Swindon Town	42	10	7	4	40	21	6	6	9	32	39	45
7. Watford	42	9	9	3	34	21	4	9	8	20	27	44
8. Aberdare Athletic	42	11	6	4	38	18	6	4	11	19	33	44
9. Brentford	42	15	2	4	41	17	1	9	11	11	26	43
10. Swansea Town	42	11	8	2	40	19	2	7	12	10	28	41
11. Merthyr Town	42	14	2	5	33	15	3	4	14	12	41	40
12. Millwall	42	6	13	2	22	10	4	5	12	16	32	38
13. Reading	42	10	5	6	28	15	4	5	12	12	32	38
14. Bristol Rovers	42	8	8	5	32	24	6	2	13	20	43	38
15. Norwich City	42	8	10	3	29	17	4	3	14	21	45	37
16. Charlton Athletic	42	10	6	5	28	19	3	5	13	15	37	37
17. Northampton Town	42	13	3	5	30	17	0	8	13	17	54	37
18. Gillingham	42	11	4	6	36	20	3	4	14	11	40	36
19. **ALBION**	42	9	6	6	33	19	4	3	14	12	32	35
20. Newport County	42	8	7	6	22	18	3	5	13	22	43	34
21. Exeter City	42	7	5	9	22	29	4	7	10	16	30	34
22. Southend United	42	7	5	9	23	23	1	6	14	11	51	27

the next decade Huddersfield won the First Division title in three successive years, 1924, 1925 and 1926; were runners-up in 1927 and 1928; won the Cup this season; and were losing finalists in 1928 and 1930.

The attendance record was broken yet again with a crowd of 22,241 (£1,856) present to witness a goal-less draw. Huddersfield dominated the early exchanges, but the Albion soon settled and should have won the game. The star-studded Yorkshire side made no mistake in the replay, scoring two second-half goals to win through to the third round on a pitch described as a 'swamp'. Despite these three big Cup games, Albion announced a loss of £1,000 at the end of the campaign.

At a meeting held at the Oddfellows' Hall in Queen's Road on 21 July 1922, the Supporters' Club was re-formed, the original having disbanded on the outbreak of the Great War. The chairman was Mr F. G. Baker, and the honorary secretary was John Talbot Nanson, an auctioneer and estate agent who was Mayor of Brighton from 1938 to 1941. Nanson also became chairman of the National Federation of Supporters' Clubs when that organisation (motto: *To help — not hinder*) was formed in 1927 by Albion, Bournemouth & B.A., Brentford, Charlton Athletic, Northampton Town and Plymouth Argyle S.C.s, and remained in that office until his death in 1949. The club's first headquarters were at the Belvedere Mansions Hotel in King's Road.

SEASON 1922–23

What a difference a year makes! In May 1922 the Albion were in a 'slough of despond', but twelve months later all at the Goldstone were in buoyant mood. After a poor start, in which only five points were gained from seven matches, results improved steadily with only four more defeats coming before Christmas. The management splashed out £275 in transfer fees during the summer and there were several changes in personnel at the outset of the season. In came Jack Jenkins (Pontypridd) at right-back, Abe Jones (Reading) at inside-right, Jimmy Moore (Leeds United) at inside-left and Jimmy Jones (Welbeck Colliery) at outside-left, but after the mediocre opening the team reverted to roughly the same line-up as that which had played at the end of the previous season.

The prolific Jack Doran had been transferred to Manchester City for £1,050 in August and the centre-forward spot became something of a problem. Edgar Saunders and Abe Jones were tried initially with little success, and eventually the role went to the admirable Eddie Fuller, a half-back signed from London Caledonians in 1921. Another youngster to make his mark was 21-year-old Tommy Cook who came into the side at inside-left in September. Equally at home on the cricket field – he played as a batsman with the Sussex C.C.C. for many years – Tommy later switched to centre-forward and scored many spectacular goals; indeed, he still holds the aggregate (peacetime) record for the Albion with 114 in the League and 9 in the F.A. Cup. In October, Ernie Wilson made his League début on the left wing in the 2–1 defeat of Brentford at the Goldstone. Signed from Denaby United in May, 'Tug' went on to play 509 League matches for the club, another record that remains intact.

George Coomber was at his very best during this, his benefit season, and he inspired the rest of the team with his popular personality and skilful play at centre-half. A good team spirit developed which became evident in the performances and results. On Christmas Day the visitors to Hove were Portsmouth and the biggest League gate of the season (15,000) saw

Albion 1922–23

Back row left to right: Jack Thompson, Jack Jenkins, H. Baker, Billy Hayes, Reg Phillips.
Middle row left to right: Alf Nelmes (trainer), Edgar Saunders, Jack Woodhouse, George Coomber, Charlie Webb (manager), George Moorhead, Wally Little, Jimmy Jones, Dickie Meades (assistant trainer).
Front row left to right: Jack Nightingale, Abe Jones, Billy McAllister, Andy Neil, Jack Feebery (captain), Fred Groves, Jimmy Moore, Tug Wilson, Arnold Broadhead.

SEASON 1922–23

Date	Comp.	Ven.	Opponents	Result	HT	Pos.	Scorers	Atten.	Cook T	Coomber G	Feebery J	Fuller E	Groves F	Hayes W	Hopkins J	Jenkins J	Jones A	Jones J	Little W	McAllister W	Moore J	Moorhead G	Neil A	Nightingale J	Saunders E	Thompson J	Wilson E	Woodhouse J
Aug 26	FL D3(S)	(h)	Norwich City	D 0–0	0–0	7=		11,500			3	7		1		2	8	11	6		10	5	4		9			
30	FL D3(S)	(a)	Exeter City	L 0–1	0–1	21		2,000		5	3	7		1		2	8	11	6		10		4		9			
Sep 2	FL D3(S)	(a)	Norwich City	L 0–1	0–1	21		10,000		5	3	7		1		2	9	11	6	8	10		4					
6	FL D3(S)	(h)	Exeter City	W 3–0	2–0	13=	A Jones, McAllister, Moore	9,000		5	3	7		1		2	9	11	6	8	10		4					
9	FL D3(S)	(a)	Luton Town	D 1–1	1–0	13	Moore	9,000		5	3	7		1		2	9	11	6	8	10		4					
16	FL D3(S)	(h)	Luton Town	L 0–1	0–0	17		8,000		5	3	7		1		2	9	11	6	8	10		4					
23	FL D3(S)	(a)	Queen's Park R.	D 0–0	0–0	17		15,000	10	5	3	9	7	1		2		11	6				8					4
30	FL D3(S)	(h)	Queen's Park R.	W 2–0	1–0	15	Fuller, J Jones	10,000	10	5	3	9	7	1		2		11	6				8					4
Oct 7	FL D3(S)	(h)	Gillingham	W 3–0	1–0	13	Neil, Feebery (pen), Cook	9,000	10	5	3	9	7	1		2		11	6				8					4
14	FL D3(S)	(a)	Gillingham	L 0–2	0–2	14		7,000	10	5	3	9	7	1		2		11	6				8					4
21	FL D3(S)	(h)	Brentford	W 2–1	1–0	11	Fuller 2	8,000	10	5	3	9	7	1		2			6				8				11	4
28	FL D3(S)	(a)	Brentford	W 2–1	1–1	9	Neil, Fuller	8,000	10	5	3	9	7	1		2			6				8				11	4
Nov 4	FL D3(S)	(h)	Swansea Town	L 1–3	0–2	12	Feebery (pen)	9,000	10	5	3	9	7	1		2			6				8				11	4
11	FL D3(S)	(a)	Swansea Town	D 0–0	0–0	12		15,000	10	5	3	9	7	1		2			6				8				11	4
18	FL D3(S)	(a)	Swindon Town	L 0–3	0–1	12		6,000	10	5	3	9	7	1		2			6				8				11	4
25	FL D3(S)	(h)	Swindon Town	D 1–1	0–0	12	Fuller	9,000	10	5	3	9	7	1		2			6				8				11	4
Dec 9	FL D3(S)	(h)	Aberdare Athletic	W 3–1	2–1	12	Cook, Fuller, Own goal	6,500	10	5	3	9	7	1		2			6				8				11	4
16	FL D3(S)	(a)	Newport County	L 0–1	0–1	12		8,000	10	5		9	7	1		3			6				8			2	11	4
23	FL D3(S)	(h)	Newport County	W 2–1	2–0	11	Neil, Fuller	7,000	10	5		9	7	1		3			6				8			2	11	4
25	FL D3(S)	(h)	Portsmouth	W 7–1	2–1	8	Fuller 2, J Jones, Little (pen), Cook 2, Neil	15,000	10	5		9	7	1		3		11	6				8			2		4
26	FL D3(S)	(a)	Portsmouth	W 2–1	1–0	7	Neil, Little (pen)	19,603	10	5		9	7	1		3			6				8			2	11	4
30	FL D3(S)	(a)	Northampton T.	D 0–0	0–0	7		10,000	10	5		9	7	1		3			6				8			2	11	4
Jan 6	FL D3(S)	(h)	Northampton T.	W 1–0	0–0	5	J Jones	9,000	10	5		9	7	1		3		11	6				8			2		4
13	FAC R1	(h)	Corinthians	D 1–1	0–0	–	Neil	23,642	10	5		9	7	1		3		11	6				8			2		4
17	FAC R1 Rep	(a*)	Corinthians	D 1–1*	1–0	–	Cook	9,350	10	5		9	7	1		3		11	6				8			2		4
20	FL D3(S)	(h)	Bristol City	W 2–1	1–0	6	Cook 2	7,200	9	5			7	1	10	3			6				8			2	11	4
22	FAC R1 2Rep(n*)		Corinthians	W 1–0	0–0	–	Cook	43,760	9	5			7	1	10	3			6				8			2	11	4
27	FL D3(S)	(a)	Bristol City	L 1–3	0–1	7	Little (pen)	16,000		5		9	7	1	10	3			6				8			2	11	4
Feb 3	FAC R2	(h)	West Ham United	D 1–1	0–0	–	Cook	19,531	9	5	3		7	1	10				6				8			2	11	4
7	FAC R2 Rep	(a)	West Ham United	L 0–1	0–1	–		20,000	10	5			7	1		3			6				8		9	2	11	4
10	FL D3(S)	(a)	Watford	W 2–1	1–0	5=	Wilson, Neil	5,000		5		9		1	10	3			6				8	7		2	11	4
17	FL D3(S)	(h)	Charlton Athletic	W 1–0	0–0	5	Hopkins	7,750		5		9		1	10	3			6				8	7		2	11	4
21	FL D3(S)	(a)	Watford	W 3–0	1–0	3	Neil, Fuller, Hopkins	6,250		5		9		1	10	3			6				8	7		2	11	4
Mar 3	FL D3(S)	(h)	Plymouth Argyle	W 1–0	1–0	3	Fuller	10,500		5		9		1	10	3			6				8	7		2	11	4
10	FL D3(S)	(a)	Plymouth Argyle	D 2–2	1–1	3	Nightingale 2	5,000		5		9		1	10	3			6				8	7		2	11	4
17	FL D3(S)	(a)	Bristol Rovers	D 0–0	0–0	4		8,000		5		9		1	10	3			6				8	7		2	11	4
24	FL D3(S)	(h)	Bristol Rovers	W 2–1	0–0	4	Hopkins 2	7,500		5		9		1	10	3			6				8	7		2	11	4
30	FL D3(S)	(a)	Millwall	L 1–2	1–0	4	Fuller	20,000		5		9		1	10	3			6				8	7		2	11	4
31	FL D3(S)	(a)	Reading	D 0–0	0–0	4		7,000		5		9		1	10	3			6				8	7		2	11	4
Apr 2	FL D3(S)	(h)	Millwall	W 2–1	1–0	4	Neil 2	13,000		5		9		1	10	3			6				8	7		2	11	4
7	FL D3(S)	(h)	Reading	W 3–1	2–0	3	Little (pen), Fuller, Hopkins	7,073		5		9		1	10	3			6				8	7		2	11	4
14	FL D3(S)	(a)	Southend United	D 0–0	0–0	4		8,000		5		9		1	10	3			6				8	7		2	11	4
16	FL D3(S)	(a)	Charlton Athletic	W 1–0	1–0	3	Wilson	3,000		5		9		1	10	3			6				8	6		2	11	4
21	FL D3(S)	(h)	Southend United	L 0–1	0–0	4		5,000		5		9		1	10	3			6				8	7		2	11	4
28	FL D3(S)	(a)	Merthyr Town	L 0–2	0–1	4		4,000		5		9		1	10	3			6				8	7		2	11	4
May 1	FL D3(S)	(a)	Aberdare Athletic	W 1–0	1–0	4	Neil	8,000		5		9		1	10	3			6				8	7		2	11	4
5	FL D3(S)	(h)	Merthyr Town	D 0–0	0–0	4		5,000		5		9		1	10	3			6				8	7		2	11	4
League appearances									18	41	17	34	26	42	17	42	6	16	41	8	6	1	42	17	2	25	25	36
League goals								OG – 1	6		2	13			5		1	3	4	1	2		10	2			2	

Notes: Jan 17 – played at The Crystal Palace.
– after extra time.
Jan 22 – played at Stamford Bridge, Chelsea FC.

Albion thrash their great rivals 7–1. Twenty-four hours later almost 20,000 turned out at Fratton Park to see Brighton complete the double over Pompey by winning 2–1.

In January, Charlie Webb signed Arsenal's speedy Irish inside-left Jimmy Hopkins to bolster the promotion challenge. From Christmas, Albion were very much the form team in the Southern Section, losing just four of the last 24 matches, but the moderate start to the campaign meant there was little margin for error. Defeat at Ashton Gate, when Albion were reduced to ten men after Jack Jenkins was injured with the scores still level, ended any real hopes of catching the highly consistent Bristol City side which went on to win the championship by six points.

The English Cup brought yet another series of memorable matches when Albion were drawn at home to the legendary amateur club Corinthians in the first round. The Corinthians were formed by N. L. 'Pa' Jackson in 1882 to counter the lack of success of the England team against Scotland. The England side comprised mainly public-school and university men at the time, and Jackson's idea was to give these players regular practice together in order to improve teamwork. They played friendly matches all over the British Isles and frequently toured abroad, and within 20 years became the most famous club in the land. They regularly beat the top professional sides, sometimes by enormous scores, the most famous victory being a 10–3 drubbing of Cup holders Bury in the Sheriff of London's Charity Shield match (forerunner of the F.A. Charity Shield) in March 1904. All the great university players represented the club, and on two occasions the England team was made up entirely of Corinthians. It was a club rule that it would not take part in competitive matches, but in 1922 this was amended to

Football League Division 3 (South) 1922–23

		P	W	D	L	F	A	W	D	L	F	A	Pts
1.	Bristol City	42	16	4	1	43	13	8	7	6	23	27	59
2.	Plymouth Argyle	42	18	3	0	47	6	5	4	12	14	23	53
3.	Swansea Town	42	13	6	2	46	14	9	3	9	32	31	53
4.	**ALBION**	42	15	3	3	39	13	5	8	8	13	21	51
5.	Luton Town	42	14	4	3	47	18	7	3	11	21	31	49
6.	Millwall	42	9	10	2	27	13	5	8	8	18	27	46
7.	Portsmouth	42	10	5	6	34	20	9	3	9	24	32	46
8.	Northampton Town	42	13	6	2	40	17	4	5	12	14	27	45
9.	Swindon Town	42	14	4	3	41	17	3	7	11	21	39	45
10.	Watford	42	10	6	5	35	23	7	4	10	22	31	44
11.	Queen's Park R.	42	10	4	7	34	24	6	6	9	20	25	42
12.	Charlton Athletic	42	11	6	4	33	14	3	8	10	22	37	42
13.	Bristol Rovers	42	7	9	5	25	19	6	7	8	10	17	42
14.	Brentford	42	9	4	8	27	23	4	9	9	18	28	38
15.	Southend United	42	10	6	5	35	18	2	7	12	14	36	37
16.	Gillingham	42	13	4	4	38	18	2	3	16	13	41	37
17.	Merthyr Town	42	10	4	7	27	17	1	10	10	12	31	36
18.	Norwich City	42	8	7	6	29	26	5	3	13	22	45	36
19.	Reading	42	9	8	4	24	15	1	6	14	12	40	34
20.	Exeter City	42	10	4	7	27	18	3	3	15	20	66	33
21.	Aberdare Athletic	42	6	8	7	25	23	3	3	15	17	47	29
22.	Newport County	42	8	6	7	28	21	0	5	16	12	49	27

Gentlemen v. Players
The historic meeting between the amateur Corinthians and the Albion professionals enthralled the nation. The tie went to a second replay at Chelsea's Stamford Bridge, with Tommy Cook scoring the winning goal for the pro's. Here the two teams tussle below the distinctive gable of Archibald Leitch's East Stand before a crowd of over 43,000, the largest ever to watch the Albion until 1930.

allow entry into the English Cup, so the Goldstone match on 13 January took on a historic context, being the first appearance of the Corinthians in the competition.

There was nationwide interest in the tie, and a 'moving-picture' was taken which was shown in cinemas all over the country. The Goldstone attendance record was bettered once again with 23,642 packing the ground. Charlie Webb was in no doubt as to the task confronting his team: the players representing the Corinthians had amassed a total of 126 amateur caps, and Ben Howard-Baker, Arthur Knight, Baishe Bower, Kenneth Hegan, Norman Creek, Graham Doggart, Claude Ashton and Freddie Ewer won full England honours while Robin Moulsdale won a full Welsh cap; so Albion were very much the second favourites. A thrillingly close contest ended at 1–1, Andy Neil equalising Norman Creek's second-half opener for the amateurs, and the replay was arranged for the following Wednesday afternoon at The Crystal Palace ground, scene of the English Cup finals from 1895 to 1914.

On the day of the match the whole of south-eastern England was enveloped in dense fog and there was some doubt whether it would be played, but after an arduous journey the Albion party was astonished to find the ground completely clear. The weather had an effect on the gate, though, and only 9,350 saw the game. The referee was delayed in the 'pea-souper', not arriving until half time, and in his absence one of the linesmen took the whistle.

Another stirring encounter ensued. Tommy Cook opened Albion's account after 30 minutes, but Miles Howell levelled the scores in the second half to send the game into extra time. There was no further scoring during the additional 30 minutes and the tie went to a second replay. The Corinthian secretary sportingly left the choice of venue to the Albion and the match was staged at Stamford Bridge. Some measure of the interest in the game can be judged by the attendance: a crowd of 43,760 turned out, a huge assembly for a midweek afternoon match on a neutral ground. The game never came up to the high standard of the first two meetings and a somewhat scrappy affair ended in favour of the Albion, with Tommy Cook touching in a rebound off a post for the only goal in the second half. In the evening both teams dined at the Café Royal in London's Regent Street, a splendid affair attended by officials of the Football Association and many famous Corinthians of the past.

West Ham United, at the Goldstone Ground, was Albion's reward in the second round. The Hammers won promotion to the First Division this season and were a tough proposition for Charlie Webb's team. Another big crowd created a wonderful atmosphere inside the ground. Once again thick fog covered the area throughout the day, but it lifted sufficiently to enable the game to start on schedule. Tommy Cook scored his third goal of the competition to give Albion a 33rd-minute lead, somewhat against the run of play, only for West Ham's sharpshooter Vic Watson to equalise with a quarter of an hour remaining. The replay at West Ham was played on a quagmire and consequently the defences dominated throughout. Albion performed superbly but bowed out to a Billy Moore goal two minutes before the interval. There was little to choose between the teams and it was no disgrace to lose to a side of West Ham's stature. Playing at right-back for the Hammers was Billy Henderson who was on Albion's staff in the last Southern League season. The Essex club went all the way in the competition, only to lose 2–0 to Bolton Wanderers in the first final to be staged at the new Wembley Stadium.

Throughout the season the defence was consistently brilliant and conceded a mere 34 League goals, still a record for Albion in the Football League to this day (equalled in 1984–85). Jack Jenkins made a big contribution, playing in all 42 matches; his thoughtful, constructive play gave a good deal of poise to the back line. Goalkeeper Billy Hayes and Andy Neil were also ever-present.

The Lambs had a reasonable season, finishing seventh in the Southern League, but they accumulated 96 goals in the process with crushing Goldstone wins over Reading (6–0), Watford (7–0), Yeovil and Petters United (8–0), Southend United (8–2) and Coventry City (9–0).

Thanks mainly to the two English Cup ties, a profit of £2,035 was achieved, enabling The Brighton and Hove Albion F.C., Limited, to pay its shareholders a dividend of 5 per cent for the first time since its formation in 1904.

SEASON 1923–24

After such a promising season, all the first-team players were retained and Webb introduced an additional three professionals to the club: full-back Redvers 'Reg' Smith from Midland League Scunthorpe United, centre-forward Fred Brown from Sheffield United, and Steve Wright, a wing-half from Norwich City.

As in the previous season, Brighton got off to an uninspiring start, winning only one of the first five matches, but followed up with seven wins in the next eight games which put them amongst the leaders. Portsmouth were among the early pace-setters, but on 6 October the Albion brought a temporary halt to the Hampshire club's progress, winning splendidly by three goals to one at Fratton Park. In the five seasons following the Great War the Football League fixtures were arranged so that clubs met one another home and away in consecutive matches, so Pompey arrived at Hove the following Saturday to return the compliment with interest by thumping Brighton 4–0. This was Albion's only home defeat of the season and there were some big wins registered at the Goldstone. Of the total of 68 League goals, 56 were scored at home, and a marginally better away record would have seen the club challenging for promotion. Portsmouth were champions with 59 points, four more than runners-up Plymouth Argyle with Albion back in fifth place.

It should be said that only one team was promoted from each of the two Third Division sections, which meant heartbreak for many a club, none more so than Plymouth Argyle. The Pilgrims were the outstanding team in the Southern Section throughout the 1920s, finishing runners-up in six successive seasons from 1922 to 1927. They eventually gained promotion in 1930 after finishing third and fourth in 1928 and 1929 respectively.

Once again the Albion defence was almost faultless, conceding just 37 goals, a total bettered only by Portsmouth and Plymouth. Goalkeeper Bill Hayes kept a clean sheet on 22 occasions (including seven in a row), while Tommy Cook was maturing into an excellent centre-forward; he led the goalscorers with 28, including five hat-tricks, followed by Jimmy Hopkins on 20. With Andy Neil pulling the strings, the attack developed into a far more cohesive unit than in recent years, but in March he was transferred to Arsenal for £3,000, by far the highest fee received by Albion up to that time. Average gates fell, but the 15,457 crowd that saw Albion thump Luton Town 4–0 on Boxing Day set a new Goldstone record in the League. (The actual figure was somewhat higher as a number of eager spectators broke down the Goldstone Lane fences to gain entry.)

In January, Albion were drawn to play Second Division Barnsley in the first round of the English Cup. The party travelled up to Sheffield on the preceding Thursday, followed on the Friday by several directors and the Mayor of Brighton, Councillor Hugh Milner Black. His Worship donated two handsome watercolours of the Brighton coat of arms – one framed in Albion's blue and white, the other in Barnsley red – to be presented to the player-of-the-match on each team.

The pitch was so heavy that the coin was tossed up four times before it fell flat, much to the amusement of the crowd! Albion were the more polished

Albion 1923–24

At rear: Billy Hayes, H. Baker.
Third row left to right: Jack Feebery, George Harvey, Jack Thompson, Fred Groves, Steve Wright, Billy McAllister.
Second row left to right: Alf Nelmes (trainer), Jack Jenkins, Edgar Saunders, Wally Little, John Bradford, Jimmy Jones, Fred Brown, Jack Woodhouse, Reg Smith, Dickie Meades (assistant trainer).
Front row left to right: Jack Nightingale, Andy Neil, Eddie Fuller, George Coomber (captain), Tommy Cook, Jimmy Hopkins, Tug Wilson.

SEASON 1923–24

Date	Comp.	Ven.	Opponents	Result	HT	Pos.	Scorers	Atten.	Brown F	Cook T	Coomber G	Feebery J	Fuller E	Groves F	Hayes W	Hopkins J	Jenkins J	Jones J	Little W	McAllister W	Neil A	Nightingale J	Smith R	Thompson J	Wilson E	Woodhouse J	Wright S
Aug 25	FL D3(S)	(a)	Northampton T.	L 0–3	0–1	18=		14,000	9		5				1	10	3		6	4		8	7		2	11	
29	FL D3(S)	(h)	Gillingham	D 2–2	2–1	19	Brown, Hopkins	5,000	9		5				1	10	3		6	4		8	7		2	11	
Sep 1	FL D3(S)	(h)	Northampton T.	W 2–0	0–0	13	Hopkins (pen), Nightingale	10,000	9		5				1	10	3		6	4		8	7		2	11	
5	FL D3(S)	(a)	Gillingham	D 1–1	1–1	12	Nightingale	6,000	9		5				1	10	3		6	4		8	7		2	11	
8	FL D3(S)	(a)	Bristol Rovers	L 0–2	0–1	17		14,000	9		5				1	10	3		6	4		8	7		2	11	
15	FL D3(S)	(h)	Bristol Rovers	W 2–1	2–1	14	Neil, Coomber	6,500	9		5				1	10	3		6	4	8		7		2	11	
22	FL D3(S)	(a)	Brentford	W 2–1	1–0	8	Little (pen), Brown	5,000	9		5				1	10	3		6	4	8		7		2	11	
29	FL D3(S)	(h)	Brentford	W 2–0	2–0	6	Hopkins, Neil	9,000	9		5				1	10	3		6	4	8		7		2	11	
Oct 6	FL D3(S)	(a)	Portsmouth	W 3–1	0–0	5	Hopkins 3	12,475	9		5				1	10	3		6	4	8		7		2	11	
13	FL D3(S)	(h)	Portsmouth	L 0–4	0–3	8		13,000	9		5				1	10	3		6	4	8		7		2	11	
20	FL D3(S)	(h)	Exeter City	W 1–0	1–0	7	Nightingale	7,000	9		5	3			1	10			6	4		8	7		2	11	
27	FL D3(S)	(a)	Exeter City	W 1–0	1–0	5	Little (pen)	5,000	9		5				1	10	3		6	4	8		7		2	11	
Nov 3	FL D3(S)	(h)	Aberdare Athletic	W 5–0	2–0	4	Cook 3, Hopkins, Nightingale	6,500	9		5				1	10	3		6	4	8		7		2	11	
10	FL D3(S)	(a)	Aberdare Athletic	L 1–3	0–1	4	Hopkins	7,000	8	9	5	3			1	10			6	4			7		2	11	
17	FL D3(S)	(a)	Swansea Town	L 0–1	0–1	5		12,000	9		5				1	10	3		6	4	8		7		2	11	
24	FL D3(S)	(h)	Swansea Town	W 4–1	1–0	4	Nightingale 2, Neil 2	11,500	9		5				1	10			6	4	8		7	3	2	11	
Dec 1	FL D3(S)	(a)	Millwall	D 0–0	0–0	4		14,000	9		5				1	10	3		6	4	8		7		2	11	
8	FL D3(S)	(h)	Millwall	D 2–2	1–1	4	Little (pen), Cook	9,000	9		5				1	10	3		6	4	8		7		2	11	
15	FL D3(S)	(a)	Bournem'th & B.A.	L 0–1	0–1	6		5,000	9		5				1	10	3		6	4	8		7		2	11	
22	FL D3(S)	(h)	Bournem'th & B.A.	W 5–0	1–0	5	Cook 4, Hopkins	6,500	9		5				1	10	3		6	4	8		7		2	11	
25	FL D3(S)	(a)	Luton Town	D 0–0	0–0	4		13,500	9		5			7	1	10	3		6	4	8				2	11	
26	FL D3(S)	(h)	Luton Town	W 4–0	3–0	4	Neil, Cook 2, Hopkins	15,457	9		5			7	1	10			6	4	8			3	2	11	
29	FL D3(S)	(a)	Reading	W 1–0	0–0	4	Cook	7,000	9		5			7	1	10			6	4	8			3	2	11	
Jan 5	FL D3(S)	(h)	Reading	W 4–0	2–0	3	Cook 3, Groves	8,750	9		5			7	1	10			6	4	8			3	2	11	
12	FAC R1	(a)	Barnsley	D 0–0	0–0	–		18,490	9		5				1	10	3		6	4	8		7		2	11	
16	FAC R1 Rep	(h)	Barnsley	W 1–0	0–0	–	Hopkins	22,068	9		5				1	10	3		6	4	8		7		2	11	
19	FL D3(S)	(a)	Queen's Park R.	L 0–1	0–1	3		5,000	9		5				1	10	3		6	4	8		7		2	11	
26	FL D3(S)	(h)	Queen's Park R.	W 3–0	1–0	3	Neil, Cook 2	7,000	9		5				1	10	3		6	4	8		7		2	11	
Feb 2	FAC R2	(h)	Everton	W 5–2	2–2	–	Cook 3, Little (pen), Neil	27,450	9		5				1	10	3		6	4	8		7		2	11	
9	FL D3(S)	(h)	Plymouth Argyle	W 4–1	3–0	–	Neil, Cook 2, Hopkins	6,350	9		5				1	10	3		6	4	8		7		2	11	
16	FL D3(S)	(a)	Newport County	D 0–0	0–0	3		10,000	9		5				1	10			6	4	8		7	3	2	11	
23	FAC R3	(a)	Manchester City	L 1–5	0–1	–	Little (pen)	24,734	9		5				1	10	3		6	4	8		7		2	11	
Mar 1	FL D3(S)	(a)	Merthyr Town	L 1–2	1–2	4	Cook	8,500	9		5			6	1	10	3			4	8		7		2	11	
8	FL D3(S)	(h)	Merthyr Town	D 0–0	0–0	5		7,500	9		5			6	1	10	3			4	8		7		2	11	
15	FL D3(S)	(h)	Charlton Athletic	W 3–0	1–0	4	Brown, Hopkins, Cook	6,250	8	9	5				1	10			6	4			7	3	2	11	
22	FL D3(S)	(a)	Charlton Athletic	W 2–0	2–0	4	Nightingale, Hopkins	3,500	8	9	5				1	10	3		6	4			7		2	11	
26	FL D3(S)	(h)	Newport County	W 4–0	3–0	4	Cook 3, Hopkins	3,250	8	9	5				1	10	3		6	4			7		2	11	
29	FL D3(S)	(h)	Norwich City	W 3–0	1–0	3	Hopkins 3	6,500	8	9	5				1	10	3		6	4			7		2	11	
Apr 5	FL D3(S)	(a)	Norwich City	L 0–1	0–1	3		10,000	8	9	5				1	10	3		6	4			7		2	11	
12	FL D3(S)	(h)	Swindon Town	D 1–1	0–0	3	Hopkins	5,000	8	9	5				1	10	3	11	6	4			7	2			
18	FL D3(S)	(h)	Southend United	W 2–0	0–0	3	Cook, Hopkins	10,500	8	9	5				1	10	3		6	4			7	2		11	
19	FL D3(S)	(h)	Swindon Town	L 0–4	0–3	4		5,500	8	9	5				1	10	3		6	4			7	2		11	
21	FL D3(S)	(a)	Southend United	L 0–1	0–1	5		9,000	8	9	5				1	10	3		6	4			7	2		11	
26	FL D3(S)	(h)	Watford	W 3–0	1–0	4	McAllister 2, Cook	5,000	8	9	5		4		1	10	3		6	8			7	2		11	
30	FL D3(S)	(a)	Plymouth Argyle	L 0–3	0–2	4		8,000		9	5		4		1	10	3		6	8			7	2		11	
May 3	FL D3(S)	(a)	Watford	D 0–0	0–0	5		4,000	9		5	3	4		1	10	2		6	8			7			11	
League appearances									19	33	42	3	5	4	42	42	35	1	35	41	29	38	12	34	41	2	4
League goals									3	25	1			1		19			3	2	7	7					

Football League Division 3 (South) 1923–24

		P	W	D	L	F	A	W	D	L	F	A	Pts
1.	Portsmouth	42	15	3	3	57	11	9	8	4	30	19	59
2.	Plymouth Argyle	42	13	6	2	46	15	10	3	8	24	19	55
3.	Millwall	42	17	3	1	45	11	5	7	9	19	27	54
4.	Swansea Town	42	18	2	1	39	10	4	6	11	21	38	52
5.	**ALBION**	42	16	4	1	56	12	5	5	11	12	25	51
6.	Swindon Town	42	14	5	2	38	11	3	8	10	20	33	47
7.	Luton Town	42	11	7	3	35	19	5	7	9	15	25	46
8.	Northampton Town	42	14	3	4	40	15	3	8	10	24	32	45
9.	Bristol Rovers	42	11	7	3	34	15	4	6	11	18	31	43
10.	Newport County	42	15	4	2	39	15	2	5	14	17	49	43
11.	Norwich City	42	13	5	3	45	18	3	15	15	41	40	40
12.	Aberdare Athletic	42	9	9	3	35	18	3	5	13	10	40	38
13.	Merthyr Town	42	11	8	2	33	19	0	8	13	12	46	38
14.	Charlton Athletic	42	8	7	6	26	20	3	8	10	12	25	37
15.	Gillingham	42	11	6	4	27	15	1	7	13	16	43	37
16.	Exeter City	42	14	4	3	33	17	1	4	16	4	35	37
17.	Brentford	42	9	8	4	33	21	5	0	16	21	50	36
18.	Reading	42	12	2	7	35	20	1	7	13	16	37	35
19.	Southend United	42	11	7	3	35	19	1	3	17	18	65	34
20.	Watford	42	8	8	5	35	18	1	7	13	10	36	33
21.	Bournemouth & B.A.	42	6	8	7	19	19	5	3	13	21	46	33
22.	Queen's Park R.	42	9	6	6	28	26	2	3	16	9	51	31

Spectators on the East Banking at the Manchester City cup-tie, 23 February 1924
Crowd scenes were very popular with photographers as those in view were always liable to buy the resulting postcard. The smiles on the faces of these fans presumably means the photograph was taken before the 5–1 Albion defeat. The crowd numbered 24,734.

side and most of the action took place in Barnsley's half of the pitch, but a series of amazing saves by their amateur goalkeeper, Harold Cope, earned the Colliers a goal-less draw and Cope the man-of-the-match award; Albion's award went to the industrious Jimmy Hopkins. Barnsley almost stole the match in the second half: Ernie Hine missed a penalty after Jack Thompson had handled in the box, and also hit the bar in the dying seconds.

A record midweek crowd was attracted to the Goldstone for the replay: 22,066 spectators (£1,747) packed into the ground knowing that victory would see Everton as the visitors to Hove in the second round. As expected, a dour, hard-tackling game resulted, with Barnsley adopting the rugged style for which they were renowned, and everything remained equal until Jimmy Hopkins broke the deadlock with only six minutes left to play.

The Albion were blessed with some wonderful Cup draws between the wars and the visit of Everton was one of the best. Though failing to win any trophies, the Everton team of the early 1920s was recognised as the most entertaining side in the League. To quote the *Athletic News* of the period, 'No team in the country has served up more delightful football.' The Liverpool newspapers were confident of an Everton win, and, with six internationals in the team, who could blame them? With men like goalkeeper Alf Harland (Ireland), centre-half Neil McBain (Scotland), right-winger Sam Chedgzoy (England), inside-right Bobby Irvine (Ireland), centre-forward Jack Cock (England) and outside-left Alec Troup (Scotland) on view, the attendance record was understandably exceeded for the fifth time in four seasons. An amazing 27,450 (£2,177) watched the game, and the magical attraction of the Cup can be gauged by the crowd at the Goldstone on the following Saturday when the highly promising League match with Plymouth Argyle was attended by just 6,350.

Everton made a good start with Jack Cock scoring in the seventh minute, but Albion equalised through Tommy Cook three minutes later. Wilf Chadwick put the First Division side back in front on 25 minutes, but Wally Little scored from the penalty spot to send the teams in level at 2–2. In the second half everything went Albion's way and they were soon ahead, Tommy Cook latching on to a loose ball and steering it into the net. Eighteen minutes after the break Tommy scored his third and, with the Everton defence on its heels, Andy Neil added a fifth late in the game to complete the rout. The football world was stunned and Albion were through to the last sixteen for the second time in their history. Some 23 years later Charlie Webb wrote of this side: 'They gave the best Cup exhibition of any Albion team under my management' — praise indeed!

In the third round Manchester City were the opponents at the Goldstone, yet another attractive tie. City also had a fair sprinkling of internationals in their team with the legendary Welshman Billy Meredith on the right wing. Meredith was just five months short of his 50th birthday and had played for Manchester United against the Albion in the English Cup fifteen years earlier at the tender age of 34 — a truly incredible character.

There was another big turn-out for the game, but fate was against the Albion and little went their way. In the third minute Jimmy Hopkins had what appeared to be a good goal disallowed for offside and that set the pattern. Territorially the game was even throughout, but uncharacteristic defensive errors gave the scoreline a somewhat false look. City led at half time with a goal from right-half Sammy Sharp. Soon after the interval Meredith scored with an inswinging corner which hit Billy Hayes on its way into the net. The Albion 'keeper was involved again when he brilliantly saved Horace Barnes's penalty only to see the rebound crashed past him. Tommy Browell added a fourth for City before Wally Little opened Albion's account from the penalty spot when Tommy Cook was up-ended in the area. There was no way back, however, and when Browell added a fifth the destruction was complete.

The outstanding form of Jack Jenkins at left-back came to the notice of the Welsh selectors, and in only his second season in senior football he won the first of his eight caps at the age of 31. The Welsh eleven was a formidable combination at this time, the foundation of the team being the excellent Cardiff City side. Skippered by their great half-back Fred Keenor, Wales won the Home Championship, beating Scotland 2–0 at Ninian Park, England 2–1 at Blackburn and Ireland 1–0 in Belfast. Jack played his part in all three games.

As a result of another excellent English Cup run, a record profit of £2,606 16s. 4d. was announced at the a.g.m. held at the Old Ship Hotel, which meant that the club was in the black to the enormous amount of £3,549. The board took great pleasure in recommending that the shareholders should receive a 5-per-cent dividend for the second year running.

SEASON 1924–25

Two old favourites left for pastures new during the summer: Billy Hayes and Jack Woodhouse. Jack, a veteran of some twelve years, retired to become a licensee; he, George Coomber and George Beech were the last playing links with the pre-war side. Hayes moved on to Southend United having missed just one game in his five years at the Goldstone, the home match with Grimsby Town on 29 September 1920. On his return he played in 175 consecutive League and Cup games, a record which stood until Eric Gill broke it in September 1956.

Hayes's replacement was Walter Cook from Plymouth Argyle, one of several new faces. Wing-half Reg Wilkinson was signed from Sunderland; he was to render magnificent service to the Albion over the next ten years, making nearly 400 first-team appearances before retiring. Other newcomers were Bob Dennison, a free-scoring inside-forward from Norwich City; Jack Smith from Swansea Town; Syd Bedford from Northampton Town; and last, but by no means least, right-back Dickie Downs from Everton. Dickie had appeared in two English Cup finals with Barnsley before the Great War, gaining a winner's medal in 1912, and won an England cap in 1920 at the age of 34. Unfortunately, an injury forced his retirement in December but not before he had turned in some excellent performances for the Albion.

Compared with the happenings of recent years this turned out to be a moderate season. A splendid 4–2 win at Brentford in the opening game, and a sequence of good results in late September and early October, flattered to deceive, and from second place after nine matches the team rapidly plunged into the lower half of the table. In the lead-up to Christmas, Albion failed to register a goal in six successive League games, but a revival over Christmas and the New Year brought an improvement which eventually saw the club into a respectable eighth place. Plymouth were again the bridesmaids, losing out to Swansea Town on the last day of the season.

SEASON 1924–25

Date	Comp.	Ven.	Opponents	Result	HT	Pos.	Scorers	Atten.	Bedford S	Beech G	Bradford J	Bunting J	Cook T	Cook W	Coomber G	Dennison R	Downs D	Fuller E	Hopkins J	Hoyland F	Jenkins J	Jennings S	Little W	McAllister W	McKenna H	Mulhall J	Nightingale J	Smith JW	Smith R	Wilkinson R	Wilson E
Aug 30	FL D3(S)	(a)	Brentford	W 4–2	3–0	7=	Dennison, Hopkins, J Smith 2	8,500					1		5	8	2		10				3		6	4		7	9		11
Sep 6	FL D3(S)	(h)	Millwall	D 3–3	2–1	11	Dennison 3	14,000					1		5	8	2		10				3		6	4		7	9		11
8	FL D3(S)	(a)	Norwich City	D 2–2	1–2	9	Hopkins 2	6,000					1		5	8	2		10				3		6	4		7	9		11
13	FL D3(S)	(a)	Luton Town	L 1–3	1–1	14=	Nightingale	8,000					1		5	8	2		10				3		6	4		7	9		11
20	FL D3(S)	(h)	Gillingham	W 2–0	1–0	10	T Cook, Hopkins	11,000				1	9		5	8	2		10				3		6	4		7			11
27	FL D3(S)	(a)	Bournem'th & B.A.	D 0–0	0–0	13		7,000				1	9		5	8	2		10				3		6	4		7			11
Oct 2	FL D3(S)	(a)	Aberdare Athletic	W 2–1	2–1	8	Hopkins, Dennison	6,000				1	9		5	8	2		10				3		6	4		7			11
4	FL D3(S)	(h)	Newport County	W 4–1	2–0	5	Dennison, T Cook 3	10,000				1	9		5	8	2		10				3		6	4		7			11
8	FL D3(S)	(h)	Merthyr Town	W 3–1	3–0	2	T Cook 3	6,500				1	9		5		8		10				3		6	4		7		2	11
11	FL D3(S)	(h)	Plymouth Argyle	L 2–3	1–1	4	Little, Dennison	14,794				1	9		5	8	2		10				3		6	4		7			11
18	FL D3(S)	(a)	Bristol City	L 1–2	1–0	6	Hopkins	10,000				1	9		5	8	2		10				3		6	4		7			11
25	FL D3(S)	(a)	Southend United	L 0–2	0–1	11		7,500					9	1	5		2		10				3		6	4		7	8		11
Nov 1	FL D3(S)	(h)	Watford	W 2–0	2–0	6	T Cook, Nightingale	4,000	5				9	1			2		10				3		6	8		7		4	11
8	FL D3(S)	(a)	Northampton T.	L 0–1	0–1	10		9,500	5				9	1			2		10				3		6	8		7		4	11
15	FL D3(S)	(h)	Charlton Athletic	D 0–0	0–0	9		8,000		3			9	1		8	2		10				5		6	4		7			11
22	FL D3(S)	(a)	Queen's Park R.	L 0–2	0–2	13		8,500		3			9	1		8	2		10				5		6	4		7			11
Dec 6	FL D3(S)	(a)	Reading	D 0–0	0–0	14		6,648					9	1			2	5	10				3		6	4		7			11
13	FL D3(S)	(h)	Swansea Town	D 0–0	0–0	13		6,000					9	1				5	10				3		6	4	8	7		2	11
20	FL D3(S)	(a)	Exeter City	L 0–2	0–1	14		6,000			1		8					5	10				3		6	4		7	9	2	11
25	FL D3(S)	(a)	Bristol Rovers	W 2–1	0–1	13	Dennison 2	19,000					9	1		8		5	10				3		6			7		2	4	11
26	FL D3(S)	(h)	Bristol Rovers	W 1–0	0–0	12	Little (pen)	15,732	4				9	1		8		5	10				3		6			7		2		11
27	FL D3(S)	(h)	Brentford	W 4–1	2–0	9	Dennison, T Cook 2, Hopkins	2,500	4				9	1		8		5	10				3		6			7		2		11
Jan 3	FL D3(S)	(a)	Millwall	D 1–1	0–1	8	T Cook	15,000					9	1		8		5	10				3		6			7		2	4	11
10	FAC R1	(a)	Watford	D 1–1	1–1	–	Hopkins	13,602	4				9	1		8		5	10				3		6			7		2		11
14	FAC R1 Rep	(a)	Watford	W 4–3*	1–1	–	Dennison 3, Hopkins	10,500	4				9	1		8		5	10				3		6			7		2		11
17	FL D3(S)	(h)	Luton Town	W 2–1	1–0	8	Hopkins, T Cook	7,246	5				9	1		8			10				3		6			7		2	4	11
24	FL D3(S)	(a)	Gillingham	L 0–2	0–1	9		7,000	5				9	1		8			10				3		6			7		2	4	11
31	FAC R2	(a)	Southampton	L 0–1	0–1	–		17,795	4				9	1		8			10				3		6		5	7		2		11
Feb 7	FL D3(S)	(a)	Newport County	D 0–0	0–0	10		12,000	4					1		8			10				3		6		5	7	9	2		11
14	FL D3(S)	(a)	Plymouth Argyle	L 0–1	0–0	11		10,000	3				9	1		8			10						6		5	7		2	4	11
21	FL D3(S)	(h)	Bristol City	W 1–0	0–0	10	Hopkins	7,570	5				9	1		8			10				3		6			7		2	4	11
28	FL D3(S)	(h)	Southend United	W 2–1	0–0	10	J Smith, Little (pen)	10,000						1		8			10	7	3		6				5		9	2	4	11
Mar 7	FL D3(S)	(a)	Watford	W 1–0	0–0	10	T Cook	5,000	4		10		9	1		8				7	3		6				5		2			11
11	FL D3(S)	(h)	Bournem'th & B.A.	L 0–1	0–0	10		2,712	4		10		9	1		8				7	3		6				5		2			11
14	FL D3(S)	(h)	Northampton T.	L 0–1	0–1	10		6,000	4		10		9	1							3	8	6				5	7		2		11
21	FL D3(S)	(a)	Charlton Athletic	L 0–1	0–1	10		5,000	4				9	1							3	8	6				5	7	10	2		11
25	FL D3(S)	(h)	Aberdare Athletic	W 4–1	1–1	9	Little (pen), Jennings 3	2,200					9	1				5			3	8	6					7	10	2	4	11
28	FL D3(S)	(h)	Queen's Park R.	W 5–0	1–0	9	Jennings, J Smith, Little (pen), T Cook 2	6,500					9	1				5			3	8	6					7	10	2	4	11
Apr 4	FL D3(S)	(a)	Merthyr Town	W 2–1	0–0	8	Nightingale, Jennings	3,000					9	1				5	10		3	8	6					7		2	4	11
10	FL D3(S)	(a)	Swindon Town	W 3–1	0–0	8	Hopkins, T Cook, Jennings	11,781					9	1				5	10		3	8	6					7		2	4	11
11	FL D3(S)	(h)	Reading	L 0–1	0–0	8		7,709					9	1				5	10		3	8	6					7		2	4	11
13	FL D3(S)	(a)	Swindon Town	L 0–3	0–2	8		10,000						1				5	10	7	3	8	6						9	2	4	11
18	FL D3(S)	(a)	Swansea Town	L 0–1	0–1	10		18,000	3					1				5	10			8	6					7	9	2	4	11
25	FL D3(S)	(h)	Exeter City	W 2–0	1–0	9	T Cook 2	5,700					9	1				5	10		3	8	6					7		2	4	11
May 2	FL D3(S)	(h)	Norwich City	W 3–1	2–1	8	Jennings 2, Hopkins	6,000						1				5	10		3	8	6					7	9	2	4	11
			League appearances						14	2	3	8	33	34	12	25	16	16	36	4	40	11	42	19	7	2	38	14	26	18	42
			League goals										18			10			11			8	5				3	4			

Note: Jan 14 – after extra time (90-minute score 3–3).

Football League Division 3 (South) 1924–25

		P	W	D	L	F	A	W	D	L	F	A	Pts
1.	Swansea Town	42	17	4	0	51	12	6	7	8	17	23	57
2.	Plymouth Argyle	42	17	3	1	55	12	6	7	8	22	26	56
3.	Bristol City	42	14	5	2	40	10	8	4	9	20	31	53
4.	Swindon Town	42	17	2	2	51	13	3	9	9	15	25	51
5.	Millwall	42	12	5	4	35	14	6	8	7	23	24	49
6.	Newport County	42	13	6	2	35	12	7	3	11	27	30	49
7.	Exeter City	42	13	4	4	37	19	6	5	10	22	29	47
8.	**ALBION**	42	14	3	4	43	17	5	5	11	16	28	46
9.	Northampton Town	42	12	3	6	34	18	8	3	10	17	26	46
10.	Southend United	42	14	1	6	34	18	5	4	12	17	43	43
11.	Watford	42	12	3	6	22	20	5	6	10	16	27	43
12.	Norwich City	42	10	8	3	39	18	4	5	12	14	33	41
13.	Gillingham	42	11	8	2	25	11	2	6	13	10	33	40
14.	Reading	42	9	6	6	28	15	4	5	12	9	23	38
15.	Charlton Athletic	42	12	6	3	31	13	1	6	14	15	35	38
16.	Luton Town	42	9	10	2	34	15	1	7	13	15	42	37
17.	Bristol Rovers	42	10	5	6	26	13	2	8	11	16	36	37
18.	Aberdare Athletic	42	13	4	4	40	21	1	5	15	14	46	37
19.	Queen's Park R.	42	10	6	5	28	19	4	2	15	14	44	36
20.	Bournem'th & B.A.	42	10	5	6	25	17	5	2	14	20	41	34
21.	Brentford	42	8	7	6	28	26	1	0	20	10	65	25
22.	Merthyr Town	42	8	3	10	24	27	0	2	19	11	50	21

George Coomber displaced a cartilage in his right knee during the match at Southend in October, causing him to retire. He did make a brief come-back in the reserves after an operation to remove the offending cartilage, but at the end of the season decided to call it a day. The Albion players were insured under the Workmen's Compensation Act at the time, but on receiving Coomber's claim the insurance company refused payment as he had played subsequent to recovery. George, through the club, took the company to court and eventually received his money. For many years after, he ran a building company in Portslade and carried out much work on behalf of the club at the Goldstone. His firm laid the drainage system for the North Stand and built the turnstiles and toilets behind the north-east terracing, all without payment. George was a truly great servant to the Albion.

In March, Charlie Webb secured the transfer of Sam Jennings from West Ham United. A proven goalscorer, Sam netted eight times in the remaining eleven games, including three in a 4–1 defeat of Aberdare Athletic at the Goldstone. The team averaged more than two goals a game at home, but failed to score in 12 of the 21 away fixtures.

This was very much a defensive period in the game's evolution with many teams exploiting the offside law to perfection. Up to and including this season, the law required that *three* opponents be between the foremost attacker and the goal,

which made it extremely difficult to penetrate a well-organised defence. The situation became so bad that the law was amended to *two* on the completion of this season. (Huddersfield Town conceded only 28 goals in winning the First Division championship this season compared with 60 in 1925–26 when they completed their hat-trick of titles under the new ruling.) Nevertheless, three Albion marksmen attained double figures: Tommy Cook with eighteen, Jimmy Hopkins with eleven (plus two in cup-ties) and Bob Dennison with thirteen in League and Cup.

Abion 1924–25

Back row left to right: Billy McAllister, Dickie Downs, John Bunting, Walter Cook, Jack Jenkins, George Beech.
Middle row left to right: Alf Nelmes (trainer), Sid Bedford, Fred Hoyland, Reg Smith, Wally Little, Reg Wilkinson, John Bradford, Eddie Fuller,
  Dickie Meades (assistant trainer).
Front row left to right: Ernie Ison, Jack Nightingale, Bob Dennison, Jack Smith, George Coomber (captain), Tommy Cook, Jimmy Hopkins,
  Tug Wilson.

On 6 June 1925, when the rest of the country was playing cricket, the Brighton Boys team entertained Sheffield Boys in the final of the English Schools Trophy at the Goldstone Ground. It was the first appearance of the Brighton, Hove and District Schools F.A. in the final, and an enthusiastic crowd of 10,831 turned out to cheer them on. There was no fairytale ending, however, as Sheffield won by a goal to nil.

Tommy Cook received the ultimate accolade when he was selected to lead England's attack against Wales at Swansea on 28 February, a tremendous achievement for a Third Division player that brought scouts from the leading clubs 'sniffing' around the Goldstone. Jack Jenkins missed the Swansea match but played against Scotland and Ireland in Wales's other two internationals of the season.

On the face of things the English Cup was something of a failure on Albion's part, yet the team performed well in the competition. Old friends Watford were beaten at the Goldstone after a 1–1 draw at Vicarage Road. The replay ended 4–3 after extra time in a cracking match in which the fortunes ebbed and flowed throughout. The second-round draw paired Albion with another old protagonist, Southampton, at The Dell. The Saints, now a Second Division side, won by the only goal of the match scored by full-back Tom Parker from a penalty in the fourth minute; the ball had bounced wickedly, hitting Syd Bedford on the arm, and, to the Albion's consternation, referee Butler awarded the spot kick. Mr Butler was the linesman who took over the whistle in the replay with the Corinthians two years earlier and had also officiated the Everton tie last season, so he was well known and respected by most of the Albion players.

Wally Little was awarded a testimonial this season for five years' outstanding service to the club, and he inevitably scored from the penalty spot in his benefit match, the 5–0 League win over Queen's Park Rangers in March. Wally was deadly from the spot and rarely missed; he was the team's 'penalty king' until his departure in 1929, converting 26 in League and Cup. Appropriately, along with Tug Wilson, he did not miss a game this term. The shareholders were also rewarded with a 5-percent dividend for the third consecutive year.

The Lambs were pulling in the crowds at Hove. They took third place in the Eastern Section of the Southern League and the average home attendance was an astonishing 3,406.

SEASON 1925–26

There were quite a number of comings and goings during the summer months. Bob Dennison moved on to Manchester City, Syd Bedford went to Luton Town, and Jack Thompson was forced out of the game through injury. The most significant signings were Paul Mooney, a tall, raw-boned Scot from the East Stirlingshire club; Fred Hawley, a very experienced and much-travelled centre-half from Bristol City; and full-back Jack Curran from Glenavon. Curran had been capped by Ireland on four occasions, and had represented both the Irish League and, during a spell with Pontypridd, the Welsh League. Mooney was to make over 300 appearances for the Albion and Curran almost 200.

It was some time before defences came to terms with the new offside law and consequently goals were scored in abundance throughout the Football League. Albion's opening match was at Newport, and the Somerton Park crowd had its appetite whetted with a sensational 4–3 victory for County with all the goals coming in the second half. The effect that the revised offside law had on events can best be illustrated by quoting some statistics.

❒ No fewer than five clubs scored over 100 goals. Prior to this season the century had been achieved on just five occasions since the inception of the Football League in 1888: by Sunderland in 1893, Small Heath in 1894, Liverpool in 1896, and West Bromwich Albion and Spurs in 1920.

SEASON 1925–26

Date	Comp.	Ven.	Opponents	Result	HT	Pos.	Scorers	Atten.	Cheetham J	Cook T	Cook W	Curran J	Edmonds A	Fuller E	Gilgun P	Goord G	Gough A	Hawley F	Hopkins J	Hoyland F	Ison E	Jenkins J	Jennings S	Kelly J	Little W	Mackay T	Mooney P	Neil A	Nightingale J	Smith R	Webb S	Wilkinson R	Wilson E
Aug 29	FL D3(S)	(a)	Newport County	L 3–4	0–0	12=	Jennings, Little (pen), Hopkins	11,232	1	9								5	10			3	8		6				7		2	4	11
Sep 5	FL D3(S)	(h)	Watford	W 3–1	0–1	14	T Cook 2, Jennings	12,110	1	9								5	10	7		3	8		6						2	4	11
12	FL D3(S)	(a)	Brentford	W 6–1	2–1	14	T Cook 2, Jennings 2, Hopkins, Nightingale	8,803	1	9								5	10			3	8		6				7		2	4	11
14	FL D3(S)	(a)	Norwich City	W 2–1	1–1	6	Hawley, T Cook	7,381	1	9	2							5	10			3	8		6				7			4	11
19	FL D3(S)	(h)	Crystal Palace	W 3–2	2–2	6	T Cook, Little 2 (2 pens)	11,738	1	9								5	10			3	8		6				7		2	4	11
26	FL D3(S)	(a)	Bristol City	L 0–1	0–1	10		10,531	1	9								5	10			3	8		6				7		2	4	11
Oct 3	FL D3(S)	(h)	Plymouth Argyle	L 1–2	1–0	16	Hopkins	15,417	1	9								5	10			3	8		6				7		2	4	11
10	FL D3(S)	(a)	Southend United	L 0–4	0–2	18		8,276	1							8		5	10			3	9		6				7		2	4	11
14	FL D3(S)	(h)	Millwall	W 3–1	3–1	13	Hopkins, T Cook, Jennings	6,499		9		1						5	10			3	8		6				7		2	4	11
17	FL D3(S)	(a)	Luton Town	D 3–3	2–2	12=	Goord, Jennings, Hopkins	7,522				1				9		5	10			3	8		6				7		2	4	11
24	FL D3(S)	(h)	Queen's Park R.	W 2–1	2–1	8	T Cook, Nightingale	8,816		9		1						5	10			3	8		6				7		2	4	11
28	FL D3(S)	(h)	Norwich City	D 1–1	1–1	4	Gilgun	5,171				1			9			5	10			3	8		6				7		2	4	11
31	FL D3(S)	(a)	Gillingham	L 1–3	0–3	10	Nightingale	6,814				1					9	5	10			3	8		6				7		2	4	11
Nov 7	FL D3(S)	(h)	Merthyr Town	W 3–1	1–0	6	Hawley, Gilgun 2	6,988				1			9			5	10			3	8		6				7		2	4	11
14	FL D3(S)	(a)	Exeter City	W 4–2	1–0	6	Hawley, Hopkins, Gough, Wilson	5,525				1					9	5	10			3	8		6				7		2	4	11
21	FL D3(S)	(h)	Reading	D 2–2	1–2	5	Gough, Nightingale	9,597				1					9	5	10			3	8		6				7		2	4	11
28	FAC R1	(h)	Watford	D 1–1	1–0	–	Little (pen)	11,503		9		1						5	10			3	8		6				7		2	4	11
Dec 2	FAC R1 Rep	(a)	Watford	L 0–2	0–0	–		5,601				1					9	5	10			3			6				7		2	4	11
5	FL D3(S)	(h)	Charlton Athletic	W 1–0	0–0	4	Hopkins	5,288			2	1					9	5	10			3	8		6				7			4	11
12	FL D3(S)	(a)	Bristol Rovers	L 0–4	0–2	4		5,008			2	1					9	5	10			3	8		6				7			4	11
19	FL D3(S)	(h)	Swindon Town	W 3–1	1–0	4	Jennings, Fuller, Little (pen)	6,098			2	1		9				5	10			3	8		6				7			4	11
25	FL D3(S)	(h)	Aberdare Athletic	W 6–2	3–1	4	Nightingale 2, Wilkinson, Fuller 3	9,285			2	1		9				5	10			3	8		6				7			4	11
26	FL D3(S)	(a)	Aberdare Athletic	D 2–2	2–2	4	Fuller, Jennings	8,075			2			9					10			3	8	5	6				7			4	11
Jan 2	FL D3(S)	(h)	Newport County	W 2–1	2–0	4	Hopkins, Wilson	7,398			2	1		9				5	10			3	8		6				7			4	11
16	FL D3(S)	(a)	Watford	D 3–3	1–3	4	Fuller, Little, Nightingale	3,647			2	1		9				5	10			3	8		6				7			4	11
23	FL D3(S)	(h)	Brentford	W 3–2	3–2	4	Jennings, Little, Nightingale	6,107			2	1		9				5	10			3	8		6				7		2	4	11
Feb 6	FL D3(S)	(h)	Bristol City	D 0–0	0–0	4		9,890			2	1		9				5	10			3	8		6				7			4	11
13	FL D3(S)	(a)	Plymouth Argyle	L 3–5	3–4	4	Jennings 2, Nightingale	13,049	8		2	1						5	10			3	8		6				7			4	11
24	FL D3(S)	(a)	Bournem'th & B.A.	W 3–0	1–0	4	Nightingale 3	4,181	8			1	3	4				5	10				9		6				7	2			11
27	FL D3(S)	(h)	Luton Town	W 2–0	1–0	4	Nightingale, Jennings	7,721	8			4						5	10			3	9		6				7	2	1		11
Mar 6	FL D3(S)	(a)	Queen's Park R.	W 2–0	1–0	4	Jennings 2	8,799	8			2	4					5	10			3	9		6				7	1			11
10	FL D3(S)	(a)	Crystal Palace	L 1–2	0–1	4	Nightingale	5,871	8			4						5	10			3	9		6				7	2	1		11
13	FL D3(S)	(h)	Gillingham	L 1–2	0–0	4	Neil	9,612			2	4						5	10			3	9		6			8	7	1		11
20	FL D3(S)	(a)	Merthyr Town	W 1–0	1–0	4	Jennings	3,823			2	6							10			3	9		4	5		8	7	1		11
22	FL D3(S)	(a)	Millwall	L 0–2	0–2	5		4,383			2							5	10				9		6	3	8	7	1		4	11
27	FL D3(S)	(h)	Exeter City	L 1–3	1–3	5	Wilson	5,913			2	6						5	10			3	9			5	8	7	1		4	11
Apr 2	FL D3(S)	(h)	Northampton T.	D 2–2	2–1	5	Jennings, Neil	10,450	8			2	6					5				3	9				10	7	1		4	11
3	FL D3(S)	(a)	Reading	D 0–0	0–0	5		17,132	8			2					9	5	10			3						6	7	1	4	11
6	FL D3(S)	(a)	Northampton T.	W 2–1	0–0	5	Gough 2	8,434			2						9	5	10			3	8					6	7	1	4	11
10	FL D3(S)	(h)	Bourn'm'th & B.A.	L 3–4	1–2	5	Jennings (pen), Hopkins, Own goal	6,403			2						9	5	10			3	8					6	7	1	4	11
17	FL D3(S)	(a)	Charlton Athletic	D 1–1	0–0	5	Jennings	4,792	8									5	10			3	9	1				6	7	2	4	11
21	FL D3(S)	(h)	Southend United	W 3–2	3–0	5	Hawley, Jennings 2	3,722										5	10	11	3	9	1	6			8	7	2		4	
24	FL D3(S)	(h)	Bristol Rovers	L 2–3	1–2	5	Little 2 (2 pens)	6,059										5	10	11	3	9		6			8	7	2	1	4	
May 1	FL D3(S)	(a)	Swindon Town	L 0–1	0–0	5		4,616											10		3	9		6			5	8	7	2	1	4	11
League appearances									8	9	18	31	5	8	3	1	8	37	39	1	2	38	41	2	36	1	7	12	41	16	22	36	40
League goals								OG – 1		8				6	3	1	4	4	9				20		8			2	14			1	3

□ Manchester City were relegated to the Second Division despite scoring 89 goals. Last season Huddersfield Town managed only 69 in winning the championship.

□ Albion's total of 84 goals was the best to date, beating the 73 scored in the Southern League in 1911–12.

□ In 1924–25 the average number of goals per game in the 42 matches involving the Albion was 2·48. This season the average was 3·74, representing an increase of 53 goals.

The goals were shared amongst thirteen players, Sam Jennings leading the way with 20 and Jack Nightingale on 14. Tommy Cook was injured in October and played in only nine League games, but the team still managed to score three or more goals on sixteen occasions, with big wins at Brentford (6–1) and at home to Aberdare Athletic on Christmas Day (6–2). The thrashing imposed on Brentford was marred by crowd problems among the home supporters and Griffin Park was subsequently closed for two weeks by the authorities.

The team struggled in the early matches and after eight games were as low as eighteenth in the section. Things slowly improved, and from late November a place in the top five was maintained. Plymouth were again pipped on the last day of the campaign, this time by Reading; the Pilgrims broke the Football League scoring record with 107 goals and were extremely unfortunate to miss out on promotion. Large crowds watched Albion's home and away draws with Reading and also the two matches with Plymouth, Argyle coming out on top in both encounters. In March, Andy Neil made a welcome return from Arsenal.

The English Cup took on a different format this year. Up to this point the majority of the Southern Section clubs were not called upon to enter the

Football League Division 3 (South) 1925–26

		P	W	D	L	F	A	W	D	L	F	A	Pts
1.	Reading	42	16	5	0	49	16	7	6	8	28	36	57
2.	Plymouth Argyle	42	16	2	3	71	33	8	6	7	36	34	56
3.	Millwall	42	14	6	1	52	12	7	5	9	21	27	53
4.	Bristol City	42	14	3	4	42	15	7	6	8	30	36	51
5.	**ALBION**	42	12	4	5	47	33	7	5	9	37	40	47
6.	Swindon Town	42	16	2	3	48	22	4	4	13	21	42	46
7.	Luton Town	42	16	4	1	60	25	2	3	16	20	50	43
8.	Bournemouth & B.A.	42	10	5	6	44	30	7	4	10	31	61	43
9.	Aberdare Athletic	42	11	6	4	50	24	6	2	13	24	42	42
10.	Gillingham	42	11	4	6	36	19	6	4	11	17	30	42
11.	Southend United	42	13	2	6	50	20	6	2	13	28	53	42
12.	Northampton Town	42	13	5	3	47	26	4	4	13	35	54	41
13.	Crystal Palace	42	16	1	4	50	21	2	4	15	25	58	41
14.	Merthyr Town	42	13	3	5	51	25	1	8	12	18	50	39
15.	Watford	42	12	5	4	47	26	3	4	14	26	63	39
16.	Norwich City	42	11	5	5	35	26	4	4	13	23	47	39
17.	Newport County	42	11	5	5	39	27	3	5	13	25	47	38
18.	Brentford	42	12	4	5	44	22	4	2	15	25	62	38
19.	Bristol Rovers	42	9	4	8	44	28	6	2	13	22	41	36
20.	Exeter City	42	13	2	6	54	25	2	3	16	18	45	35
21.	Charlton Athletic	42	9	7	5	32	23	2	6	13	16	45	35
22.	Queen's Park R.	42	5	7	9	23	32	1	2	18	14	52	21

Season-ticket rates for 1925–26:

	£	s.	d.
Admitting to ground only	1	1	0
Admitting to Enclosure and South Stand	1	15	0
ditto (Ladies)	1	7	6
Admitting to ground and reserved seats, West Stand	2	12	6
ditto (Ladies)	2	2	0

Albion 1925–26

Back row left to right: Albert Hunter, Reg Smith, Walter Cook, Stan Webb, Jack Curran, Sam Jennings.
Middle row left to right: Alf Nelmes (trainer), George Beech, Reg Wilkinson, Eddie Fuller, Wally Little, Paul Mooney, Fred Hawley, Eddie Edmonds, Dickie Meades (assistant trainer).
Front row left to right: Jack Nightingale, Fred Hoyland, Pat Gilgun, Tommy Cook, Jack Jenkins (captain), Tommy Mackay, Ernie Ison, Jimmy Hopkins, Tug Wilson.

From 1922 to 1928 the Albion competed each May for the Berks and Bucks Hospital Charity Cup with the host club, Reading. This season the match was cancelled because of the General Strike and the consequent lack of public transport.

tournament until they went into the hat with the First and Second Division sides for the first round proper. This caused unrest among the Northern Section clubs who had to take part in the qualifying competition. The Football Association therefore altered the rules so that all the Third Division clubs, with the exception of three who had performed well the previous season, came in at the first round proper, but the number of rounds was increased by two (with the qualifying rounds reduced from six to four), and the First and Second Division clubs now came in at the new third round which was the last-64 stage as it is today.

As in the previous season, Albion drew Watford in the first round, this time at the Goldstone, and the tie again went to a replay. Wally Little had given Albion a half-time lead from the penalty spot, but Fred Pagnam equalised for the Brewers with five minutes of the match remaining. Albion were without their two main spearheads for the replay at Vicarage Road, Sam Jennings and Tommy Cook picking up injuries in the first game, and the team lacked its usual punch and understanding. They played well under the circumstances but lost to two goals scored in the last ten minutes.

Three internationals: Jack Jenkins (Wales), Tommy Cook (England) and Jack Curran (Ireland).
These three were joined by a fourth this season: Jimmy Hopkins, who won an Irish cap in October against England. Jenkins brought his collection up to seven this term, while Cook had to be content with just the one cap from 1924–25; he remained the only Albion player to make the full England side for 55 years. Curran made his appearances for Ireland while with Glenavon and Pontypridd, but having three players capped while actually playing for the Albion was quite remarkable for a Third Division side.

The Supporters' Club published a handbook for this season, the first in a long line of such publications both before and after the Second World War. The price was 2d.

ALBION'S BIG STEP

In 1926, Brighton and Hove Albion F.C. became its own master at the Goldstone Ground. Since the amateurs of Hove returned to the old Hove Park in 1904, Alderman John Clark had sublet the ground to the Albion on a lease which was renewed from time to time during the intervening years, but the arrangement was a stumbling-block to any ambition to develop the facilities as all the stands, dressing-rooms and other structures remained the property of Clark.

On Wednesday, 29 September 1926, Albion chairman Charles Brown came to an agreement with Alderman Clark in which the club undertook to pay compensation for the outstanding five years of Clark's lease from the Stanford Estate, and also to purchase his interests on the property. The transaction meant that the Albion were now the owners of the ground on a 99-year lease from the Stanford Estate, with the option of obtaining the freehold during the next eight years on the payment of the balance of the agreed purchase price. It was an eminently satisfactory arrangement for all concerned.

Negotiations for such an agreement had been going on for some years without success, so this was truly a red-letter day in the Albion's history. The club was now free to carry out alterations as and when it liked, with one important proviso: no structure could be erected on the eastern side of the ground that would project above the boundary fence (Clark's home overlooked the Goldstone on that side), a restraint which has severely restricted the development of the ground, as any visitor can see. There was one other restriction that was not thought to be problematic: no structure could exceed a height of 50 feet above ground level.

Charles Brown hoped this great step would bring about the ultimate acquisition of the freehold and called on the Sussex public to rally round the club, adding that attendances at the Goldstone were not commensurate with the high standard of football being provided. An appeal was launched throughout the county in an attempt to interest the public and local businesses in the 5,600 remaining five-shilling shares of the original 16,000 that were offered. Within ten days more than 1,400 had been snapped up, and the list of new shareholders was published weekly in the local Press. The whole project became something of a crusade, and the Supporters' Club added its weight to the campaign, doubling its holding to 200 shares.

Brown revealed the improvement scheme that the board had provisionally drawn up: the covering of the North Terrace, the construction of a new West Stand stretching the whole length of the ground, and the covering of the popular east side. The ground would become an 'island' surrounded by roads. The cost of this work, together with the purchase of the freehold, was estimated at £20,000.

With the exception of the North Stand and the road scheme, most of the plans remained a dream when the austerity of the Depression hit the club's finances severely, but the intention of making the Goldstone Ground 'one of the best in southern England' showed that the board had the prosperity of the club at heart.

SEASON 1926–27

In recent years the Albion had gained a reputation as one of the best sides in the Southern Section, and this season was another in which the team excelled. A poor display in the first match at Brentford enabled the Bees to win comfortably 4–0, but this proved a minor setback as the team suffered only one more defeat before the turn of the year. Nine straight wins in October and November saw Albion at the top of the table; added to this record run was a 3–0 defeat of Athenian League amateurs Barnet at the Goldstone in the first round of the English Cup.

On 18 September, Albion ran riot at the Goldstone and thrashed Swindon Town 9–3, with goals from Jennings (4), Cook (2), Neil, Nightingale and the predictable penalty from Wally Little, an amazing scoreline which stood as the club's biggest League win until Newport County were beaten 9–1 in April 1951. Home form was tremendous, with another crushing victory recorded in January when Bristol Rovers were trounced 7–0. Albion averaged almost three goals a game at Hove, scoring 61 in the 21 League matches, and the fans derived a great deal of pleasure and entertainment throughout the campaign. Only Plymouth and Bournemouth won at the Goldstone and the gates increased accordingly, averaging 9,452, a new high.

Though scoring only eighteen goals in the away matches, results were good, with four successive wins being recorded in October, and the visit to Ashton Gate on 9 April saw Albion inflict Bristol City's only home defeat of the season. Despite this fine 2–0 victory, form in the latter stages of the season found promotion hopes diminishing, and just one point from the three Easter-holiday fixtures sealed Albion's fate. Only five of the final fifteen matches were won. Nevertheless, a creditable fourth place was achieved, nine points behind the runaway champions Bristol City.

Sam Jennings had a great season, notching 25 League goals, and Tommy Cook was back to his best with 21. A strange incident occurred just before Christmas when certain clandestine visitors arrived at Cook's Haywards Heath home by motor car. The affair was not given a great deal of publicity, but it was disclosed that the shady characters had 'threatened and tried to influence Cook'; the police were called in and the matter was reported to the Football Association. Tommy was awarded a benefit this season and was presented with £437 from the League match with Gillingham on 5 March. Jack Nightingale was also granted a testimonial, the League fixture against Charlton Athletic on 2 April.

SEASON 1926–27

Date	Comp.	Ven.	Opponents	Result	HT	Pos.	Scorers	Atten.	Cook T	Curran J	Edmonds A	Gough A	Hopkins J	Ison E	James D	Jenkins J	Jennings S	Little W	Mellon J	Mooney P	Neil A	Nightingale J	O'Rawe F	Oswald W	Smith R	Sykes A	Webb S	Wilkinson R	Williams R	Wilson E
Aug 28	FL D3(S)	(a)	Brentford	L 0–4	0–4	19=		12,057	10				11			3	9	6			8	7	5		2			4	1	
Sep 1	FL D3(S)	(h)	Crystal Palace	D 1–1	1–0	17	Jennings	7,209		3			10	11			9	6		5	8	7			2			4	1	
4	FL D3(S)	(h)	Millwall	W 3–1	1–0	11	Cook, Jennings, Little (pen)	10,406	9	3			10				8	6		5		7			2			4	1	11
11	FL D3(S)	(a)	Bristol Rovers	D 0–0	0–0	14		9,390	9	3			10				8	6		5		7			2			4	1	11
18	FL D3(S)	(h)	Swindon Town	W 9–3	5–3	11	Neil, Jennings 4, Cook 2, Little (pen), Nightingale	10,303	9	3							8	6		5	10	7			2			4	1	11
25	FL D3(S)	(a)	Exeter City	D 0–0	0–0	11		7,539	9	3							8	6		5	10	7			2			4	1	11
Oct 2	FL D3(S)	(h)	Merthyr Town	W 4–0	0–0	11	Jennings, Nightingale, Cook 2	9,944	9	3							8	6		5	10	7			2			4	1	11
6	FL D3(S)	(h)	Norwich City	W 3–2	1–0	7	Cook 2, Jennings	5,499	9	3							8	6	4	5	10	7			2				1	11
9	FL D3(S)	(a)	Southend United	W 1–0	0–0	5	Cook	7,369	9	3							8	6		5	10	7			2			4	1	11
16	FL D3(S)	(a)	Gillingham	W 3–2	2–0	4	Neil, Mooney, Cook	6,385	9	3							8	6		5	10	7			2			4	1	11
23	FL D3(S)	(h)	Watford	W 4–1	2–1	3	Neil 2, Jennings 2	10,043	9	3							8	6		5	10	7			2			4	1	11
28	FL D3(S)	(a)	Norwich City	W 2–0	0–0	2	Jennings, Cook	3,893	9	3							8	6		5	10	7			2			4	1	11
30	FL D3(S)	(a)	Coventry City	W 2–1	1–1	2	Little (pen), Wilson	7,144	9	3							8	6		5	10	7			2			4	1	11
Nov 6	FL D3(S)	(h)	Queen's Park R.	W 4–1	2–1	1	Hopkins, Own goal, Cook 2	10,875	9	3			10				8	6		5		7			2			4	1	11
20	FL D3(S)	(h)	Bristol City	W 3–0	1–0	1	Jennings 2, Little	9,958	9	3							8	6		5	10	7			2			4	1	11
27	FAC R1	(h)	Barnet	W 3–0	2–0	–	Jennings 2, Cook	13,874	9	3							8	6		5	10	7			2			4	1	11
Dec 4	FL D3(S)	(h)	Plymouth Argyle	L 1–2	1–0	1	Cook	8,954	9	3							8	6		5	10	7			2			4	1	11
11	FAC R2	(a)	Watford	W 1–0	1–0	–	Cook	15,789	9	3							8	6		5	10	7			2			4	1	11
18	FL D3(S)	(h)	Aberdare Athletic	W 3–1	2–1	2	Cook 2, Little (pen)	11,789	9	3							8	6		5	10	7			2			4	1	11
25	FL D3(S)	(h)	Northampton T.	W 2–0	2–0	2	Jennings, Nightingale	12,991	9	3							8	6		5	10	7			2			4	1	11
27	FL D3(S)	(a)	Northampton T.	D 0–0	0–0	2		12,782	9	3							8	6		5	10	7			2			4	1	11
Jan 1	FL D3(S)	(a)	Crystal Palace	L 0–2	0–1	3		14,346	9	3							8	6		5	10	7			2			4	1	11
8	FAC R3	(a)	Sheffield Wed.	L 0–2	0–1	–		24,696	9	3			10					6		5	8	7			2			4	1	11
15	FL D3(S)	(h)	Brentford	D 1–1	0–0	3	Own goal	9,517	9	3			10							5	8	7			2	6		4	1	11
22	FL D3(S)	(h)	Millwall	D 1–1	1–0	4		9,755	8	3			10				9			5		7			2	6		4	1	11
29	FL D3(S)	(h)	Bristol Rovers	W 7–0	2–0	3	Jennings 2, Hopkins 3, Mooney, Cook	7,472	8	3			10				9	6		5		7			2			4	1	11
Feb 5	FL D3(S)	(a)	Swindon Town	D 2–2	2–1	4	Jennings 2	15,317	8	3			10				9	6		5		7			2			4	1	11
12	FL D3(S)	(h)	Exeter City	W 5–2	1–0	3	Jennings 2, Wilson 2, Hopkins	10,245	8	3			10				9	6		5		7			2			4	1	11
19	FL D3(S)	(a)	Merthyr Town	L 0–1	0–1	3		3,172	8	3			10				9	6		5		7			2			4	1	11
26	FL D3(S)	(h)	Southend United	W 2–1	1–0	2	Cook (pen), Jennings	10,676	8	3			10				9	6		5		7			2			4	1	11
Mar 2	FL D3(S)	(a)	Bournem'th & B.A.	L 0–1	0–1	2		3,153	8	3			10				9	6		5		7			2			4	1	11
5	FL D3(S)	(h)	Gillingham	W 3–2	2–1	2	Hopkins, Wilson, Cook	9,447	8	3			10				9			5		7			2	6		4	1	11
12	FL D3(S)	(a)	Watford	L 0–1	0–1	3		6,598	9	3			10			2	8			5		7				6		4	1	11
19	FL D3(S)	(h)	Coventry City	D 1–1	0–1	3	Own goal	8,150	9	3			10			2	8			5		7				6		4	1	11
23	FL D3(S)	(a)	Charlton Athletic	L 0–1	0–0	3		1,721	9	3			10			2	8	6		5		7					1	4		11
26	FL D3(S)	(a)	Queen's Park R.	D 2–2	2–1	3	Own goal, Hopkins	8,401	9	3			10			2	8	6		5		7					1	4		11
31	FL D3(S)	(h)	Newport County	W 1–0	0–0	4	Cook	2,956	9	3			10			2	8	6		5		7					1	4		11
Apr 2	FL D3(S)	(h)	Charlton Athletic	W 3–2	2–1	2	Own goal, Cook, Hopkins	7,823	9	3			10			2	8	6		5		7						4	1	11
9	FL D3(S)	(a)	Bristol City	W 2–0	1–0	2	Nightingale, Jennings	21,905		3						2	9	6		5	10	7		8				4	1	11
15	FL D3(S)	(h)	Luton Town	D 1–1	0–0	2	Jennings	12,581	9	3						2	8	6		5	10	7						4	1	11
16	FL D3(S)	(a)	Bournem'th & B.A.	L 0–2	0–0	3		8,567	10	3						2	9	6		5	8	7						4	1	11
18	FL D3(S)	(a)	Luton Town	L 0–4	0–1	3		9,353	10	3		5				2	9	6			8	7						4	1	11
23	FL D3(S)	(a)	Plymouth Argyle	L 0–2	0–1	4		12,658		3	9					8	10	6		5	2	7						4	1	11
30	FL D3(S)	(h)	Newport County	W 1–0	0–0	4	Jennings	6,045		3				11		2	9	6		5	8	7						4	1	10
May 7	FL D3(S)	(a)	Aberdare Athletic	D 2–2	1–0	4	Jennings, Oswald	1,242		3				11		2	9	6		5		7		8				4	1	10
League appearances									36	41	1	1	21	4	2	13	41	37	1	40	26	28	1	11	30	5	3	41	39	40
League goals								OG – 5	21				8				25	5		2	4	4		1						4

Albion 1926–27

Inset: Reg Williams (captain).
Back row left to right: A. Knight, Eddie Fuller, Jack Jenkins, Paul Mooney.
Second row left to right: Bill Jones (assistant trainer), Dickie Meades (trainer), Albert Sykes, Reg Wilkinson, Reg Smith, Jimmy Mellon, Stan Webb, Bert Chamberlain, Frank O'Rawe, Eddie Edmonds, Sam Jennings, George Beech (assistant trainer).
Seated left to right: Jack Nightingale, Andy Neil, Wally Little, Tommy Cook, Willie Oswald, Tug Wilson, Jack Curran.
On ground: Jimmy Hopkins, Jack Cheetham, Tony Gough, Ernie Ison.

		P	W	D	L	F	A	W	D	L	F	A	Pts
	Football League Division 3 (South) 1926–27												
1.	Bristol City	42	19	1	1	71	24	8	7	6	33	30	62
2.	Plymouth Argyle	42	17	4	0	52	14	8	6	7	43	47	60
3.	Millwall	42	16	2	3	55	19	7	8	6	34	32	56
4.	**ALBION**	42	15	4	2	61	24	6	7	8	18	26	53
5.	Swindon Town	42	16	3	2	64	31	5	6	10	36	54	51
6.	Crystal Palace	42	12	6	3	57	33	6	3	12	27	48	45
7.	Bournemouth & B.A.	42	13	2	6	49	24	5	6	10	29	42	44
8.	Luton Town	42	12	9	0	48	19	3	5	13	20	47	44
9.	Newport County	42	15	4	2	40	20	4	2	15	17	51	44
10.	Bristol Rovers	42	12	4	5	46	28	4	5	12	32	52	41
11.	Brentford	42	10	9	2	46	20	3	5	13	24	41	40
12.	Exeter City	42	14	4	3	46	18	1	6	14	30	55	40
13.	Charlton Athletic	42	13	5	3	44	22	3	3	15	16	39	40
14.	Queen's Park R.	42	9	8	4	41	27	6	1	14	24	44	39
15.	Coventry City	42	11	4	6	44	33	4	3	14	27	53	37
16.	Norwich City	42	10	5	6	41	25	2	6	13	18	46	35
17.	Merthyr Town	42	11	5	5	42	25	2	4	15	21	55	35
18.	Northampton Town	42	13	4	4	36	23	2	1	18	23	64	35
19.	Southend United	42	12	3	6	44	25	2	3	16	20	52	34
20.	Gillingham	42	10	5	6	36	26	1	5	15	18	46	32
21.	Watford	42	9	6	6	36	27	3	2	16	21	60	32
22.	Aberdare Athletic	42	8	2	11	38	48	1	5	15	24	53	25

After the defeat of Barnet in the opening stage of the English Cup, Albion were drawn to play Watford for the third successive season. The two sides were sick of the sight of each other, but the fans loved it and 15,499 turned up at Vicarage Road. Albion's skipper, goalie Reg Williams, had played for Watford in the cup-ties of the previous two seasons before moving to Hove in the summer. Tommy Cook scored the only goal of the game in the fourth minute and Albion went through to meet First Division Sheffield Wednesday at Hillsborough in the third round.

Charlie Webb took the players up to Baslow in Derbyshire for special training in the week leading up to the game and the stay was enjoyed by all, although the hotel left something to be desired. On the day of the match Albion were confident of their chances. There were memories of the last time the sides had met each other in the Cup – in 1914 when the Owls trimmed Albion 3–0 – and a crowd of 24,696 filled the stadium. There was

to be no giant-killing act this time either, Wednesday running out 2–0 victors with a goal in each half. Webb was particularly impressed with the Yorkshire club's inside-right Dan Kirkwood; a year later he paid £500 for Kirkwood's transfer and the big Scot went on to star for the Albion for more than five years.

It was not only the League side that was thrilling the crowds at the Goldstone this term. The Lambs had another terrific campaign, winning the Southern League's Eastern Section, and they clinched the League championship in October 1927, defeating Western Section winners Torquay United 4–0. The reserves also took part in the enlarged London Combination, forerunner of the Football Combination, and finished ninth of 22 clubs in a very strong competition. Big crowds followed the progress of the Lambs at the Goldstone, where they were undefeated until mid December, and, on 27 December, 7,144 spectators watched the Southern League match with lowly Folkestone.

In October, Jack Jenkins received what was to be his eighth and final Welsh cap in the 3–0 defeat by Scotland in Glasgow. It was also during this season that the 'Penny-on-the-Ball' competition was introduced by the Supporters' Club: raffle tickets were sold on the ground at 1*d.* apiece and the winner of the draw was awarded the match-ball. The competition was a huge success and lasted until the late 1950s.

On 6 December 1926, with the ground development plans in mind, the capital of The Brighton and Hove Albion F.C., Limited, was increased by £6,000 with the creation of an additional 24,000 five-shilling shares. Added to the original 16,000 shares that were offered, the authorised capital of the company now amounted to £10,000, although by 1933 only 17,897 shares (£4,474 5*s.*) had been taken up.

SEASON 1927–28

In 1926–27 the Albion had been in brilliant form during the first half of the season with a marked falling-off in the New Year. This time it was the exact opposite, with the club occupying thirteenth position on Boxing Day but improving tremendously to finish fourth.

Andy Neil and Jack Nightingale left the club during the summer, and Norman Thomson (Clapton Orient) and Tommy Simpson (Dundee United) were enlisted as replacements. The team got off to a terrific start, beating Brentford 5–2 at the Goldstone and winning by a similar margin at Luton a week later, but they were unusually slack at home with three defeats coming before Christmas. There were some good performances, the 4–1 defeat of Plymouth Argyle in November being among the best. The Pilgrims were something of a bogey-team to Albion, having won the last seven meetings between the sides.

The leadership of the division changed hands frequently early on, with Queen's Park Rangers, Norwich City, Charlton Athletic and Northampton Town on top at various times. Then, in mid December, Millwall broke through the pack and could not be shifted for the rest of the season. They went on to win the title with a record 65 points, ten ahead of Northampton in second place, scoring 127 goals in the process. Brighton inflicted a rare defeat on them in September, winning 3–1 at the Goldstone, but the Dockers got their revenge in January by drubbing Albion 6–0 at The Den.

After the defeat at Bournemouth on Boxing Day the team went from strength to strength and lost only five of the remaining 23 matches. Tommy Cook was the main marksman with 26 in League and Cup, while Jimmy Hopkins registered 13. The skipper, goalkeeper Reg Williams, was ever-present along with right-half Reg Wilkinson and left-winger Tug Wilson, who enjoyed a testimonial this season, the goal-less draw with Gillingham in March. Jack Jenkins also had a benefit, the Merthyr Town game, and he celebrated by scoring two penalty goals within a two-minute spell in the second half.

With the quest to boost the club's finances still in full swing, everyone was hoping for a good F.A. Cup run, but it was not to be. Incredibly, Albion's name came out of the hat with that of Watford for a fourth successive season, and there was a certain amount of gloom at the Goldstone and no doubt at Vicarage Road as well. With 88 League clubs, plus the non-Leaguers, in the competition, the odds on this occurring have been calculated at over 9 million to 1!

Even the weather was against the Albion. On the day of the match thick fog enveloped southern England and it took the team and supporters four hours to complete the journey to Watford, but there was no way the game could take place. On the same afternoon a crowd of over 3,000 waited in vain for the arrival of Sheppey United for a Southern League fixture with the Lambs, but the Kent side were stranded *en route*, much to

SEASON 1927–28

Date	Comp.	Ven.	Opponents	Result	HT	Pos.	Scorers	Atten.	Chamberlain H	Cook T	Curran J	Hopkins J	James D	Jenkins J	Jennings S	Little W	Mace S	Mooney P	Oswald W	Readman J	Simpson T	Smith R	Sykes A	Thomson N	Wilkinson R	Williams R	Wilson E
Aug 27	FL D3(S)	(h)	Brentford	W 5–2	2–0	7=	Wilson, Jennings 3, Thomson	13,164			3	10			9	6		5			7	2		8	4	1	11
Sep 1	FL D3(S)	(a)	Newport County	L 1–3	0–1	9	Thomson	6,146			3	10			9	6		5			7	2		8	4	1	11
Sep 3	FL D3(S)	(a)	Luton Town	W 5–2	2–2	5	Cook, Simpson, Mooney 2, Hopkins	9,468		9	3	10			8		6	5			7	2			4	1	11
Sep 10	FL D3(S)	(h)	Millwall	W 3–1	2–0	5	Cook 3	12,984		9	3	10			8		6	5			7	2			4	1	11
Sep 14	FL D3(S)	(h)	Newport County	L 1–4	1–3	9	Cook	3,700		9	3	10			8		6	5			7	2			4	1	11
Sep 17	FL D3(S)	(a)	Crystal Palace	D 1–1	0–1	9	Hopkins	13,557		9	3	10			8		6	5			7	2			4	1	11
Sep 24	FL D3(S)	(h)	Exeter City	L 0–2	0–0	10		10,076		9	3	10			8		6	5			7	2			4	1	11
Oct 1	FL D3(S)	(h)	Torquay United	D 1–1	1–1	12	Wilson	2,156		9	3					6		5	10	8	7	2			4	1	11
Oct 8	FL D3(S)	(h)	Norwich City	W 1–0	0–0	11	Oswald	9,286			3				8	6		5	10	9	7	2			4	1	11
Oct 15	FL D3(S)	(a)	Northampton T.	L 0–1	0–0	12		13,214		10	3				8	6		5		9	7	2			4	1	11
Oct 22	FL D3(S)	(h)	Walsall	D 0–0	0–0	12		2,737		10	3				8	6		5		9	7	2			4	1	11
Oct 29	FL D3(S)	(a)	Gillingham	W 1–0	1–0	11	Jennings	4,681	3	9		10	7		8	6		5				2			4	1	11
Nov 5	FL D3(S)	(h)	Coventry City	W 3–0	1–0	10	Cook, Jennings, Wilson	7,153		9	3	10	7		8	6		5				2			4	1	11
Nov 12	FL D3(S)	(a)	Merthyr Town	L 2–4	1–4	10	James, Hopkins	3,111		9	3	10	7		8	6		5				2			4	1	11
Nov 19	FL D3(S)	(a)	Plymouth Argyle	W 4–1	2–0	8	Wilson, James, Cook, Smith	5,552		9	3	10	7		8	6		5				2			4	1	11
Nov 30	FAC R1	(a)	Watford	W 2–1	0–1	—	James, Cook	6,058		9	2	10	7	3	8	6		5							4	1	11
Dec 3	FL D3(S)	(h)	Charlton Athletic	D 2–2	2–1	8	Jennings, Cook	7,992		9	3	10	7	2	8	6		5							4	1	11
Dec 10	FAC R2	(a)	Northampton T.	L 0–1	0–1	—		16,092		9	3	10	7	2	8	6		5							4	1	11
Dec 17	FL D3(S)	(h)	Queen's Park R.	L 1–3	1–0	10	Cook	5,835		9	3	10	7	2	8	6		5							4	1	11
Dec 24	FL D3(S)	(a)	Swindon Town	L 3–4	1–1	12	Cook 2, Simpson	7,445		9	3	10	8	2		6		5			7				4	1	11
Dec 26	FL D3(S)	(a)	Bournem'th & B.A.	L 1–3	1–1	13	James	2,288		9	3	10	8	2		6		5			7				4	1	11
Dec 27	FL D3(S)	(h)	Bournem'th & B.A.	W 3–2	1–2	10	Simpson, Cook, Hopkins	6,381		9	3	10	8	2		6		5			7				4	1	11
Dec 31	FL D3(S)	(h)	Brentford	W 3–1	2–1	9	Hopkins, Cook, Simpson	6,061		9	3	10	8	2		6		5			7				4	1	11
Jan 7	FL D3(S)	(h)	Luton Town	W 3–1	1–0	7	Cook 2, Wilson	5,707		9	3	10	8	2		6		5			7				4	1	11
Jan 14	FL D3(S)	(a)	Watford	D 3–3	2–1	7	Cook 2, Hopkins	5,912		9	3	10	8	2		6		5			7				4	1	11
Jan 21	FL D3(S)	(a)	Millwall	L 0–6	0–3	9		20,696		9	3	10	8	2		6		5			7				4	1	11
Jan 28	FL D3(S)	(h)	Crystal Palace	W 4–2	2–1	7	James, Wilson 2, Cook	4,494		9	3	10	8	2				5			7		6		4	1	11
Feb 4	FL D3(S)	(a)	Exeter City	W 3–0	2–0	6	Cook, Hopkins 2	6,916		9	3	10	8	2				5			7		6		4	1	11
Feb 11	FL D3(S)	(h)	Torquay United	W 3–0	1–0	5	Cook, Hopkins, Jenkins (pen)	7,430		9	3	10	8	2				5			7		6		4	1	11
Feb 18	FL D3(S)	(a)	Norwich City	D 0–0	0–0	5		8,131		9	3	10	8	2				5			7		6		4	1	11
Feb 25	FL D3(S)	(a)	Northampton T.	W 2–1	0–0	5	Cook (pen), Simpson	12,631		9	3	10	8	2				5			7		6		4	1	11
Mar 3	FL D3(S)	(a)	Walsall	D 3–3	1–2	4	Mooney, Cook, James	6,170		9	3	10	8	2				5			7		6		4	1	11
Mar 10	FL D3(S)	(h)	Gillingham	D 0–0	0–0	4		7,860		9	3	10	8	2				5			7		6		4	1	11
Mar 17	FL D3(S)	(a)	Coventry City	D 2–2	0–2	5	Hopkins, Little (pen)	10,695			3	10		2	9	6		5			7			8	4	1	11
Mar 24	FL D3(S)	(h)	Merthyr Town	W 5–0	2–0	5	Thomson 2, Cook, Jenkins 2 (2 pens)	7,663		9	3	10		2		6		5			7			8	4	1	11
Mar 31	FL D3(S)	(a)	Plymouth Argyle	L 0–2	0–2	6		6,289		9	3	10	8	2		6		5			7				4	1	11
Apr 6	FL D3(S)	(h)	Southend United	W 1–0	1–0	5	Simpson	11,742		9	3	10		2				5			7		6	8	4	1	11
Apr 7	FL D3(S)	(h)	Watford	D 1–1	0–1	4	Hopkins	7,969		9	3	10		2				5			7		6	8	4	1	11
Apr 9	FL D3(S)	(a)	Southend United	W 1–0	1–0	4	Hopkins	10,407		9	3	10		2				5			7		6	8	4	1	11
Apr 14	FL D3(S)	(a)	Charlton Athletic	L 0–3	0–1	5		5,930		9	3	10		2				5			7		6	8	4	1	11
Apr 21	FL D3(S)	(h)	Bristol Rovers	W 5–0	2–0	4	Hopkins, Thomson, Cook 2, James	4,118	3	9		10	7	2		6		5						8	4	1	11
Apr 23	FL D3(S)	(a)	Bristol Rovers	L 0–1	0–0	4		4,155	3	9		10	7	2		6		5						8	4	1	11
Apr 28	FL D3(S)	(a)	Queen's Park R.	L 0–5	0–3	6		5,594	3	9		10	7	2		6		5						8	4	1	11
May 5	FL D3(S)	(h)	Swindon Town	W 4–2	3–1	4	Jennings 2, James 2	5,757			3	10	8	2	9	6		5			7				4	1	11
League appearances									4	37	37	38	26	28	17	31	5	37	3	6	30	15	11	11	42	42	42
League goals										25		13	8	3	8	1		3	1		6	1		5			7

Albion 1927–28

Back row left to right: Tommy Cook, Reg Smith, Stan Webb, Reg Williams (captain), Stan Mace, Eddie Edmonds, Albert Sykes.
Middle row left to right: Bill Jones (assistant trainer), George Beech (assistant trainer), Willie Oswald, Jack Jenkins, Bert Chamberlain, Reg Wilkinson, Paul Mooney, Wally Little, Jack Curran, Ernie Ison, Tommy Simpson, Dickie Meades (trainer).
Front row left to right: Tony Gough, Roy, Norman Thomson, Joe Readman, Sam Jennings, Andy Campbell, Dai James, Jimmy Hopkins, Tug Wilson.

Football League Division 3 (South) 1927–28												
		P	W	D	L	F	A	W	D	L	F	A	Pts
1.	Millwall	42	19	2	0	87	15	11	3	7	40	35	65
2.	Northampton Town	42	17	3	1	67	23	6	6	9	35	41	55
3.	Plymouth Argyle	42	17	2	2	60	19	6	5	10	25	35	53
4.	ALBION	42	14	4	3	51	24	5	6	10	30	45	48
5.	Crystal Palace	42	15	3	3	46	23	3	9	9	33	49	48
6.	Swindon Town	42	12	6	3	60	26	7	3	11	30	43	47
7.	Southend United	42	14	2	5	48	19	6	4	11	32	45	46
8.	Exeter City	42	11	6	4	49	27	6	6	9	21	33	46
9.	Newport County	42	12	5	4	52	38	6	4	11	29	46	45
10.	Queen's Park R.	42	8	5	8	37	35	9	4	8	35	36	43
11.	Charlton Athletic	42	12	5	4	34	27	3	8	10	26	43	43
12.	Brentford	42	12	4	5	49	30	4	4	13	27	44	40
13.	Luton Town	42	13	5	3	56	27	3	2	16	38	60	39
14.	Bournemouth & B.A.	42	12	6	3	44	24	1	6	14	28	55	38
15.	Watford	42	10	5	6	42	34	4	5	12	26	44	38
16.	Gillingham	42	10	3	8	33	26	3	8	10	29	55	37
17.	Norwich City	42	9	8	4	41	26	1	8	12	25	44	36
18.	Walsall	42	9	6	6	52	35	3	3	15	23	66	33
19.	Bristol Rovers	42	11	3	7	41	36	3	1	17	26	57	32
20.	Coventry City	42	5	8	8	40	36	6	1	14	27	60	31
21.	Merthyr Town	42	7	6	8	38	40	2	7	12	15	51	31
22.	Torquay United	42	4	10	7	27	36	4	4	13	26	67	30

the embarrassment of the Goldstone officials. The Watford tie was rearranged for the following Wednesday when a much-reduced crowd of 6,058 turned up for the afternoon kick-off. Watford went ahead in the first period, but within sixteen minutes of the restart Albion scored twice through Dai James and Tommy Cook and held out for the victory.

Ten days later Albion travelled to Northampton for the second-round tie, where they lost by a goal to nil. There was some consolation in the size of the attendance, 16,092 (£1,080), one of the largest at Northampton since the Great War. The Cobblers fully deserved their win having played most of the match with ten men after centre-forward Harry Loasby had broken a leg in a collision with Reg Williams early in the game.

Attendances were a huge disappointment to the directors this season with the average at the Goldstone being 7,630, almost 2,000 down on 1926–27. With the finances in a delicate state this was a serious blow and, from the distance of time, it is difficult to understand why there was such a drop in what was a relatively successful campaign.

In a golden era for the local schools' representative side, Brighton Boys reached the final of the English Schools Trophy competition for the second time in four seasons, and a magnificent crowd filled the Goldstone on 19 May to see them play North Staffordshire. The match ended 2–2, but the 13,815 spectators certainly got their money's-worth. In the second match, played at Stoke's Victoria Ground on 26 May, the North Staffs. side won another fine match 3–1. Two of the Brighton lads went on to win fame with the Albion: left-half Jack Dugnolle and centre-forward Eric Townsend, both from the Connaught Road School in Hove.

Record holder
Ernie 'Tug' Wilson played more games for Albion than any other player. Between 1922 and 1936, the little Yorkshireman played in 509 Football League matches. He received the first of two benefits this season.

SEASON 1928–29

After six years of modest achievement, in which Albion finished lower than fifth only once, this season was very disappointing with the team ending up in fifteenth place in the Southern Section. There were constant changes in attack which upset the rhythm of the whole side and, with Tommy Cook out for long periods through injury, only 58 goals were scored, 23 fewer than last term. This put extra pressure on the defence which became uncharacteristically leaky, conceding 76 goals, the highest total since joining the Football League.

The dynamic Sam Jennings had been snapped up by Nottingham Forest after scoring 63 goals in 115 League and Cup games for the Albion. The management brought Dan Kirkwood from Sheffield Wednesday as his replacement and he responded brilliantly, scoring 21 goals in League and Cup. Other newcomers, all forwards, were Hector Lawson (Aberdeen), Joe Pointon (Luton Town), Jimmy Townley (Spurs) and Bobby Farrell (Portsmouth). Dundee-born Farrell joined the Albion on his release after a trial at Fratton Park and became one of the most popular players in the club's history. He played until

his retirement during the Second World War, making well over 400 appearances, and the fans took him to their hearts.

Albion began with three successive 1–0 defeats, won only one of the opening eight fixtures, and by late September were propping up the rest of the division. Home form was generally good, although the 5–1 defeat by Crystal Palace in December was the biggest Goldstone reverse since Portsmouth won 5–0 in December 1905. On the credit side Bristol Rovers were beaten 4–0 in January. Rovers must have dreaded their visits to Hove around this time: in the six seasons 1926–32 they lost each time at the Goldstone, conceding 23 goals and scoring none.

There were some heavy defeats on the road – 5–1 at Torquay, 4–1 at Brentford and 4–1 at bottom-placed Exeter – and only

On 16 February the Goldstone Ground was honoured with its second amateur international match when 4,500 spectators witnessed a 1–1 draw between England and Wales.

SEASON 1928–29

Date	Comp.	Ven.	Opponents	Result	HT	Pos.	Scorers	Atten.	Carruthers J	Chamberlain H	Cook T	Curran J	Edmonds A	Farrell R	Gordon L	Hopkins J	Ison E	James D	Jenkins J	Kirkwood D	Lawson H	Little W	Mooney P	Osborne J	Pointon J	Smith R	Townley J	Turnbull W	Webb S	Wilkinson R	Williams J	Williams R	Wilson E
Aug 25	FL D3(S)	(a)	Luton Town	L 0–1	0–1	19=		10,256				3	9						2	8		6	5				10	7		4		1	11
27	FL D3(S)	(a)	Merthyr Town	L 0–1	0–1	22		4,674				3	9						2	8		6	5				10	7		4		1	11
Sep 1	FL D3(S)	(h)	Coventry City	L 0–1	0–1	22		9,571				3						9	2	8		6	5		7		10			4		1	11
5	FL D3(S)	(h)	Merthyr Town	W 2–1	2–0	20	Mooney, Little (pen)	6,352			9	3							2	8		6	5		7		10			4		1	11
8	FL D3(S)	(a)	Northampton T.	D 1–1	1–0	19	Cook	11,214			9	3							2	8		6	5		7		10			4		1	11
15	FL D3(S)	(h)	Charlton Athletic	L 2–3	1–3	22	Wilson, Pointon	9,191			9	3							2	8		6	5		7		10			4		1	11
22	FL D3(S)	(a)	Norwich City	L 1–3	1–3	22	Kirkwood	7,425			9	3				7			2	8		6	5				10			4		1	11
29	FL D3(S)	(h)	Swindon Town	D 2–2	2–2	21	Cook 2	9,338			9								2	8		6	5	3	7		10			4		1	11
Oct 6	FL D3(S)	(h)	Exeter City	W 3–2	2–1	19	Cook 2, Hopkins	8,456			9					7			2	8		6	5	3			10			4		1	11
13	FL D3(S)	(h)	Southend United	D 1–1	0–0	18	Kirkwood	7,756			9					7			2	8		6	5	3			10			4		1	11
20	FL D3(S)	(a)	Torquay United	L 1–5	0–3	21	Cook	5,137			9					7			2	8		6	5	3			10			4		1	11
27	FL D3(S)	(h)	Gillingham	W 3–1	2–0	18	Hopkins, Kirkwood, Cook	6,558			9			10	6	7			3	8			5			2				4		1	11
Nov 3	FL D3(S)	(a)	Plymouth Argyle	L 0–1	0–0	20		10,244			9			10	6	7			3	8			5			2				4		1	11
10	FL D3(S)	(h)	Fulham	W 2–0	1–0	18	Kirkwood, Wilkinson	10,351			9			10	6	7			3	8			5			2				4		1	11
17	FL D3(S)	(a)	Queen's Park R.	L 2–3	0–2	19	Jenkins (pen), Kirkwood	11,065			9			10	6	7			3	8			5			2				4		1	11
24	FAC R1	(a)	Brentford	L 1–4	0–3	–	Kirkwood	9,439			9			10	6	7			3	8			5			2				4		1	11
Dec 1	FL D3(S)	(a)	Watford	L 1–2	1–1	18	Cook	9,256			9			10	6	7			3	8						2				4	5	1	11
15	FL D3(S)	(a)	Newport County	W 2–1	0–0	16	Kirkwood, Hopkins	2,174			9			10	6	7			3	8						2				4	5	1	11
22	FL D3(S)	(h)	Crystal Palace	L 1–5	0–4	17	Kirkwood	3,899			9			10	6	7			3	8						2				4	5	1	11
25	FL D3(S)	(h)	Brentford	W 3–2	2–1	16	Kirkwood 2, Own goal	8,600			9			10	6	7			3	8			5			2				4		1	11
26	FL D3(S)	(a)	Brentford	L 1–5	1–2	17	Kirkwood	5,117			9			10	6	7			3	8			5			2				4		1	11
29	FL D3(S)	(h)	Luton Town	W 1–0	1–0	15	Kirkwood	6,824		3	9			10	6	7				8			5			2			1	4			11
Jan 5	FL D3(S)	(a)	Coventry City	L 0–3	0–2	17		14,232	9	3					6	7	11			8	10		5			2			1	4			
12	FL D3(S)	(h)	Bristol Rovers	W 4–0	2–0	15	Mooney, Pointon, Kirkwood 2	4,837		3					6	7				8	10		5		9	2			1	4			11
19	FL D3(S)	(h)	Northampton T.	L 0–3	0–2	16		7,197		3	10				6	7				8			5		9	2			1	4			11
26	FL D3(S)	(a)	Charlton Athletic	L 0–3	0–1	17		8,469		3	10				6	7				8			5		9	2			1	4			11
Feb 2	FL D3(S)	(h)	Norwich City	W 3–0	1–0	16	Kirkwood, Farrell, Wilson	2,093				3		6	10	7				8					9	2			1	4	5		11
9	FL D3(S)	(a)	Swindon Town	D 2–2	2–1	16	Farrell, Pointon	3,093				3		6	10	7				8					9	2			1	4	5		11
23	FL D3(S)	(h)	Southend United	W 2–1	2–0	16	Hopkins, Pointon	4,964				3		6	10	7				8					9	2			1	4	5		11
Mar 2	FL D3(S)	(h)	Torquay United	L 1–2	1–1	16	Wilkinson (pen)	5,589				3		6	10	7				8					9	2			1	4	5		11
9	FL D3(S)	(a)	Gillingham	D 1–1	1–1	15	Kirkwood	3,961				3		6	10	7				8					9	2			1	4	5		11
16	FL D3(S)	(h)	Plymouth Argyle	W 2–1	1–0	15	Wilson, Cook	7,487			10	3		6		7				8					9	2			1	4	5		11
23	FL D3(S)	(h)	Fulham	L 1–3	0–0	16	Farrell	17,183			10	3		6		7				8					9	2			1	4	5		11
29	FL D3(S)	(a)	Bournem'th & B.A.	W 1–0	1–0	15	Kirkwood	9,494				3		6	10	7				8					9	2			1	4	5		11
30	FL D3(S)	(h)	Queen's Park R.	W 2–1	1–0	15	Hopkins, Farrell	9,413				3		6	10	7				8					9	2			1	4			11
Apr 1	FL D3(S)	(a)	Bournem'th & B.A.	L 2–3	0–1	15	Kirkwood, Cook	6,247			9	3		6	10	7				8						2			1	4	5		11
6	FL D3(S)	(a)	Bristol Rovers	L 0–3	0–2	16		4,849				3		6	10	7				8					9	2			1	4	5		11
13	FL D3(S)	(h)	Watford	D 1–1	0–0	15	Wilson	5,682	9			3		6	10	7				8						2			1	4	5		11
17	FL D3(S)	(a)	Exeter City	L 1–4	1–1	15	Hopkins	2,352	9			3		6	10	7				8						2			1	4	5		11
20	FL D3(S)	(a)	Walsall	W 2–1	0–1	15	Pointon, Kirkwood	4,088				3		6	10	7				8					9	2			1	4			11
27	FL D3(S)	(h)	Newport County	W 2–1	1–0	15	Kirkwood, Hopkins	4,759				3		6	10	7				8					9	2			1	4			11
May 1	FL D3(S)	(h)	Walsall	W 2–1	1–0	15	Cook, Kirkwood	3,640			9	3		6	10	7				8						2			1	4			11
4	FL D3(S)	(a)	Crystal Palace	L 0–1	0–0	15		22,146				3		6	10	7				8					9	2			1	4			11
League appearances									3	5	24	25	8	32	18	27	6	2	20	40	7	19	29	3	16	31	9	5	22	39	16	20	36
League goals								OG – 1			11			4		7			1	20		1	2		5					2			4

Albion 1928–29

Back row left to right: Reg Williams (captain), Reg Smith, Bert Chamberlain, Paul Mooney, Eddie Edmonds, Stan Webb, Jack Jenkins, Bobby Farrell, Hector Lawson.

Middle row left to right: George Beech (assistant trainer), Bill Brown, Joe Pointon, F. Panther, Les Gordon, Dan Kirkwood, Wally Little, John Fox, Tommy Cook, Jimmy Townley, Jimmy Hopkins, Dickie Meades (trainer).

Front row left to right: Bill Jones (assistant trainer), Dan Resoli, Jack Osborne, Billy Turnbull, Jack Curran, Dai James, Ernie Ison, Tug Wilson.

		P	W	D	L	F	A	W	D	L	F	A	Pts
	Football League Division 3 (South) 1928–29												
1.	Charlton Athletic	42	14	5	2	51	22	9	3	9	35	38	54
2.	Crystal Palace	42	14	2	5	40	25	9	6	6	41	42	54
3.	Northampton Town	42	14	6	1	68	23	6	6	9	28	34	52
4.	Plymouth Argyle	42	14	6	1	51	13	6	6	9	32	38	52
5.	Fulham	42	14	3	4	60	31	7	7	7	41	40	52
6.	Queen's Park R.	42	13	7	1	50	22	6	7	8	32	39	52
7.	Luton Town	42	16	3	2	64	28	3	8	10	25	45	49
8.	Watford	42	15	3	3	55	31	4	7	10	24	43	48
9.	Bournemouth & B.A.	42	14	4	3	54	31	5	5	11	30	46	47
10.	Swindon Town	42	12	5	4	48	27	3	8	10	27	45	43
11.	Coventry City	42	9	6	6	35	23	5	8	8	27	34	42
12.	Southend United	42	10	7	4	44	27	5	4	12	36	48	41
13.	Brentford	42	11	4	6	34	21	3	6	12	22	39	38
14.	Walsall	42	11	7	3	47	25	2	5	14	26	54	38
15.	**ALBION**	42	14	2	5	39	28	2	4	15	19	48	38
16.	Newport County	42	8	6	7	37	28	5	3	13	32	58	35
17.	Norwich City	42	12	3	6	49	29	2	3	16	20	52	34
18.	Torquay United	42	10	3	8	46	36	4	3	14	20	48	34
19.	Bristol Rovers	42	9	6	6	39	28	4	1	16	21	51	33
20.	Merthyr Town	42	11	6	4	42	28	0	2	19	13	75	30
21.	Exeter City	42	7	6	8	49	40	2	5	14	18	48	29
22.	Gillingham	42	7	8	6	22	24	3	1	17	21	59	29

two away wins were recorded. The section was a very tight affair with no fewer than eight clubs heading the table during the campaign, but Charlton Athletic timed their run-in to perfection, going top for the first time at the end of April with only two matches remaining and winning the title on goal-average from Crystal Palace. Only seven points separated the top nine teams.

At the end of December, Stan Webb took over between the posts from Reg Williams. Stan was signed from Sussex County League side Hove as a teenager in 1924 whilst employed at the Portslade gas-works, but with the wealth of goalkeeping talent at the club he was loaned to Tunbridge Wells Rangers. He was to become one of a rare breed: a locally produced player who made over 200 appearances for the Albion.

Brentford ended any ambition of a run in the F.A. Cup, winning 4–1 at Griffin Park in the first round. The day of the second-round ties found Albion without a fixture and an attractive friendly was arranged with the Corinthians at the Goldstone. A full-strength Brighton side was soundly beaten 6–4 by the amateurs who fielded eight of the team that played in the three Cup games of 1923.

The average attendance at the Goldstone slumped even further to 6,871 and, with the absence of a rewarding cup-run, the financial position worsened dramatically. The match with Norwich City on Saturday, 2 February, was attended by just 2,093 spectators, the smallest crowd ever to witness a Football League game at the Goldstone.

SEASON 1929–30

Following the traumas of 1928–29, the playing staff was drastically changed before the start of the new season. Tommy Cook left to take a cricket-coaching post in South Africa, Reg Williams hung up his gloves and Jack Jenkins his boots, Wally Little was transferred to Clapton Orient, and Jimmy Hopkins moved into the Southern League with Aldershot. At a stroke the club had lost three internationals and two other senior professionals. Replacing them proved difficult, but Charlie Webb signed a number of new men: Harry Marsden (Nottingham Forest), Geordie Nicol (Manchester United), Harold Sly (Gillingham), Potter Smith (Cardiff City), Hugh Vallance (Queen's Park Rangers) and Dave Walker (Walsall).

Potter Smith possessed a wealth of experience and, at only 28 years old, was to render magnificent service, making well over 300 appearances for the Albion. Walker also went on to play in excess of 300 games for the club. Vallance had been a reserve at Q.P.R. and started out as such on his arrival at the Goldstone, but, after winning the centre-forward spot from Geordie Nicol after three matches, he turned out to be a goalscoring phenomenon, creating a club record with 30 goals in the League (which stood until 1977) and scoring another two in the Cup. Hugh grabbed four hat-tricks before Christmas and formed a superb twin spearhead with Dan Kirkwood who notched 31 goals in League and Cup.

Albion 1929–30
Back row left to right: Ernie Ison, Hugh Vallance, Geordie Nicol, Jimmy Newton, Stan Webb, Harold Sly, Les Gordon, Jack Williams.
Middle row left to right: Bill Jones (assistant trainer), Jack Curran, Harry Dutton, Reg Wilkinson, Paul Mooney, Jack Jenkins, Jimmy Townley, John Fox, Dan Kirkwood, Dickie Meades (trainer).
Front row left to right: Hudson, Harry Marsden, George Webb, Bobby Farrell, Reg Smith (captain), Dave Walker, Potter Smith, Ralph Jasper, Tug Wilson.

The reserve team's London Combination match with Luton Town at the Goldstone on 16 November was abandoned after 30 minutes because of the atrociously wet conditions with the Lambs 3–0 up. The reported attendance figure was nil!

SEASON 1929–30

Date	Comp.	Ven.	Opponents	Result	HT	Pos.	Scorers	Atten.	Curran J	Dutton H	Farrell R	Fuller E	Ison E	Kirkwood D	McDonald M	Marsden H	Mooney P	Newton J	Nicol G	Sly H	Smith R	Smith P	Thompson S	Vallance H	Walker D	Webb S	Wilkinson R	Williams J	Wilson E
Aug 31	FL D3(S)	(a)	Bristol Rovers	L 0–1	0–0	18=		10,229	3		7			8			5		9	6	2	10					1	4	11
Sep 4	FL D3(S)	(h)	Watford	W 2–1	2–1	10=	P Smith 2	6,368	3		7			8			5		9	6	2	10					1	4	11
7	FL D3(S)	(a)	Norwich City	W 6–3	3–1	6	Wilson, Kirkwood 4, Wilkinson (pen)	7,546	3		7			8					9	6	2	10				5	1	4	11
14	FL D3(S)	(h)	Swindon Town	W 3–0	2–0	6	Kirkwood, Farrell, Vallance	9,641	3		7			8						6	2	10		9		5	1	4	11
18	FL D3(S)	(a)	Watford	L 0–3	0–1	8		6,763	3		7			8						6	2	10		9		5	1	4	11
21	FL D3(S)	(a)	Plymouth Argyle	D 1–1	0–1	8	Vallance	11,530	3		7			8						6	2	10		9		5	1	4	11
25	FL D3(S)	(h)	Clapton Orient	W 1–0	1–0	7	Vallance	6,046	3		7			8						6	2	10		9		5	1	4	11
28	FL D3(S)	(h)	Merthyr Town	W 4–1	3–1	7	Vallance 3, P Smith	8,384	3		7			8						6	2	10		9		5	1	4	11
Oct 5	FL D3(S)	(a)	Torquay United	L 2–5	0–1	7	Kirkwood 2	3,934	3		7			8						6	2	10		9		5	1	4	11
12	FL D3(S)	(a)	Newport County	W 3–2	2–2	7	Kirkwood, Farrell, Williams	7,877	3		7			8						6	2	10		9		5	1	4	11
19	FL D3(S)	(a)	Crystal Palace	D 2–2	1–1	7	Kirkwood, Vallance	13,882	3	6	7			8							2	10		9		5	1	4	11
26	FL D3(S)	(h)	Gillingham	W 2–0	2–0	6	Vallance, Wilkinson (pen)	7,504	3	6	7			8		2						10		9		5	1	4	11
Nov 2	FL D3(S)	(a)	Northampton T.	W 3–1	1–0	5	Vallance 3	4,704	3	6	7					2						8		9	10	5	1	4	11
9	FL D3(S)	(h)	Exeter City	D 1–1	0–1	5	Kirkwood	9,186	3	6	7			8		2						10		9		5	1	4	11
16	FL D3(S)	(a)	Southend United	D 0–0	0–0	5		3,553	3	6	7			8		2						10		9		5	1	4	11
23	FL D3(S)	(h)	Luton Town	W 4–1	1–0	4	Vallance 3, Wilson	4,827	3	6	7			8		2						10		9		5	1	4	11
30	FAC R1	(h)	Peterboro' & F.U.	W 4–0	0–0	—	Farrell, Kirkwood 2, P Smith	10,519	3	6	7			8		2						10		9		5	1	4	11
Dec 7	FL D3(S)	(h)	Walsall	W 4–0	3–0	3	Vallance 2, Wilson, Kirkwood	6,360	3	6	7			8		2						10		9		5	1	4	11
14	FAC R2	(h)	Barry Town	W 4–1	4–0	—	P Smith 2, Kirkwood, Thompson	9,361	3	6				8		2						10	7	9		5	1	4	11
21	FL D3(S)	(h)	Fulham	W 5–0	2–0	3	Vallance 3, Farrell 2	4,206	3	6	7			8		2						10		9		5	1	4	11
25	FL D3(S)	(a)	Brentford	L 2–5	0–4	3	Vallance, Kirkwood	14,612	3	6	7			8		2						10		9		5	1	4	11
26	FL D3(S)	(h)	Brentford	W 2–0	0–0	3	P Smith, Vallance	19,193	3	6	7	4		8		2						10		9		5	1		11
28	FL D3(S)	(h)	Bristol Rovers	W 1–0	1–0	3	Dutton	6,494	3	6	7	4		8		2						10		9		5	1		11
Jan 4	FL D3(S)	(a)	Norwich City	L 0–2	0–0	4		9,654	3	6	7			8		2	5					10		9			1	4	11
11	FAC R3	(h)	Grimsby Town	D 1–1	0–0	—	Dutton	21,563	3	6	7			8		2						10		9		5	1	4	11
14	FAC R3 Rep	(a)	Grimsby Town	W 1–0	0–0	—	Vallance	15,000	3	6	7			8		2						10		9		5	1	4	11
18	FL D3(S)	(a)	Swindon Town	W 1–0	0–0	4	Walker	6,617	3	6	7		11			2	5					10		9	8		1	4	
25	FAC R4	(a)	Portsmouth	W 1–0	0–0	—	Vallance	37,522	3	6	7			8		2						10		9		5	1	4	11
Feb 1	FL D3(S)	(a)	Merthyr Town	W 8–2	5–1	3	Kirkwood 4, Wilson, Vallance 2, Farrell	1,984	3	6	7			8		2						10		9		5	1	4	11
8	FL D3(S)	(h)	Torquay United	W 5–0	2–0	3	P Smith, Vallance 2, Kirkwood 2	9,964	3	6	7			8		2						10		9		5	1	4	11
15	FAC R5	(a)	Newcastle United	L 0–3	0–2	—		56,469	3	6	7			8		2						10		9		5	1	4	11
22	FL D3(S)	(h)	Crystal Palace	L 1–2	1–2	3	Kirkwood (pen)	11,530	3	6	7			8		2						10		9		5	1	4	11
Mar 1	FL D3(S)	(a)	Gillingham	D 2–2	1–2	3	Nicol, Dutton	5,035	3	6	7			8		2			9			10				5	1	4	11
3	FL D3(S)	(h)	Newport County	D 2–2	1–2	3	Nicol 2	2,670	3	6	7			8		2	5		9			10					1	4	11
8	FL D3(S)	(h)	Northampton T.	W 2–1	2–1	3	Wilson, Kirkwood	10,622	3	6	7			8		2	5					10		9			1	4	11
12	FL D3(S)	(a)	Bournem'th & B.A.	D 1–1	0–1	3	Farrell	3,476	3	6	7			8		2	5					10		9			1	4	11
15	FL D3(S)	(a)	Exeter City	W 4–1	2–0	3	Wilson 2, P Smith, Kirkwood	5,863	3	6				8	7	2	5					10		9			1	4	11
22	FL D3(S)	(h)	Southend United	W 1–0	1–0	3	Vallance	10,223	3	6				8	7	2	5					10		9			1	4	11
27	FL D3(S)	(a)	Queen's Park R.	L 1–3	0–3	3	Kirkwood	6,578	3	6				8	7	2						10		9		5	1	4	11
29	FL D3(S)	(a)	Luton Town	L 0–1	0–1	3		7,199	3	6	7			8	10	2								9		5	1	4	11
Apr 2	FL D3(S)	(a)	Plymouth Argyle	L 0–1	0–1	3		9,791	3	6	7			8		2						9			10	5	1	4	11
5	FL D3(S)	(h)	Bournem'th & B.A.	W 4–3	1–0	3	Kirkwood 3, Vallance	6,753	3	6	7			8		2	5					9			10		1	4	11
12	FL D3(S)	(a)	Walsall	L 0–2	0–0	3		4,447	3	6	7			8		2	5					10		9			1	4	11
18	FL D3(S)	(h)	Coventry City	D 1–1	0–0	3	Vallance	9,100	3	6	7			8		2	5					10		9			1	4	11
19	FL D3(S)	(a)	Queen's Park R.	L 2–3	1–1	3	Dutton (pen), Kirkwood	6,411	3	6	7			8		2	5					10		9			1	4	11
22	FL D3(S)	(a)	Coventry City	W 2–0	1–0	3	Kirkwood, Vallance	14,618	3	6				8	7	2	5					10		9			1	4	11
26	FL D3(S)	(a)	Fulham	L 1–5	0–2	3	Kirkwood	10,511	3	6				8	7	2	5					10		9			1	4	11
May 3	FL D3(S)	(a)	Clapton Orient	L 1–4	1–2	5	Vallance	8,763	3	6	7			8		2	5					10		9		1		4	11
League appearances									42	32	37	2	1	40	6	29	16	1	5	10	13	37	0	37	6	41	40	26	41
League goals										3	6			28					3			6		30	1		2	1	7

The League campaign proved a great success with Albion scoring a club-record 87 goals. From December, third place was maintained behind the runaway leaders Plymouth Argyle and Brentford. It was obvious very early on that the title would be a two-horse race. Albion were never in serious contention, but there were some outstanding moments. Norwich City were beaten 6–3 at the Goldstone in September (Kirkwood 4), Fulham 5–0 in December (Vallance 3) and Torquay United 5–0 in February (Vallance 2, Kirkwood 2). There were only three home defeats, but this could not compare with Brentford's incredible home form: they never dropped a point at Griffin Park and chalked up some huge scores. A young centre-forward by the name of Billy Lane netted 33 times for the Bees some 20 years before he became popular on the South Coast as an Albion manager.

The match with Brentford on Boxing Day attracted the largest crowd ever to see a League match at the Goldstone up to that point, 19,193, but, in the crush to gain admittance, the south-east gate and several barriers were broken down, and damage was done to scaffolding on the nearby St Agnes's Church by supporters hoping to gain a view. Several people were taken to hospital, but the day ended on a bright note with Albion winning 2–0.

There was a big improvement in away results with five wins and sixteen points being gained. When Albion beat Northampton Town 3–1 in November (Vallance 3), it was the Cobblers' first home defeat for more than a year, and on 1 February Merthyr Town were crushed 8–2 (Kirkwood 4) which remains Albion's biggest away win in the League. The hapless Welsh club conceded 135 goals and finished bottom this season, to be voted out of the Football League in favour of the short-lived Thames club (based at the West Ham greyhound stadium). There were also some poor performances on the road, though, with five goals being conceded on three occasions, and the heavy defeats at Fulham and Clapton Orient in the final two games of the campaign saw Albion drop from third to fifth.

Plymouth Argyle at last won promotion to Division Two, winning the championship with 68 points, the highest total in the Southern Section until the number of clubs was increased to 24 in 1950. They set a terrific pace, finishing seven points ahead of Brentford and seventeen in front of third place.

Jack Curran did not miss a match this season. Reg Smith, Reg Wilkinson and Ernie Ison received benefits, but, with the club's finances in a poor state, they were unfortunate not to be granted a match and had to make do with the proceeds of a collection at one of the Eastertide games.

Football League Division 3 (South) 1929–30															
		P	W	D	L	F	A	W	D	L	F	A	Pts
1.	Plymouth Argyle	42	18	3	0	63	12	12	5	4	35	26	68
2.	Brentford	42	21	0	0	66	12	7	5	9	28	32	61
3.	Queen's Park R.	42	13	5	3	46	26	8	4	9	34	42	51
4.	Northampton Town	42	14	6	1	53	20	7	2	12	29	38	50
5.	**ALBION**	42	16	2	3	54	20	5	6	10	33	43	50
6.	Coventry City	42	14	3	4	54	25	5	6	10	34	48	47
7.	Fulham	42	12	6	3	54	33	6	5	10	33	50	47
8.	Norwich City	42	14	4	3	55	28	4	6	11	33	49	46
9.	Crystal Palace	42	14	5	2	56	26	3	7	11	25	48	46
10.	Bournemouth & B.A.	42	11	6	4	47	24	4	7	10	25	37	43
11.	Southend United	42	11	6	4	41	19	4	7	10	28	40	43
12.	Clapton Orient	42	10	8	3	38	21	4	5	12	17	41	41
13.	Luton Town	42	13	4	4	42	25	1	8	12	22	53	40
14.	Swindon Town	42	10	7	4	42	25	3	5	13	31	58	38
15.	Watford	42	10	4	7	37	30	5	4	12	23	43	38
16.	Exeter City	42	10	6	5	45	29	2	5	14	22	44	35
17.	Walsall	42	10	4	7	45	24	3	4	14	26	54	34
18.	Newport County	42	9	9	3	48	29	3	1	17	26	56	34
19.	Torquay United	42	9	6	6	50	38	1	5	15	14	56	31
20.	Bristol Rovers	42	11	3	7	45	31	0	5	16	22	62	30
21.	Gillingham	42	9	5	7	38	28	2	3	16	13	52	30
22.	Merthyr Town	42	5	6	10	39	49	1	3	17	21	86	21

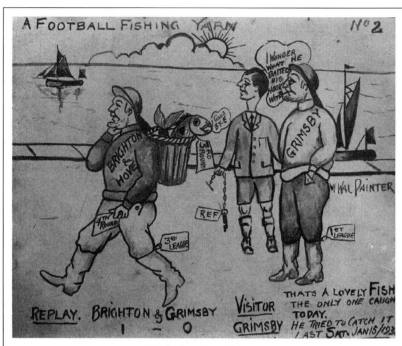

A fishy tale from Grimsby

This cartoon was published to commemorate Albion's first-ever victory over a First Division side on their own ground.

Fortunately, another great F.A. Cup run came to the aid of the financial situation. The first two rounds saw Albion account for Southern League opposition in the shape of Peterborough & Fletton United and Barry, both played at the Goldstone. Albion were now in with the big boys and were drawn at home to Grimsby Town. The Mariners had won promotion to the First Division the previous season but were struggling to avoid relegation this time round and missed the drop by a single point. Defensively they were no marvels, but in attack they possessed a lot of skill with Jackie Bestall (later capped by England) and Tim Coleman (subsequently of Arsenal fame) outstanding.

A huge crowd of 21,563 squeezed into the ground to witness a tough, goal-less first half. Nine minutes after the restart Jack Prior put the First Division side in front and, with left-half Harry Dutton injured and limping down the left wing, things did not look too bright for the Albion, but in a curious twist of fate Harry became the hero of the hour, fastening onto a long clearance and scoring the equaliser with only ten minutes remaining.

For the replay on Tuesday afternoon, Albion were unchanged, Dutton passing a late fitness test. Another dour game resulted with neither side giving an inch, and again there was no score at the interval. With the second half in its infancy, Grimsby's left-back, Hugh Jacobson, fisted out a goal-bound Kirkwood effort, but, much to the disappointment of the Brighton contingent, Reg Wilkinson missed the resultant penalty. With time running out it looked as though extra time would be required. Then, in the 87th minute, Tug Wilson beat his full-back and swung over a perfect cross from the left. Hughie Vallance rose amid a clutch of players and guided the ball wide of the goalkeeper with a glancing header. As was the custom after famous Cup victories, the team was met by an ecstatic crowd at Brighton Central Station when they arrived around midnight. Vallance and Kirkwood were carried shoulder-high to the station entrance, and it was some time before the crowd dispersed.

Albion knew their fourth-round opponents before travelling to Grimsby: Portsmouth at Fratton Park. Since joining the Third Division with the other Southern League clubs in 1920, Pompey had forced their way into the First Division and, after struggling initially to stay in the top flight, they now possessed a fine team. They had appeared at Wembley nine months earlier but lost 2–0 to Bolton Wanderers. The tie caught the imagination of the public and an estimated 8,000 supporters travelled from all over Sussex. It turned out to be a memorable match, watched by a crowd of 37,522, just short of the Fratton record at the time. As in the Grimsby tie, goals were at a premium, and it was not until the 62nd minute that Vallance scored what was to be the winner from a Tug Wilson pass. Despite an injury to Harry Marsden which virtually cut Albion down to ten men, the Pompey onslaught was magnificently repulsed, and at the final whistle there was much rejoicing. Renderings of 'Sussex by the Sea' could be heard all the way back to Fratton Station.

The fifth round saw Albion travel north to face the might of Newcastle United, supported by six train-loads of followers leaving Brighton at midnight. The Magpies were bottom of the First Division at the time, but, with their great traditions to spur them on, they were a very different proposition in the F.A. Cup. Inspired by an enormous 56,469 crowd, their all-Scottish forward line of Jimmy Boyd, Andy Cunningham, Hughie Gallacher, Tommy McDonald and Tommy Lang made short work of the Albion. The seasiders were never allowed to get into their stride and were well beaten by a Gallacher hat-trick to nil; the little man was in irresistible form and threatened to score every time he touched the ball. Albion never stopped trying and left the North-East with their reputation as a good footballing side intact.

The six Cup matches were attended by 147,434 spectators, and Albion's share of the £9,664 receipts gave a much-needed boost to the club's funds. It was over 50 years before Albion played in front of a crowd bigger than that at Newcastle in February 1930.

The reserves' 4–0 defeat at Folkestone on 30 April brought the curtain down on an era: it was the club's last match in the Southern League after 25 seasons of competition, both first-team and reserve, and three League championships. The Lambs would now concentrate on the all-reserve London Combination after playing in both competitions for the last four seasons, but the club remained as honorary members of the Southern League until after the Second World War.

SEASON 1930–31

During the summer the club finally made the Goldstone its own by purchasing the freehold of the ground from the Stanford Estate, a momentous occasion in Albion history and a very wise investment. The balance of £5,120 16s. was raised with a bank-loan on substantial securities.

A number of significant ground improvements were also made. At the end of the previous season Hove Corporation had threatened to remove the wooden West Stand, which was still listed as a temporary structure and considered dangerous by the municipal authorities. The club carried out work to improve the stand, and also built new terracing behind the north goal and at the top of the east side.

The improvements did not stop there. The board and the Supporters' Club got together to open a fund for the building of a roof over three-quarters of the north terracing. The cost of the project was estimated at £1,075, but was later increased to £1,325 when Hove Corporation insisted that the foundations should be deeper. Work commenced towards the end of the year and by January 1931 the first North Stand was ready. The Supporters' Club raised £625 towards the scheme, but on completion there was still £525 outstanding. On 29 April two matches were staged at the Goldstone in aid of the fund – Brighton Boys versus Southampton Boys, followed by an Old Albion XI versus the Press – and over £100 was raised. The rest of the sum owing was raised by supporters over the next few years.

Three new recruits joined the staff for this season: full-back Frank Brett (Northampton Town), goalkeeper Joe Duckworth

The Goldstone Ground area in the 1930s

The recently built North Stand can be seen in this bird's-eye view from above Hove Station, along with the extension of Newtown Road behind the West Stand to the Old Shoreham Road. These two features were the only major realisations of the ambitious ground-rebuilding programme launched in 1926. Newtown Road can also be seen winding its way through the remaining buildings of Goldstone Farm to St Agnes's Church.

SEASON 1930–31

Date	Comp.	Ven.	Opponents	Result	HT	Pos.	Scorers	Atten.	Brett F	Carruthers J	Curran J	Duckworth J	Dutton H	Farrell R	Ison E	Kirkwood D	McDonald M	Marsden H	Moffatt W	Mooney P	Nicol G	Sly H	Smith P	Thompson S	Vallance H	Walker D	Webb S	Wilkinson R	Wilson E
Aug 30	FL D3(S)	(a)	Gillingham	D 0–0	0–0	10=		5,325			3		6	7		8		2		5			10		9		1	4	11
Sep 3	FL D3(S)	(h)	Southend United	L 1–2	1–1	18=	Smith	7,035			3		6	7		8		2		5			10		9		1	4	11
6	FL D3(S)	(h)	Exeter City	W 3–2	2–1	8=	Vallance, Farrell, Walker	8,819	2		3			7		8			6	5					9	10	1	4	11
8	FL D3(S)	(a)	Luton Town	D 2–2	0–1	7=	Vallance, Kirkwood (pen)	7,849	2		3		6	7		8				5			10		9		1	4	11
13	FL D3(S)	(a)	Queen's Park R.	L 1–4	0–4	16	Wilson	6,582	3				6	7		8		2		5			10		9		1	4	11
17	FL D3(S)	(h)	Luton Town	W 2–0	1–0	12	Kirkwood 2 (1 pen)	4,088	3				6	7		8		2		5			10		9		1	4	11
20	FL D3(S)	(a)	Torquay United	L 1–3	0–2	14	Kirkwood	4,789	3				6	7		8		2		5			10		9		1	4	11
27	FL D3(S)	(h)	Northampton T.	D 1–1	1–1	16	Nicol	10,105	3				6	7		8		2		5	9		10				1	4	11
Oct 4	FL D3(S)	(a)	Brentford	L 2–3	1–3	18	Walker, Nicol	9,348	3				6	7		8		2		5	9					10	1	4	11
8	FL D3(S)	(h)	Swindon Town	W 1–0	1–0	12	Kirkwood	3,716	3				6	7	11	8		2		5	9		10				1	4	
11	FL D3(S)	(h)	Crystal Palace	D 1–1	1–0	12	Nicol	9,730	3				6	7	11	8		2		5	9		10				1	4	
18	FL D3(S)	(h)	Norwich City	W 1–0	0–0	13	Kirkwood	8,641	3				6	7	11	8		2		5	9		10				1	4	
25	FL D3(S)	(a)	Thames	D 0–0	0–0	11		1,621	3	6				7		8		2		5	9		10				1	4	11
Nov 1	FL D3(S)	(h)	Clapton Orient	W 3–1	1–1	6	Nicol, Smith, Kirkwood	3,699	3				6	7		8		2		5	9		10				1	4	11
8	FL D3(S)	(a)	Notts County	D 2–2	2–2	9	Farrell 2	12,362	3				6	7		8		2		5	9		10				1	4	11
15	FL D3(S)	(h)	Watford	W 1–0	1–0	8	Smith	6,034	3	4			6	7		8		2		5	9		10				1		11
22	FL D3(S)	(a)	Bournem'th & B.A.	W 2–1	1–0	6	Carruthers 2	4,934	3	9			6	7		8		2	4	5			10				1		11
Dec 6	FL D3(S)	(h)	Fulham	W 1–0	0–0	5	Carruthers	8,743	3	9			6	7		8		2	4	5			10				1		11
20	FL D3(S)	(a)	Walsall	D 0–0	0–0	5		5,821	3	9			6	7		8		2		5			10				1	4	11
25	FL D3(S)	(a)	Bristol Rovers	D 3–3	2–1	7	Farrell, Kirkwood, Wilson	13,229	3	9			6	7		8		2		5			10				1	4	11
26	FL D3(S)	(h)	Bristol Rovers	W 4–0	2–0	5	Carruthers 3, Wilson	9,133	3	9			6	7		8		2		5			10				1	4	11
27	FL D3(S)	(h)	Gillingham	W 5–0	4–0	4	Nicol 4, Kirkwood	7,610	3				6	7		8		2		5	9		10				1	4	11
Jan 3	FL D3(S)	(a)	Exeter City	D 2–2	0–2	4	Nicol 2	4,702	3				6	7		8		2		5	9		10				1	4	11
10	FAC R3	(a)	Leicester City	W 2–1	0–1	—	Smith 2	25,722	3				6	7		8		2		5	9		10				1	4	11
17	FL D3(S)	(h)	Queen's Park R.	D 1–1	0–1	4	Kirkwood	10,532	3				6	7		8		2		5	9		10				1	4	11
24	FAC R4	(h)	Watford	L 0–2	0–2	—		22,700	3	9			6	7		8		2		5			10				1	4	11
28	FL D3(S)	(h)	Torquay United	W 3–0	2–0	2	Kirkwood, Carruthers, Mooney	4,763	3	9				7		8		2	6	5			10				1	4	11
31	FL D3(S)	(a)	Northampton T.	L 1–2	1–1	5	Smith	5,868	3	9				7		8		2	4	5	6		10				1		11
Feb 7	FL D3(S)	(h)	Brentford	W 1–0	0–0	2	Smith	9,451	3	9			6	7		8		2		5			10				1	4	11
14	FL D3(S)	(h)	Crystal Palace	W 1–0	0–0	2	Wilson	16,986	3	9			6	7		8		2		5			10				1	4	11
21	FL D3(S)	(a)	Norwich City	D 2–2	1–1	2	Carruthers, McDonald	7,570	3	9			6	7			8	2		5			10				1	4	11
28	FL D3(S)	(h)	Thames	L 2–4	1–2	3	Mooney, Kirkwood	7,060	3	9			6	7		8		2		5			10				1	4	11
Mar 7	FL D3(S)	(a)	Clapton Orient	L 0–1	0–1	3		2,218	3			1	6	7		8		2		5	9		10					4	11
14	FL D3(S)	(a)	Notts County	L 1–3	0–1	6	Walker	14,037	3			1	6	7		8		2		5			10			9		4	11
21	FL D3(S)	(a)	Watford	L 0–5	0–3	7		5,441	3			1	6			8		2	4	5			10	7		9			11
28	FL D3(S)	(h)	Bournem'th & B.A.	W 3–1	1–0	7	Nicol 2, Walker	5,524	3			1	6	7		8		2		5	9					10		4	11
Apr 3	FL D3(S)	(h)	Newport County	W 5–0	2–0	5	Wilson, Walker 2, Nicol 2	5,992	3			1	6	7				2		5	9		10			8		4	11
4	FL D3(S)	(a)	Swindon Town	D 1–1	1–0	5	Walker	6,123	3			1	6	7				2		5	9		10			8		4	11
6	FL D3(S)	(a)	Newport County	L 0–2	0–0	6		3,346	3			1	6	7				2		5	9		10			8		4	11
11	FL D3(S)	(h)	Fulham	D 1–1	1–0	7	Nicol	6,701	3			1	6	7				2		5	9		10			8		4	11
18	FL D3(S)	(a)	Coventry City	D 0–0	0–0	7		5,329	3			1	6	7		8		2		5	9		10					4	11
22	FL D3(S)	(h)	Coventry City	W 2–0	2–0	6	Farrell, Nicol	3,809	3			1	6	7		8		2		5	9		10					4	11
25	FL D3(S)	(h)	Walsall	D 3–3	1–3	6	Nicol 2 (1 pen), Kirkwood	2,965	3			1	6	7		8		2		5	9		10					4	11
May 2	FL D3(S)	(a)	Southend United	W 2–0	1–0	4	Nicol, Wilson	5,758	3			1	6	7		8		2		5	9					10		4	11
League appearances									40	13	4	12	38	38	3	36	4	28	18	41	22	1	35	1	7	14	30	38	39
League goals										8				5		13	1			2	19		5		2	7			6

(Reading) and defender Billy Moffatt (Portsmouth). Brett and Duckworth had made more than 200 appearances for their respective clubs and were valuable additions to the playing strength. Brett was to skipper the side for some five years.

The team began the campaign in poor form, winning only two out of nine matches, and by October were eighteenth. At this point the club lost the considerable services of Hugh Vallance and Jack Curran, the pair departing following a serious misdemeanour, the details of which were not disclosed. Vallance tried his luck in the French League and Curran returned to Ireland with Linfield. Ironically, following the loss of the two stars, there was a remarkable reversal of fortune with Albion going sixteen games unbeaten, and by the end of January they were second, six points behind Notts County; this superb run included an excellent 2–2 draw at Meadow Lane. At this stage reserve half-back Jack Carruthers was given a run at centre-forward in the League team and he did a grand job, scoring eight goals in eleven outings up front, including a hat-trick in the 4–0 home win over Bristol Rovers on Boxing Day.

Four successive defeats in February and March ended any promotion ambitions, and the 4–2 home defeat by struggling Thames was the low point of the season; up to then Albion had conceded only eight goals at the Goldstone. Fifteen draws, more than any other team in the League, were far too many to make any real impression; even so, a useful fourth place was attained. The defensive record was amongst the best in the section with only two sides conceding fewer, but in attack just 68 goals were scored compared with champions Notts County (97), runners-up Crystal Palace (107) and Brentford in third place (90). Geordie Nicol and Dan Kirkwood were Albion's leading marksmen with nineteen and thirteen respectively.

As reward for the good showing in the previous season's F.A. Cup, the Albion were exempted until the third-round stage where they were drawn to face Leicester City at Filbert Street. City occupied a mid-table position in the First Division and had one of the best teams in the club's history. They were runners-up behind Sheffield Wednesday in 1928–29 and possessed a

Football League Division 3 (South) 1930–31

		P	W	D	L	F	A	W	D	L	F	A	Pts
1.	Notts County	42	16	4	1	58	13	8	7	6	39	33	59
2.	Crystal Palace	42	17	2	2	71	20	5	5	11	36	51	51
3.	Brentford	42	14	3	4	62	30	8	3	10	28	34	50
4.	ALBION	42	13	5	3	45	20	4	10	7	23	33	49
5.	Southend United	42	16	0	5	53	26	6	5	10	23	34	49
6.	Northampton Town	42	10	6	5	37	20	8	6	7	40	39	48
7.	Luton Town	42	15	3	3	61	17	4	5	12	15	34	46
8.	Queen's Park R.	42	15	0	6	57	23	5	3	13	25	52	43
9.	Fulham	42	15	3	3	49	21	3	4	14	28	54	43
10.	Bournemouth & B.A.	42	11	7	3	39	22	4	6	11	33	51	43
11.	Torquay United	42	13	3	5	56	26	4	4	13	24	58	43
12.	Swindon Town	42	15	5	1	68	29	3	1	17	21	65	42
13.	Exeter City	42	12	6	3	55	35	5	2	14	29	55	42
14.	Coventry City	42	11	4	6	55	28	5	5	11	20	37	41
15.	Bristol Rovers	42	12	3	6	49	36	4	5	12	26	56	40
16.	Gillingham	42	10	6	5	40	29	4	4	13	21	47	38
17.	Walsall	42	9	5	7	44	38	5	4	12	34	57	37
18.	Watford	42	9	4	8	41	29	5	3	13	31	46	35
19.	Clapton Orient	42	12	3	6	47	33	2	4	15	16	58	35
20.	Thames	42	12	5	4	34	20	1	3	17	20	73	34
21.	Newport County	42	10	5	6	45	31	1	1	19	24	80	28
22.	Norwich City	42	10	7	4	37	20	0	1	20	10	56	28

Albion 1930–31

Back row left to right: Geordie Nicol, Potter Smith, Harry Marsden, Stan Webb, Jack Williams, Joe Duckworth, Almeric Hall, Harry Dutton, Billy Moffatt.

Middle row left to right: Bill Jones (assistant trainer), Reg Wilkinson, Tom Charlton, Reg Smith, Frank Brett (captain), Paul Mooney, Eric Townsend, Tug Wilson, Dickie Meades (trainer).

Front row left to right: Jack Carruthers, Stan Thompson, Murdoch McDonald, Dan Kirkwood, Bobby Farrell, Harold Sly, Ernie Webster, Dave Walker, Ernie Ison.

> During excavation work being carried out for the building of the North Stand, an eighteenth-century cannonball was unearthed.

> The Supporters' Club staged a grand fête and motor-cycle gymkhana at the Goldstone in June 1931 in aid of the North Stand fund. There were numerous events – fancy dress parades, lovely-ankle contests, children's races, brass band and motor-bike displays, etc. – and a good turnout raised £24 7s. 11d. The fête was opened by one of the M.P.s for Brighton, Sir Cooper Rawson.

very strong set of forwards, with a trio of England players in outside-right Hughie Adcock, inside-right Ernie Hine (who had played for Barnsley against Albion in the cup-tie of 1923–24) and left-winger Len Barry. Centre-forward Arthur Chandler became a Leicester legend, scoring a total of 273 goals for the club in a long career.

Four special trains carried the Albion supporters north, but they were delayed by fog and did not arrive until ten minutes after the kick-off. By that time City were already in the lead, Arthur Lochhead scoring in the fifth minute. The pitch was rock-hard and devoid of grass, and it took the Albion some time to settle. At half time the score remained 1–0 in favour of the home team, but after the break Albion began to press and within ten minutes Potter Smith scored two 'beauties' to put them in front. City seemed to tire after these early setbacks and had no answer to Albion's inspired play. There was no further scoring and the team and its supporters returned to Brighton in high spirits.

The elation dimmed somewhat when the draw for the fourth round was made: Watford at Vicarage Road, the fifth time in seven years that the clubs were paired in the F.A. Cup. The Brewers were having a poor season and finished eighteenth in the Southern Section, but they enjoyed an excellent cup-run. They beat Albion 2–0, both goals coming in a two-minute spell midway through the second half, and qualified to meet Birmingham in the fifth round.

Paul Mooney and Stan Webb took benefits this term, and a collection was made on their behalf at the Notts County match on 14 March when the biggest attendance of the season, 14,037, saw Albion lose 3–1 to the champions-elect. It was a big setback to a player not to be awarded a match for his testimonial – a good turn-out could set him up when his playing days were over – but at the time the club just could not afford it. There had been large outlays on the ground improvements and purchase of the freehold, and in a very wet winter average attendances were down to just over 7,000, resulting in a loss on the season of £1,981 17s. 11d.

On 4 November, Noah Clark, an Albion director and one of the founders of the club, passed away. Noah was a man of Sussex, born in Billingshurst, and was in his 84th year. A wholesale fish merchant by profession, at one time he owned a fleet of boats operating out of Brighton. His passion for football dated from the early days of professionalism in the town and he was a shareholder of the Brighton United club. After United folded, Noah was one of the leading figures in the formation of the Albion, and in the intervening years gained a reputation throughout the game as a knowledgeable and generous man. His special love was the reserve team and he followed them on their travels for many years; indeed, he always referred to them as 'my lambs', which resulted in the nickname by which they were known until after the Second World War. The story goes that in the old days, when sheep still grazed on the Goldstone pitch during the week, the gambolling of the spring lambs prompted a friend to telephone Clark with the message that his favourite reserves were chasing around the pitch! At a dinner in 1925 celebrating the 21st anniversary of both the limited company and of Clark's directorate, Albion chairman Charles Brown referred to Noah as 'the father of the club' and presented him with an illuminated address. When Albion carried off the Southern League Championship Shield and the F.A. Charity Shield in 1910, Clark had plaster replicas of the two trophies built into the gables of his new house, 'Wincombe' in Dyke Road (now no.238), where they can be seen to this day, splendidly highlighted in blue and white.

SEASON 1931–32

During the summer break Charlie Webb employed some of the players to widen and heighten the popular east side of the Goldstone; for many years after, the northern end of this part of the ground was known as the 'Spion Kop', while the central section, fenced off with a higher admission charge, was the 'Chicken Run'. The Supporters' Club also did its bit, opening a fund to build a players' and supporters' recreation hut in the north-west corner of the ground, and by the end of October the wooden structure was opened. A neat and colourful garden situated in front of it was said to have been groundsman Dick Whittington's pride and joy; one wonders what would be its fate in modern times. The building served in various capacities for many years and was eventually demolished in 1984.

The summer also saw the passing of 70-year-old John Jackson, the man who had founded the club in 1901 and was its first manager. He had been landlord of the Running Horse in King Street, Brighton, for many years.

Jack Eyres (Walsall), Sam Brown (Bournemouth & B.A.) and Ernie King (West Bromwich Albion) joined Albion for this campaign, and in November Arthur Attwood arrived from Bristol Rovers to lead the attack. Attwood had played for Rovers at Hove in September and created a great impression. He had scored three goals at Eastville prior to coming to the Goldstone and went on to net 29 League and Cup goals for the Albion in only 30 matches. He made a terrific start: after drawing a blank in his first game for the club, Arthur then notched an amazing fourteen goals in the next eight games.

Football League Division 3 (South) 1931–32

		P	W	D	L	F	A	W	D	L	F	A	Pts
1.	Fulham	42	15	3	3	72	27	9	6	6	39	35	57
2.	Reading	42	19	1	1	65	21	4	8	9	32	46	55
3.	Southend United	42	12	5	4	41	18	9	6	6	36	35	53
4.	Crystal Palace	42	14	7	0	48	12	6	4	11	26	51	51
5.	Brentford	42	11	6	4	40	22	8	4	9	28	30	48
6.	Luton Town	42	16	1	4	62	25	4	6	11	33	45	47
7.	Exeter City	42	16	3	2	53	16	4	4	13	24	46	47
8.	**ALBION**	42	12	4	5	42	21	5	8	8	31	37	46
9.	Cardiff City	42	14	2	5	62	29	5	6	10	25	44	46
10.	Norwich City	42	12	7	2	51	22	5	5	11	25	45	46
11.	Watford	42	14	4	3	49	27	5	4	12	32	52	46
12.	Coventry City	42	17	2	2	74	28	1	6	14	34	69	44
13.	Queen's Park R.	42	11	6	4	50	30	4	6	11	29	43	42
14.	Northampton Town	42	12	3	6	48	26	4	4	13	21	43	39
15.	Bournemouth & B.A.	42	8	8	5	42	32	5	4	12	28	46	38
16.	Clapton Orient	42	7	8	6	41	35	5	3	13	36	55	35
17.	Swindon Town	42	12	2	7	47	31	2	4	15	23	53	34
18.	Bristol Rovers	42	11	6	4	46	30	2	2	17	19	62	34
19.	Torquay United	42	9	6	6	49	39	3	3	15	23	67	33
20.	Mansfield Town	42	11	5	5	54	45	0	5	16	21	63	32
21.	Gillingham	42	8	6	7	26	26	2	2	17	14	56	28
22.	Thames	42	6	7	8	35	35	1	2	18	18	74	23

SEASON 1931–32

Date	Comp.	Ven.	Opponents	Result	HT	Pos.	Scorers	Atten.	Ansell G	Attwood A	Brett F	Brown S	Duckworth J	Dutton H	Eyres J	Farrell R	King E	Kirkwood D	Marsden H	Moffatt W	Mooney P	Nicol G	Sly H	Smith P	Thompson S	Townsend E	Walker D	Watson H	Webb S	Wilkinson R	Wilson E
Aug 29	FL D3(S)	(h)	Norwich City	W 2–1	1–1	5=	Smith, Kirkwood	10,195		3		1	6					8	2		5	9		10	7					4	11
31	FL D3(S)	(a)	Cardiff City	D 1–1	0–1	3	Thompson	10,435		3		1	6					8	2	4		9		10	7					5	11
Sep 5	FL D3(S)	(a)	Swindon Town	W 2–1	0–1	2	Smith, Nicol	5,643		3		1	6					8	2	4		9		10	7					5	11
9	FL D3(S)	(h)	Crystal Palace	L 0–3	0–1	6=		11,175		3		1	6					8	2	4		9		10	7					5	11
12	FL D3(S)	(h)	Clapton Orient	D 1–1	1–0	7	Townsend	5,988		3		1	6			7		8	2		5			10		9				4	11
16	FL D3(S)	(a)	Crystal Palace	L 0–2	0–1	11		12,071		3		1				7		8	2		5			10		9	6			4	11
19	FL D3(S)	(a)	Torquay United	D 1–1	0–0	10	Farrell	4,590		3		1				7		8	2		5			10		9	6			4	11
26	FL D3(S)	(h)	Bristol Rovers	W 2–0	0–0	7	Wilson, Kirkwood	8,197		3		1				7		8	2		5	9		10		6				4	11
30	FL D3(S)	(a)	Exeter City	L 1–3	1–2	8	Walker	3,886		3		1	6			7		8	2		5			10		9				4	11
Oct 3	FL D3(S)	(a)	Queen's Park R.	D 1–1	1–1	11	Kirkwood	13,813			3	1	6			7		8	2		5			10		9				4	11
10	FL D3(S)	(h)	Bournem'th & B.A.	W 4–1	1–0	9	Wilson, Kirkwood 2, Farrell	9,134		3		1	6			7		8	2		5			10		9				4	11
17	FL D3(S)	(h)	Northampton T.	W 1–0	0–0	7	Walker	5,714		3		1	6			7		8	2		5			10		9				4	11
24	FL D3(S)	(h)	Reading	W 2–0	2–0	5	Smith, Walker	9,732		3		1	6			7		8	2		5			10		9				4	11
31	FL D3(S)	(a)	Southend United	L 0–2	0–1	7		10,488		3		1	6			7		8	2		5			10		9				4	11
Nov 7	FL D3(S)	(h)	Fulham	L 2–3	2–2	10	Smith, Kirkwood	10,370	9	3		1	6			7		8	2		5			10						4	11
14	FL D3(S)	(a)	Thames	W 2–1	1–1	9	Wilson, Attwood	1,889	9	3		1	6			7		8	2		5			10						4	11
21	FL D3(S)	(h)	Brentford	L 1–2	0–1	11	Attwood	9,582	9	3		1	6			7		8	2		5			10						4	11
28	FAC R1	(a)	Folkestone	W 5–2	2–0	–	Farrell, Wilson, Attwood, Smith, Kirkwood	5,557	9	3		1	6			7		8	2		5			10						4	11
Dec 5	FL D3(S)	(h)	Coventry City	W 4–1	1–0	6	Attwood 3 (1 pen), Smith	6,981	9	3		1	6			7		8	2		5			10						4	11
12	FAC R2	(h)	Doncaster Rovers	W 5–0	2–0	–	Wilson, Attwood 2 (1 pen), Kirkwood, Farrell	14,369	9	3		1	6			7		8	2		5			10						4	11
19	FL D3(S)	(h)	Luton Town	W 3–2	2–2	6	Attwood 2, Kirkwood	6,628	9	3		1	6			7		8	2		5			10						4	11
25	FL D3(S)	(a)	Mansfield Town	D 3–3	1–1	8	Farrell, Attwood 2	10,848	9	3		1	6			7		8	2		5			10						4	11
26	FL D3(S)	(h)	Mansfield Town	W 4–0	2–0	7	Attwood 2, Smith, Dutton	16,516	9	3		1	6			7		8	2		5			10						4	11
Jan 2	FL D3(S)	(a)	Norwich City	L 1–2	1–0	7	Wilson	9,088	9	3		1	6					8	2		5			10		8				4	11
9	FAC R3	(h)	Port Vale	L 1–2	0–1	–	Attwood	21,690	9	3		1	6			7		8	2		5			10						4	11
16	FL D3(S)	(h)	Swindon Town	W 1–0	1–0	9	Attwood	6,388	9	3		1	6			7		8	2		5			10						4	11
23	FL D3(S)	(a)	Clapton Orient	D 2–2	1–1	7	Own goal, Smith	5,284	9	3		1	6			7		8	2		5			10						4	11
30	FL D3(S)	(h)	Torquay United	L 0–2	0–0	9		7,079	9	3		1	6			7		8	2		5			10						4	11
Feb 6	FL D3(S)	(a)	Bristol Rovers	W 4–0	2–0	8	Wilson, Kirkwood, Attwood, Eyres	8,711	9	3					10	7		8	2		5			6				1		4	11
13	FL D3(S)	(h)	Queen's Park R.	W 1–0	1–0	6	Eyres	7,033	9	3					10	7		8	2		5			6				1		4	11
20	FL D3(S)	(h)	Bournem'th & B.A.	W 2–1	0–1	7	Farrell, Attwood (pen)	4,597	9	3					10	7		8	2		5			6				1		4	11
27	FL D3(S)	(h)	Northampton T.	D 0–0	0–0	7		7,966	9	3					10	7		8	2		5			6				1		4	11
Mar 5	FL D3(S)	(a)	Reading	L 1–3	1–0	7	Attwood	10,596	9	3				6	11	7		8	2		5			10				1		4	
12	FL D3(S)	(h)	Southend United	L 1–2	1–1	8	Walker	7,021	9	3						7		8	2		5			6			10	1		4	11
19	FL D3(S)	(a)	Fulham	L 0–3	0–0	10		20,460	9						7	3	8	2		5			6			10	1		4	11	
25	FL D3(S)	(h)	Watford	W 2–1	1–0	8	Walker, Farrell	10,528	9	3						7		8	2		5			6			10	1		4	11
26	FL D3(S)	(h)	Thames	W 4–1	4–0	7	Attwood 3, Wilson	5,181	9		3					7		8	2		5			10				6	1	4	11
28	FL D3(S)	(a)	Watford	D 2–2	1–1	8	Kirkwood, Eyres	7,012	9		3				10	7		8	2		5			6				4	1		11
Apr 2	FL D3(S)	(a)	Brentford	D 2–2	0–1	7	Attwood, Walker	9,107	9	3						7		8	2		5			6			10		1	4	11
9	FL D3(S)	(h)	Exeter City	D 1–1	1–1	8	Wilson	4,792	9	3						7		8	2		5			6			10		1	4	11
13	FL D3(S)	(a)	Gillingham	D 0–0	0–0	7		2,174	9		3				10	7		8	2		5			6					1	4	11
16	FL D3(S)	(h)	Coventry City	L 3–4	1–3	10	Farrell 2, Attwood	7,587	9	3					10	7		8	2		5			6					1	4	11
23	FL D3(S)	(a)	Gillingham	W 7–0	3–0	7	Attwood 4, Kirkwood 2, Farrell	4,583	9	3					10	7		8	2		5			6					1	4	11
30	FL D3(S)	(a)	Luton Town	L 2–3	1–1	9	Kirkwood, Attwood	6,328	9	3					10	7		8	2		5		4	6					1		11
May 7	FL D3(S)	(h)	Cardiff City	D 0–0	0–0	8		5,447	9	3					10	7		8	2		5		4	6					1		11
			League appearances						1	27	37	4	25	23	11	38	1	41	42	3	39	4	3	42	4	3	15	2	17	39	41
			League goals				OG – 1			25				1	3	8		12				1		7	1	1	6				7

Another débutant was seventeen-year-old Eric Townsend, a former star with Brighton Boys. He made his first appearance on 12 September, scoring Albion's goal in the 1–1 draw with Clapton Orient at the Goldstone, and a tremendous future was predicted for him.

The team began well, gaining five points from three games, then came down to earth with a bump, losing 3–0 to Crystal Palace at the Goldstone. There was much chopping and changing of the side in the early part of the season, especially in attack where four players were tried at centre-forward before the arrival of Attwood. Then, from 7 November until Boxing Day, the team remained unchanged for nine matches. The first of these games was against Fulham at the Goldstone, the Londoners winning a thriller 3–2. Fulham's first goal was scored by their inside-right Jim Hammond, a local lad who represented Brighton Schools before graduating into the Sussex County League with Lewes. While at the Dripping Pan he won an England amateur cap against Wales in 1928, a very rare achievement for a Sussex-based player, and subsequently went to Craven Cottage where he gave fine service up to 1938. Jim also played cricket for Sussex as an all-rounder from 1928 until 1946.

Albion kept pace with the leaders for most of the season despite unfortunate slip-ups at home, losing to most of the top sides; indeed, only Reading of the leading five were conquered at the Goldstone. On 23 April, Arthur Attwood had a field day, scoring four goals in the 7–0 hammering of Gillingham. Away form was very encouraging with five wins and eight draws being recorded, and the team failed to score in only four of the 21 away games. The biggest win on the road came at Bristol Rovers in February; Tommy Cook led the Rovers attack but was powerless to prevent Albion winning 4–0.

Southend United led the section up to early December, then a disastrous decline saw them plummet into mid table before recovering to finished third. Brentford took over the leadership until February, when Fulham gained pole position and held on to take the championship by two points from Reading. After winning five points from the three Easter games, Albion finished eighth.

The first round of the F.A. Cup found Albion travelling to Kent to play Southern League Folkestone and they ran out comfortable 5–2 winners with a goal apiece from each of the

Albion on Civvy Street
A pre-season line-up preparing to take on St Anne's Well Gardens Bowling Club.
Back row left to right: Bobby Farrell, Paul Mooney, Harry Marsden, Dave Walker, Stan Thompson, Joe Duckworth, Dan Kirkwood.
Front row left to right: Harry Dutton (standing), Tug Wilson, Frank Brett (captain), Geordie Nicol, Sam Brown, Jack Eyres, Harold Sly.

forwards. The tie attracted a record 5,557 crowd to the small Folkestone ground. The home team had the former Everton and England star Jack Cock at inside-right. Jack had played for Everton against the Albion in the memorable cup-tie of 1924.

The second round brought Doncaster Rovers to Hove. Albion cruised through 5–0, the highest score of the round, and drew Second Division Port Vale at the Goldstone at the next stage. Vale were struggling and only avoided the drop into the Third Division on goal-average, but they proved too strong for the Albion, winning by two Wilf Nolan goals to one. Arthur Attwood grabbed Albion's consolation goal ten minutes from time.

Although there was an improvement in the Goldstone attendances, the average was still only 8,119, resulting in a loss for the season of £1,027 16s. 11d. In his speech at the a.g.m., club president and chairman William Goodwin said that he was dumbfounded that a club representing an area the size of Brighton and Hove, with a population of a quarter of a million, could not draw an average gate of 9,000 when a city the size of Norwich, with a population of half that amount, could rely on average crowds of 11,000. He went on to comment: 'I wonder if the town really wants a professional football club.'

SEASON 1932–33

What a sensational season this was to be, although no one could have predicted it in April 1932 when it was revealed that Albion's application for entry into this season's F.A. Cup had not been received until after the deadline on 20 March, an unbelievable gaffe by secretary Albert Underwood. Instead, the club would be required to participate in the qualifying competition. All was to end well, but there was much gnashing of teeth at the time.

The result of Underwood's oversight was what must be one of the strangest cup-runs of all time. There were thoughts of

scratching from the competition, but there was a lot of interest locally and it was decided to keep faith with the public. The campaign started on 1 October rather than the usual late November when Shoreham were the visitors to Hove for the first match, and an inquisitive crowd of over 5,000 turned up to see how the amateurs would fare. The Musselmen's left-back and captain was none other than Albion's old stalwart Reg Smith, but he was powerless to prevent the ensuing massacre. Five-nil up at the interval, Albion ran out 12–0 victors with Arthur Attwood grabbing six of the goals.

Worthing were entertained next at the Goldstone. The tie was originally drawn to be played at Worthing Sports Ground (now Woodside Road), but for financial reasons the two clubs agreed to switch to the larger arena. Worthing were one of the leading teams in the Sussex County League but could find no answer to the superior speed and fitness of the professionals, Albion winning 7–1. In the third qualifying round Albion travelled to Hastings & St Leonards and walloped the Southern Amateur League side 9–0. Albion again offered to stage the tie at the Goldstone, but there was a great deal of enthusiasm generated in Hastings and the game was attended by a record 7,723 crowd at the Pilot Field.

The team had to travel again for the fourth-round qualifier with Barnet. The Hertfordshire side were challenging for the Athenian League title and also reached the quarter-final stage of the F.A. Amateur Cup, but they were no match for the Albion, losing by four goals to nil. So Brighton came through four easy qualifiers unscathed to reach the stage at which they should have entered the competition, the first round proper. Crystal Palace were the opponents and were convincingly beaten at Selhurst Park with second-half goals from Stan Thompson and Arthur Attwood, Palace scoring a late consolation goal.

In the second round Albion were drawn at home to Wrexham and a fairly uninspiring game ended in a goal-less draw, but the replay was anything but dull; with the winners due to meet Chelsea at home, the game was played at a cracking pace. Wrexham took an early lead through their Welsh international centre-forward Tom Bamford and added a second before the break. Charlie Webb switched the team around for the second-half and Albion tore into their opponents. Potter Smith pulled one back eight minutes after the restart, but it was not until the 85th minute that Dave Walker scored the equaliser, sending

the game into extra time. Brighton lasted the pace on the heavy pitch much better than Wrexham, and with twelve minutes remaining the tenacious Bobby Farrell shook off several challenges and drove home the winner. The match took its toll on the players and both Attwood and Mooney received injuries which sidelined them for some time.

Full-back Frank Brett had been out with an injury, but, with Paul Mooney indisposed, he returned to the team at centre-half and played so well that he could not be shifted for the rest of the season. His performance against Chelsea in the third-round tie had much to do with the Albion's tremendous victory over the First Division side. Though without their England centre-half Peter O'Dowd, Chelsea had some famous names in their line-up: goalkeeper Vic Woodley, later to win nineteen England caps and to guest briefly for Albion in the war; outside-right Jackie Crawford of England; inside-right George Mills, also later capped by England; and centre-forward Hughie Gallacher of Scotland, who had terrorised the Albion defence in the Newcastle tie three years earlier. There were to be no heroics from the wee Scot this time, however, as Brett was detailed to follow him all over the park and carried out his role with such effect that Gallacher hardly got a kick.

Albion opened in sensational manner, Attwood scoring after just 30 seconds, and the early success inspired both the crowd and the players. Albion's vigorous, bustling methods never allowed the Pensioners to settle into their normal game and in the second half there were several heated exchanges. After Tug Wilson increased Albion's lead in the 65th minute, the referee was called upon to calm things down. George Barber scored a late goal for Chelsea, but the final whistle found Albion still on the attack. This terrific result did not get the nationwide acclaim that it deserved, for, on the same day, Walsall defeated

It's there!
West Ham United goalkeeper George Watson, under pressure from Arthur Attwood, watches in despair as Reg Wilkinson's lob from the touchline finds its way into the Hammers' net to put Albion 1–0 up after just ten minutes of the F.A. Cup fifth-round tie on 18 February. Twenty minutes later it was 2–0 as Attwood scored in front of the North Stand. This was Brighton's ninth tie in the most memorable cup-run the club enjoyed until 1983, but, as the crowd anticipated a first Albion appearance in the quarter-finals, Second Division West Ham fought back to force a replay. The huge audience numbered 32,310, beating the previous best by almost 5,000. The figure remained a record until 1958.

SEASON 1932–33

Date	Comp.	Ven.	Opponents	Result	HT	Pos.	Scorers	Atten.	Ansell G	Attwood A	Brett F	Carruthers J	Farrell R	Harrison J	King E	Kirkwood D	Marsden H	Martin E	Mooney P	Sly H	Smith P	Thompson S	Townsend E	Varco P	Walker D	Watson H	Webb S	Wilkinson R	Wilson E	Wright J
Aug 27	FL D3(S)	(h)	Gillingham	W 1–0	1–0	1=	Attwood	9,517		9	3		7			8	2				5	6			10		1		4	11
31	FL D3(S)	(a)	Crystal Palace	L 0–5	0–2	15		13,704		9	3		7			8	2				5	6			10	4	1		4	11
Sep 3	FL D3(S)	(a)	Watford	W 4–0	2–0	8	Ansell, Farrell 2, Attwood	7,995	10	9			7			8	2				5	3	6				4	1			11
7	FL D3(S)	(h)	Crystal Palace	L 1–2	1–0	10	Attwood	9,302	10	9			7			8	2				5	3	6				4	1			11
10	FL D3(S)	(h)	Cardiff City	W 1–0	1–0	7	Kirkwood	7,790	10	9			7			8	2				5	3	6				4	1			11
17	FL D3(S)	(a)	Reading	L 0–3	0–1	12		11,593	10	9			7			8	2				5	3	6				4	1			11
22	FL D3(S)	(a)	Northampton T.	D 0–0	0–0	8		3,784		9	3		7			8	2				5	6	10					1		4	11
24	FL D3(S)	(h)	Norwich City	D 1–1	1–0	8	Wilson	5,486		9	3		7			8	2				5	6	10					1		4	11
Oct 1	FAC Q1	(h)	Shoreham	W 12–0	5–0	–	Attwood 6, Smith 3, Kirkwood 2, Farrell	5,500		9	3		7			8	2				5	6	10					1		4	11
8	FL D3(S)	(a)	Bristol Rovers	L 3–5	1–2	16	Farrell 2, Attwood	8,889		9	3		7			8	2				5	6	10					1		4	11
15	FAC Q2	(h*)	Worthing	W 7–1	4–0	–	Ansell, Farrell, Wilson, Attwood 2, Smith 2	5,952	8	9	3		7				2				5	4	10			6	1			11
19	FL D3(S)	(h)	Aldershot	L 0–2	0–0	19		3,600	8	9	3		7				2				5	6	10				1		4	11
22	FL D3(S)	(h)	Clapton Orient	D 0–0	0–0	18		4,119		9	3		6		8		2		5		10	7					1		4	11
29	FAC Q3	(a)	Hastings & St L.	W 9–0	2–0	–	Farrell 3, Thompson 2, Attwood 2, Smith 2 (1 pen)	7,723		9	3		6		8		2		5		10	7			4		1			11
Nov 2	FL D3(S)	(a)	Swindon Town	L 1–5	0–3	19	Attwood	2,689		9	3				8		2		5		10	7			6		1		4	11
5	FL D3(S)	(h)	Bournem'th & B.A.	W 3–0	2–0	17	Attwood, Wilson, Carruthers	4,767		9		6	7		8		2	3	5		10				4		1			11
12	FAC Q4	(a)	Barnet	W 4–0	3–0	–	Smith, Thompson 2, Attwood	4,000		9		6	8				2	3	5		10	7			4		1			11
17	FL D3(S)	(a)	Newport County	L 2–5	0–3	17	Wilson, Attwood	3,750		9		6					2	3	5		10	7			8		1		4	11
19	FL D3(S)	(h)	Luton Town	W 2–0	0–0	17	Walker, Attwood	4,102		9			8			2			3	5		6	7		10		1		4	11
26	FAC R1	(a)	Crystal Palace	W 2–1	0–0	–	Thompson, Attwood	15,500		9			8			3			2	5		6	7		10		1		4	11
Dec 3	FL D3(S)	(a)	Torquay United	D 1–1	1–1	17	Attwood	5,417		9			8			3			2	5		6	7		10		1		4	11
10	FAC R2	(h)	Wrexham	D 0–0	0–0	–		10,352					9	8		3			2	5		6	7		10		1		4	11
14	FAC R2 Rep	(a)	Wrexham	W 3–2*	0–2	–	Smith, Walker, Farrell	10,000		9			8			3			2	5		6	7		10		1		4	11
17	FL D3(S)	(h)	Coventry City	W 1–0	0–0	13	Smith	5,837			5		8			3			2			10	7	9	6		1		4	11
24	FL D3(S)	(a)	Bristol City	W 4–3	3–2	12	Wilson, Farrell, Townsend	6,992			5		8			3			2			10	7	9	6		1		4	11
26	FL D3(S)	(a)	Queen's Park R.	W 1–0	0–0	9	Thompson	9,177			5	2	8			3						10	7	9	6				4	11	1
27	FL D3(S)	(h)	Queen's Park R.	W 4–1	1–0	7	Thompson 2, Townsend, Wilson	14,544			5	2	8			3						10	7	9	6				4	11	1
31	FL D3(S)	(a)	Gillingham	L 0–2	0–0	8		5,818			5	2	8			3						10	7	9	6				4	11
Jan 7	FL D3(S)	(h)	Watford	W 3–0	2–0	7	Attwood, Thompson, Wilkinson (pen)	6,516		9	5		8			3			2			10	7		6		1		4	11
14	FAC R3	(h)	Chelsea	W 2–1	1–0	–	Attwood, Wilson	23,580		9	5		8			3			2			10	7		6		1		4	11
18	FL D3(S)	(a)	Exeter City	L 1–4	0–2	9	Wilkinson (pen)	3,739		9	5		8			3			2			10	7		6		1		4	11
21	FL D3(S)	(a)	Cardiff City	W 2–1	0–0	7	Townsend 2	4,185			5		8			3			2			10	7	9	6		1		4	11
28	FAC R4	(h)	Bradford (P.A.)	W 2–1	2–0	–	Attwood, Smith	18,248		9	5		8			3			2			10	7		6		1		4	11
Feb 1	FL D3(S)	(h)	Reading	W 5–3	4–1	6	Thompson, Smith, Farrell, Attwood 2	8,027		9	5		8			3			2			10	7		6		1		4	11
4	FL D3(S)	(a)	Norwich City	L 0–1	0–1	7		10,385		9	5		8			3			2			10	7		6		1		4	11
11	FL D3(S)	(h)	Northampton T.	W 2–1	2–0	6	Farrell, Attwood	6,755		9	5		8			3			2			10	7		6		1		4	11
18	FAC R5	(h)	West Ham United	D 2–2	2–1	–	Wilkinson, Attwood	32,310		9	5		8			3			2			10	7		6		1		4	11
22	FAC R5 Rep	(a)	West Ham United	L 0–1*	0–0	–		36,742		9	5		8			3			2			10	7		6		1		4	11
Mar 1	FL D3(S)	(h)	Bristol Rovers	L 0–3	0–1	9		4,020		9	5		8			3			2			10	7		6		1		4	11
4	FL D3(S)	(a)	Clapton Orient	L 0–2	0–2	9		6,143		9	5	2	10			3	8						7		6		1		4	11
11	FL D3(S)	(h)	Swindon Town	W 5–1	2–1	8	Townsend 2, Thompson, Farrell, Wilson	5,813			5		8			2					3	10	7	9	6		1		4	11
18	FL D3(S)	(a)	Bournem'th & B.A.	D 1–1	1–1	9	Attwood	4,209		9			8			3			2		5	10	7		6		1		4	11
25	FL D3(S)	(h)	Newport County	W 1–0	1–0	9	Farrell	5,045		9	5		8			3			2			10	7		6		1		4	11
29	FL D3(S)	(a)	Aldershot	D 1–1	1–0	8	Wilkinson (pen)	3,357		9	5		8			3			2			10	7		6		1		4	11
Apr 1	FL D3(S)	(a)	Luton Town	D 0–0	0–0	7		4,240		9	5		8			3			2			10	7		6		1		4	11
8	FL D3(S)	(h)	Exeter City	W 2–1	2–1	5	Townsend, Farrell	6,627			5		8			3			2			10	7	9	6		1		4	11
14	FL D3(S)	(h)	Southend United	L 1–2	0–2	8	Wilkinson (pen)	8,996			5		8			3			2			10	7	9	6		1		4	11
15	FL D3(S)	(a)	Torquay United	L 0–1	0–1	9		3,937		9	5		8			3			2			10	7		6		1		4	11
17	FL D3(S)	(h)	Southend United	L 1–2	1–1	12	Wilson	8,372		9	5		8			3			2			10	7		6		1		4	11
22	FL D3(S)	(h)	Brentford	L 1–2	0–1	13	Attwood	8,659		9	5		8			3			2			10	7		6		1		4	11
26	FL D3(S)	(a)	Brentford	L 1–2	0–1	13	Own goal	12,638		9	5		8			3			2			10	7		6				4	11	1
29	FL D3(S)	(a)	Coventry City	D 2–2	1–1	13	Attwood 2	10,822		9	5		8	11	3				2			10	7		6				4		1
May 6	FL D3(S)	(h)	Bristol City	W 7–0	2–0	12	Attwood 3, Smith, Thompson, Harrison 2	3,645		9	5		8	11	3				2			10	7		6				4		1
League appearances									5	33	33	7	41	2	28	11	36	4	17	8	41	31	8	1	36	4	37	34	40	5
League goals								OG – 1	1	20			10	2	1	1					3	7	8		1			4	7	

Notes: Oct 15 – tie drawn away but switched to the Goldstone Ground.

Dec 14 – after extra time.

Feb 22 – after extra time.

the mighty Arsenal in one of the greatest upsets of all time, a feat that overshadowed all others.

A fortnight later Bradford (P.A.) were beaten 2–1 at the Goldstone in the fourth round. Albion built up a two-goal half-time lead and the result was never really in doubt. In the fifth round Albion were drawn at home to Second Division West Ham United. The Hammers were having a mediocre season and avoided relegation to Division Three by one point. Nevertheless, the tie caught the public's imagination and a big crowd was anticipated. In the week before the game the following hints for spectators appeared in the local Press:

1. Wear a cap if you can.
2. Get there soon.
3. Do your bit to pack.
4. Have ready the exact amount of admission money.

Football League Division 3 (South) 1932–33

		P	W	D	L	F	A	W	D	L	F	A	Pts
1.	Brentford	42	15	4	2	45	19	11	6	4	45	30	62
2.	Exeter City	42	17	2	2	57	13	7	8	6	31	35	58
3.	Norwich City	42	16	3	2	49	17	6	10	5	39	38	57
4.	Reading	42	14	5	2	68	30	5	8	8	35	41	51
5.	Crystal Palace	42	14	4	3	51	21	5	4	12	27	43	46
6.	Coventry City	42	16	1	4	75	24	3	5	13	31	53	44
7.	Gillingham	42	14	4	3	54	24	4	4	13	18	37	44
8.	Northampton Town	42	16	5	0	54	11	2	3	16	22	55	44
9.	Bristol Rovers	42	13	5	3	38	22	2	9	10	23	34	44
10.	Torquay United	42	12	7	2	51	26	4	5	12	21	41	44
11.	Watford	42	11	8	2	37	22	5	4	12	29	41	44
12.	**ALBION**	42	13	3	5	42	20	4	5	12	24	45	42
13.	Southend United	42	11	5	5	39	27	4	6	11	26	55	41
14.	Luton Town	42	12	8	1	60	32	1	5	15	18	46	39
15.	Bristol City	42	11	5	5	59	37	1	8	12	24	53	37
16.	Queen's Park R.	42	9	8	4	48	32	4	3	14	24	55	37
17.	Aldershot	42	11	6	4	37	21	2	4	15	24	51	36
18.	Bournemouth & B.A.	42	10	7	4	44	27	2	5	14	16	54	36
19.	Cardiff City	42	12	4	5	48	30	0	3	18	21	69	31
20.	Clapton Orient	42	7	8	6	39	35	1	5	15	20	58	29
21.	Newport County	42	9	4	8	42	42	2	3	16	19	63	29
22.	Swindon Town	42	7	9	5	36	29	2	2	17	24	76	29

Albion line-up v. West Ham United, F.A. Cup fifth round
Standing left to right: Harry Marsden, Reg Wilkinson, Stan Webb, Ernie King, Frank Brett (captain), Dave Walker.
Seated left to right: Stan Thompson, Bobby Farrell, Arthur Attwood, Potter Smith, Tug Wilson.

Quite why a cap was deemed necessary cannot be imagined as the match took place in February and nobody was likely to suffer sunstroke! It was also announced that no cars would be allowed inside the ground as was the normal custom at the time. People travelled from far and near to attend the tie; one couple flew from Paris to Croydon Airport and completed the journey by motor car.

The huge crowd numbered 32,310 (£2,903 3s. 1d.), almost 5,000 more than the previous best, to establish a ground record that lasted 25 years. A contemporary explanation for the excessive turn-out was that it was the only cup-tie being played south of Derby, and it is a reasonable assumption that the majority of spectators were not Albion supporters as the next home match, a League fixture with Bristol Rovers, was attended by a miserable 4,020.

A temporary uncovered stand was erected and the seating capacity was increased to 2,500. In the crush many people did not see the play and caught only fleeting glimpses of the ball when it was ballooned skyward. Amid incredible scenes, Albion took the lead on ten minutes when Reg Wilkinson lobbed the ball in off the far post. Twenty minutes later Arthur Attwood collected the ball on the halfway line and dashed between the backs to drive home a second. To quote the reporter from the *Sussex Daily News*: 'Half an hour after the start I was wondering who the Albion would draw in the next round.' West Ham's master goalscorer, Vic Watson, pulled one back just before the interval and in the second half the Hammers began to press strongly. It was only a matter of time before they equalised, but they left it late, left-half Joe Musgrave scoring direct from a free kick with only ten minutes left on the clock. It had been a scrappy match and there were no complaints about the result from either side.

An even bigger crowd squeezed into Upton Park for the Tuesday-afternoon replay, and 36,742 (£2,776) saw Albion push West Ham all the way. The lads played gallantly and at times produced some brilliant football, but they lost out to a Jackie Morton goal scored in the first period of extra time. The Hammers went through to beat Birmingham 4–0 in the sixth round before losing 2–1 in the semi-finals to the eventual winners, Everton.

Nine ties and eleven matches, an incredible run from the beginning of October to late February! As a point of interest, Albion's nine opponents came from seven different competitions: First Division, Second Division, Third Division (South), Third Division (North), Athenian League, Southern Amateur League and Sussex County League.

While Cup form was excellent, the League performances can be summed up in one word: Inconsistent. Lack of thrust up front was the biggest problem. With the exception of Arthur Attwood, who scored 24 goals in League and Cup (not counting an additional eleven in the qualifying competition), no other player found the net regularly, although young Eric Townsend did marvellously well, scoring eight goals in his eight outings in the first team. Percy Varco, signed from Norwich City during the summer with a reputation as a sharpshooter, failed to hold a place in the League side.

The 5–1 defeat at Swindon on 2 November saw Albion as low as nineteenth in the Southern Section with Frank Brett and Potter Smith hospitalised after a bruising encounter; Brett had played on with a broken rib and was out of action for a month. Because of the F.A. Cup qualifiers, several League matches had to be rearranged for midweek and the losses at the turnstiles were enormous; only 3,600 spectators paid to watch the 2–0 home defeat by Aldershot in October. In the run-up to Christmas, Albion conceded eighteen goals in four successive away games, then came an improvement with a maximum six points coming from the Christmas-holiday programme. By early April they were fifth, but because of the extended Cup escapades Albion had played some nine or ten more games than most of the other Southern Section sides and they began to flag. Any mathematical chances of promotion disappeared with five consecutive defeats, which included a point-less Easter and two defeats by Brentford. The Bees went on to win the title by four points from Exeter City and within two years won promotion to the First Division. Albion saved their finest League display for the final day of the campaign when Bristol City were trounced 7–0 at the Goldstone; sadly, only 3,645 people witnessed the game.

Tug Wilson received his second benefit in May, and rather than being granted the proceeds of a League fixture he was rewarded with a testimonial match against Birmingham. A good crowd turned out for the popular little winger and saw Albion beat the First Division side 2–1.

Six-shooter
Arthur Attwood bagged a club-record six goals in the 12–0 F.A. Cup first-qualifying-round victory over Shoreham.

SEASON 1933–34

In reviewing Albion's performance during the 1932–33 season, a reporter wrote in reference to the disappointing gates: 'The moral is: Support the Albion next season and they will yet bring Second Division football to the Goldstone Ground. They have the players; give them the support.' It was not to be. With unemployment at record levels and the Depression at its deepest, the average gate fell further still, to a record low for the club in the Football League of just 6,309.

New signings included Bert Jepson, a right-winger from Fulham; Wolverhampton's Welsh international full-back Albert Lumberg; Jimmy Short, an inside-forward from Sheffield Wednesday; and Len Darling, a young wing-half from Gillingham. The only important departure was that of Dan Kirkwood who left for Luton Town in October.

The season opened in mediocre fashion with only one win in six starts. The 5–1 defeat of Bristol City at the Goldstone on 16 October brought the poor run to an end, but by then Albion were firmly rooted in the wrong half of the table. While home performances gave little cause for concern, the first six away matches ended in defeat, and when victory eventually came at Aldershot in mid October the team was in eighteenth place.

The club was plagued by injuries throughout the season. Great things were expected from Lumberg, but injury and then a dispute with the management kept him out of the side. The unfortunate Eric Townsend was advised by a heart specialist to retire in late October; he was only nineteen, a tragedy for both Eric and the club. Potter Smith was hurt during the Christmas games and missed most of the remainder of the season, and Arthur Attwood was struck down with appendicitis in February. Consequently the team was changed from match to match.

Bobby Farrell was due a testimonial but because of the financial situation it was held over for twelve months. Albion remained in the lower reaches for most of the season, doing well against the top sides but often failing against the weaker teams. On 21 April, Bournemouth were beaten 6–0 with a hat-trick from Oliver 'Buster' Brown. With Attwood missing from the scene there was no recognised centre-forward, and in March Charlie Webb secured the services of Brown from West Ham United. The burly leader proved to be worth his weight in gold: in only eight League outings he scored eleven goals and, incredibly, was top scorer for the season. He also netted four times in the newly introduced Third Division (South) Cup, bringing his total to fifteen in just ten games.

Albion did well in the new competition, winning through to the semi-finals before bowing out 4–3 (Brown 3) to the eventual winners, Exeter City, in a second replay. Brown's arrival came too late to make a big difference to the League season, but his goal-burst helped the team into tenth place, the highest position of the campaign. In January, Webb brought in 21-year-old Harry Egan from the Notts. club Sutton Town to fill the gap left by the injured Potter Smith and he performed with great credit, so much so that within a few weeks Sunderland offered a four-figure fee for his transfer, but the club refused to release him.

The F.A. Cup programme was somewhat less distinguished than that of the previous season. In contrast, Albion were exempted until the third round where they eased through comfortably with a 3–1 victory over Swindon Town in vile weather at the Goldstone. Bolton Wanderers were the visitors to Hove for the fourth-round tie. The Trotters had been relegated from the First Division at the end of the previous season

Albion 1933–34

Back row left to right: Reg Wilkinson, Frank Brett (captain), Jack Trees, Bobby Farrell, Stan Webb, Joe Wright, Ted Martin, Paul Mooney, Jack Carruthers.
Middle row left to right: Bill Jones (assistant trainer), Albert Lumberg, John Callender, Ernie King, Arthur Attwood, Jim Short, Jack Harrison, Almeric Hall, Stan Thompson, Dickie Meades (trainer).
Front row left to right: Bert Jepson, Helliwell, Harry Marsden, Dave Walker, Eric Townsend, Potter Smith, Tug Wilson, Len Darling.

The Southern Section Cup was never a big draw for the public and the matches involving the Albion only attracted an average of around 3,000 spectators over the competition's six seasons. The game at Newport County's Somerton Park on 22 February 1934 was attended by a crowd estimated at just 1,000, the smallest ever to watch Albion in a senior match in peacetime since the club joined the Football League in 1920. The receipts amounted to a pitiful £12 2s.

SEASON 1933–34

Match-by-match record (player columns give shirt numbers; blank = did not play):

Date	Comp	Ven	Opponents	Result	HT	Pos	Scorers	Atten.
Aug 26	FL D3(S)	(a)	Queen's Park R.	L 0–2	0–2	19=		11,986
30	FL D3(S)	(h)	Torquay United	W 3–1	2–1	8=	Wilkinson (pen), Attwood, Harrison	6,404
Sep 2	FL D3(S)	(h)	Newport County	D 1–1	0–1	11=	Farrell	6,878
6	FL D3(S)	(a)	Torquay United	L 0–3	0–1	14		3,609
9	FL D3(S)	(a)	Norwich City	L 3–4	1–3	17	Smith, Wilkinson, Wilson	14,933
13	FL D3(S)	(h)	Exeter City	L 0–3	0–2	17		5,304
16	FL D3(S)	(h)	Bristol City	W 5–1	0–0	15	Wilson, Attwood 2, Thompson 2	7,308
23	FL D3(S)	(a)	Clapton Orient	L 1–2	0–1	17	Smith	6,486
30	FL D3(S)	(h)	Swindon Town	W 3–0	2–0	15	Smith, Thompson, Wilkinson (pen)	6,609
Oct 7	FL D3(S)	(a)	Reading	L 0–2	0–0	18		10,808
14	FL D3(S)	(a)	Aldershot	W 1–0	1–0	16	Attwood	4,407
21	FL D3(S)	(h)	Coventry City	D 1–1	0–0	16	Wilson	7,376
28	FL D3(S)	(a)	Southend United	D 0–0	0–0	16		5,803
Nov 4	FL D3(S)	(h)	Bristol Rovers	L 0–2	0–0	17		6,653
11	FL D3(S)	(a)	Crystal Palace	L 1–2	0–2	17	Short	10,562
18	FL D3(S)	(h)	Gillingham	W 5–2	3–0	15	Smith, Attwood 2, Short, Wilson	5,186
Dec 2	FL D3(S)	(h)	Cardiff City	W 4–0	2–0	12	Smith, Attwood 2, Wilkinson (pen)	5,012
16	FL D3(S)	(h)	Charlton Athletic	W 1–0	0–1	11	Wilson	6,377
23	FL D3(S)	(a)	Watford	L 0–2	0–0	11		5,346
25	FL D3(S)	(a)	Northampton T.	D 1–1	1–1	11	Farrell	11,978
26	FL D3(S)	(h)	Northampton T.	D 3–3	0–1	11	Wilson, Wilkinson (pen), Short	7,907
30	FL D3(S)	(a)	Queen's Park R.	L 0–1	0–0	12		6,579
Jan 6	FL D3(S)	(a)	Newport County	D 2–2	0–1	13	Wilson, Thompson	4,694
13	FAC R3	(h)	Swindon Town	W 3–1	1–0	–	Short, Walker, Farrell	13,650
20	FL D3(S)	(h)	Norwich City	D 1–1	1–1	13	Farrell	8,894
27	FAC R4	(h)	Bolton Wanderers	D 1–1	1–0	–	Wilkinson (pen)	25,535
31	FAC R4 Rep	(a)	Bolton Wanderers	L 1–6	1–3	–	Own goal	24,047
Feb 3	FL D3(S)	(h)	Clapton Orient	D 0–0	0–0	14		5,308
7	FL D3(S)	(a)	Bristol City	L 0–5	0–4	14		4,556
10	FL D3(S)	(a)	Swindon Town	D 1–1	0–1	15	Attwood	8,288
17	FL D3(S)	(h)	Reading	D 1–1	1–0	14	Wilson	5,621
22	SSC R2	(h)	Newport County	W 1–0	0–0	–	Attwood	1,000
24	FL D3(S)	(h)	Aldershot	W 3–1	2–1	13	Egan 2, Short	4,675
Mar 3	FL D3(S)	(a)	Coventry City	L 0–2	0–1	14		14,003
8	SSC R3	(a)	Queen's Park R.	W 2–1	1–1	–	Short, Egan	4,000
10	FL D3(S)	(h)	Southend United	W 1–0	0–0	13	Egan	5,440
17	FL D3(S)	(h)	Bristol Rovers	D 1–1	0–1	12	Egan	7,792
24	FL D3(S)	(h)	Crystal Palace	W 4–1	2–0	11	Farrell, Egan, Short 2	5,356
30	FL D3(S)	(h)	Luton Town	D 1–1	0–0	12	Farrell	10,134
31	FL D3(S)	(a)	Gillingham	L 0–3	0–1	12		6,690
Apr 2	FL D3(S)	(a)	Luton Town	W 2–1	1–0	12	Brown 2	10,133
7	FL D3(S)	(h)	Exeter City	W 2–1	1–0	12	Brown 2	5,799
12	SSC SF	(n*)	Exeter City	D 1–1*	0–1	–	Egan	2,221
14	FL D3(S)	(a)	Cardiff City	W 4–1	3–0	11	Brown 2, Walker, Own goal	4,237
18	FL D3(S)	(a)	Bournem'th & B.A.	D 1–1	0–1	11	Jepson	2,148
21	FL D3(S)	(h)	Bournem'th & B.A.	W 6–0	3–0	11	Brown 3, Own goal, Jepson, Egan	4,291
23	SSC SF Rep	(a)	Exeter City	D 1–1*	1–1	–	Brown	4,000
26	SSC SF 2Rep	(h)	Exeter City	L 3–4	1–1	–	Brown 3	5,486
28	FL D3(S)	(a)	Charlton Athletic	L 3–4	1–4	10	Brown 2, Farrell	5,761
May 5	FL D3(S)	(h)	Watford	W 2–0	1–0	10	Walker, Egan	4,692

Players (columns in order): Attwood A, Brett F, Brown O, Darling L, Egan H, Farrell R, Harrison J, Jepson A, King E, Lumberg A, Marsden H, Martin E, Mooney P, Short J, Smith P, Thompson S, Townsend E, Walker D, Webb S, Wilkinson R, Wilson E, Wright J.

League appearances	21	13	8	9	13	41	3	15	34	21	29	0	29	25	25	17	4	41	33	34	39	9
League goals (OG – 2)	9		11		7	6	1	2						6	5	4		2		5	8	

Notes: Apr 12 – played at Craven Cottage, Fulham FC. / – after extra time. / Apr 23 – after extra time.

---

and narrowly missed out on promotion at the first attempt, finishing third. They possessed a good all-round team with a particularly brilliant left-wing duo in Willie Cook and Ray Westwood: Cook played for Scotland against England in April and Westwood became one of England's finest inside-forwards of the 1930s.

Football League Division 3 (South) 1933–34

		P	W	D	L	F	A	W	D	L	F	A	Pts
1.	Norwich City	42	16	4	1	55	19	9	7	5	33	30	61
2.	Coventry City	42	16	3	2	70	22	5	9	7	30	32	54
3.	Reading	42	17	4	0	60	13	4	8	9	22	37	54
4.	Queen's Park R.	42	17	2	2	42	12	7	4	10	28	39	54
5.	Charlton Athletic	42	14	5	2	53	27	8	3	10	30	29	52
6.	Luton Town	42	14	3	4	55	28	7	7	7	28	33	52
7.	Bristol Rovers	42	14	4	3	49	21	6	7	8	28	26	51
8.	Swindon Town	42	13	5	3	42	25	4	6	11	22	43	45
9.	Exeter City	42	12	5	4	43	18	4	6	11	25	38	43
10.	**ALBION**	42	12	7	2	47	18	3	6	12	21	42	43
11.	Clapton Orient	42	14	4	3	60	25	2	6	13	15	44	42
12.	Crystal Palace	42	11	6	4	40	25	5	3	13	31	42	41
13.	Northampton Town	42	10	6	5	45	32	4	6	11	26	46	40
14.	Aldershot	42	8	6	7	28	27	5	6	10	24	44	38
15.	Watford	42	12	4	5	43	16	3	3	15	27	47	37
16.	Southend United	42	9	6	6	32	27	3	4	14	19	47	34
17.	Gillingham	42	8	8	5	49	41	3	3	15	26	55	33
18.	Newport County	42	9	6	6	25	23	2	8	11	24	47	33
19.	Bristol City	42	7	8	6	33	22	3	5	13	25	63	33
20.	Torquay United	42	10	4	7	32	28	3	3	15	21	65	33
21.	Bournemouth & B.A.	42	7	7	7	41	37	2	2	17	19	65	27
22.	Cardiff City	42	6	4	11	32	43	3	2	16	25	62	24

When Albion took the field, instead of the usual burst of cheering they were greeted with howls of laughter from the 25,535 crowd: a local company had sponsored the club for a new set of socks with a blue-and-white chequered design perhaps more suited to a music-hall comedian! It was the first – and last – time they were displayed. Despite their outrageous hosiery, Albion led at half time through a Reg Wilkinson penalty, but five minutes after the break Westwood equalised with a fluke goal; he intended a cross but sliced his kick and the ball sailed on the wind over Stan Webb's head into the net. Though it was a lucky goal, there was no doubt that Bolton deserved the draw.

In the replay at Burnden Park, Wanderers proved far too good for Brighton and cantered to a 6–1 win. Albion equalised an early Jack Milsom effort with an own-goal from Bolton's veteran full-back Alec Finney, but two further goals from Milsom and one apiece from George T. Taylor, Ken Cameron and Ray Westwood inflicted Albion's heaviest F.A. Cup defeat up to that date. In the next round Bolton beat Liverpool 3–0 at Anfield before losing 3–0 at home to Portsmouth in the sixth round.

SEASON 1934–35

Albion started this campaign in championship style, winning four of the first five games. The initial Goldstone attendances were around the 10,000 mark, but wet weather, together with a loss of form up to Christmas, took its toll and gates fell alarmingly. The average for the season was 6,570, and the club's philosophy of 'Give us the support and we will give you the football' seemed to be in direct contrast to the fans' attitude. Even the spectacular 6–0 defeat of Exeter City on 27 October failed to generate much enthusiasm, the next home game attracting a pitiful 2,728 spectators.

Last season's sensational late signing, Buster Brown, lost his wife during the summer, missed pre-season training, and in the opening matches appeared overweight and sluggish. Though failing to maintain his incredible rate of success, he remained the only consistent goalscorer, netting 25 in League and Cup. There was no lack of skill among the forwards, with Bobby Farrell, Potter Smith and Tug Wilson among the cleverest in the Third Division, but the smart approach work could not be converted into goals.

In contrast the defence performed wonderfully well. With new goalkeeper Charlie Thomson from Falkirk and the veteran ex-England star Herbert Jones from Blackburn Rovers at left-back, only one goal was conceded at Hove before the 2–0 defeat by Millwall on 22 December. The Dockers and Northampton Town were the only visitors to take both points from the Goldstone, but there were occasional defensive lapses and the 6–0 hiding at Clapton Orient in April was the poorest display of the season. Jones and Ernie King formed an excellent rearguard; the experience and intelligence of the balding Jones was the perfect foil to the dash and robust play of the giant King. Right-half Len Darling also had a great season and was the subject of interest from several First Division clubs.

Jones was injured at Gillingham in April and young Ernie Marriott stepped into the side to great effect. Ernie had been recommended to the club by Harry Burrows, a football agent operating from the Nottingham district. Harry was the brother of Sheffield Wednesday's England wing-half Horace Burrows and was responsible for the signing of a large number of young players from the Nottinghamshire area in the 1930s.

In the New Year the team was hit by a series of injuries to key players, Paul Mooney and Potter Smith among them. Mooney's absence opened the way for Jack Stevens, signed from Stockport County during the close season, and like Marriott he quickly settled into the side. Mooney was innocently involved in a tragic accident during the match at Gillingham on 1 December when, after half an hour, a sickening clash of heads with

Entente cordiale

Albion and Arsenal enjoy an eve-of-match visit to the Astoria Cinema in Gloucester Place, Brighton, to see Anna Neagle – herself an Arsenal fan – in Nell Gwyn. *The third-round cup-tie with the most glamourous club in England was the highlight of an otherwise drab season, and the two clubs struck up a splendid rapport before the match. Standing side-by-side at the front of the group are the two managers, Charlie Webb and George Allison, who enjoyed some good-natured banter on the stage during the evening.*

SEASON 1934–35

Date	Comp.	Ven.	Opponents	Result	HT	Pos.	Scorers	Atten.	Attwood A	Barber S	Brett F	Brown O	Darling L	Egan H	Farrell R	Jepson A	Jones H	King E	Marriott E	Mooney P	Payne J	Short J	Smith P	Stevens J	Thompson S	Thomson C	Walker D	Wilson E
Aug 25	FL D3(S)	(h)	Bristol Rovers	W 3–1	3–1	4=	Mooney, Brown 2	11,123				9			8	7	3	2		5	11		10	4		1	6	
29	FL D3(S)	(a)	Watford	W 1–0	1–0	2	Brown	5,660				9			8	7	3	2		5	11		10	4		1	6	
Sep 1	FL D3(S)	(a)	Charlton Athletic	L 1–3	1–1	7=	Payne	12,769				9			8	7	3	2		5	11		10	4		1	6	
5	FL D3(S)	(h)	Watford	W 2–0	0–0	3	Jepson 2	6,557				9			8	7	3	2		5	11		10	4		1	6	
8	FL D3(S)	(h)	Crystal Palace	W 3–0	0–0	2	Brown 2, Egan	10,560				9	4	10	8	7	3	2		5	11					1	6	
15	FL D3(S)	(a)	Queen's Park R.	L 1–2	0–0	4	Walker	9,410				9	4		8	7	3	2		5	11		10			1	6	
19	SSC R1	(a)	Southend United	D 1–1	0–0	–	Mooney	5,000				9	4		8		3	2		5	11		10		7	1	6	
22	FL D3(S)	(h)	Torquay United	D 0–0	0–0	6		3,944				9	4		7		3	2		5	11	8	10			1	6	
26	SSC R1 Rep	(h)	Southend United	W 3–1	1–1	–	Brown, Egan, Jepson	3,185	6			9	4	10	8	7	3	2		5						1		11
29	FL D3(S)	(a)	Swindon Town	D 4–4	2–1	5=	Brown 3, Farrell	7,369				9			8	7	3	2		5			10	4		1	6	11
Oct 6	FL D3(S)	(h)	Aldershot	W 3–0	2–0	3	Wilson, Brown, Smith	6,438				9	4		8	7	3	2		5			10			1	6	11
13	FL D3(S)	(a)	Cardiff City	D 0–0	0–0	4		8,959			5	9	4		8	7	3	2					10			1	6	11
20	FL D3(S)	(a)	Newport County	L 0–1	0–0	4		3,696			5	9	4		8	7	3	2					10			1	6	11
27	FL D3(S)	(h)	Exeter City	W 6–0	3–0	3	Jepson, Brown 2, Walker, Smith 2	7,281				9	4		8	7	3	2		5			10			1	6	11
29	SSC R2	(a)	Millwall	L 1–2	1–1	–	Jepson	1,800				9	4		8	7	3	2		5			10			1	6	11
Nov 3	FL D3(S)	(a)	Northampton T.	L 1–4	0–3	5	Farrell	7,366			5	9	4		8	7	3	2					10			1	6	11
10	FL D3(S)	(h)	Bournem'th & B.A.	W 2–0	1–0	5	Smith, Brown	2,728				9	4		8	7	3	2					10	5		1	6	11
17	FL D3(S)	(a)	Coventry City	W 2–0	0–0	4	Jepson, Farrell	16,839				9	4		8	7	3	2		5			10			1	6	11
24	FAC R1	(h)	Folkestone	W 3–1	1–0	–	Smith, Jepson, Brown (pen)	9,400				9	4		8	7	3	2		5			10			1	6	11
Dec 1	FL D3(S)	(a)	Gillingham	D 0–0	0–0	5		4,115				9	4		8	7	3	2		5			10			1	6	11
8	FAC R2	(a)	Queen's Park R.	W 2–1	1–1	–	Brown, Farrell	14,738				9	4		8	7	3	2		5			10			1	6	11
15	FL D3(S)	(a)	Bristol City	L 0–1	0–1	5		9,981				9	4		8	7	3	2		5			10			1	6	11
22	FL D3(S)	(h)	Millwall	L 0–2	0–1	9		7,796				9	4		8	7	3	2		5			10			1	6	11
25	FL D3(S)	(a)	Luton Town	L 0–4	0–1	9		12,964				9	4		8	7	3	2		5			10			1	6	11
26	FL D3(S)	(h)	Luton Town	W 4–1	2–1	8	Wilson 2, Brown, Smith	13,577				9	4		8	7	3	2		5			10			1	6	11
29	FL D3(S)	(h)	Bristol Rovers	D 0–0	0–0	7		10,987				9	4		8	7	3	2		5			10			1	6	11
Jan 5	FL D3(S)	(h)	Charlton Athletic	W 2–1	1–0	7	Darling, Farrell	11,476				9	4		8	7	3	2		5			10			1	6	11
12	FAC R3	(h)	Arsenal	L 0–2	0–1	–		22,343				9	4		8	7	3	2		5			10			1	6	11
16	FL D3(S)	(h)	Clapton Orient	W 3–0	1–0	7	Brown 2 (1 pen), Own goal	4,862				9	4		8		3	2		5			10		7	1	6	11
19	FL D3(S)	(a)	Crystal Palace	L 0–3	0–1	6		11,189				9	4		8		3	2		5		7	10			1	6	11
26	FL D3(S)	(h)	Queen's Park R.	W 5–1	3–1	6	Wilson 2, Thompson, Smith, Brown	5,098				9	4		8		3	2		5			10		7	1	6	11
Feb 2	FL D3(S)	(a)	Torquay United	L 0–3	0–3	6		3,480				9	4		8		3	2		5			10		7	1	6	11
9	FL D3(S)	(h)	Swindon Town	D 2–2	2–1	6	Thompson, Brown	5,831				9	4				3	2		5		8	10		7	1	6	11
16	FL D3(S)	(a)	Aldershot	L 0–1	0–0	8		3,642				9	4		8		3	2		5			10		7	1	6	11
23	FL D3(S)	(h)	Cardiff City	W 3–1	0–1	7	Short (pen), Wilson, Smith	5,828					4		8	7	3	2		5		9	10			1	6	11
Mar 2	FL D3(S)	(h)	Newport County	W 3–1	1–1	7	Wilson 2, Short	5,687					4		8	7	3	2		5		9	10			1	6	11
9	FL D3(S)	(a)	Exeter City	L 1–3	1–2	7	Brown (pen)	3,755				9	4		8	7	3	2		5			10			1	6	11
16	FL D3(S)	(h)	Northampton T.	L 2–3	1–3	8	Wilson, Attwood	5,550	7			9	4		8		3	2		5			10			1	6	11
20	FL D3(S)	(h)	Reading	W 1–0	1–0	7	Farrell	3,782	7		5	9	4		8		3	2					10			1	6	11
23	FL D3(S)	(a)	Bournem'th & B.A.	L 0–1	0–0	7		4,503	7		5	9	4		8		3	2					10			1	6	11
30	FL D3(S)	(h)	Coventry City	W 2–0	1–0	7	Wilson, Brown	6,154	7		5	9	4		8		3	2					10			1	6	11
Apr 6	FL D3(S)	(a)	Clapton Orient	L 0–6	0–4	7		6,614	7		5	9	4				3	2				8	10			1	6	11
13	FL D3(S)	(h)	Gillingham	D 1–1	1–0	8	Brown	5,227				9	4				3	2	8			7	10	5		1	6	11
19	FL D3(S)	(h)	Southend United	D 2–2	1–1	7	Smith, Jepson	4,594				9	4			7	3	2	8				10	5		1	6	11
20	FL D3(S)	(a)	Reading	D 4–4	2–2	7	Short 2, Brown, Wilson	8,278				9	4				3	2	8			7	10	5		1	6	11
22	FL D3(S)	(h)	Southend United	L 2–3	1–0	9	Brown 2	9,692				9	4				3	2	8			7	10	5		1	6	11
27	FL D3(S)	(h)	Bristol City	W 2–0	1–0	8	Jepson, Smith	3,873				9	4			7	3	2	8				10	5		1	6	11
May 4	FL D3(S)	(a)	Millwall	L 1–3	1–1	9	Short	6,740				9	4				3	2	8			7	10	5		1	6	11
			League appearances						6	0	8	40	37	2	36	30	37	41	6	27	8	12	36	12	5	42	42	35
			League goals				OG – 1		1			23	1	1	5	6				1	1	5	9		2		2	11

centre-forward Simeon Raleigh resulted in the Gillingham player leaving the field. He returned before the break and continued for some 40 minutes, but, with a quarter of an hour remaining, he collapsed and again left the pitch. He died later that week.

Albion finished up in ninth position, a long way behind champions Charlton Athletic who won the title by eight points from runners-up Reading.

Football League Division 3 (South) 1934–35

		P	W	D	L	F	A	W	D	L	F	A	Pts
1.	Charlton Athletic	42	17	2	2	62	20	10	5	6	41	32	61
2.	Reading	42	16	5	0	59	23	5	6	10	30	42	53
3.	Coventry City	42	14	5	2	56	14	7	4	10	30	36	51
4.	Luton Town	42	12	7	2	60	23	7	5	9	32	37	50
5.	Crystal Palace	42	15	3	3	51	14	4	7	10	35	50	48
6.	Watford	42	14	2	5	53	19	5	7	9	23	30	47
7.	Northampton Town	42	14	3	4	40	21	5	4	12	25	46	46
8.	Bristol Rovers	42	14	6	1	54	27	3	4	14	19	50	44
9.	**ALBION**	42	15	4	2	51	16	2	5	14	18	46	43
10.	Torquay United	42	15	2	4	60	22	3	4	14	21	53	42
11.	Exeter City	42	11	5	5	48	29	5	4	12	22	46	41
12.	Millwall	42	11	4	6	33	26	6	3	12	24	36	41
13.	Queen's Park R.	42	14	6	1	49	22	2	3	16	14	50	41
14.	Clapton Orient	42	13	3	5	47	21	2	7	12	18	44	40
15.	Bristol City	42	14	3	4	37	18	1	6	14	15	50	39
16.	Swindon Town	42	11	7	3	45	22	2	5	14	22	56	38
17.	Bournemouth & B.A.	42	10	5	6	36	26	5	2	14	18	45	37
18.	Aldershot	42	12	6	3	35	20	1	4	16	15	55	36
19.	Cardiff City	42	11	6	4	42	27	2	3	16	20	55	35
20.	Gillingham	42	10	7	4	36	25	1	6	14	19	50	35
21.	Southend United	42	10	4	7	40	29	1	5	15	25	49	31
22.	Newport County	42	7	4	10	36	40	3	1	17	18	72	25

For the second time in four seasons Albion were paired with Southern League Folkestone in the first round of the F.A. Cup, and, as in the previous meeting, went through without too much bother, winning 3–1 at the Goldstone. The Folkestone defence played well and after the match Charlie Webb signed their left-back Bill Long. Long played for the reserves but was released at the end of the season.

Two weeks later Albion went to Queen's Park Rangers and won the second-round tie 2–1. When the draw for the third round took place, the club became the envy of every side in the country: Arsenal at home! The north London side were on their way to a third successive League title and were the most famous, the most admired and the most feared club in the land. It was their custom at this time to train in Brighton and Hove before Cup games and this tie was to be no exception. The Albion management gave them permission to use the Goldstone and the teams trained together, creating a splendid rapport between the two clubs.

Another record turn-out was anticipated and precautions were taken accordingly, but many people avoided the match because of the advance publicity of a huge attendance and in the event only 22,343 saw the game. If the gate was something of a disappointment, so too was the football. Arsenal fielded ten current internationals, including seven of the England team which had beaten Italy 3–2 in the so-called 'Battle of Highbury' two months earlier: goalkeeper Frank Moss, full-backs George Male and Eddie Hapgood, left-half Wilf Copping, and forwards Ray Bowden, Ted Drake and Cliff Bastin. Alex James missed the tie: the little Scottish genius picked up an injury and withdrew at the eleventh hour.

Despite all the expectations, the match never reached the high quality that was hoped for, but with so many famous players on view it did not really matter. The Gunners won with goals scored late in each half, Joe Hulme at 45 minutes and Ted Drake two minutes from time, and went through to defeat Leicester City and Reading before losing to Sheffield Wednesday, the eventual winners, 2–1 in the sixth round at Hillsborough.

Albion 1934–35

Back row left to right: Jack Stevens, Stan Webb, Paul Mooney, Charlie Thomson, Frank Brett, Potter Smith, Arthur Attwood.
Middle row left to right: Dickie Meades (trainer), Ernie King, Ernie Marriott, Stan Barber, Charlie Webb (manager), Jim Short, Jack Dugnolle, Herbert Jones (captain), Ted Martin, Bill Jones (assistant trainer).
Front row left to right: Bert Jepson, Bobby Farrell, Stan Thompson, Len Darling, Tug Wilson, Buster Brown, Harry Egan, John Payne.

Charlie Thomson and Dave Walker played in every match this term, and Ernie King was absent only once. Bobby Farrell's deferred benefit match took place on 1 May when a crowd of almost 4,000 saw Albion lose 3–2 to First Division Portsmouth.

SEASON 1935–36

This was to be another season in which the club was hit by injuries. Most of the recognised first-team players were out for varying periods, and despite a number of new signings the lack of reserve strength became a serious factor in Albion's failure to mount a realistic challenge for promotion.

Among the new men were outside-right Billy Richards from Fulham, a Welsh international; centre-forward Alec Law, a Scot from Sheffield Wednesday; inside-forward Tommy Prest, who had seen lengthy service with Burnley; and left-winger Bert Stephens from Brentford. Stephens had been at Griffin Park for four years without gaining a regular place in the League team, yet on coming to the Goldstone he developed into a very successful goalscorer. Two great favourites departed in the early days of the campaign: goalkeeper Stan Webb and skipper Frank Brett both joined Tunbridge Wells Rangers in the Southern League.

Potter Smith inherited the captaincy and had a big influence on the younger players in his benefit season. Potter was now 34, but his form throughout the season was inspirational. After playing at inside-left during most of his long career, he switched to half-back in December when both Darling and Walker were absent, and remained in the middle line for the rest of his playing days.

Once again the team was exasperatingly inconsistent. On 21 September they lost 5–0 at Coventry, then bounced back seven days later to trounce Newport County 7–1 at Hove

(Brown 3). On 26 October, Notts County were beaten 5–1 at the Goldstone (Alec Law 4), and a week later Albion crashed 5–2 at Bristol Rovers. At Christmas there were 3–0 home and away victories over Bristol City, and after a 4–0 defeat at Crystal Palace in January a splendid of run of seven wins in eight games lifted the club to sixth, but there were only two more wins in the last eleven fixtures.

The team was frequently shuffled around because of the spate of injuries – outside-left Tug Wilson appeared at right-half on one occasion – and in consequence the final seventh placing represented a fairly successful campaign. The section was a much closer affair than in recent seasons with Coventry City winning the title by just one point from Luton Town. For the first time since the days of Vallance and Kirkwood, Albion now possessed two reliable goalscorers: Alec Law, with 27 goals in League and Cup, provided the spearhead and formed a tremendous partnership with Bert Stephens, who popped up all over the place and netted 21 times.

The F.A. Cup found Albion playing non-League opposition in both the opening rounds. Southern League Cheltenham Town performed brilliantly to gain a goal-less draw at the Goldstone in the first round, but collapsed to a 6–0 hiding on their own ground in the replay. In the second round Midland League Scarborough equalised an early Bobby Farrell effort with an 85th-minute penalty to earn a replay at the Goldstone, which Albion won comfortably by three goals to nil.

SEASON 1935–36

Date	Comp.	Ven.	Opponents	Result	HT	Pos.	Scorers	Atten.	Bellamy W	Brown O	Clarke W	Darling L	Dugnolle J	Egan H	Farrell R	King E	Law A	McCarthy T	Marriott E	Martin E	Mee G	Mooney P	Prest T	Richards W	Smith P	Stephens H	Stevens J	Thomson C	Walker D	Wilson E
Aug 31	FL D3(S)	(h)	Torquay United	W 3–2	1–2	5=	Law, Walker, Farrell	10,499				4			8	3	9		2						10	7	5	1	6	11
Sep 4	FL D3(S)	(h)	Queen's Park R.	D 1–1	0–1	3=	Law	8,303				4			8	3	9		2						10	7	5	1	6	11
7	FL D3(S)	(a)	Aldershot	L 0–1	0–1	13=		5,651				4			8	3	9		2						10	7	5	1	6	11
12	FL D3(S)	(a)	Queen's Park R.	L 2–3	2–3	16	Law 2	6,236	11			4			8	3	9	1	2						10	7	5		6	
14	FL D3(S)	(h)	Swindon Town	L 0–2	0–1	20		8,463	11			4			8	3	9		2						10	7	5	1	6	
18	FL D3(S)	(h)	Watford	W 2–1	1–0	17	Stephens, Smith	4,831	11	9		4			8				2	3	1				10	7	5		6	
21	FL D3(S)	(a)	Coventry City	L 0–5	0–3	20		18,776		9		4			8				2	3	1				10	7	5		6	11
28	FL D3(S)	(h)	Newport County	W 7–1	1–1	16	Richards 2, Brown 3, Stephens 2	7,246		9		4							2	3	1		8	7	10	11	5		6	
Oct 5	FL D3(S)	(a)	Exeter City	D 3–3	3–2	17	Stephens, Richards, Walker	4,432		9		4							2	3	1		8	7	10	11	5		6	
12	FL D3(S)	(h)	Bournem'th & B.A.	L 0–1	0–0	20		8,482		9		4							2	3	1		8	7	10	11	5		6	
19	FL D3(S)	(a)	Luton Town	L 1–2	1–2	20	Stephens	10,679				4			8	2	9			3				7	10	11	5	1	6	
23	SSC R2	(h)	Queen's Park R.	W 2–1	2–1	–	Prest, Own goal	2,222				4				2	9			3			8	7	10	11	5	1	6	
26	FL D3(S)	(h)	Notts County	W 5–1	2–1	19	Smith, Law 4	8,158				4				2	9			3			8	7	10	11	5	1	6	
Nov 2	FL D3(S)	(a)	Bristol Rovers	L 2–5	1–2	20	Richards, Smith	7,997				4	6			2	9			3			8	7	10	11	5	1		
9	FL D3(S)	(h)	Gillingham	D 1–1	0–0	18	Law	6,220				4			8	2	9			3				7	10	11	5	1	6	
13	SSC R3	(a)	Swindon Town	L 1–2	0–0	–	Farrell	1,700				4			8	2	9			3				7	10		5	1	6	11
16	FL D3(S)	(a)	Southend United	D 0–0	0–0	18		6,403				4			8	2	9			3				7	10		5	1	6	11
23	FL D3(S)	(h)	Northampton T.	W 5–1	3–0	17	Farrell 2, Stephens 2, Smith	5,886		9		4			8	2				3				7	10	11	5	1	6	
30	FAC R1	(h)	Cheltenham Town	D 0–0	0–0	–		7,280				4			8	2	9			3				7	10	11	5	1	6	
Dec 4	FAC R1 Rep	(a)	Cheltenham Town	W 6–0	2–0	–	Law 3, Stephens 2, Farrell	5,000				4			8	2	9			3				7	10	11	5	1	6	
7	FL D3(S)	(h)	Reading	W 4–2	2–1	15	Richards 2, Farrell, Wilson	8,326				4			8	2	9			3				7	10		5	1	6	11
14	FAC R2	(a)	Scarborough	D 1–1	1–0	–	Farrell	7,344				4			8	2	9			3				7	10		5	1	6	11
18	FAC R2 Rep	(h)	Scarborough	W 3–0	1–0	–	Law, Farrell, Darling (pen)	5,457				4			8	2	9			3				7	10		5	1	6	11
21	FL D3(S)	(h)	Clapton Orient	L 1–3	1–3	15	Stephens	5,400				4			8	2	9			3				7	10	11	5	1	6	
25	FL D3(S)	(h)	Bristol City	W 3–2	0–3	13	Stephens	8,634				4			8	2	9			3				7	10	11	5	1	6	
26	FL D3(S)	(a)	Bristol City	W 3–0	2–0	11	Stephens, Law 2	13,175				4			8	2	9			3				7	10	11	5	1	6	
28	FL D3(S)	(a)	Torquay United	L 0–1	0–0	13		4,354							8	2	9			3			10	7	6	11	5	1	4	
Jan 4	FL D3(S)	(h)	Aldershot	W 2–1	1–1	11	Law, Prest	6,637			6				8	2	9			3			10	7	4	11	5	1		
11	FAC R3	(a)	Fulham	L 1–2	1–1	–	Farrell	29,328				4			8	2	9			3				7	10	11	5	1	6	
15	FL D3(S)	(a)	Crystal Palace	L 0–4	0–3	11		3,030				4			8	2	9			3				7	10	11	5	1	6	
18	FL D3(S)	(a)	Swindon Town	W 2–1	0–0	10	Stephens, Law	4,720							8	2	9			3			10	7	4	11	5	1	6	
25	FL D3(S)	(h)	Coventry City	W 2–1	0–1	9	Farrell, Law	8,202							8	2	9			3			10	7	4	11	5	1	6	
Feb 1	FL D3(S)	(a)	Newport County	W 2–0	1–0	6	Law, Stephens	4,751						10	8	2	9			3				7	4	11	5	1	6	
8	FL D3(S)	(a)	Exeter City	W 3–1	1–1	7	Farrell, Stephens 2	7,209						10	8	2	9			3				7	4	11	5	1	6	
15	FL D3(S)	(a)	Bournem'th & B.A.	W 2–1	2–1	7	Law, Stephens	5,689						10	8	2	9			3				7	4	11	5	1	6	
22	FL D3(S)	(h)	Luton Town	D 1–1	0–1	6	Walker	10,111						10	8	2	9			3				7	4	11	5	1	6	
29	FL D3(S)	(a)	Gillingham	W 2–1	1–1	6	Law 2 (1 pen)	4,931							8	2	9			3			10	7	4	11	5	1	6	
Mar 7	FL D3(S)	(h)	Cardiff City	W 1–0	1–0	6	Prest	8,198							8	2	9			3			10	7	4	11	5	1	6	
14	FL D3(S)	(a)	Notts County	D 1–1	0–1	6	Stephens	5,263							8	2	9			3			10	7	4	11	5	1	6	
18	FL D3(S)	(a)	Cardiff City	L 0–1	0–1	6		4,268							8	2	9			3			10	7	4	11	5	1	6	
21	FL D3(S)	(h)	Southend United	L 1–3	0–2	7	Law	8,260							8	2	9			3			10	7	4	11	5	1	6	
28	FL D3(S)	(a)	Northampton T.	L 0–1	0–1	7		6,306				4			8	2	9			3				7	10	11	5	1	6	
Apr 4	FL D3(S)	(h)	Crystal Palace	W 2–1	1–1	7	Law, Stephens	5,879				4			8	2	9			3				7	10	11	5	1	6	
10	FL D3(S)	(a)	Millwall	D 0–0	0–0	7		17,226				4			8	2				3			10	7		11	5	1	6	9
11	FL D3(S)	(a)	Reading	L 0–3	0–1	7		9,806				4			8	2				3			10	7		11	5	1	6	9
13	FL D3(S)	(h)	Millwall	D 0–0	0–0	7		10,243				4			8	2				3			10	7		11	5	1	6	9
18	FL D3(S)	(h)	Bristol Rovers	W 4–1	0–1	7	Brown, Prest, Stephens 2	5,646		9		4			8	2				3			10	7		11	5	1	6	
25	FL D3(S)	(a)	Clapton Orient	L 1–3	0–0	7	Stephens	3,421		9		4			7	2				3			8		10	11	5	1	6	
May 2	FL D3(S)	(a)	Watford	L 1–2	0–0	7	Richards	5,685		9		4			8	2				3				7	10	11	5	1	6	
League appearances									3	9	1	30	2	4	35	39	32	1	8	37	7	1	21	29	41	41	40	35	38	8
League goals										4					6		23						3	7	4	19			3	1

Fulham staged the third-round tie at Craven Cottage before an excellent 29,328 crowd (£1,920). The Londoners took the lead after 20 minutes, but Albion equalised through Farrell within 60 seconds. A goal from Jim Hammond midway through the second half gave the Cottagers victory and a home tie with Blackpool in the fourth round. Though holding only a mid-table berth in the Second Division, Fulham went on to reach the semi-finals where they were beaten 2–1 by Sheffield United.

In the third competition, the Southern Section Cup, Albion went out to runners-up Swindon Town having defeated Queen's Park Rangers 2–1 at the Goldstone.

After fourteen years of brilliant displays on the Albion left wing, Tug Wilson finally called it a day at the end of the season, although he continued to play locally with Vernon Athletic in the Sussex County League. The little Yorkshireman had played 509 League games, an all-time club record, but there was now a natural successor in Bert Stephens.

Tug's retirement came too late to enable him to play in an end-of-season fund-raising match at the Goldstone between an Old Albion side and an Old Portsmouth XI. Most of Albion's team had only recently retired and some were still playing in junior football, but the star was undoubtedly Bullet Jones, the club's assistant trainer and an old favourite from the Southern League days. Now in his mid 50s, he delighted the crowd with his legendary shooting powers and scored a goal in the Old Albion's 2–0 victory. (Earlier in the season, on 25 September, the Old Albion XI had drawn 2–2 with the Old Pompey XI in aid of the Supporters' Club fund, a game watched by 1,011 fans.)

Football League Division 3 (South) 1935–36

		P	W	D	L	F	A	W	D	L	F	A	Pts
1.	Coventry City	42	19	1	1	75	12	5	8	8	27	33	57
2.	Luton Town	42	13	6	2	56	20	9	6	6	25	25	56
3.	Reading	42	18	0	3	52	20	8	2	11	35	42	54
4.	Queen's Park R.	42	14	4	3	55	19	8	5	8	29	34	53
5.	Watford	42	12	3	6	47	29	8	6	7	33	25	49
6.	Crystal Palace	42	15	4	2	64	20	7	1	13	32	54	49
7.	**ALBION**	42	13	4	4	48	25	5	4	12	22	38	44
8.	Bournemouth & B.A.	42	13	6	2	66	36	2	5	9	24	30	43
9.	Notts County	42	10	5	6	40	25	5	7	9	20	32	42
10.	Torquay United	42	14	4	3	41	27	2	5	14	21	35	41
11.	Aldershot	42	9	6	6	29	21	5	6	10	24	40	40
12.	Millwall	42	9	8	4	33	21	5	4	12	25	50	40
13.	Bristol City	42	11	5	5	32	21	4	5	12	16	38	40
14.	Clapton Orient	42	13	2	6	34	15	3	4	14	21	46	38
15.	Northampton Town	42	12	5	4	38	24	3	3	15	24	64	38
16.	Gillingham	42	9	5	7	34	25	5	4	12	32	52	37
17.	Bristol Rovers	42	11	6	4	48	31	3	3	15	21	64	37
18.	Southend United	42	8	7	6	38	21	5	3	13	23	41	36
19.	Swindon Town	42	10	5	6	43	33	4	3	14	21	40	36
20.	Cardiff City	42	11	5	5	37	23	2	5	14	23	50	36
21.	Newport County	42	8	4	9	36	44	3	5	13	24	67	31
22.	Exeter City	42	7	5	9	38	41	1	6	14	21	52	27

Plenty of room inside!

League gates slumped in the late 1920s and early '30s to levels unknown since 1945. As the country – and Albion's football – emerged from depression, so attendances rose. The average was up to 7,659 in 1935–36, but this Southern Section Cup tie with Queen's Park Rangers on 23 October attracted just 2,222 fans, one of the lowest gates ever for a senior match at Hove. Even more sparsely occupied than the rest of the East Side is the Chicken Run, a fenced-off area with a higher admission charge. The picture shows Rangers' goalie Bill Mason clearing his lines from Albion's Tommy Prest (left) and Alec Law.

The 1935–36 season saw the infamous 'Pools War' come to a head. Littlewoods Pools had started in February 1923; others followed a few years later, and after a few brushes with the law the pools became a popular success. However, the Football League management committee objected to the use of its fixtures for purposes of gambling, and tried everything in its power to thwart the pools companies and 'cleanse the game' — against the wishes of many clubs. The result was that for two Saturdays, 29 February and 7 March 1936, the published fixtures were scrapped and others substituted. The clubs were notified who their opponents would be at short notice, presenting obvious problems for teams and supporters travelling to away matches.

In Albion's case, an away match at Notts County turned into a trip to Gillingham, and Cardiff City were guests at the Goldstone rather than Bristol Rovers. Not surprisingly, gates slumped, news of the rearranged fixtures was in any case leaked to the Press, and the 'war' was an emphatic defeat for the League. Normal service was soon resumed both on the pitch and on the coupons. Twenty-three years later, in April 1959, the League finally took the matter to court to establish that its fixtures were protected by copyright, and ever since the pools companies have paid for the fixtures, generating much income for the League.

Albion 1935–36

Back row left to right: Gordon Mee, Ernie King, Charlie Thomson.
Middle row left to right: Billy Richards, Bill Jones (assistant trainer), Ernie Marriott, Jack Stevens, Ted Martin, Charlie Webb (manager), Dave Walker, Harry Egan, Paul Mooney, Tom McCarthy, Dickie Meades (trainer).
Front row left to right: Bobby Farrell, Jack Dugnolle, Len Darling, Billy Clarke, Tommy Prest, Buster Brown, Alec Law, Potter Smith (captain), Tug Wilson.

SEASON 1936–37

This was Albion's most successful season since joining the Football League in 1920, with third place being achieved and several club records surpassed:

- Highest placing in Third Division — 3rd, previous best 4th
- Highest number of wins — 24, previous best 21
- Highest number of away wins — 9, previous best 5
- Highest total of 'doubles' — 8, previous best 5
- Highest average home gate — 10,667, previous best 9,452

Alec Law had broken a leg towards the end of the previous season and was out of the side for a considerable time. Jock Davie was recruited from Margate to fill the vacant centre-forward spot, and other signings included Joe Wilson, an inside-forward from Newcastle United; full-back Billy Burton and utility forward Jimmy Cargill from Nottingham Forest; and Stan Risdon, a half-back from Exeter City. Joe Wilson needs no introduction to older Albion fans; his association with the club was to last for 38 years as player, trainer, assistant manager, caretaker manager and chief scout. He made an immediate impact at the Goldstone and had a magnificent season. Paul Mooney had retired during the summer and moved into the Sussex County League to play for the Brighton side Vernon Athletic.

Albion gave notice that they meant business by winning four of the first five games, at which stage they headed the section. Potter Smith was injured in the opening match at Gillingham and did not reappear until mid October; in his absence Dave Walker assumed the role of skipper. After the terrific start came something of a collapse – only one point came from the next five games and the team sank to thirteenth – but then came a splendid run of five consecutive wins and eleven games without defeat. The 4–0 Boxing Day win over Gillingham at Hove saw the team back into top spot where they remained for five weeks until defeat at Northampton on 6 February. That gave the Cobblers a noteworthy double as they were the only team to win at the Goldstone this season.

Second place was maintained behind leaders Notts County with Luton Town handily placed in third spot. On Good Friday, Southend United were beaten 1–0 at the Goldstone in front of the biggest crowd of the season (17,227), but this success was followed by defeat at Reading on the Saturday and again at Southend on Easter Monday, two setbacks which enabled Luton to leap-frog Albion into second place. Two more impressive home wins over Queen's Park Rangers (4–1) and Torquay United (5–1) kept Albion among the leaders, but, to the huge disappointment of the Sussex public, the poor Easter had ended any dreams of promotion.

Albion were scheduled to play Notts County at Meadow Lane in the penultimate fixture on 24 April. County had led the section since the middle of March and were red-hot favourites for the title. With Brighton now out of the race they were expected to win comfortably, but Albion never read the script and gave their finest performance of the campaign to win 1–0 with a second-half goal from Joe Wilson; 29,516 hopeful fans had come to see their favourites strengthen their claim to the title, the biggest audience Albion had ever played to in a League match. The defeat caused an adverse reaction in the Magpies' team, and on the last day of the season they were beaten 2–1 at Walsall while Luton were accounting for Torquay United 2–0 at Kenilworth Road to snatch the championship by two points in an exciting finale.

Albion 1936–37

Back row left to right: Ernie Marriott, Gordon Mee, Jack Stevens, Charlie Thomson, Dave Walker, Jimmy Cargill, Clarrie Murfin, Bill Jones (assistant trainer).
Middle row left to right: Dickie Meades (trainer), Billy Burton, Ernie King, Jock McNaughton, Wally Pollard, Charlie Webb (manager), Potter Smith (captain), Hunt, Ted Martin, Jock Davie.
Front row left to right: Billy Richards, Stan Risdon, Buster Brown, Joe Wilson, Tommy Prest, Alec Law, Bobby Farrell.

> For the match at Bristol Rovers on 26 September, Albion wore a change strip of red-and-white hooped shirts for the first time. The strip was a present from Arsenal, who had worn the shirts on three occasions during their successful run to the F.A. Cup final in 1936 when it brought them 'an abundance of luck'. Albion lost 2–0.

SEASON 1936–37

Date	Comp.	Ven.	Opponents	Result	HT	Pos.	Scorers	Atten.	Brophy H	Brown O	Burton W	Cargill J	Darling L	Davie J	Dugnolle J	Farrell R	King E	Law A	McNaughton J	Marriott E	Martin E	Mee G	Prest T	Richards W	Risdon S	Smith P	Stephens H	Stevens J	Thomson C	Walker D	Wilson JA
Aug 29	FL D3(S)	(a)	Gillingham	L 0–1	0–1	19=		7,338				7	4	9		2					3					10	11	5	1	6	8
Sep 2	FL D3(S)	(h)	Newport County	W 2–0	2–0	7	Davie 2	7,738				7	4	9		10	2				3						11	5	1	6	8
5	FL D3(S)	(h)	Aldershot	W 1–0	0–0	5	Wilson	10,248				7	4	9		10	2				3						11	5	1	6	8
10	FL D3(S)	(a)	Newport County	W 4–1	1–0	1	Davie, Walker, Stephens, Darling (pen)	7,005				7	4	9		10	2		3								11	5	1	6	8
12	FL D3(S)	(a)	Swindon Town	W 2–1	2–0	1=	Cargill, Stephens	9,060				7	4	9		10	2		3								11	5	1	6	8
17	FL D3(S)	(a)	Clapton Orient	L 0–2	0–0	5		6,153				7	4	9		10	2		3								11	5	1	6	8
19	FL D3(S)	(h)	Millwall	D 2–2	1–1	4	Richards, Davie	12,888		2			4	9		10					3			7			11	5	1	6	8
26	FL D3(S)	(a)	Bristol Rovers	L 0–2	0–1	9		10,435		2	7		4	9		10					3						11	5	1	6	8
30	SSC R1	(a)	Crystal Palace	L 2–3	0–1	–	Stephens 2	2,822	5	2	7			9		10					3				4		11		1	6	8
Oct 3	FL D3(S)	(a)	Northampton T.	L 1–2	0–1	12	Farrell	10,499				7	4	9		10	2				3						11	5	1	6	8
10	FL D3(S)	(a)	Bournem'th & B.A.	L 0–1	0–1	13		9,630			9	7	4		6	8	2				3		10				11	5	1		
17	FL D3(S)	(a)	Walsall	W 4–1	2–0	10	Smith, Davie, Wilson, Stephens	6,321						9		10	2				3			7		4	11	5	1	6	8
24	FL D3(S)	(h)	Luton Town	W 2–1	2–0	8	Davie, Farrell	14,652						9		10	2				3			7		4	11	5	1	6	8
31	FL D3(S)	(a)	Cardiff City	W 2–1	0–0	7	Davie, Stephens	17,805						9		10	2				3			7		4	11	5	1	6	8
Nov 7	FL D3(S)	(h)	Crystal Palace	W 1–0	0–0	4	Walker	7,768						9		10	2				3			7		4	11	5	1	6	8
14	FL D3(S)	(a)	Exeter City	W 4–0	1–0	4	Davie 3, Stephens	5,500						9		10	2				3			7		4	11	5	1	6	8
21	FL D3(S)	(h)	Reading	D 1–1	1–1	2	Stephens	13,509						9		10	2				3			7		4	11	5	1	6	8
28	FAC R1	(a)	Queen's Park R.	L 1–5	0–1	–	Davie	16,000						9		10	2				3			7		4	11	5	1	6	8
Dec 5	FL D3(S)	(h)	Bristol City	W 2–0	0–0	2	Stephens 2	8,101						9		10	2				3			7		4	11	5	1	6	8
12	FL D3(S)	(a)	Torquay United	W 2–0	1–0	2	Stephens 2	2,908						9		8	2				3		10	7		4	11	5	1	6	
19	FL D3(S)	(h)	Notts County	D 2–2	1–0	2	Prest, Stephens	10,989								8	2	9			3		10	7		4	11	5	1	6	
25	FL D3(S)	(h)	Watford	D 1–1	1–0	2	Davie	14,923						9		8	2				3	1	10	7		4	11	5		6	
26	FL D3(S)	(h)	Gillingham	W 4–0	2–0	1	Law, Cargill 2, Stephens	13,977				7	4			10	2	9			3	1					11	5		6	8
28	FL D3(S)	(a)	Watford	L 0–1	0–1	1		6,055		2		10	4					9			3	1		7			11	5		6	8
Jan 2	FL D3(S)	(a)	Aldershot	W 1–0	1–0	1	Law	3,641						9			2	10			3			7		4	11	5	1	6	8
9	FL D3(S)	(h)	Swindon Town	W 2–0	1–0	1	Cargill, Stephens	10,864				7	4	9			2	10			3						11	5	1	6	8
21	FL D3(S)	(a)	Queen's Park R.	W 3–2	2–0	1	Stephens 2, Law	4,742		2			10			7		9			3					4	11	5	1	6	8
23	FL D3(S)	(a)	Millwall	L 0–3	0–1	1		17,351		2			10			7		9			3					4	11	5	1	6	8
30	FL D3(S)	(h)	Bristol Rovers	W 5–2	3–2	1	Law, Wilson 2, Farrell, Stephens	6,443					10			7	2	9			3					4	11	5	1	6	8
Feb 6	FL D3(S)	(a)	Northampton T.	L 0–2	0–2	2		13,034					10			7	2	9		11	3					4		5	1	6	8
13	FL D3(S)	(h)	Bournem'th & B.A.	W 1–0	1–0	1	Farrell	10,778					10			7	2	9			3					4	11	5	1	6	8
20	FL D3(S)	(h)	Walsall	W 3–0	1–0	1	Stephens 3	10,898					4			7	2	9			3					10	11	5	1	6	8
27	FL D3(S)	(a)	Luton Town	L 1–2	0–1	2	Law	19,488					4			7	2	9			3					10	11	5	1	6	8
Mar 6	FL D3(S)	(h)	Cardiff City	W 7–2	4–2	1	Farrell, Cargill 2, Walker, Law, Stephens 2	10,632				7	4			10	2	9			3						11	5	1	6	8
13	FL D3(S)	(a)	Crystal Palace	L 0–2	0–1	2		16,255				7	4			10	2	9			3						11	5	1	6	8
20	FL D3(S)	(h)	Exeter City	W 1–0	0–0	2	Law	10,268					10			7	2	9			3					4	11	5	1	6	8
26	FL D3(S)	(h)	Southend United	W 1–0	1–0	2	Stephens	17,227					10			7	2	9			3					4	11	5	1	6	8
27	FL D3(S)	(a)	Reading	L 0–2	0–2	2		9,570		2			10			7		9			3					4	11	5	1	6	8
29	FL D3(S)	(a)	Southend United	L 1–2	1–0	3	Wilson	14,551					4	9						2	3		7			10	11	5	1	6	8
Apr 3	FL D3(S)	(h)	Queen's Park R.	W 4–1	2–1	3	Davie, Farrell 2, Stephens	9,176						9		7		10		2	3					4	11	5	1	6	8
10	FL D3(S)	(a)	Bristol City	L 0–1	0–1	3		8,817						9		7	2	10			3					4	11	5	1	6	8
17	FL D3(S)	(h)	Torquay United	W 5–1	3–0	3	Cargill, Wilson, Davie, Stephens, Prest	6,801				7		9			2				3		10			4	11	5	1	6	8
24	FL D3(S)	(a)	Notts County	W 1–0	0–0	3	Wilson	29,516				7		9		10	2				3					4	11	5	1	6	8
May 1	FL D3(S)	(h)	Clapton Orient	D 1–1	1–0	3	Cargill	5,629				7		9		10	2				3					4	11	5	1	6	8
			League appearances						0	1	6	30	19	24	1	35	34	18	3	4	37	3	6	15	3	25	41	40	39	40	38
			League goals									8	1	13		7		7					2	1		1	24			3	7

The Hatters deserved the honours overall. Their attack scored 103 goals, 29 more than both Notts County and Brighton, and Joe Payne created a new Southern Section record with a staggering 55 goals. Left-winger Bert Stephens led Albion's list with 26 in League and Cup, followed by Jock Davie on 14.

Albion crashed out of both cup competitions at the first hurdle, losing 5–1 at Queen's Park Rangers in the F.A. Cup and 3–2 at Crystal Palace in the Southern Section tournament.

After the disappointment of missing out on promotion at the eleventh hour, a good deal of criticism was levelled at team selection at crucial stages of the campaign. At Christmas, certain directors had urged the recall of the experienced Alec Law to lead the attack and won their case to the exclusion of the younger Jock Davie. Popular opinion was that Davie should have been retained, and results seemed to support this view: with Davie leading the line seven away wins were recorded in which Jock scored six goals, while after Law's return only two victories came away from the Goldstone. There was also much dissatisfaction with the decision to play Bobby Farrell, a natural right-winger, at inside-left during the early part of the season against the player's wishes and to the detriment of his form; and again after errors in selection were made for the Easter matches. Letters to the Press suggested a lack of appreciation by the directors regarding the form of the reserve-team players and called for the manager to be allowed greater freedom in picking the team.

Football League Division 3 (South) 1936–37

		P	W	D	L	F	A	W	D	L	F	A	Pts
1.	Luton Town	42	19	1	1	69	16	8	3	10	34	37	58
2.	Notts County	42	15	3	3	44	23	8	7	6	30	29	56
3.	**ALBION**	42	15	5	1	49	16	9	0	12	25	27	53
4.	Watford	42	14	4	3	53	21	5	7	9	32	39	49
5.	Reading	42	14	5	2	53	23	5	6	10	23	37	49
6.	Bournemouth & B.A.	42	17	3	1	45	20	3	6	12	20	39	49
7.	Northampton Town	42	15	4	2	56	22	5	2	14	29	46	46
8.	Millwall	42	12	4	5	43	24	6	6	9	21	30	46
9.	Queen's Park R.	42	12	2	7	51	24	6	7	8	22	28	45
10.	Southend United	42	10	8	3	49	23	7	3	11	29	44	45
11.	Gillingham	42	14	5	2	36	18	4	3	14	16	48	44
12.	Clapton Orient	42	10	8	3	29	17	4	7	10	23	35	43
13.	Swindon Town	42	12	4	5	52	24	2	7	12	23	49	39
14.	Crystal Palace	42	11	7	3	45	20	2	5	14	17	41	38
15.	Bristol Rovers	42	14	3	4	49	20	2	1	18	22	60	36
16.	Bristol City	42	13	3	5	42	20	2	3	16	16	50	36
17.	Walsall	42	11	3	7	38	34	2	7	12	25	51	36
18.	Cardiff City	42	10	5	6	35	24	4	2	15	19	63	35
19.	Newport County	42	7	7	7	37	28	5	3	13	30	70	34
20.	Torquay United	42	9	5	7	42	32	2	5	14	15	48	32
21.	Exeter City	42	9	5	7	36	37	1	7	13	23	51	32
22.	Aldershot	42	5	6	10	29	29	2	3	16	21	60	23

The criticisms were aimed at the board and did not detract from the achievements of the players. The team served up some brilliant football with the pivotal play of Jack Stevens – and the defence in general – being a feature. Only 43 goals were conceded in the 42 League matches, the second lowest total in the entire Football League; the Northern Section champions, Stockport County, conceded just 39. Attendances were up by just over 3,000 on the previous term's average, representing a seasonal increase of some £3,500 in cash terms.

Albert Underwood, the club's long-serving secretary, died in January and a benefit match was arranged on behalf of his widow in October 1937. Albert had been at the Goldstone since 1910 and was largely instrumental in keeping football going in the area during the Great War with the formation of the Brighton and Hove club. Left-half Dave Walker also enjoyed a testimonial match, a 1–1 draw with Southampton on 28 April.

In the mid to late 1930s there was a good deal of speculation regarding a move to the Brighton and Hove greyhound stadium in Nevill Road, a rumour that has echoed down the years. However, the board announced that it was not prepared to support the idea for reasons of tradition and sentiment, and instead had plans drawn up for large-scale improvements to the Goldstone in line with the proposals of ten years earlier. In particular, a scheme was revealed in November 1936 for a 'colossal stand' along the entire western side of the ground with new offices, bars and training facilities underneath. The noble structure would have accommodated around 10,000 spectators, both seated and standing, but the stumbling-block was, of course, the cost. This was estimated to be around £18,000 and the lavish new stand remained firmly on the drawing-board.

SEASON 1937–38

This season saw the club come closer to gaining promotion than ever before. Although Albion finished two places lower than in 1936–37, the section was a much closer affair and they were in with a very good chance until the final two matches. Unfortunately, both of them were away from home and neither ended in victory.

As usual, nothing much was conceded at the Goldstone with only nine points being dropped, yet ironically it was a 2–1 home defeat by Watford on 26 March and a 1–1 Goldstone draw with lowly Torquay United on 15 April which effectively cost the club promotion. Away results in the early part of the season kept the team below the halfway mark, the first point not being won until 13 November after six successive defeats. Subsequently only three matches were lost on the road and Albion remained unbeaten from mid January until late April, a sequence of nine away matches. The run included a superb 3–0 win over Notts County at Meadow Lane. County headed the table at Christmas, but a remarkable decline saw them drop to an eventual eleventh place.

From January, Watford and Queen's Park Rangers had vied for top spot, but Millwall made a late run and enhanced their leadership by beating Albion 2–0 at The Den in the penultimate

Waiting at Hove for the train to South Liverpool, F.A. Cup second round, 11 December 1937
From left to right: Ernie Marriott, Dickie Meades (trainer), Ted Martin, Jock Davie, Bobby Farrell, Stan Risdon, Len Darling, Dave Walker (captain), Jack Stevens, William Goodwin (chairman and president), Charlie Thompson, Charlie Webb (manager), Joe Wilson, unknown, unknown, Bert Goffey.

SEASON 1937–38

Date	Comp.	Ven.	Opponents	Result	HT	Pos.	Scorers	Atten.	Bowden O	Cargill J	Darling L	Davie J	Dugnolle J	Farrell R	Goffey H	Hall E	Hurst S	King E	Law A	McNaughton J	Marriott E	Martin E	Mee G	Murfin C	Risdon S	Stephens H	Stevens J	Thomson C	Walker D	Wilson JA
Aug 28	FL D3(S)	(a)	Queen's Park R.	L 1–2	1–1	15	Cargill	16,090		10	4	9		7				2				3				11	5	1	6	8
Sep 1	FL D3(S)	(h)	Southend United	W 3–1	2–0	7=	Davie, Stephens, Martin (pen)	9,492		10	4	9		7				2				3				11	5	1	6	8
4	FL D3(S)	(h)	Reading	D 1–1	1–1	9	Davie	12,343		10	4	9		7				2				3				11	5	1	6	8
8	FL D3(S)	(a)	Southend United	L 1–2	0–2	12=	Stephens	5,460		10	4	9		7				2				3				11	5	1	6	8
11	FL D3(S)	(h)	Bournem'th & B.A.	W 3–1	2–1	11	Davie, Cargill 2	9,483		10		9		7				2				3			4	11	5	1	6	8
15	FL D3(S)	(h)	Mansfield Town	W 2–0	1–0	7	Wilson, Farrell	6,294		10		9		7				2				3			4	11	5	1	6	8
18	FL D3(S)	(a)	Cardiff City	L 1–4	1–2	12	Davie	28,034		10		9		7				2				3			4	11	5	1	6	8
25	FL D3(S)	(h)	Walsall	W 1–0	0–0	8=	Cargill	8,801		10		9		7				2				3		11	4		5	1	6	8
29	SSC R1	(a)	Gillingham	L 1–3	0–1	–	Risdon	2,000			4			7		5		2		9	3				10	11		1	6	8
Oct 2	FL D3(S)	(a)	Northampton T.	L 1–3	0–3	11=	Martin (pen)	7,998		10		9		7				2				3			4	11	5	1	6	8
9	FL D3(S)	(h)	Bristol Rovers	W 3–0	2–0	10	Davie, Hurst, Walker	9,229		10	4	9		7			11				2	3					5	1	6	8
16	FL D3(S)	(a)	Crystal Palace	L 2–3	2–1	11	Wilson, Davie	19,121		10	4	9		7		5	11				2	3						1	6	8
23	FL D3(S)	(h)	Notts County	L 0–1	0–0	12		9,231		10	4	9		7			11				2	3					5	1	6	8
30	FL D3(S)	(a)	Newport County	L 0–1	0–0	14		7,999		10	4			7			11		9		2	3					5	1	6	8
Nov 6	FL D3(S)	(h)	Bristol City	D 1–1	0–0	17	Martin (pen)	8,256	10		4			7			11				2	3	9				5	1	6	8
13	FL D3(S)	(a)	Watford	D 1–1	0–0	16	Stephens	9,281		10	4			7		5					2	3	9			11		1	6	8
20	FL D3(S)	(a)	Gillingham	W 1–0	1–0	13	Cargill	7,701		10	4			7		5					2	3	9			11		1	6	8
27	FAC R1	(h)	Tunbridge Wells R.	W 5–1	1–0	–	Davie 3, Wilson, Farrell	9,801		10	4	9		7							2	3				11	5	1	6	8
Dec 4	FL D3(S)	(h)	Swindon Town	W 3–1	2–0	13	Davie, Goffey, Stephens	6,824			4	9		7	10						2	3				11	5	1	6	8
11	FAC R2	(a)	South Liverpool	D 1–1	0–1	–	Wilson	9,063			4	9		7	10						2	3				11	5	1	6	8
15	FAC R2 Rep	(h)	South Liverpool	W 6–0	3–0	–	Davie 4, Stephens, Farrell	7,073			4	9		7	10						2	3				11	5	1	6	8
18	FL D3(S)	(h)	Millwall	W 1–0	0–0	9	Stephens	10,657			4	9		7	10						2	3				11	5	1	6	8
27	FL D3(S)	(h)	Clapton Orient	W 2–1	1–0	9	Stephens, Davie	18,327			4	9		7	10						2	3				11	5	1	6	8
28	FL D3(S)	(a)	Clapton Orient	W 3–0	0–0	6	Goffey, Farrell, Wilson	4,634			4	9	6	7	10						2	3				11	5	1		8
Jan 1	FL D3(S)	(h)	Queen's Park R.	W 3–1	2–0	6	Stephens 2, Davie	13,244			4	9		7	10						2	3				11	5	1	6	8
8	FAC R3	(a)	Bury	L 0–2	0–1	–		17,559			4	9		7	10					3	2					11	5	1	6	8
12	FL D3(S)	(a)	Exeter City	L 0–4	0–3	5		3,093			4	9		7	10						2	3				11	5	1	6	8
15	FL D3(S)	(a)	Reading	L 1–2	0–2	8	Martin (pen)	7,844			4	9	6	7	10						2	3				11	5	1		8
22	FL D3(S)	(a)	Bournem'th & B.A.	D 0–0	0–0	8		7,698			4	9	6	7	10						2	3				11	5	1		8
29	FL D3(S)	(h)	Cardiff City	W 2–1	2–0	8	Davie, Stephens	9,802			4	9	6	7	10						2	3				11	5	1		8
Feb 5	FL D3(S)	(a)	Walsall	W 3–0	1–0	7	Davie, Walker, Farrell	4,440				9		7	10						2	3			4	11	5	1	6	8
12	FL D3(S)	(h)	Northampton T.	L 1–2	0–0	7	Davie	8,447			4	9		7	10						2	3				11	5	1	6	8
19	FL D3(S)	(h)	Bristol Rovers	D 0–0	0–0	8		7,140			4	9		7	10						2	3	1			11	5		6	8
26	FL D3(S)	(h)	Crystal Palace	W 2–1	1–0	6	Davie, Stephens	9,707			4	9		7	10						2	3	1			11	5		6	8
Mar 5	FL D3(S)	(a)	Notts County	W 3–0	2–0	5	Stephens 2, Davie	14,816		7		9			10						2	3	1		4	11	5		6	8
12	FL D3(S)	(h)	Newport County	W 1–0	1–0	3	Cargill	9,345		7		9			10						2	3	1		4	11	5		6	8
19	FL D3(S)	(a)	Bristol City	D 1–1	0–1	3	Stephens	20,127		7		9			10						2	3	1		4	11	5		6	8
23	FL D3(S)	(a)	Aldershot	W 2–1	2–1	2	Davie 2	2,303		7		9			10						2	3	1		4	11	5		6	8
26	FL D3(S)	(h)	Watford	L 1–2	0–1	3	Stephens	14,781		7		9			10						2	3	1		4	11	5		6	8
Apr 2	FL D3(S)	(h)	Gillingham	D 1–1	0–1	5	Stephens	6,450				9		7	10						2	3	1		4	11	5		6	8
9	FL D3(S)	(h)	Exeter City	W 6–0	3–0	4	Cargill, Stephens 3, Davie, Hurst	7,722		10		9					7				2	3	1		4	11	5		6	8
15	FL D3(S)	(h)	Torquay United	D 1–1	1–1	4	Stephens	14,376		10		9					7				2	3	1		4	11	5		6	8
16	FL D3(S)	(a)	Swindon Town	W 1–0	0–0	4	Hurst	13,954				9			10		7				2	3	1		4	11	5		6	8
18	FL D3(S)	(a)	Torquay United	W 1–0	0–0	4	Stephens	3,978				9		7	10						2	3	1		4	11	5		6	8
23	FL D3(S)	(h)	Aldershot	W 2–1	2–0	4	Stephens 2	9,380				9		7	10						2	3	1		4	11	5		6	8
30	FL D3(S)	(a)	Millwall	L 0–2	0–1	5		32,914				9		7	10						2	3	1		4	11	5		6	8
May 7	FL D3(S)	(a)	Mansfield Town	D 1–1	0–1	5	Marriott (pen)	4,417				9		7	10						2	3	1		4	11	5		6	8
			League appearances						1	22	23	38	4	39	24	3	8	9	1	0	33	42	15	1	17	36	39	27	38	42
			League goals							7		17	3	2	3		3				1	4				22			2	3

match of the season; witnessed by a tremendous crowd of 32,914, the result ended Albion's promotion push. A week later the Dockers made sure of the title with a crushing 5–1 win at Exeter to finish one point ahead of runners-up Bristol City and five clear of the Albion in fifth place.

The dynamic Jock Davie led Albion's goalscorers with 24 in League and Cup, while Bert Stephens netted 23, bringing his total to 70 in three seasons since arriving at the Goldstone, a remarkable scoring rate for a winger. However, quite the outstanding player of the season was Ernie Marriott at right-back. Recalled to the side when Ernie King was injured at the beginning of October, Marriott turned in some impressive performances and retained his place through sheer merit. King was granted a benefit this year but, because of the injury, he was unable to play in his testimonial match on 4 May, a 5–1 defeat at the hands of First Division Bolton Wanderers.

There were constant team changes throughout the campaign and only eight players made more than 30 League appearances, with left-back Ted Martin and inside-right Joe Wilson ever-present. Once again the directors were heavily criticised for forcing manager Webb's hand in the matter of team selection. The public were mystified in particular at the exclusion of winger Stan Hurst. Signed from Watford during the close season, Stan appeared in only eight League games despite playing well and scoring three goals, and the fans demanded to know why.

With the success of the team at the Goldstone, the average attendance was 10,164, around 500 down on 1936–37 but nevertheless reflecting a healthy interest in the promotion effort.

Football League Division 3 (South) 1937–38

		P	W	D	L	F	A	W	D	L	F	A	Pts
1.	Millwall	42	15	3	3	53	15	8	7	6	30	22	56
2.	Bristol City	42	14	6	1	37	13	7	7	7	31	27	55
3.	Queen's Park R.	42	15	3	3	44	17	7	6	8	36	30	53
4.	Watford	42	14	4	3	50	15	7	7	7	23	28	53
5.	**ALBION**	42	15	3	3	40	16	6	6	9	24	28	51
6.	Reading	42	17	2	2	44	21	3	9	9	27	42	51
7.	Crystal Palace	42	14	4	3	45	17	4	8	9	22	30	48
8.	Swindon Town	42	12	4	5	33	19	5	6	10	16	30	44
9.	Northampton Town	42	12	4	5	30	19	5	5	11	21	38	43
10.	Cardiff City	42	13	7	1	57	22	2	5	14	10	32	42
11.	Notts County	42	10	6	5	29	17	6	3	12	21	33	41
12.	Southend United	42	12	5	4	43	23	3	5	13	27	45	40
13.	Bournemouth & B.A.	42	8	10	3	36	20	6	2	13	20	37	40
14.	Mansfield Town	42	12	5	4	46	26	3	4	14	16	41	39
15.	Bristol Rovers	42	10	7	4	28	20	3	6	12	18	41	39
16.	Newport County	42	9	10	2	31	15	2	6	13	12	37	38
17.	Exeter City	42	10	4	7	37	32	3	8	10	20	38	38
18.	Aldershot	42	11	4	6	23	14	4	1	16	16	45	35
19.	Clapton Orient	42	10	7	4	27	19	3	0	18	15	42	33
20.	Torquay United	42	7	5	9	22	28	2	7	12	16	45	30
21.	Walsall	42	10	4	7	34	37	1	3	17	18	51	29
22.	Gillingham	42	9	5	7	25	25	1	1	19	11	52	26

Though reaching the third round of the F.A. Cup, there was to be no money-spinning glamour tie. Tunbridge Wells Rangers were beaten 5–1 at the Goldstone in the first round, with the aid of a hat-trick from Jock Davie. (Playing in goal for the Southern League side was the son of Albion's pre-Great War 'keeper Bob Beale.) In the second round South Liverpool were drawn away and a ground-record 9,063 crowd squeezed into the cramped arena to see the locals hold Albion to a 1–1 draw. South Liverpool were members of the Lancashire Combination and were on their way to the second of three successive championships, but they could not stem the tide in the Goldstone replay when four goals from Jock Davie helped Albion to a 6–0 victory. The big win saw Albion qualify for an away tie with Bury in the third round. The Shakers were a moderate Second Division side, but Albion could make little impression on them, losing 2–0 to goals scored in each half.

The Southern Section Cup was a disappointment, Gillingham winning the first-round tie at Priestfield 3–1.

In contrast to the League side, the reserve team had its worst season to date, finishing last of the 24 teams in the London Combination and conceding 123 goals in the process. There was talk of pulling out of the Combination and returning to the Southern League, but it was wisely decided to stay put.

Trainer Dickie Meades announced his retirement in May after nineteen years with the club; aged 45, he had decided to concentrate on his business as a masseur. The height of Dickie's career came in 1929 when he was chosen to act as trainer to the England team on the end-of-season tour of France, Belgium and Spain. His loyalty was rewarded with a benefit match.

SEASON 1938–39

What was to be the last regular football season for seven years was one of continued frustration for the Albion and their supporters: a season that promised so much saw the team miss out in the closing stages yet again. With the higher running-costs of the Second Division, rumour was rife – and not for the last time – that the club did not want promotion.

The whole season was played out against a background of political and military rumblings across Europe. The infamous Munich Agreement, signed by Chamberlain, Daladier, Hitler and Mussolini on 29 September, was followed by the German annexation of Czechoslovakia in March 1939, and by the Italian seizure of Albania in April. On 27 April conscription was introduced in Britain. As had happened in 1914–15, the season at the start of the First World War, attendances fell. The home average this season dropped to 8,392, and the last two matches at the Goldstone attracted crowds of under 3,000 after it had become obvious that the Albion were not going to win the section.

During the summer the North Stand was extended to the full width of the pitch and the enlarged structure was christened on 27 August when Walsall were defeated 3–1 in the initial fixture. Also on show for the first time were new signings Peter Trainor from Preston North End and Jack Philbin from Torquay United. Other new recruits were Bob Vasey (Notts County), Freddie Green (Torquay United) and Jack Atherton (Preston North End).

With the retirement of Dickie Meades, the vacant trainer's job went to Sam Cowan. In a splendid playing career with Doncaster Rovers, Manchester City and Bradford City, Sam played in 474 League matches, and appeared in three F.A. Cup finals while at Maine Road, skippering the victorious team of 1934. In addition he had won three England caps, so he was more than qualified for the post.

In the first half of the season Albion maintained a comfortable place in the top half of the table without giving much cause for excitement. Exeter City were beaten 6–1 at the Goldstone in September and home form was again impressive, with only nine

Albion 1938–39

Back row left to right: Gordon Mee, Jack Philbin, Jock McNaughton, Charlie Thomson, Peter Trainor, Jock Davie.
Middle row left to right: Bill Jones (assistant trainer), Bert Goffey, Freddie Green, Jack Stevens, Ernie Hall, Jimmy Cargill, Albert Day, Jack Atherton, Des Broomfield, Vic Saunders, Sam Cowan (trainer).
Front row left to right: Alec Law, Ernie Marriott, Len Darling, Joe Wilson, Bob Vasey, Dave Walker (captain), Stan Risdon, Stan Hurst, Ted Martin, Bobby Farrell.

SEASON 1938–39

Date	Comp.	Ven.	Opponents	Result	HT	Pos.	Scorers	Atten.	Atherton J	Cargill J	Darling L	Davie J	Farrell R	Goffey H	Green F	Hurst S	Law A	McNaughton J	Marriott E	Martin E	Mee G	Philbin J	Risdon S	Stephens H	Stevens J	Thomson C	Trainor P	Vasey R	Walker D	Wilson JA
Aug 27	FL D3(S)	(h)	Walsall	W 3–1	1–1	3=	Law, Stephens 2	10,850		4						7	9		2	3		10		11		1	5		6	8
30	FL D3(S)	(a)	Bristol Rovers	W 1–0	0–0	1=	Law	10,436		4						7	9		2	3		10		11		1	5		6	8
Sep 3	FL D3(S)	(a)	Mansfield Town	L 2–4	1–2	9	Hurst 2	5,830		4				10		7	9		2	3				11		1	5		6	8
7	FL D3(S)	(h)	Reading	D 2–2	1–0	10	Stephens 2	8,285		4						7	9		2	3		10		11		1	5		6	8
10	FL D3(S)	(h)	Queen's Park R.	W 3–1	2–1	8	Stephens, Cargill, Hurst	11,708	10	4						7	9		2	3				11		1	5		6	8
14	FL D3(S)	(a)	Reading	L 0–3	0–2	9		7,473	10	4						7	9		2	3				11		1	5		6	8
17	FL D3(S)	(a)	Southend United	D 1–1	1–0	7	Law	8,274		4				10		7	9		2	3				11		1	5		6	8
24	FL D3(S)	(h)	Exeter City	W 6–1	2–1	6	Goffey, Law 2, Hurst, Stephens, Wilson	9,372		4				10		7	9		2	3				11		1	5		6	8
Oct 1	FL D3(S)	(a)	Cardiff City	L 1–4	1–2	8	Law	17,393		4				10		7	9		2	3				11		1	5		6	8
8	FL D3(S)	(h)	Ipswich Town	W 2–0	0–0	7	Hurst 2	10,482		4				10		7	9		2	3				11	5	1			6	8
15	FL D3(S)	(a)	Aldershot	L 0–3	0–0	7		12,203		4				10		7	9		2	3				11	5	1			6	8
22	FL D3(S)	(a)	Crystal Palace	L 0–1	0–0	9		18,899		4				10		7	9		2	3				11		1	5		6	8
29	FL D3(S)	(h)	Northampton T.	W 1–0	0–0	7	Stephens	9,204		4				10		7	9		2	3				11		1	5		6	8
Nov 5	FL D3(S)	(a)	Newport County	L 0–2	0–0	7		11,290		4				10		7	9		2	3				11		1	5		6	8
12	FL D3(S)	(h)	Clapton Orient	W 2–0	2–0	7	Davie, Wilson	7,630	10		4	9	7						2	3				11		1	5		6	8
19	FL D3(S)	(a)	Torquay United	W 2–0	0–0	6	Wilson, Hurst	3,563	10		4	9				7			2	3				11		1	5		6	8
26	FAC R1	(a)	Yeovil & Petters U.	L 1–2	1–1	–	Marriott (pen)	8,200	10		4	9				7			2	3				11		1	5		6	8
Dec 3	FL D3(S)	(a)	Port Vale	D 1–1	1–1	7	Stephens	8,015	10	7	4	9							2	3				11		1	5		6	8
10	SSC R2	(h*)	Crystal Palace	L 2–3	1–0		Davie, Cargill	3,877	10	7		9			8				2	3				11		1	5	4	6	
17	FL D3(S)	(a)	Notts County	L 3–4	1–1	7	Atherton 2, Vasey	8,073	10	7		9							2	3				11	5	1		4	6	8
24	FL D3(S)	(a)	Walsall	W 2–0	2–0	6	Stephens 2	4,925	10	7		9							2	3				11	5	1		4	6	8
26	FL D3(S)	(a)	Bristol City	L 0–2	0–2	9		9,958	10	7		9							2	3				11		1	5	4	6	8
27	FL D3(S)	(h)	Bristol City	W 1–0	1–0	7	Cargill	12,071	10	7		9							2	3				11		1	5	4	6	8
31	FL D3(S)	(h)	Mansfield Town	W 3–0	3–0	6	Goffey, Stephens, Hurst	7,084				9		10		7			2	3				11		1	5	4	6	8
Jan 7	FL D3(S)	(h)	Swindon Town	W 4–0	3–0	3	Farrell, Davie	5,224				9	7	10					2	3				11		1	5	4	6	8
14	FL D3(S)	(h)	Queen's Park R.	W 2–1	2–1	3	Goffey, Own goal	11,387				9		10		7			2	3				11		1	5	4	6	8
28	FL D3(S)	(a)	Exeter City	D 2–2	1–1	3	Davie 2	5,152				9		10		7			2	3				11		1	5	4	6	8
Feb 4	FL D3(S)	(h)	Cardiff City	L 1–2	0–2	4	Stephens	9,770				9		10		7			2	3				11		1	5	4	6	8
8	FL D3(S)	(h)	Southend United	W 3–0	2–0	2	Cargill, Stephens, Davie	4,508		7	4	9			8				2	3	1			11			5		6	10
11	FL D3(S)	(h)	Ipswich Town	D 0–0	0–0	2		13,373		7	4	9			8				2	3	1			11			5		6	10
18	FL D3(S)	(a)	Aldershot	D 1–1	1–1	3	Walker	5,403			4	9		10		7			2	3	1			11			5		6	8
25	FL D3(S)	(h)	Crystal Palace	D 0–0	0–0	4		7,146			4	9		10		7			2	3	1			11			5		6	8
Mar 4	FL D3(S)	(a)	Northampton T.	W 4–1	2–0	3	Davie 2, Wilson, Stephens	5,044			4	9		10		7			2	3	1			11			5		6	8
11	FL D3(S)	(a)	Newport County	D 0–0	0–0	2		15,157		7	4	9		10					2	3	1			11			5		6	8
18	FL D3(S)	(a)	Clapton Orient	L 0–2	0–0	2		7,333		7	4			10				9	2	3	1			11			5		6	8
25	FL D3(S)	(h)	Torquay United	W 2–0	1–0	2	Davie 2	6,469			4	9		10	8				2	3	1			11			5		6	7
Apr 1	FL D3(S)	(a)	Swindon Town	L 2–3	1–0	3	Wilson, Stephens	9,111			4	9		10	8				2	3	1			11			5		6	7
7	FL D3(S)	(h)	Bournem'th & B.A.	D 1–1	0–1	3	Goffey	10,320			4	9		10					2	3	1	5		11					6	7
8	FL D3(S)	(h)	Port Vale	W 1–0	1–0	3	Goffey	7,807			4	9		10					2	3	1	5		11					6	7
10	FL D3(S)	(a)	Bournem'th & B.A.	L 0–2	0–1	4		7,528			4	9	5	10			7		2	3	1			11					6	8
15	FL D3(S)	(a)	Watford	D 1–1	1–0	3	Cargill	6,339		7	4	9		10					2		1		5	11				3	6	8
22	FL D3(S)	(a)	Notts County	W 2–0	2–0	3	Philbin, Farrell	5,508			4	9	7	10					2		1	5		11				3	6	8
26	FL D3(S)	(h)	Watford	D 0–0	0–0	3		2,620			4	9	7	10		8			2		1	5		11				3	6	
29	FL D3(S)	(h)	Bristol Rovers	W 6–3	3–1	3	Stephens 2, Goffey 2, Farrell 2	2,806			4	9	7	10		8			2		1	5		11				3	6	
			League appearances						9	14	33	27	10	28	2	25	15	3	40	35	16	6	1	40	6	26	34	15	40	37
			League goals				OG – 1		2	4		9	6	7		8	6					1		17				1	1	5

Note: Dec 10 – tie drawn away but switched to the Goldstone Ground.

points forfeited; Aldershot and Cardiff City were the only victors at Hove.

Because of cup commitments by both Albion and prospective opponents, there was just one first-team fixture at the Goldstone in an incredible seven-week period from 12 November to 27 December. The exception was a Southern Section Cup match against Crystal Palace on 10 December which the Palace management generously allowed to be switched from Selhurst. The Glaziers were not as forthcoming on the pitch, though, winning the tie 3–2 before a crowd of 3,877.

During this period of absence Albion were drawn away in the first round of the F.A. Cup to Yeovil and Petters United of the Southern League. The Somerset side were laying the foundations of their reputation as giant-killers *par excellence*. They had reached the third round in 1934–35 when, after accounting for Crystal Palace and Exeter City, they were soundly beaten 6–2 on their own ground by Liverpool; and again in 1937–38, when they lost 3–0 to Manchester United at Old Trafford. This season Albion provided the cannon-fodder by losing 2–1 on the famous Huish slope. Ernie Marriott equalised an early Yeovil opener with a penalty just before half time, but the home team regained the lead in the 60th minute and ran out deserved winners, the first non-League side to beat Albion since their entry into the Football League. Yeovil went on to beat Folkestone in the second round before losing to Sheffield Wednesday

Football League Division 3 (South) 1938–39

		P	W	D	L	F	A	W	D	L	F	A	Pts
1.	Newport County	42	15	4	2	37	16	7	7	7	21	29	55
2.	Crystal Palace	42	15	4	2	49	18	5	8	8	22	34	52
3.	**ALBION**	42	14	5	2	43	14	5	6	10	25	35	49
4.	Watford	42	14	6	1	44	15	3	6	12	18	36	46
5.	Reading	42	12	6	3	46	23	4	8	9	23	36	46
6.	Queen's Park R.	42	10	8	3	44	15	5	6	10	24	34	44
7.	Ipswich Town	42	14	3	4	46	21	2	9	10	16	31	44
8.	Bristol City	42	14	5	2	42	19	2	7	12	19	44	44
9.	Swindon Town	42	15	5	2	53	25	3	4	14	19	52	44
10.	Aldershot	42	13	6	2	31	15	3	6	12	22	51	44
11.	Notts County	42	12	6	3	36	16	5	3	13	23	38	43
12.	Southend United	42	14	5	2	38	13	2	4	15	23	51	41
13.	Cardiff City	42	12	1	8	40	28	3	10	8	21	37	41
14.	Exeter City	42	9	9	3	40	32	4	5	12	25	50	40
15.	Bournemouth & B.A.	42	10	8	3	38	22	3	5	13	14	36	39
16.	Mansfield Town	42	10	8	3	33	19	2	7	12	11	43	39
17.	Northampton Town	42	13	5	3	41	20	2	3	16	10	38	38
18.	Port Vale	42	10	5	6	36	23	4	4	13	16	35	37
19.	Torquay United	42	7	5	9	27	28	7	4	10	27	42	37
20.	Clapton Orient	42	10	9	2	40	16	1	4	16	13	39	35
21.	Walsall	42	9	6	6	47	23	2	5	14	21	46	33
22.	Bristol Rovers	42	8	8	5	30	17	2	5	14	25	44	33

2–1 in a third-round replay after holding the First Division side to a thrilling 1–1 draw at Hillsborough.

There was no really outstanding side in the Southern Section this term and it was generally felt that the standard was the poorest for many years. The surprise of the season was the emergence of Newport County. Since joining the Football League in 1920, the Monmouthshire club had struggled for survival and never finished higher than sixth. In 1931 they failed to gain re-election after finishing one place off the bottom, only to be voted back a year later on the demise of Thames. Since then they had been placed 21st, 18th, 22nd, 21st, 19th and 16th, hardly the pedigree for promotion, yet they won the section with 55 points despite registering only 58 goals.

From the turn of the year Albion were never out of the top four, but deficiencies in attack gave cause for concern. The problem positions were outside-right and inside-left where numerous players were tried without real success, and the team failed to score in 11 of the 42 League games. In contrast the defence was as sound as ever, keeping a clean sheet on no fewer than seventeen occasions, but, with only five of the last fifteen matches ending in victory, promotion hopes gradually faded and the final third placing was seen by the fans as failure. The club received £100, to be shared among the players, under the talent-money scheme.

Ted Martin received scant reward for five years of consistency at the Goldstone when only 794 spectators watched the Albion beat West Ham United 2–0 in his testimonial match on 19 April.

A sign of things to come

In August 1938 the Sussex Police met their counterparts from Wuppertal in a challenge football match during a short visit to Hove by the German force. The game was played in a friendly and sporting manner with the local bobbies winning 3–2, but there were signs of things to come when the German party insisted on giving the Nazi salute on their arrival at Hove Station, again at the civic reception, and, as this chilling photograph shows, prior to the kick-off at the Goldstone Ground.

SEASON 1939–40

The season opened with a friendly match against Crystal Palace at the Goldstone. Played in aid of the Football League's Jubilee Fund – to benefit players, former players and clubs in times of hardship – local derbies were arranged all over the country for the second year running, this season seeing the return fixtures of the previous term. Palace had thrashed Albion 5–1 at Selhurst Park in August 1938, but this time an exciting game ended with the teams sharing six goals. It was also the first occasion on which Albion appeared in numbered shirts, under the Football League's new directive.

A week later, with the political situation worsening daily, the League programme began with a goal-less draw against Port Vale at Hove. There had been numerous changes to the playing staff during the summer: Alec Law had moved to Chester, Stan Hurst to Aldershot, Jimmy Cargill to Barrow and goalkeeper Charlie Thomson to Exeter City, while Dave Walker had retired after ten years at Hove. In came nineteen-year-old goalkeeper Harry Baldwin and outside-right Geoff Spencer from West Bromwich Albion, inside-left Bill Isaac (Newcastle United), left-half Joe Harris (Doncaster Rovers), centre-forward Frank Hindley (Nottingham Forest), wing-half Charlie Longdon (Brentford) and 21-year-old right-winger Tony James (Folkestone).

SEASON 1939–40

Date	Comp.	Ven.	Opponents	Result	HT	Pos.	Scorers	Atten.
Aug 26	FL D3(S)*	(h)	Port Vale	D 0-0	0-0	7		7,554
30	FL D3(S)*	(h)	Aldershot	W 2-1	1-0	3=	Hindley, Stephens	5,269
Sep 2	FL D3(S)*	(a)	Bristol City	D 3-3	3-2	5	Davie 2, J Wilson	7,694
Oct 21	FL (South 'B')	(h)	Aldershot	W 4-0	1-0	1=	Davie 2, Goffey, Isaac	2,696
28	FL (South 'B')	(a)	Bournem'th & B.A.	L 1-6	0-2	6	Davie	2,000
Nov 4	FL (South 'B')	(h)	Chelsea	W 5-1	0-1	4	Davie, Farrell 3, J Wilson	4,053
11	FL (South 'B')	(a)	Southampton	L 2-3	0-3	6	Risdon, Marriott (pen)	3,000
18	FL (South 'B')	(h)	Brentford	L 1-4	1-2	8	Farrell	3,533
25	FL (South 'B')	(a)	Reading	L 1-2	0-1	8	Kay	1,996
Dec 2	FL (South 'B')	(h)	Fulham	L 4-7	2-4	8	J Wilson, Farrell 2, Own goal	5,000
9	FL (South 'B')	(h)	Portsmouth	L 1-2	1-1	9	Risdon	3,000
16	FL (South 'B')	(a)	Queen's Park R.	L 2-3	1-0	9	Davie 2	2,000
23	FL (South 'B')	(a)	Aldershot	L 1-5	1-2	9	Risdon	1,000
25	FL (South 'B')	(h)	Bournem'th & B.A.	L 1-3	1-1	10	Risdon	4,000
26	FL (South 'B')	(a)	Chelsea	L 2-3	0-3	10	Stephens, Davie	3,000
30	FL (South 'B')	(h)	Southampton	W 9-4	5-1	9	J Wilson 3, Farrell 3, Davie 3	944
Jan 6	FL (South 'B')	(a)	Brentford	W 3-2	0-1	9	Own goal, Davie 2 (1 pen)	2,701
13	FL (South 'B')	(h)	Reading	L 0-1	0-0	9		2,000
20	FL (South 'B')	(a)	Fulham	D 1-1	1-1	9	Stephens	1,375
27	FL (South 'B')	(a)	Portsmouth	L 1-5	1-5	9	Risdon	1,718
Feb 10	FL (South 'D')	(h)	Crystal Palace	L 1-3	1-0	7=	Risdon	1,739
24	FL (South 'D')	(h)	Reading	W 3-0	1-0	5	Stephens 2, Farrell	2,120
Mar 2	FL (South 'D')	(a)	Clapton Orient	L 1-5	0-5	8	Davie	2,000
9	FL (South 'D')	(a)	Queen's Park R.	L 1-2	0-0	9	Davie	2,500
16	FL (South 'D')	(a)	Southend United	L 2-8	2-4	10	Davie 2	2,000
22	FL (South 'D')	(a)	Norwich City	D 3-3	1-1	10	Farrell, Davie	3,297
23	FL (South 'D')	(h)	Bournem'th & B.A.	L 0-5	0-0	10		3,560
25	FL (South 'D')	(a)	Norwich City	L 0-3	0-0	10		8,535
30	FL (South 'D')	(a)	Watford	L 2-4	1-3	10	Stephens 2	3,174
Apr 6	FL (South 'D')	(a)	Crystal Palace	L 0-10	0-5	10		7,500
10	FL (South 'D')	(h)	Southend United	L 1-3	1-3	10	J Kelly	506
13	FLWC Prelim.	(h)	Clapton Orient	L 1-2	0-0	–	Stephens	2,445
17	FL (South 'D')	(h)	Bournem'th & B.A.	D 3-3	2-2	10	Stephens 2, Bott	522
20	FL (South 'D')	(h)	Queen's Park R.	L 4-5	2-2	10	Davie 2, Stephens 2	3,000
27	FL (South 'D')	(a)	Aldershot	L 1-4	1-0	10	Darling	2,200
May 4	FL (South 'B')	(h)	Queen's Park R.	W 3-1	0-1	9	Davie 2, Bott	1,100
13	FL (South 'D')	(h)	Aldershot	D 2-2	1-2	10	Bott (pen), Collins	600
18	FL (South 'D')	(h)	Reading	L 1-3	1-2	10	Cothliff	1,299
Jun 1	FL (South 'D')	(h)	Watford	D 2-2	2-0	10	Stephens 2	587
8	FL (South 'D')	(a)	Clapton Orient	W 3-0	3-0	10	Stephens, Own goal, Harman	450

Football League (South 'B') appearances		
Football League (South 'B') goals	OG – 2	
Football League (South 'D') appearances		
Football League (South 'D') goals	OG – 1	

Notes: The Football League Division Three (South) was cancelled upon the outbreak of war on Sep 3.

Apr 6 – Clifford made up the side after 10 minutes, taking over in goal from Mee; they swapped back at half time.

The following additional players each made one appearance in the Football League (South 'D') – Apr 10: Layton, W. (no.10) and Swinfen, R. (no.7).

Two more League games were played, a 2–1 win over Aldershot at the Goldstone and a 3–3 draw at Bristol City. With German forces invading Poland on 1 September, compulsory military service for all men between the ages of 18 and 41 was announced the following day. On 3 September 1939, Prime Minister Neville Chamberlain broadcast to the nation that a state of war would exist between the United Kingdom and Germany as from 5 p.m. So, for the second time in 25 years, Europe plunged into bloody conflict and three days later the *Luftwaffe* staged its first air-raid on mainland Britain.

The Football League season was immediately suspended and the assembly of crowds was banned by the Government, but within two weeks the restriction was lifted and the clubs started playing friendly matches until a decision could be made regarding the immediate future of the game. The London Combination was also aborted and the Albion reserve team was dropped for the duration.

Players' contracts were suspended and a new maximum wage of thirty shillings (£1.50) per week was introduced. Many footballers were called into the armed forces, while others joined the auxiliary services. Unlike the Great War period, the Albion board decided to keep the club running, in line with the vast majority of clubs throughout the land. On 2 October the Football League met at Crewe and agreed on plans for regional competitions to commence on 21 October. For the remainder of the season the League clubs would be divided into eight divisions, viz.: South 'A', South 'B', South-West, Midlands, East Midlands, West, North-West, and North-East. Two further competitions, South 'C' for First and Second Division clubs, and South 'D' for Third Division sides, were organised by the League for the second half of the season after the London-based clubs had threatened to form their own competition. The metropolitan teams were unhappy about the League's regionalisation which had split the capital in two, a disagreement which would simmer for two more seasons.

Albion were to play in the South 'B' and 'D' sections and initially fielded a team comprising the club's own players, but, as service commitments took them away from the area, Charlie Webb took advantage of the 'guest-player' system. This enabled men stationed in a particular district to make up the numbers for the local club, having first obtained the permission of their commanding officer. The system was absolutely vital for the continuance of football during the war but was often abused by clubs, star players with 'box-office appeal' being brought in to the exclusion of registered players. Nevertheless, there were also to be many occasions over the next seven seasons when Albion had to resort to recruiting opposition players or even spectators to make up a team.

With the absence of organised training, and the players often being strangers to one another, there were some remarkable scorelines: Fulham 7 Albion 4; Albion 9 Southampton 4; Southend 8 Albion 2; and Crystal Palace 10 Albion 0 were among the more outrageous. The club fared badly in this first wartime season, finishing ninth of ten in section 'B' and last of ten in section 'D', with a goal tally of 72–118 in the 36 matches. Every match away from home was lost. The F.A. Cup was cancelled, but the Football League ran a War Cup competition. Albion's involvement was minimal as they lost at home to Clapton Orient in the preliminary round.

The visits of teams such as Chelsea and Portsmouth afforded Goldstone regulars the opportunity of seeing some top-class First Division players in action, but with minds on greater things the gates were disastrously low, especially in the latter stages of the season when attendances of under 1,000 became

Football League (South 'B') 1939–40

		P	W	D	L	F	A	W	D	L	F	A	Pts
1.	Queen's Park R.	18	8	1	0	27	11	4	1	4	22	15	26
2.	Bournemouth & B.A.	18	7	2	0	27	9	4	0	5	25	28	24
3.	Chelsea	18	6	3	0	23	12	3	2	4	21	25	23
4.	Reading	18	7	1	1	33	17	3	1	5	14	25	22
5.	Brentford	18	6	1	2	27	21	2	1	6	15	20	18
6.	Fulham	18	6	0	3	33	26	1	4	4	17	25	18
7.	Portsmouth	18	6	0	3	26	16	1	2	6	11	26	16
8.	Aldershot	18	4	3	2	24	17	1	1	7	14	32	14
9.	**ALBION**	18	5	1	3	28	16	0	0	9	14	37	11
10.	Southampton	18	4	0	5	26	23	0	0	9	15	41	8

Football League (South 'D') 1939–40

		P	W	D	L	F	A	W	D	L	F	A	Pts
1.	Crystal Palace	18	7	1	1	41	11	6	0	3	23	19	27
2.	Queen's Park R.	18	7	1	1	26	12	3	2	4	12	16	23
3.	Watford	18	6	3	0	29	10	1	4	4	12	19	21
4.	Southend United	18	6	2	1	27	10	2	1	6	14	27	19
5.	Aldershot	18	6	1	2	23	13	1	2	6	15	23	17
6.	Clapton Orient	18	6	1	2	25	16	1	2	6	8	29	17
7.	Bournemouth & B.A.	17	6	1	1	24	7	1	1	7	14	33	16
8.	Norwich City	17	6	1	2	24	16	0	3	5	8	18	16
9.	Reading	18	5	1	3	19	16	1	1	7	12	26	14
10.	**ALBION**	18	2	4	3	19	18	0	0	9	11	47	8

Note: The match Bournemouth & B.A. v. Norwich City was not played within the season.

the norm. The biggest turn-out was 4,083 for the visit of Chelsea on 4 November, but only around 450 attended the final match of the season, a 3–0 victory over Clapton Orient on 8 June as the season was extended by an extra month. Two days earlier Frank Hindley became Albion's first casualty of the war, shot through the shoulder.

At the end of the campaign the club's finances were in very bad shape: crippling debts of £5,635 16s. 1d. were disclosed and Albion were very close to liquidation. Indeed, it was only the initiative of the vice-chairman, Councillor Albert Hillman (Mayor of Hove 1936–40) who approached the board of the Brighton and Hove Stadium Company with a view to them

Albion's saviour
Albert Hillman, Mayor of Hove 1936–40, who brought in greyhound stadium directors Charles Wakeling and Carlo Campbell to rescue the club from liquidation. 'That to me would have been one of the most serious blows and disappointments of my life,' he told the a.g.m. just a few weeks before his death in November 1940. 'I feel that having got a professional football club in Hove we don't want to go into liquidation and give somebody else the chance to start elsewhere. Sooner than that such a thing should happen I think the Albion flag should be kept flying if it is anyhow possible.'

taking over the club, that saved the day. The greyhound stadium directors, Charles Wakeling and Major 'Carlo' Campbell, responded admirably and were appointed to the Albion board in May, Wakeling making out a cheque to cover the most pressing debts. Hillman himself became chairman and, together with former chairman William Goodwin, came up with £3,500 to meet an urgent demand from the bank. Goodwin, who had served as a director, president and chairman at various times for some 35 years, resigned 'for the good of the club' along with fellow directors Henry Miles (30 years on the board), William Neal and Hubert Service.

The new board hoped, by careful management and prudent expenditure, to pay its way during the war and even build up a reserve fund. Sadly, Councillor Hillman passed away in November 1940 in his fifth term as mayor. His enterprise had undoubtedly rescued the club from liquidation. Hillman's death left Wakeling and Campbell in control, a partnership which was to bring an up-beat air of vigour and life to the Goldstone throughout the war. Part of their rescue package was an agreement to remove the club – 'at an opportune moment' – to the greyhound stadium with the Goldstone Ground put up for sale, but the scheme never came to fruition because dog-racing was also held on Saturday afternoons during the conflict. The

plan was raised again in October 1943, this time with the intention of retaining the Goldstone for junior and schoolboy matches, but once again nothing came of the idea.

One splendid initiative that was a great success was the formation of an Albion junior side, to encourage and develop talent among the youth of Sussex. The youngsters played their first game on 10 May, a 3–1 defeat of Hove, and five of the lads were drafted into the first team three weeks later for the final two League games of the season, a 2–2 draw with Watford and a 3–0 victory over Clapton Orient. With the enthusiastic backing of the new board, the juniors played an extensive programme of friendly matches during the war. They were also entered in the Sussex Wartime Cup in the four seasons 1941–45 and the Sussex County Emergency League in 1945–46, and did much to keep local football alive throughout the war. They won the Cup (which was played on a league basis) in 1942–43 and completed a double by lifting the R.U.R. Cup, beating Worthing 4–3 at Woodside Road. Charlie Chase, Bernard Moore, Stan Willemse, Charlie Burtenshaw, Jess Willard and Jack Ball all graduated into post-war League football from the Albion junior side, which was managed by Bullet Jones's son Leslie.

Boys 2 Men 2
The five lads from the Albion junior team fielded against Watford in the Football League's South 'D' competition on 1 June 1940. The team came out with a creditable 2–2 draw. Left to right, they are: Bert Austen (17 years old), Charlie Chase (16), Charlie Harman (16), Roy Watts (17) and Stan Hickman (18).

SEASON 1940–41

The previous season had been played amid the so-called 'phoney war', but there was nothing false about the conflict when the 1940–41 campaign began. August saw the start of the Battle of Britain, and while Brighton and Hove were not in the direct firing line they did suffer from many daylight raids. Over the next four years of the war there were 86 air-raids on the twin towns, with 222 civilians killed and nearly 300 houses

completely destroyed. On 14 September 1940, 55 people were killed in a single raid on Kemp Town, including 6 in the Odeon Cinema in St George's Road which received a direct hit.

Played against the background of air-raids and warnings, football at times struggled to continue. The Football League was split into north and south regions, and, because of the widely differing numbers of matches each club was expecting to

All in a day's work

Or rather three-and-a-half minutes' work during the Battle of Britain. That's how long the Goldstone fixture with Southampton on 21 September lasted before it was curtailed by an air-raid. The line-up for the club's shortest-ever game was (left to right): Bobby Farrell, Stan Willemse, Len Darling, Charlie Harman, Charlie Chase, Roy Watts, Stan Hickman, Gordon Mee, Joe Wilson, Ted Martin and Stan Risdon. The two teams tried again on 12 October and managed a total of 45 minutes. but with enemy aircraft buzzing around, it was not easy to concentrate on the football and neither side managed to score.

play, goal-average was used as the fairest means of differentiating between teams in the tables.

The air-raids led to many farcical situations as play had to be suspended as soon as the warning was sounded. Albion's home match with Portsmouth on 14 September lasted only 40 minutes before it was abandoned with Pompey leading 2–1, and the goal-less draw with Southampton at Hove on 12 October consisted of two halves of 20 and 25 minutes duration; both results were allowed to stand. The match with Southampton on 21 September, attended by only 250 fans, was abandoned after just over three minutes; this game did not count in the table!

Brighton had been left out of the 'stipulated fixtures' which meant that they had to organise their own matches. Bournemouth and Clapton Orient both cancelled Goldstone fixtures because they were unable to put teams together, and by November Albion, desperate for games, appealed for help from the Football League, stating that the club was willing to pay opponents' travel and match expenses. There was enormous disappointment when Arsenal failed to raise a side to play at the Goldstone on 9 November for what should have been the most attractive fixture of the season. To their credit, Albion kept going under the most adverse circumstances and never failed to fulfil an engagement. On Christmas Eve, Charlie Webb travelled with just four players – Joe Wilson and juniors Roy Watts, Charlie Chase and Charlie Harman – for the Christmas-morning fixture at Norwich. In the event Bolton Wanderers' Jimmy Ithell turned out at centre-half and the remaining six places were filled by Norwich City youngsters and servicemen. Strengthened by four other Bolton players, the Canaries proceeded to win by a staggering eighteen goals to nil, which did their League placing a power of good! It was to remain the highest score throughout wartime football, but Webb was truly proud of his men who never gave up.

By the New Year, Albion had failed to win any games, had been bottom of the South Region since 5 October, and were still having difficulty in arranging matches. The London clubs organised their own cup competition for the second half of the season, leaving Brighton and the other teams in the South-East out on a limb, so Albion director Charles Wakeling fostered a new competition, the Football League South, to run alongside the South Regional competition. Results were to count in both

leagues, a somewhat complicated arrangement, but the new competition, which was decided on the traditional points basis, received official Football League sanction.

There was also the War Cup competition, and Albion received a fair measure of compensation for Arsenal's failure to appear in November by drawing them in the first round, which was played on a two-legged basis. Around 12,000 spectators turned up for the first leg at Hove on 15 February to witness a match that was relayed to the nation on BBC radio by commentator Raymond Glendenning. The Gunners cruised to a 4–1 win with two goals from Alf Kirchen and one apiece from the Compton brothers, Leslie and Dennis, against an Albion side with just one guest, Torquay United's George Devonport. For the second leg Arsenal recalled Ted Drake to bolster their attack, but Brighton put up a great fight, holding the London side in a goal-less first half before losing 3–1. Arsenal went all the way to the final where they were beaten 2–1 by Preston North End in a replay at Blackburn after a 1–1 draw at Wembley.

It was 1 February before Albion won their first match of the season, against fellow strugglers Bournemouth, but then came a remarkable change of fortune. In March the King's Liverpool Regiment was posted to Newhaven. It happened that the majority of Liverpool's players were serving with the regiment, manna from heaven for hard-pressed manager Charlie Webb, and the subsequent line-ups had a distinct 'Anfield' look about them. From the arrival of the 'Liverpools' only Portsmouth managed to beat the Albion, and a series of big wins took the club to the top of the Football League South competition and to a final 27th position out of 34 in the League's South Region.

> Arsenal played their home matches at White Hart Lane, Tottenham, throughout the war as Highbury was requisitioned for use as a first-aid post and air-raid patrol centre. However, Albion centre-half Peter Trainor was unaware of this situation on 22 February when he turned up for the second-leg War Cup match — at Highbury! Fortunately, Albion had a 'spare man' in Jack Westby, the Blackburn Rovers pivot who had guested for the club earlier in the season.

SEASON 1940–41

Date	Comp.	Ven.	Opponents	Result	HT	Pos.	Scorers	Atten.
Aug 31	FL (South)	(a)	Southampton	L 1–3	1–2	26=	Willemse	1,200
Sep 7	FL (South)	(a)	Crystal Palace	L 2–5	1–3	29	Stephens, Colborn	1,508
14	FL (South)*	(h)	Portsmouth	L 1–2	–	31	Willemse	1,000
21	FL (South)*		Southampton	– –	– –	30	–	250
Oct 5	FL (South)	(a)	Portsmouth	L 1–5	0–3	34	Harman	1,643
12	FL (South)*	(a)	Southampton	D 0–0	0–0	34	–	500
Nov 2	FL (South)	(a)	Aldershot	L 1–5	0–2	34	Risdon	3,000
23	FL (South)	(h)	Watford	D 1–1	0–1	34	Gunn	700
30	FL (South)	(h)	Aldershot	D 1–1	1–0	34	J Wilson	500
Dec 7	FL (South)	(a)	Watford	L 0–4	0–2	34	–	1,500
14	FL (South)	(h)	Charlton Athletic	D 1–1	1–1	34	Isaac	300
25	FL (South)	(a)	Norwich City	L 0–18	0–10	34	–	1,419
28	FL (South)	(h)	Crystal Palace	L 1–5	1–2	34	Risdon	1,000
Jan 25	FL (South) †(a')		Southend United	L 0–2	0–2	34 6	–	850
Feb 1	FL (South) †(h)		Bourem'th & B.A.	W 2–1	1–0	34 4	Isaac, Harman	1,000
8	FL (South) †	(a)	Watford	D 2–2	1–2	34 5	Harman, Devonport	1,500
15	FLWC R1 Lg1(h)		Arsenal	L 1–4	0–3	– –	Stephens	12,000
22	FLWC R1 Lg2(a')		Arsenal	L 1–3	0–0	– –	Stephens	3,846
Mar 1	FL (South) †	(h)	Portsmouth	W 4–0	1–0	33 3	Stephens 2, Welsh 2	2,400
8	FL (South) †	(h)	Southampton	W 3–1	2–0	32 2	Own goal, Welsh 2	2,500
15	FL (South) †	(a)	Bourem'th & B.A.	W 3–1	1–1	32 2	Laney, Davie, Balmer	1,000
22	FL (South) †	(h)	Luton Town	W 7–4	4–1	31 1	Welsh 6, J Wilson	2,000
29	FL (South) †	(a)	Portsmouth	L 2–3	1–1	31 3	Stephens, Davie	2,149
Apr 5	FL (South) †	(a)	Southend United	D 2–2	1–1	31 3	Balmer 2	2,000
12	FL (South) †	(a)	Luton Town	D 3–3	2–1	31 2	Stephens, Balmer, Welsh	1,000
14	FL (South) †	(h)	Southampton	W 6–3	1–2	31 2	Stephens 3, Welsh 2 (2 pens), Balmer	4,000
19	FL (South) †	(h)	Southampton	W 3–1	2–0	29 1	R Jones, Welsh 2	2,000
May 3	FL (South) †	(h)	Watford	W 4–2	4–2	28 1	Balmer 2, Stephens 2	2,700
31	FLS Chall.	(h)	Watford	W 4–1	0–0	– –	Stephens 2, Balmer 2	2,695

Football League (South) appearances — OG – 1
Football League (South) goals

Notes Matches marked † in the Football League (South) regional competition also counted towards a subsidiary competition, the Football League South. Positions in this secondary league are shown to the right of those in the main competition.

Sep 14 – match abandoned after 40 minutes because of possible air-raid.
  – result allowed to stand; appearances and goal included in end-of-season statistics.

Sep 21 – match abandoned after 3 minutes because of possible air-raid with score 0–0; appearances not included in the main competition.

Oct 12 – first half abandoned after 20 minutes, second half abandoned after 25 minutes, because of possible air-raids.
  – result allowed to stand; appearances included in end-of-season statistics.

Jan 25 – match played at New Writtle Street, Chelmsford City FC.

Feb 1 – match duration 70 minutes total as visitors arrived late.

Feb 22 – match played at White Hart Lane, Tottenham Hotspur FC.

Football League (South) 1940–41

		P	W	D	L	F	A	W	D	L	F	A	G Ave
1.	Crystal Palace	27	9	2	3	55	23	7	2	4	31	21	1.954
2.	West Ham United	25	9	2	4	48	24	5	4	1	22	15	1.794
3.	Coventry City	10	2	2	1	15	9	3	1	1	13	7	1.750
4.	Arsenal	19	5	3	0	28	12	5	2	4	38	26	1.736
5.	Cardiff City	24	9	5	1	58	26	3	0	6	17	24	1.500
6.	Reading	26	11	1	3	53	23	3	4	4	20	28	1.431
7.	Norwich City	19	9	1	0	60	16	0	1	8	13	39	1.327
8.	Watford	35	10	5	4	62	29	5	1	10	34	44	1.315
9.	Portsmouth	31	12	1	4	74	28	4	1	9	18	43	1.295
10.	Tottenham Hotspur	23	6	2	6	38	23	3	3	3	15	18	1.292
11.	Millwall	31	10	2	1	33	11	6	3	9	40	46	1.280
12.	Walsall	32	13	2	3	78	42	1	5	8	22	38	1.250
13.	West Bromwich A.	28	9	1	5	49	29	4	4	5	34	40	1.202
14.	Leicester City	33	14	3	2	57	24	3	2	9	30	49	1.191
15.	Northampton Town	30	12	2	2	61	27	2	1	11	23	44	1.183
16.	Bristol City	20	9	1	0	39	6	1	1	8	16	42	1.145
17.	Mansfield Town	29	10	4	3	56	31	2	2	8	21	37	1.132
18.	Charlton Athletic	19	4	1	4	25	17	3	3	4	12	17	1.088
19.	Aldershot	24	10	1	4	55	32	4	1	4	18	36	1.073
20.	Brentford	23	6	3	4	36	27	3	0	7	15	24	1.000
21.	Chelsea	23	6	2	1	27	11	4	2	8	30	47	0.982
22.	Birmingham	16	4	0	2	17	11	3	1	6	21	32	0.883
23.	Fulham	30	5	2	4	30	19	5	5	9	32	54	0.849
24.	Luton Town	35	9	4	4	50	36	2	3	13	32	64	0.820
25.	Stoke City	36	7	5	4	45	25	2	4	14	31	71	0.791
26.	Queen's Park R.	23	5	2	4	26	26	3	1	8	21	34	0.783
27.	**ALBION**	25	7	5	2	36	24	1	2	8	15	51	0.680
28.	Nottingham Forest	25	5	1	4	25	24	2	2	11	25	53	0.649
29.	Bournemouth & B.A.	27	9	3	4	49	36	0	0	11	10	56	0.641
30.	Notts County	21	5	1	2	19	18	3	2	8	23	48	0.636
31.	Southend United	29	9	2	4	44	35	3	2	9	20	66	0.633
32.	Southampton	31	2	0	6	17	24	2	4	17	36	87	0.477
33.	Swansea Town	10	2	0	2	7	6	1	0	5	5	27	0.363
34.	Clapton Orient	15	1	1	3	7	12	0	2	8	12	54	0.287

Football League South 1940–41

		P	W	D	L	F	A	W	D	L	F	A	Pts
1.	**ALBION**	13	7	1	0	31	14	1	2	2	10	11	19
2.	Watford	14	6	1	2	39	13	2	0	3	15	20	17
3.	Portsmouth	13	7	0	1	46	11	0	0	5	2	18	14
4.	Southend United	12	5	0	2	21	16	1	1	3	9	19	13
5.	Luton Town	11	3	1	0	12	5	2	0	5	17	28	11
6.	Bournemouth & B.A.	12	5	1	2	23	17	0	0	4	3	22	11
7.	Norwich City	6	3	0	0	14	8	0	0	3	3	14	6
8.	Southampton	13	0	0	0	0	0	1	1	11	25	54	3

Because of the incompletion of fixtures in the Football League South – Luton Town and Norwich City had both entered the competition late – second-placed Watford disputed Brighton's claim to the title, and so a challenge match was arranged to settle the issue. Albion won the decider 4–1 at the Goldstone with a line-up including Liverpool's Bernard Ramsden, Phil Taylor, Jimmy McInnes, Harry Eastham and Jack Balmer. Other Liverpool men to turn out this season were Bill Kinghorn, Tom Bush and Ron Jones, while John Shafto, Jack Easdale, Dirk Kemp and George Paterson also played many games for the club over the next few seasons.

Another famous face to appear in a blue-and-white striped shirt around this time was that of the Charlton Athletic and England star Don Welsh, later to become the Albion's manager. Don scored six goals in the 7–4 home defeat of Luton Town in March and ended the season with fifteen goals from only seven appearances.

SEASON 1941–42

The simmering row between the London clubs and the Football League came to a head in August when the League published its fixtures for a South Regional competition. The metropolitan sides were very unhappy with the arrangement and formed their own competition, the London War League, and also a London War Cup. Albion, otherwise geographically isolated along with Portsmouth, Aldershot and Reading, were more-or-less forced to join the rebels and were thereby deemed to have seceded from the Football League. By April a mutual understanding had been reached and the clubs were welcomed back into the Football League fold on payment of a nominal fine.

The season began well with only one defeat suffered in the first nine fixtures, at Queen's Park Rangers in the opening game. Jock Davie was loaned to Rangers and repaid Brighton's generosity by scoring a hat-trick in a 5–2 win over his club-mates. The 'Liverpools' were still in town, which accounts for the good early form, and by mid October Albion had attained the lofty height of fourth place, but then the Anfield brigade moved on and the team won just one of the subsequent eight games. Indeed, there were only three wins after Christmas.

The League was very competitive up to the Yuletide period, but, with many players in transit, the scorelines took on ridiculous proportions in the New Year: in the first six matches involving the Albion in 1942, an incredible 56 goals were scored, almost 10 a game. With 34 of them finishing in the Brighton net, Charles Wakeling appealed through the *Sussex Daily News* for any first-class players serving in the county to make themselves known to the management. The guest system reached its peak this season with Albion employing no fewer than 50 such players. Among the more prominent visitors were England internationals Arthur Cunliffe, George Eastham and Vic Woodley; 22-year-old Stan Pearson, an inside-forward from

Manchester United who went on to win eight England caps after the war; and a young Ron Burgess of Spurs, then a forward but destined to become one of Wales's greatest internationals at wing-half. Two future Albion managers made brief appearances for the club: George Curtis, the Arsenal inside-forward, and Billy Lane, who scored a goal in the 3–2 defeat at Clapton Orient in March.

For the match with Millwall on 29 November, Albion had to call upon the services of young Reg Bowles from the juniors at left-back; at the age of just 15 years and 258 days, he became the club's youngest-ever first-team player. Albion won 5–0 with the youngster playing his part in snuffing out the threat from Millwall's excellent outside-right Freddie Fisher. Reg went on to make over 50 appearances for Sussex. Two weeks later another junior, eighteen-year-old goalkeeper Jack Ball, was drafted into the side at short notice for his début at Queen's Park Rangers with regular custodian Gordon Mee moving to outside-left. Although conceding three goals on his first outing, Jack went on to play many more games for Albion over the next twelve years.

Two Arsenal players who turned out regularly for the Albion this season, left-back Cyril Tooze and inside-forward Stan Morgan, were supporting troops in the daring raid on the German radar station at Bruneval in Normandy in February

The Royal Navy defeated the Army 5–3 on 13 December at the Goldstone before a crowd of 500. Sub-lieutenant Archie Hart, on a training course at *H.M.S. King Alfred*, had turned out on Albion's right wing on the eight previous Saturdays and was the star of the show. The Army XI included Albion guests Harry Eastham and Jack Westby.

SEASON 1941–42

Date	Comp.	Ven.	Opponents	Atten.	Result	HT	Pos.	Scorers
Aug 30	London WL	(h)	Queen's Park R.	3,500	L	2-5	1-2	10	Shafto, Balmer
Sep 6	London WL	(a)	Reading	4,500	W	5-4	2-1	10	Balmer 2, Tunnicliffe, Pearson, Taylor
13	London WL	(a)	Clapton Orient	2,000	D	3-3	1-1	9	Easdale, Davie 2
20	London WL	(h)	Brentford	5,000	D	2-2	0-1	11	J Wilson, Balmer
27	London WL	(h)	Crystal Palace	4,000	W	3-2	3-1	7	Balmer, Ramsden
Oct 4	London WL	(a)	Fulham	2,500	W	3-2	3-1	7	Stephens 2, Davie
11	London WL	(a)	Tottenham H'spur	4,500	W	2-1	0-1	6	Balmer 2
18	London WL	(h)	Portsmouth	5,800	W	2-1	0-1	4	Jones, Tunnicliffe
25	London WL	(h)	Chelsea	3,000	W	3-1	0-0	4	Davie 3
Nov 1	London WL	(h)	Charlton Athletic	5,900	L	3-5	1-3	5	Davie 2, Hart
8	London WL	(a)	West Ham United	5,800	L	0-4	0-0	9	
15	London WL	(h)	Watford	4,000	D	2-2	1-0	8	Davie, Cunliffe
22	London WL	(h)	Aldershot	4,000	L	1-5	0-2	9	Hart
29	London WL	(a)	Millwall	3,200	W	5-3	0-1	9	Davie 2, Cunliffe 2, J Wilson
Dec 6	London WL	(h)	Arsenal	7,500	L	2-3	1-1	9	Davie, J Wilson
13	London WL**	(a)	Queen's Park R.	3,000	L	0-3	0-3	10	
20	London WL	(h)	Reading	2,500	L	1-5	1-2	10	J Wilson
25	London WL	(h)	Clapton Orient	4,500	W	4-1	2-1	9	Peters, Morgan, Chase, Gunn
27	London WL	(a)	Brentford	5,000	L	2-4	1-2	10	Davie, J Wilson
Jan 3	London WL	(a)	Crystal Palace	5,000	L	1-10	0-3	10	Stephens
10	London WL*	(h)	Fulham	2,500	L	3-7	1-4	10	Day 2, Cunliffe
17	London WL*	(h)	Tottenham H'spur	2,000	W	5-2	1-0	10	Morgan 3, Cunliffe, Davie
24	London WL*	(a)	Portsmouth	4,190	L	3-5	2-1	10	Morgan, Welsh, Cunliffe
31	London WL*	(h)	Chelsea	3,000	W	8-2	2-1	10	Davie 5, Cunliffe 2, Morgan
Feb 7	London WL*	(a)	Charlton Athletic	900	L	2-8	0-2	10	Davie, J Wilson
14	London WL**	(h)	West Ham United	3,000	L	1-3	0-1	10	Cunliffe
21	London WL*	(a)	Watford	600	L	1-7	1-2	10	Lancelotte
28	London WL*	(h)	Aldershot	4,300	L	1-5	0-2	10	Welsh
Mar 7	London WL**	(a)	Millwall	1,800	L	0-2	0-0	11	
14	London WC*	(h)	Arsenal	7,500	L	2-4	2-2	12	Risdon (pen), Morgan
21	London WC*	(a*)	West Ham United	4,000	L	1-2	1-2	9	Davie
28	London WC	(a)	Clapton Orient	1,500	L	2-3	1-2	4	Davie, Lane
Apr 4	London WC	(a)	West Ham United	4,000	L	2-6	1-2	4	Cunliffe, Davie (pen)
6	London WC*	(h)	Clapton Orient	5,000	W	5-2	2-1	3	Cunliffe, Griffin, Davie 3
11	London WC	(h)	Arsenal	12,000	L	0-3	0-1	3	
18	London WC*	(a*)	Arsenal	8,400	L	1-5	1-2	4	Davie

Notes: Dec 13, Dec 20, Dec 25, Jan 10, Jan 31, Feb 7, Feb 14, Mar 7, Mar 21, Apr 6 and Apr 18 – the full line-ups for these matches are not confirmed; those players asterisked were expected to play and are included in the end-of-season statistics.

Mar 14 – played at White Hart Lane, Tottenham Hotspur FC.
Apr 18 – played at White Hart Lane, Tottenham Hotspur FC.
Albion finished bottom (4th) of Section One of the London War Cup and did not qualify for the next stage.

The following players each made one appearance in the London War League:
- Dec 13: Chapman, A. (no.9).
- Jan 3: Pryde, R. (no.3) and Thew (no.8).
- Jan 24: Moores, P. (no.7).
- Feb 14: Mulraney, A. (no.10) and Walker, C. (no.8).
- Feb 21: Burdett (no.9); Gregory, F. (no.5) and Simmons, L. (no.11).
- Feb 28: Woods (no.11).
- Mar 7: Buckell (no.7).
- Mar 14: Owens (no.4).

London War League 1941–42											
	P	W	D	L	F	A	W	D	L	F	A	Pts
1. Arsenal	30	14	0	1	70	17	9	2	4	38	26	48
2. Portsmouth	30	11	1	3	59	27	9	1	5	46	32	42
3. West Ham United	30	10	2	3	38	20	7	3	5	43	24	39
4. Aldershot	30	10	2	3	45	26	7	3	5	40	30	39
5. Tottenham Hotspur	30	9	4	2	34	12	6	4	5	27	29	38
6. Crystal Palace	30	10	4	1	45	16	4	2	9	25	37	34
7. Reading	30	9	3	3	46	33	4	5	6	30	25	34
8. Charlton Athletic	30	8	2	5	41	31	6	3	6	31	33	33
9. Brentford	30	10	0	5	45	38	4	2	9	35	38	30
10. Queen's Park R.	30	7	1	7	25	26	4	2	9	27	33	25
11. Fulham	30	4	2	9	36	55	6	2	7	43	44	24
12. **ALBION**	30	5	3	7	43	45	4	1	10	28	63	22
13. Chelsea	30	3	4	8	28	45	5	0	10	28	43	20
14. Millwall	30	6	3	6	31	28	1	2	12	22	54	19
15. Clapton Orient	30	4	4	7	25	38	1	3	11	17	56	17
16. Watford	30	4	2	9	24	46	2	2	11	23	68	16

and received a tremendous ovation on their next appearance at the Goldstone. Tooze was killed in action in Italy early in 1944.

Albion conceded 108 goals in the 30 London League matches and finished twelfth of the sixteen competing clubs. From March, the London War Cup competition was played. The clubs were divided into four sections, played on a league basis, with the section winners going through to the semi-final stage. Albion finished bottom of Group One with Arsenal coming out on top, but Brentford beat the Gunners in the semi-final and went on to victory in the final, defeating Portsmouth 2–0 at Wembley.

There was no stopping Jock Davie this term. Apart from the goals he scored while guesting for other clubs, he netted 27 for the Albion, including eight in the two League fixtures with Chelsea; he registered five in the home match with the Pensioners in January despite being ten minutes late for the kick-off!

With the defeat of the *Luftwaffe* in the skies over Britain, and the attraction of matches with the big London clubs, the season saw a marked increase in attendances. The League average was over 4,000, and Arsenal pulled in another 12,000 gate for the Cup match on 11 April.

SEASON 1942–43

The Football League at last settled down to a stable pattern with Albion competing in the South Region along with all the clubs in London and the South-East. The first two matches ended in narrow home defeats, but in the next game Albion were well and truly thrashed 9–4 by Brentford at Griffin Park. Only one point was gained from the opening six matches. Then, in early October, the 'Liverpools' returned to the district and the situation immediately improved with a splendid 2–1 home win over Portsmouth and a 4–2 victory at Millwall.

Aldershot gained a 3–0 win at Hove on 7 November with what was virtually a representative team containing six of the biggest names in the game: Cliff Britton (Everton and England), Stan Cullis (Wolves and England captain), Jimmy Hagan (Sheffield United and later England), Tommy Lawton (Everton and England), Dave McCulloch (Derby County and Scotland) and Jackie Cunliffe (Everton and England). The Shots often fielded such teams during the war but it failed to bring them any success. The turnover of players at the Recreation Ground

Business as usual
When Albion regulars turned up for the early home games, they were shocked to find that the North Stand had been hit by a German bomb. It landed at the western end, severely damaging the roof and some supporting girders, and also blew out four windows in the West Stand. The pitch was covered with flints, dust and other debris, and it took Bullet Jones, now trainer-cum-groundsman, and his staff a week to clear the mess. The North Stand roof was completely removed and it was several years before it was repaired. This picture shows the view from Hove Park.

SEASON 1942–43

Date	Comp.	Ven.	Opponents	Result	HT	Pos.	Scorers	Atten.	Ball J	Blackman J	Bojar F	Bowles R	Bunyon W	Cameron J	Cater R	Cook P	Darling L	Davie J	Day A	Easdale J	Eastham H	Ford F	France E	Gillespie I	Gore L	Griffin A	Griffiths M	Harlock D	Jones S	Kinghorn W	Kirkman N	Longdon C	McInnes J	Malpass S	Marriott E	Mee G	Moore B	Morgan S	Mountford G	O'Donnell F	Ohlens P	Pearson S	Reid E	Richmond	Risdon S	Shafto J	Stephens H	Stevens J	Taylor P	Thorne A	Tully F	Walker C	Watson Jack	Wilson JA	Woodward L
Aug 29	FL (South)	(h)	Reading	L	2–3	1–1	14	Davie, Stephens	2,500										4	9										10		3			5		2			1			7				6		11							8	
Sep 5	FL (South)	(h)	Chelsea	L	1–2	0–1	16	Wilson	2,800			3							4	9										7					5		2		1		10							6		11							8	
12	FL (South)	(a)	Brentford	L	4–9	0–4	17	Davie 2, Morgan, Griffiths	4,020			3							4	9							7								5		2		1		10							6		11							8	
19	FL (South)	(a)	Watford	D	1–1	0–1	17	Risdon (pen)	2,126	1		3								9					11		7		4					5													10	6	2							8		
26	FL (South)	(h)	Crystal Palace	L	1–8	1–4	18	Gore	2,600	6	3								9	8				5		7	11		4								1									10		2									
Oct 3	FL (South)	(a)	Luton Town	L	2–5	1–3	17	Davie, Risdon (pen)	3,120	1								3	9		5	7							11					4												10	8	2			6					
10	FL (South)	(h)	Portsmouth	W	2–1	0–0	16	Kinghorn, Morgan	2,000	1		6									5									7	3	4		9					10								8	2		11							
17	FL (South)	(a)	Millwall	W	4–2	1–1	15	Griffiths 2, Morgan 2	4,172	1		6									5	7				8			4					10													2	9	11								3
24	FL (South)	(h)	Queen's Park R.	L	2–3	2–3	17	Malpass, Pearson	3,200	1			3								8	7							4			9													10	6	2		11							5
31	FL (South)	(h)	Charlton Athletic	W	3–1	0–0	14	Shafto, Kinghorn 2	3,000	1								6			5	7							11			4	3													8	2	9	10							
Nov 7	FL (South)	(h)	Aldershot	L	0–3	0–0	16		3,800	1								6			5	7							11			4	3													8	2	9	10							
14	FL (South)	(a)	Southampton	D	2–2	2–0	16	Stephens, Morgan	5,800	1												7							11			4				8										5	2	9	10	6							
21	FL (South)	(h)	West Ham United	D	2–2	1–1	16	Kinghorn 2	3,500	1											5	7							11			4													9	2	10	6					8		
28	FL (South)	(a)	Reading	L	1–5	0–4	16	Darling (pen)	2,500	1								4		9	5	7										3				8									10	2		11	6							
Dec 5	FL (South)	(a)	Chelsea	D	0–0	0–0	16		4,200	1								4			5	7						3	11								8									2	9	10	6							
12	FL (South)	(h)	Brentford	W	7–2	2–0	14	Shafto 3, Pearson, Stephens 2, Morgan	4,000	1								4			5	7														8							10	3	2	9	11	6							
19	FL (South)	(h)	Watford	W	2–1	2–1	14	Davie, Shafto	3,000	1									8		5	7							11														3	2	9	10	6				4			
25	FL (South)	(a)	Clapton Orient	L	1–3	1–1	15	Ohlens	3,200	1	11	3	7	4															5									10				9		6	8	2									
26	FL (South)	(h)	Clapton Orient	W	1–0	0–0	13	Thorne	6,800	1	10	3											6			7			5									8						4	2					9	11				
Jan 2	FL (South)	(a)	Crystal Palace	W	4–1	3–1	11	Eastham, Stephens, Reid 2	2,700	1											5	7							6			3						10						8	2	9	11	4							
9	FL (South)	(a)	Luton Town	W	8–0	5–0	10	Darling 2 (1 pen), Stephens 2, Shafto 4	2,000	1								10			5	7							6			3						8							2	9	11	4							
16	FL (South)	(a)	Portsmouth	L	1–2	1–0	11	Morgan	5,099	1								4			5						7		6			3						10						8	2	9	11								
23	FL (South)	(h)	Millwall	D	3–3	2–0	11	Shafto, Wilson, Morgan	2,500	1											5						7		6			3						10						4	2	9	11					8		
30	FL (South)	(a)	Queen's Park R.	W	4–3	1–2	11	Shafto 2, Stephens, Kinghorn	3,800	1								4			5	7							11			6	3											8	2	9	10							
Feb 6	FL (South)	(h)	Charlton Athletic	W	2–0	0–0	10	Shafto 2	2,500	1								8			5	7							11			6											3	2	9	10	4							
13	FL (South)	(a)	Aldershot	L	2–3	1–3	12	Eastham, Stephens	4,800	1											5	7						3	11			6											4	2	9	10					8		
20	FL (South)	(a)	Southampton	L	2–6	2–4	12	Shafto, O'Donnell	3,000	1												7						3	6			5					10		4	2	9	11					8		
27	FL (South)	(a)	West Ham United	L	1–2	0–1	12	Kinghorn	3,000	1						5						7						3	11			6	8								9	2		10	4							
Mar 6	FL (S'th) Cup	(h)	Arsenal	L	1–5	1–5	3	Eastham	8,500	1		10									5	7							3			6											8	2		11	4	9						
13	FL (S'th) Cup	(h)	West Ham United	L	1–4	0–3	3	Stephens	3,000	1											5	7							3			6				6						10		4	2	9	11					8		
20	FL (S'th) Cup	(a)	Watford	D	1–1	0–0	3	Morgan	2,000	1											5	7							6	3								10					4	2	9	11					8		
27	FL (S'th) Cup	(a*)	Arsenal	L	0–5	0–2	4		8,000	1									9										3	7		6	4										10	2		11						5	8	
Apr 3	FL (S'th) Cup	(a)	West Ham United	L	1–7	0–7	4	Shafto	5,500	1												7							6	4			3									10	2	9	11					5	8	
10	FL (S'th) Cup	(a)	Watford	L	0–5	0–5	4		1,500		8	2												9					5	7		6	4											10*		1*		11							
League appearances									24	1	8	3	1	1	1	1		12	7	2	17	17	1	1	1	2	1	5	1	7	14	1	24	0	16	1	5	1	10	1	1	5	23	1	28	15	23	1	10	1	1	1	0	8	2
League goals											3	5							2							1		3			7						1					8		1	1	2	2		2	15	9			1			2	

Notes: Mar 27 – played at White Hart Lane, Tottenham Hotspur FC.

       Apr 10 – Reid and Risdon swapped positions for the second half.

       Albion finished bottom (4th) of Section One of the Football League (South) Cup and did not qualify for the next stage.

Football League (South) 1942–43											
	P	W	D	L	F	A	W	D	L	F	A	Pts
1. Arsenal	28	11	0	3	53	12	10	1	3	49	28	43
2. Tottenham Hotspur	28	9	4	1	42	13	7	2	5	26	15	38
3. Queen's Park R.	28	11	1	2	40	20	7	1	6	24	29	38
4. Portsmouth	28	10	2	2	38	20	6	1	7	28	32	35
5. Southampton	28	9	2	3	47	21	5	3	6	39	37	33
6. West Ham United	28	10	1	3	46	26	4	4	6	34	40	33
7. Chelsea	28	7	2	5	29	23	7	2	5	23	22	32
8. Aldershot	28	9	2	3	57	33	5	0	9	30	44	30
9. Brentford	28	8	3	3	43	26	4	2	8	21	37	29
10. Charlton Athletic	28	7	2	5	41	36	6	1	7	27	39	29
11. Clapton Orient	28	8	1	5	33	33	3	4	7	21	39	27
12. **ALBION**	28	6	2	6	35	34	4	3	7	30	39	25
13. Reading	28	5	2	7	36	37	4	4	6	31	37	24
14. Fulham	28	7	1	6	40	37	3	1	10	29	41	22
15. Crystal Palace	28	3	3	8	19	32	4	2	8	30	43	19
16. Millwall	28	4	3	7	29	32	2	2	10	37	56	17
17. Watford	28	5	1	8	35	41	2	1	11	16	47	16
18. Luton Town	28	3	4	7	25	37	1	2	11	18	63	14

was quite astonishing, the town being the focal point for the Army's activities.

On Christmas Day, Albion travelled to Leyton for a match with Clapton Orient and found themselves forced to appeal for two volunteers from the crowd to make up the numbers. They performed well in the circumstances, although losing 3–1. For the return match at the Goldstone on Boxing Day, Charlie Webb included six juniors in the team and they repaid him in fine style, winning 1–0 with a goal from young Albert Thorne.

The improved form saw Albion pull away from the bottom of the division to finish twelfth of eighteen clubs, with Arsenal winning the championship. Arsenal also headed Group One of the League's South Cup, Albion occupying the basement with just one point from the six matches. The Gunners went on to win the trophy, comfortably beating Charlton Athletic 7–1 at Wembley.

One of the features of the campaign was the excellent form of nineteen-year-old local lad Jack Ball between the posts. Jack took over from Gordon Mee early in the season and became the regular goalkeeper. He signed professional forms in February but was called into the R.A.F. a month later.

On 10 April, Albion were scheduled to meet Watford at Hove in the final fixture, but at the eleventh hour discovered that they had no goalkeeper. Full-back Stan Risdon volunteered for the unenviable job and by half time Albion were losing 5–0. During the interval it was decided that Stan should hand over the gloves to inside-right Ernie Reid and, no doubt to Ernie's delight, Watford failed to add to their score. The versatile Reid was registered with Norwich City but played for the Albion fairly regularly throughout the war years, and appeared in most positions on the team sheet — including goalkeeper!

Another guest player, Liverpool's Johnny Shafto, headed the goalscorers with sixteen, including three in the 7–2 defeat of Brentford and four in the 8–0 win over Luton Town. Skipper Stan Risdon managed to turn out in every match, a rare achievement in wartime football. Among the prominent guests this season were Mal Griffiths, a future Welsh international with Leicester City; Frank O'Donnell of Aston Villa, the holder of six Scottish caps who had gained a runner's-up medal in the 1937 F.A. Cup final with Preston North End; and Felix Bojar, a skilful, Polish international left-back, the first foreigner to play for the Albion.

> The Albion directorate's admirable proposal to let service-men and -women in free for the match with Clapton Orient on Boxing Day infringed Football League regulations and was quickly halted by the management committee, so the board generously paid for Forces in uniform at their own personal expense. The Football League's minimum admission charge had increased from 1s. to 1s. 3d. this season, the first rise since the end of the Great War. Admission charges at the Goldstone were 1s. 6d. (7·5p) generally, with a reduced entrance fee of 7d. (about 3p) for the Forces.

SEASON 1943–44

In August director Herbert Ridge passed away and Alec Whitcher was selected to fill the vacant position on the board. An avid football fan, Whitcher became a great promoter of Albion's cause and in the mid-to-late 1940s wrote four books – *The Ace of Games*, *Soccer Calling*, *The Voice of Soccer*, and *The Sportsman's Club* – donating around £1,500 from the sale of the three latter publications to club funds.

The 'Liverpools' were back in town for the first half of the campaign and Albion maintained a respectable mid-table position in the Football League (South) until the New Year. The opening match ended in a 4–0 defeat by Reading at the Goldstone. Playing between the posts for Brighton was a Polish airman, Bishek Szajna-Stankowski, who had already appeared at Hove in an R.A.F. representative side; on that occasion he was referred to by the pseudonym 'A. Pole' for fear of reprisals to his family by the Germans in his home country.

The ace of directors
Alec Whitcher presents a cheque for £300, from the proceeds of his book The Ace of Games, *to Stanley Rous, secretary of the Football Association, for the F.A. Benevolent Fund. The Albion benefited from his other three books. From left to right, Carlo Campbell, Stanley Rous, Councillor A. Rostance, Alec Whitcher and Charles Wakeling.*

SEASON 1943–44

Date	Comp.	Ven.	Opponents	Result	HT	Pos.	Scorers	Atten.
Aug 28	FL (South)	(h)	Reading	L	0-4	0-1	16=		2,000
Sep 4	FL (South)	(h)	Chelsea	L	1-3	1-0	18	J Wilson	2,900
11	FL (South)	(a)	Brentford	W	3-2	1-0	14	Stephens, Shafto, Griffiths	5,310
18	FL (South)	(h)	Clapton Orient	W	2-0	1-0	11	Reid, Taylor	3,200
25	FL (South)	(h)	Arsenal	D	1-1	1-0	11	Shafto	8,000
Oct 2	FL (South)	(a)	Luton Town	W	4-2	1-0	8	Taylor, Stephens 3	3,000
9	FL (South)	(a)	Tottenham H'spur	L	0-2	0-1	10		11,000
16	FL (South)	(h)	Millwall	L	1-2	1-0	13	J Wilson	4,000
23	FL (South)	(a)	Queen's Park R.	W	3-1	2-0	12	Eastham, Reid, Taylor	3,500
30	FL (South)	(a)	Charlton Athletic	W	4-1	1-1	8	J Wilson, Griffiths, Shafto, Taylor	4,000
Nov 6	FL (South)	(a)	Fulham	L	2-6	2-2	11	Shafto 2	4,200
13	FL (South)	(a)	Southampton	L	2-4	1-2	13	Shafto, Stephens	3,000
20	FL (South)	(h)	West Ham United	L	1-2	1-1	13	Stephens	5,000
27	FL (South)	(a)	Reading	W	3-2	1-2	13	Reid 2, Stephens	3,000
Dec 4	FL (South)	(a)	Chelsea	W	1-0	0-0	13	Hassell	7,000
11	FL (South)	(a)	Brentford	L	0-2	0-2	13		2,500
18	FL (South)	(h)	Portsmouth	W	3-2	0-1	13	Hassell, Reid 2	4,401
25	FL (South)	(h)	Crystal Palace	L	1-3	0-0	13	Hassell	5,000
27	FL (South)	(a)	Crystal Palace	L	2-6	2-1	13	Malone, Hassell	3,500
Jan 1	FL (South)*	(a)	Clapton Orient	L	0-3	0-3	14		1,500
8	FL (South)	(h)	Fulham	L	3-6	2-2	15	Davie, J Wilson, Stephens	3,000
22	FL (South)	(h)	Luton Town	W	8-0	5-0	14	Wright, Davie, J Wilson 2, McNeill 3, Hassell	1,500
29	FL (South)	(h)	Tottenham H'spur	L	0-2	0-0	14		6,100
Feb 5	FL (South)*	(a*)	Millwall	L	4-7	3-4	14	Hassell 2, Stehens 2	2,563
12	FL (South)	(a)	Queen's Park R.	L	0-1	0-1	14		7,000
19	FL (S'th) Cup	(h)	Charlton Athletic	L	1-2	0-2		Longdon	2,500
26	FL (S'th) Cup	(a)	Crystal Palace	W	3-2	1-1		2= J Wilson, Hassell 2	5,000
Mar 4	FL (S'th) Cup	(a)	Brentford	L	0-8	0-2	4		5,020
11	FL (S'th) Cup	(a)	Charlton Athletic	L	0-2	0-0	4		4,278
18	FL (S'th) Cup	(h)	Crystal Palace	L	2-4	1-1	4	Hillman, Stephens	3,500
25	FL (S'th) Cup	(h)	Brentford	W	5-0	1-0	4	Moore 2, Hassell, J Wilson, Hillman	3,000
Apr 8	FL (South)	(h)	Charlton Athletic	D	3-3	2-0	14	Hillman, Hassell, Moore	6,200
10	FL (South)	(a*)	Arsenal	L	1-3	1-2	15	J Wilson	9,000
22	FL (South)	(a)	Portsmouth	L	0-3	0-1	15		4,363
29	FL (South)	(a)	Southampton	L	0-3	0-1	15		6,000
May 6	FL (South)	(a)	West Ham United	L	2-6	1-4	16	Driver, Moore	4,000

Notes: Feb 5 – played at The Valley, Charlton Athletic FC.

Apr 10 – played at White Hart Lane, Tottenham Hotspur FC.

Albion finished bottom (4th) of Section One of the Football League (South) Cup and did not qualify for the next stage.

The following additional players each made one appearance in the Football League (South):

– Jan 1: Grier (no.6), Lawrence (no.2), Lowrie (no.9), Sanderson (no.4), Young (no.1) and an unknown guest player (no.5).

– Feb 5: Dooley, A. (no.10) and Hooper, P. (no.1).

– Apr 22: Pointon, W. (no.10) and Richardson, D. (no.5).

Player appearances table

Player	League appearances	League goals
Anderson J	3	
Ball	1	
Ball J	1	
Bentley G	0	
Boyd J	1	
Cocker J	1	
Darling L	13	2
Davie J	2	1
Driver A	1	1
Easdale J	15	
Eastham H	18	1
Edington J	1	
Fairhurst W	4	
Fox D	3	
France E	1	
Grainger J	2	
Griffiths M	7	2
Hassell T	17	8
Hickman S	1	1
Hillman D	4	2
Hollis H	0	1
Ithell J	13	
Kemp D	7	
Kinghorn W	2	
Longdon C	8	1
McInnes J	14	
McKenzie D	2	
McNeill H	2	3
Malone R	1	1
Marriott E	10	
Martin E	4	
Matthewson G	1	
Mee G	3	
Moore B	6	2
Muttitt E	2	
Reid E	23	6
Risdon S	29	
Shafto J	9	6
Sperrin W	2	
Stephens H	24	10
Szajna-St'ski B	1	
Taylor P	16	4
Tootill A	1	
Ward J	2	
Wassall J	1	
Weaver S	1	
Wilson F	9	
Wilson JA	26	4
Woodward L	4	
Wright T	4	1

126

Football League (South) 1943–44											
	P	W	D	L	F	A	W	D	L	F	A	Pts
1. Tottenham Hotspur	30	11	4	0	42	16	8	4	3	29	20	46
2. West Ham United	30	10	4	1	40	16	7	3	5	34	23	41
3. Queen's Park R.	30	9	5	1	40	26	5	7	3	29	28	40
4. Arsenal	30	9	5	1	47	20	5	5	5	25	22	38
5. Crystal Palace	30	9	3	3	39	23	7	2	6	36	30	37
6. Portsmouth	30	9	2	4	34	27	7	3	5	34	32	37
7. Brentford	30	10	1	4	38	23	4	6	5	33	28	35
8. Chelsea	30	9	2	4	42	19	7	0	8	37	36	34
9. Fulham	30	7	3	5	47	35	4	6	5	33	38	31
10. Millwall	30	7	1	7	48	42	6	3	6	22	24	30
11. Aldershot	30	6	3	6	32	33	6	3	6	32	40	30
12. Reading	30	7	1	7	43	33	5	2	8	30	29	27
13. Southampton	30	6	4	5	38	29	4	3	8	29	59	27
14. Charlton Athletic	30	5	4	6	24	29	4	3	8	33	44	25
15. Watford	30	4	4	7	35	38	2	4	9	23	42	20
16. **ALBION**	30	3	2	10	26	36	6	0	9	29	46	20
17. Luton Town	30	2	4	9	26	38	1	1	13	16	66	11
18. Clapton Orient	30	3	3	9	15	38	1	0	14	17	49	11

In September a very strong Arsenal side was held to a 1–1 draw at the Goldstone, witnessed by 8,000 fans. Albion's team contained no fewer than six Anfielders and they held the lead until fifteen minutes from time when Cliff Bastin scored the equaliser from the penalty spot. Other notable results included a 4–1 win over Charlton Athletic at The Valley, and a 1–0 defeat of Chelsea at Stamford Bridge.

In the absence of the Liverpool contingent in the New Year, manager Webb again found it difficult to field a team and only one of the last eleven League games ended in victory, a resounding 8–0 win over a depleted Luton Town side at the Goldstone. Heavy defeats against Fulham, Millwall and West Ham United saw Albion drop to sixteenth, only two places off the bottom, with Tottenham Hotspur winning the title by a five-point margin from West Ham.

From February the Football League's South Cup competition was played, but Albion fared little better, finishing last of the four teams in Group One. A remarkable reversal of fortunes came when Brentford were beaten 5–0 at the Goldstone only three weeks after thrashing the Albion 8–0 at Griffin Park. The group was headed by Charlton Athletic who went on to lift the trophy by defeating Chelsea 3–1 in the Wembley final, with Albion's future manager Don Welsh scoring one of the goals.

There were numerous changes in the line-ups from week to week, but skipper Stan Risdon was again ever-present and Joe Wilson missed only a handful of games. Bert Stephens was leading goalscorer with a total of eleven in League and Cup. Most prominent new guest this season was Chelsea's former England half-back Sam Weaver, one of the early exponents of the 'long throw'.

SEASON 1944–45

Albion started their Football League (South) campaign in abysmal fashion when, after a 6–2 hiding at Brentford and a 3–1 home win over Clapton Orient, the team lost on eleven successive occasions, conceding 56 goals in the process. There were no 'Liverpools' this season, but the guest-player system was used extensively, the club fielding no fewer than 38 during the term. Frank O'Donnell, the Scottish international, played another fourteen games, and there was a distinct north-of-the-border feel to the side as seven players with Scottish clubs also made appearances. Another player to assist the Albion was the Arsenal left-winger Cyril Hodges, later to become a permanent fixture at the Goldstone as a player and subsequently as trainer/coach.

Digging for victory
Cartoonist Reg Carter's impression of the Albion board – Alec Whitcher, Charles Wakeling and Carlo Campbell – preparing their post-war campaign.

SEASON 1944–45

Date	Comp.	Ven.	Opponents	Result	HT	Pos.	Scorers	Atten.
Aug 26	FL (South)	(a)	Brentford	L 2-6	2-2	15	Stephens, Cook	5,500
Sep 2	FL (South)	(h)	Clapton Orient	W 3-1	1-1	10	Stephens, Hassell, Risdon	2,500
9	FL (South)	(a)	Crystal Palace	L 2-5	2-3	13	Hodges 2	6,400
16	FL (South)	(h)	Fulham	L 1-7	1-4	14	Offord	4,500
23	FL (South)	(h)	Luton Town	L 2-4	2-0	15	Cook, Wilson	4,679
30	FL (South)	(h)	West Ham United	L 0-1	0-1	16		6,000
Oct 7	FL (South)	(a*)	Arsenal	L 3-6	2-4	17	Crawford, Stephens, Cook	10,581
14	FL (South)	(a)	Aldershot	L 1-3	0-1	17	Reid (pen)	3,300
21	FL (South)	(h)	Reading	L 3-9	1-5	17	McDermott 2, Crawford	4,000
28	FL (South)	(a)	Queen's Park R.	L 0-4	0-2	17		6,475
Nov 4	FL (South)	(h)	Charlton Athletic	L 1-7	0-3	17	Moore	4,000
11	FL (South)	(a)	Watford	L 1-5	0-2	17	Moore	2,833
18	FL (South)	(h)	Chelsea	L 3-5	2-2	18	Moore, O'Donnell, Stephens	6,000
25	FL (South)	(a)	Portsmouth	W 1-0	0-0	17	Reid (pen)	10,511
Dec 2	FL (South)	(a)	Brentford	L 2-7	1-5	18	Wilson, Stephens	5,000
9	FL (South)	(a)	Clapton Orient	D 2-2	2-1	17	Briscoe, Moore	2,000
16	FL (South)	(h)	Crystal Palace	L 0-3	0-1	17		3,500
23	FL (South)	(a)	Southampton	L 2-3	1-2	18	McDermott, Reid (pen)	7,000
26	FL (South)	(h)	Southampton	W 2-0	0-0	17	Townsend, Weir	6,780
30	FL (South)	(a)	Fulham	W 3-2	2-2	17	Hodges, Moore 2	4,000
Jan 6	FL (South)	(h)	Luton Town	W 3-2	2-1	16	Wilson, Reid (pen), Reece	4,500
13	FL (South)	(a)	West Ham United	L 4-5	2-1	16	Moore 2, Hodges, Stephens	5,000
20	FL (St'h Cup	(a)	Arsenal	L 3-0	3-0	16	McDermott, Hodges 2	10,000
Feb 3	FL (St'h Cup	(a)	Brentford	W 5-3	3-2	2	Stephens 2, Hodges 2, McDermott	10,000
10	FL (St'h Cup	(h)	Fulham	L 1-3	0-2	2=	O'Donnell	7,000
17	FL (St'h Cup	(h)	Millwall	W 6-2	2-1	1	Hodges 4, Reid, Frost	10,000
24	FL (St'h Cup	(h)	Brentford	L 2-4	0-2	2	O'Donnell, Moore	10,000
Mar 3	FL (St'h Cup	(a)	Fulham	L 2-5	1-1	3	Moore, Stephens	9,000
10	FL (St'h Cup	(a)	Millwall	L 0-1	0-1	3		12,200
17	FL (South)	(h)	Reading	L 2-3	2-1	17	Hodges 2	4,000
24	FL (South)	(h)	Queen's Park R.	D 1-1	1-1	17	Wilson	4,000
31	FL (South)	(a)	Charlton Athletic	L 1-2	0-0	17	Hodges	5,000
Apr 14	FL (South)	(a)	Watford	W 3-2	1-2	16	Moore 2, Day	3,000
21	FL (South)	(a)	Chelsea	W 2-0	1-0	14	Day, Cornish	9,176
28	FL (South)	(h)	Portsmouth	W 8-0	3-0	14	Stephens 3, Wilson, Moore, Day 2, Cornish	2,941
May 5	FL (South)	(h)	Aldershot	W 5-0	1-0	14	Wilson, Stephens 3, Cornish	1,500

Notes: Oct 7 – played at White Hart Lane, Tottenham Hotspur FC.

Albion finished 3rd in Section Two of the Football League (South) Cup and did not qualify for the next stage.

Football League (South) 1944–45											
	P	W	D	L	F	A	W	D	L	F	A	Pts
1. Tottenham Hotspur	30	11	3	1	44	17	12	3	0	37	13	52
2. West Ham United	30	12	1	2	56	21	10	2	3	40	26	47
3. Brentford	30	10	0	5	51	25	7	4	4	36	32	38
4. Chelsea	30	7	2	6	47	24	9	3	3	53	31	37
5. Southampton	30	8	3	4	53	33	9	0	6	43	36	37
6. Crystal Palace	30	10	2	3	48	26	5	3	7	26	44	35
7. Reading	30	8	4	3	37	31	6	2	7	41	37	34
8. Arsenal	30	11	0	4	51	27	3	9	9	26	40	31
9. Queen's Park R.	30	7	5	3	41	22	3	5	7	29	39	30
10. Watford	30	6	3	6	33	33	5	3	7	33	51	28
11. Fulham	30	6	2	7	46	45	5	2	8	33	38	26
12. Portsmouth	30	8	1	6	44	28	3	3	9	12	33	26
13. Charlton Athletic	30	6	1	8	36	41	6	1	8	36	40	26
14. **ALBION**	30	7	1	7	38	45	3	1	11	28	50	22
15. Luton Town	30	4	4	7	29	40	2	3	10	27	64	19
16. Aldershot	30	5	1	9	27	33	2	3	10	17	52	18
17. Millwall	30	2	5	8	25	36	3	2	10	25	48	17
18. Clapton Orient	30	4	6	5	22	32	1	1	13	17	54	17

Only two wins came before Christmas, but matters improved and eight wins in the final twelve games saw Albion climb off the bottom to finish fourteenth of the eighteen teams. Arsenal were beaten for the first time at Hove, 3–0 in January

(although the Gunners fielded a weakened side), and the team finished with four straight wins, left-winger Bert Stephens registering hat-tricks against Portsmouth and Aldershot.

In the latter part of the season the Football League's South Cup competition was played, but Albion again performed poorly, finishing third of four in Section Two. The highlight was a 6–2 Goldstone win over Millwall, the eventual section winners, in which Cyril Hodges notched four goals. Millwall went on to beat Arsenal 1–0 in the semi-final before losing 2–0 to Chelsea in front of a 90,000 crowd at Wembley.

Albion fielded seven goalkeepers in a total of 36 matches, including skipper and full-back Stan Risdon once again for the match at Aldershot in October; the Shots won 3–1. Stan missed only two matches during the season. Cyril Hodges and Bert Stephens headed the scoring list with fifteen apiece, while young Bernard Moore netted thirteen.

SEASON 1945–46

Throughout the previous season the Allies had been advancing on Germany from both east and west. On 2 May 1945, Berlin fell to the Soviet Army and Hitler committed suicide. Germany signed a general surrender on 7 May, and Victory in Europe was celebrated throughout Britain the following day.

With so many men scattered all over the world it was not thought possible to return to a peacetime football set-up and a transitional season was decided upon. The pre-war First and Second Divisions were combined and split into northern and southern sections, and the two Third Divisions were also divided into regional sections. There was no promotion or relegation. Albion competed in the Third Division (South) Southern Region and finished fourth of the eleven clubs in the competition, with Crystal Palace taking the title ahead of Cardiff City. Trainer Sam Cowan made up the numbers at Dean Court, Bournemouth, on 13 October and thus became, at the age of 44 years 156 days, the oldest player in Albion history.

One of the more remarkable games ever seen at the Goldstone was played on 29 December. On the half-hour Charlie Longdon knocked himself unconscious on the perimeter fencing and took no further part. Swindon Town immediately took the lead, but ten-man Albion came back well to lead 3–1 at half time. Further misfortune befell Brighton after the interval: Joe Wilson limped off and Jimmy Watson spent the rest of the game as a passenger on the wing. Effectively down to eight men, Albion succumbed to the Wiltshire side's pressure and the score was 3–3 with just three minutes left. With Swindon pressing for a winner, Bert Stephens, now one of just two Albion forwards, broke away and hit Albion's fourth, and at the final whistle the crowd spilled onto the pitch to acclaim a heroic performance.

In the New Year a Third Division (South) Cup tournament was staged, played on a league basis in two sections with the two leading sides in each section going through to the semi-finals. Albion performed disastrously, winning only one of their sixteen matches and finishing last. Bournemouth won the section and went on to beat Walsall in the final.

Among the guests this year were Alex Munro of Blackpool, the holder of three Scottish caps, and nineteen-year-old Arthur Rowley, then a full-back with West Bromwich Albion. Described in the local Press as 'the best defender for Brighton

since before the war', Arthur was later converted into a forward and went on to score an all-time record 433 goals in the Football League. He scored one of his earliest senior goals on 22 September from the penalty spot in Albion's 7–3 win over Crystal Palace.

But the biggest attraction of the season was undoubtedly the return of the F.A. Cup. At the request of the clubs it was played on a two-legged, home-and-away basis up to and including the sixth round, and only registered players were allowed to appear for a club. The Bristol Rovers full-back Jimmy Watson, who had appeared for the Albion in the season's early League matches, was signed permanently in November to enable him to play in the cup-ties.

In contrast with the Third Division competitions, Albion's F.A. Cup run was a tremendous success. They beat Romford of the Isthmian League 4–2 on aggregate in the first round; the eventual Isthmian League champions Walthamstow Avenue 5–3 in round two; Norwich City 6–2 in round three; and Aldershot 7–1 in the fourth round. This success set up a plum tie with Derby County at the fifth-round stage. The Rams were a powerful team and possessed a brilliant forward line: Sammy Crooks (England), Raich Carter (England), Jackie Stamps, Peter Doherty (Ireland) and Dally Duncan (Scotland). Stamps was to miss the fifth-round matches, but County proved to be in a different class to the Albion.

The first leg attracted a 23,456 crowd to the Goldstone, the biggest for twelve years, and Albion rose to the occasion, the result remaining in the balance until the last ten minutes when goals from Carter and Doherty gave the Rams an irredeemable 4–1 lead to take into the second leg. Four days later 32,000 spectators packed into the Baseball Ground and saw their team crush the Albion 6–0 with the superb Raich Carter grabbing a hat-trick. Derby went on to win the trophy, beating Charlton Athletic 4–1 after extra time at Wembley.

Jock Davie scored ten goals in the F.A. Cup ties, including a hat-trick in the 3–0 home defeat of Aldershot in the fourth round, but Bernard Moore was overall leading scorer with 28 in the three competitions, registering 13 in the first eight games. With Britain still effectively working under a wartime economy, average gates in the Third Division competitions were around

SEASON 1945–46

Date	Comp.	Ven.	Opponents	Result	HT	Pos.	Scorers	Atten.	Baldwin H	Ball J	Broomfield D	Chase C	Cowan S	Curtis J	Darling L	Davie J	Day A	Dugnolle J	Ford F	Green F	Gunn A	Hart A	Hassell T	Hillman D	Hindley F	Hughes H	London D	Longdon C	McDermott J	McNaughton J	Marriott E	Martin E	Martindale L	Miles	Millbank J	Moore B	Moore JB	Munro A	O'Donnell F	Parr C	Philbin J	Pugh J	Reece T	Reid E	Risdon S	Robson A	Rowley A	Sage F	Sheppard R	Stephens H	Trainor P	Watson Jimmy	Wharton F	Whent J	Willemse S	Williams W	Wilson Albert	Wilson JA
Aug 25	FL D3(S)S	(a)	Reading	W 2–1	1–1	4	Stephens, B Moore	6,540		1												7					6									10			9						2		3			11	5			4				8
Sep 1	FL D3(S)S	(h)	Reading	W 1–0	0–0	3	B Moore	5,851		1							9											6								10		7							2		3		11		5			4				8
5	FL D3(S)S	(a)	Bristol City	L 1–3	1–1	5	B Moore	7,793		1													7					6								10	11					3		4	2						5					9		8
8	FL D3(S)S	(h)	Bristol Rovers	L 3–4	2–1	5	Day, Sheppard, B Moore	6,253	1							9			5									6								10		7						3	2				11					4				8
12	FL D3(S)S	(a)	Swindon Town	L 2–3	2–2	5	B Moore 2	5,262	1										5									6								10		7	9						2			3		11				4				8
15	FL D3(S)S*	(a)	Bristol Rovers	W 4–2	1–1	5	O'Donnell, Whent, Longdon, B Moore	8,605	1						6													7								10			9						2		3			11				4				8
19	FL D3(S)S	(h)	Bristol City	W 4–3	2–0	5	B Moore 2, O'Donnell 2	2,787	1						4				5									6								10		7	9						2		3			11								8
22	FL D3(S)S	(h)	Crystal Palace	W 7–3	4–1	2	B Moore 4, O'Donnell 2, Rowley (pen)	7,423	1						4																					9		7	10						2		3			11	5			6				8
29	FL D3(S)S	(a)	Crystal Palace	L 1–5	0–3	3	O'Donnell	13,310		1					4													6								9		7	10						2					11	5			3				8
Oct 6	FL D3(S)S	(h)	Bournem'th & B.A.	W 4–2	2–2	3	J Wilson, Darling, B Moore, O'Donnell	7,243	1						4													3						7		9			10						2					11	5			6				8
13	FL D3(S)S	(a)	Bournem'th & B.A.	L 0–3	0–1	4		7,361	1			4	5															3	7							9			10						2					11				6				8
20	FL D3(S)S	(a)	Cardiff City	L 0–4	0–2	4		19,068	1																			6				3				9			10				4		2				7	11				5				8
27	FL D3(S)S	(h)	Cardiff City	L 2–3	1–2	7	B Moore, Robson	9,294	1						4													2				3				9			10				5			7								6			11	8
Nov 3	FL D3(S)S	(h)	Aldershot	W 4–2	2–1	5	Stephens, Darling 2, O'Donnell	7,182	1						7													2							5	9			10				4							11		3		6				8
10	FL D3(S)S	(a)	Aldershot	L 2–4	2–4	5	Stephens, B Moore	3,979	1			10			4													2								9													7	11	5	3		6				8
17	FAC R1 Lg1	(h)	Romford	W 3–1	0–0	–	Davie 2, Hindley	7,423	1			4			6	9									7			3								10									2					11	5							8
24	FAC R1 Lg2	(a)	Romford	D 1–1	0–0	–	Stephens	8,000	1						4		9								7			3								10									2					11	5			6				8
Dec 1	FL D3(S)S	(h)	Torquay United	W 3–0	1–0	5	Gunn 2, B Moore	5,475	1						4						9							5								10									2				7	11		3		6				8
8	FAC R2 Lg1	(a)	Walthamstow Ave	D 1–1	1–0	–	Longdon	8,338	1						4													7				3				9									2					11	5	6		10				8
15	FAC R2 Lg2	(h)	Walthamstow Ave	W 4–2	1–2	–	Longdon, Stephens, J Wilson, Davie	9,453	1						4	9												7			2					10														11	5	3		6				8
19	FL D3(S)S	(h)	Exeter City	W 3–2	0–2	4	B Moore 2, Watson	1,593	1						4						7									3	2					9									5					11		6		10				8
22	FL D3(S)S*	(a)	Exeter City	L 2–3	2–2	4	B Moore, Watson (pen)	4,578	1						4								10					7			2					9									5					11		3		6				8
29	FL D3(S)S	(h)	Swindon Town	W 4–3	1–1	4	Reece, B Moore, Hassell, Stephens	6,183	1														10					7			2					9							4		5					11		3		6				8
Jan 5	FAC R3 Lg1	(a)	Norwich City	W 2–1	2–1	–	Stephens, B Moore	16,188	1			8			3	9												7			2					10									5					11				6				4
9	FAC R3 Lg2	(h)	Norwich City	W 4–1	3–1	–	Chase, Davie 2, Stephens	9,349	1			8			3	9												7			2					10									5					11				6				4
12	FL D3(S)Cup	(h)	Crystal Palace	D 2–2	0–0	5=	Stephens, B Moore	9,832	1			10			2													7								9				8					5					11		3		6				4
19	FL D3(S)Cup	(a)	Crystal Palace	L 1–6	0–4	10	Stephens	8,488	1						3		9						10					7					8																	11		5	2	6				4
26	FAC R4 Lg1	(h)	Aldershot	W 3–0	2–0	–	Davie 3	13,321	1						2	9												7								8									5					11		3		6	10			4
30	FAC R4 Lg2	(a)	Aldershot	W 4–1	2–1	–	Davie 2, Chase, Stephens	5,226	1			8			2	9												7																	5					11		3		6	10			4
Feb 2	FL D3(S)Cup	(h)	Bournem'th & B.A.	L 1–4	0–1	11	B Moore	4,000	1						2								10					7					8			9									5					11		3		6				4
9	FAC R5 Lg1	(h)	Derby County	L 1–4	0–1	–	Willemse	23,456	1							9												7			2					8									5					11		3		6	10			4
13	FAC R5 Lg2	(a)	Derby County	L 0–6	0–4	–		32,000	1							9									7						2					8									5					11		3		6	10			4
16	FL D3(S)Cup	(h)	Aldershot	L 4–6	1–3	11	Hassell 2, Davie, Stephens	5,374	1						2	9							10					7								8									5					11		3		6				4
23	FL D3(S)Cup	(a)	Exeter City	D 0–0	0–0	11		8,500	1											9		10			11		2					8								5										3		6	7			4
Mar 2	FL D3(S)Cup	(h)	Exeter City	D 2–2	1–1	11	Davie, Stephens	2,800	1							9									8			7			2																			11	5	3		6	10			4
9	FL D3(S)Cup	(a)	Reading	L 1–4	0–3	11	Stephens	8,091	1						6	9							10								2		8																	11	5	3			7			4
16	FL D3(S)Cup	(h)	Reading	L 1–2	0–0	11	B Moore	4,000	1						4	10									7						2					9									5					11		3		6				8
23	FL D3(S)Cup	(h)	Torquay United	W 4–0	1–0	10	B Moore 2, Philbin, Davie	4,500	1						4	10				2											3					9					7				5					11				6				8
30	FL D3(S)Cup	(a)	Torquay United	L 0–1	0–0	10		4,143	1						4	9				2			11					7			3										10				5									6				8
Apr 6	FL D3(S)Cup	(h)	Southend United	D 2–2	1–1	10	Davie, B Moore	5,500	1						4	9				2											3					7					10				5					11				6				8
13	FL D3(S)Cup	(a)	Southend United	D 1–1	0–0	10	Stephens	6,822	1		10				4	9				2				7							3																			11	5			6				8
19	FL D3(S)Cup	(a)	Bournem'th & B.A.	L 0–4	0–1	10		9,419	1						4	9				2				7							3										10				5					11	6							8
20	FL D3(S)Cup	(a)	Bristol Rovers	L 1–6	0–4	11	Stephens (pen)	9,347	1							9				2				7							3										10				5					11	6			4				8
22	FL D3(S)Cup	(h)	Bristol Rovers	L 1–3	0–2	11	Day	7,000	1								9	4		3						10										7					11				2						5			6				8
27	FL D3(S)S	(a)	Torquay United	D 0–0	0–0	4		2,814	1								9			2								7			3										10				4					11	5			6				8
May 4	FL D3(S)Cup	(a)	Aldershot	D 2–2	1–1	11	Trainor, Broomfield	3,330	1		7			5	4		10			2											3																			11	9			6				8
							Football League D3(S)S appearances		16	4	0	2	1	0	11	0	3	0	3	1	2	1	3	0	0	0	1	17	1	1	4	2	0	1	1	19	1	6	11	0	1	1	4	2	17	1	5	5	1	16	8	6	0	18	0	1	1	20
							Football League D3(S)S goals								3		1				2		1					1								21			8				1			1	1	1		4		2		1				1
							Football League D3(S) Cup appearances		16	0	2	1	0	1	12	10	3	1	0	8	1	0	6	3	2	2	0	7	0	0	10	0	4	0	0	7	0	0	0	1	7	0	0	0	10	0	0	0	0	13	7	8	1	14	3	0	0	16
							Football League D3(S) Cup goals				1					4	1						2													6					1									7	1							

Notes: Dec 22 – only 40 minutes played each half as Albion arrived late.

Albion finished bottom (11th) of the southern region of the Football League Division Three (South) Cup and did not qualify for the next stage.

The following additional player made one appearance in the Football League Division Three (South) South:

– Sep 15: Alexander, F. (no.5).

the 5,700 mark, but the five F.A. Cup matches at the Goldstone attracted an average 12,600, giving a hint of the boom years to come.

There was also a welcome return for the reserves, who competed in the London Combination in the last season before it became the Football Combination. The reserves' programme was curtailed by fixture congestion and the team finished in the lower reaches of the table, but they did well to reach the semi-final of the London Combination Cup. With the juniors finishing seventh of the eight sides in the Sussex County Emergency League (East), it was the first time the club had run three teams.

> At the end of the season the Albion board had a handsome card, bearing the arms of the twin boroughs of Brighton and Hove, printed in blue and white as a token of gratitude to the many guest players that had played for the club during the war.

Football League Division 3 (South) South 1945–46

		P	W	D	L	F	A	W	D	L	F	A	Pts
1.	Crystal Palace	20	7	2	1	32	7	6	1	3	23	24	29
2.	Cardiff City	20	8	1	1	40	12	5	1	4	29	19	28
3.	Bristol City	20	7	2	1	32	13	4	0	6	19	27	24
4.	**ALBION**	20	8	0	2	35	22	2	1	7	14	28	21
5.	Bristol Rovers	20	3	4	3	21	21	4	2	4	23	23	20
6.	Swindon Town	20	5	1	4	20	19	3	2	5	15	28	19
7.	Bournemouth & B.A.	20	6	0	4	33	20	1	3	6	19	30	17
8.	Aldershot	20	3	3	4	20	27	3	2	5	18	29	17
9.	Exeter City	20	4	2	4	16	18	2	2	6	17	23	16
10.	Reading	20	4	2	4	26	21	1	3	6	17	28	15
11.	Torquay United	20	3	2	5	13	23	2	2	6	9	29	14

Football League Division 3 (South) Cup 1945–46
(South Region Qualifying Competition)

		P	W	D	L	F	A	W	D	L	F	A	Pts
1.	Bournemouth & B.A.	16	6	2	0	27	9	2	2	4	10	11	20
2.	Bristol Rovers	16	5	2	1	17	7	3	1	4	10	12	19
3.	Reading	16	6	1	1	26	7	2	1	5	20	22	18
4.	Crystal Palace	16	4	2	2	24	11	3	2	3	13	19	18
5.	Cardiff City	16	7	0	1	24	7	1	1	6	15	15	17
6.	Bristol City	16	6	1	1	18	8	1	2	5	11	19	17
7.	Torquay United	16	6	1	1	15	7	0	3	5	4	22	16
8.	Exeter City	16	4	2	2	12	7	1	2	5	10	21	14
9.	Swindon Town	16	4	3	1	14	10	1	1	6	7	25	14
10.	Aldershot	16	2	3	3	14	21	1	1	6	9	27	10
11.	**ALBION**	16	1	3	4	17	21	0	3	5	6	24	8

Welcome return of the F.A. Cup
Charlie Chase (right) scores the first goal past Norwich City goalkeeper Derek Davis in the F.A. Cup third-round second-leg match at the Goldstone on 9 January, putting Albion 3–1 ahead on aggregate. Two goals from Jock Davie and one from Bert Stephens sealed the tie 6–2. (The competition was uniquely run this season as a two-legged affair.) After beating Aldershot, Albion went out to the eventual Cup winners, First Division Derby County. The return of the F.A. Cup after an absence of six years was undoubtedly the highlight of the 1945–46 season and attracted some good crowds to Hove. Note the old West Stand in the background, considerably extended and altered in 1920 and 1930 beyond its original size. It lasted in this form until 1958 when it was replaced by the present West Stand.

SEASON 1946–47

After seven years of often chaotic and sometimes farcical wartime competition, things returned to normal at last, but it took some time for the majority of League clubs to regain their pre-war standards. Many struggled to survive and Albion were no exception. The financial situation was precarious and the Goldstone Ground, which had suffered bomb damage during the war, was in urgent need of repair. The club obtained a quantity of government-surplus 'battleship-grey' paint which was liberally daubed all round the ground, resulting in the tongue-in-cheek pseudonym *H.M.S. Goldstone*.

Because of the long lay-off there was a dearth of young talent available throughout the game. Surprisingly, no fewer than ten of Albion's pre-war staff returned to the club but most were in the twilight of their careers. The fixture list was the same as that of the abandoned 1939–40 season and Albion's line-up for the opening game with Port Vale at the Goldstone was the oldest in the history of the club with an average age of 31: Baldwin (26); Marriott (33) and Green (nine days short of 30); Darling (35), Trainor (31) and Dugnolle (32); Broomfield (24), Wilson (37), Hindley (30), Barker (35) and Hanlon (26).

The new players brought in during the summer were Dave Ridley and Don Barker from Millwall, Jim Gotts (Brentford), George Chapman (West Bromwich Albion), Wally Hanlon (Clyde) and the former Albion half-back Jack Dugnolle who returned from Plymouth Argyle. In addition, four local lads who had appeared for the club during the war were enlisted: goalkeeper Jack Ball, Des Broomfield, Jess Willard and Stan Willemse. There were injury setbacks as early as the pre-season practice match, and in October Cyril Hodges was brought in from Arsenal and Jock Sim from Kirkintilloch Rob Roy to reinforce the team.

There were more problems in November when the Players' Union threatened to strike, but the action was averted at the eleventh hour by a Government arbitration tribunal which awarded a long-overdue pay increase, the maximum wage leaping from £9 to £12 per week in the season and to £7 per week in the summer.

In contrast to the immediate pre-war period, Albion's home form was less than impressive. Six defeats and only eight wins came at the Goldstone, but a reasonable away record kept the club in a mid-table spot for most of the campaign. However, the final position of seventeenth was the lowest placing in the Third Division since 1921–22. The biggest home win came in December when Mansfield Town were thrashed 5–0 with a hat-trick from George Chapman, but the next home match on Christmas Day saw Albion embarrassed 6–1 by a fairly ordinary Exeter City side.

Back to normal
Trainer Sam Cowan, in Army fatigues, takes a coaching session as football returns to normal after the seven-year interruption. Cowan had played for the club in an emergency at the age of 44 in 1945, and later became manager of the Brighton Tigers Ice Hockey Club. The players pictured are, left to right: Tony James, George Chapman, Joe Wilson, unknown, Frank Hindley, Ernie Marriott, Jock Sim, Cyril Hodges, Peter Trainor, Wally Hanlon, Stan Willemse.

SEASON 1946–47

Date	Comp.	Ven.	Opponents	Result	HT	Pos.	Scorers	Atten.
Aug 31	FL D3(S)	(h)	Port Vale	D 0–0	0–0	8=		11,412
Sep 4	FL D3(S)	(h)	Aldershot	W 2–1	1–1	4=	Hindley 2	6,018
7	FL D3(S)	(a)	Bristol City	D 0–0	0–0	5		21,316
11	FL D3(S)	(a)	Crystal Palace	L 0–1	0–0	10		11,988
14	FL D3(S)	(h)	Swindon Town	L 1–4	1–1	16	Barker	8,601
18	FL D3(S)	(a)	Aldershot	W 3–1	0–1	11	Darling, Chapman, Barker	1,741
21	FL D3(S)	(a)	Bournem'th & B.A.	L 0–1	0–0	13		12,569
28	FL D3(S)	(h)	Cardiff City	L 0–4	0–2	18		13,193
Oct 5	FL D3(S)	(a)	Norwich City	W 3–2	1–2	16	Chapman, James, Barker	15,416
12	FL D3(S)	(h)	Notts County	W 3–2	3–2	11	Trainor 3	9,419
19	FL D3(S)	(h)	Reading	L 1–4	1–2	15	Darling	11,490
26	FL D3(S)	(a)	Walsall	D 1–1	1–0	17	Trainor	8,832
Nov 2	FL D3(S)	(h)	Watford	D 1–1	1–1	15	Hodges	9,458
9	FL D3(S)	(a)	Ipswich Town	W 2–1	1–1	11	Barker, Darling	11,854
16	FL D3(S)	(h)	Leyton Orient	W 2–1	1–1	10	Chapman, Stephens	9,044
23	FL D3(S)	(a)	Queen's Park R.	L 0–2	0–0	12		17,739
30	FAC R1	(a)	Norwich City	L 2–7	2–1	–	Hindley, Darling	19,264
Dec 7	FL D3(S)	(a)	Bristol Rovers	D 0–0	0–0	11		6,097
14	FL D3(S)	(h)	Mansfield Town	W 5–0	2–0	7	Stephens, Chapman 3, James	7,666
21	FL D3(S)	(a)	Torquay United	L 1–3	0–1	9	Ferrier	4,414
25	FL D3(S)	(h)	Exeter City	L 1–6	1–3	13	Sim	8,015
26	FL D3(S)	(h)	Exeter City	L 1–2	1–2	16	Sim	12,170
28	FL D3(S)	(a)	Port Vale	L 1–4	1–2	16	James	12,061
Jan 4	FL D3(S)	(h)	Bristol City	D 1–1	0–1	17	James	9,527
11	FL D3(S)	(h)	Torquay United	W 2–0	1–0	13	Willemse, Sim	5,458
15	FL D3(S)	(h)	Southend United	W 2–1	1–0	10	Sim, Chapman	4,146
18	FL D3(S)	(a)	Swindon Town	D 2–2	0–2	11	Hanlon, Sim	17,638
25	FL D3(S)	(h)	Bournem'th & B.A.	D 1–1	1–1	12	Stephens	7,725
Feb 1	FL D3(S)	(a)	Cardiff City	L 0–4	0–2	12		20,533
8	FL D3(S)	(h)	Norwich City	D 3–3	2–2	11	James, Hodges, Chapman	4,668
Mar 1	FL D3(S)	(h)	Walsall	W 2–0	2–0	11	Hodges, Hanlon	7,816
15	FL D3(S)	(h)	Ipswich Town	D 0–0	0–0	11		6,681
22	FL D3(S)	(a)	Leyton Orient	L 1–2	1–1	14	Hanlon	10,467
29	FL D3(S)	(h)	Queen's Park R.	L 0–2	0–1	16		8,432
Apr 4	FL D3(S)	(h)	Northampton T.	D 2–2	1–1	16	Willard, Hanlon	9,152
5	FL D3(S)	(a)	Southend United	D 0–0	0–0	15		10,594
7	FL D3(S)	(a)	Northampton T.	L 1–6	0–4	16	Liddell	8,754
12	FL D3(S)	(h)	Bristol Rovers	L 1–2	1–1	16	Willard	7,685
19	FL D3(S)	(a)	Mansfield Town	W 3–0	3–0	16	James, Hindley 2	6,938
May 3	FL D3(S)	(h)	Crystal Palace	W 1–0	0–0	16	Chapman	6,957
10	FL D3(S)	(a)	Notts County	L 0–2	0–2	18		12,926
17	FL D3(S)	(a)	Reading	L 0–2	0–2	18		7,069
24	FL D3(S)	(a)	Watford	W 4–1	3–0	17	Chapman, James 2, Stephens	5,376

League appearances / goals (by player):

Player	Apps	Goals
Baldwin H	10	
Ball J	32	
Bamford H	8	
Barker D	14	4
Broomfield D	18	
Chapman G	32	10
Darling L	27	3
Dugnolle J	32	1
Ferrier J	1	
Gotts J	2	
Grant J	1	
Green F	21	
Hanlon W	41	4
Hindley F	10	4
Hodges C	9	3
James A	23	8
Liddell J	4	1
Marriott E	36	
Ridley D	5	
Risdon S	2	
Sim J	15	5
Stephens H	20	4
Trainor P	32	4
Willard J	7	2
Willemse S	21	1
Wilson JA	39	

Another fall from grace came in the first round of the F.A. Cup when struggling Norwich City, who were forced to seek re-election at the end of the season, made a nonsense of their League form to crush the Albion 7–2 at Carrow Road with Les Eyre registering five, including four in the last quarter of an hour. The defeat remains Albion's biggest in the competition to this day.

Cardiff City were the promoted club, winning the section comfortably by nine points from Queen's Park Rangers. Albion fared poorly against the two leading teams, losing 4–0 home and away to Cardiff, and 2–0 home and away to Rangers. A very severe winter saw many postponements – mainly away from home in Albion's case – and the season was extended into June, six weeks later than scheduled. League gates in the first regular season after the war averaged 8,217.

The 54 League goals were shared among fourteen players, with George Chapman leading the way on ten. There were constant changes in the line-ups from week to week, but left-winger Wally Hanlon missed only one game while the ever-faithful Joe Wilson was absent on just three occasions. Joe retired at the end of the season and was rewarded for his loyalty when he was appointed as assistant to trainer Alex Wilson.

Football League Division 3 (South) 1946–47

		P	W	D	L	F	A	W	D	L	F	A	Pts
1.	Cardiff City	42	18	3	0	60	11	12	3	6	33	19	66
2.	Queen's Park R.	42	15	2	4	42	15	8	9	4	32	25	57
3.	Bristol City	42	13	4	4	56	20	7	7	7	38	36	51
4.	Swindon Town	42	15	4	2	56	25	4	7	10	28	48	49
5.	Walsall	42	11	6	4	42	25	6	6	9	32	34	46
6.	Ipswich Town	42	11	5	5	33	21	5	9	7	28	32	46
7.	Bournemouth & B.A.	42	12	4	5	43	20	6	4	11	29	34	44
8.	Southend United	42	9	7	5	38	22	8	3	10	33	38	44
9.	Reading	42	11	6	4	53	30	5	5	11	30	44	43
10.	Port Vale	42	14	4	3	51	28	3	5	13	17	35	43
11.	Torquay United	42	11	5	5	33	23	4	7	10	19	38	42
12.	Notts County	42	11	6	4	35	19	4	6	11	28	40	42
13.	Northampton Town	42	11	5	5	46	33	4	5	12	26	42	40
14.	Bristol Rovers	42	9	6	6	34	26	7	2	12	25	43	40
15.	Exeter City	42	11	6	4	37	27	4	3	14	23	42	39
16.	Watford	42	11	4	6	39	27	6	1	14	22	49	39
17.	**ALBION**	42	8	7	6	31	35	5	5	11	23	37	38
18.	Crystal Palace	42	9	7	5	29	19	4	4	13	20	43	37
19.	Leyton Orient	42	10	5	6	40	28	2	3	16	14	47	32
20.	Aldershot	42	6	7	8	25	26	4	5	12	23	52	32
21.	Norwich City	42	6	3	12	38	48	4	5	12	26	52	28
22.	Mansfield Town	42	8	5	8	31	38	1	5	15	17	58	28

SEASON 1947–48

In May 1947 former Albion favourite Tommy Cook returned from South Africa to take the post of team manager, with Charlie Webb, now turned 60, looking after the administrative side as secretary and general manager. Like any other season, 1947–48 opened with optimism; little did anyone associated with the Albion realise that there would soon be a second change at the helm, and that the team would finish at the bottom of the pile with the ignominy of having to apply for re-election to the Football League for the first and only time.

The chronic post-war housing shortage made it extremely difficult to sign new players, but Cook brought in Laurie Nevins from Newcastle United, Bob Hacking (Luton Town), Bob Redfern (Bournemouth), Lyn Thomas (Swansea Town) and Jack Whent from Canada. Whent had appeared in Albion's ranks during the war while serving with the Canadian forces. The first match, at Watford, resulted in a splendid 3–2 win, but it soon became apparent that heavy seas were ahead. At Bristol Rovers, Jack Dugnolle failed to arrive and trainer Alex Wilson, a goalkeeper by trade, was pressed into duty on the right wing. He performed quite well in the circumstances but Albion still lost 4–1.

A series of poor results ensued and by the end of October Albion were only two places from the bottom. The situation came to a head after a 4–0 home defeat by Walsall on 1 November when a disenchanted crowd of around 500 fans demonstrated in front of the West Stand. In order to cool things down, the directors agreed to interview a three-man delegation.

Whether or not as a result of this meeting, it was announced eleven days later that Charlton Athletic's veteran ex-England star, Don Welsh, had been appointed as the new secretary-manager. It was the end of an era: Charlie Webb had been in charge of the club's affairs since 1919, 28 years in which he had gained wide respect with players and fans alike. He was to remain at the Goldstone until the end of the season to advise and assist his successor, but team manager Tommy Cook, with just three wins in seventeen games under his belt, departed after only seven months in charge. Just over two years later, Albion's master goalscorer died in sad circumstances.

Welsh arrived only six months after lifting the F.A. Cup as Charlton's skipper at Wembley. He intended to register himself as a player in case of emergency, but Charlton would not agree to the move without the payment of a transfer fee which Albion could not afford. On taking office Welsh declared his intent to keep faith with the existing playing staff to steer the club out of the danger zone, but the win-less run which had begun on 20 September stretched to fifteen League matches and in February he was compelled to open the cheque-book. He opted for experience in the shape of his former Charlton team-mates Eric Lancelotte and Reg Hipkin, signed for £3,250 and £1,750 respectively, George Willis from Wolves (£1,000) and Reading's 35-year-old half-back Len Young (£1,000). The £7,000 spree represented a huge outlay for a Third Division club at the time. Frank Morrad (Fulham) and Micky Kavanagh (Bohemians) were also engaged, followed in March by Sammy Small, a 35-year-old utility player from West Ham United.

> The second half of Albion's match with Newport County at Somerton Park on 22 November was broadcast live on the BBC Light programme.

Albion 1947–48
Back row left to right: Laurie Nevins, Des Broomfield, Wally Hanlon.
Middle row left to right: Alex Wilson (trainer), Stan Risdon, Jack Dugnolle, Jack Ball, Peter Trainor, Stan Willemse, Joe Wilson (assistant trainer).
Front row left to right: Gerald Paling (director), Alec Whitcher (director), Jess Willard, Jock Sim, Ernie Marriott (captain), Tony James,
George Chapman, Charles Wakeling (chairman), Charlie Webb (secretary/general manager), Tommy Cook (team manager).

SEASON 1947–48

Date	Comp.	Ven.	Opponents	Result	HT	Pos.	Scorers	Atten.
Aug 23	FL D3(S)	(a)	Watford	W 3–2	1–1	7	Thomas, Redfern, Chapman	9,787
27	FL D3(S)	(h)	Queen's Park R.	L 0–5	0–3	10		14,228
30	FL D3(S)	(h)	Bournem'th & B.A.	L 0–2	0–1	20		9,525
Sep 4	FL D3(S)	(a)	Queen's Park R.	L 0–2	0–0	22		18,116
6	FL D3(S)	(h)	Norwich City	W 2–0	1–0	16	James, Willard	9,132
10	FL D3(S)	(a)	Swindon Town	D 1–1	1–1	16	Hacking	15,216
13	FL D3(S)	(a)	Bristol Rovers	L 1–4	1–3	19	James	13,833
17	FL D3(S)	(h)	Swindon Town	W 1–0	0–0	14	James	5,741
20	FL D3(S)	(h)	Northampton T.	L 2–3	0–2	16	Own goal, Willard	8,575
27	FL D3(S)	(a)	Aldershot	D 1–1	1–0	18	Vickers	6,997
Oct 1	FL D3(S)	(h)	Swansea Town	L 0–1	0–1	18		4,712
4	FL D3(S)	(h)	Crystal Palace	D 1–1	1–0	18	James	10,240
11	FL D3(S)	(a)	Ipswich Town	L 0–4	0–3	19		14,643
18	FL D3(S)	(h)	Bristol City	L 0–2	0–1	20		11,820
25	FL D3(S)	(a)	Reading	L 0–1	0–1	20		13,021
Nov 1	FL D3(S)	(h)	Walsall	L 0–4	0–0	20		8,995
8	FL D3(S)	(a)	Leyton Orient	L 1–2	1–1	21	Willard	12,480
15	FL D3(S)	(h)	Exeter City	L 0–1	0–1	21		8,822
22	FL D3(S)	(a)	Newport County	D 1–1	1–0	21	James	5,817
29	FAC R1	(a)	Trowbridge	D 1–1*	1–1	–	Willard	6,739
Dec 6	FAC R1 Rep	(h)	Trowbridge	W 5–0	5–0	–	Hacking, Sim, Chapman 2, James (pen)	12,000
13	FAC R2	(a)	Hartlepools United	D 1–1*	0–0	–	Sim	12,588
20	FAC R2 Rep	(h)	Hartlepools United	W 2–1	0–0	–	James, Willard	15,000
25	FL D3(S)	(h)	Port Vale	L 0–5	0–2	21		11,431
27	FL D3(S)	(h)	Port Vale	D 2–2	0–1	21	James, Booth	7,329
Jan 3	FL D3(S)	(a)	Bournem'th & B.A.	L 1–4	1–0	22	Booth	13,354
10	FAC R3	(a)	Portsmouth	L 1–4	1–1	–	Booth	37,646
17	FL D3(S)	(a)	Norwich City	D 2–2	0–1	21	Thomas 2	19,154
24	FL D3(S)	(h)	Ipswich Town	W 4–1	3–1	20	Booth 2, Thomas, James	9,097
31	FL D3(S)	(h)	Bristol Rovers	W 3–1	2–1	20	Clelland, Booth, Hacking	14,081
Feb 7	FL D3(S)	(a)	Northampton T.	L 0–4	0–2	22		6,661
14	FL D3(S)	(h)	Aldershot	D 1–1	0–0	21	Chapman	12,680
Mar 6	FL D3(S)	(a)	Bristol City	W 2–1	1–0	21	James 2 (2 pens)	13,383
13	FL D3(S)	(h)	Reading	W 2–0	0–0	21	Willis 2	15,046
20	FL D3(S)	(a)	Walsall	D 0–0	0–0	21		11,745
26	FL D3(S)	(h)	Torquay United	W 2–1	1–0	20	James (pen), Willis	18,425
27	FL D3(S)	(h)	Leyton Orient	D 0–0	0–0	20		19,026
29	FL D3(S)	(a)	Torquay United	W 2–1	2–1	20	Willis, Own goal	5,295
Apr 3	FL D3(S)	(a)	Exeter City	L 0–1	0–0	20		7,859
7	FL D3(S)	(h)	Southend United	W 1–0	1–0	20	James	10,194
10	FL D3(S)	(h)	Newport County	W 3–0	1–0	18	Willis, Moore 2	14,247
12	FL D3(S)	(a)	Crystal Palace	D 0–0	0–0	18		16,463
17	FL D3(S)	(a)	Southend United	D 2–2	1–0	18	Willis 2	6,428
22	FL D3(S)	(a)	Notts County	L 0–4	0–2	18		19,585
24	FL D3(S)	(a)	Notts County	L 1–3	0–1	19	James	19,572
28	FL D3(S)	(h)	Watford	L 1–3	0–1	20	Willis	9,652
May 1	FL D3(S)	(a)	Swansea Town	D 0–0	0–0	22		15,918

Notes: Nov 29 – after extra time.
Dec 13 – after extra time (90-minute score 1–1).

League appearances / League goals

Player	App.	Goals
Baldwin H	26	
Ball J	16	
Booth S	20	5
Broomfield D	2	
Chapman G	11	2
Clelland D	8	1
Darling L	21	
Dugnolle J	27	
Green F	3	
Hacking R	17	2
Hanlon W	31	
Hipkin R	10	
James A	42	12
Lancelotte E	14	
McLeod R	1	
Marriott E	36	
Moore B	8	2
Morrad F	11	
Nevins L	5	
Redfern R	5	1
Sim J	6	
Small S	10	
Stephens H	2	
Thomas L	13	4
Trainor P	5	
Vickers W	5	1
Whent J	21	
Willard J	29	3
Willemse S	34	
Willis G	15	8
Wilson Alex	1	
Young L	7	

Own goals: 2

The injection of new blood brought about a big improvement. The fight for survival was akin to a promotion battle, and a series of narrow wins and draws saw gates soar. The Notts County fixture in April attracted a new record crowd for a League match to the Goldstone, 19,572 turning up to witness the current England centre-forward, Tommy Lawton, score twice for the Magpies in a 3–1 win. Despite the good run Albion could not break away from the lower reaches and the last day of the campaign arrived with numerous permutations on the cards. This was the table before the last round of matches:

		P	W	D	L	F	A	Pts
17.	Torquay United	41	11	13	17	62	58	35
18.	Aldershot	41	10	14	17	45	67	34
19.	Leyton Orient	41	12	10	19	47	72	34
20.	ALBION	41	11	11	19	43	73	33
21.	Bristol Rovers	41	12	8	21	67	75	32
22.	Norwich City	41	12	8	21	58	75	32

A win at Swansea would see the club safe regardless of other results, but the match ended in a goal-less draw while both Norwich City and Bristol Rovers won, so an incredibly close

Football League Division 3 (South) 1947–48

		P	W	D	L	F	A	W	D	L	F	A	Pts
1.	Queen's Park R.	42	16	3	2	44	17	10	6	5	30	20	61
2.	Bournemouth & B.A.	42	13	5	3	42	13	11	4	6	34	22	57
3.	Walsall	42	13	5	3	37	12	8	4	9	33	28	51
4.	Ipswich Town	42	16	1	4	42	18	7	2	12	25	43	49
5.	Swansea Town	42	14	6	1	48	14	4	6	11	22	38	48
6.	Notts County	42	12	5	4	44	27	7	4	10	24	32	46
7.	Bristol City	42	11	4	6	47	26	7	3	11	30	39	43
8.	Port Vale	42	14	5	3	48	18	2	7	12	15	36	43
9.	Southend United	42	11	8	2	32	16	4	5	12	19	42	43
10.	Reading	42	10	5	6	37	28	5	6	10	19	30	41
11.	Exeter City	42	11	6	4	34	22	4	5	12	21	41	41
12.	Newport County	42	9	8	4	38	28	5	5	11	23	45	41
13.	Crystal Palace	42	12	5	4	34	14	1	8	12	17	35	39
14.	Northampton Town	42	10	5	6	35	28	4	6	11	23	44	39
15.	Watford	42	6	6	9	31	37	8	4	9	26	42	38
16.	Swindon Town	42	6	10	5	21	20	4	6	11	20	26	36
17.	Leyton Orient	42	8	5	8	31	32	5	5	11	20	41	36
18.	Torquay United	42	7	6	8	40	29	4	7	10	23	33	35
19.	Aldershot	42	5	10	6	22	26	5	4	12	23	41	34
20.	Bristol Rovers	42	7	3	11	39	34	6	5	10	32	41	34
21.	Norwich City	42	8	3	10	33	34	5	5	11	28	42	34
22.	**ALBION**	42	8	4	9	26	31	3	8	10	17	42	34

The England squad trained at the Goldstone in preparation for the match with Sweden at Highbury on 19 November, and the players stayed at the Grand Hotel. The locals were impressed by their new-fangled 'track suits'.

finale found Albion in the basement by virtue of a vastly inferior goal-average. Only two points separated the bottom seven teams, and Albion's 34-point total remains the highest by a side finishing last in 31 seasons of the old Southern Section.

The F.A. Cup brought some light relief with replay victories at Hove over Trowbridge Town of the Western League and Hartlepools United. The third-round draw gave Albion a plum tie at Portsmouth. A crowd of 37,646 saw Sammy Booth give the visitors an early lead, but the First Division side equalised before the break and ran out comfortable 4–1 winners.

With the mid-season changes in personnel, no fewer than 32 players appeared in the League team with Tony James the only ever-present. Tony was also leading scorer with fourteen in League and Cup. Goalkeeper Harry Baldwin played his part admirably in the battle with an amazing five successive penalty saves, and a total of seven out of nine penalties faced.

In what, on paper, was the club's worst season ever, more people watched the Goldstone matches than ever before, 241,139 at an average of 11,483 — a curious irony. Len Darling, Bert Stephens, Stan Risdon, Joe Wilson and Ernie Marriott were granted benefits this season, but in the Spartan days of post-war Britain the five stalwarts were forced to share the proceeds of three testimonial matches, poor reward for some 68 years of service. Yet in March the board made public a plan to rebuild the Goldstone at a cost of £100,000 over the next ten years or so.

In May, Charles Wakeling solicited support throughout the League for the club's re-election, making great play of the soaring attendances and the plans for rebuilding both the team and ground. The vote on 8 June was really a formality, but it was still a relief when the following figures were announced:

Brighton and Hove Albion	47	votes
Norwich City	47	votes
Colchester United	2	votes
Gillingham	1	vote
Worcester City	1	vote
'Others'	0	votes

'Others' included Bath City, Bridgend Town, Chelmsford City, Lovells Athletic, Merthyr Tydfil, Peterborough United and Yeovil Town.

The reserves also had a disastrous campaign, finishing bottom of Section 'B' of the Football Combination; at Tottenham in August the side suffered a 13–0 humiliation. Following the successful experiment with the wartime junior side, a third or 'A' team was formed during the season which played a series of friendly matches under the guidance of Sam Cowan. The initial game, on 14 February, resulted in a 3–0 defeat at Southwick.

March saw the rebirth of the Supporters' Club, which had folded on the outbreak of war. The chairman was Harry Coverdale, a fan for more than 40 years who had played a big part in keeping the Albion going during the war, often taking charge of the team on its travels; he was also a director from 1954 until 1960. Lord Broadbridge, the first chairman of directors and now club president, was also president of the new club, while among the vice-presidents were Ike de Costa, a name from the earliest days back in 1901; John Talbot-Nanson, secretary of the previous club; and Patsy Hendren, the Middlesex and England batting legend. Membership cost one shilling (5p), and a recruitment campaign began on 13 March at the Reading match when over 1,000 supporters were signed up.

Learning from the boss
Don Welsh gives a coaching session to his new players in his first week as Albion manager. The track-suited boss had hoped to continue his playing career but the requirement of a fee by his former club, Charlton Athletic, put paid to the idea.

The Olympics at the Goldstone

The XIVth Olympic Games came to Hove on 26 July 1948 when Afghanistan met Luxemburg in a preliminary-round tie before a holiday crowd of 7,000. The tall, lean Afghans disappointed the spectators by not playing in bare feet but still proved no match for the Grand Duchy which won 6–0. Hero of the hour was acrobatic goalkeeper Abdul Ghafour Assar who kept the score down considerably; the picture shows him saving a header from Luxemburg outside-right Jules Gales. The Luxemburg side was beaten 6–1 by Yugoslavia in the next round. Sweden won the Wembley final 3–1 against the Yugoslavs, Great Britain managing fourth place.

SEASON 1948–49

The heavy spending continued during the close season in an effort to improve the playing standard. A club-record £5,000 brought Johnny McNichol from Newcastle United. Harry Daniels was signed from Queen's Park Rangers (£2,000), George Lewis from Southampton (£1,100), Ron Guttridge from Aston Villa (£500) and Ken Davies from Walsall (£250). Les Jones and Des Tennant arrived from Barry Town, Paddy Brennan came from Shelbourne, Geoff Taylor from Lincoln City, and Billy Reed, a former Welsh amateur-international winger, arrived from Cardiff City. Des Broomfield and Stan Risdon were released to join the newly formed professional club Hastings United in the Southern League. A new playing strip was adopted, the first change for 44 years, as Don Welsh introduced blue shirts with white sleeves in a 'new-broom-sweeps-clean' gesture.

There was a tremendous upsurge of enthusiasm for the game this season: an all-time high of 41·2 million attended matches at an average of over 22,000 throughout the Football League. Albion's opening match saw their recently created League attendance record bettered when 21,593 spectators watched the 1–1 draw with Swindon Town. The record was to be surpassed twice more before the end of the campaign.

After six games Albion were unbeaten and in second place, but were then brought down to earth with a 6–2 hiding at Millwall. That humiliation was followed by two more defeats. Then, from 25 September, Albion remained unbeaten in fifteen League matches, a run broken only by a 3–1 reverse at Newport in the first round of the F.A. Cup. By mid January the team was back in second spot behind Swindon Town, but a loss of form brought a worrying lapse, ending in a remarkable 6–1 home defeat by Bournemouth. Third place was maintained into March, but of the last twelve matches only two ended in victory and the club had to settle for a final sixth placing, fourteen points behind champions Swansea Town. The last game of the

At the end of the season the Supporters' Club held its first 'Albion Week', a festival of fund-raising activities including concerts, quizzes, dances, and other sporting and social events. Although very popular, it did not prove to be a financial success and a small loss was incurred. The Week included exhibition football matches involving teams from the Press, the ice-hockey club Brighton Tigers, the Supporters' Club itself, and a side of former Albion players.

SEASON 1948–49

Date	Comp.	Ven.	Opponents	Result	HT	Pos.	Scorers	Atten.
Aug 21	FL D3(S)	(h)	Swindon Town	D 1–1	1–0	9=	Lewis	21,593
25	FL D3(S)	(a)	Bristol City	D 1–1	0–0	10=	Davies	24,432
28	FL D3(S)	(a)	Leyton Orient	W 3–0	1–0	6	Willis 2, Willemse (pen)	16,416
Sep 1	FL D3(S)	(h)	Bristol City	D 0–0	0–0	5		17,483
4	FL D3(S)	(h)	Port Vale	W 1–0	0–0	3=	Lancelotte	20,383
8	FL D3(S)	(h)	Norwich City	W 1–0	1–0	2	Willard	17,559
11	FL D3(S)	(a)	Millwall	L 2–6	0–2	5	Tennant, Lancelotte	23,721
15	FL D3(S)	(a)	Norwich City	L 1–2	1–1	7=	Willemse	22,277
18	FL D3(S)	(h)	Aldershot	L 0–4	0–2	12		18,281
25	FL D3(S)	(a)	Bournem'th & B.A.	W 1–0	1–0	10	Willis	17,777
Oct 2	FL D3(S)	(a)	Southend United	D 0–0	0–0	11		11,106
9	FL D3(S)	(h)	Watford	D 0–0	0–0	10		16,066
16	FL D3(S)	(a)	Crystal Palace	W 2–0	1–0	6	Tennant 2	15,170
23	FL D3(S)	(h)	Torquay United	W 3–1	1–0	5	Willis, Tennant, Booth	17,359
30	FL D3(S)	(a)	Walsall	D 0–0	0–0	4		11,407
Nov 6	FL D3(S)	(h)	Newport County	W 3–2	1–1	4	Hipkin, McNichol, Tennant	17,011
13	FL D3(S)	(a)	Bristol Rovers	D 0–0	0–0	4		21,879
20	FL D3(S)	(h)	Reading	W 2–0	1–0	3	Kavanagh, Tennant (pen)	18,834
27	FAC R1	(a)	Newport County	L 1–3	0–2	–	Tennant	14,000
Dec 4	FL D3(S)	(h)	Notts County	W 3–2	2–0	3	Kavanagh, Lewis 2	22,994
18	FL D3(S)	(a)	Swindon Town	D 0–0	0–0	3		15,823
25	FL D3(S)	(a)	Exeter City	D 1–1	0–0	3	McNichol	8,037
27	FL D3(S)	(h)	Exeter City	W 2–0	0–0	3	Lewis, Lancelotte	19,483
Jan 1	FL D3(S)	(h)	Leyton Orient	W 3–1	1–0	2	Tennant, Lancelotte, Lewis	11,992
15	FL D3(S)	(a)	Port Vale	W 4–3	3–2	2	Tennant, Lewis 2, Own goal	9,562
22	FL D3(S)	(h)	Millwall	L 1–2	0–1	2	Tennant	25,485
29	FL D3(S)	(a)	Swansea Town	L 0–3	0–1	3		26,045
Feb 5	FL D3(S)	(a)	Aldershot	D 1–1	1–1	3	Lancelotte	8,249
12	FL D3(S)	(a)	Ipswich Town	D 2–2	0–2	3	Kavanagh, Lancelotte	10,695
19	FL D3(S)	(h)	Bournem'th & B.A.	L 1–6	0–3	4	Tennant	20,859
26	FL D3(S)	(h)	Southend United	W 1–0	1–0	3	Mansell	13,893
Mar 5	FL D3(S)	(a)	Watford	D 0–0	0–0	3		8,665
12	FL D3(S)	(h)	Crystal Palace	D 1–1	0–0	3	Lewis	15,413
19	FL D3(S)	(a)	Torquay United	D 1–1	0–0	3	Lancelotte	7,324
26	FL D3(S)	(h)	Walsall	L 1–2	1–1	6	Lancelotte	13,458
Apr 2	FL D3(S)	(a)	Newport County	D 1–1	0–0	5	Roberts	11,779
9	FL D3(S)	(h)	Bristol Rovers	W 2–1	2–0	4	Roberts, McCurley	14,829
15	FL D3(S)	(h)	Northampton T.	D 0–0	0–0	5		18,271
16	FL D3(S)	(a)	Reading	L 1–6	0–5	6	Willis	18,497
18	FL D3(S)	(a)	Northampton T.	D 1–1	0–1	6	McCurley	9,184
23	FL D3(S)	(h)	Swansea Town	L 0–2	0–0	6		19,974
30	FL D3(S)	(a)	Notts County	D 1–1	1–1	6	McCurley	19,829
May 7	FL D3(S)	(h)	Ipswich Town	W 6–1	4–0	6	McCurley 2, Morrad 3 (2 pens), Roberts	11,088

League appearances (by player): Baldwin H 40, Ball J 2, Booth S 8, Brennan P 8, Daniels H 28, Davies K 14, Guttridge R 10, Hipkin R 5, James A 4, Jones LJ 3, Kavanagh M 12, Lancelotte E 32, Lewis G 24, McCurley K 7, McNichol J 33, Mansell J 9, Morrad F 16, Reed WG 8, Roberts D 9, Sim J 5, Small S 27, Taylor G 2, Tennant D 39, Whent J 39, Wilkins J 2, Willard J 26, Willemse S 36, Willis G 13, Young L 1.

League goals (by player): OG – 1; Booth S 1, Davies K 1, Hipkin R 1, Kavanagh M 3, Lancelotte E 8, Lewis G 8, McCurley K 5, McNichol J 2, Mansell J 1, Morrad F 3, Roberts D 3, Tennant D 10, Willard J 1, Willemse S 2, Willis G 5.

season saw Ipswich Town beaten 6–1 at the Goldstone with the aid of a hat-trick from Frank Morrad.

Only four away games ended in defeat, but Albion took on the mantle of draw specialists, registering thirteen on the road and a total of eighteen, the highest number in the four sections of the Football League and far too many for a serious promotion challenge to be mounted. Just six players made more than 30 appearances, and the fact that 29 players were employed made the season's endeavours even more creditable. The 55 League goals were evenly distributed among fifteen scorers, with the versatile Des Tennant leading the list with eleven in League and Cup. Des turned out in five different positions in his 39 outings.

Despite the huge improvement in the team's performance, the most outstanding feature was the incredible increase in attendances: there were five gates in excess of 20,000 and the average of 17,729 was more than 50 per cent up even on the previous term's record-breaking figure. Large-scale ground improvements were carried out during the season as the first part of the board's £100,000 plan to reconstruct the ground, and the new arrangements were inaugurated for the Bournemouth match on 19 February. The southern third of the east terracing was completely rebuilt and combined with the central 'Chicken Run' section to form a new east enclosure, while additional turnstiles were built all round the ground. The north-west terracing was raised to accommodate another 2,000 fans.

Football League Division 3 (South) 1948–49

		P	W	D	L	F	A	W	D	L	F	A	Pts
1.	Swansea Town	42	20	1	0	60	11	7	7	7	27	23	62
2.	Reading	42	17	1	3	48	18	8	4	9	29	32	55
3.	Bournemouth & B.A.	42	15	2	4	42	17	7	6	8	27	31	52
4.	Swindon Town	42	11	9	1	38	20	7	6	8	26	36	51
5.	Bristol Rovers	42	13	5	3	42	23	6	5	10	19	28	48
6.	**ALBION**	42	11	5	5	32	26	4	13	4	23	29	48
7.	Ipswich Town	42	14	3	4	53	30	4	6	11	25	47	45
8.	Millwall	42	12	7	2	42	23	5	4	12	21	41	45
9.	Torquay United	42	12	5	4	45	26	5	6	10	20	44	45
10.	Norwich City	42	11	6	4	32	10	5	6	10	35	39	44
11.	Notts County	42	15	3	3	68	19	4	2	15	34	49	43
12.	Exeter City	42	12	5	4	45	26	3	5	13	18	50	40
13.	Port Vale	42	11	3	7	32	21	3	8	10	19	33	39
14.	Walsall	42	9	9	3	34	28	6	3	12	22	36	38
15.	Newport County	42	8	6	7	41	35	6	3	12	27	57	37
16.	Bristol City	42	8	8	5	28	24	3	5	13	16	38	35
17.	Watford	42	6	9	6	24	21	4	6	11	17	33	35
18.	Southend United	42	5	10	6	18	18	4	6	11	23	28	34
19.	Leyton Orient	42	6	6	9	36	29	2	6	13	22	51	34
20.	Northampton Town	42	9	6	6	33	20	3	3	15	18	42	33
21.	Aldershot	42	6	5	10	26	29	5	6	10	22	30	33
22.	Crystal Palace	42	7	8	6	27	27	1	3	17	11	49	27

In March the death was announced of the former Albion chairman and president Mr William Goodwin at the age of 79. Goodwin served on the board for 35 years from 1905 until 1940 and was a member of the Southern League management committee in the early years. He was also the founder of the Dyke Golf Club in 1910. Another great servant of the game passed away on 6 May 1949: Edgar Everest, the 'Grand Old Man of Sussex Football', was 84. County F.A. secretary for 56 years, he was, of course, the pioneer of the professional game in Brighton and Hove with the founding of the Brighton United club in 1897.

Albion 1948–49

Back row left to right: Dave Clelland, George Lewis, Jack Whent, Ernie Marriott, Stan Willemse, Des Tennant, Johnny McNichol, Ron Rattray, Reg Hipkin, Harry Baldwin, Harry Daniels, Jack Ball, Kevin McCurley, Sammy Booth, unknown.
Middle row left to right: Willie Wakefield, George Willis, Billy Reed, Paddy Brennan, Eric Lancelotte, Jess Willard, Tony James, Jock Sim.
Seated on ground left to right: Ken Davies, Micky Kavanagh.

SEASON 1949–50

During the summer Chelsea made an offer for Albion's brilliant young full-back Stan Willemse and he was transferred to the First Division club for a £6,000 fee, by far the largest received for an Albion player at the time. The cash went a long way to covering the cost of the rebuilding work carried out at the Goldstone in the close season. The South Stand, which had remained virtually unchanged since it was acquired in 1904, was raised and re-erected behind new terracing. Improvements were also made to the West Stand and the east terracing, and new toilets were added around the ground. Most of the club's locally based players were employed by the building contractors throughout the summer.

In May 1950 the Supporters' Club held its second 'Albion Week', but again, although popular, the event did not prove to be a financial success and was subsequently dropped. The highlight was a football match at the Goldstone between an Albion Old Professionals XI and a side from the ever-popular Brighton Tigers. The footballers beat the ice-hockey men 6–4. The teams were:

Albion Veterans: Gordon Mee; Wally Little and Frank Brett; Don Welsh, Paul Mooney and Arthur Attwood; Bert Jepson, Bobby Farrell, Eric Townsend, Billy Lane and Ernie Wilson.

Brighton Tigers: Gib Hutchinson; Jean Lacroix and Al Truelove; Lefty Wilmot, Tommy Jamieson and Lorne Trottier; Johnny Evans, Lee Thorne, Bobby Lee, Andy Rochon and Lennie Baker.

Several other favourites departed before the start of the new season: Ernie Marriott to Southern League Tonbridge, Tony James to Bristol Rovers and Sammy Booth to Hastings United. Two newcomers were added to the staff: centre-forward Fred Leamon, a Channel Islander from Bristol Rovers, and Cliff Pinchbeck from Everton. Pinchbeck's Goldstone interlude was a brief one as Port Vale paid £3,500 for his signature in November.

The successful 'A'-team experiment continued with entry into the London Midweek League, and an under-18 side, the junior 'A' team, competed in the Greater London Minor Combination. One of the youngsters to graduate from the 'A' team made his first-team début in September: assistant trainer Joe Wilson's brother Glen, like Joe, was to serve the club in various capacities for many years.

The team's form up to the New Year was disappointing, particularly at home where just four of the first fifteen games were won. As in the previous season there was a plethora of drawn matches, and following three losses over the Christmas-holiday period Albion were in fifteenth place. By the end of September, Harry Baldwin had stretched his penalty-saving sequence to a remarkable ten out of fifteen. He and great rival Jack Ball enjoyed a joint benefit this term. The long-serving former manager Charlie Webb also received a testimonial for which Arsenal and Portsmouth provided a Goldstone crowd of over 13,000 with an exhibition of memorable football in September, Pompey winning 2–1.

Albion stumbled at the first hurdle in the F.A. Cup for the second season running, losing 2–1 at Ipswich. Then, from March, came a vast improvement and the run-in brought only

SEASON 1949–50

The column headings for the player appearance grid are (left to right): Baldwin H, Ball J, Brennan P, Connelly E, Daniels H, Davies K, Guttridge R, Kavanagh M, Lancelotte E, Leamon F, McCurley K, McNichol J, Mansell J, Morrad F, Morris W, Pinchbeck C, Reed W, Rees M, Roberts D, Sim J, Small S, South A, Suttle K, Tennant D, Thompson C, Vitty J, Whent J, Wilkins J, Willard J, Wilson G.

Date	Comp	Ven	Opponents	Result	HT	Pos	Scorers	Atten.
Aug 20	FL D3(S)	(h)	Notting'm Forest	D	2–2	0–2	13=	Lancelotte, Davies	21,625
24	FL D3(S)	(a)	Aldershot	W	1–0	1–0	5	Lancelotte	8,182
27	FL D3(S)	(a)	Northampton T.	D	1–1	1–1	7	Pinchbeck	18,661
31	FL D3(S)	(h)	Aldershot	D	1–1	1–1	6	Tennant (pen)	16,006
Sep 3	FL D3(S)	(h)	Norwich City	L	1–3	1–2	11=	Davies	18,716
5	FL D3(S)	(a)	Millwall	L	1–5	0–2	13	Lancelotte	18,364
10	FL D3(S)	(a)	Newport County	W	1–0	1–0	12	Pinchbeck	11,157
14	FL D3(S)	(a)	Reading	L	0–3	0–0	13		15,567
17	FL D3(S)	(h)	Bristol City	W	2–1	1–1	10	Tennant (pen), Lancelotte	16,687
24	FL D3(S)	(a)	Bournem'th & B.A.	D	2–2	1–2	12	McNichol, Pinchbeck	17,391
Oct 1	FL D3(S)	(a)	Walsall	L	2–4	1–1	13	Morris, Pinchbeck	10,714
8	FL D3(S)	(h)	Bristol Rovers	L	1–2	0–2	14	Leamon	16,031
15	FL D3(S)	(a)	Southend United	L	2–3	1–1	16	Tennant, Pinchbeck	12,605
22	FL D3(S)	(a)	Notts County	L	2–3	2–1	18	McNichol, Morris	17,411
29	FL D3(S)	(a)	Port Vale	L	0–3	0–2	21		11,189
Nov 5	FL D3(S)	(h)	Ipswich Town	W	2–1	0–1	17	Willard 2	5,471
12	FL D3(S)	(a)	Exeter City	W	3–2	2–0	15	McNichol, Connelly, Lancelotte	7,599
19	FL D3(S)	(h)	Leyton Orient	D	2–2	0–1	13	Willard, Kavanagh	13,066
26	FAC R1	(a)	Ipswich Town	L	1–2	0–1	–	Tennant (pen)	12,265
Dec 3	FL D3(S)	(h)	Watford	W	2–1	1–0	13	Tennant, Morris	9,775
17	FL D3(S)	(a)	Notting'm Forest	W	1–0	1–0	13	Leamon	13,096
24	FL D3(S)	(a)	Northampton T.	L	1–2	1–2	13	Tennant	14,958
26	FL D3(S)	(h)	Swindon Town	L	0–1	0–1	14		14,306
27	FL D3(S)	(a)	Swindon Town	L	2–4	2–2	15	McNichol, Reed	18,872
31	FL D3(S)	(h)	Norwich City	W	2–1	1–0	12	Tennant (pen), McNichol	22,871
Jan 7	FL D3(S)	(a)	Crystal Palace	D	0–0	0–0	11		13,289
14	FL D3(S)	(h)	Newport County	W	5–0	3–0	11	Davies, McNichol, Kavanagh 2, Leamon	11,502
21	FL D3(S)	(a)	Bristol City	W	2–1	0–1	11	Leamon, Kavanagh	14,811
Feb 4	FL D3(S)	(h)	Bournem'th & B.A.	D	1–1	0–1	12	Tennant (pen)	14,512
11	FL D3(S)	(a)	Crystal Palace	L	0–6	0–2	12		13,973
18	FL D3(S)	(h)	Walsall	D	1–1	1–0	12	McNichol	12,487
25	FL D3(S)	(a)	Bristol Rovers	L	0–3	0–1	14		13,149
Mar 4	FL D3(S)	(h)	Southend United	W	2–1	0–0	13	Whent, Willard	11,797
11	FL D3(S)	(a)	Notts County	L	2–4	0–2	14	Lancelotte, Thompson	34,283
18	FL D3(S)	(h)	Port Vale	W	2–1	1–0	13	Whent, McNichol	11,852
25	FL D3(S)	(a)	Ipswich Town	D	2–2	1–2	13	Whent, Thompson	10,702
Apr 1	FL D3(S)	(h)	Exeter City	D	0–0	0–0	13		11,322
7	FL D3(S)	(h)	Torquay United	W	2–1	0–1	12	Whent, McNichol	16,517
8	FL D3(S)	(a)	Leyton Orient	W	1–0	0–0	12	Thompson	10,276
10	FL D3(S)	(a)	Torquay United	D	0–0	0–0	12		7,585
15	FL D3(S)	(h)	Reading	W	2–1	1–1	11	Thompson, Davies	12,583
22	FL D3(S)	(a)	Watford	D	0–0	0–0	9		10,845
May 6	FL D3(S)	(h)	Millwall	W	1–0	0–0	8	McCurley	12,913

League appearances and goals (from the summary rows of the grid):

Player	Apps	Goals
Baldwin H	37	
Ball J	5	
Brennan P	29	
Connelly E	6	1
Daniels H	4	
Davies K	22	4
Guttridge R	7	
Kavanagh M	14	4
Lancelotte E	14	6
Leamon F	11	4
McCurley K	3	1
McNichol J	38	9
Mansell J	11	
Morrad F	8	
Morris W	17	3
Pinchbeck C	14	5
Reed W	21	1
Rees M	2	
Roberts D	8	
Sim J	6	
Small S	1	
South A	2	
Suttle K	3	
Tennant D	40	7
Thompson C	10	4
Vitty J	28	
Whent J	41	
Wilkins J	25	
Willard J	32	4
Wilson G	3	

The reserves' 2–1 Combination Cup defeat by Arsenal at Highbury on 4 February was attended by 30,000 spectators. Tickets were on sale for the Gunners' fifth-round F.A. Cup tie with Burnley the following Saturday.

one defeat in eleven games, at the hands of champions Notts County at Meadow Lane. Albion finished in a respectable eighth position.

At the end of April came the news that Billy Lane had been appointed as Don Welsh's assistant. Lane was a prolific goalscorer in his playing days and, on retiring in 1938, became assistant manager at Brentford under Harry Curtis, although he did make a guest appearance for Albion in March 1942. Prior to joining the Albion he was in charge of Guildford City in the Southern League.

Skipper Jack Whent missed just one game during the season, but a total of 30 players were used in the League games, too many to create any consistency. The club also suffered from the lack of a regular goalscorer, inside-forward Johnny McNichol leading the way with the modest total of nine.

Football League Division 3 (South) 1949–50

		P	W	D	L	F	A	W	D	L	F	A	Pts
1.	Notts County	42	17	3	1	60	12	8	5	8	35	38	58
2.	Northampton Town	42	12	6	3	43	21	8	5	8	29	29	51
3.	Southend United	42	15	4	2	43	15	4	9	8	23	33	51
4.	Nottingham Forest	42	13	0	8	37	15	7	9	5	30	24	49
5.	Torquay United	42	13	6	2	40	23	6	4	11	26	40	48
6.	Watford	42	10	6	5	26	13	6	7	8	19	22	45
7.	Crystal Palace	42	12	5	4	35	21	3	9	9	20	33	44
8.	**ALBION**	42	9	8	4	32	24	7	4	10	25	45	44
9.	Bristol Rovers	42	12	6	3	34	18	7	0	14	17	33	43
10.	Reading	42	15	2	4	48	21	2	6	13	22	43	42
11.	Norwich City	42	15	5	1	44	21	5	5	11	21	42	42
12.	Bournemouth & B.A.	42	11	6	4	38	19	5	4	12	19	37	42
13.	Port Vale	42	12	6	3	33	13	3	5	13	14	29	41
14.	Swindon Town	42	9	7	5	41	30	6	4	11	18	32	41
15.	Bristol City	42	12	4	5	38	19	3	6	12	22	42	40
16.	Exeter City	42	9	8	4	37	27	5	3	13	26	48	39
17.	Ipswich Town	42	9	6	6	36	36	3	5	13	21	50	35
18.	Leyton Orient	42	10	6	5	33	30	2	5	14	20	55	35
19.	Walsall	42	8	8	5	37	25	1	8	12	24	37	34
20.	Aldershot	42	10	6	5	30	16	3	5	13	18	44	34
21.	Newport County	42	11	5	5	50	34	2	3	16	17	64	34
22.	Millwall	42	11	1	9	39	29	3	3	15	16	34	32

Season ticket rates this season:

	£	s.	d.
West Stand:	5	5	0
South Stand:	3	10	0
Ground:	2	0	0

Albion 1949–50
Note the South Stand in the background, being raised and rebuilt behind new terracing.
Standing left to right: Paddy Brennan, Dave Clelland, Kevin McCurley, Jack Mansell, Cecil Williams, Derek Jones, Rees Thomas, Billy Reed, Fred Leamon, Eric Lancelotte, Jock Sim, Frank Morrad, Harry Baldwin.
Seated left to right: Alex Wilson (trainer), Jack Whent (captain), Jack Ball, Des Tennant, Harry Daniels, Ken Davies, Micky Kavanagh, Jess Willard, Ron Guttridge, Joe Wilson (asst. trainer).

SEASON 1950–51

This season was one of mediocrity and disappointment. That the Sussex public was tired of Third Division football was evident from the dwindling Goldstone attendances which fell to an average 11,163, the lowest for four years, while the overall average for the section reached an all-time high at 15,947.

The shortage of housing remained a severe problem; indeed the club was forced to resort to court proceedings against several former players in order to regain possession of their club accommodation. Nevertheless, there were three new signings during the summer: Ken Bennett (Guildford City), Doug Keene (Brentford) and Tommy Hassell (Aldershot). Frankie Howard, a nineteen-year-old from Guildford City, signed as a professional after being on the club's books as an amateur for some time. Skipper Jack Whent was transferred to Luton Town in a deal which brought Luton's Jim Mulvaney and Peter Walsh to the Goldstone, and Ken Davies, Jock Sim, Fred Leamon and Eric Lancelotte were released to join Chippenham Town in the Western League. As a result the playing staff was younger than in recent years with 24-year-old Des Tennant taking over as captain.

The two Third Division sections were extended to 24 teams this season, with Colchester United and Gillingham elected to the Southern Section. Yet another poor start saw Albion firmly rooted in the lower half of the table with just five victories

coming before the turn of the year. Within the space of eight days in November the team lost 7–0 at Reading and 6–0 at home to Plymouth Argyle. The label of draw specialists still dogged the club with seventeen matches finishing even; only Scunthorpe United registered more in the whole League, reflecting the defensive nature of Albion's style. A propensity to concede late goals was also a frustrating trait: on four occasions in December and January, games that were effectively won were thrown away with goals conceded in the dying seconds. One such notable occasion was the Christmas-holiday match at Norwich. Ken Bennett opened the scoring with 30 seconds left, but, amazingly, City equalised with the last kick, although no one was sure of the result until it was confirmed on the Tannoy!

At the a.g.m. on 19 May, it was disclosed that there were still 22,000 of the 40,000 five-shilling shares unsold. The club's view was that, although £5,500 could be raised by their release, it was not a significant amount compared to the £100,000 or so needed to upgrade the ground and the team for Second or First Division football. The cost of mailing all shareholders was already over £8, and it was also felt unfair to sell the shares at five shillings when, in reality, they were worth only a few pence.

SEASON 1950–51

Date	Comp.	Ven.	Opponents	Result	HT	Pos.	Scorers	Atten.	Baldwin H	Ball J	Bennett K	Brennan P	Garbutt R	Hassell T	Howard F	Johnston R	Keene D	McCoy T	McCurley K	McNichol J	Mansell J	Morrad F	Morris W	Mulvaney J	Reed WG	South A	Tennant D	Thompson C	Thompson P	Vitty J	Wilkins J	Willard J	Wilson G
Aug 19	FL D3(S)	(h)	Torquay United	D 2-2	1-1	12=	McNichol, Morris	18,650	1		10	6					7			8			11				2	9		3	5	4	
23	FL D3(S)	(a)	Notting'm Forest	L 0-4	0-2	17=		22,312	1		10	6					7			8			11				2	9		3	5	4	
26	FL D3(S)	(a)	Aldershot	D 0-0	0-0	20		9,951	1			6					7			8			11	9			2	10		3	5	4	
30	FL D3(S)	(h)	Notting'm Forest	L 1-2	0-1	22	Willard	13,665	1		10	6					7			8			11				2	9		3	5	4	
Sep 2	FL D3(S)	(h)	Swindon Town	W 1-0	0-0	18	Willard	14,204	1											8			11	9	7	5	2	10		3		4	6
4	FL D3(S)	(a)	Millwall	D 1-1	0-0	14	Wilson	21,207	1					11						8				9	7	5	2	10		3		4	6
9	FL D3(S)	(a)	Colchester United	L 1-4	0-2	20	Reed	13,729	1		10			11						8					7	5	2	9		3		4	6
13	FL D3(S)	(h)	Millwall	L 2-3	0-1	21=	C Thompson, McNichol	11,837	1		10			11						8	3				7	5	2	9				4	6
16	FL D3(S)	(h)	Bristol Rovers	D 2-2	0-2	21	C Thompson, McNichol	11,766	1					10	11		7			8	3					5	2	9				4	6
23	FL D3(S)	(a)	Crystal Palace	W 2-0	1-0	16	McNichol, C Thompson	17,800	1					10			11			8	3				7	5	2	9				4	6
30	FL D3(S)	(a)	Watford	D 1-1	1-0	18	C Thompson	9,611	1					10			11			8	3				7	5	2	9				4	6
Oct 7	FL D3(S)	(h)	Bristol City	D 1-1	1-0	19	C Thompson	11,557	1								11			8	3	10			7	5	2	9				4	6
14	FL D3(S)	(a)	Gillingham	D 1-1	1-1	17	C Thompson	15,060	1								11			8	3	10			7	5	2	9				4	6
21	FL D3(S)	(h)	Bournem'th & B.A.	W 2-1	2-1	14	C Thompson, Hassell	13,053	1					10			11			8	3				7	5	2	9				4	6
28	FL D3(S)	(a)	Exeter City	L 2-4	2-3	16	McNichol, C Thompson	10,865	1					10			11			8	3				7	5	2	9				4	6
Nov 4	FL D3(S)	(h)	Southend United	W 2-1	0-1	13	Keene 2	11,317	1					10	7		11			8	3					5	2	9				4	6
11	FL D3(S)	(a)	Reading	L 0-7	0-3	14		14,867	1					10	11		7			8	3					5	2	9				4	6
18	FL D3(S)	(h)	Plymouth Argyle	L 0-6	0-2	18		9,768	1					7	10					8	3		11				2	9			5	4	6
25	FAC R1	(a)	Tooting & Mitch.U.	W 3-2	1-1	–	Mansell, Tennant, McNichol	10,000	1					10						8	11				6	2	7	9		3	5	4	
Dec 2	FL D3(S)	(h)	Leyton Orient	W 3-0	1-0	15	C Thompson, Hassell 2	9,695	1					10				5		8	11				6	2	7	9		3		4	
9	FAC R2	(h)	Ipswich Town	W 2-0	1-0	–	Mansell, C Thompson	14,411	1					10				5		8	11				6	2	7	9		3		4	
16	FL D3(S)	(a)	Torquay United	L 1-3	1-2	17	Hassell	4,750	1					10			11	5		8					6	2	7	9		3		4	
23	FL D3(S)	(h)	Aldershot	L 1-2	1-0	19	McNichol	7,235	1					10			11	5		8					6	2	7	9		3		4	
26	FL D3(S)	(h)	Norwich City	D 1-1	0-0	19	Bennett	14,134	1		10						7	5		8	11					2	4	9		3			6
27	FL D3(S)	(a)	Norwich City	D 1-1	0-0	19	Bennett	22,893	1		10						7	5		8	11					2	4	9		3			6
30	FL D3(S)	(a)	Swindon Town	D 0-0	0-0	19		7,743	1		10						11	5	9	8	3				7		2					4	6
Jan 6	FAC R3	(h)	Chesterfield	W 2-1	1-0	–	Bennett, McNichol	17,688	1		10						11	5		8	3				7		2	9				4	6
13	FL D3(S)	(h)	Colchester United	W 3-1	3-0	17	C Thompson, Willard, Keene	11,699	1		10						11	5		8	3				7		2	9				4	6
17	FL D3(S)	(h)	Port Vale	D 2-2	1-0	17	Willard 2	5,754	1		10						11	5		8	3				7		2	9				4	6
20	FL D3(S)	(a)	Bristol Rovers	L 2-3	1-0	17	Bennett, C Thompson	17,121	1		10							5		8	3		11		7		2	9				4	6
27	FAC R4	(a)	Bristol City	L 0-1	0-0	–		28,730	1		10						11	5		8	3				7		2	9				4	6
Feb 3	FL D3(S)	(h)	Crystal Palace	W 1-0	1-0	18	Willard	6,790	1		10						11	5		8	3				7		2	9				4	6
10	FL D3(S)	(a)	Ipswich Town	L 0-3	0-1	18		10,977	1		10						11	5		8	3				7		2	9				4	6
17	FL D3(S)	(h)	Watford	D 1-1	1-1	18	Reed	7,151	1		9	6					11	5		8	3				7		2					4	10
24	FL D3(S)	(a)	Bristol City	L 0-2	0-1	19		12,748	1		9	4						5		8	3		11		7		2					6	10
Mar 3	FL D3(S)	(h)	Gillingham	D 2-2	1-2	19	Reed, McNichol	10,903	1		10	4						5	9	8	3				7		2					6	11
10	FL D3(S)	(a)	Bournem'th & B.A.	D 2-2	2-1	18	Own goal, McCurley	9,391	1			4						5	9	8	3				7		2	6	10				11
17	FL D3(S)	(h)	Exeter City	W 4-1	2-0	17	Willard, Reed, Bennett, Keene	8,305		1	10						11	5	9	8	3				7		2					4	6
23	FL D3(S)	(h)	Northampton T.	W 5-1	2-1	15	Bennett, McCurley 2, Keene, Wilkins (pen)	15,511		1	10						11		9	8	3				7		2				5	4	6
24	FL D3(S)	(a)	Southend United	L 1-3	0-2	15	Wilkins (pen)	8,966		1	10						11		9	8	3				7		2				5	4	6
27	FL D3(S)	(a)	Northampton T.	D 0-0	0-0	15		9,288		1	10						11	5	9	8	3				7		2					4	6
31	FL D3(S)	(h)	Reading	D 1-1	1-1	15	Garbutt	10,469		1	10		9				11	5		8	3				7		2					4	6
Apr 7	FL D3(S)	(a)	Plymouth Argyle	D 3-3	2-0	15	Garbutt 2, Reed	10,369		1	10		9				11	5		8	3				7		2					4	6
14	FL D3(S)	(h)	Ipswich Town	W 4-0	2-0	15	Garbutt, Willard, McNichol, Wilson	11,031		1	10		9				11	5		8	3				7		2					4	6
18	FL D3(S)	(h)	Newport County	W 9-1	2-0	15	Bennett 2, Keene, McNichol 4, Tennant (pen), Mansell (pen)	12,114		1	10		9				11	5		8	3				7		2					4	6
21	FL D3(S)	(a)	Leyton Orient	L 1-2	0-1	14	Tennant (pen)	9,405		1	10		9				11	5		8	3				7		2					4	6
23	FL D3(S)	(a)	Port Vale	W 1-0	0-0	13	Bennett	10,340		1	10		9				11	5		8	3				7		2					4	6
28	FL D3(S)	(h)	Walsall	W 1-0	0-0	12	Reed	10,144		1	10		9				11	5		8	3				7		2					4	6
May 3	FL D3(S)	(a)	Walsall	L 0-1	0-0	13		5,669		1	10		9				11	5		8	3				7		2					4	6
5	FL D3(S)	(a)	Newport County	L 0-3	0-0	13		9,274		1	10		9				11	5	9	8	3				6		7					4	6
							League appearances		33	13	29	8	9	11	6	1	33	22	11	46	39	8	11	8	25	12	42	31	1	15	17	41	34
							League goals	OG – 1			8		4	4			6		3	12	1			1	6		2	11			2	8	2

Albion also bowed out of the F.A. Cup in the last minute, through a penalty conceded at Bristol City in the fourth round. The club had reached this stage for the first time since the initial post-war tournament with wins over Tooting & Mitcham United of the Athenian League, Ipswich Town and Second Division Chesterfield.

In March, Don Welsh left to take up the managerial post vacated by George Kay at Liverpool, leaving Billy Lane to take the Albion helm in a caretaker role until such time as a successor could be appointed. Lane introduced a more attacking format which brought about an immediate improvement and a corresponding increase in attendances. From the time of his appointment, Albion remained unbeaten at home, and on 18 April inflicted a crushing 9–1 defeat on Newport County which remains the club's joint record League victory to this day. The resurgence saw Albion climb to thirteenth place.

Centre-forward Cyril Thompson created another club record which still stands when he scored a goal in eight successive Football League games early in the season, but the goals dried up and Cyril scored only four more times prior to being exchanged for Watford's Ray Garbutt in March. Though not regarded as a goalscorer, Johnny McNichol again finished as leading striker with fourteen in League and Cup. He was also the only ever-present and had a superb season, with a brand of play which won him the reputation as the finest inside-forward

> In the 51 years between the defeat of Bradford (P.A.) in January 1933 and the victory over Liverpool in January 1984, this season's defeat of Second Division Chesterfield was the only time Albion beat opponents from a higher division in the F.A. Cup, an amazing statistic considering the many notable successes prior to 1933.

> The 'A'-team's Metropolitan League match with St Neots on 3 February was watched by just one spectator. The intrepid fan was not short of company, however, as the pitch, Hove United's Grenadier Ground in Rowan Avenue, was such a quagmire that the referee decided to man one touch-line with both linesmen running the other!

Football League Division 3 (South) 1950–51													
		P	W	D	L	F	A	W	D	L	F	A	Pts
1.	Nottingham Forest	46	16	6	1	57	17	14	4	5	53	23	70
2.	Norwich City	46	16	6	1	42	14	9	8	6	40	31	64
3.	Reading	46	15	6	2	57	17	6	9	8	31	36	57
4.	Plymouth Argyle	46	16	5	2	54	19	8	4	11	31	36	57
5.	Millwall	46	15	6	2	52	23	8	4	11	28	34	56
6.	Bristol Rovers	46	15	7	1	46	18	5	8	10	18	24	55
7.	Southend United	46	15	4	4	64	27	6	6	11	28	42	52
8.	Ipswich Town	46	15	4	4	48	24	8	2	13	21	34	52
9.	Bournemouth & B.A.	46	17	5	1	49	16	5	2	16	16	41	51
10.	Bristol City	46	15	4	4	41	25	5	7	11	23	34	51
11.	Newport County	46	13	4	6	48	25	6	5	12	29	45	47
12.	Port Vale	46	13	6	4	35	24	3	7	13	25	41	45
13.	**ALBION**	46	11	8	4	51	31	2	9	12	20	48	43
14.	Exeter City	46	11	4	8	33	30	7	2	14	29	55	42
15.	Walsall	46	12	4	7	32	20	3	6	14	20	42	40
16.	Colchester United	46	12	5	6	43	25	2	7	14	20	51	40
17.	Swindon Town	46	15	4	4	38	17	3	0	20	17	50	40
18.	Aldershot	46	11	8	4	37	20	4	2	17	19	68	40
19.	Leyton Orient	46	13	2	8	36	28	2	6	15	17	47	38
20.	Torquay United	46	13	2	8	47	39	1	7	15	17	42	37
21.	Northampton Town	46	8	9	6	39	30	2	7	14	16	37	36
22.	Gillingham	46	10	7	6	41	30	3	2	18	28	71	35
23.	Watford	46	8	5	10	29	28	1	6	16	25	60	29
24.	Crystal Palace	46	6	5	12	18	39	2	6	15	15	45	27

Albion 1950-51

Back row left to right: Jack Ball, Jack Vitty, Jack Wilkins, Cyril Thompson, Kevin McCurley, Tony Sale.
Middle row left to right: Des Tennant (captain), Paddy Brennan, Jess Willard, Ken Bennett, Jack Mansell, Glen Wilson.
Front row left to right: Jack Whent, Johnny McNichol, Frankie Howard, Harry Baldwin, Micky Kavanagh, Doug Keene, Bill Morris.

Thank you, effendi
Des Tennant receives the Galatasaray club pennant from the Turkish club's skipper. This friendly in September 1950 was only the second time Albion met continental opposition (the first was in 1904) and began a long series of such matches in the 1950s and '60s. Albion beat the Istanbul side 5–2.

in the Third Division and brought the First Division scouts to the Gold-stone. Another plus in an otherwise dismal campaign was the form of Jack Mansell at left-back. Jack appeared down the left wing when he joined the Albion in 1949 but developed into an outstanding defender.

The reserve team had another awful season, propping up the rest in Section 'B' of the Football Combination. The woeful lack of reserve strength was critical and became one of Lane's priorities on taking charge. The 'A' team was entered in the Metropolitan and District League for the first time, finishing eighth of sixteen clubs. They remained in the competition for twelve seasons until 1962, playing most home matches at Rowan Avenue, the greyhound stadium or the Goldstone.

Jack Dugnolle had a testimonial this term and he shared a match with last season's beneficiaries, Baldwin and Ball, when Don Welsh brought his Liverpool side to the Goldstone to draw 1–1 with the Albion.

During the summer of 1951 the Supporters' Club cleared the bays under the South Stand for conversion into a bicycle-parking area. The price of parking one's trusty machine was 3*d*.

SEASON 1951–52

There were more than 50 applicants for the vacant managerial position, but, after due deliberation, the board announced that caretaker Billy Lane was the successful candidate. He won immediate popularity with fans by reintroducing the traditional blue-and-white striped shirts.

Under Don Welsh the team had played a defence-in-depth system, relying on swift counter-attacks to steal a goal, a technique that the players failed to master. For his first full season in charge, Lane adopted an all-out attacking style employing the traditional five forwards, which brought about a remarkable transition. The players adapted quickly to the plan with such flare that the team won admiration throughout the Southern Section.

Kevin McCurley had gone to Liverpool during the summer, Frank Morrad to Brentford and Tommy Hassell to Folkestone. The new recruits were Albert Wetton from Spurs, Paddy McIlvenny (Cardiff City) and Jimmy Sirrell (Bradford (P.A.)), but the line-up for the opening match was almost the same as that which finished the previous season. The initial fixture resulted in a resounding 5–1 victory over Colchester United at the Goldstone, followed by two away wins which took Albion to the top of the section, but then four consecutive defeats brought a slide into mid table. On 22 September, Albion set out on a sequence of fifteen League matches in which only one defeat was suffered. The run culminated in a Christmas double over Crystal Palace and the team was back in top spot.

SEASON 1951–52

Date	Comp.	Ven.	Opponents	Result	HT	Pos.	Scorers	Atten.	Baldwin H	Ball J	Bennett K	Garbutt R	Higgins R	Howard F	Keene D	McCoy T	McIlvenny P	McNichol J	Mansell J	Reed WG	Sirrell J	South A	Tennant D	Vitty J	Wetton A	Willard J	Wilson G
Aug 18	FL D3(S)	(h)	Colchester United	W 5–1	3–0	5	Willard, Bennett 2, Reed, Garbutt	17,068	1		10	9			11	5		8	3	7			2			4	6
22	FL D3(S)	(a)	Torquay United	W 1–0	0–0	1	Garbutt	9,258	1		10	9			11	5		8	3	7			2			4	6
25	FL D3(S)	(a)	Millwall	W 3–0	1–0	1	Garbutt 2, Reed	26,583	1		10	9			11	5		8	3	7			2			4	6
29	FL D3(S)	(h)	Torquay United	L 3–4	2–3	3	Willard, McNichol, Garbutt	19,108	1		10	9		11		5		8	3	7			2			4	6
Sep 1	FL D3(S)	(h)	Bournem'th & B.A.	L 0–1	0–0	4		14,255	1		10	9		11		5		8	3	7			2			4	6
5	FL D3(S)	(a)	Ipswich Town	L 0–5				13,263	1		10	9		11		5		8	3	7			2			4	6
8	FL D3(S)	(a)	Southend United	L 0–2	0–1	16		9,799	1		10	9		11		5		8	3	7			2			4	6
12	FL D3(S)	(h)	Ipswich Town	W 5–1	1–1	11	Reed 3, Garbutt, Keene	13,077	1			9			11			8	3	7		5	2		10	4	6
15	FL D3(S)	(h)	Newport County	L 1–2	0–2	14	McNichol	10,949	1		10				11	5		8	3	7			2		9	4	6
22	FL D3(S)	(a)	Reading	W 4–1	1–0		Reed, McNichol 3	16,331	1			9			11	5		8	3	7	10		2			4	6
29	FL D3(S)	(h)	Northampton T.	W 2–0	1–0	10	Sirrell 2	15,861	1			9			11	5		8	3	7	10		2			4	6
Oct 6	FL D3(S)	(a)	Swindon Town	W 2–0	0–0	6	Sirrell, Mansell	11,825	1			9			11	5		8	3	7	10		2			4	6
13	FL D3(S)	(h)	Leyton Orient	W 3–1	2–1	4	Bennett 2, Reed	17,466	1		10	9			11	5		8	3	7			2			4	6
20	FL D3(S)	(a)	Walsall	D 1–1	1–1	4	Sirrell	6,309	1			9			11	5		8	3	7	10		2			4	6
27	FL D3(S)	(h)	Shrewsbury Town	W 1–0	0–0	4	Bennett	17,025	1		10	9			11	5		8	3	7			2			4	6
Nov 3	FL D3(S)	(a)	Aldershot	W 2–0	1–0	4	Sirrell, McNichol	9,719	1			9			11	5		8	3	7	10		2			4	6
10	FL D3(S)	(h)	Watford	W 4–1	2–1	2	Reed, McNichol, Keene, Mansell	18,123	1			9			11	5		8	3	7	10		2			4	6
17	FL D3(S)	(a)	Bristol Rovers	L 0–5	0–1	4		17,980	1			9		11		5		8	3	7	10		2			4	6
24	FAC R1	(h)	Bristol City	L 1–2	1–2	–	Bennett	18,511	1			9			11	5		8	3	7	10		2			4	6
Dec 1	FL D3(S)	(a)	Norwich City	W 1–0	0–0	2	Bennett	23,122	1		9	11				5		8	3	7	10			2		4	6
8	FL D3(S)	(h)	Exeter City	W 2–1	0–0	1	Vitty, Garbutt	11,591	1			9	11			5		8	3	7	10			2		4	6
15	FL D3(S)	(h)	Port Vale	W 2–1	1–0	1	McNichol, Bennett	14,218	1		9		11			5		8	3	7	10			2		4	6
22	FL D3(S)	(h)	Millwall	D 0–0	0–0	2		18,247	1		9	11				5		8	3	7	10			2		4	6
25	FL D3(S)	(a)	Crystal Palace	W 2–1	0–1	1	Reed, Garbutt	15,323	1		9	11				5		8	3	7	10		2			4	6
26	FL D3(S)	(h)	Crystal Palace	W 4–3	0–1	1	Bennett 2, Reed, McNichol	24,228	1		9	11				5		8	3	7	10		2			4	6
29	FL D3(S)	(a)	Bournem'th & B.A.	L 1–3	0–1	2	Sirrell	12,841	1		9	11				5		8	3	7	10		2			4	6
Jan 5	FL D3(S)	(h)	Southend United	W 5–0	3–0	2	Reed 2, McNichol, Mansell (pen), Howard	19,547		1	10	9		11		5		8	3	7			2			4	6
12	FL D3(S)	(a)	Port Vale	D 1–1	0–1	2	Mansell (pen)	17,860		1	10	9		11		5		8	3	7			2			4	6
19	FL D3(S)	(a)	Newport County	D 1–1	1–1	2	Reed	10,333		1	10	9		11		5		8	3	7			2			4	6
26	FL D3(S)	(h)	Reading	W 1–0	1–0	2	Bennett	23,677		1	10	9		11		5		8	3	7			2			4	6
Feb 2	FL D3(S)	(a)	Gillingham	W 3–2	2–1	2	Reed, Bennett, Own goal	15,538		1	10	9		11				8	3	7		5	2			4	6
9	FL D3(S)	(a)	Northampton T.	L 0–3	0–1	2		14,079		1	10	9		11				8	3	7		5	2			4	6
16	FL D3(S)	(h)	Swindon Town	W 4–0	3–0	2	Garbutt, Bennett, Reed 2	18,526		1	10	9		11		5			3	7	8		2			4	6
23	FL D3(S)	(h)	Gillingham	D 0–0	0–0	3		21,669		1	10	9		11		5			3	7	8		2			4	6
Mar 1	FL D3(S)	(a)	Leyton Orient	W 3–2	1–0	3	Bennett, Garbutt, Howard	13,397		1	10	9		11		5			3	7	8		2			4	6
8	FL D3(S)	(h)	Walsall	W 5–1	2–0	3	Bennett 2, Mansell 2 (1 pen), Willard	15,847		1	10	9		11		5			3	7	8		2			4	6
15	FL D3(S)	(a)	Shrewsbury Town	D 1–1	1–1	3	Bennett	11,500		1	10	9		11		5			3	7	8		2			4	6
22	FL D3(S)	(h)	Aldershot	W 4–2	1–2	3	Reed 2, Bennett, Garbutt	19,179		1	10	9		11		5			3	7	8		2			4	6
Apr 3	FL D3(S)	(a)	Watford	L 1–3	1–2	3	Garbutt	4,488		1	10	9		11		5		8	3	7			2			4	6
5	FL D3(S)	(h)	Bristol Rovers	D 1–1	1–1	3	Own goal	14,375		1	10	9		11		5	4	8	3	7			2				6
11	FL D3(S)	(a)	Bristol City	L 1–4	0–2	3	Garbutt	17,188		1	10	9		11		5		8	3	7			2			4	6
12	FL D3(S)	(a)	Plymouth Argyle	D 2–2	2–1	3	McNichol 2	31,755		1		9		11		5		8	3	7	10		2			4	6
14	FL D3(S)	(h)	Bristol City	D 1–1	1–1	4	Sirrell	17,519		1		9		11				8	3	7	10	5	2			4	6
19	FL D3(S)	(h)	Norwich City	W 2–0	1–0	3	McNichol 2	19,410		1	9			11		5		8	3	7	10		2			4	6
23	FL D3(S)	(a)	Plymouth Argyle	L 2–3	1–2	3	Reed, Bennett	29,140		1	9			11		5		8	3	7	10		2			4	6
26	FL D3(S)	(a)	Exeter City	L 0–2	0–1	4		8,836		1	9					11	5	8	3	7	10		2			4	6
May 1	FL D3(S)	(a)	Colchester United	D 0–0	0–0	5		7,075		1	9					11	5	8	3	7	10		2			4	6
League appearances									18	28	42	23	8	26	15	42	1	41	46	46	27	4	42	4	2	45	46
League goals								OG – 2			18	13		2	2			14	6	19	7		1			3	

Albion 1951–52
Back row left to right: Jack Ball, Jack Vitty, Tim McCoy, Alec South, Jack Wilkins, Albert Wetton, Harry Baldwin.
Middle row left to right: Alex Wilson (trainer), Des Tennant, Johnny McNichol (captain), Ray Garbutt, Ken Bennett, Paddy Brennan, Doug Keene, Joe Wilson (assistant trainer).
Seated left to right: Billy Reed, Paddy McIlvenny, Glen Wilson, Billy Lane (manager), Frankie Howard, Jess Willard, Jack Mansell.

An Albion team played under floodlights for the first time on 7 November 1951 when the reserves met Hastings United in a friendly match at the Pilot Field. The lights did not function too well initially, and during the game a number of lamps exploded. Albion won the match 3–2.

In March 1952 the club employed an architect to inspect a railway shed at Newhaven with a view to converting it into a stand. The architect advised that the building was too old.

Football League Division 3 (South) 1951–52												
	P	W	D	L	F	A	W	D	L	F	A	Pts
1. Plymouth Argyle	46	19	3	1	70	19	10	5	8	37	34	66
2. Reading	46	19	2	2	73	23	10	1	12	39	37	61
3. Norwich City	46	18	1	4	55	15	8	8	7	34	35	61
4. Millwall	46	16	5	2	46	21	7	7	9	28	32	58
5. ALBION	46	15	4	4	57	24	9	6	8	30	39	58
6. Newport County	46	13	7	3	45	26	8	5	10	32	50	54
7. Bristol Rovers	46	14	5	4	60	20	6	7	10	29	33	52
8. Northampton Town	46	17	1	5	65	31	5	4	14	28	43	49
9. Southend United	46	16	6	1	56	17	3	4	16	19	49	48
10. Colchester United	46	12	7	4	32	22	5	5	13	24	55	46
11. Torquay United	46	10	3	10	53	42	7	7	9	33	56	44
12. Aldershot	46	11	4	8	40	27	7	4	12	38	62	44
13. Port Vale	46	11	11	1	33	16	3	4	16	17	50	43
14. Bournemouth & B.A.	46	11	4	8	42	30	5	6	12	27	45	42
15. Bristol City	46	13	6	4	44	26	2	6	15	14	43	42
16. Swindon Town	46	9	9	5	29	22	5	5	13	22	46	42
17. Ipswich Town	46	12	4	7	45	31	4	5	14	18	43	41
18. Leyton Orient	46	12	5	6	39	26	4	4	15	16	42	41
19. Crystal Palace	46	9	7	7	32	28	6	2	15	29	52	39
20. Shrewsbury Town	46	11	3	9	35	29	2	7	14	27	57	36
21. Watford	46	7	7	9	34	37	6	3	14	23	44	36
22. Gillingham	46	10	7	6	47	31	1	6	16	24	50	35
23. Exeter City	46	10	4	9	40	36	3	5	15	25	50	35
24. Walsall	46	11	3	9	38	31	2	2	19	17	63	31

In May 1952 the Sussex County youth team triumphed in the national knock-out competition, the F.A. County Youth Cup. Having beaten Hampshire (2–0), Berks & Bucks (4–0), Middlesex (2–1), North Riding (6–0) and Essex (3–0), Sussex defeated their Liverpool County rivals with a team that included Albion 'A'-team youngsters John Cragg, Peter Martin (captain), Steve Burtenshaw, Ernie Hughes and Gordie Howieson. Sussex won the away leg, staged at Goodison Park on 10 May and attended by 12,000 spectators, by two goals to one thanks to Alan Arnell and Ernie Hughes. The home leg followed at the Goldstone two weeks later before a crowd of 6,481, Ernie Hughes scoring in a 1–0 win. Burtenshaw, Cragg, Howieson and Hughes later turned professional with the Albion, but only Steve Burtenshaw played for the first team. Arnell turned professional with Liverpool, and later played for Tranmere Rovers and Halifax Town.

Defeat at Bournemouth in the last game of the old year allowed Plymouth Argyle to regain the leadership on goal-average, and they were to remain there for the rest of the campaign. Albion kept in close contention with some scintillating performances until April when a run of three games brought just one point, enabling the incredibly consistent Plymouth side to stretch its lead over the Albion to seven points. A 4–1 reverse at Bristol City on 11 April dashed any hopes of promotion, but in the following match a relaxed Albion gave their finest display of the season, holding Plymouth to a 2–2 draw in front of a 31,755 Home Park crowd. Johnny McNichol scored twice within a minute to give Albion a 2–0 lead on 24 minutes, but a penalty conceded on the stroke of half time allowed Argyle to claw their way back into the game.

Eleven days later Plymouth arrived at the Goldstone for the return fixture requiring a point to clinch the title. They took the honours with a 3–2 victory in a superb game watched by a 29,140 crowd, a new record League attendance. General opinion was that Argyle were the most accomplished team seen at the Goldstone for some years. Only one point from the final three matches saw Albion drop to fifth, which failed to reflect the excellence of the performances during a sparkling season.

The team met with particular success against the other leading promotion contenders, completing the double over Reading and Norwich City and taking three points from Millwall. The F.A. Cup was less rewarding, Albion going out to Bristol City for the second year running, losing 2–1 in a first-round tie at the Goldstone.

The refreshing, attacking approach resulted in a tremendous increase in attendances with a Goldstone average of 17,831, the highest thus far. The team registered 87 goals, equalling the previous best in 1929–30, and scored four or more on nine occasions. Outside-right Billy Reed notched nineteen League goals with the dashing Ken Bennett on eighteen. Skipper Johnny McNichol was again the star of the side, but there were other successes: left-half Glen Wilson was the most improved player on the staff; the thoughtful Jack Mansell added to a growing reputation as an outstanding full-back; centre-half Tim McCoy was splendid as the sheet-anchor of the team; and right-half Jess Willard, the season's beneficiary, never stopped running all winter. The management responded to the success by paying all first-team players the maximum wage (£14 per week) for the first time.

SEASON 1952–53

After such a memorable season, the new campaign was anticipated with great relish, and the public practice match was attended by more than 7,000 spectators. However, three weeks before the opening League fixture came the news that Johnny McNichol had been transferred to First Division Chelsea for £12,000 plus Jimmy Leadbetter. It was no great surprise: the brilliant Scot had been watched by several leading clubs for some time, but the fans were upset by the release of the club's best player and saw it as a retrograde step to promotion ambitions. Nevertheless, a large crowd of 23,711 turned up to see Albion wallop Crystal Palace 4–1 in the first match, the biggest gate of the term.

In addition to Leadbetter, Billy Lane brought in Les Owens from Reading, Dennis Gordon (West Bromwich Albion), Eric Gill (Charlton Athletic) and Maurice McLafferty (Sheffield United). Among those leaving were goalkeeper Harry Baldwin to Kettering Town and Jack Vitty to Workington. Baldwin was 32 and had given fine service at the Goldstone for thirteen years. Trainer Alex Wilson also left the club during the summer

and his assistant Joe Wilson was promoted to fill the post. Alex had a testimonial in September for which his former club Arsenal took on an All-Star XI at the Goldstone.

The season consisted of three distinct parts: a great start, an indifferent middle, and a grandstand finish. Albion were the early pace-setters with six unbeaten games and remained in the frame into November. Rumours regarding the imminent departure of Jack Mansell to Cardiff City had been circulating from the outset of the season and in early October the 25-year-old full-back joined the Ninian Park staff for a £15,000 fee. Fulham's Reg Fox was recruited as a replacement, but the loss of another star player resulted in heavy criticism of the board's motives and yet again the question was raised by a disenchanted public: Did the club really want promotion?

The minimum ground admission was increased this season from 1s. 6d. (7·5p) to 1s. 9d. (just under 9p) to counter an increase in the Government's Entertainment Tax.

SEASON 1952–53

Date	Comp.	Ven.	Opponents	Result	HT	Pos.	Scorers	Atten.	Addinall A	Ball J	Bennett K	Bisset T	Burtenshaw S	Foreman D	Fox R	Gilberg H	Gill E	Gordon D	Howard F	Jennings R	Keene D	Leadbetter J	McCoy T	McIlvenny P	McLafferty M	Mansell J	Medhurst H	Moffatt J	Owens L	Reed WG	Sirrell J	South A	Tennant D	Wetton A	Willard J	Wilson G
Aug 23	FL D3(S)	(h)	Crystal Palace	W 4–1	3–0	5=	Leadbetter, Owens, Reed 2	23,905		1											11	10	5			3			9	7	8		2		4	6
28	FL D3(S)	(a)	Shrewsbury Town	D 0–0	0–0	3		12,660		1											11	10	5	6		3			9	7	8		2		4	
30	FL D3(S)	(a)	Bristol City	D 2–2	1–0	4=	Keene, Sirrell	16,491		1											11	10	5	4		3			9	7	8	6	2			
Sep 3	FL D3(S)	(h)	Shrewsbury Town	W 3–1	0–0	4	Owens, Reed, Bennett	16,730		1	8										11	10	5	4		3			9	7		6	2			
6	FL D3(S)	(h)	Torquay United	W 2–1	2–1	1	Bennett, Owens	19,774		1	8										11	10	5	4		3			9	7			2			6
9	FL D3(S)	(a)	Southend United	W 2–1	1–0	1	Leadbetter, Mansell	10,463		1	8										11	10	5	4		3			9	7		6	2			
13	FL D3(S)	(a)	Northampton T.	L 3–5	1–3	3	Owens, Tennant (pen), Bennett	14,342		1	8										11	10	5	4		3			9	7		6	2			
17	FL D3(S)	(h)	Southend United	D 2–2	1–1	4=	Reed, Leadbetter	16,877		1	8								11			10	5	4		3			9	7		6	2			
20	FL D3(S)	(h)	Leyton Orient	W 3–1	1–0	2	Leadbetter, Bennett 2	20,354			8						1		11			10	5	4		3			9	7			2			6
24	FL D3(S)	(h)	Exeter City	W 4–2	0–0	1	McIlvenny 2, Tennant (pen), Reed	14,998			8						1	9	11				5	4		3				7	10		2			6
27	FL D3(S)	(a)	Ipswich Town	L 0–1	0–1	3		10,993		1	8							9	11				5	4		3				7	10		2			6
Oct 1	FL D3(S)	(a)	Bournem'th & B.A.	L 1–2	1–2	5	Tennant (pen)	9,026		1	8				3			9	11			10	5	4						7			2			6
4	FL D3(S)	(h)	Reading	D 1–1	0–0	5	Reed	20,639		1					3			9	11			10	5	4						7	8		2			6
11	FL D3(S)	(h)	Queen's Park R.	W 2–0	2–0	3	Leadbetter, Reed	18,987		1	8				3			9	11			10	5	4						7			2			6
18	FL D3(S)	(a)	Swindon Town	L 0–3	0–0	4		10,278		1	9				3				11			10	5	4						7	8		2			6
25	FL D3(S)	(h)	Aldershot	W 4–2	3–1	4	McIlvenny 2, Foreman, Leadbetter	15,412		1	9			11								10	5	8	3					7			2		4	6
Nov 1	FL D3(S)	(a)	Colchester United	D 0–0	0–0	4		8,001		1	9			11								10	5	8	3					7		4	2			6
8	FL D3(S)	(h)	Norwich City	L 2–3	1–2	5	Bennett 2	20,091		1	9			11								10	5	8	3					7		4	2			6
15	FL D3(S)	(a)	Coventry City	L 1–3	1–1	7	South	11,863			10			11									5	8	3		1			7		9	2		4	6
22	FAC R1	(a)	Yeovil Town	W 4–1	1–1	–	Howard, Owens 2, Tennant (pen)	9,955		1	10				3				11				5	8					9	7			2		4	6
29	FL D3(S)	(a)	Bristol Rovers	L 0–7	0–1	11		11,647			10				3				11				5	8			1		9	7			2		4	6
Dec 6	FAC R2	(h)	Norwich City	W 2–0	0–0	–	Bennett 2	21,265			10				3				11		7	8	5	4			1		9				2			6
13	FL D3(S)	(a)	Gillingham	W 2–1	2–0	7	Bennett 2	10,369			10				3				11		7	8	5	4			1		9				2			6
20	FL D3(S)	(a)	Crystal Palace	L 1–2	1–2	9	Keene	9,922			10				3				11		7	8	5	4			1		9				2			6
25	FL D3(S)	(a)	Newport County	W 3–0	2–0	7	Own goal, Howard, Reed	10,630			10				3				11			8	5	4			1		9	7			2			6
27	FL D3(S)	(h)	Newport County	D 2–2	1–0	7	Reed, Tennant	15,552			10								11			8	5	4	3		1		9	7			2			6
Jan 3	FL D3(S)	(h)	Bristol City	L 0–1	0–1	7		15,905		1	10								11			8	5	4	3				9	7			2			6
10	FAC R3	(a)	Barnsley	L 3–4	3–0	–	Owens, Howard, Reed	17,244			10								11			8		4	3		1		9	7			2	5		6
14	FL D3(S)	(a)	Watford	W 3–2	2–0	7	Howard, Bennett, Leadbetter	4,555			9								11			10		4	3		1			7	8		2	5		6
17	FL D3(S)	(a)	Torquay United	W 2–1	0–1	7	Reed, Addinall	7,384	9		8					10			11					4	3		1			7		5	2			6
24	FL D3(S)	(h)	Northampton T.	D 1–1	0–0	7	Tennant (pen)	18,750	9		8					10			11					4	3		1			7		5	2			6
31	FL D3(S)	(h)	Watford	L 1–2	0–0	7	Addinall	13,587	9		8					10			11	2				4	3		1			7		5				6
Feb 7	FL D3(S)	(a)	Leyton Orient	L 0–3	0–2	8		8,528	9					11		8						10	5		3		1			7		4	2			6
14	FL D3(S)	(h)	Ipswich Town	L 1–4	0–3	8	Willard	8,354	9							10				3	11	8	5				1	7					2		4	6
21	FL D3(S)	(a)	Reading	D 0–0	0–0	10		13,557	9							10	1			3	11			8				7				5	2		4	6
28	FL D3(S)	(a)	Queen's Park R.	D 3–3	1–1	9	Addinall 2, Wilson	15,136	9		8					10	1			3	11									7		5	2		4	6
Mar 7	FL D3(S)	(h)	Swindon Town	L 1–2	1–2	9	Bennett	12,824	9		8						1	7			11				3						10	5	2		4	6
14	FL D3(S)	(a)	Aldershot	W 2–1	0–1	9	Gilberg, Gordon	7,201	9		10			11		8	1	7						4	3							5	2			6
21	FL D3(S)	(h)	Colchester United	D 0–0	0–0	9		12,588	9		10			11		8	1	7						4	3							5	2			6
28	FL D3(S)	(a)	Norwich City	L 2–3	2–0	9	Gilberg, Wilson	14,226	9					11	3	8	1	7				10		4								5	2			6
Apr 3	FL D3(S)	(h)	Walsall	W 4–2	2–0	9	Foreman 2, Own goal, Addinall	13,383	9					11	3	8	1	7				10	5	4									2			6
4	FL D3(S)	(h)	Coventry City	D 1–1	1–1	9	Addinall	14,930	9					11	3	8	1	7				10	5	4								6	2			
6	FL D3(S)	(a)	Walsall	L 0–3	0–1	9		4,093			8	9		11		4	1	7				10	5		3								2			6
11	FL D3(S)	(a)	Exeter City	W 5–1	2–0	9	Foreman, Gordon 2, Leadbetter, Addinall	7,731	9				6	11		8	1	7				10	5	4	3								2			
15	FL D3(S)	(h)	Millwall	W 1–0	0–0	9	Addinall	14,052	9					11		8	1	7				10	5	4	3								2		6	
18	FL D3(S)	(h)	Bristol Rovers	W 2–1	2–0	9	Leadbetter, Addinall	22,266	9					11		8	1	7				10	5	4	3							6	2			
22	FL D3(S)	(h)	Bournem'th & B.A.	W 2–0	1–0	7	Foreman (pen), Addinall	11,889	9				4	11		8	1	7		2		10	5		3											6
25	FL D3(S)	(a)	Millwall	D 1–1	0–1	7	Addinall	20,131	9					11		8	1	7		2		10	5	4	3											6
May 2	FL D3(S)	(h)	Gillingham	W 5–0	1–0	7	Leadbetter, Foreman (pen), Own goal, Gordon, McIlvenny	10,092	9					11		8	1	7				10	5	4	3								2			6
							League appearances		19	17	30	1	2	17	11	19	17	18	18	6	13	34	36	39	21	11	12	2	15	29	9	20	43	1	10	36
							League goals	OG – 3	11		11			6		2		4	2		2	10		5		1			4	10	1	1	5		1	2

On 8 November, Albion suffered their first home defeat, losing 3–2 to Norwich City, and three weeks later crashed 7–0 at Bristol Rovers. Confidence was dented and the team failed to register a home win for an unbelievable five months during which time five away matches ended in victory. Lane was seldom without injury problems: skipper Jess Willard received a bad knee injury early in the season; centre-forward Les Owens broke five ribs; and Glen Wilson, Frankie Howard and Tim McCoy were all out for lengthy spells. The loss of Owens and the lack of inside-forward strength were solved at a stroke when Bert Addinall and Harry Gilberg were signed from Queen's Park Rangers in January. Addinall led the attack in rugged fashion, scoring in his first match and notching eleven goals in nineteen appearances to finish joint top scorer in League games with Ken Bennett.

Albion had slipped to ninth place by the time the Goldstone bogey was finally laid on Good Friday, 3 April, with a 4–2 win over Walsall, and the frustration of the Hove crowd boiled over the following day against Coventry City. The unfortunate referee, Mr Gordon Thorpe of Swindon, disallowed a Denis Foreman effort just before City equalised in the first half, and then failed to curb the strong-arm Coventry tactics in a bad-tempered game which ended 1–1. An unprecedented chorus of 'Oh My, What a Referee!' rang out around the ground, and at the final whistle Mr Thorpe was surrounded by an angry mob. Albion chairman Carlo Campbell, assisting the police guard for

Football League Division 3 (South) 1952–53

		P	W	D	L	F	A	W	D	L	F	A	Pts
1.	Bristol Rovers	46	17	4	2	55	19	9	8	6	37	27	64
2.	Millwall	46	14	7	2	46	16	10	7	6	36	28	62
3.	Northampton Town	46	18	4	1	75	30	8	6	9	34	40	62
4.	Norwich City	46	16	6	1	56	17	9	4	10	43	38	60
5.	Bristol City	46	13	8	2	62	28	9	7	7	33	33	59
6.	Coventry City	46	15	5	3	52	22	4	7	12	25	40	50
7.	**ALBION**	46	12	6	5	48	30	7	6	10	33	45	50
8.	Southend United	46	15	5	3	41	21	3	8	12	28	53	49
9.	Bournemouth & B.A.	46	15	3	5	49	23	4	6	13	25	46	47
10.	Watford	46	12	8	3	39	21	3	9	11	23	42	47
11.	Reading	46	17	3	3	53	18	2	5	16	16	46	46
12.	Torquay United	46	15	4	4	61	28	3	5	15	26	60	45
13.	Crystal Palace	46	12	7	4	40	26	3	6	14	26	56	43
14.	Leyton Orient	46	12	7	4	52	28	4	3	16	16	45	42
15.	Newport County	46	12	4	7	43	34	4	6	13	27	48	42
16.	Ipswich Town	46	10	7	6	34	28	3	8	12	26	41	41
17.	Exeter City	46	11	8	4	40	24	2	6	15	21	47	40
18.	Swindon Town	46	9	5	9	38	33	5	7	11	26	46	40
19.	Aldershot	46	8	8	7	36	29	4	7	12	25	48	39
20.	Queen's Park R.	46	9	9	5	37	34	3	6	14	24	48	39
21.	Gillingham	46	10	7	6	30	26	2	8	13	25	48	39
22.	Colchester United	46	9	9	5	40	29	3	5	15	19	47	38
23.	Shrewsbury Town	46	11	5	7	38	35	1	7	15	30	56	36
24.	Walsall	46	5	9	9	35	46	2	1	20	21	72	24

the official, was struck several times by blows intended for Mr Thorpe.

The Easter Monday return at Walsall was lost 3–0, but Albion then staged an excellent finale which saw only one point dropped in the last six matches, including superb home wins over the eventual champions Bristol Rovers (2–1) and runners-up Millwall (1–0). There were some very strong sides in the Southern Section this term and Albion ended up in seventh place, fourteen points off the lead.

The most astonishing game of the season came in the F.A. Cup when, after home wins over Yeovil Town and Norwich City, Albion were drawn away to Second Division Barnsley in the third round. On the same afternoon the reserves entertained Crystal Palace at the Goldstone and a huge cheer rang around the ground at half time when it was announced that the first team was winning 3–0 at Oakwell. There was much speculation among the crowd as to who would be the opponents in the next round, but, as they drifted away at the end, the Tannoy crackled into life with the stunning news that Barnsley had won 4–3.

Albion 1952–53
Back row left to right: B. Rees, Eric Gill, Albert Wetton, Johnny Moffatt, Alec South, George Roelich, Denis Foreman, Jack Ball, Les Owens.
Middle row left to right: Ernie Marriott (assistant trainer), Des Tennant, Frankie Howard, Johnny Dougan, Dennis Gordon, Roy Jennings, Jess Willard (captain), Jimmy Leadbetter, Tim McCoy, Maurice McLafferty, Joe Wilson (trainer).
Seated left to right: Jack Mansell, Ray Garbutt, Paddy McIlvenny, Billy Reed, Billy Lane (manager), Ken Bennett, Doug Keene, Glen Wilson, Jimmy Sirrell.

Though never reaching the heights of the previous season, the entertainment value at the Goldstone remained high and the average gate was a highly encouraging 16,171. Des Tennant regained the captaincy when Jess Willard was indisposed early in the campaign and was the only player to manage more than 40 League games. Glen Wilson had another terrific season and was the subject of scrutiny by a number of First Division clubs, but at the end of the day the loyal Albion fans were left to reflect on what might have been but for the departures of Mansell and McNichol.

There was also a marked increase in interest for the youthful reserve team. The 1–0 Combination Cup defeat by Spurs on 28 February attracted 10,000 spectators to Hove, a record for a reserve-team match played under normal circumstances (higher attendances have been recorded when first-team cup-tie tickets have been on sale). Under the guidance of former Albion skipper Ernie Marriott, the 'stiffs' had a much better season than in the previous few years and, though finishing in mid table, scored 72 goals in the 30 Combination matches.

Although not yet a permanent feature, a youth team was entered in the first F.A. Youth Cup competition. Manchester United won this initial tournament, but Albion did well to beat both Crystal Palace and Portsmouth before losing to Brentford in the fourth round. Only in 1957–58 have Albion failed to enter, but this early success remains the club's best performance in the competition, equalled just twice, in 1961–62 and 1992–93.

Albion in Europe
At the end of May, three weeks after the final ball was kicked at home, Albion set out on their first continental tour. First stop was Belgium, where eight goals were shared with F.C. Liège under a blazing sun; the two teams exchanged cuff-links and tie-pins before the game. The second match was in the Bavarian town of Fürth, Albion stepping in at the last moment after French and Belgian teams had cancelled fixtures with the West German side. Known as the 'Trefoils', Spielvereinigung Fürth won the match, which was played in continuous rain in front of 2,500 spectators, with a single Glen Wilson own-goal. Here, Alec South challenges the German 'keeper, Höger.

SEASON 1953–54

Billy Lane's third season in charge was to be the most successful the club had enjoyed since entering the Football League, with runner's-up spot attained for the first time. Lane had mustered a useful squad of players and an excellent team spirit prevailed. In August a club-record £7,000 brought Barnsley's centre-half Matt McNeil to the Goldstone, Ken Bennett went to Crystal Palace in July in a direct swap for his namesake Ron Bennett, and in the same month Lane made his most astute signing during his time with the Albion when he brought in left-back Jimmy Langley from Leeds United. During the summer the terracing of all standing areas was completed.

Albion opened the campaign in brilliant style, and after five games were the only side in England with a 100-per-cent record. The leading clubs set a terrific pace, and with thirteen points from the first seven matches Albion held only second spot. Ipswich Town proved to be the team to beat, and on 26 September the Suffolk side gained a 2–1 victory at the Goldstone, one of only three home defeats of the season and a result that was to have a big influence on the eventual destiny of the championship shield. In November the Portsmouth inside-forward Albert Mundy was signed to strengthen the forward line and he proved a great asset, quickly blending into the team and developing a fine understanding with Dennis Gordon down the right wing.

Albion maintained a healthy position in the table and were out of the top three for only a brief period in September and October, but after the first round of matches in the New Year the formidable Ipswich side had stretched its lead over Albion to eight points. The Suffolk club was then involved in a lengthy F.A. Cup run, and a superb sequence of seven wins saw Albion take over at the head of the section on 20 February, a week after beating Ipswich 3–2 at Portman Road in a pulsating match in which Albion came back from a 2–0 half-time deficit. Excitement rose and attendances at the Goldstone reached new heights, peaking in March when 31,025 attended the 2–1 victory over third-placed Southampton, the first 30,000-plus gate for a League match at the Goldstone.

The leadership was retained into April with promotion looking a very real prospect. Throughout the season the team

> The home League fixture with Queen's Park Rangers on 31 October was postponed to avoid a clash with the big rugby match being played at the nearby greyhound stadium: the visiting New Zealand All Blacks opened their tour with a 24–0 win over the Southern Counties in front of 9,000 spectators. Instead, Albion and Rangers staged a friendly match at The Saffrons in Eastbourne which Albion won 2–1.

Albion 1953–54

Back row left to right: Glen Wilson, Maurice McLafferty, Albert Wetton, Joe Carpenter, Matt McNeil, Tim McCoy, Roy Jennings, Steve Burtenshaw, Irvin Brown, Don Boxall, Arthur Dainton.
Middle row left to right: Alec South, Reg Fox, Tommy Bisset, Pat Thompson, Eric Gill, Roy Marshall, Dennis Gordon, Jimmy Offord, Jimmy Leadbetter, Des Tennant (captain).
Seated left to right: Jimmy Sirrell, Ron Bennett, Frankie Howard, Paddy McIlvenny, Roy Hollins, Johnny Dougan, Bert Addinall, Harry Gilberg, Denis Foreman, Jimmy Langley.

SEASON 1953–54

Date	Comp.	Ven.	Opponents	Result	HT	Pos	Scorers	Atten.	Addinall A	Bennett R	Bisset T	Burtenshaw S	Foreman D	Fox R	Gilberg H	Gill E	Gordon D	Howard F	Jennings R	Langley J	Leadbetter J	McCoy T	McIlvenny P	McNeil M	Moore B	Mundy A	Sirrell J	South A	Tennant D	Wilson G
Aug 19	FL D3(S)	(a)	Queen's Park R.	W 2–1	0–1	4=	Gilberg, Addinall	14,565	9				11		8	1	7			3	10	5		4					2	6
22	FL D3(S)	(a)	Torquay United	W 3–2	0–0	3	Addinall 2, Foreman	9,076	9				11			1	7			3	10	5		4				8	2	6
26	FL D3(S)	(h)	Leyton Orient	W 2–1	0–1	3	Sirrell 2	18,336	9	7			11			1				3	10	5		4			8		2	6
29	FL D3(S)	(h)	Northampton T.	W 3–2	1–1	2	Leadbetter 2, Foreman	16,709	9				11			1	7			3	10	5		4			8		2	6
Sep 3	FL D3(S)	(a)	Leyton Orient	W 2–0	1–0	1	Tennant, Addinall	13,806	9				11			1	7			3	10	5		4			8		2	6
5	FL D3(S)	(a)	Gillingham	D 0–0	0–0	2		16,203	9				11			1	7			3	10	5		4			8		2	6
9	FL D3(S)	(h)	Southend United	W 3–2	1–1	2	Leadbetter 2, Sirrell	17,790	9				11			1	7		2	3	10	5		4			8			6
12	FL D3(S)	(h)	Coventry City	W 3–1	0–1	1	Foreman (pen), Sirrell, Leadbetter	20,465	9				11			1	7		2	3	10	5		4			8			6
15	FL D3(S)	(a)	Southend United	L 0–2	0–1	1		6,980	9				11			1	7		2	3	10	5		4			8			6
19	FL D3(S)	(a)	Bourn'th & B.A.	D 1–1	1–1	2	Leadbetter	13,442	9				11			1	7		2	3	10	5	4				8			6
23	FL D3(S)	(h)	Watford	D 3–3	2–3	4	Sirrell, Gordon, Addinall	14,557	9				11			1	7			3	10	5	4				8			6
26	FL D3(S)	(h)	Ipswich Town	L 1–2	1–2	4	Foreman (pen)	23,209	9				11			1	7			3	10	5	4				8		2	6
29	FL D3(S)	(a)	Watford	D 1–1	1–0	4	Leadbetter	8,940	9	7			11			1	8			3	10		4				5		2	6
Oct 3	FL D3(S)	(a)	Millwall	W 2–0	0–0	4	Sirrell, Bisset	21,027	9		9		11			1	7			3	10		4				8	5	2	6
10	FL D3(S)	(a)	Exeter City	W 1–0	1–0	3	Leadbetter	12,044	9				11			1	7			3	10		4				8	5	2	6
17	FL D3(S)	(h)	Newport County	W 4–2	2–1	2	Wilson, Leadbetter, Foreman 2	15,936	9	7			11			1	8			3	10		4					5	2	6
24	FL D3(S)	(a)	Norwich City	L 0–1	0–1	4		23,736	9				11			1	7			3	10		4				8	5	2	6
Nov 7	FL D3(S)	(a)	Southampton	L 0–1	0–1	3		19,579	9		9		11			1	7			3	10		4				8	5	2	6
14	FL D3(S)	(h)	Colchester United	W 1–0	1–0	2	Gordon	15,624	9		9		11			1	7			3	10		4				8	5	2	6
21	FAC R1	(h)	Coventry City	W 5–1	1–1	–	Addinall 2, Leadbetter, Howard, Tennant (pen)	20,225	9							1	7	11		3	10		4				8	5	2	6
28	FL D3(S)	(h)	Bristol City	W 2–1	0–1	3	Mundy, Gordon	19,214								1	7	11		3	10		4			8		5	2	6
Dec 5	FL D3(S)	(a)	Aldershot	W 3–2	2–2	3	Addinall, Mundy, Tennant (pen)	7,245	9							1	7	11		3	10		4			8		5	2	6
12	FAC R2	(a)	Wrexham	D 1–1	1–0	–	Leadbetter	17,980								1	7	11		3	10		4			8		5	2	6
16	FAC R2 Rep	(h)	Wrexham	D 1–1*	0–1	–	Gordon	15,571								1	7	11		3	10		4			8		5	2	6
19	FL D3(S)	(a)	Torquay United	L 1–2	1–1	3	Leadbetter	13,450							7	1	9	11		3	10		4			8		5	2	6
21	FAC R2 2Rep(n*)		Wrexham	L 1–3	1–3	–	Sirrell	4,766			9					1	7	11		3		4				8	10	5	2	6
25	FL D3(S)		Walsall	L 1–3	1–0	3	Mundy	9,404	9							1	7			3			4			8	10	5	2	6
26	FL D3(S)	(h)	Walsall	W 5–3	3–1	3	Sirrell 2, Addinall, Gordon, South	17,592	9				11			1	7			3			4			8	10	5	2	6
Jan 2	FL D3(S)	(a)	Northampton T.	L 2–4	0–3	3	Addinall 3	10,989	9				11			1	7			3	10		4			8		5	2	6
9	FL D3(S)	(h)	Reading	W 3–2	3–1	3	Gordon, Leadbetter, Addinall	13,613	9			4	11			1	7			3	10					8		5	2	6
16	FL D3(S)	(h)	Gillingham	W 3–1	2–0	3	Addinall 2, Mundy	16,019	9			4	11			1	7			3	10					8		5	2	6
23	FL D3(S)	(a)	Coventry City	W 2–1	1–1	3	Addinall, Mundy	10,175	9			4	11			1	7			3	10					8		5	2	6
Feb 6	FL D3(S)	(a)	Bourn'th & B.A.	W 3–0	2–0	2	Addinall, Foreman, South	13,177	9			4	11			1	7			3	10					8		5	2	6
13	FL D3(S)	(a)	Ipswich Town	W 3–2	0–2	2	Foreman, Mundy 2	16,479	9			4	11			1	7			3	10				5	8			2	6
20	FL D3(S)	(h)	Millwall	W 4–0	1–0	1	Addinall 2, Leadbetter, Gordon	23,968	9			4	11			1	7			3	10					8		5	2	6
27	FL D3(S)	(h)	Exeter City	W 2–1	1–1	1	Tennant (pen), Mundy	20,251	9							1	7	11		3	10					8		5	2	6
Mar 6	FL D3(S)	(a)	Newport County	L 0–1	0–1	1		11,417	9			4				1	7	11		3	10					8		5	2	6
13	FL D3(S)	(h)	Crystal Palace	W 3–0	1–0	1	Addinall, Howard, Gordon	19,312	9			4				1	7	11		3	10					8		5	2	6
20	FL D3(S)	(a)	Bristol City	D 1–1	1–0	1	Gordon	21,937	9			4				1	7	11		3	10					8		5	2	6
24	FL D3(S)	(a)	Reading	L 1–2	1–2	1	Addinall	12,120	9			4				1	7	11		3	10					8		5	2	6
27	FL D3(S)	(a)	Southampton	W 2–1	1–0	1	Addinall, Gordon	31,025	9			4				1	7	11		3	10				8			5	2	6
Apr 3	FL D3(S)	(a)	Colchester United	D 1–1	0–0	1	Leadbetter	8,282	9			4	11			1	7			3	10				8			5	2	6
7	FL D3(S)	(h)	Swindon Town	D 1–1	0–0	1	Moore	19,440	9			4	11			1	7			3	10				8			5	2	6
10	FL D3(S)	(h)	Aldershot	W 3–2	1–1	1	Mundy, Tennant (pen), Gordon	22,336	9				11			1	7			3			4		10	8		5	2	6
16	FL D3(S)	(h)	Shrewsbury Town	L 2–3	2–2	2	Wilson, Leadbetter	27,925	9							1	7	11		3	10		4			8		5	2	6
17	FL D3(S)	(a)	Swindon Town	W 1–0	1–0	2	Moore	12,319				4		2		1	7	11		3	10				9		8	5		6
19	FL D3(S)	(a)	Shrewsbury Town	L 1–3	0–1	2	Addinall	11,706	9					2	4	1	7	11		3	10				8			5		6
24	FL D3(S)	(h)	Norwich City	D 0–0	0–0	2		23,790	9				11	2	4	1	7			3	10				8			5		6
28	FL D3(S)	(h)	Crystal Palace	D 1–1	0–0	2	Leadbetter	12,439	9				11	2	4	1	7			3	10				8			5		6
30	FL D3(S)	(h)	Queen's Park R.	W 3–1	0–1	2	Mundy 2, Langley	10,493	9				11		4	1	7			3	10				8			5	2	6
League appearances									41	3	3	15	34	4	6	46	45	12	4	46	43	12	18	10	7	21	19	33	38	46
League goals									20	1		8	1			10	1	1		1	15				2	11	8	2	4	2

Notes: Dec 16 – after extra time.
Dec 21 – played at Selhurst Park, Crystal Palace FC.

Football League Division 3 (South) 1953–54

		P	W	D	L	F	A	W	D	L	F	A	Pts
1.	Ipswich Town	46	15	5	3	47	19	12	5	6	35	32	64
2.	**ALBION**	46	17	3	3	57	31	9	6	8	29	30	61
3.	Bristol City	46	18	3	2	59	18	7	3	13	29	48	56
4.	Watford	46	16	3	4	52	23	5	7	11	33	46	52
5.	Northampton Town	46	18	4	1	63	18	2	7	14	19	37	51
6.	Southampton	46	17	5	1	51	22	5	2	16	25	41	51
7.	Norwich City	46	13	5	5	43	28	7	6	10	30	38	51
8.	Reading	46	14	3	6	57	33	6	6	11	29	40	49
9.	Exeter City	46	12	2	9	39	22	8	6	9	29	36	48
10.	Gillingham	46	14	3	6	37	22	5	7	11	24	44	48
11.	Leyton Orient	46	14	5	4	48	26	4	6	13	31	47	47
12.	Millwall	46	15	3	5	44	24	4	6	13	30	53	47
13.	Torquay United	46	10	10	3	48	33	7	2	14	33	56	46
14.	Coventry City	46	14	5	4	36	15	4	4	15	25	41	45
15.	Newport County	46	14	5	4	42	28	5	2	16	19	53	44
16.	Southend United	46	15	2	6	47	22	3	5	15	23	49	43
17.	Aldershot	46	11	5	7	45	31	6	4	13	29	55	43
18.	Queen's Park R.	46	10	5	8	32	25	6	5	12	18	44	42
19.	Bournemouth & B.A.	46	12	5	6	47	27	4	3	16	20	43	40
19.	Swindon Town	46	13	5	5	48	21	2	5	16	19	42	40
21.	Shrewsbury Town	46	12	8	3	48	34	2	4	17	17	42	40
22.	Crystal Palace	46	11	7	5	41	30	3	5	15	19	56	40
23.	Colchester United	46	7	7	9	35	29	3	3	17	15	49	30
24.	Walsall	46	8	5	10	22	27	1	3	19	18	60	26

Note: Bournemouth & B.A. and Swindon Town finished level in nineteenth place.

Miss Mavis Maitland, a 22-year-old from Addison Road, Hove, won the first Supporters' Club 'Miss Albion' title in 1954 and went on to become the country's first National Football Queen. Miss Albion was chosen each year until the mid 1970s.

showed a tenacious spirit, coming from behind to win on no fewer than thirteen occasions, but the crucial Easter weekend proved disastrous. Albion had an easy programme on paper, but the players suffered a dose of the jitters, scraping a narrow win at Swindon in between home and away defeats by lowly Shrewsbury Town. There remained a mathematical possibility of promotion until the penultimate match, but Ipswich retained their composure to win the section with 64 points, three more than Albion. It was an exciting race and a splendid effort, but Ipswich were worthy champions; indeed, but for their extended Cup heroics they might well have settled the issue earlier.

Albion's F.A. Cup campaign saw the club through to the second round with a convincing 5–1 win over Coventry City at the Goldstone, but they were well beaten 3–1 by Wrexham in a second replay staged at neutral Selhurst Park after two 1–1 draws.

The defence was a capable unit with Jimmy Langley an instant success. Eighteen-year-old Steve Burtenshaw showed great promise on coming into the side at right-half in January, but he was then called into the Army and lost to the club for a considerable time. Though scoring 94 goals in all competitive matches, doubts hung over the forward line. Chances spurned in the important late games proved costly, but Bert Addinall broke the post-war record with 22 goals in League and Cup while Jimmy Leadbetter registered 17.

The average attendance rose to 18,880 and, all things considered, it was a tremendous season despite the bitter disappointment for the club and its supporters. It was also a most successful season financially with profits of £1,498. In addition to the League eleven, the reserve team continued to improve, winning promotion to the First Division of the Football Combination, and at the final curtain the management announced the retention of 28 professionals.

SEASON 1954–55

A new South Stand was built during the summer, replacing the original wooden structure which had served since 1904 with some alterations and additions. The new stand had seating for 1,000 spectators behind terracing.

Following a season of high drama, the Albion and their supporters expected great things this term, but by the end of September the team were already ten points adrift of Bristol City at the head of the section. Albion were never in contention; indeed, by the turn of the year they were in the lower half of the table.

The defence was again highly consistent with the ever-present Eric Gill outstanding between the posts and wing-half Harry Gilberg, though troubled with injury, having his best period with the club. Glen Wilson was made team skipper but became unsettled later in the season and was put on the transfer list at his own request, the captaincy passing to Jimmy Langley. Ironically, the pair were chosen to represent the Southern Section against the Northern Section at Reading in March. The following week the brilliant Langley was selected for the England B side against West Germany at Hillsborough and furthered his growing reputation in a 1–1 draw.

The forward line was a different proposition with the centre-forward spot a particular headache. Bert Addinall had departed for Crystal Palace during the summer and Billy Lane laid out a big fee for Manchester City's Ken Whitfield as his replacement. The popular Addinall was a hard act to follow. Whitfield failed to impress and quickly lost his place to the veteran Bernard Moore; he spent most of the season in the reserves, but returned to the League side at centre-half in March where he proved an instant success and went on to make the position his own for several seasons.

Inside-right Albert Mundy was top scorer with 21 in League and Cup, followed by Dennis Gordon on 15 from the right wing. Two amateur forwards from the Royal Navy, Peter Harburn and Malcolm Stephens, were given their opportunity in the latter stages of the campaign and both were impressive. The duo were later to sign as professionals and proved valuable additions to the staff.

After a 3–2 setback at Southampton on New Year's Day came a vast improvement which saw only five defeats in the last 22 League games. Bristol City skated away with the title with 70 points, 9 more than Leyton Orient in second place. Albion

Albion 1954–55

Standing left to right: Bernard Moore, Dennis Gordon, Ron Hampton, Pat Thompson, Alec South, Eric Gill, Ron Dyamond, Roy Jennings, Matt McNeil, Len Edwards, Brian Meeser, Johnny Longland, Tommy Bisset.
Seated left to right: Jimmy Leadbetter, Harry Gilberg, Des Tennant, Glen Wilson (captain), Jimmy Langley, Albert Mundy, Reg Fox, Ken Whitfield, Denis Foreman, Frankie Howard.

SEASON 1954–55

Date	Comp.	Ven.	Opponents	Result	HT	Pos.	Scorers	Atten.
Aug 21	FL D3(S)	(a)	Millwall	L	0–2	0–1	21=		25,445
25	FL D3(S)	(h)	Walsall	W	3–0	0–0	11	Foreman, Whitfield, Gordon	17,336
28	FL D3(S)	(h)	Southampton	L	1–2	0–2	17	Mundy	22,258
Sep 2	FL D3(S)	(a)	Walsall	W	2–0	1–0	11	Whitfield, Howard	13,056
4	FL D3(S)	(a)	Coventry City	L	1–2	0–2	17	Mundy	20,674
8	FL D3(S)	(h)	Shrewsbury Town	D	0–0	0–0	15		14,375
11	FL D3(S)	(h)	Brentford	L	3–4	3–3	18	Langley 2, Gordon	17,361
13	FL D3(S)	(a)	Shrewsbury Town	L	0–3	0–2	20		6,418
18	FL D3(S)	(h)	Newport County	W	4–1	1–1	17	Moore, Mundy 2, Foreman	13,466
22	FL D3(S)	(h)	Reading	W	3–2	0–0	15	Mundy 2, Moore	12,860
25	FL D3(S)	(a)	Torquay United	L	1–2	1–1	16	Mundy	8,097
29	FL D3(S)	(a)	Reading	W	2–0	0–0	13	Leadbetter, Moore	6,243
Oct 2	FL D3(S)	(h)	Bristol City	L	0–1	0–1	15		21,034
9	FL D3(S)	(a)	Colchester United	W	4–2	2–2	14	Mundy, Gordon 2, Foreman	9,334
16	FL D3(S)	(h)	Norwich City	L	0–1	0–1	17		18,016
23	FL D3(S)	(a)	Southend United	L	0–4	0–3	18		9,167
30	FL D3(S)	(h)	Queen's Park R.	W	4–1	3–1	16	South, Leadbetter, Tennant (pen), Mundy	14,825
Nov 6	FL D3(S)	(a)	Swindon Town	W	2–0	1–0	15	Howard, Mundy	8,846
13	FL D3(S)	(h)	Crystal Palace	W	1–0	1–0	10	Gordon	16,440
20	FAC R1	(h)	Tunbridge Wells U.	W	5–0	2–0	–	Leadbetter, Gordon, Gilberg 2, Tennant (pen)	16,046
27	FL D3(S)	(h)	Watford	W	3–1	1–0	8	Howard 3	10,342
Dec 4	FL D3(S)	(a)	Bournem'th & B.A.	D	1–1	1–0	9	Moore	8,607
11	FAC R2	(a)	Norwich City	D	0–0	0–0	–		17,548
15	FAC R2 Rep	(h)	Norwich City	W	5–1	1–0	–	Tennant, Mundy 2, Leadbetter, Howard	10,198
18	FL D3(S)	(h)	Millwall	L	1–2	1–1	12	Tennant (pen)	13,337
27	FL D3(S)	(a)	Leyton Orient	D	0–0	0–0	12		25,054
Jan 1	FL D3(S)	(a)	Southampton	L	2–3	0–1	14	Moore, Mundy	16,164
8	FAC R3	(h)	Aston Villa	D	2–2	1–2	–	Moore, Mundy	24,822
10	FAC R3 Rep	(a)	Aston Villa	L	2–4	1–3	–	Foreman, Wilson	13,509
22	FL D3(S)	(a)	Brentford	W	3–2	1–1	14	Wilson, Gordon, Foreman	10,170
29	FL D3(S)	(a)	Exeter City	L	1–3	0–1	14	Mundy	7,042
Feb 5	FL D3(S)	(a)	Newport County	W	3–1	1–1	13	Foreman, Howard, Gordon	7,025
12	FL D3(S)	(h)	Torquay United	D	1–1	1–0	13	Gordon	13,306
19	FL D3(S)	(a)	Bristol City	L	2–3	1–2	13	Gordon 2	24,461
26	FL D3(S)	(h)	Colchester United	D	1–1	1–0	14	Moore	11,158
Mar 5	FL D3(S)	(a)	Norwich City	D	0–0	0–0	14		9,255
12	FL D3(S)	(h)	Southend United	W	2–1	1–0	12	Foreman, Mundy	9,680
19	FL D3(S)	(a)	Queen's Park R.	L	2–3	0–1	13	Gordon, Mundy	9,149
23	FL D3(S)	(h)	Exeter City	W	5–3	1–2	11	Gordon, Moore, Mundy 2, Howard	4,175
26	FL D3(S)	(h)	Swindon Town	W	3–1	1–0	10	Stephens, Tennant 2 (1 pen)	8,761
Apr 2	FL D3(S)	(a)	Crystal Palace	L	0–1	0–0	11		11,814
8	FL D3(S)	(a)	Gillingham	D	1–1	1–1	11	Foreman	13,867
9	FL D3(S)	(h)	Northampton T.	W	2–1	2–0	8	Moore, Mundy	13,120
11	FL D3(S)	(h)	Gillingham	W	1–0	0–0	8	Foreman	11,083
16	FL D3(S)	(a)	Watford	D	0–0	0–0	8		8,190
20	FL D3(S)	(h)	Leyton Orient	W	1–0	0–0	7	Harburn	11,493
23	FL D3(S)	(h)	Bournem'th & B.A.	D	1–1	1–0	6	Leadbetter	10,454
27	FL D3(S)	(a)	Northampton T.	L	0–1	0–1	7		4,211
30	FL D3(S)	(a)	Aldershot	D	2–2	1–1	7	Tennant (pen), Mundy	8,897
May 4	FL D3(S)	(h)	Aldershot	W	5–3	3–0	7	Harburn 2, Langley, Howard, Gordon	6,557
7	FL D3(S)	(h)	Coventry City	W	2–0	2–0	6	Gordon, Leadbetter	3,770

League appearances / goals (players: Bisset T, Edwards L, Foreman D, Fox R, Gilberg H, Gill E, Gordon D, Harburn P, Howard F, Langley J, Leadbetter J, Longland J, McIlvenny P, McNeil M, Moore B, Mundy A, South A, Stephens M, Tennant D, Trusler J, Whitfield K, Wilson G)

	Bisset T	Edwards L	Foreman D	Fox R	Gilberg H	Gill E	Gordon D	Harburn P	Howard F	Langley J	Leadbetter J	Longland J	McIlvenny P	McNeil M	Moore B	Mundy A	South A	Stephens M	Tennant D	Trusler J	Whitfield K	Wilson G
League appearances	1	6	25	4	39	46	43	7	36	45	30	3	2	29	22	41	10	5	45	1	22	44
League goals			8				14	3	8	3	4				8	18	1	1	5		2	1

Football League Division 3 (South) 1954–55

		P	W	D	L	F	A	W	D	L	F	A	Pts
1.	Bristol City	46	17	4	2	62	22	13	6	4	39	25	70
2.	Leyton Orient	46	16	2	5	48	20	10	7	6	41	27	61
3.	Southampton	46	16	6	1	49	19	8	5	10	26	32	59
4.	Gillingham	46	12	8	3	41	28	8	7	8	36	38	55
5.	Millwall	46	14	6	3	44	25	6	5	12	28	43	51
6.	**ALBION**	46	14	4	5	47	27	6	6	11	29	36	50
7.	Watford	46	11	9	3	45	26	7	5	11	26	36	50
8.	Torquay United	46	12	6	5	51	39	6	6	11	31	43	48
9.	Coventry City	46	15	5	3	50	26	3	6	14	17	33	47
10.	Southend United	46	13	5	5	48	28	4	7	12	35	52	46
11.	Brentford	46	11	6	6	44	36	5	8	10	38	46	46
11.	Norwich City	46	13	5	5	41	26	5	5	13	20	37	46
13.	Northampton Town	46	13	5	5	47	27	6	3	14	26	54	46
14.	Aldershot	46	12	6	5	44	23	4	7	12	31	48	45
15.	Queen's Park R.	46	13	7	3	46	25	2	7	14	23	50	44
16.	Shrewsbury Town	46	14	5	4	49	24	2	5	16	21	54	42
17.	Bournemouth & B.A.	46	7	8	8	32	29	5	10	8	25	36	42
18.	Reading	46	7	10	6	32	26	6	5	12	33	47	41
19.	Newport County	46	8	8	7	32	29	3	8	12	28	44	38
20.	Crystal Palace	46	9	11	3	32	24	2	5	16	20	56	38
21.	Swindon Town	46	10	8	5	30	19	1	7	15	16	45	37
22.	Exeter City	46	9	7	7	30	31	2	8	13	17	42	37
23.	Walsall	46	9	6	8	49	36	1	8	14	26	50	34
24.	Colchester United	46	7	6	10	33	40	2	7	14	20	51	31

Note: Brentford and Norwich City finished level in eleventh place.

finished sixth, but the excellence of the previous season's performances was never approached and the average attendance dropped drastically to 12,835. Indeed, the 3,770 recorded for the last match, with Coventry City, remains a post-war low for a Goldstone Football League game.

The finest displays were reserved for the F.A. Cup. After home wins over Tunbridge Wells United and Norwich City (in a replay), Aston Villa came out of the hat with the Albion for the third-round tie. Villa were contenders for the First Division title and the biggest crowd of the season turned up at the Goldstone to see Albion prove that they could match the best in the country by holding the famous visitors to a 2–2 draw. Villa led 2–1 with only five minutes remaining, but Albert Mundy sent the 24,822 fans home happy with a deserved equaliser. In the Monday-afternoon replay Albion were beaten 4–2 in another splendid encounter, but Villa lost to Doncaster Rovers in the fourth round after four replays.

At the end of the season Jimmy Langley received further recognition when he was selected for the F.A.'s summer tour of the West Indies.

SEASON 1955–56

Another excellent campaign, in which several club records were surpassed, saw Albion again finish as runners-up. The entertainment value at the Goldstone was simply superb. After an initial 1–1 draw with Queen's Park Rangers, the team won fourteen home League matches on the trot, during which 55 goals were scored, an average of almost 4 per game.

The section was a closely fought affair up to the turn of the year, then quickly became a three-horse race between Brighton, Leyton Orient and Ipswich Town, yet oddly the Albion never headed the table at any stage. Their fortunes hinged on the only home defeat of the season when Watford brought the winning run to an end on 25 February. Albion built up a 2–0 lead soon after the interval and the crowd were gleefully anticipating another landslide victory, but the Brewers staged an admirable come-back to run out 3–2 winners.

That defeat was the first in the League at the Goldstone for fourteen months and caused the team to fall two points behind Leyton Orient; the Essex team also had two crucial games in hand and the gap proved impossible to close. At the end of March, Albion travelled to Brisbane Road with the knowledge that nothing short of victory would give them a chance of catching the exasperatingly consistent Orient. Before a crowd of over 25,000, they came away with an excellent 1–0 win, Malcolm Stephens scoring the all-important goal late in the game.

Orient met with little success against their two main rivals, taking one point from the Albion and losing home and away to Ipswich Town, but they regularly defeated the lesser sides while Albion's attacking style sometimes left them exposed, with surprising defeats at struggling Queen's Park Rangers, Newport County and bogey-side Shrewsbury Town.

Albion kept up the pressure with a maximum six points over Easter and only one defeat in the final twelve games, 2–1 at Ipswich in the penultimate fixture, but the surrender of a point in the return match with Leyton Orient at the Goldstone on 18 April was critical. Eight days later Orient clinched the title with a 2–1 win over Millwall, then proceeded to lose their last three games to finish on 66 points, one more than Albion and two ahead of Ipswich, with fourth-placed Southend United eleven adrift of the leading bunch. Albion received the scant consolation of £220 in talent money for taking second spot.

The 65-point total was the highest the club had ever achieved, beating the 61 gained in 1953–54, and the 112 League goals remain a club record by a long way. In fact, Albion scored more goals than any other club in the Football League, Albert Mundy leading the way with 28 League goals followed by Peter Harburn with 27 in League and Cup, Denis Foreman with 15 in League and Cup, and Malcolm Stephens with 13 from only 20 League games; all four registered hat-tricks. The team scored four or more on eleven occasions, with a top League score of 6–0 against Norwich City and a magnificent 8–1 eclipse of Newport County in the first round of the F.A. Cup. Seven days after their Goldstone humiliation, the Canaries gained revenge by beating Albion 2–1 in the second round, again at Hove, to the great

> Goldstone House, the dominating building which overlooked the eastern side of the football ground, was demolished in 1955 and replaced by new houses in Goldstone Lane and Fonthill Road. It had been the residence of Albion's former landlord Alderman John Clark.

Albion 1955–56

Back row left to right: Glen Wilson, Denny Orford, Dennis Lampriere, Ken Whitfield, Bernard Sibley, Bernard Moore, Len Edwards, Don Clarke, Adrian Thorne, Tommy Bisset.
Middle row left to right: Billy Lane (manager), Reg Fox, Dennis Gordon, Matt McNeil, Roy Jennings, Roy Marshall, Eric Gill, Johnny Longland, John Trusler, Ron Clark, Peter Harburn, Joe Wilson (trainer).
Front row left to right: Harry Easton, Roy Balston, Malcolm Stephens, Albert Mundy, Jimmy Langley (captain), Frankie Howard, Denis Foreman, Des Tennant, Dave Standing.

SEASON 1955–56

Date	Comp.	Ven.	Opponents	Result	HT	Pos.	Scorers	Atten.
Aug 20	FL D3(S)	(h)	Queen's Park R.	D 1–1	0–0	13=	Langley	14,510
24	FL D3(S)	(h)	Walsall	W 3–0	3–0	6	Mundy 3	8,897
27	FL D3(S)	(a)	Northampton T.	L 0–3	0–2	11=		10,685
Sep 1	FL D3(S)	(a)	Walsall	D 2–2	0–1	12=	Mundy, Harburn	13,147
3	FL D3(S)	(h)	Aldershot	W 5–2	4–0	7	Mundy 2, Harburn, Howard, Tennant (pen)	12,722
7	FL D3(S)	(h)	Swindon Town	D 0–0	0–0	12		6,090
10	FL D3(S)	(a)	Crystal Palace	W 2–1	0–1	6	Wilson, Whitfield	20,159
14	FL D3(S)	(h)	Swindon Town	W 2–1	1–0	3	Own goal, Mundy	10,694
17	FL D3(S)	(a)	Gillingham	L 0–1	0–0	8		12,228
21	FL D3(S)	(a)	Torquay United	D 0–0	0–0	9		7,038
24	FL D3(S)	(h)	Southampton	W 5–0	2–0	7	Wilson, Howard, Mundy, Own goal, Foreman	16,169
28	FL D3(S)	(h)	Ipswich Town	W 3–0	1–0	5	Mundy 2, Harburn	13,642
Oct 1	FL D3(S)	(a)	Shrewsbury Town	L 1–2	0–1	8	Mundy	9,390
8	FL D3(S)	(h)	Reading	W 3–1	1–0	5	Stephens 2, Gordon	15,677
15	FL D3(S)	(a)	Watford	W 3–1	2–1	4	Gordon 2, Harburn	9,480
22	FL D3(S)	(h)	Brentford	W 3–0	1–0	3	Mundy, Harburn, Foreman	12,771
29	FL D3(S)	(a)	Coventry City	L 2–3	0–3	4	Harburn 2	14,734
Nov 5	FL D3(S)	(h)	Southend United	W 4–0	2–0	4	Harburn, Gordon, Foreman 2	17,708
12	FL D3(S)	(a)	Exeter City	W 5–0	1–0	2	Langley 2 (2 pens), Harburn, Foreman, Gordon	9,019
19	FAC R1	(h)	Newport County	W 8–1	5–0	–	Howard, Harburn 4, Foreman 3	18,978
26	FL D3(S)	(a)	Colchester United	D 3–3	3–1	2	Foreman, Gordon, Harburn	9,010
Dec 3	FL D3(S)	(h)	Norwich City	W 6–0	2–0	2	Langley (pen), Mundy, Howard 2, Harburn, Gordon	18,144
10	FAC R2	(h)	Norwich City	L 1–2	0–0	–	Langley	22,364
17	FL D3(S)	(a)	Queen's Park R.	L 1–2	0–1	3	Mundy	7,607
24	FL D3(S)	(h)	Northampton T.	W 4–0	1–0	2	Gordon, Mundy, Harburn, Wilson	11,004
26	FL D3(S)	(h)	Newport County	W 4–1	0–1	2	Foreman, Mundy 2, Harburn	13,536
27	FL D3(S)	(a)	Newport County	L 0–1	0–0	3		5,907
31	FL D3(S)	(a)	Aldershot	W 3–0	2–0	3	Tennant, Stephens 2	8,115
Jan 14	FL D3(S)	(h)	Crystal Palace	W 5–0	1–0	2	Stephens 3, Foreman, Own goal	13,602
21	FL D3(S)	(h)	Gillingham	W 5–0	3–0	2	Mundy 2, Stephens, Harburn 2	17,192
28	FL D3(S)	(a)	Bournem'th & B.A.	L 0–2	0–0	2		10,734
Feb 4	FL D3(S)	(a)	Southampton	W 2–1	1–1	3	Harburn 2	14,895
11	FL D3(S)	(h)	Shrewsbury Town	W 3–2	1–1	3	Mundy 2, Own goal	11,334
18	FL D3(S)	(a)	Reading	W 2–0	1–0	2	Stephens, Mundy	7,242
25	FL D3(S)	(h)	Watford	L 2–3	1–0	3	Foreman, Mundy	16,559
Mar 3	FL D3(S)	(a)	Brentford	L 1–2	1–1	3	Mundy	11,061
10	FL D3(S)	(a)	Coventry City	W 2–1	0–0	3	Langley (pen), Tennant	16,952
17	FL D3(S)	(a)	Southend United	W 2–1	1–0	3	Foreman, Harburn	12,521
24	FL D3(S)	(h)	Exeter City	W 1–0	0–0	3	Tennant	12,996
30	FL D3(S)	(a)	Millwall	W 4–2	3–0	2	Own goal, Harburn, Langley (pen), Foreman	17,079
31	FL D3(S)	(a)	Leyton Orient	W 1–0	0–0	2	Stephens	25,550
Apr 2	FL D3(S)	(h)	Millwall	W 2–1	2–0	2	Stephens, Harburn	23,076
7	FL D3(S)	(h)	Colchester United	W 2–0	0–0	2	Harburn, Langley (pen)	17,330
14	FL D3(S)	(a)	Norwich City	D 3–3	2–1	2	Wilson, Harburn, Mundy	12,444
18	FL D3(S)	(h)	Leyton Orient	D 1–1	1–1	2	Own goal	30,864
21	FL D3(S)	(h)	Bournem'th & B.A.	W 4–1	2–1	2	Mundy 3, Stephens	15,348
25	FL D3(S)	(a)	Ipswich Town	L 1–2	0–1	2	Tennant	18,233
28	FL D3(S)	(h)	Torquay United	W 3–2	2–1	2	Foreman, Gordon, Stephens	11,706

Player appearances grid (shirt numbers):

Date	Bisset T	Clarke D	Foreman D	Fox R	Gilberg H	Gill E	Gordon D	Harburn P	Howard F	Jennings R	Langley J	McNeil M	Mundy A	Neate D	Stephens M	Tennant D	Whitfield K	Wilson G
Aug 20			10	4		1	7	9	11		3		8			2	5	6
24			10		4	1	7	9	11		3		8			2	5	6
27	9		10		4	1	7		11		3		8			2	5	6
Sep 1	2		10			1	7	9	11		3		8			4	5	6
3	2		10			1	7	9	11		3		8			4	5	6
7	2		10			1	7	9	11		3		8			4	5	6
10	2					1	7	9	11		3	5	8			4	10	6
14	2		10			1	7	9	11		3		8			4	5	6
17	2		10			1	7	9	11		3	5	8			4		6
21	2					1	7		11		3	5	8		10	4	9	6
24	2		10			1	7	9	11		3	5	8			4		6
28	2		10			1	7	9	11		3	5	8			4		6
Oct 1	2		10			1	7	9	11		3	5	8			4		6
8					2	1	7	9	11		3		8		10	4	5	6
15	2					1	7	9	11		3		8		10	4	5	6
22	2		10			1	7	9	11		3		8			4	5	6
29	2		10			1	7	9	11		3		8			4	5	6
Nov 5	2		10			1	7	9	11		3	4	8				5	6
12	2		10			1	7	9	11		3	4	8				5	6
19			10			1	7	9	11	2	3	4	8				5	6
26	2		10			1	7	9	11		3	4	8				5	6
Dec 3	2		10			1	7	9	11		3	4	8				5	6
10	2		10			1	7	9	11		3	4	8				5	6
17	2		10			1	7	9	11		3		8			4	5	6
24	2		10			1	7	9	11		3		8			4	5	6
26	2		10			1	7	9	11		3		8			4	5	6
27	2		11			1	7	9			3		8		10	4	5	6
31	2		11			1	7	9			3		8		10	4	5	6
Jan 14	2		11			1	7	9			3		8		10	4	5	6
21	2		11			1	7	9			3		8		10	4	5	6
28	2		11			1	7	9			3		8		10	4	5	6
Feb 4	2		10			1	7	9	11		3		8			4	5	6
11	2		10			1	7	9	11		3	6	8			4	5	
18	2					1	7	9	11		3	6	8		10	4	5	
25	2		10			1	7	9			3	6	8		11	4	5	
Mar 3	2		10			1	7	9			3	6	8		11	4	5	
10	2		10			1	7	9	11		3		8			4	5	6
17	2		10			1	7	9	11		3		8			4	5	6
24	2		11			1	7	9			3		8		10	4	5	6
30	2		11			1	7	9			3		8		10	4	5	6
31	2		11			1	7	9			3		8		10	4	5	6
Apr 2	2		11			1	7	9			3		8		10	4	5	6
7	2		11			1	7	9			3		8		10	4	5	6
14	2		11			1	7	9			3		8		10	4	5	6
18	2		10			1	7	9			3		8	11		4	5	6
21	2		10			1	7				3		9	11	8	4	5	6
25	2		10			1	7				3		9	11	8	4	5	6
28	2		10			1	7	9			3		8		11	4	5	6
League appearances	43	2	40	1	3	46	46	41	27	2	44	14	46	4	20	42	43	42
League goals (OG – 6)			12				9	23	4		7		28		13	5	1	4

Football League Division 3 (South) 1955–56

		P	W	D	L	F	A	W	D	L	F	A	Pts
1.	Leyton Orient	46	18	3	2	76	20	11	5	7	30	29	66
2.	**ALBION**	46	20	2	1	73	16	9	5	9	39	34	65
3.	Ipswich Town	46	16	6	1	59	28	9	8	6	47	32	64
4.	Southend United	46	16	4	3	58	25	5	7	11	30	55	53
5.	Torquay United	46	11	10	2	48	21	9	2	12	38	42	52
6.	Brentford	46	11	8	4	40	30	8	6	9	29	36	52
7.	Norwich City	46	15	4	4	56	31	4	9	10	30	51	51
8.	Coventry City	46	16	4	3	54	20	5	14	19	40	49	
9.	Bournemouth & B.A.	46	13	6	4	39	14	6	4	13	24	37	48
10.	Gillingham	46	12	3	8	38	28	7	7	9	31	43	48
11.	Northampton Town	46	14	3	6	44	27	6	4	13	23	44	47
12.	Colchester United	46	14	4	5	56	37	4	7	12	20	44	47
13.	Shrewsbury Town	46	12	9	2	47	21	5	3	15	22	45	46
14.	Southampton	46	13	6	4	60	30	5	2	16	31	51	44
15.	Aldershot	46	9	9	5	36	33	3	7	13	34	57	40
16.	Exeter City	46	10	6	7	39	30	5	4	14	19	47	40
17.	Reading	46	10	2	11	40	37	5	7	11	30	42	39
18.	Queen's Park R.	46	10	7	6	44	32	4	4	15	20	54	39
19.	Newport County	46	12	2	9	32	26	3	7	13	26	53	39
20.	Walsall	46	13	5	5	43	28	2	3	18	25	56	38
21.	Watford	46	8	5	10	31	39	5	6	12	21	46	37
22.	Millwall	46	13	4	6	56	31	2	2	19	27	69	36
23.	Crystal Palace	46	7	3	13	27	32	5	7	11	27	51	34
24.	Swindon Town	46	4	10	9	18	22	4	4	15	16	56	30

On 2 May an excellent Brighton Boys side met Liverpool at the Goldstone in the first leg of the English Schools Trophy Final. A crowd of over 14,000 saw the local lads go down 3–2 in a superb match, Willie Carlin scoring two for the Merseyside team. A fortnight later the Liverpool youngsters ran away with the second leg, winning 4–0 at Goodison Park in front of an incredible 38,000 spectators.

In August, Albion made an unsuccessful attempt to purchase a 5,000-capacity stand from the Mitcham greyhound stadium for £25,000. The structure eventually found a new home at Leyton Orient's Brisbane Road ground.

disappointment of a large crowd which had come hoping for another crushing victory.

Only 50 goals were conceded in the 46 League matches and the half-back line of Tennant, Whitfield and Wilson was reckoned the best in the division. Langley and Bisset were outstanding at full-back, and the reliable Eric Gill was again ever-present in goal. Jimmy Langley was honoured with further appearances for England's B team, against Yugoslavia and Scotland, and spent the summer of 1956 on tour with the F.A. team in South Africa.

The promotion challenge aroused tremendous interest and an average crowd of 15,323 attended the Goldstone matches, with a highest of 30,864 at the Leyton Orient game in April.

Albion's secret weapon
Comedian Fred Emney leads out skipper Jimmy Langley and his team on 21 January 1956 to take on Gillingham. Kitted out in extra large shorts and shirt, Fred might have been expected to block the goal, but 'keeper Eric Gill is there behind him just in case! Anyway, he would scarcely have been needed as Gillingham were promptly dispatched with ease (5–0), as most teams were in the record-breaking 1955–56 season.

SEASON 1956–57

In summarising Albion's performances this season, a local commentator posed the question: 'Is there a more exasperating football club in the country?' For the umpteenth time, the team proved good but not good enough.

The opening fixture, a 4–3 win over Shrewsbury Town at the Goldstone, was attended by 17,430 fans, but a hesitant start found the team as low as thirteenth by the end of December and the gates fell to the lowest level for years, reflecting the utter dismay felt by the supporters.

The fans also had to suffer the considerable loss of Jimmy Langley. The 27-year-old left-back was selected as England's travelling reserve for the match with Northern Ireland at Newcastle in October, and rumblings regarding his transfer had been aired for some time. Jimmy had ambitions of furthering his international career, and in February he departed for Fulham for a £12,000 fee. It was a huge loss to the club, but his transfer was accepted as inevitable by the majority of fans and it was left to big Roy Jennings to fill the left-back berth.

Ironically, in the wake of Langley's departure the team won four successive matches and put together a series of fifteen unbeaten games, including big home wins over Northampton Town (5–0) and Reading (8–3). Earlier in the season Albion had

won 5–2 at Brentford, and they recorded another big Goldstone victory over Torquay United (6–0). The Devonians recovered to finish as runners-up to Ipswich Town, losing out on goal-average in one of the finest campaigns in their history.

The excellent late run saw Albion climb to sixth place, only seven points behind promoted Ipswich, and gates improved to give an average for the season of 11,606, nearly 4,000 down on 1955–56.

Albion went out of the F.A. Cup in the initial round for the first time in five years when Millwall won a replay 3–1 after a 1–1 draw at the Goldstone.

On 8 December, Albion became the first side to defeat the touring Hungarian club MTK Budapest, winning by five goals to three. The Soviets had recently moved into the visitors' homeland to quell the uprising and the opportunity was taken to use the proceeds for the benefit of the Hungarian Relief Fund. The MTK players had won well over 170 caps in the fabulous Hungarian side of the 1950s, and included Nandor Hidegkuti and Josef Zakarias from the 1954 World Cup Final.

SEASON 1956–57

Date	Comp.	Ven.	Opponents	Result	HT	Pos.	Scorers	Atten.	Bisset T	Burtenshaw S	Darey J	Foreman D	Gill E	Gordon D	Grant A	Harburn P	Howard F	Humphries R	Jennings R	Johnson M	Langley J	Mundy A	Neate D	Stephens M	Tennant D	Thomas R	Whitfield K	Wilson G
Aug 18	FL D3(S)	(h)	Shrewsbury Town	W 4–3	2–0	12	Foreman, Harburn, Mundy 2	17,430	2			10	1	7		9	11				3	8			4		5	6
21	FL D3(S)	(a)	Watford	L 1–2	0–1	12=	Harburn	12,472	2	4		10	1	7		9	11				3	8					5	6
25	FL D3(S)	(a)	Walsall	L 2–3	0–1	16	Mundy, Howard	10,082	2	4		10	1	7			11				3	9	8				5	6
29	FL D3(S)	(h)	Watford	D 2–2	0–0	15	Gordon, Mundy	13,052	2	4		10	1	7		9	11				3	8					5	6
Sep 1	FL D3(S)	(h)	Ipswich Town	W 3–2	2–0	13=	Langley (pen), Foreman, Harburn	15,177		4		10	1	7		9	11		2		3	8					5	6
4	FL D3(S)	(a)	Brentford	W 5–2	2–0	10	Howard, Foreman, Wilson, Harburn, Mundy	12,150		4		10	1	7		9	11		2		3	8					5	6
8	FL D3(S)	(a)	Bournem'th & B.A.	D 1–1	1–1	12	Gordon	13,941				10	1	7		9	11		2		3	8			4		5	6
12	FL D3(S)	(h)	Brentford	L 1–2	0–1	15	Langley (pen)	14,317		4		10	1	7		9	11		2		3	8					5	6
15	FL D3(S)	(h)	Torquay United	W 6–0	2–0	11	Foreman 2, Howard, Mundy 2, Harburn	15,856		4		10	1	7		9	11		2		3	8					5	6
19	FL D3(S)	(a)	Aldershot	W 4–1	0–0	8	Wilson, Harburn, Foreman, Mundy	5,668		4		10	1	7		9	11		2		3	8					5	6
22	FL D3(S)	(a)	Millwall	L 3–4	0–2	13	Harburn, Foreman, Howard	15,517		4		10	1	7		9	11		2		3	8					5	6
26	FL D3(S)	(h)	Aldershot	D 2–2	1–0	10	Howard, Foreman	11,861				10	1	7		9	11		2		3	8			4		5	6
29	FL D3(S)	(a)	Southend United	L 1–3	0–2	14	Langley (pen)	10,150				10	1	7		9	11		2		3		8		4		5	6
Oct 6	FL D3(S)	(h)	Exeter City	W 3–0	3–0	11	Bisset 2, Foreman	13,349	9			10	1	7			11		2			8			4	3	5	6
13	FL D3(S)	(a)	Southampton	L 0–1	0–1	10		22,103	9			10	1	7			11		2		3	8			4		5	6
20	FL D3(S)	(h)	Coventry City	W 2–1	0–1	10	Harburn 2	14,225				10	1	7		9	11				3	8			4	2	5	6
27	FL D3(S)	(a)	Norwich City	D 1–1	0–1	8	Mundy	11,513				10	1	7		9	11				3	8			4	2	5	6
Nov 3	FL D3(S)	(h)	Colchester United	D 0–0	0–0	8		13,550				10	1	7		9	11				3	8			4	2	5	6
10	FL D3(S)	(a)	Newport County	D 0–0	0–0	8		9,082	6			10	1	7		9		8			3		11		4	2	5	
17	FAC R1	(h)	Millwall	D 1–1	1–1	–	Wilson	15,978				10	1	7		9	11				3	8			4	2	5	6
19	FAC R1 Rep	(a)	Millwall	L 1–3	0–2	–	Langley (pen)	9,149				10	1	7		9	11				3	8			4	2	5	6
24	FL D3(S)	(a)	Plymouth Argyle	L 0–2	0–0	12		11,914				11	1	7	6			8	9		3				4	2	5	10
Dec 1	FL D3(S)	(h)	Queen's Park R.	W 1–0	1–0	9	Mundy	9,770				10	1	7			11			9	3	8			4	2	5	6
15	FL D3(S)	(a)	Shrewsbury Town	L 0–4	0–1	11		6,061	6			10	1	7		9	11	8			3				4	2	5	
22	FL D3(S)	(h)	Walsall	L 1–3	0–1	13	Harburn	6,733				10	1	7		9	11	8			3				4	2	5	6
25	FL D3(S)	(h)	Gillingham	D 0–0	0–0	12		5,237				10	1	7		9					3	8	11		4	2	5	6
26	FL D3(S)	(h)	Gillingham	W 3–1	2–1	8	Harburn, Gordon, Mundy	7,362				10	1	7		9					3	8	11		4	2	5	6
29	FL D3(S)	(a)	Ipswich Town	L 0–4	0–1	13		14,633					1	7				8		9	3		11	10	4	2	5	6
Jan 5	FL D3(S)	(h)	Swindon Town	W 2–0	2–0	10	Foreman, Tennant	6,370				10	1	7		9		8			3		11		4	2	5	6
12	FL D3(S)	(h)	Bournem'th & B.A.	D 2–2	0–2	10	Foreman, Humphries	9,027				10	1	7		9		8			3		11		4	2	5	6
19	FL D3(S)	(a)	Torquay United	L 0–1	0–0	13		5,971				10	1			9	11	8			3		7		4	2	5	6
26	FL D3(S)	(a)	Swindon Town	L 0–3	0–2	13		8,003				10	1			9	11				3	8	7		4	2	5	6
Feb 2	FL D3(S)	(h)	Millwall	W 3–2	0–1	11	Thomas, Neate, Humphries	9,439				10	1	7		9		2			3		11		4	8	5	6
9	FL D3(S)	(h)	Southend United	D 1–1	0–0	11	Neate	11,170				10	1	7		9			2		3		11		4	8	5	6
16	FL D3(S)	(a)	Exeter City	W 3–1	2–1	10	Tennant, Neate 2	6,545		4		10	1	7		9					3		8		11	2	5	6
23	FL D3(S)	(h)	Southampton	W 1–0	0–0	10	Jennings	8,213		4		10	1	7		9					3		8		11	2	5	6
Mar 2	FL D3(S)	(a)	Coventry City	W 2–1	1–1	6=	Neate, Harburn	11,655		4		10	1	7		9					3		8		11	2	5	6
9	FL D3(S)	(a)	Northampton T.	W 5–0	3–0	4	Mundy 2, Foreman, Harburn 2	11,922		4		10	1	7		9					3	8			11	2	5	6
16	FL D3(S)	(a)	Colchester United	D 0–0	0–0	5		10,459		4		10	1	7		9					3	8			11	2	5	6
23	FL D3(S)	(h)	Newport County	W 2–0	1–0	4	Jennings (pen), Mundy	12,492		4		10	1	7		9			2		3	8			11		5	6
30	FL D3(S)	(a)	Reading	D 2–2	1–0	4	Gordon, Neate	7,274		4		10	1	7		9					3		8		11	2	5	6
Apr 6	FL D3(S)	(h)	Plymouth Argyle	W 3–1	0–1	5	Mundy 2, Gordon	12,385		4		10	1	7		9					3	8			11	2	5	6
13	FL D3(S)	(a)	Queen's Park R.	D 0–0	0–0	5		6,911		4		10	1	7		9					3		11	8		2	5	6
19	FL D3(S)	(a)	Crystal Palace	D 2–2	0–0	5	Harburn, Foreman	15,514		4		10	1	7		9					3	8			11	2	5	6
20	FL D3(S)	(h)	Norwich City	W 3–0	1–0	5	Gordon, Mundy, Wilson	12,807		4		10	1	7		9	11				3	8				2	5	6
22	FL D3(S)	(a)	Crystal Palace	D 1–1	1–1	5	Foreman	11,382		4	9	10	1	7			11				3	8				2	5	6
27	FL D3(S)	(h)	Reading	W 8–3	3–3	5	Jennings (pen), Mundy 3, Foreman 2, Darey, Howard	9,051		4	9	10	1	7			11		2		3	8					5	6
30	FL D3(S)	(a)	Northampton T.	L 0–1	0–1	5		4,019		4		10	1	7			11	9			3	8				2	5	6
League appearances									6	25	2	45	46	44	1	36	27	10	29	2	31	34	20	4	32	23	45	44
League goals									2		1	16		6		15	6	2	3		3	20	6		2	1		3

Football League Division 3 (South) 1956–57

		P	W	D	L	F	A	W	D	L	F	A	Pts
1.	Ipswich Town	46	18	3	2	72	20	7	6	10	29	34	59
2.	Torquay United	46	19	4	0	71	18	5	7	11	18	46	59
3.	Colchester United	46	15	8	0	49	19	7	6	10	35	37	58
4.	Southampton	46	15	4	4	48	20	7	6	10	28	32	54
5.	Bournemouth & B.A.	46	15	7	1	57	20	4	7	12	31	42	52
6.	**ALBION**	46	15	6	2	59	26	4	8	11	27	39	52
7.	Southend United	46	14	3	6	42	20	4	9	10	31	45	48
8.	Brentford	46	12	9	2	55	29	4	7	12	23	47	48
9.	Shrewsbury Town	46	11	9	3	45	24	4	9	10	27	55	48
10.	Queen's Park R.	46	12	7	4	42	21	6	4	13	19	39	47
11.	Watford	46	11	6	6	44	32	7	4	12	28	43	46
12.	Newport County	46	15	6	2	51	18	1	7	15	14	44	45
13.	Reading	46	13	4	6	44	30	5	5	13	36	51	45
14.	Northampton Town	46	15	5	3	49	22	3	4	16	17	51	45
15.	Walsall	46	11	7	5	49	25	5	5	13	31	49	44
16.	Coventry City	46	12	5	6	52	36	4	7	12	22	48	44
17.	Millwall	46	13	7	3	46	29	3	5	15	18	55	44
18.	Plymouth Argyle	46	10	8	5	38	31	6	3	14	30	42	43
19.	Aldershot	46	11	5	7	43	35	4	7	12	36	57	42
20.	Crystal Palace	46	7	10	6	31	28	4	8	11	31	47	40
21.	Exeter City	46	8	8	7	37	29	4	5	14	24	50	37
22.	Gillingham	46	7	8	8	29	29	5	5	13	25	56	37
23.	Swindon Town	46	12	3	8	43	33	3	3	17	23	63	36
24.	Norwich City	46	7	5	11	33	37	1	10	12	28	57	31

On 13 October the England youth team drew 2–2 with Switzerland at the Goldstone. The crowd was swollen to 11,047 because of the appearance of Rodney Feist, a Brighton lad and later an Albion reserve, at right-back.

To avoid a clash of colours in the away match with Coventry City on 2 March, Albion turned out in a change strip of black shirts with white sleeves.

Eric Gill was again ever-present beneath the bar and clocked up his 200th consecutive appearance in the home match with Southampton in February. Glen Wilson, Ken Whitfield, Denis Foreman and Dennis Gordon missed only six games between them. Steve Burtenshaw returned to the side at right-half on his demob from the Army and swiftly developed into a fine player.

Modern followers of the game may find it difficult to comprehend that doubts were cast over a forward line that mustered 86 goals, yet this was the case. Inside-right Albert Mundy top-scored for the third season in a row with 20 goals but was said to be slowing down; Denis Foreman finished on 16 but was considered by some to be below his best; and the enthusiastic Peter Harburn registered 15 but had his critics as leader of the attack. With the benefit of hindsight, it would appear the criticism was the result of frustration, but how the game has changed!

Albion 1956–57

Back row left to right: Alan Grant, Ron Clark, Roy Marshall, Eric Gill, Norman Stevens, Glen Wilson.

Middle row left to right: Joe Wilson (trainer), Irvin Brown, Ken Whitfield, Don Clarke, Steve Burtenshaw, Jimmy Langley (captain), Dennis Gordon, Bernard Sibley, Peter Harburn, Tommy Bisset, Roy Jennings, Cyril Hodges (assistant trainer).

Seated left to right: Roy Hollins, Mick Johnson, Frankie Howard, Malcolm Stephens, Billy Lane (manager), Denis Foreman, Albert Mundy, Des Tennant, Mackie Reed.

SEASON 1957–58

During the summer the Government announced that the much-despised Entertainment Tax, introduced in 1917 as 'a wartime measure', was to be dropped; football clubs had been campaigning to this end for many years and the decision was greeted with huge delight. In Albion's case it meant a saving of around £10,000 a season and plans were immediately set in motion to build a new West Stand, the final piece in the club's ten-year, £100,000 ground-rebuilding jigsaw. The North Stand had been extended to its full width again during the previous season, following bomb damage to the western end in 1942.

Albion's form in the opening games was outstanding, and after four weeks they headed the table, dropping just one point in seven matches. Then came a sequence of four successive defeats which brought a decline into fifth place. At this point Billy Lane shrewdly signed Syd Ellis, Charlton Athletic's former England under-23 full-back, and Leyton Orient's experienced inside-forward Dave Sexton. Both players settled quickly with Sexton scoring on his début in the 3–2 win at Aldershot.

Two significant events took place in February: Albert Mundy, the club's leading goalscorer for the previous three seasons, left for Aldershot, and goalkeeper Eric Gill's tremendous run of 247 consecutive appearances came to an end. Eric turned up at Brighton Station for the trip to Coventry on 1 March but was obviously unwell and was sent home.

> Albion's Christmas-morning match with Swindon Town was the club's last on Christmas Day, ending a tradition that had proved a great attraction since 1902.

With the leadership changing hands from match to match, an exciting title race developed, and from late November Brighton were never out of the top three. On 15 March, Albion travelled to the current leaders Reading and achieved an excellent 1–1 draw; the gates were closed on a 25,880 crowd, leaving thousands stranded outside the ground. After an indifferent Easter-holiday programme – three points from three games – Albion led the section by a point from Plymouth Argyle with a game in hand, but the subsequent three matches harvested only two points and a prevailing sense of *déjà vu* became evident throughout Sussex.

Around this period the season had to be completed by the end of April which meant that Albion were forced to play their final four matches in eight days, three of which were away from home. On Wednesday, 23 April, Albion drew 2–2 at Port Vale and three days later Denis Foreman's last-minute goal won two priceless points at Watford to put Brighton second. This was the table on Saturday, 26 April:

		P	W	D	L	F	A	Pts
1.	Plymouth Argyle	46	25	8	13	67	48	58
2.	ALBION	44	23	12	9	82	63	58
3.	Swindon Town	46	21	15	10	79	50	57
4.	Brentford	45	23	10	12	81	56	56
5.	Reading	46	21	13	12	79	51	55

On the Monday, Albion travelled to fourth-placed Brentford knowing that a point would clinch the championship, but the Bees won by a goal to nil before a 25,700 crowd to go ahead of Albion and Plymouth at the top of the table. Albion's goal-average was the lowest of the three, but the other challengers

SEASON 1957–58

Date	Comp.	Ven.	Opponents	Result	HT	Pos.	Scorers	Atten.	Bates D	Bisset T	Brown I	Burtenshaw S	Champelovier L	Ellis S	Foreman D	Gill E	Gordon D	Harburn P	Hodge E	Hollins D	Howard F	Jennings R	Mundy A	Sexton D	Small P	Tennant D	Thomas R	Thorne A	Whitfield K	Wilson G
Aug 24	FL D3(S)	(a)	Gillingham	W 1–0	0–0	1=	Harburn	11,249	2			4			10	1		9			11	3	8		7				5	6
28	FL D3(S)	(h)	Bournem'th & B.A.	W 2–1	1–1	4=	Harburn, Mundy	17,010	2			4			10	1		9			11	3	8		7				5	6
31	FL D3(S)	(h)	Exeter City	D 2–2	0–0	4	Mundy, Small	16,036	2			4			10	1		9			11	3	8		7				5	6
Sep 4	FL D3(S)	(a)	Bournem'th & B.A.	W 3–1	1–0	2	Gordon 2, Mundy	12,875				4			10	1	7	9			11	3	8			2			5	6
7	FL D3(S)	(a)	Queen's Park R.	W 1–0	0–0	1	Harburn	10,676				4			10	1	7	9			11	3	8			2			5	6
11	FL D3(S)	(h)	Plymouth Argyle	W 3–2	1–1	1	Jennings (pen), Own goal, Harburn	13,408				4			10	1	7	9			11	3	8			2			5	6
14	FL D3(S)	(h)	Southend United	W 3–1	0–0	1	Harburn, Foreman, Mundy	20,390				4			10	1	7	9			11	3	8			2			5	6
16	FL D3(S)	(a)	Plymouth Argyle	L 1–2	0–0	1	Mundy	19,121				4			10	1	7	9			11	3	8			2			5	6
21	FL D3(S)	(h)	Norwich City	L 0–1	0–0	1		16,910				4			10	1	7	9			11	3	8			2			5	6
25	FL D3(S)	(h)	Aldershot	L 0–1	0–1	1		8,687				4			10	1	7	9			11	3	8			2			5	6
28	FL D3(S)	(a)	Southampton	L 0–5	0–2	5		18,043				4			10	1	7	9				3	8		11	2			5	6
Oct 2	FL D3(S)	(a)	Aldershot	W 3–2	2–2	4	Harburn, Sexton, Small	4,063				4		8		1	7	9				3		10	11	2			5	6
5	FL D3(S)	(h)	Newport County	W 5–3	1–2	1	Mundy, Sexton, Gordon, Harburn 2	14,560				4			11	1	7	9				3	8	10		2			5	6
12	FL D3(S)	(a)	Walsall	W 3–2	2–0	1	Mundy, Harburn, Foreman	11,080	4					6	11	1	7	9				3	8	10		2			5	
19	FL D3(S)	(h)	Coventry City	W 3–0	2–0	1	Harburn 2, Mundy	17,250				4			11	1	7	9				3	8	10		2			5	6
26	FL D3(S)	(a)	Shrewsbury Town	L 0–2	0–0	2		8,056				4			11	1	7	9				3	8	10		2			5	6
Nov 2	FL D3(S)	(h)	Reading	L 1–2	1–1	6	Small	16,549				4				1	7	9			11	3	8		10	2			5	6
9	FL D3(S)	(a)	Northampton T.	W 4–2	2–1	1	Harburn 2, Sexton, Gordon	7,088		5		4				1	7	9			11	3	8	10		2				6
16	FAC R1	(h)	Walsall	W 2–1	1–1	–	Sexton 2	15,325				4				1	7	9			11	3	8	10		2			5	6
23	FL D3(S)	(a)	Crystal Palace	W 4–2	2–2	3	Sexton 3, Mundy	15,757				4	3			1	7	9			11		8	10		2			5	6
30	FL D3(S)	(a)	Torquay United	D 1–1	0–1	3	Harburn	15,661				4				1	7	9			11	3	8	10		2			5	6
Dec 7	FAC R2	(a)	Norwich City	D 1–1	1–0	–	Foreman	19,748			3	4			10	1	7	9			11		8			2			5	6
11	FAC R2 Rep	(h)	Norwich City	L 1–2	0–1	–	Foreman	8,984			3	4			10	1	7	9			11		8			2			5	6
14	FL D3(S)	(h)	Colchester United	W 5–2	2–1	2	Gordon 2, Sexton (pen), Harburn, Howard	9,716			3	4				1	7	9			11		8	10		2			5	6
21	FL D3(S)	(h)	Gillingham	W 5–2	1–1	1	Sexton 3 (1 pen), Foreman, Gordon	10,430			3	4			10	1	7	9			11			8		2			5	6
25	FL D3(S)	(a)	Swindon Town	D 2–2	2–0	1	Mundy, Sexton	12,269				4				1	7	9			11	3	8	10		2			5	6
26	FL D3(S)	(h)	Swindon Town	W 1–0	1–0	1	Gordon	21,496				4				1	7	9			11	3	8	10		2			5	6
28	FL D3(S)	(a)	Exeter City	L 0–2	0–0	1		10,701				4				1	7	9			11	3	8	10		2			5	6
Jan 4	FL D3(S)	(h)	Port Vale	D 0–0	0–0	1		13,227	4					3	10	1	7	9			11		8			2			5	6
11	FL D3(S)	(h)	Queen's Park R.	D 1–1	1–1	1	Sexton	13,289	4					3		1	7	9			11		8	10		2			5	6
18	FL D3(S)	(a)	Southend United	W 2–0	1–0	1	Thorne, Howard	11,665	4					3	10	1	7				11		8			2		9	5	6
Feb 1	FL D3(S)	(a)	Norwich City	D 0–0	0–0	2		20,687	4					3	10	1	7				11		8			2		9	5	6
8	FL D3(S)	(h)	Southampton	D 1–1	0–1	2	Thorne	17,304	4					3	10	1	7				11		8			2		9	5	6
15	FL D3(S)	(a)	Newport County	W 2–1	1–0	1	Sexton, Harburn	9,424	4			8		3		1	7	9			11			10		2			5	6
22	FL D3(S)	(h)	Walsall	W 2–0	1–0	2	Foreman, Gordon	12,303	4			8		3	10	1	7	9			11					2			5	6
Mar 1	FL D3(S)	(a)	Coventry City	D 2–2	1–0	2	Bates, Harburn	9,073	4					3	10		7	9		1	11			8		2			5	6
8	FL D3(S)	(h)	Shrewsbury Town	W 2–1	1–0	3	Own goal, Foreman	11,134	4					3	10		7	9		1	11			8		2			5	6
15	FL D3(S)	(a)	Reading	D 1–1	0–1	3	Sexton	25,880	4					3	10		7	9		1	11			8		2			5	6
22	FL D3(S)	(h)	Crystal Palace	W 3–2	0–2	2	Foreman, Sexton, Harburn	19,517	4					3	10	1	7	9			11			8		2			5	6
29	FL D3(S)	(a)	Colchester United	W 2–1	0–1	1	Gordon 2	8,751	4					3	10	1	7	9			11			8		2			5	6
Apr 4	FL D3(S)	(a)	Millwall	D 2–2	2–1	2	Sexton, Foreman	17,810	4					3	10	1	7	9			11			8		2			5	6
5	FL D3(S)	(h)	Northampton T.	L 1–4	0–2	1	Sexton	19,933	4					3	10	1	7	9			11			8		2			5	6
7	FL D3(S)	(h)	Millwall	W 4–2	1–1	1	Wilson, Gordon, Foreman 2	19,124	4	5				3	10	1	7				11					2	8	9		6
12	FL D3(S)	(a)	Torquay United	L 0–2	0–1	3		7,693	4	5				3	10	1	7				11					2	8	9		6
19	FL D3(S)	(h)	Brentford	D 1–1	0–1	3	Harburn	25,597	4					3	10	1	7	9			11			8		2			5	6
23	FL D3(S)	(a)	Port Vale	D 2–2	1–1	3	Harburn, Sexton	7,245	4					3	10	1	7	9			11			8		2			5	6
26	FL D3(S)	(a)	Watford	W 1–0	0–0	2	Foreman	9,576	4					3	10	1	7	9			11					2		8	5	6
28	FL D3(S)	(a)	Brentford	L 0–1	0–0	3		25,700	4					3	10	1	7	9			11					2		8	5	6
30	FL D3(S)	(h)	Watford	W 6–0	5–0	1	Thorne 5, Wilson (pen)	31,038	4					3	10	1	7	9			11					2		8	5	6
League appearances									21	3	3	28	1	25	37	43	43	42	4	3	41	17	23	26	8	35	8	7	43	45
League goals							OG – 2		1						10		12	20			2	1	10	18	3			7		2

Football League Division 3 (South) 1957–58

		P	W	D	L	F	A	W	D	L	F	A	Pts
1.	**ALBION**	46	13	6	4	52	30	11	6	6	36	34	60
2.	Brentford	46	15	5	3	52	24	9	5	9	30	32	58
3.	Plymouth Argyle	46	17	4	2	43	17	8	4	11	24	31	58
4.	Swindon Town	46	14	7	2	47	16	7	8	8	32	34	57
5.	Reading	46	14	5	4	52	23	7	8	8	27	28	55
6.	Southampton	46	16	3	4	78	31	6	7	10	34	41	54
7.	Southend United	46	14	5	4	56	26	7	7	9	34	32	54
8.	Norwich City	46	11	9	3	41	28	8	6	9	34	42	53
9.	Bournemouth & B.A.	46	16	5	2	54	24	5	4	14	27	50	51
10.	Queen's Park R.	46	15	6	2	40	14	3	8	12	24	51	50
11.	Newport County	46	12	6	5	40	24	5	8	10	33	43	48
12.	Colchester United	46	13	5	5	45	27	4	8	11	32	52	47
13.	Northampton Town	46	13	1	9	60	33	6	5	12	27	46	44
14.	Crystal Palace	46	12	5	6	46	30	3	8	12	24	42	43
15.	Port Vale	46	12	6	5	49	24	4	4	15	18	34	42
16.	Watford	46	9	8	6	34	27	4	8	11	25	50	42
17.	Shrewsbury Town	46	10	6	7	29	25	5	4	14	20	46	40
18.	Aldershot	46	7	9	7	31	34	5	7	11	28	55	40
19.	Coventry City	46	10	9	4	41	24	3	4	16	20	57	39
20.	Walsall	46	10	7	6	37	24	4	2	17	24	51	37
21.	Torquay United	46	9	7	7	33	34	2	6	15	16	40	35
22.	Gillingham	46	12	5	6	33	24	1	4	18	19	57	35
23.	Millwall	46	6	6	11	37	36	5	3	15	26	55	31
24.	Exeter City	46	10	4	9	37	35	1	5	17	20	64	31

The floral clock in Palmeira Square was rearranged in the style of a football pitch bearing the legends 'Congratulations Albion' and '2nd Div' as the Borough of Hove's tribute to the club.

had now completed their fixtures while Albion had that crucial game in hand.

On Wednesday, 30 April, Watford arrived at the Goldstone to try to prevent Albion getting the required point; the match was originally scheduled for 25 January but had been postponed owing to adverse weather conditions. Interest was intense and workplaces throughout the area emptied rather earlier than usual as the enthusiastic hordes converged on the Goldstone for the six-fifteen kick-off (no floodlights in 1958). A crowd of 31,038, a new League record, crammed into the ground, while the factory roofs in Newtown Road were lined with those unable to gain admittance. Lamp-posts and trees were at a premium as every vantage point was sought, and the youngsters inside the ground were allowed on to the perimeter track to ease the crush. When Albion took the field the greeting was deafening, and what followed came straight out of a *Boy's Own* comic-strip.

Dave Sexton had picked up an injury at Port Vale so Billy Lane drafted 20-year-old Adrian Thorne into the side to play up front alongside Peter Harburn in the final three games. Thorne was a local boy who had recently been demobbed from national service with the Army. He had been with the club for four years, but the crucial Watford match was only his seventh outing in the first team.

After five minutes Thorne put Albion in front, and three minutes later he made it two-nil. Another 60 seconds and the local hero scored a third, effectively sewing up the championship. A hat-trick in four minutes! The fans were delirious, and when skipper Glen Wilson scored from the penalty spot and Thorne added his fourth to give Albion a 5–0 interval lead, the good-natured crowd spilled onto the pitch and it was some time before the playing-area was cleared to enable the second half to commence. Watford recovered some of their poise in the second period and prevented the Albion adding to the score until a minute from time when the inevitable Thorne netted his fifth and Albion's sixth.

The scenes at the final whistle were astonishing. Caps and scarfs littered the ground as the fans danced around the pitch. The players made appearances from the dressing-room in various states of undress and an hour after the game the ground was still half-full with people reluctant to go home. Caught up in the tide of emotion, Billy Lane locked himself in his office for some time. A 38-year-old dream of Second Division football had come true for everyone with the Albion's fortunes at heart.

Though there were quite a number of drawn matches, the run-in saw Albion beaten only four times in 29 League games, and a club-record eleven wins were gained on the road. Five goalscorers reached double figures: Peter Harburn and Dave Sexton with 20 apiece, Dennis Gordon and Denis Foreman with 12 each, and Albert Mundy notched 10 before his departure. The success of the team brought some of the missing fans back to the Goldstone and the average rose to 16,546. The club received £550 talent money for taking the title.

On the day following the incredible Watford match the contractors moved in to demolish the quaint, wooden West Stand which had served for so many years. A few days later the

Albion 1957–58
The champions pictured at the end of the season.
Standing left to right: Billy Lane (manager), Steve Burtenshaw, Roy Jennings, Eric Gill, Don Bates, Tommy Bisset, Joe Wilson (trainer).
Seated left to right: Des Tennant, Dennis Gordon, Dave Sexton, Peter Harburn, Ken Whitfield, Glen Wilson (captain),
On ground left to right: Peter Small, Adrian Thorne, Denis Foreman, Frankie Howard.

players and their wives departed on a five-day trip to Paris as reward for the season's efforts.

In such a momentous campaign the F.A. Cup performances were somewhat less distinguished, Norwich City winning a second-round replay at the Goldstone 2–1 after Walsall had been dispatched 2–1 in the first round.

Sadly, Albion chairman Major Carlo Campbell, who had served on the board for over seventeen years and helped save the club in 1940, did not live to see his ambition of Second Division football at the Goldstone come to fruition. He died on 26 February, just two months before the club clinched promotion. Billy Lane paid this tribute: 'I have lost more than a good chairman — I have lost a very great friend.'

We've done it!
After 38 years of frustration, the relief and joy is obvious on the faces of both those in the dressing-room and those celebrating wildly on the pitch following Albion's 6–0 demolition of Watford to clinch the Third Division (South) championship.

October 1960: amid a widespread national scandal over result-fixing and bribery within the game, allegations were made that the two Albion victories over Watford at the end of the 1957–58 promotion campaign had been arranged. The Watford skipper at the time of the matches, John Meadows, was quoted in the Press as saying that he and his team-mates shared £110, allegedly from the Albion players. Meadows was reported as making it clear that neither club was implicated and that it had been a matter entirely between the players. Albion chairman Alec Whitcher said that he was astonished and the players vigorously denied the allegations. The F.A. and the Football League referred the matter to the Director of Public Prosecutions, but the affair went no further. Nevertheless, it was something of a bombshell locally, and an element of doubt was cast over one of the most momentous occasions in the club's history.

Glen Wilson, the Albion captain at the time who had since left the club to take the player-manager's position at Exeter City, was quoted as saying: 'I have nothing to hide and nothing to be ashamed of. I am proud of the part I played in helping Albion to win promotion and very proud of the boys who played with me.'

SEASON 1958–59

The £32,330 central section of the new West Stand, or the Grand Stand as the club preferred to call it for many years, was opened in readiness for the new season, providing seated accommodation for around 1,400 fans above terracing as Albion entered the brave new world of Division Two.

Billy Lane brought only two new faces to the Goldstone during the summer, Jack Bertolini from Workington and Johnny Shepherd from Millwall, and declared his intention of giving the players who had earned promotion an opportunity to prove themselves in the higher company. Just before the season opened, however, Everton came up with £8,000 for the services of Peter Harburn, a great opportunity for the popular centre-forward but a blow to the club's hopes.

Albion fans scanned the fixture list and drooled at the prospect of first-ever League encounters with Sunderland, Liverpool, Huddersfield Town, Derby County, the two Sheffield clubs, and the first engagement, at Middlesbrough. However, the eagerly awaited fixture at Ayresome Park ended in total disaster: 5–0 down at the interval, the side collapsed to the biggest (peacetime) defeat in the club's history, eventually losing 9–0 with Brian Clough – later an Albion manager – notching five. Goalkeeper Eric Gill missed the match, no doubt to his eternal relief, and young Dave Hollins was on the receiving end. It did him no lasting harm, though, as he was soon to win Welsh under-23 honours and went on to gain eleven caps at senior level after his transfer to Newcastle United.

The first point in Division Two was gained at home to Charlton Athletic, but the next two games brought a 5–0 defeat at Liverpool and a 3–0 loss at Bristol City. Seventeen goals conceded in three away matches, and by September Albion were propping up the rest. To add to the manager's problems, an injury to Denis Foreman put him out for the remainder of the season and it quickly became apparent that the team needed strengthening to meet the challenge. Home form was quite reasonable – only eventual champions Sheffield Wednesday and Middlesbrough won at the Goldstone (Clough registering another three goals as Albion succumbed 6–4 to 'Boro) – but too many of the matches ended in draws, and by Christmas Albion had just eighteen points from 22 games and were only two places from the bottom.

Despite the appalling start Billy Lane remained calm and bought wisely. He signed three players from Arsenal: young forwards Ronnie Clayton and Freddie Jones in September, followed a month later by right-winger Mike Tiddy. October also saw the arrival of a proven goalscorer, Tommy Dixon from Reading, and Roy 'Doz' Little, an experienced full-back from Manchester City.

Brave new world
Skipper Glen Wilson leads his team out at Ayresome Park as Albion make their début in the Second Division. However, the big day turned out to be a disaster as Middlesbrough slaughtered the newcomers 9–0. Here, Brian Clough, one of the most prolific goalscorers in the history of the game and later an Albion manager, wheels away after scoring his fifth goal past a dejected Dave Hollins.

SEASON 1958–59

Date	Comp.	Ven.	Opponents	Result	HT	Pos.	Scorers	Atten.	Bertolini J	Bisset T	Burtenshaw S	Clayton R	Darey J	Dixon T	Ellis S	Foreman D	Gill E	Gordon D	Hollins D	Howard F	Jennings R	Jones F	Little R	McNeill I	Sexton D	Shepherd J	Stevens N	Tennant D	Thorne A	Tiddy M	Whitfield K	Wilson G
Aug 23	FL D2	(a)	Middlesbrough	L 0–9	0–5	21=		32,136	4						3	10		7	1	11					9	8		2			5	6
30	FL D2	(h)	Charlton Athletic	D 2–2	0–0	20	Foreman, Sexton	27,739	4	2					3	10	1	7		11					9	8					5	6
Sep 3	FL D2	(a)	Liverpool	L 0–5	0–5	21=		39,520	4	2					3	10	1	7		11					9	8					5	6
6	FL D2	(a)	Bristol City	L 0–3	0–2	22		23,377	8	2	4						1	7		11	3				10	9					5	6
10	FL D2	(h)	Grimsby Town	W 2–0	2–0	22	Shepherd, Burtenshaw	20,880		2	4	8					1	7		11	3				10	9					5	6
13	FL D2	(h)	Cardiff City	D 2–2	2–1	21	Shepherd, Wilson (pen)	25,009		2	4	8			3		1	7				11			10	9					5	6
16	FL D2	(a)	Grimsby Town	D 1–1	0–1	20	Jones	15,349		2	4	8			3		1	7				11			10	9					5	6
20	FL D2	(a)	Huddersfield Town	L 2–3	0–0	22	Sexton, Shepherd	13,244		2	4	8			3		1	7				11			10	9					5	6
24	FL D2	(h)	Liverpool	D 2–2	1–1	20	Jones, Whitfield	21,323		2	4	8					1	7			3	11				9			10		5	6
27	FL D2	(h)	Barnsley	D 1–1	1–1	20	Wilson (pen)	24,381		2	4	8					1	7			3	11				9			10		5	6
Oct 4	FL D2	(a)	Rotherham United	W 1–0	0–0	17	Thorne	7,240		2	4	8						7	1		3	11				9			10		5	6
11	FL D2	(h)	Sheffield Wed.	L 1–3	1–1	19	Thorne	26,987		2	4			9				7	1		3	11				8			10		5	6
18	FL D2	(a)	Scunthorpe United	W 3–2	1–1	18	Wilson, Shepherd 2	11,921		2	4			9					1	11		7	3			8			10		5	6
25	FL D2	(h)	Leyton Orient	D 2–2	1–2	16	Thorne, Shepherd	26,265		2	4			9					1			11	3			8			10	7	5	6
Nov 1	FL D2	(a)	Lincoln City	L 2–4	0–3	18	Thorne, Dixon	11,254			4			9					1			11	3			8		2	10	7	5	6
8	FL D2	(h)	Bristol Rovers	D 1–1	1–0	18	Clayton	22,155	4	2		10		9					1			11	3			8				7	5	6
15	FL D2	(a)	Ipswich Town	L 3–5	1–2	18	Dixon, Shepherd 2	13,009	4	2				9					1			11	3		10	8				7	5	6
22	FL D2	(h)	Swansea Town	D 2–2	2–0	20	Tiddy, Jones	18,674	4	2				9					1			11	3			8			10	7	5	6
29	FL D2	(a)	Stoke City	L 0–3	0–2	21		13,251	4	2				9				8	1			11	3			10				7	5	6
Dec 6	FL D2	(h)	Sunderland	W 2–0	1–0	20	Sexton, Jones	23,537	4	2				9			1					11	3		10	8				7	5	6
13	FL D2	(a)	Derby County	W 3–1	1–1	16	Shepherd 2, Howard	14,834	4	2				9			1			11			3		10	8				7	5	6
20	FL D2	(h)	Middlesbrough	L 4–6	0–2	20	Shepherd 2, Jones, Sexton	20,981	4	2				9			1					11	3		10	8				7	5	6
26	FL D2	(a)	Fulham	L 1–3	0–1	20	Thorne	28,639	4	2							1				5	11	3		10	8			9	7		6
27	FL D2	(h)	Fulham	W 3–0	1–0	17	Dixon 2, Thorne	36,747	4	2				10			1				5	11	3		8				9	7		6
Jan 3	FL D2	(a)	Charlton Athletic	W 3–2	1–1	17	Thorne 2, Dixon	21,539	4	2				10			1				5	11	3		8				9	7		6
10	FAC R3	(h)	Bradford City	L 0–2	0–1	–		22,169	4	2				10					1		5	11	3		8				9	7		6
17	FL D2	(h)	Bristol City	D 2–2	0–1	14	Sexton 2	18,166	4	2				10					1		5	11	3		9	8				7		6
31	FL D2	(a)	Cardiff City	L 1–3	1–2	17	Sexton	15,891	4					10	2				1		5	11	3		9	8				7		6
Feb 7	FL D2	(h)	Huddersfield Town	W 2–0	1–0	14	Jones, Dixon	19,250	4	2				10			1	7			5	11	3		9	8						6
14	FL D2	(a)	Barnsley	W 2–0	1–0	13	Jones, Gordon	8,412	4	2				10				7	1		5	11	3		9	8						6
21	FL D2	(h)	Rotherham United	W 3–0	1–0	11	Dixon 2, Gordon	18,831	4	2				10				7	1		5	11	3			9				8		6
28	FL D2	(a)	Bristol Rovers	L 0–2	0–1	13		15,785	4	2				10					1		5	11	3		8	9				7		6
Mar 7	FL D2	(h)	Scunthorpe United	W 2–1	0–0	12	Shepherd, Thorne	17,761	4					10	2		1				5	11	3			8			9	7		6
14	FL D2	(a)	Leyton Orient	D 2–2	1–0	12	Wilson, Shepherd	15,811	4					10	2		1				5	11	3			8			9	7		6
21	FL D2	(h)	Lincoln City	W 2–1	0–0	11	Own goal, Wilson (pen)	19,888	4					9	2		1	7			5	11	3	10		8						6
28	FL D2	(a)	Sheffield Wed	L 0–2	0–1	13		21,368	4					9	2		1				5	11	3	10		8				7		6
30	FL D2	(h)	Sheffield United	W 2–0	1–0	12	Shepherd, Tiddy	21,612	4					9	2		1				5	11	3	10		8				7		6
31	FL D2	(a)	Sheffield United	L 1–3	0–2	12	Dixon	16,063	4					8	2		1				5	11	3	10					9	7		6
Apr 4	FL D2	(h)	Ipswich Town	W 4–1	2–0	11	McNeill 2, Sexton, Thorne	20,931	4					8	2		1				5		3	10	9				11	7		6
11	FL D2	(a)	Swansea Town	L 2–4	1–2	14	Jones, Wilson (pen)	6,743	4					8	2		1				5	11	3	10	9					7		6
18	FL D2	(h)	Stoke City	D 2–2	0–0	13	Jones, Wilson (pen)	19,501	4				9	8			1				5	11	3	10			2			7		6
22	FL D2	(h)	Derby County	W 3–1	1–0	11	Dixon, Shepherd 2	21,037			4			10	2		1				5	11	3		9	8				7		6
25	FL D2	(a)	Sunderland	L 1–4	0–1	12	Tiddy	12,024	4				9	10	2		1				5	11	3			8				7		6
							League appearances		30	28	13	8	2	30	17	3	27	17	15	7	26	35	30	7	23	36	1	2	15	26	22	42
							League goals	OG – 1			1	1		10		1		2		1		9		2	8	17			10	3	1	7

Football League Division 2 1958–59

		P	W	D	L	F	A	W	D	L	F	A	Pts
1.	Sheffield Wednesday	42	18	2	1	68	13	10	4	7	38	35	62
2.	Fulham	42	18	1	2	65	26	9	5	7	31	35	60
3.	Sheffield United	42	16	2	3	54	15	7	5	9	28	33	53
4.	Liverpool	42	15	3	3	57	25	9	2	10	30	37	53
5.	Stoke City	42	16	2	3	48	19	5	5	11	24	39	49
6.	Bristol Rovers	42	13	5	3	46	23	5	7	9	34	41	48
7.	Derby County	42	15	1	5	46	29	5	7	9	28	42	48
8.	Charlton Athletic	42	13	3	5	53	33	5	4	12	39	57	43
9.	Cardiff City	42	12	2	7	37	26	6	5	10	28	39	43
10.	Bristol City	42	11	3	7	43	27	6	4	11	31	43	41
11.	Swansea Town	42	12	5	4	52	30	4	4	13	27	51	41
12.	**ALBION**	42	10	9	2	46	29	5	2	14	28	61	41
13.	Middlesbrough	42	9	7	5	51	26	6	3	12	36	45	40
14.	Huddersfield Town	42	12	3	6	39	20	4	5	12	23	35	40
15.	Sunderland	42	13	4	4	42	23	3	4	14	22	52	40
16.	Ipswich Town	42	12	4	5	37	27	5	2	14	25	50	40
17.	Leyton Orient	42	9	4	8	43	30	5	4	12	28	48	36
18.	Scunthorpe United	42	7	6	8	32	37	5	3	13	23	47	33
19.	Lincoln City	42	10	5	6	45	37	1	2	18	18	56	29
20.	Rotherham United	42	9	5	7	32	28	1	4	16	10	54	29
21.	Grimsby Town	42	7	7	7	41	36	2	3	16	21	54	28
22.	Barnsley	42	8	4	9	34	34	2	3	16	21	57	27

The 6–4 Goldstone defeat at the hands of Middlesbrough on 20 December was recorded by the BBC with the highlights televised that evening.

The Football League's *carte blanche* go-ahead for floodlit football in June 1958 meant Albion's first team playing under lights for the first time in the 5–0 defeat by Liverpool at Anfield on 3 September. Billy Lane was very much against floodlit League games and had refused to allow his team to appear in such matches for several seasons. He was of the opinion that, with the Goldstone not possessing lights, it would give an unfair advantage to the opposition.

Albion 2 Huddersfield Town 0, 7 February 1959

Tommy Dixon (not in picture) beats former England goalkeeper Ray Wood to clinch only the fourth home win of the term and move Albion into mid table, before a crowd of almost 20,000. In the background is the first third – or, as it turned out, half – of the new Grand Stand or West Stand.

With the influx of fresh players came a gradual improvement. On Boxing Day, Roy Jennings took over the centre-half spot from Ken Whitfield with the brief to play a 'stopper' role and the defensive pivotal play of the former full-back became one of the successes of the season. The half-back line was the strength of the side, with Jack Bertolini an unqualified success and the ever-reliable Glen Wilson playing in every match.

On 27 December promotion favourites Fulham were the visitors to Hove with an all-star line-up including George Cohen and Johnny Haynes, but the biggest attraction was the first return appearance of Albion's former skipper, the much-loved Jimmy Langley, now the proud owner of three England caps. The turn-out was a staggering 36,747 (£4,376), a ground record that will never again be approached. It was reported that there was still space on the terraces, and that the ground ought to hold 38,000 — and this with only one section of the West Stand completed! The Albion players responded magnificently, putting on their finest display of the campaign to wallop the Cottagers 3–0. Fulham went on to take the runner's-up spot behind Sheffield Wednesday.

After the turn of the year, Albion began to climb out of the danger zone with six consecutive home victories and wins at Charlton and Barnsley. Leicester City's inside-forward Ian McNeill was signed in March for a £7,000 fee and the Scot's clever scheming had a big influence on the team. The improvement continued, and the eventual twelfth placing represented a fine performance after such a calamitous beginning. Indeed, the side finished one point and one place ahead of its chief tormentor, Middlesbrough. Bob Pennington, football correspondent with the *Daily Express*, had slated the Albion's performances early in the season and challenged that if they

Albion 1958–59, with the Football League Third Division (South) Championship Shield
Back row left to right: Peter Harburn, Eric Hodge, Roy Jennings, Dave Hollins, Peter Rhodes, Alan Grant, Irvin Brown.
Third row left to right: Tommy Bisset, Bernard Sibley, Dennis Gordon, Norman Stevens, Ken Whitfield, Glen Wilson (captain), Syd Ellis, John Shepherd, Steve Burtenshaw.
Second row left to right: Joe Wilson (trainer), Keith Abbis, Ron Sleap, Jack Bertolini, Adrian Thorne, Des Tennant, Denis Foreman, Frankie Howard, Dave Sexton, Dennis Alexander, Cyril Hodges (assistant trainer).
Front row left to right: Billy Lane (manager), Dr Alexander Greig (director), Arthur Pembroke (director), Gerald Paling (director), Alec Whitcher (chairman), General Sir Leslie Hollis (director), Harry Coverdale (director), Len Holt (secretary).

finished in the top half of the table he would walk from his London office to the Goldstone. He must have watched the results of the closing matches with some trepidation!

All attendance records were surpassed with a Goldstone average of 22,460. Nearly half a million spectators attended the 21 League matches, and, to emphasise the enthusiasm surrounding the club on its elevation to the higher sphere, the average attendance at the reserve-team games was 3,850. The 'A' team also played their part by reaching the Metropolitan League Cup final where they were beaten 1–0 by Crawley Town over two legs.

Johnny Shepherd netted seventeen goals in the League games, but he missed the third-round F.A. Cup tie when Albion were beaten 2–0 at the Goldstone by Third Division Bradford City.

SEASON 1959–60

There were two significant departures from the first-team squad during the close season: Dave Sexton joined Crystal Palace and Ken Whitfield moved to Queen's Park Rangers; and two players joined the staff: Bob McNicol from Accrington Stanley and Bill Curry from Newcastle United. Curry had previously represented the England under-23 side and cost the Albion a club-record £13,000.

The southern section of the West Stand was completed during the first half of the season and opened in January. The cost of the additional structure, some £25,913, was generously guaranteed by chairman Alec Whitcher, but the expenditure on the 2,500-seat stand was far in excess of the original estimate

of £13,500 and, as a result, the northern section was never built. The Supporters' Club raised £5,000 towards the total.

As usual, public interest was initially high and the pre-season public trial match was attended by almost 7,000 spectators. The Goldstone was packed for the opening game when a crowd of 31,828, the biggest turn-out for a League match all season, home or away, witnessed a 2–1 defeat at the hands of Aston Villa. It came as no surprise to those present when the polished Midlands outfit went on to become Second Division champions.

Albion tended to produce their best football against the top sides, but most of the term was spent in the lower reaches with

SEASON 1959–60

Player columns (in order): Abbis K · Bertolini J · Bisset T · Burtenshaw S · Clayton R · Curry W · Darey J · Dixon T · Foreman D · Gill E · Gordon D · Hollins D · Jennings R · Jones F · Little R · McNeill I · McNicol R · Shepherd J · Thorne A · Tiddy M · Wilson G

Date	Comp.	Ven.	Opponents	Result	HT	Pos	Scorers	Atten.
Aug 22	FL D2	(h)	Aston Villa	L 1–2	1–1	17=	Shepherd	31,828
26	FL D2	(a)	Huddersfield Town	L 0–2	0–2	21=		15,221
29	FL D2	(a)	Sunderland	D 0–0	0–0	20		28,482
Sep 2	FL D2	(h)	Huddersfield Town	W 3–2	1–2	15	Curry, Wilson (pen), Gordon	22,558
5	FL D2	(h)	Portsmouth	W 3–1	1–1	10=	Curry	29,153
10	FL D2	(a)	Leyton Orient	L 2–3	1–2	12=	Shepherd, Gordon	13,439
12	FL D2	(a)	Stoke City	W 3–1	2–0	10	Gordon, Clayton, Curry	17,630
16	FL D2	(h)	Leyton Orient	D 1–1	1–0	10	Curry	21,500
19	FL D2	(h)	Plymouth Argyle	D 2–2	2–0	13	Wilson, Bertolini	23,163
26	FL D2	(h)	Swansea Town	L 1–2	0–0	15	Curry	20,567
Oct 3	FL D2	(a)	Bristol Rovers	W 5–4	2–2	14	Dixon, Thorne, Curry 2, Bertolini	20,058
10	FL D2	(a)	Liverpool	D 2–2	0–1	15	Jones, Curry	30,366
17	FL D2	(h)	Charlton Athletic	D 1–1	1–1	15	Tiddy	24,175
24	FL D2	(a)	Bristol City	W 1–0	0–0	10	Thorne	17,804
31	FL D2	(h)	Scunthorpe United	L 0–1	0–0	13		18,927
Nov 7	FL D2	(a)	Rotherham United	L 0–1	0–1	13		11,531
14	FL D2	(h)	Cardiff City	D 2–2	0–0	14	Bertolini, Curry	16,151
21	FL D2	(a)	Hull City	L 1–3	1–2	17	Dixon	17,107
28	FL D2	(h)	Sheffield United	L 0–2	0–2	17		16,176
Dec 5	FL D2	(a)	Middlesbrough	L 1–4	1–1	17	Foreman	19,426
12	FL D2	(h)	Derby County	W 2–0	0–0	17	Curry, Thorne	11,763
19	FL D2	(a)	Aston Villa	L 1–3	0–0	17	Gordon	25,428
26	FL D2	(a)	Ipswich Town	L 0–3	0–2	17		13,974
28	FL D2	(h)	Ipswich Town	L 1–4	1–2	18	Jennings (pen)	16,030
Jan 2	FL D2	(h)	Sunderland	W 2–1	0–1	16	Jones, Thorne	10,495
9	FAC R3	(a)	Bath City	W 1–0	0–0	–	Tiddy	18,015
16	FL D2	(a)	Portsmouth	D 2–2	1–1	17	Jones, Thorne	18,223
23	FL D2	(a)	Stoke City	W 1–0	0–0	16	Curry	12,811
30	FAC R4	(h)	Rotherham United	D 1–1	0–1	–	Thorne	24,500
Feb 3	FAC R4 Rep	(h)	Rotherham United	D 1–1*	1–0	–	Thorne	23,871
6	FL D2	(a)	Plymouth Argyle	L 2–3	2–2	16	Thorne, Abbis	18,668
8	FAC R4 2Rep(n*)		Rotherham United	W 6–0	2–0	–	Thorne 2, Curry 3, Jones	32,864
13	FL D2	(h)	Swansea Town	D 2–2	2–2	16	Curry, Jones	10,163
20	FAC R5	(a)	Preston North End	L 1–2	0–2	–	Wilson (pen)	34,543
27	FL D2	(h)	Liverpool	L 1–2	0–1	17	McNeill	21,118
Mar 2	FL D2	(h)	Bristol Rovers	D 2–2	2–1	17	Tiddy, Curry	10,451
5	FL D2	(a)	Charlton Athletic	L 1–3	1–1	18	Curry	16,465
12	FL D2	(h)	Bristol City	W 5–1	2–1	17	Clayton, Curry 3 (1 pen), Jennings (pen)	15,962
19	FL D2	(a)	Sheffield United	L 1–4	0–2	18	Curry	14,474
26	FL D2	(h)	Rotherham United	D 0–0	0–0	17		13,352
Apr 2	FL D2	(a)	Cardiff City	W 4–1	2–1	16	Curry 2, Gordon, Thorne	19,532
9	FL D2	(h)	Hull City	D 1–1	0–1	16	McNeill	14,323
15	FL D2	(a)	Lincoln City	L 1–2	0–1	17	Thorne	13,129
16	FL D2	(a)	Derby County	W 1–0	0–0	15	McNeill	14,761
18	FL D2	(h)	Lincoln City	D 3–3	0–3	16	Thorne, Own goal, McNeill	15,682
23	FL D2	(h)	Middlesbrough	W 3–2	1–0	14	Abbis 2, McNeill	17,517
30	FL D2	(a)	Scunthorpe United	W 2–1	0–0	14	Foreman, Curry	6,537

Notes: Feb 3 – after extra time.
Feb 8 – played at Highbury, Arsenal FC.

League appearances and goals

Player	League appearances	League goals
Own goals		1
Abbis K	17	3
Bertolini J	42	3
Bisset T	22	
Burtenshaw S	1	
Clayton R	6	2
Curry W	40	23
Darey J	3	
Dixon T	5	2
Foreman D	4	2
Gill E	9	
Gordon D	18	5
Hollins D	33	
Jennings R	42	2
Jones F	29	4
Little R	38	
McNeill I	35	5
McNicol R	24	
Shepherd J	9	2
Thorne A	27	9
Tiddy M	31	2
Wilson G	27	2

On 21 November the Great Britain Olympic XI defeated the Republic of Ireland 3–2 in front of a 7,557 Goldstone crowd with the aid of a hat-trick from Northern Ireland's Paddy Hasty. The match was a qualifier for the 1960 Rome Olympic tournament.

---

relegation a real threat at times. Most of the high spots came away from Hove. The game at Bristol Rovers in October saw Albion twice a goal behind but fighting back to win 5–4. At Liverpool a week later, Jimmy Melia – an Albion manager of the future – equalised for the Reds only in injury time. But the most outstanding performance came at Ninian Park in April when Albion thrashed the eventual runners-up, Cardiff City, 4–1. The team also showed its fighting qualities in the home game with Lincoln City in April when, 3–0 down at the interval, they struck back with three second-half goals to level the scores, Ian McNeill grabbing the equaliser with just two minutes to spare.

Albion finished the season in fourteenth place, but the greatest excitement was reserved for the F.A. Cup. In the best run for several years Albion were drawn away to giant-killers Bath City in the third round. The Southern League Premier Division leaders had already accounted for Millwall and Notts County, and, with cup-fever gripping the spa, were confident of

Football League Division 2 1959–60

		P	W	D	L	F	A	W	D	L	F	A	Pts
1.	Aston Villa	42	17	3	1	62	19	8	6	7	27	24	59
2.	Cardiff City	42	15	2	4	55	36	8	10	3	35	26	58
3.	Liverpool	42	15	3	3	59	28	5	7	9	31	38	50
4.	Sheffield United	42	12	5	4	43	22	7	7	7	25	29	50
5.	Middlesbrough	42	14	2	5	56	21	5	5	11	34	43	48
6.	Huddersfield Town	42	13	3	5	44	20	6	6	9	29	32	47
7.	Charlton Athletic	42	12	2	5	55	28	5	6	10	35	59	47
8.	Rotherham United	42	9	9	3	31	23	8	4	9	30	37	47
9.	Bristol Rovers	42	12	6	3	42	28	6	5	10	30	50	47
10.	Leyton Orient	42	12	4	5	47	25	3	10	8	29	36	44
11.	Ipswich Town	42	12	5	4	48	24	7	1	13	30	44	44
12.	Swansea City	42	12	6	3	54	32	3	4	14	28	52	40
13.	Lincoln City	42	11	3	7	41	25	5	4	12	34	53	39
14.	**ALBION**	42	7	8	6	35	32	6	4	11	32	44	38
15.	Scunthorpe United	42	9	7	5	38	26	4	3	14	19	45	36
16.	Sunderland	42	8	6	7	35	29	4	6	11	17	36	36
17.	Stoke City	42	8	3	10	40	38	6	4	11	26	45	35
18.	Derby County	42	9	4	8	31	28	5	3	13	30	49	35
19.	Plymouth Argyle	42	10	6	5	42	36	3	3	15	19	53	35
20.	Portsmouth	42	6	6	9	36	36	4	6	11	23	41	32
21.	Hull City	42	7	6	8	27	30	3	4	14	21	46	30
22.	Bristol City	42	8	3	10	27	31	3	2	16	33	66	27

toppling the Albion. A record 18,015 spectators squeezed into the Twerton Park ground – which resulted in the roof of one stand collapsing – but, despite a magnificent effort by the non-Leaguers, Albion went through by virtue of a 30-yarder from Mike Tiddy in the 70th minute.

In the fourth round Albion were drawn to play Rotherham United at Millmoor. The Yorkshire side were the surprise packet of the season and were making a serious push for First

Albion 1959–60

Back row left to right: Alan Grant, Dave Sexton, Syd Ellis, Roy Jennings, Glen Wilson (captain), Eric Hodge, Dennis Gordon, Steve Burtenshaw, Adrian Thorne, Denis Foreman.
Middle row left to right: Joe Wilson (trainer), Norman Stevens, John Shepherd, Keith Abbis, Eric Gill, Ronnie Clayton, Tommy Dixon, Dave Hollins, Ken Whitfield, Tony Sitford, Tommy Bisset, Cyril Hodges (assistant trainer).
Seated left to right: Des Tennant, Doz Little, Mike Tiddy, Jack Bertolini, Ian McNeill, Billy Lane (manager), Freddie Jones, Frankie Howard, Nobby Upton, Roger Wedge, Terry Tiddy.

Division status. They had held Arsenal at Highbury in the previous round before winning 2–0 at the third attempt. Albion forced a 1–1 draw at Rotherham and the Goldstone replay also finished at 1–1 after extra time. The second replay was somewhat ironically staged at Highbury on a Monday evening, and both the team and its fans responded to the still-unusual experience of playing under floodlights tremendously. A mass exodus from the South Coast swelled the attendance to 32,864, and the majority were rewarded with a superb Albion display. Two-nil up at half time, they scored three goals in a seven-minute spell early in the second period and ran out 6–0 victors, Bill Curry hitting a hat-trick.

The draw paired Albion with Preston North End, but, after the excitement of Highbury, perhaps an anti-climax was inevitable at Deepdale and the First Division team scored twice in the opening half, effectively killing off the match. Glen Wilson reduced the arrears with a last-minute penalty, but North End were worthy winners.

Once again the half-back line was Albion's strong point with Jack Bertolini and Roy Jennings ever-present. Glen Wilson notched up his 400th League match for the club during the course of the season, and at the end of the term he was released to take the post of player-manager at Exeter City.

The reserve team were beaten only twice at the Goldstone in Division One of the Football Combination and at one time appeared likely to take the championship, but there were too many drawn games and they had to settle for third place behind Chelsea and Spurs. The average home attendance for the Combination matches was 3,469; indeed, many supporters felt that the reserves gave better value for money than the seniors.

In April the Brazilian side Fluminense, champions of the Rio de Janeiro League, were entertained at the Goldstone, winning a friendly match 2–1 before a crowd of nearly 10,000. Around this period Albion played prestige games with quite a number of attractive foreign sides, and the lack of floodlighting was seen as something of an embarrassment with the games often ending in semi-darkness or having to be curtailed. With the club now playing regular floodlit games away from home, the pressure was on to light up the Goldstone.

SEASON 1960–61

Money was in short supply so, despite the poor showing of the previous season, the club signed only one player before the opening of the new campaign, Everton's left-winger Bobby Laverick. He missed the first three games because of a suspension incurred while at Goodison Park.

Albion lost their opening match 4–1 at Derby and, though there was the occasional good performance, the team struggled from start to finish. Bristol Rovers were defeated 6–1 in the second home game, but when Bill Curry left for Derby County in September the situation became serious and a poor run saw Albion bottom by the end of October. In November a club-record £15,000 brought Chelsea forward Tony Nicholas to the Goldstone and centre-forward Dennis Windross was signed from Middlesbrough, but by the time Manchester United's former Eire international full-back Joe Carolan arrived early in December the team was still only five places above the basement.

The continuing poor form prompted a takeover bid in October by Reggie Coleman-Cohen, a director of the Alliance Building Society who claimed to be the club's largest shareholder. The move was resisted by chairman Alec Whitcher, but the lively debate prompted an improvement in the club's affairs both on and off the pitch. Whitcher himself resigned on health grounds in November and was replaced as chairman by Gerald Paling.

With the arrival of Carolan, Albion climbed to twelfth place by the New Year, but, after bowing out of the F.A. Cup at the end of January, the team became unsettled and failed to win any of the subsequent eight games. Two wins out of three at Easter reduced the pressure, but with two matches to go the situation was critical. This was the table on 21 April:

		P	W	D	L	F	A	Pts
17.	Stoke City	39	11	12	16	48	53	34
18.	Leyton Orient	40	13	8	19	54	76	34
19.	Huddersfield T.	40	12	9	19	57	69	33
20.	ALBION	40	12	9	19	57	74	33
21.	Portsmouth	40	10	11	19	61	86	31
22.	Lincoln City	40	7	8	25	46	88	22

The final home fixture was against Huddersfield Town, followed by a trip to struggling Stoke City, but a win for either Huddersfield or Albion would virtually guarantee safety because of Portsmouth's vastly inferior goal-average. The Yorkshire side led 1–0 at half time and there were many taught nerves among the 13,002 crowd, but two Tony Nicholas goals

ensured a further season of Second Division fare at the Goldstone while Pompey lost 3–0 at Middlesbrough the same day and were relegated. On the last day of the campaign Albion beat Stoke City 2–0 to finish in a deceptive sixteenth place.

After the thrills of the previous season, the F.A. Cup run could well have been dull by comparison, but in fact it produced one of the most exhilarating ties seen at the Goldstone since the war. In the third round Derby County were the visitors to Hove only three weeks after the League match between the two sides. That game had seen former Goldstone favourite Bill Curry score as the Rams took a 2–1 half-time lead, only for the Albion to stage a great fight-back to win 3–2. This time Brighton led all the way to run out 3–1 winners with goals from Ian McNeill, Bobby Laverick and Dennis Windross.

The fourth round paired Albion with Burnley, the reigning League champions, at the Goldstone. The Lancashire side under Harry Potts were enjoying one of the most successful periods in their history and included full internationals Alex Elder and the great Jimmy McIlroy (both of Northern Ireland), and John Connelly and Brian Pilkington (both of England). Torrential rain before the game, coupled with apprehension regarding the likely size of the gate, put off many supporters. Nevertheless, 28,672 attended, and a large proportion of them

> The Goldstone Ground staged its third amateur international on 5 November when England beat Wales 6–1.

Albion 1960–61

Back row left to right: Jack Bertolini, Nobby Upton, Jeff Darey, Charlie Baker, Dave Hollins, Bernard Sibley, Denis Foreman, Bobby Brayne, Peter Small (assistant trainer).
Third row left to right: Des Tennant (assistant trainer), Alan Brown, Tommy Bisset, Graham Lawrence, Norman Stevens, Tony Sitford, Roy Jennings (captain), Steve Burtenshaw, Dennis Gordon, Peter Cull, Cyril Hodges (assistant trainer).
Second row left to right: Joe Wilson (trainer), Bobby Laverick, Doz Little, Mike Tiddy, Ian McNeill, Bill Curry, Keith Abbis, Adrian Thorne, Terry Tiddy, Freddie Jones.
On ground left to right: Roger Wedge, Tony Hall, David Round, Michael Harris, Alan Kingsbury, Dave Hannam.

SEASON 1960–61

Date	Comp.	Ven.	Opponents	Result	HT	Pos.	Scorers	Atten.	Abbis K	Baker C	Bertolini J	Bisset T	Burtenshaw S	Carolan J	Crowther S	Curry W	Darey J	Foreman D	Gordon D	Hollins D	Jennings R	Jones F	Laverick R	Little R	McNeill I	McNicol R	Nicholas A	Sitford A	Thorne A	Tiddy M	Windross D
Aug 20	FL D2	(a)	Derby County	L 1–4	0–2	19	Curry	14,134		4	3	6				9		11		1	5				8	2			10	7	
24	FL D2	(h)	Leyton Orient	D 1–1	1–1	17	Curry	17,797		4	3	6				9				1	5	11			8	2			10	7	
27	FL D2	(h)	Bristol Rovers	W 6–1	2–1	11	Thorne 4, Jones, Curry	15,437		4	3	6				9				1	5	11			8	2			10	7	
31	FL D2	(a)	Leyton Orient	L 1–2	0–1	15	Thorne	12,937		4	3	6				9				1	5		11		8	2			10	7	
Sep 3	FL D2	(a)	Liverpool	L 0–2	0–2	17		24,390		4	3	6				9				1	5		11		8	2			10	7	
7	FL D2	(h)	Ipswich Town	L 2–4	2–3	19	Laverick, Tiddy (pen)	12,595		4	3	6							11	11	5		10		8	2	9			7	
10	FL D2	(h)	Rotherham United	W 1–0	0–0	18	Laverick	14,409		4		6				9				1	5		10	3	8	2			11	7	
13	FL D2	(h)	Ipswich Town	L 0–4	0–3	20		14,665		4		6				9				1	5		10	3	8	2			11	7	
17	FL D2	(a)	Southampton	L 2–4	0–0	21	Laverick, Jennings (pen)	19,349		4		6				9				1	5		10	3	8	2			11	7	
24	FL D2	(h)	Leeds United	W 2–1	1–0	21	McNeill 2	15,991		4		6				9				1	5		10	3	8	2			11	7	
Oct 1	FL D2	(a)	Middlesbrough	D 2–2	0–1	19	Tiddy, Thorne	15,489		4		6					9	10		1	5			3	8	2			11	7	
8	FL D2	(a)	Norwich City	D 2–2	0–1	19	McNeill, Jennings	22,919		4		6				9				1	5		10	3	8	2			11	7	
15	FL D2	(h)	Charlton Athletic	L 3–5	1–2	20	Bisset 2, Darey	17,134		4	9	6					10			1	5			3	8	2			11	7	
20	FLC R2	(a)	Notts County	W 3–1	2–0	–	Laverick, Thorne 2	10,499	1	4		6									5		10	3	8	2	9	11	11	7	
22	FL D2	(a)	Sheffield United	L 1–2	0–0	20	Thorne	16,167	1	4	9	6									5		10	3	8	2			11	7	
29	FL D2	(h)	Stoke City	L 0–1	0–0	22		8,791	1	4		6									5	11	10	3	8	2			9	7	
Nov 5	FL D2	(a)	Swansea Town	W 3–2	2–1	21	Bertolini 2, Thorne	11,029	1	4		6									5	11		3	8	2	9		10	7	
12	FL D2	(h)	Luton Town	W 1–0	0–0	17	Thorne	14,011	1	4		6									5	11		3	8	2	9		10	7	
16	FLC R3	(h)	Wrexham	L 0–2	0–1	–		4,650		4		6					9			1	5	11		3	8	2			10	7	
19	FL D2	(a)	Lincoln City	L 1–2	1–1	20	Nicholas	4,772	1	4		6									5			3	8	2	10		11	7	9
26	FL D2	(h)	Portsmouth	D 2–2	0–1	19	Own goal, Nicholas	14,370	6	1	4										5		10	3		2	8		11	7	9
Dec 3	FL D2	(a)	Huddersfield Town	W 1–0	0–0	17	Thorne	5,860	6	1	4										5		10	3		2	8		11	7	9
10	FL D2	(h)	Sunderland	L 1–2	0–1	18	Jennings (pen)	13,888	1	4			6	3							5		10			2	8		11	7	9
17	FL D2	(h)	Derby County	W 3–2	1–2	18	Jennings (pen), Tiddy, Nicholas	12,682	1	4			6	3							5		11		8	2	10			7	9
23	FL D2	(a)	Scunthorpe United	D 2–2	0–0	15=	Nicholas 2	9,272	1	4			6	3							5		11		8	2	10			7	9
27	FL D2	(a)	Scunthorpe United	D 1–1	1–0	15	Windross	20,490	1	4			6	3							5				8	2	10		11	7	9
31	FL D2	(a)	Bristol Rovers	W 1–0	1–0	12	Laverick	12,823	1	4			6	3							5		11		8	2	10			7	9
Jan 7	FAC R3	(h)	Derby County	W 3–1	1–0	–	McNeill, Laverick, Windross	18,397	1	4			6	3							5		11		8	2	10			7	9
14	FL D2	(a)	Liverpool	W 3–1	1–0	12	Nicholas, Windross, Jennings (pen)	17,495	1	4			6	3							5		11		8	2	10			7	9
28	FAC R4	(h)	Burnley	D 3–3	1–1	–	Bertolini, McNicol, Windross	28,672	1	4			6	3							5		11		8	2	10			7	9
31	FAC R4 Rep	(a)	Burnley	L 0–2	0–1	–		22,800	1	4			6	3							5		11		8	2	10			7	9
Feb 4	FL D2	(h)	Southampton	L 0–1	0–0	12		20,640	1	4			5	3									11	6	8	2	10			7	9
10	FL D2	(a)	Leeds United	L 2–3	1–1	12	Laverick 2	12,589	1	4			6	3							5		11		8	2	10			7	9
18	FL D2	(a)	Middlesbrough	L 0–1	0–1	14		16,199	1	4			6	3							5		11		8	2	10			7	9
25	FL D2	(h)	Norwich City	D 2–2	2–2	15	Own goal, Laverick	13,130	1	4			6	3							5		11		8	2	10			7	9
Mar 4	FL D2	(a)	Charlton Athletic	L 1–3	0–1	18	McNeill	14,447		4			6	3						1	5		11		8	2	10		9	7	
11	FL D2	(h)	Sheffield United	D 0–0	0–0	17		18,059		4			6	3						1	5		11		8	2	10			7	9
18	FL D2	(h)	Sunderland	L 1–2	1–0	18	Laverick	26,782	1	4			6	3							5		11		8	2	10			7	9
25	FL D2	(h)	Swansea Town	D 0–0	0–0	19		12,903	1	4			6	3							5		11		8	2	10			7	9
31	FL D2	(h)	Plymouth Argyle	W 2–0	0–0	19	Laverick, Nicholas	19,697	1	4				3	6						5		10		7	2	9		11		8
Apr 1	FL D2	(a)	Portsmouth	L 0–4	0–2	19		20,993	1	4				3	6						5		10			2	9		11	8	7
3	FL D2	(a)	Plymouth Argyle	W 2–1	2–1	19	Thorne 2	14,826	1	4			6	3							5				8	2	9		10		7
8	FL D2	(h)	Lincoln City	W 1–0	0–0	18	Laverick	14,905	1	4			6	3							5				8	2	9		11	7	
15	FL D2	(a)	Luton Town	L 1–3	1–2	20	Nicholas	9,104	1	4				3	6			10			5		11		8	2	9			7	
18	FL D2	(a)	Rotherham United	L 2–5	1–2	20	Sitford, Nicholas	7,073	1	4			5	3	6						11	7			8	2	9	10			
22	FL D2	(h)	Huddersfield Town	W 2–1	0–1	18	Nicholas 2	13,002	1	4			6	3							11		5		8	2	9	10	7		
29	FL D2	(a)	Stoke City	W 2–0	2–0	16	Nicholas 2	5,232	1	4			6	3				10	7		5		11		8	2	9				
			League appearances						2	27	42	8	37	22	4	9	3	6	3	15	40	5	31	15	38	42	27	2	27	39	18
			League goals				OG – 2				2	2				3	1				5	1	10		4		13	1	12	3	2

Football League Division 2 1960–61

		P	W	D	L	F	A	W	D	L	F	A	Pts
1.	Ipswich Town	42	15	3	3	55	24	11	4	6	45	31	59
2.	Sheffield United	42	16	2	3	49	22	10	4	7	32	29	58
3.	Liverpool	42	14	5	2	49	21	7	5	9	38	37	52
4.	Norwich City	42	15	3	3	46	20	5	6	10	24	33	49
5.	Middlesbrough	42	13	6	2	44	20	5	6	10	39	54	48
6.	Sunderland	42	12	5	4	47	24	5	8	8	28	36	47
7.	Swansea Town	42	14	4	3	49	26	4	7	10	28	47	47
8.	Southampton	42	12	4	5	57	35	6	4	11	27	46	44
9.	Scunthorpe United	42	9	8	4	39	25	5	7	9	30	39	43
10.	Charlton Athletic	42	12	3	6	60	42	4	8	9	37	49	43
11.	Plymouth Argyle	42	13	4	4	52	32	4	4	13	29	50	42
12.	Derby County	42	9	6	6	46	35	6	4	11	34	45	40
13.	Luton Town	42	13	5	3	48	27	2	4	15	23	52	39
14.	Leeds United	42	7	7	7	41	38	7	3	11	34	45	38
15.	Rotherham United	42	9	7	5	37	24	3	6	12	28	40	37
16.	**ALBION**	42	9	6	6	33	26	5	3	13	28	49	37
17.	Bristol Rovers	42	13	4	4	52	35	2	3	16	21	57	37
18.	Stoke City	42	9	6	6	39	26	3	6	12	12	33	36
19.	Leyton Orient	42	10	5	6	31	29	4	3	14	24	49	36
20.	Huddersfield Town	42	7	5	9	33	33	6	4	11	29	38	35
21.	Portsmouth	42	10	6	5	38	27	1	5	15	26	64	33
22.	Lincoln City	42	5	4	12	30	43	3	4	14	18	52	24

Around this period a 20-year-old Liverpudlian by the name of Jimmy Tarbuck appeared as an inside-forward in Albion's 'A' team. Jimmy was on the staff at Butlin's Ocean Hotel in Saltdean as a 'redcoat' and was later to win fame as a comedian. He did eventually get to play for the Albion first team, on 17 January 1971 in a fund-raising match against Eastbourne United, but missed a penalty.

arrived early to witness the ground staff frantically forking away the puddles.

By kick-off the sun had broken through, but when left-half Brian Miller put the champions in front on 25 minutes it was pouring again. Jack Bertolini equalised with a thunderbolt just before the break, but early in the second period Joe Carolan had the misfortune to head a long throw past Charlie Baker to restore Burnley's lead. After an hour's play Albion right-back Bob McNicol picked up a clearance from 'keeper Adam Blacklaw well inside his own half and set off for the Burnley goal. From fully 35 yards, Bob unleashed a shot which flew past the stranded Blacklaw and into the net for a goal that will remain in the memories of those present for many years. And yet the tremendous roar which greeted that goal was as a whisper compared with what followed in the 68th minute when Dennis Windross drove home a Mike Tiddy cross to put Albion in front. With the big crowd chorusing 'Sussex by the Sea', a lesser team might well have buckled, but Burnley, the more polished side throughout, showed their mettle and four minutes later made it 3–3 through Jimmy Robson amid almost total silence. It was a terrific tussle, but underdogs seldom get a second chance, and at a rain-swept Turf Moor Albion lost the replay 2–0 as Burnley progressed towards a semi-final defeat by the great Spurs side, on their way to the League and Cup double.

The season saw the advent of a new midweek competition, the Football League Cup. It did not prove popular with the fans, and, after a 3–1 win at Notts County in the second round, Albion were soundly beaten 2–0 by Fourth Division Wrexham in front of just 4,650 Goldstone spectators.

In what was, overall, a poor season, Bob McNicol and the consistent Jack Bertolini played in every match, while Adrian Thorne top-scored with fourteen goals in League and Cup with Tony Nicholas and Bobby Laverick on thirteen and twelve respectively. Manager Billy Lane took full responsibility for the unimpressive League showing, and at the end of the campaign surprisingly announced his resignation on 3 May. Lane had been in charge for more than ten years and was the fourth-longest-serving manager in the Football League. Gerald Paling reluctantly accepted his decision and publicly thanked him for his services to the club. After leading Albion on a brief tour of West Germany, Billy left the Goldstone and eventually took the manager's job at Southern League Gravesend & Northfleet in December 1961.

In January the Football League, under great pressure from Jimmy Hill's Professional Footballers' Association, finally agreed to abolish the 60-year-old maximum wage (currently £20 per week) and to introduce some limited freedoms in the retain-and-transfer system to signal the end of 'soccer slavery'. The deal was morally just and averted a strike, but the game would never be quite the same again as the wealthy, big-city clubs began to attract the best players to squeeze out the small-town sides. Albion had to make cuts in staff to meet the new conditions and were forced to scrap the 'A' team in 1962.

Lit up at last

In 1961, Albion finally installed floodlights at the Goldstone Ground. Manager Billy Lane had always been opposed to night-time soccer and Albion were one of the last League clubs to 'light up', but the attraction eventually proved irresistible and the 'Drenchliting' system was installed at a cost of £13,523. The new lights were inaugurated with an attractive friendly match against the Boldklubben Frem of Copenhagen, nine times champions of Denmark, on the evening of Monday, 10 April 1961. Despite atrocious weather, 7,541 spectators turned out to see Albion win an entertaining encounter 3–1. Here, goalkeeper Charlie Baker is on the receiving end of a Danish attack.

SEASON 1961–62

Billy Lane's successor, appointed in June, was George Curtis, the 41-year-old former Arsenal and Southampton inside-forward who had guested briefly for Albion during the war. (By coincidence, his predecessors, Don Welsh and Billy Lane, had also guested for the club.) Curtis had gained coaching experience abroad and with the England youth side, and was brought in from Sunderland where he had coached the Rokerites with some success.

New players introduced during the two pre-season friendlies with Queen's Park Rangers – which replaced the traditional public practice matches – included Bobby Baxter (Darlington) and Dave Smith (Burnley). In the opening League game, at Scunthorpe United, Albion fought back admirably from a 2–0 deficit to lead 3–2, but had to settle for a 3–3 draw. Such goalscoring could not be sustained, however, and although hovering in mid table until the end of November, eight matches without a win before Christmas saw Albion sink deep into relegation trouble.

Curtis introduced the popular new 4–2–4 formation of the day, but the club did not have the players for the job and a lack of cash ruled out the possibility of buying proven replacements.

A Christmas double over Bristol Rovers eased the situation, but only one victory in the first three months of 1962 sent Albion to the bottom of the table. The relegation battle was a close affair involving some ten clubs with only a few matches remaining, but Albion seldom looked capable of avoiding the drop. Fading hopes were briefly raised when maximum points were taken from the first two Easter-holiday fixtures, but, with a very poor goal-average, defeat at Norwich City on Easter Monday confirmed the inevitable.

After four seasons of hard-won Second Division fare, the return to the obscurity of Division Three was a huge blow, but in truth the side was simply not good enough. The new manager attributed the team's failure to a general lack of determination and inadequacies in attack. Centre-forward Joe Caven, signed from Airdrieonians at the end of February to add some thrust up front, failed to register a goal in his nine outings, which just about summed up the depressing situation. For the last game of the season at Derby County, Curtis drafted in four young débutants, three of whom, John Standing, Phil Gilbert and Alistair Miller, mustered only seventeen League appearances for the Albion between them. The fourth was Brian Powney, a

SEASON 1961–62

Date	Comp.	Ven.	Opponents	Result	HT	Pos.	Scorers	Atten.	Baker C	Baxter R	Bertolini J	Brown A	Burtenshaw S	Carolan J	Caven J	Cochrane J	Gilbert P	Goodchild J	Hudson C	Jennings R	Jest S	Laverick R	McNeill I	McNicol R	Miller A	Nicholas A	Powney B	Sitford A	Smith D	Standing J	Tiddy M
Aug 19	FL D2	(a)	Scunthorpe United	D 3–3	0–2	11=	Goodchild 2, Laverick	8,068	1		4		6	3					10		5		11	8		9			2		7
22	FL D2	(h)	Leeds United	L 1–3	1–1	16=	Tiddy	22,744	1		4		6	3					10		5		11	8		9			2		7
26	FL D2	(h)	Swansea Town	D 2–2	2–1	15	Goodchild, Tiddy	16,078	1		4		6	3					10		5		11	8		9			2		7
30	FL D2	(a)	Leeds United	D 1–1	0–1	16	Goodchild	12,642	1		4		6	3					10		5		11	8		9			2		7
Sep 2	FL D2	(h)	Bury	L 0–2	0–2	18		12,522	1		4		6	3					10		5		11	8		9			2		7
5	FL D2	(h)	Stoke City	W 2–1	2–1	11	Laverick, Jennings (pen)	12,738	1		4		6						10		5		11	8	2	9			3		7
9	FL D2	(a)	Charlton Athletic	W 3–2	0–1	10	Laverick 2, Nicholas	10,242	1		4		6						10		5		11	8	2	9			3		7
12	FLC R1	(a)	Bury	L 1–5	1–2	–	Nicholas	7,827	1		4	9	6								5		11	8	2	10			3		7
16	FL D2	(h)	Liverpool	D 0–0	0–0	11		19,366	1		4		6						10		5		11	8	2	9			3		7
18	FL D2	(h)	Stoke City	W 1–0	0–0	4	McNeill	9,135	1		4		6						10		5		11	8	2	9			3		7
23	FL D2	(a)	Rotherham United	L 1–2	0–1	12	Goodchild	8,722	1		4		6						10		5		11	8	2	9			3		7
30	FL D2	(h)	Sunderland	D 1–1	0–1	14	Nicholas	17,070	1		4		6						10		5		11	8	2	9			3		7
Oct 7	FL D2	(a)	Southampton	L 1–6	1–3	16	Laverick	16,314	1		4		6	3					10		5		11	8	2	9					7
14	FL D2	(h)	Luton Town	W 2–1	0–1	13	Goodchild, Laverick	14,186	1		4		6	3					10		5		11	8	2	9					7
21	FL D2	(a)	Newcastle United	L 0–5	0–2	16		24,408	1		4	9	6	3					10		5		11	8	2						7
28	FL D2	(h)	Middlesbrough	W 2–0	0–0	13	Goodchild 2	13,387	1		4	9	6						10		5		11	8	2			3			7
Nov 4	FL D2	(a)	Walsall	D 2–2	1–0	13	Brown, Laverick	9,963	1		4	9	6						10		5		11	8	2			3			7
11	FL D2	(h)	Huddersfield Town	D 2–2	1–1	12	Goodchild, Brown	10,742	1		4	9	6						10		5		11	8	2			3			7
18	FL D2	(a)	Leyton Orient	L 1–4	0–4	15	Nicholas	10,295	1		4	9	6						10		5		11		2	8		3			7
25	FL D2	(h)	Preston North End	D 0–0	0–0	15		13,016	1	6	4	9	5						10				11		2	8		3			7
Dec 2	FL D2	(a)	Plymouth Argyle	L 0–5	0–2	17		10,414	1	6	4		5						10				11	8	2	9		3			7
9	FL D2	(a)	Derby County	L 1–2	1–1	17	Nicholas	10,782	1		4	9	6						10		5	2	11	8		7		3			
16	FL D2	(h)	Scunthorpe United	L 0–3	0–3	18		9,377	1		4		6						10		5	2	11	8		9		3			7
23	FL D2	(a)	Swansea Town	L 0–3	0–2	20		7,937	1	11	4		6						10		5			8		9		3	2		7
26	FL D2	(a)	Bristol Rovers	W 1–0	0–1	17	Nicholas	13,105	1	10	4		6								11	5		8		9		3	2		7
30	FL D2	(h)	Bristol Rovers	W 1–0	1–0	16	Own goal	8,732	1	3	4		6						10		5		11	8		9		2			7
Jan 6	FAC R3	(h)	Blackburn Rovers	L 0–3	0–1	–		20,405	1	3	4		6						10		5		11	8		9		2			7
13	FL D2	(a)	Bury	L 1–2	1–1	17	Nicholas	6,129	1	3	4		6								5		11	8	2	10		9			7
Feb 3	FL D2	(a)	Liverpool	L 1–3	1–0	18	Sitford	36,414	1	3	4		6								11		5		8	2	10		9			7
10	FL D2	(h)	Rotherham United	L 0–3	0–1	19		10,369	1	3	4		6								11		5		8	2	10		9			7
17	FL D2	(a)	Sunderland	D 0–0	0–0	17		22,575	1	3	4		6								11		5		8	2	10		9			7
24	FL D2	(h)	Southampton	D 0–0	0–0	18		11,952	1	3	4		6								11		5		8	2	10		9			7
Mar 3	FL D2	(a)	Luton Town	L 1–2	0–0	20	Bertolini	7,005	1	3	4		6		9				11			5			2		10	8				7
10	FL D2	(h)	Newcastle United	L 0–4	0–2	22		12,397	1	3	4		6		9	8			11		5				2		10					7
16	FL D2	(a)	Middlesbrough	L 0–4	0–1	22		17,465	1	3	4		6		9	8			11		5				2		10					7
24	FL D2	(h)	Walsall	W 3–2	3–2	22	Laverick 2, Jennings	9,912	1	3	4		6	2	9				8		5		11	10			7					7
31	FL D2	(a)	Huddersfield Town	L 0–2	0–0	22		8,187	1	3	4		6	2	9						5		11	10			8					7
Apr 7	FL D2	(h)	Leyton Orient	L 0–1	0–1	22		12,927	1	3	4		6	2	9						5		11	10			8					7
10	FL D2	(h)	Charlton Athletic	D 2–2	1–2	22	Nicholas, Jennings	12,616	1	3	4		6		9						5		11	10			8			2		7
14	FL D2	(a)	Preston North End	L 1–3	1–1	22	Nicholas	9,160	1	3	4		6		9				8		5		11	10	2		7					7
20	FL D2	(a)	Norwich City	W 2–1	2–1	22	Jennings, Goodchild	13,395	1	3	4		6						8		5		11	10	2		7	9				
21	FL D2	(h)	Plymouth Argyle	W 3–2	0–1	21	Nicholas, Tiddy, Laverick	13,016	1	3	4		6								5		11	10	2		8	9				7
23	FL D2	(a)	Norwich City	L 0–3	0–0	22		16,162	1	3	4		6								5		11	10	2		8	9				7
28	FL D2	(a)	Derby County	L 0–2	0–1	22		6,739	1	3	8		6		9		10				5					11	7	1		4	2	
			League appearances						41	22	42	7	42	11	9	2	1	34	1	40	2	32	36	27	1	38	1	20	15	1	37
			League goals	OG – 1							1	2							10		4		10	1		9		1			3

Football League Division 2 1961–62

		P	W	D	L	F	A	W	D	L	F	A	Pts
1.	Liverpool	42	18	3	0	68	19	9	5	7	31	24	62
2.	Leyton Orient	42	11	5	5	34	17	11	5	5	35	23	54
3.	Sunderland	42	17	3	1	60	16	5	6	10	25	34	53
4.	Scunthorpe United	42	14	4	3	52	26	7	3	11	34	45	49
5.	Plymouth Argyle	42	12	4	5	45	30	7	4	10	30	45	46
6.	Southampton	42	13	3	5	53	28	5	6	10	24	34	45
7.	Huddersfield Town	42	11	5	5	39	22	5	7	9	28	37	44
8.	Stoke City	42	13	4	4	34	17	4	4	13	21	40	42
9.	Rotherham United	42	9	6	6	36	30	7	3	11	34	46	41
10.	Preston North End	42	11	4	6	34	23	4	6	11	21	34	40
11.	Newcastle United	42	10	5	6	40	27	5	4	12	24	31	39
12.	Middlesbrough	42	11	3	7	45	29	5	4	12	31	43	39
13.	Luton Town	42	12	1	8	44	37	5	4	12	25	34	39
14.	Walsall	42	11	7	3	42	23	3	4	14	28	52	39
15.	Charlton Athletic	42	10	5	6	38	30	5	4	12	31	45	39
16.	Derby County	42	10	7	4	42	27	4	4	13	26	48	39
17.	Norwich City	42	10	6	5	36	28	4	5	12	25	42	39
18.	Bury	42	9	4	8	32	36	8	1	12	20	40	39
19.	Leeds United	42	9	6	6	24	19	3	6	12	26	42	36
20.	Swansea Town	42	10	5	6	38	30	2	7	12	23	53	36
21.	Bristol Rovers	42	11	3	7	36	31	2	4	15	17	50	33
22.	**ALBION**	42	7	7	7	24	32	3	4	14	18	54	31

seventeen-year-old goalkeeper who went on to add 385 first-team matches to this initial outing.

Albion were thrashed at the first hurdle in both cup competitions. After a 5–1 defeat at Second Division Bury in the League Cup, they went down 3–0 at the Goldstone in the F.A. Cup to First Division Blackburn Rovers who included former England skipper Ronnie Clayton and current England outside-right Bryan Douglas. The club did manage to win a trophy however, beating Hastings United 3–1 over two legs for the Sussex Professional Cup (the clubs had shared the trophy in 1960–61 after a drawn tie). Hastings finished at the bottom of the First Division of the Southern League and the meeting of two depressed sides was reflected in the play.

There were few memorable moments in such a wretched campaign, but Jack Bertolini and Steve Burtenshaw performed well at half-back, both appearing in every League match. In a lack-lustre forward line, Johnny Goodchild, Bobby Laverick and Tony Nicholas scored ten goals apiece in all League and Cup games. At the end of the season, twelve of the professional staff were not retained, including most of the club's experienced players. Inevitably the attendances fell, but the average of 13,206 in a relegation season showed the potential at the Goldstone. However, the experiment of fielding the reserves in the Football Combination's Midweek Section was a failure from both a playing and a financial viewpoint: the side finished sixteenth of eighteen clubs and the highest gate was just 977.

Trainer Joe Wilson received his second testimonial with the club when, despite a foul November evening, 12,600 spectators turned out to see an International All-Star XI, made up of London-based players, beat an Albion XI 5–0.

The bad results prompted another struggle for control of the boardroom. The 'Season Ticket Holders and Patrons Association', commonly known as the 'Pep Group', was a league of councillors and businessmen campaigning in December and the New Year 'to keep top-class football at the Goldstone'.

Offering guarantees of up to £40,000, the group demanded the release of the 20,000 unsold shares, representation on the board, and the acquisition of a proven goalscorer. The move was resisted by the directorate, but the Pep Group would be back. The club itself launched a lottery in March 1962, the 'Lucky Shot' with a top weekly prize of £10, to bring in much-needed funds, and followed that with the 'Goldstone Development Association' lottery. It was hoped that the two would bring in £14,000 annually.

On 31 January the England youth team met the Netherlands at the Goldstone. The side was: Jim Montgomery (Sunderland); Colin Huxford (Chelsea) and Eric Brookes (Barnsley); Martin Peters (West Ham United), John Sleevwenhoek (Aston Villa) and Ron Harris (Chelsea); Alan Suddick (Newcastle United), Alan Baker (Aston Villa), George Jones (Bury), John Byrom (Blackburn Rovers) and Neil Young (Manchester City). Three-nil down after 35 minutes, the England lads fought back to win 4–3 with a goal by Jones and a hat-trick from Young.

Albion line-up v. Leeds United, Football League Division Two, 22 August 1961
Standing left to right: Jack Bertolini, Dave Smith, Roy Jennings (captain), Charlie Baker, Joe Carolan, Steve Burtenshaw.
Seated left to right: Mike Tiddy, Ian McNeill, Tony Nicholas, Johnny Goodchild, Bobby Laverick.

SEASON 1962–63

Albion, the last champions of Division Three (South), now found themselves in a very different, nationwide Third Division, with the prospect of first-ever encounters with Carlisle United and Halifax Town. Phrases such as 'soccer wilderness' became the vogue, but after the disasters of last season all at the Goldstone were hopeful of a swift return to Division Two. With the departure of six seasoned professionals, George Curtis put his faith in a young side. The newcomers included 19-year-old John Dillon from Sunderland; Bobby Walker, 19, from Gateshead; David James, 19, and Ken Franks, 18, both from Blantyre Victoria; Jim Cooper, 22, from Airdrieonians; and the relatively experienced Peter Donnelly, 23, from Swansea Town.

An opening draw at Queen's Park Rangers, followed by two home wins, fuelled expectations of a promotion push and the initial attendances hovered around the 15,000 mark, but hopes were soon dashed as Albion embarked on a run of eleven League games without a victory and within a matter of weeks found themselves bottom with gates below 7,000. In the absence of experienced campaigners, an assortment of youngsters were thrust into the side and an emphasis on defence brought little tangible success. At this point Curtis made his best move during his time with the club by paying £9,000 for Tottenham Hotspur's reserve inside-forward Jimmy Collins who went on to become a great favourite for almost five years. The poor run

---

George Curtis believed in encouraging youth and flying the Albion flag around the county. On 20 November the full Albion side beat the Nevill School under-16s 13–2 a week after defeating Lancing College 8–0.

---

appeared to be ending in Collins's second game on 6 October when Albion gained a 2–0 lead over Reading after only five minutes, but when the Biscuitmen hit back to send Albion crashing to a 4–2 defeat the crowd gave vent to its frustration with roars of 'Resign!' aimed at the directors' box.

The Pep Group was prompted to raise its head again amid the crisis, calling upon the Supporters' Club to stop giving money to the parent club and asking for a general boycott of matches. The pressure on the board finally told in November when chairman Gerald Paling and vice-chairman Cyril Clarke resigned, to be replaced by Eric Courtney-King, president of the Supporters' Club, as chairman, and Tom Whiting as vice-chairman. Local builder Harold Paris, greyhound stadium chairman Frederick Arnold, business consultant Norman Dupont and the Pep Group's Len Stringer were then recruited to the new board which immediately made funds available for signings. Paris also launched the 'Albion Fund' for the purchase of new players, and at last everyone concerned united behind the common struggle as supporters raised £10,000 within two weeks.

Curtis used the new money to bring in Bill Cassidy, a hard-tackling wing-half from Rotherham United; Allan Jackson, an inside-forward from Bury; and winger George Waites from Leyton Orient. Things temporarily perked up as a more attacking format was adopted, and a fine 5–1 victory at Bradford (P.A.) was secured. Another excellent away win came at Bristol City on Boxing Day.

The New Year saw Britain in the grip of another ice age. After two Goldstone matches had been postponed – an exceptionally rare event – the club spent £1,000 on clearing the ground to enable the match with Crystal Palace to take place.

SEASON 1962–63

Date	Comp.	Ven.	Opponents	Result	HT	Pos.	Scorers	Atten.
Aug 18	FL D3	(a)	Queen's Park R.	D	2–2	2–1	8=	Cochrane 2	11,506
21	FL D3	(h)	Barnsley	W	2–0	0–0	3=	Goodchild, Donnelly	14,846
25	FL D3	(h)	Hull City	W	2–1	1–0	3	Jennings (pen), Dillon	15,573
28	FL D3	(a)	Barnsley	L	0–2	0–2	9		7,345
Sep 1	FL D3	(a)	Crystal Palace	D	2–2	1–0	9	Goodchild 2	18,464
4	FL D3	(h)	Swindon Town	D	1–1	1–1	8	Baxter	13,951
8	FL D3	(h)	Wrexham	L	1–3	0–3	13	Donnelly	11,896
11	FL D3	(a)	Swindon Town	L	1–5	0–3	16	Jennings (pen)	11,420
15	FL D3	(a)	Halifax Town	L	1–2	0–1	19	Jennings	3,667
18	FL D3	(a)	Peterborough Utd	L	0–3	0–2	20		10,784
22	FL D3	(h)	Bristol Rovers	D	1–1	1–0	21	Cochrane	7,943
25	FLC R2	(h)	Portsmouth	L	1–5	0–2	–	Bailey	5,550
29	FL D3	(a)	Watford	L	0–2	0–2	23		11,929
Oct 2	FL D3	(a)	Carlisle United	L	0–1	0–0	24		7,865
6	FL D3	(h)	Reading	L	2–4	2–2	24	Bailey, Goodchild	7,494
9	FL D3	(h)	Carlisle United	W	1–0	1–0	22	Hannam	6,556
13	FL D3	(a)	Port Vale	W	2–1	1–0	22	Donnelly, Walker	7,503
15	FL D3	(a)	Peterborough Utd	L	1–3	0–3	22	Collins	10,925
20	FL D3	(h)	Shrewsbury Town	D	1–1	1–0	22	Goodchild	8,280
27	FL D3	(a)	Millwall	D	2–2	1–0	22	Goodchild, Donnelly	13,205
Nov 3	FAC R1	(a)	Southend United	L	1–2	0–2	–	Cooper	8,705
10	FL D3	(a)	Colchester United	L	1–4	1–2	22	Hannam	3,835
17	FL D3	(h)	Notts County	L	1–3	1–2	22	Cooper	5,884
Dec 1	FL D3	(h)	Coventry City	D	2–2	1–0	22	Jennings 2 (1 pen)	9,296
8	FL D3	(a)	Bradford (P.A.)	W	5–1	2–1	20	Collins, Dillon 2, Jackson, Waites	4,765
15	FL D3	(h)	Queen's Park R.	D	2–2	2–2	21	Donnelly 2	11,282
22	FL D3	(a)	Hull City	L	1–2	1–2	21	Donnelly	8,050
26	FL D3	(a)	Bristol City	W	2–1	2–0	21	Goodchild, Donnelly	9,092
Jan 12	FL D3	(h)	Crystal Palace	L	1–2	1–1	21	Donnelly	11,807
26	FL D3	(h)	Southend United	D	0–0	0–0	20		11,633
Feb 2	FL D3	(h)	Halifax Town	L	0–1	0–1	20		6,416
9	FL D3	(a)	Bristol Rovers	L	1–4	0–1	20	Jackson	7,816
23	FL D3	(a)	Reading	W	5–4	1–2	18	Jackson 2, Jennings 2, Burtenshaw	5,934
Mar 2	FL D3	(a)	Port Vale	W	3–1	1–1	16	Bertolini 2, Jackson	9,911
9	FL D3	(a)	Shrewsbury Town	L	1–2	1–0	17	Baxter	3,656
16	FL D3	(h)	Millwall	L	0–2	0–0	20		10,818
19	FL D3	(h)	Bristol City	W	1–0	1–0	18	Donnelly	5,391
23	FL D3	(a)	Southend United	D	1–1	1–1	18	Baxter	9,082
30	FL D3	(h)	Colchester United	W	3–0	2–0	16	Baxter, Collins, Cooper	6,153
Apr 6	FL D3	(a)	Notts County	W	1–0	0–0	17	Collins	7,001
12	FL D3	(h)	Northampton T.	L	0–5	0–1	19		15,026
13	FL D3	(h)	Bournem'th & B.A.	L	0–1	0–0	21		10,061
16	FL D3	(a)	Northampton T.	L	0–3	0–1	22		17,520
20	FL D3	(a)	Coventry City	D	1–1	0–0	21	Donnelly	14,966
27	FL D3	(h)	Bradford (P.A.)	W	3–1	1–1	21	Gilbert 2, Webber	8,245
May 4	FL D3	(h)	Watford	L	1–4	1–2	22	Gilbert	9,392
8	FL D3	(a)	Bournem'th & B.A.	L	0–1	0–1	22		6,143
18	FL D3	(a)	Wrexham	D	0–0	0–0	22		5,346

Players (left→right): Bailey C, Baker C, Baxter B, Bertolini J, Burtenshaw S, Cassidy W, Caven J, Cochrane J, Collins J, Cooper J, Dillon J, Donnelly P, Franks K, Gall N, Gilbert P, Goodchild J, Hannam D, Jackson A, James D, Jennings R, Jest S, McGonigal B, Powney B, Sanders A, Standing J, Upton R, Waites G, Walker R, Webber K

League appearances	4	13	38	46	36	25	1	12	34	20	21	45	1	5	4	31	5	15	5	41	10	25	8	17	9	3	15	12	5
League goals	1		4	2	1			3	4	2	3	11			3	7	2	5		7							1	1	1

Football League Division 3 1962–63

		P	W	D	L	F	A	W	D	L	F	A	Pts
1.	Northampton Town	46	16	6	1	64	19	10	4	9	45	41	62
2.	Swindon Town	46	18	2	3	60	22	4	12	7	27	34	58
3.	Port Vale	46	16	4	3	47	25	7	4	12	25	33	54
4.	Coventry City	46	14	6	3	54	28	4	11	8	29	41	53
5.	Bournemouth & B.A.	46	11	12	0	39	16	7	4	12	24	30	52
6.	Peterborough United	46	11	5	7	48	33	9	6	8	45	42	51
7.	Notts County	46	15	3	5	46	29	4	10	9	27	45	51
8.	Southend United	46	11	7	5	38	24	8	5	10	37	53	50
9.	Wrexham	46	14	4	5	54	27	6	3	14	30	56	49
10.	Hull City	46	12	6	5	40	22	7	4	12	34	47	48
11.	Crystal Palace	46	10	7	6	38	22	7	6	10	30	36	47
12.	Colchester United	46	11	6	6	41	35	7	5	11	32	58	47
13.	Queen's Park R.	46	9	6	8	44	36	8	5	10	41	40	45
14.	Bristol City	46	10	9	4	54	38	6	4	13	46	54	45
15.	Shrewsbury Town	46	13	4	6	57	41	3	8	12	26	40	44
16.	Millwall	46	11	6	6	50	32	4	7	12	32	55	43
17.	Watford	46	12	3	8	55	40	5	5	13	27	45	42
18.	Barnsley	46	12	6	5	39	28	3	5	15	24	46	41
19.	Bristol Rovers	46	11	8	4	45	29	4	3	16	25	59	41
20.	Reading	46	13	4	6	51	30	3	4	16	23	48	40
21.	Bradford (P.A.)	46	10	9	4	43	36	4	3	16	36	61	40
22.	**ALBION**	46	7	6	10	28	38	6	12	9	30	46	36
23.	Carlisle United	46	12	4	7	41	37	1	5	17	20	52	35
24.	Halifax Town	46	8	3	12	41	51	1	9	13	23	55	30

The ground staff performed wonders and it was one of only four matches to survive, but Palace – with a natty line in yellow gloves – won 2–1. A point surrendered to Southend United in the next home match, when all the other Third Division fixtures were postponed, put Albion in deeper trouble. Now fourth from bottom, Albion were not winning and the other clubs were accumulating games in hand. When fellow strugglers Halifax

Town won 1–0 at the Goldstone on 2 February (one of only four League games played), the inevitable finally happened: four days later manager George Curtis left the club 'by mutual agreement' with sixteen months of his three-year contract still to run. Trainer Joe Wilson took over as caretaker until a replacement could be appointed and put the emphasis back on attack. A 5–4 victory at Reading and four more wins before Easter left Albion seventeenth but having played four games more than most of their rivals.

On 11 April, Albion's search for a new manager ended when Archie Macaulay, the 48-year-old former Scottish international wing-half, was appointed to the post. Macaulay had guided Third Division Norwich City to the F.A. Cup semi-finals in 1959, and had just resigned from the hot-seat at First Division West Bromwich Albion for personal reasons. However, his arrival in Hove was heralded by the eventual champions, Northampton Town, going 'nap' at the Goldstone, the first part of a goal-less and point-less three-match Easter programme for the club. Now four or five games ahead of their rivals, Albion were slowly but surely overtaken, and by the time Macaulay got stuck into his post in mid April it was too late to improve the situation. The unbelievable was confirmed by a 1–0 defeat at Dean Court, Bournemouth, on 8 May: Albion had fallen straight

Albion beat the weather — but not Palace

The coldest winter in over 200 years struck on Boxing Day 1962 and retained its icy grip for two months. The temperature in Brighton remained below freezing for 27 days, and a Pools Panel was formed because of the number of postponements. Albion, however, defeated the adverse conditions with the aid of a council tar-melting machine – seen here under the supervision of director Harold Paris – which unfortunately turned the pitch into a quagmire. The match with Crystal Palace on 12 January went ahead, but Albion were not rewarded for their initiative and went down to a 2–1 defeat.

Albion 1962–63

Back row left to right: Bobby Walker, Norman Gall, Syd Jest, Charlie Baker, David James, Jack Bertolini, Nobby Upton.
Middle row left to right: Bert McGonigal, Joe Caven, Johnny Cochrane, Phil Gilbert, Roy Jennings (captain), Craig Bailey, Steve Burtenshaw, Ken Franks, Brian Powney.
Front row left to right: Dave Hannam, Bobby Baxter, John Dillon, John Standing, Barry Fitch, Johnny Goodchild, Terry Warwick, Syd Cousins.

through the Third Division and found themselves 'down amongst the dead men'.

Cup performances were equally dismal, the team bowing out of both competitions without a win for the second season running. A weakened Portsmouth side won 5–1 at the Goldstone in the League Cup, and Southend United beat Albion 2–1 at Roots Hall in the F.A. Cup.

Popular opinion was that the club had failed to heed the lessons of last term, and that the management had been complacent in not opting for experience until the campaign was half over. Curtis's youth policy, though admirable in concept, was a failure, and the money spent lavishly in November came too late. No fewer than seventeen players made their Albion débuts in the course of the season and a total of 29 were employed. The dependable Jack Bertolini was ever-present for the fourth successive season while Peter Donnelly top-scored with eleven goals. The most encouraging aspect of another disastrous campaign was the form of the reserve team, whose whole-hearted displays saw them into fourth place in the Football Combination's Midweek Section.

SEASON 1963–64

As Albion contemplated trips to Fourth Division outposts such as Workington, Barrow, Hartlepool and Darlington, Archie Macaulay insisted on peak fitness and the pre-season training was the hardest for some years. He also introduced a new wage structure which incorporated payment for appearances and a bonus scheme according to the team's League position. The target was promotion, and, although basic salaries had been cut, Macaulay reckoned that if the team was in the top four the players could earn as much as £40 per week.

Albion were notoriously bad starters around this period; indeed, they had failed to win their opening match in the previous five seasons. This year was no exception, and when Workington left the Goldstone with two points in the bag there was much barracking and criticism. After a second home defeat at the hands of Stockport County, Albion had only one point from four games and were in 90th place in the Football League. Macaulay refused to panic and it was October before he made his first signing, Ernie Healer on a free transfer from Berwick Rangers. Hopes were pinned on Jimmy Collins as the midfield general who would lead the club back to respectability. He responded magnificently and played in every match.

After the poor start, only two of the following fourteen games ended in defeat and luckless Lincoln City took the full force of the improvement, losing 5–1 at Hove. By the end of a ten-match October, Albion had climbed to fourth place and were in contention, but a hard-fought 2–0 home win over Darlington in an ill-tempered encounter had a profound effect on the remainder of the campaign: Albion 'keeper Bert McGonigal and the Quakers' Jim Lawton were stretchered off after a sickening collision; McGonigal was out for virtually the rest of the season and the no.1 jersey was handed to young Brian Powney.

Dave Turner, a £6,000 signing from Newcastle United, made his first appearance in the Darlington match. Macaulay made two more important signings in January when he brought in Wally Gould from York City and Jack Smith from Swindon Town; the pair made their entrance in the 1–1 draw at Stockport County, and all three new boys went on to give excellent service to the Albion with over 600 appearances between them. Another loyal servant won a regular place this season, young Norman Gall taking over the centre-half role from Roy Jennings with the popular skipper moving to left-back where he had begun his career.

Despite some impressive away performances late in the season, Albion could not maintain the pressure on the leading clubs and finished in a disappointing eighth place, eight points adrift of a promotion spot and ten behind champions Gillingham.

The cup tournaments were once again undistinguished. After winning 2–1 at Torquay United, Albion were unfortunate not to beat Second Division Northampton Town in a League Cup second-round fixture at the Goldstone, and narrowly lost the replay 3–2 to a penalty conceded three minutes from time. In

Albion 1963–64
Back row left to right: Bert McGonigal, Jimmy Collins, Norman Gall, Nobby Upton, George Waites, Barry Fitch, Syd Cousins, Brian Powney.
Middle row left to right: Allan Jackson, Bill Cassidy, Syd Jest, Phil Gilbert, Roy Jennings (captain), Peter Donnelly, Allan Sanders, Steve Burtenshaw.
Front row left to right: Johnny Goodchild, Jim Cooper, Bobby Baxter, Keith Webber, Jack Bertolini, David Kydd.

> The popular match-day jackpot lottery started this season. The tickets cost 6d. (2·5p) and the prize money was 50 per cent of the pool, the club taking the other half. The jackpot continued until 1987 when it became a victim of falling gates.

SEASON 1963–64

Date	Comp.	Ven.	Opponents	Result	HT	Pos.	Scorers	Atten.	Baxter R	Bertolini J	Burtenshaw S	Cassidy W	Collins J	Cooper J	Donnelly P	Fitch B	Gall N	Gilbert P	Goodchild J	Gould W	Healer E	Jackson A	Jennings R	Knight P	McGonigal B	Powney B	Sanders A	Smith J	Turner D	Upton R	Waites G	Webber K
Aug 24	FL D4	(h)	Workington	L 1–2	0–2	18=	Cooper	9,617		4	3	6	10	7	9			8	11				5		1		2					
28	FL D4	(a)	Rochdale	D 1–1	0–0	19	Cooper	5,666	6	2			10	7	9		5		11				3		1					4		8
31	FL D4	(a)	Newport County	L 0–2	0–1	22		6,222	6	2			10		11		5		7			8	3		1					4		9
Sep 4	FLC R1	(a)	Torquay United	W 2–1	2–0	–	Cooper, Goodchild	4,242	6	2			8	7	9		5		11			10	3		1					4		
7	FL D4	(h)	Stockport County	L 1–2	0–2	22	Collins (pen)	6,582	6	2			8	7	9		5		11			10	3		1					4		
10	FL D4	(h)	Rochdale	W 3–1	2–0	19=	Goodchild 2, Collins	6,910	6	2		10	8		9		5		11				3			1				4	7	
14	FL D4	(a)	Bradford (P.A.)	L 1–2	1–1	20	Donnelly	4,974	6			10	8		9		5		11				3			1	2			4	7	
18	FL D4	(a)	Oxford United	W 3–1	0–0	18	Baxter 2, Goodchild	7,954	8		6		9		11	3	5		7			10	2			1				4		
21	FL D4	(h)	Chesterfield	D 1–1	0–0	20	Goodchild	7,880	10		6		8				5		11				3			1	2			4	7	9
25	FLC R2	(h)	Northampton T.	D 1–1	0–1	–	Baxter	5,504	11		4	6	8		10		5						3			1	2				7	9
28	FL D4	(a)	Doncaster Rovers	D 1–1	1–0	19	Donnelly	5,085	11		4	6	8		10		5						3		1		2				7	9
Oct 1	FL D4	(h)	Oxford United	W 2–1	0–0	14	Webber 2	4,755	11		4	6	8				5		10				3		1		2				7	9
5	FL D4	(a)	Hartlepools United	D 2–2	2–0	13=	Goodchild, Collins	3,123	11		4	6	8				5		10				3		1		2				7	9
7	FL D4	(a)	York City	W 3–2	2–2	10	Webber 3	4,575		4	6		8	11			5		10				3		1		2				7	9
12	FL D4	(h)	Southport	W 1–0	1–0	8	Webber	10,051		4	6		8	11			5		10				3		1		2				7	9
14	FLC R2 Rep	(a)	Northampton T.	L 2–3	1–1	–	Webber, Bertolini	5,569	10	4		6	8	7			5		11				3		1		2					9
17	FL D4	(h)	York City	W 3–0	2–0	5	Goodchild 2 (1 pen), Cooper	9,426		4	6	10	8	7			5		11				3		1		2					9
19	FL D4	(a)	Gillingham	L 0–1	0–0	9		13,351		4	6	10	8	7			5		11				3		1		2					9
23	FL D4	(a)	Chester	D 0–0	0–0	8		8,398		4	6	10	8	7			5		11				3		1		2					9
26	FL D4	(h)	Lincoln City	W 5–1	0–0	5	Cassidy, Webber, Collins, Goodchild 2 (2 pens)	9,928		4	6	10	8	7			5		11				3		1		2					9
29	FL D4	(h)	Chester	D 0–0	0–0	4		11,866		4	6	10	8	7			5		11				3		1		2					9
Nov 2	FL D4	(a)	Bradford City	L 1–3	1–2	5	Bertolini	6,237		4	6	10	8	7					11				3		1		2			5		9
9	FL D4	(h)	Aldershot	W 3–1	2–1	5	Webber, Collins 2	10,092		4	6	10	8	7			5		11				3		1		2					9
16	FAC R1	(h)	Colchester United	L 0–1	0–0	–		13,848		4	6	10	8	7			5		11				3		1		2					9
23	FL D4	(h)	Torquay United	W 3–0	1–0	4	Webber, Bertolini 2	11,108		4	6	10	8	7			5		11				3		1		2					9
30	FL D4	(a)	Halifax Town	D 2–2	1–1	6	Webber 2	2,639		4	6	10	8	7			5		11				3		1		2					9
Dec 7	FL D4	(h)	Darlington	W 2–0	2–0	4	Cooper, Collins	9,394		4		10	8	7			5		11				3		1		2		6			9
14	FL D4	(a)	Workington	L 0–1	0–0	5		3,609	11		4		8				5		7		10		3			1	2		6			9
21	FL D4	(h)	Newport County	L 1–2	0–1	6	Collins (pen)	7,552		4			8	7			5		11		10		3			1	2		6			9
26	FL D4	(h)	Exeter City	L 1–2	1–0	7	Healer	10,250		4			8	7			5		11		10		3			1	2		6			9
28	FL D4	(a)	Exeter City	D 0–0	0–0	6		9,875		4	5		8	7					11			10	3			1	2		6			9
Jan 11	FL D4	(a)	Stockport County	D 1–1	1–0	8	Bertolini	3,478		4	5		8	11					10	7			3			1	2	9	6			
18	FL D4	(h)	Bradford (P.A.)	L 0–1	0–0	9		9,501		4	5		8						10	11			3	7		1	2	9	6			
25	FL D4	(h)	Tranmere Rovers	D 1–1	0–0	8	Cassidy	8,327		4		10	8				3			11				7		1	2		6	5		9
Feb 1	FL D4	(a)	Chesterfield	L 0–1	0–0	10		3,385		4	6	10	8				3		11	7						1	2	9		5		
8	FL D4	(h)	Doncaster Rovers	W 4–0	3–0	10	Smith, Goodchild 2, Cassidy	7,519			4	10	8				3		11	7						1	2	9	6	5		
15	FL D4	(h)	Hartlepools United	W 4–1	2–0	10	Cassidy 2, Turner, Smith	8,746			4	10	8				3		11	7						1	2	9	6	5		
22	FL D4	(a)	Southport	D 3–3	1–2	10	Goodchild 2, Collins	1,974		9	4	10	8				3		11	7						1	2		6	5		
24	FL D4	(a)	Carlisle United	W 1–0	1–0	8	Collins	8,500		9	4	10	8	7			3		11							1	2		6	5		
29	FL D4	(h)	Gillingham	W 2–1	0–0	7	Collins, Smith	15,349			4	10	8				3		11	7						1	2	9	6	5		
Mar 7	FL D4	(a)	Lincoln City	W 2–0	1–0	7	Gould, Smith	5,439			4	10	8				3		11	7						1	2	9	6	5		
14	FL D4	(h)	Bradford City	L 1–2	0–2	7	Collins	9,357			4	10	8				3		11	7						1	2	9	6	5		
21	FL D4	(a)	Aldershot	L 0–1	0–0	7		5,909		4			8				3		11	7						1	2	9	6	5		10
27	FL D4	(h)	Barrow	W 2–0	0–0	7	Smith, Webber	11,628		4			8				3		11	7						1	2	9	6	5		10
30	FL D4	(a)	Barrow	D 1–1	0–0	8	Webber	2,724		4			8	7			3			11		10				1	2		6	5		9
Apr 3	FL D4	(a)	Torquay United	L 0–3	0–2	8		4,752		4			8				3		11	7		10				1	2		6	5		9
11	FL D4	(h)	Halifax Town	W 3–0	1–0	8	Smith, Gould, Turner	7,165			4	10	8				3			7						1	2	9	6	5		11
17	FL D4	(a)	Tranmere Rovers	W 2–1	1–1	8	Gould, Own goal	6,747			4	10	8				3		11	7						1	2	9	6	5		
20	FL D4	(a)	Darlington	W 2–1	2–0	6	Cassidy, Goodchild	2,526			4	10	8				3		11	7					1		2	9	6	5		
25	FL D4	(h)	Carlisle United	L 1–3	0–3	7	Burtenshaw	8,843			4	10	8				3		11	7					1		2		6	5		9
							League appearances		11	30	33	29	46	21	8	1	41	1	42	18	3	6	29	2	21	25	41	13	23	25	8	29
							League goals	OG – 1	2	4	1	6	12	4	2				14	3	1							6	2			13

Football League Division 4 1963–64

		P	W	D	L	F	A	W	D	L	F	A	Pts
1.	Gillingham	46	16	7	0	37	10	7	7	9	22	20	60
2.	Carlisle United	46	17	3	3	70	20	8	7	8	43	38	60
3.	Workington	46	15	6	2	46	19	9	5	9	30	33	59
4.	Exeter City	46	12	9	2	39	14	8	9	6	23	23	58
5.	Bradford City	46	15	3	5	45	24	10	3	10	31	38	56
6.	Torquay United	46	16	6	1	60	20	4	5	14	20	34	51
7.	Tranmere Rovers	46	12	4	7	46	30	8	7	8	39	43	51
8.	**ALBION**	46	13	3	7	45	22	6	9	8	26	30	50
9.	Aldershot	46	15	3	5	58	28	4	7	12	25	50	48
10.	Halifax Town	46	14	4	5	47	28	3	10	10	30	49	48
11.	Lincoln City	46	15	2	6	49	31	4	7	12	18	44	47
12.	Chester	46	17	3	3	47	18	2	5	16	18	42	46
13.	Bradford (P.A.)	46	13	5	5	50	34	5	4	14	25	47	45
14.	Doncaster Rovers	46	11	8	4	46	23	4	4	15	24	52	42
15.	Newport County	46	12	3	8	35	24	5	5	13	29	49	42
16.	Chesterfield	46	8	9	6	29	27	7	3	13	28	44	42
17.	Stockport County	46	12	7	4	32	19	3	5	15	18	49	42
18.	Oxford United	46	10	7	6	37	27	4	6	13	22	36	41
19.	Darlington	46	8	9	6	40	37	6	3	14	26	56	40
20.	Rochdale	46	9	8	6	36	24	3	7	13	20	35	39
21.	Southport	46	12	6	5	42	29	3	3	17	21	59	39
22.	York City	46	9	3	11	29	26	5	4	14	23	40	35
23.	Hartlepools United	46	8	7	8	30	36	4	2	17	24	57	33
24.	Barrow	46	4	10	9	30	36	2	8	13	21	57	30

In January young John Bush, a 'cool, confident defender' from Westbury, Wiltshire, became the Albion's first apprentice-professional. He never made the first team.

the F.A. Cup they were beaten 1–0 at home by Third Division Colchester United in a close and exciting game.

Johnny Goodchild led the goalscorers with fifteen in League and Cup, followed by 21-year-old Welsh striker Keith Webber with fourteen, including a splendid hat-trick in the 3–2 win at York City in October. Though Albion were never really in contention for promotion, an average crowd of over 9,000 came to the conclusion that life in the Fourth Division was not that terrible after all — as long as it was only for a short time.

One disturbing aspect of the season was the first sign of the modern scourge of hooliganism that eventually changed the face and atmosphere of football grounds all over the country. In 1961–62 the F.A. had felt it necessary to warn spectators of all clubs not to run on to the pitch, a warning which Albion had to repeat to their fans this season. On 28 September 1963, in a Football Combination fixture with Bournemouth, the referee threatened to abandon the match if the Hove crowd continued to throw objects onto the pitch following clashes between David Kydd and the Cherries' goalkeeper. The bad behaviour of a small number of mindless spectators escalated considerably in the years to come.

SEASON 1964–65

In the past Albion had obtained the services of a number of former international players who did not always put their previous experience to good effect, but in May 1964 they signed one who did. Bobby Smith cost a modest £5,000 from Tottenham Hotspur just six months after scoring in England's 8–3 win over Northern Ireland at Wembley, the last of his fifteen international appearances. At the age of 31, Bobby was a remarkable acquisition for a Fourth Division club and the football world was astonished. Season-ticket sales soared, and more than 20,000 spectators turned up to see Albion, in their new blue shirts with white sleeves (last seen when Don Welsh was manager), beat Barrow 3–1 in the opening game with Bobby scoring twice. Three days later an even bigger crowd attended the Oxford United match, but centre-half Mike Hennigan, a summer signing from Southampton, fractured an elbow and ten-man Albion did well to earn a draw.

After five unbeaten matches Albion were in fourth spot, but three successive away defeats brought a drop into mid table by the end of September and the Goldstone attendances began to diminish. In early October, Archie Macaulay signed another famous Tottenham player, full-back Mel Hopkins. The holder of 34 Welsh caps, Hopkins went straight into the side against Notts County at the Goldstone and Albion won 6–0.

Macaulay had wanted Albion in the promotion places by November, and by winning 2–0 at Aldershot on the last day of October they achieved his target, moving into fourth place five points behind Bradford (P.A.) at the head of the section. A week later a 20,645 Goldstone crowd saw the Yorkshire side hold Albion to a 2–2 draw.

The 3–1 home win over Crewe Alexandra in January was Bobby Smith's last game for six weeks because of a hamstring injury, but team-spirit was high and in Bobby's absence Albion won four League matches and drew the fifth. Wing-half Barrie Rees was brought in from Everton for just under £10,000 and scored in a 4–4 thriller with Chester at Hove.

As February became March, Albion moved into third spot on the back of a run of nine wins from eleven games. On 22 March they played a very rough 2–2 draw with Rochdale at Spotland: Norman Gall was sent off, and the Brighton players were subjected to a dreadful pelting from the crowd. A fair number of washers, coins and other objects were thrown; Brian Powney was hit by a dart and Barrie Rees just managed to avoid a china cup. The form of 21-year-old Rees, together with that of fellow half-backs Norman Gall, 22, and Dave Turner, 21, was highly impressive and the trio were seen as the backbone of the side for some time to come. However, the 3–1 home defeat of Southport on 26 March was marred by tragedy. The following morning Rees was travelling to his parents' home in Rhyl when his Mini was in collision with a lorry on the A5; he died from his injuries in the Manor Hospital, Nuneaton. Barrie had been chosen as reserve for the Welsh under-23 side on three occasions and was widely tipped as a future full international. The whole town was shocked by the tragedy. Despite the club's rise to second spot, it was one of the saddest weeks in Albion's history.

Peter Donnelly was transferred to Bradford City in March and celebrated his move with a brace of goals in a 4–1 win over the Albion at Valley Parade on 6 April. Four days later the division leaders, Tranmere Rovers, came to the Goldstone and 23,933 fans saw Barry Dyson swoop onto a poor Norman Gall back-pass to give the visitors a half-time advantage. Despite relentless second-half pressure, Albion seemed destined to relinquish their unbeaten home record, but, with little more than a quarter of an hour remaining, Bobby Smith forced home the equaliser. The crowd would have gladly settled for a share of the points, but in the last minute Norman Gall made amends for his earlier error by heading a Jimmy Collins corner into the net to send Albion to the top of the table. The unfortunate Rovers had been among the leaders all season but were to miss out on promotion at the eleventh hour.

Bobby Smith
Probably the biggest name ever to sign for the Albion, former England centre-forward Bobby Smith cost the club just £5,000 and created a huge surge in interest. He didn't disappoint the fans, scoring 20 League and Cup goals in 1964–65.

That much-loved comedian Norman Wisdom, an Albion director from 1964 until 1970, rewrote the lyrics of 'Sussex by the Sea' with an Albion theme. Wearing his famous 'gump' suit, Norman led the crowd of 20,864 in a rendition of the song during half time at the Chesterfield game in February. Albion won the match 5–0.

SEASON 1964–65

Date	Comp.	Ven.	Opponents	Result	HT	Pos.	Scorers	Atten.	Baxter R	Bertolini J	Burtenshaw S	Cassidy W	Collins J	Donnelly P	Gall N	Goodchild J	Gould W	Hennigan M	Hopkins M	Knight P	McGonigal B	McQuarrie A	Oliver J	Powney B	Rees B	Sanders A	Smith J	Smith RA	Turner D	Upton R	Webber K
Aug 22	FL D4	(h)	Barrow	W 3–1	2–0	5=	Collins (pen), R Smith 2	20,058	4				8		3	11	7		5					1		2	10	9	6		
25	FL D4	(h)	Oxford United	D 0–0	0–0	3		22,697	4				8		3	11	7		5					1		2	10	9	6		
29	FL D4	(a)	Hartlepools United	D 1–1	1–0	5	McQuarrie	6,667	2				4		5	11	7					8		1		3	10	9	6		
Sep 2	FLC R1	(h)	Millwall	D 2–2	1–1	–	J Smith, R Smith	13,352	4				8		3	11	7							1		2	10	9	6		5
5	FL D4	(h)	Rochdale	W 3–0	2–0		Collins, J Smith, Goodchild	14,356	4				8		3	11	7							1		2	10	9	6		
7	FL D4	(a)	Newport County	D 1–1	1–0	4	J Smith	6,119	4				8		3	11	7							1		2	10		6	5	9
9	FLC R1 Rep	(a)	Millwall	L 0–1	0–1	–		7,385	4				8		3	11	7						9	1		2	10		6	5	
12	FL D4	(a)	Millwall	L 0–2	0–1	8		12,181	4				8		3	11	7							1		2	10	9	6	5	
15	FL D4	(h)	Newport County	W 1–0	1–0	6	Collins	13,980	3	4		10	8		11	5				7	1					2		9			
19	FL D4	(h)	Bradford City	D 3–3	3–2	6	R Smith 2, Knight	14,559	3	4		10	8			5	11			7	1					2		9		6	
26	FL D4	(a)	Chester	L 1–3	0–1	13	J Smith	9,068	3			6	8			11	5			7	1					2	10	9		4	
28	FL D4	(a)	York City	L 1–2	0–0	13	Gould	8,925	3			6	8			5	11	7			1					2	10	9		4	
Oct 3	FL D4	(h)	Torquay United	W 3–1	0–1	13	R Smith 2, Gould	13,056	3			6	8			5	11	7			1					2	10	9		4	
6	FL D4	(a)	York City	W 3–1	2–0	8	J Smith, R Smith, Gould	15,002	3	4			8			5	11	7						1		2	10	9	6		
10	FL D4	(h)	Notts County	W 6–0	4–0	8	Gould, Collins 2, J Smith 2, R Smith	14,261	3	4			8			5	11	7		2				1			10	9	6		
14	FL D4	(a)	Lincoln City	W 1–0	0–0	6	Gould	5,604	3	4			8			5	11	7		2				1			10	9	6		
17	FL D4	(a)	Chesterfield	D 1–1	1–1	5	J Smith	9,923	3	4			8			5		7		2				1			11	9	6		
20	FL D4	(h)	Lincoln City	W 4–0	2–0	4	Cassidy, Gould 2, Goodchild	17,116	3	4		10	8			5	11	7		2				1				9	6		
24	FL D4	(h)	Doncaster Rovers	D 1–1	1–1	5	Cassidy	16,523	3	4		10	8	9		5	11	7		2				1					6		
28	FL D4	(a)	Crewe Alexandra	L 2–3	0–2	5	Cassidy 2	3,466	3	10		9	8			5	11	7		2				1					6	4	
31	FL D4	(a)	Aldershot	W 2–0	2–0	4	Gould, Turner	8,032	3	4		10	8			5	11	7		2			9	1					6		
Nov 7	FL D4	(h)	Bradford (P.A.)	D 2–2	2–1	4	J Smith, R Smith	20,645	3			8	4			5	11	7		2				1			10	9	6		
14	FAC R1	(a)	Bristol City	L 0–1	0–0	–		12,618	3	4			8			5	11	7		2				1			10	9	6		
21	FL D4	(h)	Wrexham	W 5–1	2–1	4	Goodchild, Cassidy 2, Gould, R Smith	14,423	3	4		10	8			5	11	7		2				1				9	6		
27	FL D4	(a)	Tranmere Rovers	L 2–4	0–2	4	R Smith, Cassidy	13,257	3			10	8			5	11	7		2				1				9	6	4	
Dec 12	FL D4	(h)	Barrow	W 4–1	3–0	4	Goodchild, Gould, R Smith 2	3,125	6			10	8			5	11	7		3				1	2			9	4		
19	FL D4	(h)	Hartlepools United	W 5–0	1–0	4	R Smith 2, Gould 2, Collins	12,258	6			10	8			5	11	7		3				1	2			9	4		
26	FL D4	(h)	Halifax Town	W 2–1	1–1	4	Gould, Cassidy	19,298	6			10	8			5	11	7		3				1	2			9	4		
28	FL D4	(h)	Halifax Town	D 1–1	1–0	4	J Smith	3,133	6				10			5	11	7						1	2		8	9	4		
Jan 9	FL D4	(h)	Crewe Alexandra	W 3–1	1–0	4	J Smith, Gould, Collins	14,501	3				8			5	11	7		2				1	4		10	9	6		
16	FL D4	(h)	Millwall	W 2–0	1–0	4	Own goal, Gould	18,313	3			10	8			5	11	7		2				1	4			9		6	
30	FL D4	(a)	Southport	W 2–1	0–1	4	J Smith, Collins (pen)	2,286	3			10	8			5	11	7		2				1	4		9		6		
Feb 6	FL D4	(h)	Chester	D 4–4	2–2	4	Goodchild, Rees, Collins 2	16,414	3			10	8			5	11	7		2				1	4		9		6		
13	FL D4	(a)	Torquay United	W 1–0	1–0	4	J Smith	4,868	3	4		10	8			5	11	7		2				1	6		9				
20	FL D4	(a)	Notts County	W 2–1	1–0	3	Cassidy, J Smith	5,002	3			10	8			5	11	7		2				1	4		9		6		
27	FL D4	(h)	Chesterfield	W 5–0	3–0	3	Gould, Goodchild 2, Hopkins, Turner	20,864	3				8			5	11	7		2				1	4		10	9	6		
Mar 6	FL D4	(a)	Doncaster Rovers	L 1–2	0–0	4	R Smith	10,345	3				8			5	11	7		2				1	4		10	9	6		
13	FL D4	(h)	Aldershot	W 2–0	1–0	4	Gould, Collins	18,456	3				8			5	11	7		2				10	1	4	9		6		
20	FL D4	(a)	Bradford (P.A.)	L 0–2	0–1	4		6,288	3				8			5	11	7		2				10	1	4	9		6		
22	FL D4	(a)	Rochdale	D 2–2	1–1	4	Goodchild, Collins	7,005	3				8			5	11	7		2				10	1	4	9		6		
26	FL D4	(a)	Southport	W 3–1	2–1	2	Gould, Collins 2	19,789		2			8			5	11	7		3				10	1	4	9		6		
31	FL D4	(a)	Oxford United	D 2–2	0–0	3	R Smith, J Smith	13,429	3	4			8			5	11	7		2				1			10	9	6		
Apr 3	FL D4	(a)	Wrexham	W 2–1	1–1	2	J Smith, Gould	5,879	3	4		10	8			5	11	7		2				1			9		6		
6	FL D4	(h)	Bradford City	L 1–4	1–3	2	Cassidy	4,377	3			10	4			5	11	7		2				8	1		9		6		
10	FL D4	(h)	Tranmere Rovers	W 2–1	0–1	1	R Smith, Gall	23,933	3	4			8			5	11	7		2				1			9		6		
16	FL D4	(a)	Stockport County	W 4–1	2–1	1	Goodchild, R Smith, Gould, Collins	10,125	3	4			8				11	7	5	2				1			10	9	6		
17	FL D4	(a)	Darlington	L 0–2	0–0	1		5,070	3	4			8				11	7	5	2				1			10	9	6		
19	FL D4	(h)	Stockport County	W 3–1	3–1	1	J Smith, Collins, Goodchild	21,489	3	4			8			5	11	7		2				1			10	9	6		
26	FL D4	(h)	Darlington	W 3–1	2–0	1	Collins, J Smith, Gould	31,423	3	4			8			5	11	7		2				1			10	9	6		
League appearances									39	24	2	24	45	3	44	43	43	4	34	3	5	2	5	41	12	16	35	31	40	10	1
League goals							OG – 1					10	17		1	10	21		1	1	1	1			1		17	19	2		

Football League Division 4 1964–65

		P	W	D	L	F	A	W	D	L	F	A	Pts
1.	**ALBION**	46	18	5	0	68	20	8	6	9	34	37	63
2.	Millwall	46	13	10	0	45	15	10	6	7	33	30	62
3.	York City	46	20	1	2	63	21	8	5	10	28	35	62
4.	Oxford United	46	18	4	1	54	13	5	11	7	33	31	61
5.	Tranmere Rovers	46	20	2	1	72	20	7	4	12	27	36	60
6.	Rochdale	46	15	4	4	46	22	7	10	6	28	31	58
7.	Bradford (P.A.)	46	14	8	1	52	22	6	9	8	34	40	57
8.	Chester	46	19	1	3	75	26	6	5	12	44	55	56
9.	Doncaster Rovers	46	13	6	4	46	25	7	5	11	38	47	51
10.	Crewe Alexandra	46	11	8	4	55	34	7	5	11	35	47	49
11.	Torquay United	46	11	5	7	41	33	10	2	11	29	37	49
12.	Chesterfield	46	13	5	5	36	22	7	3	13	22	48	48
13.	Notts County	46	12	7	4	43	23	3	7	13	18	50	44
14.	Wrexham	46	12	5	6	59	37	5	4	14	25	55	43
15.	Hartlepools United	46	11	10	2	44	28	4	3	16	17	57	43
16.	Newport County	46	14	5	4	54	26	3	3	17	31	55	42
17.	Darlington	46	14	2	7	52	30	4	4	15	32	57	42
18.	Aldershot	46	14	3	6	46	25	1	4	18	18	59	37
19.	Bradford City	46	9	2	12	37	36	3	6	14	33	52	32
20.	Southport	46	5	9	9	35	45	3	7	13	23	44	32
21.	Barrow	46	9	4	10	30	38	3	2	18	29	67	30
22.	Lincoln City	46	8	4	11	35	33	3	2	18	23	66	28
23.	Halifax Town	46	9	4	10	37	37	2	2	19	17	66	28
24.	Stockport County	46	8	4	11	30	34	2	3	18	14	53	27

The Albion Sportsmen's Association was launched in the New Year to run a bingo competition, with the object of giving financial assistance to the club for team-strengthening and ground improvements.

With home and away clashes to come against Stockport County and Darlington, both re-election strugglers, Albion were hopeful of ultimate success, but the promotion tussle was a close-run affair with the top eight clubs still involved. Four points were taken from the Stockport games and, despite defeat at Darlington, the club remained top, but then both York City and Oxford United went ahead on Saturday, 24 April, with victories in their last games. With the home game against Darlington to come on the Monday, Albion still needed a point to be sure of promotion; two points would clinch the title.

The final game attracted an enormous crowd of 31,423 to the Goldstone and the players rose to the occasion. Jimmy Collins registered the 100th League goal of the campaign in the nineteenth minute and Jack Smith added a second before the interval. Darlington pulled one back two minutes after the break, but when Wally Gould scored his 21st of the season it was all over bar the shouting and the frenzied fans roared their delight at the new Fourth Division champions.

Only five points were forfeited in an unbeaten home campaign and the team averaged almost three goals a game at the Goldstone. The magic 100-goal mark was reached for only the second time ever, and, thanks in no short measure to the

The match-ball used in the championship clincher with Darlington was purchased for the club by a supporter, Mr R. Camps of Southgate, Middlesex, in an early example of sponsorship. His admirable idea was eagerly taken up by the club who invited supporters and businesses to sponsor each match-ball the following season, with a printed acknowledgement in the programme.

Albion 1964–65

Back row left to right: Brian Powney, Bert Royal, John Bush, Norman Gall, Dave Turner, Nobby Upton, Peter Knight, Bobby Baxter, Bert McGonigal.
Third row left to right: Cyril Hodges (trainer), David Kydd, Keith Webber, Andy McQuarrie, Mike Hennigan, Gary Brown, Billy Forrest, Allan Sanders, Jack Bertolini, Steve Burtenshaw (player-coach).
Second row left to right: Wally Gould, Jimmy Collins (captain), Bobby Smith, Jack Smith, Bill Cassidy, Johnny Goochild.
On ground left to right: Eric Whitington, Peter Medhurst, John Duncliffe, Frank Croney.

promptings of Bobby Smith, six players reached double figures: Wally Gould 21, Bobby himself 20, Jack Smith 18, Jimmy Collins 17, Johnny Goodchild 10 and Bill Cassidy 10. There were seven gates in excess of 20,000 and the seasonal average of 17,975 was the highest in the Third and Fourth Divisions; indeed, only four Second Division clubs bettered the total. The lowest gate was 12,258 for the match with Hartlepools United in December.

As was becoming almost traditional, the cup performances were anti-climactic. In the League Cup a 2–2 home draw with promotion rivals Millwall was followed by a 1–0 defeat in the replay. In the F.A. Cup, Albion lost 1–0 at Third Division Bristol City, but escape from the Football League basement was the priority.

Club chairman Eric Courtney-King backed his manager throughout the term and the board found the cash to maintain the promotion push, but at the end of the season the club was over £100,000 in debt. It was a situation which worsened dramatically in the years to come.

SEASON 1965–66

Macaulay's ambition for the season was consolidation and a place in the middle of the Third Division. The players who had won promotion were given their chance to maintain the progress and there were only two close-season arrivals, free transfers Peter Davies (Swansea Town) and Peter Leggett (Swindon Town), but neither was to make an impact at the Goldstone. However, the campaign got off on the wrong foot even before a ball had been kicked in anger: Bobby Smith reported for training weighing fifteen stone, Jack Bertolini tore knee ligaments in a pre-season friendly, and Wally Gould was to miss the first three matches through suspension. Smith was suspended by the club for two weeks and lost a stone in weight.

Albion lost their opening match at Mansfield Town where former Goldstone favourite Bill Curry scored twice in the Stags' 3–1 win. Indeed, Albion lost their first three games and were soon in the bottom four with the inevitable demands for the manager's head. Macaulay brought in a new forward in September, the much-travelled Charlie Livesey from Northampton Town, but lost another the following month when Bobby Smith left the Goldstone under a cloud. Having broken club rules by contributing articles to a national newspaper, Smith was dismissed and ended up in the Southern League with Hastings United in a sensational turn of events.

With the team struggling around the relegation zone, new faces continued to arrive: Northern Ireland international full-back Jimmy Magill and winger Brian Tawse from Arsenal; half-back Derek Leck from Northampton Town; and Stewart Henderson, a trialist from Chelsea who went on to become a great favourite with the fans for several seasons.

An improved Albion gradually worked their way up the ladder and by Christmas were in mid table. Southend United felt the full force of the revival on 27 November when Brighton equalled their highest score in the Football League, beating the Essex side 9–1 with Jack Smith hitting three of six second-half goals. In the New Year the club maintained its mid-table position to finish fifteenth, a respectable placing after the disastrous opening. After a memorable 6–4 Goldstone victory over Mansfield Town in January, much of the interest in the latter stages concerned the new phenomenon of 'toilet-roll throwing'. Usually hurled by young fans in the North Stand in

SEASON 1965–66

Date	Comp	Ven	Opponents	Result	HT	Pos	Scorers	Atten.
Aug 21	FL D3	(a)	Mansfield Town	L 1–3	0–2	17	Cassidy	7,647
23	FL D3	(a)	Queen's Park R.	L 1–4	1–1	18	Oliver	10,531
28	FL D3	(h)	Hull City	L 1–2	0–0	24	Cassidy	16,583
Sep 1	FLC R1	(a)	Luton Town	D 1–1	1–0	–	Cassidy	3,758
3	FL D3	(a)	Reading	D 0–0	0–0	22		10,358
7	FLC R1 Rep	(h)	Luton Town	W 2–0	0–0	–	Cassidy, R Smith	11,745
11	FL D3	(h)	Exeter City	W 2–1	2–0	21	J Smith, J Collins	13,252
15	FL D3	(a)	Grimsby Town	L 1–3	0–3	23	Turner	5,140
18	FL D3	(a)	Peterborough Utd	D 2–2	0–2	22	J Smith, Turner	7,588
21	FLC R2	(a)	Ipswich Town	L 1–2	1–1	–	Kydd	13,498
25	FL D3	(h)	Millwall	D 2–2	1–1	21	Gould, Livesey	16,356
Oct 2	FL D3	(a)	Gillingham	L 1–3	0–2	22	Gould (pen)	10,078
5	FL D3	(h)	Grimsby Town	L 1–2	0–2	22	J Collins	13,858
9	FL D3	(a)	Bristol Rovers	D 0–0	0–0	23		10,418
15	FL D3	(h)	York City	W 3–1	2–1	20	Cassidy, Gould (pen), J Smith	14,067
23	FL D3	(a)	Oxford United	D 0–0	0–0	21		9,968
30	FL D3	(h)	Swansea Town	D 1–1	0–1	19=	Cassidy	13,906
Nov 6	FL D3	(a)	Walsall	L 1–2	1–2	21	Cassidy	8,529
13	FAC R1	(h)	Wisbech Town	W 10–1	3–0	–	J Smith 2, Livesey 3, Own goal, Goodchild, J Collins, Cassidy 2	12,508
20	FL D3	(a)	Bournem'th & B.A.	W 1–0	1–0	19	Turner	5,347
23	FL D3	(h)	Queen's Park R.	L 0–2	0–1	21		10,699
27	FL D3	(h)	Southend United	W 9–1	3–0	15	J Collins, Goodchild 2, Gould, J Smith 3, Livesey 2	11,124
Dec 4	FAC R2	(h)	Bedford Town	D 1–1	0–0	–	Gould	16,979
6	FAC R2 Rep	(a)	Bedford Town	L 1–2	1–0	–	Turner	11,500
11	FL D3	(h)	Shrewsbury Town	D 1–1	0–1	17	Cassidy	11,152
17	FL D3	(a)	York City	W 1–0	0–0	16	J Collins	3,787
27	FL D3	(h)	Watford	W 2–0	1–0	14	Livesey 2	19,104
Jan 1	FL D3	(h)	Bristol Rovers	W 4–3	1–0	13	Livesey 2, Tawse, Gould	14,408
7	FL D3	(a)	Workington	L 0–1	0–1	13		4,007
29	FL D3	(h)	Mansfield Town	W 6–4	5–2	14	Tawse 2, J Smith, Livesey 2, Own goal	13,068
Feb 5	FL D3	(a)	Hull City	L 0–1	0–1	16		25,774
12	FL D3	(h)	Scunthorpe United	L 0–1	0–1	16		12,658
19	FL D3	(h)	Reading	D 1–1	0–0	16	Turner	13,323
Mar 5	FL D3	(a)	Scunthorpe United	D 2–2	0–2	17	Oliver, Gould	4,482
8	FL D3	(h)	Oxford United	W 2–0	1–0	16	Oliver, Own goal	11,965
12	FL D3	(h)	Peterborough Utd	W 1–0	1–0	14	Own goal	12,682
19	FL D3	(a)	Millwall	L 2–3	0–2	16	Livesey, Gould	15,802
22	FL D3	(h)	Watford	W 1–0	1–0	12	Livesey	6,116
26	FL D3	(h)	Gillingham	L 0–1	0–0	16		7,875
Apr 2	FL D3	(h)	Walsall	W 2–1	1–0	16	J Smith, J Collins	10,757
8	FL D3	(h)	Brentford	W 2–0	2–0	16	J Smith, Gould	17,176
9	FL D3	(a)	Swindon Town	L 2–3	2–3	12	Goodchild, J Collins	13,367
11	FL D3	(a)	Brentford	L 0–2	0–1	14		7,670
16	FL D3	(h)	Bournem'th & B.A.	L 1–2	0–2	16	Tawse	9,652
22	FL D3	(h)	Southend United	D 0–0	0–0	15		6,734
30	FL D3	(h)	Swindon Town	W 1–0	0–0	15	Gould	10,733
May 3	FL D3	(a)	Exeter City	L 0–2	0–1	15		3,344
6	FL D3	(a)	Shrewsbury Town	L 1–3	1–1	16	Hopkins	2,775
13	FL D3	(h)	Oldham Athletic	W 3–1	1–0	16	Tawse, J Smith, J Collins (pen)	9,196
18	FL D3	(a)	Oldham Athletic	L 0–1	0–0	16		10,398
20	FL D3	(h)	Workington	W 3–1	1–1	15	Tawse, Cassidy, Gould	9,137
28	FL D3	(a)	Swansea Town	D 2–2	1–1	15	Turner, J Collins	5,864

	League appearances	41	2	0	24	2	40	6	43	12	41	4	0	22	4	2	21	6	28	23	38	6	38	0	22	3	46	1	0
	Substitute appearances				4							1	1	1		1			6									
	League goals	OG – 3			7		8			3	10			1			11		3		10	6	5				

Football League Division 3 1965–66

		P	W	D	L	F	A	W	D	L	F	A	Pts
1.	Hull City	46	19	2	2	64	24	12	5	6	45	38	69
2.	Millwall	46	19	4	0	47	13	8	7	8	29	30	65
3.	Queen's Park R.	46	16	3	4	62	29	8	6	9	33	36	57
4.	Scunthorpe United	46	9	8	6	44	34	12	3	8	36	33	53
5.	Workington	46	13	6	4	38	18	6	8	9	29	39	52
6.	Gillingham	46	14	4	5	33	19	8	4	11	29	35	52
7.	Swindon Town	46	11	8	4	43	18	8	5	10	31	30	51
8.	Reading	46	13	5	5	36	19	6	6	9	34	44	51
9.	Walsall	46	13	7	3	48	21	7	3	13	29	43	50
10.	Shrewsbury Town	46	13	7	3	48	22	6	4	13	25	42	49
11.	Grimsby Town	46	15	6	2	47	25	2	7	14	21	37	47
12.	Watford	46	12	4	7	33	19	5	9	9	22	32	47
13.	Peterborough United	46	13	6	4	50	26	4	6	13	30	40	46
14.	Oxford United	46	11	3	9	38	33	8	5	10	32	41	46
15.	**ALBION**	46	13	4	6	48	28	3	7	13	19	37	43
16.	Bristol Rovers	46	11	10	2	34	18	6	4	13	14	26	49	42
17.	Swansea Town	46	14	4	5	61	37	1	7	15	20	59	41
18.	Bournemouth & B.A.	46	9	8	6	24	19	4	4	15	14	37	38
19.	Mansfield Town	46	10	5	8	31	36	5	3	15	28	53	38
20.	Oldham Athletic	46	8	7	8	34	33	4	6	13	21	48	37
21.	Southend United	46	15	1	7	47	25	1	3	19	11	55	36
22.	Exeter City	46	9	6	8	36	28	3	5	15	17	51	35
23.	Brentford	46	9	4	10	34	30	1	8	14	14	39	32
24.	York City	46	5	7	11	30	44	4	2	17	23	62	27

celebration of a Brighton goal, the paper became festooned around the nets and the club was ordered to post warning-notices by the F.A.

The cup competitions provided brief but interesting diversions. Just two weeks before the 9–1 demolition of Southend United, Albion had gone one better by thrashing Southern League Wisbech Town 10–1 in the first round of the F.A. Cup. It took them 20 minutes to score the first, but then the floodgates opened and they cruised to their biggest victory in the competition since Shoreham were beaten 12–0 in the qualifying rounds of 1932–33.

In the second round 16,979 spectators turned up at the Goldstone expecting another goal-feast against Southern League opposition, but Bedford Town were a tougher nut than Wisbech. Two years earlier they had won at Second Division Newcastle United and had just beaten Exeter City in Devon. Bedford played superbly, opening the scoring just after the break, and it was well into injury time when Wally Gould saved Albion's blushes with a headed equaliser. A live sound commentary of the replay was relayed to over 2,000 fans in the Goldstone's West Stand. Albion went ahead in the opening half through Dave Turner, but, with the big crowd solidly behind the part-timers, Bedford attacked throughout the second half and deservedly took the honours with two late goals. It was only the second time since joining the Football League in 1920 that Brighton had fallen to non-League opposition. After beating fellow Southern Leaguers Hereford United in round three, Bedford went out at home to the eventual Cup winners, Everton.

In the League Cup, Fourth Division Luton Town were held to a 1–1 draw at Kenilworth Road. Bobby Smith made his only appearance of the season in the replay and scored in a 2–0 victory. David Kydd scored on his first-team début in the second-round home tie with Ipswich Town, but Albion lost 2–1 to the Second Division side.

Dave Turner was the only ever-present, while the popular Charlie Livesey top-scored with fourteen goals despite playing in only 30 of the 52 games. With a few notable exceptions it was an unspectacular season, but Jimmy Magill rounded it off nicely with two more caps to bring his total to 26. On 10 November, less than two weeks after joining the club, the Northern Ireland full-back had become Albion's first full international for 39 years when he played in the 2–1 defeat by England at Wembley.

Substitutes – for injured players only – were introduced for the first time this season. Jim Oliver grabbed a little fame when he came on for Bill Cassidy in the 2–1 home defeat by Hull City on 28 August to become Albion's first playing substitute. Peter Leggett had worn the no. 12 shirt in the two previous games but was not called upon.

Albion 1965–66
Back row left to right: Bert McGonigal, David Kydd, Jimmy Collins (captain), Jack Bertolini, Johnny Goodchild, Bobby Baxter, Peter Davies, Brian Powney.
Third row left to right: Cyril Hodges (trainer), Mike Hickman, Peter Leggett, Norman Gall, Bill Cassidy, Dave Turner, Gary Brown, Jim Oliver, Allan Sanders, Steve Burtenshaw (player-coach).
Second row left to right: Jack Smith, Mel Hopkins, Bobby Smith, Eric Whitington.
On ground left to right: John Duncliffe, Wally Gould, Frank Croney, Peter Knight.

SEASON 1966–67

During the summer Alf Ramsey's England team carried off the World Cup at Wembley and the domestic game would never quite be the same again. Ramsey's revolutionary tactics – no wingers, overlapping full-backs, 4–3–3, and all that – became the fashion, though most clubs were ill-equipped to put the new method to good effect.

There were two close-season arrivals at the Goldstone, Howard Wilkinson from Sheffield Wednesday and goalkeeper Tony Burns from Arsenal. There were no major departures although Jack Bertolini had been forced to retire through injury.

As ever the season began with high hopes, but after eight games Albion were bottom of the table and still without a win, one of their worst starts ever. On the last day of September, Archie Macaulay signed Kit Napier from Newcastle United for £9,000, a transaction which proved a tremendous piece of business. A versatile, skilful ball-player in the Scottish tradition, Kit appeared in every forward position by the end of the

SEASON 1966–67

Date	Comp.	Ven.	Opponents	Result	HT	Pos.	Scorers	Atten.	Badminton R	Baxter R	Borthwick W	Burns A	Burtenshaw S	Cassidy W	Collins J	Dear B	Duncliffe J	Gall N	Gould W	Henderson S	Hickman M	Hopkins M	Leck D	Livesey C	Magill J	Napier K	Oliver J	Powney B	Smith J	Tawse B	Templeman J	Tranter W	Turner D	Upton R	Whitington E	Wilkinson H	Woolgar P
Aug 20	FL D3	(h)	Swindon Town	D 2–2	0–1	8=	Wilkinson, Collins (pen)	10,102	3						8				10				4	9	2			1	N	11			6	5		7	
24	FLC R1	(h)	Leyton Orient	W 1–0	1–0	–	Collins (pen)	7,972	3						8			5	9			N	4	10	2			1		11			6			7	
27	FL D3	(a)	Reading	D 1–1	0–0	13=	Wilkinson	8,088	3						8			5	10			N	4	9	2			1		11			6			7	
Sep 3	FL D3	(h)	Doncaster Rovers	D 0–0	0–0	12=		10,642	3						8			5	7			N	4	10	2			1		11			6			9	
7	FL D3	(h)	Bournem'th & B.A.	L 0–3	0–0	22=		10,888	3						8			5	7			N	4	10	2			1	11				6			9	
10	FL D3	(a)	Mansfield Town	L 1–2	0–1	22	Gould	5,175	3	1					4			5	7		9	N		10	2					11			6			8	
14	FLC R2	(h)	Norwich City	W 1–0	0–0	–	Livesey	7,364	6	1					8			5	11			3		10	2		9			N			4			7	
17	FL D3	(h)	Grimsby Town	L 0–2	0–1	24		9,762	6	1					8			5	11	2		3		10			9			12			4			7†	
24	FL D3	(a)	Walsall	L 1–2	0–2	24	Own goal	8,177	3						10	4		5	11	2				9			N	1					6		8	7	
28	FL D3	(h)	Bournem'th & B.A.	L 1–2	0–2	24	Whitington	6,462	3						8	4		5	11	2				9				1		N			6		10	7	
Oct 1	FL D3	(h)	Peterborough Utd	W 5–2	0–1	22	Gould 2, Napier 2, Turner	8,598	3							4		5	11	2				8		9		1		N			6		10	7	
5	FLC R3	(h)	Coventry City	D 1–1	0–1	–	Collins	13,257	3					9	4			5	11	2				8				1		N			6		10	7	
8	FL D3	(a)	Leyton Orient	W 1–0	1–0	19	Gould	13,007	3						4			5	11	2				8		9		1		N			6		10	7	
11	FLC R3 Rep	(h)	Coventry City	W 3–1	2–1	–	Livesey, Cassidy, Wilkinson	13,437	3					9	4			5	11	2				8		9		1		N			6		10	7	
15	FL D3	(a)	Gillingham	L 0–2	0–1	21		7,758	3						10	4		5	11	2				8		9		1					6		N	7	
19	FL D3	(h)	Darlington	W 5–0	2–0	20	Whitington, Own goal, Gould, Napier, Collins	9,421	3						N	4		5	11	2				8		9		1					6		10	7	
22	FL D3	(h)	Workington	D 0–0	0–0	20		13,109	3						N	4		5	11	2				8		9		1					6		10	7	
26	FLC R4	(h)	Northampton T.	D 1–1	0–0	–	Collins	17,238	3						N	4		5	11	2				8		9		1				6			10	7	
28	FL D3	(a)	Scunthorpe Utd	W 1–0	0–0	18	Wilkinson	5,512	3						9	4		5	10	2				8				1		11		6			N	7	
Nov 1	FLC R4 Rep	(a)	Northampton T.	L 0–8	0–3	–		6,899	3						9	4		5	11	2				8		10		1				N	6			7	
5	FL D3	(h)	Oldham Athletic	W 2–0	0–1	17	Napier, Livesey	9,931	3					12	8			5	11	2				10		9†		1				4	6			7	
12	FL D3	(a)	Oxford United	W 2–1	0–0	13	Own goal, Livesey	6,169	3						8			5	11	2				10		9		1				4	6		N	7	
14	FL D3	(a)	Darlington	L 1–3	0–3	14	Wilkinson	6,351	3						8			5	11	2				10†		9		1				4	6		12	7	
19	FL D3	(h)	Bristol Rovers	W 3–2	0–1	13	Gall, Turner 2	11,542	3						8	4		2	11	N						9		1				5	6		10	7	
26	FAC R1	(h)	Newport County	W 2–1	0–0	–	Turner, Whitington	4,825	3						9	4		2	11	N						8		1				5	6		10	7	
Dec 3	FL D3	(h)	Shrewsbury Town	W 2–1	1–1	11	Livesey, Tawse	10,920	3			4		9				5	10							8	2	N	1		11			6			7	
10	FL D3	(a)	Middlesbrough	L 0–1	0–1	13		9,585	3					9	11			5	10							8	2	12	1				4	6			7†	
17	FL D3	(h)	Swindon Town	D 1–1	0–1	13	Cassidy	10,081	3					9	8			5	7							2	10		1		11		4	6		N		
26	FL D3	(a)	Queen's Park R.	L 0–3	0–3	17		17,875	3					9	8			5	7†							10	2	12	1		11		4	6				
27	FL D3	(h)	Queen's Park R.	D 2–2	2–0	15	Tawse (pen), Cassidy	22,947	3					9				2		N						10		8	7	1	11		4	5	6			
31	FL D3	(h)	Reading	L 0–1	0–0	17		12,257	3	1				9	10			2	7							8	N				11		4	5	6			
Jan 7	FAC R2	(a)	Bath City	W 5–0	2–0	–	Turner, Whitington 2, Tawse 2	7,417	3	1								2	8							N	9	7			11	4	5	6		10	
14	FL D3	(a)	Mansfield Town	W 1–0	0–0	15	Whitington	13,591	3	1								2	8							N	9	7			11	4	5	6		10	
21	FL D3	(a)	Grimsby Town	W 3–2	2–0	12	Oliver, Gould, Tawse	4,897	3	1								2	8							N	9	7			11	4	5	6		10	
28	FAC R3	(a)	Aldershot	D 0–0	0–0	–		12,812	3	1								2	8							N	9	7			11	4	5	6		10	
Feb 1	FAC R3 Rep	(h)	Aldershot	W 3–1	1–0	–	Whitington, Napier, Livesey	29,208	3	1								2	8							12	9	7			11	4	5	6		10†	
4	FL D3	(h)	Walsall	L 2–3	0–3	13	Oliver, Gould	13,411	3	1								2	10	N						8	9	7			11	4	5	6			
11	FL D3	(a)	Peterborough Utd	L 1–2	0–2	17	Whitington	6,432	3									5	8								2	9	7	1		11	4		6		10	N
18	FAC R4	(h)	Chelsea	D 1–1	0–1	–	Turner	35,000	3	1								5	8								2	9	7			11	4		6		10	N
22	FAC R4 Rep	(a)	Chelsea	L 0–4	0–2	–		54,852	3	1								5	8						N			9	7			11	4	2	6		10	N
25	FL D3	(a)	Leyton Orient	L 2–3	2–1	19	Gould, Napier	5,437	3	1								5	11						8	2	9					4	6	10		N	7
Mar 4	FL D3	(h)	Gillingham	D 2–2	1–1	19	Napier 2	11,112	3									5	8						2	9		1			11	4	N	6		10	7
8	FL D3	(h)	Swansea Town	W 3–2	2–1	16	Livesey, Tawse, Napier	8,970	3							8		5	N						10	2	9		1		11			6			7
11	FL D3	(h)	Swansea Town	D 1–1	0–0	14=	Livesey	5,702	3†						4			5	8				12	10	2	9		1		11			6			7
17	FL D3	(a)	Workington	L 1–2	0–1	16	Napier	2,563	3						4	10		5	N					8	2	9		1		11			6			7
24	FL D3	(a)	Watford	D 1–1	0–0	15	Tawse (pen)	15,584	3							N		5	9	2			4	8		10		1		11			6			7
25	FL D3	(h)	Scunthorpe Utd	D 2–2	1–1	16	Dear 2	11,624	3						8	10		5	11	2			4†	9		7		1			12		6			7
27	FL D3	(h)	Watford	W 1–0	0–0	15	Dear	13,640							12	10†	3	5	9	2			4	8				1		11			6			7
Apr 1	FL D3	(a)	Oldham Athletic	L 1–4	1–2	16	Dear	5,964	3						12	10		5	9	2			4			8†		1		11			6			7
8	FL D3	(h)	Oxford United	W 2–0	0–0	15	Collins, Dear	9,770	3	1					4	9		5	11	2			N	10		8							6			7
12	FL D3	(h)	Torquay United	L 0–1	0–1	16		11,625	3	1					8	9		5	7	2				10		11							4			6	N
15	FL D3	(a)	Bristol Rovers	D 2–2	0–1	16	Whitington 2	9,042	3	1					8			5	7	2				10		11							4		6	9	N
22	FL D3	(h)	Colchester United	D 1–1	1–1	16	Gould	10,567	3	1					8			5	7	2				10		11							4		6	9	N
26	FL D3	(a)	Torquay United	L 0–5	0–0	17		9,093	3	1†					8			5	7	2	11			9		10							4		6		12
29	FL D3	(a)	Shrewsbury Town	D 0–0	0–0	18		4,042	3						8	10		5	7	2	11			9				1				4	6			N
May 6	FL D3	(h)	Middlesbrough	D 1–1	1–0	18	Tawse (pen)	12,692	3						8			5	7	2	4			9		10		1		11			6			N
13	FL D3	(a)	Colchester United	L 2–3	1–1	20	Turner, Livesey	4,238	3						8			5	N	2	4			9		10		1		11			6			7
16	FL D3	(a)	Doncaster Rovers	D 1–1	0–0	19	Turner	3,039	2		8							3	5	11								N		4	6	10		9	7	1
League appearances									1	44	1	12	1	11	34	7	2	45	42	24	5	1	8	38	15	30	6	33	2	22	15	15	45	1	14	31	1
Substitute appearances														1	2											1		2			1	1			1	1
League goals								OG – 3						2	3	5		1	9						6		9	2		6			5		6	4	

campaign and went on to score nearly 100 goals in his Albion career. At the a.g.m. the following morning one shareholder referred to the players as 'a bunch of comedians'. Macaulay leapt to their defence, but the best response came later that day when Albion stormed to a 5–2 win over Peterborough United at the Goldstone, with two début goals from Napier.

There were precious few high spots in the League games, but Albion continued to be one of the best-supported teams in the Third Division. On a foul Wednesday evening in October, with

> The crowd at the 5–0 win over Darlington on 19 November was further entertained by the pop group The Mike Stuart Span which played before the match and at half time.

the team in 22nd place, almost 10,000 die-hards turned out for the match with lowly Darlington and were rewarded for their doggedness with a 5–0 win. The Christmas holiday provided entertaining fare with two matches against the runaway leaders and eventual champions Queen's Park Rangers, who also went on to lift the League Cup at Wembley. Albion, having lost 3–0 at Loftus Road on Boxing Day, drafted nineteen-year-old John Templeman for his début the following day to put the shackles on the dangerous Rodney Marsh in a 2–2 draw.

Albion spent the latter part of the season hovering three or four points above the bottom four, but an end-of-season run of eight matches without a win left them just two places and two points above the relegation zone in nineteenth place. A point against high-fliers Middlesbrough on 6 May saw them safe with

Football League Division 3 1966–67													
		P	W	D	L	F	A	W	D	L	F	A	Pts
1.	Queen's Park R.	46	18	4	1	66	15	8	11	4	37	23	67
2.	Middlesbrough	46	16	3	4	51	20	7	6	10	36	44	55
3.	Watford	46	15	5	3	39	17	5	9	9	22	29	54
4.	Reading	46	13	7	3	45	20	9	2	12	31	37	53
5.	Bristol Rovers	46	13	8	2	47	28	7	5	11	29	39	53
6.	Shrewsbury Town	46	15	5	3	48	24	5	7	11	29	38	52
7.	Torquay United	46	17	3	3	57	20	4	6	13	16	34	51
8.	Swindon Town	46	14	5	4	53	21	6	5	12	28	38	50
9.	Mansfield Town	46	12	4	7	48	37	8	5	10	36	42	49
10.	Oldham Athletic	46	15	4	4	51	16	4	6	13	29	47	48
11.	Gillingham	46	11	9	3	36	18	4	7	12	22	44	46
12.	Walsall	46	12	8	3	37	16	6	2	15	28	56	46
13.	Colchester United	46	14	3	6	52	30	3	7	13	24	43	44
14.	Leyton Orient	46	10	9	4	36	27	3	9	11	22	41	44
15.	Peterborough United	46	12	4	7	40	31	2	11	10	26	40	43
16.	Oxford United	46	10	8	5	41	29	5	5	13	20	37	43
17.	Grimsby Town	46	13	5	5	46	23	4	4	15	15	45	43
18.	Scunthorpe United	46	13	4	6	39	26	4	4	15	19	47	42
19.	**ALBION**	46	10	8	5	37	27	3	7	13	24	44	41
20.	Bournemouth & B.A.	46	8	10	5	24	24	4	7	12	15	33	41
21.	Swansea Town	46	9	9	5	50	30	3	6	14	35	59	39
22.	Darlington	46	8	7	8	26	28	5	4	14	21	53	37
23.	Doncaster Rovers	46	11	6	6	40	40	1	2	20	18	77	32
24.	Workington	46	9	3	11	35	35	3	4	16	20	54	31

two games to spare. The average attendance was down on the previous season, but overall income was up owing to long-overdue runs in both cup competitions.

Albion reached the fourth round of the League Cup for the first time ever. After beating Leyton Orient, they gained another 1–0 victory over Second Division Norwich City before holding Coventry City to a draw at the Goldstone. Jimmy Hill's Sky Blues won the Second Division championship this season, but Albion won the Highfield Road replay 3–1 with probably the best performance of the campaign, despite going behind after just nine minutes. In the fourth-round tie at the Goldstone, Albion were just seven minutes away from a place in the last eight, but Second Division strugglers Northampton Town equalised and in the replay at the County Ground embarrassed Albion 8–0 to earn a home tie with First Division West Bromwich Albion.

The club also reached the fourth round of the F.A. Cup. A fine 2–1 win at Newport County was followed by a 5–0 victory at Southern League Bath City. The third round saw a clash with

Aldershot at the Recreation Ground. The club chartered a train to take around 500 fans to Hampshire and they were rewarded with a 0–0 draw. With the prize for the winners being a plum home tie against First Division Chelsea, the replay attracted 29,208 fans (£6,250) to the Goldstone. Albion beat the Fourth Division side 3–1, but amid the celebrations it was evident that the hooligan problem was worsening: several bottles were thrown from the North Stand and there was much obscene chanting, but the F.A. took no action on either count.

Star-studded Chelsea, managed by Tommy Docherty, were a huge attraction at the start of one of their most successful periods. They included internationals Peter Bonetti and Bobby Tambling (England), and Eddie McCreadie and Charlie Cooke (Scotland); up front was £100,000 centre-forward Tony Hateley.

A 35,000 sell-out crowd (£8,500), the second largest in Goldstone history, saw Tambling give Chelsea a fifth-minute lead. John Boyle received his marching orders in the first half for kicking Wally Gould, but the Londoners still held the advantage at the break. Four minutes into the second period Albion's skipper Dave Turner levelled the scores. Towards the end Brian Tawse beat Bonetti with a tremendous volley, but the deafening roar was silenced when the effort was disallowed for an infringement. The Wednesday-evening replay attracted an enormous crowd of 54,852 to Stamford Bridge with the gates shut on many more. Had Jim Oliver been able to connect with a Wally Gould cross with the score at 0–0 the outcome might have been different, but in the end Chelsea won a hard-fought match 4–0 and progressed to the final, only to lose 2–1 to Spurs.

Norman Gall and Dave Turner missed only one game each, but, with injury problems and with Jimmy Collins and Jimmy Magill missing for lengthy spells in the New Year after requesting transfers, Albion used a total of 29 players. Kit Napier and Eric Whitington top-scored with ten goals apiece all-told. Brian Dear, a late-season loan signing from West Ham United, scored five goals in just seven games.

Cup fever
Fans queue for Chelsea cup-tie tickets which were also rather craftily put on sale at the Football Combination fixture with Notts County; a crowd of 22,229 paid for admission to create a somewhat dubious record for a Goldstone reserve-team fixture. The glamorous Chelsea side attracted a crowd of 35,000 to the Goldstone, the second largest in history. (The rather ramshackle frontage in Newtown Road was bricked in when the present offices and dressing-rooms were built in 1972.)

Albion 1966–67

Back row left to right: Wally Gould, Wilf Tranter, Jimmy Collins, Bill Cassidy, Jack Smith, Norman Gall, Bob Socha.
Third row left to right: Steve Burtenshaw (coach), Derek Leck, Mel Hopkins, Charlie Livesey, Brian Powney, Tony Burns, Eric Whitington, Roger Badminton, Mike Hickman, Cyril Hodges (trainer).
Second row left to right: Jim Oliver, Dave Turner, Jimmy Magill (captain), Bobby Baxter, Nobby Upton, Bill Bannister, Howard Wilkinson, John Templeman, Paul Bence.
Front row left to right: John Duncliffe, Stewart Henderson, Frank Croney, Brian Tawse.

SEASON 1967–68

Four great favourites left the club during the summer: Bobby Baxter moved to Torquay United, Bill Cassidy to Chelmsford City, Jimmy Collins to Wimbledon and Mel Hopkins to Canterbury City. Newcomers included George Dalton, a full-back from Newcastle United, and Paul Flood, a forward from the Bohemians club of Dublin. Two days prior to the opening match another Irishman arrived when Archie Macaulay splashed out a club-record £25,000 fee for Bolton Wanderers' centre-half John Napier, the holder of one full cap for Northern Ireland and another at under-23 level.

The early signs were promising, Albion winning their first three home games without conceding a goal, and in late September Macaulay invested another £10,000 in Preston North End's former Cup final skipper Nobby Lawton, a midfield playmaker. Lawton settled in quickly and the team celebrated his début with a handsome 2–1 win at Orient. Albion were fourth at this point, but the campaign rapidly turned sour with two consecutive home defeats and a run of five matches without victory which brought a plunge into the relegation area.

With all the money spent on new players, club chairman Eric Courtney-King warned that 'heads would roll' if the challenge for promotion was not maintained, but team morale continued to decline while the belief grew amongst the supporters that the club was happy to remain in Division Three. Despite a slight improvement in the New Year, gates fell below the 6,000 mark and there were repeated calls for both a new manager and for the resignation of the board. In February, Eric Courtney-King accommodated his critics by resigning as chairman, to be replaced by Tom Whiting. In an unhappy period for the club, it was also necessary to issue a final warning to the young fans who continued to throw toilet-rolls and to run onto the pitch.

The second half of the season was spent mostly just above mid table, although the club did climb to fifth spot in early April, but two home defeats at Easter ensured a mediocre finish. In the final game, at Walsall, Kit Napier brought his personal tally for the season to 28 goals, equalling the post-war record held by Albert Mundy. It was a terrific achievement in an otherwise forgettable season and he was presented with a gold wrist-watch. Albion finished tenth, rather surprisingly only eight points short of promotion in a poor division.

The two cup tournaments brought little solace. After defeating Colchester United 4–0 at the Goldstone, Albion lost 3–0 to Second Division Blackburn Rovers at Ewood Park in the second round of the League Cup. In the F.A. Cup, Southend United were beaten 1–0 at the Goldstone in the first round, but Albion were second-best to an Ivor Allchurch-inspired Swansea Town in the next round, losing 2–1 to the Fourth Division side at the Vetch Field. The 38-year-old Welsh international was in superb form and in a class of his own.

Bobby Smith was back in town in November to play in a testimonial match for the joint benefits of Jack Bertolini and trainer Cyril Hodges, and scored for an All-Star XI in a 6–5 win over the Albion. The game attracted a superb attendance of 15,768, which remains a record for a non-competitive Albion match at the Goldstone. Bertolini, who had been looking after the youth team on a part-time basis, left the club in January with former player Glen Wilson returning to supervise the juniors.

Kit Napier missed only one of Albion's 50 matches, while his namesake, John, was absent only twice and added a second under-23 cap to his collection when he was chosen against Wales in March. The centre-half was also selected for the senior

SEASON 1967–68

Date	Comp.	Ven.	Opponents	Result	HT	Pos.	Scorers	Atten.	Badminton R	Bence P	Burns A	Dalton G	Duncliffe J	Flood P	Fuller R	Gall N	Gould W	Henderson S	Hickman M	Lawton N	Livesey C	Magill J	Napier K	Napier J	Oliver J	Powney B	Tawse B	Templeman J	Tranter W	Turner D	Whitington E	Wilkinson H
Aug 19	FL D3	(a)	Swindon Town	L 1–2	1–0	16=	Livesey	15,790		1	3					2	8				10		9	5			11	4	N	6		7
23	FLC R1	(h)	Colchester United	W 4–0	1–0	—	Livesey, K Napier 2, Flood	10,455	5†	1	3			12		4	7				10		9				11	8	2	6		
26	FL D3	(h)	Shrewsbury Town	W 3–0	1–0	8	Livesey, K Napier 2	12,833		1	3			12		4	7				10		9	5			11	8†	2	6		
Sep 2	FL D3	(h)	Bury	W 3–0	1–0	5	K Napier	13,465		1	3			12		4	7				10		9	5			11†	8	2	6		
6	FL D3	(a)	Torquay United	D 1–1	1–0	7	K Napier	8,291		1	3			12		4†	7				10		9	5			11	8	2	6		
8	FL D3	(a)	Stockport County	L 0–2	0–0	9=		9,276		1	3			N			7	8			10		9	5			11	4	2	6		
13	FLC R2	(a)	Blackburn Rovers	L 1–3	1–1	—	K Napier	10,257		1	3						11	8			10		9	5			7	4	2	6	N	
16	FL D3	(h)	Tranmere Rovers	W 2–0	0–0	6	Livesey, Wilkinson	12,705		1	3						11		8†		10		9	5			7	4	2	6		12
23	FL D3	(a)	Orient	W 2–1	1–1	4	Tawse (pen), K Napier	4,646		1	3						12			10	8		9	5			11†	4	2	6		
25	FL D3	(h)	Torquay United	L 0–1	0–1	5		19,689		1	3					4†				10	8	2	9	5			11			6	12	7
30	FL D3	(h)	Northampton T.	L 0–2	0–1	11		13,540		1	3						7			8	10			5			11	4	2	6	9†	12
Oct 4	FL D3	(a)	Grimsby Town	L 2–4	1–2	16	K Napier, Wilkinson	4,834	1†		3						8			10		2	9	5	7		11	4		6		12
7	FL D3	(a)	Colchester United	D 0–0	0–0	17		5,075			3						7			8	10	2	9	5	N	1	11			6		
14	FL D3	(a)	Peterborough Utd	D 1–1	0–0	15	J Napier	10,905			3					4	7			8	10	2	9	5		1	11	N		6		
21	FL D3	(a)	Mansfield Town	W 3–1	2–1	11	Livesey, Tranter, Templeman	5,231			3		11			4				8	10†		9	5		1		12	2	6		7
23	FL D3	(h)	Grimsby Town	W 3–1	1–1	7	Wilkinson, Livesey 2	13,185				3	11			4				8	10		9	5		1		N	2	6		7
28	FL D3	(h)	Watford	W 1–0	0–0	6	Flood	12,806				3	11			4				8	10		9	5		1		N	2	6		7
Nov 4	FL D3	(a)	Southport	L 0–1	0–0	9		5,069				3	11			4				8			9	5		1		10	2	6	12	7†
11	FL D3	(h)	Scunthorpe Utd	W 3–1	0–0	6	K Napier, Lawton, Flood	11,251		1	3					4	11	N		8	10		9	5			7		2	6		
18	FL D3	(a)	Oldham Athletic	L 0–3	0–1	13		7,852		1	3					4	11†	12		8	10		9	5			7		2	6		
25	FL D3	(h)	Bristol Rovers	D 1–1	1–0	13	Gould	10,373		1	3					4	N	7			10		9	5			11		2	6		
Dec 2	FL D3	(h)	Barrow	D 1–1	0–0	14	K Napier	6,076			3						7	10	8				9	5		1	11	4	2	6	N	
13	FAC R1	(h)	Southend United	W 1–0	0–0	—	K Napier	12,296			3						7	10†	8	12			9	5		1	11	4	2	6		
16	FL D3	(h)	Swindon Town	D 0–0	0–0	13		9,142			3					4	11		8		10		9	5		1		N	2	6		
23	FL D3*	(a)	Shrewsbury Town	D 0–0	0–0	15		5,132			3					4	11		8		10		9	5		1		6	2			7
26	FL D3	(h)	Gillingham	W 3–0	2–0	10	K Napier 2, Wilkinson	12,896			3					4	11	6	8†		10		9	5		1		12	2			7
30	FL D3	(a)	Gillingham	D 1–1	0–0	10	K Napier	6,154			3					4	10	6			8		9	5		1	11	2		N		7
Jan 6	FAC R2	(a)	Swansea Town	L 1–2	1–0	—	Hickman	9,520			3					4	10	6	8				9	5		1	11†	2	12			7
17	FL D3	(a)	Bury	L 0–4	0–2	11		6,085			3					4	11				10		9	5		1		N	2	6		7
19	FL D3	(a)	Tranmere Rovers	D 2–2	2–0	10	K Napier, Turner	8,203		1	3					4	11				8		9	5			7†	10	2	6		12
27	FL D3	(h)	Oxford United	D 0–0	0–0	8		10,612			3†					4	11				10		9	5		1	7	8	2	6		12
Feb 3	FL D3	(h)	Orient	D 1–1	1–0	10	Gould	8,882			3					4	11	6		10†			9	5	7	1	8		2	12		
10	FL D3	(a)	Northampton T.	D 2–2	0–2		K Napier, Oliver	7,882		1		3		N		2	4				8	10	9	5	7		11			6		
24	FL D3	(h)	Colchester United	D 0–0	0–0	13		6,512		1		3	10			4†							9	5			11	8	2	6	12	7
28	FL D3	(h)	Walsall	W 1–0	1–0	9	Wilkinson	6,447		1		3	N							10	2	9	5			11	8	4	6		7
Mar 2	FL D3	(a)	Peterborough Utd	W 3–2	1–0	8	Magill, K Napier 2	4,580		1		3								10	2	9	5			11	8†	4	6	12	7
9	FL D3	(a)	Reading	L 0–1	0–1	10		6,272		1		3								10	2	9	5			11		4	6		7
16	FL D3	(h)	Mansfield Town	W 3–0	0–0	9	K Napier, Turner, Tawse	7,756		1		3				2	12				10		9	5			11	8	4	6†		7
20	FL D3	(h)	Reading	D 1–1	1–0	6	K Napier	9,188		1		3				5	12				10		9				11	8	4	6†		7
23	FL D3	(a)	Watford	L 0–4	0–1	11		6,344		1		3				2					10		9	5			11	8	6		N	7
30	FL D3	(h)	Southport	W 1–0	1–0	7	K Napier	5,813		1		3	8	N		2					10		9	5			11	6			4	7
Apr 6	FL D3	(a)	Scunthorpe Utd	W 3–1	2–0	5	K Napier 2, Wilkinson	2,715		1		3				N	2			8	10		9	5			11	6			4	7
12	FL D3	(a)	Bournem'th & B.A.	D 2–2	0–2	5	Lawton, K Napier	8,464		1		3				12	2			8	10		9	5			11	6†			4	7
13	FL D3	(h)	Oldham Athletic	L 0–1	0–1	9		11,598		1			3			2				8	10		9	5			11	12		6	4	7†
15	FL D3	(h)	Bournem'th & B.A.	L 2–3	2–2	10	Own goal, Livesey	8,957				3				4	2			8†	10		9	5			11			12	6	7
20	FL D3	(a)	Bristol Rovers	L 1–3	1–3	13	K Napier	6,846				3				6				2	10	N	9	5		1	11	4		8		7
27	FL D3	(h)	Barrow	D 1–1	0–1	14	Whitington	6,183				3				4				2			11			1	7	8	12	6†	10	
May 1	FL D3	(h)	Stockport County	W 3–0	2–0	12	Flood, K Napier, Whitington	5,792	N		3			8		4							9	5			11		6		10	7
4	FL D3	(a)	Oxford United	L 0–2	0–1	12		12,918				3		8		4				2	N		9	5			11	6			10	7
11	FL D3	(a)	Walsall	W 2–1	1–1	11	K Napier, Wilkinson	5,385	12			8		3†		2	10						9	5			11	6			4	7
							League appearances		0	0	27	24	20	11	0	31	22	13	7	22	40	7	45	45	3	19	37	32	28	34	12	27
							Substitute appearances			1			3	1	2	2											1	2	1	2	4	5
							League goals	OG – 1						3			2			2	7	1	24	1	1		2	1	1	2	2	7

Note: Dec 23 – no substitute selected because of illness in squad.

Football League Division 3 1967–68

		P	W	D	L	F	A	W	D	L	F	A	Pts
1.	Oxford United	46	18	3	2	49	20	4	10	9	20	27	57
2.	Bury	46	19	3	1	64	24	5	5	13	27	42	56
3.	Shrewsbury Town	46	14	6	3	42	17	6	9	8	19	32	55
4.	Torquay United	46	15	6	2	40	17	6	5	12	20	39	53
5.	Reading	46	15	5	3	43	17	6	4	13	27	43	51
6.	Watford	46	15	3	5	59	20	6	5	12	15	30	50
7.	Walsall	46	12	7	4	47	22	7	5	11	27	39	50
8.	Barrow	46	14	6	3	43	13	7	2	14	22	41	50
9.	Swindon Town	46	13	8	2	51	16	3	9	11	23	35	49
10.	**ALBION**	46	11	8	4	31	14	5	8	10	26	41	48
11.	Gillingham	46	13	6	4	35	19	5	6	12	24	44	48
12.	Bournemouth & B.A.	46	13	7	3	39	17	3	8	12	17	34	47
13.	Stockport County	46	16	5	2	49	22	3	4	16	21	53	47
14.	Southport	46	13	6	4	35	22	4	6	13	30	43	46
15.	Bristol Rovers	46	14	3	6	42	25	3	6	14	30	53	43
15.	Oldham Athletic	46	11	3	9	37	32	7	4	12	23	33	43
17.	Northampton Town	46	10	8	5	40	25	4	5	14	18	47	41
18.	Orient	46	10	6	7	27	24	2	11	10	19	38	41
19.	Tranmere Rovers	46	10	7	6	39	28	4	5	14	23	46	40
20.	Mansfield Town	46	8	7	8	32	31	4	6	13	19	36	37
21.	Grimsby Town	46	10	7	6	33	21	4	2	17	19	48	37
22.	Colchester United	46	6	8	9	29	40	3	7	13	21	47	33
23.	Scunthorpe United	46	8	9	6	36	34	2	3	18	20	53	32
24.	Peterborough United	46	14	4	5	46	23	6	6	11	33	44	31

Notes: Peterborough United had nineteen points deducted at the end of the season for illegal payments; Bristol Rovers and Oldham Athletic finished level in fifteenth place.

Northern Ireland team against Wales but had to cry off because of Albion's rearranged League fixture with Walsall at the Goldstone, played on the same February evening.

The reserve team had an appalling season, finishing bottom of Division Two of the Football Combination, and in April the club announced that it was to be dropped for financial reasons; the saving was estimated at between £10,000 and £15,000 a season. For 1968–69 the club would rely on a first-team squad of seventeen players, with a youth side retained in the South East Counties League. Several other clubs had tried this set-up, pioneered by Portsmouth three years earlier, in an effort to cut expenses, but most Albion followers saw it as a retrograde step.

The 501 Executive Club, superseded soon after by the Albion Sporting Club, commenced this season for some of the more affluent fans, with all profits going towards the development of the ground. Both clubs held regular dinner evenings at the greyhound stadium.

Albion 1967–68

Back row left to right: Brian Tawse, Stewart Henderson, Andy Tasker, Paul Bence, George Dalton, Wally Gould, John Duncliffe, Paul Flood.
Middle row left to right: Cyril Hodges (trainer), Charlie Livesey, Kit Napier, Roger Badminton, Brian Powney, Tony Burns, Eric Whitington, John Templeman, Jimmy Magill, Steve Burtenshaw (coach).
Front left to right: Wilf Tranter, Norman Gall, Mike Hickman, Howard Wilkinson, Bob Fuller, Jim Oliver, Stewart Ogden, Dave Turner (capt.).

SEASON 1968–69

Of the seven players transfer-listed at the end of 1967–68, only Wilf Tranter had made much of an impact at the Goldstone; he left for the United States to play for Baltimore Bays. Mike Hickman, 21, joined Grimsby Town in June on a free transfer after only eighteen appearances in Albion's first team, but went on to play in 253 League matches for the Mariners. The summer signings were Mike Everitt, a £2,500 buy from Plymouth Argyle, and another Bobby Smith, a free transfer from Grimsby Town.

Fewer than 10,000 were at the Goldstone for the opening match against Mansfield Town, the lowest attendance for an initial home fixture since the return to peacetime competition in 1946, and as Albion lost 2–1 there were already calls from the terraces of 'Macaulay out!'. A win at Southport and a crushing

Albion 1968–69

Standing left to right: Cyril Hodges (trainer), Brian Powney, Nobby Lawton (captain), Norman Gall, John Templeman, John Napier, Roger Badminton, Kit Napier, Charlie Livesey, Jimmy Magill, Tony Burns, Archie Macaulay (manager).
Seated left to right: George Dalton, Bobby Smith, Ken Blackburn, Stewart Henderson, Brian Tawse, Paul Flood, Howard Wilkinson, Mike Everitt, Dave Turner.

SEASON 1968–69

Date	Comp.	Ven.	Opponents	Result	HT	Pos.	Scorers	Atten.	Armstrong D	Blackburn K	Burns A	Dawson A	Everitt M	Flood P	Gall N	Henderson S	Lawton N	Livesey C	Napier K	Napier J	Powney B	Sidebottom G	Smith RW	Spearitt E	Tawse B	Templeman J	Turner D	Wilkinson H	Wright B
Aug 10	FL D3	(h)	Mansfield Town	L 1–2	1–2	18	J Napier	9,647			1		3		4†	2	10		9	5			12		11	8	6	7	
14	FLC R1	(h)	Oxford United	W 2–0	0–0	–	Templeman, K Napier	7,304			1		3	11		2	8	10	9	5			N			4	6	7	
17	FL D3	(a)	Southport	W 3–2	1–1	12=	Lawton, Livesey 2	3,794			1		3	11	12	2	8	10	9	5						4	6†	7	
24	FL D3	(h)	Oldham Athletic	W 6–0	4–0	3	Flood, Henderson, Livesey, Wilkinson, K Napier, Templeman	8,336			1		3†	11	12	2	8	10	9	5						4	6	7	
28	FL D3	(h)	Torquay United	D 1–1	1–0	3	Templeman	14,821			1		3	11	N	2	8	10	9	5						4	6	7	
31	FL D3	(a)	Barrow	D 1–1	1–0	5	Flood	5,779			1			11	3	2		10	9	5			8		12	4	6	7†	
Sep 4	FLC R2	(h)	Luton Town	D 1–1	0–1	–	Lawton	15,305			1			11	3	2	8	10	9	5			N			4	6	7	
7	FL D3	(h)	Rotherham United	D 2–2	1–1	6	Turner, Flood	10,164			1			11	3	2	10	9		5			8		N	4	6	7	
11	FLC R2 Rep	(a)	Luton Town	L 2–4	0–0	–	Livesey, K Napier	18,679			1			11	3	2	8	10	9	5			N			4	6	7	
14	FL D3	(a)	Gillingham	L 0–5	0–1	13		4,445	7		1		3	10†		2	8		9	5					11	4	6	12	
16	FL D3*	(a)	Orient	– –	1–1	14	Lawton	5,518	11						3	2	8	10	9	5	1		6		N		4	7	
21	FL D3	(h)	Luton Town	W 1–0	1–0	10	Wilkinson	11,689	11		1				3	2	8	10	9	5			6		N		4	7	
28	FL D3	(a)	Barnsley	L 0–4	0–0	15		9,189	11		1			N	3	2	8	10	9	5			6				4	7	
Oct 5	FL D3	(a)	Bournem'th & B.A.	L 0–2	0–1	17		7,842	7		1			N	3	2	8	10	9	5			4		11		6		
9	FL D3	(a)	Torquay United	D 1–1	0–1	18	K Napier	7,697			1		3	11	4	2	8†	12	9	5					7	10	6		
12	FL D3	(h)	Swindon Town	L 1–3	0–1	19	Lawton	7,355	7		1			11	3	2	8	10	9	5					12	4	6†		
14	FL D3	(a)	Tranmere Rovers	W 2–0	1–0	15	Templeman, K Napier	6,482	N					11	3	2	10	8	9	5	1		6		7	4			
18	FL D3	(a)	Reading	L 0–1	0–0	15		7,047	11		N			8		2	3	6	9	5	1		10		7	4			
21	FL D3	(a)	Orient	L 2–3	1–2	18	Armstrong, K Napier	5,510	12		1			11	3	2	8	10	9	5			6		7	4†			
26	FL D3	(h)	Watford	L 0–1	0–0	20		8,335					9	11	3	2	8	10†		5	1		6		7		4	12	
Nov 1	FL D3	(a)	Stockport County	L 1–3	0–0	20	Turner	8,174	N					10	3	2	8		9	5	1		4		11		6	7	
6	FL D3	(a)	Crewe Alexandra	L 0–1	0–1	23		3,811	11					10	3	2	4		9	5	1		6		12		8†	7	
9	FL D3	(h)	Bristol Rovers	W 3–1	2–0	21	K Napier 3	6,175	N				6	3	9	2	10		8	5	1		4		11			7	
16	FAC R1	(h)	Kidderminster Har.	D 2–2	2–0	–	Livesey, Lawton	9,244					6	3†	12	2	10	9	8	5	1		4		11			7	
20	FAC R1 Rep	(a)	Kidderminster Har.	W 1–0	1–0	–	K Napier	8,442			1		3		N	2	10	9	8	5			4		11		6	7	
23	FL D3	(h)	Northampton T.	D 1–1	0–1	21	J Napier	6,613			1		3		N	2	10	9	8	5			4		11		6	7	
30	FL D3	(a)	Walsall	L 0–4	0–1	22		4,892			1		3		N	2	10	9	8	5			4		11		6	7	
Dec 7	FAC R2	(h)	Northampton T.	L 1–2	0–0	–	K Napier	8,839	N		1		3	11	6	2		9	8	5			4			7	10		
14	FL D3	(a)	Swindon Town	L 0–1	0–0	23		10,914	12			9	10	3†	6	2		11	8	5	1		4			7			
20	FL D3	(h)	Reading	W 2–0	0–0	22	Dawson, Wilkinson	6,868	10†			9	3		6	2		11	8	5	1		4			7		12	
26	FL D3	(h)	Bournem'th & B.A.	W 4–1	2–0	19	Dawson, Smith, K Napier, Livesey	14,693				9	3		6	2	10	11	8	5	1		4			N	7		
28	FL D3	(a)	Watford	L 0–1	0–0	21		12,533				9	3		6	2	10		8	5	1		4			N	7	11	
Jan 4	FL D3	(a)	Plymouth Argyle	D 1–1	1–1	19	Dawson	6,774				9	3			2	10	11†	8	5	1		4				6	7	12
11	FL D3	(h)	Stockport County	D 1–1	0–0	20	K Napier	10,645				9	4		6	2		12	8	5		1			11†		10	7	3
18	FL D3	(a)	Bristol Rovers	D 1–1	0–1	18	Everitt (pen)	8,002	11			9	2		6		10	N	8	5		1					4	7	3
25	FL D3	(h)	Crewe Alexandra	W 3–1	2–0	16	Armstrong, K Napier, Dawson	11,269	11			9	3		2		4	N	8	5		1		10			6	7	
Feb 1	FL D3	(h)	Shrewsbury Town	W 3–0	1–0	17	Lawton, Gall, Dawson	11,716	11			9		3	6		4	N	8	5	1			10		2		7	
15	FL D3	(h)	Walsall	W 3–0	0–0	11	Dawson 2, Own goal	10,018	11			9			6	3	4		8	5		1		10		2	N	7	
22	FL D3	(a)	Hartlepool	W 5–2	2–2	10	Dawson 4, Wilkinson	2,923	11			9			6	3	4		8	5		1		10		2	N	7	
25	FL D3	(a)	Northampton T.	D 1–1	0–1	8	K Napier	4,554	11			9†			6	3	4		8	5		1		10		2	12	7	
Mar 1	FL D3	(a)	Mansfield Town	L 2–3	1–1	10	Armstrong, Spearitt (pen)	13,595	11						6	3	4		8	5		1		10	N	2	9	7	
5	FL D3	(h)	Plymouth Argyle	D 0–0	0–0	11		13,295	11			9			N				8	5	1		4	10		2	6	7	3
8	FL D3	(h)	Southport	W 4–0	3–0	10	Wilkinson, Dawson 2, K Napier	11,397	11			9†			12				8	5	1		4	10		2	6	7	3
12	FL D3	(a)	Shrewsbury Town	W 2–1	1–0	9	Spearitt, Blackburn	2,854	11	9					12				8	5	1		4	10		2	6†	7	3
15	FL D3	(a)	Oldham Athletic	L 0–2	0–1	8		3,995	11			9			6	2			8	5		1	4	10		3		7	N
19	FL D3	(h)	Hartlepool	D 1–1	0–0	8	Armstrong	11,206	11			9				2	N		8	5		1	4	10		3	6	7	
22	FL D3	(h)	Barrow	W 4–1	1–0	8	K Napier, Armstrong, Dawson 2	9,997	11			9				2	N		8	5	1		4	10		3	6	7	
29	FL D3	(a)	Rotherham United	D 1–1	0–0	9	K Napier	7,568	11			9				2	N		8	5	1		4	10		3	6	7	
Apr 4	FL D3	(h)	Orient	W 2–0	1–0	7	Dawson, Lawton	16,007	11			9			12	2	8		7	5	1		4	10		3	6†		
5	FL D3	(h)	Barnsley	W 4–1	1–0	6	Armstrong, Spearitt, Turner, Dawson	11,410	11			9			12	2	8			5	1		4†	10	7	3	6		
12	FL D3	(a)	Luton Town	L 0–3	0–1	8		11,965	11			9			6	2			8	5	1			10	N	3	4	7	
16	FL D3	(h)	Tranmere Rovers	D 2–2	0–1	8	Spearitt 2	10,749	11			9			N	2	8		7	5	1		4	10		3	6		
19	FL D3	(h)	Gillingham	L 0–2	0–0	8		11,749	11			9			12	2	8		7	5	1			10†		3	6	4	
								League appearances	27	1	15	23	18	17	28	40	34	19	43	46	22	9	29	18	14	31	35	32	5
								Substitute appearances	2						7			2					1		3		1	3	1
								League goals OG – 1	6	1		17	1	3	1	1	4	4	14	2			1	5		3	3	5	

Note: Sep 16 – abandoned at half time because of muddy pitch and worsening conditions. Appearances and goal not included in end-of-season statistics.

Football League Division 3 1968–69

		P	W	D	L	F	A	W	D	L	F	A	Pts
1.	Watford	46	16	5	2	35	7	11	5	7	39	27	64
2.	Swindon Town	46	18	4	1	38	7	9	6	8	33	28	64
3.	Luton Town	46	20	3	0	57	14	5	8	10	17	24	61
4.	Bournemouth & B.A.	46	16	2	5	41	17	5	7	11	19	28	51
5.	Plymouth Argyle	46	10	8	5	34	25	7	7	9	19	24	49
6.	Torquay United	46	13	4	6	35	18	5	8	10	19	28	48
7.	Tranmere Rovers	46	12	3	8	36	31	7	7	9	34	37	48
8.	Southport	46	14	8	1	52	20	3	5	15	19	44	47
9.	Stockport County	46	14	5	4	49	25	2	9	12	18	43	46
10.	Barnsley	46	13	6	4	37	21	3	8	12	21	42	46
11.	Rotherham United	46	12	6	5	40	21	4	7	12	16	29	45
12.	**ALBION**	46	12	7	4	49	21	4	6	13	23	44	45
13.	Walsall	46	10	9	4	34	18	4	7	12	16	31	44
14.	Reading	46	13	3	7	41	25	2	10	11	26	41	43
15.	Mansfield Town	46	14	5	4	37	18	2	6	15	21	44	43
16.	Bristol Rovers	46	12	6	5	41	27	4	5	14	22	44	43
17.	Shrewsbury Town	46	11	8	4	28	17	5	3	15	23	50	43
18.	Orient	46	10	8	5	31	19	4	6	13	20	39	42
19.	Barrow	46	11	6	6	30	23	6	2	15	26	52	42
20.	Gillingham	46	10	10	3	35	20	3	5	15	19	43	41
21.	Northampton Town	46	9	8	6	37	30	5	4	14	17	31	40
22.	Hartlepool	46	6	12	5	25	29	4	7	12	15	41	39
23.	Crewe Alexandra	46	11	4	8	40	31	2	5	16	12	45	35
24.	Oldham Athletic	46	9	6	8	33	27	4	3	16	17	56	35

6–0 home victory over Oldham Athletic found the team amongst the leaders, but it was not to last. Points were squandered, and within the space of a few weeks Albion were in the relegation zone. The midweek match at Orient on 16 September was abandoned at half time with the score at 1–1 because of the waterlogged state of the pitch; the unfortunate referee was escorted from the ground by the police after the angry Brisbane Road crowd rioted. In the rearranged match held on 21 October, Nobby Lawton was sent off for kicking an opponent and received a three-match suspension from the F.A.

Archie Macaulay had paid £5,000 for Millwall's speedy winger Dave Armstrong in September, but results continued to be poor. Only two wins from twelve games left Albion just above the bottom four and the pressure finally told on Macaulay

Owing to a last-minute injury to Norman Gall, goalkeeper Tony Burns was named as substitute for the match at Reading on 18 October, a very rare occurrence. In the event his services were not called upon, but, had he come on, Brian Powney, who later served as an outfield player while managing Southwick, would have come out of goal.

who quit his post after five-and-a-half years in charge on Friday, 25 October, just 24 hours before the annual meeting of shareholders. The home match with Watford was lost 1–0, and as Albion began the search for a new manager the club took the unusual step of appointing a team-selection committee, including skipper Nobby Lawton, to look after playing matters.

There were some well-known names among the applicants – Don Howe, John Bond, Ron Saunders, Gordon Jago, and former Albion stars Jack Mansell and, rather surprisingly, Bobby Smith – but the early favourite was former 'Busby Babe' Freddie Goodwin, recently returned from two years in the U.S.A. where he had been in charge of the New York Generals; he had previously managed Scunthorpe United and was known as a fine tactician. After watching Albion lose their two games under committee control to drop to 23rd, Goodwin was officially appointed as the new boss. Only 6,175 spectators, the smallest crowd of the season, attended his first game in charge, but they saw Kit Napier score a hat-trick as Bristol Rovers were beaten 3–1.

Goodwin's first dealing in the transfer market came in December when he paid Bury around £9,000 for his former Manchester United colleague Alex Dawson. Twice a loser in F.A. Cup finals, Dawson was a real character and quickly won the admiration of the fans with his belligerent, swashbuckling style. At this point Albion were just two places off the bottom, but Dawson's arrival lifted the team and the situation slowly improved. Barrie Wright and goalkeeper Geoff Sidebottom were added to the staff in January – the pair had played for Goodwin in New York – and Eddie Spearritt was signed from Ipswich Town for £20,000 to further reinforce the side. Trainer Cyril Hodges left the club in December, while Mike Yaxley, a familiar figure for many seasons to come, joined the club full-time as youth coach in March.

Points were accumulated, and eight games without defeat brought a climb to eighth place by the end of February as Dawson found the Hartlepool mud to his liking, hitting the net four times in a 5–2 win. From the arrival of Goodwin, Albion went fifteen home games without defeat and gates doubled. The 16,007 attendance at the 2–0 Good Friday victory over Orient was the best turn-out of the season, but the excellent home run was ended by Gillingham who won the final fixture 2–0 and Albion dropped to a final twelfth place as the clubs behind played their games in hand. At the turn of the year Albion had appeared likely candidates for Division Four, but by the end of the campaign they looked a promotion side as the new manager turned the tide.

The cup matches were all played before the improvement came about, but Albion beat Division Two strugglers Oxford United 2–0 at home in the first round of the League Cup before going out to Luton Town 4–2 in a second-round replay.

Kidderminster Harriers, on their way to the championship of the West Midlands League, were the opponents at Hove in the F.A. Cup first round. Albion cruised to a 2–0 half-time advantage but paid the price of easing up when the part-timers came back superbly with two goals in two minutes midway through the second period. In the replay Kit Napier scored just before the break and Albion desperately held out for victory, the unlucky Worcestershire side twice hitting the woodwork. Fewer than 9,000 fans were at the Goldstone to see Albion play fellow Third Division strugglers Northampton Town in the second round. The Cobblers were relegated this season, but they beat the Albion 2–1 and went through to meet Bolton Wanderers at the third stage. When Kit Napier's second-half opening goal was equalised within a minute, a replay had looked odds-on, but Northampton, despite having player-manager Ron Flowers carried off ten minutes from time, snatched the winner four minutes into injury time.

Centre-half John Napier played consistently well at the heart of the defence and appeared in all 52 competitive matches. Kit Napier led the scorers with eighteen goals in League and Cup, one ahead of the splendid Alex Dawson who hit seventeen in just 23 games.

The rise of the hooligan continued, and there was full-scale fighting in the North Stand at the Northampton Town cup-tie. The police resorted to closed-circuit television for crowd supervision, and there were a number of arrests and convictions in the latter months. In April, Albion were again ordered to post warning-notices around the ground after missiles and toilet-rolls were thrown onto the pitch against Hartlepool.

Player of the Season
John Napier receives the club's first Player of the Season award, an innovation suggested by supporters Ron and Winn Carr.

SEASON 1969–70

Charlie Livesey left for Crawley Town during the close season and Freddie Goodwin brought in Alan Gilliver, a free transfer from Rotherham United, as a replacement striker. Leicester City's former Scottish international full-back Willie Bell arrived as player-coach, also without the payment of a fee.

The opening fixture, a home match with Walsall, ended in a 1–1 draw with nineteen-year-old goalkeeper Phil Parkes, later to win renown with Queen's Park Rangers, West Ham United and England, keeping the Saddlers in the game with a series of fine saves. After seven matches Albion were unbeaten in third place and talk amongst the fans was of almost certain promotion, but the early form was not maintained and by mid December the team were as low as twelfth in the table.

A feature of the season was the chaos that Kit Napier was able to create in opposition defences with his beautifully flighted, inswinging corners from either flag, and against Bury on 27 December he scored direct to set Albion up for a 2–0 win. That was the first of a sequence of six consecutive victories and part of an overall run of fourteen games unbeaten which saw Albion climb up the table again.

In January the squad was strengthened by the addition of 20-year-old forward Alan Duffy, signed from Newcastle United for £10,000, and he immediately repaid part of that fee with a début goal against Bradford City. The 3–0 victory over Walsall on 25 February saw Albion into first place, but defeats at Southport and Torquay United temporarily knocked them off the top. By the time the crucial Easter games came around Albion were still leading the section by a couple of points, although their closest rivals had up to four games in hand.

On Good Friday fellow promotion contenders Reading came to the Goldstone with 5,000 travelling supporters, swelling the attendance to 32,036. Albion rose to the occasion with a 2–1 win to remain top of the section:

		P	W	D	L	F	A	Pts
1.	ALBION	41	22	9	10	52	33	53
2.	Orient	37	20	11	6	56	27	51
3.	Bristol Rovers	39	18	13	8	72	49	49
4.	Luton Town	38	18	12	8	64	40	48
5.	Barnsley	41	17	13	11	59	50	47
6.	Reading	39	18	10	11	69	63	46

However, the side's chances were completely blown by defeat at Halifax Town on the Saturday, and then by a 4–1 drubbing at Fulham on Easter Monday. Albion still held second spot at this point, but a third successive defeat, at Rochdale, saw any hope disappear. As the chasing group overtook them, Brighton dropped to a final fifth place, a real anti-climax to a most promising finale. Just two points from the last ten cost the club dear as they finished five points behind a promotion place.

Albion had an excellent run in the League Cup with Goldstone wins over lowly Second Division opposition in the opening two rounds, Portsmouth (1–0) and Birmingham City (2–0), both games attracting big gates. The third-round tie, a first-ever clash with Wolverhampton Wanderers, was an all-ticket affair. The famous Wolves were destined to finish thirteenth in the First Division this season, but Albion tore into them from the start and gained a 2–1 lead at the interval thanks to Alan Gilliver and Eddie Spearritt. However, the vast majority of the 32,539 crowd went home bitterly disappointed as two late goals from Hugh Curran gave Wolves a 3–2 victory.

In the F.A. Cup, Enfield were the visitors to Hove in the first round. The Middlesex club were a strong side, winning the F.A. Amateur Cup and the Isthmian League championship this term, and with seven amateur internationals in their line-up they proved stern opposition. Albion narrowly won 2–1 with both goals coming from Alan Gilliver, a victory which led to a

Albion 1969–70

Back row left to right: Mike Yaxley (coach), Terry Stanley, George Dalton, Barrie Wright, Bobby Smith, Mike Everitt, Dave Armstrong, Ken Blackburn, Joe Wilson (trainer).
Third row left to right: Tom Whiting (chairman), Brian Powney, Andy Marchant, Stewart Henderson, Dave Turner, John Napier, Norman Gall, John Templeman, Paul Flood, Geoff Sidebottom, Harold Paris (vice-chairman).
Second row left to right: Howard Wilkinson, Alex Dawson, Kit Napier, Eddie Spearritt, Freddie Goodwin (manager), Nobby Lawton (captain), Willie Bell, Alan Gilliver, Brian Tawse.
On ground left to right: Martin Tew, Keith Watkins, Mick Stanley, Gary Parsons.

With a blizzard raging in the area on 29 November, fans arriving at Brighton and Hove railway stations were disappointed to read notices that the match with Torquay United was off. They were even more disappointed to discover later that the notices were premature and that the match had in fact been played to a 2–2 draw. The crowd was kept down to just 5,640.

SEASON 1969–70

Date	Comp.	Ven.	Opponents	Result	HT	Pos.	Scorers	Atten.	Armstrong D	Bell W	Dawson A	Duffy A	Everitt M	Gall N	Gilliver A	Henderson S	Lawton N	Napier K	Napier J	Powney B	Sidebottom G	Smith RW	Spearritt E	Stanley T	Tawse B	Templeman J	Turner D	Wilkinson H	Wright B
Aug 9	FL D3	(h)	Walsall	D 1–1	1–1	14=	Dawson	11,250	N	3	9				10	2	8	7	5		1	4	11				6		
13	FLC R1	(h)	Portsmouth	W 1–0	0–0	–	Dawson	19,787	N	3	9				10	2	8	7	5		1	4	11				6		
16	FL D3	(a)	Plymouth Argyle	W 1–0	0–0	6=	Gilliver	11,237		3	9				10	2	8	7	5		1	4	11			N	6		
23	FL D3	(h)	Bournem'th & B.A.	D 1–1	1–0	9	K Napier	13,961	12	3	9			6	10	2	8	7	5		1	4	11†				6		
27	FL D3	(h)	Rochdale	W 2–0	1–0	4	Spearritt (pen), Gilliver	13,690	7	3	9				10	2	8		5		1	4	11		N		6		
30	FL D3	(a)	Bury	W 2–1	1–1	4	Gilliver, K Napier	5,634	7†	3	9				10	2	8	12	5		1	4	11				6		
Sep 3	FLC R2	(h)	Birmingham City	W 2–0	1–0	–	Gilliver, K Napier	24,232	N	3	9				10	2	8	7	5		1	4	11				6		
6	FL D3	(h)	Gillingham	W 3–1	3–0	2	Dawson, Gilliver, K Napier	13,400	12	3	9				10	2	8	7†	5		1	4	11				6		
13	FL D3	(a)	Orient	D 1–1	1–1	3	Dawson	8,040	N		9		3		10	2	8	7	5		1	4	11				6		
15	FL D3	(a)	Mansfield Town	L 0–1	0–0	4=		6,304			9		3	12	10	2	8	7	5	1		4			11		6†		
20	FL D3	(h)	Barrow	W 2–0	1–0	3	Lawton, Spearritt	21,190	12	3	9				10	2	8	7†	5		1	4	11				6		
24	FLC R3	(h)	Wolverhampton W.	L 2–3	2–1	–	Gilliver, Spearritt	32,539	N	3	9				10	2	8	7	5		1	4	11				6		
27	FL D3	(a)	Bradford City	L 0–1	0–1	5		9,715		3	9			12	10	2	8	7	5		1	4	11				6†		
30	FL D3	(a)	Doncaster Rovers	L 0–2	0–1	9		10,779	11	3				6	9	2	8	7†	5		1	4	10						12
Oct 4	FL D3	(h)	Bristol Rovers	L 0–3	0–3	10		11,417		3	9			5	10	2	8	7	N	1		4	11				6		
7	FL D3	(h)	Plymouth Argyle	W 2–0	0–0	9	K Napier 2	10,967	11	3			4		10	2	8	9	5	1			7			N	6		
11	FL D3	(a)	Shrewsbury Town	D 2–2	1–1	9	Lawton, Own goal	3,921	11	3			4	N	10	2	8	9	5	1			7				6		
18	FL D3	(h)	Luton Town	L 1–2	0–1	10	Bell	18,722	11	3	10†		4	12		2	8	9	5	1			7				6		
25	FL D3	(a)	Tranmere Rovers	L 0–2	0–2	12		3,764	7†	3			4		10		8		5		1		12		11	2	6	9	
Nov 1	FL D3	(h)	Fulham	W 2–1	1–1	10	Gilliver, K Napier	17,760	11	3				6	9†	2	7	8	5		1		4			12	10		
8	FL D3	(a)	Reading	L 0–1	0–0	11		7,420	12	3				6	9	2	7	8	5		1		4			11†	10		
15	FAC R1	(h)	Enfield	W 2–1	1–1	–	Gilliver 2	11,276	11	3	9		N	6	8	2		7	5		1		4				10		
22	FL D3	(a)	Barnsley	W 2–1	1–1	10	J Napier, Gilliver	11,243	11†	3	9		12	6	8	2		7	5		1		4						10
25	FL D3	(a)	Rotherham United	L 0–2	0–1	10		5,984	11	3	9		12	6	8	2		7	5		1		4†						10
29	FL D3	(h)	Torquay United	D 2–2	1–1	10	K Napier, Gilliver	5,640		3	9			6	8	2	7†	11	5		1		4				10	12	
Dec 6	FAC R2	(h)	Walsall	D 1–1	1–0	–	Dawson	10,231		3	9			6	8	2	7	11	5		1†		4				10	12	
9	FAC R2 Rep	(a)	Walsall	D 1–1*	0–1	–	Dawson	9,621		3	9			6	8	2	7	11	5	1			4				10†	12	
13	FL D3	(h)	Orient	D 0–0	0–0	12		9,274		3			12	6	8	2		9	5	1			4	7				11	10†
15	FAC R2 2Rep(n*)		Walsall	D 0–0*	0–0	–		4,299		3	9			6	8†	2	7	11	5	1			4				10	12	
17	FAC R2 3Rep(n*)		Walsall	L 1–2	0–0	–	Lawton	2,241		3	9			6	8	2	7	11	5	1			4			10†		12	
20	FL D3	(a)	Gillingham	W 1–0	1–0	9	Dawson	3,930		3	9			6		2	7†	8	5	1			4	12			10	11	
26	FL D3	(a)	Bournem'th & B.A.	D 0–0	0–0	9=		7,763		3	9			6		2	8	7	5	1			4	N			10	11	
27	FL D3	(h)	Bury	W 2–0	2–0	9	K Napier, Spearritt	13,383		3	9			6	N	2	7	8	5	1			4				10	11	
Jan 3	FL D3	(h)	Doncaster Rovers	W 1–0	0–0	7	Gilliver	10,833		3	9			6	12	2	7†	8	5	1			4				10	11	
17	FL D3	(h)	Bradford City	W 2–1	1–0	8	Duffy, Dawson	14,552		3	9	8		5	N	2		7		1		10	4				6	11	
23	FL D3	(a)	Stockport County	W 1–0	1–0	4	Smith	5,109		3	9	8		5		2	7	11			1	10	4	N			6		
31	FL D3	(a)	Bristol Rovers	W 2–0	1–0	3	Dawson 2	11,820		3	9	8		5		2	7	11			1	10	4	N			6		
Feb 7	FL D3	(h)	Shrewsbury Town	W 1–0	1–0	3	Dawson	15,554		3	9	8		6	N	2	7	11	5		1		4				10		
16	FL D3	(a)	Barrow	D 1–1	1–0	4	Turner	3,892		3	9	8		6	N	2	7	11	5		1		4				10		
21	FL D3	(h)	Tranmere Rovers	W 2–0	1–0	3	Duffy, Dawson	16,324		3	9	8		6		2	4	11	5		1	12		7			10†		
25	FL D3	(a*)	Walsall	W 3–0	1–0	1	Turner 2, K Napier	7,535		3	12	8		6	9	2		11	5		1		4	7†			10		
28	FL D3	(a)	Luton Town	D 1–1	1–0	1	Own goal	17,584		3	N	8		6	9	2		11	5		1	7	4				10		
Mar 3	FL D3	(a)	Southport	L 0–2	0–0	2		3,963		3	9	8		6	N	2	7	11	5		1		4				10		
7	FL D3	(h)	Barnsley	W 2–0	0–0	1	Spearritt (pen), Turner	15,622	11	3	9	8		6		2	4		5	1			7				10	N	
11	FL D3	(h)	Halifax Town	W 4–0	1–0	1	Turner, Gilliver 3	16,759		3		8		6	9	2	4	11	5	1			7				10	N	
14	FL D3	(a)	Torquay United	L 1–2	0–2	2=	Gall	4,807		3		8		6	9	2	4	11	5	1			7				10	N	
18	FL D3	(h)	Stockport County	W 1–0	1–0	1	Gilliver	16,667		3		8		6	9	2	4	11	5	1			7				10	N	
21	FL D3	(h)	Southport	W 1–0	0–0	1	K Napier	14,655		3		8†		6	9	2	4	11	5	1			7	12			10		
27	FL D3	(h)	Reading	W 2–1	1–0	1	Duffy 2	32,036		3		8		6	9	2	4	11	5	1		10	7	N					
28	FL D3	(a)	Halifax Town	L 0–1	0–1	1		4,006		3		8		6	9	2	4	11	5		1	10	7†	12					
30	FL D3	(a)	Fulham	L 1–4	0–3	2	Wilkinson	17,988		3	9†	8		6		2		12	5	1		10	4	7				11	
Apr 4	FL D3	(a)	Rochdale	L 1–2	0–1	3	Own goal	4,735		3	12	8		6	9†	2	4	7	5	1		10						11	
8	FL D3	(h)	Rotherham United	W 2–1	0–1	3	Duffy 2 (1 pen)	11,297		3	12	9		6		2	8	7†	5	1		4					10	11	
15	FL D3	(h)	Mansfield Town	L 1–2	0–0	4	Own goal	10,274		6		8	N		9	2	10	7	5	1		4	3					11	
			League appearances						11	44	28	20	6	32	31	45	39	41	42	21	25	22	41	4	2	2	36	11	3
			Substitute appearances						4		3		3	3	1			2				1	1	3		1		1	1
			League goals					OG – 4		1	9	6		1	12		2	10	1			1	4				5	1	

Notes: Dec 9 – after extra time.
Dec 15 – played at Craven Cottage, Fulham FC.
– after extra time.
Dec 17 – played at Highfield Road, Coventry City FC.
Feb 25 – played at The Hawthorns, West Bromwich Albion FC, as the Fellows Park pitch was unfit.

Football League Division 3 1969–70

		P	W	D	L	F	A	W	D	L	F	A	Pts
1.	Orient	46	16	5	2	43	15	9	7	7	24	21	62
2.	Luton Town	46	13	8	2	46	15	10	6	7	31	28	60
3.	Bristol Rovers	46	15	5	3	51	26	5	11	7	29	33	56
4.	Fulham	46	12	9	2	43	26	8	6	9	38	29	55
5.	**ALBION**	46	16	4	3	37	16	7	5	11	20	27	55
6.	Mansfield Town	46	14	4	5	46	22	7	7	9	24	27	53
7.	Barnsley	46	14	6	3	43	24	5	9	9	25	35	53
8.	Reading	46	16	3	4	52	29	5	8	10	35	48	53
9.	Rochdale	46	11	6	6	39	24	7	4	12	30	36	46
10.	Bradford City	46	11	6	6	37	22	6	6	11	20	28	46
11.	Doncaster Rovers	46	13	4	6	31	19	4	8	11	21	35	46
12.	Walsall	46	11	4	8	33	31	6	8	9	21	36	46
13.	Torquay United	46	9	9	5	36	22	5	8	10	26	37	45
14.	Rotherham United	46	10	8	5	36	19	5	6	12	26	35	44
15.	Shrewsbury Town	46	10	12	1	35	17	3	6	14	27	46	44
16.	Tranmere Rovers	46	10	8	5	38	29	4	8	11	18	43	44
17.	Plymouth Argyle	46	10	7	6	32	23	6	4	13	24	41	43
18.	Halifax Town	46	10	9	4	31	25	4	6	13	16	38	43
19.	Bury	46	13	4	6	47	29	2	7	14	28	51	41
20.	Gillingham	46	7	6	10	28	33	6	7	10	24	31	39
21.	Bournemouth & B.A.	46	8	9	6	28	27	4	6	13	20	44	39
22.	Southport	46	11	5	7	31	22	3	5	15	17	44	38
23.	Barrow	46	7	9	7	28	27	1	5	17	18	54	30
24.	Stockport County	46	4	7	12	17	30	2	4	17	10	41	23

remarkable, marathon, second-round tie with Walsall. In the first game at the Goldstone, goalkeeper Geoff Sidebottom was stretchered off with concussion on 65 minutes with Albion leading 1–0; Eddie Spearritt took over the jersey and did well as the side held out for a 1–1 draw. The replay at Fellows Park also ended at one-apiece after extra time, and the tie went to a third match, played at neutral Craven Cottage. The game again ended in stalemate, remaining goal-less after 120 minutes. The third replay was staged at Coventry City's ground and, with the scores level at 1–1, looked likely to require a further 30 minutes, but with only two minutes left on the watch left-winger Colin Taylor netted the winner and the Saddlers went through to the third round after seven hours play.

Albion fielded virtually a full-strength side in the Sussex Professional Cup final for the first time since 1964, but amazingly lost 1–0 to Crawley Town – Charlie Livesey *et al.* – for their first defeat in nine years of the competition.

The popular right-back Stewart Henderson missed only one game throughout the campaign and was voted Player of the Season by the supporters. Alan Gilliver also showed fine form, top-scoring with sixteen goals in League and Cup in his first season with the club. The re-formed reserve team played in the London Midweek Football League and performed admirably, losing only 7 of the 28 League and Cup matches. Indeed, they were beaten only once between 10 December and 24 April, and won the League Cup at the first time of asking.

One damper on the season was the first real 'aggro' seen at the Goldstone as the hooligans' reign of terror began in earnest. The clashes with Luton Town were particularly notorious, with bottles and 'bovver boots' flying in the North Stand. The return match at Kenilworth Road was marred by Albion 'yobs' damaging turnstiles, spraying paint, fighting on the terraces and throwing smoke-bombs. They even tried to overturn Malcolm Macdonald's car, with the Hatters' centre-forward and his baby inside.

From a damper to a bombshell: after returning from the club's four-match, post-season tour of Spain, Freddie Goodwin was approached with an exceptional offer by Second Division Birmingham City who had parted company with manager Stan Cullis two months earlier. With eighteen months of his contract outstanding and a new three-year contract on offer, the board

initially refused to release Goodwin, but on 28 May they reluctantly agreed to the move with City paying around £4,500 in compensation. Further acrimony arose when coach Willie Bell followed Goodwin to St Andrews. Bell was still registered as an Albion player with a year left on his contract, and City were fined £5,000 for making an illegal approach. The pair were then joined by Albion's former full-back George Dalton who had been coaching the junior team. So Albion, having found a manager who looked capable of leading the club back to Division Two, had been unable to hold on to him and the search was on again.

> Albion's post-season tour of Spain got off to an unusual start when they played Paiporta, a Third Division club from Valencia, on probably the most unusual pitch they had ever seen. It was actually in the middle of a dried-up river bed: no grass, very dusty, dotted with pebbles, and with steel pipes for corner flags! Every October the football would cease as the rains fell and the river came to life again!

SEASON 1970–71

While most of the footballing world's attention was directed towards the Mexico World Cup, the Albion board was drawing up a short-list for the managerial vacancy. The names included former Blackpool and England 'keeper Tony Waiters and an old Brighton favourite, Steve Burtenshaw, currently Arsenal coach, but the unanimous choice was Pat Saward, the 41-year-old assistant manager and chief coach of Coventry City who had been the second choice when Goodwin was appointed in 1968. Taking up his post at the end of June, the new manager's confidence and zest for the job created quite a stir,

while the players found their pre-season training under Saward, new coach Peter Dinsdale and trainer Mike Yaxley to be the hardest ever. The summer saw no important departures from the squad, but there were two newcomers: Peter O'Sullivan from Manchester United, Goodwin's last signing; and trialist Alex Sheridan from the Scottish amateur side Queen's Park. O'Sullivan went on to play nearly 500 games for the club.

In contrast to the fine form of the previous term, the League season saw a struggle against relegation. By December the team, which played in a new all-white strip, had sunk to 21st place with just three wins, a run which included a miserable sequence of six games in a row without scoring a goal. Injuries and illness added to the manager's difficulties, and Saward returned to Coventry City to sign Ian Goodwin on loan, the first of the many such signings which earned him the nickname 'The Loan Ranger'!

With a shortage of cash at his disposal, Pat Saward launched the 'Buy-a-Player Fund' on 7 December to raise £50,000 for strengthening the squad. In just two days £500 was raised, but criticism of the club and its finances was running high. The protests were led by sausage manufacturer Ron Laver backed by a consortium ready to inject £100,000, but the takeover attempt was totally rejected by the directorate. By early

Albion 1970–71
Back row left to right: Joe Wilson (chief scout), Howard Wilkinson, John Templeman, John Napier (captain), Keith Watkins, Alan Gilliver, Alex Sheridan, Alex Dawson, Eddie Spearritt, Peter O'Sullivan.
Third row left to right: Stewart Henderson, Terry Stanley, Bobby Smith, Geoff Sidebottom, Brian Powney, Paul Flood, Alan Duffy, Andy Marchant.
Second row left to right: Mike Yaxley (trainer), Kit Napier, Nobby Lawton, Pat Saward (manager), Dave Turner, Norman Gall, Peter Dinsdale (coach).
On ground left to right: Martin Tew, Gary Parsons, Mark Douglas, Mick Stanley.

SEASON 1970–71

Date	Comp.	Ven.	Opponents	Result	HT	Pos.	Scorers	Atten.
Aug 15	FL D3	(h)	Torquay United	D 0–0	0–0	9=		11,493
18	FLC R1	(a)	Bristol Rovers	L 0–1	0–0	—		7,276
22	FL D3	(a)	Mansfield Town	L 0–1	0–1	21		7,988
29	FL D3	(h)	Rotherham United	D 1–1	0–1	19	Gilliver	9,849
Sep 2	FL D3	(a)	Plymouth Argyle	D 1–1	1–1	20	Spearritt	9,729
5	FL D3	(a)	Bury	W 2–0	1–0	13	Spearritt, Gilliver	3,416
12	FL D3	(h)	Bradford City	L 1–2	0–0	16	Turner	9,223
19	FL D3	(a)	Halifax Town	W 1–0	0–0	12	Gilliver	3,424
23	FL D3	(a)	Fulham	L 0–1	0–0	15		13,856
26	FL D3	(h)	Bristol Rovers	D 0–0	0–0	14=		10,118
29	FL D3	(a)	Doncaster Rovers	L 0–2	0–1	17		3,447
Oct 3	FL D3	(a)	Aston Villa	D 0–0	0–0	17		26,189
10	FL D3	(h)	Port Vale	D 0–0	0–0	17		9,383
16	FL D3	(a)	Torquay United	L 0–1	0–1	18		5,519
21	FL D3	(a)	Rochdale	D 1–1	0–1	19	O'Sullivan	7,532
24	FL D3	(h)	Wrexham	W 2–0	0–0	17	K Napier, Lawton	8,043
31	FL D3	(a)	Preston North End	D 1–1	1–0	17		12,567
Nov 7	FL D3	(h)	Chesterfield	L 1–2	1–0	19	Own goal	8,023
14	FL D3	(a)	Gillingham	D 1–1	1–0	18	Templeman	3,008
21	FAC R1	(h)	Cheltenham Town	W 4–0	2–0	—	Gilliver, O'Sullivan, K Napier (pen), Woffinden	8,348
25	FL D3	(h)	Swansea City	D 2–2	2–1	17	Gilliver, K Napier (pen)	6,578
28	FL D3	(a)	Walsall	L 0–1	0–0	21		3,957
Dec 5	FL D3	(h)	Barnsley	L 1–2	1–2	21	Flood	7,685
12	FAC R2	(a)	Hereford United	W 2–1	0–0	—	Lawton, K Napier	12,769
19	FL D3	(h)	Mansfield Town	W 2–0	1–0	19	Lawton, K Napier (pen)	6,583
Jan 2	FAC R3	(a)	Cardiff City	L 0–1	0–1	—		19,338
9	FL D3	(h)	Doncaster Rovers	W 3–0	2–0	20	K Napier, Lawton, Sheridan	7,811
16	FL D3	(a)	Rochdale	D 3–3	3–2	20	Wilkinson, Gilliver 2	4,984
30	FL D3	(h)	Walsall	D 2–2	2–1	20	Gilliver, K Napier	8,333
Feb 6	FL D3	(a)	Barnsley	L 0–1	0–0	21		4,840
13	FL D3	(h)	Shrewsbury Town	L 1–2	0–0	23	Lawton	8,241
20	FL D3	(a)	Swansea City	L 0–1	0–0	23		7,661
27	FL D3	(h)	Preston North End	D 0–0	0–0	23		9,957
Mar 10	FL D3	(h)	Fulham	W 3–2	2–2	23	O'Sullivan, Irvine, K Napier	14,413
13	FL D3	(h)	Gillingham	W 3–1	3–0	23	Irvine, Murray 2	10,794
15	FL D3	(a)	Tranmere Rovers	L 0–3	0–0	23		3,243
20	FL D3	(a)	Chesterfield	L 1–2	0–1	23	Own goal	8,101
24	FL D3	(a)	Shrewsbury Town	W 1–0	0–0	22	Irvine	3,089
27	FL D3	(h)	Bury	W 1–0	1–0	21	Irvine	9,212
31	FL D3	(h)	Tranmere Rovers	D 0–0	0–0	18		9,766
Apr 3	FL D3	(a)	Rotherham United	L 0–2	0–2	21		5,072
9	FL D3	(h)	Aston Villa	W 1–0	0–0	18	K Napier	22,687
10	FL D3	(h)	Reading	W 2–0	1–0	15	K Napier (pen), Turner	10,866
12	FL D3	(a)	Bradford City	W 3–2	1–2	14	K Napier, Duffy 2	4,109
17	FL D3	(a)	Port Vale	L 1–2	1–1	15	Murray	3,749
21	FL D3	(a)	Reading	W 3–0	0–0	15	Templeman, Irvine, Spearritt	5,980
24	FL D3	(h)	Halifax Town	L 0–2	0–1	15		10,671
28	FL D3	(h)	Plymouth Argyle	D 1–1	0–0	16	Irvine	8,202
May 1	FL D3	(a)	Bristol Rovers	W 3–1	1–0	14	Murray, K Napier 2	5,530
7	FL D3	(a)	Wrexham	D 1–1	1–1	14	Sheridan	4,523

Appearance summary (by player):

	League appearances	Substitute appearances	League goals
			OG – 2
Dawson A	2	1	
Dovey A	2		
Duffy A	14	7	2
Flood P	4	1	1
Gall N	43	2	
Gilliver A	23	1	7
Goodwin I	19		
Henderson S	36		
Irvine W	14	2	6
Lawton N	17		4
Murray A	17		4
Napier K	43		11
Napier J	46	2	
O'Sullivan P	35		2
Powney B	35		
Seymour I	3		
Sheridan A	12	3	2
Sidebottom G	6	1	
Smith RW	21	4	
Spearritt E	38	3	3
Stanley T	12	1	
Templeman J	31	1	2
Turner D	18	3	3
Wilkinson H	15	3	1
Woffinden C	0		

Football League Division 3 1970–71

		P	W	D	L	F	A	W	D	L	F	A	Pts
1.	Preston North End	46	15	8	0	42	16	7	9	7	21	23	61
2.	Fulham	46	15	6	2	39	12	9	6	8	29	29	60
3.	Halifax Town	46	16	2	5	46	22	6	10	7	28	33	56
4.	Aston Villa	46	13	7	3	27	13	6	8	9	27	33	53
5.	Chesterfield	46	13	8	2	45	12	4	9	10	21	26	51
6.	Bristol Rovers	46	11	5	7	38	24	8	8	7	31	26	51
7.	Mansfield Town	46	13	7	3	44	28	5	8	10	20	34	51
8.	Rotherham United	46	12	10	1	38	19	5	6	12	26	41	50
9.	Wrexham	46	12	8	3	43	25	6	5	12	29	40	49
10.	Torquay United	46	12	6	5	37	26	7	5	11	17	31	49
11.	Swansea City	46	11	5	7	41	25	4	11	8	18	31	46
12.	Barnsley	46	12	6	5	30	19	5	5	13	19	33	45
13.	Shrewsbury Town	46	11	6	6	37	28	5	7	11	21	34	45
14.	**ALBION**	46	8	10	5	28	20	6	6	11	22	27	44
15.	Plymouth Argyle	46	6	12	5	39	33	6	7	10	24	30	43
16.	Rochdale	46	8	8	7	29	26	6	7	10	32	42	43
17.	Port Vale	46	11	6	6	29	18	4	6	13	23	41	42
18.	Tranmere Rovers	46	8	11	4	27	18	2	11	10	18	37	42
19.	Bradford City	46	7	6	10	23	26	6	8	9	26	37	40
20.	Walsall	46	10	1	12	30	27	4	10	9	21	30	39
21.	Reading	46	10	7	6	32	33	4	4	15	16	52	39
22.	Bury	46	7	9	7	30	23	5	4	14	22	37	37
23.	Doncaster Rovers	46	8	5	10	28	27	5	4	14	17	39	35
24.	Gillingham	46	6	9	8	22	29	4	4	15	20	38	33

> In March two of the fund-raising staff were charged with offences concerning the club's lotteries in something of a minor scandal.

January supporters had become heavily involved in fund-raising schemes, but Albion were losing £400 per week and performances had to improve to increase money at the gates.

One of the few bright spots on the pitch was the consistent play of Peter O'Sullivan who, after a few early-season troubles, was called into the Welsh under-23 squad in January. However, the team continued to play poorly and by February, with the club next to bottom, home gates had fallen to around 8,000. Goalkeeper Geoff Sidebottom was forced to retire because of head injuries and Fulham's Ian Seymour was brought in on loan as Brian Powney was also injured. Two other important departures were those of Nobby Lawton and Alan Gilliver who both joined Lincoln City in February.

The turning point came in early March when Bert Murray, on loan from Birmingham City but apparently about to sign for Fulham, agreed to join Albion for £10,000 of Saward's fund and thus became known as 'The People's Player'. Together with Willie Irvine, an experienced Northern Ireland international centre-forward on loan from Preston North End, Bert played a major part in the 3–2 defeat of second-placed Fulham on

We love our Albion!
More than 3,000 school-children and other supporters from all over Sussex march along Madeira Drive, Brighton, on St Valentine's Day, 14 February, in a sponsored walk to raise money for Pat Saward's Buy-a-Player Fund. The two top fund-raising schools contested the Pat Saward Cup at the Goldstone at Easter.

10 March before a 14,413 Goldstone crowd. Gillingham, bottom of the table, were beaten in the next game, and although the following two matches were lost, Albion then put together a run of seven victories and only three defeats in climbing to the respectability of fourteenth place, five points clear of relegation. Maximum points over Easter saw Saward rewarded with the Division Three Manager of the Month award as the club made its position safe.

The League Cup saw a quick exit at the hands of Bristol Rovers who went on to the quarter-finals, but the team reached the third round of the F.A. Cup with wins over Southern Leaguers Cheltenham Town and Hereford United before going out at Second Division Cardiff City in a narrow 1–0 defeat.

Pat Saward's first season in charge therefore ended on an upbeat note, the arrival of Murray and Irvine providing a welcome boost to a forward line that was lacking in thrust for

most of the season. Top-scorer Kit Napier managed only thirteen goals, and it was defender Norman Gall who scooped the fans' Player of the Season award. A number of players were placed on the close-season transfer list, mainly reserves but also including Paul Flood, Howard Wilkinson, Bobby Smith and Alex Dawson.

The club programme on 9 January 1971 carried a full-page advertisement for Pat Saward's Appeal Fund which referred to a fictitious First Division match, Albion v. Liverpool, to be staged at the Goldstone on '12 November 197?'. Described as 'not a dream but a reality we all want', the advert turned out to be a remarkable prophesy as Albion played Liverpool in the First Division at home on 10 November 1979.

SEASON 1971–72

After an absence of seven years, the traditional blue-and-white striped shirts made a welcome return this season. Also back at the club, to assist with the reserves and juniors, was former skipper Glen Wilson, but chief coach Peter Dinsdale had left owing to ill health and Mike Yaxley was the manager's new right-hand man. On-loan striker Willie Irvine joined the club permanently during the summer.

To counter the previous season's lack of scoring power, Pat Saward decided on an entertaining policy of all-out attack using Kit Napier and Willie Irvine as the main strikers with support from wingers Peter O'Sullivan and Bert Murray. The plan reaped a rich harvest early on with big wins at Mansfield

Town (3–0) and Rotherham United (4–2), but inconsistency during September and October dropped the club to twelfth. Saward's appeal for money to sign players continued, and he also bolstered the squad with several loan signings; the first was Northern Ireland international Bertie Lutton (Wolves) who took over from the injury-plagued Dave Turner. Another was Brian Bromley, a midfield general from Portsmouth who also took over from Turner in December and immediately had a profound influence on the team.

By Christmas, after a good run of six wins from seven League games, Albion were challenging the front-runners once again. The visitors on Boxing Day were second-placed Bournemouth,

189

SEASON 1971–72

Date	Comp.	Ven.	Opponents	Result	HT	Pos.	Scorers	Atten.	Beamish K	Bromley B	Dobson C	Dovey A	Duffy A	Gall N	Goodwin I	Henderson S	Irvine W	Lutton B	Murray A	Napier K	Napier J	O'Sullivan P	Powney B	Spearritt E	Stanley T	Templeman J	Turner D
Aug 14	FL D3	(a)	Port Vale	D 1–1	0–1	13=	Templeman	4,384					12	6		2	9		7	8†	5	11	1	3		4	10
17	FLC R1	(a)	Swansea City	W 1–0	0–0	–	Spearritt	5,680					N	6		2	9		7	8	5	11	1	3		4	10
21	FL D3	(h)	Bradford City	W 3–1	1–0	4=	Irvine, K Napier, Turner	10,350					12	6		2	9		7	8	5	11	1	3		4	10†
28	FL D3	(a)	Mansfield Town	W 3–0	1–0	1	K Napier 3	4,131					N	6		2	9		7	8	5	11	1	3		4	10
31	FL D3	(a)	Rotherham United	W 4–2	3–1	2	K Napier, Murray, Turner 2	4,782					12	6		2	9		7	8†	5	11	1	3		4	10
Sep 4	FL D3	(h)	York City	L 0–2	0–1	4		14,360					12	6	8†	2	9		7		5	11	1	3		4	10
8	FLC R2	(a)	Norwich City	L 0–2	0–1	–		11,659				1	10	6		2	9		7	8	5	11		3	N	4	
11	FL D3	(a)	Aston Villa	L 0–2	0–0	7		25,809					N	6		2	9	7	10	8	5	11	1	3		4	
18	FL D3	(h)	Notts County	D 1–1	0–0	9	O'Sullivan	13,443					12	6		2	9		7†	8	5	11	1	3		4	10
25	FL D3	(a)	Torquay United	D 2–2	1–0	9	Lutton, Irvine	5,439						6		2	9	7	12	8	5	11	1	3		4	10†
29	FL D3	(h)	Bristol Rovers	W 3–1	1–0	6	Lutton, K Napier (pen), Murray	12,649					N	5		2	9	7	10	8	4	11	1	3			6
Oct 2	FL D3	(h)	Barnsley	D 0–0	0–0	7		12,127					N	6		2	9	7	10	8	5	11	1	3		4	
8	FL D3	(a)	Tranmere Rovers	L 0–2	0–2	7		3,731						6	12	2	9	7†	10	8	5	11	1	3		4	
16	FL D3	(a)	Port Vale	D 1–1	1–0	11	O'Sullivan	9,007						6		2	9	7†	4	8	5	11	1	3		12	10
19	FL D3	(a)	Swansea City	L 1–2	0–1	12	Murray (pen)	6,206					N	6		2	9		7	8	5	11	1	3		4	10
23	FL D3	(a)	Walsall	W 1–0	1–0	11	Irvine	3,719					12	6		2	9		7	8	5	11	1	3		4	10†
30	FL D3	(h)	Shrewsbury Town	W 2–0	1–0	7	K Napier, O'Sullivan	9,778						6		2	9	12	7	8	5	11	1	3		4†	10
Nov 6	FL D3	(a)	Plymouth Argyle	W 2–1	1–0	7	Murray (pen), O'Sullivan	11,429						6		2	9	N	4	7	5	11	1	3		10	8
13	FL D3	(h)	Halifax Town	W 2–1	1–0	7	O'Sullivan, Irvine	9,896					N	6		2	9		7	8	5	11	1	3		4	10
20	FAC R1	(h)	Hillingdon Borough	W 7–1	2–0	–	Spearritt, K Napier 2, O'Sullivan 2, Own goal, Murray	9,836					N	6		2	9		7	8	5	11	1	3		4	10
27	FL D3	(a)	Chesterfield	W 2–1	1–0	6	K Napier, Irvine	10,179						6		2	9		7	8	5	11	1	3		4	10†
Dec 4	FL D3	(h)	Bolton Wanderers	D 1–1	1–1	5	Irvine	5,209		10				6	N	2	9		7	8	5	11	1	3		4	
11	FAC R2	(h)	Walsall	D 1–1	0–0	–	Irvine	12,797		10			12	6		2	9		7	8	5	11	1	3		4†	
14	FAC R2 Rep	(a)	Walsall	L 1–2	1–1	–	K Napier	8,014		10			12	6		2†	9		7	8	5	11	1	3		4	
18	FL D3	(a)	York City	W 2–1	0–0	6	Murray, Templeman	3,451		10		1		6	N	2	9		7	8	5	11		3		4	
27	FL D3	(h)	AFC Bournemouth	W 2–0	1–0	6	K Napier, O'Sullivan	30,600		10			12	6		2	9		7	8†	5	11	1	3		4	
Jan 1	FL D3	(a)	Notts County	L 0–1	0–0	5		16,401		10			N	6		2	9		7	8	5	11	1	3		4	
8	FL D3	(h)	Mansfield Town	W 1–0	0–0	5	Bromley	10,616		10			12	6		2†	9		7	8	5	11	1	3		4	
15	FL D3	(h)	Oldham Athletic	W 4–2	3–2	4	Murray, O'Sullivan, Spearritt 2	6,907		10			12	6		2	9		7†	8	5	11	1	3		4	
22	FL D3	(a)	Bristol Rovers	D 2–2	1–1	4	J Napier, Irvine	9,744		10	12			6		2	9		7	8	5	11	1	3		4†	
29	FL D3	(h)	Swansea City	W 1–0	0–0	4	Murray	13,083		10	12			6		2	9†		7	8	5	11	1	3		4	
Feb 5	FL D3	(a)	Wrexham	W 2–1	1–0	4	O'Sullivan, Irvine	3,771		10				6		2	9	12	7	8	5	11	1	3		4†	
12	FL D3	(h)	Walsall	L 1–2	0–1	4	Spearritt	14,437		10				6		2	9	12	7	8†	5	11	1	3		4	
19	FL D3	(a)	Shrewsbury Town	W 5–3	0–0	4	O'Sullivan 2, K Napier, Own goal, Irvine	3,966		10†				6		2	9		7	8	5	11	1	3		4	12
26	FL D3	(h)	Plymouth Argyle	W 3–0	3–0	4	Murray 2, K Napier	15,198		10				6		2	9		7	8	5	11	1	3	N	4	
Mar 4	FL D3	(a)	Halifax Town	W 5–0	3–0	4	Irvine, Murray, K Napier, Templeman 2	2,432		10				6	N	2	9		7	8	5	11	1	3		4	
11	FL D3	(a)	Tranmere Rovers	W 2–0	1–0	3	Bromley, Templeman	17,439		10				6		2	9	N	7	8	5	11	1	3		4	
15	FL D3	(h)	Oldham Athletic	L 0–1	0–0	3		17,916	12	10		1		6		2	9†		7	8	5	11				4	
18	FL D3	(a)	Bradford City	L 1–2	0–2	3	K Napier	4,804	12	10				6		2†	9		7	8	5	11	1	3		4	
25	FL D3	(h)	Aston Villa	W 2–1	1–0	2	Irvine, K Napier	28,833	8	10				5	6	2	9	N	7			11	1	3		4	
31	FL D3	(h)	Torquay United	W 3–1	0–1	2	Murray (pen), Beamish, Lutton	27,513	8	10				5	6	2		9†	12	7		11	1	3		4	
Apr 1	FL D3	(a)	AFC Bournemouth	D 1–1	0–1	3	Lutton	22,540	9	10†				5	6	2			7	8		11	1	3		4	12
4	FL D3	(a)	Barnsley	W 1–0	0–0	2	Templeman	6,541	9	10				5	6	2			7	8		11	1	3		4	N
8	FL D3	(a)	Wrexham	W 3–2	1–0	2	Beamish 2, Irvine	18,156	8	10				5	6	2	9†	12	7			11	1	3		4	12
12	FL D3	(a)	Blackburn Rovers	D 2–2	1–1	2	Irvine 2	8,558	8	10				5	6		9		7†			11	1	3		4	12
15	FL D3	(a)	Chesterfield	W 1–0	1–0	2	K Napier	6,325	8	10				5	6		9			2	7	11†	1	3		4	12
19	FL D3	(h)	Blackburn Rovers	W 3–0	2–0	2	Irvine, Beamish, Bromley	23,269	8	10				5	6	2†	9		12		7	11	1	3		4	
22	FL D3	(h)	Bolton Wanderers	W 2–1	0–0	2	Murray (pen)	25,074	8	10				5	6	2	9	N			7	11	1	3		4	
26	FL D3	(h)	Rotherham United	W 2–1	1–1	2	Irvine, Beamish	27,928	8	10				5	6	2	9		12		7	11	1	3			4†
29	FL D3	(a)	Rochdale	W 2–1	0–0	2	K Napier, Beamish	4,283	8	10				5	6	2	9		12		7	11	1	3			4†
May 3	FL D3	(h)	Rochdale	D 1–1	1–0	2	Templeman	34,766	8	10				5	6	2	9		12		7†	11	1	3			4
League appearances									12	28	2	2	0	46	13	34	41	11	44	44	34	46	44	46	0	44	15
Substitute appearances									2	1	2		9		1			3	6		1					1	4
League goals					OG – 1				6	3							16	4	12	16	1	10		3		7	3

Football League Division 3 1971–72

		P	W	D	L	F	A	W	D	L	F	A	Pts
1.	Aston Villa	46	20	1	2	45	10	12	5	6	40	22	70
2.	**ALBION**	46	15	5	3	39	18	12	6	5	43	29	65
3.	AFC Bournemouth	46	16	6	1	43	13	7	10	6	30	24	62
4.	Notts County	46	16	4	4	42	19	9	9	5	32	25	62
5.	Rotherham United	46	12	8	3	46	25	8	7	8	23	27	55
6.	Bristol Rovers	46	17	2	4	54	26	4	10	9	21	30	54
7.	Bolton Wanderers	46	14	4	5	41	25	6	8	9	26	28	50
8.	Plymouth Argyle	46	13	6	4	43	26	7	4	12	31	38	50
9.	Walsall	46	12	8	3	38	16	3	10	10	24	41	48
10.	Blackburn Rovers	46	14	4	5	39	22	5	5	13	15	35	47
11.	Oldham Athletic	46	11	4	8	37	35	6	7	10	22	28	45
12.	Shrewsbury Town	46	13	5	5	50	29	4	5	14	23	36	44
13.	Chesterfield	46	10	5	8	25	23	8	3	12	32	34	44
14.	Swansea City	46	10	6	7	27	21	7	4	12	19	38	44
15.	Port Vale	46	10	10	3	27	21	3	5	15	16	38	41
16.	Wrexham	46	10	5	8	33	26	6	3	14	26	37	40
17.	Halifax Town	46	11	6	6	31	22	2	6	15	17	39	38
18.	Rochdale	46	11	7	5	35	26	1	6	16	22	57	37
19.	York City	46	8	8	7	32	22	4	4	15	25	44	36
20.	Tranmere Rovers	46	9	7	7	34	30	1	9	13	16	41	36
21.	Mansfield Town	46	5	12	6	19	26	3	8	12	22	37	36
22.	Barnsley	46	6	10	7	23	30	3	8	12	9	34	36
23.	Torquay United	46	8	6	9	31	31	2	6	15	10	38	32
24.	Bradford City	46	6	8	9	27	32	5	2	16	18	45	32

> Groundsman Frankie Howard admitted painting bare patches of the pitch green to make it look better on television.

close rivals along the coast hoping that the management of John Bond and the phenomenal goalscoring of Ted MacDougall and Phil Boyer would take the club from the Fourth Division to the Second in two years. Some 30,600 fans assembled to see the Cherries outclassed 2–0. Kit Napier scored one of the best goals ever seen on the ground, while the Bournemouth forward threat was snuffed out by Albion's central defensive combination of John Napier and Norman Gall. Brighton finished the year in fifth place and Saward was rewarded with his second divisional Manager of the Month award.

There followed a narrow defeat (0–1) at Notts County on New Year's Day, but by the end of January Albion had joined a breakaway group of Notts, Bournemouth and the glamour club of the section, Aston Villa. The attacking policy then produced some more amazing results away from home: Oldham Athletic (4–2), Shrewsbury Town (5–3, with all the goals in 27 second-half minutes) and Halifax Town (5–0, the team arriving in the nick of time after a trip from Manchester in four taxis!). Bromley was signed permanently for £14,000 in January and March saw Lutton sign for £5,000, but another on-loan player,

Huddersfield Town's Colin Dobson, suffered a broken ankle against Walsall and returned to Leeds Road.

Despite the glut of goals, Saward still attempted to strengthen his strike-force. After looking at the rather overweight, former England forward Fred Pickering, he finally settled on Tranmere Rovers' Ken Beamish who cost a club-record £25,000 fee plus Alan Duffy in early March. His biggest decision, though, came in mid March following two defeats in the run-up to the Goldstone clash with leaders Aston Villa. Defenders Stewart Henderson and John Napier were dropped, with Bert Murray and Ian Goodwin, who had been injured for most of the season, taking their places; Brian Bromley took over as skipper. The Villa match, highlighted on *Match of the Day*, was attended by an all-ticket crowd of 28,833 which saw Albion triumph 2–1. Willie Irvine scored a magnificent, team-worked goal that was a runner-up in the BBC's Goal of the Season competition.

That victory heralded a twelve-match unbeaten run-in that saw Albion finish as runners-up to Villa, but the sequence was not without drama. With a never-say-die attitude, the side scored decisive goals in the last ten minutes in no fewer than seven of those twelve games. With four of the last five games at home, expectations rose as Albion edged ahead of Bournemouth and Notts County, and Ken Beamish's amazing winner against Rotherham United, a 25-yarder well into injury-time, sent Albion into the last two games against lowly Rochdale needing three points to secure second place. Beamish again scored a late winning goal at Spotland to set up the climax at the Goldstone on 3 May.

The culmination of a tremendous season saw 34,766 spectators, the third biggest crowd in Goldstone history, gather to see Brighton gain that vital point. When John Templeman scored in the just the fourth minute, memories flashed back to April 1958 and Albion's 6–0 hammering of Watford under similar

> On 20 November international athlete Dave Bedford ran 30 circuits of the Goldstone pitch in half an hour before the match with Hillingdon Borough to raise money for a party for Albion's pensioner supporters.

circumstances. The goal-rush didn't materialise, though. Rochdale, who required a point to avoid relegation, scored a second-half equaliser and the game became a lack-lustre affair with both sides settling for a draw, but it really didn't matter and at the end thousands of happy fans swarmed onto the pitch to acknowledge the team.

Albion finished on 65 points, equalling their best-ever total in 1955–56, but it was the incredible away record that stood out: twelve wins and only five defeats, 43 goals (four more than at home), the best away record in the entire Football League. Saward's option for attack had certainly been justified. The people's Player of the Season was the People's Player, Bert Murray, but the key to success was the consistency of the whole team: eight players made more than 40 League appearances and four players scored more than ten goals. Home crowds averaged 17,679, a most healthy figure.

Cup games provided little diversion from the main task. Southern League Hillingdon Borough were knocked for seven in the F.A. Cup, but Albion fell in the second round to their bogey-side, Walsall. In the League Cup, after winning at Swansea City, they put up a good display but went out 2–0 at Second Division Norwich City.

Coincidentally, but also perhaps symbolically as Albion entered a hopeful new era in Division Two, the old, squalid dressing-rooms under the West Stand were torn down in May 1972, part of a scheme to replace the club facilities that had begun the previous December. It included new toilets, a new boardroom and offices, a new entrance and the completion in brick of the Newtown Road frontage to replace the old iron fence. The scheme was largely financed by the sale of club houses.

The only black mark was the non-stop rise of terrace thuggery. Albion were fined £350 after Roy Brown, the Hove-born Notts County 'keeper, was hit on the head by a can thrown from the South Stand. Television cameras were installed for crowd control at the Boxing Day match against Bournemouth, but there were still 29 arrests in what was described as a 'near riot'. There were also 23 arrests at the Aston Villa match in March.

Albion 1971–72

Back row left to right: Ian Goodwin, Willie Irvine, Steve Piper, Terry Stanley, Stewart Henderson, Brian Powney, Alan Dovey, Alan Boorn, Peter O'Sullivan, John Templeman, Alex Sheridan, Kit Napier.
Middle row left to right: Glen Wilson (trainer), Norman Gall, Eddie Spearritt, John Napier (capt.), Pat Saward (man.), Dave Turner, Alan Duffy, Bert Murray, Mike Yaxley (coach).
On ground left to right: Ricky Sopp, Kevin Worsfold, Stephen Barrett, Julio Grato, Tony Paris, Tony Towner, Mark Douglas, Billy Wylie, John Rodkin.

SEASON 1972–73

After the outstanding and somewhat unexpected success of 1971–72, Albion's second taste of Division Two football was to prove an unmitigated disaster. Public interest was high, but Pat Saward's attempts to strengthen the squad for the new challenge were defeated by the inflated transfer market. He made his thinking clear, however, by putting former stalwarts Stewart Henderson, Dave Turner and both Napiers on the transfer list. Brian Bromley was appointed club captain.

The season started in earnest with a hard-fought draw at home to Bristol City. The first away game, a 6–2 defeat at Blackpool, was seen as a hiccup as Albion forced creditable draws at home to Sunderland and away to Aston Villa, but it took six games to register a first League win, a rousing 2–1 defeat of Fulham. There was now plenty of transfer activity as Saward rebuilt the side. After a season of all-out attack it was vital to shore up the defence, so in came two new full-backs, Graham Howell (Bradford City) and George Ley (Portsmouth). The experienced ex-England forward Barry Bridges (Millwall) arrived for a club-record £29,000, while Dave Turner and Kit Napier moved on to Blackburn Rovers, and John Napier signed for Bradford City.

Saward's dealings in the loan market continued with Lewes-born midfielder Stan Brown (Fulham), and defenders John Moore (Luton Town) and John McGrath (Southampton) joining the club temporarily in a bid to stem the basic defensive errors that were costing vital points: in the first ten League matches, Albion had taken the lead seven times but had won only once.

October started with Albion next to bottom, but they remained unbeaten throughout the month and rose to sixteenth. A crowd of 16,387 saw the 2–2 draw with Cardiff City at Hove on 4 November, but little did the spectators realise that it was the last point the club would collect until February, a miserable sequence of twelve consecutive League defeats which saw the club plummet to the bottom of the table and remain there. The side managed just five goals in the run — including an own-goal

and two Eddie Spearritt penalties! Team morale completely collapsed as heavy defeats were suffered at Preston North End (0–4), Carlisle United (1–5), Oxford United (0–3), Sunderland (0–4) and Fulham (1–5). The manager, dismayed by the attitude of some of his players, announced a new 'get tough' policy after Christmas – the players were made to smarten up and had their hair cut – and the ever-willing Ian Goodwin was made club captain. Norman Gall, Bertie Lutton and Alan Dovey were transfer-listed as a bleak January left the club seven points behind 21st-placed Cardiff City.

The dreadful, three-month losing streak was finally halted on 10 February when Saward gave League débuts to youngsters Tony Towner and Pat Hilton, and was rewarded with a refreshing 2–0 win over Luton Town. Two more defeats were then followed by the best run of the season, five home wins and two away draws which enabled Albion to close the gap to 20th place and safety to just three points by mid April, but defeats at the two runaway leaders, Burnley and Queen's Park Rangers, condemned Brighton to a swift return to the Third Division.

Even the diversion of an F.A. Cup tie with Chelsea proved disastrous. The star-studded First Division side, winners of the trophy in 1970, included England internationals John Hollins and Peter Osgood in their line-up, and were a huge draw. A

> A 1973 Albion plan for 20 maisonettes in the north-eastern corner of the ground was by no means the club's first attempt to make full use of its 5·7-acre Goldstone plot. The space behind the North Stand was the proposed site of a petrol station in 1957 and of a car showroom in 1963, when there was also a plan for an office block in Goldstone Lane. All the club's plans were rejected by Hove Borough Council, but permission for a four-storey office block in the north-eastern corner was given in the 1980s.

Albion 1972–73
Back row left to right: Ian Goodwin, Kit Napier, Steve Piper, Brian Bromley (captain), Stewart Henderson, Alan Dovey, Brian Powney, Eddie Spearritt, Tommy Armstrong, John Templeman, Steve Breach, John Napier.
Middle row left to right: Glen Wilson (youth-team manager), Bert Murray, Norman Gall, Willie Irvine, Mike Yaxley (trainer/physio), Ken Beamish, Pat Saward (manager), Bertie Lutton, Peter O'Sullivan, Alan Boorn, Ray Crawford (coach).
On ground left to right: Tony Towner, Ray Brockwell, Terry Harvey, Stephen Barrett, Tony Paris, Julio Grato, Ricky Sopp, Leslie Nelson, Trevor Bryson.

SEASON 1972–73

Date	Comp.	Ven.	Opponents	Result	HT	Pos.	Scorers	Atten.	Beamish K	Boorn A	Bridges B	Bromley B	Brown S	Conway M	Dovey A	Gall N	Goodwin I	Henderson S	Hilton P	Howell G	Hughes T	Irvine W	Ley G	Lutton B	McGrath J	Moore J	Murray A	Napier K	Napier J	O'Sullivan P	Piper S	Powney B	Robertson L	Spearritt E	Templeman J	Towner A
Aug 12	FL D2	(h)	Bristol City	D 1–1	1–1	9=	Irvine	16,839	8†		10					5	6					9		12			4	7		11		1		3	2	
16	FLC R1	(h)	Exeter City	W 2–1	0–1	–	Irvine, Beamish	10,155	8		10			1			6					9		N			4	7	5	11		1		3	2	
19	FL D2	(a)	Blackpool	L 2–6	1–3	18=	Irvine 2	10,984	8		10					5	6					9		12			4	7		11		1		3†	2	
26	FL D2	(h)	Sunderland	D 2–2	0–2	18	Murray, Irvine	15,906	9							5	6			2		10		12			7	8		11		1		3		4†
29	FL D2	(a)	Notting'm Forest	L 0–1	0–1	20		10,659	8†							5	6			2		9		10			7	12		11		1		3		4
Sep 2	FL D2	(a)	Aston Villa	D 1–1	0–0	19	O'Sullivan	30,175	8†		7					5				2				9	10		6		12	11	1	1		3		4
5	FLC R2	(a)	Bristol Rovers	L 0–4	0–0	–		9,530			7						6			2				9	10		8		5	11	N	1		3		4
9	FL D2	(h)	Fulham	W 2–1	2–1	15	Templeman, Murray (pen)	15,615	9		8						6			2				N	10		7		5	11		1		3		4
16	FL D2	(a)	Luton Town	L 1–2	1–1	18	Templeman	11,627	9		8	10					6			2				12			7		5	11†		1		3		4
20	FL D2	(h)	Millwall	L 1–3	1–2	20	Bridges	17,404	9		8	10					6			2		N					7		5	11		1		3		4
23	FL D2	(h)	Oxford United	D 2–2	2–2	20	Murray (pen), Irvine	15,455	7		8	10					6			2		9	3				4		5	11		1		N		
27	FL D2	(a)	Cardiff City	D 1–1	1–1	19	Spearritt	9,531	12		8	10					5			2		9†	3				7			11		1		4	6	
30	FL D2	(a)	Portsmouth	L 0–2	0–1	21		15,726	12		7	10					5					9†	3	4			2					1		8	6	
Oct 7	FL D2	(h)	Hull City	D 1–1	0–1	19	Murray	14,330	12		8						6			2		9	3				7		5	11		1		10	4†	
14	FL D2	(a)	Huddersfield Town	W 2–0	1–0	18	Spearritt, Bridges	7,935	9		8		4				5						3				6	7		11		1		10	N	
21	FL D2	(h)	Sheffield Wed.	D 3–3	0–1	16=	Murray 2, Beamish	18,699	9		8	12	4				5						3				6	7		11		1		10	2†	
28	FL D2	(a)	Swindon Town	D 2–2	2–1	16=	Spearritt, Beamish	10,286	9		8	N	4				5						3				6	7		11		1		10	2	
Nov 4	FL D2	(h)	Cardiff City	D 2–2	2–1	18	Beamish, Murray	16,387	9		8	N	4				5			2			3				6	7		11		1		10		
11	FL D2	(a)	Millwall	L 0–3	0–1	20		10,386	9		8	12	4†				5			2			3				6	7		11		1		10		
18	FL D2	(h)	Burnley	L 0–1	0–0	21		17,470	12		8	10†	4				5			2		9	3				6	7		11	6	1				
25	FL D2	(a)	Preston North End	L 0–4	0–2	22		8,005	9		8	10	4			1	5			2		9	6				7			11†		1		3		
Dec 2	FL D2	(h)	Middlesbrough	L 0–2	0–0	22		11,116	9		8		4				6			2†			3	12	5		7			11		1		10		
9	FL D2	(a)	Orient	L 0–1	0–0	22		5,387	9		8		4				6					7		3	N	5	2			11		1		10		
16	FL D2	(a)	Carlisle United	L 1–5	0–3	22	Spearritt (pen)	5,671			8						12	6	2			7		3	9	5	4			11	1†	1		10		
23	FL D2	(h)	Queen's Park R.	L 1–2	1–2	22	Bridges	13,735			9						5	6				10		3	7		2			11		1	8	4		N
26	FL D2	(a)	Oxford United	L 0–3	0–1	22		9,730			9						5†	6				10		3	7		2			11		1	8	4		12
30	FL D2	(h)	Blackpool	L 1–2	0–0	22	Spearritt (pen)	18,001	12	4	8†	10					5						7	3						11		1	9	6	2	
Jan 6	FL D2	(a)	Sunderland	L 0–4	0–2	22		12,573	12	4†	8	10					6						7	3						11	5		9		2	
13	FAC R3	(h)	Chelsea	L 0–2	0–1	–		29,287	9		8	10					6					7	3			N				11	5	1		4	2	
20	FL D2	(h)	Aston Villa	L 1–3	0–2	22	Own goal	12,212	9		8	10					6			7†			3				12			11	5	1		4	2	
27	FL D2	(a)	Fulham	L 1–5	1–2	22	Murray	12,008	9		8	10					6			2†			7							11	5	1	12	3	4	
Feb 10	FL D2	(h)	Luton Town	W 2–0	0–0	22	Beamish 2	11,404	9				4				6		7	12	1						8			10	5			3	2	11†
17	FL D2	(a)	Bristol City	L 1–3	1–1	22	O'Sullivan	11,116	9†		7		4				6			12	1						8			10	5			3	2	11
Mar 2	FL D2	(h)	Hull City	L 0–2	0–1	22		7,781	9								6†			12	1		3				8			10	5		7	4	2	11
10	FL D2	(h)	Huddersfield Town	W 2–1	2–1	22	Towner, Robertson	10,053	9		12					5				4†			3				8			10			1	7	6	2	11
17	FL D2	(a)	Sheffield Wed.	D 1–1	0–1	22	Beamish	16,122	9		12					5				4			3				8			10			1	7	6	2	11†
21	FL D2	(h)	Carlisle United	W 1–0	0–0	22	Beamish	11,008	9		N					5				4			3				8			10			1	7	6	2	11
24	FL D2	(h)	Swindon Town	W 3–1	2–1	22	Murray, Beamish 2	10,276	9		12					5				4			3				8			10			1	7	6	2	11†
31	FL D2	(h)	Preston North End	W 2–0	0–0	22	Towner, Robertson	12,047	9		N					5				4			3				8			10			1	7	6	2	11
Apr 7	FL D2	(a)	Middlesbrough	D 1–1	1–0	22	Robertson	6,816	9†		12					5				4			3				8			10			1	7	6	2	11
14	FL D2	(h)	Orient	W 2–1	0–1	22	Own goal, Robertson	14,744	9		12					5				4			3				8			10			1	7†	6	2	11
21	FL D2	(a)	Burnley	L 0–3	0–1	22		15,698	9		12					5				4			3				8			10			1	7	6	2	11†
23	FL D2	(h)	Portsmouth	D 1–1	0–0	22	Bridges	15,535	9		12					5				4†			3				8			10			1	7	6	2	11
24	FL D2	(a)	Queen's Park R.	L 0–2	0–1	22		16,625			12		4						7				3				8			10	5		9†	6	2	11
28	FL D2	(h)	Notting'm Forest	D 2–2	0–2	22	Spearritt (pen), Conway	9,709	9				4		7		N				8	2		3						10	5	1		6		11
			League appearances						31	2	25	17	9	1	2	32	14	2	3	32	3	11	31	7	3	5	38	3	5	42	9	37	15	39	30	14
			Substitute appearances						7		8	2					1			3						5				1	1	1			1	1
			League goals OG – 2						9		4											5					9			2				4	6	2	2

Football League Division 2 1972–73

		P	W	D	L	F	A	W	D	L	F	A	Pts
1.	Burnley	42	13	6	2	44	18	11	8	2	28	17	62
2.	Queen's Park R.	42	16	4	1	54	13	8	9	4	27	24	61
3.	Aston Villa	42	12	5	4	27	17	6	9	6	24	30	50
4.	Middlesbrough	42	12	6	3	29	15	5	7	9	17	28	47
5.	Bristol City	42	10	7	4	34	18	7	5	9	29	33	46
6.	Sunderland	42	12	6	3	35	17	5	6	10	24	32	46
7.	Blackpool	42	12	6	3	37	17	6	4	11	19	34	46
8.	Oxford United	42	14	2	5	36	18	5	5	11	16	25	45
9.	Fulham	42	11	6	4	32	16	5	6	10	26	33	44
10.	Sheffield Wednesday	42	14	4	3	40	20	3	6	12	19	35	44
11.	Millwall	42	12	5	4	33	18	4	5	12	22	29	42
12.	Luton Town	42	6	9	6	24	23	9	2	10	20	30	41
13.	Hull City	42	9	7	5	39	22	5	5	11	25	37	40
14.	Nottingham Forest	42	12	5	4	32	18	2	7	12	15	34	40
15.	Orient	42	11	6	4	33	18	1	6	14	16	35	36
16.	Swindon Town	42	8	9	4	28	23	2	7	12	18	37	36
17.	Portsmouth	42	7	6	8	21	22	5	5	11	21	37	35
18.	Carlisle United	42	10	5	6	40	24	1	7	13	10	35	34
19.	Preston North End	42	6	8	7	19	25	5	4	12	18	39	34
20.	Cardiff City	42	11	4	6	32	21	0	7	14	11	37	33
21.	Huddersfield Town	42	7	9	5	21	20	1	8	12	15	36	33
22.	**ALBION**	42	7	8	6	32	31	1	5	15	14	52	29

29,287 all-ticket Goldstone crowd saw the Londoners win with two Osgood goals, but a game of cynical fouling, five cautions, the dismissals of George Ley and Chelsea's Ron 'Chopper' Harris, and a particularly brutal last 20 minutes made it a day of shame for both clubs. There were 25 arrests as the violence spread onto the Goldstone terraces.

Having scraped past Exeter in the first round, Albion made an ignominious exit from the League Cup at the hands of Third Division Bristol Rovers (0–4) in a foretaste of what was to come.

Ken Beamish was top scorer with just ten goals as Albion were simply outclassed on so many occasions. Bad luck and injuries accounted for some of the team's failings, but basic defensive errors were the real culprits and Pat Saward's task for the coming season was to stop the rot. Albion fans were left to wonder if their team was destined always to be a Third Division 'also-ran'.

In hindsight, the most far-reaching event of the season was the change in boardroom personnel at the New Year. It was revealed that the overdraft had grown to £200,000, a financial burden which prompted Mike Bamber, the youngest member of the board, and fellow director Norman Hyams to propose a property-development company based at the Goldstone, the club benefiting from the profits; Suncombe Investments Ltd became a subsidiary of the club in 1973–74. However, chairman Tom Whiting and director Tony de Boer felt unable to make the required commitment and quit the board. Bamber and Len Stringer were elected joint-chairmen, and in January the new board was strengthened by the appointment of Keith Wickenden and Dudley Sizen as directors. A property tycoon and former jazz-drummer, Bamber had been introduced to the board in July 1970 by Norman Wisdom following an appeal for new directors, and was soon to be in sole charge. The Albion were to enjoy a golden era under his dynamic leadership.

SEASON 1973–74

Back in the Third Division once more, Albion supporters were to experience a real roller-coaster of a season which heralded the most successful period in the club's history. Mike Bamber was left as sole chairman when Len Stringer resigned from the board at the beginning of October for personal reasons, but the club was still suffering from the perennial lack of cash: Pat Saward's only new signings were Mick Brown (Crystal Palace) and Ronnie Howell (Swindon Town), both on free transfers. One sad note from the summer was the passing on 13 June of 86-year-old Charlie Webb, the former player and manager who was associated with the club from 1909 until 1948.

In a bizarre opening to the League season, Albion were unbeaten away from home for five games, but the first five Goldstone fixtures, plus a League Cup encounter with Charlton Athletic, all ended in defeat. Former skippers Bert Murray and Brian Bromley departed for pastures-new while John Boyle arrived on loan from Chelsea as Saward tried desperately to find a winning formula.

Just 6,228 fans watched a dreadful 1–0 home defeat by Halifax Town on 13 October and, with Albion in the bottom four, the gate dipped below 6,000 a week later as a first Goldstone victory, 2–0 over Shrewsbury Town, was recorded. It was not enough to save Saward, though, and two days later, on 22 October, he was sacked with over three years left on his contract. (Saward received 'reasonably substantial compensation' from the club late in 1975.) There was considerable public sympathy for the man who had unexpectedly taken the club into Division Two, and at the following game, a 4–0 victory over Southport with trainer Glen Wilson in charge, around 150 supporters staged a demonstration for his return. Former Albion half-back Steve Burtenshaw, who had recently resigned

Commercial manager Ron Pavey launched an important new lottery on 9 March. Three'n'Easy was expected to bring in around £1,000 each week.

as Arsenal coach, was an early favourite for the vacancy, but Mike Bamber had his eyes on bigger fish.

On 15 October, Brian Clough and his assistant Peter Taylor resigned from First Division Derby County, mainly because of restrictions placed on Clough's media activities. The pair had started in management at Hartlepools United, but it was at Derby that Clough established himself as the most dynamic and controversial manager in England while leading the Rams to their first League Championship in 1972.

Mike Bamber and vice-chairman Harry Bloom met Clough and Taylor for the first time on 27 October at London's Waldorf Hotel as Albion returned from defeat at Hereford. News of the mutual interest leaked and suddenly the club became the centre of attention. Negotiations between the parties were prolonged, but eventually the news broke on 1 November: Brian Clough and Peter Taylor had signed a five-year contract to manage an ailing Third Division club, Brighton and Hove Albion!

The whole football world was astounded by Bamber's coup; it was the chairman who had sold the club's potential to Clough and, in particular, Taylor. Significantly, he asked for no restriction on their media activities. Pat Saward was now a forgotten man as Albion fans rushed to buy up the remaining season tickets. Clough's first game in charge, a goal-less home draw with York City, was attended by 16,017, almost 10,000 up on the previous gate.

The new management team took stock of the Albion squad on an overnight stay at the White Hart Hotel in Lewes, and, in Taylor's words, soon realised they were dealing with 'a bunch of amateurs and layabouts'. Strengthening the squad was a priority, and Clough's first signing was cover for Brian Powney in the form of Ron Hillyard, on-loan from York City.

The manager tried to stem the supporters' new-found optimism: 'Forget promotion, just be happy to avoid relegation.' The point was hammered home in no uncertain terms in the F.A. Cup first round by Isthmian League side Walton & Hersham.

Albion 1973–74

Back row left to right: Ray Crawford (coach), Ian Goodwin, George Ley, Steve Piper, Mick Brown, Brian Powney, Grenville Millington, Norman Gall, Trevor Bryson, John Templeman, Ken Beamish, Glen Wilson (youth-team trainer).
Middle row left to right: Pat Hilton, Brian Bromley, Bert Murray, Alan Boorn, Peter O'Sullivan, Pat Saward (manager), Eddie Spearritt (captain), Tony Towner, Graham Howell, Ronnie Howell, Barry Bridges.
On ground left to right: Lee Plummer, Frank Fraser, Stephen Barrett, Terry Norton, Dave Busby, Ricky Sopp, Terry Harvey, Mick Conway, Biz Russell.

SEASON 1973–74

Date	Comp.	Ven.	Opponents	Result	HT	Pos.	Scorers	Atten.	Beamish K	Boyle J	Bridges B	Bromley B	Brown M	Busby D	Conway M	Downsborough P	Fuschillo P	Gall N	Goodeve K	Goodwin I	Grummitt P	Hilton P	Howell G	Howell R	Ley G	McEwan W	Murray A	Norton T	O'Sullivan P	Piper S	Powney B	Robertson L	Spearritt E	Templeman J	Towner A	Welch R	Wilson H
Aug 25	FL D3	(a)	Rochdale	D 1–1	1–0	12=	Bridges	2,306	9		8	10	12					5					2		3				11		1		6	4	7†		
29	FLC R1	(h)	Charlton Athletic	L 1–2	1–1	–	Templeman	8,452	9		8	10						5					2	4	3				11		1	12	6†	7			
Sep 1	FL D3	(h)	AFC Bournemouth	L 0–2	0–1	17=		9,835	9		8	10	6					5					2†	4	3				11		1	12		7			
8	FL D3	(a)	Plymouth Argyle	W 1–0	1–0	14	Towner	7,011			8					1		5		12		10	2	4	3				11			9	6		7†		
10	FL D3	(a)	Southport	D 1–1	0–0	10=	Beamish	3,462	7		8		N			1		5		6		10		4	3				11			9		2			
15	FL D3	(h)	Charlton Athletic	L 1–2	1–1	18	Bridges	9,379	7		8†					1		5		6		10		4	3				11			9	12	2			
19	FL D3	(h)	Oldham Athletic	L 1–2	1–1	21	Robertson (pen)	6,870	7†		8							5		6		10		4	3				11		1	9	12	2			
22	FL D3	(a)	Grimsby Town	D 0–0	0–0	20		7,797	12	8	9							5		6		10		4	3				11		1		2		7†		
29	FL D3	(h)	Watford	L 0–1	0–1	22		7,645	10	8	9							5				12	2	4†					11		1		6	3	7		
Oct 2	FL D3	(a)	Oldham Athletic	W 1–0	0–0	18	Beamish	6,929	8	4								5		3		9					N		11	6	1		10	2	7		
6	FL D3	(a)	Blackburn Rovers	L 1–3	1–0	19	Beamish	6,526	8	4								5		3†		9					12		11	6	1		10	2	7		
13	FL D3	(h)	Halifax Town	L 0–1	0–1	21		6,228	9	8	12							5				10	2†						11	6	1		3	4	7		
20	FL D3	(h)	Shrewsbury Town	W 2–0	1–0	19	R Howell, Beamish	5,308	9	4†	7			12				5						10	3				11	6	1		8	2			
24	FL D3	(h)	Southport	W 4–0	1–0	18	R Howell (pen), O'Sullivan, Spearritt, Bridges	6,417	9	4	7							5						10	3				11	6	1	N	8	2			
27	FL D3	(a)	Hereford United	L 0–3	0–2	19		8,139	9	8	7							5				12	4†	10	3				11	6	1			2			
Nov 3	FL D3	(h)	York City	D 0–0	0–0	19		16,017	9	4	7							5				N		8	3				11	6	1	10		2			
10	FL D3	(a)	Huddersfield Town	D 2–2	0–1	19	Beamish, Bridges	6,057	8	4	7							5		12		9			3				11	6	1	10†	2				
13	FL D3	(a)	Walsall	W 1–0	0–0	17	Hilton	5,116	8	N	7							5				9			3				11	6	1	10	4	2			
17	FL D3	(h)	Chesterfield	D 0–0	0–0	18		14,148	8†		7				12			5				9			3				11	6	1	10	4	2			
24	FAC R1	(a)	Walton & Hersh'm	D 0–0	0–0	–		6,500			7							5				9	N	8	3				11	6	1	10	4	2			
28	FAC R1 Rep	(h)	Walton & Hersh'm	L 0–4	0–1	–		9,657			7							5				9		8	3				11	6†	1	10	4	2	12		
Dec 1	FL D3	(h)	Bristol Rovers	L 2–8	1–5	18	O'Sullivan, R Howell	10,762	8									5				9	12	6	3†				11		1	10	4	2	7		
8	FL D3	(a)	Tranmere Rovers	L 1–4	0–2	18	Hilton	4,458	8									5	6		1	9	2	N	3				11			10	4		7		
22	FL D3	(a)	Watford	L 0–1	0–1	20		5,909	8									5	4		1	9	3					N	11	6		10		2	7		
26	FL D3	(h)	Aldershot	L 0–1	0–1	20		14,769	9									5	8		1	10	N						11	6		7		2		4	3
29	FL D3	(h)	Plymouth Argyle	W 1–0	0–0	20	Beamish	11,181	8									5	N		1			10					11	6		9		2	7	4	3
Jan 1	FL D3	(a)	AFC Bournemouth	D 0–0	0–0	20		17,094	8									5	N		1			10					11	6		9		2	7	4	3
12	FL D3	(a)	Charlton Athletic	W 4–0	0–0	20	R Howell 3 (1 pen), O'Sullivan	6,878	8									5	N		1			10					11	6		9		2	7	4	3
20	FL D3	(h)	Rochdale	W 2–1	2–0	17	Towner, Beamish	18,885	8									5	12		1			10					11	6		9		2	7	4†	3
27	FL D3	(a)	Cambridge United	D 1–1	0–0	18	Brown	7,749	8				12					5			1								11	6		9	10	2	7†	4	3
Feb 2	FL D3	(a)	Port Vale	L 1–2	0–2	18	Beamish	3,728	8		9		12					5			1								11†	6		7	10	2		4	3
9	FL D3	(h)	Grimsby Town	D 1–1	0–1	18	Bridges	10,469	8		9							5			1								11	6		N	10	2	7	4	3
16	FL D3	(a)	Halifax Town	D 2–2	0–2	18	Robertson (pen), Templeman	2,767	N		9		5								1								11	6		8	10	2	7	4	3
23	FL D3	(h)	Blackburn Rovers	W 3–0	1–0	18	Welch (pen), Bridges 2	12,120	8		9		5								1			12					11	6			10	2	7†	4	3
27	FL D3	(h)	Wrexham	W 2–1	2–1	15	R Howell (pen), O'Sullivan	7,510	8		9						2	5			1			7		4			11	6			10		N		3
Mar 3	FL D3	(a)	Aldershot	W 1–0	1–0	15	Beamish	9,837	8		9						2	5			1			7		10			11	6		12				4†	3
10	FL D3	(h)	Hereford United	W 2–1	0–1	10	Beamish, Piper	17,061	8		9						2	5			1			7		4			11	6		12	10†				3
16	FL D3	(a)	Shrewsbury Town	L 0–1	0–1	12		2,077	8		9						2	5			1†			10		4			11	6		7			12		3
20	FL D3	(h)	Port Vale	W 2–1	2–0	9	Bridges, McEwan	9,365	8		9						2	5						10		7			11	6	1				N	4	3
23	FL D3	(h)	Huddersfield Town	L 1–2	1–1	13	McEwan	12,564	8		9						2	5						10		7			11	6	1				N	4	3
25	FL D3	(a)	Wrexham	L 0–1	0–1	15		5,925	8		9							5	2					10		7			11	6	1				N	4	3
30	FL D3	(a)	York City	L 0–3	0–2	17		6,708	8		12		6					5†	2					10		7			11		1	9				4	3
Apr 3	FL D3	(h)	Cambridge United	W 4–1	2–1	14	Bridges, Welch, McEwan, R Howell (pen)	9,851	8		9		5				6							10		7			11		1	N		2		4	3
6	FL D3	(h)	Walsall	W 2–1	1–1	12	Bridges, Robertson	10,574	8		9						6									7			11	5	1	10		2	N	4	3
12	FL D3	(a)	Southend United	W 2–0	0–0	10	Beamish 2	9,772	8		9						6									7			11	5	1	10		2	N	4	3
13	FL D3	(a)	Chesterfield	L 0–1	0–1	12		6,917	8		9†						6									7			11	5	1	10		2	12	4	3
15	FL D3	(h)	Southend United	L 0–2	0–2	13		12,943	8		9						6									7			11	5	1	10		2	12	4†	3
20	FL D3	(h)	Tranmere Rovers	L 1–3	1–2	16	R Howell (pen)	9,593	9								6							4		8			10	5	1	11		2	7	N	3
27	FL D3	(a)	Bristol Rovers	D 1–1	1–0	18	Robertson	19,137	9								6							N		7			11	5	1	10		2	8	4	3
League appearances									43	10	31	2	5	0	0	3	13	37	5	6	16	15	8	26	16	15	0	0	46	34	27	27	21	34	20	21	25
Substitute appearances									1		2		3	1	1				1	2		2	1	1			1					3	2		3		
League goals									12		10		1									2		9		3			4	1		4	1	1	2	2	

Football League Division 3 1973–74

		P	W	D	L	F	A	W	D	L	F	A	Pts
1.	Oldham Athletic	46	13	6	4	50	23	12	6	5	33	24	62
2.	Bristol Rovers	46	15	6	2	37	15	7	11	5	28	18	61
3.	York City	46	13	8	2	37	15	8	11	4	30	23	61
4.	Wrexham	46	15	6	2	44	15	7	6	10	19	28	56
5.	Chesterfield	46	14	6	3	31	16	7	8	8	24	26	56
6.	Grimsby Town	46	14	6	3	48	21	4	9	10	19	29	51
7.	Watford	46	12	6	5	34	21	7	6	10	30	35	50
8.	Aldershot	46	13	6	4	47	22	6	5	12	18	30	49
9.	Halifax Town	46	9	11	3	23	15	5	10	8	25	36	49
10.	Huddersfield Town	46	14	5	4	37	16	3	8	12	19	39	47
11.	AFC Bournemouth	46	11	5	7	25	23	5	10	8	29	35	47
12.	Southend United	46	10	7	6	40	30	6	7	10	22	32	46
13.	Blackburn Rovers	46	13	4	6	38	21	5	6	12	24	43	46
14.	Charlton Athletic	46	13	5	5	43	29	6	3	14	23	44	46
15.	Walsall	46	11	7	5	37	19	5	6	12	20	29	45
16.	Tranmere Rovers	46	10	8	5	31	15	5	7	11	19	29	45
17.	Plymouth Argyle	46	13	6	4	37	17	4	4	15	22	37	44
18.	Hereford United	46	10	5	8	31	25	4	10	9	22	32	43
19.	**ALBION**	46	10	3	10	31	31	6	8	9	21	27	43
20.	Port Vale	46	12	6	5	37	23	2	8	13	15	35	42
21.	Cambridge United	46	11	7	5	36	27	2	2	19	12	54	35
22.	Shrewsbury Town	46	7	7	9	24	24	3	4	16	17	38	31
23.	Southport	46	4	14	5	19	20	2	2	19	16	62	28
24.	Rochdale	46	1	12	10	24	38	1	5	17	14	56	21

On 20 October 1973, Dave Busby came on as a substitute, the first black player to represent Albion in a senior match.

The Amateur Cup holders, who included former Albion reserve Colin Woffinden, forced a 0–0 draw on their tiny Stompond Lane ground, but thrashed Albion 4–0 in the Goldstone replay with a hat-trick in the last eight minutes by joiner Clive Foskett in what is undoubtedly the club's worst-ever Cup defeat. The very name of Walton & Hersham still causes a shudder in most Brighton fans. Amid the media glare surrounding Clough, further humiliation came just three days later at the hands of the Third Division leaders, Bristol Rovers, who won 8–2 at the Goldstone in front of ITV's *Big Match* cameras. After one of the most infamous weeks in the club's history, a 4–1 defeat at Tranmere Rovers and 1–0 defeats at the hands of Watford and Aldershot seemed minor in comparison, but left Albion in 20th place.

Clough, ashamed of his new team's lack of heart, signed goalkeeper Peter Grummitt on loan from Sheffield Wednesday and immediately selected him for first-team duties. In came Ken Goodeve from Luton Town, and a pair of young Burnley players, Harry Wilson and Ronnie Welch, for a joint fee of £70,000. Results began to pick up and only two games were lost in fourteen as the club climbed to ninth place. Ever-hopeful fans started to talk of possible promotion, but the rest of the season rather fell flat and the club dropped to a final placing of nineteenth. The new signings continued in the latter half of the season, mainly through the efforts of Peter Taylor, and in came Paul Fuschillo and Billy McEwan from Blackpool for £15,000.

It was Clough that attracted all the attention, though. Quotes abounded. 'Of course I'm bigger than Brighton — I was bigger than Derby, too', ran one headline. Throughout the season Bamber had to deny that his manager would be leaving for Derby County, Aston Villa, or even Iran, where he was offered the post of national manager.

The season ended in a welter of activity. Steve Govier, Andy Rollings and Ian Mellor, the latter for a club-record £40,000, were all signed from Norwich City, and in early May Fred Binney, a prolific goalscorer for Exeter City, joined the club with John Templeman and Lammie Robertson going in the opposite direction. Twelve players were placed on the transfer list as part of the rebuilding operation. With a new team costing around £200,000 in his charge, the manager assured his chairman of promotion next time round. The arrival of Brian Clough captured the headlines and the imagination of the Sussex public. An exciting new era under the leadership of Mike Bamber had begun.

This season was notable for the advent of Sunday football. Amid oil shortages, a miners' overtime ban, a rail strike and a power-station work-to-rule, three-day working was introduced and a State of Emergency declared by the Conservative Government. In November a ban on floodlights necessitated early kick-offs: the Walton & Hersham replay started at 1.45 p.m. – perhaps fortunately restricting the size of the crowd – and two-fifteen became the regular Saturday kick-off time. Senior Sunday football was sanctioned for the duration of the emergency just before Christmas and Albion were soon involved with the Rochdale match chosen as an experiment. Special arrangements were made to circumvent legal restrictions as charging to watch the match was illegal on a Sunday. Spectators paid the usual admission prices as a subscription to the 'Dolphins Club', and received a membership card and entrance to the ground; season-ticket holders were deemed to be honorary members. There was a turnstile provided for free admission, but it was reported to be little-used. An 18,885 crowd, the biggest of the season, witnessed a 2–1 victory and justified Mike Bamber's view that Sunday matches could halt falling gates. Other Sunday games were played at Cambridge United and Aldershot, and a second home game, against Hereford United, when 17,061 spectators attended.

Planning the future
New manager Brian Clough (left) discusses his plans for the club with chairman Mike Bamber (centre) and assistant Peter Taylor (right). However, the Goldstone career of one member of this triumvirate was to be brief indeed.

SEASON 1974-75

Many familiar faces left the Goldstone in the summer, leaving only four players – Peter O'Sullivan, Tony Towner, Micky Conway and Dave Busby – who had played in the pre-Clough era eight months or so earlier. As ever, the manager was both outspoken and optimistic. 'If I've turned Brighton upside down and inside out, I don't apologise,' he wrote in the Supporters' Club handbook; 'Now we are looking forward to a great start from a new team.' Assistant manager Peter Taylor wrote: 'Those who have been supporters for a good number of years could well feel that a bomb has dropped on the Goldstone Ground recently. The place has stirred a little since our arrival, hasn't it!' However, another 'bomb' was about to explode in the Old Shoreham Road and in the football world in general.

On 20 July the Leeds United chairman, Manny Cussins, announced that the replacement for his former manager Don Revie, now in charge of the England team, was — Brian Clough! Attracted by one of the biggest clubs of the era and a £20,000 salary – he was reported to be on £7,500 at Brighton – Clough had negotiated a release from his Albion contract. It was apparently agreed with Cussins that Leeds would pay Albion £75,000 in compensation and play a friendly at the Goldstone. More importantly, Peter Taylor was to stay on as team manager. It was felt locally that Albion may have got the better part of the deal as Clough had, perhaps, been biding his time in Hove, whereas Taylor, who later admitted that he had pushed his ex-partner into the Goldstone job, assured everyone that *he* was fully committed to the club.

However, Leeds United allegedly reneged on the agreement, and on 4 September Albion issued writs against Clough, for breach of contract, and Leeds, for compensation for the loss of the manager's services. The matter was subsequently settled out of court in Albion's favour in December 1975, Leeds paying compensation of £45,000. (As it turned out, Clough's tenure at Elland Road lasted just 44 days, the changes he made proving too extreme for the board, and on 6 January 1975 he joined Nottingham Forest. Before moving to the City Ground, Clough admitted that he had let Mike Bamber down badly, but the Albion chairman was quick to scotch rumours that he could return to the Goldstone.)

Despite the loss of Brian Clough, season tickets were snapped up quickly by expectant supporters. Taylor, in full charge of a team for the first time, completed his close-season signings with Ricky Marlowe (Shrewsbury Town) and a new midfield general in Ernie Machin (Plymouth Argyle). For reasons best known to the club, the blue-and-white stripes were again dropped in favour of an all-white strip.

The season opened with a rare visit from Crystal Palace, to renew a rivalry from the old Third Division (South) days; the competition between the two sides intensified greatly over the next few years. Managed by Malcolm Allison, Palace had just been relegated from the Second Division and were something of a glamour club, but with them came the spectre of large-scale crowd disturbances. Eighty-five police officers plus dogs, horses and motor-bikes were detailed to control the 26,235 crowd, but there were still 20 arrests and the rival fans were shepherded out of separate entrances. Brighton won with a goal from Ian Mellor, one of five players making his full début, in the club's first opening-day victory for ten years.

Results thereafter fell well below expectations, and by the end of October Albion were in the bottom four with attendances considerably under the 'break-even' figure of 14,000. There was a 6–0 hiding at Walsall, and a 4–0 home defeat at the hands of player-manager Bobby Charlton and his Preston North End team. To shore up a leaky defence, Taylor brought in Graham Winstanley on loan from Carlisle United and things started to pick up as, first, Andy Rollings and then Steve Piper rapidly improved alongside the experienced Winstanley who was soon signed permanently; he was also made skipper while still on loan. In came Ken Tiler, a full-back from Chesterfield, while Peter O'Sullivan, initially played as a

Albion 1974–75

Inset: Ernie Machin (captain).
Back row left to right: Harry Wilson, Ronnie Welch, Ricky Sopp, Derek Forster, Tommy Barden, Peter Grummitt, Paul Fuschillo, Ricky Marlowe.
Middle row left to right: Glen Wilson (trainer), Fred Binney, Steve Piper, Steve Cooper, Billy McEwan, Andy Rollings, Steve Govier, Ian Mellor, Peter O'Sullivan, Gerry Clarke (coach).
Seated left to right: Lee Plummer, Tony Towner, Mick Conway, Peter Taylor (manager), Biz Russell, Dave Busby, Frank Fraser.

SEASON 1974–75

Player columns (left to right): Binney F, Busby D, Conway M, Fell G, Forster D, Fuschillo P, Govier S, Grummitt P, Lewis A, McEwan W, Machin E, Marlowe R, Mason T, Mellor I, O'Sullivan P, Piper S, Rollings A, Smith W, Tiler K, Towner A, Walker J, Welch R, Wilson H, Winstanley G

Date	Comp.	Ven.	Opponents	Result	HT	Pos.	Scorers	Atten.
Aug 17	FL D3	(h)	Crystal Palace	W 1–0	0–0	1=	Mellor	26,235
21	FLC R1	(a)	Reading	D 0–0	0–0	–		7,567
24	FL D3	(a)	Peterborough Utd	L 0–2	0–0	16=		9,324
28	FLC R1 Rep	(h)	Reading	D 2–2*	0–0	–	Binney (pen), Rollings	11,803
31	FL D3	(h)	Chesterfield	W 2–1	1–1	8=	Mellor, Binney	11,527
Sep 3	FLC R1 2Rep	(a)	Reading	D 0–0*	0–0	–		8,527
5	FLC R1 3Rep	(h)	Reading	L 2–3	1–1	–	Marlowe 2	7,257
7	FL D3	(a)	Blackburn Rovers	L 0–1	0–0	14=		5,858
14	FL D3	(h)	Watford	W 2–0	1–0	9	Marlowe, Welch	11,606
18	FL D3	(h)	Port Vale	D 1–1	1–0	7=	Marlowe	12,319
21	FL D3	(a)	AFC Bournemouth	L 0–2	0–1	15		7,951
24	FL D3	(a)	Charlton Athletic	L 1–2	0–1	16	Walker	6,443
28	FL D3	(h)	Bury	D 0–0	0–0	17		10,622
Oct 1	FL D3	(a)	Walsall	L 0–6	0–2	18		5,291
5	FL D3	(h)	Wrexham	D 3–3	0–2	19	Binney (pen), Mellor, Govier	8,900
8	FL D3	(a)	Grimsby Town	L 2–3	0–0	19	Towner, Binney	4,795
12	FL D3	(a)	Huddersfield Town	L 0–1	0–0	20		6,544
16	FL D3	(h)	Grimsby Town	W 3–1	0–1	18	Welch, Walker, Mellor	8,172
19	FL D3	(h)	Preston North End	L 0–4	0–2	20		16,413
26	FL D3	(a)	Gillingham	L 1–2	1–0	22	Fuschillo	5,985
Nov 2	FL D3	(a)	Tranmere Rovers	W 2–1	2–1	20	Marlowe, Mason	2,134
9	FL D3	(h)	Swindon Town	D 1–1	1–1	21	Mellor (pen)	8,761
16	FL D3	(a)	Hereford United	L 0–2	0–1	22		7,016
23	FAC R1	(h)	Aldershot	W 3–1	2–0	–	Binney 2, Mellor	11,970
30	FL D3	(a)	Halifax Town	L 0–1	0–1	23		1,961
Dec 7	FL D3	(h)	Southend United	W 2–0	2–0	22	Mason, Walker	10,035
14	FAC R2	(h)	Brentford	W 1–0	1–0	–	Binney	13,281
21	FL D3	(h)	Plymouth Argyle	D 2–2	0–2	21	Binney, Towner	9,913
26	FL D3	(a)	Watford	D 1–1	0–1	22	Binney	6,639
28	FL D3	(h)	Aldershot	W 2–0	2–0	19	Towner, Mellor	12,668
Jan 4	FAC R3	(h)	Leatherhead	L 0–1	0–0	–		20,491
11	FL D3	(a)	Southend United	L 0–1	0–0	21		5,846
25	FL D3	(h)	Colchester United	W 2–0	1–0	21	Binney 2	9,937
Feb 4	FL D3	(a)	Swindon Town	L 0–1	0–0	22		9,561
8	FL D3	(h)	Tranmere Rovers	W 3–1	1–0	19	Towner, O'Sullivan 2	9,997
15	FL D3	(a)	Colchester United	D 2–2	1–2	18	Binney, Towner	4,161
22	FL D3	(h)	Hereford United	W 2–1	1–0	19	Piper, Towner	11,541
Mar 1	FL D3	(a)	Chesterfield	W 4–2	0–2	17	Fell, Walker, Wilson, Binney	4,622
8	FL D3	(h)	Charlton Athletic	D 1–1	1–0	17	Winstanley	13,898
15	FL D3	(a)	Bury	L 1–2	0–0	19	Towner	4,037
18	FL D3	(a)	Crystal Palace	L 0–3	0–2	19		18,799
22	FL D3	(h)	Blackburn Rovers	L 0–1	0–0	20		13,470
26	FL D3	(h)	AFC Bournemouth	W 2–1	0–1	19	Marlowe, O'Sullivan	10,319
29	FL D3	(a)	Plymouth Argyle	D 2–2	2–1	19	Fell, Own goal	19,396
31	FL D3	(a)	Aldershot	L 1–2	0–0	19	Winstanley	7,985
Apr 5	FL D3	(h)	Gillingham	W 4–3	3–1	20	Fell, O'Sullivan, Wilson (pen), Towner	10,487
9	FL D3	(h)	Walsall	W 1–0	0–0	19	Towner	10,898
12	FL D3	(a)	Wrexham	L 1–2	1–2	19	Towner	3,223
16	FL D3	(h)	Halifax Town	D 0–0	0–0	19		10,309
19	FL D3	(h)	Huddersfield Town	W 2–0	0–0	17	Marlowe, Fell	10,822
23	FL D3	(h)	Peterborough Utd	W 2–0	1–0	17	Wilson (pen), Fell	11,509
26	FL D3	(a)	Preston North End	L 0–1	0–1	19		6,222
28	FL D3	(a)	Port Vale	L 0–1	0–1	19		2,754

Notes: Aug 28 – after extra time (90-minute score 1–1).
Sep 3 – after extra time.

Player totals:

	Binney F	Busby D	Conway M	Fell G	Forster D	Fuschillo P	Govier S	Grummitt P	Lewis A	McEwan W	Machin E	Marlowe R	Mason T	Mellor I	O'Sullivan P	Piper S	Rollings A	Smith W	Tiler K	Towner A	Walker J	Welch R	Wilson H	Winstanley G
League appearances	24	1	0	20	3	4	12	43	3	12	28	24	23	26	39	37	25	5	28	41	23	14	42	29
Substitute appearances	2	1												1	2	2					4	1		
League goals (OG – 1)	9			5		1	1					5	2	6	4	1				10	4	2	3	2

Football League Division 3 1974–75

		P	W	D	L	F	A	W	D	L	F	A	Pts
1.	Blackburn Rovers	46	15	7	1	40	16	7	9	7	28	29	60
2.	Plymouth Argyle	46	16	5	2	38	19	8	6	9	41	39	59
3.	Charlton Athletic	46	15	5	3	51	29	7	6	10	25	32	55
4.	Swindon Town	46	18	3	2	43	17	3	8	12	21	41	53
5.	Crystal Palace	46	14	8	1	48	22	4	7	12	18	35	51
6.	Port Vale	46	15	6	2	37	19	3	9	11	24	35	51
7.	Peterborough United	46	10	9	4	24	17	9	3	11	23	36	50
8.	Walsall	46	15	5	3	46	13	3	8	12	21	39	49
9.	Preston North End	46	16	5	2	42	19	6	14	21	49	49
10.	Gillingham	46	14	6	3	43	23	8	12	22	37	48
11.	Colchester United	46	13	7	3	45	22	4	6	13	25	41	47
12.	Hereford United	46	14	6	3	42	21	8	13	22	45	46
13.	Wrexham	46	10	8	5	41	23	5	7	11	24	32	45
14.	Bury	46	13	6	4	38	17	3	6	14	15	33	44
15.	Chesterfield	46	11	7	5	37	25	5	5	13	25	41	44
16.	Grimsby Town	46	12	8	3	35	19	3	5	15	20	45	43
17.	Halifax Town	46	11	10	2	33	20	2	7	14	16	45	43
18.	Southend United	46	11	9	3	32	17	2	7	13	18	42	42
19.	**ALBION**	46	14	7	2	38	21	2	3	18	18	43	42
20.	Aldershot	46	13	5	5	40	21	4	6	13	42	38
21.	AFC Bournemouth	46	9	6	8	27	25	4	6	13	17	33	38
22.	Tranmere Rovers	46	12	4	7	39	21	2	5	16	16	36	37
23.	Watford	46	9	7	7	30	31	1	10	12	22	44	37
24.	Huddersfield Town	46	9	6	8	32	29	2	4	17	15	47	32

Note: Aldershot had one point deducted on 9.9.1974 for fielding an unregistered player.

winger and then dropped after 194 consecutive first-team games, patched up his differences with the manager and impressed in a new midfield role.

Albion, in 23rd place, defeated Southend United 2–0 on 7 December and went through the month unbeaten to move out of the relegation places, but the battle continued into 1975. Staying just ahead of the bottom four from February onwards and with games in hand, they made sure of their status with a 2–0 win over Peterborough United on 23 April with two matches to spare. Home results were good all season with only two League defeats, but away performances were generally dreadful: just seven points were gained on the road, the worst record in the entire Football League. A big disappointment was the failure of both Ian Mellor and Fred Binney to find the net regularly, and the top scorer in the League was winger Tony Towner with ten goals.

Home wins over Aldershot and Brentford in the F.A. Cup set up a third-round Goldstone tie with Isthmian Leaguers Leatherhead. With Albion anticipating a useful cup-run, Chris Kelly, the 'Leatherhead Lip', scored the only goal to knock out Brighton in front of 20,491 fans, the second time in two seasons that the club had been humiliated by non-League opposition. Colin Woffinden, the former Albion reserve who had been in the winning Walton & Hersham side, was also in the triumphant Leatherhead team. Leatherhead went on to a tie at First Division Leicester City and were 2–0 up before eventually succumbing 3–2.

The League Cup saw a seven-hour marathon with Reading which was eventually won at Hove by the Berkshire side.

In December 1974, with the club's liabilities approaching £500,000, the share capital of the company was increased by £375,000 through a new, two-tiered issue: 400,000 ordinary shares at 25p and 275,000 'A' ordinary (non-voting) shares at £1. Added to the initial £4,000 issue in 1904 and the £6,000 increase in 1926, the nominal capital of the company was now £385,000. The huge increase reflected both the ambition of Mike Bamber to see the club succeed, and the rapidly escalating cost of running a football club in inflationary times.

SEASON 1975–76

After the previous season's close shave at the wrong end of the table, nobody at the Goldstone was making bold predictions this time round. Two experienced players were signed, defender Phil Beal (Tottenham Hotspur) and striker Neil Martin (Nottingham Forest), and once again the traditional blue-and-white stripes were restored. Public interest was reasonably high, and over 12,000 Three'n'Easy tickets were being sold each week in addition to the Albion Bingo game, bringing in substantial funds.

An excellent 3–0 home win over Rotherham United got the season off to a good start, but two home defeats followed and after five matches Albion were tenth. The next two games epitomised the rest of the season: a 6–0 thrashing of Chester at the Goldstone, followed by a 2–0 defeat at bottom-placed Colchester United. Albion, to their credit, bounced back from the Layer Road defeat with a 1–0 win at unbeaten Crystal Palace, and followed with three more wins to move into third place. From that point the season took shape: sparkling home performances in front of large crowds, but a lack of resolve and determination letting the club down badly away from the Goldstone.

Dennis Burnett arrived from Hull City to bolster the promotion push and performed well enough to oust skipper Graham Winstanley from the side, forming a sound defensive pairing with Andy Rollings. Ernie Machin and Peter O'Sullivan were both performing well in midfield while, up front, Fred Binney was at last knocking in the goals.

Second-placed Hereford United were despatched 4–2 before a crowd of 17,811, a match notable for the bravery of Binney who returned to the fray with a bandaged head-wound. The New Year saw a splendid win at third-placed Cardiff City, but it was the last win of the season on the road and only four more away points were gained. In contrast, only three more home points were dropped and a second 6–0 home win was recorded, at the expense of Colchester United. On 24 February, Crystal Palace visited the Goldstone for an all-ticket clash in front of 33,300 fans. A tremendous Albion performance saw Palace, one

> On 1 October 1975, Albion played First Division Stoke City in a friendly to commemorate the 75th anniversary of the formation of the club as the amateur side Brighton and Hove Rangers in 1900. (It was then believed that Rangers were the same club as Albion, but the authors of this work have shown that this was not the case and that Albion were formed separately in June 1901.) An excellent programme was produced for the occasion with articles on the club's history. The game was drawn 1–1.

Albion 1975–76
Back row left to right: Allen Lewis, Ricky Sopp, Andy Rollings, Whittaker, Robin Madden, Frank Fraser, Tommy Mason.
Third row left to right: Ken Gutteridge (coach), Graham Winstanley (captain), Harry Wilson, Ken Tiler, Peter Grummitt, Tommy Barden, Derek Forster, Steve Piper, Jim Walker, Ian Mellor, Peter Ward, Ricky Marlowe, Glen Wilson (physio).
Seated left to right: Ernie Machin, Fred Binney, Peter O'Sullivan, Neil Martin, Peter Taylor (manager), Brian Daykin (assistant manager), Tony Towner, Phil Beal, Gerry Fell.
On ground left to right: Mick Conway, Stephen Branch, Carmine Porpora, Kevin Deakin, Stephen Ward, Micky Jones, Lee Plummer.

SEASON 1975–76

Date	Comp.	Ven.	Opponents	Result	HT	Pos.	Scorers	Atten.
Aug 16	FL D3	(h)	Rotherham United	W 3–0	3–0	1=	Binney, Machin, Martin	10,138
19	FLC R1 Lg1	(a)	Brentford	L 1–2	1–0	–	Own goal	5,560
23	FL D3	(a)	Sheffield Wed.	D 3–3	1–2	5	Martin 2, Towner	10,326
27	FLC R1 Lg2	(h)	Brentford	D 1–1	1–1	–	Binney (pen)	11,016
30	FL D3	(h)	Cardiff City	L 0–1	0–0	10		11,353
Sep 6	FL D3	(a)	Port Vale	D 1–1	1–0	10	Binney	3,289
10	FL D3	(h)	Walsall	L 1–2	1–1	12	Binney	8,592
13	FL D3	(h)	Chester	W 6–0	2–0	7	Binney 2, O'Sullivan, Mellor, Fell 2	7,924
20	FL D3	(a)	Colchester United	L 0–2	0–0	11		3,176
23	FL D3	(a)	Crystal Palace	W 1–0	1–0	7	Butlin	25,606
27	FL D3	(h)	Chesterfield	W 3–0	2–0	6	O'Sullivan, Butlin, Binney	8,784
Oct 4	FL D3	(a)	Shrewsbury Town	W 2–1	2–0	3	Binney, O'Sullivan	4,198
11	FL D3	(h)	Preston North End	W 1–0	1–0	3	Rollings	14,375
18	FL D3	(a)	Grimsby Town	L 1–2	0–0	4	Martin	4,938
25	FL D3	(h)	Wrexham	W 3–2	1–1	5	Towner, Martin, Fell	12,059
Nov 1	FL D3	(a)	Peterborough Utd	L 0–1	0–1	5		8,630
4	FL D3	(h)	Bury	W 2–1	2–1	4	Binney 2	14,603
8	FL D3	(h)	Southend United	W 2–0	1–0	3	O'Sullivan, Fell	13,720
15	FL D3	(a)	Halifax Town	W 3–1	1–1	2	Martin, Binney, Fell	2,201
22	FAC R1	(a)	Watford	W 3–0	1–0	–	Martin, Binney 2	9,283
29	FL D3	(a)	Swindon Town	L 2–3	1–0	3	Binney, Mellor	6,792
Dec 6	FL D3	(h)	Hereford United	W 4–2	2–1	2	Binney, Mellor, Martin 2	17,811
13	FAC R2	(a)	Gillingham	W 1–0	0–0	–	Fell	10,579
20	FL D3	(a)	Walsall	L 0–2	0–0	4		5,435
27	FL D3	(a)	Gillingham	L 0–1	0–1	6		9,294
30	FL D3	(h)	Aldershot	W 4–1	3–1	2	O'Sullivan 2, Mellor, Binney	18,818
Jan 3	FAC R3	(a)	Southend United	L 1–2	1–1	–	Binney	9,878
10	FL D3	(a)	Cardiff City	W 1–0	0–0	3	Mellor	17,728
17	FL D3	(h)	Colchester United	W 6–0	3–0	2	Mellor, Rollings, Binney 2, Fell 2	16,302
24	FL D3	(a)	Chester	L 0–3	0–0	4		5,099
31	FL D3	(h)	Mansfield Town	W 1–0	0–0	3	Own goal	11,918
Feb 3	FL D3	(h)	Millwall	W 1–0	0–0	2	Binney	15,332
7	FL D3	(a)	Bury	D 1–1	0–0	3	Mellor	6,217
17	FL D3	(a)	Southend United	L 0–4	0–1	4		4,784
21	FL D3	(h)	Halifax Town	W 1–0	0–0	3	Binney	13,686
24	FL D3	(h)	Crystal Palace	W 2–0	1–0	2	Morgan 2	33,300
28	FL D3	(a)	Wrexham	L 0–3	0–1	2		4,662
Mar 1	FL D3	(a)	Mansfield Town	L 0–1	0–0	2		8,321
6	FL D3	(h)	Peterborough Utd	W 5–0	2–0	2	Binney 2, Mellor, Rollings, Morgan	16,397
10	FL D3	(h)	Shrewsbury Town	D 2–2	0–2	2	Morgan, Binney	21,423
13	FL D3	(a)	Preston North End	L 0–1	0–0	2		6,720
17	FL D3	(h)	Grimsby Town	W 4–2	1–2	2	Morgan, Wilson (pen), Binney (pen), O'Sullivan	17,384
20	FL D3	(h)	Swindon Town	W 2–0	0–0	2	Morgan 2	18,208
27	FL D3	(h)	Hereford United	D 1–1	1–0	2	Ward	12,160
Apr 3	FL D3	(a)	Rotherham United	D 1–1	1–0	2	Ward	4,309
7	FL D3	(a)	Chesterfield	L 1–2	0–1	4	Kinnear (pen)	5,156
10	FL D3	(h)	Port Vale	W 3–0	1–0	3	Binney, Mellor, Ward	19,171
16	FL D3	(a)	Millwall	L 1–3	0–2	4	Binney	23,008
17	FL D3	(h)	Aldershot	D 1–1	0–0	4	Ward	11,666
19	FL D3	(h)	Gillingham	D 1–1	0–1	4	Ward	19,142
24	FL D3	(h)	Sheffield Wed.	D 1–1	0–1	4	Ward	11,859

Players (columns): Beal P, Binney F, Burnett D, Butlin B, Fell G, Grummitt P, Horton B, Kinnear J, Machin E, Martin N, Mason T, Mellor I, Morgan S, O'Sullivan P, Piper S, Rollings A, Tiler K, Towner A, Walker J, Ward P, Wilson H, Winstanley G

	Beal	Binney	Burnett	Butlin	Fell	Grummitt	Horton	Kinnear	Machin	Martin	Mason	Mellor	Morgan	O'Sullivan	Piper	Rollings	Tiler	Towner	Walker	Ward	Wilson	Winstanley
League appearances	8	38	36	5	25	46	11	15	36	13	0	33	18	46	19	36	30	28	1	8	46	8
Substitute appearances	1			4				1		4		1			2			1				1
League goals (OG – 1)		23		2	7			1	1	8		9	7	7		3		2		6	1	

of the season's F.A. Cup semi-finalists, beaten by two goals from £30,000 signing Sammy Morgan, but the tension of the occasion released the hooligan elements and referee Ron Challis threatened to abandon the game if Palace fans continued to throw smoke-bombs and other missiles.

By March, Albion were second to Hereford United, but then Shrewsbury Town managed to end a brilliant run of fourteen consecutive home victories with a 2–2 draw. The next game saw the début of 27-year-old Brian Horton, the midfield dynamo who was to have such an important influence on the team over the next five years. Signed from Port Vale for a bargain £27,000, 'Nobby' took over from Machin and also assumed the captaincy before the season was out. Three games later, at Hereford, came another important début, that of Peter Ward in place of Fred Binney — and what a début! A slightly-built, 20-year-old forward signed for £4,000 from Burton Albion in May 1975, Ward scored with his first touch after just 50 seconds and impressed with his whole performance in a 1–1 draw. That point kept the Seagulls in second place as the race entered the final furlong. Only two points from three away games allowed Cardiff City to move into the runner's-up position, but, with the top *three* now promoted (since 1974), Albion were still excellently placed although the Good Friday match with Millwall was crucial. This was the table prior to the clash at the Den:

> With an eye to the club's future and the burgeoning crowds, the board made a bid for the nearby greyhound stadium in 1976, but were defeated in their attempt to give the club a new home by the leisure group Corals.

		P	W	D	L	F	A	Pts
1.	Hereford United	42	23	10	9	77	51	56
2.	Cardiff City	43	21	11	11	68	48	53
3.	ALBION	42	22	6	14	74	47	50
4.	Millwall	43	17	16	10	47	42	50
5.	Crystal Palace	42	17	15	10	58	43	49
6.	Walsall	43	17	13	13	70	56	47
7.	Wrexham	41	18	10	13	57	46	46

Football League Division 3 1975–76

		P	W	D	L	F	A	W	D	L	F	A	Pts
1.	Hereford United	46	14	6	3	45	24	12	5	6	41	31	63
2.	Cardiff City	46	14	7	2	38	13	8	6	9	31	35	57
3.	Millwall	46	16	6	1	35	14	4	10	9	19	29	56
4.	**ALBION**	46	18	3	2	58	15	4	6	13	20	38	53
5.	Crystal Palace	46	7	12	4	30	20	11	5	7	31	26	53
6.	Wrexham	46	13	6	4	38	21	7	6	10	28	34	52
7.	Walsall	46	11	8	4	43	22	7	6	10	31	39	50
8.	Preston North End	46	15	4	4	45	23	4	6	13	17	34	48
9.	Shrewsbury Town	46	14	2	7	36	25	5	8	10	25	34	48
10.	Peterborough United	46	12	7	4	37	23	3	11	9	26	40	48
11.	Mansfield Town	46	8	11	4	31	22	8	4	11	27	30	47
12.	Port Vale	46	10	10	3	33	21	5	6	12	22	33	46
13.	Bury	46	11	7	5	33	16	3	9	11	18	30	44
14.	Chesterfield	46	11	5	7	45	30	6	4	13	24	39	43
15.	Gillingham	46	10	8	5	38	27	2	11	10	20	41	43
16.	Rotherham United	46	11	6	6	35	22	4	6	13	19	43	42
17.	Chester	46	13	7	3	34	19	2	5	16	9	43	42
18.	Grimsby Town	46	13	7	3	39	21	2	3	18	23	53	40
19.	Swindon Town	46	11	4	8	42	31	5	4	14	20	44	40
20.	Sheffield Wednesday	46	12	6	5	34	25	0	10	13	14	34	40
21.	Aldershot	46	10	8	5	34	26	3	5	15	25	49	39
22.	Colchester United	46	9	6	8	25	27	3	8	12	16	38	38
23.	Southend United	46	9	7	7	40	31	3	6	14	25	44	37
24.	Halifax Town	46	6	5	12	22	32	5	8	10	19	29	35

The Lions were on a twelve-match unbeaten run which Albion were unable to dent, going down 3–1 before 23,008 fans. All was not lost as Brighton, now two points behind Millwall but with a game in hand and a much better goal-average, had a match at lowly Aldershot the following day. They could only draw that game, though, and followed it with another draw at home to Gillingham to end any hope of promotion.

What a frustrating season for the Goldstone regulars — and there were plenty of them, an average of 15,317. How could a team which had dropped only seven points at home perform so abysmally away, gaining just fourteen points? Perhaps the players were swept along by the fervour of the Goldstone as support took off at the start of the club's golden era. Fred Binney scored 27 goals in all competitions, but no one else managed double figures. Grummitt, Wilson and O'Sullivan were ever-present, but no other player managed 40 League appearances.

> Terry Venables, the coach of arch-rivals Crystal Palace, played for an Albion XI against Tottenham Hotspur in Joe Kinnear's testimonial on 23 March 1976. The Albion side also included Dave Mackay, Jimmy Greaves and Rodney Marsh.

For the third season in a row Albion were in trouble with the F.A. for accumulating 100 disciplinary points.

The League Cup saw the customary early exit, this time over two legs to Fourth Division Brentford, but the F.A. Cup provided wins at Watford and Gillingham before Albion disappointingly went out at Third Division strugglers Southend United. The Watford tie was notable for the first of a long series of charter-trains to away venues. The club had run trains before – to Aldershot in January 1967, for example – but the success of this trip led to the chartering of trains to the other cup-ties and to seven League matches. The alcohol-free trains, which became known as the 'Seagull Specials', were a regular and popular feature of the following four seasons and often conveyed the team as well as around 500 supporters.

Despite the disappointment, the foundations of a fine team had been laid. The omens were good for the next campaign, none more so than the sparkling talent of Peter Ward who had scored six goals in his eight games at the end of the season. 'He's the hottest property in English football', proclaimed Taylor, who would not contemplate his new star moving from the club. Instead, it was the manager who sensationally left the Goldstone, resigning on 15 July for 'failing to win promotion in two years'. Two days later he ended speculation by rejoining his former partner Brian Clough at Nottingham Forest, leaving Albion to find their sixth manager in just eight years.

At the start of the season it appeared that the club had a new nickname. In 1974–75 each match-day programme had sported a photograph of a dolphin, and the first of the rather small-sized programmes this term had the new club badge on the front cover, a silhouette of the friendly aquatic mammal with the legend 'The Dolphins'. It was not the first attempt to foist a nickname on supporters. In October 1950 the *Brighton Standard*, the unofficial organ of the Supporters' Club, launched a competition for one. 'Dolphins' was among the suggestions then, along with 'Holidaymakers' and 'Seasiders', but the winner was 'Brovions', derived from <u>Br</u>ighton and <u>Hov</u>e Alb<u>ion</u>. The new name was used by the crowd on 9 December 1950 but, needless to say, didn't catch on. Some old books specify the club's nickname as 'Shrimps', but this has never been the case. 'Seasiders' was occasionally used by the Press and the fans, but this applied generally to all coastal teams. However, this season saw the birth of a genuine new alternative to 'Albion'. Said to have been 'invented' by supporter Lee Philips in a West Street pub on Christmas Eve as a response to the Crystal Palace chant of 'Eagles, Eagles!', the cry 'Seagulls, Seagulls!' rapidly caught on with other supporters, coming into its own at the big clash with Palace on 24 February, and the team has been known as 'The Seagulls' ever since. The Seagull image and rallying cry helped to cement the growing bond between the club and its burgeoning support over the next few years, and in 1977 the club badge was officially changed to a seagull silhouette.

Four generations of Albion badge
The traditional coat-of-arms design, of the twin towns of Brighton (left) and Hove (right), was used after the Second World War until about 1974; there was also a hybrid design employing the shield of Hove and the dolphin crest of Brighton. The calligraphic shield was worn on shirts in the latter 1950s. The dolphin design was used, as noted above, for a brief period in the mid 1970s before giving way in 1977 to the familiar seagull logo. Note that other badges, employing just lettering, have also been used on shirts.

SEASON 1976–77

Mike Bamber acted quickly in inviting former England midfielder Alan Mullery, jobless since retiring from Fulham at the end of 1975–76, to the Goldstone for an interview the day after Taylor resigned. The chairman's mind had drifted back to January 1973 when Albion took on Fulham at Craven Cottage. He recalled Mullery striking his full-back colleague Jimmy Dunne after an argument on the pitch, and hitting him for a second time after Albion scored their only goal. A man so determined to win must surely make a successful manager, Bamber mused, and after meeting the board Mullery was offered the position at a salary of around £7,500 p.a. Thus, on 16 July 1976, less than 24 hours after Taylor's resignation, Brighton and Hove Albion had a new manager.

The cheery self-confidence of 34-year-old Mullery contrasted with the dour persona of his predecessor, who, before leaving, had brought in two experienced defenders on free transfers, Chris Cattlin (Coventry City) and Graham Cross (Leicester City), and also a new new assistant coach, George Aitken from Grimsby Town. Ernie Machin had been released to join Coventry City's coaching staff.

After four League games Albion were unbeaten and top, but lost the next match 2–0 at Grimsby Town with skipper Brian Horton sent off. That was the only defeat in September, and Mullery was doubly rewarded with a four-year contract and a Manager of the Month award. Albion bounced back from Blundell Park to hammer York City 7–2 on *Match of the Day* with five second-half goals. October opened with a disappointing draw against Crystal Palace, and three days later Albion's bogey-team, Walsall, were holding the Seagulls goal-less at half time. The team received one of Mullery's famous 'rocket' team-talks and came out to demolish the Saddlers 7–0, with Peter Ward hitting four goals and Ian Mellor three in just 28 minutes, sweet revenge for a 6–0 thrashing at Fellows Park two years earlier. Ward had now scored nine League goals and was attracting rave reviews. Ian Mellor, in for Fred Binney, was proving the perfect foil for his lightning-quick partner.

The Seagulls maintained their position in the top three, but on New Year's Day found themselves 4–0 down after 67 minutes at Swindon when referee Alan Robinson abandoned the game with the pitch unplayable. Lucky Albion defeated Northampton Town 2–0 two days later and moved back to the top knowing they would have a second chance at Swindon.

Graham Cross, who had been given the spot-kicking job following Horton's vital miss at Portsmouth on 27 December, made his penalty début at home to Chester. His first attempt was saved but the 'keeper was ruled to have moved, and his second effort went in off the post. Two weeks later, at home to Lincoln City, Cross again took two attempts to open the scoring from the spot. The 4–0 victory took Brighton four points clear of Mansfield Town, Wrexham, Rotherham United and Sheffield Wednesday, but Mullery ordered Peter Ward to take any future penalties. His star striker had now hit seventeen League goals and had Hugh Vallance's club record – 30 League goals in 1929–30 – firmly in his sights.

Peter Grummitt, who had impressed as the best Albion no.1 for some years, received the injury that ended his League career against Tranmere Rovers on 5 March, and so Eric Steele, signed for £19,000 from Peterborough United five weeks earlier, made his Brighton début in the cauldron of Selhurst Park, the fifth Albion–Palace clash of the season. A 3–1 defeat dropped the Seagulls to third, and when the new leaders, Mansfield Town, came to the Goldstone on 2 April to dominate the early play, Albion supporters were justifiably anxious. However, Peter Ward equalised with a penalty in the 35th minute, Gerry Fell scored a second before half time and Ward then sealed victory with his second goal. Top spot was regained, and Portsmouth were then sent packing 4–0 before an all-ticket 25,451 crowd.

Easter saw wins at Gillingham and at home to Reading, and Albion were still in top spot when they went to second-placed Wrexham. A goal-less draw at the Racecourse Ground put Brighton in an enviable position: if they beat Sheffield Wednesday on Tuesday, 3 May, in the last home game the season, and if Rotherham United lost at home to Reading, then the Seagulls would be promoted; there were still two games to follow in case of disaster. Seventh-placed Wednesday were no push-overs and a 30,756 crowd saw them take

Albion 1976–77

Back row left to right: Dennis Burnett, Gerry Fell, Graham Cross, Andy Rollings, Peter Grummitt, Ian Mellor, Chris Cattlin, Sammy Morgan, Graham Winstanley.

Front row left to right: Tony Towner, Ken Tiler, Harry Wilson, Peter Ward, Alan Mullery (manager), Brian Horton (captain), Peter O'Sullivan, Fred Binney, Steve Piper, Joe Kinnear.

On 19 May 1977 the board acquired, at auction, two stuffed seagulls in a glass display case which were subsequently exhibited in the boardroom.

SEASON 1976–77

Date	Comp.	Ven.	Opponents	Result	HT	Pos.	Scorers	Atten.	Beal P	Binney F	Burnett D	Cattlin C	Cross G	Elliott M	Fell G	Grummitt P	Horton B	Mellor I	Morgan S	O'Sullivan P	Piper S	Rollings A	Steele E	Tiler K	Towner A	Ward P	Wilson H	Winstanley G
Aug 14	FLC R1 Lg1	(a)	Southend United	D 1–1	0–0	–	Horton (pen)	6,254		9	N	3	6		7	1	4			11	10	5		2		8		
17	FLC R1 Lg2	(h)	Southend United	W 2–1	1–1	–	Horton 2 (1 pen)	11,907		9	N	3	6		7	1	4			11	10	5		2		8		
21	FL D3	(h)	Oxford United	W 3–2	2–0	5	Binney 2, Horton (pen)	13,446		9	12	3	6		7	1	4			11	10	5†		2		8		
24	FL D3	(a)	Chester	W 1–0	0–0	2	Ward	4,573		9	N	3	6		7	1	4			11	10	5		2		8		
28	FL D3	(a)	Preston North End	D 1–1	1–0	3	Ward	6,265	2	9	4	3	6		7	1		N		11	10	5				8		
31	FLC R2	(a)	Ipswich Town	D 0–0	0–0	–		16,055		9†	4	2	6			1		12		11	10	5			7	8	3	
Sep 4	FL D3	(h)	Rotherham United	W 3–1	1–0	1	Towner, Mellor, Binney	16,059		9		2	6			1	4	12		11	10	5†			7	8	3	
7	FLC R2 Rep	(h)	Ipswich Town	W 2–1	0–0	–	Binney, Cross	26,748	2	9	6		5			1	4	12		11	10				7†	8	3	
11	FL D3	(a)	Grimsby Town	L 0–2	0–1	4=		4,481		9	6		5			1	4	12		11	10			2	7†	8	3	
18	FL D3	(h)	York City	W 7–2	2–2	1	Ward 2, Piper, O'Sullivan, Mellor 2, Fell	15,605		9†	6		5		12	1	4	7		11	10			2		8	3	
22	FLC R3	(a)	West Bromwich A.	W 2–0	2–0	–	Ward 2	18,455			6	N	5		7	1	4	9		11	10			2		8	3	
25	FL D3	(a)	Tranmere Rovers	W 3–1	1–1	1	Ward, Horton, Burnett	4,223			12		6		7	1	4	9		11†	10	5		2		8	3	
Oct 2	FL D3	(h)	Crystal Palace	D 1–1	0–0	2	Own goal	27,054			11	N	6		7	1	4	9			10	5		2		8	3	
5	FL D3	(h)	Walsall	W 7–0	0–0	1	Mellor 3, Ward 4	14,128			N		6		7	1	4	9		11	10	5		2		8	3	
9	FL D3	(a)	Bury	L 0–3	0–1	1		8,915			12		6		7	1	4	9		11	10	5		2		8	3†	
16	FL D3	(h)	Peterborough Utd	W 1–0	1–0	1	Cross	18,276			N		6			1	4	9		11	10	5		2	7	8	3	
23	FL D3	(a)	Mansfield Town	D 1–1	1–0	1	Cattlin	7,240			N	3	6			1	4	9		11	10	5		2	7	8		
26	FLC R4	(h)	Derby County	D 1–1	1–1	–	Ward	33,500				3	6		N	1	4	9		11	10	5		2	7	8		
30	FL D3	(a)	Northampton T.	W 2–0	1–0	1	Ward, Towner	7,782				3	6		N	1	4	9		11	10	5		2	7	8		
Nov 3	FL D3	(a)	Reading	W 3–2	1–1	1	Ward, Horton 2	12,097			N	3	6			1	4	9		11	10	5		2	7	8		
6	FL D3	(h)	Swindon Town	W 4–0	3–0	1	Rollings, Mellor 2, Ward	18,761				3	6		12	1	4	9		11	10	5		2	7†	8		
8	FLC R4 Rep	(a)	Derby County	L 1–2	0–2	–	Mellor	25,880			5	3	6		12	1	4	9		11	10			2	7†	8		
13	FL D3	(a)	Port Vale	D 2–2	0–1	1	Towner, Ward	6,449			6	3	5			1	4	9		11	10			2	7	8		N
20	FAC R1	(h)	Crystal Palace	D 2–2	1–0	–	Ward, Mellor	29,510				3	6		12	1	4	9		11	10	5		2	7†	8		
23	FAC R1 Rep	(a)	Crystal Palace	D 1–1*	1–1	–	Mellor	29,174				3	6			1	4	9	12	11	10	5†		2	7	8		
27	FL D3	(h)	Wrexham	L 0–2	0–1	1		22,682				3	6			1	4	9	12	11†	10			2	7	8		5
Dec 4	FL D3	(a)	Shrewsbury Town	L 0–1	0–1	3		9,121				3	6			1	4	9	12	11	10	5		2	7	8†		
6	FAC R1 2Rep(n*)		Crystal Palace	L 0–1	0–1	–		14,118				2	6			1	4	9	12	11	10†	5			7	8	3	
18	FL D3	(h)	Chesterfield	W 2–1	0–1	1	Ward, Morgan	14,043				2	6			1	4	9	12	11	10†	5			7	8	3	
27	FL D3	(a)	Portsmouth	L 0–1	0–1	3		32,368				2	6			1	4	9	12	11†	10	5			7	8	3	
29	FL D3	(h)	Gillingham	W 2–0	1–0	2	Horton, Fell	16,880			N	2	6		7	1	4	11	9		10					8	3	5
Jan 1	FL D3*	(a)	Swindon Town	– –	0–2	2		12,369			7†	2	6		12	1	4	11	9		10					8	3	5
3	FL D3	(h)	Northampton T.	W 2–0	1–0	1	Towner, Ward	22,504				2	6			1	4	9	12	11	10†				7	8	3	5
8	FL D3	(a)	Sheffield Wed.	D 0–0	0–0	1		17,177				3	6			1	4	9	N	11	10			2	7	8		5
15	FL D3	(h)	Chester	W 3–0	1–0	1	Cross (pen), Ward 2	16,495				3	6			1	4	9	N	11	10	5		2	7	8		
22	FL D3	(a)	Oxford United	L 0–1	0–0	1		8,155				3	6			1	4	9	12	11	10	5		2	7†	8		
29	FL D3	(h)	Lincoln City	W 4–0	1–0	1	Cross (pen), Mellor, Towner, O'Sullivan	18,632				3	6			1	4	9	N	11	10	5		2	7	8		
Feb 5	FL D3	(h)	Preston North End	W 2–0	1–0	1	Ward, Towner	21,338				3	6			1	4	9	N	11	10	5		2	7	8		
12	FL D3	(a)	Rotherham United	D 0–0	0–0	1		9,303				3	6			1	4	9	N	11	10	5		2	7	8		
19	FL D3	(h)	Grimsby Town	W 3–0	1–0	1	Mellor, Ward 2 (1 pen)	20,412				3	6			1	4	9	12	11†	10	5		2	7	8		
26	FL D3	(a)	York City	W 1–0	1–0	1	Ward	4,415				3	6			1	4	9	N	11	10	5		2	7	8		
Mar 5	FL D3	(h)	Tranmere Rovers	D 1–1	1–1	1	Horton	20,263				3	6			1	4	9	12	11	10	5		2	7†	8		
12	FL D3	(a)	Crystal Palace	L 1–3	0–1	3	Rollings	28,677				3	6				4	9	12	11	10†	5	1	2	7	8		
15	FL D3	(h)	Shrewsbury Town	W 4–0	0–0	1	Horton, Ward 2 (1 pen), Mellor	17,494				3	6	7	12		4	9		11†	10	5	1	2		8		
19	FL D3	(h)	Bury	D 1–1	1–0	1	Rollings	20,630				3	6	7†	12		4	9		11	10	5	1	2		8		
26	FL D3	(a)	Peterborough Utd	L 0–2	0–0	3		7,851				3	6	7†			4	9	12	11	10	5	1	2		8		
Apr 2	FL D3	(h)	Mansfield Town	W 3–1	2–1	1	Ward 2 (1 pen), Fell	23,594				3	6		7		4	9	N	11	10	5	1	2		8		
6	FL D3	(h)	Portsmouth	W 4–0	2–0	1	Ward 2, Rollings, Piper	25,451				3	6		7		4	9	N	11	10	5	1	2		8		
9	FL D3	(a)	Gillingham	W 1–0	0–0	1	Mellor	11,588				2	6		7		4	9	N	11	10	5	1			8	3	
12	FL D3	(h)	Reading	W 2–0	1–0	1	Ward 2 (1 pen)	26,253				2	6		7		4	9†	12	11	10	5	1			8	3	
16	FL D3	(a)	Walsall	L 0–1	0–0	1		7,591				3	6		7		4	9†	12	11	10	5	1	2		8		
20	FL D3	(a)	Lincoln City	D 2–2	2–1	1	Piper, Horton	7,512				3	6		7		4	9	N	11	10	5	1	2		8		
23	FL D3	(h)	Port Vale	W 1–0	0–0	1	Fell	23,446				3	6		7		4	9	12	11†	10	5	1	2		8		
30	FL D3	(a)	Wrexham	D 0–0	0–0	1		20,005					6		7		4	9	N	11	10	5	1	2		8	3	
May 3	FL D3	(h)	Sheffield Wed.	W 3–2	0–1	1	Ward, Horton (pen), Piper	30,756					6		7†		4	9	12	11	10	5	1	2		8	3	
10	FL D3	(a)	Swindon Town	L 1–2	1–1	2	Ward	8,526				3	6		7		4	9	12		10	5	1	2		8	11†	
14	FL D3	(a)	Chesterfield	D 1–1	0–1	2	Ward	8,212				3	6		7		4	9	12	11†	10	5	1	2		8		
							League appearances		1	6	5	37	46	3	19	31	45	41	1	43	46	39	15	38	23	46	17	4
							Substitute appearances				3				4			2	16									
							League goals	OG – 1		3	1	1	3		4		9	12	1	2	4	4			6	32		

Notes: Nov 23 – after extra time.
Dec 6 – played at Stamford Bridge, Chelsea FC.
Jan 1 – abandoned after 67 minutes because of waterlogged pitch with score 0–4. Appearances not included in end-of-season statistics.

Football League Division 3 1976–77

		P	W	D	L	F	A	W	D	L	F	A	Pts
1.	Mansfield Town	46	17	6	0	52	13	11	2	10	26	29	64
2.	**ALBION**	46	19	3	1	63	14	6	8	9	20	26	61
3.	Crystal Palace	46	17	5	1	46	15	6	8	9	22	25	59
4.	Rotherham United	46	11	9	3	30	15	11	6	6	39	29	59
5.	Wrexham	46	15	6	2	47	22	9	4	10	33	32	58
6.	Preston North End	46	15	4	4	48	21	6	8	9	16	22	54
7.	Bury	46	15	2	6	41	21	8	6	9	23	38	54
8.	Sheffield Wednesday	46	15	4	4	39	18	7	5	11	26	37	53
9.	Lincoln City	46	12	9	2	50	30	7	5	11	27	40	52
10.	Shrewsbury Town	46	13	7	3	40	21	5	4	14	25	38	47
11.	Swindon Town	46	12	6	5	48	33	3	9	11	20	42	45
12.	Gillingham	46	11	8	4	31	21	5	4	14	24	43	44
13.	Chester	46	14	3	6	28	20	4	5	14	20	38	44
14.	Tranmere Rovers	46	10	7	6	31	23	3	10	10	20	30	43
15.	Walsall	46	8	7	8	39	32	5	8	10	18	33	41
16.	Peterborough United	46	11	4	8	33	28	2	11	10	22	37	41
17.	Oxford United	46	9	8	6	34	29	3	7	13	21	36	39
18.	Chesterfield	46	10	6	7	30	20	4	4	15	26	44	38
19.	Port Vale	46	9	7	7	29	28	2	9	12	18	43	38
20.	Portsmouth	46	8	9	6	28	26	3	5	15	25	44	36
21.	Reading	46	10	5	8	29	24	3	4	16	20	49	35
22.	Northampton Town	46	9	4	10	33	29	4	4	15	27	46	34
23.	Grimsby Town	46	10	6	7	29	22	2	3	18	16	47	33
24.	York City	46	7	8	8	25	34	3	4	16	25	55	32

a first-minute lead which was preserved until the 57th minute. Peter Ward, who had missed a penalty just after half time, hit his 30th League goal of the season to put Albion level. The news of defeat for Rotherham United, who had kicked off half an hour earlier, gave the team a fillip, and a second penalty on 71 minutes was put away by Brian Horton. Steve Piper scored a third goal four minutes from time and, although Wednesday pulled one back, Albion held on to clinch promotion to the Second Division for the third time amid the traditional pitch invasion.

Two questions remained: Could Albion clinch the championship and could Ward break the scoring record? The answer to the first question was No as Albion took only one point from their last two games, allowing Mansfield Town to take the title by three points – Crystal Palace sneaked into the third promotion place – but Ward made sure of his place in Brighton's history with two more goals to total 32 in the League and 36 overall, eclipsing both Hugh Vallance and Arthur Attwood (who scored 35 goals in 1932–33 including eleven in the F.A. Cup qualifying rounds). Ward was the leading scorer in the entire Football League.

In a season that had it all, Albion even managed a decent run in the League Cup, the first for seven years. After defeating Southend United over two legs, they travelled to First Division Ipswich Town in the second round. The Suffolk club, under Bobby Robson, were one of the leading sides of the day and their team was packed with current and future internationals. A solid Albion defensive display brought the Town back to the Goldstone and the replay again showed the Seagulls' fighting qualities. Facing the prospect of extra time with ten men – Phil Beal was carried off late in the game – Graham Cross scored the winner two minutes from time to set up a first-ever competitive meeting with the other Albion, West Bromwich, at The Hawthorns. The win over Ipswich was Brighton's first competitive victory over a First Division club for 43 years.

The 1976–77 season was

That's my boy!
Alan Mullery and his star striker Peter Ward celebrate with a beer after holding First Division Derby County to a 1–1 draw in the fourth round of the League Cup. 'Wardy' had just scored his twelfth goal of the season, well on the way to breaking the club's goalscoring record and topping the Football League's scoring charts.

West Bromwich Albion's first back in Division One and they were destined to finish seventh, but the Third Division Albion ran the First Division Albion ragged, and two goals from Ward won the match. The Throstles' frustration boiled over when

Willie Johnston was sent off for the tenth time in his career. Next on the list were Derby County, League champions of 1975 who counted England's Roy McFarland, Colin Todd and Charlie George among their seven internationals. A capacity, all-ticket

Flashpoint!
One of the most memorable matches of a memorable season was the F.A. Cup first-round second replay with Crystal Palace at Stamford Bridge in December. With Palace leading 1–0, Brian Horton tucked away this penalty only for referee Ron Challis, who had already disallowed one Brighton 'goal', to order the kick to be taken again because of encroachment by an Albion player. After the ensuing uproar had died down, Paul Hammond saved Horton's second attempt and the Eagles held out to defeat the Seagulls. The rather volatile Alan Mullery, unhappy with the decision, is pictured here discussing the incident with the official at the final whistle. He also made a rude gesture to jeering Palace fans, an incident for which he was fined £75.

Goldstone crowd of 33,500, paying a record £25,500, saw Ward fire past County's Graham Moseley after just 37 seconds, but the Rams equalised to force a replay. Three charter-trains, a plane and numerous coaches assisted the exodus of Albion supporters to the Baseball Ground, but the fans were disappointed by a 2–1 defeat although the Seagulls certainly fought hard for an equaliser after Ian Mellor's 56th-minute goal.

Albion made a first-round exit from the F.A. Cup at the hands of arch-rivals Crystal Palace after an epic three-match series. Two draws were played before near-30,000 crowds at the Goldstone and Selhurst, and a second replay at neutral Stamford Bridge was twice postponed as the rains came after a record-breaking summer drought. The third match was a controversial affair which ended 1–0 to Palace before a crowd of 14,118.

But it was promotion that mattered above all else. The entertainment on offer at the Goldstone was quite superb and gates averaged over 20,000 for only the second time ever, while the Seagull Special charter-trains and many coaches took Albion supporters to away games in unprecedented numbers. Peter Ward was voted Player of the Season by the Third Division managers. His pace and skill made him the most exciting Brighton player for years, and the modest young man was now among the most-talked-about players in the country. Opposing defenders were bemused by his skills and Albion were awarded eight penalties after fouls on him. However, he was beaten for the supporters' own accolade by an overwhelming vote for skipper Brian Horton.

> On 12 October 1976 the Albion reserves beat Charlton Athletic 3–0 in a Midweek League game watched by a crowd of 17,554. Most had come to the match to purchase tickets for the Derby County League Cup tie a fortnight later.

The board prepared for a promising future by announcing in February that a new parent company, Brighton and Hove Sports and Leisure Limited, had been formed to provide the club with much-needed funds from off-the-field activities in property-dealing. The loss in 1975–76 had fallen to £37,000 and around £1,000 was coming into the club weekly from commercial activities, but the overdraft was now standing at £418,000 and the plans were seen to be of long-term benefit to the club. There was opposition from some of the 300 or so smaller shareholders who thought the club would be divorced from the public, but the new company had acquired all Albion shares by 10 March 1977, thus bringing 76 years of running the club openly to an end.

The critics' justifiable fears were further fuelled when the Supporters' Club, founded in 1912 and re-formed in 1924 and 1948, was told by the parent club to wind up its operations. Around £100,000 had been raised by the Supporters' Club over the previous ten years, but all its activities were taken over by Albion's commercial department in a streamlining that was considered to be in the best interests of the football club.

SEASON 1977–78

This season saw Albion challenge for a place in Division One for the very first time, and supporters came to the Goldstone in record numbers to witness the attempt. Alan Mullery and his board made their ambitions clear in late June when the club's transfer record was smashed in capturing Preston North End's Mark Lawrenson from under the nose of Liverpool; the 20-year-old central defender, already a Republic of Ireland cap, signed for £112,000 in what proved to be an exceptional investment. John Ruggiero (Stoke City), Eric Potts (Sheffield Wednesday) and Gary Williams (Preston North End) also arrived, with the dependable but aging Graham Cross and left-back Harry Wilson moving on to Deepdale. Peter Ward confirmed his future with the club by signing a four-year contract but was the subject of transfer speculation throughout the term. There was an unprecedented demand for season tickets despite a rise in admission prices – the cost of a terrace place rose 35p to £1 – but fans eagerly anticipated clashes with the likes of Sheffield United, Sunderland and Spurs, and looked forward to the opening

> On 13 March 1978, at the Brighton Trades and Labour Club in Lewes Road, the first draw was made in the popular Seagull Lottery. Fifty thousand 20-pence tickets rapidly sold out each week – there was even a waiting-list – and a first-prize of £1,000 was offered. The lottery brought in around £4,700 each week and further cemented the growing bond between club and supporters with the draw made at pubs and other venues throughout the county. It continued for 675 weeks until the launch of Seagull Bingo in February 1991.

fixture, the first clash with South Coast rivals Southampton for fifteen years.

Around 5,000 Brighton fans were rewarded with a creditable 1–1 draw at The Dell, but the visit of Millwall to the Goldstone was marred by their notorious hooligan following, an aspect of promotion that had worried many people. Albion's response was to announce the construction of a pen for 3,800 away supporters in the north-east corner, but it was to be another year before it was ready. The Lions led 2–0 at half time, but the Seagulls won the day with three second-half goals. Albion then ended Mansfield Town's 38-match unbeaten home run to gain some measure of revenge for being pipped for the Third Division championship.

The great start continued through September, and a home win over Luton Town saw Albion move into second place. The Seagulls then flew up to Sunderland to win 2–0 and take over at the top, one point clear of Spurs. Never before had Albion occupied such a lofty position in the Football League. However, the first League defeat of the season was then inflicted by Charlton Athletic. Albion, 2–0 down, fought back to lead 3–2 with the help of a three-times-taken penalty, but the Valiants staged their own come-back to win 4–3 in a superb game. Bolton Wanderers moved into top spot and then gave Albion a footballing lesson in winning 2–1 at the Goldstone in the next outing. Four games without a win dropped the Seagulls to sixth, but then victories over Cardiff City and Orient set up a first-ever Football League clash with second-placed Tottenham Hotspur. The cauldron of White Hart Lane was filled with 48,613 fans, easily the largest crowd to have seen Albion in a League game at the time. Paul Clark, a nineteen-year-old midfield power-house

SEASON 1977–78

Date	Comp.	Ven.	Opponents	Result	HT	Pos.	Scorers	Atten.	Cattlin C	Clark P	Fell G	Horton B	Lawrenson M	Maybank E	Mellor I	Moseley G	O'Sullivan P	Piper S	Poskett M	Potts E	Rollings A	Ruggiero J	Sayer P	Steele E	Tiler K	Towner A	Ward P	Williams G	Winstanley G
Aug 13	FLC R1 Lg1	(a)	Cambridge United	D	0–0 0–0	–	–	5,486	3			4	6		9		5†	10		7		11		1	2		8	12	
16	FLC R1 Lg2	(h)	Cambridge United	D	0–0 0–0	–	–	18,273	3	12		4	6		9		5	10		7		11†		1	2		8		
20	FL D2	(a)	Southampton	D	1–1 0–1	7=	Ruggiero	24,306	3			4	6		9		11†	10		7	5	12		1	2		8		
23	FLC R1 Rep	(h)	Cambridge United	W	3–1 1–0	–	Horton 2 (1 pen), Ward	19,297	3			4	6		9		11	10		7	5	N		1	2		8		
27	FL D2	(h)	Millwall	W	3–2 0–2	10	Ward, Own goal, Piper	18,924	3			4	6		9		11†	10		7	5	12		1	2		8		
30	FLC R2	(h)	Oldham Athletic	D	0–0 0–0	–	–	20,218	3	12		4	6		9†			10		7	5	11		1	2		8		
Sep 3	FL D2	(a)	Mansfield Town	W	2–1 1–0	6	Ruggiero, Piper	8,622	3	12		4	6					10		7	5	11		1	2	8†			
10	FL D2	(h)	Hull City	W	2–1 0–1	6	Fell, Mellor	20,692	3	8		4	6		9			10		7	5	11†		1	2	12			
13	FLC R2 Rep	(h)	Oldham Athletic	D	2–2* 0–0	–	Potts, Cattlin	7,787	3	8†		4	6		9			10		7	5	11		1	2	12			
17	FL D2	(h)	Burnley	D	0–0 0–0	5	–	9,199	3			4	6		9			10		7	5	11		1	2	N	8		
20	FLC R2 2Rep(n*)		Oldham Athletic	L	1–2* 0–0	–	Ward	1,840	3			4	6†		9		11	10		7	5			1	2	12	8		
24	FL D2	(h)	Sheffield United	W	2–1 1–0	4	Ward 2	21,666	3	N		4	6		9		11	10		7	5			1	2		8		
27	FL D2	(h)	Luton Town	W	3–2 0–0	2	Ward, Fell 2	25,132	3	12		4	6		9		11	10†		7				1	2		8		
Oct 1	FL D2	(a)	Sunderland	W	2–0 0–0	2	Piper, Ward	24,013	6			4			9		11	10		7				1	2		8	3	5
4	FL D2	(a)	Charlton Athletic	L	3–4 1–2	6	Ward 2 (1 pen), Winstanley	18,998	6	12		4			9†		11	10		7				1	2		8	3	5
8	FL D2	(h)	Bolton Wanderers	L	1–2 1–1	3	Mellor	27,430	3	12		4	6		9		11	10		7	5†			1	2		8		
15	FL D2	(a)	Stoke City	L	0–1 0–0	5	–	16,290	2			4	6		9		11	10		7†		12		1			8	3	5
22	FL D2	(a)	Crystal Palace	D	1–1 1–0	5	Mellor	28,208	2	12		4	6		9		11	10		7				1		8†		3	5
29	FL D2	(h)	Cardiff City	W	4–0 2–0	3	O'Sullivan 2, Mellor, Ward	22,704	2	N		4	6		9		11	10		7				1		8		3	5
Nov 5	FL D2	(a)	Notts County	L	0–1 0–0	5	–	9,549	2	12		4	6		9		11	10		7†				1		8		3	5
12	FL D2	(h)	Orient	W	1–0 0–0	3	Horton (pen)	20,389	2			4			9		11	10†		7			12	1		8		3	5
19	FL D2	(a)	Tottenham H'spur	D	0–0 0–0	4	–	48,613	2	10		4	6		9		11			N				1		7	8	3	5
26	FL D2	(h)	Blackburn Rovers	D	2–2 2–1	5	Maybank, Towner	26,467	2	10		4	6	9	N		11							1		7	8	3	5
Dec 3	FL D2	(a)	Blackpool	W	1–0 1–0	4	Maybank	9,704	2	10		4	6	9	N		11				5			1		7	8	3	
10	FL D2	(h)	Oldham Athletic	D	1–1 0–0	3	Horton (pen)	22,339	2	10†		4	6	9			11			12	5			1		7	8	3	
17	FL D2	(h)	Orient	W	1–0 0–0	3	Clark	9,374	2	10		4	6	9†			11			12	5			1		7	8	3	
26	FL D2	(h)	Bristol Rovers	D	1–1 0–1	5	Horton	25,509	2†	10		4	6	9			11				5			1		7	8	3	
28	FL D2	(a)	Fulham	L	1–2 0–2	5	Maybank	21,695	2†	10		4	6	9		12	11				5			1		7	8	3	
31	FL D2	(a)	Luton Town	L	0–1 0–1	5	–	13,109	2	10		4	6	9			11			12	5			1		7	8	3	
Jan 2	FL D2	(h)	Southampton	D	1–1 0–0	5	Lawrenson	32,979	2	10†		4	6	9			11			12	5			1		7	8	3	
7	FAC R3	(h)	Scarborough	W	3–0 2–0	–	Ward, Potts, Horton	23,748		10		4	6	9	12		11			2†				1		7	8	3	5
14	FL D2	(a)	Millwall	W	1–0 0–0	5	Ward	9,534	2	10		4	6	9			11			N	5			1		7	8	3	
21	FL D2	(h)	Mansfield Town	W	5–1 3–0	4	Ward 3 (1 pen), Maybank, Horton	22,647	2	10		4	6	9			11			N	5			1		7	8	3	
31	FAC R4	(h)	Notts County	L	1–2 0–2	–	Towner	23,590	2†	10		4	6		9		11			12	5			1		7	8	3	
Feb 4	FL D2	(a)	Hull City	D	1–1 1–1	4	Poskett	4,543	2	10†		4	6				11		9	N	5			1		7	8	3	
11	FL D2	(h)	Burnley	W	2–1 1–0	4	Poskett, Horton (pen)	22,694	2†	10		4	6				11		9	12	5			1		7	8	3	
25	FL D2	(h)	Sunderland	W	2–1 0–0	4	Potts 2	25,771	2			4	6				11		9	12	5		10	1		7	8	3†	
Mar 4	FL D2	(a)	Bolton Wanderers	D	1–1 0–1	4	Horton (pen)	21,405	2			4	6	9			11			7	5		10	1		12	8†	3	
11	FL D2	(h)	Stoke City	W	2–1 2–0	4	Potts, Sayer	24,797	2			4	6	9			11		12	7	5		10	1		8†		3	
18	FL D2	(a)	Crystal Palace	D	0–0 0–0	4	–	26,305	2			4	6	9			11		8	7	5		10	1		N		3	
24	FL D2	(a)	Cardiff City	L	0–1 0–0	4	–	10,222	2	10		4	6	9			11†		12		5		7	1			8	3	
25	FL D2	(h)	Fulham	W	2–0 1–0	4	O'Sullivan, Clark	24,601	2	10		4	6	9			11†		12					1		7	8	3	5
Apr 1	FL D2	(h)	Notts County	W	2–1 0–1	4	Horton, O'Sullivan	20,315	2†	10		4	6	9			11			12	5			1		7	8	3	
4	FL D2	(a)	Sheffield United	L	0–2 0–0	4	–	13,342		10		4	6				11†				8			1	2	7		3	5
8	FL D2	(h)	Blackburn Rovers	W	1–0 0–0	4	Potts	10,178		10†		4	6						9	11	12				2	7	8	3	5
15	FL D2	(h)	Tottenham H'spur	W	3–1 2–1	4	Clark, Winstanley, Potts	32,647		10		4	6				11		9	12				1	2	7†	8	3	5
18	FL D2	(a)	Bristol Rovers	W	4–0 2–0	4	Poskett 3, Ward	9,789		10		4	6			1	11		9	N					2	7	8	3	5
22	FL D2	(a)	Oldham Athletic	D	1–1 0–1	4	Towner	10,249		10		4	6			1	11†		9	12					2	7	8	3	5
25	FL D2	(a)	Charlton Athletic	W	1–0 0–0	3	Potts	31,203		10†		4	6			1	11		9	12					2	7	8	3	5
29	FL D2	(h)	Blackpool	W	2–1 0–0	5	Ward, Horton (pen)	33,431				4	6			1	11		9	12			10†		2	7	8	3	5
League appearances									31	26	1	42	40	16	16	4	38	15	11	19	24	4	6	38	17	23	39	34	18
Substitute appearances										6					1				2	14		4				3			
League goals							OG – 1			3	3	8	1	4	4		4	3	6	5		2	1		2	1	2	14		2

Notes: Sep 13 – after extra time (90-minute score 1–1).
Sep 20 – played at Filbert Street, Leicester City FC.
 – after extra time (90-minute score 1–1).

Football League Division 2 1977–78

		P	W	D	L	F	A	W	D	L	F	A	Pts
1.	Bolton Wanderers	42	16	4	1	39	14	8	6	7	24	19	58
2.	Southampton	42	15	4	2	44	16	7	9	5	26	23	57
3.	Tottenham Hotspur	42	13	7	1	50	19	7	9	5	33	30	56
4.	**ALBION**	42	15	5	1	43	21	7	7	7	20	17	56
5.	Blackburn Rovers	42	12	4	5	33	16	4	9	8	23	44	45
6.	Sunderland	42	11	6	4	36	17	3	10	8	31	42	44
7.	Stoke City	42	13	5	3	38	16	3	5	13	15	33	42
8.	Oldham Athletic	42	9	10	2	32	20	4	6	11	22	38	42
9.	Crystal Palace	42	9	7	5	31	20	4	8	9	19	27	41
10.	Fulham	42	9	8	4	32	19	5	5	11	17	30	41
11.	Burnley	42	11	6	4	35	20	4	4	13	21	44	40
12.	Sheffield United	42	13	4	4	38	22	3	4	14	24	51	40
13.	Luton Town	42	11	4	6	35	20	3	6	12	19	32	38
14.	Orient	42	8	12	1	30	20	2	7	12	13	29	38
15.	Notts County	42	10	9	2	36	22	1	7	13	18	40	38
16.	Millwall	42	8	8	5	23	20	4	6	11	26	37	38
17.	Charlton Athletic	42	11	6	4	38	27	2	6	13	17	41	38
18.	Bristol Rovers	42	10	7	4	40	26	3	5	13	21	51	38
19.	Cardiff City	42	12	6	3	32	23	1	6	14	19	48	38
20.	Blackpool	42	7	8	6	35	25	5	5	11	24	35	37
21.	Mansfield Town	42	6	6	9	30	34	4	5	12	19	35	31
22.	Hull City	42	6	6	9	23	25	2	6	13	11	27	28

from Southend United, made his début in place of Steve Piper, but it was largely thanks to goalkeeper Eric Steele that Mullery's men held his old team to a goal-less draw, the first home point dropped by Spurs.

Having paid over £100,000 for Lawrenson, who was fully justifying his fee, Mullery then staggered Albion fans further by paying over £200,000 for Fulham centre-forward Teddy Maybank. Ten days later it was revealed that the club's parent company, Brighton and Hove Sports and Leisure Limited, had brought off its first property deal to wipe out the debt on Maybank. Mike Bamber emphasised that Albion had never been so financially and operationally viable, with the parent company generating funds to allow the club to enter the transfer market without jeopardising its financial position. Maybank took over the no.9 shirt from Ian Mellor and made a great start with goals in his first two games.

Albion, in fifth place, met third-placed Southampton on 2 January before a 32,979 all-ticket Goldstone crowd. The game was marred by the dismissal of Andy Rollings for two bad fouls, but ten-man Albion won a point with a Lawrenson reply to Alan Ball's opener to keep the Seagulls four points behind the three promotion places. Peter Ward hit his first League goal since October against Millwall, and followed it with a hat-trick at home to Mansfield Town, the second of his Albion career. An injury to Maybank, who was now coming under heavy criticism, prompted Mullery to sign Hartlepool striker Malcolm Poskett for £60,000, and he repaid his new manager with a début goal to win a point at Hull. The strengthening continued with the purchase of Cardiff City's Welsh international midfielder Peter Sayer for £100,000. He made his début at home to Sunderland but found his new team a goal down and being out-played. Alan Mullery substituted Eric Potts for full-back Gary Williams and was rewarded with two goals in the last three minutes from the man who was thereafter dubbed 'supersub'.

Five clubs – Albion, Blackburn Rovers, Bolton Wanderers, Southampton and Tottenham Hotspur – were now four points clear of the rest. The game at Ewood Park on 8 April was critical as the losers would be out

Albion 1977–78

Back row left to right: Mark Elliott, Gary Phillips, Mark Andrews, Phil Smith, Paul Hubbard, Stephen Ward, Vaughan Woolley.
Third row left to right: Ken Gutteridge (assistant manager), Ken Tiler, Mark Lawrenson, Ian Mellor, Andy Rollings, Eric Steele, Peter Grummitt, Chris Cattlin, Gary Williams, Sammy Morgan, Graham Winstanley, George Aitken (coach).
Second row left to right: Glen Geard, Tony Towner, Eric Potts, Peter Ward, Brian Horton (captain), Steve Piper, John Ruggiero, Peter O'Sullivan, Russell Cox, Glen Wilson (physio).
On ground left to right: Martin Cox, Mike Ring, Ian Liddle.

of the run-in to promotion. Blackburn and Albion threw everything at each other for 90 minutes, but it was Eric Potts who hit the only goal five minutes from time to set up another 'four-pointer' with leaders Tottenham Hotspur at the Goldstone.

The all-ticket visit of Spurs was the most glamourous match of the season, but it brought the worst football-related violence the town had ever seen. Mobs from London invaded Brighton on the Friday night, and the 'aggro' continued at the Goldstone the following day with 51 arrests and 85 casualties, 20 ending up in hospital. Tottenham supporters, supposed to be confined to the East and North-East Terraces, infiltrated the North Stand in large numbers. The resultant fighting spilled onto the pitch and referee Alan Turvey was forced to take the teams off for fourteen minutes. There were five further minutes of interruption throughout the match, but eventually Albion ran out worthy winners. Leading 2–1 at the interval with a solo effort from Paul Clark and a Graham Winstanley volley, Albion wrapped the match up with a 72nd-minute goal from supersub Potts. However, the violence of that notorious day prompted the F.A. to order the erection of a perimeter fence around the Goldstone pitch the following season.

Albion were now four points behind Bolton, Tottenham and Southampton, but the latter two had played a game more and Spurs had won only once since 22 March. Former Derby County goalkeeper Graham Moseley made his début at Bristol Rovers where Malcolm Poskett secured victory with a hat-trick to close the gap to just two points. A point was dropped at Oldham, but the Seagulls still gained on the leaders as Bolton went down at Cardiff City and Spurs amazingly lost at home to Sunderland. The excitement throughout Sussex had now reached fever pitch, and 31,203 fans saw Albion move above Spurs into third place with a 1–0 victory over Charlton Athletic. However, Southampton's draw at Orient the same evening virtually ensured their promotion, and the following night Bolton Wanderers also clinched their place in Division One while Tottenham moved one point ahead of Albion with a 1–0 win over Hull City. The third promotion place therefore depended on the last

Saturday of the season. Assuming an Albion victory over relegation-threatened Blackpool, Tottenham needed a draw from Southampton to edge out the Seagulls on goal-difference.

A capacity Goldstone crowd of 33,431, the largest of the season and the third 30,000-plus attendance in two weeks, saw the Seagulls force a 2–1 victory over Blackpool, but nobody was really surprised to hear that Southampton and Spurs had played out a goal-less draw, a result which ensured promotion for both clubs. Albion therefore lost out by a difference of just nine goals. There were brave words from Mike Bamber and Alan Mullery about the determination to make it next time, but the immense disappointment felt by the whole of Sussex was matched by the equally great pride of all supporters in the achievement of their hitherto largely insignificant club which had at last established itself as a footballing power.

Cup performances were a contrast to League form. Albion played six League Cup matches, but after struggling to beat Cambridge United they went out in the second round to Oldham Athletic. In the F.A. Cup another Division Two side, Notts County, won at the Goldstone after Albion had disposed of Northern Premier League Scarborough.

The outstanding Player of the Season was Peter O'Sullivan whose midfield vision created so many opportunities. Top scorer was Peter Ward who, although unable to maintain the previous season's high standard, hit seventeen goals and came third in a national poll for the country's most popular footballer (behind Steve Coppell and Glenn Hoddle). On 6 September he made his international début when the England under-21 side beat Norway under-21s 6–0 at the Goldstone Ground. Ward delighted the 18,431 crowd with a hat-trick and was named in the full England squad for a World Cup qualifier in Luxemburg on 12 October by acting England manager Ron Greenwood, but he failed to make even the bench on that occasion.

Never before had Brighton finished so high in the Football League – the previous best was a modest twelfth in Division Two – generated so much excitement and interest, nor played to such crowds. Over 635,000 passed through the Goldstone

Next time

The bitter disappointment of missing out on promotion to the First Division on goal-difference is apparent on these faces in the West Stand after the final match of the season. Alan Mullery reassured 33,000 fans that the team would double its efforts in the following season, but the vast crowd could take heart from the fact that their club had, at last, made a real impression in the Football League.

turnstiles, and the average home League crowd of 25,264 set an all-time Albion record. The club responded by unveiling plans for ground improvements to befit their new status. The first of several schemes in the 1970s and '80s that never came to fruition, the plan included a 3,240-seat East Stand and a second tier for an extended, 6,300-seat West Stand at a cost of £600,000. It would have given the Goldstone 10,500 seats and 48 luxury boxes; it currently had just 3,400 seats.

SEASON 1978–79

Albion started the League season at Wrexham with the same squad that had finished fourth, and played out a goal-less draw in a heatwave. Newly promoted Cambridge United were the first visitors to the Goldstone and left with a 2–0 victory, courtesy of two gift goals. The first win of the season was gained four days later at home to Sunderland, and was followed by a sparkling 4–1 win over Millwall at The Den; it was a memorable day for the county as Sussex won the Gillette Cup with a five-wicket victory over Somerset at Lord's.

After a bad defeat at the hands of Leicester City, Alan Mullery signed his first new player since February, Derby County's Republic of Ireland international winger Gerry Ryan for £80,000. The signing prompted Tony Towner to join Millwall in October for £65,000 after nearly eight years at the Goldstone. Ryan impressed straight away and the Seagulls hammered Preston North End 5–1 – with the Lilywhites' Mick Baxter

contributing two own-goals – but after being well beaten at Selhurst by an undefeated Crystal Palace, Albion were left in ninth position, four points adrift of Palace at the top.

A 3–0 win over Fulham and a 3–0 defeat at Burnley were as different as chalk and cheese as the season continued in topsyturvy fashion. The first-ever Football League visit of West Ham United on 28 October was a great attraction, but Albion were beaten by two 'Pop' Robson goals to one by Peter Sayer. The game was marred by the Hammers' hooligans. The away

It was hoped that around £250,000 would be brought in annually by the new Wishbone Lottery. Launched on 26 March 1979 under the management of former star player Johnny McNichol, the instant scratch-off tickets cost 25p and offered a first prize of £1,000.

SEASON 1978–79

Date	Comp.	Ven.	Opponents	Result	HT	Pos.	Scorers	Atten.	Cattlin C	Chivers M	Clark P	Geard G	Horton B	Lawrenson M	Maybank E	Moseley G	O'Sullivan P	Poskett M	Rollings A	Ruggiero J	Ryan G	Sayer P	Steele E	Tiler K	Towner A	Ward P	Williams G	Winstanley G
Aug 19	FL D2	(a)	Wrexham	D 0–0	0–0	14=		14,008		10	4		6	9	1		11					7†		2	12	8	3	5
22	FL D2	(h)	Cambridge United	L 0–2	0–0	17		21,548		10	4		6	9			11					7	1	2	12	8	3	5†
26	FL D2	(h)	Sunderland	W 2–0	1–0	12	Ward 2	19,885		10	4		6	9			11	N	5			1		2	7	8	3	
29	FLC R2	(h)	Millwall	W 1–0	1–0	–	O'Sullivan	16,748		10	4		6	9			11	12	5			1		2	7†	8	3	
Sep 2	FL D2	(a)	Millwall	W 4–1	1–1	5	Maybank 2, Horton, Poskett	9,238		10†	4		6	9			11	8	5		12	1		2	7		3	
9	FL D2	(h)	Oldham Athletic	W 1–0	1–0	3	Own goal	19,735		10	4		6	9			11	12	5			1		2	7	8†	3	
23	FL D2	(a)	Leicester City	L 1–4	0–2	10	Williams	14,307		10†	4		6	9			11				12	1		2	7	8	3	
27	FL D2	(a)	Stoke City	D 2–2	0–1	4	Ward, Maybank	22,203		10†	4		6	9			11		5		7	12	1	2		8	3	
30	FL D2	(h)	Preston North End	W 5–1	4–0	3	Own goals 2, Ryan, Ward, Clark	19,217		10	4		6	9				5	N	7	1	1	2		8	3	
Oct 3	FLC R3	(a)	Burnley	W 3–1	1–0	2	Maybank, Ward 2	9,056		10	4		6	9			11		5			7	1		N	8	3	
7	FL D2	(a)	Crystal Palace	L 1–3	0–0	9	Horton	33,685		10	4		6	9			11		5		7	12	1	2†		8	3	
14	FL D2	(h)	Fulham	W 3–0	1–0	4	Ryan 2, Horton	24,606		10	4		6	9	1		11		5		7	N		2		8	3	
21	FL D2	(a)	Burnley	L 0–3	0–0	10		10,271		10	4†		6	9	1		11		5		7	12		2		8	3	
28	FL D2	(h)	West Ham United	L 1–2	1–2	12	Sayer	32,634		10	4		6	9	1		11		5†		7	12		2		8	3	
Nov 4	FL D2	(a)	Sheffield United	W 1–0	1–0	8	Poskett	16,683		12	4		6	9	1		11	8			7†	10		2			3	5
7	FLC R4	(h)	Peterborough Utd	W 1–0	1–0	–	Lawrenson	21,421		10	4		6	9†	1		11	8			7			2	12		3	5
11	FL D2	(h)	Wrexham	W 2–1	1–0	6	Ryan, Horton	19,659		N	4		6	9	1		11	8	5		7	6		2			3	
18	FL D2	(a)	Sunderland	L 1–2	1–1	11	Poskett	22,738		11	4		6	9	1			8	5		7	10†		2		12	3	
21	FL D2	(h)	Millwall	W 3–0	2–0	6	Ryan, Poskett 2	19,408	11		4		6	9	1			8	5		7	10		2		N	3	
25	FL D2	(a)	Notts County	L 0–1	0–0	12		8,851	11	10	4		6	9	1			8	5		7†			2		12	3	
Dec 2	FL D2	(h)	Orient	W 2–0	1–0	7	Horton (pen), Sayer	16,691	2		4		6	9†	1		11	7	5		12	10				8	3	
9	FL D2	(h)	Blackburn Rovers	D 1–1	1–1	7	Ryan	8,046	2		4		6	12	1		11	9†	5		7	10				8	3	
13	FLC R5	(a)	Notting'm Forest	L 1–3	0–1	–	Ward	30,672	2	12	4		6	9†	1		11	7	5			10				8	3	
16	FL D2	(h)	Luton Town	W 3–1	2–1	4	Horton (pen), Rollings, Sayer	16,252	2	12	4		6		1		11	9†	5		7	10				8	3	
23	FL D2	(a)	Charlton Athletic	W 3–0	0–4	5	Poskett 3	10,135	2	N	4		6	9	1		11	8	5		7	10					3	
26	FL D2	(h)	Cardiff City	W 5–0	3–0	3	Williams, Maybank 3, Horton (pen)	20,172	2	12	4		6†	9	1		11	8	5		7	10					3	
30	FL D2	(h)	Newcastle United	W 2–0	1–0	3	Poskett, O'Sullivan	25,812	2	N	4		6	9	1		11	8	5		7	10					3	
Jan 9	FAC R3	(h)	Wolverhampton W.	L 2–3	1–1	–	Lawrenson, Ryan	25,217	2	12	4		6	9†	1		11	8	5		7	10					3	
20	FL D2	(h)	Stoke City	D 1–1	1–1	2	Poskett	23,076	2		4		6	9	1		11	8	5		7†	10			12		3	
Feb 3	FL D2	(h)	Leicester City	W 3–1	2–1	1	Maybank, Sayer, Ward	19,973	2		4		6	9	1		11	8	5		7†	10			12		3	
10	FL D2	(a)	Preston North End	L 0–1	0–0	2		11,649	2	12	4		6	9			11	8	5		7†	10	1				3	
17	FL D2	(h)	Crystal Palace	D 0–0	0–0	1		23,795	2		4		6	9			11	8†	5		7	10	1		12		3	
24	FL D2	(a)	Fulham	W 1–0	1–0	1	Clark	18,640	2	12	4		6	9			11		5		7	10†	1			8	3	
Mar 3	FL D2	(h)	Burnley	W 2–1	0–0	2	Horton (pen), Lawrenson	19,402	2	10	4		6	9			11	N	5		7		1			8	3	
6	FL D2	(a)	Oldham Athletic	W 3–1	1–0	1	Ward, Rollings, Ryan	4,637	2	10	4		6	9			11	N	5		7		1			8	3	
10	FL D2	(a)	West Ham United	D 0–0	0–0	1		35,802	2	10	4		6	9			11	12	5		7		1			8†	3	
17	FL D2	(h)	Sheffield United	W 2–0	1–0	1	Lawrenson, Ryan	20,091	2	10	4		6	9			11†	12	5		7		1			8	3	
20	FL D2	(a)	Bristol Rovers	W 2–1	1–0	1	Ward 2	8,290	2	10	4		6				11	9	5		7	N	1			8	3	
24	FL D2	(a)	Cambridge United	D 0–0	0–0	1		8,453	2	10	4		6	12			11	9	5		7		1			8†	3	
31	FL D2	(h)	Notts County	D 0–0	0–0	1		21,398	2	9	10		6				11	12	5		7	4	1			8†	3	
Apr 7	FL D2	(a)	Orient	D 3–3	2–2	1	Sayer, Chivers, Clark	11,567	2	9	10		6				11	8	5		7	4	1			N	3	
13	FL D2	(a)	Charlton Athletic	W 2–0	1–0	1	Clark, Own goal	30,859	2	9	10		12	6			11	8	5		7†	4	1				3	
14	FL D2	(a)	Cardiff City	L 1–3	1–2	1	Ward	12,613	2	10†	4		6	9			11	12			7		1			8	3	
16	FL D2	(h)	Bristol Rovers	W 3–0	3–0	1	Horton 2 (1 pen), Maybank	23,204	2	5	4		6†	9			11	12			7	10	1			8	3	
21	FL D2	(h)	Luton Town	D 1–1	0–1	2	Maybank	13,132	2		6			9			11	12			7	10	1			8	3†	5
28	FL D2	(h)	Blackburn Rovers	W 2–1	1–0	1	Maybank, Rollings	26,141	2		6	N	4	9				11	5		7	10	1			8	3	
May 5	FL D2	(a)	Newcastle United	W 3–1	3–0	1	Horton, Ward, Ryan	28,425	2		6		4	9			11	12	5		7†	10	1			8	3	
League appearances									27	3	28	0	39	39	35	17	37	21	37	0	34	26	25	17	4	27	42	4
Substitute appearances									5	1	2				2			8				1	6			2		5
League goals							OG – 4			1	4		11	2	10		1	10	3		9	5				10	2	

supporters' pen in the north-east corner had been in use since August, but the perimeter fencing was not yet complete. West Ham followers invaded areas intended for Albion fans and there were nearly 80 arrests. A 72-year-old Albion supporter died after being crushed on the East Terrace.

Two home defeats in the first three months — Albion had suffered only four in the previous three seasons! A defeat at Notts County on 25 November dropped the Seagulls to twelfth place and attendances fell below 17,000 in December. The form of the team was a factor, but many fans pointed to the 30-per-cent rise in charges that had taken terrace admission to £1.30, the second highest in the country.

While League form was mixed, Albion progressed to the last eight of the League Cup for the first – and only – time. Millwall fell victim to a Peter O'Sullivan 25-yarder in round two; with the north-eastern pen in use for the first time, peace was maintained on the terraces despite the very real threat of violence. A 3–1 win over Burnley at Turf Moor set up a home tie with Third Division Peterborough United. Albion cruised to victory, but the margin was narrow, a single Mark Lawrenson goal. Albion's first-ever game in the fifth round was a City Ground clash with Nottingham Forest. In 1977–78, Forest had won both the League Championship and the League Cup, and

Football League Division 2 1978–79

		P	W	D	L	F	A	W	D	L	F	A	Pts
1.	Crystal Palace	42	12	7	2	30	11	7	12	2	21	13	57
2.	ALBION	42	16	3	2	44	11	7	7	7	28	28	56
3.	Stoke City	42	11	7	3	35	15	9	9	3	23	16	56
4.	Sunderland	42	13	3	5	39	19	9	8	4	31	25	55
5.	West Ham United	42	12	7	2	46	15	6	7	8	24	24	50
6.	Notts County	42	8	10	3	23	15	6	6	9	25	45	44
7.	Preston North End	42	7	11	3	36	23	5	7	9	23	34	42
8.	Newcastle United	42	13	3	5	35	24	4	5	12	16	31	42
9.	Cardiff City	42	12	5	4	34	23	4	5	12	22	47	42
10.	Fulham	42	10	7	4	35	19	3	8	10	15	28	41
11.	Orient	42	11	5	5	32	18	4	5	12	19	33	40
12.	Cambridge United	42	7	10	4	22	15	5	6	10	22	37	40
13.	Burnley	42	11	6	4	31	22	3	6	12	20	40	40
14.	Oldham Athletic	42	11	7	3	40	17	3	6	12	16	38	39
15.	Wrexham	42	10	6	5	31	16	2	8	11	14	26	38
16.	Bristol Rovers	42	10	6	5	34	23	4	4	13	14	37	38
17.	Leicester City	42	7	8	6	28	23	3	9	9	15	29	37
18.	Luton Town	42	11	5	5	46	24	2	5	14	14	33	36
19.	Charlton Athletic	42	6	8	7	28	28	5	5	11	32	41	35
20.	Sheffield United	42	9	6	6	34	24	2	6	13	18	45	34
21.	Millwall	42	7	4	10	22	29	4	6	11	20	32	32
22.	Blackburn Rovers	42	5	8	8	24	29	5	2	14	17	43	30

The Seagull Line, Brighton 8049, was set up by the Post Office on 13 April 1979 to provide information on the club 24 hours a day by telephone. In 1987–88 it was replaced by a more general, premium-rate service, the Sussex Sportsline, but returned as a premium-rate service itself on 1 July 1989 on 0898–800609 (later 0891–800609).

were on their way to European Cup success this season under former Albion managers Brian Clough and Peter Taylor. Supported by around 5,000 fans, Albion gave a great performance with Peter Ward equalising John McGovern's opener four minutes after half time. Forest came back with two more goals to seal the match by the 66th minute and went on to retain their trophy, but the manner of the Brighton display gave supporters renewed heart.

The Forest cup-tie proved something of a watershed. Suddenly Albion found their old form and won the four other matches in December with some great displays, including hat-tricks for Malcolm Poskett and Teddy Maybank. An icy blast from the Arctic played havoc with the New Year schedule and several games were postponed. There was a tremendous F.A. Cup third-round tie with Wolves which the First Division side shaded 3–2, but the match was particularly memorable for Mark Lawrenson's ninth-minute solo goal when he ran with the ball from deep inside his own half. Lawrenson was now a regular in the Republic of Ireland side and was currently outstanding in the Albion defence; his vision and ball-winning skills were matched by his ability to bring the ball forward from the back to great effect.

A 3–1 win over Leicester City on 3 February took Albion to the top of Division Two for only the second time ever. The Seagulls were able to maintain their position near the top and victory at Fulham on 24 February opened a gap between the top five – Albion, Stoke City, Crystal Palace, West Ham United and Sunderland – and the sixth-placed Cottagers. February also saw the arrival of Juan Carlos Oblitas and Percy Rojas, two Peruvian World Cup stars on trial. Oblitas was apparently about to sign in a tie-up with American side Tampa Bay Rowdies, but the deal fell through and the pair, who would have cost £400,000, returned home.

March saw Albion unbeaten, six points clear of fourth-placed Sunderland, but they had played at least two games more than their rivals. With Teddy Maybank suspended, Mullery brought in his former Spurs colleague Martin Chivers as a stop-gap centre-forward. He played only three games this season, but made his mark with a classic header in a 3–3 draw at Orient on 7 April. The second-largest home crowd of the season, 30,859, watched a routine 2–0 win over Charlton Athletic on Good Friday, but for the second Easter running Albion crashed at Ninian Park, Cardiff. Although still top, it was a serious blow to promotion hopes.

Easter Monday saw Albion's fortunes restored with a 3–0 win over Bristol Rovers while Stoke City and West Ham United could only draw, and Sunderland lost at home to bottom side Blackburn Rovers. However, the Seagulls paid a great price for victory with Lawrenson breaking his arm. Paul Clark, already in for the injured Andy Rollings, and Graham Winstanley were therefore at the heart of the

defence at Luton. With a Gary Williams own-goal giving the Hatters a first-half lead, Alan Mullery gambled by playing just three at the back for the last 25 minutes. The tactic worked, and a Teddy Maybank goal seven minutes from time gave Albion a precious point. Nevertheless, a point dropped knocked Brighton off top spot and gave the advantage to the others. This was the situation:

		P	W	D	L	F	A	Pts
1.	Stoke City	40	19	15	6	57	31	53
2.	ALBION	40	21	10	9	67	37	52
3.	Sunderland	39	20	11	8	61	39	51
4.	Crystal Palace	39	16	19	4	46	24	51
5.	West Ham United	37	17	12	8	65	34	46

The last home game saw Albion beat Blackburn Rovers 2–1. Teddy Maybank opened the scoring through a cloud, the result of a smoke-bomb thrown from the South Stand, but the football

Albion 1978–79

Back row left to right: Glen Wilson (physio), Chris Cattlin, Teddy Maybank, Ken Tiler, Malcolm Poskett, Eric Potts, George Aitken (coach).
Middle row left to right: Ken Craggs (assistant manager), Tony Towner, Graham Winstanley, Eric Steele, Andy Rollings, Graham Moseley, Mark Lawrenson, Gary Williams, Alan Mullery (manager).
Seated left to right: Paul Clark, Peter Ward, Brian Horton (captain), Mike Bamber (chairman), Harry Bloom (vice-chairman), Peter O'Sullivan, Peter Sayer, John Ruggiero.

authorities took no action over an isolated incident. As the team ran a lap of honour in front of 26,141 hopeful fans, the dramatic news filtered through that West Ham had only managed a draw and then, amazingly, that Sunderland had lost at home to Cardiff City. Those sensational results meant that an Albion win in their last match at Newcastle would give them 56 points, the same as last year, but this time would guarantee a place in Division One for the first time.

The team travelled to Tyneside on the Wednesday and were joined by nearly 10,000 fans travelling by car, coach, train and plane on the Saturday to transform the Leazes End into a sea of blue and white. With just two defeats in the last 24 League games, the Albion supporters were confident and were rewarded with a devastating first-half display: goals from Brian Horton, Peter Ward and Gerry Ryan put Albion 3–0 up at the

> Ron Pavey's commercial department was very active and produced autographed plaques at £3.50 each to commemorate promotion. Albion also launched a range of men's toiletries in October, 'created exclusively for the club' by Panache Cosmetics. An advertisement showed the manager and four players sampling Seagulls Sport Splash, Seagulls Talc and Seagulls Deodorant.

break. The Magpies hit the woodwork twice and reduced the deficit ten minutes from the end, but the triumphant Seagulls rode out the remaining minutes to win the coveted place in Division One.

The clincher
Gerry Ryan scores just before half time in the final game of the season at Newcastle. Needing a victory to ensure promotion, Albion went in at the break 3–0 up and virtually certain of clinching a coveted place in the First Division. Final score was 3–1.

It was an unforgettable climax to the season. Champagne flowed on the Seagull Special charter-train which arrived in Brighton at 2 a.m. to be greeted – in a scene reminiscent of past triumphs – by 500 cheering supporters. The celebrations continued the following day when thousands of fans acclaimed their heroes at the Goldstone, and many thousands more – some estimates said 100,000 – watched an open-top bus tour ending at Hove Town Hall where a civic reception was held.

Left-back Gary Williams was the only ever-present, and Peter Ward was top scorer with thirteen in League and Cup; Brian Horton, Malcolm Poskett, Teddy Maybank and Gerry Ryan also reached double figures and Albion were the division's highest scorers. Mark Lawrenson was the outstanding Player

of the Season. Crowds were down on last season's record figures, but the average was still a very healthy 22,074.

On 11 May arch-rivals Crystal Palace beat Burnley 2–0 before a record 51,801 crowd at Selhurst Park to pip the Seagulls for the championship. Albion had flown off to California for a holiday the same day, but the trip was not a great success. Fixtures were difficult to arrange during a fuel crisis and manager Alan Mullery found himself in hot water for arguing with the referee in San Diego.

With Albion supporters relishing trips to Old Trafford, Anfield, Goodison Park, Highbury, etc., attention turned to the state of the Goldstone Ground. Because of objections by Goldstone Lane residents, the plans for a new East Stand had been reduced to a simple roof structure over the terrace, but the entire £1·5 million scheme, which included an extended West Stand and a new South Stand, was shelved in February because of possible interference with match arrangements. By April the club's policy had changed to seeking a completely new ground. It was never to happen: the Goldstone remained undeveloped and fourteen years later the club was still desperately seeking a new venue away from the home it had occupied since 1902.

Unable to arrange fixtures in the U.S.A. because of the fuel crisis, Albion played a group of local ex-patriots in San Diego on 28 May 1979 in a six-a-side game; the club won 4–2. During the tour Brighton played their first full match on an artificial surface when they beat Portland Timbers 2–1 at the Civic Stadium, Portland, Oregon, on 16 May.

Civic pride
The mayors of Brighton (Alfred Feld, left) and Hove (Les Hamilton, right), along with thousands of fans, greet the team outside Hove Town Hall. After a tour of the twin towns, the club were fêted by the two councils and enjoyed a civic reception at the Town Hall in the greatest display of local pride for many years.

SEASON 1979–80

Since 1920, when the club joined the Football League, every Brighton supporter had dreamed of the day their favourites would play in the First Division. That 59-year-old dream was about to come true, the culmination of a rapid rise from Division Three, but, after four years of unprecedented success, Albion now faced their biggest challenge ever. Strengthening the defence was the priority, and in came Steve Foster (Portsmouth) for £150,000 and the versatile John Gregory (Aston Villa) for a record £250,000.

Terrace admission rose again to £1.50 and over 6,000 supporters purchased the newly available terrace season tickets. Large-scale ground improvements had been ruled out, but 980 extra seats were provided in a temporary stand which was erected to the north of the West Stand. Soon dubbed the 'Lego Stand', the West Stand Extension cost £200,000 and brought the total number of seats to around 4,500. The opening fixture was a highly attractive encounter with Arsenal, a club with which Albion had forged close links in the past. A pay dispute threatened to ruin the opening, but on the eve of the game most of the rebels signed new contracts leaving just Graham Moseley and Chris Cattlin out in the cold.

And so the great day arrived, Saturday, 18 August 1979. Seagull supporters everywhere relished the prospect, but many were also wary of the very real hooligan threat associated with the big clubs and the attendance turned out to be a disappointing 28,604, some 5,000 short of capacity. There were 33 arrests

Albion's new status rather went to chairman Mike Bamber's head in 1979 when he had a sign installed outside the club's main entrance proclaiming 'This is the Goldstone', mimicking Liverpool's sign at Anfield. It was removed under Brian Bedson in 1984 and donated to the Goldstone Middle School.

overnight and another 19 at the ground, but the presence of over 300 policemen prevented any great disruption. The teams lined up thus:

Brighton and Hove Albion: Eric Steele; John Gregory; Gary Williams; Brian Horton (captain); Andy Rollings; Mark Lawrenson; Gerry Ryan; Peter Ward; Teddy Maybank; Peter Sayer; Peter O'Sullivan; sub. Malcolm Poskett.

Arsenal: Pat Jennings; Pat Rice (captain); Sammy Nelson; Brian Talbot; David O'Leary; Willie Young; Liam Brady; Alan Sunderland; Frank Stapleton; David Price; Graham Rix; sub. John Hollins.

Albion kicked off towards the south goal and nearly made a dream start, Arsenal 'keeper Pat Jennings just preventing a first-minute goal from Gerry Ryan, but the Gunners then proceeded to give a lesson in finishing, notching three goals in a twelve-minute spell before half time. With Liam Brady adding a fourth in the second half to inflict Albion's biggest defeat for over three years, it was clear that the challenge of the First Division would be a far, far tougher proposition than that of the Second Division two years earlier.

Teddy Maybank hit the club's first goal in the top flight at Aston Villa. The first three games were lost, but then the first win was recorded, a 3–1 home victory over Bolton Wanderers. Albion missed a hatful of chances in defeat at Tottenham, but suffered greater disaster when star defender Mark Lawrenson was stretchered off with a leg injury. For the visit of Ipswich Town, therefore, Alan Mullery gave a début to seventeen-year-old Gary Stevens, once an apprentice with the Suffolk club, and the youngster gave a sound performance as Albion won 2–0. The season's first away point, at West Bromwich, augured well, and at the beginning of October the Seagulls found themselves in sixteenth place.

Next stop was Old Trafford where a crowd of 52,641, the largest ever to watch Albion in a regular-season League match, saw Manchester United triumph 2–0. As Albion's morale withered, Eric Steele and Gary Williams added insult to injury by indulging in fisticuffs in front of the Stretford End. Mullery took no direct action (perhaps recalling the similar incident that caused Mike Bamber to offer him the manager's job) but placed Steele on the transfer list and promoted the now-settled Graham Moseley to first-choice 'keeper. The popular Steele made an unexpected final appearance at home to Leeds United when Moseley fell ill, but was soon on his way to Watford for £100,000.

Albion 1979–80

Back row left to right: Glen Wilson (equipment manager), Teddy Maybank, Malcolm Poskett, Mark Lawrenson, Martin Chivers, Giles Stille, Mike Yaxley (physio).
Middle row left to right: Ken Craggs (assistant manager), Steve Foster, Andy Rollings, Graham Moseley, Eric Steele, Gary Williams, John Gregory, Gerry Ryan, George Aitken (coach).
Seated left to right: Paul Clark, Peter Sayer, Brian Horton (captain), Alan Mullery (manager), Peter O'Sullivan, Peter Ward, Mick Kerslake.

SEASON 1979–80

Date	Comp.	Ven.	Opponents	Result	HT	Pos.	Scorers	Atten.	Cattlin C	Chivers M	Clark P	Clarke R	Foster S	Geard G	Gregory J	Horton B	Lawrenson M	McNab N	Maybank E	Moseley G	O'Sullivan P	Poskett M	Rollings A	Ryan G	Sayer P	Steele E	Stevens G	Stille G	Suddaby P	Ward P	Williams G
Aug 18	FL D1	(h)	Arsenal	L	0–4	0–3	20		28,604							2	4	6		9†		11	12	5	7	10	1				8	3
22	FL D1	(a)	Aston Villa	L	1–2	1–1	21	Maybank	28,803							2	4	6		9		11	12	5	7†	10	1				8	3
25	FL D1	(a)	Manchester City	L	2–3	1–2	21	Maybank, Ward	34,557		12					2	4	6		9		11		5†	7	10	1				8	3
28	FLC R2 Lg1	(h)	Cambridge United	W	2–0	1–0	–	Horton, Ward	15,370			7		5		2	4	6		9	1	11		12	10†						8	3
Sep 1	FL D1	(h)	Bolton Wanderers	W	3–1	2–0	19	Ward, Clark, Horton	20,171			7†		5		2	4	6		9	1	11		12	10						8	3
4	FLC R2 Lg2	(a)	Cambridge United	W	2–1	1–0	–	Maybank, Ward	4,952			7		5		2	4†	6		9	1	11		12	10						8	3
8	FL D1	(a)	Tottenham H'spur	L	1–2	0–1	21	Horton	34,107			7		5		2	4	6†		9		11		12	10		1				8	3
15	FL D1	(h)	Ipswich Town	W	2–0	1–0	17	Clark, Ryan	23,608			7†		5		2	4			9		11		12	10		1	6			8	3
22	FL D1	(h)	Southampton	D	0–0	0–0	17		26,918			7		5		2	4			9		11		12	10†		1	6			8	3
25	FLC R3	(a)	Northampton T.	W	1–0	1–0	–	Poskett	7,105			7		5		2	4					11†	9	12	10		1	6			8	3
29	FL D1	(a)	West Bromwich A.	D	2–2	0–2	16	Poskett, O'Sullivan	20,024			7†		5		2	4					11	9	12	10		1	6			8	3
Oct 6	FL D1	(a)	Manchester United	L	0–2	0–1	19		52,641			7		5		2	4			9		11		12	10		1	6			8†	3
13	FL D1	(h)	Leeds United	D	0–0	0–0	21		27,002			7		5		2				9		11		2	12	10†	1	6			8	3
20	FL D1	(a)	Coventry City	L	1–2	1–1	21	Rollings	17,328	12				5			4			9	1	11		2	7	10		6			8†	3
27	FL D1	(h)	Norwich City	L	2–4	1–1	22	Foster, Ryan	23,180		9†	12		5			4				1	11		2	7	10		6			8	3
30	FLC R4	(h)	Arsenal	D	0–0	0–0	–		25,231	8	2			5			4			9	1	11			7	10		6			N	3
Nov 3	FL D1	(a)	Arsenal	L	0–3	0–0	22		34,400					8	5				9†		1	11		2	7	10		6			12	3
10	FL D1	(h)	Liverpool	L	1–4	0–1	22	Clarke	29,682		12		9	5		2	4				1	11			7	10†		6			8	3
13	FLC R4 Rep	(a)	Arsenal	L	0–4	0–2	–		30,351	2		10	9	5	7†		4				1	11	8		12			6				3
17	FL D1	(a)	Notting'm Forest	W	1–0	1–0	21	Ryan	25,837		N		9	5			4	10			1	11			7			6		2	8	3
24	FL D1	(a)	Middlesbrough	D	1–1	0–0	21	Williams	16,010		12		9	5			4	10			1	11			7			6†		2	8	3
Dec 1	FL D1	(h)	Derby County	W	2–0	1–0	21	Ward, Clarke	22,980				9	5			4	10			1	11			7			2	N	6	8	3
8	FL D1	(a)	Everton	L	0–2	0–2	21		23,534				9	5		2	4	10			1	11			7			N		6	8	3
15	FL D1	(h)	Stoke City	D	0–0	0–0	21		18,392				9	5		2	4	10			1	11†			7			12		6	8	3
21	FL D1	(a)	Wolverhampton W.	W	3–1	2–1	21	Ward 3	15,807				9			2	4	10			1	11			7			5	N	6	8	3
26	FL D1	(h)	Crystal Palace	W	3–0	2–0	19	Horton (pen), Ward, Ryan	28,358				9	5		2	4	10			1	11			7			6	N		8	3
29	FL D1	(h)	Manchester City	W	4–1	3–1	18	Clarke 2, Ward, Ryan	28,093				9	5		2	4†	10			1	11			7			6	12		8	3
Jan 1	FL D1	(a)	Bristol City	D	2–2	0–1	18	Clarke, Own goal	19,259				9	5		2	4	10			1	11			7			6	N		8	3
5	FAC R3	(a)	Mansfield Town	W	2–0	0–0	–	Ryan, Clarke	8,204				9	5		2	4	10			1	11			7			N		6	8	3
12	FL D1	(a)	Bolton Wanderers	W	2–0	1–0	17	Ward 2	13,963				9	5		2	4	10			1	11			7			N		6	8	3
19	FL D1	(h)	Tottenham H'spur	L	0–2	0–2	17		29,417				9	5†			4	10			1	11			7	12		2		6	8	3
26	FAC R4	(a)	Arsenal	L	0–2	0–1	–		43,202				9	5			4	10			1	11†			7	12		2		6	8	3
Feb 2	FL D1	(a)	Ipswich Town	D	1–1	0–0	17	Stevens	22,494				9	5			4	10			1	11			7†			12		6	8	3
9	FL D1	(h)	Southampton	L	1–5	0–2	19	Ward	21,853				9†	5		2	4	10	12		1	11			7			6			8	3
16	FL D1	(h)	West Bromwich A.	D	0–0	0–0	18		22,633				9	5		2	4	10	7		1	11			N			6			8	3
23	FL D1	(a)	Leeds United	D	1–1	0–0	17	Ward	17,216				9	5		2	4	10	7		1	11			12			6†			8	3
Mar 1	FL D1	(h)	Coventry City	D	1–1	1–1	18	Clarke	21,605				9	5		2	4	10†	7		1	11			12			6			8	3
3	FL D1	(h)	Aston Villa	D	1–1	1–1	16	Clarke	23,377				9	5		2	4	10	7		1	11			N			6			8	3
8	FL D1	(a)	Norwich City	D	2–2	2–0	16	Horton, Lawrenson	15,640				9	5		2	4	10	7		1	11†			12			6			8	3
15	FL D1	(h)	Manchester United	D	0–0	0–0	17		29,670				9	5		2	4	10	7		1	11†			12			6			8	3
22	FL D1	(a)	Liverpool	L	0–1	0–0	17		42,747				9	5		2	4†	10	7		1	11			6			12			8	3
29	FL D1	(h)	Notting'm Forest	W	1–0	1–0	17	Williams	25,128				9	5		2	4	10	7		1	11			6†			12			8	3
Apr 5	FL D1	(a)	Crystal Palace	D	1–1	1–0	16	Ward	31,466				9	5		2	4	10	7		1	11			6†					12	8	3
7	FL D1	(h)	Bristol City	L	0–1	0–0	16		23,171				9†	5		2	4	10	7		1	11			6					12	8	3
8	FL D1	(h)	Wolverhampton W.	W	3–0	1–0	16	Ward 2, Own goal	27,026				9	5		2	4	10	7		1						N			11	8	3
12	FL D1	(a)	Derby County	L	0–3	0–0	16		17,257				9	5		2	4	10	7		1	12								11	6	8	3†
19	FL D1	(h)	Middlesbrough	W	2–1	0–0	16	Clarke, Ward	20,427				9	5		2	4	10	7		1	11†			12					2	6	8	3
26	FL D1	(a)	Stoke City	L	0–1	0–1	16		14,442				9	5		2	4	10†	7		1				12					11	6	8	3
May 3	FL D1	(h)	Everton	D	0–0	0–0	16		21,243				9	5		2	4†	10	7		1				11	12					6	8	3
League appearances									0	1	7	30	38	0	33	42	33	15	11	33	38	1	7	25	14	9	21	0	21	41	42
Substitute appearances										1	4							1				1	2	11	3		5	1	2	1	
League goals	OG – 2										2	8	1			4	1		2		1	1	5			1			16	2

The 'Lego Stand'
The West Stand Extension seated 980 spectators and lasted six years from 1979 until 1985.

Football League Division 1 1979–80

		P	W	D	L	F	A	W	D	L	F	A	Pts
1.	Liverpool	42	15	6	0	46	8	10	4	7	35	22	60
2.	Manchester United	42	17	3	1	43	8	7	7	7	22	27	58
3.	Ipswich Town	42	14	4	3	43	13	8	5	8	25	26	53
4.	Arsenal	42	8	10	3	24	12	10	6	5	28	24	52
5.	Nottingham Forest	42	16	4	1	44	11	4	4	13	19	32	48
6.	Wolverhampton W.	42	9	6	6	29	20	10	3	8	29	27	47
7.	Aston Villa	42	11	5	5	29	22	5	9	7	22	28	46
8.	Southampton	42	14	2	5	53	24	4	7	10	12	29	45
9.	Middlesbrough	42	11	7	3	31	14	5	5	11	19	30	44
10.	West Bromwich A.	42	9	8	4	37	23	2	11	8	17	27	41
11.	Leeds United	42	10	7	4	30	17	3	7	11	16	33	40
12.	Norwich City	42	10	8	3	38	30	3	6	12	20	36	40
13.	Crystal Palace	42	9	9	3	26	13	3	7	11	15	37	40
14.	Tottenham Hotspur	42	11	5	5	30	22	4	5	12	22	40	40
15.	Coventry City	42	12	2	7	34	24	4	5	12	22	42	39
16.	**ALBION**	42	8	8	5	25	20	3	7	11	22	37	37
17.	Manchester City	42	8	8	5	28	25	4	5	12	15	41	37
18.	Stoke City	42	9	4	8	27	26	4	6	11	17	32	36
19.	Everton	42	7	7	7	28	25	2	10	9	15	26	35
20.	Bristol City	42	6	6	9	22	30	3	7	11	15	36	31
21.	Derby County	42	9	4	8	36	29	2	4	15	11	38	30
22.	Bolton Wanderers	42	5	11	5	19	21	0	4	17	19	52	25

The visit of the Canaries saw the Seagulls take a 2–1 lead over their avine opponents, but Norwich City scored three times in 28 minutes to take the match and send Albion to the bottom of the table. Ray Clarke, a £175,000 centre-forward from Belgian side Bruges, arrived to strengthen the squad, but heavy defeats at Arsenal and at home to reigning champions

Albion reached the final of the *Daily Express* national five-a-side tournament at the Wembley Arena on 28 November but lost 2–0 to Sunderland.

Liverpool left the Seagulls bottom, hopelessly outclassed, and written off by most pundits.

The League Cup only added to the gloom. After straightforward victories over Cambridge United and Northampton Town, Albion came up against Arsenal in the fourth round. A fighting performance earned a 0–0 draw at the Goldstone, but the replay was lost 4–0 with the worst display for many years. Out of the League Cup, bottom of the table, without a League win for two months and apparently devoid of inspiration, Albion now faced a daunting trip to the City Ground, Nottingham, where Forest, the champions of Europe, were unbeaten since April 1977.

Peter Ward had managed only two First Division goals, and in early November Alan Mullery tried unsuccessfully to swap his out-of-touch striker for Derby County's Gerry Daly. Nottingham Forest then came in with a £600,000 bid, but the confirmation from Forest manager Brian Clough never came and so Ward remained an Albion player as the team headed for the City Ground. Also in the party were Peter Suddaby, an experienced defender signed from Blackpool on a free transfer, and a fit-again Mark Lawrenson who took over from Sayer in midfield. Apparently unwanted, Ward positively sparkled and caused havoc in the Forest defence. On twelve minutes Gerry Ryan gave Brighton the lead by wrong-footing Peter Shilton.

The turning point
The faces of former Albion managers Brian Clough (left) and Peter Taylor say it all: Brighton have just beaten European champions Nottingham Forest on their own ground. The match was undoubtedly the turning point of the season. The boost to morale enabled the club to survive its first campaign in Division One.

The Albion defence then fought a splendid rear-guard action to hold the Nottingham forwards at bay. Peter Suddaby brought steadiness to a back-four in which Steve Foster was outstanding, while Graham Moseley brought off a splendid penalty save just before half time. The Seagulls weathered the second-half storm to hold on for a thrilling victory which nudged them above Bolton Wanderers on goal-difference. Mike Bamber thanked Clough, his former manager, for unwittingly rejuvenating Ward, while the *Evening Argus* summed the day up nicely with its headline: 'Miracles can still happen'.

Eleven months earlier a match at Forest had appeared to be the turning point of the season; this time there was no doubt. The gloom immediately vanished from the Goldstone, a point was gained at Middlesbrough, and fellow strugglers Derby County were sent packing 2–0. Defeat by a brutal Everton side was the only loss in December as Albion enjoyed a marvellous Yuletide: there was a second away win, at a frozen Wolverhampton (Ward 3); a first victory over Crystal Palace in ten attempts; and a 4–1 drubbing of Manchester City, memorable for Gerry Ryan's remarkable 75-yard run with the ball to score. The win over Palace lifted Albion above Bristol City, Derby County and Bolton Wanderers, the three clubs who were eventually relegated. At last the Seagulls were establishing themselves in the top flight and audacious attempts were made to sign Rainer Bonhof, the West German international star, and Kevin Keegan, but both rejected the personal terms.

Albion got the New Year off to a good start, drawing at lowly Bristol City and winning at bottom club Bolton Wanderers, but Spurs emphasised a gulf in class by winning 2–0 at the Goldstone with the Argentine World Cup stars Osvaldo Ardiles and Riccardo Villa particularly outstanding. Mullery bolstered his midfield with the £230,000 purchase of Neil McNab from Bolton Wanderers, but six consecutive draws provoked criticism from some fans. The manager's response was 'Just look at who we've drawn with!' after a goal-less match with Manchester United. That draw left Albion seven points clear of the relegation places and, barring disasters, looking forward to a second season in the First Division.

There were still ups and downs, though. There was a row with the Press over the facilities offered, and the club was snubbed by Oxford United's seventeen-year-old midfielder Kevin Brock. On the plus side were a home win over Nottingham Forest, Albion thereby registering a double over the European champions, and a sparkling second win over Wolves. Defeats by Bristol City and Derby County gave cause for concern, but more for the manner of defeat than for any lingering fears of relegation.

The F.A. Cup saw a 2–0 win at Third Division Mansfield Town before Albion came up against Arsenal for the fifth time in the season. The Gunners again proved too strong and won the fourth-round tie 2–0, a comfortable step on their way to the final where they lost 1–0 to Second Division West Ham United.

A cigarette-end, carelessly discarded by a spectator at the Middlesbrough match on 19 April, was the probable cause of the fire which gutted the 26-year-old South Stand that night, and it was closed for the final game. In January it had been revealed that the Goldstone, which was now subject to the 1975 Safety of Sports Grounds Act, required considerable work,

The redundant Church of St Agnes at the corner of Goldstone Lane and Newtown Road was purchased by the club for £17,500 and converted into a gymnasium by March 1980.

especially on the East Terrace, to gain a certificate for a 30,000 capacity. With hopes for a new ground fading, a £2·5 million scheme was revealed for new North and South Stands, both with 3,500 seats above terracing for another 3,500, and for a roof over the East Terrace. Permission was granted for the North Stand, but the whole scheme was shelved in May when it was found that covenants, made in 1926 when the club purchased a lease and not thought now to be a problem, in fact prohibited the development. The covenants were ruled unenforceable in the High Court in November 1982, but the proposed new stands were never built. Instead, the gutted South Stand was successfully converted into an all-seated facility for 2,436 fans by Christmas 1980, and 200 extra seats and a new Press box were built at the front of the West Stand in the summer.

The season ended with a testimonial match against Southampton for the benefit of midfielder Peter O'Sullivan; after ten years and 465 Albion games, a total bettered only by Ernie Wilson, 'Sully' was off to the sunshine of California with the San Diego Sockers. The supporters' Player of the Season was the commanding Steve Foster, while the emergence of Gary Stevens and the all-round ability of Mark Lawrenson augured well for the future. Home and away attendances topped the million mark for the first time ever, and the home average of 24,795 was the second highest on record. Curiously though, there was not a single 30,000 attendance. With the Sussex public having become accustomed over the last few seasons to seeing their team at the top and winning virtually every home match, perhaps the novelty of the First Division had worn off quickly.

The South Stand fire

This dramatic photograph, taken on the evening of 19 April by a Goldstone Lane resident, shows a fireman on the South Stand terrace fighting the blaze in the seating at the rear. Just a few hours earlier a 20,427 crowd had watched the game with Middlesbrough. The roof of the stand remained intact, but the wooden seating and supporting structure were destroyed. The stand reopened as an 'all-seater' the following season.

SEASON 1980–81

When Albion opened their second season in the First Division against Wolves at the Goldstone, several old friends were missing. The most obvious absentee was the 50-year-old North Stand, demolished in the summer after failing a safety test. The ground's certified capacity was reduced to 24,000 but increased throughout the season as work continued on the terracing and on the gutted South Stand. The popular Seagull Special charter-train had made its last journey, a victim of rising costs and operational problems. Gone, too, were the traditional blue-and-white stripes, replaced by an all-blue strip bearing the name of the club's new sponsor, British Caledonian Airways, in a three-year deal worth £180,000. Even

'Sussex by the Sea' had disappeared; the team ran out to the theme from the film *Rocky*, but the old fanfare was soon restored after pressure from supporters. Many fans were also missing and the attendance failed to reach 20,000. The country was in a deepening recession, terrace admission had risen to £2, and season tickets were still available for the first time for several years.

Ray Clarke and Andy Rollings were among those to have left the club. Into the side came Gordon Smith, a ball-playing, £400,000 midfielder from Glasgow Rangers; Michael Robinson, the Manchester City centre-forward, also for £400,000; and Ray McHale from Swindon Town. Steve Foster and Mark Lawrenson had both signed long-term contracts along with Peter Ward, who had gained a full England cap with a brief appearance as substitute in Australia during the summer.

A 2–0 victory over Wolves augured well for the season. Gordon Smith marked his début with a goal, bagged a brace at Tottenham in a 2–2 draw, and was instrumental in gaining an unexpected point at Coventry in October: Albion trailed 3–0 after 64 minutes, but then the elegant Scot hit a nineteen-minute hat-trick to save the game. Peter O'Sullivan rejoined the club in October and replaced McHale in midfield, but form generally was very poor. Only two wins were recorded before November and, with just eight points from sixteen games, Albion were bottom once again.

Peter Ward took ten matches to open his League account and the on-off deal with Nottingham Forest was resurrected in October at £400,000, but the Forest manager, Brian Clough, again dithered over a final decision. The next game, coincidentally at home to Forest, was Ward's best of the season and the transfer was confirmed the following week. Alan Mullery had already lined up Manchester United's nineteen-year-old Andy Ritchie, at a club-record £500,000, as a replacement, and so Albion's top goalscorer and longest-serving player left the club with barely a murmur from supporters.

When the Republic of Ireland played France in Paris on 28 October, the Irish line-up included Mark Lawrenson and Michael Robinson, with Gerry Ryan coming on as substitute. It was the first time three Albion players had ever played in the same international match.

Another trauma in October was the sudden death of vice-chairman Harry Bloom *en route* to Stoke City. Bloom's calming influence had been a vital buffer between Mike Bamber and Alan Mullery, and by the end of the month there were already rumours that a rift was growing between the chairman and his manager, although both denied it.

The gate fell to just 12,112 for the visit of Middlesbrough, well below the 20,000 break-even figure and the lowest for over four years. Some fans hankered for the more open play of the Third Division days when the Seagulls ruled the roost, but crowd violence, the lack of a decent stadium and high admission prices were also blamed. The gloom was dispelled when, for the third year in a row, Albion enjoyed a splendid Christmas. After defeating the League-leaders, Aston Villa, before a fully-open, all-seated South Stand, victories were recorded over fellow strugglers Leicester City and Crystal Palace.

Michael Robinson was now scoring regularly, but basic defensive errors were proving costly. Mullery publicly admonished Graham Moseley, asserting that the goalkeeper had cost the club six points, and brought in Perry Digweed from Fulham for £150,000, a player who went on to give more than twelve years service to the club. Perry did his bit, but the Christmas respite was now long-forgotten as the dismal displays continued. Only two more matches were won by mid April, but, fortunately, Crystal Palace were much worse and made 22nd place their own with Albion hovering just above Norwich and Leicester. Despite their lowly position, the Seagulls should

Albion 1980–81
Back row left to right: Paul Clark, Gary Williams, Mark Lawrenson, Gary Stevens, Peter Suddaby, Peter Sayer.
Middle row left to right: Glen Wilson (equipment manager), Ken Craggs (assistant manager), Moshe Gariani, Neil McNab, Graham Moseley, John Phillips, Steve Foster, George Aitken (coach), Mike Yaxley (physio).
Seated left to right: Peter Ward, Gordon Smith, Brian Horton (captain), Alan Mullery (manager), John Gregory, Gerry Ryan, Ray McHale.

SEASON 1980–81

Date	Comp.	Ven.	Opponents	Result	HT	Pos.	Scorers	Atten.
Aug 16	FL D1	(h)	Wolverhampton W.	W 2–0	0–0	6=	Smith, Gregory	19,307
19	FL D1	(a)	Ipswich Town	L 0–2	0–1	12		21,568
23	FL D1	(a)	Tottenham H'spur	D 2–2	1–1	9	Smith 2	39,763
26	FLC R2 Lg1	(h)	Tranmere Rovers	W 3–1	3–0	–	Foster, Robinson, Ward	10,055
30	FL D1	(h)	West Bromwich A.	L 1–2	1–0	13=	Robinson	18,162
Sep 3	FLC R2 Lg2	(a)	Tranmere Rovers	W 4–2	1–1	–	Robinson 2, Foster, Williams	4,390
6	FL D1	(a)	Southampton	L 1–3	0–2	18	Smith	22,225
13	FL D1	(h)	Birmingham City	D 2–2	1–1	17	McNab, Lawrenson	15,788
20	FL D1	(h)	Norwich City	W 2–0	0–0	14	Robinson, Stevens	14,877
23	FLC R3	(h)	Coventry City	L 1–2	1–1	–	Ryan	14,426
27	FL D1	(a)	Liverpool	L 1–4	0–1	16	Horton (pen)	35,836
Oct 4	FL D1	(a)	Coventry City	D 3–3	0–2	16	Smith 3	11,462
7	FL D1	(h)	Everton	L 1–3	0–0	16	Ward	16,523
11	FL D1	(h)	Notting'm Forest	L 0–1	0–1	18		17,420
18	FL D1	(a)	Stoke City	D 0–0	0–0	18		13,079
22	FL D1	(a)	Aston Villa	L 1–4	1–1	18	Gregory	27,367
25	FL D1	(h)	Manchester City	L 1–2	0–0	20	Robinson	18,368
Nov 1	FL D1	(a)	Arsenal	L 0–2	0–0	22		28,569
8	FL D1	(h)	Middlesbrough	L 0–1	0–0	22		12,112
11	FL D1	(h)	Ipswich Town	W 1–0	0–0	20	Robinson	17,055
15	FL D1	(a)	Wolverhampton W.	W 2–0	1–0	19	Robinson 2	15,946
22	FL D1	(h)	Manchester United	L 1–4	0–3	20	Ritchie	23,277
29	FL D1	(a)	Leeds United	L 0–1	0–0	20		14,333
Dec 6	FL D1	(h)	Sunderland	W 2–1	1–0	20	Robinson, Ritchie	13,903
13	FL D1	(a)	Everton	L 3–4	2–2	20	O'Sullivan, Ritchie, Robinson	19,157
20	FL D1	(a)	Aston Villa	W 1–0	1–0	20	Robinson	16,425
26	FL D1	(a)	Leicester City	W 1–0	0–0	20	Gregory	19,570
27	FL D1	(h)	Crystal Palace	W 3–2	1–1	18	O'Sullivan, Robinson 2	27,367
Jan 3	FAC R3	(a)	Manchester United	D 2–2	2–0	–	Horton, Ritchie	42,199
7	FAC R3 Rep	(h)	Manchester United	L 0–2	0–1	–		26,928
10	FL D1	(a)	Manchester United	L 1–2	0–1	19	Ritchie	42,208
17	FL D1	(a)	West Bromwich A.	L 0–2	0–1	19		15,643
31	FL D1	(h)	Tottenham H'spur	L 0–2	0–1	19		23,354
Feb 7	FL D1	(a)	Birmingham City	L 1–2	0–1	19	Robinson	13,691
21	FL D1	(h)	Liverpool	D 2–2	2–1	19	Robinson, Smith	23,275
24	FL D1	(h)	Southampton	W 2–0	0–0	19	Williams (pen), Stille	23,715
28	FL D1	(a)	Norwich City	L 1–3	0–2	19	Robinson	16,199
Mar 7	FL D1	(h)	Coventry City	W 4–1	2–1	19	Robinson 2, Stille, Smith	14,063
14	FL D1	(a)	Notting'm Forest	L 1–4	1–2	19	Stille	20,688
21	FL D1	(h)	Stoke City	D 1–1	1–1	19	Robinson	13,583
28	FL D1	(a)	Manchester City	D 1–1	0–0	19	Gregory	30,122
Apr 4	FL D1	(h)	Arsenal	L 0–1	0–1	19		21,015
11	FL D1	(a)	Middlesbrough	L 0–1	0–0	20		11,076
18	FL D1	(a)	Crystal Palace	W 2–0	2–0	20	Gregory 2, Smith	18,792
20	FL D1	(h)	Leicester City	W 2–1	1–0	19	Robinson, Gregory	21,179
25	FL D1	(a)	Sunderland	W 2–1	1–0	18	Robinson, Williams	22,317
May 2	FL D1	(h)	Leeds United	W 2–0	1–0	18	Foster, Ritchie	27,577

Players: Clark P, Cohen J, Digweed P, Foster S, Gariani M, Gregory J, Horton B, Lawrenson M, McHale R, McNab N, Moseley G, O'Sullivan P, Phillips J, Ramsey C, Ritchie A, Robinson M, Ryan G, Sayer P, Smith G, Stevens G, Stille G, Vessey A, Ward P, Williams G

	Clark P	Cohen J	Digweed P	Foster S	Gariani M	Gregory J	Horton B	Lawrenson M	McHale R	McNab N	Moseley G	O'Sullivan P	Phillips J	Ramsey C	Ritchie A	Robinson M	Ryan G	Sayer P	Smith G	Stevens G	Stille G	Vessey A	Ward P	Williams G
League appearances	8	3	15	42	0	39	38	40	9	33	26	22	1	3	23	42	2	0	36	33	9	1	11	26
Substitute appearances	1	3		1		2				2		2		3				8					1	2
League goals				1		7	1	1		1		2			5	19			10	1	3		1	2

Football League Division 1 1980–81

		P	W	D	L	F	A	W	D	L	F	A	Pts
1.	Aston Villa	42	16	3	2	40	13	10	5	6	32	27	60
2.	Ipswich Town	42	15	4	2	45	14	8	6	7	32	29	56
3.	Arsenal	42	13	8	0	36	17	6	7	8	25	28	53
4.	West Bromwich A.	42	15	4	2	40	15	5	8	8	20	27	52
5.	Liverpool	42	13	5	3	38	15	4	12	5	24	27	51
6.	Southampton	42	15	4	2	47	22	5	6	10	29	34	50
7.	Nottingham Forest	42	15	3	3	44	20	4	9	8	18	24	50
8.	Manchester United	42	9	11	1	30	14	6	7	8	21	22	48
9.	Leeds United	42	10	5	6	19	19	7	5	9	20	28	44
10.	Tottenham Hotspur	42	9	9	3	44	31	5	6	10	26	37	43
11.	Stoke City	42	8	9	4	31	23	4	9	8	20	37	42
12.	Manchester City	42	10	7	4	35	25	4	4	13	21	34	39
13.	Birmingham City	42	11	5	5	32	23	2	7	12	18	38	38
14.	Middlesbrough	42	14	4	3	38	16	2	1	18	15	45	37
15.	Everton	42	8	6	7	32	25	5	4	12	23	33	36
16.	Coventry City	42	9	6	6	31	30	4	4	13	17	38	36
17.	Sunderland	42	10	4	7	32	19	4	3	14	20	34	35
18.	Wolverhampton W.	42	11	2	8	26	20	2	7	12	17	35	35
19.	**ALBION**	42	10	3	8	30	26	4	4	13	24	41	35
20.	Norwich City	42	9	7	5	34	25	4	0	17	15	48	33
21.	Leicester City	42	7	5	9	20	23	6	1	14	20	44	32
22.	Crystal Palace	42	6	4	11	32	37	0	3	18	15	46	19

Supporters were given an unwelcome Christmas present in the form of a proposal by Mike Bamber to develop a 'super stadium' in the Gatwick area in a joint venture with Crystal Palace, but the plans were dropped a month later as Palace pursued a link-up with Wimbledon.

have buried Liverpool when, after being 2–0 up in just eight minutes, they allowed the League champions to snatch a draw.

After beating Coventry City on 7 March, Albion collected just two points from five games to drop to 20th position with four games to play. Not even four victories could guarantee safety and relegation looked probable. Easter Saturday saw Albion win 2–0 at already-demoted Crystal Palace. However, Norwich City won at Tottenham to leave Albion in deep trouble. This was the situation:

		P	W	D	L	F	A	Pts
16.	Sunderland	39	13	7	19	49	49	33
17.	Wolves	37	12	8	17	39	49	32
18.	Coventry City	39	11	9	19	45	67	31
19.	Norwich City	39	12	7	20	46	69	31
20.	ALBION	39	11	7	21	48	65	29
21.	Leicester City	39	11	6	22	35	63	28
22.	Crystal Palace	39	6	6	27	43	76	18

The first of two 'four-pointers' came on Easter Monday, a home match with Leicester City. The Seagulls found themselves 1–0 down at half time but came back in the second period to win 2–1 against a nine-man City side, virtually sealing

Leicester's fate. Norwich City, though, maintained a two-point lead over the Albion by defeating second-placed Ipswich Town.

The penultimate Saturday saw Albion, on 31 points, travel to Sunderland. With the Canaries favourites to beat Leicester City on the last day of the season and thereby total at least 35 points, anything but a win at Roker meant probable relegation for the Seagulls. However, an Albion win would make Sunderland, whose last game was at Liverpool, odds-on to go down. Brighton took a first-half lead through Michael Robinson, but the Rokerites equalised on 62 minutes. Albion left it very late, but in the last minute a cross from Gordon Smith was fired into the net by left-back Gary Williams for the most dramatic and the most vital goal of the season.

Norwich City lost at Manchester United to leave themselves, Sunderland and Albion all on 33 points with one game to play, so an Albion victory over Leeds United would see them to safety ahead of the Canaries by virtue of a much better goal-difference. The largest crowd of the season, 27,577, saw Steve Foster give the Seagulls a 1–0 half-time lead. An Andy Ritchie goal in the 80th minute sealed Albion's fourth successive victory, and at the final whistle there was a great outburst of joy

in celebration of a truly remarkable escape under extreme pressure. Amazingly, Norwich lost at home to Leicester and Sunderland won at Liverpool, leaving the Canaries as the third relegated team.

Cup performances were indifferent with the exception of the first half at Old Trafford in the F.A. Cup third round. Albion overwhelmed Manchester United to lead 2–0, only for United to come back for a draw and then outplay the Seagulls in the Goldstone replay. Mark Lawrenson was sent off as the side cruised past Tranmere Rovers in the League Cup, but Albion then disappointingly went out at home to the eventual semi-finalists, Coventry City, in round three.

Michael Robinson was Player of the Season for his 22 goals in League and Cup, and for his all-round effort in traditional centre-forward style. Second-highest scorer was Gordon Smith with ten, but Andy Ritchie disappointed with just six goals in his 28 games. Average attendances fell to 18,969, the lowest for five years. With a huge wage-bill to meet, the falling support caused alarm in the boardroom, but the hard-won First Division status had been preserved and the club could surely hope for better things in the season ahead.

Lifeline
Left-back Gary Williams scores the last-minute winner in the penultimate fixture at Sunderland to maintain a slender lifeline to safety. The most vital goal of the campaign, this strike allowed Albion to continue their magnificent, four-victory climax to the season.

SEASON 1981–82

In the week following the great escape, manager Alan Mullery was offered, and accepted, a three-year contract, but the paperwork never materialised. The manager/chairman relationship was further strained when Mullery found that Mike Bamber was preparing to sell star defender Mark Lawrenson to Liverpool, while he himself had arranged a deal with the new Manchester United boss, Ron Atkinson.

The situation came to a head on 12 June when the manager met Bamber and his fellow directors Tom Appleby and Dudley Sizen. Apparently asked to make changes to his coaching staff of Ken Craggs, George Aitken and Jimmy Melia, Mullery refused point-blank and alleged later that there was then indecision over his own future at the club. The board's version was that they had made no such request and that the meeting had ended amicably. It may have been one big misunderstanding, but, whatever happened, Mullery announced that he had resigned, apparently to the great surprise of Bamber. 'I am shocked, but I will not stand in his way,' said the chairman. Neither party contacted the other, and so the five-year reign of Albion's most successful manager was over.

Applications poured in for the vacant post, but the board interviewed only one man, the Charlton Athletic manager Mike Bailey who had just led the Valiants to promotion from the Third Division. On 19 June, Bailey was confirmed as the new Albion manager; there was some confusion as Charlton alleged that he was still under contract, but Bailey insisted he had never signed a contract at The Valley. In what turned out to be a managerial 'swap', Mullery then took over the reins at Charlton together with his long-time confidant Ken Craggs.

The transfer of John Gregory, to Queen's Park Rangers for £300,000, was completed, and the new manager began rebuilding. Tony Grealish was signed from Luton Town as replacement for Brian Horton, the influential skipper, now 32, moving in the reverse direction; and full-back Don Shanks joined on a free transfer from Queen's Park Rangers. Mark Lawrenson, probably the most complete Albion player ever, signed for Liverpool in August for £900,000, by far the largest fee ever paid for a Brighton player; he went on to win a host of medals with the Anfield club. In the opposite direction came Jimmy Case, the experienced Liverpool midfielder, for £350,000. Steve Foster was made club captain on the departure of Lawrenson.

For the first time since its formation, a change was made to the Football League's point-scoring system with three points now being awarded for a win instead of two. Albion picked up their first three-point haul with a 2–0 win over Middlesbrough in the third game, and after a second win, at Wolves on 22 September, the Seagulls briefly occupied fifth place, their highest-ever position in the Football League. Mike Bailey's squad-building continued with the signing of two Arsenal players, midfielder Steve Gatting for £200,000 and Northern Ireland left-back Sammy Nelson for around £30,000. In the absence of Gary Stevens, Gatting was immediately drafted into the defence at Everton and remained a defender for virtually his entire ten-year Albion career.

The good form was underlined by the 4–1 destruction of Manchester City with Andy Ritchie, who had been the target of criticism, scoring twice. A crowd of 26,320 witnessed a tremendous Albion fight-back against European champions Liverpool: 3–1 down with eleven minutes remaining, Jimmy Case and Andy Ritchie scored the goals to force a 3–3 draw, and the Seagulls followed that with a first Football League victory at Tottenham. The only clouds on the Albion horizon were poor attendances: gates were down all around the country, and Liverpool were the only side to attract more than 20,000 to the Goldstone before Christmas. The fence in front of the West Terrace was

> Albion beat the Nigerian national side 5–1 in a Goldstone friendly in August, and a reserve side made the return trip the following month. The Nigerian World Cup team beat Albion reserves 5–0 in Lagos and 4–0 in Ibadan in front of crowds reported as 35,000 and 40,000 respectively.

Albion 1981–82

Back row left to right: Gary Williams, Mark Lawrenson, Perry Digweed, Graham Moseley, Steve Foster (captain), Gary Stevens, Michael Robinson.
Middle row left to right: John Collins (coach), Tony Vessey, Chris Ramsey, Giles Stille, Mike Ring, Paul Clark, Tony Grealish, Mike Yaxley (physio).
Seated left to right: Andy Ritchie, Moshe Gariani, Tommy Mason, Mike Bailey (man.), Neil McNab, Gordon Smith, Gerry Ryan.

> Sussex played Surrey in a 25-over, floodlit cricket match at the Goldstone on 7 September 1981. Sussex won by three wickets with Imran Khan hitting dozens of white cricket balls all around the ground in his 123 not out, but the match attracted a very poor attendance.

SEASON 1981–82

Date	Comp.	Ven.	Opponents	Result	HT	Pos.	Scorers	Atten.	Case J	Digweed P	Foster S	Gatting S	Grealish A	McNab N	Moseley G	Nelson S	Ring M	Ritchie A	Robinson M	Ryan G	Shanks D	Smith G	Stevens G	Stille G	Thomas M	Vessey A	Williams G
Aug 29	FL D1	(a)	West Ham United	D 1–1	0–0	12=	McNab (pen)	30,468	7		5		4	10	1			8†	9	11	2	12	6				3
Sep 1	FL D1	(h)	Swansea City	L 1–2	1–2	14	Ritchie	19,885	7		5		4†	10	1			8	9	11	2	12	6				3
5	FL D1	(h)	Middlesbrough	W 2–0	1–0	8=	Case, Own goal	13,386	7		5		4	10	1			8†	9	11	2	12	6				3
12	FL D1	(a)	Everton	D 1–1	0–0	10	Robinson	27,352	7		5	6		4	10	1		8	9		2	11				N	3
19	FL D1	(h)	Coventry City	W 2–2	1–1	12	Robinson, McNab (pen)	15,262	7		5	6	4	10	1			8†	9		2	11	12				3
22	FL D1	(a)	Wolverhampton W.	W 1–0	5		Ritchie	12,586	7		5	6	4	10	1			8†	9		2	11	12				3
26	FL D1	(a)	Notting'm Forest	L 1–2	1–0	10	Smith	19,220	7		5	6	4	10	1			8	9		2	11	N				3
Oct 3	FL D1	(h)	Manchester City	W 4–1	0–0	8	Robinson, Ritchie 2, Williams	18,284	7		5	6	4†	10	1			8	9		2	11	12				3
6	FLC R2 Lg1		Huddersfield Town	L 0–1	0–0	–		9,803	7		5	6			1		8		9	11	2	N	4				3
10	FL D1	(a)	West Bromwich A.	D 0–0	0–0	7		13,704	7		5	6	4†	10	1			8	9		2	11	12				3
17	FL D1	(h)	Liverpool	D 3–3	0–2	9	Foster, Case, Ritchie	26,320	7	1	5	6		4	10			8	9		2	11	N				3
24	FL D1	(a)	Tottenham H'spur	W 1–0	0–0	8	Robinson	37,294	7		5	6	4	10	1			8	9		2	11	N				3
27	FLC R2 Lg2		Huddersfield Town	W 2–0	0–0	–	Ritchie, Grealish	14,192	7		5	6	4	10	1	3		8	9	12	2	11†					
31	FL D1	(h)	Stoke City	D 0–0	0–0	7		17,862	7		5	6	4†	10	1			8	9		2	11	12				3
Nov 7	FL D1	(h)	Birmingham City	D 1–1	0–1	9	Robinson	18,392	7		5	6	4	10	1			8†	9		2	11			12		3
10	FLC R3	(a)	Barnsley	L 1–4	1–2	–	Gatting	19,534	7		5	6	4	10	1	3		8†	9		2	11	12				
21	FL D1	(h)	Notts County	D 2–2	0–2	11	Case, Gatting	13,854	7		5	4		10	1	3		9	12	2	8	6†		11			
24	FL D1	(a)	Swansea City	D 0–0	0–0	10		14,459	7		5	6	4	10	1	3		9		2	8			11		N	
28	FL D1	(a)	Manchester United	L 0–2	0–1	11		41,911	7		5	6	4	10	1	3		9		2	8			11		N	
Dec 5	FL D1	(h)	Sunderland	W 2–1	1–1	11	Smith, Ritchie	14,251			5	6	4	10	1	3	12	9†	7	2	8			11			
8	FL D1	(a)	Southampton	W 2–0	0–0	6	Ritchie, Gatting	22,128			5	6	4	10	1	3		9		7	2	8	N		11		
28	FL D1	(h)	Aston Villa	L 0–1	0–0	9		24,287	7		5	6	4	10	1	3		8		2	9	12	11†				
Jan 2	FAC R3	(a)	Barnet	D 0–0	0–0	–		4,800	7		5	6	4	10†	1	3		8	9		2		12		11		
5	FAC R3 Rep	(h)	Barnet	W 3–1	0–0	–	Thomas, Case, McNab (pen)	15,885	7		5	6	4	10	1	3		8	9†	12	2				11		
16	FL D1	(a)	West Ham United	W 1–0	0–0	8	Ritchie	22,620			5	6	4	10	1	3		8		7	2	9	N		11		
23	FAC R4	(a)	Oxford United	L 0–3	0–2	–		17,898			5	6	4	10	1	3		8		7	2	9	N		11		
26	FL D1	(a)	Arsenal	D 0–0	0–0	9		17,992			5	6	4	10	1	3		8		7†	2	9	12		11		
30	FL D1	(a)	Coventry City	W 1–0	1–0	7	Ritchie	11,023			6	4	10	1	3		8		7	2	9	5		11		N	
Feb 6	FL D1	(h)	Everton	W 3–1	1–0	8	Grealish, Ryan, Foster	16,148	7		5	6	4	10	1	3		8		9	N	11	2				
13	FL D1	(a)	Manchester City	L 0–4	0–2	8		30,038	7		5	6	4	10	1	3		8		9	N	11	2				
20	FL D1	(h)	Notting'm Forest	L 0–1	0–1	9		17,175	7		5	6	4†	10	1	3		8	12	9			2		11		
27	FL D1	(h)	West Bromwich A.	D 2–2	1–0	9	Ritchie, Robinson	14,553	7		5	6	4	10	1	3		8	9†	12			2		11		
Mar 2	FL D1	(h)	Leeds United	W 1–0	1–0	9	Stille	12,857	7		5	6	4			1	3	8	9	N			2	10	11		
6	FL D1	(a)	Liverpool	W 1–0	1–0	8	Ritchie	28,574	7	1	5	6	4			3		8	9	11	12		2	10†			
9	FL D1	(h)	Tottenham H'spur	L 1–3	0–1	9	Gatting	27,090	7	1	5	6	4		12	3		8	9	11			2	10†			
20	FL D1	(a)	Stoke City	D 0–0	0–0	9		9,120	7	1		6	4†	10		3		8	9	12	2	11	5				
27	FL D1	(a)	Birmingham City	L 0–1	0–0	10		13,234		1	5	6	4	10			8	9	7†	3	11	2			12		
30	FL D1	(a)	Ipswich Town	L 1–3	0–1	11	Robinson	19,361		1	5	6	4†	10		3		8	9		2		7	12	11		
Apr 3	FL D1	(h)	Southampton	D 1–1	1–0	11	McNab (pen)	20,977		1	5	6	4	10		3		8	9		2		7	N	11		
10	FL D1	(h)	Arsenal	W 2–0	0–0	10	Ritchie, Robinson	21,019	4	1	5	6		10		3		8	9	N	2		7		11		
12	FL D1	(a)	Aston Villa	L 0–3	0–0	11		22,731		1	5	6	4	10†		3		8	9		2		7	12	11		
17	FL D1	(a)	Notts County	L 1–4	0–2	12	Robinson	7,920	7	1	5	6	N	10		3		8	9		2	11	4				
20	FL D1	(a)	Middlesbrough	L 1–2	1–1	13	Ritchie	9,788	7	1	5	6	N	10		3		8	9	11	2		4				
24	FL D1	(h)	Manchester United	L 0–1	0–0	13		20,755	7	1	5	6	N	10		3		8	9	11	2		4				
May 1	FL D1	(a)	Sunderland	L 0–3	0–1	13		16,224	7		5	6	12	10		1	3	8†	9	11	2		4				
4	FL D1	(h)	Wolverhampton W.	W 2–0	2–0	11	Robinson, Nelson	10,429	7†		5	6	12	10		1	3	11	8	9		2		4			
8	FL D1	(h)	Ipswich Town	L 0–1	0–1	12		17,786	7		5	6	12	10†		1	3	8	9		2		4		11		
15	FL D1	(a)	Leeds United	L 1–2	1–0	13	Robinson	19,831	7		5	10	4	12		1	8†	9	11	2		6			11	3	
			League appearances						33	12	40	39	34	38	30	27	1	38	34	17	35	24	25	3	18	0	14
			Substitute appearances									3	2						1	1	3	1	3	7	2	2	
			League goals				OG – 1		3		2	3	1	3		1		13	11	1		2		1			1

replaced by less-obtrusive bars as a compromise after the club had applied to remove all fences in a bid to win back supporters.

The side then did nothing to help its cause by playing three dismal home draws with Stoke City, Birmingham City and Notts County, and questions were asked about the lack-lustre performances and Bailey's defensive tactics in general. In early November, Everton's Welsh international midfielder Mickey Thomas signed for £350,000 and he helped the team to a first victory over Southampton at The Dell for 26 years, with the commanding Steve Foster subduing Kevin Keegan to press his case for an England opportunity. His chance came in February, against Northern Ireland at Wembley, and the Albion skipper had a sound game alongside Stoke City's Dave Watson. Sammy Nelson made his 48th appearance in an emerald-green shirt in the same match.

Former Albion favourite Peter Ward was outstanding for Nottingham Forest and scored the only goal in their Goldstone victory on 20 February, but March opened with a home win over Leeds United and was followed by a first win at Liverpool. Andy Ritchie scrambled a goal close to half time, and a resolute defence then held out with a huge slice of luck: Tony Grealish's short back-pass in the 80th minute was hit past Perry Digweed

Football League Division 1 1981–82

		P	W	D	L	F	A	W	D	L	F	A	Pts
1.	Liverpool	42	14	3	4	39	14	12	6	3	41	18	87
2.	Ipswich Town	42	17	1	3	47	25	9	4	8	28	28	83
3.	Manchester United	42	12	6	3	27	9	10	6	5	32	20	78
4.	Tottenham Hotspur	42	12	6	3	41	26	8	7	6	26	22	71
5.	Arsenal	42	13	5	3	27	15	7	6	8	21	22	71
6.	Swansea City	42	13	3	5	34	16	8	3	10	24	35	69
7.	Southampton	42	15	2	4	49	30	4	7	10	23	37	66
8.	Everton	42	11	7	3	33	21	6	6	9	23	29	64
9.	West Ham United	42	9	10	2	42	29	5	6	10	24	28	58
10.	Manchester City	42	9	7	5	32	23	6	6	9	17	27	58
11.	Aston Villa	42	9	6	6	28	24	6	6	9	27	29	57
12.	Nottingham Forest	42	7	7	7	19	20	8	5	8	23	28	57
13.	**ALBION**	42	8	7	6	30	24	5	6	10	13	28	52
14.	Coventry City	42	9	4	8	31	24	4	7	10	25	38	50
15.	Notts County	42	8	5	8	32	33	5	3	13	29	36	47
16.	Birmingham City	42	8	6	7	29	35	2	8	11	24	36	44
17.	West Bromwich A.	42	6	6	9	24	25	5	5	11	22	32	44
18.	Stoke City	42	9	2	10	27	28	3	6	12	17	35	44
19.	Sunderland	42	6	5	10	19	26	5	6	10	19	32	44
20.	Leeds United	42	6	11	4	23	20	4	1	16	16	41	42
21.	Wolverhampton W.	42	8	8	5	19	20	2	5	14	13	43	40
22.	Middlesbrough	42	5	9	7	20	24	3	6	12	14	28	39

On 6 March the Albion squad launched 'In Brighton' and 'Brighton Rap', a double-A-side disc on Howard Kruger's Energy Records label. The single made the Peter Powell show on Radio One. Steve Foster was also to be heard on the England World Cup squad's hit, 'This Time'.

by Welsh international Ian Rush, but the ball stuck in the Anfield mud and Steve Foster cleared to confirm a famous Brighton victory.

The Seagulls were now eighth and hopeful of a UEFA Cup place – clubs down to seventh place eventually qualified – but a rapid decline set in and they won only two of the remaining fourteen games to drop to a disappointing final position of thirteenth. Bailey's dour defensive methods reached their nadir in defeat at Birmingham City. Under pressure from all quarters, the manager then threw away the shackles and allowed the team to play. A home draw followed against championship contenders Southampton and then a cherished first League win over Arsenal, but seven out of the last eight games were lost including heavy defeats at Aston Villa, Notts County and Sunderland as Albion slipped down the table. The pressure on Bailey was increased by the unsettled Mickey Thomas who went 'AWOL' for the third time in April.

Once again cup form was poor. Twice outplayed by Third Division Huddersfield Town in the Milk Cup, Albion conjured up two goals in the the last five minutes to set up a tie at Second Division Barnsley. This time the Seagulls' luck did not hold and they crashed 4–1. The F.A. Cup saw a third-round tie at muddy Underhill, the home of Alliance Premier League side Barnet. The crowd was depleted by the Bees' trebling of prices, but they saw Albion held to a goal-less draw. The Seagulls easily won the replay and later signed the non-Leaguers' left-back Graham Pearce, but were then humbled 3–0 in the fourth round at the Goldstone by a lively Oxford United side from the Third Division which tore Albion's ponderous defence apart.

No player stood out, but Andy Ritchie was voted Player of the Season for his fourteen goals in League and Cup. Steve Foster received a second England cap in May, and made a third appearance against Kuwait in the World Cup in Spain where Sammy Nelson played two games for Northern Ireland. Tony Grealish, barracked for much of the season, captained his country, the Republic of Ireland, against Algeria in May and remains the only Albion player so honoured.

Despite many good results, leading to a highest-ever finish, it was not a happy season and the late decline did not augur well; perhaps Bailey's ultra-cautious tactics had been right after all. The average attendance was still over 18,000 despite a deepening recession and doubts about the fare on offer, but the club was falling further into debt to meet a huge wage-bill which rose to £970,000, prompting Mike Bamber to declare that 'We cannot survive if we have to pay the sort of wages that are being asked.' A scheme for a new, £600,000 North Stand with hospitality boxes was put on ice, and a plan for a giant electronic score-board in the north-eastern corner also came to nothing.

> On 28 April 1982, Michael Robinson, Tony Grealish and substitute Gerry Ryan all played for the Republic of Ireland against Algeria in Algiers, while Sammy Nelson represented Northern Ireland against Scotland in Belfast. It was the first time four Albion players had made international appearances on the same day. The following day Mickey Thomas played for Wales against England in Cardiff with Steve Foster a member of the English squad.

SEASON 1982–83

The 1982–83 season will always be remembered by those fans who witnessed it for one thing: the F.A. Cup. Although the club was now in its fourth season in the First Division, supporters found it hard to believe that Albion had really made it all the way to Wembley to take on the most famous club in the land, Manchester United, for the best-loved prize in football. When seen in the context of a disastrous League season, the feat seems all the more amazing.

During the summer, to the relief of all concerned, Mickey Thomas moved to Stoke City for £200,000. Paul Clark and Gary Williams also left the Goldstone, while new arrivals were Neil Smillie (Crystal Palace) and Gary Howlett (Coventry City). At one stage the signing of ex-England forward Charlie George seemed on the cards, but Albion were unable to meet his demands. Disenchantment with the previous season's performances and another rise in admission charges led to a large surplus of season tickets for the first time for several years.

The League season opened with an entertaining 1–1 home draw with Ipswich Town, but the 13,641 crowd was a long way short of the 22,000 break-even figure. The first two away games ended in heavy defeats, at West Bromwich (0–5) and Nottingham Forest (0–4), putting pressure on the Seagulls to get a result against Arsenal. Mike Bailey made some bold changes and the new centre-forward, Gerry Ryan, grabbed the winner on 31 minutes in a rousing performance. Two home victories sandwiched another 5–0 thrashing at Luton Town, but then Albion gained a first away point, at Everton, and were in a respectable eleventh position because of their good home record.

It was an unhappy time for the club, though. The gate for Birmingham City was just 9,845; Albion, now around £500,000 in debt and with some hefty, long-term contracts to support, could not survive in the First Division with such small crowds. Terrace admission was reduced by 50p to £2 for the visits of Notts County and Norwich City, but both games attracted only around 10,000 spectators. On a happier note, the Supporters' Club was re-established on 17 September after a break of five years, although it was never to be the same fund-raising force it had been in the past.

The Seagulls urgently needed a fillip and found one in Peter Ward, the former Goldstone favourite who had not been a success at Nottingham Forest. Mike Bailey took Ward on loan for four months and his presence put another 5,000 on the gate for his first match, against West Ham. Peter was the star as Albion gained a 3–1 victory, and he scored the only goal of the match in the club's first-ever win over Manchester United.

However, the dismal away performances continued, and after a first home League defeat of the season, 2–0 to Notts County, the pressure on Mike Bailey, who was not on contract, was intense. On 4 December, Albion lost 2–0 at Coventry and the matter came to a head: manager and club parted company on the Monday 'by mutual consent' with coaches John Collins

> Albion and Manchester City were forced to leave the Maine Road pitch for six minutes on 18 December when a stray dog defied the stewards' attempts to capture it.

SEASON 1982–83

Date	Comp.	Ven.	Opponents	Result	HT	Pos.	Scorers	Atten.
Aug 28	FL D1	(h)	Ipswich Town	D	1–1	1–1	11=	Ritchie	13,641
Sep 1	FL D1	(a)	West Bromwich A.	L	0–5	0–0	20		11,546
4	FL D1	(a)	Notting'm Forest	L	0–4	0–2	21		13,704
7	FL D1	(h)	Arsenal	W	1–0	1–0	16	Ryan	13,507
11	FL D1	(h)	Sunderland	W	3–2	0–2	18	Smith, Ryan, Grealish	10,264
18	FL D1	(a)	Luton Town	L	0–5	0–1	18		11,342
25	FL D1	(h)	Birmingham City	W	1–0	0–0	11	Gatting	9,845
Oct 2	FL D1	(a)	Everton	D	2–2	1–1	11	Robinson, Case	17,539
6	FLC R2 Lg1	(a)	Tottenham H'spur	L	1–1	1–0	–	Grealish	20,416
9	FL D1	(h)	Swansea City	D	1–1	1–1	12	Foster	11,050
16	FL D1	(a)	Stoke City	L	0–3	0–2	16		13,936
23	FL D1	(h)	West Ham United	W	3–1	1–0	12	Smith, Gatting, Robinson	20,490
26	FLC R2 Lg2	(h)	Tottenham H'spur	L	1–0	0–0	–		20,763
30	FL D1	(a)	Liverpool	L	1–3	1–3	14	Ryan	27,929
Nov 6	FL D1	(h)	Manchester United	W	1–0	0–0	12	Ward	18,398
13	FL D1	(a)	Aston Villa	L	0–1	0–0	15		18,834
20	FL D1	(a)	Watford	L	1–4	0–1	17	Ryan	16,520
27	FL D1	(h)	Notts County	L	0–2	0–1	17		10,008
Dec 4	FL D1	(a)	Coventry City	L	0–2	0–2	18		8,054
11	FL D1	(h)	Norwich City	W	3–0	1–0	18	Case, Ritchie, Robinson	9,994
18	FL D1	(a)	Manchester City	D	1–1	0–1	18	Ritchie	20,615
27	FL D1	(h)	Southampton	L	0–1	0–0	19		21,794
28	FL D1	(a)	Tottenham H'spur	L	0–2	0–1	19		23,944
Jan 1	FL D1	(h)	Watford	D	1–1	0–0	20	Ward	15,139
3	FL D1	(a)	Notting'm Forest	D	1–1	0–1	18	Robinson	10,402
8	FAC R3	(h)	Newcastle United	D	1–1	0–0	–	Ritchie	17,711
12	FAC R3 Rep	(a)	Newcastle United	W	1–0	0–0	–	Ward	32,134
15	FL D1	(a)	Ipswich Town	L	0–2	0–1	21		17,092
22	FL D1	(h)	Luton Town	L	2–4	0–2	21	Ritchie, Grealish	11,785
29	FAC R4	(h)	Manchester City	W	4–0	2–0	–	Case, Smillie, Robinson 2	16,804
Feb 5	FL D1	(a)	Arsenal	L	1–3	1–2	22	Robinson	17,972
12	FL D1	(a)	West Bromwich A.	D	0–0	0–0	22		9,902
20	FAC R5	(a)	Liverpool	W	2–1	1–0	–	Ryan, Case	44,868
26	FL D1	(h)	Stoke City	L	1–2	1–2	22	Ritchie	14,937
Mar 1	FL D1	(a)	Swansea City	W	2–1	1–1	20	Robinson, Case	8,825
5	FL D1	(a)	West Ham United	L	1–2	0–2	21	Ryan	16,850
12	FAC R6	(h)	Norwich City	W	1–0	0–0	–	Case	28,800
19	FL D1	(a)	Manchester United	D	1–1	1–0	22	Gatting	36,700
22	FL D1	(h)	Liverpool	D	2–2	2–0	–	Robinson, Howlett	25,030
26	FL D1	(h)	Aston Villa	L	1–2	0–1	22	Smith	14,657
Apr 2	FL D1	(h)	Tottenham H'spur	W	2–1	0–1	22	Gatting, Ryan	20,359
5	FL D1	(a)	Southampton	D	0–0	0–0	20		18,253
9	FL D1	(h)	Everton	L	1–2	0–1	21	Smith (pen)	14,534
16	FAC SF	(n*)	Sheffield Wed.	W	2–1	1–0	–	Case, Robinson	54,627
19	FL D1	(a)	Sunderland	D	1–1	1–1	22	Smith	13,414
23	FL D1	(h)	Coventry City	W	1–0	0–0	21	Connor	14,674
30	FL D1	(a)	Notts County	L	0–1	0–0	21		7,349
May 2	FL D1	(a)	Birmingham City	L	1–2	0–1	22	Smith	15,977
7	FL D1	(h)	Manchester City	L	0–1	0–0	22		17,794
14	FL D1	(a)	Norwich City	L	1–2	0–1	22	Smith	20,306
21	FAC F	(n*)	Manchester United	D	2–2*	1–0	–	Smith, Stevens	100,000
26	FAC F Rep	(n*)	Manchester United	L	0–4	0–3	–		92,000

Player columns (in order): Case J, Connor T, Digweed P, Foster S, Gatting S, Grealish A, Howlett G, McNab N, Moseley G, Nelson S, O'Regan K, Pearce G, Ramsey C, Ring M, Ritchie A, Robinson M, Rodon C, Ryan G, Shanks D, Smillie N, Smith G, Stevens G, Stille G, Ward P

	Case J	Connor T	Digweed P	Foster S	Gatting S	Grealish A	Howlett G	McNab N	Moseley G	Nelson S	O'Regan K	Pearce G	Ramsey C	Ring M	Ritchie A	Robinson M	Rodon C	Ryan G	Shanks D	Smillie N	Smith G	Stevens G	Stille G	Ward P
League appearances	35	5	15	35	40	38	9	14	27	13	1	13	23	0	21	35	0	16	10	22	26	41	7	16
Substitute appearances		2	1									1		1	3	1	1	10		3	3			2
League goals	3	1		1	4	2	1								5	7		6			6			2

Notes: Apr 16 – played at Highbury, Arsenal FC.

May 21 – played at Wembley Stadium.
 – after extra time (90-minute score 2–2).

May 26 – played at Wembley Stadium.

The Football League Cup was sponsored as the Milk Cup.

Football League Division 1 1982–83

		P	W	D	L	F	A	W	D	L	F	A	Pts
1.	Liverpool	42	16	4	1	55	16	8	6	7	32	21	82
2.	Watford	42	16	2	3	49	20	6	3	12	25	37	71
3.	Manchester United	42	14	7	0	39	10	5	6	10	17	28	70
4.	Tottenham Hotspur	42	15	4	2	50	15	5	5	11	15	35	69
5.	Nottingham Forest	42	12	5	4	34	18	8	4	9	28	32	69
6.	Aston Villa	42	17	2	2	47	15	4	3	14	15	35	68
7.	Everton	42	13	6	2	43	19	5	4	12	23	29	64
8.	West Ham United	42	13	3	5	41	23	7	1	13	27	39	64
9.	Ipswich Town	42	11	3	7	39	23	4	10	7	25	27	58
10.	Arsenal	42	11	6	4	36	19	5	4	12	22	37	58
11.	West Bromwich A.	42	11	5	5	35	20	4	7	10	16	29	57
12.	Southampton	42	11	5	5	36	22	4	7	10	18	36	57
13.	Stoke City	42	13	4	4	34	21	4	5	13	19	43	57
14.	Norwich City	42	10	6	5	30	18	4	6	11	22	40	57
15.	Notts County	42	12	4	5	37	25	3	3	15	18	46	52
16.	Sunderland	42	7	10	4	30	22	5	4	12	18	39	50
17.	Birmingham City	42	9	7	5	29	24	3	7	11	11	31	50
18.	Luton Town	42	7	7	7	34	33	5	6	10	31	51	49
19.	Coventry City	42	10	5	6	29	17	3	4	14	19	42	48
20.	Manchester City	42	9	5	7	26	23	4	3	14	21	47	47
21.	Swansea City	42	10	4	7	32	29	0	7	14	19	40	41
22.	**ALBION**	42	8	7	6	25	22	1	6	14	13	46	40

and Brian Eastick also leaving the Goldstone. Bailey's tactics had been based on a cautious, ultra-defensive approach, a system which Mike Bamber justifiably claimed had bored the spectators and reduced income. The chairman admitted that Bailey's system would probably have borne fruit over three or four years, but, with Albion falling ever deeper into debt, time was not on the club's side. However, the board was not unanimous in this view and director Dudley Sizen resigned over the issue.

Chief coach George Aitken and chief scout Jimmy Melia, both with managerial experience in the lower divisions, were put in temporary charge, but, although they were in joint control, it was Melia who grabbed the limelight. Both agreed that Albion should attack, and their first line-up included all three principal strikers, Ritchie, Robinson and Ward. Chris Ramsey was recalled at right-back after nineteen months in the wilderness and Steve Gatting was moved to midfield; Neil McNab was dropped and soon went on loan to Leeds United. Albion won that game against Norwich City 3–0 and followed it with only their second away point, at Manchester City. However, an unhappy Yuletide landed the Seagulls in the relegation places for the first time. One hopeful sign was the marked improvement of Jimmy Case since Aitken and fellow 'scouse' Melia had been in charge.

Albion 1982–83

Standing left to right: John Collins (coach), Neil McNab, Andy Ritchie, Sammy Nelson, Graham Moseley, Perry Digweed, Steve Foster (captain), Gordon Smith, Tony Grealish, Mike Yaxley (physio).
Seated left to right: Mickey Thomas, Jimmy Case, Gary Stevens, Gerry Ryan, Mike Bailey (manager), Don Shanks, Steve Gatting, Michael Robinson, Neil Smillie.

Albion went through the first two months of 1983 without a League victory and became firmly rooted in the bottom three. Peter Ward played his last game on loan against Stoke City in a 2–1 home defeat; 'Wardy' had managed only two goals in his sixteen League games, but with Albion said to be losing £6,000 a week the club could not afford the £125,000 asking-price anyway. The first away win of the season came on 1 March at Swansea City, and two weeks later, largely on the strength of performances in the F.A. Cup, Jimmy Melia was confirmed as manager. The team responded with improved form, moving up to 20th place with creditable draws against Manchester United, Liverpool, Aston Villa and Southampton, and a thrilling victory over Spurs. However, defeat at the hands of Everton was a severe setback: Albion equalised three minutes from time but, in their all-out effort to secure three points, allowed Kevin Sheedy to snatch a last-minute winner.

In March, Melia unexpectedly swapped Andy Ritchie, who had scored just six goals, for Leeds United's Terry Connor. The bustling black striker scored his first Albion goal in a 1–0 win over Coventry City on 23 April, only the third League victory of the year, but the game was marred by the sending-off of Chris Ramsey – his second dismissal in three weeks – and City's Steve Jacobs for fighting. Albion's fate was virtually sealed by defeat

at Notts County and a draw at fellow strugglers Birmingham City, but a victory in the final home match could still have provided a slender lifeline. Defender Gary Stevens was presented with the Player of the Season award before the game, but Manchester City's 1–0 win condemned Albion to relegation in bottom place. After four years in the top flight it was a huge blow – indeed, the club has never really recovered from the setback – but the bitter pill was, of course, sweetened for supporters by forthcoming events at Wembley, and, in an unusual reversal of the normal situation, the club was now free to concentrate on the Cup!

Top League scorer was Michael Robinson with just seven goals and the average League attendance fell to 14,676, over 10,000 down on the Division One début season just three years earlier. Curiously, the home record was identical to the previous season's, but the Seagulls won four more away matches in 1981–82 when finishing thirteenth.

The League Cup, now sponsored by the Milk Marketing Board as the Milk Cup, saw a second-round exit at the hands of Tottenham Hotspur. Spurs were decidedly fortunate to be on level terms after the first leg at White Hart Lane, but won the Goldstone leg 1–0 with a goal from Garth Crooks. Sadly, once again, some of their fans rampaged through the town.

THE WEMBLEY TRAIL 1983

Albion's F.A. Cup record in recent years was woeful, but they had once been renowned cup-fighters. Twice while in the Southern League and seven times between 1921 and 1933 they had knocked out First Division opposition, but since that great run of 1932–33 a victory over Second Division Chesterfield in 1951 was the only instance of Albion 'giant-killing'. Indeed, defeats by Bedford Town, Walton & Hersham, Leatherhead and Oxford United were still fresh in the memory. On six occasions Albion had reached the last sixteen but they had never progressed to the quarter-finals.

The third round saw Second Division Newcastle United, six-time winners of the trophy, at a muddy Goldstone, and when Terry McDermott equalised Andy Ritchie's opener, many thought Brighton's Cup interest would, as usual, soon be over. Anyway, First Division survival was more important, for, as John Vinicombe put it in the *Evening Argus*, 'Can anyone seriously imagine them winning the Cup, or even reaching the final?' Albion entered the red-hot atmosphere of St James's Park without the suspended Steve Foster but grabbed the lead in the 62nd minute through Peter Ward and survived the ensuing onslaught, including two disallowed home 'goals' in the last four minutes.

Four-time winners Manchester City were the visitors to the Goldstone in the fourth round. In complete contrast with their League form, Albion despatched City 4–0, a result that prompted manager John Bond to quit Maine Road. Jimmy Case, Neil Smillie and Michael Robinson (2) scored as Albion progressed to the fifth round for the first time in 23 years where the reward was a daunting visit to the Anfield citadel of Liverpool.

The Football League champions, twice winners of the F.A. Cup, were in their accustomed position at the top of the League, on the way to a fourteenth championship, and were favourites for the Cup. Albion were bottom of the First Division and 9/1 against winning the tie, but supporters were confident, perhaps because Brighton were the last away side to win at Anfield. Staged on a Sunday (because Everton were at home to Spurs the previous day), the match was attended by over 4,000 fans from Sussex who saw Albion take the game to the home side. In the 32nd minute Michael Robinson beat former team-mate Mark Lawrenson (one of Liverpool's eight internationals) and centred for Gerry Ryan to score in front of the Kop. The Seagulls then weathered the Red storm until the 70th minute when Craig Johnston produced a scissor-kick shot to beat Perry Digweed. The home crowd now settled back expecting victory, but within a minute a 25-yarder from ex-Red Jimmy Case took a wicked deflection off Ronnie Whelan to sail past Bruce Grobbelaar. The excitement continued four minutes later when the normally reliable Phil Neal hit a penalty past Digweed's left post. Albion then repelled wave after wave of Liverpool attacks – Chris Ramsey headed off the line from Lawrenson – and five minutes later referee Alf Grey blew the final whistle on what is probably the club's most famous victory. While the players acknowledged the ecstatic Albion fans, ex-Liverpool man Jimmy Melia accepted the applause of the Kop which had just seen its first home Cup defeat since 1974.

Take that!
Jimmy Case's rocket is about to deflect off his former Liverpool colleague Ronnie Whelan (no.5) and into the net. This strike, less than a minute after the Reds' equaliser, clinched one of the greatest victories in Albion history.

With Albion in the quarter-finals for the first time, the ebullient Melia, still joint acting-manager, declared himself the man for the job and there were few to disagree. The balding, slightly comical figure in the white disco-shoes was now not only a local hero but also a national celebrity. Albion, 80/1 to win the Cup before the Liverpool match, were now just 9/1 with a home tie against fellow strugglers Norwich City to come.

The quarter-final was not all-ticket and the gates were closed just before kick-off with a capacity 28,800 inside the Goldstone, including 7,000 from East Anglia who were given the north-east corner and half the North Terrace. The match itself was not a classic with defences largely on top, but both sides went full pelt for a result. Jimmy Case, already booked for a foul, was rather fortunate still to be on the pitch when he decided the match in the 66th minute. As he ran on to an Andy Ritchie pass, Albion's midfielder bore down on the Canaries' goal alongside Paul Haylock and the linesman flagged furiously, but Jimmy went on to bury the ball in Chris Woods's net. City protested, but the linesman had been flagging for a foul *on* Case and referee Alan Robinson had played advantage. With Albion now in the semi-finals, the performance was good enough for Jimmy Melia, effectively in charge already, to be formalised in the role of manager on 16 March with George Aitken as his assistant.

The semi-final draw paired Arsenal with favourites Manchester United, while Brighton, now just 5/1 to lift the trophy, would play either Burnley or Sheffield Wednesday, both from the Second Division. The Owls, three-time winners of the Cup, won their replay 5–0 to set up a clash on 16 April at Highbury.

Gerry Ryan, the preferred striker in place of the cup-tied Terry Connor, was injured against Everton, so Gordon Smith was given the forward role alongside Michael Robinson. Chris Ramsey was suspended, so Gary Stevens was switched to right-back with Steve Gatting moving into the centre of defence and Graham Pearce returning at left-back. With Neil McNab cup-tied during his loan period at Leeds United, the no.12 shirt was given to Kieran O'Regan, a nineteen-year-old full-back who had yet to make his first-team début. The teams were:

Brighton and Hove Albion: Graham Moseley; Gary Stevens; Graham Pearce; Tony Grealish; Steve Foster (captain); Steve Gatting; Jimmy Case; Gary Howlett; Michael Robinson; Gordon Smith; Neil Smillie; sub. Kieran O'Regan.

Sheffield Wednesday: Bob Bolder; Mel Sterland; Pat Heard; Mark Smith; Mike Lyons (captain); Gary Shelton; Gary Megson; Simon Mills; Gary Bannister; Andy McCulloch; Ante Mirocevic; sub. Peter Shirtliff.

On a brilliantly sunny day, Brighton supporters occupied the uncovered Clock End with the Wednesday faithful on the Highbury North Bank. It was the Yorkshire fans who made most of the noise prior to the match, but as Albion ran out in their all-yellow strip the Seagull supporters released hundreds of blue, white and yellow balloons to steal their rivals' thunder.

In a splendid attacking game, Albion took the lead on fourteen minutes through Jimmy Case, who beat Bob Bolder with a swerving shot from 35 yards in-off the bar for his fourth goal in four Cup games. Albion continued to dominate until half time, but Wednesday came back strongly in the second half and equalised on 57 minutes when Ante Mirocevic scrambled the ball over the line. Both sides then threw everything at each

Wembley, here we come
Michael Robinson, supported by Gordon Smith, turns and fires home the winning goal in the semi-final against Sheffield Wednesday to secure the club's first-ever visit to the famous old stadium.

Around 26,000 fans made the trip to Highbury for the semi-final in five charter trains and 113 coaches, but a single coach-load of just 30 supporters made the trip to Sunderland the following Tuesday evening. The loyal fans were rewarded with a guarantee of tickets for the Cup final.

other and Steve Foster, playing with a poisoned elbow, was magnificent at repelling the Owls' attacks. The tie was decided in the 78th minute. Jimmy Case put Gordon Smith through, but his shot was blocked by Bolder. The ball rebounded back to the Scot who passed inside to Michael Robinson. Albion's centre-forward seemed to take an age to turn and shoot, but his effort was good enough to beat the desperate attempt of Mel Sterland to save on the line. It was then down to Graham Moseley to produce a great save from Mike Lyons to confirm the Seagulls' first visit to Wembley. George Courtney's final whistle signalled the start of tremendous Albion celebrations before thoughts turned to the forthcoming clash with Manchester United who had beaten Arsenal 2–1 at Villa Park.

The run-up to the big day was far from smooth, though. There was a relegation battle to fight – a battle which was lost two weeks before the final – and there was Steve Foster's impending suspension. A booking for dissent at Notts County meant the skipper would miss Albion's attempt to become the first side to win the Cup in a relegation season. An appeal to the F.A. was in vain and so the club took action in the High Court, on the grounds that the ban was against the Association's own rules because representations were not allowed. Foster thus became only the third footballer to take the F.A. to court, following in the footsteps of George Eastham and Ernie Machin. On 16 May, Mr Justice Vinelott decided that the rules were 'fair and consistent', and that any interference on his part would destroy the basis of the competition and would be unfair to other clubs. After all, United would be without Remi Moses and Norwich had been without Steve Walford for the same reason. Foster thus lost his case and decided not to appeal.

Two days later Melia announced his team which was largely as expected; only Jimmy Case and Tony Grealish had played at Wembley before. The only surprise in United's side was the inclusion of the inexperienced Alan Davies. Going for their fifth F.A. Cup triumph, United, who had finished third in Division One, fielded nine full internationals in their line-up.

Brighton and Hove Albion: Graham Moseley; Chris Ramsey; Graham Pearce; Tony Grealish (capt.); Gary Stevens; Steve Gatting; Jimmy Case; Gary Howlett; Michael Robinson; Gordon Smith; Neil Smillie; sub. Gerry Ryan.

Manchester United: Gary Bailey; Mike Duxbury; Arthur Albiston; Ray Wilkins; Kevin Moran; Gordon McQueen; Bryan Robson (captain); Arnold Muhren; Frank Stapleton; Norman Whiteside; Alan Davies; sub. Ashley Grimes.

Amid criticism of Albion's 25,000-ticket allocation, the following figures were released: 16,500 to season-ticket holders, and Christmas and Stoke City match-voucher holders; 1,750 to new season-ticket holders for 1983–84; 1,750 to players, officials and staff; 4,200 to fund-raising agents and sponsors; and 800 sundries to fans outside the Sussex area. None were released for general sale.

On the Friday, Albion left for an overnight stop at Selsdon Park near Croydon. They awoke on Saturday morning to headlines such as 'Landslide Ahead!' in the *Daily Express*, which predicted the most one-sided final for years because of the limitations of the Albion defence. 'The Joke's on You, Jimmy!', screamed the *Sun*. The *Daily Mail* reckoned Brighton's only chance was a flaw in the United performance. The betting public backed the Press's view: United were firm favourites at 3/1 on; Albion were 9/4 and the draw was 11/4. Favourite results were 1–0 or 2–0 wins for the Red Devils, while a 2–2 draw was 20/1 and a 3–2 Albion victory was 50/1. The winners would also, of course, have a place in the following season's European Cup-Winners' Cup.

THE 1983 F.A. CUP FINAL — THEIR GREATEST DAY

The Seagulls flew to the stadium by helicopter, courtesy of sponsors British Caledonian, to greet the main accumulation of Albion fans in the upper tier of the tunnel end, which was a riot of blue and white; the lower tier was distinctly red though, and other pockets of United fans fuelled speculation about the destination of some tickets. After 'Abide with Me', the teams came out to a thunderous roar with stand-in skipper Tony Grealish sporting a white headband, a mark of sympathy for the suspended Foster.

At 3 p.m. the great moment came as Great Yarmouth's Alf Grey signalled United to kick off towards their own supporters. In the first minute Michael Robinson nearly latched onto a short back-pass; after a week of rain the pitch cut up quickly and the ball often held up in the wetter parts. It was all United for the first ten minutes, but there was no direct threat to Graham Moseley's goal. Albion launched their first attack on twelve minutes and won a corner. The ball was not effectively cleared and fell to Steve Gatting. It then went via Tony Grealish and Neil Smillie to Gary Howlett near the right corner of the

penalty area who floated a delicate cross towards the far post. Gordon Smith got his head to the ball before Kevin Moran and sent it beyond Gary Bailey's reach into the far corner of the net: Albion 1 Manchester United 0, with thirteen minutes on the watch!

United soon regained their territorial dominance and a terrific scramble in front of goal on eighteen minutes was their first real threat. Moseley made his first real save, from Frank Stapleton, in the 28th minute and United were now putting considerable pressure on a Brighton defence that was confounding the critics. The closest shave yet came on 31 minutes when Chris Ramsey headed off the line from Gordon McQueen and Bryan Robson's follow-up was well saved by Moseley. Five minutes from the break Albion nearly went 2–0 up as Neil Smillie put in a similar cross to Howlett's and Bailey was forced to palm over from Robinson. There was a definite weakness in the heart of the United defence and, with one goal scored via that route already, there lay Albion's best chance. Tony Grealish hit another cross diagonally across the box; Moran and McQueen

Hero ...
Gordon Smith rises behind Kevin Moran to head Gary Howlett's pinpoint cross into the far corner of the United net to give Albion the lead.

both left it and Steve Gatting just failed at the far post. At half time it was Ron Atkinson who hurried his players into the dressing-room while the blue-and-white flags flew. It had been an entertaining 45 minutes played at a fast pace.

The second half opened with Norman Whiteside beating Chris Ramsey and shooting into the net, but Alf Grey spotted the Irishman's handball. After seven minutes of fairly even play, Whiteside went in high on Ramsey's shin as the Albion full-back cleared, and then trod on his ankle. The referee had a strong word with the United forward but did not signal a foul. Ramsey received attention from Mike Yaxley but was in obvious difficulty from a twisted ankle and, two minutes later, was unable to challenge for a far-post ball which Frank Stapleton fired into the net for the equaliser. Chris was immediately replaced by Gerry Ryan; the Irish international forward let nobody down in his emergency role as full-back, and was soon holding off Frank Stapleton to feed the ball back to Moseley.

In the fastest-flowing final for many years, United still had the majority of possession although Albion also threatened. After 71 minutes Arnold Muhren found Ray Wilkins on the United right with a long cross-field ball. Cutting inside Graham Pearce, the England midfielder hit a left-foot curler from the edge of the box around a despairing Moseley and into the left corner of the net for a tremendous goal. The Wembley stands were now a sea of red and white. With one hand on the Cup, surely United would not let go now.

United kept up the pressure for the next ten minutes as Albion desperately tried to mount an attack, but on 86 minutes

the Seagulls won a corner. Jimmy Case played the ball to Tony Grealish on the edge of the area who sent a speculative low ball into the box. Gary Stevens controlled the ball near the penalty spot and fired it into the net from ten yards without a United challenge. The Albion supporters and team all went wild with delight. What a time to score your first goal of the season! Another six minutes were played, but when Mr Grey blew his whistle for time it was the United players who looked the more tired after a match of sustained pace and excitement. The Reds had had sixteen goal attempts to the Blues' eight, but the score was 2–2 and extra time was required. Albion had certainly confounded the pundits.

With the sun now shining brightly, Albion attacked the tunnel end. Although the pace inevitably slowed, both sides played attacking football but neither managed a direct attempt on goal in the first half of extra time.

The teams changed round for the last fifteen minutes, and the majority of the Manchester players now had their socks rolled down with only Gary Howlett looking similarly tired for the Albion. For ten minutes it was all United, but good work by Stevens and Gatting prevented a goal. With two minutes remaining, Norman Whiteside again netted after handling. Into the last minute and a long ball from Kevin Moran was intercepted by Graham Pearce for Jimmy Case to chip a through-ball for Michael Robinson to chase. Albion's hard-running centre-forward shrugged off Moran and then held the ball back to beat McQueen. Now inside the penalty area, 'Robbo' passed across the box to the unmarked Gordon Smith, ten yards

... or villain?
The last minute of extra-time and Gordon Smith has the chance to win the Cup for Albion, but Gary Bailey is poised to make an excellent save.

from goal. 'And Smith must score!', declared radio commentator Peter Jones as the Scot trapped the ball and fired his shot. Alas! the ball struck the legs of the oncoming Gary Bailey as he spread himself and the grateful 'keeper dived on the ball to prevent Smith getting to the rebound. Twenty-one seconds later the final whistle went. It was probably the most memorable and most talked-about incident in the club's history. Smith – certainly according to all Albion fans present – should have scored, but it was, in truth, an excellent save by the United goalkeeper.

Thus Albion failed to take the Cup and land a place in Europe by the width of Gary Bailey's leg, but a splendid match

In the run-up to the Cup final, Albion released a second record, 'The Boys in the Old Brighton Blue', again on Howard Kruger's Energy Records label. The flip-side was a solo by Gordon Smith, 'When Seagulls are Flying'. In August 1983 the club received a 'silver disc' for its sales. Local songster Johnny Wakelin released 'Where Seagulls Fly' in April.

had enjoyed two dramatic climaxes from the Seagulls, who had showed themselves to be Manchester United's equals on the day, and the two teams ran a deserved lap of honour together.

HONOUR IN DEFEAT — THE REPLAY

Albion flew home that evening by helicopter to a celebration banquet at the Brighton Centre. Curiously, although Wembley's night-time capacity was reduced to 92,000, Albion's ticket allocation was actually increased to 30,000. Fans queueing for replay tickets the following day, were disappointed to read a story in the *Evening Argus* that former Manchester City boss John Bond could well become Brighton manager with Melia stepping down to no.2, a rumour vigorously denied by Mike Bamber.

Most of the media's interest concerned Gary Stevens, who had been voted Man of the Match. His future was being openly discussed, although he had no desire to leave. Melia also had a selection problem: Ramsey was injured and Foster was available for the replay, but who should play right-back? The obvious answer was to switch Stevens from the centre, but Gary had played so well in the no.5 shirt. Melia's solution was to play Gatting, a decidedly left-footed player, at right-back with Foster and Stevens in the centre. United were unchanged.

Thursday, 26 May, and 92,000 fans assembled for the third F.A. Cup final replay in a row. This time both tiers at the tunnel end were full of blue-and-white colours. Albion kicked off and enjoyed plenty of the early play, but Foster's white headband was prominent in the Albion box clearing several crosses. With 25 minutes gone it was clear that Albion had come to attack this time, but it was Manchester who took the lead when Arthur Albiston hit a low cross into the left side of the penalty area. Alan Davies laid the ball back to Bryan Robson on the edge of the box and the England international shot through Graham Pearce's legs and past an unsighted Graham Moseley into the far right-hand corner. Four minutes later Albion went 2–0 down when a Davies cross from the left was headed past Moseley by an unmarked Norman Whiteside eight yards out.

With the fillip of a two-goal lead, it was all United now. They were much more purposeful than on Saturday, and McQueen and Moran looked steadier. For Albion, Jimmy Case was playing better than in the first match and he nearly reduced the lead a few minutes from the break with a 25-yard rocket that deflected up off Kevin Moran; Gary Bailey, already moving for the ball, was forced to leap backwards and just managed to palm it over the bar at full stretch. Albion's chances disappeared with that splendid save as, on 44 minutes, United went three-up courtesy of Robson, who fired home at the far post after the ball was headed back across goal by Frank Stapleton. Wembley was now a sea of red as the teams went off for the interval. Albion had had five goal attempts to United's six but were 3–0 down and out of it.

The second half was without any real meaning, although both teams still strived for goals. 'Stevie Foster, what a difference you have made!' sang a cruel red army, but perhaps they were right and the splitting of Stevens and Gatting had been wrong. United increased their lead on 62 minutes when Arnold Muhren scored from the spot after Stevens had held Robson.

The pace was relentless and on 74 minutes Gerry Ryan came on for the tiring Gary Howlett. The Seagull fans ought to have been as quiet as mice at 4–0 down — not a bit of it! The Albion masses were out-singing their red rivals, just as they had on Saturday, and blue-and-white banners and flags were flying around the stadium. 'We're proud of you', they sang, and they could also take pride in their own performance amid such adversity. At the final whistle the Brighton players sank to their knees. It may have been the largest winning margin ever at Wembley, but it was, after all, a replay after Albion went so close on Saturday, and the two matches had produced the most open, entertaining and exciting final for many years. The team's performance, and that of its supporters, brought only credit to the name of Brighton and Hove Albion, and they were far from disgraced in front of a huge, worldwide TV audience.

Bryan Robson led his side up the steps to collect the trophy from H.R.H. Princess Michael of Kent, then Steve Foster led his weary troops up to collect their runner's-up medals. Behind him came Gatting, Smillie, Smith, Moseley, Ryan, Stevens, Pearce, Grealish, Case, Howlett and Robinson, the last two sobbing uncontrollably. They then found the energy for a well-deserved final lap of honour. The heavens opened the following evening (Friday), but the wet weather did not prevent around 40,000 fans from singing the praises of their team on a tour of the twin towns before a civic reception at Hove Town Hall.

The repercussions of the F.A. Cup final were to drag on for some time as various claims were made over how Albion had benefited financially. The club said that it took £384,000 from both games, £160,000 of which had gone to the players in bonuses. Seven years later Ron Pavey was still having to deny that Albion gave more than 1,000 tickets to United. But the biggest question at the end of a dramatic season was: Could Albion keep their star players and their magnificent Cup-final support to bounce straight back into Division One?

Thanks for the memory
Jimmy Case, Gerry Ryan, Gordon Smith, Neil Smillie and Michael Robinson lead the way on a final lap of honour. Although well beaten in the end, Albion were far from disgraced and received a tremendous ovation from all in the stadium for their performance over the two games.

SEASON 1983–84

For the first time since 1968–69, Albion played out a season largely in mid table with no real incentive, but it was far from dull. As the F.A. Cup final faded into memory, the board felt it necessary to sell some prized assets. Despite a trading profit of £332,000 in the previous year, the club could no longer support the lucrative, long-term contracts of the last few years in the top flight – the wage-bill had risen to over £1·2 million – and so Gary Stevens moved to Tottenham Hotspur for £300,000, Michael Robinson went to Liverpool for £200,000, and Neil McNab was sold to Manchester City for just £30,000. In came a new centre-forward, Sheffield United's Alan Young, for £140,000 and midfielder Dean Wilkins, the younger brother of Manchester United's Ray, from Queen's Park Rangers.

Back at the club after three years out of the game was Albion's former full-back Chris Cattlin, who was appointed chief coach by Mike Bamber in July while Jimmy Melia was on holiday. Cattlin and Melia were to liaise on team matters, with George Aitken concentrating on scouting and Sammy Nelson managing the reserves. The appointment of Cattlin was seen as an attempt to strengthen club discipline in the relaxed atmosphere under Melia, but would the manager and his new coach get along? The answer was an emphatic No.

In July tragedy struck the club when vice-chairman Keith Wickenden was killed in a plane crash at Shoreham. The two remaining directors, Mike Bamber and Tom Appleby, were joined before the end of the year by local businessmen Bryan Bedson and John Campbell, and by the former England manager Ron Greenwood, a local resident.

After a trip to Majorca and a clash with the fabulous Real Madrid – Albion lost narrowly 1–0 – the real action began with defeats at Oldham Athletic and Leeds United. The next fixture was a first-ever League meeting with Chelsea. Alan Young made his début, but the match will be remembered for events other than the Scot's brilliant scissor-kick goal in a 2–1 Albion defeat. Friday night saw running battles between Chelsea followers, police and local youths, and the game was played in a brooding atmosphere before 20,874 people, 8,000 of them from London. Chelsea supporters infiltrated all parts of the ground, and at the final whistle the hooligans invaded the pitch from all unfenced areas to launch a vicious attack on the hopelessly outnumbered police. By the time a police horse had managed to clear the pitch, seven constables were injured and the north goal was broken. It was the worst outbreak of violence ever seen at the Goldstone; the 1978 Spurs match was described as 'trivial' in comparison. The Minister of Sport, Neil Macfarlane, called for reports and both clubs were charged by the F.A. but cleared of blame. However, the Chelsea left-back, Chris Hutchings, was charged with threatening and abusive behaviour for swearing at police trying to clear the pitch. The forthcoming match with Portsmouth, also seen as a potentially explosive encounter, was rapidly made all-ticket with the North and North-East Terraces allocated to Pompey fans.

Albion lifted the gloom with wins over Derby County and Swansea City, and Melia brought in former England 'keeper Joe Corrigan for £20,000 from Seattle Sounders to bolster the last line of defence. However, the club's state of affairs prompted a takeover campaign by two local impresarios, Jeffrey Kruger and son Howard, and their associate Jon Rosemann. 'Brighton F.C. not Bamber F.C.' was their slogan as they demanded to know where the club's Wembley profits had gone; where were the new North Stand, better facilities for spectators and the accommodation for the Supporters' Club? The 'Stop the Rot' campaign claimed substantial American backing, but the Albion board completely rejected the approach.

Unbeaten Charlton Athletic arrived at the Goldstone on 1 October, but a quite brilliant Albion display sent them packing 7–0; Jimmy Case stole the show with a hattrick, and Terry Connor won over his Goldstone detractors with a tremendous performance. The takeover group's proposed demonstration fizzled out, but when it later emerged that it was Cattlin who had decided upon both

Day of shame
Chelsea thugs invade the Goldstone pitch on 3 September to launch a vicious attack on the police. It was the worst outbreak of spectator violence ever seen at the ground and, thankfully, one of the last. By the late 1980s, the 20-year-old cancer of hooliganism had largely been excised from matches at Hove.

SEASON 1983–84

Date	Comp.	Ven.	Opponents	Result	HT	Pos.	Scorers	Atten.	Case J	Connor T	Corrigan J	Digweed P	Foster S	Gatting S	Grealish A	Howlett G	Hutchings C	Jones M	Kraay H	Lambert M	Moseley G	Muir I	O'Regan K	Pearce G	Penney S	Ramsey C	Ring M	Ryan G	Smillie N	Smith G	Steele S	Stille G	Wilkins D	Wilson D	Young A	Young E	Young W
Aug 27	FL D2	(a)	Oldham Athletic	L 0–1	0–0	15=		5,750	7	10			5	6	4	8†					1		2	3				9	11	12							
29	FL D2	(a)	Leeds United	L 2–3	1–2	20	Grealish, Connor	13,303	7	10			5	6	4	N				9			2	3					11	8	1						
Sep 3	FL D2	(h)	Chelsea	L 1–2	0–1	21	A Young	20,874	7	10		1	5	6	4†					12			2	3					11	8					9		
6	FL D2	(h)	Derby County	W 1–0	1–0	18	Smith (pen)	10,891	7	10		1	5	6		4							2	3					11	8					9	N	
10	FL D2	(a)	Swansea City	W 3–1	2–0	12	A Young, Connor 2	7,643	7	10		1	5	6	12	4†							2	3					11	8					9		
17	FL D2	(h)	Carlisle United	D 1–1	0–1	11	Own goal	11,735	7	10	1		5	6	4†	12							2	3					11	8					9		
24	FL D2	(a)	Blackburn Rovers	D 2–2	1–1	12	Case, Smith (pen)	5,060	7	10	1			6	4	12							2	3					11†	8					9	5	
Oct 1	FL D2	(h)	Charlton Athletic	W 7–0	5–0	9	Ryan 2, Smith, Case 3, Connor	11,517	7†	10	1			6	4	11							2	3			12	9		8						5	
4	FLC R2 Lg1	(h)	Bristol Rovers	W 4–2	2–2	–	Ryan, Connor, Smith 2	9,417	7	10	1			6	4	11							2	3			N	9		8						5	
8	FL D2	(h)	Portsmouth	L 0–1	0–1	12		17,582	7	10	1				4	11							2	3			12	9		8		6†				5	
15	FL D2	(a)	Grimsby Town	L 0–5	0–3	14		5,469	7	10	1			6		11							2	3		4†		9		8		12				5	
22	FL D2	(h)	Sheffield Wed.	L 1–3	0–2	16	Ryan	14,827	7	10	1			6	4	N							2	3				9	11	8						5	
25	FLC R2 Lg2	(a)	Bristol Rovers	L 1–2*	0–1	–	Connor	9,936	7	10	1			6	4								2	3				9	11	12					8	5†	
29	FL D2	(a)	Cambridge United	W 4–3	3–1	14	A Young 2, Grealish, Pearce	3,905	7	10	1			6	4								2	3				9	11†	12					8	5	
Nov 5	FL D2	(h)	Huddersfield Town	W 3–1	0–1	12	Gatting (pen), Connor, A Young	11,063		10	1			6	4	11							7	3		2		9		N					8	5	
8	FLC R3	(a)	West Ham United	L 0–1	0–0	–		17,082		10	1			6	4	11							7	3		2		9		12					8†	5	
12	FL D2	(a)	Manchester City	L 0–4	0–3	16		24,562	5	10	1			6	4	11							7	3		2		9†		12					8		
19	FL D2	(h)	Shrewsbury Town	D 2–2	1–0	16	Connor, A Young	9,746	8	10†	1			6	4	11							7	3		2	12								9	5	
26	FL D2	(a)	Barnsley	L 1–3	1–3	17	A Young	7,705	8	10†	1		5	6	4		3						11		7					12					9	2	
Dec 3	FL D2	(h)	Cardiff City	W 3–1	1–0	14	Wilson 2, Connor	9,924	8	10	1		5	6	4†		3						2		12			11						7	9		
10	FL D2	(a)	Middlesbrough	D 0–0	0–0	14		6,037	8	10	1		5	6			3						2		11			9†					4	7	12		
17	FL D2	(h)	Newcastle United	L 0–1	0–0	14		13,896		10	1		5	6	4†		3			9			2		11			12					8	7			
26	FL D2	(a)	Crystal Palace	W 2–0	0–0	12	Wilson, Smillie	13,781	8	10	1		5		2		3						N		11			9	4					7		6	
27	FL D2	(h)	Fulham	D 1–1	0–0	14	Ryan	15,076	8	10	1		5				3		2						11			9	4					7	N	6	
31	FL D2	(a)	Chelsea	L 0–1	0–0	14		18,542	8	10	1			6	2		3								11			9	4					7	N	5	
Jan 2	FL D2	(h)	Blackburn Rovers	D 1–1	0–1	14	Wilson (pen)	9,844	8	10	1		5	6	2		3								11				4					7	9	N	
7	FAC R3	(h)	Swansea City	W 2–0	0–0	–	Own goal, Connor	11,330	8	10	1		5	6	2		3								11			12					4	7	9†		
14	FL D2	(h)	Oldham Athletic	W 4–0	1–0	13	Connor, Wilson, Ryan, Foster	10,203		10	1		5	6		4			12				2		11			9	8					7†		3	
21	FL D2	(a)	Carlisle United	W 2–1	2–0	10	Wilson, Connor	5,169		10	1			5		8	3						2		11			9	4					7	N	6	
29	FAC R4	(h)	Liverpool	W 2–0	0–0	–	Ryan, Connor	19,057		10	1		5	3	4		2								11			9	8					7	N	6	
Feb 4	FL D2	(a)	Charlton Athletic	L 0–2	0–0	10		7,435		10	1		5	3	4		2								11			9	8					7	N	6	
11	FL D2	(h)	Swansea City	D 1–1	0–0	11	Gatting	11,979	N	10	1		5	3	4		2								11			9	8					7		6	
18	FAC R5	(a)	Watford	L 1–3	0–2	–	Wilson (pen)	28,000	12	10	1		5	3	4		2								11			9†	8					7		6	
25	FL D2	(h)	Sheffield Wed.	L 1–2	0–1	13	O'Regan	21,614	8	10†	1			6	4		3		12				2		11									7	9	5	
28	FL D2	(h)	Cambridge United	W 3–0	2–0	11	Connor, Gatting, Wilson	8,167	4	10	1			6	12		3						2		11				8					7	9	5†	
Mar 3	FL D2	(a)	Huddersfield Town	W 1–0	1–0	9	A Young	6,985	4	10	1			6	8	11	3						2		12									7	9†	5	
10	FL D2	(h)	Manchester City	D 1–1	0–0	10	Grealish	14,132	4	10†	1				8	11	3						2		12									7	9	5	6
17	FL D2	(a)	Derby County	W 3–0	0–0	10	Penney, A Young, Smith	11,560	4			1				8	3						2		11				N	10				7	9	5	6
24	FL D2	(h)	Leeds United	W 3–0	2–0	9	Wilson (pen), E Young, Connor	12,605	4	10	1						3					N	2		11				8					7	9	5	6
31	FL D2	(a)	Portsmouth	L 1–5	1–0	9	Wilson (pen)	12,724	4	10	1			5			3		N			9	2		11				8					7			6
Apr 7	FL D2	(h)	Grimsby Town	W 2–0	1–0	9	A Young 2	10,610	4	10†	1			6			3	2							11			12	8					7	9	5	
14	FL D2	(a)	Shrewsbury Town	L 1–2	0–1	9	E Young	3,332	4		1			6			3	2				10			11†			12	8					7	9	5	
21	FL D2	(h)	Crystal Palace	W 3–1	2–0	9	A Young, Connor, E Young	15,214	4	10	1			6			3						2		11			12	8†					7	9	5	
23	FL D2	(a)	Fulham	L 1–3	0–3	9	Connor	7,742	4	10	1			6			3		N				2		11			8						7	9	5	
28	FL D2	(h)	Barnsley	W 1–0	0–0	9	Gatting	8,955		10	1			6		4	3	2	12						11				8†					7	9	5	
May 5	FL D2	(a)	Cardiff City	D 2–2	0–1	9	Hutchings, Wilson	4,366	4	10	1			6			3	2					12	8	11†									7	9	5	
7	FL D2	(h)	Middlesbrough	W 3–0	1–0	8	Smillie, Own goal, E Young	9,168	4	10	1						3	2	6				N	11				9	8					7		5	
12	FL D2	(a)	Newcastle United	L 1–3	1–1	9	Ryan	36,415	4	10†	1			6			3	2						11				8	12					7	9	5	
							League appearances		35	40	36	4	16	35	23	15	26	6	2	2	1	2	30	18	22	4	0	20	25	11	1	1	2	26	25	30	4
							Substitute appearances								2	2			3	1			1		3		3	4	1	4		1			1		
							League goals	OG – 2	4	13			1	4	3		1						1	1	1			6	2	4				10	12	4	

Notes: Oct 25 – after extra time (90-minute score 0–2).
The Football League was sponsored as the Canon League, and the Football League Cup was sponsored as the Milk Cup.

Canon League Division 2 1983–84

		P	W	D	L	F	A	W	D	L	F	A	Pts
1.	Chelsea	42	15	4	2	55	17	10	9	2	35	23	88
2.	Sheffield Wednesday	42	16	4	1	47	16	10	6	5	25	18	88
3.	Newcastle United	42	16	2	3	51	18	8	6	7	34	35	80
4.	Manchester City	42	13	3	5	43	21	7	7	7	23	27	70
5.	Grimsby Town	42	13	6	2	36	15	6	7	8	24	32	70
6.	Blackburn Rovers	42	9	11	1	35	19	8	5	8	22	27	67
7.	Carlisle United	42	10	9	2	29	13	6	7	8	19	28	64
8.	Shrewsbury Town	42	13	5	3	34	18	4	5	12	15	35	61
9.	**ALBION**	42	11	6	4	42	17	6	3	12	27	43	60
10.	Leeds United	42	13	4	4	33	16	3	8	10	22	40	60
11.	Fulham	42	9	6	6	35	24	6	6	9	25	29	57
12.	Huddersfield Town	42	8	6	7	27	20	6	9	6	29	29	57
13.	Charlton Athletic	42	13	4	4	40	26	3	5	13	13	38	57
14.	Barnsley	42	9	6	6	33	23	6	1	14	24	30	52
15.	Cardiff City	42	11	3	7	32	27	4	3	14	21	39	51
16.	Portsmouth	42	8	3	10	46	32	6	4	11	27	32	49
17.	Middlesbrough	42	9	8	4	26	18	2	5	13	15	29	49
18.	Crystal Palace	42	8	5	8	18	18	4	6	11	24	34	47
19.	Oldham Athletic	42	10	6	5	33	27	3	2	16	14	46	47
20.	Derby County	42	9	5	7	26	26	2	4	15	10	46	42
21.	Swansea City	42	7	4	10	20	28	0	4	17	16	57	29
22.	Cambridge United	42	4	7	10	20	33	0	5	16	8	44	24

An anonymous supporter took out a four-page advert in the *Evening Argus* on 2 September appealing for more support and, in particular, for more vocal support; he wanted the game the following day to be a fun afternoon for everyone. He should not have wasted his money — it was the Chelsea match!

the tactics and the line-up, questions were asked about Jimmy Melia's position. Bamber confirmed that Melia was team manager, but Cattlin continued to pick the side, a selection that lost 5–0 at Grimsby just two weeks later.

Melia could take no more and resigned on 19 October. The man who took the team to Wembley in May had only seven League victories under his belt in ten months and, although not on contract, was reported to have received £15,000 in compensation. The parting was not amicable: the tabloid Press carried spiteful quotes by Melia against Cattlin, while Bamber countered with allegations that his former manager was a 'mole' for the takeover group. Cattlin was put in charge of all team matters, but the next match, a 3–1 defeat by Division Two leaders Sheffield Wednesday, was notable mainly for Melia's appearance on the North Terrace to the acclaim of the fans there. As he was chaired shoulder-high the chants rang out – 'Melia in, Bamber out!' – but the former manager lost a good deal of sympathy with his farcical display amongst Albion's noisiest supporters.

Cattlin was soon confirmed as manager with Sammy Nelson as his assistant, and he began rebuilding in November. In came

Albion's new shirts, bearing the name of the Phoenix Brewery Company, made their début at home to Portsmouth in October. The £30,000 sponsorship was seen as a natural extension to the brewery's five-year-old association with the club in a coaching scheme for schools, but it was also a tie-up with a long-standing supporter of the Albion. As Tamplins Brewery, the company had been a shareholder of the club from 1904 until the boardroom buy-up of 1977 and had also held shares in Brighton United.

Albion 1983–84

Back row left to right: Terry Connor, Gary Howlett, Gerry Ryan, Giles Stille, Graham Pearce, Kieran O'Regan, Chris Ramsey.
Middle row left to right: Mike Yaxley (physio), George Aitken (assistant manager), Gordon Smith, Graham Moseley, Perry Digweed, Sammy Nelson, Chris Cattlin (coach), Glen Wilson (equipment manager).
Seated left to right: Steve Foster (captain), Jimmy Case, Tony Grealish, Jimmy Melia (manager), Steve Gatting, Michael Robinson, Neil Smillie.

Steve Penney (Ballymena United), Chris Hutchings (Chelsea) and Danny Wilson (on loan from Nottingham Forest), three players who went on to give splendid service although Hutchings, of course, still had an appointment at Hove Magistrates Court. Another arrival was Dutch trialist Hans Kraay who was the subject of a lengthy ban in his home country.

Results continued to be mixed and the club hovered around fourteenth place, but chairman Mike Bamber put himself firmly behind the new manager with an article in the club programme: 'We probably had our success too fast; the solid foundations and right base from which to progress long-term weren't established, so we have decided to rebuild for the future.' Cattlin was offered a three-year contract in December but rejected it: he was eager to prove himself first and would review the situation in May.

The team had to settle for a mid-table spot in the New Year, but the personnel changes continued. The impressive Danny Wilson signed for £45,000, but several experienced – and highly paid – players left. With the emergence of Eric Young, signed from Slough Town by Mike Bailey in 1982, the obvious rift between Cattlin and Steve Foster was finally resolved when the latter was transferred to Aston Villa in March. He was soon followed by Tony Grealish (to West Bromwich Albion) and Gordon Smith (to Manchester City). The disciplinary record was of some concern: Steve Gatting, Alan Young, Eric Young, Chris Hutchings and Jimmy Case were all sent off before the New Year. Case won the Player of the Season award and Terry Connor was top scorer with seventeen League and Cup goals. Gates were down by over 2,000 on 1982–83 at 12,286.

After a rather fortunate, two-legged victory over Bristol Rovers, Albion's Milk Cup hopes were dashed by a single goal at First Division West Ham United. However, the club's new-found tradition in the F.A. Cup was maintained as Albion despatched Swansea City 2–0 to set up a fourth-round Goldstone tie with — Liverpool! Hopes of another victory over the League champions aroused great interest both locally and nationally, and the match was switched to the Sunday for live television coverage (which somewhat reduced the attendance). The League-leaders had ex-Seagulls Mark Lawrenson and Michael Robinson in their ranks, but once again Albion rose to the occasion. Joe Corrigan and Steve Foster were magnificent as Liverpool dominated before the break, but Brighton took the lead on 57 minutes when Gerry Ryan ran through a square defence to clip the ball past Bruce Grobbelaar. Unbelievably, just a minute later, it was Terry Connor's turn, clean through and firing past the startled Grobbelaar from the edge of the penalty area. Twice in the First Division Albion had allowed Liverpool to come back from 2–0 down, but this time the team deservedly held on to win the tie.

The fifth round saw an all-ticket clash at First Division Watford, but the 6,500 Albion fans in the capacity 28,000 crowd were dismayed to watch an Albion performance that threatened only briefly when Danny Wilson's penalty reduced the deficit to 2–1. Thus the previous season's losing finalists went out 3–1 to this year's runners-up, the Hornets progressing to their first final only to lose 2–0 to Everton.

The events of a season of turmoil took their toll on chairman Mike Bamber who suffered a heart-attack at the end of March, and there was further pressure on him in June 1984 when director Ron Greenwood resigned. A month later, at a meeting on 24 July with fellow board members Tom Appleby, Bryan Bedson and John Campbell, Bamber resigned as chairman and director of the club 'as a result of major and mutual disagreements on policy.' It was the end of an era. Sole chairman since November 1973, Bamber's forceful and dynamic personality, and his ambition for the club, had led Albion to unprecedented success, but all good things come to an end and many supporters agreed it was time for a change. There was also sadness on 3 April 1984 when Joe Wilson, a much-loved servant of the Albion for 38 years from 1936 until 1974, passed away.

SEASON 1984–85

The new club chairman was 46-year-old printing-company director Bryan Bedson, and he was joined by four new directors: Peter Kent, Richard Crown, Ray Bloom (son of former vice-chairman Harry Bloom) and former director Dudley Sizen. The newly constituted board inherited debts in the region of £1·3 million and a loss running at £13,000 a week. By January 1985 Mike Bamber was prompted to launch his own takeover bid, but the matter was resolved amicably in March with all shares back in the hands of the board. However, the massive debt spawned by the sky-high expenditure of the glory years was to weigh heavily on the club in the seasons to come.

The main summer signings were veteran ex-England striker Frank Worthington (Southampton), who was joining his eighth Football League club, and midfielder-cum-defender Steve Jacobs (Coventry City). For the first time in 27 years Albion won their opening fixture away from home, 3–0 at Carlisle, and after nine games the club was in fifth place. Graham Moseley, still on the free-transfer list, was back to his best between the posts and went on to play in every game. In the centre of defence were Eric Young and, on loan from Newcastle United, Jeff Clarke, but supporters were astonished to find that hard-up Albion were apparently unable to afford a £7,500 down-payment for the experienced Clarke. Gary O'Reilly, who had arrived from Spurs for £45,000 a few weeks earlier, then switched from full-back to central defence to form a sound partnership with Young. Alan Young was sold to Notts County for £50,000 in September to ease the financial position, while another £30,000 came in as Birmingham City signed full-back Mark Jones with striker Mike Ferguson travelling to the Goldstone.

Despite the cash limitations, the playing side of the club was now healthy and Chris Cattlin felt the time was right to sign a three-year contract. However, the worst run of the season followed and Terry Connor's goal at Oxford was the club's last for 589 minutes of play until he scored again in the 2–1 home defeat by Middlesbrough. A goal-less draw with Barnsley was so bad that Cattlin fined himself a week's wages! It was also a terrible way to inaugurate the splendid, 6,000-capacity North Stand, built at a cost of £200,000 but a much simpler design than had been planned a few years earlier, in effect just a roof. The one bright spot was the full-international début of Steve Penney, the first of seventeen caps for Northern Ireland the young winger would win while at the Goldstone, a club record.

The spell was broken at Molineux on 1 December when Eric Young scored the only goal to maintain the Seagulls' 100-percent League record against Wolves. Albion then climbed back up the table with a fine second half to the season that saw only three more defeats. A happy Christmas was followed by an almost blank January, and on 9 February, with ice closing the East Terrace, the lowest home crowd for over eleven years, just 7,337, saw a 1–0 win over Cardiff City.

To strengthen the promotion push, Cattlin took Arsenal's eighteen-year-old reserve defender – and future England international – Martin Keown on loan, and then signed Portsmouth striker Alan Biley for £50,000 in March, but in a completely unexpected move Jimmy Case was sold to Southampton for £30,000 where he was to give over six years of excellent service in the First Division. The popular Case was the third member of the F.A. Cup final side to leave this season, Chris Ramsey having moved to Swindon Town on a free transfer and Gary Howlett having joined Bournemouth for £15,000,

Albion were in sixth position when they arrived at Selhurst Park at the start of April, but the 1–1 draw with lowly Crystal Palace will be remembered only for the sickening broken leg suffered by Gerry Ryan in an appalling tackle by Henry Hughton, who was immediately dismissed. To his eternal credit, Albion's genial Irishman refused to condemn Hughton, but he never played another game for the club.

The biggest home crowd of the season, 17,279, witnessed a draw with Leeds United that damaged both clubs' promotion chances, and when Albion lost for the first time since 2 February, at Middlesbrough, any hope of going up seemed to have disappeared with the Seagulls now seven points behind third-placed Manchester City. After despatching Wolves 5–1, Albion found renewed hope with the faltering progress of Blackburn Rovers and Manchester City, but nearly slipped up themselves at Grimsby: 2–0 down with fifteen minutes left, Hans Kraay scored the Seagulls' opening goal and the team then hit another three in a sensational last

Albion 1984–85

Back row left to right: Mark Jones, Steve Penney, Steve Jacobs, Alan Young, Graham Pearce, Kieran O'Regan, Gary Howlett.
Middle row left to right: Sammy Nelson (coach), Hans Kraay, Eric Young, Joe Corrigan, Perry Digweed, Frank Worthington, Terry Connor, George Petchey (assistant manager).
Seated left to right: Neil Smillie, Chris Hutchings, Jimmy Case (capt.), Chris Cattlin (man.), Steve Gatting, Gerry Ryan, Danny Wilson.

> In an effort to raise funds, Albion entered the mail-order business in conjunction with several other clubs in September, issuing a glossy, 64-page catalogue under the banner 'Family Focus'.

SEASON 1984–85

Date	Comp.	Ven.	Opponents	Result	HT	Pos.	Scorers	Atten.
Aug 25	FL D2	(a)	Carlisle United	W 3–0	3–0	1=	Connor, Penney, Wilson	4,721
28	FL D2	(h)	Notts County	W 2–1	1–0	1	Jacobs, Worthington	13,484
Sep 1	FL D2	(h)	Huddersfield Town	L 0–1	0–0	4=		12,493
8	FL D2	(a)	Cardiff City	W 4–2	2–0	4	Worthington, Connor, Penney, Howlett	4,634
15	FL D2	(h)	Crystal Palace	W 1–0	0–0	2	O'Reilly	15,044
22	FL D2	(a)	Oldham Athletic	L 0–1	0–1	7		3,368
25	FLC R2 Lg1	(h)	Aldershot	W 3–1	3–0	–	Connor 2, Worthington	8,024
29	FL D2	(h)	Fulham	W 2–0	0–0		Connor, Ryan	12,395
Oct 2	FL D2	(a)	Wimbledon	L 0–1	0–0	7		6,531
6	FL D2	(h)	Birmingham City	W 2–0	1–0	5	Jacobs, Penney	13,697
9	FLC R2 Lg2	(a)	Aldershot	L 0–3*	0–0	–		4,675
13	FL D2	(a)	Oxford United	L 1–2	1–1	5	Connor	10,581
20	FL D2	(h)	Barnsley	D 0–0	0–0	5		10,941
27	FL D2	(a)	Shrewsbury Town	D 0–0	0–0			4,524
Nov 3	FL D2	(h)	Manchester City	D 0–0	0–0	7		14,035
10	FL D2	(a)	Blackburn Rovers	L 0–2	0–0	11		7,341
17	FL D2	(a)	Leeds United	L 0–1	0–1	12		13,127
24	FL D2	(h)	Middlesbrough	L 1–2	0–0	12	Connor	9,083
Dec 1	FL D2	(a)	Wolverhampton W.	W 1–0	1–0	11	Young	7,463
8	FL D2	(h)	Grimsby Town	D 0–0	0–0	11		9,347
15	FL D2	(a)	Sheffield United	D 1–1	0–0	11	Connor	9,835
22	FL D2	(a)	Huddersfield Town	W 2–1	0–0	11	Ryan 2	6,876
26	FL D2	(h)	Portsmouth	D 1–1	1–1	11	Ryan	14,854
29	FL D2	(h)	Wimbledon	W 2–1	0–1	10	Wilson, Worthington	11,106
Jan 1	FL D2	(a)	Charlton Athletic	W 1–0	1–0	10	O'Reilly	7,249
5	FAC R3	(h)	Hull City	W 1–0	0–0	–	Hutchings	11,681
26	FAC R4	(a)	Barnsley	L 1–2	0–1	–	Ryan	8,860
Feb 2	FL D2	(a)	Fulham	L 0–2	0–0	12		6,990
5	FL D2	(h)	Carlisle United	W 4–1	1–0	8	Connor, Wilson (pen), Young, Ryan	7,610
9	FL D2	(h)	Cardiff City	W 1–0	0–0	7	Hutchings	7,337
23	FL D2	(a)	Manchester City	L 0–2	0–1	8		20,227
Mar 2	FL D2	(h)	Shrewsbury Town	W 1–0	0–0	8	Wilson (pen)	8,519
6	FL D2	(h)	Blackburn Rovers	W 3–1	1–0	5	Young, Connor 2	11,126
13	FL D2	(a)	Barnsley	D 0–0	0–0	6		5,342
16	FL D2	(h)	Oxford United	D 0–0	0–0	7		15,409
23	FL D2	(a)	Birmingham City	L 0–1	1–0	7	Worthington	8,983
29	FL D2	(h)	Oldham Athletic	W 2–0	0–0	6	Biley, Connor	10,005
Apr 2	FL D2	(a)	Crystal Palace	D 1–1	0–1	6	Wilson	8,025
6	FL D2	(a)	Portsmouth	D 1–1	1–1	6	Ferguson	22,867
8	FL D2	(h)	Charlton Athletic	W 2–1	0–1	6	Worthington (pen), Connor	12,036
14	FL D2	(a)	Notts County	W 2–1	0–0	6	O'Reilly, Kraay	4,671
20	FL D2	(h)	Leeds United	D 1–1	1–1	6	Biley	17,279
27	FL D2	(a)	Middlesbrough	L 1–2	1–2	7	Kraay	4,413
May 4	FL D2	(h)	Wolverhampton W.	W 5–1	3–1	7	Worthington 2 (1 pen), Penney, Biley, Connor	8,581
7	FL D2	(a)	Grimsby Town	W 4–2	0–1	7	Kraay, Biley, Connor 2	4,034
11	FL D2	(h)	Sheffield United	W 1–0	0–0	6	Own goal	13,184

Notes: Oct 9 – after extra time (90–minute score 0–2).

The Football League was sponsored as the Canon League, and the Football League Cup was sponsored as the Milk Cup.

	Biley A	Case J	Clarke J	Connor T	Ferguson M	Gatting S	Howlett G	Hutchings C	Jacobs S	Jones M	Keown M	Kraay H	Moseley G	Muir I	O'Regan K	O'Reilly G	Pearce G	Penney S	Ryan G	Smillie N	Wilson D	Worthington F	Young E
League appearances	12	21	4	37	8	8	6	42	18	3	16	17	42	1	11	36	24	24	17	15	38	27	35
Substitute appearances	1	3	1												1		1	4		2	5	9	4
League goals	OG – 1 / 4			14	1			1	1	2		3				3		4	5		5	7	3

Canon League Division 2 1984–85

	P	W	D	L	F	A	W	D	L	F	A	Pts
1. Oxford United	42	18	2	1	62	15	7	7	7	22	21	84
2. Birmingham City	42	12	6	3	30	15	13	1	7	29	18	82
3. Manchester City	42	14	4	3	42	16	7	7	7	24	24	74
4. Portsmouth	42	11	6	4	39	25	9	8	4	30	25	74
5. Blackburn Rovers	42	14	3	4	38	15	7	7	7	28	26	73
6. ALBION	42	13	6	2	31	11	7	6	8	23	23	72
7. Leeds United	42	12	7	2	37	11	7	5	9	29	32	69
8. Shrewsbury Town	42	12	6	3	45	22	6	5	10	21	31	65
9. Fulham	42	13	3	5	35	26	6	5	10	33	38	65
10. Grimsby Town	42	13	1	7	47	32	5	7	9	25	32	62
11. Barnsley	42	11	7	3	27	12	3	9	9	15	30	58
12. Wimbledon	42	9	8	4	40	29	7	2	12	31	46	58
13. Huddersfield Town	42	9	5	7	28	29	6	5	10	24	35	55
14. Oldham Athletic	42	10	4	7	27	23	5	4	12	22	44	53
15. Crystal Palace	42	8	7	6	25	27	4	5	12	21	38	48
16. Carlisle United	42	8	5	8	27	23	5	3	13	23	44	47
17. Charlton Athletic	42	8	7	6	34	30	3	5	13	17	33	45
18. Sheffield United	42	7	6	8	31	28	3	8	10	23	38	44
19. Middlesbrough	42	8	7	6	22	26	4	2	15	19	31	40
20. Notts County	42	6	5	10	25	32	4	4	15	20	41	37
21. Cardiff City	42	5	3	13	24	42	4	5	12	23	37	35
22. Wolverhampton W.	42	5	4	12	18	32	3	5	13	19	47	33

Forty former players assembled on the Goldstone pitch before the game with Grimsby Town on 8 December to celebrate Albion's 2,500th game in the Football League. The oldest ex-player present was 80-year-old Harold Sly who made 24 appearances for the club in the period 1929–33.

five minutes. That amazing win gave Brighton an unexpected chance of promotion which depended heavily on other results. It was a slim hope and Albion did their bit, beating Sheffield United 1–0, but Manchester City's 5–1 demolition of Charlton Athletic ensured their place in the First Division alongside the leading pair, Oxford United and Birmingham City.

So Albion just failed to regain their lost place in Division One by a mere three points. It was a rather unexpected finish to the season, and promotion-fever certainly never got to the supporters with the average attendance lower than the previous year's. The strength of the side was undoubtedly the defence which conceded just 34 goals, equalling the record of 1922–23, and goalkeeper Graham Moseley won the Player of the Season award. The team's failing had been in front of goal, with only Terry Connor managing double figures, and the key to promotion surely lay in strengthening the attack. But at last there was some stability at the club.

Cup form reverted to the pre-1983 standard. Fourth Division Aldershot deservedly repeated a pre-season friendly victory by putting Albion out of the Milk Cup in the second round. The Seagulls beat Hull City, managed by former skipper Brian Horton, in the F.A. Cup on a snow-covered Goldstone, but were well beaten at Barnsley in the fourth round.

SEASON 1985–86

This was to be a vital season for English football. With the appalling tragedies of May 1985 – at Bradford City and the Heysel Stadium – still fresh in the memory, everyone concerned with the national game was praying for a renaissance from the scourge of the hooligan and for an end to unsafe grounds.

Albion's efforts to present a welcoming face included a new Junior Seagulls club for under-14s, but the six-year-old 'Lego Stand' had gone. Frank Worthington, Hans Kraay, Martin Lambert, Ian Muir and Neil Smillie had also departed, the last to Watford for an unexpected £100,000, and Chris Cattlin used the money to bring in former £1 million striker Justin Fashanu from Notts County as a new target man. Other newcomers included Dennis Mortimer, skipper of Aston Villa's European Cup-winning side, and Dean Saunders, a young forward released by Swansea City. Martin Keown was back on loan along with Sheffield Wednesday's central-defender Gavin Oliver.

The season's main interest was provided by the F.A. Cup. The third round saw the Seagulls at Newcastle, currently eleventh in the First Division and with future England internationals Peter Beardsley and Paul Gascoigne in their line-up, but the Magpies were ineffective against a resolute Albion who repeated their triumph of three years earlier. Eric Young scored in the first minute and Dean Saunders clinched the tie with a breakaway goal five minutes from time. Perry Digweed was magnificent between the posts.

The red strip Albion wore on Tyneside was now thought to be lucky and it was used again at Boothferry Park, Hull, in the fourth round. The Seagulls established a 2–0 lead after 20 minutes through Dean Saunders and Terry Connor, but the Tigers pulled it back to 2–2 with half an hour remaining, only for Connor to win the tie with a great header. With two excellent Cup wins behind him, Chris Cattlin was rewarded with the Division Two Manager of the Month nomination for January.

Now in the fifth round for the third time in four years, Albion were drawn away once again, this time at Fourth Division Peterborough United. Five thousand fans wearing red favours travelled to London Road and saw Albion snatch a 2–2 draw on a snow-covered pitch, thanks largely to substitute Steve Jacobs who came on for the ineffective Justin Fashanu. The replay was eventually staged sixteen days later after 400 loyal fans had helped to clear the pitch and terraces of snow. The Posh proved very stubborn, but a 78th-minute strike by Dean Saunders, his fourth goal in the competition, saw Brighton into the quarter-finals for only the second time in their history.

At last the draw rewarded Albion with a home tie: First Division Southampton on the following Saturday. The Saints included England internationals Peter Shilton, Mark Wright, Dave Armstrong and Danny Wallace, and also had former Seagulls skipper Jimmy Case in their side. Cattlin dropped Chris Hutchings for the game, moved Steve Jacobs from midfield

Deano strikes

Dennis Mortimer salutes as Dean Saunders scores Albion's first goal on the snow-bound Peterborough United pitch in a 2–2 draw. The Seagulls won this fifth-round F.A. Cup tie in a Goldstone replay to enter the quarter-finals for only the second time in history. Saunders scored four goals in the run and was one of the most exciting players to play for the club in recent years, but, with Albion desperate for cash, he was sold to Oxford United in March 1987 for a paltry £60,000. In 1991 he cost Liverpool a British-record £2·9 million.

SEASON 1985–86

Date	Comp.	Ven.	Opponents	Result	HT	Pos.	Scorers	Atten.	Biley A	Connor T	Digweed P	Edwards S	Fashanu J	Ferguson M	Gatting S	Hutchings C	Jacobs S	Keown M	Massimo F	Mortimer D	Moseley G	Newman D	Oliver G	O'Regan K	O'Reilly G	Pearce G	Penney S	Saunders D	Wilson D	Young E
Aug 17	FL D2	(h)	Grimsby Town	D 2–2	0–1	9=	Biley, Connor	9,787	8	10			9			3†		2		11	1		5		6		7	12	4	
20	FL D2	(a)	Barnsley	L 2–3	1–2	15	Connor, Saunders	5,051	8†	10			9					2		11	1		5	3	6		7	12	4	
24	FL D2	(h)	Bradford City	W 2–1	1–1	7	Wilson (pen), Connor	9,263	8†	10	1		9							11			2		6	3	12	7	4	5
27	FL D2	(h)	Sheffield United	D 0–0	0–0	10		10,128		10	1		9					12		11			2		6	3	7	8	4	5†
31	FL D2	(a)	Middlesbrough	W 1–0	1–0	9	Wilson (pen)	5,543		10	1		9†				8			11			5	2	6	3	7	12	4	
Sep 4	FL D2	(h)	Leeds United	L 0–1	0–0	9		9,798	9	10†	1						4	2		11			5	12	6	3	7	8		
7	FL D2	(h)	Blackburn Rovers	W 3–1	1–1	7	Biley, Ferguson, Saunders	8,159	10		1			9			7	2		11			5		6	3	N	8	4	
14	FL D2	(a)	Millwall	W 1–0	0–0	4	Ferguson	8,013	10†		1			9			7			11			6		2	3	12	8	4	5
21	FL D2	(h)	Wimbledon	W 2–0	1–0	4	Wilson, Ferguson	9,973	10		1			9			7			11			6		2	3	N	8	4	5
25	FLC R2 Lg1	(h)	Bradford City	W 5–2	3–1	–	Wilson 3, Keown, Penney	6,664	10†		1			9			7	2		11				12	6	3	8		4	5
28	FL D2	(a)	Fulham	L 0–1	0–0	4		5,861			1			9			7			11			6	12	2†	3	8	10	4	5
Oct 2	FMC Group	(h)	West Bromwich A.	L 1–2	1–2	–	Wilson (pen)	4,649			1					12	7	9		11‡			2†	14	6	3	8	10	4	5
5	FL D2	(h)	Carlisle United	W 6–1	2–0	4	Ferguson, Biley, Wilson, Jacobs, Saunders, Mortimer	8,608	10†		1			9		2	7			11			6		5	3	12	8	4	
8	FLC R2 Lg2	(a*)	Bradford City	W 2–0	1–0	–	Biley, Ferguson	5,368	10		1			9		2	7	N		11					6	3		8	4	5
12	FL D2	(a)	Stoke City	D 1–1	1–0	5	Hutchings	7,662	10†		1			9		2	7			11			12		6	3		8	4	5
16	FMC Group	(a)	Crystal Palace	W 3–1	2–0	–	O'Regan, Wilson, Keown	2,207				12				2†	7	9		11	1	N		10	6	3		8	4	5
19	FL D2	(h)	Charlton Athletic	L 3–5	1–1	7	Saunders, Keown, Wilson (pen)	11,546	10		1					2	7	9		11†			5	12	6	3		8	4	
26	FL D2	(a)	Oldham Athletic	L 0–4	0–1	8		4,970						9		2†	7			11	1		10		6	3	12	8	4	5
29	FLC R3	(a)	Liverpool	L 0–4	0–1	–		15,291	12				9				6	2		11	1			10		3	7†	8	4	5
Nov 2	FL D2	(h)	Norwich City	D 1–1	0–0	8	Saunders	10,423	10†				9			8		12		11	1		2		6	3		7	4	5
9	FL D2	(a)	Shrewsbury Town	L 1–2	1–2	10	Fashanu	2,942	10	4			9			2				11	1		6	12		3	8	7†		5
16	FL D2	(h)	Huddersfield Town	W 4–3	2–1	10	Ferguson, Biley (pen), Young, Saunders	7,952	10	4				9		2	6			11	1	N				3	8	7		5
23	FL D2	(a)	Sunderland	L 1–2	0–1	11	Connor	14,712		10			9			2	12			11	1				6	3	8	7†	4	5
30	FL D2	(h)	Hull City	W 3–1	2–1	8	Connor, Wilson, Fashanu	8,478		10			9			2	6			11	1			N		3	8	7	4	5
Dec 7	FL D2	(h)	Barnsley	L 0–1	0–0	8		8,819		10			9			2	6			11	1			N		3	8	7	4	5
14	FL D2	(a)	Grimsby Town	W 2–0	2–0	8	Connor 2	5,320		10	1		9			2				11				12	6	3	8	7	4	5†
20	FL D2	(a*)	Bradford City	L 2–3	0–2	8	Wilson (pen), Saunders	4,318		10	1		9				2			11				N	6	3	8	7	4	5
26	FL D2	(a)	Portsmouth	W 2–1	1–1	8	Saunders, Connor	15,265		10	1		9		N		2			11					6	3	8	7	4	5
28	FL D2	(a)	Leeds United	W 3–2	1–0	7	Connor, Own goal, Pearce	13,110		10	1		9		N		2			11					6	3	8	7	4	5
Jan 1	FL D2	(h)	Crystal Palace	W 2–0	1–0	5	Saunders, Wilson (pen)	15,469		10†	1		9		12		2			11					6	3	8	7	4	5
4	FAC R3	(a)	Newcastle United	W 2–0	1–0	–	Young, Saunders	24,643		10	1		9		N		2			11					6	3	8	7	4	5
18	FL D2	(h)	Middlesbrough	D 3–3	1–2	5	Connor 2, Saunders	10,106		10	1		9		N	2				11					6	3	8	7	4	5
25	FAC R4	(a)	Hull City	W 3–2	2–1	–	Saunders, Connor 2	12,228		10	1		9		N	2				11					6	3	8	7	4	5
Feb 1	FL D2	(a)	Sheffield United	L 0–3	0–0	7		7,367		10	1			9	12	2				11†					6	3	8	7	4	5
4	FL D2	(a)	Charlton Athletic	D 2–2	1–0	7	Penney, Saunders	5,932	N	10	1				11	2	7								6	3	8	9	4	5
15	FAC R5	(a)	Peterborough Utd	D 2–2	0–0	–	Saunders, Jacobs	15,812		10	1		9†			2	12			11					6	3	8	7	4	5
22	FL D2	(a)	Wimbledon	D 0–0	0–0	6		5,797	9	10	1				3	2	11					N			6		8	7	4	5
Mar 3	FAC R5 Rep	(h)	Peterborough Utd	W 1–0	0–0	–	Saunders	19,010	12	10	1				11†	2	7								6	3	8	9	4	5
8	FAC R6	(h)	Southampton	L 0–2	0–2	–		25,069	12	10	1			9			2†			11					6	3	8	7	4	5
15	FL D2	(h)	Stoke City	W 2–0	1–0	7	Wilson, Mortimer	8,783	9	10	1				12	3	2			11					6		8	7	4	5†
18	FL D2	(a)	Blackburn Rovers	W 4–1	1–0	6	Connor 2, Wilson, Saunders	3,616	9†	10	1				3	2	8			11					6		12	7	4	5
22	FL D2	(h)	Millwall	W 1–0	0–0	5	Young	9,370	9	10	1				3	2†	8			11					6		12	7	4	5
29	FL D2	(a)	Crystal Palace	L 0–1	0–1	5		9,124	9	10	1				3	2	8†			11					6		12	7	4	5
31	FL D2	(h)	Portsmouth	L 2–3	0–3	6	Saunders, O'Regan	16,640	9	10	1				3	2				11				12	6		8	7	4†	5
Apr 2	FL D2	(h)	Oldham Athletic	D 1–1	0–1	6	Saunders	8,200	9	10	1				6	2				11		N		4		3	8	7		5
5	FL D2	(a)	Norwich City	L 0–3	0–0	8		15,155	9†	10	1				6	2	4			11				12		3	8	7		5
12	FL D2	(h)	Shrewsbury Town	L 0–2	0–0	8		7,210	9†	10	1				6	2			12	11		5		4		3	8	7		
16	FL D2	(h)	Fulham	L 2–3	1–1	8	Wilson, Connor	6,255		10	1				3	2	7			11		N			6		8	9	4	5
19	FL D2	(a)	Huddersfield Town	L 0–1	0–0	9		5,469		10	1				3	2	7			11				12	6		8	9	4†	5
26	FL D2	(h)	Sunderland	W 3–1	1–0	9	Own goal, Saunders, Penney	9,189		10	1				3	2	7			11				12	6	4	8	9		5†
29	FL D2	(a)	Carlisle United	L 0–2	0–1	9		4,854		10	1				3	2	7			11		N		5	6	4	8	9		
May 2	FL D2	(a)	Hull City	L 0–2	0–0	11		5,459		10	1				3	2	7			11		N		5	6	4	8	9		
							League appearances		22	33	33	0	16	9	14	29	29	5	0	40	9	1	15	6	35	32	30	39	33	32
							Substitute appearances								3		1	2	1				1	9			7	3		
							League goals	OG – 2	4	14			2	5		1	1	1		2				1		1	2	15	11	2

Notes: Oct 8 and Dec 20 – matches played at Odsal Stadium, Bradford.

The Football League was sponsored as the Canon League, and the Football League Cup was sponsored as the Milk Cup.

Albion finished 2nd in Group 8 of the Full Members Cup and did not qualify for the next stage.

Canon League Division 2 1985–86

		P	W	D	L	F	A	W	D	L	F	A	Pts
1.	Norwich City	42	16	4	1	51	15	9	5	7	33	22	84
2.	Charlton Athletic	42	14	5	2	44	15	8	6	7	34	30	77
3.	Wimbledon	42	13	6	2	38	16	8	7	6	20	21	76
4.	Portsmouth	42	13	4	4	43	17	9	3	9	26	24	73
5.	Crystal Palace	42	12	3	6	29	22	7	6	8	28	30	66
6.	Hull City	42	11	7	3	39	19	6	6	9	26	36	64
7.	Sheffield United	42	10	7	4	36	24	7	4	10	28	39	62
8.	Oldham Athletic	42	13	4	4	40	28	4	5	12	22	33	60
9.	Millwall	42	12	3	6	39	24	5	5	11	25	41	59
10.	Stoke City	42	8	11	2	29	16	6	4	11	19	34	57
11.	**ALBION**	42	10	5	6	42	30	6	3	12	22	34	56
12.	Barnsley	42	9	6	6	29	26	5	8	8	18	24	56
13.	Bradford City	42	14	1	6	36	24	2	5	14	15	39	54
14.	Leeds United	42	9	7	5	30	22	6	1	14	26	50	53
15.	Grimsby Town	42	11	4	6	35	24	3	6	12	23	38	52
16.	Huddersfield Town	42	10	6	5	30	23	4	4	13	21	44	52
17.	Shrewsbury Town	42	11	5	5	29	20	3	4	14	23	44	51
18.	Sunderland	42	10	5	6	33	29	3	6	12	14	32	50
19.	Blackburn Rovers	42	10	4	7	30	20	2	9	10	23	42	49
20.	Carlisle United	42	10	2	9	30	28	3	5	13	17	43	46
21.	Middlesbrough	42	8	6	7	26	23	4	3	14	18	30	45
22.	Fulham	42	8	3	10	29	32	2	3	16	16	37	36

Home-videos – of the two F.A. Cup matches against Peterborough United – were made available to the public for the first time following a change in regulations.

to right-back, and selected Mike Ferguson at no.9 for his first senior game in five weeks. It was a controversial line-up and the manager later admitted it was a mistake. Before a crowd of 25,069, the tie was dominated by Southampton who opened up a 2–0 lead in 31 minutes. An ineffective Albion were well beaten and the Saints went through to the semi-final where they lost to eventual winners Liverpool.

In the Milk Cup competition, two wins over Bradford City sent Albion to Anfield for a third-round tie with Liverpool. Unlike 1983 and 1984 there were no heroics this time and the Seagulls went down 4–0. Albion also made their début in the new Full Members Cup competition – for First and Second Division teams only – but went out in the group stage to West Bromwich Albion despite winning at Crystal Palace.

The Seagulls got off to a good start in the League, losing just three of their first twelve games. With Terry Connor and Justin Fashanu side-lined, Cattlin turned to Mike Ferguson to partner Saunders and Biley up front, and the much-criticised centre-forward responded with five goals in eight games in his best spell at the club. A poor run in October caused some dissatisfaction, but wins at Grimsby, Portsmouth and Leeds restored confidence in the team which occupied seventh place at the turn of the year.

There was no money available to strengthen the squad, though, and two defeats at Easter, by promotion rivals Crystal Palace and Portsmouth, completely deflated the club. Albion had been lying fifth, four points behind third place with ten games to play, but only one win was gained from the remaining eight matches as the season fell apart. When bottom club Fulham triumphed 3–2 at the Goldstone before just 6,255 spectators, rumours were rife that Cattlin was ready to quit. Chairman Bryan Bedson dismissed the talk as speculation, but it was notable that former manager Alan Mullery was back at the Goldstone to see the game.

Dean Saunders was presented with the Player of the Season award before the last home game. The live-wire Welshman, who had lit up the season with nineteen goals, signed a three-year contract and made his international début in March. His form was a revelation, in stark contrast to that of Justin Fashanu who scored just two goals and was plagued by injury; he never kicked a ball for Brighton again after the Peterborough cup-tie.

A disappointing season was fizzling out when Albion lost their penultimate game 2–0 at Carlisle United. Two days later Chris Cattlin was dismissed and his former assistant George Petchey took charge for the last game at Hull City. The ex-manager kept tight-lipped as the club made allegations of gross misconduct, but his many supporters were far from silent: more than 100 attended a protest-meeting in Hove Park; then, on 11 May, 500 marched through Hove to be addressed by Cattlin himself. The protesters also gathered a 2,000-signature petition. It all proved to no avail as the following day Alan Mullery was reappointed manager, with former player Peter Suddaby returning as coach and Barry Lloyd, the successful Worthing manager, joining the staff as reserve- and youth-team coach. George Petchey and chief scout George Aitken left by mutual consent, while Glen Wilson, a long-time Albion servant and currently kit-man, and some lottery staff were made redundant as an economic cutback.

Albion 1985–86
Back row left to right: Mike Ferguson, Justin Fashanu, Eric Young, Gary O'Reilly, Terry Connor.
Middle row left to right: George Petchey (coach), Steve Gatting, Graham Moseley, Steve Jacobs, Perry Digweed, Dean Saunders, Mike Yaxley (physio).
Seated left to right: Steve Penney, Chris Hutchings, Danny Wilson (captain), Chris Cattlin (manager), Dennis Mortimer, Alan Biley, Kieran O'Regan.

Cattlin launched a legal action alleging wrongful dismissal; the club countered with its own allegations of negligence and breach of duty. The affair was to drag on for three years until April 1989 when an out-of court settlement was made in Cattlin's favour at a sum estimated at between £40,000 and £60,000 with Albion also agreeing to withdraw all allegations.

And so one of the most traumatic fortnights in the history of the club ended with Alan Mullery back in charge after a gap of five years, but most supporters looked forward to the 1986–87 season only with trepidation. Home crowds, averaging just 9,722, were already at their lowest since the Fourth Division days of 1963–64, and many of those who had attended this season were now disaffected following the events of May. With the club falling deeper into debt by the week – the total current liability stood at £1·39 million – the question now was not whether Albion could get back to Division One but could the club survive at all. It did, but only because of large cash injections by generous directors.

In November, Albion were forced to pull out of the Top Score football pool, operated in conjunction with the majority of Football League clubs since September, after running up a loss of around £20,000.

SEASON 1986–87

G raham Moseley, Graham Pearce, Steve Jacobs and Dennis Mortimer all left the Goldstone during the summer of 1986, but Alan Mullery found his hands tied by the lack of cash as he attempted to strengthen the squad. Three players, Dale Jasper (Chelsea), Les Berry (Charlton Athletic) and Gerry Armstrong (Chesterfield), joined the club on free transfers, while John Keeley (Chelmsford City) was signed for a bargain £1,500 as back-up for goalkeeper Perry Digweed, the only player remaining from Mullery's earlier régime. There were new shirt-sponsors, director Peter Kent's Nobo Visual Aids, and the Trustees Savings Bank was backing the popular Junior Seagulls, now nearly 650 strong, in addition to the club's schools coaching scheme.

Albion played Spurs on 8 August for the benefit of the injured Gerry Ryan, now retired from the League ranks, and the presence of former stars Peter Ward, Ian Mellor and Brian

SEASON 1986–87

Player columns (left to right): Armstrong G, Berry L, Brown K, Campbell G, Chapman I, Connor T, Crumplin J, Digweed P, Edwards S, Gatting S, Gipp D, Hughes D, Hutchings C, Isaac R, Jasper D, Keeley J, Massimo F, O'Regan K, O'Reilly G, Penney S, Rowell G, Saunders D, Tillman R, Wilson D, Young E

Date	Comp.	Ven.	Opponents	Result	HT	Pos.	Scorers	Atten.
Aug 23	FL D2	(h)	Portsmouth	D 0–0	0–0	14=		13,723
30	FL D2	(a)	Sunderland	D 1–1	0–1	14=	Connor	14,990
Sep 3	FL D2	(h)	Birmingham City	W 2–0	1–0	10=	Saunders, Connor	9,750
6	FL D2	(h)	Grimsby Town	L 0–1	0–1	12		7,791
13	FL D2	(a)	Plymouth Argyle	D 2–2	0–0	14	Connor, Penney	9,423
16	FL D2	(a)	Shrewsbury Town	L 0–1	0–0	15		2,684
20	FL D2	(h)	West Bromwich A.	W 2–0	1–0	9	Wilson (pen), Connor	8,766
24	FLC R2 Lg1	(h)	Notting'm Forest	D 0–0	0–0	–		13,266
27	FL D2	(a)	Oldham Athletic	D 1–1	0–0	16	Wilson	5,654
Oct 1	FMC R1	(h)	Birmingham City	L 0–3	0–1	–		3,794
4	FL D2	(h)	Stoke City	W 1–0	1–0	7	Wilson (pen)	8,316
8	FLC R2 Lg2	(a)	Notting'm Forest	L 0–3	0–1	–		16,036
11	FL D2	(a)	Ipswich Town	L 0–1	0–0	8		11,215
18	FL D2	(h)	Barnsley	D 1–1	1–0	11	Own goal	7,923
25	FL D2	(a)	Derby County	L 1–4	0–2	15	Jasper	10,768
Nov 1	FL D2	(h)	Hull City	W 2–1	0–1	11	Connor 2	7,330
8	FL D2	(a)	Huddersfield Town	L 1–2	1–1	13	Jasper	4,463
15	FL D2	(a)	Reading	L 1–2	1–1	17	Penney	7,407
22	FL D2	(h)	Blackburn Rovers	L 0–2	0–1	19		7,326
29	FL D2	(a)	Sheffield United	W 1–0	1–0	17	Saunders	8,840
Dec 6	FL D2	(h)	Bradford City	D 2–2	0–0	16	Saunders (pen), Hughes	7,135
13	FL D2	(a)	Leeds United	L 1–3	0–1	17	Armstrong	12,014
21	FL D2	(h)	Shrewsbury Town	W 3–0	2–0	15	Saunders 2 (1 pen), Armstrong	8,220
26	FL D2	(a)	Crystal Palace	L 0–2	0–0	16		10,365
27	FL D2	(h)	Reading	D 1–1	0–0	16	Penney	10,523
Jan 1	FL D2	(h)	Millwall	L 0–1	0–1	16		7,645
3	FL D2	(a)	Grimsby Town	W 2–1	2–1	15	Saunders, Armstrong	4,729
10	FAC R3	(a)	Sheffield United	D 0–0	0–0	–		9,556
21	FAC R3 Rep	(h)	Sheffield United	L 1–2	0–0	–	Jasper	7,019
24	FL D2	(a)	Portsmouth	L 0–1	0–1	16		12,992
Feb 7	FL D2	(h)	Sunderland	L 0–3	0–1	19		7,820
14	FL D2	(a)	Birmingham City	L 0–2	0–0	20		6,439
21	FL D2	(h)	Oldham Athletic	L 1–2	0–0	21	Connor	6,585
28	FL D2	(a)	West Bromwich A.	D 0–0	0–0	21		8,359
Mar 7	FL D2	(h)	Derby County	L 0–1	0–0	22		9,100
14	FL D2	(a)	Barnsley	L 1–3	1–1	22	Tiltman	4,733
21	FL D2	(h)	Ipswich Town	L 1–2	1–0	22	Gatting	8,393
28	FL D2	(a)	Stoke City	D 1–1	1–0	22	Wilson	10,216
Apr 3	FL D2	(h)	Huddersfield Town	D 1–1	1–0	22	Connor	7,515
7	FL D2	(h)	Plymouth Argyle	D 1–1	1–1	22	Armstrong	6,483
18	FL D2	(a)	Millwall	L 1–3	1–3	22	Young	3,851
20	FL D2	(h)	Crystal Palace	W 2–0	0–0	22	Wilson, Hughes	10,062
25	FL D2	(a)	Blackburn Rovers	D 1–1	1–1	22	Wilson (pen)	6,509
28	FL D2	(a)	Hull City	L 0–1	0–0	22		5,219
May 2	FL D2	(h)	Sheffield United	W 2–0	1–0	22	Wilson, Connor	5,377
4	FL D2	(a)	Bradford City	L 0–2	0–1	22		10,902
9	FL D2	(a)	Leeds United	L 0–1	0–0	22		8,139

Season totals (per player column, in order listed above):

	Arm	Ber	Bro	Cam	Cha	Con	Cru	Dig	Edw	Gat	Gip	Hug	Hut	Isa	Jas	Kee	Mas	ORe	ORy	Pen	Row	Sau	Til	Wil	You
League appearances	27	22	15	0	5	38	5	22	0	40	0	26	36	11	32	20	0	21	7	27	8	27	9	35	29
Substitute appearances	4	1		2								3			3			3	1		2	3	3	3	
League goals (OG – 1)	4					9				1		2			2					3		6	1	7	1

Notes: The Football League was sponsored as the Today League from October, and the Football League Cup was sponsored as the Littlewoods Challenge Cup.

Today League Division 2 1986–87

		P	W	D	L	F	A	W	D	L	F	A	Pts
1.	Derby County	42	14	6	1	42	18	11	3	7	22	20	84
2.	Portsmouth	42	17	2	2	37	11	6	7	8	16	17	78
3.	Oldham Athletic	42	13	6	2	36	16	9	3	9	29	28	75
4.	Leeds United	42	15	4	2	43	16	4	7	10	15	28	68
5.	Ipswich Town	42	12	6	3	29	10	5	7	9	30	33	64
6.	Crystal Palace	42	12	4	5	35	20	7	1	13	16	33	62
7.	Plymouth Argyle	42	12	6	3	40	23	4	7	10	22	34	61
8.	Stoke City	42	11	5	5	40	21	5	5	11	23	32	58
9.	Sheffield United	42	10	8	3	31	19	5	5	11	19	30	58
10.	Bradford City	42	10	5	6	36	27	5	5	11	26	35	55
11.	Barnsley	42	8	7	6	26	23	6	6	9	23	29	55
12.	Blackburn Rovers	42	11	4	6	30	22	4	6	11	15	33	55
13.	Reading	42	11	4	6	33	23	3	7	11	19	36	53
14.	Hull City	42	10	6	5	25	22	3	8	10	16	33	53
15.	West Bromwich A.	42	8	6	7	29	22	5	6	10	22	27	51
16.	Millwall	42	10	5	6	27	16	4	4	13	12	29	51
17.	Huddersfield Town	42	9	6	6	38	30	4	6	11	16	31	51
18.	Shrewsbury Town	42	11	3	7	24	14	4	3	14	17	39	51
19.	Birmingham City	42	8	9	4	27	21	3	8	10	20	38	50
20.	Sunderland	42	8	6	7	25	23	4	6	11	24	36	48
21.	Grimsby Town	42	5	8	8	18	21	5	6	10	21	38	44
22.	**ALBION**	42	7	6	8	22	20	2	6	13	15	34	39

After many years of training in public parks and on college pitches, Albion finally established a permanent training-centre on part of the Worthing Rugby Club's grounds at Angmering in April 1987. The club remained there until 1990–91 when a move was made to the University of Sussex following problems with the pitches.

Horton attracted an excellent crowd of 10,759. The match programme carried an intriguing invitation to 'one of the most important meetings in the club's history' at The Dome on 20 August. It was the launch of Albion Lifeline, a fund-raising scheme which could net the club up to £120,000 a year purely for the purpose of acquiring new players. Members would have regular draws for prizes plus other benefits. Five hundred fans signed up at the meeting, and by the time of the first draw in October there were around 1,800 members.

With Albion hovering around the middle of the table, the new Lifeline allowed Mullery to bring in the experienced Gary Rowell from Middlesbrough and left-back/midfielder Darren Hughes from Shrewsbury Town. There were obvious problems, though. Last season's top scorer, Dean Saunders, was now a marked man, while centre-forward Gerry Armstrong failed to score before December. One bonus was the form of John Keeley who proved a more-than-capable deputy for Perry Digweed.

With attendances falling regularly below 8,000, Albion tried Sunday football at the Goldstone on 21 December for the first time in the League since 1974, and were rewarded with a 3–0 win over Shrewsbury Town before a crowd of 8,220. Juniors and senior citizens were allowed in free in a goodwill gesture which was repeated for the visit of Reading the following Saturday.

A roof was provided in the south-west corner of the Goldstone Ground – courtesy of Cobsen-Davies Roofing, the Supporters' Club and Mr Hugh Franks – for the benefit of those disabled supporters who watch matches from the area. It was inaugurated at the Blackburn Rovers game on 22 November 1986.

Albion 1986–87

Back row left to right: Danny Carter, Ian Chapman, Steve Gatting, Trevor Wood, Gerry Armstrong, Franco Massimo, Perry Digweed, Terry Spinks, Paul Arscott, Philip Lovell.
Middle row left to right: Peter Suddaby (coach), Chris Harris, Dale Jasper, Terry Connor, Gary O'Reilly, Eric Young, Sean Edwards, David Gipp, Mike Yaxley (physio), Barry Lloyd (coach).
Seated left to right: Daren Newman, Kieran O'Regan, Steve Penney, Dean Saunders, Alan Mullery (manager), Danny Wilson (captain), Dennis Mortimer, Chris Hutchings, Paul Dobinson.

On 3 January, Albion won 3–1 at Grimsby to move into fifteenth place, eight points clear of the bottom three, but on the same day Gary O'Reilly was sold to Crystal Palace for £40,000. It was a great surprise, but the club had to raise cash to pay the wage-bill. Two days later there was an even bigger surprise as Alan Mullery was sacked after just eight months for an alleged lack of commitment. Youth-team coach Barry Lloyd was named as manager the following day, 6 January, with Peter Suddaby staying on as coach, but Mullery, who was not on contract, said he had been 'stabbed in the back after being given five years to rebuild the club.'

It was an extraordinary turn of events which was never entirely explained, but the transfer of power was swift and Barry Lloyd, Albion's sixth manager in as many years, was now firmly in charge. Making his name as a midfielder with Fulham, Lloyd had successfully managed Yeovil and Worthing, but this was his first time at the helm of a Football League club — and an ailing one at that. His first result was a creditable 0–0 draw at Sheffield United in the F.A. Cup, but Albion lost the replay 2–1 with a dreadful performance. The facts of Second Division life were hammered home by Sunderland who won 3–0 at the Goldstone, a defeat which saw the start of a vicious hate campaign from the terraces against the chairman, Bryan Bedson. The board responded by giving Lloyd a three-year contract and making all players available for transfer.

The dreadful performances continued and Albion sank rapidly to the foot of the table; they were never to leave it. Five consecutive home matches were lost and it was fifteen games before Lloyd had the satisfaction of a win. As the team headed for Division Three with barely a murmur, there were loud calls for the return of Chris Cattlin. Dean Saunders, who four years later cost Liverpool almost £3 million, was sold to First Division Oxford United in March for just £60,000 to raise cash, but Lloyd seemed to prefer the untried Richard Tiltman to the popular Welsh international anyway. Other inexperienced players were brought in – Kevan Brown (Southampton), Robert Isaac (Chelsea) and John Crumplin (Bognor Regis Town) – as Lloyd tried to find a winning formula. In the match at Birmingham City he was forced to play sixteen-year-old Ian Chapman at left-back, Albion's youngest player ever in a peacetime Football League match.

By March most supporters were resigned to relegation which was finally confirmed on 5 May at Bradford City. The final game brought Leeds United and their dreaded hooligans to the Goldstone. The police operation was huge, but there was a great deal of trouble in the town, and at the end of the match many of the Yorkshire side's 3,000 followers scaled the fences to attack the police and Albion fans. Peace was eventually restored, but the incident will be remembered alongside the infamous games with Spurs and Chelsea as one of the worst outbreaks of violence ever seen at the Goldstone. Thankfully, it was also one of the last.

With Albion succumbing 3–0 at home to Birmingham City in the Full Members Cup, the one highlight of the season was a Littlewoods Cup tie with First Division leaders Nottingham Forest. Albion did well to force a goal-less draw at the Goldstone in an entertaining game, but the second leg was lost 3–0 with Perry Digweed suffering a broken cheekbone before half time and Steve Gatting taking over in goal.

So Albion were left to contemplate a disastrous campaign which had seen the lowest average crowd since 1946–47, just 8,282. To add to the gloom, the reserves finished bottom of the Football Combination. In March the board made an approach to Corals with a view to sharing the greyhound stadium and selling the Goldstone for around £8 million – an idea first mooted in 1938 – but nothing came of it. However, much of the club's financial burden was relieved in April by the injection of nearly £1 million from director Greg Stanley. Other members of the board took similar steps to cover another large chunk of the £1·6 million debt with the result that, for the moment, the club was no longer crippled by high interest payments said to be running at £3,000 a week. Mr Stanley, a multi-millionaire director of a do-it-yourself retail group who had joined the board in November 1985, was made president in October 1989 as a token of the club's gratitude.

SEASON 1987–88

With Albion at rock-bottom, there was little cause for optimism among the Goldstone faithful, but Barry Lloyd was determined to rebuild the team and the summer of 1987 was the busiest for many years. The sale of Terry Connor, Danny Wilson and Eric Young realised £410,000, with which Lloyd purchased a new strike-force, Kevin Bremner (Reading) and Garry Nelson (Plymouth Argyle); a new skipper, Doug Rougvie (Chelsea); and a new left-back, Keith Dublin (Chelsea). Rotherham United's midfielder Mike Trusson arrived on a free transfer, while back at the club after three seasons abroad was Dean Wilkins; his second spell was to prove considerably more successful than his first. Gerry Armstrong, Steve Gatting and Chris Hutchings were all made available.

The much-abused Bryan Bedson stepped down from the chairmanship in June to be replaced by Dudley Sizen, and Martin Hinshelwood was appointed as Lloyd's new right-hand man. There was a welcome return for the fans' favourite colours of blue-and-white stripes after seven years of all-blue shirts.

A membership scheme for supporters was introduced, initially as part of the Government's attempt to stem hooliganism. All the home supporters' areas except the North Stand and West Terrace North were made members-only from 19 September, with the North-East Terrace and the eastern block of the South Stand reserved for away fans. The scheme proved both popular and successful, and, together with efficient policing and changing attitudes, contributed to the rapid decline of 'aggro' at the ground in the late 1980s. Indeed, the hooligan problem had largely disappeared from grounds throughout the country by the early '90s.

The League season got off to a good start with two wins and two draws, but with the opening fixture attracting only 6,068 fans to Hove and just 2,286 spectators attending the match at Chesterfield, the realities of Third Division football rapidly sank in. Lloyd continued building, paying £32,500 for midfielder Alan Curbishley (Charlton Athletic) and £80,000 for Paul Wood

(Portsmouth) as a stand-in for the injured Garry Nelson. Defeat at Port Vale on 28 September dropped Albion to thirteenth, but it was their last for three months as a new club record of seventeen League and Cup matches without defeat was set. Six League wins and seven draws saw Albion climb steadily to fourth place, but the bubble burst on 28 December at Ashton Gate when Bristol City hammered the Seagulls 5–2.

At the New Year, Albion found themselves fifth. Far from being candidates for Division Four, Barry Lloyd had produced a new team pushing for a place in the promotion play-offs and the public was now showing support for the manager. By the beginning of April, Albion were sixth, just behind the three play-off positions, with some vital clashes against the leading sides to come:

		P	W	D	L	F	A	Pts
1.	Notts County	39	20	12	7	72	41	72
2.	Sunderland	38	20	12	6	72	42	72
3.	Walsall	40	19	12	9	60	44	69
4.	Wigan Athletic	38	19	11	8	62	47	68
5.	Northampton T.	39	15	17	7	57	37	62
6.	ALBION	38	16	14	8	52	42	62

Victories over Gillingham, Walsall, away to Notts County – the best performance of the season – and at home to Wigan Athletic put them into fourth place. At last the Sussex public started to believe in its team and 14,421 turned out for the visit of fifth-placed Northampton Town, the third 'six-pointer' in a row, to be rewarded with a 3–0 Albion victory. Six wins out of six with the pressure really on made April a memorable month and earned Barry Lloyd his second divisional Manager of the Month award of the season, the first having come in February.

A win over Mansfield Town lifted Albion to third, just a point behind Walsall, and guaranteed the Seagulls at least a play-off place. A 2–0 lead was squandered at Chester, but the dismay at coming away with only a point was tempered by the news that Walsall had gone down at Bristol Rovers and Notts County had sensationally lost at home to Port Vale. Thus Albion moved into second place behind the runaway leaders, Sunderland, with one game to go, and a home win over Bristol Rovers on 7 May would virtually ensure promotion ahead of third-placed Walsall. The biggest

Albion 1987–88

Back row left to right: Mark Leather (physio), Richard Tiltman, Trevor Wood, Gerry Armstrong, Grant Horscroft, Mike Trusson, Garry Nelson, Dale Jasper, John Keeley, Damien Webber, Ted Streeter (youth development officer).
Middle row left to right: Barry Lloyd (manager), Steve Gatting, Chris Hutchings, Robert Isaac, Perry Digweed, David Gipp, Ian Chapman, John Crumplin, Martin Hinshelwood (coach).
Seated left to right: Kevan Brown, Darren Hughes, Kevin Bremner, Doug Rougvie (captain), Gary Rowell, Dean Wilkins, Steve Penney.

Albion launched a new lottery, the Sussex Cashline, on 25 January 1988 with a daily prize of £100 for a weekly stake of 50 pence. Another competition, the popular match-day jackpot lottery, was no longer run this season after 24 years, a victim of falling gates.

SEASON 1987–88

Date	Comp.	Ven.	Opponents	Result	HT	Pos	Scorers	Atten.	Armstrong G	Bremner K	Brown K	Chapman I	Chivers G	Cooper G	Crumplin J	Curbishley A	Dineen J	Dublin K	Gatting S	Gipp D	Horscroft G	Hutchings C	Isaac R	Jasper D	Keeley J	Nelson G	Owers A	Penney S	Rougvie D	Rowell G	Tiltman R	Trusson M	Wilkins D	Wood P
Aug 15	FL D3	(h)	York City	W 1–0	0–0	5=	Nelson	6,068		9	2							3	6		N	8		N	1	10	7	5	4				11	
18	FLC R1 Lg1	(a)	Gillingham	L 0–1	0–0	–		4,162		9	2					14		3				8	6	12	1	10‡	7	5	4†				11	
22	FL D3	(a)	Chesterfield	D 0–0	0–0	6=		2,286	14		2					7	4	3	6	10		8		N	1			5		9‡			11	
26	FLC R1 Lg2	(h)	Gillingham	W* 1–0*	1–0	–	Hutchings	5,479	9		2					7	4	3	6	10‡		8		N	1			5		14			11	
29	FL D3	(h)	Fulham	W 2–0	1–0	4	Bremner 2	8,773	N	9	2	N			7	4		3	6			8			1			5					11	10
31	FL D3	(a)	Northampton T.	D 1–1	0–0	5	Armstrong	7,934	14	9	2				7‡	4		3	6			8	N		1			5					11	10
Sep 5	FL D3	(h)	Blackpool	L 1–3	0–1	10	Curbishley (pen)	7,166	14	9	2				7‡	4		3	6			8	N		1			5					11	10
12	FL D3	(a)	Aldershot	W 4–1	2–1	5	Nelson 2, Own goal, Gatting	3,970		9	2				N	4		3	6			8			1	7			5	N			11	10
16	FL D3	(h)	Rotherham United	D 1–1	0–1	8	Bremner	6,945	12	9	2				14	4		3	6			8			1	7‡			5				11	10†
19	FL D3	(h)	Sunderland	W 3–1	2–0	4	Nelson, Hutchings, Rougvie	8,949	N	9	2					4		3	6			8			1	7			5	N			11	10
26	FL D3	(a)	Southend United	L 1–2	0–0	9	Wood	3,789	12	9	2‡					4		3	6			8			1	7			5	14			11†	10
28	FL D3	(a)	Port Vale	L 0–2	0–0	10		3,789	N	9	2				14	4		3	6			8			1	7			5				11‡	10
Oct 3	FL D3	(h)	Bury	W 2–1	1–1	8	Curbishley (pen), Nelson	6,509	12	9	2				11	4		3	6			8			1	7†			5				N	10
10	FL D3	(a)	Walsall	D 1–1	0–1	9	Nelson	5,020	12	9	2				11‡	4		3	6			8			1	7			5				14	10‡
17	FL D3	(h)	Preston North End	D 0–0	0–0	10		6,043	12	9	2				11	4		3	6			8			1	7			5	N				10†
20	FL D3	(a)	Wigan Athletic	D 3–3	0–1	10	Wilkins, Bremner 2	2,392	N	9	2				11	4		3	6			8			1	7			5	N			10	
24	FL D3	(a)	Brentford	W 2–1	0–1	8	Curbishley, Bremner	7,600	12	9	2				11	4		3	6			8‡		14	1	7		5†					10	
27	AMC Group	(a)	Fulham	W 6–1	5–0	–	Bremner 2, Crumplin, Wilkins, Nelson 2	2,272		9	2				11	4		3	6					8	1	7		5	N			10	
31	FL D3	(a)	Grimsby Town	W 1–0	5	Bremner	2,711	N	9	2				11	4		3	6			8		N	1	7			5				10	
Nov 4	FL D3	(h)	Doncaster Rovers	W 2–0	1–0	5	Nelson 2	7,142	N	9	2				11	4		3	6			8		N	1	7			5				10	
7	FL D3	(h)	Gillingham	D 1–1	0–0	5	Dublin	6,437	N	9	2				11	4		3	6			8		N	1	7			5				10	
14	FAC R1	(a)	Brentford	W 2–0	0–0	–	Nelson 2 (1 pen)	6,358		9	2				11†	4‡		3	6			8		14	1	7			5				10	12
21	FL D3	(a)	Mansfield Town	D 1–1	0–1	6	Nelson	3,284	12	9	2							3	6			8		4	1	7			5			N	10	11†
25	AMC Group	(h)	Southend United	W 3–2	3–1	–	Jasper, Bremner, Nelson	3,565		9	2					N		3	6			8		4	1	7			5			N	10	11
28	FL D3	(a)	Notts County	D 1–1	0–0	6	Dublin	8,725	N	9	2							3	6			8		4	1	7			5			N	10	11
Dec 5	FAC R2	(a)	Northampton T.	W 2–1	0–0	–	Bremner, Nelson	6,444	N	9	2							3	6			8		4	1	7			5	N		8	10	11
12	FL D3	(h)	Chester City	W 1–0	0–0	4	Trusson	6,738	N	9	2					N		3	6			8		4	1	7			5			8	10	11
19	FL D3	(a)	Bristol Rovers	W 2–1	1–1	4	Jasper, Nelson	3,589	N	9	2					N		3	6		5			4	1	7						8	10	11
26	FL D3	(h)	Southend United	D 0–0	0–0	4		11,147	12	9	2					N		3	6		5			4†	1	7						8	10	11
28	FL D3	(a)	Bristol City	L 2–5	0–3	5	Nelson, Wood	16,058	N	9	2					N		3	6					4	1	7			5			8	10	11
Jan 1	FL D3	(a)	Fulham	W 2–1	0–1	5	Trusson, Jasper	6,530	N	9	2					14		3	6					4	1	7			5			8	10	11‡
2	FL D3	(h)	Aldershot	D 1–1	0–1	5	Dublin	9,420		9	2					11		3	6					4	1	7	N		5			8	10	N
9	FAC R3	(h)	AFC Bournemouth	W 2–1	–	Rougvie, Nelson	14,411		9	2					11	4	3	6					N	1	7			5			8	10	N
16	FL D3	(a)	Sunderland	L 0–1	0–1	7		17,404		9	2					11	4	3	6					N	1	7			5			8	10†	12
20	AMC R1	(h)	Southend United	W 4–2	2–2	–	Nelson 2, Wilkins, Bremner	6,654		9	2		14		11	4‡	3	6						1	7			5			8	10	N
30	FAC R4	(a)	Arsenal	L 1–2	1–1	–	Nelson	26,467		9	2					11	4	3	6					N	1	7			5			8	10	N
Feb 6	FL D3	(a)	Blackpool	W 3–1	0–0	6	Crumplin, Nelson 2	4,081		9	2				11	4	3	6					N	1	7			5			8	10	N
10	AMC S QF	(a)	Hereford United	W 1–0*	0–0	–	Armstrong	2,345	14		2‡				11	4	3	6			12		1	7			5		8†	10	9
13	FL D3	(a)	Bristol City	W 3–2	1–0	5	Nelson 2, Rougvie	8,781		9	2				11	4	3	6					N	1	7			5			8	10	N
17	FL D3	(h)	Chesterfield	D 2–2	1–1	5	Nelson, Jasper	8,182		9	2				11	4	3	6					14	1	7			5			8‡	10	N
20	FL D3	(a)	York City	W 2–0	1–0	5	Jasper, Nelson	2,576		9	2				N	11†	4	3	6					8	1	7			5				10	12
27	FL D3	(a)	Bury	L 1–2	0–0	5	Nelson	2,557		9	2				11†	4	3	6					8	1	7			5			N	10	12
Mar 2	FL D3	(h)	Port Vale	W 2–0	0–0	5	Curbishley (pen), Crumplin	7,296		9	2				N	12	4	3	6					8	1	7			5				10	11†
5	FL D3	(a)	Preston North End	L 0–3	0–3	6		5,834		9†	2				14	12	4	3	6					8	1	7			5				10†	11
9	AMC S SF	(h)	Notts County	L 1–5	1–3	–	Gatting	8,499	12	9†	2					4	3	6					8‡	1	7	14	5				10	11
12	FL D3	(h)	Walsall	W 2–1	1–0	6	Dublin, Wood	8,345		N	2‡		14			4	3	6						1	7	11	5			8	10	9
16	FL D3	(a)	Rotherham United	L 0–1	0–0	6		2,562	12				N			4	3	6				2		1	7†	11	5			8	10	9
19	FL D3	(h)	Grimsby Town	D 0–0	0–0	6		7,269	12			2	14			4	3	6				5		1	7	11†				8‡	10	9
26	FL D3	(a)	Brentford	D 1–1	1–0	6	Penney	5,331	9		2					N	4	3	6	N				5	1	7	8	11				10	
Apr 2	FL D3	(h)	Gillingham	W 2–0	2–0	6	Penney, Curbishley (pen)	9,256	9		2					N	4	3	6	N					1	7	8	11	5			10	
4	FL D3	(a)	Notts County	W 2–1	1–1	6	Owers, Nelson	7,522	9		2					N	4	3	6	N				5	1	7	8	11				10†	
9	FL D3	(h)	Wigan Athletic	W 2–0	0–0	4	Curbishley	9,423	9†		2					14	4	3	6	12				5	1	7	8	11				10‡	
15	FL D3	(h)	Northampton T.	W 3–0	1–0	4	Owers, Gatting, Nelson	14,421	9		2					N	4†	3	6					5	1	7	8	11				10	12
23	FL D3	(a)	Doncaster Rovers	W 2–0	0–0	4	Nelson, Wood	1,683	9		2					N		3	6					5	1	7	8	11			N	10	4
30	FL D3	(h)	Mansfield Town	W 3–1	2–1	3	Penney, Gatting (pen), Dublin	11,493	9		2					N		3	6					5	1	7	8	11			12	10	4†
May 2	FL D3	(a)	Chester City	D 2–2	2–1	2	Wilkins 2	3,345	9†		2					N		3	6					5	1	7	8	11			12	10	4
7	FL D3	(h)	Bristol Rovers	W 2–1	1–0	2	Bremner, Nelson	19,800	9		2					N	4‡	3	6					5	1	7	8	11				10	12
League appearances									0	42	35	0	10	0	19	34	0	46	46	1	2	20	10	12	46	42	9	13	35	1	1	13	43	26
Substitute appearances									11	2			2	7						1		2						1				2	1	5
League goals							OG – 1		1	8					2	6		5	3			1		4		22	2	3	2			2	3	4

Notes: Aug 26 – after extra time (90–minute score 1–0).
— tie lost 4–5 on penalties.
Feb 10 – after extra time.

Albion finshed top of their preliminary group in the Associate Members Cup and qualified for the first round.

The Football League was sponsored as the Barclays League, the Football League Cup was sponsored as the Littlewoods Challenge Cup, and the Associate Members Cup was initially sponsored as the Freight Rover Trophy and then as the Sherpa Van Trophy.

League crowd for nearly five years, 19,800, saw Kevin Bremner open the scoring with a diving header in the fourteenth minute, his first League goal for six months. Just 20 seconds into the second half Garry Nelson ran clear to slot the ball through the legs of the Rovers goalkeeper. The Bristol side pulled one back on 67 minutes, but Albion held on to the lead to secure second spot and automatic promotion amid the usual scenes of jubilation.

It was an amazing transformation from the utter despondency of just a year earlier, and Barry Lloyd and his staff deserved the highest praise for turning the club around in one season. The public had only caught promotion-fever late in the day and crowds averaged just under 9,000, but they were now fully behind the team and manager. The problem for Lloyd now was to strengthen the squad for the challenge ahead. Garry Nelson was the 32-goal Player of the Season, just four short of Peter Ward's club record; played as an out-and-out striker for the first time in his career, he dazzled with his pace, skill and all-round contribution. Also outstanding were ever-present

Albion's own hooligan following caused a number of problems this season, but a happier note was struck by the 'Caveman Crew', a group of young supporters determined to put a smile back into Saturday afternoons. Their celery-throwing antics at away matches both amazed and amused the home fans.

Barclays League Division 3 1987–88											
	P	W	D	L	F	A	W	D	L	F	A	Pts
1. Sunderland	46	14	7	2	51	22	13	5	5	41	26	93
2. **ALBION**	46	15	7	1	37	16	8	8	7	32	31	84
3. Walsall	46	15	6	2	39	22	8	7	8	29	28	82
4. Notts County	46	14	4	5	53	24	9	8	6	29	25	81
5. Bristol City	46	14	6	3	51	30	7	6	10	26	32	75
6. Northampton Town	46	12	8	3	36	18	6	11	6	34	33	73
7. Wigan Athletic	46	11	8	4	36	23	9	4	10	34	38	72
8. Bristol Rovers	46	14	5	4	43	19	4	7	12	25	37	66
9. Fulham	46	10	5	8	36	24	9	4	10	33	36	66
10. Blackpool	46	13	4	6	45	27	4	10	9	26	35	65
11. Port Vale	46	12	8	3	36	19	6	3	14	22	37	65
12. Brentford	46	9	8	6	27	23	7	6	10	26	36	62
13. Gillingham	46	8	9	6	45	21	6	8	9	32	40	59
14. Bury	46	9	7	7	33	26	6	7	10	25	31	59
15. Chester City	46	9	8	6	29	30	5	8	10	22	32	58
16. Preston North End	46	10	6	7	30	23	5	7	11	18	36	58
17. Southend United	46	10	6	7	42	33	4	7	12	23	50	55
18. Chesterfield	46	10	5	8	25	28	5	5	13	16	42	55
19. Mansfield Town	46	10	6	7	25	21	4	6	13	23	38	54
20. Aldershot	46	12	3	8	45	32	3	5	15	19	42	53
21. Rotherham United	46	8	8	7	28	25	4	8	11	22	41	52
22. Grimsby Town	46	6	7	10	25	29	6	7	10	23	29	50
23. York City	46	4	7	12	27	45	4	2	17	21	46	33
24. Doncaster Rovers	46	6	5	12	25	36	2	4	17	15	48	33

'keeper John Keeley, and defender Steve Gatting who had started the season on the transfer list.

Good progress was made in two of the three cup competitions. After wins at Third Division Brentford and Northampton Town, Albion saw off Second Division Bournemouth 2–0 at the Goldstone in the third round of the F.A. Cup to set up a home tie with Arsenal. The match was all-ticket, but the police insisted on the allocation of the entire East Terrace to Arsenal fans who were to have 10,500 of the 29,000 tickets. The Gunners, holders of the Littlewoods Cup, were on the rise again under manager George Graham, finishing sixth in the First Division this season, and fielded England internationals Kenny Sansom, Steve Williams, Tony Adams and Graham Rix. A crowd of 26,467 saw an even game in which Albion missed several chances. Kevin Richardson put Arsenal ahead, but Garry Nelson equalised before half time. The First Division side won the match with a Perry Groves strike eleven minutes from time.

The Associate Members Cup, currently sponsored as the Sherpa Van Trophy, saw Albion thrash Fulham 6–1 at Craven Cottage. Wins over Southend United (twice) and Hereford

Nelson takes on the Gunners
Garry Nelson fires a spectacular equaliser in the F.A. Cup fourth-round tie against Arsenal, his 21st goal of the season. The match attracted a crowd of 26,467 to the Goldstone, the largest since the F.A. Cup run of 1983.

United set up a southern semi-final with promotion rivals Notts County. A win would have put Brighton just one tie from Wembley, but County took the Seagulls apart and ran out impressive 5–1 winners in Albion's heaviest home defeat since 1973. Interest in the Littlewoods Cup was brief, the Seagulls going out in a penalty shoot-out at Hove to emergency goalkeeper Paul Haylock after Gillingham's regular no.1, Phil Kite, had been sent off.

There was a cup success, though. The reserves won the Sussex Senior Challenge Cup for the first time on 2 May, skipper Grant Horscroft lifting the trophy after a 3–0 win over his former club Lewes in the Goldstone final. Albion had competed regularly for the county's premier trophy since 1978, but had previously only reached the semi-final stage twice.

SEASON 1988–89

On 11 July 1988, Mike Bamber, the 57-year-old former chairman of the club, passed away at his home in Jersey. The man who guided Albion through their most successful era suffered terribly at the end, but was comforted by the support of his family and many friends; they included Brian Clough, who always regarded Bamber as the best chairman he had known in his long career.

Despite spending over £700,000 on the Goldstone Ground in the last ten years – much of the money coming from the Football Grounds Improvement Trust – Albion had to close the crumbling North-East Terrace and the capacity was reduced to just over 23,000. Away fans were accommodated on the East Terrace North in a new pen more in keeping with *Stalag 17* than the Goldstone Ground. East Terrace regulars were also disgruntled, but were reassured that the whole terrace would eventually be renewed. Terrace admission rose to £3.50 for members and £4 for non-members, the first rises for three years.

Barry Lloyd kept the same squad that won promotion, but the Seagulls made a disastrous start, losing the first six League games. Strengthening the squad was essential, and Lloyd signed centre-half Nicky Bissett and midfielder Robert Codner from non-League Barnet for a total of £230,000. A more experienced player, Sheffield Wednesday's Larry May, also arrived for around £200,000 and immediately tightened up the defence as the Seagulls broke their duck with a 2–1 home victory over Leeds United on 1 October.

The team found some form in October, and a 3–0 victory over Sunderland on 26 November lifted Albion out of the bottom three for the first time, but the battle against relegation continued into 1989. Fortunately, Shrewsbury Town, and in particular Birmingham City and Walsall, were even worse than the Albion and those three clubs occupied the relegation

> This was the season when supporters everywhere joined in the craze for inflatable toys. Said to have been started by Manchester City fans sporting blow-up bananas, Albion followers, of course, responded with inflatable seagulls.

SEASON 1988–89

Date	Comp.	Ven.	Opponents	Result	HT	Pos.	Scorers	Atten.	Armstrong G	Bissett N	Bremner K	Brown K	Chapman I	Chivers G	Codner R	Coles D	Cooper G	Crumplin J	Curbishley A	Digweed P	Dineen J	Dublin K	Fearon R	Gatting S	Gipp D	Isaac R	Keeley J	May L	Nelson G	Owers A	Penney S	Trusson M	Wilkins D	Wood P
Aug 27	FL D2	(h)	Bradford City	L 1–3	1–1	22	Nelson	9,730				2		3				N	4					6		5	1		7	8	11	N	10	9
30	FLC R1 Lg1	(a)	Southend United	L 0–2	0–1	–		3,072				2		3			N	N						6		5	1		7	8	11	4	10	9
Sep 3	FL D2	(a)	Oxford United	L 2–3	0–2	24	Chivers, Armstrong	6,004	12					2					4			3		6		5	1		7	8	11†	N	10	9
7	FLC R1 Lg2	(h)	Southend United	L 0–1	0–0	–		4,649	12					2				N	4			3		6		5	1		7	8	11		10	9†
10	FL D2	(h)	AFC Bournemouth	L 1–2	0–2	23	Chivers	8,247	9					2	11				4‡			3		6		5	1		7	8	12		10†	14
17	FL D2	(a)	Manchester City	L 1–2	0–1	24	Bremner	16,033			9			2	11			N	4			3		6		5	1		7	8			10†	12
21	FL D2	(h)	West Bromwich A.	L 0–1	0–0	24		7,395			9			2	11‡			14	4	1†		3		6		5			7	8			10	12
24	FL D2	(a)	Swindon Town	L 0–3	0–1	24		6,585			9	12		2	11			N				3	1	6		5			7	8†			10	4
Oct 1	FL D2	(h)	Leeds United	W 2–1	0–1	22	Nelson, Bremner	7,109			9	N		2	11							3	1	6		4		5	7	14		8‡		10
5	FL D2	(h)	Barnsley	L 0–1	0–0	23		7,327			9	3		2	11				12				1	6		4‡		5	7			8	14	10†
8	FL D2	(a)	Leicester City	L 0–1	0–0	24		9,201	9					2	11				N			3	1	6		4		5	7			8	N	10
15	FL D2	(a)	Watford	D 1–1	0–0	24	Own goal	12,126	9					2	11		N		N			3	1	6				5	7			8	4	10
22	FL D2	(h)	Oldham Athletic	W 2–0	2–0	23	Gatting, May	7,699	N		9		3	2	11				8				1	6				5	7	14			4	10‡
26	FL D2	(h)	Walsall	D 2–2	1–2	23	Bremner, Curbishley	8,311	N		9			2	11				8			3	1	6				5	7	N			4	10
29	FL D2	(a)	Chelsea	L 0–2	0–1	23		15,406	12		9			2	11				8			3		6			1	5	7	N			4	10†
Nov 5	FL D2	(h)	Shrewsbury Town	W 3–1	0–0	23	Chivers, Nelson, Wood	7,365	N		9			2	11		N		8			3		6			1	5	7				4	10
9	FMC R1	(a)	Bradford City	L 1–3	0–0	–	Nelson	3,145	9	5				2	11		N		8†			3		6			1		7	12			4	10
12	FL D2	(a)	Blackburn Rovers	L 1–2	1–2	23	Curbishley (pen)	6,980		N	9			2	11			10	8			3		6			1	5	7	N			4	
19	FL D2	(a)	Ipswich Town	W 3–2	1–2	22	Curbishley, May, Bremner	12,386	N		9			2				N	8			3		6			1	5	7	10	11		4	
26	FL D2	(h)	Sunderland	W 3–0	1–0	21	Chivers, Penney, Bremner	10,039	N		9			2				N	8			3		6			1	5	7	10	11		4	
Dec 3	FL D2	(a)	Hull City	L 2–5	1–3	21	Bremner, Gatting	5,686			9			2				14	8‡			3		6			1	5	7	10	11†		4	12
6	FL D2	(a)	Plymouth Argyle	L 0–3	0–1	21		8,133			9			2	14			11†	8			3		6			1	5	7	10‡			4	12
10	FL D2	(h)	Stoke City	D 1–1	0–1	22	Gatting	7,443		5	9			2	11		N	10	8			3		6			1		7	N			4	
17	FL D2	(a)	Portsmouth	L 0–2	0–1	22		12,467		5	9			2	10			N	8			3		6			1		7		11	N	4	
26	FL D2	(h)	Crystal Palace	W 3–1	2–0	22	Bremner, Chivers, Nelson	13,515		5	9			2	11†		12	N	8			3		6			1		7		10		4	
31	FL D2	(h)	Birmingham City	W 4–0	0–0	20	Chivers, Bremner 3	9,324		5	9			2			11†	N	8			3		6			1		7		10		4	12
Jan 2	FL D2	(a)	AFC Bournemouth	L 1–2	1–0	21	Nelson	10,627		5	9			2			11†	N	8			3		6			1		7		10		4	12
7	FAC R3	(h)	Leeds United	L 1–2	0–0	–	Curbishley (pen)	10,914			9			2			11	N	8			3		6			1	5	7	N			4	10
14	FL D2	(h)	Plymouth Argyle	D 2–2	1–1	20	Bremner, May	8,504			9			2			12	14	8			3		6			1	5	7	10†			4	11‡
21	FL D2	(a)	Bradford City	W 1–0	1–0	20	Owers	8,183			9		N	2				N				3		6			1	5	7	10		8	4	11
Feb 4	FL D2	(a)	Barnsley	D 2–2	1–1	20	Nelson, Bremner	12,498			9			2				N	N			3		6			1	5	7	10		8	4	11
11	FL D2	(h)	Leicester City	D 1–1	0–1	20	Nelson	9,572			9		14	2					12			3		6‡			1	5	7	10		8†	4	11
18	FL D2	(a)	Oldham Athletic	L 1–2	1–2	21	Owers	5,918		6	9		N	2					12			3					1	5	7	10		8†	4	11
25	FL D2	(h)	Watford	W 1–0	1–0	20	Bremner	9,522		6	9		5	2				N	12			3					1		7	10		8†	4	11
28	FL D2	(a)	Walsall	L 0–1	0–0	21		4,613		6	9		5	2				14	N			3					1		7	10		8	4	11‡
Mar 4	FL D2	(h)	Blackburn Rovers	W 3–0	0–0	20	Nelson 2, Bremner	8,075		6	9		5	2				11	N			3					1		7	10		8	4	N
11	FL D2	(a)	Shrewsbury Town	D 1–1	1–0	20	Nelson	4,029			9		5	2		1		11	N			3			N			6	7	10		8	4	
15	FL D2	(h)	Chelsea	L 0–1	0–1	20		12,600			9		6	2				11†	12			3					1	5	7	10		8‡	4	14
18	FL D2	(a)	West Bromwich A.	L 0–1	0–0	21		11,586			9		6	2				11	10			3					1	5	7	N		8	4	N
25	FL D2	(h)	Oxford United	W 2–1	0–1	21	Curbishley (pen), Nelson	9,077			9		6	2	12				10			3					1	5	7	N		8†	4	11
27	FL D2	(a)	Crystal Palace	L 1–2	0–2	21	Curbishley (pen)	14,384			9		6	2	12				10			3					1	5	7	N		8	4	11†
Apr 1	FL D2	(h)	Manchester City	W 2–1	1–0	20	Curbishley (pen), Own goal	12,072			9		6	2	12				10			3					1	5†	7	N		8	4	11
5	FL D2	(h)	Portsmouth	W 2–1	0–1	18	Bremner, Nelson	10,100		5	9		6	2	12				10			3					1		7	N		8†	4	11
8	FL D2	(a)	Birmingham City	W 2–1	2–1	17	Nelson 2	4,579		5	9		6	2	12			N	10			3					1		7			8†	4	11
15	FL D2	(a)	Leeds United	L 0–1	0–1	17		14,915		5	9		6	2	8†			14	10			3					1		7	12			4‡	11
22	FL D2	(h)	Swindon Town	L 0–2	0–0	18		9,510		5	9		6	2	8†		12		10		N	3					1		7	4				11
29	FL D2	(a)	Sunderland	L 0–1	0–1	20		12,856		5	9		6	2	8		N		10			3					1		7	N			4	11
May 1	FL D2	(h)	Hull City	D 1–1	0–0	19	Codner	6,750		5	9		6	2	8				10			3					1		7	N		14	4	11‡
6	FL D2	(h)	Ipswich Town	L 0–1	0–1	20		8,616		5	9		6	2	8				10		N	3					1		7	N		11	4	
13	FL D2	(a)	Stoke City	D 2–2	1–1	19	Nelson, Wilkins	5,841			9		6	2	8				10		N	3		5			1		7	N		11	4	
							League appearances		3	16	41	2	18	46	22	1	2	7	32	1	0	43	7	29	0	9	37	24	46	21	9	21	42	27
							Substitute appearances		2			1	1		6		3	5	5											3	1	1	1	8
							League goals	OG – 2	1		15			6	1				6					3				3	15	2	1		1	1

Note: The Football League was sponsored as the Barclays League, the Football League Cup was sponsored as the Littlewoods Challenge Cup, and the Full Members Cup was sponsored as the Simod Cup.

Barclays League Division 2 1988–89

		P	W	D	L	F	A	W	D	L	F	A	Pts
1.	Chelsea	46	15	6	2	50	25	14	6	3	46	25	99
2.	Manchester City	46	12	8	3	48	28	11	5	7	29	25	82
3.	Crystal Palace	46	15	6	2	42	17	8	6	9	29	32	81
4.	Watford	46	14	5	4	41	18	8	7	8	33	30	78
5.	Blackburn Rovers	46	16	4	3	50	22	6	7	10	24	37	77
6.	Swindon Town	46	13	8	2	35	15	7	8	8	33	38	76
7.	Barnsley	46	12	8	3	37	21	8	6	9	29	37	74
8.	Ipswich Town	46	13	3	7	42	23	9	4	10	29	38	73
9.	West Bromwich A.	46	13	7	3	43	18	5	11	7	22	23	72
10.	Leeds United	46	12	6	5	34	20	5	10	8	25	30	67
11.	Sunderland	46	12	8	3	40	23	4	7	12	20	37	63
12.	AFC Bournemouth	46	13	3	7	32	20	5	5	13	21	42	62
13.	Stoke City	46	10	9	4	33	25	5	5	13	24	47	59
14.	Bradford City	46	8	11	4	29	22	5	6	12	23	37	56
15.	Leicester City	46	11	6	6	31	20	2	10	11	25	43	55
16.	Oldham Athletic	46	9	10	4	49	32	2	11	10	26	40	54
17.	Oxford United	46	11	6	6	40	34	3	6	14	22	36	54
18.	Plymouth Argyle	46	11	4	8	35	22	3	8	12	20	44	54
19.	**ALBION**	46	11	5	7	36	24	3	4	16	21	42	51
20.	Portsmouth	46	10	6	7	33	21	3	6	14	20	41	51
21.	Hull City	46	7	9	7	31	25	4	5	14	21	43	47
22.	Shrewsbury Town	46	4	11	8	25	31	4	7	12	15	36	42
23.	Birmingham City	46	6	4	13	21	33	2	7	14	10	43	35
24.	Walsall	46	3	10	10	27	42	2	6	15	14	38	31

places for the rest of the season; the Seagulls generally hovered a few points clear in 20th or 21st place. Three successive wins in April virtually guaranteed safety, but the season ended with just two points from six matches.

> In May 1989 the club launched 'Sports Express', to sell sports- and leisure-wear in aid of club funds. It was a natural extension to 'Albion Trophies', a service to local clubs and societies which had started in November 1988.

Highlights were few and far between. Third-placed Blackburn Rovers were despatched 3–0, and Albion were unlucky to lose by a single goal to Chelsea, the season's champions. The most memorable game was the Easter Monday clash with Crystal Palace at Selhurst. Referee Kelvin Morton sent off Mike Trusson and awarded five penalties, a Football League record. Palace had four of the five but missed three, while Alan Curbishley scored from Albion's single spot kick; the final score was 2–1 to Palace. The Manchester City game was also memorable. Albion scored a late winner with an own-goal, but, as City pushed for an equaliser, the ball was headed further out of play by chief 'ball-boy' Keith Cuss. The incident, whether accidental or not, embarrassed the club and 41-year-old Cuss, something of a cult figure, was dismissed.

The biggest crowd at the Goldstone in 1988–89 didn't watch the Albion. Indeed, the 15,000 people in the ground on 25 September didn't see a football match at all. They were worshippers at a Roman Catholic service. The Bishop of Arundel and Brighton preached from a platform in the middle of the pitch while the musical accompaniment was provided by an organ mounted in front of the West Stand.

Albion 1988–89

Back row left to right: Mark Leather (physio), Jack Dineen, Geoff Cooper, Robert Isaac, Doug Rougvie, Gerry Armstrong, Grant Horscroft, Gary Chivers, Roy Hales, Mike Trusson, Ted Streeter (reserve-team manager).
Middle row left to right: Barry Lloyd (manager), Paul Wood, Kevan Brown, Perry Digweed, Ian Chapman, John Keeley, John Crumplin, David Gipp, Martin Hinshelwood (coach).
Front left to right: Alan Curbishley, Keith Dublin, Kevin Bremner, Steve Gatting (capt.), Garry Nelson, Dean Wilkins, Steve Penney, Adrian Owers.

There was further embarrassment in a Sussex Senior Cup tie at Southwick when Gerry Armstrong, now reserve-team player-coach, was sent off. After receiving considerable verbal abuse from a section of the crowd, the normally genial Irish international assaulted a spectator. He was immediately suspended by the club but resigned shortly after.

All four cup matches were lost, the worst performance being a 3–0 aggregate defeat by Third Division Southend United in the Littlewoods Cup.

Goalkeeper John Keeley won the Player of the Season award while defender Gary Chivers was the only ever-present. Garry Nelson just stole the scoring honours with sixteen in League and Cup to Kevin Bremner's fifteen. It was a mediocre season, but gates rose slightly to average just over 9,000. Barry Lloyd admitted that new players were badly needed, but money was hard to come by: the loss for the financial year 1988–89 was £806,582, the worst to date, and left the club's total deficit at around £1·7 million.

On 15 April 1989, 95 Liverpool supporters lost their lives at Sheffield Wednesday's Hillsborough stadium in the nation's worst-ever sporting disaster, a tragedy that had enormous ramifications for football and the design of its stadia. Albion and the various local-authority services were able to pronounce the Goldstone safe, although the fences were to stay with the gates left open. A sombre Hove crowd observed a minute's

Making their first appearances at the start of the season were two 'fanzines', alternative voices to the club's official programme. 'Gulls Eye' was a low-cost and occasionally scurrilous production which brought disgrace to the club by association after publishing a cartoon in the wake of the Kegworth air disaster. It was later sued for libel by a number of directors, a matter which was settled out of court in the board's favour, and was behind the BISA movement in 1992. 'And Smith Must Score', which lasted until 1992, was slightly more 'up-market' and took its name from BBC radio commentator Peter Jones's words at the end of the 1983 F.A. Cup final. The Albion programme itself, which now cost 80 pence, was reasonable value and, to its credit, included a correspondence page which sometimes heavily criticised the club, especially over the arrangements on the East Terrace.

silence at the following match with Swindon Town and contributed nearly £7,000 to the Relief Fund. Shortly after, Albion announced plans for an all-seated family stand with executive boxes as an extension to the West Stand at a cost of more than £1 million, but, like so many plans for the ground, it never materialised. The board added that an all-seated Goldstone was not envisaged in the foreseeable future, but assured fans that the renewal of the East Terrace would commence shortly with money from the Football Grounds Improvement Trust.

SEASON 1989–90

For the second successive summer Barry Lloyd spent not a penny on new players. The club did spend £150,000 on the East Terrace though, creating a new area in the southern section for 3,000 away fans. Apart from the upper section of the East Terrace North, which now held just 2,040 home fans, the rest of the terrace was closed on safety grounds. Terrace capacities throughout the country were reduced by 15 per cent

following the recommendation of Lord Justice Taylor's preliminary report on the Hillsborough disaster, and the capacity of the Goldstone was now 18,493, only half its record attendance.

To the surprise of most of their supporters, Albion got off to an excellent start. The visit to Bramall Lane on 9 September was an amazing affair. Sheffield United took a 3–0 lead, but Albion came back to lead 4–3 before finally succumbing 5–4.

SEASON 1989–90

Date	Comp.	Ven.	Opponents	Result	HT	Pos.	Scorers	Atten.
Aug 19	FL D2	(h)	AFC Bournemouth	W 2–1	0–0	7	Bissett, Codner	9,719
23	FLC R1 Lg1	(h)	Brentford	L 0–3	0–2	–		6,045
26	FL D2	(a)	Barnsley	L 0–1	0–0	13		5,920
29	FLC R1 Lg2	(a)	Brentford	D 1–1	1–1	–	Wilkins	4,306
Sep 2	FL D2	(h)	Port Vale	W 2–0	0–0	9	Nelson, Codner (pen)	7,218
9	FL D2	(a)	Sheffield United	L 4–5	1–3	10=	Wood 2, Bremner 2	12,653
12	FL D2	(h)	Wolverhampton W.	W 4–2	4–1	4	Nelson, Bremner 2, Codner	12,338
16	FL D2	(h)	West Ham United	W 3–0	3–0	2	Bremner, Codner, Nelson	12,689
23	FL D2	(a)	Leicester City	L 0–1	0–0	3		8,926
27	FL D2	(h)	Ipswich Town	W 1–0	0–0	2	Wilkins	9,770
30	FL D2	(a)	Plymouth Argyle	L 1–2	0–1	6	Wood	7,610
Oct 7	FL D2	(a)	Bradford City	L 0–2	0–1	8		7,933
14	FL D2	(h)	Watford	W 1–0	1–0	7	Bissett	9,260
18	FL D2	(a)	Middlesbrough	D 2–2	0–0	6	Curbishley, Bremner	13,551
21	FL D2	(h)	Newcastle United	L 0–3	0–1	10		10,756
28	FL D2	(a)	Hull City	W 2–0	1–0	7	Bissett, Codner	4,756
Nov 1	FL D2	(h)	Swindon Town	L 1–2	0–1	9	Wilkins	8,070
4	FL D2	(h)	Blackburn Rovers	L 1–2	1–1	12	Bremner	7,445
11	FL D2	(a)	Stoke City	L 2–3	1–3	12	Codner, Bremner	10,346
18	FL D2	(a)	Oldham Athletic	D 1–1	0–1	12	Codner	7,066
25	FL D2	(a)	Sunderland	L 1–2	1–1	13	Bissett	8,681
29	FMC R2	(a)	Norwich City	L 0–5	0–2	–		5,704
Dec 2	FL D2	(a)	AFC Bournemouth	W 2–0	2–0	12	Nelson, Chapman	6,890
9	FL D2	(h)	Wolverhampton W.	D 1–1	0–0	11	Wilkins	9,817
16	FL D2	(a)	Leeds United	L 0–3	0–3	15		24,070
26	FL D2	(a)	Portsmouth	D 0–0	0–0	14		10,800
30	FL D2	(h)	Oxford United	L 0–1	0–1	17		7,738
Jan 1	FL D2	(a)	West Bromwich A.	L 0–3	0–2	18		9,407
6	FAC R3	(h)	Luton Town	W 4–1	0–0	–	Dublin, Nelson, Codner, Curbishley	10,361
13	FL D2	(a)	Barnsley	D 1–1	0–0	18	Barham	6,856
20	FL D2	(a)	Port Vale	L 1–2	0–0	20	Codner	8,666
27	FAC R4	(a)	Oldham Athletic	L 1–2	0–0	–	Barham	11,034
Feb 10	FL D2	(a)	West Ham United	L 1–3	1–0	22	Nelson	19,101
17	FL D2	(h)	Leicester City	W 1–0	1–0	19	Bremner	7,498
24	FL D2	(a)	Sunderland	L 1–2	0–2	19	Chivers	14,528
28	FL D2	(h)	Middlesbrough	W 1–0	0–0	18	Barham	5,504
Mar 3	FL D2	(h)	Oldham Athletic	D 1–1	0–0	18	Gotsmanov	8,229
7	FL D2	(h)	Plymouth Argyle	W 2–1	1–0	16	Own goal, Gotsmanov	7,418
10	FL D2	(a)	Ipswich Town	L 1–2	1–1	16	Wilkins	10,886
14	FL D2	(h)	Sheffield United	D 2–2	2–1	16	Own goal, Chivers	8,703
17	FL D2	(h)	Bradford City	W 2–1	0–0	16	Wilkins 2	6,831
20	FL D2	(a)	Watford	L 2–4	0–3	15	Crumplin, Bissett	8,487
31	FL D2	(a)	Newcastle United	L 0–2	0–0	18		18,746
Apr 6	FL D2	(h)	Hull City	W 2–0	0–0	16	Own goal, Gotsmanov	6,789
10	FL D2	(a)	Swindon Town	W 2–1	2–0	15=	Bremner, Chivers	8,444
14	FL D2	(a)	West Bromwich A.	L 0–3	0–2	17		8,371
16	FL D2	(a)	Portsmouth	L 0–3	0–0	17		10,924
21	FL D2	(h)	Leeds United	D 2–2	0–1	19	Gotsmanov, Crumplin	11,359
25	FL D2	(a)	Oxford United	W 1–0	0–0	18	Codner	3,864
28	FL D2	(h)	Stoke City	L 1–4	0–0	17	Bremner	9,614
May 5	FL D2	(a)	Blackburn Rovers	D 1–1	0–0	18	Bremner	9,283

Player appearance/number grid (column headers as listed top of table):

Barham M, Bissett N, Bremner K, Chapman I, Chivers G, Codner R, Cormack L, Crumplin J, Curbishley A, Dick A, Digweed P, Dublin K, Edwards A, Gabbiadini R, Gatting S, Gotsmanov S, Keeley J, Lambert M, McCarthy P, McGrath D, Nelson G, Owers A, Robinson J, Stemp W, Trusson M, Wilkins D, Wood P

League appearances: Barham M 16, Bissett N 28, Bremner K 42, Chapman I 41, Chivers G 41, Codner R 45, Cormack L 0, Crumplin J 14, Curbishley A 45, Dick A 0, Digweed P 11, Dublin K 43, Edwards A 1, Gabbiadini R 0, Gatting S 19, Gotsmanov S 14, Keeley J 35, Lambert M 0, McCarthy P 2, McGrath D 1, Nelson G 32, Owers A 0, Robinson J 4, Stemp W 2, Trusson M 0, Wilkins D 46, Wood P 24

Substitute appearances: Barham M 1, Bissett N 1, Bremner K 1, Crumplin J 11, Gatting S 1, Gotsmanov S 2, Lambert M 1, McCarthy P 1, Nelson G 1, Owers A 4, Robinson J 1, Wood P 2

League goals: OG – 3, Barham M 2, Bissett N 5, Bremner K 12, Chapman I 1, Chivers G 3, Codner R 9, Crumplin J 2, Curbishley A 1, Gotsmanov S 4, Nelson G 5, Wilkins D 6, Wood P 3

Note: The Football League was sponsored as the Barclays League, the Football League Cup was sponsored as the Littlewoods Challenge Cup, and the Full Members Cup was sponsored as the Zenith Data Systems Cup.

Barclays League Division 2 1989–90

		P	W	D	L	F	A	W	D	L	F	A	Pts
1.	Leeds United	46	16	6	1	46	18	8	7	8	33	34	85
2.	Sheffield United	46	14	5	4	43	27	10	8	5	35	31	85
3.	Newcastle United	46	17	4	2	51	26	5	10	8	29	29	80
4.	Swindon Town	46	12	6	5	49	29	8	7	30	30	74	
5.	Blackburn Rovers	46	10	9	4	43	30	9	8	6	31	29	74
6.	Sunderland	46	10	8	5	41	32	10	6	7	29	32	74
7.	West Ham United	46	14	5	4	50	22	6	7	10	30	35	72
8.	Oldham Athletic	46	15	7	1	50	23	4	7	12	20	34	71
9.	Ipswich Town	46	13	7	3	38	22	6	5	12	29	44	69
10.	Wolverhampton W.	46	12	5	6	37	20	6	8	9	30	40	67
11.	Port Vale	46	11	9	3	37	20	4	7	12	25	37	61
12.	Portsmouth	46	9	8	6	40	34	6	9	8	22	31	61
13.	Leicester City	46	10	8	5	34	29	5	6	12	33	50	59
14.	Hull City	46	7	8	8	27	31	7	8	8	31	34	58
15.	Watford	46	11	6	6	41	28	3	9	11	17	32	57
16.	Plymouth Argyle	46	9	8	6	30	23	5	5	13	28	40	55
17.	Oxford United	46	8	7	8	35	31	7	2	14	22	35	54
18.	ALBION	46	10	6	7	28	27	5	5	13	28	45	54
19.	Barnsley	46	7	9	7	22	23	6	6	11	27	48	54
20.	West Bromwich A.	46	8	6	9	35	37	6	7	10	32	34	51
21.	Middlesbrough	46	10	3	10	33	29	3	8	12	19	34	50
22.	AFC Bournemouth	46	8	6	9	30	31	4	6	13	27	45	48
23.	Bradford City	46	9	6	8	26	24	6	8	15	18	44	41
24.	Stoke City	46	4	11	8	20	24	2	8	13	15	39	37

Undeterred, the Seagulls travelled to Wolves and hit another four goals to maintain their immaculate record at Molineux. Back to the Goldstone and 12,689 fans, the biggest home attendance of the season, saw Albion thrash West Ham United 3–0 to move into second place behind Sheffield United.

After twelve games Albion lay sixth with a 100-per-cent home record, but on 21 October the bubble burst when Newcastle United won 3–0 at the Goldstone and it was then downhill all the way. There were demonstrations calling for Lloyd's head, and defeat in the return fixture with West Ham in February put Albion in the bottom three for the first time. The manager's hands were tied by the lack of cash: the club was around £2·5 million in debt and the board had to find money to pay back former director Frank Shannon or face the possibility of a winding-up order. Then, out of the blue, came former England international Mark Barham, and a few weeks later Lloyd brought in a Soviet international, Sergei Gotsmanov, on trial from Dinamo Minsk. It was an inspired acquisition.

A win over Leicester City on 17 February was the first home victory for four months, and the emergence of Barham and in particular Gotsmanov coincided with a general upsurge in home form. Normally a midfielder, Sergei came into the side when Garry Nelson succumbed to injury and immediately impressed with his skill and pace; the Belorussian was clearly a cut above most of those around him.

Albion 1989–90

Back row left to right: Nicky Bissett, Larry May, John Keeley, Mike Trusson, Perry Digweed, Robert Codner.
Third row left to right: Barry Lloyd (manager), Gary Chivers, Ted Streeter (youth development officer), Paul McCarthy, Steve Penney, John Robinson, Garry Nelson, Martin Lambert,
*   Dean Wilkins, Jack Dineen, Ian Chapman, Robert Isaac, Malcolm Stuart (physio), Keith Dublin, Martin Hinshelwood (coach).*
Second row left to right: Brian McKenna, John Crumplin, Alan Curbishley, Wayne Stemp, Steve Gatting (captain), Paul Wood, Kevin Bremner, Adrian Owers, Jimmy Jones.
On ground left to right: Andy Nimmo, Matthew Bown, Stuart Danbury, Dwayne Rhone, Derek McGrath, Mark Gumpright, Spencer Rush, Jason Mummery, David Coldwell, Chris Lyons,
*   Tim Smith, Stuart Munday, Greg O'Dowd, Michael Barrett.*

The biggest crowd of the season at the Goldstone watched a 1–1 draw between England B – including full caps Paul Parker, Michael Thomas, Tony Adams, Gary Pallister, Paul Gascoigne and Steve Bull – and an Italian under-21 side on 14 November. Although the attendance of 16,125 was well short of the ground's reduced capacity, over 2,000 spectators were locked out when the police shut the gates fearing a late surge. The kick-off was delayed by eight minutes to allow as many in as possible.

At the start of April, Albion were in eighteenth place, four points clear of the relegation zone, and a win at Oxford meant the club was virtually safe with two games to play.

The F.A. Cup paired Albion with First Division strugglers Luton Town in the third round. The Hatters included former Seagull skipper Danny Wilson, but his old team won the day with a sparkling 4–1 victory which rather put the dampers on a proposed demonstration against the board. Despite taking the lead on Oldham Athletic's plastic pitch, Albion went down 2–1 in the fourth round to the eventual semi-finalists.

Third Division Brentford won 3–0 at the Goldstone to knock Albion out of the Littlewoods Cup over two legs, while Norwich City put five past John Keeley to end any further interest in the Zenith Data Systems Cup at Carrow Road.

And so a season which had started so well left the fans as unhappy and fearful for the future as ever. Gotsmanov had shone like a beacon in the last two months, but Keith Dublin, a revelation on moving to the centre of defence, took the Player of the Season award. At least Barry Lloyd's youngsters were starting to come through with Paul McCarthy, Derek McGrath, John Robinson and Wayne Stemp all making their débuts, but the manager was surely going to have to open the cheque-book in the summer.

On 29 January, Mr Justice Taylor's final report into football spectator safety was published with enormous consequences for all clubs. Accepted by the F.A. and the Government, the main requirement was for every First and Second Division stadium to be all-seated by the start of the 1994–95 season, with Third and Fourth Division grounds to follow by 1999 (although this was later relaxed). While the move towards all-seaters was unwelcome to many fans throughout the country, the Albion board accepted the proposals with enthusiasm. As it was considered unrealistic to convert the Goldstone – which has just 5,110 seats – because of its lack of access and room for development, thoughts turned to a new, out-of-town stadium, possibly at Waterhall as proposed by Mike Bamber in 1983, but the obvious questions over the finance and precise location for such a project remained unanswered. The urgent quest for a new home put an end to hopes of refurbishing the East Terrace.

One definite investment for the future was the establishment of the Seagulls Community Scheme. Launched on 3 March, the project, funded jointly by the club, the Football Association, the Sports Council, and Hove and Worthing Borough Councils, was designed to forge links between the Albion and the local community. Steve Ford, a former Albion reserve player, was appointed Community Development Officer.

Many of Albion's former stars gathered at the ground on 3 April 1990 as the 1983 F.A. Cup final side lost 3–0 to a full-strength Tottenham Hotspur side in former goalkeeper Graham Moseley's testimonial. The side included Paul Clark, Steve Foster, Brian Horton, Gary Howlett, Mark Lawrenson, Graham Pearce, Chris Ramsey, Michael Robinson, Andy Rollings, Gerry Ryan, Neil Smillie, Gordon Smith and Gary Stevens. The 6,410 attendance in pouring rain was a great tribute to Moseley who banked around £18,000 from the night.

SEASON 1990–91

With the Football League shuffling its numbers, four promotion places were available from the Second Division for the first time – three automatic and one via the play-offs – but most Albion supporters were looking to the other end of the table. Their fears were fuelled by the departures of defender Keith Dublin to Watford for £275,000 and goalkeeper John Keeley to Oldham Athletic for £240,000, and the failure to secure Sergei Gotsmanov who joined First Division Southampton. Kevin Bremner and Alan Curbishley had also departed. Barry Lloyd made three signings: Mike Small (PAOK Salonika), an English centre-forward who had spent the last seven years on the Continent; winger Clive Walker (Fulham); and left-back Russel Bromage (Bristol City).

After an opening defeat at Barnsley, Albion gave the Goldstone faithful little cause for optimism by only drawing at home with their traditional whipping-boys, Wolves, but by the end of September, with wins at Watford and Blackburn and entertaining 3–2 home victories over Portsmouth and Charlton Athletic under their belts, the Seagulls were in a respectable seventh place.

By now Lloyd had landed a second new striker, Republic of Ireland international John Byrne for £125,000 from Le Havre. The season continued in topsyturvy fashion: torn to shreds by Sheffield Wednesday and horrible defeats at Oxford and Oldham, but excellent wins at Ipswich and Port Vale. With Mike Small proving to be the best centre-forward for some years and Byrne providing skilful support, Albion's away performances were usually in marked contrast to those of the previous two seasons, and Barry Lloyd was rewarded for the general good form with a three-year extension of his contract until summer 1994.

On Wednesday, 16 January, ex-Swansea City forward Bryan Wade, who had been unemployed until offered a trial by Lloyd, made his full home début and scored all four goals against Newcastle United, the first such haul by an Albion player since Peter Ward against Walsall in 1976; the 4–2 victory lifted the club back into a play-off position. By winning their fifth successive League match, against Leicester City on 20 February, the Seagulls were now sixth, but only two points were gained from the next five games. Following an injury to Paul McCarthy, Lloyd brought in Arsenal's experienced defender Colin Pates on loan, and Albion put together another good run of four wins which lifted them to fourth place and in touch with Sheffield Wednesday for an automatic promotion spot.

However, the wheels started to come off in a 2–1 home defeat by Port Vale, and the only success in a dismal run of seven matches was a rousing 1–0 defeat of leaders West Ham United. Vital games were lost at home to Oxford United and promotion rivals Bristol City, who won with a last-minute goal. That Albion were still in the hunt was largely due to the equally faltering progress of others. West Ham and Oldham were already assured of promotion; Sheffield Wednesday were clear favourites to win third place, and Notts County and Millwall were reasonably sure of play-off berths. That left Albion and three others to chase the final two play-off places. This was the table on 23 April before the visit to Hull City:

		P	W	D	L	F	A	Pts
1.	West Ham United	41	23	13	5	55	27	82
2.	Oldham Athletic	42	22	13	7	76	48	79
3.	Sheffield Wed.	40	19	14	7	69	44	71
4.	Notts County	42	19	11	12	65	53	68
5.	Millwall	43	18	13	12	63	47	67
6.	ALBION	43	19	7	17	60	66	64
7.	Middlesbrough	42	18	9	15	62	44	63
8.	Bristol City	42	19	6	17	62	61	63
9.	Barnsley	41	17	11	13	58	41	62

Mark Barham's late winner gave Albion victory at Boothferry Park, the first win in five games. Defeat at Middlesbrough left the Seagulls seventh, but midweek results meant that everything depended on the last day of the regular season with Albion at home to Ipswich Town. Middlesbrough were at Barnsley to complicate the permutations, but a Brighton victory would secure a play-off place.

The Seagulls took a first-half lead with a Mike Small penalty, his fifteenth League goal of the season but his first since February. Fifteen minutes from time Town were also awarded a penalty. Perry Digweed, the Player of the Season, pushed away Chris Kiwomya's kick amid scenes of great jubilation, but the drama was just starting. Eight minutes later Kiwomya netted an equaliser and the news filtered through that Barnsley were leading Middlesbrough, a situation that would have eliminated Albion. With less than two minutes left John Byrne was brought down outside the penalty area. Dean Wilkins took the resulting free kick and floated the ball beautifully into the far corner of Phil Parkes's net to send the largest home League crowd of the season, just 12,281, into rapture.

A second Albion team appeared on the local scene in 1990: the Brighton and Hove Albion Women's Football Club. Founded originally as Brighton GPO in 1967 and later known as C & C Sports, the Albion Women receive the official backing of the men's club through the Seagulls Community Scheme and play their regular home fixtures, in the same colours, at Withdean Stadium. A prestige match was staged at the Goldstone on 15 September 1991 when 300 spectators attended a match with Milton Keynes. Competing initially in the South East Counties League, the team were promoted to the National League Division One South in 1991. (There had been an Albion Ladies team in the 1970s, run as part of the Supporters' Club and competing in the Sussex Martlet Women's Football League along with C & C Sports.)

Barclays League Division 2 1990–91

		P	W	D	L	F	A	W	D	L	F	A	Pts
1.	Oldham Athletic	46	17	5	1	55	21	8	8	7	28	32	88
2.	West Ham United	46	15	6	2	41	18	9	9	5	19	16	87
3.	Sheffield Wednesday	46	12	10	1	43	23	10	6	7	37	28	82
4.	Notts County	46	14	4	5	45	28	9	7	7	31	27	80
5.	Millwall	46	11	6	6	43	28	9	7	7	27	23	73
6.	ALBION	46	12	4	7	37	31	9	3	11	26	38	70
7.	Middlesbrough	46	12	4	7	36	17	8	5	10	30	30	69
8.	Barnsley	46	13	7	3	39	16	6	5	12	24	32	69
9.	Bristol City	46	14	5	4	44	28	6	2	15	24	43	67
10.	Oxford United	46	10	9	4	41	29	4	10	9	28	37	61
11.	Newcastle United	46	8	10	5	24	22	6	7	10	25	34	59
12.	Wolverhampton W.	46	11	6	6	45	35	2	13	8	18	28	58
13.	Bristol Rovers	46	11	7	5	29	20	4	6	13	27	39	58
14.	Ipswich Town	46	9	8	6	32	28	4	10	9	28	40	57
15.	Port Vale	46	10	4	9	32	24	5	8	10	24	40	57
16.	Charlton Athletic	46	8	6	9	27	25	5	10	8	30	36	56
17.	Portsmouth	46	10	6	7	34	27	4	5	14	24	43	53
18.	Plymouth Argyle	46	10	10	3	36	20	2	7	14	18	48	53
19.	Blackburn Rovers	46	8	6	9	26	27	6	4	13	25	39	52
20.	Watford	46	5	8	10	24	32	7	7	9	21	27	51
21.	Swindon Town	46	8	6	9	31	30	4	8	11	34	43	50
22.	Leicester City	46	12	4	7	41	33	2	4	17	19	50	50
23.	West Bromwich A.	46	7	11	5	26	21	3	7	13	26	40	48
24.	Hull City	46	6	10	7	35	32	4	5	14	22	53	45

SEASON 1990–91

Date	Comp.	Ven.	Opponents	Result	HT	Pos.	Scorers	Atten.	Barham M	Beeney M	Bissett N	Bromage R	Byrne J	Chapman I	Chivers G	Codner R	Coldwell D	Cormack L	Crumplin J	Digweed P	Gatting S	Gurinovich I	Iovan S	McCarthy P	McGrath D	McGuinness P	McKenna B	Meola A	Nelson G	Owers A	Pates C	Robinson J	Small M	Stemp W	Wade B	Walker C	Wilkins D
Aug 25	FL D2	(a)	Barnsley	L 1–2	1–0	17=	Nelson	6,885	8			3			6	10			2	1				5					7			14	9	N		11	4‡
29	FLC R1 Lg1	(h)	Northampton T.	L 0–2	0–1	–		3,834				3		14	6	10		N	2	1				5					7			8‡	9			11	4
Sep 1	FL D2	(h)	Wolverhampton W	D 1–1	0–1	20=	Small (pen)	9,820						3	6	10	N	N	2					5				1	7			8	9			11	4
4	FLC R1 Lg2	(a)	Northampton T.	D 1–1	0–0	–	Small	4,760	8					3	6	10			2					5				1	7	N		N	9			11	4
8	FL D2	(a)	Watford	W 1–0	0–0	15	Nelson	7,847	8					3	6	10			2	1	N			5					7	N			9			11	4
15	FL D2	(h)	Charlton Athletic	W 3–2	1–1	10	Small, Codner, Wilkins	8,281	7†				12	3		10			2	1	6			5					8	N			9			11	4
19	FL D2	(h)	Portsmouth	W 3–2	3–1	6	Small, Codner, Wilkins	9,117	8				12	3‡		10			2	1	6			5					7†	14			9			11	4
22	FL D2	(a)	Bristol City	L 1–3	0–2	10	Small	11,522	8				12	3		10			2	1	6			5					7†	N			9			11	4
29	FL D2	(a)	Blackburn Rovers	W 2–1	1–1	7	Byrne, Chivers	6,027	7				8		3	10			2	1	6			5					N	N			9			11	4
Oct 3	FL D2	(h)	Sheffield Wed.	L 0–4	0–2	10		10,379	7†				8		6	10			2	1	3			5					12	N			9			11	4
6	FL D2	(h)	Swindon Town	D 3–3	3–1	11	Gatting, Small, Byrne	7,940	7				8		6	10			2	1	3			5					N	N			9			11	4
13	FL D2	(a)	West Bromwich A.	D 1–1	1–0	11	Byrne	9,833	7				8		6				2	1	3			5					N	10			9		N	11	4
20	FL D2	(a)	Oxford United	L 0–3	0–1	12		4,733	7†				8	14	6				2	1	3			5‡					12	10			9			11	4
24	FL D2	(h)	Hull City	W 3–1	1–0	9	Byrne, Wilkins, Walker	5,354	7				8	5	6	10			2	1	3					N			N				9			11	4
27	FL D2	(h)	Middlesbrough	L 2–4	2–3	11	Wilkins, Small	7,532	7				8	5	6	10			2†		3					N	1						9		12	11	4
Nov 3	FL D2	(a)	Ipswich Town	W 3–1	2–0	9	Byrne, Small 2 (1 pen)	11,437	7				8	5	6	10			2	1	3					N							9		N	11	4
10	FL D2	(h)	Plymouth Argyle	W 3–2	1–1	8	Barham, Small, Codner	7,305	7				8	3	6	10			2	1	5					N							9		N	11	4
17	FL D2	(a)	West Ham United	L 1–2	1–0	9	Small	23,082	7				8	3	6	10			2	1	5					N							9		N	11	4
20	FMC R1	(a)	Plymouth Argyle	D* 0–0*	0–0	–		3,596	7			N	8	3		10			2	1	5	N		6									9			11	4
24	FL D2	(h)	Millwall	D 0–0	0–0	9		9,638				N	8		6	10			2	1	5	N		3								7	9			11	4
Dec 1	FL D2	(a)	Oldham Athletic	L 1–6	0–2	12	Wilkins	11,426	7				8†	3	2	10			14	1	5	12		6									9			11‡	4
15	FL D2	(h)	Barnsley	W 1–0	0–0	10	Barham	5,829	7				8†	N	2	10			3	1	5			6					12				9			11	4
19	FMC R2	(h)	Charlton Athletic	W 3–1	1–0	–	Codner, Small 2	2,588	7					14	6	10‡			2	1	3	8		5					N				9			11	4
22	FL D2	(a)	Port Vale	W 1–0	0–0	7	Small	6,750	7					N	2	10			3	1	5	8		6					N				9			11	4
26	FL D2	(h)	Bristol Rovers	L 0–1	0–1	9		6,936	7					3‡		10			2	1	5	8		6	14				12				9			11†	4
Jan 1	FL D2	(a)	Notts County	L 1–2	1–2	11	Gurinovich	8,276				N			2	10			3	1	5	8		6	N				7				9			11	4
5	FAC R3	(h)	Scunthorpe Utd	W 3–2	2–1	–	Barham 2, Gurinovich	7,785	7†					N	6	10			2	1	3	8		5								12	9			11	4
12	FL D2	(a)	Wolverhampton W.	W 3–2	2–1	10	Wade, Codner, Barham	12,788	7					14	6	10			2	1	3			5					N				9		8	11	4‡
16	FL D2	(h)	Newcastle United	W 4–2	1–0	7	Wade 4	7,684	7					N	6	10			2	1	3			5					N				9		8	11	4
19	FL D2	(h)	Watford	W 3–0	2–0	6	Small (pen), Codner 2 (1 pen)	8,339	7				12	14	6	10			2	1	3			5									9‡		8†	11	4
26	FAC R4	(a)	Liverpool	D 2–2	0–0	–	Small (pen), Byrne	32,670	7‡				10	14	6				2	1	3			5	12								9		8†	11	4
30	FAC R4 Rep	(h)	Liverpool	L 2–3*	1–1	–	Small, Byrne	14,440	7				8	14	6	10			2	1	3			5									9		N	11‡	4
Feb 2	FL D2	(a)	Charlton Athletic	W 2–1	1–0	6	Small (pen), Codner	7,178	7				8	N	6	10			2	1	3			5									9		N	11	4
18	FMC S QF	(h)	Crystal Palace	L 0–2*	0–0	–		9,633	7				8	14	6†	10			2	1	3			5‡									9		12	11	4
20	FL D2	(h)	Leicester City	W 3–0	1–0	6	Small, Wilkins, Wade	6,455					8	6		10			2	1	3				N							7	9†	5	12	11	4
23	FL D2	(a)	Plymouth Argyle	L 0–2	0–2	6		5,384	7†				8	6		10			2	1	3				14							12		5	9‡	11	4
27	FL D2	(a)	Newcastle United	D 0–0	0–0	6		12,692					8	6	5	10			2	1	3			N	N							7			9	11	4
Mar 2	FL D2	(h)	Oldham Athletic	L 1–2	0–1	6	Chivers	9,496					8	N	6	10			2	1	3										5	7	9†		12	11	4
9	FL D2	(a)	Millwall	L 0–3	0–2	9		9,824					8	12	6	10			2†	1	3				11				N		5	7	9				4
13	FL D2	(a)	Sheffield Wed.	D 1–1	0–1	8	Byrne	23,969					8	14	6	10			2	1	3								12		5	7	9†			11‡	4
16	FL D2	(h)	Blackburn Rovers	W 1–0	0–0	7	Chivers	6,468					8	14	6	10			2	1	3								12		5	7‡	9†			11	4
20	FL D2	(h)	West Bromwich A.	W 2–0	1–0	5	Nelson 2	6,676					8	N	6	10			2	1	3				N				9		5	7				11	4
23	FL D2	(a)	Swindon Town	W 3–1	1–1	4	Walker, Codner (pen), Nelson	7,342					8	N	6	10			2	1	3				14				9		5	7‡				11	4
30	FL D2	(a)	Bristol Rovers	W 3–1	2–1	4	Byrne 2, Walker	6,276					8‡		6	10	N		2	1	3				14				9		5	7				11	4
Apr 3	FL D2	(h)	Port Vale	L 1–2	1–1	5	Chivers	9,733					8		6	10			2	1	3				N				9		5	7†			12	11	4
6	FL D2	(a)	Leicester City	L 0–3	0–2	6		8,444					8	N	6	10			2	1	3								9‡		5	7			14	11	4
10	FL D2	(h)	West Ham United	W 1–0	1–0	6	Byrne	11,904	7‡				8	N	6	10			2	1	3								14		5		9			11	4
13	FL D2	(h)	Notts County	D 0–0	0–0	5		9,864	7				8		6	10			2	1	3		N						N		5		9			11	4
16	FL D2	(a)	Portsmouth	L 0–1	0–1	5		12,271	7‡				8		6	10			2	1	3		12						14		5		9			11	4†
20	FL D2	(h)	Oxford United	L 0–3	0–1	6		8,118	7†	1			8		6	10			2		3		12						14		5		9‡			11	4
23	FL D2	(h)	Bristol City	L 0–1	0–0	6		7,738	7				8	N	6	10			2	1	3								N		5		9			11	4
27	FL D2	(a)	Hull City	W 1–0	0–0	6	Barham	4,037	7	1	10		8	N	6				2		3								12		5		9†			11	4
May 4	FL D2	(a)	Middlesbrough	L 0–2	0–0	7		18,054	7		10		8†	14	6				2	1	3‡								12		5		9			11	4
11	FL D2	(h)	Ipswich Town	W 2–1	1–0	6	Small (pen), Wilkins	12,281	7		6†		8‡	12		10			2	1	3										5		9		14	11	4
19	FL D2 PO Lg1	(h)	Millwall	W 4–1	1–1	–	Barham, Small, Walker, Codner	15,390	7		6			N	2	10				1	3		8								5	14	9			11‡	4
22	FL D2 PO Lg2	(a)	Millwall	W 2–1	0–1	–	Codner, Robinson	17,370	7†		6			12	2	10				1	3		8						11‡		5	14	9				4
Jun 2	FL D2 PO F	(n*)	Notts County	L 1–3	0–1	–	Wilkins	59,940	7		5		14	12	2	10				1	3†		8‡								6		9			11	4
							League appearances		35	2	6	1	34	15	42	45	0	0	45	45	46	3	3	21	1	0	1	1	13	2	20	13	42	2	5	47	49
							Substitute appearances						5	10					1			1	2		4				11	1		4			6		
							League goals		5				9		4	10					1	1							5			1	16		6	4	8

Notes: Nov 20 – after extra time.
– tie won 3–1 on penalties.
Jan 30 – after extra time (90-minute score 1–1).
Feb 18 – after extra time.
Jun 2 – played at Wembley Stadium.
The Football League play-offs are included in the end-of-season statistics.
The Football League was sponsored as the Barclays League, the Football League Cup was sponsored as the Rumbelows League Cup, and the Full Members Cup was sponsored as the Zenith Data Systems Cup.

They left it very, very late, but Albion had secured a play-off place in sixth position and a two-legged meeting with Millwall. The team had far exceeded expectations, but curiously support actually fell and the home average was a paltry 8,386. The outstanding performers were goalkeeper Perry Digweed; John Crumplin, a revelation at full-back; the consistent Gary Chivers; and Mike Small, a player of strength and skill who had looked capable of more goals until he received an injury in February. Amazingly, Albion's goal-difference was *minus* six, reflecting some heavy defeats home and away, and they aimed to become the first team in history to win promotion with a negative goal-difference.

The Millwall games were all-ticket with the Lions firm favourites. The first leg was staged on Sunday, 19 May, at Hove and Lloyd was forced to make changes because of injuries. Stefan Iovan, a very experienced £60,000 import from Romania, was brought in as sweeper and Small was played as a lone striker. For half an hour the outlook was bleak, the Lions taking

As part of their community programme, Albion launched *Seagull News* in August 1990, a regular newspaper with features on the community scheme, the club in general, the county football scene and other matters of interest.

Albion 1990–91

Back row left to right: David Coldwell, Paul McCarthy, Perry Digweed, Nicky Bissett, Brian McKenna, Wayne Stemp, Steve Gatting.
Third row left to right: Greg O'Dowd, Jonathan Lockhart, Larry May (reserve-team coach), John Robinson, Derek McGrath, Chris Lyons, John Crumplin, Adrian Owers, Gary Chivers, Stuart Munday, Lee Cormack, Ted Streeter (youth development officer), Tim Smith, Billy Logan.
Seated left to right: Malcolm Stuart (physio), Garry Nelson, Mark Barham, Dean Wilkins (capt.), Barry Lloyd (man.), Robert Codner, Ian Chapman, Steve Penney, Martin Hinshelwood (coach).
On ground left to right: Mark Gumpright, Spencer Rush, Jamie Williams, Michael Barrett, Scott McDonald, Jonathan Norris, Stuart Danbury, Andy Nimmo, Simon Funnell, Mark Sherriff.

the lead on fourteen minutes, but the Seagulls then came back and Mark Barham equalised five minutes before the break. The tie was virtually settled in seven incredible second-half minutes as Mike Small suddenly rediscovered his old form. Mike himself scored in the 53rd minute following a defensive mistake, laid on the third for Clive Walker two minutes later, and then set up Robert Codner for the fourth in the 59th minute. A 4–1 lead going into the second leg looked to be enough and the Seagulls' supporters in the 15,390 crowd celebrated wildly.

Every Albion home match was filmed by Video Sport Limited and made available to the public in the form of home-videos with full commentary for the first time. A compilation of the whole season was later made available.

There was a red-hot atmosphere in The Den on the Tuesday night, and when the Lions opened the scoring in the sixteenth minute the 2,500 Albion followers were apprehensive. Shortly afterwards Perry Digweed produced a fingertip save from David Thompson that probably turned the match; a Millwall goal then would have put enormous pressure on Albion, but they held out until half time and nearly scored themselves. Two minutes into the second half Small and Barham set up Robert Codner for the equaliser. That knocked the stuffing out of Millwall and it was Albion who dominated the rest of the match. John Robinson scored his first goal for the club on 72 minutes to win the match 2–1 and give Albion a magnificent 6–2 aggregate victory.

THE 1991 DIVISION TWO PLAY-OFF FINAL — SO NEAR AND YET ...

Albion thus secured their third appearance at Wembley eight years after their F.A. Cup final appearances against Manchester United. This time the opponents were Notts County, with the prize a place in the First Division and matches against United, Liverpool, Arsenal, Tottenham, etc. For Albion that would mean a return to the élite company they shared for four seasons from 1979 to 1983 and a financial reward estimated at over £1 million, vital to a club as debt-ridden as Brighton.

County had finished the regular season on a winning streak and gained fourth place, ten points clear of the Seagulls; they had defeated Middlesbrough 2–1 on aggregate to reach the final. Albion were slight underdogs, but their tremendous performances against Millwall gave everyone cause for optimism.

The two sides lined up thus:

Brighton and Hove Albion: Perry Digweed; Gary Chivers; Steve Gatting; Dean Wilkins (captain); Nicky Bissett; Colin Pates; Mark Barham; Stefan Iovan; Mike Small; Robert Codner; Clive Walker; subs. Ian Chapman and John Byrne.

Notts County: Steve Cherry; Charlie Palmer; Alan Paris; Chris Short; Dean Yeates; Don O'Riordan; Dean Thomas; Phil Turner (captain); Dave Regis; Mark Draper; Tommy Johnson; subs. Paul Harding and Kevin Bartlett.

The launch of Seagull Bingo on 25 February saw the end of the popular Seagull Lottery after nearly thirteen years and the Sussex Cashline after three. The new competition offered three games for 50 pence with top prizes of £2,000.

Around 32,400 supporters made the journey from Sussex to the now all-seated Wembley Stadium on Sunday, 2 June 1991; it was the greatest exodus of Albion fans ever, quite a revelation in an otherwise poorly-supported season. County had about 26,000 fans in a crowd of 59,940.

County kicked off defending the tunnel end, but it was the Seagulls, in a dazzling, red-and-white 'paint-splash' change strip, who took the early honours. On three minutes Robert Codner fired a left-footer wide from just outside the box, then Steve Cherry was forced into a desperate save with his feet from Clive Walker. Albion were making most of the running, but County looked dangerous on the break and the live-wire Tommy Johnson gave the Magpies the lead on 29 minutes, unmarked inside the goal area to head home after a short corner that had confused the Albion defence. Back came Brighton, and just before half time Clive Walker headed a Barham cross against the near post from twelve yards out with Cherry beaten.

The second period was just three minutes old when Dean Wilkins curled a free kick from 33 yards against the top of the crossbar, but County nearly made it 2–0 through Johnson as the game swung back and forth. Then, on 59 minutes, the danger man struck again: Tommy Johnson received the ball on the left edge of the Albion penalty area and fired an acute shot on the turn that had enough pace to beat the despairing Perry Digweed. Almost immediately John Byrne and Ian Chapman were brought on for Stefan Iovan and Steve Gatting. Byrne soon had a chance from 22 yards, but fired his right-foot shot badly wide. The County defence was now on top of the Albion attack. Mike Small, so effective against Millwall, hardly got a look-in and Robert Codner was restricted on his forward runs by the experienced Don O'Riordan.

The game was sealed in the 71st minute when Dave Regis chested a centre into the net at the far post for County's third. Albion had just one more chance, John Byrne's tricky run setting up Dean Wilkins to make it 3–1 in the last minute, but when Mr Elleray blew the final whistle the Seagulls were left to reflect on what might have been. Phil Turner and his men received the play-off trophy, then a tearful Dean Wilkins led his side up to the royal box and on a lap of honour to the unstinting applause of the Brighton supporters.

It was a disappointing day for the Seagulls. County deserved their victory for their better finishing, but few Albion fans could ever have imagined at the start of the season how close their favourites would have come to reaching the First Division with such meagre resources.

End of a dream

Notts County's Dave Regis raises his arm in triumph after scrambling the ball into Albion's net. With County now 3–0 up and less than 20 minutes left on the watch, this was the moment the Seagulls knew their dream of a return to Division One was at an end. The Magpies' flirtation with the élite lasted just one season as they were relegated in 1992.

Wembley 1991: how it was

Some of the 32,400 Albion fans who supported the team so splendidly in the play-off final. It was the biggest 'awayday' following in the history of the club, but the average attendance for the regular League matches was a miserable 8,386. As has always been said, the potential is there, but it is has so rarely been realised.

SEASON 1990–91 — OTHER MATTERS

In a season of constant interest, Albion's F.A. Cup run was short but sweet. After disposing of stubborn Scunthorpe United 3–2 at the Goldstone, the Seagulls were drawn at League champions Liverpool to revive memories of 1983 and 1984 when the Reds were twice sent tumbling out of the competition. Around 5,000 Albion supporters saw their favourites hold Liverpool goal-less at half time, with John Crumplin performing magnificently to negate the threat from England's John Barnes. Two goals from Ian Rush soon after the break looked to have wrapped the game up, but, with tremendous support from their followers, Albion stormed back with a Mike Small penalty and then equalised with a John Byrne header thirteen minutes from time. The Seagulls then came close to repeating their famous triumphs, and it was Liverpool who were glad to hear the final whistle.

With the Goldstone's capacity down to just 17,677, the replay was made members-only for Albion supporters and a 14,440 crowd saw a tremendous contest. England midfielder Steve McMahon, back from injury, gave Liverpool the lead, but Mike Small equalised before half time. Small appeared unlucky to have a second-half effort disallowed and the game went to

extra time. John Byrne latched on to a short back-pass to fire Albion ahead in the 99th minute, but a superb shot from Ian Rush and another goal from the inspirational McMahon in the second period of extra time won the match for Liverpool. Thus the Merseysiders finally laid their Brighton bogey, but they went out in the next round to Everton after another tremendous tussle.

The Zenith Data Systems Cup saw Albion progress past Charlton Athletic and then Plymouth Argyle – courtesy of a penalty shoot-out – to a southern quarter-final tie with Crystal Palace. The First Division side's robust aerial bombardment won them no friends at the Goldstone, but they took the match 2–0 in extra time after both of Albion's central defenders, Gary Chivers and Paul McCarthy, had gone off injured. Palace went on to lift the trophy at Wembley with victory over Everton. In the Rumbelows League Cup, Albion went out tamely to Fourth Division Northampton Town who triumphed 2–0 in the Hove leg.

It had been a tremendously entertaining season, but at the end of it Albion were still in Division Two and facing an uncertain future. Money was still desperately short: around

£109,000 was banked from the trip to Wembley, but the wage-bill had risen by 70 per cent in the last two years to a massive £1·25 million, the total debt had risen to £2·6 million, the club was losing around £1,000 a day in interest charges, and gates had continued to be fall despite the success of the team. The search for a new home continued, and in November, together with with local development company Wyncote, the club launched an £18 million scheme for a multi-purpose sports, leisure and shopping complex to include a 25,000-capacity, all-seated stadium as required by the Football Licensing Authority

by 1994 (in the top two divisions). The artist's impression was splendid, but the reality was that there was no agreed site and little hope of finding the funding with the country in a deep recession. Negotiations with Brighton Council for Waterhall proved fruitless – as they had in Mike Bamber's day – on environmental grounds, and the club looked to the only possible site in Hove, at Toad's Hole (between King George VI Avenue and the bypass). Without the sale of the Goldstone and the extra revenue to be generated from commercial concerns associated with a new stadium, the board believed the outlook was bleak.

SEASON 1991–92

It's been said before: 'What a difference a year makes!' — but never was it more apt. In June 1991, Albion just failed to make the First Division; eleven months later they found themselves relegated as the never-ending cycle of success and failure took another turn. There is rarely a dull moment following the fortunes of Brighton and Hove Albion, and supporters certainly run the full gamut of emotions.

The club was obliged to cash in on last season's find, top scorer Mike Small who moved on to West Ham United for a £400,000 fee; it was an excellent profit but a major setback to hopes for a successful season. Garry Nelson joined Charlton Athletic for £50,000 after four years in Hove, while leaving on free transfers were Steve Gatting (Charlton Athletic) after 369 games for the club, the last link with the 1983 F.A. Cup final side, and the injury-plagued Steve Penney (Hearts). Barry Lloyd added only the experienced former Millwall captain Les Briley and an old favourite, Crystal Palace's Gary O'Reilly, to the first-team squad, both on free transfers.

This year's variation in the colours – blue-and-white striped shorts – was a real eye-opener and caused much amusement wherever it was seen! The new shirt sponsors were the TSB

Bank. At the Goldstone the more relaxed atmosphere apparent throughout the Football League resulted in the removal of all perimeter fences after thirteen years and the opening of most areas to non-members.

By the end of September the Seagulls were twelfth, and had shown glimpses of impressive form and excellent character, especially in the Lions' Den at Millwall. Perry Digweed was injured in the warm-up; reserve 'keeper Mark Beeney, watching from the stand, was called into action as an emergency substitute, but for the first eight minutes defender Gary Chivers stood guard between the Albion goalposts. The Seagulls ran out 2–1 winners on a memorable night.

Scoring his seventh goal of the season at Millwall was John Byrne, but seven weeks later the popular striker was sold to Sunderland for £225,000, an offer hard-up Albion could not ignore. Having already seen Mike Small depart, it was a great

> England lost 3–1 to the U.S.S.R. at the Goldstone on 8 September in the first-ever women's international staged at Hove.

Albion 1991–92

Back row left to right: Greg O'Dowd, John Robinson, Bryan Wade, Gary Chivers, Nicky Bissett, Stefan Iovan, Robert Codner, Clive Walker.
Middle row left to right: Larry May (reserve-team coach), Malcolm Stuart (physio), David Clarkson, Garry Nelson, Gary O'Reilly, Perry Digweed, Mark Beeney, Mike Small, John Byrne, Ted Streeter (youth development officer), Wayne Stemp, Martin Hinshelwood (coach), Stuart Munday.
Front row left to right: John Crumplin, Ian Chapman, Russel Bromage, Barry Lloyd (manager), Dean Wilkins (captain), Derek McGrath, Mark Barham.

SEASON 1991–92

Player columns (left→right): Barham M, Beeney M, Bissett N, Briley L, Byrne J, Chapman I, Chivers G, Clarkson D, Codner R, Crumplin J, Digweed P, Farrington M, Funnell S, Gall M, Gallacher B, Iovan S, McCarthy P, McGrath D, Meade R, Munday S, O'Dowd G, O'Reilly G, Reed P, Robinson J, Sommer J, Wade B, Walker C, Wilkins D

Date	Comp	Ven	Opponents	Result	HT	Pos	Scorers	Atten.
Aug 17	FL D2	(h)	Tranmere Rovers	L	0–2	0–2 22=		9,679
20	FL D2	(a)	Bristol City	L	1–2	0–1 23	Bissett	11,299
24	FL D2	(a)	Barnsley	W	2–1	1–1 16	Wade, Barham	6,066
31	FL D2	(h)	Wolverhampton W.	D	3–3	2–2 17	O'Reilly, Barham, Robinson	10,621
Sep 4	FL D2*	(a)	Millwall	W	2–1	1–1 13	Byrne, Codner	9,266
7	FL D2	(a)	Portsmouth	D	0–0	0–0 14		10,567
14	FL D2	(h)	Watford	L	0–1	0–0 16		8,741
18	FL D2	(h)	Port Vale	W	3–1	3–0 13	Byrne, Meade, Robinson	5,790
21	FL D2	(a)	Derby County	L	1–3	0–1 16	Meade	12,004
24	FLC R2 Lg1	(a)	Brentford	L	1–4	0–3 –	Robinson	4,927
28	FL D2	(h)	Bristol Rovers	W	3–1	1–1 12	Codner 2, Byrne	6,392
Oct 5	FL D2	(a)	Sunderland	L	2–4	2–1 14	Byrne, Robinson	15,119
9	FLC R2 Lg2	(h)	Brentford	W	4–2*	3–1 –	Byrne 2, Codner, Meade	4,502
12	FL D2	(h)	Ipswich Town	D	2–2	0–1 15	Byrne, Chivers	9,010
19	FL D2	(a)	Charlton Athletic	L	0–2	0–2 18		5,598
23	FMC R2	(h)	Wimbledon	W	3–2	2–1 –	Barham, Robinson, Chivers	2,796
26	FL D2	(h)	Swindon Town	L	0–2	0–1 19		7,370
30	FL D2	(h)	Leicester City	L	1–2	0–1 19	Codner	6,424
Nov 2	FL D2	(a)	Blackburn Rovers	L	0–1	0–0 20		9,877
6	FL D2	(h)	Grimsby Town	W	3–0	3–0 20	Meade 2, Gall	4,420
9	FL D2	(h)	Middlesbrough	D	1–1	1–0 20	Gall	8,720
16	FL D2	(a)	Cambridge United	D	0–0	0–0 17		7,625
23	FL D2	(a)	Oxford United	L	1–3	0–1 19	Gall	4,563
26	FMC S QF	(a)	West Ham United	L	0–2	0–2 –		8,146
30	FL D2	(h)	Plymouth Argyle	W	1–0	0–0 18	O'Reilly	6,713
Dec 7	FL D2	(a)	Southend United	L	1–2	0–0 22	Wade	6,303
14	FL D2	(h)	Newcastle United	D	2–2	1–2 20	O'Reilly, Farrington	7,658
21	FL D2	(a)	Millwall	L	3–4	0–1 21	Gall 2, Chapman	7,598
26	FL D2	(a)	Leicester City	L	1–2	0–1 23	Gallacher	16,767
28	FL D2	(a)	Wolverhampton W.	L	0–2	0–2 23		13,606
Jan 1	FL D2	(h)	Bristol City	D	0–0	0–0 23		7,555
4	FAC R3	(h)	Crawley Town	W	5–0	3–0 –	Gall, Walker, Chapman 2 (1 pen), Meade	18,031
11	FL D2	(h)	Barnsley	W	3–1	2–0 23	Robinson, Wade, Chapman	6,107
17	FL D2	(a)	Tranmere Rovers	D	1–1	0–0 21	Meade	7,179
25	FAC R4	(a)	Bolton Wanderers	L	1–2	0–0 –	Meade	12,635
Feb 1	FL D2	(h)	Charlton Athletic	L	1–2	1–1 22	Walker	8,870
8	FL D2	(a)	Swindon Town	L	1–2	1–0 23	Gall	9,127
15	FL D2	(h)	Oxford United	L	1–2	1–2 24	Robinson	6,096
22	FL D2	(a)	Plymouth Argyle	D	1–1	0–1 24	Gall	5,259
29	FL D2	(h)	Southend United	W	3–2	1–1 24	Meade, Codner, Munday	8,271
Mar 7	FL D2	(a)	Newcastle United	W	1–0	0–0 20	Gall	24,597
10	FL D2	(a)	Grimsby Town	W	1–0	0–0 18	Walker	4,583
14	FL D2	(h)	Blackburn Rovers	L	0–3	0–2 20		10,845
21	FL D2	(a)	Middlesbrough	L	0–4	0–3 23		13,054
28	FL D2	(h)	Cambridge United	D	1–1	0–1 23	Gall	7,702
31	FL D2	(h)	Watford	W	1–0	0–0 21	Meade	7,589
Apr 11	FL D2	(a)	Port Vale	L	1–2	0–0 23	Gall	6,441
15	FL D2	(h)	Derby County	L	1–2	0–0 23	Gall	8,159
20	FL D2	(a)	Bristol Rovers	L	1–4	0–2 24	Gall	6,092
25	FL D2	(a)	Sunderland	D	2–2	2–2 24	Gall, Codner	9,851
29	FL D2	(h)	Portsmouth	W	2–1	1–0 23	Robinson, Meade	11,647
May 2	FL D2	(a)	Ipswich Town	L	1–3	1–2 23	Meade	26,803

Player totals:

	Barham M	Beeney M	Bissett N	Briley L	Byrne J	Chapman I	Chivers G	Clarkson D	Codner R	Crumplin J	Digweed P	Farrington M	Funnell S	Gall M	Gallacher B	Iovan S	McCarthy P	McGrath D	Meade R	Munday S	O'Dowd G	O'Reilly G	Reed P	Robinson J	Sommer J	Wade B	Walker C	Wilkins D
League appearances	22	24	11	11	13	35	36	4	44	27	20	8	0	30	31	4	20	0	35	14	0	28	0	34	1	7	23	24
Substitute appearances	2	1	2	4		2	2	9	1	2		6	1	1		5		1		2				2				2
League goals	2		1		5	2	1		6			1		13	1				9	1		3		6		3	2	

Notes: Sep 4 – Following a pre-match injury to Digweed, Chivers (wearing no.5) started the match in goal with Crumplin (wearing no.12) at right-back. Beeney, an emergency substitute, replaced Crumplin and took over in goal after eight minutes.

Oct 9 – after extra time (90-minute score 4–1).

The Football League was sponsored as the Barclays League, the Football League Cup was sponsored as the Rumbelows League Cup, and the Full Members Cup was sponsored as the Zenith Data Systems Cup.

Barclays League Division 2 1991–92

		P	W	D	L	F	A	W	D	L	F	A	Pts
1.	Ipswich Town	46	16	3	4	42	22	8	9	6	28	28	84
2.	Middlesbrough	46	15	6	2	37	13	8	5	10	21	28	80
3.	Derby County	46	11	4	8	35	24	12	5	6	34	27	78
4.	Leicester City	46	14	4	5	41	24	9	4	10	21	31	77
5.	Cambridge United	46	10	9	4	34	19	9	8	6	31	28	74
6.	Blackburn Rovers	46	14	5	4	41	17	7	6	10	29	32	74
7.	Charlton Athletic	46	9	7	7	25	23	11	4	8	29	25	71
8.	Swindon Town	46	15	3	5	38	22	3	12	8	31	33	69
9.	Portsmouth	46	15	6	2	41	12	4	6	13	24	39	69
10.	Watford	46	9	5	9	25	23	9	6	8	26	25	65
11.	Wolverhampton W.	46	11	6	6	36	24	7	4	12	25	30	64
12.	Southend United	46	11	5	7	37	26	6	6	11	26	37	62
13.	Bristol City	46	11	9	3	43	29	5	5	13	17	34	62
14.	Tranmere Rovers	46	9	9	5	37	32	5	10	8	19	24	61
15.	Millwall	46	10	4	9	32	32	7	6	10	32	39	61
16.	Barnsley	46	11	4	8	27	25	5	7	11	19	32	59
17.	Bristol City	46	10	8	5	30	24	3	7	13	25	47	54
18.	Sunderland	46	10	6	7	36	24	4	5	14	25	42	53
19.	Grimsby Town	46	7	5	11	25	28	7	6	10	22	34	53
20.	Newcastle United	46	9	8	6	38	30	4	5	14	28	54	52
21.	Oxford United	46	10	6	7	39	30	3	5	15	27	43	50
22.	Plymouth Argyle	46	11	5	7	26	26	2	4	17	16	38	48
23.	**ALBION**	46	7	7	9	36	37	5	4	14	20	40	47
24.	Port Vale	46	7	8	8	23	25	3	7	13	19	34	45

blow for fans to lose Byrne who went on to enjoy a successful Cup run with Sunderland. By this time Lloyd had acquired two new strikers: Raphael Meade, a former Arsenal youngster who had spent several years on the Continent; and Mark Farrington, a player of similar pedigree from Dutch club Feyenoord for a potential fee of £100,000. Meade scored nine League goals but rarely impressed. The unfortunate Farrington, plagued by injury problems, never showed any form in his few outings and became a target of the crowd's frustration.

After the departure of Byrne, Lloyd signed a third new striker, Maidstone United's Mark Gall for £45,000. The ever-willing and speedy Gall quickly became a crowd favourite in a struggling side and top-scored with fourteen goals in League and Cup to scoop the Player of the Season award.

In December, Albion fell into the relegation places for the first time and also suffered a first-ever League defeat at the hands of Wolverhampton Wanderers — at the fourteenth attempt! As 1991 gave way to '92 it became obvious that the rest of the season was to be a struggle against the drop. A good run in late February and early March saw the club rise off the bottom to eighteenth place, but there were only two more victories in the last ten games and the Seagulls' fate was sealed.

The side managed just seven home wins and lost 23 times, both equalling worst-ever figures. Much was made about the sale of Small and Byrne and the weakness of the forward line, but the defence was equally culpable. The injury list was the longest for many years – only Robert Codner managed 40 League games – but after the arrival of Gall there was little chance of bringing in any other new faces as the financial crisis bit deeper. While crowds all over the country rose for the fifth successive season, the Goldstone League average fell for the third year in a row to just 8,010, a level unheard of in peacetime since the great Depression of the 1930s. On 6 November, with live football on television, just 4,420 watched the 3–0 defeat of Grimsby Town, the lowest League gate at Hove since 1955.

The one highlight was a third-round F.A. Cup tie at home to Sussex Senior Cup holders Crawley Town. Having twice reached the first round proper in the early '70s, it was the Reds' first-ever excursion this far into the competition. They defeated Fourth Division Northampton Town 4–2 at Town Mead in the first round and then won 2–0 at Hayes to set up the first-ever clash between two Sussex sides in the competition proper in 111 seasons of the Cup. It was also Albion's first meeting with a Sussex side in the competition since the administrative blunder of 1932.

In the Crawley side were Tony Vessey, who had once played for the Albion in the First Division, and Damian Webber, a former Brighton reserve, but the biggest cheer was reserved for 36-year-old substitute Tony Towner who made 183 appearances on the Albion wing from 1973 until 1978.

A crowd of 18,031 gathered on 4 January to see Crawley dominate the game for the first 20 minutes, but Mark Gall's opener against the run of play knocked the stuffing out of the Reds and the Seagulls ran out comfortable 5–0 winners. However, the north Sussex side left with a sizeable profit from the record £109,428 receipts. The reward for the Albion was a trip to Bolton, but a tame performance saw the Third Division side triumph 2–1 to end the Sussex interest.

Brentford, the eventual Third Division champions, were Albion's opponents in the Rumbelows League Cup. Inspired by Brighton's former Cup final winger Neil Smillie, the Bees coasted the opening leg 4–1 at Griffin Park. The second leg saw a rousing Albion come-back to level the tie at 90 minutes, but Brentford won through with a goal in extra time.

The Zenith Data Systems Cup saw Albion account for First Division Wimbledon 3–2 with Gary Chivers firing home a last-minute winner from just outside the box. The Seagulls went out 2–0 to West Ham United in the southern area quarter-final.

The reserves won the Sussex Senior Cup for the second time in five seasons, skipper Greg O'Dowd lifting the trophy after a 1–0 defeat of the Eastbourne-based side Langney Sports.

With little to shout about on the pitch, the Goldstone faithful turned their attention to manager Barry Lloyd who had now been in charge for well over five years. In December, Lloyd was appointed to the board as managing director in complete charge of the day-to-day running of the club, but by the end of the season the calls from the terraces for the his head had become intense. He was emphatically supported by 46-year-old Greg Stanley, the club's president and greatest benefactor who had taken over as chairman in December from Dudley Sizen (who resigned the next day). He asserted that the club would have folded if not for the profit – around £550,000 – from Lloyd's transfer dealings.

The dissatisfaction felt by many supporters materialised in the form of the 'Brighton Independent Supporters Association' (BISA). An offshoot of the 'Gulls Eye' 'fanzine', the group staged a peaceful demonstration on the pitch after the Southend United match on 29 February to call for a dialogue with the board. A few days later Greg Stanley, together with fellow directors Barry Lloyd and Dennis Sullivan, met a BISA delegation to explain the club's predicament. The welcome (but long overdue) display of *glasnost* continued with a public meeting on 12 May, an event which allowed supporters to question the chairman directly, a notion almost unheard of since the 1977 buy-up of shares by the board. (Two public meetings were held by Mike Bamber in 1981 and '82). It was intended as the first of a series of regular meetings, but the idea soon fizzled out.

The search for a new ground continued and received a large boost in May when Hove Borough Council voted overwhelmingly in favour of inviting an application from the club for a sporting complex at the Toad's Hole site off King George VI Avenue, but the idea met with much local opposition.

In a Victory Shield international at the Goldstone on 10 April, England's under-15 schoolboys defeated their Northern Ireland counterparts 3–0 before a crowd of 3,944. Jamie Howell from Worthing, already on Arsenal's books, skippered the side and scored twice.

BRIGHTON INDEPENDENT SUPPORTERS ASSOCIATION

TO ALL BRIGHTON FANS

LAST HOME GAME THE CLUB LOCKED THE DOORS WHEN CONFRONTED BY THE LOYAL FANS.

HOW LONG ARE WE GOING TO PUT UP WITH THIS INSULTING AND UNCONSTRUCTIVE POLICY.

WHATEVER HAPPENS TODAY (*EVEN IF WE WIN 4-1*), WE INTEND TO OCCUPY THE PITCH AFTER THE GAME. WE WILL REMAIN THERE UNTIL A CLUB DIRECTOR MEETS US AND AGREES TO SOME KIND OF DIALOGUE.

IF YOU CARE ABOUT THE WAY THIS CLUB IS GOING DON'T SKULK OFF AFTER THE GAME. FAN POWER IS A TELLING FORCE. WEST HAM AND ARSENAL FANS HAVE PROVED THAT!

GET BEHIND THE TEAM DURING THE GAME AND UNITE ON THE PITCH PEACEFULLY AFTERWARDS!

WE HAVE BEEN ASSURED THAT NO ONE WILL BE ARRESTED

IF YOU CARE YOU'LL BE OUT THERE

Strong words from BISA
This leaflet was distributed before the match on 29 February and resulted in a demonstration by around 1,000 supporters.

SEASON 1992–93

Despite being relegated, Albion found themselves still in Division Two — but only because of the formation of the new F.A. Premier League. While the élite wallowed in a satellite-television windfall, supporters were left in little doubt that Albion were among the poorest relations with the whole season played out to a backdrop of financial uncertainty which threatened the very existence of the club. The years of living beyond its means – paying wages for better-quality players while gates plummeted – finally caught up with the club, resulting in the most traumatic season in 92 years of history.

It was obvious in the close season, when there was great difficulty paying players and other staff, that this was to be a make-or-break year. The board's hopes rested upon a 'financial restructuring', in essence the borrowing of more money against the value of the Goldstone Ground in a commercial mortgage; this value was to be enhanced to around £4 million by obtaining planning permission for a commercial development which would only come to fruition when the club moved to a new ground. The plan for a 'non-food retail park', designed by developers Wyncote plc, was put to Hove Council in August, but the planning committee finally rejected it in November against the advice of its professional officers. The scheme was debated by the full council in January but received the same fate.

The urgent need for financial restructuring and, in particular, the planning consent, had been made that much greater in November – Friday the 13th to be precise – when the Inland Revenue issued a petition in the High Court to have the club wound up for non-payment of £398,000 in PAYE. Managing director Barry Lloyd heartened supporters: 'Rest assured, the Albion will be carrying on.' He was proved right — just.

In order to meet the short-term problem of Albion's tax demand, Wyncote made an offer to buy the Goldstone, a deal which would have required Albion to move to another ground two or three years later. With a new local stadium looking a long way off, that meant a spell of ground-sharing with perhaps Portsmouth or Millwall. The board rejected the approach by Wyncote and dropped any notion of a £23 million development with them at Toad's Hole, looking instead to a £30 million development on one of three unnamed sites to the west of Hove.

With an adjournment won in the High Court on 16 December, Albion returned to Hove Council with a modified scheme which was similarly rejected on 2 February, just eight days before the next court appearance. (After discussions between the parties, and facing the prospect of a public inquiry, the council eventually passed the plan on 29 June.) This time Lloyd was 'no more than hopeful', but the Seagulls won a second stay of execution until 21 April. Some supporters claimed that liquidation would be beneficial; that with the debts cleared and a new board in control the club could prosper. But that could only happen if a buyer could be found. There were rumours of a consortium waiting in the wings, but no one came forward. Together with a lack of definite information from the Goldstone, it all left the lay fan baffled and immensely concerned.

A second winding-up petition, brought by an Australian club claiming money for the transfer of Dave Clarkson, was dismissed, but still the tax-man had to be satisfied. There was an alternative: bringing in an administrator, with the approval of creditors, to slash spending and seek a buyer. Such an action would have staved off the threat of winding-up, but a split board

rejected the move with the result that directors Bernard Clarke and Dennis Sullivan resigned in February to deepen the crisis.

As the High Court date approached, nothing was heard from the Goldstone to reassure supporters as to the future of their club and it became clear that without an immediate cash injection Albion were going to fold. The administration option was ruled out because of the £200,000 costs involved.

Against this background of doom, the team had performed creditably, none more so than goalkeeper Mark Beeney. Signed in March 1991 for £30,000 from Maidstone United, Beeney had been tracked by Howard Wilkinson, manager of League champions Leeds United. On 20 April, the eve of the fateful showdown with the Revenue, Beeney signed for Leeds in a deal which gave Albion an immediate payment of £350,000 with more to come depending on his progress at Elland Road. Barry Lloyd whisked the bank draft to the Worthing tax offices to avert the danger, and the following day the case was dismissed.

It was the greatest save by an Albion goalkeeper in history! There is little room for sentiment in modern football, but perhaps Howard Wilkinson, who made 147 appearances for Brighton in the period 1966–71, was doing his old club a very big favour while obtaining the services of an excellent player.

The fee enabled the Seagulls to pay off the original tax bill, but the sum owed had risen to around £600,000 and there were also police and VAT bills to meet. Although the immediate threat had been lifted, the club was still in a perilous situation which prompted its best-known fan, BBC TV presenter Des Lynam, to set up an 'S.O.S.' ('Save Our Seagulls') fund in an attempt to pay off the creditors. In conjunction with the radio station Southern *fm*, Des raised around £28,500 in a marathon broadcast on Sunday, 25 April, with more events to follow.

Thus the club had survived through its most dire times, but with all the uncertainty – particularly the late payment of wages – it seemed inevitable that morale would collapse. However, to the credit of all concerned, the side performed commendably and challenged for a play-off place for much of the season. There were, of course, no new players other than free-transfers, one of which was the redoubtable Steve Foster who returned to Hove after eight years away; the 35-year-old England international, who played more games for the club in the First Division than anyone else, had a superb season at the heart of the defence and won the Player of the Season award.

		P	W	D	L	F	A	W	D	L	F	A	Pts
	Barclays League Division 2 1992–93												
1.	Stoke City	46	17	4	2	41	13	10	8	5	32	21	93
2.	Bolton Wanderers	46	18	2	3	48	14	9	7	7	32	27	90
3.	Port Vale	46	14	7	2	44	17	12	4	7	35	27	89
4.	West Bromwich A.	46	17	3	3	56	22	8	7	8	32	32	85
5.	Swansea City	46	12	7	4	38	17	8	6	9	27	30	73
6.	Stockport County	46	11	11	1	47	18	8	4	11	34	39	72
7.	Leyton Orient	46	16	4	3	49	20	5	5	13	20	33	72
8.	Reading	46	14	4	5	44	20	4	11	8	22	31	69
9.	**ALBION**	46	13	4	6	36	24	7	5	11	27	35	69
10.	Bradford City	46	12	5	6	36	24	6	9	8	33	43	68
11.	Rotherham United	46	9	7	7	30	27	8	7	8	30	33	65
12.	Fulham	46	9	9	5	28	22	7	8	8	29	33	65
13.	Burnley	46	11	8	4	38	21	4	8	11	19	38	61
14.	Plymouth Argyle	46	11	6	6	38	28	5	6	12	21	36	60
15.	Huddersfield Town	46	10	6	7	30	22	7	3	13	24	39	60
16.	Hartlepool United	46	8	6	9	19	23	6	6	11	23	37	54
17.	AFC Bournemouth	46	7	10	6	28	24	5	7	11	17	28	53
18.	Blackpool	46	9	9	5	40	30	3	6	14	23	45	51
19.	Exeter City	46	5	8	10	26	30	6	9	8	28	39	50
20.	Hull City	46	9	5	9	28	26	4	6	13	18	43	50
21.	Preston North End	46	8	5	10	41	47	5	3	15	24	47	47
22.	Mansfield Town	46	7	8	8	34	34	4	3	16	18	46	44
23.	Wigan Athletic	46	6	6	11	26	34	4	5	14	17	38	41
24.	Chester City	46	6	2	15	30	47	2	3	18	19	55	29

SEASON 1992–93

Date	Comp.	Ven.	Opponents	Result	HT	Pos.	Scorers	Atten.	Beeney M	Bissett N	Byrne J	Chapman I	Chivers G	Codner R	Cotterill S	Crumplin J	Digweed P	Edwards M	Farrington M	Foster S	Funnell S	Gallacher B	Kennedy A	McCarthy P	Macciochi D	Moulden P	Munday S	Myall S	Nogan K	Robinson J	Tuck S	Walker C	Wilkins D	Wilkinson D	Wosahlo B
Aug 15	FL D2	(a)	Leyton Orient	L 2–3	0–1	17	Moulden, Cotterill	5,614	1	5		3	2	10	9†	N				6	12					8				7		11	4		
18	FLC R1 Lg1	(a)	Colchester United	D 1–1	0–0	–	Wilkins	3,817	1	5		3	2	10		N		9		6	8									7		11	4	N	
22	FL D2	(h)	Bolton Wanderers	W 2–1	1–1	10	Cotterill, Chapman	6,205	1			3	2	10‡	9	5		14		6	N					8				7		11	4		
26	FLC R1 Lg2	(h)	Colchester United	W 1–0	0–0	–	Wilkins	4,125	1			3	2	10†		5		9‡		6	8									7		11	4	12	14
29	FL D2	(a)	Bradford City	D 1–1	0–0	11	Foster	5,151	1			3	2	10	9	5		N		6	N					8				7		11		4	
Sep 1	FL D2	(a)	Exeter City	W 3–2	2–2	7	Foster, Cotterill, Wilkinson	3,035	1			3	2	10	9	5		14		6	N					8				7		11‡		4	
5	FL D2	(h)	Preston North End	W 2–0	0–0	5	Moulden 2	6,026	1			3	2	10	9	5		N		6						8				7		11	N	4	
12	FL D2	(h)	Huddersfield Town	W 2–1	1–1	3	Foster, Moulden	6,141	1			3	2	10	9	5		14		6						8				7		11‡	N	4	
16	FL D2	(a)	Stoke City	D 1–1	0–1	4	Wilkins	10,867	1			3	2	10	9	5		7		6	N				14	8							11	4‡	
19	FL D2	(a)	Blackpool	D 2–2	0–1	5	Moulden, Codner	4,618	1			3		10	9	5		7		6				2	14	8						11‡	4	N	
23	FLC R2 Lg1	(h*)	Manchester United	D 1–1	0–1	–	Edwards	16,649	1			3	2	10		7		8		6	N		9	5								11	4	N	
26	FL D2	(h)	Reading	L 0–1	0–1	7		7,341	1			3	2†	10	9‡	12		7		6			14	5		8						11	4		
Oct 3	FL D2	(a)	Port Vale	L 1–3	1–1	9	Wilkins	5,731	1			3		10	9	2‡		7		6			12	5		8						11†	4	14	
7	FLC R2 Lg2	(a*)	Manchester United	L 0–1	0–1	–		25,405	1			3	2	10		7		8†		6	12		9	5								11	4	N	
10	FL D2	(h)	Wigan Athletic	W 1–0	1–0	6	Cotterill	5,784	1			3	2	10	9	7		N	N	6				5		8						11	4		
17	FL D2	(a)	Rotherham United	L 0–1	0–1	10		4,404	1			3	2	10		7		12	14	6			9	5					8‡			11†	4		
24	FL D2	(h)	Hartlepool United	D 1–1	0–0	12	Foster	5,918	1			3	2			7		12		6		N	9	5					10			11†	4	8	
31	FL D2	(a)	Chester City	L 1–2	0–2	13	Edwards	2,735	1			3	2			7		10	9	6		N		5					N			11	4	8	
Nov 3	FL D2	(a)	AFC Bournemouth	D 1–1	0–1	13	Wilkins	4,828	1			3	2			7		10	9†	6		N	12	5								11	4	8	
7	FL D2	(h)	Stockport County	W 2–0	1–0	12	Kennedy 2	5,742	1			3	2	10		7		9		6			8	5					N			11	4	N	
14	FAC R1	(h)	Hayes	W 2–0	1–0	–	Kennedy, Codner	5,879	1			3	2	10		7		9	N	6			8	5								11	4	N	
20	FL D2	(a)	Swansea City	W 1–0	0–0	9	Kennedy	4,645	1			3	2	10		7		9	N	6			8	5								11	4	N	
28	FL D2	(h)	Fulham	L 0–2	0–0	13		7,894	1	6		3	2	10		7		9	12				8	5								11†	4	N	
Dec 1	AMC Group	(a)	Reading	D 1–1	1–0	–	Wilkinson	1,209	1	6		3	2	10		7		9					8	5			N						4	11	N
5	FAC R2	(h)	Woking	D 1–1	1–0	–	Kennedy	9,208	1	6		3‡	2	10		7†		9					8	5					12			11	4	14	
9	AMC Group	(h)	AFC Bournemouth	W 3–2	3–2	–	Wilkinson, Walker, Nogan	1,607	1	6				10				9			N	3		5	N		2		8			11	4	7	
12	FL D2	(a)	Mansfield Town	W 3–1	1–0	9	Kennedy, Own goal, Wilkinson	2,869	1	6			2	10							N	3	8	5			N		9			11	4	7	
16	FAC R2 rep	(a)	Woking	W 2–1	1–1	–	Codner, Crumplin	5,870	1	6		3	2	10		12		N					8	5					9			11	4	7†	
19	FL D2	(h)	Plymouth Argyle	W 2–1	1–0	7	Nogan, Codner	5,962	1	6		3	2	10		7		14				N	8‡	5					9			11	4		
26	FL D2	(h)	Burnley	W 3–0	1–0	6	Nogan 2, Crumplin	8,741		6		3	2	10		7‡	1	14				N	8	5					9			11	4		
28	FL D2	(a)	Hull City	L 0–1	0–0	9		4,785	1	6		3	2	10		7					N	N	8	5					9			11	4		
Jan 2	FAC R3	(h)	Portsmouth	W 1–0	1–0	–	Edwards	17,581	1	6			2	10		7		11‡		5	14	3	8				N		9				4		
9	FL D2	(h)	Stoke City	D 2–2	0–0	8	Nogan, Own goal	8,622	1	6			2	10		7		N		5		3	8				N		9			11	4		
16	FL D2	(a)	Reading	L 0–3	0–2	9		4,400	1	6		14	2	10		7				5		3	8‡				N		9			11	4		
18	AMC R2	(h)	Walsall	W 4–2*	1–0	–	Walker, Nogan, Chivers, Kennedy	1,664	1			3	2	14		7‡		N		5			8	6			10		9			11	4		
23	FAC R4	(a)	Manchester United	L 0–1	0–0	–		33,610	1	6		3	2	10		N		14		5			8‡				7		9			11	4		
27	FL D2	(h)	Bradford City	D 1–1	0–0	10	Walker	5,141	1	6		3	2	10‡		14				5			8				7	N	9			11	4		
30	FL D2	(a)	Bolton Wanderers	W 1–0	0–0	8	Nogan	8,929	1	6		3	2	10		14							8	5			7	N	9‡			11	4		
Feb 6	FL D2	(h)	Leyton Orient	L 1–3	0–2	9	Kennedy	7,850	1	6		3	2	10		14		N					8	5			7		9			11	4‡		
13	FL D2	(a)	Preston North End	L 0–1	0–0	9		4,334	1	6		3	2	10				8			N			5			7		9			11	4	N	
17	AMC S QF	(h)	Exeter City	L 0–1	0–0	–		1,875	1			3		10		7‡		8		6			14	5			2		9			11	4	N	
20	FL D2	(h)	Exeter City	W 3–0	0–0	10	Nogan, Kennedy, Walker	5,585	1			3		10				7		6	N		8	5			2		9			11	4	N	
27	FL D2	(a)	Wigan Athletic	W 2–1	1–0	8	Nogan 2	2,033	1			3	2	10				7		6	N		8	5					9		N	11		4	
Mar 3	FL D2	(a)	Huddersfield Town	W 2–1	1–0	6	Nogan, Walker	3,563	1			3	2	10				7		6	N	N	8	5					9			11		4	
6	FL D2	(h)	Port Vale	L 0–2	0–0	7		7,294	1			3	2	10				7		6	N	N	8	5					9			11		4	
10	FL D2	(h)	West Bromwich A.	W 3–1	0–0	7	Nogan, Kennedy 2	7,440	1				2	10†				7		6	N	3	8	5					9			11	12	4	
13	FL D2	(a)	Stockport County	D 0–0	0–0	7		5,298	1				2	10				7		6	N	3	8	5			N		9				11	4	
20	FL D2	(h)	AFC Bournemouth	W 1–0	1–0	7	Nogan	7,059	1				2	10				7‡		6		3	8	5			N		9			14	11	4	
23	FL D2	(a)	Fulham	L 0–2	0–1	8		5,402	1				2	10						6	14	3‡	8	5			N		9			7	11	4	
27	FL D2	(h)	Swansea City	L 0–2	0–1	9		7,558	1		14	3	6	10				12					8‡	5			2		9			7†	11	4	
31	FL D2	(h)	Blackpool	D 1–1	0–0	7	Nogan	5,170	1			3†	6	10				12					8	5			2	N	9			7	11	4	
Apr 3	FL D2	(a)	West Bromwich A.	L 1–3	0–0	9	Codner	13,002	1		14		6	10				N				3	8‡	5				2	9			7	11	4	
7	FL D2	(h)	Mansfield Town	W 3–1	2–0	8	Edwards, Nogan, Wilkinson	4,731	1				2	10		7		11	14	6		3	8‡	5				N	9					4	
10	FL D2	(a)	Burnley	W 3–1	2–1	6	Nogan 2, Farrington	9,424	1				6	10		7		11	8	5	N	3						2	9				N	4	
14	FL D2	(h)	Hull City	W 2–0	1–0	6	Nogan, Farrington	7,776	1		8‡		6	10		7		11	14	5		3						2	9				N	4	
17	FL D2	(a)	Plymouth Argyle	L 2–3	1–2	7	Nogan 2	4,924	1		8		6	10		7†		11‡	14	5		3						2	9				12	4	
24	FL D2	(h)	Rotherham United	L 1–2	0–0	9	Nogan	7,841			8		6	10		7	1	11‡		5		3						2	9			14	N	4	
May 1	FL D2	(a)	Hartlepool United	L 0–2	0–0	10		2,693			8	14	6	10		7	1	11†		5		3‡						2	9				12	4	
8	FL D2	(h)	Chester City	W 3–2	2–2	9	Nogan, Byrne 2	6,247			8	3	6	10‡		12	1	7		5			14					2	9				11†	4	
							League appearances		42	12	5	32	43	43	11	27	4	24	3	35	0	14	26	30	0	11	7	7	30	6	0	36	32	26	0
							Substitute appearances				2	2				5		9	5		2		4		2							2	3	1	
							League goals	OG – 2			2	1		3	4	1		2	2	4			8			5			20			3	3	3	

Notes: Sep 23 and Oct 7 – the legs were drawn the other way round but were reversed at the request of the police.

Jan 18 – after extra time (90-minute score 2–2).

The Football League was sponsored as the Barclays League, the Football League Cup was sponsored as the Coca-Cola Cup, and the continuation of the Associate Members Cup was sponsored as the Autoglass Trophy. (The Football League no longer distinguishes between full and associate members.)

It was some time before the line-up settled down. Centre-forward Mark Gall had sustained a serious knee injury which eventually forced his retirement. The initial strike-force therefore comprised two loan players, Steve Cotterill (Wimbledon) and Paul Moulden (Oldham Athletic), both of whom impressed but could not be purchased. Barry Lloyd and his assistant Martin Hinshelwood – the latter largely in charge of team affairs as Lloyd becoming increasingly embroiled in financial matters – then turned to two free-transfer signings, Matthew Edwards and Andy Kennedy, before Edwards gave way to Kurt Nogan. A former Welsh under-21 international, Nogan had been released by Luton Town and looked a fish out of water initially, but blossomed as the season progressed to end up top scorer with an impressive 20 goals in his 30 League appearances. Kennedy was next on the list with eight League goals.

Albion spent much of the season in seventh, eighth or ninth place. Three wins in a row in April moved the Seagulls up to sixth, but it proved only a brief flirtation with the play-off positions as three consecutive defeats ended any hopes of a fourth trip to Wembley and promotion. Six home games were lost, too many to mount a sustained challenge without performing wonders away from Hove. Nevertheless, ninth place, only three points adrift of the play-off places, represented a much better performance than many followers had feared.

Most of the interest came in the cups. Albion won a League Cup tie for the first time since 1985, 2–1 on aggregate against

Colchester United. The Premier League sides, although no longer members of the Football League, still competed in the Football League Cup, and the competition, now sponsored by Coca-Cola, added some fizz to Albion's season by pairing them with mighty Manchester United. The first leg attracted 16,649 fans to Hove who saw the Seagulls hold the inaugural Premier League champions to a 1–1 draw. The second leg was won 1–0 by United, but Albion were happy to make around £92,000 from the tie, a timely sum enabling the club to meet a VAT demand.

The F.A. Cup saw two new opponents at the Goldstone: Hayes and Woking. Hayes, members of the Diadora (Isthmian) Premier Division, were beaten 2–0, but Conference side Woking proved sterner opposition, drawing the match at Hove 1–1. The Surrey side took an early lead in the replay and a 5,870 crowd packed into the Kingfield Stadium anticipated an upset, but an equaliser by Robert Codner before half time and a late winner from John Crumplin sealed the game for the League side.

In the third round, Albion staged a home tie against First Division promotion candidates Portsmouth before the largest crowd of the season, 17,581, which generated record receipts of £115,577. Missing phenomenal goalscorer Guy Whittingham, Pompey still dominated the match but Albion won the day with a tremendous defensive performance and a 27th-minute goal from Matthew Edwards. The reward could hardly have been better: another tie with Manchester United at Old Trafford. With Albion deep in financial trouble, the match could not have been better timed and a turnout of 33,610 meant a reward of around £100,000. Again the result was close, but United, fielding ten internationals, won the tie with a goal from the precocious Ryan Giggs in an otherwise lack-lustre display.

In the third cup competition, the Autoglass Trophy, Albion progressed past Reading, Bournemouth and Walsall before rather disappointingly going out at home to Exeter City. The attendances were pitiful, though, the highest being just 1,875.

Indeed, home attendances in general were very poor, falling again to a League average of just 6,699, not far off the lowest on

> Zacky March, the winger from Bosham who played 97 games for the Albion in the period 1913–22, celebrated his 100th birthday on 25 October in Bognor Regis. He is believed to be the oldest ex-professional footballer in the country.

record in the mid 1930s. The best League gate was 8,741 for the Boxing Day visit of Burnley.

And so the curtain fell on another season, but this was a season like no other. Although ultimately disappointed by the team's performance, fans were relieved that they still had a club to support. Albion have faced the possibility of liquidation before, but the sheer scale of the debt now poses the greatest threat ever. Apart from monies owed in PAYE, VAT, etc., the club stands in debt to the bank and building society to the tune of £2 million. In 1940 new directors came in to rescue the club, but there appears to be no fresh blood ready to come in now. So Albion must look, like so many other clubs, to nurturing young players and selling them; indeed, only from the mid 1960s to the mid '80s – a period which spawned the current crisis – has it been anything other than a 'selling club'. Barry Lloyd's extensive youth policy and nose for a bargain must continue to bear dividends. Debts must be paid off, not allowed to accumulate, and a similar situation must never be allowed to arise again. The club must raise its profile in the local community, doing everything possible to gain more supporters. New investment must be attracted and the ground problems must be resolved.

It can be done; other clubs have proved that. If everyone with the interest of the Albion at heart – and that should include the local councils – can rally together and communicate their good ideas, then Brighton and Hove Albion Football Club can once again climb the football pyramid and continue to bring both joy and heartbreak, pleasure and anger, exhilaration and despair to its followers for many years to come, just as it has every season since the pioneering John Jackson and his colleagues founded the club 92 eventful years ago.

Albion 1992–93

Back row left to right: Larry May (reserve-team coach), Stuart Myall, John Crumplin, Simon Funnell, Nicky Bissett, Gary O'Reilly, Paul McCarthy, Robert Codner, Ted Streeter (youth development officer).
Middle row left to right: Malcolm Stuart (physio), Mark Farrington, Andy Polston, Perry Digweed, Gary Chivers (captain), Mark Beeney, Mark Gall, Billy Logan, Martin Hinshelwood (coach).
Front row left to right: Dean Wilkins, Bernard Gallacher, John Robinson, Barry Lloyd (managing director), Clive Walker, Matthew Edwards, Ian Chapman.

CLUB HONOURS

Football Association Challenge Cup			**Western League**	
Finalists	1983		Division One Section A winners & championship finalists	1909
Football League			**Southern Alliance**	
Division Two runners-up & promoted	1979		Winners	1914
Division Two Play-Off finalists	1991		Runners-up	1913
Division Three (South) champions	1958			
Division Three (South) runners-up	1954, 1956		**Football League South**	
Division Three runners-up & promoted	1972, 1977, 1988		Champions	1941
Division Four champions	1965			
			Berks & Bucks Hospital Charity Cup	
Football Association Charity Shield			Winners	1922 (joint), 1923 (joint),
Winners	1910			1927, 1935 (joint)
Southern League			**Oxfordshire Benevolent Cup**	
Champions	1910		Winners	1985
Division Two champions	1903 (joint)			
Test match winners	1903		**La Magdalena Trophy**	
			Winners	1970
Southern Professional Charity Cup				
Winners	1910		**Jewish Chronicle Cup**	
Finalists	1909, 1911, 1913		Winners	1980
United League			**American Express Challenge Cup**	
Runners-up	1907		Winners	1986

Reserves

Southern League			**London Midweek League and Midweek League**	
Champions	1921, 1927		Champions	1978, 1981
			Runners-up	1977
South Eastern League			Cup winners	1970, 1975, 1978
Division One runners-up	1910		Cup finalists	1979
Runners-up	1912, 1921			
Football Combination				
Fourth, Division Two, & promoted	1954			

'A' team

Metropolitan & District League	
Cup finalists	1959

Youth team

South East Counties League			**Southern Youth League**	
Division Two runners-up	1982		Champions	1976, 1978, 1979
Cup winners	1990		West Section runners-up	1980
Cup finalists	1963		Cup finalists	1976, 1980
Division Two Cup winners	1985			
			Hampshire Youth League	
Worthing & District League			Champions	1981
Division Two champions	1960		Cup winners	1981
Third, Division One, & promoted	1961			
Junior Charity Cup winners	1961		**John Ullman (Kent Youth League) Invitation Cup**	
Benevolent Fund Cup winners	1960		Finalists	1989
Sussex Sunday League			**Gonfreville L'Orcher (Le Havre) Under-17 Tournament**	
Minor Division champions	1970, 1971, 1972, 1973		Winners	1991
Minor Cup winners	1970, 1971, 1972, 1973		Finalists	1992
Southern Counties Combination				
Runners-up	1973			
Cup finalists	1972			

Local competitions

Sussex Professional Challenge Cup			**Sussex (Royal Ulster Rifles) Charity Cup**	
Winners	1961 (joint), 1962, 1963,		Winners	1943, 1960, 1961 (joint)
	1964, 1965, 1967,		Finalists	1945
	1968 (joint), 1969, 1971,			
	1972, 1973, 1975		**Brighton Charity Cup**	
Finalists	1970, 1974		Winners	1952 (joint), 1953, 1956,
				1957, 1958, 1959, 1961
Sussex Senior Challenge Cup			**Hastings Charity Cup**	
Winners	1988, 1992		Winners	1926
			Finalists	1925
Roy Haydon Memorial Trophy				
Winners	1988		**Richards Hospital Cup**	
Finalists	1992		Winners	1984
Sussex Floodlit Challenge Cup			**Sussex Wartime Cup**	
Finalists	1976, 1977		Winners	1943
			Runners-up	1945

OTHER FIRST-TEAM MATCHES

The following abbreviations have been used to indicate countries of origin:

BEL	Belgium	HKG	Hong Kong	SCO	Scotland
BRA	Brazil	HUN	Hungary	SPA	Spain
CRO	Croatia	ISR	Israel	SWE	Sweden
CZE	Czechoslovakia	ITA	Italy	TUR	Turkey
DEN	Denmark	NET	Netherlands	USR	Union of Soviet
FRA	France	POR	Portugal		Socialist Republics
FRG	West Germany	ROM	Romania		

Mini-tournaments

Date		Opponents		Scorers
1979–80 Tennent Caledonian Cup				
Played at Ibrox, Glasgow				
3.8.1979	R1	Kilmarnock (SCO)	1–1	Ward
Albion lost 6–5 on penalties				
5.8.1979	3rd pl.	West Ham United	3–1	Poskett, Rollings, Horton (pen.)
1980–81 Dordrecht Tournament				
Played at Dordrecht, Netherlands				
5.8.1979	R1	RWD Molenbeek (BEL)	5–0	Ward 2, Robinson, Horton (pen.), Gregory
7.8.1979	F	Twente Enschede (NET)	1–1	Gregory
Albion lost 3–0 on penalties				
1981–82 Dordrecht Tournament				
Played at Dordrecht, Netherlands				
7.8.1981	R1	Utrecht (NET)	0–3	
9.8.1981	3rd pl.	Excelsior Rott'rdam (NET)	0–0	
Albion won 5–4 on penalties				
1982–83 Townsend-Thoresen Tournament				
Played at Eindhoven, Netherlands				
13.8.1982	R1	PSV Eindhoven (NET)	0–3	
15.8.1982	3rd pl.	Ipswich Town	1–1	Thomas
Albion lost 3–4 on penalties				
1983–84 Liège Tournament				
Played at Liège, Belgium				
30.7.1983	R1	Standard Liège (BEL)	0–3	
31.7.1983	3rd pl.	FC Liège (BEL)	2–4	Case, Connor

Date		Opponents		Scorers
1983–84 City of Palma Tournament				
Played at Palma, Majorca				
18.8.1983	R1	Real Madrid (SPA)	0–1	
20.8.1983	3rd pl.	Vasas Diosgyori (HUN)	3–2	Gatting, Grealish, Connor (pen.)
1988–89 Alliance Cup				
Played in Portugal				
23.7.1988	Group	Estoria Praia (POR)	1–1	Chivers
25.7.1988	Group	Montijo (POR)	4–0	Crumplin, Wood, Trusson, Rougvie
27.7.1988	Group	Amadora (POR)	3–1	Owers, Cooper, Bremner
29.7.1988	Group	Barreirensesa (POR)	2–0	Isaac, Penney
30.7.1988	F	Barreirensesa (POR)	1–3	Nelson
1989–90 Arundel Centenary Cup				
Played at Arundel, Sussex. The matches were not of 90-minute duration.				
27.7.1989	Group	Bognor Regis Town	3–0	Dineen 2, Wood
28.7.1989	Group	Bristol Rovers	0–0	
29.7.1989	SF	Wimbledon	1–1	Nelson
Albion won 6–5 on penalties				
29.7.1989	F	Bristol Rovers	3–4	Nelson 3
1990–91 Bucharest Tournament				
Played at Bucharest, Romania				
2.8.1990	R1	Dinamo Bucharest (ROM)	2–5	Small, Augustine
3.8.1990	3rd pl.	Heart of Midlothian (SCO)	2–2	Small, Nelson
Albion lost 4–2 on penalties				

Miscellaneous competitive matches

Date	Opponents			Scorers
1969–70 La Magdalena Trophy				
7.5.1970	Novelda (Alicante, SPA)	(a)	0–0	
Albion won on toss of coin				
1980–81 Jewish Chronicle Cup				
29.7.1980	Maccabi Nethanya (ISR)	(h)	2–0	McHale, Sayer
1981–82 Trofeo Barilla				
15.11.1981	AS Roma (ITA)	(a)	1–4	Smith

Date	Opponents			Scorers
1983–84 Townsend-Thoresen Cup				
9.8.1983	Manchester United	(h)	0–0	
Albion lost 3–4 on penalties				
1985–86 American Express Challenge Cup				
25.5.1986	Seiko (HKG)	(a)	3–1	Connor 2, Wilson (pen.)

Other tour matches

Date	Opponents		Scorers
1952–53 Belgium and West Germany			
25.5.1953	FC Liège (BEL)	4–4	Sirrell 2, Leadbetter, Wetton
27.5.1953	SV Fürth (FRG)	0–1	
1954–55 Channel Islands			
14.5.1955	Jersey Saturday League XI	4–5	Tennant (pen.), Gordon, Mundy, Gilberg
16.5.1955	Jersey & Guernsey XI	6–1	Trusler 2, Bisset 2, Gordon, Howard
1955–56 Channel Islands			
Inauguration of new ground at Boulivot, Jersey:			
10.8.1955	Grouville	9–3	Tennant, Mundy, Howard, Bisset 3, Clarke 2, Balston
11.8.1955	Jersey Saturday League XI	6–1	Howard, Gordon, Mundy, Bisset 2, Balston
1959–60 Cornwall			
6.5.1960	Newquay	4–0	Curry, Tiddy, Bertolini, Thorne
7.5.1960	Helston Athletic	4–1	Tiddy, Thorne, Bertolini, Jones
1960–61 West Germany			
11.5.1961	SSV Reutlingen	1–5	McNeill
13.5.1961	Wormatia Worms	3–0	Laverick 2, Tiddy
14.5.1961	Heilbronn	1–0	Laverick
1968–69 Northern England and Scotland			
27.7.1968	Crewe Alexandra	2–6	K. Napier, Flood
1.8.1968	Falkirk	1–1	Flood
3.8.1968	Stirling Albion	1–1	Templeman
1969–70 Republic of Ireland			
25.7.1969	Dundalk	3–0	Dawson 2, Gilliver
28.7.1969	Cork Hibernians	1–0	Dawson
29.7.1969	Limerick	0–1	
1969–70 Spain			
(See also La Magdalena Trophy)			
3.5.1970	Paiporta CF (near Valencia)	2–0	Duffy 2
10.5.1970	Benidorm	1–0	Duffy
Above date approximate only			
San Isidro Fiesta, Madrid:			
15.5.1970	CD Carabanchel (Madrid)	3–1	Duffy (pen.), Flood, K. Napier
1973–74 Majorca, Spain			
9.5.1974	Son Servera	8–2	Mellor 5, Binney, Welch, Rollings
Date approximate only			
1974–75 Northern England			
5.8.1974	Darlington	1–2	Own goal
7.8.1974	Hartlepool	0–0	
1974–75 Majorca, Spain			
9.5.1975	Son Servera	4–1	Fell 2, Marlowe, Rollings
1978–79 U.S.A.			
14.5.1979	California Surf (Anaheim)	1–1	Poskett
16.5.1979	Portland Timbers	2–1	Maybank, Sayer
3.6.1979	San Diego Sockers	2–2	O'Sullivan, Poskett
Albion won exhibition shoot-out 2–1			

Date	Opponents		Scorers
1979–80 Netherlands			
6.8.1979	East German Olympic XI	0–2	
Above match played at Beneden-Leeweden			
8.8.1979	Sparta Rotterdam	2–3	Ryan, Maybank
11.8.1979	Den Haag	1–0	Ward
1979–80 Israel			
26.2.1980	Israel XI	2–1	Lawrenson, Ward
Played at Ashkelon Stadium			
1980–81 Netherlands			
(See also Dordrecht Tournament)			
3.8.1980	NAC Breda	1–0	Robinson
9.8.1980	Groningen	0–0	
1981–82 Netherlands			
(See also Dordrecht Tournament)			
1.8.1981	Vitesse Arnhem	1–0	Robinson
4.8.1981	Den Haag	1–1	Robinson
1982–83 Belgium and Netherlands			
(See also Townsend-Thoresen Tournament)			
10.8.1982	KB Mechelen (BEL)	2–1	Ritchie, Ryan
1982–83 U.S.A.			
5.6.1983	San Diego Sockers	1–3	Rodon
Above match played at San Fernando			
6.6.1983	San Diego Sockers	0–1	
8.6.1983	San Jose Earthquakes	1–4	Rodon
1983–84 Belgium and Netherlands			
(See also Liège Tournament)			
2.8.1983	De Graafschap (NET)	2–2	Smillie, Smith
1983–84 Balearic Islands, Spain			
(See also City of Palma Tournament)			
21.8.1983	SD Ibiza	5–2	Ryan, Lambert 2, Ring 2
1984–85 Northern Ireland			
1.8.1984	Glentoran	0–0	
3.8.1984	Ballymena United	1–0	Own goal
4.8.1984	Tobermore United	5–0	Howlett, Connor, Penney, Wilson, Muir
1989–90 Republic of Ireland			
3.8.1989	Shamrock Rovers	3–0	Nelson, Codner, Bremner
5.8.1989	Shelbourne	2–1	Nelson, Dineen
8.8.1989	Drogheda United	2–1	Chivers, Lambert
1989–90 U.S.S.R.			
16.5.1990	Molodejnaja (Minsk)	0–1	
18.5.1990	Dinamo Minsk	1–1	Crumplin
A third match was played by a team consisting largely of Albion reserves:			
21.5.1990	Dinamo Moscow (res.)	6–0	Wilkins, Foloronso, Cormack, Nelson, McGrath, Bremner
1991–92 Netherlands			
30.7.1991	VCV Zealand	4–2	Small 3, Cockram
1.8.1991	Roosendaal	3–1	Nelson 2, Robinson
4.8.1991	EVV Eindhoven	2–1	Byrne 2

Friendly and benefit matches 1901–31

*Home matches played at Goldstone Ground except where noted. * Dyke Road Field † County Ground*

Date	Opponents		Score	Scorers
1901–02				
7.9.1901	Shoreham	(h*)	2–0	Barker, McAvoy (pen.)
14.9.1901	Woolwich Polytechnic	(h*)	4–2	Barker, Colclough, Mendham, Baker
2.10.1901	Southampton (res.)	(h†)	0–0	
12.10.1901	Oxford City	(h†)	0–0	
9.11.1901	London Welsh	(h†)	5–0	Russell, McAvoy, Smith, Colclough, Caldwell
16.11.1901	HMS Pembroke (Chatham)	(h†)	1–1	Frewin
20.11.1901	Eastbourne	(a)	1–2	Barker
26.12.1901	Blackpool	(h†)	1–3	McAvoy (pen.)
11.1.1902	New Brompton (res.)	(h†)	1–2	Thair
18.1.1902	Richmond Association	(h†)	0–1	
22.2.1902	Southampton Wanderers	(h)	7–1	Thair 3, Hill, Blunden 2, P. King
15.3.1902	Shoreham	(h)	4–1	Baker, Thair 3
28.3.1902	Southampton (res.)	(a)	0–2	
29.3.1902	Clapton	(h†)	2–3	Caldwell (pen.), Clarke
31.3.1902	HMS Excellent (Portsmouth)	(h†)	0–1	
19.4.1902	New Brompton	(a)	0–4	
26.4.1902	Northampton Town	(h)	1–0	Baker
30.4.1902	Hove	(a)	5–1	Craven 2, Baker, Thair, Caldwell (pen.)
1902–03				
6.9.1902	Hove	(h)	13–0	Scott 6, Lee, Thair, Broughton 2, Garfield 2, Own goal
29.11.1902	Tottenham Hotspur (res.)	(a)	1–1	Thair
25.12.1902	Tunbridge Wells	(a)	3–2	?, Lamb, Scott
26.12.1902	Sheffield Wycliffe	(h)	3–2	Scott, Smith 2
10.1.1903	West Norwood	(a)	2–7	Own goal, ?
7.3.1903	Queen's Park Rangers (res.)	(h)	1–3	Caldwell (pen.)
18.3.1903	Woolwich Arsenal	(h)	1–3	Scott
28.3.1903	Leicester Fosse	(h)	5–4	Scott, Garfield 2, Caldwell (pen.), Own goal
10.4.1903	West Norwood	(h)	3–0	Robey, Scott 2
13.4.1903	New Brompton	(h)	3–2	Thair, Smith 2
25.4.1903	Brentford	(h)	2–3	Caldwell (pen.), Garfield
29.4.1903	Everton	(h)	1–2	Thair
1903–04				
25.12.1903	Fulham	(a)	1–2	McAteer
26.12.1903	Sheffield Wycliffe	(h)	6–0	McAteer, Hyde 2, Rushton, McCairns, Pryce
16.4.1904	Crouch End Vampires	(h)	2–1	Hyde, Garfield
27.4.1904	West Bromwich Albion	(h)	3–2	White, Parsons, Pryce
30.4.1904	Burgess Hill	(a)	3–1	Roberts, Lamb, Pryce
1904–05				
12.9.1904	Tottenham Hotspur	(a)	1–3	Good
26.12.1904	Athletic Parisien (FRA)	(h)	9–1	Hulse 2, Good, Lyon, Robertson 3, Livingstone 2
24.4.1905	New Brompton	(a)	0–3	

For Albion's former manager John Jackson (also played for the 'Jackson Souvenir Cup' which was donated afterwards for an annual match between Brighton and Tottenham schoolboys):

Date	Opponents		Score	Scorers
25.4.1905	Tottenham Hotspur	(h)	3–3	Lyon, Leach 2
1905–06				
18.10.1905	3rd Coldstream Guards	(h)	4–0	Fisher, Graham, J. Kennedy, Kent
20.12.1905	S.S. Harris's Corinthian XI	(h)	5–0	Fisher, C. Buckley 2, W. Kennedy
28.3.1906	S.S. Harris's Corinthian XI	(h)	3–0	Hall, J. Kennedy, Allsopp
1906–07				

For Albion's Summer-Wage Fund:

Date	Opponents		Score	Scorers
6.4.1907	Sheffield United	(h)	1–2	Allsopp
15.4.1907	Bolton Wanderers	(h)	2–2	Kent, Lewis
1907–08				
22.2.1908	Notts County	(h)	3–1	Longstaff, Burnett, Joynes

Date	Opponents		Score	Scorers
1908–09				
26.12.1908	Hastings & St Leonards Utd	(a)	2–0	Robertson, Langley
1909–10				

For Edgar Everest, long-time secretary of the Sussex County F.A. (and founder of Brighton United):

Date	Opponents		Score	Scorers
10.11.1909	Sussex County F.A. XI	(h)	4–1	Coleman, Featherstone, Connor, Haworth
1911–12				
18.10.1911	Portsmouth	(a)	5–0	Needham 4, Smith
13.3.1912	Portsmouth	(h)	1–2	Smith
1914–15				

For Battalion funds:

Date	Opponents		Score	Scorers
10.3.1915	Footballers' Battalion	(h)	2–0	Reed, Beech
1919–20				

Victory match on Peace Day:

Date	Opponents		Score	Scorers
19.7.1919	Portsmouth	(a)	1–1	Jones
27.10.1919	Mid Rhondda	(a)	1–4	Beech
10.1.1920	Norwich City	(h)	3–3	Beech 2, Woodhouse
1920–21				
18.12.1920	Corinthians	(h)	2–4	Ritchie, Coomber
1921–22				

For Albion's Jack Bollington:

Date	Opponents		Score	Scorers
30.11.1921	Cardiff City	(h)	0–3	

For the local unemployed:

Date	Opponents		Score	Scorers
3.12.1921	Luton Town	(h)	1–1	McAllister
17.12.1921	Portsmouth	(a)	1–0	Doran
13.3.1922	Ebbw Vale	(a)	1–2	Neil
1922–23				

For the Royal Sussex County Hospital:

Date	Opponents		Score	Scorers
25.10.1922	Littlehampton & District XI	(a)	4–1	Neil, Beech, McAllister, A. Jones
22.11.1922	Amateur F.A. XI	(h)	1–1	Broadhead
2.12.1922	Fulham	(h)	1–0	Neil
6.12.1922	Royal Navy XI	(h)	2–1	A. Jones, Cook
1923–24				
17.10.1923	Amateur F.A. XI	(h)	3–1	Cook, McAllister, Hopkins
1924–25				
5.11.1924	Amateur F.A. XI	(h)	4–0	Hopkins, Cook, Ison, Dennison
29.11.1924	Bristol City	(h)	2–1	Hopkins, Mulhall
3.12.1924	Cambridge University	(h)	5–2	Little 2 (1 pen.), Hopkins, Cook, Nightingale
1925–26				
11.11.1925	Oxford University	(h)	5–3	Nightingale, Cheetham, Little, Gough 2
20.2.1926	Corinthians	(h)	2–1	Jennings, Cheetham

For Albion's Jack Thompson:

Date	Opponents		Score	Scorers
3.3.1926	Portsmouth	(h)	4–4	Hopkins, Jennings 3

For Portsmouth's James Mackie:

Date	Opponents		Score	Scorers
14.4.1926	Portsmouth	(a)	1–3	Jennings
1928–29				
8.12.1928	Corinthians	(h)	4–6	Cook 2, Jenkins (pen.), Farrell
1930–31				
29.11.1930	Corinthians	(h)	4–0	McDonald, Kirkwood, Carruthers 2
13.12.1930	Corinthians	(a)	1–4	Wilson

Friendly and benefit matches 1931–61

Date	Opponents			Scorers
1931–32				
28.12.1931	Corinthians	(h)	2–1	Own goal, Farrell
For Albion's Jack Williams:				
27.4.1932	Portsmouth	(h)	0–2	
1932–33				
For Albion's Ernie Wilson:				
4.5.1933	Birmingham	(h)	2–1	Attwood, Farrell
1934–35				
For Albion's Bobby Farrell:				
1.5.1935	Portsmouth	(h)	2–3	Wilson, Brown
1935–36				
For Albion's Potter Smith:				
29.4.1936	Brentford	(h)	1–2	Stephens
1936–37				
For Albion's Dave Walker:				
28.4.1937	Southampton	(h)	1–1	Stephens
1937–38				
For Albion's Ernie King:				
4.5.1938	Bolton Wanderers	(h)	1–5	Stephens
1938–39				
For the Football League Jubilee Fund:				
20.8.1938	Crystal Palace	(a)	1–5	Stephens
For Albion's Ted Martin:				
19.4.1939	West Ham United	(h)	2–0	Wilson 2
For Albion trainer Dickie Meades:				
3.5.1939	Brentford	(h)	0–1	
1939–40				
For the Football League Jubilee Fund:				
19.8.1939	Crystal Palace	(h)	3–3	Spencer, Stephens 2
16.9.1939	Fulham	(h)	3–3	?
23.9.1939	Millwall	(h)	6–1	Isaac 2, Davie 2, J. Wilson, Risdon
30.9.1939	Southampton	(a)	1–4	Day
7.10.1939	Crystal Palace	(a)	2–2	Stephens, Darling
14.10.1939	Southend United	(h)	0–4	
25.5.1940	Brentford	(a)	1–4	Stephens
1940–41				
10.5.1941	Army XI (Liverpool Reg.)	(h)	3–2	Stephens 2, Welsh
24.5.1941	Army XI (Liverpool Reg.)	(h)	4–1	Own goal, Devonport 2, J. Wilson
27.5.1941	Army XI (Liverpool Reg.)	(a)	3–7	?
Above match played at Seaford				
7.6.1941	Allied Army XI	(h)	7–1	Balmer 3, Shafto, J. Wilson 2, Harman
1942–43				
17.4.1943	Fulham	(h)	0–9	
1943–44				
1.4.1944	Clapton Orient	(h)	4–2	Hillman, Fox 2, Moore
1944–45				
2.4.1945	Southampton	(a)	2–2	Hodges, Reid (pen.)
1947–48				
28.2.1948	Portsmouth	(h)	1–1	Lancelotte
For Albion's Len Darling, Ernie Marriott, Bert Stephens, Stan Risdon and Joe Wilson:				
26.4.1948	Notts County	(h)	1–7	Welsh
1948–49				
For Albion's Len Darling, Ernie Marriott, Bert Stephens, Stan Risdon and Joe Wilson:				
27.9.1948	Wolverhampton Wanderers	(h)	1–4	Willis
11.12.1948	Bristol Rovers	(h)	2–1	James, Clelland
For Albion's Len Darling, Ernie Marriott, Bert Stephens, Stan Risdon and Joe Wilson:				
25.4.1949	Charlton Athletic	(h)	1–3	McCurley

Date	Opponents			Scorers
1949–50				
10.12.1949	Lincoln City	(a)	1–3	Roberts
20.4.1950	Army XI	(h)	2–2	McCurley, Whent
28.4.1950	Heart of Midlothian (SCO)	(h)	1–1	Whent
1950–51				
21.9.1950	Galatasaray (TUR)	(h)	5–2	Wilson 2, McNichol, Hassell, Thompson
For Albion's Harry Baldwin and Jack Ball:				
28.9.1950	All-Star XI	(h)	4–3	Own goal, Willard, McNichol, McCurley
12.4.1951	St Johnstone (SCO)	(h)	4–1	Reed 2, McCurley 2
For Albion's Harry Baldwin, Jack Ball and Jack Dugnolle:				
30.4.1951	Liverpool	(h)	1–1	McNichol
Festival of Britain celebration match:				
9.5.1951	Nancy (FRA)	(h)	2–1	Howard, Garbutt
Festival of Britain celebration match:				
12.5.1951	Hamborn 07 (FRG)	(h)	3–2	Jackson 2, Willard
Festival of Britain celebration match:				
19.5.1951	Ayr United (SCO)	(h)	5–1	McNichol, Barbutt 2, Howard, Willard
1951–52				
For Albion's Jess Willard:				
2.5.1952	Nottingham Forest	(h)	5–4	Bennett, Dougal, Willard (pen.), McNichol, Reed
1953–54				
31.10.1953	Queen's Park Rangers	(n)	2–1	Addinall, Bisset
Played at The Saffrons, Eastbourne				
1954–55				
6.5.1955	Burnley	(h)	2–3	Moore, Orford
1955–56				
7.1.1956	Derby County	(h)	3–4	Langley, Stephens, Halley
1956–57				
For the Hungarian Relief Fund:				
8.12.1956	MTK Budapest (HUN)	(h)	5–3	Gordon 2, Foreman, Langley (pen.), Harburn
13.3.1957	Banik Ostrava (CZE)	(h)	3–1	Clarke, Foreman, Stephens
For the Albion Players' Benefit Fund:				
3.5.1957	Liverpool	(h)	0–2	
1958–59				
24.1.1959	West Ham United	(h)	3–3	Shepherd, Whitfield, Wilson
For the Albion Players' Benefit Fund:				
14.4.1959	Kilmarnock (SCO)	(h)	3–1	Jones, Foreman, Wilson (pen.)
For the Albion Players' Benefit Fund:				
1.5.1959	Newcastle United	(h)	1–1	Gordon
1959–60				
For the Albion Players' Benefit Fund:				
30.3.1960	Djurgarden (SWE)	(h)	0–0	
27.4.1960	Fluminense (BRA)	(h)	1–2	Own goal
1960–61				
Goldstone Ground floodlight inauguration:				
10.4.1961	Frem (DEN)	(h)	3–1	Laverick 2, Bertolini
2.5.1961	Wormatia Worms (FRG)	(h)	3–1	Laverick, Foreman, Own goal

Friendly and benefit matches 1961–79

Date	Opponents			Scorers
1961–62				
12.8.1961	Queen's Park Rangers	(a)	2–3	Goodchild, Laverick
15.8.1961	Queen's Park Rangers	(h)	3–1	Laverick 2, Goodchild
3.10.1961	Hamilton Academical (SCO)	(h)	4–1	Goodchild, Cochrane, Tiddy, Laverick
17.10.1961	SSV Reutlingen (FRG)	(h)	1–1	Laverick
Inauguration of social club:				
30.10.1961	Chelmsford City	(a)	1–1	Laverick
For Albion trainer Joe Wilson:				
14.11.1961	G. Gunn International XI	(h)	0–5	
27.1.1962	West Ham United	(h)	3–1	Bertolini, Sitford 2
1962–63				
11.8.1962	Chelsea	(h)	1–1	Goodchild
For Albion's Frankie Howard:				
12.11.1962	G. Gunn International XI	(h)	5–5	Goodchild 2, Cooper, Upton, Collins
24.11.1962	Hastings United	(a)	0–2	
23.1.1963	Arsenal	(h)	2–1	Donnelly, Jackson
1963–64				
14.8.1963	Lewes	(a)	9–0	Webber 3, Cooper, Donnelly 3, Gilbert, Jackson
For Albion's Steve Burtenshaw:				
11.11.1963	G. Gunn International XI	(h)	3–7	Goodchild, Collins, Burtenshaw (pen.)
Abandoned at 85 minutes when crowd invaded pitch thinking final whistle had been blown				
4.1.1964	Reading	(h)	2–2	Collins 2
1964–65				
15.8.1964	Charlton Athletic	(h)	3–1	R. Smith, J. Smith, Collins (pen.)
1965–66				
10.8.1965	Leyton Orient	(h)	1–1	J. Smith
14.8.1965	Charlton Athletic	(h)	0–3	
17.8.1965	Leyton Orient	(a)	3–1	J. Smith, Cassidy, Oliver
21.1.1966	Spartak Brno (CZE)	(h)	3–1	Collins 2, Livesey
1966–67				
10.8.1966	Tel Aviv Maccabi (ISR)	(h)	0–1	
13.8.1966	Sheffield United	(h)	1–1	Own goal
1967–68				
5.8.1967	Andover	(a)	2–0	Hickman, Livesey
8.8.1967	Brentford	(a)	1–2	Livesey
9.8.1967	Guildford City	(a)	2–1	K. Napier, Oliver
12.8.1967	Southampton	(h)	0–2	
For Albion's Jack Bertolini and coach Cyril Hodges:				
13.11.1967	All-Star XI	(h)	5–6	K. Napier, Templeman, Gould
17.2.1968	Ipswich Town	(h)	0–1	
1968–69				
5.8.1968	Coventry City	(h)	1–2	Templeman
1969–70				
2.8.1969	Gibraltar XI	(h)	6–0	Bell, Dawson 4, Gilliver
Inauguration of new ground:				
19.10.1969	Seaford Sunday XI	(a)	11–1	?
1970–71				
1.8.1970	Southampton	(h)	0–1	
5.8.1970	Portsmouth	(a)	1–0	K. Napier
9.8.1970	Bournemouth & B.A.	(h)	2–3	Turner, Gilliver
For Pat Saward's Buy-a-Player Appeal and for Eastbourne United funds (the team was billed as Pat Saward's XI but consisted of nine Albion players, the manager and comedian Jimmy Tarbuck):				
17.1.1971	Eastbourne United	(a)	2–3	Dawson, Wilkinson
23.2.1971	Queen's Park Rangers	(h)	0–1	
For Albion's Norman Gall and Brian Powney:				
11.5.1971	Wolverhampton Wanderers	(h)	0–2	
For Albion's Norman Gall and Brian Powney (played at the Greyhound Stadium):				
16.5.1971	International Club	(h)	?–?	

Date	Opponents			Scorers
1971–72				
31.7.1971	Coventry City	(h)	1–2	Templeman
4.8.1971	Millwall	(h)	0–0	
7.8.1971	Orient	(h)	2–2	Turner, Murray
18.1.1972	Huddersfield Town	(h)	0–1	
For Albion's Norman Gall and Brian Powney:				
5.5.1972	Chelsea	(h)	2–3	Beamish, Templeman
For Albion's Geoff Sidebottom:				
11.5.1972	Birmingham City	(h)	2–2	Steele (pen.), Spearritt
1972–73				
29.7.1972	Queen's Park Rangers	(h)	1–2	Beamish
1.8.1972	Southampton	(h)	0–0	
5.8.1972	Charlton Athletic	(a)	1–1	Beamish
3.2.1973	Stoke City	(h)	0–2	
23.2.1973	Moscow Spartak (USR)	(h)	1–0	Goodwin
1973–74				
11.8.1973	Crystal Palace	(h)	2–1	Beamish, Templeman
13.8.1973	Gillingham	(a)	1–2	Robertson
15.8.1973	Portsmouth	(a)	1–4	Robertson
18.8.1973	Portsmouth	(h)	2–2	Bridges, Beamish
For Albion chief scout Joe Wilson:				
3.5.1974	All-Star XI	(h)	2–2	Powney (pen.), O'Sullivan
1974–75				
3.8.1974	Ipswich Town	(h)	0–3	
For Albion groundsman Frankie Howard:				
3.3.1975	Queen's Park Rangers	(h)	2–1	Binney, McCalliog
1975–76				
2.8.1975	Portsmouth	(a)	1–2	O'Sullivan
7.8.1975	Wolverhampton Wanderers	(h)	0–2	
Albion 75th anniversary match:				
1.10.1975	Stoke City	(h)	1–1	Binney
13.2.1976	Ipswich Town	(h)	3–1	Mellor 2, Rollings
For Albion's Joe Kinnear:				
23.3.1976	Tottenham Hotspur	(h)	1–6	Kinnear (pen.)
27.4.1976	Norwich City	(h)	2–2	Binney, O'Sullivan
1976–77				
6.8.1976	Torquay United	(a)	1–1	Piper
9.8.1976	Luton Town	(h)	1–1	Rollings
16.5.1977	Norwich City	(h)	1–2	P. Ward
Worthing floodlight inauguration:				
17.5.1977	Rediffusion All-Star XI	(a)	5–3	P. Ward 2, O'Sullivan, Winstanley, S. Ward
1977–78				
2.8.1977	Brentford	(a)	3–2	Mellor, P. Ward 2
6.8.1977	Wolverhampton Wanderers	(h)	1–0	P. Ward
For Albion's Chris Cattlin:				
9.8.1977	Coventry City	(h)	3–1	P. Ward (pen.), Potts, Lawrenson
For Albion's Peter Grummitt:				
2.5.1978	Alan Mullery's All-Star XI	(h)	8–7	Poskett 3, Sayer 2, Ruggiero 2, Moseley (pen.)
For Worthing's Peter Cull, a former Albion youngster (played at Worthing F.C.):				
11.5.1978	David Hamilton's All-Star XI	(a)	3–8	P. Ward 2 (1 pen.), Powell
1978–79				
1.8.1978	Reading	(a)	0–0	
4.8.1978	Southend United	(a)	3–1	Maybank, Sayer, Winstanley
7.8.1978	Brentford	(a)	4–1	Rollings, Ward, Maybank, Potts
12.8.1978	Queen's Park Rangers	(h)	2–1	Rollings, Maybank
For Swansea City's Mick Conway, a former Albion player:				
8.5.1979	Swansea City	(a)	3–1	Poskett, Ryan, Maybank

Friendly and benefit matches 1979–93

Date	Opponents			Scorers
1979–80				
24.10.1979	Den Haag (NET)	(h)	1–0	Ward
For Albion's Peter O'Sullivan:				
22.4.1980	Southampton	(h)	1–3	Mullery (pen.)
5.5.1980	Portsmouth	(a)	0–1	
1980–81				
11.8.1980	Sparta Rotterdam (NET)	(h)	1–1	Stille
25.11.1980	NAC Breda (NET)	(h)	0–2	
23.1.1981	Chelsea	(a)	2–2	Ritchie, Stevens
6.3.1981	Groningen (NET)	(h)	1–1	Ritchie
1981–82				
18.8.1981	Brentford	(a)	3–1	McNab, Case, Ryan
21.8.1981	Fulham	(h)	2–1	Robinson, Foster
24.8.1981	Nigeria XI	(h)	5–1	Grealish, Foster, Ritchie, McNab (pen.), Smith
14.11.1981	Crystal Palace	(a)	1–1	Smith
19.12.1981	Luton Town	(h)	1–0	Ritchie
1982–83				
7.8.1982	Crystal Palace	(a)	0–1	
18.8.1982	Queen's Park Rangers	(h)	2–2	Own goal, Ritchie
21.8.1982	Cambridge United	(a)	2–0	Ritchie, Gatting (pen.)
1983–84				
12.8.1983	Tottenham Hotspur	(h)	0–0	
For Whitehawk's Gary Williams, a former Albion player:				
14.5.1984	Ex-Albion XI	(h)	3–3	A. Young, Connor, Russell
For the dependants of Lewes's Dave Standing, a former Albion youngster:				
16.5.1984	Sussex Select XI	(a)	6–2	Connor 2, A. Young, E. Young, Ryan, Wilson
For Royal Sussex County Hospital Diabetic Unit (in memory of Upper Beeding's Peter Ashdown):				
18.5.1984	Upper Beeding	(a)	11–2	?
1984–85				
8.8.1984	Gillingham	(a)	2–0	Connor 2
10.8.1984	Aldershot	(a)	3–1	Connor
17.8.1984	Arsenal	(h)	1–1	E. Young
21.8.1984	Dorking	(a)	1–0	Worthington
1985–86				
29.7.1985	Aldershot	(a)	5–0	Fashanu 2, Biley, Connor, Saunders
2.8.1985	Arsenal	(h)	1–2	Mortimer
5.8.1985	Liverpool	(h)	1–4	Jacobs
9.8.1985	Nottingham Forest	(h)	5–2	Biley, Jacobs, Saunders, Wilson, O'Reilly
Lewes centenary match:				
18.9.1985	Lewes	(a)	5–0	Jacobs, Ferguson, Biley, Saunders, Edwards
1986–87				
For Albion's Gerry Ryan:				
8.8.1986	Tottenham Hotspur	(h)	0–4	
11.8.1986	Charlton Athletic	(h)	0–0	
24.2.1987	Lewes	(a)	3–0	Tiltman, Saunders, Wilson
1987–88				
28.7.1987	Barnstaple Town	(a)	2–1	Own goal, Armstrong
31.7.1987	AFC Bournemouth	(h)	0–2	
5.8.1987	Arsenal	(h)	2–7	Penney, Bremner
7.8.1987	Colchester United	(a)	0–2	
For Sussex cricketer Paul Parker and Middlesex cricketer Mike Gatting:				
29.3.1988	International Cricketers XI	(h)	10–2	Bremner 3, Dineen 2, Cooper 2, Nelson, Gipp, Chivers
Haywards Heath floodlight inauguration:				
19.4.1988	Haywards Heath	(a)	6–1	Wood, Isaac, Penney, Cooper, Bremner 2
1988–89				
5.8.1988	Bognor Regis Town	(a)	6–1	Own goal, Nelson 3, Wood, Penney
Seaford Town centenary match:				
8.8.1988	Seaford Town	(a)	5–1	Crumplin 2, Rougvie, Gipp, Wilkins
11.8.1988	West Ham United	(h)	1–0	Rougvie
16.8.1988	Millwall	(a)	2–2	Rougvie, Nelson
19.8.1988	Gillingham	(a)	0–2	
1989–90				
11.8.1989	Charlton Athletic	(h)	1–0	Crumplin
15.8.1989	Shoreham	(a)	2–2	Gatting, Lambert
Inauguration of Worthing Sports Centre artificial pitch:				
1.10.1989	Charlton Athletic	(n)	2–3	Bremner, Wood
Selsey floodlight opening:				
22.3.1990	Selsey	(a)	5–2	Gotsmanov, Bremner 2, Uzokwe 2
For Southwick's Trevor Dove:				
8.5.1990	Southwick	(a)	1–1	Barham
1990–91				
27.7.1990	Shoreham	(a)	0–0	
11.8.1990	Fisher Athletic	(a)	6–0	McCarthy, Nelson 2, Small, Coldwell, Foloronso
For Albion's Steve Gatting:				
17.8.1990	Arsenal	(h)	2–2	Codner, Nelson
For St Catherine's Hospice (former Albion youngster Micky Edmonds's testimonial match, played at Burgess Hill Town F.C.):				
20.8.1990	Micky Edmonds's XI	(a)	0–0	
8.10.1990	Pagham	(a)	6–1	Small, Gatting, Wade 2, Cormack, Nelson
29.10.1990	Dinamo Minsk (USR)	(h)	1–2	Small
For Albion's Steve Gatting:				
12.11.1990	Eastbourne Select XI	(a)	6–0	Gurinovich, Codner 3, Wade, McGrath
For Crawley Town's Cliff Cant:				
16.5.1991	Crawley Town	(a)	3–1	Small, Own goal, Coldwell
1991–92				
7.8.1991	Dorchester Town	(a)	3–0	Byrne, Nelson, Wade
9.8.1991	Steaua Bucharest (ROM)	(h)	5–4	Own goal, Walker 3, Crumplin
Folkestone Invicta ground inauguration:				
26.8.1991	Folkestone Invicta	(a)	7–0	Byrne, White, Sherriff, Lockhart, Robinson, Gardner, ?
10.2.1992	New Zealand	(h)	0–2	
1992–93				
22.7.1992	Charlton Athletic	(a)	2–2	Funnell 2
25.7.1992	Horsham	(a)	7–0	Chapman 2, Edwards, Funnell, Barham, Walker, Wosahlo
28.7.1992	Dorchester Town	(a)	0–0	
29.7.1992	Tottenham Hotspur	(h)	1–1	Funnell
31.7.1992	Sittingbourne	(a)	1–0	Chapman
4.8.1992	Wimbledon	(h)	0–3	
For Albion's Gary Chivers:				
7.8.1992	Crystal Palace	(h)	0–1	
11.8.1992	Inker Zapresic (CRO)	(h)	3–2	Robinson 2, Foster

Berks & Bucks Hospital Charity Cup

Contested annually at Elm Park by Albion and Reading in the 1920s, with the proceeds going to the Royal Berkshire Hospital, Reading.

Date		Opponents		Score	Scorers	Date		Opponents		Score	Scorers
1921–22						**1925–26**					
13.5.1922	F	Reading	(a)	1–1	Doran	8.5.1926		Cancelled owing to travelling difficulties during General Strike			
Each club held the trophy for six months						**1926–27**					
1922–23						14.5.1927	F	Reading	(a)	1–0	Jennings
12.5.1923	F	Reading	(a)	0–0		**1927–28**					
Each club held the trophy for six months						12.5.1928	F	Reading	(a)	1–3	Ross
1923–24						**1934–35 King George V Silver Jubilee match**					
10.5.1924	F	Reading	(a)	1–2	Coomber	6.5.1935	F	Reading	(a)	1–1	Attwood
1924–25						*Each club held the trophy for six months*					
9.5.1925	F	Reading	(a)	0–1							

Brentford Hospital Cup

Date		Opponents		Score	Scorers
1935–36					
30.4.1936	F	Brentford	(a)	0–1	

Oxfordshire Benevolent Cup

Date		Opponents		Score	Scorers
1985–86					
7.8.1985	F	Oxford United	(a)	1–1	Mortimer
Albion won 5–4 on penalties					

Other miscellaneous matches played by the first team

The following matches would normally have been played by the reserves or were local competitions. See pages 267–284 for more details.

Date	Competition	Opponents	Venue	Score	Scorers
The following matches in the South Eastern League were played by the first team largely for practice:					
2.9.1903	South Eastern League	War Office Sports Club	(h)	6–3	Scott, Thair, Roberts, McAteer, Garfield 2
7.10.1903	South Eastern League	Tottenham Hotspur	(h)	4–3	Rushton 3, McAteer
11.11.1903	South Eastern League	New Brompton	(h)	2–1	Thair, Own goal
28.11.1903	South Eastern League	Tottenham Hotspur	(a)	0–7	
2.9.1904	South Eastern League	Southern United	(h)	6–1	Gilhooly 3, Good 2 (1 pen.), Hulse
28.9.1904	South Eastern League	Watford	(a)	3–1	Good, Garfield 2
12.10.1904	South Eastern League	Watford	(h)	4–0	Garfield 2, Robertson (pen.), Lyon
15.2.1905	South Eastern League	Hastings & St Leonards	(h)	2–0	Gilhooly, Hulse
13.9.1905	South Eastern League D1	Watford	(a)	2–0	Hall, W. Kennedy
25.4.1906	South Eastern League D1	Woolwich Arsenal	(h)	6–1	W. Kennedy 2, Fisher 2, Kent (pen.), Allsopp
2.2.1907	South Eastern League D1	Watford	(h)	5–0	Lewis 2, Hall 3
Played by the first team as part of the Hastings Charity Festival:					
30.4.1908	Freeman-Thos. Ch. Shield	Hastings & St L. United	(a)	1–3 aet	Longstaff
Played by the two first teams for the benefit of the family of Norwich City's Henrie Reid, who died during the original, abandoned game on 5.2.1910:					
19.2.1910	South Eastern League D1	Norwich City	(h)	6–0	Middleton 3, Coleman, Webb, Booth
Played at Woodside Road, Worthing F.C., by the first team in order to boost the monies raised for charity:					
12.5.1960	Sussex (R.U.R.) Cup F	Arundel	(n*)	6–0	Abbis, Curry 3, McNicol, Little
For the first four seasons, 1960–64, Albion's first team contested the Sussex Professional Challenge Cup, but did so only once thereafter:					
24.4.1961	Sussex Pro. Cup F Lg1	Hastings United	(h)	2–2	Brown 2
1.5.1961	Sussex Pro. Cup F Lg2	Hastings United	(a)	2–2	Windross, Laverick
26.3.1962	Sussex Pro. Cup F Lg1	Hastings United	(h)	1–0	Laverick
30.4.1962	Sussex Pro. Cup F Lg2	Hastings United	(a)	2–1	Hodges 2
22.5.1963	Sussex Pro. Cup F	Hastings United	(a)	3–1	Cassidy, Goodchild, Gilbert
7.4.1964	Sussex Pro. Cup SF	Hastings United	(h)	1–1 aet	Turner
22.4.1964	Sussex Pro. Cup SF Rep	Hastings United	(a)	3–0	Cassidy 2, Gall
24.11.1964	Sussex Pro. Cup F	Crawley Town	(h)	3–1	Kydd, Baxter, McQuarrie
30.4.1970	Sussex Pro. Cup F	Crawley Town	(a)	0–1	
Albion's first-team twice opposed the local side for the Richards Hospital Cup, in aid of the Queen Victoria Hospital, East Grinstead:					
13.5.1984	Richards Hospital Cup	East Grinstead	(a)	3–0	Muir 2, Wilson
12.5.1985	Richards Hospital Cup	East Grinstead	(a)	0–1	
Albion's first team contested this match as a 'learning experience' following a particularly poor display in the previous Football League match:					
25.11.1986	Sussex Senior Cup R2	Eastbourne United	(h)	2–0	Saunders, Armstrong

RESERVES, 'A' TEAM, YOUTH TEAM AND LOCAL COMPETITIONS

The Albion reserve team originated in the second season of the club, 1902–03, when it was forced to field a second eleven in the South Eastern League – then a first-team competition – on 18 October against St Albans Amateurs; the fixture clashed with an F.A. Cup qualifying game. A reserve side was again fielded in the League in April 1903 against Grays United and also played four friendly games that season.

It was in 1903–04, with the club having ascended to the First Division of the Southern League, that a reserve side was formed in earnest and entered in the South Eastern League. The Lambs, as the reserves became affectionately known, continued in the South Eastern League until 1921 with the exception of one season, 1907–08, when the club withdrew after failing to gain re-election to the First Division. The Southern League Second Division was contested that season, as it had been in 1904–05.

The South Eastern League disbanded in 1921 and the principal competition in the 1920s was the Southern League, the Lambs twice winning the championship, 1921 and 1927. After playing four seasons in the London Combination as well (and therefore up to 78 fixtures a year!), they left the Southern League in 1930 in favour of the latter competition. An all-reserve league which had originated as a first-team competition for clubs in the capital during the Great War, the London Combination continued until the outbreak of the Second World War in 1939. It reformed in 1944–45 but Albion re-entered in 1945–46, the last season before it became the Football Combination. Guest players were allowed in this transitional season, the fixtures of which were not completed.

The Football Combination and its cup competition were the mainstays of the reserve side for many years. The most successful seasons were 1953–54 when promotion was gained from Division Two, and 1959–60 when the team finished third in Division One. In 1968, though, the second eleven was disbanded as an economy measure. The cutback lasted just one season and the reserves were resurrected for 1969–70, contesting the London Midweek League, a second-best option to the Football Combination. They won the League championship twice and the Cup on three occasions.

After thirteen years in the Midweek League, Albion were elected to the Football Combination again in 1982 and have contested it ever since.

Some competitive records:

Biggest win — 10–0, Grays Thurrock United, Southern League, 21.12.1927
Biggest defeat — 0–13, Tottenham Hotspur, Football Combination, 25.8.1947
Biggest home attendance — 22,229, Notts County, Football Combination, 11.2.1967
  (First-team cup tickets on sale)
  — c. 10,000, Tottenham H., Football Comb. Cup, 28.2.1953
  (Normal conditions)
Biggest away attendance — c. 40,000, Nigeria XI, Friendly, c. 30.9.1981
  — c. 30,000, Arsenal, Football Combination Cup, 4.2.1950
  (First-team cup tickets on sale)
Most career appearances — 284+, Ernie Ison, 1924–31
Most career goals — 127+, Bill Miller, 1910–22

Reserve team league summary 1903–21														
Season	*Competition*	*P*	*W*	*D*	*L*	*F*	*A*	*W*	*D*	*L*	*F*	*A*	*Pts*	*Position/ No. of clubs*
1903–04	South Eastern League	24	9	0	3	36	20	4	3	5	20	29	29	5/13
1904–05	South Eastern League	24	10	0	2	37	11	8	1	3	37	30	37	3/13
" "	Southern League Div. 2	22	7	2	2	35	13	2	1	8	13	36	21	6/12
1905–06	South Eastern League Div. 1	24	7	1	4	33	14	4	2	6	18	18	25	6/13
1906–07	South Eastern League Div. 1	24	5	1	6	27	23	0	2	10	7	45	13	13/13
1907–08	Southern League Div. 2	18	3	3	3	21	16	1	1	7	13	31	12	9/10
1908–09	South Eastern League Div. 1	38	15	2	2	45	15	5	3	11	28	48	45	7/20
1909–10	South Eastern League Div. 1	34	14	2	1	45	15	5	6	6	25	33	46	2/18
1910–11	South Eastern League	36	10	4	4	57	22	5	5	8	26	31	39	5/19
1911–12	South Eastern League	38	17	1	1	76	18	7	7	5	34	29	56	2/20
1912–13	South Eastern League	36	11	3	4	58	22	4	2	12	28	41	35	8/19
1913–14	South Eastern League	40	12	2	6	56	26	6	6	8	18	36	44	8/21
1914–15	South Eastern League	40	9	3	8	39	31	4	4	12	25	49	33	14/21
1915–19	Did not compete													
1919–20	South Eastern League	28	10	2	2	50	25	3	3	8	20	35	31	4/8
1920–21	South Eastern League	14	7	0	0	20	5	2	1	4	11	12	19	2/8
" "	Southern League – English section	24	11	1	0	46	12	5	2	5	17	17	35	1/13

Albion beat Barry, the Welsh section winners, in October 1921 to clinch the 1920–21 Southern League championship

Reserve team league summary 1921–93

Season	Competition	P	W	D	L	F	A	W	D	L	F	A	Pts	Position/No. of clubs
1921–22	Southern League – English section	36	8	7	3	38	22	4	6	8	22	30	37	10/19
1922–23	Southern League – English section	38	17	1	1	73	11	3	2	14	23	49	43	7/20
1923–24	Southern League – Eastern section	30	11	2	2	39	14	2	5	8	16	28	33	6/16
1924–25	Southern League – Eastern section	32	10	5	1	43	16	5	5	6	25	26	40	3/17
1925–26	Southern League – Eastern section	34	15	0	2	69	27	6	4	7	42	42	46	3/18
1926–27	Southern League – Eastern section	32	14	2	0	52	14	7	4	5	34	33	48	1/17
	Albion beat Torquay United, the Western section winners, in October 1927 to clinch the 1926–27 Southern League championship													
" "	London Combination	42	14	3	4	63	25	3	7	11	30	57	44	9/22
1927–28	Southern League – Eastern section	34	13	0	4	62	23	7	0	10	28	40	40	4/18
" "	London Combination	42	14	5	2	57	24	8	5	8	41	48	54	4/22
1928–29	Southern League – Eastern section	36	13	4	1	63	25	6	5	7	28	31	47	3/19
" "	London Combination	42	16	2	3	49	22	3	3	15	24	70	43	10/22
1929–30	Southern League – Eastern section	32	10	1	5	41	30	2	1	3	15	49	26	13/17
" "	London Combination	42	8	5	8	45	36	2	5	14	24	69	30	21/22
1930–31	London Combination Div. 1	42	14	3	4	54	32	3	1	17	26	66	38	14/22
1931–32	London Combination Div. 1	42	11	3	7	42	33	3	2	16	18	59	33	18/22
1932–33	London Combination Div. 1	46	13	4	6	64	33	4	3	16	19	71	41	15/24
1933–34	London Combination	46	11	3	9	37	29	5	6	12	29	49	41	16/24
1934–35	London Combination	46	14	5	4	50	24	3	3	17	15	57	42	12/24
1935–36	London Combination	46	9	7	7	42	35	2	1	20	25	84	30	23/24
1936–37	London Combination	46	12	4	7	43	35	3	8	12	29	55	42	13/24
1937–38	London Combination	46	5	10	8	38	45	5	2	16	32	78	32	24/24
1938–39	London Combination	46	13	5	5	43	19	9	2	12	32	51	51	7/24
1939–40	London Combination					*Albion played two matches before the London Combination was cancelled upon the outbreak of war*								
1940–45	Did not compete													
1945–46	London Combination	28	5	3	6	33	33	2	4	8	26	56	21	c. 16/18
	The season's programme was not completed and six matches were left outstanding													
1946–47	Football Combination section B	30	4	6	5	36	35	3	3	9	19	42	23	13/16
1947–48	Football Combination section B	30	3	2	10	27	35	0	2	13	11	56	10	16/16
1948–49	Football Combination section A	30	9	3	3	24	14	3	3	9	20	33	30	8/16
1949–50	Football Combination section B	30	8	2	5	30	19	5	3	7	26	31	31	8/16
1950–51	Football Combination section B	30	6	3	6	23	20	1	1	13	20	53	18	16/16
1951–52	Football Combination section B	30	5	5	5	30	29	3	3	9	15	39	24	13/16
1952–53	Football Combination Div. 2	30	7	5	3	47	25	3	4	8	25	40	29	8/16
1953–54	Football Combination Div. 2	30	10	1	4	37	21	4	5	6	20	25	34	4/16
1954–55	Football Combination Div. 1	30	8	2	5	42	32	4	4	7	21	34	30	9/16
1955–56	Football Combination	42	8	7	6	53	37	9	1	11	26	45	42	15/32
1956–57	Football Combination	42	13	3	5	50	32	4	3	14	32	64	40	17/32
1957–58	Football Combination	42	12	3	6	41	23	11	2	8	32	25	51	7/32
1958–59	Football Combination Div. 1	34	7	3	7	35	21	4	5	8	32	37	30	10/18
1959–60	Football Combination Div. 1	34	9	6	2	33	16	7	6	4	31	28	44	3/18
1960–61	Football Combination Div. 1	34	5	4	8	30	36	4	1	12	22	49	23	17/18
1961–62	Football Combination – Midweek section	34	6	5	6	25	26	1	3	13	17	51	22	16/18
1962–63	Football Combination – Midweek section	34	12	1	4	38	26	6	3	8	15	27	40	4/18
1963–64	Football Combination Div. 2	34	6	3	8	32	45	2	5	10	20	43	24	15/18
1964–65	Football Combination Div. 2	36	10	3	5	44	24	3	7	8	20	35	36	10/19
1965–66	Football Combination Div. 2	38	13	1	5	46	25	9	3	7	43	34	48	4/20
1966–67	Football Combination Div. 2	24	7	3	2	27	14	3	5	4	20	20	28	5/13
1967–68	Football Combination Div. 2	40	8	3	9	37	32	5	2	13	17	45	31	11/11
1968–69	Did not compete													
1969–70	London Midweek League	14	4	1	2	17	7	2	2	3	10	9	15	4/8
1970–71	London Midweek League	18	4	3	2	17	9	2	2	5	10	24	17	610
1971–72	Midweek League	22	5	2	4	15	18	2	2	7	11	39	18	9/12
1972–73	Midweek League	20	3	4	3	16	14	4	3	3	15	19	21	5/11
1973–74	Midweek League	24	5	3	4	22	11	3	4	5	18	21	23	7/13
1974–75	Midweek League	26	4	5	4	28	22	7	0	6	20	28	27	8/14
1975–76	Midweek League	26	7	3	3	29	13	3	4	6	19	31	27	7/14
1976–77	Midweek League	20	5	2	3	20	14	5	1	4	16	12	23	2/11
1977–78	Midweek League	22	7	2	2	24	12	7	1	3	20	15	31	1/12
1978–79	Midweek League	22	7	1	3	23	15	6	3	2	19	11	30	3/12
1979–80	Midweek League	24	4	4	4	24	28	4	1	7	16	27	21	10/13
1980–81	Midweek League	24	7	3	2	36	16	7	3	2	17	7	34	1/13
1981–82	Midweek League	26	7	1	5	19	14	4	3	6	12	22	26	7/14
1982–83	Football Combination	42	7	9	5	30	26	3	6	12	23	39	35	14/22
1983–84	Football Combination	42	14	2	5	48	19	5	5	11	26	46	45	12/22
1984–85	Football Combination	42	11	4	6	46	33	4	8	9	25	39	42	12/22
1985–86	Football Combination	42	6	6	9	25	28	3	3	15	15	65	27	17/22
1986–87	Football Combination	38	5	2	12	27	42	1	2	16	17	50	16	20/20
1987–88	Sunday Mirror Football Combination	38	8	5	6	33	28	7	3	9	25	44	38	14/20
1988–89	Ovenden Papers Football Combination	38	4	7	8	18	27	3	6	10	25	54	27	15/20
1989–90	Ovenden Papers Football Combination	38	10	4	5	29	20	5	2	12	23	46	51	9/20
1990–91	Ovenden Papers Football Combination	38	7	5	7	34	27	4	1	14	13	42	39	17/20
1991–92	Neville Ovenden Football Combination	38	7	2	10	31	29	1	6	12	15	38	32	19/20
1992–93	N. Ovenden Football Combination Div. 1	38	5	6	8	27	37	4	1	14	11	44	34	19/20

South Eastern League results 1903–21

Team	1903–04	1904–05	1905–06 D1	1906–07 D1	1908–09 D1	1909–10 D1	1910–11	1911–12	1912–13	1913–14	1914–15	1919–20	1920–21
Arsenal (res.)*	1–2 N7 / 0–4 F15	0–3 A21 / 2–5 D26	6–1 A25† / 0–1 N27	2–4 D1 / 2–8 M9	4–2 M17 / 2–0 A26	1–0 A20 / 1–1 S1	4–0 D10 / 2–2 S17	3–1 O14 / 2–1 F3	2–4 S28 / 2–2 J25	2–4 S6 / 2–1 A11	0–2 D12 / 2–4 A17		
Aylesbury United	3–2 J9 / 1–1 F20		7–2 M4 / 7–4 O29										
Boscombe											2–2 S2 / 3–0 O28		
Brentford (res.)									4–0 A5 / 7–1 F1	6–1 D20 / 1–1 D6			
Bristol City (res.)							1–1 F18 / 0–1 O1	3–0 J13 / 3–1 F17	3–0 S14 / 1–2 O5	3–0 A14 / 0–3 J31	1–2 F3 / 0–4 A6		
Cardiff City (res.)											3–2 S19 / 0–3 J23		
Charlton Athletic													3–2 A13 / 0–0 J27
Chelsea (res.)			1–1 O7 / 1–3 F10	3–3 J5 / 1–7 O25	4–1 S12 / 2–3 N7	1–4 S4 / 0–0 J8	1–3 J21 / 1–4 A15	2–4 S30 / 1–0 D30	1–0 A19 / 2–3 S2	8–1 F14 / 1–5 O11	3–2 S12 / 2–1 A28		
Chesham Generals	5–0 A1 / 1–0 A5												
Clapton Orient (res.)				3–0 A10 / 0–2 D5	2–1 F16 / 1–5 A18	2–2 M22 / 2–2 A29	1–0 F10 / 3–0 O7	8–1 N30 / 3–1 S7		1–1 O29 / 1–3 S25	1–2 M13 / 1–4 N7		
Coventry City (res.)					4–1 J22 / 1–3 S11	0–1 O8 / 1–0 F11	5–2 J6 / 2–3 S9						
Croydon Common (res. 1909–10 & 1912–15)					0–2 F27 / 0–5 A17	2–1 O30 / 2–2 M12	3–1 S1 / 2–3 S14	6–2 J3 / 2–4 J31	2–0 D7 / 1–4 J1	6–3 M21 / 0–0 N15	4–0 M27 / 5–2 N21		
Crystal Palace (res.)					1–0 S19 / 3–2 J23	1–1 A30 / 1–1 D18							
Eastbourne			–* / 2–2 F3*										
Eastbourne Old Town		2–0 J21 / 4–3 N5	8–1 O21* / –*										
Fulham (res.)					2–0 J16 / 2–4 S26	2–0 M5 / 1–0 N20	2–3 M4 / 2–4 O15	1–1 M9 / 1–1 D2	1–1 F8 / 1–2 M15	0–1 N8 / 0–3 N29	0–2 N14 / 1–1 M20		
Gillingham (res.)*	2–1 N11† / 4–2 M5									0–2 J24 / 1–0 S27	7–0 J2 / 2–0 S5		
Grays United	0–4 O10 / 0–0 D12	4–0 S14 / 2–1 M22	3–0 J10 / 2–0 S2										
Hastings & St Leonards*		2–0 F15† / 2–4 D31	3–2 N11 / 3–2 O14	4–2 M6 / 0–2 M27	4–1 O31 / 2–5 M6	2–1 A2 / 1–1 M25							
Hitchin Town	1–2 D5 / 4–2 F6	2–0 J7 / 3–1 M8	4–0 S23 / 4–0 A14	0–2 N17 / 1–4 M23									
Leicester Fosse (res.)										7–0 A4 / 2–2 S18			
Leyton (res. 1906–12)			0–4 A17 / 2–3 F22	2–3 S1 / 0–5 A18	0–0 A12 / 0–3 D28	2–0 F23 / 0–2 O9	4–1 D31 / 1–2 S3	3–0 S16 / 0–1 J20					
Luton Town (res.)	4–1 O24 / 2–2 S19	2–0 A1 / 6–0 D3	5–0 S9 / 0–1 J6	1–3 D15 / 0–3 A20	3–2 O3 / 0–4 F6	2–1 A13 / 3–0 J1	3–1 M18 / 1–2 N12	7–0 A5 / 3–1 A8		4–0 O3 / 1–9 F6	4–4 O11 / 2–2 S20	3–0 A10 / 1–1 F21	2–1 O6 / 1–2 S22
Maidstone United			4–1 S7 / 3–2 J25	0–1 F17 / 1–3 A16	3–2 N3 / 0–2 S8	5–1 S1 / 0–0 O24							
Northampton Town (res.)							5–0 J14 / 1–1 N26	4–3 D26 / 3–2 D28	8–0 M22 / 3–1 N16	1–2 O4 / 1–0 F7			
Norwich City (res.)			0–1 A13 / 0–5 D8		2–0 A24 / 2–1 D19	6–0 F19† / 1–1 S25	0–0 D3 / 2–0 A8	3–1 J27 / 2–2 S23	7–0 M8 / 0–2 N2	1–0 S20 / 2–1 J17	0–2 A5 / 0–0 A2		
Peterborough City							10–2 S24 / 1–2 O29	4–0 A20 / 2–2 M16	7–1 J11 / 0–1 F15	3–3 J10 / 1–0 D27			
Portsmouth (res.)					5–1 J30 / 1–1 F20	4–0 D4 / 3–1 M28		1–3 D26 / 0–3 D25	3–0 O25 / 1–1 F28	2–1 F13 / 2–1 O10	1–3 D13 / 0–6 D25	5–2 D26 / 1–2 A24	1–0 F12 / 0–1 M26
Queen's Park Rangers (res.)	2–1 N21 / 2–6 M19	0–1 F18 / 2–1 O22	0–1 N25 / 1–1 M31	0–1 M2 / 0–1 O27	2–0 N28 / 2–2 J9				2–5 N23 / 3–0 M29	1–3 F21 / 2–5 O18	1–4 N25 / 1–2 M6		
Reading (res. 1911–21)							4–2 F15 / 1–1 J28	4–2 F24 / 4–0 O21	4–2 O26 / 2–2 M1	1–1 N28 / 0–0 D25	7–4 a30 / 1–7 S6	3–1 N8 / 3–1 F7	2–0 N20 / 3–2 M2
St Albans Amateurs	4–0 A9 / 5–0 A23												
Sittingbourne				5–1 M16 / 2–7 N10	3–0 M24 / 0–2 M20								
Southampton (res.)									3–2 A13 / 1–0 A10	1–2 A10 / 0–4 D5	1–4 F14 / 2–7 O4	4–1 M27 / 0–1 J3	3–0 S11 / 1–3 m7
Southend United (res. 1908–10 & 1914–20)					2–0 N14 / 4–2 F3	2–1 O2 / 2–1 F12			9–0 A6 / 1–1 M30		1–0 F27 / 1–2 O24	2–2 S13 / 3–0 A2	3–1 A5 / 5–0 m1
Southern United		6–1 S2† / 1–1 J12											
Swindon Town (res.)					2–1 N21 / 2–3 O10	3–1 D11 / 3–4 A23	6–2 A22 / 1–2 D17	4–0 D23 / 0–0 A27	1–1 D21 / 0–1 A26	4–2 N22 / 0–0 M28	3–2 O17 / 1–1 F20		
Thorneycrofts											6–2 D27 / 0–3 O18	3–1 F28 / 1–1 J24	5–1 D28 / 5–1 N13
Tottenham Hotspur (res.)	4–3 O7† / 0–7 N28†	4–3 M18 / 2–7 N19	0–2 J20 / 0–2 S16	2–1 M30 / 0–0 A6	2–1 D26 / 0–6 A13	1–1 O16 / 2–3 A11	0–1 N19 / 1–0 F25	2–0 N25 / 1–5 N4	1–1 N9 / 0–2 A12	3–0 M7 / 1–2 N1	1–2 M3 / 1–4 S26		
Tunbridge Wells Rangers					1–1 A21 / 5–1 D25		7–0 D27 / 3–2 D26	6–0 S2 / 2–2 D25	3–1 D28 / 2–3 O19				
War Office Sports Club	6–3 S2† / 0–1 A4*												
Watford (res.)	4–1 S5 / 1–4 A16	4–0 O12† / 3–1 S28†	3–1 F14 / 2–0 S13†	5–0 F2† / 1–1 O13	4–1 S18 / 1–0 J29	4–1 S10 / 2–2 J7	7–1 O28 / 1–1 M2	2–0 J18 / 0–1 D19	3–0 J3 / 1–0 O19	2–1 J20 / 0–1 D19	2–0 N22 / 0–1 S24	6–0 A17 / 1–3 D6	4–1 S25 / 1–3 O2
West Ham United (res.)					0–2 J2 / 1–2 S5	6–1 D25 / 2–8 D27	1–1 N5 / 1–1 A13	2–1 D9 / 1–7 M24	1–2 M21 / 0–2 D13	1–0 A18 / 3–3 F1	2–2 N11		

Notes: Home matches are given above away matches. Albion score given first. a – August, A – April; M – March, m – May.

Matches marked with a dagger (†) were played by the Albion first team. (Note that the 1902–03 South Eastern League was competed for by the first team; see "Season 1902–03", page 32.)

1903–04 v. War Office Sports Club (away) – played at the Goldstone Ground as part of the War Office Sports Club's tour.

1905–06 – Eastbourne took over Eastbourne Old Town's fixtures on D2 when the latter club disbanded following an F.A. censure for mismanagement.

1909–10 v. Norwich City (home) – match originally played F5 but abandoned in the second half when City's Henrie Reid died of heart failure with the score 3–1.

1914–15 v. Brentford (home 1–2 O14, and away 3–1 S14) were deleted from the record when Brentford withdrew from the League.

Arsenal were known as Woolwich Arsenal until 1913; Gillingham were known as New Brompton until 1913; and Hastings & St Leonards, now Hastings Town, combined with St Leonards United in 1906 to form Hastings & St Leonards United.

Southern League results (reserves only)	1904–05 D2	1907–08 D2	1920–21 Eng.	1921–22 Eng.	1922–23 Eng.	1923–24 E.	1924–25 E.	1925–26 E.	1926–27 E.	1927–28 E.	1928–29 E.	1929–30 E.
Aldershot Town										4–2 A25 0–2 M21	4–0 D12 0–1 J12	1–1 O9 1–4 M26
Bath City				0–0 N12 1–4 N5	3–2 J24 2–1 D23							
Bournem'th & BA (res. 1923–30)*			7–0 J1 2–3 J22	0–0 M11 0–0 M4	3–0 F24 1–4 F17	5–2 D15 1–1 D22	0–1 S27 0–2 J31	4–2 J9 2–2 A10	2–1 A9 3–1 A16	2–1 F16 1–4 D27	5–4 S26 2–0 M29	4–2 J1 2–1 D11
Bristol City (res.)				3–6 N26 2–0 N19	2–0 J27 2–4 J20							
Bristol Rovers (res.)				4–0 D26 2–2 D27	2–2 M17 2–2 M24							
Charlton Athletic (res. from 1921)			4–3 J15 1–3 S4		2–2 O22 1–3 O29							
Chatham Town			6–1 a28 2–1 N27							0–1 N30 2–1 M24	6–1 J23 2–2 O17	
Clapton Orient (res.)	1–2 N12 0–0 O8											
Coventry City (res.)						9–0 S23 1–4 S30	4–2 D1 2–2 D8	3–0 S10 1–2 S29	4–0 S12 4–1 J23			
Croydon Common		2–2 O19 1–2 F29										
Dartford									4–3 m4 1–0 N27	5–2 N16 0–1 S7	7–1 O24 1–2 N14	1–3 D12 2–1 A5
Exeter City (res.)				0–1 a31 1–1 S7	2–0 O18 1–3 m5							
Folkestone						2–1 J19 0–3 N24	4–4 D20 1–1 S6	6–1 D26 5–4 D25	3–1 D27 5–0 D25	6–0 J18 3–2 F22	2–2 F27 1–6 O10	4–0 J8 0–4 A30
Fulham (res.)	0–0 O15 1–7 A12								4–1 O31 1–1 M25			
Gillingham			4–1 M12 3–1 M19	4–1 A15 1–0 A22						4–2 N12 1–3 M10	1–1 S12 0–3 D8	
Grays Thurrock United*	1–1 F4 1–3 S24							6–0 J30 2–4 O24	3–0 S8 5–1 S1	10–0 D21 5–3 A11	5–2 J16 4–2 N7	1–3 M27 2–3 O2
Guildford City*				2–2 F15 0–1 J21	1–0 A28 0–1 D9	1–2 A21 0–1 A18	1–1 A13 5–1 A10	8–3 A5 0–2 A2	4–0 m7 6–2 D4	4–1 D7 2–0 J25	3–2 A24 1–1 F13	3–2 M5 3–8 D18
Hastings & St Leonards Utd		3–0 A13 1–2 F19										
Kettering Town						4–1 N10 1–2 S15	1–0 M21 1–2 M5	2–5 M6 2–2 N7	4–1 O16 0–4 D18	0–2 M22 2–3 O22	1–1 A10 0–2 A4	1–2 M20 2–3 A7
Leicester City (res.)						0–0 N17 0–4 S10	1–1 S24 2–1 S16	3–2 a29 2–1 J2	2–0 M16 5–3 F24			
Luton Town (res.)			2–2 O23 1–1 O30	5–0 M25 1–1 M18	3–1 S9 1–2 S16	3–1 D25 2–1 D26	9–1 S13 1–1 J17	4–1 O17 2–3 F27	4–0 A18 1–1 A15			
Millwall (res.)			1–0 N17 1–0 M14	1–0 A29 1–2 m6	3–0 M30 1–5 A2	3–1 O31 1–3 F18	7–3 D25 0–5 D26	2–3 S23 1–2 S7	0–0 S29 0–0 O11	1–2 S28 2–1 F27	2–1 J30 1–1 N26	1–5 F12 0–2 D2
Northampton Town (res.)						6–1 a25 1–1 S1	5–1 J3 1–1 M14					1–0 M12 0–8 N21
Northfleet United										3–1 N2 0–4 M7	2–2 J2 2–2 J9	2–0 A9 1–3 A18
Norwich City (res.)			2–1 M28 0–1 M25	5–0 D17 2–2 D24	3–0 S2 0–1 a26	1–0 A5 1–1 M29	4–1 F14 3–0 m2	4–2 F13 4–2 A22	4–1 O20 2–8 S22	3–0 F18 1–4 O8	4–0 D19 2–1 M14	4–2 N6 0–2 F27
Nuneaton Town							2–1 N22 2–1 O23	5–1 D12 2–4 D19				
Peterborough & Fletton Utd						0–1 A19 0–1 S29	1–0 O25 0–4 F28	2–1 O10 1–3 M13	4–2 J1 0–3 N20	2–6 N23 0–3 A30	6–1 M6 3–4 S6	6–1 J22 0–2 S19
Plymouth Argyle (res.)				1–1 F25 0–1 F18	4–0 M10 0–2 M3							
Poole									4–0 O27 2–2 D1	6–1 F29 1–2 F25	4–2 F20 4–2 O31	
Portsmouth (res.)	4–3 A22 2–5 D24	0–3 N23 3–1 A27*	3–1 A16 1–1 A9	2–2 A14 2–0 A17	3–0 D26 1–4 D25	1–0 O6 1–4 O13	0–0 A4 1–1 A25	4–2 N14 0–2 D5	5–2 D15 0–2 M19			
Reading (res.)	4–0 D10 0–1 A8		4–1 O9 0–3 O16	1–0 D31 2–3 J14	6–0 M31 2–0 A7	1–0 D29 4–0 J5	2–1 D6 4–0 A11	5–1 A3 5–3 N21	6–1 D8 1–1 J12			
Salisbury City		1–2 F8 2–6 O26										
Sheppey United										4–0 J4 2–1 F1	2–0 M20 0–1 O3	2–3 J29 1–1 D14
Sittingbourne										2–1 M28 0–2 S21	1–3 F6 3–0 m1	4–2 O23 0–3 A2
Southall	4–1 S17 1–0 J14											
Southampton (res.)	2–0 O1 1–6 J28	3–3 O5 1–7 D28	6–2 A27 0–2 F5	1–4 S24 1–4 O1	3–2 O28 1–3 O21	2–2 F16 1–3 M26	3–1 O18 1–2 M11	2–1 S26 4–4 O3	1–0 M30 1–0 A27	6–1 J11 6–4 F15	3–2 D5 1–1 O1	4–3 A30 1–2 M19
Southend United (res. 1921–23)			2–3 A6 1–3 M4	4–1 S3 2–4 a27	8–2 A14 1–2 A21							
Swindon Town (res.)	2–5 D17 2–4 A15		2–2 M7 1–3 D7	2–2 A1 2–1 A8	2–0 N18 3–4 N25							
Thames											5–0 N21 1–0 a30	2–1 F5 0–2 S30
Thorneycrofts			2–0 A2 2–1 F19									
Torquay United					1–2 O14 0–4 J6							
Tunbridge Wells Rangers		5–0 S7 3–3 D25										
Watford (res.)	7–0 A29 1–2 F25		5–0 A30 4–0 A23	1–0 O8 1–1 O15	7–0 F10 1–0 F3	6–0 m3 1–1 A12	0–0 M7 2–2 N1	4–1 J16 5–2 S5	2–2 M12 2–5 O23			
West Ham United (res.)	4–1 D27 0–6 M25											
Wycombe Wanderers	6–0 S3 4–2 M11		3–1 M14 0–4 A1									
Yeovil & Petters United					8–0 D30 3–3 A3							

Notes: Home matches are given above away matches. Albion score given first. a – August, A – April; M – March, m – May.

1907–08 v. Portsmouth (away) – match originally played A25 but abandoned after 5 minutes because of snow on pitch with score 0–0.

1920–21 Championship match v. Barry played S22 1921 at The Den, Millwall FC. Result 1–1 after double extra time.
    Replay O19 1921 at Ninian Park, Cardiff City FC. Result 2–1.

1926–27 Championship match v. Torquay United played O5 1927 at the Goldstone Ground. Result 4–0.

1929–30 v. Poole (home 4–0 F19, away 2–1 O16) were deleted from the record when Poole withdrew from the League.

Bournemouth & Boscombe Athletic, now AFC Bournemouth, were known as Boscombe until 1923; Grays Thurrock United were known as Grays United in 1904–05; and Guildford City were known as Guildford United until 1927.

London Combination results	1926–27	1927–28	1928–29	1929–30	1930–31 D1	1931–32 D1	1932–33 D1	1933–34	1934–35	1935–36	1936–37	1937–38	1938–39	1945–46
Aldershot							7–0 m3 / 0–3 O26	1–0 F10 / 0–5 S27						4–6 D8 / 0–9 J12
Arsenal	1–0 J8 / 2–2 J15	1–0 F4 / 1–4 S24	0–6 a29 / 1–4 O6	3–3 m1 / 0–3 M10	2–5 A18 / 0–2 D13	1–4 N28 / 0–4 A9	3–4 F8 / 1–7 A22	0–1 D25 / 0–3 S13	1–2 D25 / 2–1 D26	1–1 F1 / 1–5 S28	0–5 J23 / 0–4 S19	3–3 O30 / 0–4 M12	0–2 M18 / 1–0 N12	
Bournemouth & B.A.								6–2 S23 / 2–5 M19*	2–2 M6 / 0–1 J12	2–1 F15 / 0–2 O12	2–0 N4 / 0–1 M3	3–3 S18 / 1–5 D27	1–1 O26 / 0–2 F15	
Brentford	4–0 a28 / 1–5 m2	2–1 D31 / 1–1 a27	2–2 D26 / 0–2 D25	2–2 D25 / 1–5 D26	0–2 F14 / 0–4 O11	0–2 N14 / 0–8 M26	0–3 M15 / 0–4 S10	0–3 M31 / 1–0 N18	1–3 N3 / 0–1 M16	0–1 D14 / 0–2 A18	2–3 J2 / 1–5 S5	1–1 M5 / 3–2 O23	2–1 N5 / 0–2 M11	1–3 O13 / 0–5 N3
Bristol City							1–3 D26 / 0–3 D27	0–1 F14 / 1–1 S16	3–1 D1 / 0–0 A13	0–0 D26 / 6–2 D25	3–0 F27 / 2–3 O24	1–2 A16 / 0–4 D4	3–0 D17 / 0–7 A22	
Cardiff City	2–0 S25 / 0–0 F12	0–0 O13 / 1–3 S5	1–0 D1 / 0–3 M8	2–4 N2 / 2–0 A25	2–1 D20 / 1–1 m7	2–1 S2								
Charlton Athletic	1–1 N13 / 0–1 A2	4–2 A14 / 3–3 D3	6–1 J26 / 3–3 S15	1–0 A3 / 2–2 A19	2–1 M21 / 4–0 N15	2–1 D25 / 1–0 F29	3–1 D31 / 2–1 a27	1–0 M3 / 1–2 O21	4–1 S1 / 0–1 J5	3–2 F26 / 0–4 A4	3–1 M27 / 0–1 N21	1–2 J15 / 1–2 S4	0–0 J28 / 4–3 S24	1–0 m1 / 1–6 F16
Chelsea	2–3 F5 / 1–1 N11	2–0 M3 / 1–1 F8	4–0 A1 / 3–2 M21	1–0 a31 / 1–10 D28	1–1 O4 / 0–6 F7	1–1 S19 / 1–4 J30	5–0 S3 / 1–1 M29	3–0 O5 / 1–1 A7	3–2 S15 / 0–2 J26	6–1 O16 / 1–4 A21	1–3 M13 / 1–1 N7	2–0 O6 / 0–3 F23	1–2 S17 / 2–2 M1	3–4 a25 / 8–4 A5
Clapton Orient	1–2 M23 / 0–2 M10	2–0 O26 / 2–1 S15	2–1 S22 / 4–1 F2	6–1 m3 / 0–1 S23	2–3 A4 / 3–5 N29	4–1 J23 / 0–2 S12	2–2 O1		2–1 a29 / 0–3 S29	1–1 J16 / 2–2 N23	3–3 D25 / 1–3 A8	3–0 N19 / 1–3 F5	/ 0–2 M25	–* / –*
Coventry City	6–0 O30 / 2–4 M5	2–2 M17 / 3–4 N5	2–0 S8 / 0–2 J19	3–1 A21 / 0–4 S2	4–3 O25 / 2–1 F28	1–2 O31 / 1–0 M12	3–1 J21 / 0–3 F11		2–5 S21 / 1–2 m5	2–2 F6 / 1–5 M30	2–2 M16 / 4–6 J25	0–1 m6 / 1–6 O3	/ 2–3 O28	/ 1–0 F2
Crystal Palace	1–1 M2 / 5–0 N3	3–3 S17 / 6–1 J28	1–2 O20 / 1–1 M2	1–2 A26 / 2–2 D21	4–2 J31 / 1–4 S27	1–1 S9	2–3 S21 / 3–1 S14	3–0 A14 / 3–0 D2	2–0 J19 / 1–5 S8	2–4 N2 / 1–9 M7	0–0 D12 / 1–1 A17	1–3 A30 / 1–5 a31	3–2 S28	4–2 S15 / 0–0 D29
Fulham	6–1 A23 / 2–1 F3	4–0 O15 / 2–1 m3	2–1 A20 / 1–3 D6	1–4 O19 / 1–4 F22	2–2 N8 / 0–4 M14	5–3 A2 / 3–5 N21	2–1 D24 / 0–7 m6	0–1 J6 / 3–3 S2	2–0 M23 / 3–2 N10	1–0 A25 / 1–2 D21	3–2 S12 / 1–1 J9	0–0 m7 / 1–2 N18	5–0 M4 / 0–5 O29	1–1 A20 / 1–3 A27
Ipswich Town														0–1 J19 / 0–8 O6
Leicester City	4–1 N24 / 2–6 D28	1–1 D10 / 2–4 N19	3–0 N3 / 4–1 M16	5–0 O5 / 2–5 F8	1–0 M7 / 1–5 N1	1–1 J2 / 1–3 a29	4–0 O8 / 1–5 F18	1–1 M17 / 2–4 N4	2–1 F16 / 0–2 O6	4–0 J18 / 0–3 S14	3–1 O17 / 1–4 F20	2–1 F2 / 2–1 A7	3–1 A10 / 1–3 M13	
Luton Town	2–1 A6 / 0–7 J5	3–2 S3 / 2–0 J7	2–1 a25 / 1–3 D29	3–2 F26* / 1–0 M22	2–0 A6 / 0–1 A3	3–1 O17 / 0–3 F27	1–0 A1 / 1–1 N19	2–0 A2 / 1–4 M30	3–0 O3 / 1–2 O24	0–1 A11 / 0–7 D7	2–3 A26 / 2–1 D19	1–1 F19 / 2–6 O9	3–0 D24 / 1–2 a27	–* / –*
Millwall	5–0 J22 / 0–3 S4	7–0 J21 / 4–3 S10	2–0 M9 / 0–6 O27	4–5 S21 / 1–4 A24	4–0 D25 / 1–6 D26	0–0 M5 / 0–1 O24	1–0 A8 / 2–2 O2		3–1 A6 / 2–4 m2	4–2 S11 / 4–3 A12	2–0 S26 / 0–6 F26	0–2 O16 / 1–6 F25	1–1 O22	/ 0–2 O27
Northampton Town								5–2 M4 / 1–3 O22	1–1 N1 / 1–1 J13	2–1 O20 / 1–1 M2	1–2 O2 / 0–5 N9	1–1 F13 / 0–2 F12	/ 5–2 D10	
Portsmouth	3–0 S11 / 2–2 S18	1–4 M31 / 0–2 A21	5–1 J5 / 0–2 S1	3–1 A12 / 4–3 D7	3–2 D6 / 1–3 A11	2–4 M19 / 2–3 N7	6–0 F25 / 0–4 O15	0–0 D9 / 1–1 A21	1–1 A20 / 2–0 D8	0–4 N28 / 0–4 S18	1–3 A18 / 1–1 A3	3–0 J21 / 3–1 N26		2–2 O20 / 2–2 S22
Queen's Park Rangers	4–3 M26 / 1–8 A30	4–0 A28 / 3–2 D17	1–1 A6 / 1–1 N24	0–0 M1 / 2–2 O26	3–0 S13 / 0–1 J17	2–4 O3 / 1–3 F13	2–4 O29 / 1–3 J14	3–4 a26 / 2–0 D30	4–0 F2 / 3–3 S22	1–4 A10 / 2–0 A13	2–1 O31 / 2–5 M6	1–5 a28 / 1–1 J1	2–0 J14 / 0–3 S10	0–6 J5 / 1–6 F2
Reading	0–0 J19 / 4–6 J26	2–1 M14 / 1–1 O12	5–2 D15 / 2–4 A27	0–1 J4 / 0–3 S7	5–3 S20 / 1–1 J24	2–0 M9 / 0–5 A23	1–2 S17 / 1–4 J28	1–3 O7 / 2–4 O26	2–2 M9 / 1–1 D5	0–0 F29 / 3–1 S11	4–1 A10 / 3–1 D27	2–2 J22 / 0–4 S1	3–0 D26	1–3 D22
Southampton	5–3 S15 / 2–2 O6	2–3 O19 / 0–0 N9	2–0 N17 / 1–3 M30	1–2 F15 / 2–2 O12	1–3 a30 / 3–4 M11	3–2 F20 / 0–0 O10	3–2 A29 / 2–0 D17	0–2 O17 / 2–0 J20	3–0 D29 / 0–3 a25	2–1 O5 / 1–2 F8	1–3 a29 / 2–1 D26	4–1 M19 / 1–5 N6	0–0 F11 / 2–0 O8	4–2 N10 / 3–3 S8
Southend United	5–3 O9 / 2–0 F26	5–1 A9 / 2–1 A6	2–3 O13 / 1–6 F23	4–0 M29 / 2–2 J15*	5–0 m2 / 2–3 S1	5–1 A16 / 0–4 D5	2–2 A17 / 1–0 A14	4–1 A28 / 0–1 D16	0–0 A22 / 1–3 A19	0–0 N16 / 0–5 M21	1–1 S8 / 3–3 m1	1–3 S3 / 2–2 S1	/ 1–1 D31	2–2 N24 / 3–3 N17
Swansea Town	3–2 F16 / 1–1 N6	3–3 O1 / 2–0 F11	0–1 A17 / 0–3 S20	1–1 M15 / 0–5 N9	5–0 F21 / 1–3 O18	4–1 A30 / 1–4 D19	0–0 N12 / 0–4 M25	3–0 O14 / 0–1 F24	0–1 F23 / 1–2 J4		1–2 O15 / 1–6 A23	1–2 J7		
Tottenham Hotspur	1–2 D11 / 1–1 J29	3–0 O18 / 4–8 a29	2–0 m4 / 0–8 D22	1–2 F1 / 0–2 S28	1–2 J3 / 2–5 S6	2–1 S5 / 1–3 J16	3–1 S6 / 1–5 S24	4–4 N11 / 1–4 M24	1–1 M7 / 0–6 O15	2–1 O20 / 1–3 F22	0–0 M29 / 2–2 M20	1–2 A2 / 1–4 S13	1–1 F18 / 2–0 F4	
Watford	6–0 N17 / 2–3 F9	6–0 J14 / 0–4 A7	1–0 M23 / 0–4 N10	2–3 S18 / 0–3 S11	2–1 N22 / 1–4 M28	2–1 M28 / 1–2 M25	5–2 a31 / 3–1 J14	2–3 S7 / 3–1 a30	2–1 a30 / 0–5 A27	7–0 D15 / 0–5 O2	2–4 M11 / 0–1 M26	1–2 A2 / 2–2 N20	1–1 F18 / 3–1 O15	6–1 S29 / 7–1 D26
West Ham United	1–2 F19 / 0–2 O2	2–1 D24 / 1–4 m5	3–1 F9 / 0–7 S29	1–3 J18 / 3–4 S14	3–2 O1 / 1–4 A16	0–1 F6 / 1–3 S26	2–2 M18 / 0–5 N5	2–0 O28 / 1–5 M10	2–4 m4 / 0–4 D22	4–2 D28 / 0–2 a31	2–0 S9 / 1–4 S2	2–1 N13 / 6–2 M26	2–1 D3 / 1–6 A8	4–0 D25 / –*

Notes: Home matches are shown above away matches. Albion score given first. a – August, A – April; M – March, m – May.

1929–30 v. Luton Town (home) – match originally played N16 but abandoned after 30 minutes because of waterlogged pitch with score 3–0.

1929–30 v. Southend United (away) – match originally played N23 but abandoned after 72 minutes because of a thunderstorm with score 1–1.

1933–34 v. Bournemouth & B.A. (away) – match originally played M14 but abandoned after 17 minutes because of heavy rain with score 0–0.

1939–40 v. Bristol City (away 3–2 a26) and Arsenal (home 0–0 S2) were deleted from the record when the London Combination was cancelled upon the outbreak of war on S3.

1945–46 – the season's programme was not completed and six matches were left outstanding. Guest players were allowed.

London Combination Cup

Date		Opponents		Score
1945–46				
23.2.1946	R1	Watford	(h)	3–1
9.3.1946	R2	Crystal Palace	(h)	3–1
30.3.1946	R3	Southend United	(h)	3–2
19.4.1946	SF	Clapton Orient	(a)	0–3

Football Combination results 1946–63

	1946–47 B	1947–48 B	1948–49 A	1949–50 B	1950–51 B	1951–52 B	1952–53 D2	1953–54 D2	1954–55 D1	1955–56	1956–57	1957–58	1958–59 D1	1959–60 D1	1960–61 D1	1961–62 Mid.	1962–63 Mid.
Aldershot	8-0 N30 / 1-2 S25	1-5 S24 / 1-1 D26		5-0 D17 / 4-1 a20	1-3 D30 / 4-2 a19		5-0 N29 / 1-1 D6	4-1 M6 / 0-3 O17		6-2 M30 / 0-2 N19	3-4 D15 / 2-2 a18	1-2 S4 / 1-0 O5				3-2 O24 / 1-1 F28	3-0 S29 / 2-0 A6
Arsenal		1-1 N8 / 1-2 a30				1-3 D25 / 0-1 D26			4-1 F5 / 1-5 D18	1-3 S5 / 0-6 S11	4-2 A16 / 3-0 J4	4-2 A25 / 2-2 O11	1-0 S12 / 0-4 J23	2-1 S3 / 2-2 D27		0-2 a19 / 0-1 F7	0-0 D8 / 0-5 A27
Birmingham City			0-3 A30 / 1-2 S4					1-2 M3 / 2-2 A10	5-2 F9 / 0-3 J8		4-2 S22 / 1-2 F2	1-0 M15 / 2-1 N2	0-1 M14 / 1-2 N8	4-0 D5 / 3-0 O17	1-2 D24 / 0-3 M15		
Bournemouth & B.A.	2-4 O5 / 3-3 O9			0-1 O15 / 0-1 O8	1-0 N25 / 2-2 D23	2-1 S8 / 2-3 a29	2-0 O8 / 0-0 O15		2-2 A2 / 1-1 N13		1-1 a25 / 1-2 D22			1-0 D19 / 1-1 a22	3-1 O8 / 0-2 D10	1-0 O10 / 1-5 F14	2-0 S1 / 1-0 M2
Brentford	1-6 S18 / 0-4 J4	1-4 S13 / 1-3 N15	3-1 N13 / 3-1 O9	3-2 A22 / 0-1 O8	0-1 S23 / 2-2 D23		5-1 N22 / 1-3 a27	1-2 F13 / 2-3 F20		0-1 F18 / 0-3 O8	4-2 S29 / 4-2 F9	4-0 A23 / 1-0 D26				2-0 M27 / 2-7 m2	3-2 A30 / 0-2 D18
Bristol City	4-4 D28 / 1-1 N9	2-2 a23 / 0-5 N1		2-1 S24 / 1-1 a27	2-0 a26 / 1-0 O21	0-1 D29 / 0-1 S1	2-2 S13 / 2-1 D27	4-2 A3 / 1-1 N14	1-2 F19 / 1-2 J29		1-0 N24 / 0-3 A6	0-2 A12 / 0-2 N30	1-0 S6 / 3-1 J17	2-0 A2 / 2-0 N28	1-1 A26 / 2-0 O15		
Bristol Rovers	1-2 D21 / 1-6 O12	5-1 S27 / 0-1 S15				1-1 N17 / 1-1 O13	3-3 S27 / 2-2 N8	2-1 A28 / 2-2 F6		1-1 A26 / 1-4 A21		5-1 N1 / 5-5 M7					
Cardiff City									6-2 A30 / 0-1 M5	2-2 M17 / 1-2 N5		5-0 O12 / 1-0 F22	7-0 S20 / 2-1 F7		0-5 A29 / 0-2 O1		
Charlton Athletic		0-1 O11 / 1-3 A10		4-3 N12 / 1-2 O22	1-1 S30 / 1-5 F7	2-2 O6 / 0-4 N10			3-2 N6 / 0-1 F12	3-0 S10 / 3-0 J14	1-0 A26 / 2-0 D14	1-2 J1 / 3-1 a30	2-0 J9 / 1-2 S19	1-3 M18 / 2-3 N12	1-0 J9 / 1-4 F10	1-4 D22 / 1-0 m9	
Chelsea	1-2 A19 / 3-1 O19	2-3 N29 / 1-2 A7	0-0 A18 / 3-2 A15	0-0 S7 / 2-0 S3	1-3 J24 / 1-3 O7				0-3 D27 / 1-4 A12	1-1 O15 / 1-5 F25	1-3 D29 / 1-7 S1	0-4 O26 / 1-4 A14	2-2 D26 / 0-0 O31	2-4 M5 / 1-7 O29	1-4 M4	2-5 D26 / 1-5 J17	1-3 M9 / 1-1 O27
Coventry City	2-2 N23 / 1-4 A12	2-3 O25 / 0-2 O18						2-2 J2 / 2-1 D12	4-0 A16 / 3-2 J15			4-0 M1 / 1-1 O19				1-2 N28 / 0-4 A11	2-0 D4 / 2-1 A17
Crystal Palace							2-2 J10 / 1-2 S6	3-1 M20 / 1-2 O31		2-4 D31 / 1-0 S3	1-1 O27 / 2-3 M9	4-0 M29 / 2-4 N16					
Fulham	2-0 S7 / 1-2 m28									2-4 S7 / 3-2 a31	2-0 M16 / 1-1 N3	1-0 a24 / 3-3 D21	1-0 A11 / 1-1 A18			3-2 M20 / 1-1 A21	2-1 J15 / 0-1 a22
Ipswich Town			2-1 S25 / 0-1 A23	3-1 O29 / 1-1 A30	3-1 O14 / 0-2 D2	5-4 S5 / 1-0 J19	2-2 J17 / 1-0 S20				3-1 D27 / 2-2 D6	1-1 S7 / 0-2 O2	1-3 O18 / 1-2 F20	0-0 O3 / 2-1 S17	2-2 a31		
Leicester City	3-3 D26 / 1-1 D25	0-1 N22 / 0-4 S20					3-4 N1 / 2-6 O11		1-6 J22 / 3-4 A25	5-1 O1 / 1-2 F11	3-0 J19 / 0-6 S15		0-1 N29 / 0-0 A4	3-2 S23 / 1-2 M26	3-1 A1 / 3-2 N26		
Leyton Orient			1-0 a28 / 1-4 O7				2-2 a30 / 2-3 J3	4-0 m1 / 0-3 J23	1-2 M31 / 0-0 A19		1-3 N23 / 1-0 m1	6-2 M28 / 4-3 A18	2-3 S14 / 2-5 A15	2-3 S14 / 1-1 S13		2-1 D26 / 0-3 N28	
Luton Town			3-1 S22 / 0-5 S18			4-4 S19 / 3-2 S15		3-6 O1 / 4-4 S3	3-1 J1 / 1-1 A18	2-2 a27 / 2-1 D24			1-1 N15 / 2-4 M21	2-2 a26 / 2-1 A30		1-1 N11 / 0-4 M14	2-1 O23 / 1-1 m20
Millwall									5-3 m5 / 2-0 N8	6-0 O29 / 4-1 M10		0-0 D28 / 1-4 a31					
Northampton Town			1-0 a25 / 0-0 S9					1-3 A19 / 3-0 J16			6-3 S8 / 3-2 J12	– / 1-0 F15					
Norwich City			1-1 D25 / 0-1 D27	2-1 A10 / 0-5 S17	0-3 S20 / 1-3 a30	2-0 a25 / 1-2 D22			3-4 A8 / 1-0 O16	1-1 N26 / 0-0 A7	1-0 N10 / 2-2 M23	1-2 S18 / –		5-2 N19 / 3-4 M25			
Nottingham Forest													1-2 O4 / 1-2 F21	5-1 a29 / 0-0 J2	0-1 D31 / 1-5 a27		
Plymouth Argyle				2-0 D18 / 1-3 a21	1-2 D10 / 3-4 N19	1-3 O28 / 1-7 J13	0-1 O20 / 0-4 N24					2-2 F1 / 0-1 S21					
Portsmouth	2-1 S21 / 0-3 S4	0-2 m1 / 1-1 O8		4-2 N26 / 1-2 N5	2-1 S27 / 3-5 D16	3-4 a22 / 0-7 S26			3-0 M19 / 0-5 D11	1-1 N12 / 0-3 M24	3-0 D24 / 3-2 D26	2-1 N9 / 1-0 M22	4-0 J31 / 1-2 S13	1-3 J16 / 3-3 S5	3-3 A19 / 2-0 F25	1-1 S7 / 1-5 A14	3-1 A15 / 3-0 m11
Queen's Park Rangers	1-4 S11 / 0-5 N2		0-1 A16 / 2-4 D11				0-1 S10 / 3-1 S15	3-1 O24 / 0-1 M13			1-1 D17 / 1-0 a20	1-0 M2 / 3-0 O20	3-0 A4 / 4-1 A7			0-0 M6 / 3-2 A16	5-1 A3 / 0-4 O8
Reading			2-0 O2 / 1-3 D4						4-0 M3 / 0-6 O22							1-1 a29 / 1-4 D13	4-1 M25 / 4-0 S26
Southampton	1-1 O26 / 4-3 A26	0-5 S10 / 2-6 O1		1-2 D24 / 2-2 O5	0-1 S6 / 1-6 S16	1-1 S22 / 2-5 S29		1-2 A17 / 1-0 J21		3-2 S17 / 1-0 J21	1-3 A13 / 3-3 D1		2-2 O24 / 1-0 F27	1-1 A3 / 0-4 S21		2-2 A3 / 0-5 m8	1-5 N6
Southend United							6-0 D25 / 2-7 O4	2-1 M8 / 3-2 J9		7-6 J28 / 0-1 J7	4-0 m1 / 0-3 F23	– / 6-1 J11	0-0 M19 / 5-1 N23			1-2 S26 / 1-2 M28	5-4 F9 / 0-3 S15
Swansea Town				5-3 D7 / 1-4 S28	3-0 A3 / 2-8 S6	2-1 S15 / 2-6 N6	3-2 D13 / 5-5 S25	2-1 D5 / 2-2 A24					2-0 S28 / 2-0 F8	1-1 F28 / 2-3 O25	0-0 F13 / 2-2 S26		
Swindon Town				3-4 S11 / 2-2 N27	0-1 D27 / 2-3 D26	1-1 S9 / 0-5 S13	6-3 N3 / 1-1 D8	8-0 D20 / 1-3 a23	4-1 N7 / 0-2 M27			1-0 J26 / 1-2 J5	1-2 J18 / 0-1 S14			3-0 A17 / 2-4 D5	1-0 M23 / 0-1 N10
Tottenham Hotspur		2-3 D25 / 0-13 a25		2-2 O1 / 3-2 S19	1-1 J20 / 1-3 N11	0-3 D1 / 0-4 O27			3-1 F2 / 2-2 F26	3-2 M30 / 2-5 N17	2-3 D7		0-2 a23 / 0-2 D20	2-0 O10 / 2-2 D12	3-1 a20 / 2-5 S10		
Watford	1-1 m10 / 2-1 a31	1-2 S3 / 1-3 A17		1-1 O30 / 4-2 O23	3-0 S10 / 3-2 D3	1-1 D12 / 4-5 N18	1-0 O18 / 1-3 a18	3-1 D25 / 1-2 N15		2-3 A14 / 1-4 D3	4-2 A19 / 1-2 A22					1-2 m1 / 0-1 F18	1-3 F20 / 1-3 O17
West Ham United	2-2 O2 / 2-2 S14		3-0 O16 / 0-1 m2	0-1 a24 / 2-1 S12	6-0 O4 / 1-3 D26	2-0 O3			1-1 D4 / 0-9 S24	0-2 A30 / 2-4 A20	2-2 D8		0-1 F14 / 2-0 S27	5-1 N7 / 2-6 M12	1-3 A12 / 0-3 M11		

Notes: Home matches are shown above away matches. Albion score given first. a – August, A – April; M – March, m – May.

Football Combination Cup results 1946–55

	1946–47	1947–48	1948–49	1949–50	1950–51	1951–52	1952–53	1953–54	1954–55
Arsenal			0-3 J3 / 0-1 M27	0-1 J21 / 1-2 F4	0-3 A7 / 0-3 M3	0-0 F2 / 0-3 M16	1-0 A6 / 1-5 A26	2-0 O10 / 1-7 a29	1-2 S15 / 1-3 S7
Brentford			5-1 M5 / 2-0 A9	2-1 M11 / 0-2 F18	1-1 A21 / 0-2 A18	3-2 M1 / 4-1 M22	0-3 A30 / 3-0 A11	5-1 S19 / 6-2 O1	2-1 O13 / 2-0 S25
Charlton Athletic	3-3 M8 / 2-1 m14								
Chelsea	3-1 A7 / 0-1 M5	2-0 M24 / 0-3 M6	1-1 A2 / 1-3 M12	0-0 F11 / 1-2 J14	1-0 F24 / 0-4 M31	2-4 O24 / 0-4 F23	2-1 A25 / 1-2 J21	1-1 O3 / 0-2 S7	2-1 S4 / 1-5 S11
Crystal Palace	3-0 A5 / 0-2 M29	1-1 F7 / 1-2 J31		4-0 F25 / 2-5 A1	0-0 J27 / 0-2 F10	4-1 M15 / 2-4 A19	5-0 F7 / 2-1 J31	1-0 O2 / 2-1 S23	3-0 S1 / 0-4 a25
Fulham	0-4 M12 / 2-4 m3	4-0 M20 / 1-2 M8	7-2 F12 / 2-3 J29						
Leyton Orient	2-0 M22 / 2-1 M15	7-1 F21 / 1-1 M13	1-3 F5 / 1-2 F19						
Millwall	3-0 F15 / 0-4 m24	2-6 J10 / 1-3 M15							
Queen's Park Rangers		1-2 M29 / 1-3 M18	2-0 J15 / 1-4 J22	3-2 D31 / 2-3 M2	0-0 M24 / 1-1 M17	1-2 A12 / 2-3 A23	6-0 M14 / 1-3 A3	1-1 O7 / 0-3 a24	3-0 a21 / 1-0 a28
Reading				5-1 J8 / 1-3 M26					
Southend United				1-2 M25 / 5-0 M4	5-2 M10 / 1-2 A14	2-1 F9 / 1-2 J26	0-0 F21 / 0-2 F16	1-3 a22 / 1-2 S5	2-1 O9 / 2-1 O6
Tottenham Hotspur			1-3 M19 / 0-1 F26	0-2 J28 / 2-4 M20	0-2 M26 / 1-1 M23	0-2 m3 / 0-2 F16	0-1 F28 / 1-1 M7	0-2 S16 / 1-2 S5	1-2 S29 / 0-2 S22
West Ham United	1-4 J18 / 1-1 J25								

Notes: Home matches are shown above away matches. Albion score given first.
a – August, A – April; M – March, m – May.

Football Combination results 1963–93

Team	1963–64 D2	1964–65 D2	1965–66 D2	1966–67 D2	1967–68 D2	1982–83	1983–84	1984–85	1985–86	1986–87	1987–88	1988–89	1989–90	1990–91	1991–92	1992–93 D1
Aldershot	2–0 M10 / 0–0 A29	3–0 F20 / 1–0 O24	1–3 J8 / 5–1 O30													
Arsenal						3–1 S21 / 0–3 J22	0–0 S27 / 0–2 J28	4–0 O16 / 0–5 M9	0–3 S14 / 0–3 J18	0–1 F3 / 0–7 J3	1–1 M26 / 0–4 N14	1–3 F1 / 2–2 a27	0–3 F14 / 1–3 M20	1–3 D5 / 1–1 a25	3–4 D18 / 2–2 N16	0–3 A20 / 0–5 S1
Birmingham City	1–4 O5 / 0–3 F15	1–1 J23 / 0–5 S19	3–1 A23 / 3–2 N27	2–4 N12 / 1–1 O8					5–0 J17 / 1–3 a28	3–1 J10 / 0–5 N10	3–1 M19 / 3–0 A11	1–2 A7 / 0–1 S28				
Bournemouth & B.A.	1–3 S28 / 0–0 J25	3–0 A22 / 1–2 N4	3–3 D18 / 0–3 O16	2–4 N11 / 1–2 F4	5–0 M6 / 2–1 F17	2–3 m4 / 1–1 M30										
Brentford	0–1 F11 / 0–1 M3	0–2 D12 / 1–1 a25	3–1 m10 / 1–4 A16	4–0 D10 / 1–3 M7												
Bristol City			5–2 a21 / 2–0 J29	1–1 J28 / 3–0 D31	2–1 a19 / 3–2 S19	2–1 S13 / 3–0 D16										1–1 S24 / 0–0 M24
Bristol Rovers		3–1 A3 / 1–1 O10	1–0 A9 / 2–3 N11	4–2 O29 / 2–2 D3	1–1 O7 / 0–1 N11	0–2 A6 / 0–1 F24			2–2 J11 / 1–1 A12	0–2 a30 / 4–1 F15	3–2 M25 / 1–4 D6	0–1 J25 / 0–5 S7	5–0 S10 / 2–3 J27	4–3 A20 / 1–7 D8		
Cardiff City				2–1 M29 / 0–0 F15	2–2 F10 / 1–1 S6	4–1 A2 / 0–1 S30										
Charlton Athletic	3–1 J11 / 1–1 S10	3–1 O31 / 0–0 F27	1–3 N6 / 0–3 J15			0–0 N16 / 1–3 M29	6–2 F7 / 1–2 S20	3–0 D1 / 0–1 A27	0–1 F1 / 0–4 D18	4–0 D2 / 2–2 A16	1–0 N6 / 1–2 M29	2–1 a31 / 1–0 F14	4–2 O11 / 3–1 M6	1–1 S5 / 1–3 A30	4–0 F25 / 1–2 M13	2–1 a27 / 0–1 M31
Chelsea	1–6 M7 / 0–2 N9					0–0 m12 / 3–0 O12	2–0 F23 / 2–3 S29	1–4 D11 / 1–1 m7	1–1 A5 / 0–1 N2	0–3 A22 / 0–2 N29	2–3 F24 / 0–4 S29	1–2 S5 / 1–1 F7	0–1 S6 / 2–3 N23	1–0 N19 / 1–6 S18	1–4 O16 / 0–0 A13	3–2 S9 / 0–3 M8
Colchester United				3–0 M19 / 2–1 S25												
Coventry City	1–5 F1 / 0–8 S25	3–3 J30 / 0–3 M9														
Crystal Palace						4–2 O21 / 1–2 N25	1–3 A20 / 1–2 A15	3–3 N2 / 1–2 M15	3–1 m3 / 0–0 A13	0–0 S18 / 3–0 O17	2–2 A22 / 0–0 A13	0–2 S25 / 4–2 a30	2–0 S12 / 0–3 O22	1–3 M6 / 2–2 S16	1–4 N27 / 2–2 S16	1–3 N11 /
Fulham	0–6 a31 / 2–2 F8					1–2 O19 / 0–2 M1	2–1 J31 / 1–1 D6	1–2 A13 / 0–5 D13	2–1 N20 / 2–1 m6	0–2 M4 / 1–3 A9	4–3 D2 / 2–1 A26	2–0 S28 / 0–1 M1	2–1 N15 / 0–3 S27	5–2 m1 / 0–1 A3	2–0 a28 / 0–1 N6	1–0 A30 / 3–1 N18
Gillingham			0–1 S18 / 5–2 M12													
Ipswich Town						1–0 m2 / 2–2 S25	1–0 A3 / 0–1 S3	2–3 A30 / 2–5 D18	0–1 a31 / 0–5 J11	4–1 N12 / 4–3 M24	0–1 N18 / 1–0 A5	0–2 M8 / 5–3 O6	4–1 N8 / 0–0 J10	0–3 S29 / 1–2 M25	1–3 D11 / 0–1 A25	1–3 O21 / 1–4 S30
Leicester City						1–0 N23 / 1–1 J26	1–0 M21 / 1–4 D19									
Leyton Orient	3–0 S14 / 1–1 J18	3–3 O17 / 0–0 D5	3–2 N20 / 1–1 M30													
Luton Town		2–4 N28 / 2–2 M27	4–0 J22 / 2–1 M5			1–1 F5 / 0–1 S13	0–0 M6 / 0–4 N5	0–5 J23 / 4–0 S11	0–2 O9 / 0–0 F13	0–2 M14 / 1–3 S6	1–1 D16 / 2–1 m5	2–2 J4 / 0–3 O11	2–1 N29 / 1–5 J27	2–1 O10 / 0–1 A11	1–0 A22 / 1–2 D2	1–1 O7 / 2–1 O26
Mansfield Town			4–0 A11 / 1–1 m7	5–0 A29 / 2–2 M18												
Millwall	1–1 N30 / 0–2 M28	3–1 J2 / 2–0 S5	3–2 S4 / 4–1 F19			3–1 A26 / 1–1 J5	3–0 N2 / 2–4 O19	1–0 a25 / 2–4 N13	0–1 A19 / 0–3 N5	4–0 A1 / 1–1 S15	1–1 F3 / 2–2 M21	0–3 O19 / 1–0 A10	1–0 J3 / 1–0 F4	1–1 M23 / 1–0 O31	4–1 D23 / 0–1 M11	1–3 m4 / 2–4 A26
Norwich City				1–0 O15 / 3–0 N19	2–5 D2 / 2–1 O28	0–1 M23 / 0–3 A27	2–2 A19 / 1–2 S29	4–1 m8 / 0–0 O22	6–1 S4 / 0–2 F28	2–0 N23 / 0–6 A12	1–4 F26 / 1–2 O1	1–1 M1 / 1–4 S4	2–2 D14 / 0–4 m2	1–0 O31 / 1–5 A26	0–1 M11 / 1–3 O11	1–1 D23 / 2–1 A23
Notts County		4–1 N14 / 1–1 M13	5–0 m17 / 3–3 a28	0–1 F11 / 2–2 A5												
Oxford United		3–0 A5 / 4–5 M24	1–0 O23 / 0–3 J1	3–1 N26 / 1–0 O22	4–1 M2 / 3–2 A29	1–3 m16 / 1–0 N10	2–0 N29 / 2–1 M17	2–1 O9 / 1–1 M14	5–3 N6 / 0–1 A2	0–8 a27 / 0–1 F21	8–0 A13 / 1–2 N25	0–0 M29 / 3–4 O26	1–1 J17 / 1–3 J31	0–1 J23 / 2–0 D17	1–2 O21 / 1–2 N20	4–2 N4 / 0–2 J6
Portsmouth	1–3 A4 / 1–0 O16								0–0 O2 / 2–2 A17*	0–0 J7 / 0–0 M12	0–3 a19 / 1–2 a23	1–0 N1 / 2–2 A18	2–1 M15 / 3–0 M15	1–2 O17 / 4–2 F26	1–3 J8 / 0–6 a31	2–1 D9 / 0–2 J26
Queen's Park Rangers	4–3 O19 / 2–3 D9	2–4 a29 / 0–2 D19	1–4 D28 / 1–2 a30			1–1 O4* / 0–2 M17	1–2 O25 / 2–1 F28	0–1 J29 / 2–2 M17	1–1 M27 / 2–2 J20	2–3 F12 / 0–5 O1	1–2 S23 / 3–3 S16	0–1 A19 / 2–1 A2	5–0 F21 / 3–7 O17	2–1 N14 / 1–1 A22	1–1 M4 / 1–5 O1	1–2 M13 / 0–1 F23
Reading	0–4 D14 / 4–3 a24	4–0 S12 / 1–3 A12	0–2 A26 / 0–1 O13		1–2 S9 / 0–3 J17	2–0 m6 / 0–2 F21	1–1 A15 / 4–1 A9	4–1 N24 / 1–6 m13	5–2 A1 / 4–0 S9	3–0 D14 / 0–2 O11	0–0 M18 / 3–2 S26	2–1 O21 / 0–2 O11	0–0 N30 / 3–2 M16	1–0 m4 / 3–1 S11	0–0 F23 / 1–0 N17	5–0 a14 / 2–3 M7
Southampton	3–3 A18 / 1–3 A15	2–0 F13 / 1–3 O3				1–3 F22 / 0–5 O9	1–2 m1 / 0–0 F25	4–2 F26 / 2–4 N10	1–1 O26 / 2–7 M4	1–2 O29 / 3–4 A11	0–0 M23 / 0–5 O31	0–0 D3 / 1–0 N18	0–2 m10 / 1–7 M9	5–0 S24 /	1–0 M25 / 1–0 O14	1–3 M22 / 1–0 O14
Southend United	4–2 N2 / 3–4 F29	1–2 S26 / 3–3 F6	2–1 O9 / 7–1 D11													
Swansea City*					1–1 F25 / 5–2 N5	3–1 S23 / 0–8 F1	0–2 M9 / 0–4 F8	0–0 m23 / 1–3 D11	4–0 A14 / 1–6 S13	2–2 M7 / 0–0 O27	5–1 O12 / 5–2 M15					
Swindon Town	5–1 F22 / 3–7 O26	0–1 A28 / 0–3 N21				2–0 A30 / 2–3 N30	7–1 A17 / 1–1 N22	5–1 A9 / 1–2 m9	1–4 m3 / 2–0 N30	1–6 O15 / 1–4 M11	0–3 S9 / 1–3 J26	2–2 J18 / 0–5 D20	0–2 J24 / 0–2 D6	3–2 A17 / 0–2 N7	1–2 N13 / 0–0 A27	2–2 M17 / 0–2 a19
Tottenham Hotspur						1–1 D18 / 1–1 m7	2–1 N15 / 0–3 A9	2–0 O30 / 1–1 M4	1–1 D11 / 1–1 M4	5–1 S13 / 0–9 A26	3–2 M21 / 1–3 a29	1–4 N9 / 1–7 A8	2–3 m2 / 0–1 O28	2–3 N28 / 0–1 M16	1–1 F19 / 0–4 a17	1–1 F3* / 0–6 D16
Walsall				1–2 M24 / 0–5 J14												
Watford	2–2 M21 / 2–3 N23	4–0 A17 / 2–1 A20	3–0 O2 / 4–1 M26			0–3 D4 / 1–1 A23	1–2 O13 / 0–4 m16	2–1 N27 / 2–2 M30	0–0 M29 / 0–1 a17	3–1 D17 / 1–1 M12	2–1 O26 / 0–2 A29	1–1 J11 / 0–6 F4	0–1 A25 / 0–6 M17	5–0 D20 / 2–1 S11	0–2 A1 / 1–0 J13	0–2 A8 / 0–2 S15
West Ham United						0–2 M8 / 1–2 M28	1–2 S8 / 2–2 A7	0–3 N13 / 0–0 A23	1–0 A17 / 1–6 S3	1–2 m6 / 1–3 D13	0–2 M5 / 2–1 F27	0–0 D7 / 1–1 F28	0–0 O4 / 1–1 a17	1–1 M27 / 2–0 S11	2–0 S11 / 1–1 A7	1–3 F27 / 0–2 D1
Wimbledon												3–1 F22 / 4–1 S20	1–0 F10 / 0–3 a22	1–3 M12 / 1–3 A13	0–2 D7 / 1–1 S25	3–3 A17 / 0–4 J20

Notes: Home matches are shown above away matches. Albion score given first. a – August, A – April; M – March, m – May.

1982–83 v. Queen's Park Rangers (home) – the match was played at Loftus Road.

1984–85 v. Portsmouth (away) – the match was played at the Goldstone Ground.

1992–93 v. Tottenham Hotspur (home) – played at Nyewood Lane, Bognor Regis Town FC.

Swansea City were known as Swansea Town until 1970.

The Football Combination was sponsored in 1987–88 as the Sunday Mirror Football Combination; in 1988–91 as the Ovenden Papers Football Combination; and in 1991–93 as the Neville Ovenden Football Combination.

Football Combination Cup results 1966–68

Team	1966–67	1967–68
Bournemouth & B.A.	0–0 S10 / 1–2 S17	
Brentford	3–2 S14 / 0–3 a23	
Bristol City	2–0 a27 / 0–2 a20	
Bristol Rovers	1–0 S24 / 0–3 O1	
Cardiff City		1–2 S27*

Notes: Home matches are shown above away matches. Albion score given first. a – August, A – April.

The 1967–68 tournament was played on a knock-out basis. Albion's match was in Round 1.

Football Combination Cup summary

Season		P	W	D	L	F	A	Pts	Position/No. of clubs
1946–47	Qualifying group	14	6	2	6	22	26	14	4/8
1947–48	Qualifying group	14	3	2	9	24	28	8	8/8
1948–49	Qualifying group	14	5	1	8	30	27	11	6/8
1949–50	Qualifying group	14	3	1	10	18	31	7	8/8
1950–51	Qualifying group	14	2	5	7	10	23	9	8/8
1951–52	Qualifying group	14	4	1	9	22	33	9	5/8
1952–53	Qualifying group	14	7	2	5	25	15	16	3/8
1953–54	Qualifying group	14	5	2	7	22	27	12	6/8
1954–55	Qualifying group	14	8	0	6	21	16	16	4/8
1966–67	Qualifying group	8	3	1	4	7	12	7	4/5

Albion failed to qualify for the next stage in every season

Midweek League results

	1949–50	1969–70	1970–71	1971–72	1972–73	1973–74	1974–75	1975–76	1976–77	1977–78	1978–79	1979–80	1980–81	1981–82
Aldershot		0–0 N19 / 1–2 D3	2–0 S2 / 2–2 N18	1–1 F16 / 2–2 N10								3–2 O3 / 3–1 D11	1–1 O29 / 3–0 a26	3–1 N24 / 1–0 N10
Arsenal	1–0 F8 / 2–1 J18													
AFC Bournemouth														3–0 N17 / 1–1 F4
Brentford	2–3 N2 / 0–3 J4						5–0 A14 / 2–0 M25	2–3 F10 / 1–2 a26	0–2 A26 / 2–3 J4	3–1 N1 / 3–2 M13	1–0 F20 / 3–0 m1	3–3 M20 / 2–1 N15	2–1 J20 / 4–1 N4	2–0 A13 / 0–2 m12
Cambridge United				2–0 M1 / 0–2 D15	0–0 A4 / 1–0 N15	2–0 A29 / 0–2 S12	0–1 A1 / 1–3 a26	0–1 S16 / 2–2 S8	1–2 F15 / 4–0 D15	1–0 A18 / 2–1 F28	2–2 O31 / 3–3 a23	4–3 A28 / 3–0 a30	6–0 N27 / 1–0 D31	0–1 S15 / 0–1 S8
Charlton Athletic	3–0 J11 / 0–0 N16	4–1 A24 / 1–1 F24	1–1 D23 / 2–4 O20	1–2 F2 / 1–7 S14	1–2 O25 / 1–1 J16	1–1 F13 / 1–1 O23	3–0 F12 / 4–2 N5	4–2 A5 / 0–4 S30	5–3 S9 / 1–2 M21	5–2 O11 / 1–4 F21	0–3 F6 / 2–0 F27	3–3 A12 / 1–4 J15	2–2 D9 / 3–0 A7	0–1 M22 / 0–4 O31
Colchester United		1–2 J21 / 4–2 S17	1–2 m10 / 2–2 m13	3–0 M8 / 2–1 S29	2–2 J3 / 3–1 O4	5–1 M5 / 2–1 J29	2–2 M12 / 1–2 S10	4–1 J20 / 0–2 M29						
Crystal Palace	1–6 F1 / 0–2 N30													
Exeter City														2–0 S21 / 0–2 J26
Fulham	3–0 A12 / 4–1 A26													
Gillingham					1–1 S27 / 1–1 O17	6–1 N7 / 2–1 S19	2–1 F24 / 0–3 O30	1–1 S23 / 1–2 J12	4–0 F28 / 2–1 a25	2–2 F27 / 2–1 A5	2–0 M12 / 1–1 A5	1–3 D18 / 1–2 S19	6–1 M24 / 1–1 F11	2–1 F10 / 1–0 O14
Leyton Orient*	1–3 N23 / 0–1 D15	3–0 N12 / 2–0 a20	2–0 S16 / 0–2 N4	1–4 D29 / 0–3 D1	3–0 D13 / 1–2 A11	1–1 N21 / 2–2 F20	1–1 A10 / 1–2 D11	1–2 D11 / 2–1 J28						
Luton Town	3–0 m3 / 1–6 D21		2–3 O7 / 0–5 N10	1–0 O6 / 1–5 O26	0–1 a30 / 0–5 J10	1–3 M13 / 3–1 S24	4–4 N27 / 1–4 A28	3–1 O21 / 1–1 O6						
Millwall	1–0 A5 / 0–0 A20	2–1 O22 / 2–3 O15	1–1 J13 / 1–0 D9	2–1 N3 / 2–1 N24	3–3 N8 / 3–2 N1	0–0 D18 / 2–3 N28	5–3 O9 / 3–1 O2	2–0 O28 / 2–2 M2	2–0 A25 / 1–1 F23	5–2 M2 / 1–2 A12	2–1 M20 / 1–1 J17	3–0 m6 / 0–2 J29	4–4 S2 / 2–0 O1	1–1 D1 / 1–2 S1
Northampton Town				0–3 a25 / 0–8 a31	1–3 S13 / 2–6 A24	0–2 O3 / 2–3 O11	1–3 m2 / 1–0 J15	8–1 J6 / 5–4 N5	2–2 S21 / 1–0 N3	0–1 N15 / 1–1 S7	1–0 M6 / 2–0 S5	1–1 O18 / 4–0 J22	3–1 O15 / 1–0 O7	2–1 M18 / 3–2 M10
Peterborough United			3–1 O28 / 1–0 a24	2–2 S22 / 1–7 O11		5–0 S5 / 1–2 J16	2–2 M19 / 2–1 M5	0–2 O14 / 0–6 F17	2–2 J18 / 2–0 F9	2–8 S13 / 0–2 a24	4–0 S11 / 1–2 m3	2–2 J3 / 0–3 N28	1–0 F3 / 0–0 A3	0–5 O26
Portsmouth	3–0 F15 / 0–2 M16					1–0 D5 / 1–1 M11	1–2 J8 / 1–9 a21	2–0 D10 / 2–1 N26	1–0 A19 / 0–2 O27	1–0 M6 / 4–1 O19	4–1 N14 / 3–0 D27	3–2 N20 / 1–1 O10	3–0 A14 / 0–2 S18	1–3 A29 / 2–2 A24
Queen's Park Rangers	1–4 O12 / 1–8 S28													
Reading	5–1 D7 / 0–0 J25													
Southend United	3–3 O13 / 1–3 N26	6–1 D22 / 0–0 O1	4–0 a19 / 2–3 O14	2–0 N17 / 2–1 D8	1–3 m2 / 1–1 N29	0–1 A10 / 0–2 m2	1–2 O23 / 2–1 S18	0–0 A13 / 2–2 M24	2–1 M8 / 2–1 D8	3–1 A6 / 4–1 S21	0–1 D5 / 0–3 N28	0–4 D4 / 1–2 S11	2–3 a19 / 0–2 S9	1–2 J19 / 1–1 M24
Watford	6–5 M22 / 2–0 F22	1–2 S10 / 0–1 N5	1–1 S30 / 0–6 D2	0–5 A26 / 1–1 M27	3–0 O11 / 2–0 F21	0–1 J23 / 2–2 A3	1–1 A24 / 1–0 D18	0–0 S2 / 2–2 M31	1–2 D2 / 1–2 S15	3–0 M14 / 0–1 M20	5–4 S19 / 1–0 S27	1–3 S25 / 1–6 F27	1–3 F26 / 0–0 A24	
Wimbledon										1–1 A14 / 1–0 A20	2–3 A3 / 2–1 D19	0–2 S5 / 3–1 A10	5–0 J8 / 2–1 A9	0–2 A15 / 2–0 J5

Notes: Home matches are shown above away matches. Albion score given first. a – August, A – April; M – March, m – May.

The 1949–50 London Midweek League was contested by Albion's senior 'A' team. All other seasons were contested by the reserve team.

Leyton Orient were known as Orient from 1966 until 1987.

London Midweek League Cup 1969–71

1969–70

The competition was played on a league basis

Date		Opponents		Score
29.10.1969	league	Southend United	(h)	3–2
10.12.1969	league	Orient	(a)	3–1
31.12.1969	league	Aldershot	(a)	0–0
14.1.1970	league	Millwall	(a)	3–2
28.1.1970	league	Aldershot	(h)	2–0
11.2.1970	league	Orient	(h)	2–0
17.3.1970	league	Charlton Athletic	(a)	1–1
1.4.1970	league	Charlton Athletic	(h)	3–1
13.4.1970	league	Watford	(a)	2–0
16.4.1970	league	Southend United	(a)	2–0
20.4.1970	league	Colchester United	(h)	3–0
22.4.1970	league	Watford	(h)	1–0
27.4.1970	league	Millwall	(h)	1–3
29.4.1970	league	Colchester United	(a)	0–4

P	W	D	L	F	A	Pts	Pos.	No. of clubs
14	10	2	2	26	14	22	1	8

1970–71

The competition was played on a league basis

Date		Opponents		Score
8.9.1970	league	Charlton Athletic	(a)	0–3
20.1.1971	league	Aldershot	(h)	4–2
3.2.1971	league	Peterborough United	(h)	0–3
10.2.1971	league	Colchester United	(a)	3–2
17.2.1971	league	Charlton Athletic	(h)	2–1
24.2.1971	league	Millwall	(a)	0–4
3.3.1971	league	Orient	(a)	1–0
8.3.1971	league	Peterborough United	(a)	1–4
17.3.1971	league	Orient	(h)	1–3
24.3.1971	league	Watford	(a)	1–1
5.4.1971	league	Aldershot	(a)	1–1
7.4.1971	league	Southend United	(a)	0–0
14.4.1971	league	Luton Town	(h)	1–1
19.4.1971	league	Southend United	(h)	1–1
21.4.1971	league	Colchester United	(h)	4–0
26.4.1971	league	Millwall	(h)	4–1
29.4.1971	league	Luton Town	(a)	1–1
5.5.1971	league	Watford	(h)	2–1

P	W	D	L	F	A	Pts	Pos.	No. of clubs
18	7	6	5	27	29	20	4	10

Midweek League Cup 1971–82

Date		Opponents		Score
1971–72				
23.2.1972	Group	Aldershot	(a)	1–0
21.3.1972	Group	Charlton Athletic	(h)	1–4
12.4.1972	Group	Aldershot	(h)	1–1
18.4.1972	Group	Charlton Athletic	(a)	0–1
Albion did not qualify for the next stage				
1972–73				
7.3.1973	R1 Lg1	Gillingham	(a)	0–2
14.3.1973	R1 Lg2	Gillingham	(h)	0–3
1973–74				
20.3.1974	Group	Portsmouth	(a)	2–3
27.3.1974	Group	Millwall	(h)	2–2
17.4.1974	Group	Millwall	(a)	1–0
22.4.1974	Group	Portsmouth	(h)	0–2
Albion did not qualify for the next stage				
1974–75				
4.12.1974	R1	Northampton Town	(a)	1–0
26.2.1975	R2	Cambridge United	(h)	2–1
8.4.1975	SF	Charlton Athletic	(a)	3–0
21.4.1975	F Lg1	Luton Town	(a)	0–2
30.4.1975	F Lg2	Luton Town	(h)	3–0 aet
1975–76				
11.11.1975	R1	Southend United	(h)	2–1
2.2.1976	R2	Northampton Town	(a)	1–0
22.3.1976	SF	Watford	(h)	1–2
1976–77				
12.10.1976	Group	Charlton Athletic	(h)	3–0
1.2.1977	Group	Charlton Athletic	(a)	1–3
2.3.1977	Group	Portsmouth	(a)	3–0
13.4.1977	Group	Portsmouth	(h)	0–1
Albion did not qualify for the next stage				
1977–78				
25.10.1977	Group	Millwall	(h)	3–1
9.11.1977	Group	Gillingham	(h)	3–1
14.12.1977	Group	Millwall	(a)	4–1
21.12.1977	Group	Gillingham	(a)	4–3
16.2.1978	SF	Charlton Athletic	(h)	3–0
10.4.1978	F Lg1	Peterborough United	(h)	4–0
26.4.1978	F Lg2	Peterborough United	(a)	1–0
1978–79				
3.10.1978	Group	Gillingham	(h)	0–1
17.10.1978	Group	Northampton Town	(h)	7–1
24.10.1978	Group	Northampton Town	(a)	1–0
22.11.1978	Group	Gillingham	(a)	2–0
29.1.1979	SF	Southend United	(h)	6–3
19.4.1979	F Lg1	Peterborough United	(h)	1–1
23.4.1979	F Lg2	Peterborough United	(a)	0–1
1979–80				
8.1.1980	R1	Charlton Athletic	(h)	0–3
1980–81				
15.1.1981	R1	Millwall	(h)	1–0
5.2.1981	R2	Gillingham	(h)	0–1 aet
1981–82				
12.10.1981	R1	Wimbledon	(a)	0–2

The 'A' team, which was run by the club in the late 1940s, '50s and early '60s as a third eleven for promising young players, was a consequence of the wartime Albion junior side, a team which was formed in 1940 to promote the game amongst the youth of Sussex .

In 1948 the 'A' team was formed under the guidance of ex-England international Sam Cowan and played its first match, a friendly at Southwick, on 14 February. The next season also consisted of friendly matches only, but in 1949–50 the side was entered into the London Midweek League, then a combination of Football League clubs' 'A' sides (see above for results).

The following season, 1950–51, saw Albion contest the Metropolitan and District League, a competition they remained in until 1962. This League was a mixed bag comprising the third elevens of Football League clubs, Southern League clubs' reserve sides, and amateur clubs throughout south-eastern England. There was a League Cup and, from 1951–52, a cup for the professional sides only (there was also an amateur cup).

The team played most home games at either the Goldstone, the greyhound stadium or the Grenadier Ground in Rowan Avenue (also at Hailsham in 1949–50). It lasted until 1962 when it was disbanded largely because of the abolition of the maximum wage, which resulted in increased running-costs for all Football League clubs.

Biggest win — 8–0, Luton Town, Metropolitan League Professional Cup, 10.12.1955
Biggest defeat — 0–9, St Neots & District, Metropolitan League, 20.8.1960

'A' team league summary

Season	Competition	P	W	D	L	F	A	Pts	Position/ No. of clubs
1949–50	London Midweek League	26	11	4	11	44	52	26	8/14
1950–51	Metropolitan & District League	30	10	10	10	56	53	30	8/16
1951–52	Metropolitan & District League	26	8	3	15	54	70	19	12/14
1952–53	Metropolitan & District League	30	16	2	12	78	59	34	6/16
1953–54	Metropolitan & District League	34	14	5	15	58	65	33	10/18
1954–55	Metropolitan & District League	32	13	6	13	82	74	32	10/17
1955–56	Metropolitan & District League	32	8	5	19	48	71	21	15/17
1956–57	Metropolitan & District League	34	8	3	23	46	104	19	17/18
1957–58	Metropolitan & District League	34	7	2	25	39	81	16	18/18
1958–59	Metropolitan & District League	36	18	7	11	71	61	43	4/19
1959–60	Metropolitan & District League	38	14	6	18	67	86	34	13/20
1960–61	Metropolitan & District League	34	7	6	21	45	93	20	16/18
1961–62	Metropolitan & District League	32	11	5	16	58	73	27	12/17

Metropolitan & District League results	1950–51	1951–52	1952–53	1953–54	1954–55	1955–56	1956–57	1957–58	1958–59	1959–60	1960–61	1961–62
Arsenal ('A')									2–3 J17 / 1–0 J31	2–0 D26 / 1–5 O24	4–3 F11 / 1–3 J7	3–0 O21 / 3–4 S16
Bedford Town (res.)						4–1 m3 / 1–3 S10	0–1 N3 / 1–4 a25	0–2 A28 / 0–5 A7	4–1 N22 / 1–1 A23	0–1 S26 / 3–2 A20	1–2 N12 / 0–3 F18	2–0 J13 / 0–7 a19
Bexleyheath & Welling (res.)												1–2 N4 / 0–4 D9
Callenders Athletic	1–3 J27 / 2–2 S2	2–2 D1‡ / 1–0 M8‡	3–1 M21 / 3–0 N29									
Canterbury City										0–8 M26 / 0–4 F13		
Chelsea ('A')				1–3 D19 / 1–0 S19	4–4 D18 / 1–2 a25	0–4 a25 / 0–1 S14	0–3 O20 / 1–5 S29	1–3 F22† / 2–5 N2†	2–0 J10 / 1–5 S6	0–4 J23 / 0–3 M5		
Chingford Town	2–0 S9 / 3–0 J20											
Crawley Town							0–7 S22‡ / 0–2 A20‡	0–1 O12‡ / 0–4 A26‡	3–0 D26‡ / 1–2 m2‡	2–1 A23 / 4–2 N21	3–3 S3‡ / 1–2 A17‡	0–1 M13 / 0–4 D26
Croydon Rovers	0–1 O14‡ / 1–2 J13‡											
Dagenham	0–3 F10 / 3–3 M10											
Dartford (res.)				0–2 M13 / 1–0 O24	4–0 N13 / 2–2 S1	1–3 F25 / 2–0 O15	0–4 S15 / 1–3 A13	3–4 D21 / 1–2 S7	5–1 S13 / 2–1 M27	0–1 S19 / 2–1 D5	0–1 O29 / 3–1 D31	1–2 N18 / 0–3 J6
Dickinson (Apsley)	1–0 S23 / 7–0 F24											
Didcot Town								1–0 A21 / 3–3 N23	2–0 A18 / 5–3 M30	2–0 M12 / 2–3 S12	1–1 D17 / 0–2 A1	0–0 A14 / 3–3 a26
Dunstable Town	2–2 M3 / 3–1 S30	3–1 m3 / 2–3 F2	1–3 N15 / 1–2 J10	1–2 J9 / 2–1 N28	2–2 O30 / 1–4 A16	0–7 O22 / 3–4 F18	2–1 A10 / 4–3 D1	2–3 N30 / 3–2 M29	1–0 D6 / 3–3 N29	1–0 m7 / 1–1 O10	1–2 a27 / 3–4 D10	
Eastbourne United							2–2 m4 / 1–2 M2	0–1 J4 / 1–2 M15	0–3 D27 / 2–3 J3	2–2 O31 / 0–0 S9	1–6 N26 / 2–2 D27	1–0 M17 / 1–3 S20
Fulham ('A')								2–3 F15† / 1–0 D7†	2–2 F7† / 1–5 M21†	2–4 J30† / 3–3 O3†		
Gravesend & Northfleet (res.)				3–0 O31 / 1–1 M20	2–3 A30 / 6–1 J1	0–0 J14 / 5–3 D17						
Guildford City (res.)				1–1 a29 / 1–5 O10	0–3 M26 / 2–9 M5	7–1 D24 / 0–1 a27	1–7 S1 / 3–1 J12	1–3 a31 / 2–1 S25	1–2 O25 / 1–2 F28	1–4 a22 / 3–5 J16	4–1 S24 / 2–3 O22	1–2 J27 / 3–5 O28
Hastings United (res.)	4–2 D26 / 1–0 D23	0–1 S8‡ / 4–1 J5‡	4–1 J3 / 3–7 N1	1–1 D12 / 1–5 N14	4–4 a21 / 2–5 D4	0–3 S1 / 1–2 S21	0–6 F9 / 4–1 A19	2–1 S14 / 2–2 A11	0–2 a28 / 2–5 S16	4–0 S3 / 0–3 a24	1–4 S22	
Haywards Heath			0–1 J31 / 1–6 S3	2–3 S16‡ / 4–0 a27‡	5–5 M19‡ / 2–1 A11‡	2–3 A2‡ / 3–1 M3‡	3–0 A6 / 4–1 A19	0–2 a24 / 1–4 M1	1–1 S25 / 1–1 S3	4–0 O17 / 4–0 a26	1–1 S1 / 4–0 D24	
Horsham		0–5 a25‡ / 0–1 A24‡	4–1 A23‡ / 2–4 A16‡	4–2 A29‡ / 2–1 F13‡	2–1 A25‡ / 1–2 D27‡	2–3 A25‡ / 0–3 D26‡	3–2 D26‡ / 0–0 A16‡					
Hove United	3–3 M26 / 1–1 D25											
Leatherhead	2–2 D2‡ / 2–2 F17‡											
Luton Town ('A')	0–2 N11 / 2–3 O18	0–2 J26 / 1–5 O17	5–3 O11† / 4–1 S6†	2–3 S5 / 0–2 A19	6–0 J29† / 4–1 S11†	1–4 N19 / 0–3 J28	2–5 O6† / 1–3 O27†	0–5 S21 / 0–3 D28	1–3 S27 / 2–1 F14	2–2 A15 / 0–2 N7	1–0 A15 / 0–2 N19	
Metropolitan Police											1–1 F4 / 4–2 D3	2–0 F17 / 4–2 D16
Millwall ('A')		4–0 F23 / 3–3 O13										
Newbury Town			2–2 O4 / 1–1 F21	1–3 S26 / 3–2 J2	2–3 O2 / 0–1 F19	1–1 a20 / 0–1 M17	1–5 a18 / 0–2 N10	1–1 M22 / 2–3 D14	4–1 F21 / 2–1 N1	2–2 F27 / 1–2 A16	1–3 A22 / 1–5 M4	4–1 F3 / 0–1 F24
Oxford United (res.)*	3–1 D16 / 1–0 O28	8–2 A11 / 1–6 O20	1–4 D6 / 0–2 A11	1–4 F6 / 4–2 D26	0–2 A21 / 1–0 S18	0–2 N5 / 0–4 O1	2–2 J5 / 0–5 D8	1–2 S28 / 0–2 N9	3–1 D20 / 0–3 a23	0–1 N28 / 3–0 M19	0–5 O15 / 0–8 N5	2–1 M31 / 1–1 A20
Rainham Town												1–1 M3 / 1–0 N25
St Neots Town*	1–1 F3 / 0–4 O21										2–2 A8 / 0–9 a20	6–3 D2 / 2–3 S30
Skyways		1–3 M1‡ / 0–1 N10‡										
Southwick				0–2 a28 / 2–0 A29	3–0 S24 / 2–0 S2							
Tonbridge (res.)		0–3 F9 / 0–4 S29	2–0 J24 / 3–2 A20	2–2 S12 / 1–5 J30	2–3 S16 / 1–3 S8	1–2 A21 / 0–5 A7	0–2 M23 / 0–1 S8	1–5 S5 / 1–2 a28	2–0 A4 / 1–0 A6	3–0 F20 / 1–4 J2	1–0 O1 / 0–3 M11	3–5 S9 / 4–4 D30
Tottenham Hotspur ('A')			2–5 D22 / 2–6 O6	0–4 O25 / 4–0 D13	1–2 A24 / 0–4 F20							
Twickenham	2–1 a26 / 2–2 A7	2–2 O27‡ / 3–2 S15‡	8–1 M7 / 7–1 D20									
Vickers	0–1 D30‡ / 2–4 D9‡	6–2 J19 / 3–4 S22	2–0 a23 / 5–0 A25	0–0 a22 / 2–3 M27	1–1 M12 / 5–1 S4							
West Ham United ('A')			2–1 M28† / 5–1 S13†	2–1 M6 / 4–2 O3	3–5 S25† / 2–0 J8†	2–2 M24† / 1–0 A11†	0–8 F23 / 2–0 A27	2–0 O19† / 2–1 A12†	2–2 O11 / 4–2 J24	2–8 J9† / 2–1 D12†	0–3 S10† / 1–3 J21†	3–4 D23 / 0–5 F10
Windsor & Eton	1–3 O7‡ / 4–4 J6‡	4–2 A14‡ / 2–4 S1‡	2–3 F28 / 1–5 a30	2–1 S3 / 3–1 A16	6–3 a28 / 3–0 m5		1–2 N17 / 1–4 N24	1–2 F8 / 0–1 D26	4–3 a30 / 2–1 O18	5–0 A30 / 1–5 a29		
Wokingham Town						1–0 O16 / 5–3 F26	6–0 A28 / 1–1 N12	4–2 D22 / 4–5 M9				
Woodford Town												3–2 S23 / 3–0 N11

Notes: Home matches are shown above away matches. Albion score given first. a – August, A – April; M – March, m – May.

Matches marked † were both played at home, and matches marked ‡ were both played away; it is not known which was officially home and away.

1950–51 v. Chipperfield (away 2–2 S16) was deleted from the record when Chipperfield withdrew from the League in February.

1958–59 v. Portsmouth (home 1–1 S18) was deleted from the record when Portsmouth withdrew from the League in December.

1960–61 v. Didcot Town (away) – match originally played J28 but abandoned after 38 minutes because of snow with score 1–0.

Oxford United were known as Headington United until 1960; and St Neots Town were known as St Neots & District until 1961.

Metropolitan & District League Challenge Cup

Date		Opponents		Score	Date		Opponents		Score
1950–51					**1956–57**				
Albion did not enter the competition					29.2.1956	R2	Wokingham Town	(a)	3–0
					2.2.1956	R3	Dunstable Town	(a)	2–5
1951–52					**1957–58**				
8.12.1951	R1	Millwall ('A')	(a)	4–0	16.11.1957	R2	Hastings United (res.)	(a)	4–5
12.1.1952	R2	Skyways	(a)	0–8	**1958–59**				
1952–53					8.11.1958	R2	Fulham ('A')	(h)	2–1
18.10.1952	R1	Headington United (res.)	(a*)	1–2	7.3.1959	R3	Chelsea ('A')	(h)	3–1
Tie drawn at home but switched to Oxford					28.3.1959	SF	Bedford Town (res.)	(a)	2–1
1953–54					25.4.1959	F Lg1	Crawley Town	(a)	0–1
7.11.1953	R2	Gravesend & Northfleet (res.)	(a)	0–3	27.4.1959	F Lg2	Crawley Town	(h)	0–0
1954–55					**1959–60**				
20.11.1954	R2	Wokingham Town	(a*)	1–0	5.9.1959	R1	Fulham ('A')	(h)	2–6
12.2.1955	R3	Windsor & Eton	(a)	0–5	**1960–61**				
Second-round tie drawn at home but switched to Wokingham					8.10.1960	R1	Bedford Town (res.)	(a*)	2–3
1955–56					*Tie drawn at home but switched to Bedford*				
24.9.1955	R2	West Ham United ('A')	(h*)	0–0	**1961–62**				
3.12.1955	R2 rep	West Ham United ('A')	(h)	1–1 aet	12.9.1961	R2	Crawley Town	(h)	1–2
7.1.1956	R2 2rep	West Ham United ('A')	(h)	0–1					
Tie drawn away but switched to Hove									

Metropolitan & District League Professional Challenge Cup

Date		Opponents		Score	Date		Opponents		Score
1951–52					**1957–58**				
2.4.1952	R1	Hastings United (res.)	(a)	2–1	5.10.1957	R1 Lg1	Fulham ('A')	(h*)	0–1
21.4.1952	SF	Tonbridge (res.)	(a)	0–5	11.1.1958	R1 Lg2	Fulham ('A')	(h)	2–1
1952–53					?	R1 rep	Fulham ('A')	?	?–?
27.9.1952	R1	Hastings United (res.)	(a*)	4–5	8.3.1958	R2 Lg1	Dartford (res.)	(h)	2–2
Tie drawn at home but switched to Hastings					19.3.1958	R2 Lg2	Dartford (res.)	(a)	2–1 aet
1953–54					26.3.1958	SF Lg1	Hastings United (res.)	(a)	0–1
5.12.1953	R2	Tottenham Hotspur ('A')	(a)	1–4	4.4.1958	SF Lg2	Hastings United (res.)	(a)	0–5
1954–55					*First round first leg drawn away but switched to Hove*				
9.10.1954	R1	Guildford City (res.)	(a)	0–2	**1958–59**				
1955–56					4.10.1958	R1	Portsmouth ('A')	(a)	1–4
10.12.1955	R2	Luton Town ('A')	(h*)	8–0	**1959–60**				
10.3.1956	SF	Hastings United (res.)	(a)	0–3	14.11.1959	R2	West Ham United ('A')	(h*)	1–2
Second-round tie drawn away but switched to Hove					*Tie drawn away but switched to Hove*				
1956–57					**1960–61**				
13.10.1956	R1	Headington United (res.)	(a)	4–2	17.9.1960	R1	Hastings United (res.)	(h)	0–2
15.12.1956	R2	Dartford (res.)	(a)	0–4	**1961–62**				
Second-round tie drawn at home but switched to Dartford					7.10.1961	R2 Lg1	Dartford (res.)	(h)	2–3
					14.10.1961	R2 Lg1	Dartford (res.)	(a)	2–1
					7.11.1961	R2 rep	Dartford (res.)	(h)	0–2

Although a 'junior' side was organised during the Second World War, Albion's youth team strictly originated in 1948–49 as the junior 'A' team, a side for players under eighteen years of age. On 19 March the first friendly was played, a 2–1 win over a Medway Towns representative side, and the following term an under-18 eleven was entered in the Greater London Minor Combination. No more competitive football was played until 1952–53, the first year of the F.A.'s Youth Cup in which Albion reached the last sixteen. Only twice since that first tournament, in 1961–62 and 1992–93, have they matched that initial achievement.

After just one season, 1954–55, in the initial term of the South East Counties League, the Albion youth team re-entered league competition in 1959. A rapid climb through the divisions of the Worthing League – against adult opponents – was followed by re-entry into the South East Counties League. In 1969, however, the club left the premier youth league in the South to contest a number of local leagues throughout the 1970s. Having dominated several of these competitions, Albion were elected to the South East Counties League again in 1981. Note that, in 1962–63, 1971–73 and 1981–82, the club has run two youth sides (for different age groups) in separate league competitions.

Biggest win — 21–0, Eastbourne Town, Southern Youth League, 17.9.1978
Biggest defeat — 0–10, Southampton, South East Counties League Div. 2, 12.4.1986

Youth team league summary

Season	Competition	P	W	D	L	F	A	Pts	Position/ No. of clubs
1949–50	Greater London Minor Combination	10	4	2	4	21	20	10	?/6
1950–54	Did not compete								
1954–55	South East Counties League	20	6	2	12	29	64	14	10/11
1955–59	Did not compete								
1959–60	Worthing & District League Div. 2	18	17	0	1	111	14	34	1/10
1960–61	Worthing & District League Div. 1	22	16	1	5	104	26	33	3/12
1961–62	Worthing & D. Lge Intermediate Div.	22	9	4	9	47	42	22	7/12
1962–63	Worthing & D. Lge Intermediate Div.				Albion withdrew from the League in March				
" "	South East Counties League	30	11	3	16	57	64	25	12/16
1963–64	South East Counties League	30	5	3	22	44	90	13	15/16
1964–65	South East Counties League Div. 1	30	14	3	13	60	82	31	8/16
1965–66	South East Counties League Div. 1	30	4	7	19	41	86	15	15/16
1966–67	South East Counties League Div. 1	30	6	5	19	34	78	17	15/16
1967–68	South East Counties League Div. 1	30	8	6	16	59	97	22	11/16
1968–69	South East Counties League Div. 1	32	7	4	21	50	84	18	16/17
1969–70	Sussex Sunday League Minor Div.	22	17	2	3	111	23	36	1/12
1970–71	Sussex Sunday League Minor Div.	20	18	1	1	132	15	37	1/11
1971–72	Sussex Sunday League Minor Div.	18	15	3	0	99	22	33	1/10
" "	Southern Counties Combination	20	12	5	3	42	19	29	3/11
1972–73	Sussex Sunday League Minor Div.	20	19	1	0	130	18	39	1/11
" "	Southern Counties Combination	30	20	7	3	97	34	47	2/16
1973–74	South East Counties League Div. 1	32	10	3	19	57	75	23	13/17
1974–75	Did not compete								
1975–76	Southern Youth League	14	13	1	0	44	3	27	1/8
1976–77	Did not compete								
1977–78	Southern Youth League	16	13	2	1	52	14	27	1/9
1978–79	Southern Youth League	22	18	4	0	111	18	40	1/12
1979–80	Southern Youth League – West	14	?	?	?	?	?	?	2/8
1980–81	Hampshire Youth League	24	22	1	1	89	18	45	1/13
1981–82	Hampshire Youth League				Albion withdrew from the League in February				
" "	South East Counties League Div. 2	28	15	6	7	65	36	36	2/15
1982–83	South East Counties League Div. 2	24	7	2	15	45	59	16	11/13
1983–84	South East Counties League Div. 2	20	4	8	8	31	42	16	10/11
1984–85	South East Counties League Div. 2	22	9	5	8	37	29	23	5/12
1985–86	South East Counties League Div. 2	26	8	4	14	28	55	20	12/14
1986–87	South East Counties League Div. 2	28	11	4	13	49	56	26	9/15
1987–88	South East Counties League Div. 2	28	5	6	17	46	77	16	15/15
1988–89	South East Counties League Div. 2	28	7	9	12	40	54	23	10/15
1989–90	South East Counties League Div. 2	30	13	4	13	45	39	30	7/16
1990–91	South East Counties League Div. 2	30	7	11	12	43	52	25	10/16
1991–92	South East Counties League Div. 2	26	12	4	10	51	38	28	7/14
1992–93	South East Counties League Div. 2	26	11	6	9	48	49	28	5/14

Youth team cup summary (see also F.A. Youth Challenge Cup)

London Invitation Youth Cup

1952–53	?

South East Counties League Cup

1954–55	?
1962–63	Final
1963–64	R1
1964–65	R1
1965–66 (D1 Cup)	R1
1966–67 (D1 Cup)	R1
1967–68 (D1 Cup)	R2
1968–69 (D1 Cup)	R1
1973–74 (D1 Cup)	R1
1981–82 (D2 Cup)	R1
1982–83 (D2 Cup)	R1
1983–84 (D2 Cup)	R2
1984–85 (D2 Cup)	Winners
1985–86 (D2 Cup)	Semi-final
1986–87	Semi-final
1987–88	R1
1988–89	R1
1989–90	Winners
1990–91	R1
1991–92	R2
1992–93	R1

Southern Junior Floodlit Cup

1955–56	R1
1962–63	R2
1963–64	?
1964–65	R1
1965–66	R1
1966–67	R1
1967–68	Prelim.
1968–69	R1
1972–73	R1
1973–74	?
1974–75	R1
1975–76	Prelim.
1976–77	R?
1977–78	R1
1978–79	R1
1979–80	R1
1980–81	R3
1981–82	R2
1982–83	R2
1983–84	R2
1984–85	R1
1985–86	R3
1986–87	R1
1987–88	R1
1988–89	R2
1989–90	R2
1990–91	R1
1991–92	R1
1992–93	R1

Worthing & District Junior Charity Cup

1959–60	Semi-final
1960–61	Winners
1961–62	R4
1962–63	R1

Worthing Benevolent Fund Cup

1959–60	Winners

Worthing (Crowshaw) Cup

1960–61	Semi-final
1961–62	R2
1962–63	R1

Vernon-Wentworth Junior Challenge Cup

1961–62	R2

Sussex Sunday League Minor Cup

1969–70	Winners
1970–71	Winners
1971–72	Winners
1972–73	Winners

Southern Counties Combination Cup

1971–72	Final
1972–73	Semi-final

Southern Youth League Cup

1975–76	Final
1977–78	?
1978–79	R?
1979–80	Final

Hampshire Youth League Cup

1980–81	Winners
1981–82	R?

John Ullman (Kent Youth League) Invitation Cup

1987–88	Semi-final
1988–89	Final
1989–90	R1
1990–91	R2
1991–92	Semi-final

Gonfreville L'Orcher (Le Havre) Tournament

1990–91	Winners
1991–92	Final
1992–93	5th

F.A. Youth Challenge Cup 1952–88

Date		Opponents		Score	Date		Opponents		Score
1952–53					**1970–71**				
25.10.1952	R2	Crystal Palace	(h)	1–0	2.11.1970	R1	Aldershot	(a)	3–3
29.11.1952	R3	Portsmouth	(a)	2–1	16.11.1970	R1 rep	Aldershot	(h)	0–4
17.1.1953	R4	Brentford	(a)	0–1	**1971–72**				
1953–54					1.11.1971	R1	Southampton	(a)	1–0
10.12.1953	R1	Hastings United	(h)	0–2	**1972–73**				
1954–55					28.10.1972	R1	Slough Town	(h)	3–1
25.10.1954	R1	Portsmouth	(a)	2–4	28.11.1972	R2	Arsenal	(a)	0–5
1955–56					**1973–74**				
29.9.1955	R1	Aldershot	(a)	1–3	5.11.1973	R1	Redhill	(a)	1–1
1956–57					12.11.1973	R1 rep	Redhill	(h)	5–2
22.9.1956	R1	Eastbourne United	(a*)	0–5	10.12.1973	R2	Watford	(a)	2–1
Tie drawn at home but switched to Eastbourne					29.12.1973	R3	Ipswich Town	(a)	2–2
1957–58					5.1.1974	R3 rep	Ipswich Town	(h)	1–2
Albion did not enter the competition					**1974–75**				
1958–59					2.10.1974	R1	Southampton	(a)	0–2
8.10.1958	R1	Aldershot	(a)	4–1	**1975–76**				
19.11.1958	R2	Portsmouth	(a)	1–7	22.11.1975	R1	Millwall	(a)	1–3
1959–60					**1976–77**				
16.11.1959	R2	Southampton	(a)	2–5	1.11.1976	R1	Gillingham	(h)	4–1
1960–61					9.12.1976	R2	Camberley Town	(a*)	1–2
19.10.1960	R1	Aldershot	(a*)	5–3	*Second-round tie drawn at home but switched to Camberley*				
21.11.1960	R2	Millwall	(a)	0–2	**1977–78**				
First-round tie drawn at home but switched to Aldershot					7.11.1977	R1	Croydon	(a)	2–3
1961–62					**1978–79**				
16.11.1961	R2	Worthing	(h*)	2–0	2.11.1978	R1	Reading	(a)	3–1
15.1.1962	R3	Crystal Palace	(a)	1–0	7.12.1978	R2	Gillingham	(h)	3–0
13.2.1962	R4	Bristol City	(a)	0–2	10.1.1979	R3	Portsmouth	(a)	0–2
Second-round tie drawn away but switched to Goldstone Ground					**1979–80**				
1962–63					21.11.1979	R1	Wimbledon	(h)	1–3
17.12.1962	R2	West Ham United	(h)	3–3	**1980–81**				
18.2.1963	R2 rep	West Ham United	(a)	1–6	20.10.1980	R1	Dagenham	(h)	2–2
1963–64					5.11.1980	R1 rep	Dagenham	(a)	3–2
11.11.1963	R1	Bournemouth & B.A.	(h)	3–0	1.12.1980	R2	Millwall	(h)	1–0
16.12.1963	R2	Southampton	(a)	1–1	3.1.1981	R3	Orient	(h)	0–2
30.12.1963	R2 rep	Southampton	(h)	2–0	**1981–82**				
28.1.1964	R3	Swindon Town	(h)	2–4	2.11.1981	R1	Sutton United	(h)	2–1
1964–65					26.11.1981	R2	Cambridge United	(a)	0–2
11.11.1964	R1	Aldershot	(a)	1–2	**1982–83**				
1965–66					28.10.1982	R1	Maidstone United	(a)	1–2
3.11.1965	R1	Southampton	(a)	1–1	**1983–84**				
9.11.1965	R1 rep	Southampton	(h)	2–4 aet	8.12.1983	R2	Norwich City	(h)	0–2
1966–67					**1984–85**				
5.11.1966	R1	Aldershot	(a)	0–1	15.11.1984	R1	Folkestone Town	(h)	10–0
1967–68					4.12.1984	R2	Charlton Athletic	(h)	2–5
11.11.1967	R1	Aldershot	(h)	2–2	**1985–86**				
20.11.1967	R1 rep	Aldershot	(a)	1–4	4.11.1985	R1	Southend United	(a)	2–3
1968–69					**1986–87**				
6.11.1968	R1	Southampton	(a)	0–3	3.11.1986	R1	Staines Town	(h)	6–0
1969–70					11.12.1986	R2	AFC Bournemouth	(a)	1–3
5.11.1969	R1	Gillingham	(h)	1–0	**1987–88**				
26.11.1969	R2	Swaythling Athletic	(h)	2–2 aet	10.11.1987	R1	Croydon	(h)	2–0
8.12.1969	R2 rep	Swaythling Athletic	(h*)	1–0	30.11.1987	R2	Staines Town	(h)	2–1
15.1.1970	R3	Bournemouth & B.A.	(a)	0–6	16.1.1988	R3	Leyton Orient	(h)	1–2
Second-round replay switched to Goldstone Ground									

F.A. Youth Challenge Cup 1988–93

Date		Opponents		Score	Date		Opponents		Score
1988–89					**1991–92**				
14.11.1988	R1	Sutton United	(h)	5–0	29.10.1991	R1	Wokingham Town	(a)	2–0
5.12.1988	R2	Charlton Athletic	(h)	1–7	25.11.1991	R2	Arsenal	(h)	2–5
1989–90					**1992–93**				
7.11.1989	R1	Erith & Belvedere	(h)	4–0	4.11.1992	R1	St Albans	(a)	4–0
5.12.1989	R2	Leyton Orient	(a)	2–2	7.12.1992	R2	Charlton Athletic	(a)	1–1
11.12.1989	R2 rep	Leyton Orient	(h)	1–2	15.12.1992	R2 rep	Charlton Athletic	(h)	3–2
1990–91					5.1.1993	R3	Wycombe Wanderers	(a)	1–1
					21.1.1993	R3 rep	Wycombe Wanderers	(h)	9–0
29.10.1990	R1	Peterborough United	(a)	0–3	10.2.1993	R4	Millwall	(a)	0–3

Albion have entered several Sussex County competitions and local charity cups over the years. Apart from a few invitations to charity events in Hastings, this involvement in the local competitive scene began during the Second World War when the newly formed junior team became a mainstay of county football throughout the conflict.

Since the war, the youth team has competed in the Worthing & District League for four seasons in the late 1950s and early '60s, and in a number of other local leagues from 1969 to 1982; see page 278.

Most of the entries into the County's knock-out competitions have been by the reserves, but the first team did contest the first four seasons of the Sussex Professional Cup and have made a few appearances in the other trophies. There have also been a number of invitations to local charity cup competitions.

The results in all these competitions are given below.

Sussex Professional Challenge Cup

Contested by the professional clubs in the county from 1961 until the distinction between amateurs and professionals was abolished in 1975. Initially only Albion and Hastings United were involved. Other professional clubs to join in were Crawley Town (1963), Bognor Regis Town (1972) and Horsham (1974). Albion fielded a first team for four seasons but, because of Crawley Town's strong-arm tactics in the 1963–64 final, played the first eleven only once thereafter, in the 1969–70 final — ironically the club's first defeat in the competition.

Date		Opponents		Score	Scorers	Date		Opponents		Score	Scorers
1960–61						**1968–69**					
24.4.1961	F Lg1	Hastings United	(h)	2–2	Brown 2	5.2.1969	SF	Hastings United	(h)	4–0	Wilkinson, Priestly 2, Livesey
1.5.1961	F Lg2	Hastings United	(a)	2–2	Windross, Laverick	24.4.1969	F	Crawley Town	(a)	1–0	Wilkinson
Extra time was not possible because of bad light and each club held the trophy for six months						**1969–70**					
1961–62						30.4.1970	F	Crawley Town	(a)	0–1	
26.3.1962	F Lg1	Hastings United	(h)	1–0	Laverick	**1970–71**					
30.4.1962	F Lg2	Hastings United	(a)	2–1	Hodges 2	25.1.1971	SF	Hastings United	(a)	3–1	Woffinden 2, O'Leary
1962–63						3.5.1971	F	Crawley Town	(a)	2–1 aet	Dawson, Wilkinson
22.5.1963	F	Hastings United	(a)	3–1	Cassidy, Goodchild, Gilbert	**1971–72**					
1963–64						27.4.1972	F	Crawley Town	(h)	2–1	Bryson, Brockwell
7.4.1964	SF	Hastings United	(h)	1–1 aet	Turner	**1972–73**					
22.4.1964	SF rep	Hastings United	(a)	3–0	Cassidy 2, Gall	30.9.1972	SF	Bognor Regis Town	(a)	5–1	Bryson 2, Conway, Brockwell, Crawford
24.11.1964	F	Crawley Town	(h)	3–1	Kydd, Baxter, McQuarrie	17.4.1973	F	Crawley Town	(a)	3–0	Armstrong 2, Crawford
The final was played the following season						**1973–74**					
1964–65						13.11.1973	SF	Crawley Town	(a)	0–0 aet	
14.12.1965	F	Crawley Town	(a)	2–1	J. Smith, Oliver	25.3.1974	SF rep	Crawley Town	(a)	2–2 aet	Templeman, G. Howell
The final was played the following season						4.4.1974	SF 2rep	Crawley Town	(a)	2–1 aet	Cooper, Bryson
1965–66						26.4.1974	F	Bognor Regis Town	(a)	0–1	
No competition held						**1974–75**					
1966–67						6.1.1975	SF	Bognor Regis Town	(h)	4–0	Marlowe 2, Rollings, Machin
3.5.1967	F	Hastings United	(a)	3–1	K. Napier 2, Tawse	17.4.1975	F	Crawley Town	(a)	3–3 aet	Slaughter, Russell 2
1967–68						18.8.1975	F rep	Crawley Town	(h)	3–2 aet	Marlowe, Fell 2
22.4.1968	F	Hastings United	(a)	0–0 aet		*The final was replayed the following season*					
Each club held the trophy for six months											

Sussex Senior Challenge Cup

The county's premier trophy was first played for in the 1882–83 season when it was won by Brighton Rangers. Albion's forerunners, Brighton and Hove Rangers, reached the final in 1900–01 but lost out to Eastbourne. Albion themselves tried to enter the competition in 1905 but had to withdraw because of clashing dates with the question of professional involvement deferred. During the Second World War the Senior Cup was presented to the winners of the Sussex Wartime Cup tournament, which was played on a league basis. Albion's junior side won it as such in 1942–43 (see wartime results), but the club's first entry into the normal competition was in 1945–46. Albion entered again in 1975–76 following the abolition of the professional/amateur distinction, but then opted for the less onerous Floodlight Cup until 1978, since when they have competed every season, winning the trophy twice. The reserves have been fielded except where noted.

Date		Opponents		Score	Scorers
1945–46					
9.2.1946	R2 Lg1	Hastings & St L.	(a)	0–5	
16.2.1946	R2 Lg2	Hastings & St L.	(a)	2–5	Bromley, King
Both matches played by Albion Juniors					
1975–76					
18.11.1975	R2	Crawley Town	(a)	4–0	Winstanley, P. Ward, Marlowe, Deakin
17.1.1976	R3	Eastbourne Town	(a)	1–1	P. Ward
24.1.1976	R3 rep	Eastbourne Town	(a)	0–1	
1978–79					
4.11.1978	R1	Southwick	(a)	1–3	Stevens
1979–80					
3.11.1979	R1	Sidley United	(h)	7–1	Ring 3, Poskett, Gent, Clark, Geard
12.1.1980	R2	Hastings Town	(a)	2–0	Young, Geard (pen.)
9.2.1980	R3	Steyning Town	(a)	2–1	Ring, McAlear
8.3.1980	SF	Lewes	(a*)	0–1	
The semi-final was drawn at home but switched to the Dripping Pan					
1980–81					
1.11.1980	R1	Horsham	(a)	0–2	
1981–82					
28.11.1981	R1	Eastbourne United	(h)	0–2	
1982–83					
20.11.1982	R1	Crawley Town	(a)	3–0	Smith, Ritchie, Deans
8.1.1983	R2	Bognor Regis Town	(a*)	3–3	Howlett, O'Regan 2
15.1.1983	R2 rep	Bognor Regis Town	(a)	1–2	Ryan
The second-round tie was drawn at home but switched to Nyewood Lane					
1983–84					
29.10.1983	R1	Hastings Town	(a)	3–1	Lambert 3
10.12.1983	R2	Midhurst & E. Utd	(a)	2–0	Howlett, Wakefield
21.1.1984	R3	Peacehaven & T.	(a)	1–2	Smith
1984–85					
25.10.1984	R2	Lewes	(h)	3–3	Wakefield, Ryan 2
1.11.1984	R2 rep	Lewes	(a)	1–2 aet	Muir
1985–86					
9.11.1985	R2	Storrington	(a)	2–2	Arscott 2
11.11.1985	R2 rep	Storrington	(h)	4–0	Massimo 2, Connor 2
2.12.1985	R3	Worthing	(h)	0–3	

Date		Opponents		Score	Scorers
1986–87					
25.11.1986	R2	Eastbourne United	(h)	2–0	Saunders, Armstrong
24.1.1987	R3	Newhaven	(h)	4–0	Webber 2, Massimo, Arscott
16.2.1987	R4	Hastings Town	(h)	1–1	Gatting
23.2.1987	R4 rep	Hastings Town	(a)	4–1	Gipp 2, Saunders 2 (1 pen.)
21.3.1987	SF	Arundel	(n*)	0–2	
The second-round tie was played by Albion's first team.					
The semi-final was played at the Dripping Pan, Lewes F.C.					
1987–88					
28.11.1987	R2	Burgess Hill Town	(a)	4–3	Gipp 3, Tiltman
23.1.1988	R3	Peacehaven & T.	(a)	2–1	Own goal, Tiltman
20.2.1988	R4	Pagham	(a)	3–1	Gipp 2, Own goal
19.3.1988	SF	Southwick	(n*)	3–1 aet	Gipp 2, Tiltman
2.5.1988	F	Lewes	(n*)	3–0	Gipp, Dineen, Smith
The semi-final was played at the Dripping Pan, Lewes F.C. Final played at the Goldstone.					
Team for final: Digweed; Brown; Harris; Jasper (sub. Robinson); Horscroft; Rougvie; Armstrong; Webber; Gipp (sub. Smith); Tiltman; Dineen.					
1988–89					
21.11.1988	R2	Eastbourne United	(h)	3–1	Bissett 2, Chapman (pen.)
21.1.1989	R3	Southwick	(h)	0–0	
28.1.1989	R3 rep	Southwick	(a)	1–2 aet	Cooper
1989–90					
21.11.1989	R2	Southwick	(h)	1–3	Dineen
1990–91					
24.11.1990	R2	Lewes	(a)	1–2	McGrath
1991–92					
23.11.1991	R2	Lancing	(a)	4–1	Wade 2, Clarkson, McGrath
15.1.1992	R3	Hastings Town	(h)	0–0	
28.1.1992	R3 rep	Hastings Town	(a)	2–2 aet	Codner, Barham
5.2.1992	R3 2rep	Hastings Town	(h)	3–2 aet	Barham, Gall, Williams
22.2.1992	R4	Burgess Hill Town	(h)	4–2	Funnell, Wade 3
18.3.1992	SF	Lewes	(n*)	1–0	McDonald
4.5.1992	F	Langney Sports	(n*)	1–0	Savage
The semi-final was played at Woodside Road, Worthing F.C. Final played at the Goldstone.					
Team for final: Beeney; Crumplin; Stemp (sub. Simmonds); O'Dowd; Iovan; Reed; Briley; Wade; Funnell (sub. Wosahlo); Williams; Savage.					
1992–93					
21.11.1992	R2	Lewes	(h)	1–1	Myall
23.11.1992	R2 rep	Lewes	(a)	2–0	Farrington 2
23.1.1993	R3	Pagham	(a)	1–2	Funnell

Roy Haydon Memorial Trophy

Played for annually as a curtain-raiser to the season by the Senior Cup holders and the County League champions, with the proceeds going towards the County F.A.'s Benevolent Fund for injured players. Albion reserves contested it in 1988 and 1992 as Cup holders.

Date	Opponents		Score	Scorers
1988–89				
24.8.1988	Pagham	(a)	7–2	Crumplin 3, Walkington 2, Chapman, Cooper

Date	Opponents		Score	Scorers
1992–93				
11.8.1992	Peacehaven & T.	(a)	0–1	

Sussex Floodlight Challenge Cup

Played by those clubs with floodlights following the abandonment of the Sussex Professional Challenge Cup. Albion entered a reserve side in the three seasons of the competition which was then scrapped to force the re-entry of Albion, Hastings United, Crawley Town, Horsham *and Eastbourne United into the more important but more onerous Senior Cup. (It is a rule that clubs must enter a county competition to be eligible for the F.A.'s national competitions.)*

Date		Opponents		Score	Scorers	Date		Opponents		Score	Scorers
1975–76						**1976–77**					
1.12.1975	R1	Lewes	(h)	7–0	Deakin, P. Ward 3, Marlowe, Own goal, Mason	23.11.1976	R1	Bognor Regis Town	(a)	5–2	Lewis 2 (1 pen.), S. Ward, Binney, Elliott
16.2.1976	SF	Horsham	(h)	2–1	Marlowe, Lewis	24.3.1977	SF	Crawley Town	(h)	4–0	Fell, Binney, Own goal, Madden
12.4.1976	F	Hastings United	(a)	1–3	Deakin	4.5.1977	F	Lewes	(h)	0–2	
						1977–78					
						17.11.1977	R1	Worthing	(a)	2–3	Tiler, Ruggiero

Sussex (Royal Ulster Rifles) Charity Cup

The R.U.R. Cup, initially known as the Royal Irish Rifles Cup, was donated to the County F.A. in 1897 by that regiment when it departed from its station at Preston Barracks. In the early days the Cup was contested by the champions of the East and West Sussex Senior Leagues – Southwick beat North End Rangers to become the first *winners – but it has had a variety of formats since. During the Second World War it was awarded to the victors of a match between the winners of the Sussex Wartime Cup (played on a league basis) and runners-up, hence the junior team's involvement in 1943 and 1945. In latter years it has been contested as a normal knock-out trophy.*

Date		Opponents		Score	Scorers	Date		Opponents		Score	Scorers
1942–43						**1960–61**					
8.5.1943	F	Worthing	(a)	4–3	Thorne 2, Own goal, Chase	21.1.1961	R1	Whitehawk	(h)	3–2 aet	Brayne, Brown, Thorne
Match played by Albion Juniors						25.2.1961	R2	Haywards Heath	(h*)	2–0	T. Tiddy 2
1944–45						25.3.1961	SF	Rye United	(a)	1–1 aet	Own goal
12.5.1945	F	Worthing	(a)	1–3	Thorne	1.4.1961	SF rep	Rye United	(a)	1–1 aet	T. Tiddy
Match played by Albion Juniors						17.4.1961	SF 2rep	Rye United	(h)	2–1	Brown, Wood
1958–59						11.5.1961	F	Chichester City	(a)	3–3	Sitford 2, Hannam
13.12.1958	R2	A.P.V. Athletic	(a)	4–5	Bennetti, Sitford 2, Ratcliffe	*The cup was held jointly by Albion and Chichester City.*					
Match played by 'A' team						*The second-round tie was drawn away but switched to the Goldstone.*					
1959–60						*First match and last two were played by reserves, others played by 'A' team.*					
21.11.1959	R1	East Grinstead	(a)	1–0	Foreman						
30.1.1960	R2	Haywards Heath	(h)	8–3	Brayne 3, Clayton 3, Dixon, Sitford						
27.2.1960	R3	Rye United	(a)	6–1	Small, Horner 2, Hobbs, Hannam 2						
26.3.1960	SF	Chichester City	(a)	3–0	Sitford, Brayne, Hannam						
12.5.1960	F	Arundel	(n*)	6–0	Abbis, Curry 3, McNicol, Little						
Final played at Woodside Road, Worthing F.C.											
First two matches played by reserves, next two by the youth team, final by the first team.											

282

Brighton Charity Cup

An invitation tournament first contested in 1896 when the Royal Irish Rifles regimental side lifted the trophy. Initially the final was played as part of an annual charity football festival in Preston Park at Easter. In the 1950s and early '60s, Albion reserves contested the Cup in a

one-off match against a local side, the final usually being played at the Goldstone. The Brighton Charity Cup is now contested annually by local sides in a knock-out competition organised by the Brighton, Hove, Worthing and District Football Association.

Date		Opponents		Score	Scorers
1951–52					
28.4.1952	F	Whitehawk & M.F. O.B.	(h)	1–1	Moffatt
The Cup was jointly held					
1952–53					
6.5.1953	F	Whitehawk & M.F. O.B.	(h)	4–1	Douglas, Sirrell 2, Bisset
1953–54					
Albion were due to play Worthing for the Cup but the latter withdrew because of RUR Cup commitments					
1954–55					
9.5.1955	F	Hastings United	(h)	0–3	
1955–56					
7.5.1956	F	Sussex County F.A. XI	(h)	3–2	Johnson, Stephens 2

Date		Opponents		Score	Scorers
1956–57					
6.5.1957	F	Eastbourne United	(a)	3–1	Bisset, Darey 2
1957–58					
5.5.1958	F	Eastbourne United	(a)	3–0	Thorne 2, Darey
1958–59					
4.5.1959	F	Eastbourne United	(h)	3–0	Brayne, Dixon, Jones
1959–60					
9.5.1960	F	Whitehawk	(h)	1–3	Laffar
1960–61					
3.5.1961	F	Whitehawk	(h)	?–?	
Albion won the tie but the score is not known					

Freeman-Thomas Charity Shield

Donated by Major Freeman-Thomas, M.P. for Hastings, in 1900–01 and played by the first team as part of the Hastings Charity Festival.

Date		Opponents		Score	Scorers
1907–08					
30.4.1908	F	Hastings & St L. Utd	(a)	1–3 aet	Longstaff

Eastbourne Charity Cup

First contested in the 1897–98 season and revived by the Eastbourne Gazette and Herald in 1979. The 1989 match was contested by Albion reserves.

Date		Opponents		Score	Scorers
1988–89					
1.5.1989	F	Eastbourne Town	(a)	1–2	Brown

Hastings Charity Cup

Contested by Albion reserves.

Date		Opponents		Score	Scorers	Date		Opponents		Score	Scorers
1924–25						**1925–26**					
13.12.1924	SF	Hastings & St Leonards	(a)	9–1	Dennison 3, Green 2, Hoyland 2, Wilkinson (pen), Smith	19.9.1925	SF	Bognor	(a)	9–1	Gough, Gilgun 3, Ison 3, Edmonds 3, Hoyland
22.4.1925	F	Folkestone	(n*)	0–1		28.5.1926	F	Folkestone	(n*)	1–0	Ison
Final played at the Pilot Field, Hastings & St Leonards F.C.						*Final played at the Pilot Field, Hastings & St Leonards F.C.*					

Richards Hospital Cup

Donated in 1947 by the late Mr F. E. Richards, to be played for annually in aid of the Queen Victoria Hospital, East Grinstead. The cup, actually a silver rose bowl, was contested each year until 1955, but the

charity match was revived in 1981. Albion's first team have been the Wasps' opponents on two occasions.

Date		Opponents		Score	Scorers	Date		Opponents		Score	Scorers
1983–84						**1984–85**					
13.5.1984	F	East Grinstead	(a)	3–0	Muir 2, Wilson	12.5.1985	F	East Grinstead	(a)	0–1	

During the Second World War the reserves were disbanded and a new Albion junior side was formed to promote the game amongst the youth of the county. Comprising a mixture of youngsters and experienced guest players, the team entered the Sussex Wartime Cup (which was played on a league basis) in the four seasons 1941–45, and contested the first post-war season of the Sussex County League, 1945–46. The juniors' results in these competitions are reproduced below.

See also the Sussex (Royal Ulster Rifles) Charity Cup, which was competed for by the winners and runners-up of the Sussex Wartime Cup.

Sussex wartime results	1941–42 WC	1942–43 WC	1943–44 WC	1944–45 WC	1945–46 CLE
Bexhill Wanderers					2–2 M30 1–3 N3
CADM & TC (Eastbourne)				3–2 D23 4–1 F24	2–5 D1 –*
Crawley Town					1–5 J5 3–0 D15
East Grinstead	2–0 M14 2–1 A25	2–0 M20 5–2 N7			1–4 D22 2–6 D29
Haywards Heath	2–1 A18 1–3 F14	2–0 N14 5–3 A10	1–1 F12 2–4 J8	1–0 M10 5–2 F3	2–8 D8 1–8 F2
Lewes				7–1 D30 5–2 D2	1–3 N10 2–6 N17
Newhaven					3–3 O27 4–6 O20
R.A.F. (Eastbourne)		5–2 J16 3–2 F20			
R.A.F. (Ford)			0–3 D18 1–3 J8	4–0 A7 5–3 F10*	
R.A.F. (Tangmere)				1–0 A21 2–1 A28	
Southwick	3–0 F21 3–1 J31			6–0 M11 3–2 F19	7–0 D29 3–1 M24
Worthing	3–4 F7 1–2 F28	5–5 J30 5–1 M13	1–0 F26 0–5 M4	0–2 M17 0–1 A2	

Notes: Home matches are shown above away matches. Albion score given first. a – August, A – April; M – March, m – May.

The competitions were the Sussex Wartime Cup, 1941–45; and the Sussex County (Emergency) League (Eastern Section), 1945–46.

1944–45 v. R.A.F. (Ford) (away) – played at Worthing.

1945–46 v. CADM & TC (away) – CADM & TC withdrew from the League in early December. Their remaining matches were awarded as '0–0 victories' to their opponents and were counted in the table along with their legitimate results.

Sussex wartime league summary

Season	Competition	P	W	D	L	F	A	Pts	Position/ No. of clubs
1941–42	Sussex Wartime Cup	8	5	0	3	17	12	10	3/5
1942–43	Sussex Wartime Cup	8	7	1	0	32	15	15	1/5
1943–44	Sussex Wartime Cup	8	3	1	4	14	18	7	3/5
1944–45	Sussex Wartime Cup	14	12	0	2	47	16	24	2/8
1945–46	Sussex Co. Emerg'cy League – East	14*	2*	2	10	25	59	6*	7/8

Albion actually played 13 games in 1945–46. The remaining match, the away game with CADM & TC, was awarded to Albion as a '0–0 victory'.

Baldwin Cup

Donated in 1938 by Horace Baldwin, the honorary secretary and treasurer of the Sussex County League, on the occasion of his retirement. Albion juniors, members of the Sussex County League in 1945–46, were invited to compete for the Cup that season. In 1954–55 it was renamed the Division One Invitation Cup, and became the Division One Challenge Cup in 1973.

Date		Opponents		Score	Scorers
1945–46					
6.4.1946	R2 Lg1	Southwick	(a)	2–3	Bromley 2
20.4.1946	R2 Lg2	Southwick	(h)	2–4	King, Goodings

RECORDS AND REFERENCE

Complete record in first-team competitions 1901–93

Competition	Seasons	P	Home W	D	L	F	A	Away & Neutral W	D	L	F	A	Best
FL D1	4	168	34	25	25	110	92	13	23	48	72	152	13th, 1981–82
FL D2 (pre 1992)	15	646	152	91	80	531	379	77	64	182	350	604	2nd, 1978–79
FL D2 (post 1992)	1	46	13	4	6	36	24	7	5	11	27	35	9th, 1992–93
FL D3	13	598	168	75	56	524	279	71	84	144	318	460	2nd, 1971–72 1976–77 1987–88
FL D4	2	92	31	8	7	113	42	14	15	17	60	67	1st, 1964–65
FL D3(S)	31	1334	411	141	115	1423	707	166	183	318	748	1138	1st, 1957–58
FL Total	66	2884	809	344	289	2737	1523	348	374	720	1575	2456	13th D1, 1981–82
FL Play-Offs	1	3	1	0	0	4	1	1	0	1	3	4	Finalists D2 PO, 1990–91
FAC	82	247	65	29	28	293	139	42	28	55	172	185	Finalists, 1982–83
FLC	33	92	21	13	11	67	49	11	11	25	45	85	R5, 1978–79
FMC	6	10	2	0	3	7	10	1	1	3	4	11	S QF, 1990–91 1991–92
AMC	2	9	4	0	2	15	14	2	1	0	8	2	S SF, 1987–88
SSC	6	13	2	0	2	10	9	2	3	4	11	14	SF, 1933–34
Wartime	7	243	48	21	55	308	304	22	12	85	193	436	–
SL D1	13	492	148	53	45	470	237	44	65	137	205	405	1st, 1909–10
SL D2	2	26	13	0	0	41	9	5	1	7	27	19	1st=, 1902–03
SL Total	15	518	161	53	45	511	246	50	66	144	237	427	1st D1, 1909–10
SL Test	1	1	0	0	0	0	0	1	0	0	5	3	Winners, 1902–03
FA Ch. Shield	1	1	0	0	0	0	0	1	0	0	1	0	Winners, 1910–11
Utd League	2	32	9	4	3	40	22	3	6	7	21	32	2nd, 1906–07
WL D1 'A'	2	24	10	1	1	28	9	3	3	6	14	23	1st, 1908–09
WL Champ.	1	2	0	0	0	0	0	0	1	1	2	3	Finalists, 1908–09
S Alliance	2	32	11	4	1	45	11	8	3	5	22	23	1st, 1913–14
SCC	8	27	7	1	2	22	10	7	5	5	18	22	Winners, 1909–10
SE League	1	22	7	1	3	33	12	4	1	6	12	27	5th, 1902–03
Total	88	4160	1157	471	445	4120	2359	505	515	1067	2338	3750	–

Note that six other matches were abandoned – see page 9 – and three Football League matches in August and September 1939 were deleted from the record when the competition was cancelled upon the outbreak of war.

Record against other clubs — Aberdare Athletic to Carlisle United

Club	First encounter	Competition	P	W	D	L	F	A	W	D	L	F	A
				Home					Away & Neutral				
Aberdare Athletic	10.9.1921	FL	12	5	0	1	22	7	2	2	2	8	10
Aldershot	19.10.1932	FL	50	15	4	6	51	35	14	7	4	40	21
		FAC	5	3	0	0	9	2	1	1	0	4	1
		FLC	2	1	0	0	3	1	0	0	1	0	3
		Wartime	16	3	2	3	21	19	0	1	7	11	31
Arsenal	12.1.1935	FL	8	2	0	2	3	6	0	1	3	1	8
		FAC	3	0	0	2	1	4	0	0	1	0	2
		FLC	2	0	1	0	0	0	0	0	1	0	4
		Wartime	12	1	1	4	8	16	0	0	6	8	26
Aston Villa	5.9.1910	FL	16	3	2	3	7	8	0	2	6	4	16
		FAC	2	0	1	0	2	2	0	0	1	2	4
		FA Ch. Shield	1	0	0	0	0	0	1	0	0	1	0
Barnet	27.11.1926	FAC	4	2	0	0	6	1	1	1	0	4	0
Barnsley	12.1.1924	FL	28	6	5	3	17	9	4	2	8	14	23
		FAC	4	1	0	0	1	0	0	1	2	4	6
		FLC	1	0	0	0	0	0	0	0	1	1	4
Barrow	27.3.1964	FL	10	4	1	0	12	3	1	4	0	8	5
Barry Town	14.12.1929	FAC	1	1	0	0	4	1	0	0	0	0	0
Bath City	9.1.1960	FAC	2	0	0	0	0	0	2	0	0	6	0
Bedford Queen's Engineering Works	27.9.1902	SE League	2	1	0	0	4	0	0	1	0	2	2
Bedford Town	4.12.1965	FAC	2	0	1	0	1	1	0	0	1	1	2
Birmingham City/	30.1.1915	FL	12	4	2	0	12	3	1	2	3	5	8
Birmingham		FAC	2	0	1	0	0	0	0	0	1	0	3
		FLC	1	1	0	0	2	0	0	0	0	0	0
		FMC	1	0	0	1	0	3	0	0	0	0	0
Blackburn Rovers	6.1.1962	FL	26	7	2	4	22	14	3	5	5	16	18
		FAC	1	0	0	1	0	3	0	0	0	0	0
		FLC	1	0	0	0	0	0	0	0	1	1	3
Blackpool	19.8.1972	FL	8	1	1	2	5	7	2	1	1	8	9
Bolton Wanderers	12.1.1907	FL	8	2	1	1	7	5	2	2	0	5	2
		FAC	4	0	1	0	1	1	0	0	3	3	11
AFC Bournemouth/	15.12.1923	FL	80	21	6	13	74	51	8	15	17	38	51
Bournemouth & Boscombe Athletic		FAC	1	1	0	0	2	0	0	0	0	0	0
		AMC	1	1	0	0	3	2	0	0	0	0	0
		Wartime	10	2	1	2	11	13	1	0	4	4	19
Bradford (Park Avenue)	30.11.1907	FL	6	1	1	1	5	4	1	0	2	6	5
		SL	2	0	1	0	1	1	1	0	0	2	0
		FAC	1	1	0	0	2	1	0	0	0	0	0
Bradford City	10.1.1959	FL	20	4	3	3	18	17	2	1	7	10	20
		FAC	1	0	0	1	0	2	0	0	0	0	0
		FLC	2	1	0	0	5	2	1	0	0	2	0
		FMC	1	0	0	0	0	0	0	0	1	1	3
Brentford	21.3.1903	FL	38	13	2	4	43	22	7	2	10	36	45
		SL	22	8	1	2	24	9	0	3	8	5	21
		FAC	3	1	0	0	1	0	1	0	1	3	4
		FLC	6	1	1	1	5	6	0	1	2	3	7
		SE League	2	1	0	0	3	0	1	0	0	3	0
		WL	2	0	1	0	0	0	0	0	1	1	2
		SCC	1	0	0	1	0	2	0	0	0	0	0
		S Alliance	4	2	0	0	10	2	1	1	0	3	1
		Wartime	14	3	1	3	21	19	2	0	5	17	36
Brighton Amateurs	4.10.1902	FAC	1	1	0	0	14	2	0	0	0	0	0
Brighton Athletic	21.9.1901	FAC	1	1	0	0	6	2	0	0	0	0	0
Bristol City	20.1.1923	FL	56	14	9	5	46	20	7	6	15	33	53
		FAC	3	0	0	1	1	2	0	0	2	0	2
		Wartime	2	1	0	0	4	3	0	0	1	1	3
Bristol Rovers	12.9.1903	FL	88	28	8	8	104	56	13	13	18	54	81
		SL	26	7	5	1	26	11	3	3	7	13	22
		FAC	1	0	0	1	1	2	0	0	0	0	0
		FLC	4	1	0	0	4	2	0	0	3	1	7
		Wartime	4	0	0	2	4	7	1	0	1	5	8
Burnley	28.1.1961	FL	8	3	0	1	7	3	1	1	2	3	7
		FAC	2	0	1	0	3	3	0	0	1	0	2
		FLC	1	0	0	0	0	0	1	0	0	3	1
Bury	8.1.1938	FL	16	5	2	1	9	5	2	1	5	8	15
		FAC	1	0	0	0	0	0	0	0	1	0	2
		FLC	1	0	0	0	0	0	0	0	1	1	5
Cambridge United	27.1.1974	FL	8	2	1	1	8	4	1	3	0	5	4
		FLC	5	2	1	0	5	1	1	1	0	2	1
Cardiff City	23.10.1912	FL	34	10	4	3	38	18	6	4	7	25	30
		SL	6	2	1	0	5	3	1	1	1	1	2
		FAC	3	0	1	0	0	0	0	0	2	0	2
		S Alliance	4	2	0	0	8	1	2	0	0	3	1
		Wartime	2	0	0	1	2	3	0	0	1	0	4
Carlisle United	2.10.1962	FL	12	4	1	1	14	6	3	0	3	7	9

Record against other clubs — Charlton Athletic to Halifax Town

Club	First encounter	Competition	P	Home					Away & Neutral				
				W	D	L	F	A	W	D	L	F	A
Charlton Athletic	22.10.1921	FL	46	12	6	5	46	31	8	2	13	32	40
		FLC	1	0	0	1	1	2	0	0	0	0	0
		FMC	1	1	0	0	3	1	0	0	0	0	0
		Wartime	11	1	2	3	11	18	2	0	3	10	14
Chelsea	14.1.1933	FL	4	0	0	2	1	3	0	0	2	0	3
		FAC	4	1	1	1	3	4	0	0	1	0	4
		Wartime	10	2	0	3	18	13	3	1	1	8	4
Cheltenham Town	30.11.1935	FAC	3	1	1	0	4	0	1	0	0	6	0
Chesham Generals	3.1.1903	SE League	2	1	0	0	3	0	1	0	0	2	0
Chesham Town	14.12.1901	SL	4	2	0	0	9	0	2	0	0	11	3
Chester City/ Chester	23.10.1963	FL	12	4	2	0	17	6	1	2	3	5	10
Chesterfield	6.1.1951	FL	18	5	3	1	18	8	2	3	4	9	10
		FAC	1	1	0	0	2	1	0	0	0	0	0
Clapton	2.11.1901	FAC	1	0	0	1	2	3	0	0	0	0	0
Colchester United	9.9.1950	FL	26	8	5	0	29	6	2	7	4	16	22
		FAC	1	0	0	1	0	1	0	0	0	0	0
		FLC	3	2	0	0	5	0	0	1	0	1	1
Corinthians	13.1.1923	FAC	3	0	1	0	1	1	1	1	0	2	1
Coventry City	28.11.1908	FL	42	13	7	1	40	16	6	6	9	29	39
		SL	12	4	2	0	16	6	1	2	3	6	8
		FAC	3	1	1	0	5	1	0	0	1	0	2
		FLC	3	0	1	1	2	3	1	0	0	3	1
Crawley Town	4.1.1992	FAC	1	1	0	0	5	0	0	0	0	0	0
Crewe Alexandra	28.10.1964	FL	4	2	0	0	6	2	0	0	2	2	4
Croydon Common	16.9.1908	SL	4	2	0	0	5	1	1	0	1	4	1
		WL	2	1	0	0	5	0	0	1	0	1	1
		SCC	1	0	0	0	0	0	0	0	1	0	3
		S Alliance	4	1	1	0	5	0	0	0	2	1	4
Crystal Palace	11.10.1905	FL	80	24	10	6	72	40	9	9	22	39	68
		SL	20	5	1	4	16	10	1	6	3	8	15
		FAC	4	0	1	0	2	2	1	1	1	3	3
		Utd League	4	0	1	1	5	6	1	1	0	4	2
		WL	2	1	0	0	2	0	0	0	1	1	3
		SSC	2	0	0	1	2	3	0	0	1	2	3
		FMC	2	0	0	1	0	2	1	0	0	3	1
		Wartime	18	1	2	6	17	33	2	0	7	16	50
Darlington	13.1.1912	FL	6	3	0	0	10	1	1	0	2	3	6
		FAC	1	0	0	0	0	0	0	0	1	1	2
Derby County	9.2.1946	FL	16	5	0	3	13	8	3	0	5	10	17
		FAC	3	1	0	1	4	5	0	0	1	0	6
		FLC	2	0	1	0	1	1	0	0	1	1	2
Doncaster Rovers	12.12.1931	FL	12	4	2	0	11	1	1	2	3	5	8
		FAC	1	1	0	0	5	0	0	0	0	0	0
Eastbourne	5.10.1901	FAC	1	1	0	0	3	1	0	0	0	0	0
Enfield	15.11.1969	FAC	1	1	0	0	2	1	0	0	0	0	0
Everton	1.2.1913	FL	8	1	1	2	5	6	0	2	2	6	9
		FAC	3	1	1	0	5	2	0	0	1	0	1
Exeter City	24.10.1908	FL	68	24	5	5	82	39	12	6	16	55	58
		SL	16	5	1	2	10	8	2	0	6	8	15
		FLC	1	1	0	0	2	1	0	0	0	0	0
		SSC	3	0	0	1	3	4	0	2	0	2	2
		AMC	1	0	0	1	0	1	0	0	0	0	0
		Wartime	4	1	1	0	5	4	0	1	1	2	3
Folkestone	28.11.1931	FAC	2	1	0	0	3	1	1	0	0	5	2
Fulham	30.11.1901	FL	30	10	2	3	32	14	3	0	12	11	35
		SL	12	3	1	2	9	8	0	0	6	1	11
		FAC	1	0	0	0	0	0	0	0	1	1	2
		AMC	1	0	0	0	0	0	1	0	0	6	1
		Wartime	10	0	1	4	9	24	2	0	3	14	22
Gillingham/ New Brompton	7.11.1903	FL	74	25	8	4	88	30	8	14	15	27	46
		SL	26	10	2	1	34	8	2	3	8	13	22
		FAC	2	0	0	0	0	0	2	0	0	2	0
		FLC	2	1	0	0	1	0	0	0	1	0	1
		Utd League	4	1	1	0	3	1	0	0	2	2	6
		SSC	1	0	0	0	0	0	0	0	1	1	3
Glossop	9.12.1905	FAC	1	0	0	0	0	0	1	0	0	1	0
Grays United	7.12.1901	SL	4	2	0	0	6	3	0	0	2	0	4
		FAC	2	0	1	0	5	5	1	0	0	3	0
		SE League	2	1	0	0	2	1	0	0	1	0	5
		Utd League	2	1	0	0	9	2	0	1	0	1	1
Grimsby Town	29.9.1920	FL	30	7	4	4	25	15	6	3	6	22	27
		FAC	2	0	1	0	1	1	1	0	0	1	0
Halifax Town	15.9.1962	FL	18	5	1	3	12	6	3	3	3	15	10

Record against other clubs — Hartlepool United to Newcastle United

Club	First encounter	Competition	Home						Away & Neutral				
			P	W	D	L	F	A	W	D	L	F	A
Hartlepool United/	13.12.1947	FL	8	2	2	0	11	3	1	2	1	8	7
Hartlepool/		FAC	2	1	0	0	2	1	0	1	0	1	1
Hartlepools United													
Hastings & St Leonards/	19.10.1901	FAC	2	1	0	0	5	0	1	0	0	9	0
Hastings & St Leonards United		Utd League	2	1	0	0	1	0	0	0	1	1	6
Hayes	14.11.1992	FAC	1	1	0	0	2	0	0	0	0	0	0
Hereford United	12.12.1970	FL	6	3	0	0	8	4	0	1	2	1	6
		FAC	1	0	0	0	0	0	1	0	0	2	1
		AMC	1	0	0	0	0	0	1	0	0	1	0
Hillingdon Borough	20.11.1971	FAC	1	1	0	0	7	1	0	0	0	0	0
Hitchin Town	25.3.1903	SE League	2	1	0	0	9	1	1	0	0	1	0
Huddersfield Town	28.1.1922	FL	24	8	2	2	24	15	5	1	6	13	15
		FAC	2	0	1	0	0	0	0	0	1	0	2
		FLC	2	1	0	0	2	0	0	0	1	0	1
Hull City	21.11.1959	FL	22	7	3	1	20	10	2	1	8	8	18
		FAC	2	1	0	0	1	0	1	0	0	3	2
Ilford	15.11.1902	FAC	2	1	0	0	5	1	0	0	1	0	1
Ipswich Town	8.10.1938	FL	46	13	3	7	48	29	4	4	15	23	55
		FAC	2	1	0	0	2	0	0	0	1	1	2
		FLC	3	1	0	1	3	3	0	1	0	0	0
Kettering Town	14.11.1903	SL	2	1	0	0	3	1	0	1	0	1	1
Kidderminster Harriers	16.11.1968	FAC	2	0	1	0	2	2	1	0	0	1	0
Leatherhead	4.1.1975	FAC	1	0	0	1	0	1	0	0	0	0	0
Leeds City	14.1.1911	FAC	1	0	0	0	0	0	1	0	0	3	1
Leeds United	24.9.1960	FL	22	5	3	3	14	10	1	2	8	11	21
		FAC	1	0	0	1	1	2	0	0	0	0	0
Leicester City	10.1.1931	FL	12	4	1	1	11	5	1	0	5	3	11
		FAC	1	0	0	0	0	0	1	0	0	2	1
Leyton	6.9.1905	SL	12	5	1	0	13	3	1	3	2	5	8
		Utd League	4	0	1	1	1	3	1	0	1	3	3
		WL	4	2	0	0	4	1	0	0	2	2	8
Leyton Orient/	31.1.1906	FL	64	17	12	3	48	25	8	5	19	40	61
Orient/		FAC	1	1	0	0	3	1	0	0	0	0	0
Clapton Orient		Utd League	2	0	1	0	0	0	0	1	0	0	0
		FLC	1	1	0	0	1	0	0	0	0	0	0
		Wartime	13	6	0	1	19	6	0	2	4	9	19
Lincoln City	9.1.1915	FL	12	5	1	0	19	5	2	1	3	9	10
		FAC	1	1	0	0	2	1	0	0	0	0	0
Liverpool	1.2.1908	FL	16	1	5	2	14	16	1	1	6	6	20
		FAC	6	1	0	2	4	6	1	2	0	5	4
		FLC	1	0	0	0	0	0	0	0	1	0	4
Luton Town	17.9.1902	FL	50	17	5	3	49	23	2	7	16	25	52
		SL	22	5	4	2	18	14	1	1	9	5	20
		FAC	2	1	0	1	4	2	0	0	0	0	0
		FLC	4	1	1	0	3	1	0	1	1	3	5
		SE League	2	0	0	1	1	2	0	0	1	0	3
		Utd League	4	2	0	0	9	3	0	2	0	3	3
		WL	2	1	0	0	2	0	0	1	0	1	1
		S Alliance	4	1	1	0	3	2	0	0	2	0	8
		Wartime	8	4	0	0	26	6	1	1	2	11	14
Maidenhead	21.12.1901	SL	2	1	0	0	2	1	1	0	0	3	2
Manchester City	23.2.1924	FL	14	3	2	2	12	7	0	2	5	5	17
		FAC	2	1	0	1	5	5	0	0	0	0	0
Manchester United	16.1.1909	FL	8	1	1	2	2	5	0	1	3	2	7
		FAC	6	0	0	1	0	2	0	2	3	4	10
		FLC	2	0	1	0	1	1	0	0	1	0	1
Mansfield Town	25.12.1931	FL	32	14	0	2	44	12	5	4	7	26	24
		FAC	1	0	0	0	0	0	1	0	0	2	0
Merthyr Town	28.9.1912	FL	20	6	3	1	22	7	3	0	7	16	19
		SL	6	2	1	0	7	3	1	0	2	2	3
Middlesbrough	3.2.1906	FL	30	6	3	6	25	24	1	5	9	10	35
		FAC	3	0	1	0	1	1	0	1	1	2	4
Millwall	1.4.1904	FL	66	17	7	9	55	39	8	8	17	38	66
		FL Play-off	2	1	0	0	4	1	1	0	0	2	1
		SL	26	7	3	3	21	12	3	1	9	12	31
		FAC	2	0	1	0	1	1	0	0	1	1	3
		FLC	3	1	1	0	3	2	0	0	1	0	1
		WL Champ.	2	0	0	0	0	0	0	1	1	2	3
		S Alliance	2	0	1	0	2	2	0	1	0	0	0
		SSC	1	0	0	0	0	0	0	0	1	1	2
		Wartime	8	2	1	1	15	7	1	0	3	8	12
Newcastle United	15.2.1930	FL	12	2	1	3	8	12	2	1	3	5	11
		FAC	4	0	1	0	1	1	2	0	1	3	3

Club	First encounter	Competition	P	W	D	L	F	A	W	D	L	F	A
					Home					Away & Neutral			
Newport County	2.10.1913	FL	62	25	3	3	87	29	10	9	12	37	38
		SL	2	1	0	0	3	1	0	0	1	0	1
		FAC	3	1	0	0	8	1	1	0	1	3	4
		S Alliance	2	0	0	1	0	1	1	0	0	2	1
		SSC	1	0	0	0	0	0	1	0	0	1	0
Northampton Town	3.10.1903	FL	72	18	9	9	71	46	6	10	20	33	64
		SL	26	6	3	4	24	20	1	4	8	11	21
		FAC	3	0	0	1	1	2	1	0	1	2	2
		FLC	7	0	2	1	2	4	1	1	2	4	12
Norwich City	30.9.1905	FL	64	17	9	6	60	32	5	12	15	36	54
		SL	22	6	4	1	24	12	3	4	4	10	14
		FAC	10	4	0	2	14	6	1	2	1	5	9
		FLC	2	0	0	0	0	0	1	0	1	1	2
		Utd League	2	1	0	0	4	3	0	1	0	1	1
		FMC	1	0	0	0	0	0	0	0	1	0	5
		Wartime	3	0	1	0	3	3	0	0	2	0	21
Nottingham Forest	20.8.1949	FL	14	1	3	3	7	9	2	0	5	4	15
		FLC	3	0	1	0	0	0	0	0	2	1	6
Notts County	8.11.1930	FL	38	7	6	6	34	28	6	3	10	22	31
		FL Play-off	1	0	0	0	0	0	0	0	1	1	3
		FAC	1	0	0	1	1	2	0	0	0	0	0
		FLC	1	0	0	0	0	0	1	0	0	3	1
		AMC	1	0	0	1	1	5	0	0	0	0	0
Oldham Athletic	10.1.1914	FL	30	7	3	5	26	12	3	3	9	14	30
		FAC	4	2	0	0	5	1	0	1	1	2	3
		FLC	3	0	1	0	0	0	0	1	1	3	4
Oxford United	18.9.1963	FL	24	5	4	3	14	12	3	2	7	12	21
		FAC	1	0	0	1	0	3	0	0	0	0	0
		FLC	1	1	0	0	2	0	0	0	0	0	0
Peterborough & Fletton United	30.11.1929	FAC	1	1	0	0	4	0	0	0	0	0	0
Peterborough United	18.9.1962	FL	14	5	1	1	15	6	1	1	5	7	14
		FAC	2	1	0	0	1	0	0	1	0	2	2
		FLC	1	1	0	0	1	0	0	0	0	0	0
Plymouth Argyle	19.12.1903	FL	58	16	7	6	52	38	4	9	16	31	61
		SL	26	7	3	3	17	12	2	4	7	13	21
		WL	2	1	0	0	3	2	0	1	0	0	0
		FMC	1	0	0	0	0	0	0	1	0	0	0
Port Vale	9.1.1932	FL	40	11	7	2	29	15	4	6	10	22	38
		FAC	1	0	0	1	1	2	0	0	0	0	0
Portsmouth	26.9.1903	FL	32	8	5	3	33	18	3	4	9	11	28
		SL	24	5	4	3	14	15	3	2	7	7	17
		FAC	4	1	0	0	1	0	2	0	1	4	5
		FLC	2	1	0	1	2	5	0	0	0	0	0
		WL	2	1	0	0	3	1	0	0	1	1	3
		SCC	2	0	0	0	0	0	2	0	0	3	1
		S Alliance	4	2	0	0	7	0	2	0	0	5	1
		Wartime	14	4	0	3	18	9	2	0	5	12	22
Preston North End	11.1.1908	FL	18	5	3	1	12	5	0	2	7	3	16
		FAC	4	0	1	0	1	1	1	1	1	3	3
Queen's Park Rangers	22.11.1902	FL	62	18	6	7	64	38	6	6	19	31	64
		SL	26	9	1	3	27	15	4	4	5	9	13
		FAC	2	0	0	0	0	0	1	0	1	3	6
		SE League	2	0	1	0	1	1	0	0	1	2	3
		SCC	2	1	0	0	3	1	0	0	1	1	4
		WL	4	1	0	1	4	4	2	0	0	4	2
		SSC	2	1	0	0	2	1	1	0	0	2	1
		Wartime	12	2	1	3	12	13	1	0	5	10	19
Reading	28.12.1903	FL	70	18	12	6	70	44	8	10	18	34	62
		SL	24	6	4	2	21	13	2	2	8	9	24
		FLC	4	0	1	1	4	5	0	2	0	0	0
		WL	2	1	0	0	2	1	1	0	0	2	1
		SCC	7	3	0	1	8	4	1	1	1	1	5
		AMC	1	0	0	0	0	0	0	1	0	1	1
		Wartime	16	2	0	6	12	25	3	0	5	15	23
Rochdale	28.8.1963	FL	12	4	2	0	12	4	1	4	1	10	10
Romford	17.11.1945	FAC	2	1	0	0	3	1	0	1	0	1	1
Rotherham United	4.10.1958	FL	24	6	4	2	19	12	2	3	7	10	18
		FAC	3	0	1	0	1	1	1	1	0	7	1
St Albans Amateurs	18.10.1902	SE League	2	1	0	0	2	0	1	0	0	1	0
Scarborough	14.12.1935	FAC	3	2	0	0	6	0	0	1	0	1	1
Scunthorpe United	18.10.1958	FL	14	2	2	3	8	10	4	3	0	16	11
		FAC	1	1	0	0	3	2	0	0	0	0	0
Sheffield United	7.1.1922	FL	18	5	3	1	11	5	2	1	6	10	20
		FAC	3	1	0	1	2	2	0	1	0	0	0

Record against other clubs — Sheffield Wednesday to West Bromwich Albion

Club	First encounter	Competition	P	Home W	D	L	F	A	Away & Neutral W	D	L	F	A
Sheffield Wednesday	21.2.1914	FL	12	1	2	3	9	16	0	4	2	6	9
		FAC	3	0	0	0	0	0	1	0	2	2	6
Shepherd's Bush	28.9.1901	SL	2	1	0	0	3	1	1	0	0	2	0
Shoreham	18.10.1902	FAC	3	2	0	0	19	1	1	0	0	12	0
Shrewsbury Town	27.10.1951	FL	46	15	5	3	46	22	4	7	12	20	35
South Liverpool	11.12.1937	FAC	2	1	0	0	6	0	0	1	0	1	1
Southall	8.2.1902	SL	4	2	0	0	6	3	1	0	1	8	1
Southampton	21.11.1903	FL	28	4	6	4	15	10	2	2	10	12	34
		SL	26	9	1	3	29	15	3	3	7	15	26
		FAC	3	0	0	2	0	3	0	0	1	0	1
		WL	2	1	0	0	3	0	0	0	1	1	2
		SCC	5	3	0	0	11	3	0	2	0	2	2
		S Alliance	4	1	1	0	3	2	0	1	1	3	5
		Wartime	13	5	1	2	27	19	0	1	4	7	14
Southend United	24.2.1909	FL	76	26	6	6	72	33	8	11	19	30	54
		SL	12	4	2	0	12	2	3	2	1	6	4
		FAC	3	1	0	0	1	0	0	0	2	2	4
		FLC	4	1	0	1	2	2	0	1	1	1	3
		S Alliance	4	2	0	0	7	1	2	0	0	5	2
		SSC	2	1	0	0	3	1	0	1	0	1	1
		AMC	2	2	0	0	7	4	0	0	0	0	0
		Wartime	6	0	2	1	5	7	0	1	2	3	11
Southern United	2.11.1905	Utd League	2	1	0	0	3	1	0	0	1	1	4
Southport	12.10.1963	FL	12	6	0	0	14	1	2	2	2	9	10
Stockport County	7.9.1963	FL	12	4	1	1	11	4	2	2	2	7	7
Stoke City/ Stoke	2.9.1911	FL	30	5	7	3	17	16	3	7	5	15	19
		SL	4	2	0	0	7	1	0	0	2	2	6
Sunderland	6.12.1958	FL	32	10	3	3	31	20	2	4	10	13	28
Swansea City/ Swansea Town	25.10.1919	FL	38	3	10	6	21	25	4	7	8	18	26
		SL	2	1	0	0	4	2	0	1	0	1	1
		FAC	2	1	0	0	2	0	0	0	1	1	2
		FLC	1	0	0	0	0	0	1	0	0	1	0
Swindon Town	19.9.1903	FL	88	24	11	9	86	48	10	13	21	52	81
		SL	26	8	2	3	21	9	1	3	9	8	25
		FAC	2	2	0	0	6	1	0	0	0	0	0
		Utd League	2	1	0	0	1	0	0	0	1	0	3
		SCC	3	0	0	0	0	0	1	1	1	3	1
		SSC	1	0	0	0	0	0	0	0	1	1	2
		Wartime	2	1	0	0	4	3	0	0	1	2	3
Thames	25.10.1930	FL	4	1	0	1	6	5	1	1	0	2	1
Tooting & Mitcham United	25.11.1950	FAC	1	0	0	0	0	0	1	0	0	3	2
Torquay United	1.10.1927	FL	64	17	9	6	67	33	8	8	16	29	54
		FLC	1	0	0	0	0	0	1	0	0	2	1
		Wartime	4	2	0	0	7	0	0	1	1	0	1
Tottenham Hotspur	24.9.1902	FL	10	2	0	3	6	9	1	2	2	4	6
		SL	10	3	1	1	8	3	0	3	2	5	10
		FLC	2	0	0	1	0	1	0	1	0	1	1
		SE League	2	0	0	1	1	3	0	0	1	0	3
		Wartime	4	1	0	1	5	4	1	0	1	2	3
Tranmere Rovers	25.1.1964	FL	22	5	4	2	16	11	4	2	5	15	21
		FLC	2	1	0	0	3	1	1	0	0	4	2
Trowbridge	29.11.1947	FAC	2	1	0	0	5	0	0	1	0	1	1
Tunbridge Wells United/ Tunbridge Wells Rangers	27.11.1937	FAC	2	2	0	0	10	1	0	0	0	0	0
Walsall	22.10.1927	FL	66	21	6	6	74	38	10	9	14	40	50
		FAC	7	1	0	0	4	3	0	2	2	3	5
		AMC	1	1	0	0	4	2	0	0	0	0	0
Walthamstow Avenue	8.12.1945	FAC	2	1	0	0	4	2	0	1	0	1	1
Walton & Hersham	24.11.1973	FAC	2	0	0	1	0	4	0	1	0	0	0
Watford	14.2.1903	FL	86	23	11	9	73	40	12	14	17	47	61
		SL	24	7	1	4	26	12	2	3	7	11	25
		SL Test	1	0	0	0	0	0	1	0	0	5	3
		FAC	9	1	1	0	5	4	3	1	3	8	9
		SE League	2	1	0	0	5	1	0	0	1	1	6
		Utd League	4	1	0	1	4	3	1	0	1	5	3
		SCC	3	0	0	0	0	0	3	0	0	5	2
		Wartime	15	4	3	1	18	16	0	3	4	8	24
Wellingborough Town	5.9.1903	SL	4	2	0	0	8	1	1	0	1	6	3
West Bromwich Albion	22.9.1976	FL	18	3	3	3	10	9	0	4	5	4	17
		FLC	1	0	0	0	0	0	1	0	0	2	0
		FMC	1	0	0	1	1	2	0	0	0	0	0

Record against other clubs — West Ham United to York City

Club	First encounter	Competition	P	Home W	Home D	Home L	Home F	Home A	Away & Neutral W	Away & Neutral D	Away & Neutral L	Away & Neutral F	Away & Neutral A
West Ham United	1.10.1902	FL	10	4	0	1	9	3	0	2	3	4	8
		SL	24	8	3	1	22	7	1	6	5	7	17
		FAC	6	0	2	0	3	3	1	0	3	2	7
		FLC	1	0	0	0	0	0	0	0	1	0	1
		SE League	2	0	0	1	2	3	0	0	1	0	5
		SCC	3	0	1	0	0	0	0	1	1	3	4
		FMC	1	0	0	0	0	0	0	0	1	0	2
		Wartime	12	0	1	5	6	14	0	0	6	10	30
West Hampstead	26.10.1901	SL	2	1	0	0	4	0	0	0	1	1	3
Wigan Athletic	20.10.1987	FL	4	2	0	0	2	0	1	1	0	5	4
Wimbledon	2.10.1984	FL	4	2	0	0	4	1	0	1	1	0	1
		FMC	1	1	0	0	3	2	0	0	0	0	0
Wisbech Town	13.11.1965	FAC	1	1	0	0	10	1	0	0	0	0	0
Woking	5.12.1992	FAC	2	0	1	0	1	1	1	0	0	2	1
Wolverhampton Wanderers	24.9.1969	FL	14	4	3	0	17	6	6	0	1	14	7
		FAC	1	0	0	1	2	3	0	0	0	0	0
		FLC	1	0	0	1	2	3	0	0	0	0	0
Workington	24.8.1963	FL	6	1	1	1	4	3	0	0	3	1	4
Worthing	15.10.1932	FAC	1	1	0	0	7	1	0	0	0	0	0
Wrexham	10.12.1932	FL	18	6	1	2	21	15	2	4	3	6	9
		FAC	5	0	2	0	1	1	1	1	1	5	6
		FLC	1	0	0	1	0	2	0	0	0	0	0
Wycombe Wanderers	8.3.1902	SL	4	2	0	0	6	0	0	1	1	1	3
Yeovil Town/ Yeovil & Petters United	26.11.1938	FAC	2	0	0	0	0	0	1	0	1	5	3
York City	7.10.1963	FL	14	5	1	1	17	6	5	0	2	10	8

Longest sequences of ...

§ indicates a record extending over more than one season; the record within one season only is also shown in these instances. Some records were set in the abnormal conditions of wartime football. In these cases the peacetime record is shown in brackets. The date given is for the first match of the sequence.

	Wins		Draws		Defeats		Goals for		Goals against	
Home	14	13.9.1975	4	20.1.1934	7	16.9.1944	51§	30.10.1954	20§	6.12.1941
			"	12.10.1940	(6	18.11.1972)	25	20.8.1955	(18§	22.4.1972)
			"	23.9.1972	(6	29.8.1973)			15	12.8.1972
			"	26.11.1977	(6	1.1.1987)				
			"	16.2.1980						
Away & Neutral	5	9.10.1926	5	5.2.1949	25§	28.10.1939	15§	4.2.1956	61§	18.2.1939
					18	28.10.1939	"	9.1.1960	(31§	14.4.1928)
					(10§	1.4.1905)	13	9.1.1960	22	25.8.1928
					(10§	27.3.1982)	"	13.10.1962	"	7.9.1974
					(9	11.11.1972)				
					(9	16.12.1989)				
All matches	10	2.10.1926	6	16.2.1980	13	11.11.1972	31§	4.2.1956	36§	6.12.1941
							19	27.10.1945	22	6.12.1941
							(18	14.11.1953)	(19§	2.5.1925)
									(18	3.10.1903)
									(18	29.8.1925)

Longest sequences without a ...

§ indicates a record extending over more than one season; the record within one season only is also shown in these instances. Some records were set in the abnormal conditions of wartime football. In these cases the peacetime record is shown in brackets. The date given is for the first match of the sequence.

	Win		Draw		Defeat		Goal for		Goal against	
Home	11	20.9.1972	27§	24.12.1904	31§	13.9.1975	4	6.1.1962	6	7.2.1970
			21	24.8.1955	24	22.8.1964			"	17.1.1976
									"	29.12.1976
Away & Neutral	31§	18.3.1939	33§	11.4.1936	9§	7.3.1910	6	12.3.1921	5	25.9.1948
	18	28.10.1939	23	29.8.1936	9	22.1.1938	"	15.12.1934		
	(20§	15.12.1934)			"	10.10.1987	"	24.11.1956		
	(20§	20.3.1982)					"	4.12.1976		
	(16	10.10.1903)								
	(16	7.9.1991)								
All matches	16	21.10.1972	27§	22.11.1941	17	3.10.1987	6§	22.4.1922	7	22.12.1923
			26	2.10.1943			6	8.11.1924		
			"	10.9.1975			"	23.9.1970		

291

Most in a season ...

Qualification is 42 or more games of a regular Football League or Southern League season. Where the best (or an equal) record in proportion to the number of games played is different, this is shown in brackets even if the season consisted of fewer than 42 games. The Football League record is shown in brackets when the club record comes from the Southern League.

	Wins		Draws		Defeats		Goals for		Goals against		Points	
Home	20 (8 (5	1955–56 1901–02) 1902–03)	10	1970–71	10	1962–63 1973–74	73 (21	1955–56 1902–03)	38 (29	1962–63 1903–04)	42 (2/win) (16 (10 52 (3/win)	1955–56 1901–02 1902–03 1987–88
Away	12	1971–72	13 (14	1948–49 1905–06)	18	1974–75	43 (13	1971–72 1902–03)	61	1958–59	30 (2/win) 32 (3/win)	1971–72 1987–88
Home & Away	29 (7	1955–56 1902–03)	18	1948–49	23 (18	1988–89 1991–92 1905–06)	112 (34	1955–56 1902–03)	90	1958–59	65 (2/win) (15 84 (3/win)	1955–56 1971–72 1902–03 1987–88

Fewest in a season ...

Qualification is 42 or more games of a regular Football League or Southern League season. Where the best (or an equal) record in proportion to the number of games played is different, this is shown in brackets even if the season consisted of fewer than 42 games. The Football League record is shown in brackets when the club record comes from the Southern League.

	Wins		Draws		Defeats		Goals for		Goals against		Points	
Home	7 (5	1959–60 1961–62 1962–63 1972–73 1986–87 1991–92 1903–04)	2 (0 (0	1909–10 1928–29 1929–30 1955–56 1901–02) 1902–03)	0 (0 (0	1964–65 1901–02) 1902–03)	22	1986–87	11 (4	1909–10 1978–79 1984–85 1901–02)	20 (2/win) 27 (3/win) (28	1947–48 1962–63 1986–87 1991–92)
Away	1	1972–73 1982–83	0 (0	1936–37 1901–02)	4	1948–49	12 (6	1921–22 1923–24 1905–06)	17	1909–10 1977–78	7(2/win) (4 9 (3/win)	1972–73 1974–75 1905–06) 1982–83
Home & Away	8 (6	1972–73 1903–04)	5 (0	1936–37 1901–02)	6 (FL 8 (FL 8 (FL 8	1909–10 1971–72 1977–78 1987–88)	37	1986–87	28 (FL 34 (FL 34	1909–10 1922–23) 1984–85)	29 (2/win) 39 (3/win)	1972–73 1986–87

Most frequent opponents

Comp	Games	Club
All comps	144	Watford
FL D1	8	13 clubs
FL D2	24	Sunderland
FL D3	24	Walsall
FL D4	4	19 clubs
FL D3(S)	62	Exeter City
"	"	Northampton Town
"	"	Southend United
"	"	Swindon Town
"	"	Watford
FL total	88	Bristol Rovers
"	"	Swindon Town
FAC	10	Norwich City
FLC	7	Northampton Town
Wartime	18	Crystal Palace
SL total	26	Bristol Rovers
"	"	Gillingham/New Brompton
"	"	Millwall
"	"	Northampton Town
"	"	Plymouth Argyle
"	"	Queen's Park Rangers
"	"	Southampton
"	"	Swindon Town

Most league 'doubles'

	Doubles	Season
For	8 " "	1936–37 1957–58 1964–65
Against	6 " "	1943–44 1980–81 1991–92

Most games in a season

Games	Season	Competitions			
63	1912–13	38 SL	3 FAC	16 S Alliance	6 SCC
59	1907–08	38 SL	5 FAC	12 WL	4 SCC
"	1913–14	38 SL	4 FAC	16 S Alliance	1 SCC
"	1992–93	46 FL	5 FAC	4 FLC	4 AMC
58	1908–09	40 SL	1 FAC	14 WL	3 SCC
"	1966–67	46 FL	6 FAC	6 FLC	

Most and least settled line-ups

Within one season only. The date given is the first game of the sequence.

	Games	Date
Most settled	11 without a change	17.11.1934
Least settled (peacetime)	36 with a change	21.10.1939
	35 with a change †	20.9.1902

† two matches played on the same day (18.10.1902) are counted once only

Albion scores of 8 or more

Score	Opponents	Comp	Ven	Date
14–2	Brighton Amateurs	FAC Q1	(h)	4.10.1902
12–0	Shoreham	FAC Q2	(a)	18.10.1902
"	Shoreham	FAC Q1	(h)	1.10.1932
10–1	Wisbech Town	FAC R1	(h)	13.11.1965
9–0	Hastings & St L.	FAC Q3	(a)	29.10.1932
9–1	Hitchin Town	SE League	(h)	25.3.1903
"	Newport County	FL D3(S)	(h)	18.4.1951
"	Southend United	FL D3	(h)	27.11.1965
9–2	Grays United	Utd League	(h)	30.4.1906
9–3	Swindon Town	FL D3(S)	(h)	18.9.1926
9–4	Southampton	Wartime	(h)	30.12.1939
8–0	Southall	SL D2	(a)	28.2.1903
"	Luton Town	Wartime	(h)	9.1.1943
"	Luton Town	Wartime	(h)	22.1.1944
"	Portsmouth	Wartime	(h)	28.4.1945
8–1	Newport County	FAC R1	(h)	19.11.1955
8–2	Merthyr Town	FL D3(S)	(a)	1.2.1930
"	Chelsea	Wartime	(h)	31.1.1942
8–3	Reading	FL D3(S)	(h)	27.4.1957

Opponents' scores of 8 or more

Score	Opponents	Comp	Ven	Date
0–18	Norwich City	Wartime	(a)	25.12.1940
0–10	Crystal Palace	Wartime	(a)	6.4.1940
1–10	Crystal Palace	Wartime	(a)	3.1.1942
0–9	Middlesbrough	FL D2	(a)	23.8.1958
3–9	Reading	Wartime	(h)	21.10.1944
4–9	Brentford	Wartime	(a)	12.9.1942
0–8	Brentford	Wartime	(a)	4.3.1944
"	Northampton Town	FLC R4 rep	(a)	1.11.1966
1–8	Crystal Palace	Wartime	(h)	26.9.1942
2–8	Southend United	Wartime	(a)	16.3.1940
"	Charlton Athletic	Wartime	(a)	7.2.1942
"	Bristol Rovers	FL D3	(h)	1.12.1973

Draws with 8 or more goals

Score	Opponents	Comp	Ven	Date
5–5	Grays United	FAC Q3	(h)	1.11.1902
4–4	Swindon Town	FL D3(S)	(a)	29.9.1934
"	Reading	FL D3(S)	(a)	20.4.1935
"	Chester	FL D4	(h)	6.2.1965

Biggest victories by competition

* played at neutral venue

Comp	Home			Away & Neutral		
	Score	Opponents	Date	Score	Opponents	Date
FL D1	4–1	Manchester City	29.12.1979	3–0	Crystal Palace	18.4.1981
	"	Coventry City	7.3.1981			
	"	Manchester City	3.10.1981			
FL D2	7–0	Charlton Athletic	1.10.1983	5–4	Bristol Rovers	3.10.1959
FL D3	9–1	Southend United	27.11.1965	5–0	Halifax Town	4.3.1972
FL D4	6–0	Notts County	10.10.1964	4–1	Barrow	12.12.1964
	"			"	Stockport County	16.4.1965
FL D3(S)	9–1	Newport County	18.4.1951	8–2	Merthyr Town	1.2.1930
FAC	14–2	Brighton Amateurs	4.10.1902	12–0	Shoreham	18.10.1902
(proper)	10–1	Wisbech Town	13.11.1965	6–0	Cheltenham Town	4.12.1935
				"	Rotherham United*	8.2.1960
FLC	5–2	Bradford City	25.9.1985	4–2	Tranmere Rovers	3.9.1980
Wartime	9–4	Southampton	30.12.1939	5–3	Brentford	3.2.1945
SL D1	7–0	New Brompton	4.11.1911	5–0	Wellingborough T.	17.9.1904
SL D2	5–0	Chesham Town	25.10.1902	8–0	Southall	28.2.1903
	"	Wycombe Wand.	27.12.1902			

Biggest defeats by competition

Comp	Home			Away & Neutral		
	Score	Opponents	Date	Score	Opponents	Date
FL D1	0–4	Arsenal	18.8.1979	0–5	West Bromwich A.	1.9.1982
				"	Luton Town	18.9.1982
FL D2	4–6	Middlesbrough	20.12.1958	0–9	Middlesbrough	23.8.1958
FL D3	2–8	Bristol Rovers	1.12.1973	0–6	Walsall	1.10.1974
FL D4	1–3	Carlisle United	25.4.1964	1–4	Bradford City	6.4.1965
FL D3(S)	0–6	Plymouth Argyle	18.11.1950	0–7	Reading	11.11.1950
				"	Bristol Rovers	29.11.1952
FAC	1–5	Manchester City	23.2.1924	2–7	Norwich City	20.11.1946
FLC	1–5	Portsmouth	25.9.1962	0–8	Northampton Town	1.11.1966
Wartime	3–9	Reading	21.10.1944	0–18	Norwich City	25.12.1940
SL D1	0–5	Portsmouth	16.12.1905	0–5	West Ham United	13.2.1904
				"	Portsmouth	21.4.1906
				"	Millwall	10.4.1920
SL D2		No home defeats		0–3	Grays United	8.11.1902

Average league attendances

Figures include all regular-season Southern League and Football League matches. Wartime seasons 1939–46 include league matches only.
Season 1939–40 includes the Football League South 'B' and South 'D' competitions. An asterisk (*) indicates one unknown attendance.

Season	Home agg.	Home ave.	Away ave.	Season	Home agg.	Home ave.	Away ave.	Season	Home agg.	Home ave.	Away ave.
1901–02	**10,600	**1,767	?	1935–36	160,833	7,659	7,276	1964–65	413,414	17,975	7,138
1902–03	12,900	2,580	?	1936–37	224,008	10,667	10,723	1965–66	292,731	12,727	8,510
1903–04	85,200	5,012	*4,531	1937–38	213,442	10,164	10,847	1966–67	270,128	11,745	7,272
1904–05	81,233	4,778	5,671	1938–39	176,224	8,392	8,800	1967–68	240,530	10,458	6,918
1905–06	80,500	4,735	6,118	1939–40	34,186	1,899	3,140	1968–69	244,154	10,615	6,971
1906–07	124,620	6,559	6,263	1940–41	22,600	1,614	1,524	1969–70	335,227	14,575	7,703
1907–08	101,000	5,316	6,605	1941–42	60,700	4,047	3,619	1970–71	225,463	9,802	6,695
1908–09	103,000	5,150	5,600	1942–43	44,200	3,157	3,681	1971–72	406,617	17,679	7,590
1909–10	143,500	6,833	6,022	1943–44	60,263	4,018	5,032	1972–73	297,945	14,188	11,659
1910–11	128,500	6,763	*9,230	1944–45	68,221	4,548	5,764	1973–74	249,494	10,848	7,056
1911–12	113,500	5,974	7,421	1945–46	59,284	5,928	7,931	1974–75	270,358	11,755	6,806
1912–13	96,000	5,053	7,579	1946–47	172,563	8,217	11,262	1975–76	352,299	15,317	8,422
1913–14	105,600	5,558	8,342	1947–48	241,139	11,483	12,247	1976–77	464,202	20,183	10,545
1914–15	60,200	3,168	*4,461	1948–49	372,308	17,729	15,137	1977–78	530,545	25,264	15,669
1919–20	193,335	9,206	8,729	1949–50	296,529	14,120	14,199	1978–79	463,558	22,074	15,399
1920–21	196,000	9,333	10,981	1950–51	256,752	11,163	12,362	1979–80	520,685	24,795	24,733
1921–22	170,000	8,095	9,476	1951–52	410,105	17,831	14,104	1980–81	398,345	18,969	21,886
1922–23	180,273	8,584	9,219	1952–53	371,939	16,171	10,836	1981–82	383,192	18,247	20,236
1923–24	165,557	7,884	8,499	1953–54	434,231	18,880	13,213	1982–83	308,204	14,676	16,986
1924–25	165,944	7,902	8,936	1954–55	295,207	12,835	11,791	1983–84	258,008	12,286	10,909
1925–26	170,282	8,109	7,519	1955–56	352,433	15,323	11,842	1984–85	247,565	11,789	8,181
1926–27	198,494	9,452	8,435	1956–57	266,940	11,606	10,299	1985–86	204,156	9,722	7,407
1927–28	160,231	7,630	7,572	1957–58	380,569	16,546	12,804	1986–87	173,922	8,282	8,180
1928–29	144,295	6,871	8,140	1958–59	471,655	22,460	17,020	1987–88	205,491	8,934	5,248
1929–30	178,026	8,477	7,458	1959–60	383,702	18,272	17,258	1988–89	207,902	9,039	9,610
1930–31	149,444	7,116	6,854	1960–61	323,625	15,411	14,041	1989–90	199,135	8,658	10,626
1931–32	170,516	8,119	8,111	1961–62	277,324	13,206	12,909	1990–91	192,887	8,386	10,264
1932–33	138,584	6,599	6,972	1962–63	228,638	9,941	9,002	1991–92	184,239	8,010	10,408
1933–34	132,499	6,309	7,596	1963–64	211,846	9,211	5,528	1992–93	154,068	6,699	5,360
1934–35	137,966	6,570	8,000								

Home attendance records

All matches played at the Goldstone ground except
* Dyke Road Field   † County Ground

Att	Opponents	Date	Comp
?	Shoreham*	7.9.1901	Friendly
1,200	Brighton Athletic †	21.9.1901	FAC Prelim.
2,000	Eastbourne †	5.10.1901	FAC Q1
"	Hastings & St L. †	19.10.1901	FAC Q2
2,500	Clapton †	2.11.1901	FAC Q3
3,500	Blackpool †	26.12.1901	Friendly
4,200	Fulham	31.1.1903	SL D2
4,500	Bristol Rovers	12.9.1903	SL D1
5,000	Swindon Town	19.9.1903	SL D1
"	Northampton Town	3.10.1903	SL D1
7,000	Reading	28.12.1903	SL D1
8,500	Portsmouth	23.1.1904	SL D1
9,000	Portsmouth	24.9.1904	SL D1
10,500	Portsmouth	8.9.1906	SL D1
11,000	Fulham	9.3.1907	SL D1
12,000	Liverpool	5.2.1908	FAC R2 rep
"	Crystal Palace	26.12.1910	SL D1
13,000	Coventry City	4.2.1911	FAC R2
15,727	Clapton Orient	31.1.1914	FAC R2
16,972	Oldham Athletic	8.1.1921	FAC R1
20,260	Cardiff City	29.1.1921	FAC R2
22,241	Huddersfield Town	28.1.1922	FAC R2
23,642	Corinthians	13.1.1923	FAC R1
27,450	Everton	2.2.1924	FAC R2
32,310	West Ham United	18.2.1933	FAC R5
36,747	Fulham	27.12.1958	FL D2

Home league attendance records

All matches played at the Goldstone Ground except
† County Ground

Att	Opponents	Date
1,500	West Hampstead †	26.10.1901
1,900	Fulham †	30.11.1901
2,000	Grays United †	7.12.1901
"	Southall †	8.2.1902
2,200	Southall	13.9.1902
3,000	Wycombe Wand.	27.12.1902
4,200	Fulham	31.1.1903
4,500	Bristol Rovers	12.9.1903
5,000	Swindon Town	19.9.1903
"	Northampton Town	3.10.1903
7,000	Reading	28.12.1903
8,500	Portsmouth	23.1.1904
9,000	Portsmouth	24.9.1904
10,500	Portsmouth	8.9.1906
11,000	Fulham	9.3.1907
"	Swindon Town	23.4.1910
12,000	Crystal Palace	26.12.1910
12,300	Crystal Palace	10.4.1914
13,000	Cardiff City	20.3.1920
14,000	Southend United	2.4.1920
"	Crystal Palace	25.12.1920
"	Norwich City	25.3.1921
15,000	Portsmouth	25.12.1922
15,457	Luton Town	26.12.1923
15,732	Bristol Rovers	26.12.1924
19,193	Brentford	26.12.1929
19,572	Notts County	24.4.1948
21,593	Swindon Town	21.8.1948
22,994	Notts County	4.12.1948
25,485	Millwall	22.1.1949
29,140	Plymouth Argyle	23.4.1952
31,025	Southampton	27.3.1954
31,038	Watford	30.4.1958
36,747	Fulham	27.12.1958

Home attendances over 30,000

Att	Opponents	Date	Comp
36,747	Fulham	27.12.1958	FL D2
35,000	Chelsea	18.2.1967	FAC R4
34,766	Rochdale	3.5.1972	FL D3
33,500	Derby County	26.10.1976	FLC R4
33,300	Crystal Palace	24.2.1976	FL D3
33,431	Blackpool	29.4.1978	FL D2
32,979	Southampton	2.1.1978	FL D2
32,647	Tottenham Hotspur	15.4.1978	FL D2
32,634	West Ham United	28.10.1978	FL D2
32,539	Wolverhampton W.	24.9.1969	FLC R3
32,310	West Ham United	18.2.1933	FAC R5
32,036	Reading	27.3.1970	FL D3
31,828	Aston Villa	22.8.1959	FL D2
31,423	Darlington	26.4.1965	FL D4
31,203	Charlton Athletic	25.4.1978	FL D2
31,038	Watford	30.4.1958	FL D3(S)
31,025	Southampton	27.3.1954	FL D3(S)
30,864	Leyton Orient	18.4.1956	FL D3(S)
30,859	Charlton Athletic	13.4.1979	FL D2
30,756	Sheffield Wed.	3.5.1977	FL D3
30,600	AFC Bournemouth	27.12.1971	FL D3

Away attendances over 40,000

* played at neutral venue

Att	Opponents	Date	Comp
100,000	Manchester United*	21.5.1983	FAC F
92,000	Manchester United*	26.5.1983	FAC F rep
59,940	Notts County*	2.6.1991	FL D2 PO F
56,469	Newcastle United	15.2.1930	FAC R5
54,852	Chelsea	22.2.1967	FAC R4 rep
54,627	Sheffield Wed.*	16.4.1983	FAC SF
52,641	Manchester United	6.10.1979	FL D1
48,613	Tottenham Hotspur	19.11.1977	FL D2
44,868	Liverpool	20.2.1983	FAC R5
43,760	Corinthians*	22.1.1923	FAC R1 2rep
43,202	Arsenal	26.1.1980	FAC R4
42,747	Liverpool	22.3.1980	FL D1
42,208	Manchester United	10.1.1981	FL D1
42,199	Manchester United	3.1.1981	FAC R3
41,911	Manchester United	28.11.1981	FL D1
40,000	Nigeria XI	c. 30.9.1981	Res friendly

Home attendances under 3,000 since 1920

Not including wartime games

Att	Opponents	Date	Comp
1,607	AFC Bournemouth	9.12.1992	AMC Group
1,664	Walsall	18.1.1993	AMC R2
1,875	Exeter City	17.2.1993	AMC S QF
2,093	Norwich City	2.2.1929	FL D3(S)
2,200	Aberdare Athletic	25.3.1925	FL D3(S)
2,222	Queen's Park R.	23.10.1935	SSC R2
2,500	Brentford	27.12.1924	FL D3(S)
2,588	Charlton Athletic	19.12.1990	FMC R2
2,620	Watford	26.4.1939	FL D3(S)
2,712	Bournemouth & B.A.	11.3.1925	FL D3(S)
2,728	Bournemouth & B.A.	10.11.1934	FL D3(S)
2,737	Walsall	22.10.1927	FL D3(S)
2,796	Wimbledon	23.10.1991	FMC R2
2,806	Bristol Rovers	29.4.1939	FL D3(S)
2,965	Walsall	25.4.1931	FL D3(S)

Home attendances under 5,000 since 1946

Att	Opponents	Date	Comp
1,607	AFC Bournemouth	9.12.1992	AMC Group
1,664	Walsall	18.1.1993	AMC R2
1,875	Exeter City	17.2.1993	AMC S QF
2,588	Charlton Athletic	19.12.1990	FMC R2
2,796	Wimbledon	23.10.1991	FMC R2
3,565	Southend United	25.11.1987	AMC Prelim
3,770	Coventry City	7.5.1955	FL D3(S)
3,794	Birmingham City	1.10.1986	FMC R1
3,834	Northampton Town	29.8.1990	FLC R1 Lg1
4,125	Colchester United	26.8.1992	FLC R1 Lg2
4,146	Southend United	15.1.1947	FL D3(S)
4,175	Exeter City	23.3.1955	FL D3(S)
4,420	Grimsby Town	6.11.1991	FL D2
4,502	Brentford	9.10.1991	FLC R2 Lg2
4,649	West Bromwich A.	2.10.1985	FMC Prelim
4,649	Southend United	7.9.1988	FLC R1 Lg2
4,650	Wrexham	16.11.1960	FLC R3
4,668	Norwich City	8.2.1947	FL D3(S)
4,712	Swansea Town	1.10.1947	FL D3(S)
4,731	Mansfield Town	7.4.1993	FL D2
4,755	Oxford United	1.10.1963	FL D4

Away attendances under 2,000 since 1920

Not including wartime games.   * played at neutral venue.

Att	Opponents	Date	Comp
1,000	Newport County	22.2.1934	SSC R2
1,209	Reading	1.12.1992	AMC Group
1,242	Aberdare Athletic	7.5.1927	FL D3(S)
1,621	Thames	25.10.1930	FL D3(S)
1,683	Doncaster Rovers	23.4.1988	FL D3
1,700	Swindon Town	13.11.1935	SSC R2
1,721	Charlton Athletic	23.3.1927	FL D3(S)
1,741	Aldershot	18.9.1946	FL D3(S)
1,800	Millwall	29.10.1934	SSC R2
1,840	Oldham Athletic*	20.9.1977	FLC R2 2rep
1,889	Thames	14.11.1931	FL D3(S)
1,961	Halifax Town	30.11.1974	FL D3
1,974	Southport	22.2.1964	FL D4
1,984	Merthyr Town	1.2.1930	FL D3(S)

Home attendance records by competition

Comp	Highest			Lowest		
	Att	Opponents	Date	Att	Opponents	Date
FL D1	29,682	Liverpool	10.11.1979	9,845	Birmingham City	25.9.1982
FL D2 (pre 1992)	36,747	Fulham	27.12.1958	4,420	Grimsby Town	6.11.1991
FL D2 (post 1992)				4,731	Mansfield Town	7.4.1993
FL D3	34,766	Rochdale	3.5.1972	5,308	Shrewsbury Town	20.10.1973
FL D4	31,423	Darlington	26.4.1965	4,755	Oxford United	1.10.1963
FL D3(S)	31,038	Watford	30.4.1958	2,093	Norwich City	2.2.1929
FAC	35,000	Chelsea	18.2.1967	1,200	Brighton Athletic	21.9.1901
(proper)				5,457	Scarborough	18.12.1935
FLC	33,500	Derby County	26.10.1976	3,834	Northampton Town	29.8.1990
Wartime	12,000	Arsenal	15.2.1941	300	Charlton Athletic	14.12.1940
	"	Arsenal	11.4.1942			
SL D1	14,000	Southend United	2.4.1920	1,000	Luton Town	17.3.1915
				"	Reading	3.4.1915
SL D2	4,200	Fulham	31.1.1903	meagre	Maidenhead	1.2.1902

Away attendance records by competition

* played at a neutral venue; the record for a non-neutral venue is also given.

Comp	Highest			Lowest		
	Att	Opponents	Date	Att	Opponents	Date
FL D1	52,641	Manchester United	6.10.1979	7,349	Notts County	30.4.1983
FL D2	48,613	Tottenham Hotspur	19.11.1977	2,033	Wigan Athletic	27.2.1993
(pre 1992)				2,684	Shrewsbury Town	16.9.1986
FL D3	32,368	Portsmouth	27.12.1976	1,683	Doncaster Rovers	23.4.1988
FL D4	13,429	Oxford United	31.3.1965	1,974	Southport	22.2.1964
FL D3(S)	34,283	Notts County	11.3.1950	1,242	Aberdare Athletic	7.5.1927
FAC	100,000	Manchester United*	21.5.1983	1,200	Glossop	9.12.1905
	56,469	Newcastle United	15.2.1930			
(proper)				2,241	Walsall*	17.12.1969
				4,800	Barnet	2.1.1982
FLC	30,672	Nottingham Forest	13.12.1978	1,840	Oldham Athletic*	20.9.1977
				3,072	Southend United	30.8.1988
Wartime	19,068	Cardiff City	20.10.1945	600	Watford	21.2.1942
SL D1	25,000	Millwall	22.10.1910	1,000	Northampton Town	30.1.1904
				"	Southampton	17.2.1906
				"	Reading	17.4.1912
SL D2	several 1,000s	Fulham	23.3.1902	?		

Lowest admission price

Lowest cost of adult terrace admission.
Prices apply to club members from 1988.

Seasons	Cost	Seasons	Cost
1901–15	6d.	1973–75	50p
1919–41	1s.	1975–77	65p
1941–42	1s. 1d.	1977–78	£1
1942–46	1s. 6d.	1978–79	£1.30
1946–51	1s. 3d.	1979–80	£1.50
1951–52	1s. 6d.	1980–82	£2
1952–55	1s. 9d.	1982–85	£2.50
1955–60	2s.	1985–88	£3
1960–64	2s. 6d.	1988–89	£3.50
1964–68	4s.	1989–90	£4
1968–70	5s.	1990–91	£4.50
1970–72	6s./30p	1991–93	£5
1972–73	40p		

Cup victories over clubs of a higher standard

Opponents	Status	Score	Ven	Comp	Date
Glossop	FL D2	1–0	(a)	FAC Q4	9.12.1905
Preston North End	FL D1	1–0	(n)	FAC R1 2rep	20.1.1908
Aston Villa	FL D1	1–0	(n)	FA Ch. Shield	5.9.1910
Leeds City	FL D2	3–1	(a)	FAC R1	14.1.1911
Oldham Athletic	FL D1	1–0	(h)	FAC R1 rep	14.1.1914
Clapton Orient	FL D2	3–1	(h)	FAC R2	31.1.1914
Lincoln City	FL D2	2–1	(h)	FAC R1	9.1.1915
Oldham Athletic	FL D1	4–1	(h)	FAC R1	8.1.1921
Sheffield United	FL D1	1–0	(h)	FAC R1	7.1.1922
Barnsley	FL D2	1–0	(h)	FAC R1 rep	16.1.1924
Everton	FL D1	5-2	(h)	FAC R2	2.2.1924
Grimsby Town	FL D1	1–0	(a)	FAC R3 rep	14.1.1930
Portsmouth	FL D1	1–0	(a)	FAC R4	25.1.1930
Leicester City	FL D1	2–1	(a)	FAC R3	10.1.1931
Chelsea	FL D1	2–1	(h)	FAC R3	14.1.1933
Bradford (P.A.)	FL D2	2–1	(h)	FAC R4	28.1.1933
Chesterfield	FL D2	2–1	(h)	FAC R3	6.1.1951
Norwich City	FL D2	1–0	(a)	FLC R2	14.9.1966
Coventry City	FL D2	3–1	(a)	FLC R3 rep	11.10.1966
Oxford United	FL D2	2–0	(h)	FLC R1	14.8.1968
Portsmouth	FL D2	1–0	(h)	FLC R1	13.8.1969
Birmingham City	FL D2	2–0	(h)	FLC R2	3.9.1969
Ipswich Town	FL D1	2–1	(h)	FLC R2 rep	7.9.1976
West Bromwich A.	FL D1	2–0	(a)	FLC R3	22.9.1976
Liverpool	FL D1	2–0	(h)	FAC R4	29.1.1984
Newcastle United	FL D1	2–0	(a)	FAC R3	4.1.1986
AFC Bournemouth	FL D2	2–0	(h)	FAC R3	9.1.1988
Luton Town	FL D1	4–1	(h)	FAC R3	6.1.1990
Wimbledon	FL D1	3–2	(h)	FMC R2	23.10.1991
Portsmouth	FL D1	1–0	(h)	FAC R3	2.1.1993

Cup defeats by clubs of a lower standard

Opponents	Status	Score	Ven	Comp	Date
Darlington	N. Eastern Lge	1–2	(a)	FAC R1	13.1.1912
Yeovil & Petters Utd	Southern League	1–2	(a)	FAC R1	26.11.1938
Bradford City	FL D3	0–2	(h)	FAC R3	10.1.1959
Wrexham	FL D4	0–2	(h)	FLC R3	16.11.1960
Bedford Town	Southern League	1–2	(a)	FAC R2 rep	6.12.1965
Swansea Town	FL D4	1–2	(a)	FAC R2	6.1.1968
Northampton Town	FL D4	1–2	(h)	FAC R2	7.12.1968
Bristol Rovers	FL D3	0–4	(a)	FLC R2	5.9.1972
Walton & Hersham	Isthmian League	0–4	(h)	FAC R1 rep	28.11.1973
Leatherhead	Isthmian League	0–1	(h)	FAC R3	4.1.1975
Brentford	FL D4	1–2	(a)	FLC R1 Lg1	19.8.1975
Barnsley	FL D2	1–4	(a)	FLC R3	10.11.1981
Oxford United	FL D3	0–3	(h)	FAC R4	23.1.1982
Aldershot	FL D4	0–3	(a)	FLC R2 Lg2	9.10.1984
Southend United	FL D3	0–2	(a)	FLC R1 Lg1	30.8.1988
Southend United	FL D3	0–1	(h)	FLC R1 Lg2	7.9.1988
Brentford	FL D3	0–3	(h)	FLC R1 Lg1	23.8.1989
Northampton Town	FL D4	0–2	(h)	FLC R1 Lg1	29.8.1990
Brentford	FL D3	1–4	(a)	FLC R2 Lg1	24.9.1991
Bolton Wanderers	FL D3	1–2	(a)	FAC R4	25.1.1992

Colours

Seasons	Shirts	Shorts	Seasons	Shirts	Shorts
1901–04	Blue	White	1974–75	White, blue trim	White, blue trim
1904–05	Blue-and-white stripes	White	1975–77	Blue-and-white stripes	Blue
1905–06	Blue-and-white stripes, white collar	White	1977–80	Blue-and-white stripes, white sleeves, blue trim	Blue, white trim
1906–10	Blue-and-white stripes	White	1980–83	Blue, white trim	Blue, white trim
1910–14	Blue-and-white stripes, blue collar	White		(sponsored by British Caledonian)	
1914–48	Blue-and-white stripes	White	1983–86	Blue, white trim	White, blue trim
1948–51	Blue, white sleeves and collars	White		(sponsored by Phoenix Brewery)	
1951–58	Blue-and-white stripes	White	1986–87	Blue, white trim	White, blue trim
1958–59	Narrow blue stripes on white	White		(sponsored by Nobo)	
1959–63	Blue-and-white stripes	White	1987–89	Blue-and-white stripes	Blue, white trim
1963–64	Blue-and-white stripes, blue collars	White		(sponsored by Nobo)	
1964–70	Blue, white sleeves and collars	White	1989–91	Blue-and-white stripes, white sleeves, blue trim	Blue, red trim
1970–71	White, blue trim	White, blue trim		(sponsored by Nobo)	
1971–72	Blue-and-white stripes	Blue, white trim	1991–93	Blue-and-white stripes, white trim	Blue-and-white stripes
1972–74	Blue-and-white stripes	Blue		(sponsored by TSB Bank)	

Managerial records

The Southern League and Football League totals do not include test and play-off matches.

Manager	Career		P	W	D	L	F	A	W	D	L	F	A
John Jackson	June 1901 – March 1905	All	125	38	10	16	169	80	19	12	30	96	111
		SL	87	25	8	11	88	51	10	11	22	61	75
Frank Scott-Walford	March 1905 – April 1908	All	168	46	21	16	147	91	16	20	49	83	157
		SL	109	30	13	12	87	59	10	9	35	45	97
Jack Robson	April 1908 – December 1914	All	345	114	31	19	366	126	45	53	83	155	256
		SL	262	90	25	14	282	99	25	42	66	101	192
Alf Nelmes (acting)	December 1914 – May 1915	All	21	6	3	3	13	10	1	1	7	8	19
		SL	18	5	2	3	11	9	1	1	6	8	16
Charlie Webb	June 1919 – May 1947	All	1215	349	121	136	1348	790	137	131	341	719	1277
		SL	42	11	5	5	43	28	3	3	15	17	44
		FL	840	266	85	69	889	411	95	106	219	440	717
Tommy Cook	May 1947 – November 1947	All (FL)	17	2	1	6	6	18	1	2	5	7	17
Don Welsh	November 1947 – March 1951	All	152	36	23	16	122	92	15	31	31	78	147
		FL	141	32	23	16	111	90	14	29	27	70	133
Billy Lane	March 1951 – May 1961	All	493	144	60	43	572	298	76	59	111	344	448
		FL	462	137	55	38	531	275	72	55	105	319	425
George Curtis	June 1961 – February 1963	All	75	10	13	15	42	64	6	7	24	40	91
		FL	71	10	13	13	41	56	6	7	22	38	84
Joe Wilson (acting)	February 1963 – April 1963	All (FL)	9	3	0	1	7	3	2	1	2	9	11
Archie Macaulay	April 1963 – October 1968	All	286	75	37	30	277	144	32	43	69	160	245
		FL	254	68	30	28	245	131	27	41	60	139	213
selection committee	November 1968	All (FL)	2	0	0	0	0	0	0	0	2	1	4
Freddie Goodwin	November 1968 – May 1970	All	85	29	11	6	85	37	10	11	18	36	51
		FL	74	26	9	4	74	28	9	9	17	33	48
Pat Saward	June 1970 – October 1973	All	159	34	24	21	118	84	23	20	37	88	124
		FL	146	31	23	19	103	77	21	20	32	84	113
Glen Wilson (acting)	October 1973	All (FL)	2	1	0	0	4	0	0	0	1	0	3
Brian Clough	November 1973 – July 1974	All	34	8	3	6	23	27	4	6	7	16	19
		FL	32	8	3	5	23	23	4	5	7	16	19
Peter Taylor	July 1974 – July 1976	All	104	34	12	6	105	44	8	11	33	44	85
		FL	92	32	10	4	96	36	6	9	31	38	81
Alan Mullery	July 1976 – June 1981	All	249	76	27	21	229	108	33	39	53	137	173
		FL	214	68	22	17	205	92	27	33	47	114	149
Mike Bailey	June 1981 – December 1982	All	67	15	9	9	46	36	5	9	20	19	63
		FL	59	13	9	7	41	31	5	7	18	17	57
George Aitken & Jimmy Melia (acting)	December 1982 – March 1983	All	18	3	4	3	14	10	3	1	4	8	12
		FL	13	1	3	3	8	9	1	1	4	5	11
Jimmy Melia	March 1983 – October 1983	All	26	5	3	4	20	12	2	6	6	15	25
		FL	22	4	3	4	16	10	1	5	5	11	18
Chris Cattlin	October 1983 – April 1986	All	134	38	16	12	120	61	22	12	34	80	106
		FL	115	32	16	10	105	54	18	11	28	65	86
George Petchey (acting)	May 1986	All (FL)	1	0	0	0	0	0	0	0	1	0	2
Alan Mullery	May 1986 – January 1987	All	27	5	5	4	14	12	2	3	8	11	23
		FL	24	5	4	3	14	9	2	3	7	11	20
Barry Lloyd	January 1987 –	All	345	85	37	52	270	210	43	37	91	184	281
		FL	293	69	35	42	215	168	37	30	80	158	245

Manager of the Month awards
(Inaugurated 1969)

Pat Saward: Apr. 1971, Dec. 1971, Apr. 1972, Mar. 1973
Alan Mullery: Sep. 1976 (entire League), Feb. 1977, Apr. 1978, Dec. 1978
Chris Cattlin: Jan. 1984, Jan. 1986
Barry Lloyd: Feb. 1988, Apr. 1988

Directors of
The Brighton and Hove Albion Football Club, Limited

* original member of the board

Director	Description	Service
ALDERTON, Reginald Thomas*	Commercial traveller, Hove	1904–05
BROADBRIDGE, George Thomas*	Chartered secretary, London; later Lord Broadbridge of Brighton	1904–05 & 1905–06
BUNKER, Charles Bew*	Fishmonger, Hove	1904
COOTER, Thomas William*	Tailor, Brighton	1904–05
GRINYER, Albert William*	Landlord of Albion Inn, Hove	1904
PARKER, Benjamin*	Landlord of Cliftonville Hotel, Hove	1904–05 & 1905
STEVENS, Frederick S.*	Jeweller and watchmaker, Hove	1904–05
BAKER, William Frederick	Landlord of Standard Hotel, Brighton	1904–05
GADD, Harry	Hotelier, Albion Hotel, Queen's Road, Brighton	1904–05
CLARK, Noah	Fishmonger, Brighton	1904–05 & 1906–30
COHEN, Meyer	Finanacier, Brighton	1904
MERRIMAN, Richard N.C.D.	Brighton	1904 & 1904–05
SMITH, Francis Salter	Merchant, Hove Park Stores	1905
GOODWIN, William Faulkner	Fishmonger, Brighton	1905–40
BLOGG, William Reynolds	Printer, Hove	1905
CARDWELL, Charles John Pullen	Ironmonger and engineer, Brighton	1905
BUTCHER, Cecil Frank	Accountant's clerk, Hove	1905–29
MILES, Henry James	Electrician, Brighton	1905–40
VEY, Peter Thomas	Draper, Brighton	1905–31
BROWN, Charles Frederick	Tailor, Brighton	1906–30 & 1931–36
BANFIELD, Thomas Watts	Ironmonger, Brighton	1906–12
STAFFORD, William Henry	Store owner, Western Road, Brighton	1911–14
HARRINGTON, Thomas	Coachbuilder, Brighton	1914–28
FARR, John Grossmith	Tailor, Brighton	1923–35
BALL, Alfred Ernest	Tax collector, Hove	1923–39
BRAZIER, Henry Percy	Builder and fruit grower, Worthing	1926–33
RIDGE, Luther Herbert Archibald	Solicitor, Hove	1930–43
HILLMAN, Albert Walter	Contractor; Mayor of Hove 1936–40	1933–40
BAYLIS, Charles Horton	Retired gentleman, Hove; ex-director of Reading F.C.	1934–40
NEAL, William Edwin	Company director, Hove	1937–40
SERVICE, Hubert Stanley	Company director, Eastbourne	1939–40
WAKELING, Charles Edward	Accountant; director of greyhound stadium, Hove	1940–51
CAMPBELL, William Charles 'Carlo'	Director of food companies and of greyhound stadium, Hove	1940–58
WHITCHER, Alexander Edward	Mechanical engineer and company director, Haywards Heath	1943–60
PALING, Gerald Richard	Civil servant, Hove	1946–62
HOLLIS, General Sir Leslie Chasemore	Company director, Haywards Heath	1954–60
COVERDALE, Harry	Jeweller, Hove	1954–60
PEMBROKE, Arthur Vaughan	Architect, Hove	1954–63
GREIG, Alexander Hinshelwood	Medical practioner, Hove	1956–62
CLARKE, Cyril Alexander	Company director; Mayor of Hove 1956–58	1958–62
COURTNEY-KING, Eric	Company director, Shoreham-by-Sea	1960–68
WHITING, Thomas Edward	Solicitor, Hove	1960–73
BRAZIER, Anthony David Percy	Company director and son of Henry Brazier, Findon	1960–67
PARIS, Harold James	Building company director, Hove	1962–71
DUPONT, Alfred Norman	Business consultant and director of greyhound stadium, Hove	1962–65 & 1966–67
STRINGER, Leonard Harold	Funeral company director, Hove	1962–73
ARNOLD, Frederick Vernon	Company director, Brighton	1962–64
WISDOM, Norman Joseph	Company director and entertainer, West Chiltington	1964–70
STEVENS, Victor Samuel	Chartered accountant, Dorking	1968–70
DE BOER, Anthony Peter	Company director, Ditchling Common	1968–73
HUTCHISON, George Henry	Farmer, Hove	1969–74
BAMBER, Michael Kelway	Farmer, estate agent and surveyor, property developer, Piddinghoe	1970–84
BLOOM, Harry	Car sales company director, Brighton	1970–80
APPLEBY, Thomas Herbert	Cattle and general haulage contractor, Piltdown	1971–85 & 1990–91
HYAMS, Norman John	Development and investment company director, Wimbledon	1972–83
SMITH, William	Building company director, Hove	1972–79
SIZEN, Dudley Charles	Plastics company director,Lindfield	1973–83 & 1984–91
WICKENDEN, Keith David	Ferry company director; M.P. for Dorking 1979–83	1973–83
BEDSON, Bryan Stanley	Printing company director	1983–89
GREENWOOD, Ronald	Former England manager, Hove	1983–84
CAMPBELL, John Leslie	Marine consultant, Chelwood Gate	1983–92 & 1992–
KENT, Peter Frederick	Visual aids company director, Cuckfield	1984–90 & 1990–92
CROWN, Richard Willard Stanley	Computer company director, Hove	1985
BLOOM, Raymond A.	Company director and hotelier; son of Harry Bloom	1985–
APPLEBY, Gene Queenie May	Wife of Tom Appleby, Little Horsted	1985–90
STANLEY, Gregory Alexander	D.I.Y. company director, Angmering	1985–
SHANNON, Frank	Motor company financial director, Hove	1985–89
CLARKE, Bernard Edward	Accountant, Hove	1988–93
SULLIVAN, Dennis	Advertising executive, Hove	1990–93
ARCHER, William Ernest	D.I.Y. company director, Blackburn	1990–
LLOYD, Barry David	Manager, Brighton and Hove Albion F.C.	1991–

Chairmen

Years	Chairman
Chairmen of club committee:	
1901–02	Daniel Bott
1902–04	Harry Callaghan
Chairmen of Board of Directors:	
1904–05	George Broadbridge
1905–09	William Goodwin
1909–14	Peter Vey
1914–19	Henry Miles
1919–30	Charles Brown
1930–40	William Goodwin
1940	Albert Hillman
1940–51	Charles Wakeling
1951–58	Carlo Campbell
1958–60	Alec Whitcher
1960	Cyril Clarke (acting only)
1960–62	Gerald Paling
1962–68	Eric Courtney-King
1968–72	Tom Whiting
1972–73	Len Stringer & Mike Bamber
1973–84	Mike Bamber
1984–87	Bryan Bedson
1987–91	Dudley Sizen
1991–	Greg Stanley

Presidents

Years	President
1909–c.46	William Goodwin
c.1946–52	Lord Broadbridge
1958–75	The Duke of Norfolk
1989–91	Greg Stanley

Albion players 1901–93 — Abbis to Brand

Appearances as substitute are shown following a plus (+) sign. Players marked with a dagger (†) also made appearances for Albion in the wartime competitions; see the list of wartime players for details. Football League statistics include the play-offs, Southern League statistics include the test match, and Western League statistics include the championship play-offs.

Player	Career	FL		SL		FAC		FLC		Other		
ABBIS, Keith	1957–61	19	3 gls	–		–		–		–		
ADDINALL, Bert	1953–54	60	31 gls	–		3	2 gls	–		–		
ALLEN	1903	–		–		–		–		1		SE League
ALLSOPP, Tommy	1905–07	–		72	7 gls	6		–		25	4 gls	Utd League
ANSELL, George	1930–33	6	1 gl	–		1	1 gl	–		–		
ANTHONY, Walter	1905–08	–		80	8 gls	11		–		18	4 gls	Utd League
										8	1 gl	WL
										2		SCC
ARCHER, Arthur	1907–08	–		28		5		–		2		WL
										4		SCC
ARMSTRONG, Arthur	1909–10	–		2		–		–		1		SCC
ARMSTRONG, Dave	1966–70	38+6	6 gls	–		1		–		–		
ARMSTRONG, Gerry	1986–89	30+17	6 gls	–		–		3+1		2		FMC
										0+2	1 gl	AMC
ASPDEN, Tommy	1904–05	–		7		–		–		–		
ATHERTON, Jack	1938–39	9	2 gls	–		–		–		1		SSC
ATKINSON, Jimmy	1908–09	–		32	1 gl	1		–		10		WL
										3		SCC
ATTWOOD, Arthur	1931–35	87	55 gls	–		16	19 gls	–		1	1 gl	SSC
AULT, Alfred	1913	–		–		–		–		1	1 gl	S Alliance
BADMINTON, Roger	1966–68	1		–		–		1		–		
BAILEY, Craig	1961–63	4	1 gl	–		–		1	1 gl	–		
BAKER, Charlie	1960–64	81		–		4		2		–		
BAKER, Herbert 'Bert'	1901–06	–		13	3 gls	7	3 gls	–		–		
BALDWIN, Harry †	1939–52	164		–		19		–		–		
BALL, Jack †	1940–53	113		–		5		–		–		
BAMFORD, Harry	1946–47	8		–		–		–		–		
BARBER, Stan	1934–35	–		–		–		–		1		SSC
BARHAM, Mark	1989–92	73+3	9 gls	–		5	3 gls	3		4	1 gl	FMC
BARKER, Charles	1901–02	–		5	4 gls	3	4 gls	–		–		
BARKER, Don	1946–47	14	4 gls	–		–		–		–		
BATES, Don	1950–62	21	1 gl	–		–		–		–		
BATEY, Jasper	1913–15	–		29	1 gl	1		–		9	3 gls	S Alliance
										1		SCC
BAXTER, Bobby	1961–67	195	6 gls	–		12		13	1 gl	–		
BEAL, Phil	1975–77	9+1		–		–		2		–		
BEALE, Bob	1905–08	–		10		–		–		8		Utd League
										3		WL
BEAMISH, Ken	1972–74	86+10	27 gls	–		1		2	1 gl	–		
BEDFORD, Sid	1924–25	14		–		3		–		–		
BEECH, George	1914–20 & 1924–26	2		6		–		–		–		
BEENEY, Mark	1991–93	68+1		–		7		6		2		FMC
										4		AMC
BELL, Willie	1969–70	44	1 gl	–		5		3		–		
BELLAMY, Walter	1935–36	3		–		–		–		–		
BENCE, Paul	1965–68	0+1		–		–		–		–		
BENNETT, Ken	1950–53	101	37 gls	–		6	4 gls	–		–		
BENNETT, Ron	1953–54	3		–		–		–		–		
BENTLEY, Harry	1920–22	64		–		6		–		–		
BERRY, Les	1986–87	22+1		–		2		2		1		FMC
BERTOLINI, Jack	1958–66	258	12 gls	–		13	1 gl	8	1 gl	–		
BEST, Jack	1919–20	–		17	2 gls	–		–		–		
BILEY, Alan	1985–86	34+1	8 gls	–		0+2		2+1	1 gl	–		
BINNEY, Fred	1974–77	68+2	35 gls	–		6	6 gls	9	3 gls	–		
BIRDSALL, George	1913	–		–		–		–		1		SCC
BISSET, Tommy	1952–62	115	5 gls	–		8		–		–		
BISSETT, Nicky	1988–	73+3	6 gls	–		6		4		3		FMC
										2		AMC
BLACKBURN, Ken	1968–70	1	1 gl	–		–		–		–		
BLACKMAN, Fred	1909–11	–		76		4		–		1		FA Ch. Shield
										7		SCC
BLUNDEN, Bertie	1901–02	–		7	2 gls	–		–		–		
BOLLINGTON, Jack	1920–21	14		–		2		–		–		
BOORN, Alan	1971–74	2		–		–		–		–		
BOOTH, Billy	1908–20	–		303	8 gls	17	1 gl	–		1		FA Ch. Shield
										12	1 gl	WL
										19	1 gl	S Alliance
										17	1 gl	SCC
BOOTH, Sammy	1938–39 & 1947–49	28	6 gls	–		1	1 gl	–		–		
BORTHWICK, Walter	1967	1		–		–		–		–		
BOULTON, Bill	1903–04	–		6		–		–		–		
BOWDEN, Ossie	1937–38	1		–		–		–		–		
BOYLE, John	1973	10		–		–		–		–		
BRADFORD, John	1923–25	3		–		–		–		–		
BRAND, W. J.	1919–20	–		2		–		–		–		

Albion players 1901–93 — Bremner to Colclough

Appearances as substitute are shown following a plus (+) sign. Players marked with a dagger (†) also made appearances for Albion in the wartime competitions; see the list of wartime players for details. Football League statistics include the play-offs, Southern League statistics include the test match, and Western League statistics include the championship play-offs.

Player	Career	FL		SL		FAC		FLC		Other		
BREMNER, Kevin	1987–90	125+3	35 gls	–		7	1 gl	2		4	4 gls	AMC
BRENNAN, Jimmy	1908–09	–		10	1 gl	–		–		8	2 gls	WL
BRENNAN, Paddy	1948–52	45		–		2		–		–		
BRETT, Frank	1930–35 & 1936	131		–		12		–		–		
BRIDGE, Mick	1913	–		–		–		–		2		S Alliance
BRIDGES, Barry	1972–74	56+10	14 gls	–		3		2		–		
BRILEY, Les	1991–92	11+4		–		–		–		2		FMC
BROADHEAD, Arnold	1921–24	8	2 gls	–		–		–		–		
BROMAGE, Russel	1990–92	1		–		–		1		–		
BROMLEY, Brian	1971–73	47+3	3 gls	–		3		2		–		
BROOMFIELD, Des †	1938–48	20		–		2		–		–		
BROPHY, Harry	1936–38	–		–		–		–		1		SSC
BROUGHTON, F.	1902–03	–		1		–		–		8		SE League
BROWN, Alan	1958–62	7	2 gls	–		–		1		–		
BROWN, Fred	1923–24	19	3 gls	–		–		–		–		
BROWN, Gary	1962–65	–		–		–		1		–		
BROWN, Irvin	1951–58	3		–		–		–		–		
BROWN, Kevan	1987–88	52+1		–		4		3		5		AMC
BROWN, Mick	1973–74	5+3	1 gl	–		–		–		–		
BROWN, Oliver 'Buster'	1934–37	58	38 gls	–		3	2 gls	–		5	5 gls	SSC
BROWN, Sam	1931–32	4		–		–		–		–		
BROWN, Stan	1972	9		–		–		–		–		
BROWN, Tom	1920–21	14		16	1 gl	–		–		–		
BROWN, William 'Bill'	1913–14	–		6		–		–		10	9 gls	S Alliance
										3	1 gl	SCC
BUCKLEY, Chris	1905–06	–		19	1 gl	4		–		9	2 gls	Utd League
BUCKLEY, Frank	1905–06	–		25	2 gls	1		–		8		Utd League
BUNTING, John	1924–25	8		–		–		–		–		
BURNETT, Dennis	1975–77	41+3	1 gl	–		3		4		–		
BURNETT, Jimmy	1907–08	–		16	2 gls	5		–		8	2 gls	WL
										2	1 gl	SCC
BURNHAM, Jack	1920–21	1		–		–		–		–		
BURNS, Tony	1966–69	54		–		7		6		–		
BURTENSHAW, Steve	1951–67	237	3 gls	–		10		5		–		
BURTON, Billy	1936–37	6		–		–		–		1		SSC
BUSBY, Dave	1973–75	1+2		–		–		0+1		–		
BUTLIN, Barry	1975	5	2 gls	–		–		–		–		
BYRNE, John	1990–91 & 1993	52+7	16 gls	–		2	2 gls	2	2 gls	2		FMC
CALDWELL, Jock	1901–05	–		38	10 gls	9	3 gls	–		18	2 gls	SE League
CALLOW, J. W.	1902	–		3		–		–		–		
CAMERON	1903–04	–		19		1		–		–		
CAMPBELL, Greg	1987	0+2		–		–		–		–		
CARGILL, Jimmy	1936–39	66	19 gls	–		2		–		2	1 gl	SSC
CAROLAN, Joe	1960–62	33		–		3		–		–		
CARRUTHERS, Jack	1926–34	23	9 gls	–		4		–		–		
CARTER, W.	1913	–		–		–		–		1		S Alliance
CASE, Jimmy	1981–85	124+3	10 gls	–		13+1	5 gls	8		–		
CASSIDY, Bill	1962–67	113+5	25 gls	–		3	2 gls	8	3 gls	–		
CATTLIN, Chris	1976–80	95	1 gl	–		5		14	1 gl	–		
CAVEN, Joe	1962	10		–		–		–		–		
CHAMBERLAIN Bert	1926–29	9		–		–		–		–		
CHAMPELOVIER, Les	1956–58	1		–		–		–		–		
CHANNON, Vic	1921–24	2		–		–		–		–		
CHAPMAN, George	1946–48	43	12 gls	–		5	2 gls	–		–		
CHAPMAN, Ian	1986–	146+16	4 gls	–		8+2	2 gls	9+1		3+2		FMC
										3		AMC
CHASE, Charlie †	1940–46	–		–		4	2 gls	–		–		
CHEETHAM, John	1925–27	8		–		–		–		–		
CHIVERS, Gary	1988–93	218+2	14 gls	–		12		12		6	1 gl	FMC
										2	1 gl	AMC
CHIVERS, Martin	1979–80	4+1	1 gl	–		–		1		–		
CLARE, Edwin	1905–06	–		15		1		–		12		Utd League
CLARK, Paul	1977–82	69+10	9 gls	–		4+1		8+1		–		
CLARKE, Don 'Nobby'	1955–58	2		–		–		–		–		
CLARKE, Jeff	1984	4		–		–		1		–		
CLARKE, Ray	1979–80	30	8 gls	–		2	1 gl	1		–		
CLARKE, William 'Billy'	1935–36	1		–		–		–		–		
CLARKSON, David	1991–92	4+9		–		2		–		–		
CLAYTON, Ronnie	1958–60	14	3 gls	–		–		–		–		
CLELLAND, Dave	1948–49	8	1 gl	–		–		–		–		
COCHRANE, Johnny	1961–63	14	3 gls	–		–		1		–		
CODNER, Robert	1988–	199+7	29 gls	–		9+1	3 gl	10	1 gl	7	1 gl	FMC
										3+1		AMC
COHEN, Jacob	1980–81	3+3		–		–		–		–		
COLCLOUGH, Ephraim	1900–01	–		3	1 gl	4	2 gls	–		–		

Albion players 1901–93 — Coleman to Egan

Appearances as substitute are shown following a plus (+) sign. Players marked with a dagger (†) also made appearances for Albion in the wartime competitions; see the list of wartime players for details. Football League statistics include the play-offs, Southern League statistics include the test match, and Western League statistics include the championship play-offs.

Player	Career	FL	SL	FAC	FLC	Other	
COLEMAN, Jimmy	1909–12 & 1915	–	47 6 gls	–	–	1	FA Ch. Shield
						2 1 gl	SCC
COLES, David	1989	1	–	–	–	–	
COLES, Donald	1901–03	–	18 2 gls	–	–	7	SE League
COLLINS, Edwin 'Ned'	1901–02	–	4	4	–	–	
COLLINS, Glyn	1966	2	–	–	–	–	
COLLINS, Jimmy	1962–67	199+2 44 gls	–	7 1 gl	13 3 gls	–	
CONNELLY, Eddie	1949–50	6 1 gl	–	1	–	–	
CONNOR, Terry	1983–87	153+3 51 gls	–	10+1 4 gls	7 4 gls	–	
CONNOR, William 'Bill'	1909–10	–	9 4 gls	1	–	1	SCC
CONWAY, Mick	1972–75	1+1 1 gl	–	–	–	–	
COOK, Tommy	1921–29	190 114 gls	–	19 9 gls	–	–	
COOK, Walter	1924–26	52	–	3	–	–	
COOMBER, George	1913–25	168 1 gl	75 4 gls	18 1 gl	–	9	S Alliance
						2	SCC
COOPER, Geoff	1987–89	2+5	–	1	–	0+1	AMC
COOPER, Jim	1962–65	41 6 gls	–	2 1 gl	2 1 gl	–	
CORRIGAN, Joe	1983–85	36	–	3	3	–	
COTTERILL, Steve	1992	11 4 gls	–	–	–	–	
CRAVEN, W.	1902	–	–	–	–	1	SE League
CRINSON, Bill	1909–13	–	5	–	–	3	S Alliance
						5	SCC
CROSS, Graham	1976–77	46 3 gls	–	3	7 1 gl	–	
CROWTHER, Stan	1961	4	–	–	–	–	
CRUMP, Fred	1908–09	–	11 2 gls	–	–	8 3 gls	WL
						1	SCC
CRUMPLIN, John	1987–93	144+31 5 gls	–	11+1 1 gl	8+1	6	FMC
						6 1 gl	AMC
CURBISHLEY, Alan	1987–90	111+5 13 gls	–	6 2 gls	4	2	FMC
						4	AMC
CURRAN, Jack	1925–30	180	–	13	–	–	
CURRY, Bill	1959–60	49 26 gls	–	5 3 gls	–	–	
DALTON, Edward 'Ted'	1908–09	–	6	–	–	7	WL
						2	SCC
DALTON, George	1967–70	24	–	2	2	–	
DANIELS, Harry	1948–50	32	–	1	–	–	
DAREY, Jeff	1957–61	10 2 gls	–	–	1	–	
DARLING, Len †	1933–48	199 5 gls	–	23 2 gls	–	6	SSC
DAVIE, Jock †	1936–46	89 39 gls	–	14 18 gls	–	2 1 gl	SSC
DAVIES, Ken	1948–50	36 5 gls	–	–	–	–	
DAVIES, Peter	1965–66	6	–	–	2	–	
DAWSON, Alex	1968–71	53+4 26 gls	–	5 2 gls	3 1 gl	–	
DAY, Albert †	1938–46	–	–	1	–	–	
DEAR, Brian	1967	7 5 gls	–	–	–	–	
DENNETT, J. W.	1903–04	–	2	–	–	–	
DENNISON, Bob	1924–25	25 10 gls	–	3 3 gls	–	–	
DEXTER, Charlie	1914–15	–	33	3	–	–	
DIGWEED, Perry	1981–93	182	–	9	5	5	FMC
DILLON, John	1962–63	21 3 gls	–	1	–	–	
DIXON, Tommy	1958–60	35 12 gls	–	1	–	–	
DOBSON, Colin	1972	2+2	–	–	–	–	
DODD, George	1913–14	–	17 2 gls	2	–	–	
DOLLMAN, Frank	1902	–	2	–	–	–	
DONNELLY, Peter	1962–65	56 13 gls	–	1	2	–	
DORAN, Jack	1920–22	71 44 gls	10 10 gls	4 1 gl	–	–	
DOUGAL, Dave	1908	–	14 1 gl	–	–	–	
DOVEY, Alan	1971–73	6	–	–	2	–	
DOWNS, Dickie	1924–25	16	–	–	–	–	
DOWNSBOROUGH, Peter	1973	3	–	–	–	–	
DUBLIN, Keith	1987–90	132 5 gls	–	7 1 gl	5	2	FMC
						5	AMC
DUCKWORTH, Joe	1930–32	37	–	3	–	–	
DUFFY, Alan	1970–72	34+16 8 gls	–	0+2	2	–	
DUGNOLLE, Jack †	1933–38 & 1946–48	66	–	6	–	–	
DUNCLIFFE, John	1963–68	22	–	–	–	–	
DUTTON, Harry	1929–33	93 4 gls	–	11 1 gl	–	–	
EACOCK, Fred	1919–20	–	13 3 gls	–	–	–	
EACOCK, Jack	1908–10	–	1	–	–	–	
EDMONDS, Alfred 'Eddie'	1922–29	14	–	–	–	–	
EDWARDS, Alistair	1989–90	1	–	–	–	–	
EDWARDS, Len	1954–55	6	–	–	–	–	
EDWARDS, Matthew	1992–	24+9 2 gls	–	3+1 1 gl	4 1 gl	3	AMC
EDWARDS, Sean	1984–87	–	–	–	–	0+1	FMC
EDWARDS, W. G.	1906	–	–	–	–	1	Utd League
EGAN, Harry	1934–36	19 8 gls	–	–	–	4 3 gls	SSC

Albion players 1901–93 — Elliott to Grayer

Appearances as substitute are shown following a plus (+) sign. Players marked with a dagger (†) also made appearances for Albion in the wartime competitions; see the list of wartime players for details. Football League statistics include the play-offs, Southern League statistics include the test match, and Western League statistics include the championship play-offs.

Player	Career	FL		SL		FAC		FLC		Other		
ELLIOTT, Edward 'Teddy'	1907–15	–		5	2 gls	–		–		1		WL
ELLIOTT, Mark	1977–79	3		–		–		–		–		
ELLIS, Syd	1957–59	42		–		2		–		–		
EVANS, Tom	1921–22	5		–		–		–		–		
EVERITT, Mike	1968–70	24+3	1 gl	–		3		1		–		
EYRES, Jack	1931–32	11	3 gls	–		–		–		–		
FARRELL, Paddy	1901–04	–		28		10		–		13	1 gl	SE League
FARRELL, Robert 'Bobby' †	1928–42	382	66 gls	–		38	17 gls	–		10	1 gl	SSC
FARRINGTON, Mark	1991–	11+11	3 gl	–		–		0+2		2		FMC
FASHANU, Justin	1985–86	16	2 gls	–		3		1		–		
FEARON, Ron	1988	7		–		–		–		–		
FEATHERSTONE, George	1909–10	–		21	8 gls	–		–		1	1 gl	SCC
FEEBERY, Jack	1921–24	62	3 gls	–		5		–		–		
FELL, Gerry	1974–77	65+14	19 gls	–		3+1	1 gl	4+4		–		
FERGUSON, Mick	1984–86	17	6 gls	–		1		3	1 gl	–		
FERRIER, John	1946–47	1	1 gl	–		–		–		–		
FFENNELL, Edgar	1901–03	–		–		–		–		1		SE League
FISHER, Albert	1905–06	–		8		–		–		12	8 gls	Utd League
FITCH, Barry	1961–64	1		–		–		–		–		
FITCHIE, Tom	1907	–		–		–		–		1		WL
FLANNERY, Tom	1912–13	–		5	2 gls	–		–		3	2 gls	S Alliance
										6	5 gls	SCC
FLOOD, Paul	1967–71	32+3	7 gls	–		2		3+1	1 gl	–		
FORD, G. W.	1911–12	–		1		–		–		–		
FOREMAN, Denis	1952–62	211	63 gls	–		8	6 gls	–		–		
FORSTER, Derek	1974–76	3		–		–		–		–		
FOSTER	1906	–		–		–		–		1		Utd League
FOSTER, Steve	1979–84 & 1992–	206+1	10 gls	–		19		17	2 gls	2		AMC
FOX, Reg	1952–56	20		–		3		–		–		
FRANKS, Ken	1962–63	1		–		–		–		–		
FULLER, Eddie	1921–27 & 1929–31 & 1932–33	74	20 gls	–		4		–		–		
FUNNELL, Simon	1990–	0+3		–		0+1		2+1		–		
FUSCHILLO, Paul	1974–75	17	1 gl	–		–		–		–		
GABBIADINI, Ricardo	1990	0+1		–		–		–		–		
GALL, Mark	1991–93	30+1	13 gls	–		1	1 gl	–		1		FMC
GALL, Norman	1962–74	427+13	4 gls	–		26+1		21		–		
GALLACHER, Bernard	1991–93	45	1 gl	–		3		–		1		FMC
										1		AMC
GARBUTT, Ray	1951–52	32	17 gls	–		–		–		–		
GARDINER, J. J.	1901–06	–		5		–		–		2		SE League
GARDNER, Andy	1904–05	–		23	10 gls	5	3 gls	–		–		
GARFIELD, Ben	1902–05	–		39	17 gls	7	5 gls	–		18	7 gls	SE League
GARIANI, Moshe	1980–81	0+1		–		–		–		–		
GATTING, Steve	1981–91	316+3	19 gls	–		26		14	1 gl	5		FMC
										5	1 gl	AMC
GEARD, Glen	1976–81 & 1983	–		–		–		1		–		
GILBERG, Harry	1953–56	67	3 gls	–		5	2 gls	–		–		
GILBERT, Phil	1962–64	6	3 gls	–		–		–		–		
GILGUN, Pat	1925–26	3	3 gls	–		1		–		–		
GILHOOLY, Paddy	1904–05	–		15	5 gls	1		–		–		
GILL, Eric	1952–60	280		–		16		–		–		
GILLIVER, Allan	1969–71	54+3	19 gls	–		7	3 gls	4	2 gls	–		
GIPP, David	1984–89	1+4		–		–		1		–		
GOFFEY, Bert †	1937–42	52	9 gls	–		3		–		1		SSC
GOOCH, A.	1902	–		–		–		–		3	1 gl	SE League
GOOD, Micky	1904–05	–		25	5 gls	4	1 gl	–		–		
GOODCHILD, Johnny	1961–66	162+1	44 gls	–		7	1 gl	6	1 gl	–		
GOODEVE, Ken	1973–74	5+1		–		–		–		–		
GOODWIN, Fred	1911–13	–		49	12 gls	3	–	–		7	3 gls	S Alliance
										4	1 gl	SCC
GOODWIN, Ian	1970–74	52+4		–		3		1		–		
GOORD, George	1923–26	1	1 gl	–		–		–		–		
GORDON, Dennis	1952–61	277	62 gls	–		16	2 gls	–		–		
GORDON, Les	1928–30	18		–		–		–		–		
GOTSMANOV, Sergei	1990	14+2	4 gls	–		–		–		–		
GOTTS, Jim	1946–47	2		–		–		–		–		
GOUGH, Tony	1925–28	9	4 gls	–		1		–		–		
GOULD, Wally	1964–68	166+2	45 gls	–		12	1 gl	13		–		
GOULDING	1902	–		–		–		–		1		SE League
GOVIER, Steve	1974	12	1 gl	–		–		4		–		
GRAHAM, John	1905	–		1		–		–		–		
GRANT, Alan	1956–60	1		–		–		–		–		
GRANT, Jim	1946–47	1		–		–		–		–		
GRAYER, S.	1903	–		–		–		–		2		SE League

Albion players 1901–93 — Grealish to Hughes

Appearances as substitute are shown following a plus (+) sign. Players marked with a dagger (†) also made appearances for Albion in the wartime competitions; see the list of wartime players for details. Football League statistics include the play-offs, Southern League statistics include the test match, and Western League statistics include the championship play-offs.

Player	Career	FL	SL	FAC	FLC	Other	
GREALISH, Tony	1981–84	95+5 6 gls	–	14	7 2 gls	–	
GREEN, Freddie †	1938–48	26	–	–	–	–	
GREGORY, John	1979–81	72 7 gls	–	3	6	–	
GREGORY, Julius	1906–08	–	64	1	–	11 2 gls	Utd League
						8	WL
						3	SCC
GRIERSON, Tom	1908–09	–	5 1 gl	–	–	1	WL
						1	SCC
GROVES, Freddie	1921–24	53 2 gls	–	7	–	–	
GROVES, Henry	1919–20	–	5	–	–	–	
GRUMMITT, Peter	1973–77	136	–	9	13	–	
GURINOVICH, Igor	1990–91	3+1 1 gl	–	1 1 gl	–	1	FMC
GUTTRIDGE, Ron	1948–50	17	–	–	–	–	
HACKING, Bob	1947–48	17 2 gls	–	5 1 gl	–	–	
HAIG-BROWN, Alan	1903–05	–	–	1	–	2	Utd League
HALL, Ernie	1937–39	3	–	–	–	1	SSC
HALL, Fretwell	1920–21	12	–	–	–	–	
HALL, John E.	1908–09	–	20 3 gls	1	–	4	WL
						2	SCC
HALL, John H. 'Jack'	1906–08	–	67 38 gls	6 2 gls	–	9 6 gls	Utd League
						7 5 gls	WL
						4 3 gls	SCC
HALL, Proctor	1905–06	–	27 7 gls	5 1 gl	–	8	Utd League
HAMMOND, Harry	1903	–	–	–	–	1	SE League
HANLON, Wally	1946–48	72 4 gls	–	6	–	–	
HANNAM, Dave	1959–63	5 2 gls	–	–	1	–	
HARBURN, Peter	1951–52 & 1955–58	126 61 gls	–	7 4 gls	–	–	
HARDING, F.	1905–06	–	–	–	–	1	Utd League
HARDMAN, J.	1902–04	–	7 1 gl	3	–	11	SE League
HARKER, Frank	1905–06	–	–	–	–	1	Utd League
HARLAND, Alf	1902–03	–	9	5 2 gls	–	14	SE League
HARRISON, Jack	1931–34	5 3 gls	–	–	–	–	
HASSELL, Tommy †	1950–51	11 4 gls	–	2	–	–	
HASTINGS, Bill	1909–12	–	85 11 gls	3	–	1	FA Ch. Shield
						11 4 gls	SCC
HAWLEY, Fred	1925–26	37 4 gls	–	2	–	–	
HAWORTH, Jack	1909–12	–	81 7 gls	5 1 gl	–	1	FA Ch. Shield
						12 1 gl	SCC
HAYES, Billy	1919–24	167	42	16	–	–	
HEALER, Ernie	1963–64	3 1 gl	–	–	–	–	
HENDERSON, Crosby	1911–12	–	12	–	–	1	SCC
HENDERSON, Stewart	1965–73	198 1 gl	–	14	14	–	
HENDERSON, William 'Billy'	1919–20	–	2	–	–	–	
HENNIGAN, Mike	1964–65	4	–	–	–	–	
HICKMAN, Mike	1964–68	12+3	–	2 1 gl	1	–	
HIGGINS, Ron	1951–53	8	–	–	–	–	
HIGHAM, Tom 'Gunner'	1907–20	–	124	8 1 gl	–	4	WL
						23	S Alliance
HILL, W.	1902	–	5	–	–	1 1 gl	SE League
HILTON, Pat	1973–74	18+2 2 gls	–	2	–	–	
HINDLEY, Frank †	1939–47	10 4 gls	–	4 2 gls	–	–	
HIPKIN, Reg	1948–49	15 1 gl	–	–	–	–	
HODGE, Eric	1956–59	4	–	–	–	–	
HODGE, William 'Bill'	1912–14	–	14	–	–	13	S Alliance
						6	SCC
HODGES, Cyril †	1946–47	9 3 gls	–	–	–	–	
HOLLEY, George	1919–20	–	12 5 gls	1	–	–	
HOLLINS, Dave	1956–61	66	–	6	1	–	
HOPKINS, Jimmy	1923–29	220 72 gls	–	13 3 gls	–	–	
HOPKINS, Mel	1964–67	57+1 2 gls	–	1	3	–	
HORSCROFT, Grant	1987–88	2	–	–	–	–	
HORTON, Brian	1976–81	217+1 33 gls	–	10 2 gls	24 6 gls	–	
HOUGHTON, F.	1912	–	–	–	–	1	S Alliance
HOWARD, Frankie	1949–59	200 26 gls	–	19 5 gls	–	–	
HOWELL, Graham	1972–74	40+4	–	1	1	–	
HOWELL, Ronnie	1973–74	26+1 9 gls	–	2	1	–	
HOWES, Arthur	1902–04	–	35	4	–	10	SE League
HOWLETT, Gary	1982–84	30+2 2 gls	–	3	2	–	
HOYLAND, Fred	1924–26	5	–	–	–	–	
HUDSON, Colin	1961–62	1	–	–	–	–	
HUGHES, Darren	1986–87	26 2 gls	–	2	–	1	FMC
HUGHES, Tommy	1973	3	–	–	–	–	

Albion players 1901–93 — Hulme to Lawrenson

Appearances as substitute are shown following a plus (+) sign. Players marked with a dagger (†) also made appearances for Albion in the wartime competitions; see the list of wartime players for details. Football League statistics include the play-offs, Southern League statistics include the test match, and Western League statistics include the championship play-offs.

Player	Career	FL	SL	FAC	FLC	Other	
HULME, Arthur	1902–09	–	113 2 gls	12 1 gl	–	17 1 gl	SE League
						21 2 gls	Utd League
						9 1 gl	WL
						2	SCC
HULSE, Ben	1904–05	–	26 7 gls	4 3 gls	–	–	
HUMPHRIES, Bob	1956–57	10 2 gls	–	–	–	–	
HURST, Stan	1937–39	33 11 gls	–	1	–	–	
HUTCHINGS, Chris	1983–87	153 4 gls	–	11 1 gl	7 1 gl	2+1	FMC
						1	AMC
HYDE, Len	1903–04	–	29 4 gls	–	–	–	
INNES, Bob	1905–06	–	15 1 gl	1	–	13	Utd League
IOVAN, Stefan	1991–92	7+2	–	–	–	1	FMC
IRVINE, Willie	1971–72	66+3 27 gls	–	3 1 gl	4 1 gl	–	
ISAAC, Robert	1987–90	30	–	–	3	–	
ISHERWOOD, Bob	1908–09	–	–	–	–	2	WL
ISON, Ernie	1924–31	16	–	–	–	–	
JACKSON, Allan	1962–64	21 5 gls	–	–	1	–	
JACOBS, Steve	1984–86	47+1 3 gls	–	5+1 1 gl	5	2	FMC
JAMES, Dai	1926–29	30 8 gls	–	2 1 gl	–	–	
JAMES, David	1962–63	5	–	–	1	–	
JAMES, Tony	1939–49	69 20 gls	–	5 2 gls	–	–	
JASPER, Dale	1986–88	44+5 6 gls	–	2+1 1 gl	2+1	1	FMC
						3+1 1 gl	AMC
JEE, Joe	1908–09	–	31 5 gls	1	–	10 2 gls	WL
						2	SCC
JENKINS, Jack	1922–29	216 4 gls	–	15	–	–	
JENNINGS, Roy	1952–64	276 22 gls	–	14	7	–	
JENNINGS, Sam	1925–28	110 61 gls	–	5 2 gls	–	–	
JEPSON, Bert	1933–35	45 8 gls	–	3 1 gl	–	6 2 gls	SSC
JEST, Syd	1961–64	12	–	–	–	–	
JOHNSON, Mick	1955–57	2	–	–	–	–	
JOHNSTON, Ron	1950–51	1	–	–	–	–	
JONES, Abe	1922–23	6 1 gl	–	–	–	–	
JONES, Freddie	1958–60	69 14 gls	–	6 1 gl	1	–	
JONES, Herbert	1934–35	37	–	3	–	3	SSC
JONES, Jimmy	1922–24	17 3 gls	–	2	–	–	
JONES, Les J.	1948–50	3	–	–	–	–	
JONES, Mark	1984	9	–	–	–	–	
JONES, William 'Bill'	1909–12 & 1913–20	–	156 63 gls	11 4 gls	–	1	FA Ch. Shield
						11 2 gls	SCC
JOYNES, Dickie	1905–08	–	70 10 gls	8 2 gls	–	22 10 gls	Utd League
						9	WL
						3	SCC
KAVANAGH, Micky	1948–50	26 7 gls	–	1	–	–	
KEELEY, John	1986–90	138	–	9	6	2	FMC
						5	AMC
KEENE, Doug	1950–53	61 10 gls	–	4	–	–	
KELLY, John	1926	2	–	–	–	–	
KELLY, Willie	1904–05	–	3	–	–	–	
KENNEDY, Andy	1992–	26+4 8 gls	–	5 2 gls	2	2+1 1 gl	AMC
KENNEDY, Jimmy	1905–06	–	11 1 gl	4 1 gl	–	7 1 gl	Utd League
KENNEDY, Willie	1905–06	–	6	–	–	5	Utd League
KENT, Harry	1905–08	–	104 11 gls	11	–	22 5 gls	Utd League
						10	WL
						4	SCC
KEOWN, Martin	1985	21+2 1 gl	–	–	2 1 gl	2 1 gl	FMC
KING, Eddie	1901–02	–	3	–	–	–	
KING, Ernie	1931–38	186	–	20	–	11	SSC
KING, P.	1902	–	1	–	–	–	
KINNEAR, Joe	1975–76	15+1 1 gl	–	1+1	–	–	
KIRKWOOD, Dan	1928–33	168 74 gls	–	13 8 gls	–	–	
KITCHEN, Sid	1913	–	–	–	–	1 1 gl	S Alliance
KITTO, Dick	1906–07	–	–	–	–	1	Utd League
KNIGHT, Peter	1956–57 & 1964–66	9+1 1 gl	–	–	1	–	
KRAAY, Hans	1983–85	19+4 3 gls	–	–	–	–	
KYDD, David	1963–66	2	–	–	1 1 gl	–	
LAMB, Billy	1902–04	–	17 1 gl	5	–	17 2 gls	SE League
LAMBERT, Martin	1982–85 & 1989	2+2	–	–	0+1	–	
LANCELOTTE, Eric †	1948–50	60 14 gls	–	1	–	–	
LANGLEY, E.	1905–09	–	–	–	–	1	Utd League
LANGLEY, Jimmy	1953–57	166 14 gls	–	12 2 gls	–	–	
LANHAM, Charlie	1902	–	–	–	–	1	SE League
LAVERICK, Bobby	1960–62	63 20 gls	–	4 1 gl	2 1 gl	–	
LAW, Alec	1935–39	66 36 gls	–	5 4 gls	–	3	SSC
LAWRENSON, Mark	1977–81	152 5 gls	–	7 1 gl	15 1 gl	–	

Albion players 1901–93 — Lawson to McNab

Appearances as substitute are shown following a plus (+) sign. Players marked with a dagger (†) also made appearances for Albion in the wartime competitions; see the list of wartime players for details. Football League statistics include the play-offs, Southern League statistics include the test match, and Western League statistics include the championship play-offs.

Player	Career	FL	SL	FAC	FLC	Other	
LAWSON, Hector	1928–29	7	–	–	–	–	
LAWTON, Nobby	1967–71	112 12 gls	–	9 3 gls	6 1 gl	–	
LEACH, George	1904–05 & 1908–09	–	4	–	–	1 1 gl	SCC
LEADBETTER, Jimmy	1952–55	107 29 gls	–	8 4 gls	–	–	
LEAMON, Fred	1949–50	11 4 gls	–	–	–	–	
LECK, Derek	1965–67	29+1	–	2	1	–	
LEE, Barney	1902–03	–	8 2 gls	3 7 gls	–	8	SE League
LEEMING, Joe	1908–14	–	193	13	–	1	FA Ch. Shield
						8	WL
						12	S Alliance
						11	SCC
LEGGETT, Peter	1965–66	2+1	–	–	1	–	
LEWIS, Allen	1975–77	3	–	–	–	–	
LEWIS, John 'Jack'	1906–07	–	32 8 gls	1	–	10 4 gls	Utd League
LEWIS, George	1948–49	24 8 gls	–	1	–	–	
LEY, George	1972–74	47	–	3	1	–	
LIDDELL, John	1947–48	4 1 gl	–	–	–	–	
LITTLE, Roy 'Doz'	1958–61	83	–	6	2	–	
LITTLE, Wally	1919–29	285 32 gls	23	24 4 gls	–	–	
LIVESEY, Charlie	1965–69	124+2 28 gls	–	7+2 5 gls	11 4 gls	–	
LIVINGSTONE, Archie	1904–05	–	26	5 1 gl	–	–	
LLOYD, Arthur	1908–09	–	10	–	–	2	WL
						1	SCC
LONGDON, Charlie †	1939–46	–	–	9 2 gls	–	–	
LONGHURST, G.	1913	–	–	–	–	1	SCC
LONGLAND, Johnny	1954–56	3	–	–	–	–	
LONGSTAFF, Bert	1906–22	41 4 gls	315 59 gls	20 1 gl	–	1	FA Ch. Shield
						4 1 gl	Utd League
						18 8 gls	WL
						26 10 gls	S Alliance
						18 3 gls	SCC
LONGSTAFF, Harvey	1909–13	–	5 2 gls	–	–	1	S Alliance
						3 2 gls	SCC
LOWE, Harry	1913–14	–	2 1 gl	–	–	5 4 gls	S Alliance
						1	SCC
LUMBERG, Albert	1933–34	21	–	–	–	–	
LUMLEY, Joe	1905–08 & 1909–12	–	25	1	–	19 2 gls	Utd League
						4	WL
						3	SCC
LUTTON, Bertie	1971–73	18+11 4 gls	–	–	1	–	
LYON, Bertie	1904–05	–	29 5 gls	5	–	–	
McALLISTER, Billy	1921–25	89 6 gls	–	6	–	–	
McATEER, Tom	1903–04	–	33 6 gls	1	–	–	
McAVOY, Frank	1901–02	–	11 6 gls	4 3 gls	–	–	
McCAIRNS, Tom	1903–04	–	17 5 gls	–	–	–	
McCARTHY, Paul	1988–	73+1	–	7	4	3	FMC
						4	AMC
McCARTHY, Tom	1935–36	1	–	–	–	1	SSC
MACCIOCHI, David	1992	0+2	–	–	–	–	
McCOY, Wilf 'Tim' †	1951–54	112	–	5	–	–	
McCURLEY, Kevin	1948–51	21 9 gls	–	–	–	–	
MacDONALD, Hugh	1906–08	–	69	6	–	14	Utd League
						9	WL
						4	SCC
McDONALD, Murdoch	1930–31	10 1 gl	–	–	–	–	
McDONALD, Willie	1906–08	–	68	6	–	12 1 gl	Utd League
						9	WL
						4	SCC
MACE, Stan	1927–28	5	–	–	–	–	
McEWAN, Billy	1974	27 3 gls	–	–	1	–	
McGHIE, Joe	1909–13	–	133 3 gls	7	–	1	FA Ch. Shield
						9	S Alliance
						6	SCC
McGONIGAL, Bert	1962–66	57	–	2	3	–	
McGRATH, Derek	1988–92	2+4	–	0+1	–	–	
McGRATH, John	1972	3	–	–	–	–	
McHALE, Ray	1980–81	9+2	–	–	2	–	
MACHIN, Ernie	1974–76	64 1 gl	–	3	5	–	
McILVENNY, Paddy	1951–55	60 5 gls	–	6	–	–	
MACKAY, Tommy	1925–26	1	–	–	–	–	
McKENNA, Brian	1989–91	1	–	–	–	–	
McKENNA, Harold	1924–25	7	–	1	–	–	
McLAFFERTY, Maurice	1952–54	21	–	1	–	–	
McLEOD, Bob	1947–48	1	–	–	–	–	
McNAB, Neil	1980–83	100+3 4 gls	–	5 1 gl	7	–	

Albion players 1901–93 — McNaughton to Nelson

Appearances as substitute are shown following a plus (+) sign. Players marked with a dagger (†) also made appearances for Albion in the wartime competitions; see the list of wartime players for details. Football League statistics include the play-offs, Southern League statistics include the test match, and Western League statistics include the championship play-offs.

Player	Career	FL		SL		FAC		FLC		Other		
McNAUGHTON, Jock †	1936–46	6		–		–		–		1		SSC
McNEIL, Matt	1953–56	53		–		7		–				
McNEILL, Ian	1959–62	116	12 gls	–		9	1 gl	3		–		
McNICHOL, Johnny	1948–52	158	37 gls	–		7	2 gls	–		–		
McNICOL, Bob	1959–62	93		–		3	1 gl	3		–		
McQUARRIE, Andy	1964–65	2	1 gl	–		–		1		–		
MAGILL, Jimmy	1965–68	50	1 gl	–		4		2		–		
MANSELL, Jack	1949–52	116	9 gls	–		6	2 gls	–		–		
MANSFIELD, W.	1901–03	–		1		–		–		1		SE League
MARCH, Zacky	1913–22	56		29	6 gls	7	2 gls	–		4	1 gl	S Alliance
										1		SCC
MARLOWE, Ricky	1974–76	24+1	5 gls	–		0+1		2+1	2 gls	–		
MARRIOTT, Ernie †	1933–49	163	1 gl	–		16	1 gl	–		1		SSC
MARSDEN, Harry	1929–34	164		–		23		–		4		SSC
MARTIN, Edward 'Ted' †	1932–46	155	4 gls	–		12		–		5		SSC
MARTIN, Jack	1908–09	–		37	18 gls	1		–		12	6 gls	WL
										2	1 gl	SCC
MARTIN, Neil	1975–76	13+4	8 gls	–		3	1 gl	2		–		
MASON, Tommy	1974–76	23+2	2 gls	–		3		–		–		
MASSIMO, Franco	1985–87	0+1		–		–		0+1		–		
MATTHEWS, Charlie	1912–14	–		1		–		–		6		S Alliance
										5	1 gl	SCC
MAY, Larry	1988–89	24	3 gls	–		1		–		–		
MAYBANK, Teddy	1977–79	62+2	16 gls	–		2		7	2 gls	–		
MEADE, Raphael	1991–92	35+5	9 gls	–		2	2 gls	2	1 gl	2		FMC
MEDHURST, Harry	1952–53	12		–		2		–		–		
MEE, Gordon †	1935–45	41		–		–		–		–		
MELLON, Jimmy	1926–27	1		–		–		–		–		
MELLOR, Ian	1974–78	116+6	31 gls	–		10+1	3 gls	14+3	1 gl	–		
MELLORS, Mark	1904–06	–		63		10		–		10		Utd League
MENDHAM, C. J.	1901–02	–		3	4 gls	2	3 gls	–		–		
MEOLA, Tony	1990	1		–		–		1		–		
MIDDLETON, Harry	1909–11	–		33	5 gls	1		–		4		SCC
MIDDLETON William 'Billy'	1912–13	–		1		1		–		3	1 gl	S Alliance
										5		SCC
MILLAR, Arthur	1904–05	–		31		5	1 gl	–		–		
MILLARD, A.	1903	–		–		–		–		1		SE League
MILLER, Alistair	1962	1		–		–		–		–		
MILLER, Bill	1910–22	7		84	40 gls	5	1 gl	–		12	11 gls	S Alliance
										4		SCC
MITCHELL, F.	1901–03	–		15	1 gl	3		–		2		SE League
MOCHAN, Charlie	1905–06	–		2		–		–		6		Utd League
MOFFATT, Johnny	1951–52	2		–		–		–		–		
MOFFATT, William 'Billy'	1930–32	21		–		2		–		–		
MOONEY, Paul	1925–36	283	10 gls	–		24		–		8	1 gl	SSC
MOORE, Bernard †	1942–48 & 1954–55	37	12 gls	–		14	2 gls	–		–		
MOORE, Jimmy	1922–23	6	2 gls	–		–		–		–		
MOORE, John	1972	5		–		–		–		–		
MOORHEAD, George	1922	1		–		–		–		–		
MOORHOUSE, Ben	1919–20	–		4		–		–		–		
MORGAN, Sammy	1975–77	19+16	8 gls	–		0+2		–		–		
MORRAD, Frank	1948–51	43	3 gls	–		2		–		–		
MORRIS, Tom	1907–09	–		29	3 gls	6		–		9	1 gl	WL
										2		SCC
MORRIS, William 'Billy'	1949–51	28	4 gls	–		3		–		–		
MORTIMER, Dennis	1985–86	40	2 gls	–		4		3		2		FMC
MOSELEY, Graham	1977–86	189		–		17		17		1		FMC
MOULDEN, Paul	1992	11	5 gls	–		–		–		–		
MUIR, Ian	1984–85	3+1		–		–		–		–		
MULHALL, John	1924–25	2		–		–		–		–		
MULVANEY, Jimmy	1950–51	8		–		2		–		–		
MUNDAY, Stuart	1989–	21	1 gl	–		1		–		3		AMC
MUNDY, Albert	1953–58	165	87 gls	–		13	3 gls	–		–		
MURFIN, Clarrie	1936–38	1		–		–		–		–		
MURRAY, Bert	1971–73	99+3	25 gls	–		3	1 gl	4		–		
MYALL, Stuart	1991–	7		–		–		–		–		
NAPIER, Christopher 'Kit'	1966–72	249+7	84 gls	–		22	9 gls	13	6 gls	–		
NAPIER, John	1967–72	218+1	5 gls	–		16		12		–		
NASH, H.	1912	–		–		–		–		1		S Alliance
NEATE, Derek	1955–59	24	6 gls	–		–		–		–		
NEEDHAM, Archie	1911–15	–		98	11 gls	6		–		25		S Alliance
										2	3 gls	SCC
NEIL, Andy	1920–24 & 1926–27	167	28 gls	–		18	2 gls	–		–		
NELSON, Garry	1987–91	133+12	47 gls	–		7	6 gls	7		2	1 gl	FMC
										5	5 gls	AMC

Albion players 1901–93 — Nelson to Robertson

Appearances as substitute are shown following a plus (+) sign. Players marked with a dagger (†) also made appearances for Albion in the wartime competitions; see the list of wartime players for details. Football League statistics include the play-offs, Southern League statistics include the test match, and Western League statistics include the championship play-offs.

Player	Career	FL	SL	FAC	FLC	Other	
NELSON, Sammy	1981–83	40 1 gl	–	3	2	–	
NEVINS, Laurie	1947–48	5	–	–	–	–	
NEWMAN, Daren	1985–86	1	–	–	–	–	
NEWTON, Jimmy	1929–30	1	–	–	–	–	
NICHOLAS, Tony	1960–62	65 22 gls	–	4	1 1 gl	–	
NICOL, Geordie	1929–32	31 23 gls	–	1	–	–	
NIGHTINGALE, Jack	1921–28	182 33 gls	–	13	–	–	
NOGAN, Kurt	1992–	30 20 gls	–	3+1	–	3 2 gls	AMC
O'BRIEN, Joe	1904–05	–	28	5	–	–	SCC
O'DOWD, Greg	1988–92	0+1	–	–	–	–	
OLIVER, Gavin	1985	15+1	–	–	–	1	FMC
OLIVER, Jim	1965–68	37+6 6 gls	–	5	2	–	
O'RAWE, Frank	1926–27	1	–	–	–	–	
O'REGAN, Kieran	1982–87	69+17 2 gls	–	3	6+1	2+1 1 gl	FMC
O'REILLY, Gary	1984–87 & 1991–93	106+1 6 gls	–	7	6	3	FMC
OSBORNE, Fred	1919–20	–	3	–	–	–	
OSBORNE, John	1927–29	3	–	–	–	–	
O'SULLIVAN, Peter	1970–80 & 1980–81	432+3 39 gls	–	25 3 gls	31 1 gl	–	AMC
OSWALD, Willie	1926–28	14 2 gls	–	–	–	–	
OWEN, F.	1902–03	–	–	–	–	4	SE League
OWENS, Les	1952–53	15 4 gls	–	3 3 gls	–	–	
OWERS, Adrian	1987–91	32+8 4 gls	–	–	2	0+1	FMC
PADDINGTON, Albert	1903–04	–	31	1	–	–	
PARKER, J.	1912	–	1	–	–	–	
PARKES, David	1913–14	–	33	4	–	5	S Alliance
						5	SCC
PARLETT, Frank	1910–14	–	4	–	–	1	S Alliance
						5	SCC
PARSONS, Ted	1903–05	–	37 1 gl	–	–	–	
PATERSON, H.	1914	–	–	–	–	1	S Alliance
PATES, Colin	1991	20	–	–	–	–	
PAYNE	1903	–	–	–	–	1	SE League
PAYNE, John	1934–35	8 1 gl	–	–	–	1	SSC
PEARCE, Graham	1982–86	87+1 2 gls	–	12	7	2	FMC
PENNEY, Steve	1983–91	125+13 14 gls	–	12	9 1 gl	2	FMC
						0+1	AMC
PERKINS, Bill	1911	–	1	–	–	–	
PHILBIN, Jack †	1938–46	6 1 gl	–	–	–	–	
PHILLIPS, Reg	1921–23	3	–	–	–	–	
PHILLIPS, T. John	1980–81	1	–	–	–	–	
PIGGIN, Lionel	1912	–	2	–	–	–	
PINCHBECK, Cliff	1949	14 5 gls	–	–	–	–	
PINDER, W.	1913	–	–	–	–	1	S Alliance
PIPER, Steve	1970–78	160+2 9 gls	–	9	19	–	
POINTON, Joe	1928–29	16 5 gls	–	–	–	–	
PORTER, W.	1907	–	–	–	–	1	WL
POSKETT, Malcolm	1978–80	33+12 17 gls	–	1	4+1 1 gl	–	
POTTS, Eric	1977–78	19+14 5 gls	–	1+1 1 gl	6 1 gl	–	
POWNEY, Brian	1960–74	351	–	20	15	–	
PREST, Tommy	1935–37	27 5 gls	–	–	–	1 1 gl	SSC
PRYCE, Jack	1903–05	–	23 5 gls	–	–	–	
PUGH, Jimmy	1919–20	–	22	1	–	–	
RAMSEY, Chris	1980–84	30	–	6	1	–	
RANDALL, Ossie	1919–22	1	–	–	–	–	
READMAN, Joe	1927–28	6	–	–	–	–	
REDFERN, Bob	1947–48	5 1 gl	–	–	–	–	
REED, Walter	1903	–	–	–	–	1	SE League
REED, William F. 'Billy'	1914–15	–	18 9 gls	3	–	–	
REED, William G. 'Billy'	1948–53	129 36 gls	–	3 1 gl	–	–	
REES, Barrie	1965	12 1 gl	–	–	–	–	
REES, Mal	1949–50	2	–	–	–	–	
REGAN, J.	1913	–	–	–	–	1	S Alliance
RICHARDS, Billy	1935–37	44 8 gls	–	6	–	1	SSC
RIDLEY, Dave	1946–47	5	–	–	–	–	
RING, Mike	1977–84	1+4	–	–	1	–	
RISDON, Stan †	1936–48	23	–	10	–	2 1 gl	SSC
RITCHIE, Andy	1980–83	82+7 23 gls	–	9 2 gls	3+1 1 gl	–	
RITCHIE, George	1919–21	3	18 6 gls	–	–	–	
ROBERTS, Doug	1949–51	17 3 gls	–	–	–	–	
ROBERTS, J.	1913	–	–	–	–	1	S Alliance
ROBERTS, Willliam 'Billy'	1903–05	–	67 15 gls.	6 2 gls	–	–	
ROBERTSON, A. Lammie	1972–74	42+4 8 gls	–	2	0+1	–	
ROBERTSON, Jimmy	1908–09	–	23 5 gls	1	–	11 5 gls	WL
						2	SCC
ROBERTSON, Tom	1904–06	–	26 1 gl	5	–	–	

Albion players 1901–93 — Robinson to Steele

Appearances as substitute are shown following a plus (+) sign. Players marked with a dagger (†) also made appearances for Albion in the wartime competitions; see the list of wartime players for details. Football League statistics include the play-offs, Southern League statistics include the test match, and Western League statistics include the championship play-offs.

Player	Career	FL		SL		FAC		FLC		Other		
ROBINSON, G. L.	1904–05	–		2		–		–		–		
ROBINSON, John	1987–92	57+7	7 gls	–		2+1		5	1 gl	1	1 gl	FMC
ROBINSON, Michael	1980–83	111+2	37 gls	–		12	3 gls	8	3 gls	–		
RODGER, Tom	1908	–		15	1 gl	–		–		–		
RODGERSON, Ted	1920–22	53	11 gls	–		4		–		–		
RODON, Chris	1983–84	0+1		–		–		–		–		
ROLLINGS, Andy	1974–80 & 1986–87	168	11 gls	–		9		15	1 gl	–		
RONALDSON, Duncan	1907–08	–		19	6 gls	2		–		9	1 gl	WL
										3	2 gls	SCC
ROUGVIE, Doug	1987–88	35	2 gls	–		4	1 gl	2		5		AMC
ROUTLEDGE, Ralph	1909–15	–		50		1		–		6		SCC
ROWELL, Gary	1986–88	9+3		–		–		1		0+1		FMC
RUGGIERO, John	1977–79	4+4	2 gls	–		–		4		–		
RULE, Arthur	1905	–		1		–		–		–		
RUSHTON, George	1903–04	–		21	4 gls	1		–		–		
RUSSELL, Jock	1901–02	–		13	2 gls	4	1 gl	–		–		
RUTHERFORD, Jim	1920–21	26		–		3		–		–		
RUTHERFORD, John 'Jack'	1920–21	29	2 gls	–		3		–		–		
RYAN, Gerry	1978–86	131+42	32 gls	–		10+4	5 gls	6+6	2 gls	–		
SALT, Harold	1921–22	6	2 gls	–		–		–		–		
SANDERS, Allan	1963–65	80		–		1		5		–		
SAUNDERS, Dean	1985–87	66+6	21 gls	–		7	4 gls	4		3		FMC
SAUNDERS, Edgar	1922–23	2		–		1		–		–		
SAYER, Peter	1978–80	46+9	6 gls	–		1+1		7		–		
SCHOOLEY, Herbert	1904–07	–		–		–		–		1		Utd League
SCOTT, Frank	1902–04	–		25	14 gls	5	9 gls	–		20	11 gls	SE League
SEAR	1902	–		2	1 gl	–		–		–		
SEXTON, Dave	1957–59	49	26 gls	–		4	2 gls	–		–		
SEYMOUR, Ian	1971	3		–		–		–		–		
SHANKS, Don	1981–83	45+1		–		3		5		–		
SHARP, Alf	1901	–		1		–		–		–		
SHARPE, Ivan	1911	–		–		2		–		–		
SHEPHERD, John	1958–60	45	19 gls	–		–		–		–		
SHERIDAN, Alex	1970–72	12+3	2 gls	–		–		1		–		
SHORT, Jimmy	1933–35	37	11 gls	–		2	1 gl	–		3	1 gl	SSC
SIDEBOTTOM, Geoff	1969–71	40		–		2		3		–		
SIM, Jock	1946–50	32	5 gls	–		3	2 gls	–		–		
SIMPSON, Bobby	1912–14	–		30	11 gls	3		–		5	1 gl	S Alliance
SIMPSON, Tommy	1927–28	30	6 gls	–		–		–		–		
SIRRELL, Jimmy	1951–54	55	16 gls	–		3	1 gl	–		–		
SITFORD, Tony	1958–62	22	2 gls	–		1		1		–		
SLY, Harold	1929–33	22		–		2		–		–		
SMALL, Mike	1990–91	42	16 gls	–		3	2 gls	2	1 gl	3	2 gls	FMC
SMALL, Peter	1957–59	8	3 gls	–		–		–		–		
SMALL, Sammy	1948–50	38		–		2		–		–		
SMART, Freddie	1909–15	–		12	1 gl	–		–		3		S Alliance
										3		SCC
SMILLIE, Neil	1982–85	62+13	2 gls	–		8+1	1 gl	2		–		
SMITH, Albert	1901–03	–		8	4 gls	–		–		8	2 gls	SE League
SMITH, Alec	1906–07	–		12		–		–		8	1 gl	Utd League
SMITH, Dave	1961–62	15		–		–		1		–		
SMITH, Gordon	1980–84	97+12	22 gls	–		5+1	1 gl	8+2	2 gls	–		
SMITH, Jimmy	1911–12	–		56	36 gls	3	1 gl	–		3	1 gl	S Alliance
										3	2 gls	SCC
SMITH, John 'Jack'	1964–66	88	33 gls	–		4	2 gls	4	1 gl	–		
SMITH, John W. 'Jack'	1924–25	14	4 gls	–		–		–		–		
SMITH, Reg	1923–32	143	1 gl	–		7		–		–		
SMITH, Robert A. 'Bobby'	1964–65	31	19 gls	–		1		2	2 gls	–		
SMITH, Robert W. 'Bobby'	1968–71	72+3	2 gls	–		6		4		–		
SMITH, T. Potter	1929–37	281	40 gls	–		32	17 gls	–		6		SSC
SMITH, W.	1903	–		–		–		–		1		SE League
SMITH, Wally	1906–07	–		36	5 gls	1	1 gl	–		5	3 gls	Utd League
SMITH, Wilf	1974	5		–		–		–		–		
SOMMER, Jeurgen	1991	1		–		–		–		–		
SOUTH, Alex	1948–54	81	4 gls	–		4		–		–		
SPEARRITT, Eddie	1969–74	203+7	22 gls	–		13	1 gl	9	2 gls	–		
SPENCER, Frank	1912–20	–		109		11		–		19		S Alliance
										3		SCC
SPOONER, Billy	1913–14	–		1		–		–		4	1 gl	S Alliance
										1		SCC
STANDING, John	1961–62	10		–		–		–		–		
STANLEY, Terry	1969–72	16+6		–		0+1		–		–		
STARKS, T.	1902	–		–		–		–		1		SE League
STEELE, Eric	1977–79	87		–		2		9		–		
STEELE, Simon	1983–84	1		–		–		–		–		

Albion players 1901–93 — Stemp to Watson

Appearances as substitute are shown following a plus (+) sign. Players marked with a dagger (†) also made appearances for Albion in the wartime competitions; see the list of wartime players for details. Football League statistics include the play-offs, Southern League statistics include the test match, and Western League statistics include the championship play-offs.

Player	Career	FL		SL		FAC		FLC		Other		
STEMP, Wayne	1986–92	4		–		–		–		–		
STEPHENS, Bert †	1935–48	180	86 gls	–		20	8 gls	–		5	2 gls	SSC
STEPHENS, Malcolm	1955–57	29	14 gls	–		–		–		–		
STEVENS, Gary	1978–83	120+13	2 gls	–		11+1	1 gl	6+1		–		
STEVENS, Jack †	1934–43	137		–		10		–		1		SSC
STEVENS, Norman	1955–61	1		–		–		–		–		
STEWART, Tom	1908–09	–		39		1		–		12	1 gl	WL
										2		SCC
STILLE, Giles	1979–84	20+7	4 gls	–		2		–		–		
STOTT, T.	1911–12	–		1	1 gl	–		–		1		SCC
SUDDABY, Peter	1979–81	21+2		–		2		–		–		
SULSTON, Cecil	1911–20	–		1		–		–		–		
SUTHERLAND, Jim	1901–03	–		15	1 gl	4		–		1		SE League
SUTTLE, Ken	1949	3		–		–		–		–		
SWEETMAN, Tom	1903–05	–		–		–		–		1		SE League
SYKES, Albert	1926–28	16		–		–		–		–		
TAWSE, Brian	1965–70	97+5	14 gls	–		9	2 gls	3		–		
TAYLOR, A. J.	1902–04	–		7	2 gls	–		–		9	3 gls	SE League
TAYLOR, Geoff	1948–49	2		–		–		–		–		
TAYLOR, H. E.	1912	–		–		–		–		1		S Alliance
TELFORD, J.	1902	–		1		–		–		–		
TEMPLEMAN, John	1966–74	219+7	16 gls	–		18		10+1	2 gls	–		
TENNANT, Des	1948–59	400	40 gls	–		24	7 gls	–		–		
THAIR, Sid	1901–04	–		29	7 gls	5	4 gls	–		15	8 gls	SE League
THOMAS, D. Lyn	1947–49	13	4 gls	–		1		–		–		
THOMAS, John 'Jack'	1910–11	–		1		–		–		2	1 gl	SCC
THOMAS, Mickey	1981–82	18+2		–		3	1 gl	–		–		
THOMAS, Rees	1949 & 1956–58	31	1 gl	–		2		–		–		
THOMPSON, A. Stan	1929–35	58	14 gls	–		13	6 gls	–		2		SSC
THOMPSON, Cyril	1950–51	41	15 gls	–		4	1 gl	–		–		
THOMPSON, Jack	1921–25	94		–		12		–		–		
THOMPSON, Pat	1951–55	1		–		–		–		–		
THOMSON, Charlie	1934–39	169		–		14		–		8		SSC
THOMSON, Norman	1927–28	11	5 gls	–		–		–		–		
THORNE, Adrian	1954–61	76	38 gls	–		6	4 gls	2	2 gls	–		
TIDDY, Mike	1958–62	133	11 gls	–		10	1 gl	3		–		
TILER, Ken	1974–79	130		–		6		15		–		
TILTMAN, Richard	1986–88	10+3	1 gl	–		0+2		0+1		–		
TOWNER, Tony	1970–78	153+9	24 gls	–		8+1	1 gl	10+2		–		
TOWNLEY, Jimmy	1928–30	9		–		–		–		–		
TOWNSEND, Eric	1930–34	15	9 gls	–		–		–		–		
TOWNSHEND, A.	1907–08	–		–		–		–		2		WL
TRAINOR, Peter †	1938–48	71	4 gls	–		5		–		1		SSC
TRANTER, Wilf	1966–68	46+1	1 gl	–		6+1		3		–		
TRUSLER, Johnny	1954–56	1		–		–		–		–		
TRUSSON, Mike	1987–89	34+3	2 gls	–		3		1		2		AMC
TURNBULL, Billy	1928–29	5		–		–		–		–		
TURNER	1913	–		–		–		–		1		S Alliance
TURNER, Dave	1963–72	292+8	30 gls	–		18	4 gls	20		–		
TURNER, Tom	1905–09	–		91		10		–		19		Utd League
										14		WL
										2		SCC
TUSTIN, Bill	1908–09	–		3		–		–		1		WL
TYLER, Alfie	1913–15	–		50	1 gl	5		–		13		S Alliance
										1		SCC
UPTON, Nobby	1958–66	40		–		1		3		–		
VALLANCE, Hugh	1929–30	44	32 gls	–		6	2 gls	–		–		
VARCO, Percy	1932–33	1		–		–		–		–		
VASEY, Bob	1938–39	15	1 gl	–		–		–		1		SSC
VESSEY, Tony	1978–82	1		–		–		–		–		
VICKERS, Wilf	1947–48	5	1 gl	–		–		–		–		
VITTY, Jack	1949–52	47	1 gl	–		3		–		–		
WADE, Bryan	1990–92	12+6	9 gls	–		2+1		–		0+1		FMC
WAITES, George	1962–65	23	1 gl	–		–		1		–		
WAKE, Tom	1910–13	–		15		1		–		1		S Alliance
										5		SCC
WALKER, Clive	1990–93	106+2	9 gls	–		9	1 gl	6		3+1		FMC
										3	2 gls	AMC
WALKER, Dave	1929–39	310	28 gls	–		27	2 gls	–		12		SSC
WALKER, Jim	1974–76	24+4	4 gls	–		3		1		–		
WALKER, Robert 'Bob'	1962–63	12	1 gl	–		–		1		–		
WARD, Alf	1904–05	–		3		2	3 gls	–		–		
WARD, Peter	1975–80 & 1982–83	188+6	81 gls	–		10	3 gls	22+1	11 gls			
WARD, W.	1903	–		–		–		–		3	5 gls	SE League
WATSON, Harold	1931–33	6		–		–		–		–		

Albion players 1901–93 — Watson to Young

Appearances as substitute are shown following a plus (+) sign. Players marked with a dagger (†) also made appearances for Albion in the wartime competitions; see the list of wartime players for details. Football League statistics include the play-offs, Southern League statistics include the test match, and Western League statistics include the championship play-offs.

Player	Career	FL	SL	FAC	FLC	Other	
WATSON, Jimmy †	1945–46	–	–	6	–	–	
WEBB, Charlie	1908–15	–	219 64 gls	12 3 gls	–	1 1 gl	FA Ch. Shield
						3	WL
						26 9 gls	S Alliance
						14 2 gls	SCC
WEBB, Stan	1924–35	205	–	24	–	5	SSC
WEBBER, Keith	1963–64	35 14 gls	–	1	2 1 gl	–	
WELCH, Ronnie	1973–74	35+1 4 gls	–	–	4	–	
WEST, C. H.	1902–03	–	1	2 3 gls	–	7 1 gl	SE League
WETTON, Albert	1951–53	3	–	1	–	–	
WHENT, Jack †	1945–46 & 1947–50	101 4 gls	–	13	–	–	
WHITE, Tom	1904–06	–	29 1 gl	2 2 gls	–	4	Utd League
WHITEHOUSE, W.	1914	–	–	–	–	1	S Alliance
WHITEHURST, Squire	1901–04	–	16	6	–	10	SE League
WHITFIELD, Ken	1954–59	175 4 gls	–	7	–	–	
WHITING, Bob	1908–15	–	253	13	–	1	FA Ch. Shield
						13	WL
						24	S Alliance
						16	SCC
WHITINGTON, Eric	1964–68	26+6 8 gls	–	6 4 gls	3	–	
WHITTINGTON, George 'Dick'	1908–24		1	–	–	7	S Alliance
						6	SCC
WICKHAM, Alfred	1902	–	–	–	–	1	SE League
WILCOCK, George	1913–15	–	11	3	–	5	S Alliance
						2	SCC
WILKINS, Dean	1983–84 & 1987–	238+7 21 gls	–	16+1	14 3 gl	5	FMC
						9 2 gls	AMC
WILKINS, Jack	1948–52	44 2 gls	–	3	–	–	
WILKINSON, Darron	1992–	26+1 3 gls	–	1+1	0+1	2 2 gls	AMC
WILKINSON, Howard	1966–71	116+13 18 gls	–	5+4	9 1 gl	–	
WILKINSON, Reg	1924–34	361 14 gls	–	30 2 gls	–	5	SSC
WILLARD, Jess	1946–51	190 22 gls	–	12 2 gls	–	–	
WILLEMSE, Stan †	1946–49	91 3 gls	–	11 1 gl	–	–	
WILLIAMS, D. H.	1913	–	1	–	–	1 1 gl	S Alliance
WILLIAMS, Dave	1920–21	20 2 gls	10 3 gls	1	–	–	
WILLIAMS, Gary	1977–82	158 7 gls	–	5	13+1 1 gl	–	
WILLIAMS, Reg	1926–29	101	–	6	–	–	
WILLIAMS, W. John 'Jack'	1928–31	42 1 gl	–	6	–	–	
WILLIAMSON	1913	–	–	–	–	2 1 gl	S Alliance
						2 1 gl	SCC
WILLIS, George	1948–49	28 13 gls	–	–	–	–	
WILSON, Alex	1947	1	–	–	–	–	
WILSON, Danny	1983–87	132+3 33 gls	–	10 1 gl	7 3 gls	3 2 gls	FMC
WILSON, Ernie 'Tug'	1922–36	509 67 gls	–	49 4 gls	–	8	SSC
WILSON, Glen	1948–60	409 25 gls	–	27 3 gls	–	–	
WILSON, Harry	1973–77	130 4 gls	–	7	9	–	
WILSON, Joe	1908–09	–	25	–	–	8 1 gl	WL
						2	SCC
WILSON, Joe A. †	1936–47	156 15 gls	–	17 3 gls	–	2	SSC
WINDROSS, Dennis	1960–61	18 2 gls	–	3 2 gls	–	–	
WINSTANLEY, Graham	1974–79	63+1 4 gls	–	4	3	–	
WISDEN, Alan	1920–21	1	–	–	–	–	
WOFFINDEN, Colin	1970–71	0+3	–	0+1 1 gl	–	–	
WOMBWELL, Dick	1907–08	–	19 3 gls	5 1 gl	–	9 3 gls	WL
						2	SCC
WOOD, Paul	1987–90	77+15 8 gls	–	2+2	4	2	FMC
						3	AMC
WOODHAMS, W. H.	1902	–	2	–	–	–	
WOODHOUSE, Jack	1912–24	117	85 16 gls	15	–	20 6 gls	S Alliance
		–				4	SCC
WOOLGAR, Phil	1966–67	1	–	–	–	–	
WOOLVEN, Harold	1906–07	–	–	–	–	3 2 gls	Utd League
WORTHINGTON, Frank	1984–85	27+4 7 gls	–	2	1+1 1 gl	–	
WOSAHLO, Bradley	1991–	–	–	–	0+1	–	
WRAGG, Billy	1905–06	–	4	–	–	6	Utd League
WRIGHT, Barrie	1969–70	8+2	–	–	–	–	
WRIGHT, Joe	1932–34	14	–	–	–	–	
WRIGHT, Steve	1923–24	4	–	–	–	–	
YATES, Billy	1905–06	–	33 4 gls	5 3 gls	–	13 2 gls	Utd League
YOUNG, Alan	1983–84	25+1 12 gls	–	1	2	–	
YOUNG, Eric	1982–87	126 10 gls	–	11 1 gls	8+1	2	FMC
YOUNG, Len	1948–49	8	–	–	–	–	
YOUNG, Willie	1984	4	–	–	–	–	

Albion wartime players 1939–46 — Abel to Matthewson

This list includes the emergency league and cup competitions only from 1939 to 1946; the 1945–46 F.A. Cup is not included. Guest players were allowed and their registered club is given where known. Players marked with a dagger (†) also played in peacetime matches for the Albion; see list of Albion players 1901–93 for details.

Player	Club			Player	Club		
ABEL, Sammy	Queen's Park Rangers	1		FLACK, Doug	Fulham	1	
ADAMS, Billy	Tottenham Hotspur	1		FORD, Fred	Charlton Athletic	12	
ALEXANDER, Fred	Queen's Park Rangers	1		FOX, Dan	Albion	4	
ANDERSON, Jock	Portsmouth	3		FRANCE, Ernie	Albion	2	
AUSTEN, Herbert	Albion	6		FRANCIS, Vic	Hastings & St Leonards	1	
BALDWIN, Harry †	Albion	32		FROST, Arthur	New Brighton	3	1 gl
BALL		1		GILLESPIE, Ian	Crystal Palace	1	
BALL, Jack †	Albion	46		GOFFEY, Bert †	Albion	4	1 gl
BALMER, Jack	Liverpool	14	16 gls	GORE, Les	Clapton Orient	2	1 gl
BARBER		1		GRAINGER, Jack	Southport	2	
BARLOW, K.	Southampton	1		GREEN, Freddie †	Albion	9	
BARTRAM, A.	emergency player	1		GREGORY, Fred	Crystal Palace	1	
BENTLEY, George	Albion	1		GREGORY, Jack	Southampton	1	
BIRD, S.	emergency player	1		GRIER		1	
BLACKMAN, John	Crystal Palace	1		GRIFFIN, Albert	Albion	4	1 gl
BOJAR, Felix	Polish guest	10		GRIFFITHS, Mal	Leicester City	12	5 gls
BOTT, Wilf	Queen's Park Rangers	15	3 gls	GROVES, Ken	Preston North End	1	
BOWLES, Reg	Albion	6		GRUNDY, Arnold	Newcastle United	1	
BOYD, Jimmy	Grimsby Town	1		GUNN, Alfie	Albion	15	4 gls
BRATLEY, George	Crystal Palace	14		HANCOCK, John	Albion	1	
BRIGGS, Vic	Southwick	6		HARLOCK, Des	Tranmere Rovers	1	
BRISCOE, Jimmy	Heart of Midlothian	3	1 gl	HARMAN, Charlie	Albion	18	4 gls
BROOMFIELD, Des †	Albion	4	1 gl	HART, Archie	Third Lanark	15	2 gls
BROWN, Jimmy	Motherwell	1		HASSELL, Tommy †	Southampton	39	15 gls
BROWN, James R.	Romford Town	15		HAWORTH		3	
BROWNING, Charlie	Albion	8		HENLEY, Les	Arsenal	1	
BUCKELL	emergency player	1		HICKMAN, S.		1	
BUNYON, W.	Clapton Orient	1		HICKMAN, Stan L.	Albion	12	
BURDETT		1		HILLMAN, Dennis	Albion	12	3 gls
BURGESS, Ron	Tottenham Hotspur	4		HINDLEY, Frank †	Albion	2	
BURTENSHAW, Charlie	Albion	3		HODGES, Cyril †	Arsenal	19	15 gls
BUSH, Tom	Liverpool	3		HODGSON, Sam	Grimsby Town	9	
BUTLER, Malcolm	Blackpool	1		HOLLIS, Harry	Chester	1	
CAMERON, Jock	Albion	1		HOOPER, Percy	Tottenham Hotspur	1	
CATER, Ron	West Ham United	1		HUGHES, Horace	Albion	2	
CHAPMAN, A.		1		ISAAC, Bill	Albion	11	3 gls
CHASE, Charlie †	Albion	22	1 gl	ITHELL, Jimmy	Bolton Wanderers	2	
CHESTERS, Arthur	Crystal Palace	7		JACKSON, Les	Bradford Park Avenue	1	
CHRISTIE		1		JONES, Leslie	Albion	1	
CLARKSON, George	Blackburn Rovers	2		JONES, Ron	Liverpool	1	1 gl
CLATWORTHY, Les	Chelsea	1		JONES, Syd	Arsenal	21	1 gl
CLIFFORD, John	Northampton Town	1		KAY, John	Brentford	3	1 gl
COCKER, Joe	Arsenal	1		KEEN, Eric	unattached guest	1	
COLBORN, Harold	Albion	3	1 gl	KELLY, Jimmy	Queen's Park Rangers	1	1 gl
COLLINS, John	Albion	1	1 gl	KELLY, Lawrie	Aldershot	3	
COOK, P. R.	Luton Town	1		KEMP, Dirk	Liverpool	13	
COOK, R.	St Johnstone	9	3 gls	KINGHORN, Bill	Liverpool	20	7 gls
CORNISH, Dennis	Albion	4	3 gls	KIRKMAN, Norman	Burnley	1	
COTHLIFF, Harold	Torquay United	1	1 gl	KYLE		1	
COURT, Dick	unattached	1		LANCELOTTE, Eric †	Charlton Athletic	1	1 gl
COWAN, Sam	Albion's trainer	3		LANE, Billy	unattached guest	1	1 gl
CRAWFORD, Ted	Clapton Orient	6	2 gls	LANEY, Les	Southampton	1	1 gl
CROFT, Charlie	Huddersfield Town	1		LAWRENCE		1	
CUNLIFFE, Arthur	Hull City	19	11 gls	LAYTON, Billy	Reading	1	
CURTIS, George	Arsenal	3		LEWIS, Doug	Southampton	1	
CURTIS, J. W.	Army	1		LEWIS, Bill	West Ham United	1	
DARLING, Len †	Albion	113	7 gls	LOBB, Fred	Albion	1	
DAVIE, Jock †	Albion	86	62 gls	LONDON, Dermot	Albion	1	
DAY, Albert †	Albion	16	8 gls	LONGDON, Charlie †	Albion	101	2 gls
DEVINE, John	Queen's Park Rangers	1		LOWE, Henry	Queen's Park Rangers	1	
DEVONPORT, George	Torquay United	5	1 gl	LOWRIE		1	
DOOLEY, A.		1		LYLE		1	
DRIVER, Allenby	Sheffield Wednesday	1	1 gl	McCOY, Tim †	Albion	7	
DUGNOLLE, Jack †	Plymouth Argyle	2		McDERMOTT, Joe	Gateshead	18	5 gls
DUKE, George	Luton Town	2		McFARLANE, D. L.	Crystal Palace	1	
DYE, Derek	Norwich City	1		McINNES, Jimmy	Liverpool	30	
EASDALE, Jack	Liverpool	37	1 gl	McKENZIE, Duncan	Middlesbrough	12	
EASTHAM, George	Blackpool	3		McNAUGHTON, Jock †	Albion	7	
EASTHAM, Harry	Liverpool	50	4 gls	McNEILL, Hamilton	Bury	2	3 gls
EDINGTON, John	Arsenal	1		MALONE, Ron	Albion	1	1 gl
EVANS, Tommy	Albion	25		MALPASS, Sam	Fulham	29	1 gl
FAIRHURST, Billy	Bury	33		MARRIOTT, Ernie †	Albion	66	1 gl
FARMER, Alex	Queen's Park Rangers	1		MARTIN, Ted †	Albion	65	
FARRELL, Bobby †	Albion	36	11 gls	MARTINDALE, Len	Burnley	4	
FELTON, Bob	Port Vale	1		MATTHEWSON, George	Bury	1	

Albion wartime players 1939–46 — Mee to Young

This list includes the emergency league and cup competitions only from 1939 to 1946; the 1945–46 F.A. Cup is not included. Guest players were allowed and their registered club is given where known. Players marked with a dagger (†) also played in peacetime matches for the Albion; see list of Albion players 1901–93 for details.

Player	Club			Player	Club		
MEE, Gordon †	Albion	93		SPERRIN, Bill	Tottenham Hotspur	2	
MILES		1		SPRY		1	
MILLBANK, Joe	Crystal Palace	1		STACEY, W. A.		1	
MOORE, Bernard †	Albion	62	44 gls	STEAR, Jimmy	Southampton	1	
MOORE, J. Beriah	Cardiff City	1		STEPHENS, Bert †	Albion	161	78 gls
MOORES, Peter	Portsmouth	1		STEVENS, Jack †	Albion	38	
MORGAN, Stan	Arsenal	31	16 gls	SWINFEN Reg	Queen's Park Rangers	1	
MOUNTFORD, George	Stoke City	1		SZAJNA-STANKOWSKI, Bishek	Polish guest	1	
MUIR, Bob	Rochdale	2		TAIT, Tommy	Torquay United	1	
MULRANEY, Ambrose	Ipswich Town	1		TAPKEN, Norman	Manchester United	2	
MUNRO, Alex	Blackpool	6		TAYLOR, Phil	Liverpool	39	5 gls
MUTTITT, Ernie	Brentford	2		THEW	emergency player	1	
NEEDHAM, Fred	Stockport County	3		THORNE, Albert	Albion	3	1 gl
NIXON		1		TOOTILL, Alf	Crystal Palace	1	
O'DONNELL, Frank	Aston Villa	26	12 gls	TOOZE, Cyril	Arsenal	17	
OFFORD, Stan	Bradford Park Avenue	1	1 gl	TOWNSEND, Len	Brentford	1	1 gl
OHLENS, P. W.	Southwick	1	1 gl	TRAINOR, Peter †	Albion	17	1 gl
OWENS	emergency player	1		TULLY, Fred	Clapton Orient	1	
PACKHAM, Wally	Hastings & St Leonards	2		TUNNICLIFFE, Bill	Bournemouth	5	2 gls
PARR, Charlie	Haywards Heath	1		WALKER, Cyril	Sheffield Wednesday	2	
PATERSON, George	Liverpool	2		WALLER, Henry	Arsenal	5	
PEARSON, Stan	Manchester United	8	3 gls	WALLIS, John	Tottenham Hotspur	3	
PETERS, Cyril 'Bill'	Albion	1	1 gl	WARD, Jack	Nottingham Forest	2	
PHILBIN, Jack †	Albion	8	1 gl	WASSALL, John	Manchester United	4	
PINCHBECK, F.		1		WATSON, Jimmy †	Bristol Rovers	14	2 gls
PINKERTON, Harry	Falkirk	3		WATSON, Jack	Bury	2	
POINTON, Bill	Port Vale	1		WATTS, Royston	Albion	6	
POULTER, J.	unattached	1		WEAVER, Sam	Chelsea	1	
PRYDE, Bob	Blackburn Rovers	1		WEIR, J.	Hibernian	3	1 gl
PUGH, John	Cardiff City	1		WELSH, Don	Charlton Athletic	9	17 gls
RAMSDEN, Barney	Liverpool	9	1 gl	WESTBY, Jack	Blackburn Rovers	16	
REECE, Tom	Crystal Palace	30	2 gls	WHARTON, F.	Hibernian	1	
REID, Ernie	Norwich City	87	13 gls	WHENT, Jack †	Albion	35	1 gl
RICHARDSON, Dave	Bradford City	1		WILLEMSE, Stan †	Albion	8	2 gls
RICHMOND	emergency player	1		WILLIAMS, S.	Cardiff City	7	
RISDON, Stan †	Albion	216	12 gls	WILLIAMS, Walter	Cardiff City	1	
ROBSON, Bert	Crystal Palace	1	1 gl	WILSON, Albert	Crystal Palace	1	
ROSS, George	Dundee United	1		WILSON, Alec	Huddersfield Town	1	
ROWLEY, Arthur	West Bromwich Albion	5	1 gl	WILSON, Fred	Bournemouth	24	
SAGE, Frank	Cardiff City	1		WILSON, Joe A. †	Albion	178	31 gls
SANDERSON	emergency player	1		WINNING, Alex	Clyde	17	
SCRIMSHAW, Stan	Bradford City	2		WOODLEY, Vic	Chelsea	1	
SHAFTO, John	Liverpool	28	23 gls	WOODS		1	
SHEPPARD, Richard	Albion	5	1 gl	WOODWARD, Laurie	Bournemouth	6	
SIMMONS, L.	emergency player	1		WRIGHT, Tommy	Manchester City	9	1 gl
SLATER		1		YOUNG		1	
SMITH, A.		1		unknown emergency player		1	

Note that two players made first-team appearances only in the fixtures of the cancelled 1939–40 Football League season and are not included in the preceding lists:

HARRIS, Joe	1939 & 1945–46
SPENCER, Geoff	1939

Note also that nine players have been named as substitutes only for first-team games but have not been called upon (the figure given is the number of occasions in the season stated):

FULLER, Bob	1, 1967–68
NORTON, Terry	1, 1973–74
DINEEN, Jack	1, 1987–88 & 3, 1988–89
CORMACK, Lee	5, 1989–90 & 2, 1990–91
DICK, Alistair	1, 1989–90
COLDWELL, David	2, 1990–91
McGUINNESS, Paul	5, 1990–91
REED, Paul	1, 1991–92
TUCK, Stuart	1, 1992–93

Players with 250 or more appearances

Totals include appearances as substitute

Apps	Player	Competitions			
566	Ernie Wilson	509 FL	49 FAC	8 SSC	
491	Peter O'Sullivan	432+3 FL	25 FAC	31 FLC	
488	Norman Gall	427+13 FL	26+1 FAC	21 FLC	
466	Bobby Farrell	382 FL	38 FAC	10 SSC	36 wartime
443	Bert Longstaff	315 SL	41 FL	20 FAC	4 Utd League
		18 WL	26 S Alliance	18 SCC	1 FA Ch. Shield
436	Glen Wilson	409 FL	27 FAC		
424	Des Tennant	400 FL	24 FAC		
396	Reg Wilkinson	361 FL	30 FAC	5 SSC	
386	Brian Powney	351 FL	20 FAC	15 FLC	
369	Billy Booth	303 SL	17 FAC	12 WL	19 S Alliance
		17 SCC	1 FA Ch. Shield		
"	Steve Gatting	316+3 FL	26 FAC	14 FLC	5 FMC
		5 AMC			
366	Bert Stephens	180 FL	20 FAC	5 SSC	161 wartime
353	Joe Wilson	156 FL	17 FAC	2 FLC	178 wartime
349	Dave Walker	310 FL	27 FAC	12 SSC	
341	Len Darling	199 FL	23 FAC	6 SSC	113 wartime
338	Dave Turner	292+8 FL	18 FAC	20 FLC	
332	Wally Little	23 SL	285 FL		24 FAC
320	Bob Whiting	253 SL	13 FAC	13 WL	24 S Alliance
		16 SCC	1 FA Ch. Shield		
319	Potter Smith	281 FL	32 FAC	6 SSC	
315	Paul Mooney	283 FL	24 FAC	8 SSC	
297	Roy Jennings	276 FL	14 FAC	7 FLC	
296	Eric Gill	280 FL	16 FAC		
293	Dennis Gordon	277 FL	16 FAC		
291	Kit Napier	249+7 FL	22 FAC	13 FLC	
290	Dean Wilkins	238+7 FL	16+1 FAC	14 FLC	5 FMC
		9 AMC			
279	Jack Bertolini	258 FL	13 FAC	8 FLC	
275	Charlie Webb	219 SL	12 FAC	3 WL	26 S Alliance
		14 SCC	1 FA Ch. Shield		
272	George Coomber	75 SL	168 FL	18 FAC	9 S Alliance
		2 SCC			
255	John Templeman	219+7 FL	18 FAC	10+1 FLC	
252	Steve Burtenshaw	237 FL	10 FAC	5 FLC	
"	Brian Horton	217+1 FL	10 FAC	24 FLC	
"	Gary Chivers	218+2 FL	12 FAC	12 FLC	6 FMC
		2 AMC			
251	Stan Risdon	23 FL	10 FAC	2 SSC	216 wartime

Players with 100 or more consecutive appearances

The date given is the first game of the sequence

Apps	Player	Date
247	Eric Gill	21.2.1953
194	Peter O'Sullivan	16.10.1970
193	Jack Bertolini	25.4.1959
175	Billy Hayes	2.10.1920
146	Gary Williams	15.10.1977
143	Billy Booth	28.10.1908
139	Brian Horton	4.9.1976
124	Peter Grummitt	9.11.1974
123	Dean Wilkins	29.4.1989
115	Reg Wilkinson	9.10.1926
113	Jimmy Collins	2.10.1962
112	Johnny McNichol	22.10.1949
106	John Napier	7.2.1970
105	Bob Whiting	6.3.1909
104	George Coomber	30.8.1922
101	Jack Mansell	13.9.1950
100	Garry Nelson	12.9.1987

Consecutive-appearance record holders

Apps	Player	Date of record
24	Jock Caldwell	–
35	Frank Scott	14.2.1903
73	Billy Roberts	3.9.1904
143	Billy Booth	12.2.1910
175	Billy Hayes	17.11.1923
247	Eric Gill	26.9.1956

Most-selected substitutes

Player	Selected	Used
John Crumplin	82	33
Gerry Ryan	73	52
Adrian Owers	46	9
Gerry Armstrong	42	20
Ian Chapman	39	21
Alan Duffy	31	18
Howard Wilkinson	30	17
Sammy Morgan	29	18
Kieran O'Regan	"	19
Paul Wood	28	17
Gerry Fell	27	19
Gary Stevens	"	15
Mark Farrington	26	13
Tony Towner	25	12

Appearance record holders

Apps	Player	Date of record	Competitions		
65	Jock Caldwell	–	38 SL	9 FAC	18 SE League
174	Arthur Hulme	14.1.1905	113 SL	12 FAC	17 SE League
			21 Utd League	9 WL	2 SCC
443	Bert Longstaff	1.4.1911	315 SL	41 FL	20 FAC
			4 Utd League	18 WL	26 S Alliance
			18 SCC	1 FA Ch. Shield	
566	Ernie Wilson	31.12.1932	509 FL	49 FAC	8 SSC

Most appearances by competition

Totals include appearances as substitute

Comp	Apps	Player
FL D1	156	Steve Foster
FL D2	207	Gary Chivers
(pre 1992)	191	Steve Gatting
FL D3	322	Norman Gall
FL D4	91	Jimmy Collins
FL D3(S)	509	Ernie Wilson
FAC	49	Ernie Wilson
(proper)	45	Ernie Wilson
FLC	31	Peter O'Sullivan
Wartime	216	Stan Risdon
SL D1	315	Bert Longstaff
SL D2	26	Jock Caldwell

Most games in a season

Games	Player	Season
57	Norman Gall	1966–67
"	Keith Dublin	1987–88
"	John Keeley	1987–88
"	Dean Wilkins	1990–91
56	Bobby Baxter	1966–67
"	Dave Turner	1966–67
"	Graham Cross	1976–77
"	Steve Piper	1976–77
"	Peter Ward	1976–77
"	Steve Gatting	1987–88
55	Billy Booth	1908–09
"	Dean Wilkins	1987–88
"	Clive Walker	1990–91

Most-substituted players

Player	Subbed	Started
Peter O'Sullivan	28	488
Gerry Ryan	24	147
Dave Turner	23	330
Tony Towner	21	171
John Crumplin	"	175
Paul Wood	20	88
Terry Connor	18	170
Mark Barham	16	85
Clive Walker	"	125
John Templeman	"	247
Tony Grealish	15	116
Dean Wilkins	"	280
Raphael Meade	13	41

Players with 50 or more goals

Goals	Goals /game	Player	Competition		
174	0·48	Bert Stephens	86 FL 78 wartime	8 FAC	2 SSC
123	0·59	Tommy Cook	114 FL	9 FAC	
120	0·63	Jock Davie	39 FL 62 wartime	18 FAC	1 SSC
99	0·34	Kit Napier	84 FL	9 FAC	6 FLC
95	0·42	Peter Ward	81 FL	3 FAC	11 FLC
"	0·20	Bobby Farrell	66 FL 11 wartime	17 FAC	1 SSC
90	0·51	Albert Mundy	87 FL	3 FAC	
86	0·19	Bert Longstaff	59 SL 1 Utd League 3 SCC	4 FL 8 WL	1 FAC 10 S Alliance
82	0·45	Dan Kirkwood	74 FL	8 FAC	
79	0·29	Charlie Webb	64 SL 2 SCC	3 FAC 1 FA Ch. Shield	9 S Alliance
75	0·72	Arthur Attwood	55 FL	19 FAC	1 SSC
"	0·32	Jimmy Hopkins	72 FL	3 FAC	
71	0·13	Ernie Wilson	67 FL	4 FAC	
69	0·39	Bill Jones	63 SL	4 FAC	2 SCC
"	0·32	Denis Foreman	63 FL	6 FAC	
65	0·49	Peter Harburn	61 FL	4 FAC	
64	0·22	Dennis Gordon	62 FL	2 FAC	
63	0·55	Sam Jennings	61 FL	2 FAC	
59	0·36	Garry Nelson	47 FL 5 AMC	6 FAC	1 FMC
"	0·34	Terry Connor	51 FL	4 FAC	4 FLC
58	0·51	Bernard Moore	12 FL	2 FAC	44 wartime
57	0·18	Potter Smith	40 FL	17 FAC	
55	0·65	Jack Doran	10 SL	44 FL	1 FAC
54	0·58	Jack Hall	38 SL 5 WL	2 FAC 3 SCC	6 Utd League
52	0·46	Bill Miller	40 SL	1 FAC	11 S Alliance

Aggregate goal record holders

Goals	Player	Date of record	Competitions		
3	Bert Baker	–	3 FAC		
4	Clem Barker	5.10.1901			
7	Frank McAvoy	26.10.1901			
8	Clem Barker	21.12.1901	4 SL	4 FAC	
9	Frank McAvoy	8.2.1902	6 SL	3 FAC	
34	Frank Scott	1.11.1902	14 SL	9 FAC	11 SE League
54	Jack Hall	23.10.1907	38 SL 5 WL	2 FAC 3 SCC	6 Utd League
57	Bert Longstaff	23.12.1911			
58	Charlie Webb	15.1.1913			
66	Bert Longstaff	12.3.1913			
79	Charlie Webb	4.2.1914	64 SL 2 SCC	3 FAC 1 FA Ch. Shield	9 S Alliance
86	Bert Longstaff	7.2.1920	59 SL 1 Utd League 3 SCC	4 FL 8 WL	1 FAC 10 S Alliance
123	Tommy Cook	3.9.1927	114 FL	9 FAC	
174	Bert Stephens	9.1.1943	86 FL 78 Wartime	8 FAC	2 SSC

League goals in a season record holders

Southern League and Football League games only

Games	Player	Season
6	Frank McAvoy	1901–02
11	Frank Scott	1902–03
22	Jack Hall	1906–07
25	Jimmy Smith	1911–12
"	Tommy Cook	1923–24
"	Sam Jennings	1926–27
"	Tommy Cook	1927–28
30	Hugh Vallance	1929–30
32	Peter Ward	1976–77

Most goals by competition

Comp	In a career		In a season			In a game			
	Goals	Player	Goals	Player	Season	Goals	Player	Opponents	Date
FL D1	37	Michael Robinson	19	Michael Robinson	1980–81	3	Peter Ward	Wolverhampton W.	21.12.1979
						"	Gordon Smith	Coventry City	4.10.1980
FL D2	50	Terry Connor	23	Bill Curry	1959–60	4	Adrian Thorne	Bristol Rovers	27.8.1960
						"	Bryan Wade	Newcastle United	16.1.1991
FL D3	84	Kit Napier	32	Peter Ward	1976–77	4	Alex Dawson	Hartlepools United	22.2.1969
						"	Peter Ward	Walsall	5.10.1976
FL D4	29	Jimmy Collins	21	Wally Gould	1964–65	3	Keith Webber	York City	7.10.1963
FL D3(S)	114	Tommy Cook	30	Hugh Vallance	1929–30	5	Jack Doran	Northampton Town	5.11.1921
						"	Adrian Thorne	Watford	30.4.1958
FAC (proper)	19	Arthur Attwood	15	Arthur Attwood	1932–33	6	Arthur Attwood	Shoreham	1.10.1932
	18	Jock Davie	10*	Jock Davie	1945–46	4	Jock Davie	South Liverpool	15.12.1937
			7	Jock Davie	1937–38	"	Peter Harburn	Newport County	19.11.1955
FLC	11	Peter Ward	3	Jimmy Collins	1966–67	3	Danny Wilson	Bradford City	25.9.1985
			"	Kit Napier	1967–68				
			"	Brian Horton	1976–77				
			"	Peter Ward	1976–77				
			"	Peter Ward	1978–79				
			"	Michael Robinson	1980–81				
			"	Danny Wilson	1985–86				
Wartime	78	Bert Stephens	27	Jock Davie	1941–42	6	Don Welsh	Luton Town	22.3.1941
			27†	Bernard Moore	1945–46				
SL D1	64	Charlie Webb	25	Jimmy Smith	1911–12	4	Jimmy Smith	Stoke	30.12.1911
						"	Charlie Webb	Southampton	19.10.1912
SL D2	11	Frank Scott	11	Frank Scott	1902–03	5	Frank Scott	Southall	28.2.1903

* The 1945–46 F.A. Cup competition was a unique, two-legged affair. The record for the normal competition proper is therefore given as well.
† Bernard Moore also scored one goal in the 1945–46 FA Cup to total 28 for the season. (The FA Cup is not counted as a 'wartime' competition in this book.)

Top scorers each season

Season	Goals	Player	Season	Goals	Player	Season	Goals	Player
1901–02	9	Frank McAvoy	1936–37	26	Bert Stephens	1962–63	11	Peter Donnelly
1902–03	31	Frank Scott	1937–38	24	Jock Davie	1963–64	15	John Goodchild
1903–04	9	Billy Roberts	1938–39	17	Bert Stephens	1964–65	21	Wally Gould
1904–05	13	Andy Gardner	1939–40	22	Jock Davie	1965–66	14	Charlie Livesey
1905–06	9	Billy Yates	1940–41	15	Don Welsh	1966–67	10	Kit Napier
	"	Dickie Joynes	1941–42	27	Jock Davie		"	Eric Whitington
1906–07	28	Jack Hall	1942–43	16	John Shafto	1967–68	28	Kit Napier
1907–08	26	Jack Hall	1943–44	11	Bert Stephens	1968–69	18	Kit Napier
1908–09	25	Jack Martin		"	Tommy Hassell	1969–70	16	Alan Gilliver
1909–10	22	Bill Jones	1944–45	15	Bert Stephens	1970–71	13	Kit Napier
1910–11	19	Bill Jones		"	Cyril Hodges	1971–72	19	Kit Napier
1911–12	27	Jimmy Smith	1945–46	28	Bernard Moore	1972–73	10	Ken Beamish
1912–13	13	Charlie Webb	1946–47	10	George Chapman	1973–74	12	Ken Beamish
1913–14	20	Bill Miller	1947–48	14	Tony James	1974–75	13	Fred Binney
1914–15	13	Bill Jones	1948–49	11	Des Tennant	1975–76	27	Fred Binney
1919–20	10	Jack Doran	1949–50	9	Johnny McNichol	1976–77	36	Peter Ward
1920–21	22	Jack Doran	1950–51	14	Johnny McNichol	1977–78	17	Peter Ward
1921–22	23	Jack Doran	1951–52	19	Billy Reed	1978–79	13	Peter Ward
1922–23	13	Eddie Fuller		"	Ken Bennett	1979–80	18	Peter Ward
1923–24	28	Tommy Cook	1952–53	13	Ken Bennett	1980–81	22	Michael Robinson
1924–25	18	Tommy Cook	1953–54	22	Bert Addinall	1981–82	14	Andy Ritchie
1925–26	20	Sam Jennings	1954–55	21	Albert Mundy	1982–83	10	Michael Robinson
1926–27	27	Sam Jennings	1955–56	28	Albert Mundy	1983–84	17	Terry Connor
1927–28	26	Tommy Cook	1956–57	20	Albert Mundy	1984–85	16	Terry Connor
1928–29	21	Dan Kirkwood	1957–58	20	Peter Harburn	1985–86	19	Dean Saunders
1929–30	32	Hugh Vallance		"	Dave Sexton	1986–87	9	Terry Connor
1930–31	19	Geordie Nicol	1958–59	17	John Shepherd	1987–88	32	Garry Nelson
1931–32	29	Arthur Attwood	1959–60	26	Bill Curry	1988–89	16	Garry Nelson
1932–33	35	Arthur Attwood	1960–61	14	Adrian Thorne	1989–90	12	Kevin Bremner
1933–34	15	Oliver Brown	1961–62	10	John Goodchild	1990–91	21	Mike Small
1934–35	26	Oliver Brown		"	Bobby Laverick	1991–92	14	Mark Gall
1935–36	27	Alec Law		"	Tony Nicholas	1992–93	22	Kurt Nogan

Players scoring 4 or more goals in a match

Goals	Player	Date	Score	Opponents	Comp
6	Arthur Attwood	1.10.1932	12–0	Shoreham	FAC Q1
"	Don Welsh	22.3.1941	7–4	Luton Town	Wartime
5	Frank Scott	28.2.1903	8–0	Southall	SL D2
"	Jack Doran	5.11.1921	7–0	Northampton Town	FL D3(S)
"	Jock Davie	31.1.1942	8–2	Chelsea	Wartime
"	Adrian Thorne	30.4.1958	6–0	Watford	FL D3(S)
4	Frank Scott	18.10.1902	12–0	Shoreham	FAC Q2
"	Ben Garfield	27.4.1903	5–3	Watford	SL Test
"	Jimmy Smith	30.12.1911	4–0	Stoke	SL D1
"	Charlie Webb	19.10.1912	5–2	Southampton	SL D1
"	Tommy Cook	22.12.1923	5–0	Bournemouth & B.A.	FL D3(S)
"	Sam Jennings	18.9.1926	9–3	Swindon Town	FL D3(S)
"	Dan Kirkwood	7.9.1929	6–3	Norwich City	FL D3(S)
"	Dan Kirkwood	1.2.1930	8–2	Merthyr Town	FL D3(S)
"	Geordie Nicol	27.12.1930	5–0	Gillingham	FL D3(S)
"	Arthur Attwood	23.4.1932	7–0	Gillingham	FL D3(S)
"	Alec Law	26.10.1935	5–1	Notts County	FL D3(S)
"	Jock Davie	15.12.1937	6–0	South Liverpool	FAC R2 rep
"	John Shafto	9.1.1943	8–0	Luton Town	Wartime
"	Cyril Hodges	17.2.1945	6–2	Millwall	Wartime
"	Bernard Moore	22.9.1945	7–2	Crystal Palace	Wartime
"	Johnny McNichol	18.4.1951	9–1	Newport County	FL D3(S)
"	Peter Harburn	19.11.1955	8–1	Newport County	FAC R1
"	Adrian Thorne	27.8.1960	6–1	Bristol Rovers	FL D2
"	Alex Dawson	22.2.1969	5–2	Hartlepools United	FL D3
"	Peter Ward	5.10.1976	7–0	Walsall	FL D3
"	Bryan Wade	16.1.1991	4–2	Newcastle United	FL D2

Players scoring in 5 or more consecutive games

The date shown is the first game of the sequence

Games	Goals	Player	Date	Competitions	
8	14	Arthur Attwood	14.11.1931	6 FL	2 FAC
"	13	Bernard Moore	25.8.1945	8 wartime	
"	12	Peter Harburn	15.10.1955	7 FL	1 FAC
"	9	Arthur Attwood	29.10.1932	5 FL	3 FAC
"	8	Cyril Thompson	13.9.1950	8 FL	
6	10	Jack Martin	22.3.1909	4 SL	1 WL
				1 SCC	
"	8	Bert Addinall	26.12.1953	6 FL	
"	7	Frank McAvoy	28.9.1901	3 FL	3 FAC
5	7	Frank O'Donnell	15.9.1945	5 wartime	
"	"	Peter Ward	20.9.1977	4 FL	1 FLC
"	"	Kurt Nogan	7.4.1993	5 FL	
"	6	Frank Scott	20.12.1902	3 SL	2 SE League
"	"	Dan Kirkwood	15.12.1928	5 FL	
"	5	Andy Gardner	22.10.1904	3 SL	2 FAC
"	"	Bert Stephens	29.12.1945	2 FAC	3 wartime
"	"	Bert Addinall	11.4.1953	5 FL	
"	"	Wally Gould	28.9.1964	5 FL	

Players scoring 3 or more hat-tricks

Hat-tricks	Player	Competitions		
8	Tommy Cook	7 FL	1 FAC	
"	Jock Davie	1 FL	3 FAC	4 wartime
6	Bert Stephens	2 FL	4 wartime	
5	Arthur Attwood	4 FL	1 FAC	
4	Jimmy Smith	4 SL		
"	Jack Doran	1 SL	3 FL	
"	Hugh Vallance	4 FL		
"	Bobby Farrell	1 FL	1 FAC	2 wartime
"	Oliver Brown	3 FL	1 SSC	
3	Ben Garfield	1 SL Test	1 FAC	1 SE League
"	Jimmy Hopkins	3 FL		
"	Sam Jennings	3 FL		
"	Dan Kirkwood	3 FL		
"	Alec Law	2 FL	1 FAC	
"	Albert Mundy	3 FL		
"	Bill Curry	2 FL	1 FAC	
"	Peter Ward	3 FL		

Top penalty scorers

Penalties	Player
26	Wally Little
23	Des Tennant
17	Brian Horton
15	Danny Wilson
13	Jock Caldwell
"	Roy Jennings
12	Reg Wilkinson
10	Jimmy Langley

Players known to have played aged 36 or older

* made appearances in wartime games only

Age	Player	Last game
44–156	Sam Cowan*	13.10.1945
38–357	Reg Williams	26.12.1928
38–319	Alex Wilson	13.9.1947
38–271	Bill Jones	20.12.1919
38–200	Bert Stephens	29.11.1947
38–131	Herbert Jones	13.4.1935
38–115	Dickie Downs	6.12.1924
38–50	Joe Wilson	17.5.1947
38 or 37	Fred Tully*	26.12.1942
37–356	Ted Crawford*	21.10.1944
37–296	Les Jones	23.4.1949
37–195	Sammy Small	26.11.1949
37–156	Billy Lane*	28.3.1942
37–9	Harry Medhurst	14.2.1953
37–0	James Boyd*	29.4.1944
36–326	Dennis Gordon	29.4.1961
36–259	Len Darling	24.4.1948
c. 36–220	Jack Jenkins	26.12.1928
36–191	Len Young	1.9.1948
36–169	Frank Worthington	11.5.1985
36–27	Frank Brett	6.4.1935
36–13	Bert Longstaff	22.10.1921
36 or 37	Ernie Wilson	13.4.1936
36 or 37	Joe Leeming	25.4.1914

Players known to have played aged 17 or younger

* played aged 17 or younger in wartime games only

Age	Player	First game
15–258	Reg Bowles*	29.11.1941
16–8	Stan Willemse*	31.8.1940
16–122	Charlie Chase*	1.6.1940
16–259	Ian Chapman	14.2.1987
16–?	John Collins*	13.5.1940
16–?	Charlie Harman*	1.6.1940
17–0	Bert Griffin*	6.4.1942
17–48	Mick Conway	28.4.1973
17–85	Dave Busby	20.10.1973
17–139	Steve Burtenshaw	11.4.1953
17–169	Gary Stevens	15.9.1979
17–194	Bradley Wosahlo	26.8.1992
17–201	Franco Massimo	12.4.1986
17–203	Brian Powney	28.4.1962
17–206	Eric Townsend	12.9.1931
17–229	Phil Gilbert	28.4.1962
17–241	Daren Newman	12.4.1986
17–268	Simon Funnell	2.5.1992
17–284	Tony Towner	10.2.1973
17–286	David Gipp	25.4.1987
17–303	John Cochrane	10.3.1962
" "	Ken Blackburn	12.3.1969
17–339	Martin Lambert	29.8.1983
17–352	Sean Edwards	16.10.1985
17–355	Charlie Burtenshaw*	5.10.1940
17–360	Mark Elliott	15.3.1977
17–?	Bert Austen*	1.6.1940
17–?	Roy Watts*	1.6.1940

Oldest and youngest known line-ups

	Ave. age	Opponents	Comp	Ven	Score	Date
Oldest	32–147	Crystal Palace	FL D3(S)	(a)	0–1	11.9.1946
Youngest	21–300	Doncaster Rovers	FL D3	(a)	1–1	16.5.1967

Player age records by competition

Comp	Oldest known player			Youngest known player		
	Age	Player	Last game	Age	Player	First game
FL D1	34–183	Martin Chivers	27.10.1979	17–169	Gary Stevens	15.9.1979
FL D2	36–326	Dennis Gordon	29.4.1961	16–259	Ian Chapman	14.2.1987
FL D2 (post 1992)	35–333	Clive Walker	24.4.1993			
FL D3	35–106	Neil Martin	3.2.1976	17–85	Dave Busby	20.10.1973
FL D4	32–63	Bobby Smith	26.4.1965	18–338	Brian Powney	10.9.1963
FL D3(S)	38–357	Reg Williams	26.12.1928	17–139	Steve Burtenshaw	11.4.1953
FAC	38–325	Reg Williams	24.11.1928	17–302	Gary Stevens	26.1.1980
FLC	35–321	Frank Worthington	9.10.1984	17–179	Gary Stevens	25.9.1979
Wartime	44–156	Sam Cowan	13.10.1945	15–258	Reg Bowles	29.11.1941
SL D1	38–250	Bill Jones	29.11.1919	19–46	Chris Buckley	25.12.1905
SL D2	c. 31–230	Ned Collins	1.4.1902	c. 21–0	Bertie Blunden	25.1.1902

Players of the Season

Voted for by the fans, this award was inaugurated in 1969 at the suggestion of two supporters, Ron and Winn Carr. After a two-season gap it was revived in 1976, and was sponsored from 1979 to 1985 by Rediffusion. Since 1986 it has been backed by Granada TV Rental.

Season	Player	Season	Player	Season	Player
1968–69	John Napier	1977–78	Peter O'Sullivan	1985–86	Dean Saunders
1969–70	Stewart Henderson	1978–79	Mark Lawrenson	1986–87	Terry Connor
1970–71	Norman Gall	1979–80	Steve Foster	1987–88	Garry Nelson
1971–72	Bert Murray	1980–81	Michael Robinson	1988–89	John Keeley
1972–73	Eddie Spearritt	1981–82	Andy Ritchie	1989–90	Keith Dublin
1973–74	Norman Gall	1982–83	Gary Stevens	1990–91	Perry Digweed
1974–75	not chosen	1983–84	Jimmy Case	1991–92	Mark Gall
1975–76	not chosen	1984–85	Graham Moseley	1992–93	Steve Foster
1976–77	Brian Horton				

Captains

The following list shows the players who were captains at the beginning of each season, and those who took over for lengthy periods throughout that season

Season	Captain(s)	Season	Captain(s)	Season	Captain(s)	Season	Captain(s)
1901–02	Frank McAvoy	1930–31	Frank Brett	1956–57	Jimmy Langley	1973–74	Eddie Spearritt
	Jock Caldwell	1931–32	Frank Brett		Ken Whitfield		Norman Gall
1902–03	Jock Caldwell	1932–33	Frank Brett	1957–58	Ken Whitfield	1974–75	Ernie Machin
1903–04	Tom McAteer	1933–34	Frank Brett		Glen Wilson		Billy McEwan
1904–05	Tom Robertson		Reg Wilkinson	1958–59	Glen Wilson		Graham Winstanley
1905–06	Arthur Hulme	1934–35	Herbert Jones	1959–60	Glen Wilson	1975–76	Graham Winstanley
1906–07	Harry Kent	1935–36	Potter Smith	1960–61	Roy Jennings		Ernie Machin
1907–08	Harry Kent	1936–37	Potter Smith	1961–62	Roy Jennings	1976–77	Brian Horton
1908–09	Tom Stewart		Ernie King	1962–63	Roy Jennings	1977–78	Brian Horton
1909–10	Joe Leeming	1937–38	Dave Walker	1963–64	Roy Jennings	1978–79	Brian Horton
1910–11	Joe Leeming	1938–39	Dave Walker		Jimmy Collins	1979–80	Brian Horton
1911–12	Joe Leeming	1939–40	Len Darling	1964–65	Jimmy Collins	1980–81	Brian Horton
1912–13	Joe Leeming	1940–41	Len Darling		Bobby Smith	1981–82	Steve Foster
1913–14	Joe Leeming	1941–42	Stan Risdon		Mel Hopkins	1982–83	Steve Foster
1914–15	Billy Booth	1942–43	Stan Risdon	1965–66	Jimmy Collins	1983–84	Steve Foster
1919–20	Billy Booth	1943–44	Stan Risdon		Jimmy Magill		Jimmy Case
1920–21	Jack Rutherford	1944–45	Stan Risdon	1966–67	Jimmy Magill	1984–85	Jimmy Case
	Jack Woodhouse	1945–46	Stan Risdon		Jimmy Collins		Danny Wilson
1921–22	Jack Feebery	1946–47	Len Darling		Dave Turner	1985–86	Danny Wilson
1922–23	Jack Feebery	1947–48	Ernie Marriott	1967–68	Dave Turner	1986–87	Danny Wilson
	George Coomber	1948–49	Sammy Small		Nobby Lawton	1987–88	Doug Rougvie
1923–24	George Coomber		Jack Whent		John Napier	1988–89	Steve Gatting
1924–25	George Coomber	1949–50	Jack Whent	1968–69	Nobby Lawton		Gary Chivers
	Jack Jenkins	1950–51	Des Tennant		Dave Turner	1989–90	Steve Gatting
1925–26	Jack Jenkins	1951–52	Johnny McNichol	1969–70	Nobby Lawton		Alan Curbishley
1926–27	Reg Williams	1952–53	Jess Willard	1970–71	John Napier	1990–91	Dean Wilkins
1927–28	Reg Williams		Des Tennant	1971–72	John Napier	1991–92	Dean Wilkins
1928–29	Reg Williams	1953–54	Des Tennant		Brian Bromley		Gary Chivers
	Dan Kirkwood	1954–55	Glen Wilson	1972–73	Brian Bromley	1992–93	Gary Chivers
1929–30	Reg Smith		Jimmy Langley		Bert Murray		
	Jack Curran	1955–56	Jimmy Langley				

Incoming transfer records since 1919

Fee	Player	Selling club	Date
£200	George Holley	Sunderland	July 1919
"	David Williams	Luton Town	Feb. 1920
£250	Harry Bentley	Sheffield Wed.	c.s. 1920
£500	Fred Groves	Arsenal	Aug. 1921
£650	Sam Jennings	West Ham United	March 1925
£3,250	Eric Lancelotte	Charlton Athletic	Feb. 1948
£5,000	Johnny McNichol	Newcastle United	Aug. 1948
£7,000	Matt McNeil	Barnsley	July 1953
"	Ian McNeill	Leciester City	March 1959
£13,000	Bill Curry	Newcastle United	July 1959
£15,000	Tony Nicholas	Chelsea	Nov. 1960
£25,000	John Napier	Bolton Wanderers	Aug. 1967
£25,000 + Alan Duffy	Ken Beamish	Tranmere Rovers	March 1972
£29,000	Barry Bridges	Millwall	Aug. 1972
£35,000‡	Ronnie Welch	Burnley	Dec. 1973
" ‡	Harry Wilson	Burnley	Dec. 1973
£40,000	Ian Mellor	Norwich City	April 1974
£45,000 *	Ken Tiler	Chesterfield	Nov. 1974
£112,000	Mark Lawrenson	Preston North End	June 1977
£238,000	Teddy Maybank	Fulham	Nov. 1977
£250,000	John Gregory	Aston Villa	July 1979
£400,000	Gordon Smith	Rangers	June 1980
"	Michael Robinson	Manchester City	June 1980
£500,000	Andy Ritchie	Manchester United	Oct. 1980
" †	Terry Connor	Leeds United	March 1983

‡ *combined fee of £70,000*
* *£45,000-rated in swap for Ronnie Welch and Billy McEwan*
† *£500,000-rated in swap for Andy Ritchie*

Outgoing transfer records since 1908

Fee	Player	Buying club	Date
£700*	Jack Hall	Middlesbrough	April 1908
£735 + Bobby Simpson	Jimmy Smith	Bradford (P.A.)	Nov. 1912
£1,500 + George Beech	David Parkes	Sheffield Wed.	March 1914
£3,000	Andy Neil	Arsenal	March 1924
£6,000	Stan Willemse	Chelsea	July 1949
£12,000 + Jimmy Leadbetter	Johnny McNichol	Chelsea	Aug. 1952
£15,000	Jack Mansell	Cardiff City	Oct. 1952
£16,000	Steve Govier	Grimsby Town	Dec. 1974
£26,000	Ken Beamish	Blackburn Rovers	May 1974
£30,000	Ian Mellor	Chester	Feb. 1978
£37,000	Eric Potts	Preston North End	Aug. 1978
£65,000	Tony Towner	Millwall	Oct. 1978
£100,000	Eric Steele	Watford	Oct. 1979
£150,000	Teddy Maybank	Fulham	Dec. 1979
£175,000	Ray Clarke	Newcastle United	July 1980
£450,000	Peter Ward	Nottingham Forest	Oct. 1980
£900,000	Mark Lawrenson	Liverpool	Aug. 1981

* *maximum fee at time of £350; Hall and a 'makeweight', Harry Kent, left for combined fee of £700*

Full international appearances

* Home International championship   † World Cup qualifier   ‡ World Cup finals   § European Championship qualifier   g goal scored

Charlie Webb (Ireland) – 3 games

Date	Opponents		Venue
15.3.1909	Scotland*	0–5	Glasgow
20.3.1909	Wales*	2–3	Belfast
18.3.1911	Scotland*	0–2	Glasgow

Jack Doran (Ireland) – 3 games

Date	Opponents		Venue
23.10.1920	England*	0–2	Sunderland
22.10.1921	England*	1–1	Belfast
1.4.1922	Wales*	1–1	Belfast

Jack Jenkins (Wales) – 8 games

Date	Opponents		Venue
16.2.1924	Scotland*	2–0	Cardiff
3.3.1924	England*	2–1	Blackburn
15.3.1924	Ireland*	1–0	Belfast
14.2.1925	Scotland*	1–3	Edinburgh
18.4.1925	Ireland*	0–0	Wrexham
31.10.1925	Scotland*	0–3	Cardiff
1.3.1926	England*	3–1	Selhurst Pk.
30.10.1926	Scotland*	0–3	Glasgow

Tommy Cook (England) – 1 game

Date	Opponents		Venue
28.2.1925	Wales*	2–1	Swansea

Jimmy Hopkins (Ireland – 1 game)

Date	Opponents		Venue
24.10.1925	England*	0–0	Belfast

Jimmy Magill (Northern Ireland) – 5 games

Date	Opponents		Venue
10.11.1965	England*	1–2	Wembley
24.11.1965	Albania†	1–1	Tirana
30.3.1966	Wales*	4–1	Cardiff
7.5.1966	West Germany	0–2	Belfast
22.6.1966	Mexico	4–1	Belfast

Willie Irvine (Northern Ireland) – 3 games

Date	Opponents		Venue
20.5.1972	Scotland*	0–2	Glasgow
23.5.1972	England*	1–0	Wembley
27.5.1972	Wales*	0–0	Wrexham

Peter O'Sullivan (Wales) – 3 games

Date	Opponents		Venue
12.5.1973	Scotland (sub.)*	0–2	Wrexham
6.5.1976	Scotland*	1–3	Glasgow
25.10.1978	Malta (sub.)§ (1 g)	7–0	Wrexham

Joe Kinnear (Rep. of Ireland) – 1 game

Date	Opponents		Venue
29.10.1975	Turkey (sub.)§	4–0	Dublin

Sammy Morgan (N. Ireland) – 2 games

Date	Opponents		Venue
8.5.1976	Scotland*	0–3	Glasgow
14.5.1976	Wales (sub.)*	0–1	Swansea

Mark Lawrenson (R. of Ireland) – 14 games

Date	Opponents		Venue
12.10.1977	Bulgaria†	0–0	Dublin
12.4.1978	Poland	0–3	Lodz
21.5.1978	Norway (sub.)	0–0	Oslo
24.5.1978	Denmark§	3–3	Copenhagen
20.9.1978	Northern Ireland§	0–0	Dublin
25.10.1978	England§	1–1	Dublin
6.2.1980	England§	0–2	Wembley
26.3.1980	Cyprus† (1 g)	3–2	Nicosia
30.4.1980	Switzerland	2–0	Dublin
10.9.1980	Netherlands† (1 g)	2–1	Dublin
15.10.1980	Belgium†	1–1	Dublin
28.10.1980	France†	0–2	Paris
19.11.1980	Cyprus†	6–0	Dublin
23.5.1981	Poland	0–3	Bydgoszcz

Gerry Ryan (Rep. of Ireland) – 16 games

Date	Opponents		Venue
25.10.1978	England§	1–1	Dublin
22.5.1979	West Germany (1 g)	1–3	Dublin
11.9.1979	Wales	1–2	Swansea
26.3.1980	Cyprus (sub.)†	3–2	Nicosia
30.4.1980	Switzerland	2–0	Dublin
16.5.1980	Argentina (sub.)	0–1	Dublin
28.10.1980	France (sub.)†	0–2	Paris
21.5.1981	West Germany 'B'	0–3	Bremen
23.5.1981	Poland (sub.)	0–3	Bydgoszcz
9.9.1981	Netherlands (sub.)†	2–2	Rotterdam
28.4.1982	Algeria (sub.)	0–2	Algiers
22.5.1982	Chile (sub.)	0–1	Santiago
30.5.1982	Trindad & Tobago	1–2	Port of Spain
23.5.1984	Poland	0–0	Dublin
3.6.1984	China	1–0	Sapporo
8.8.1984	Mexico	0–0	Dublin

Peter Ward (England) – 1 game

Date	Opponents		Venue
31.5.1980	Australia (sub.)	2–1	Sydney

Moshe Gariani (Israel) – 3 games

Date	Opponents		Venue
18.6.1980	Sweden†	1–1	Stockholm
12.11.1980	Sweden†	0–0	Tel Aviv
17.12.1980	Portugal†	0–3	Lisbon

Michael Robinson (R. of Ireland) – 13 games

Date	Opponents		Venue
28.10.1980	France†	0–2	Paris
19.11.1980	Cyprus† (1 g)	6–0	Dublin
25.3.1981	Belgium†	0–1	Brussels
21.5.1981	West Germany 'B'	0–3	Bremen
23.5.1981	Poland	0–3	Bydgoszcz
9.9.1981	Netherlands† (1 g)	2–2	Rotterdam
14.10.1981	France† (1 g)	3–2	Dublin
28.4.1982	Algeria	0–2	Algiers
22.5.1982	Chile	0–1	Santiago
22.9.1982	Netherlands§	1–2	Rotterdam
13.10.1982	Iceland§	2–0	Dublin
17.11.1982	Spain§	3–3	Dublin
30.3.1983	Malta§	1–0	Valletta

Jacob Cohen (Israel) – 4 games

Date	Opponents		Venue
12.11.1980	Sweden†	0–0	Tel Aviv
17.12.1980	Portugal†	0–3	Lisbon
25.2.1981	Scotland†	0–1	Tel Aviv
28.4.1981	Scotland†	1–3	Glasgow

Tony Grealish (Rep. of Ireland) – 11 games

Date	Opponents		Venue
9.9.1981	Netherlands†	2–2	Rotterdam
28.4.1982	Algeria	0–2	Algiers
22.5.1982	Chile	0–1	Santiago
27.5.1982	Brazil	0–7	Uberlandia
30.5.1982	Trinidad & Tobago	1–2	Port of Spain
22.9.1982	Netherlands§	1–2	Rotterdam
13.10.1982	Iceland§ (1 g)	2–0	Dublin
17.11.1982	Spain§	3–3	Dublin
27.4.1983	Spain§	0–2	Zaragoza
21.9.1983	Iceland§	3–0	Reykjavik
12.10.1983	Netherlands§	2–3	Dublin

Micky Thomas (Wales) – 5 games

Date	Opponents		Venue
18.11.1981	U.S.S.R. (sub.)†	0–3	Tbilisi
24.3.1982	Spain	1–1	Valencia
27.4.1982	England*	0–1	Cardiff
24.5.1982	Scotland (sub.)*	0–1	Glasgow
27.5.1982	N. Ireland (sub.)*	3–0	Wrexham

Steve Foster (England) – 3 games

Date	Opponents		Venue
23.2.1982	Northern Ireland*	4–0	Wembley
25.5.1982	Netherlands	2–0	Wembley
25.6.1982	Kuwait‡	1–0	Bilbao

Sammy Nelson (N. Ireland) – 4 games

Date	Opponents		Venue
23.2.1982	England*	0–4	Wembley
28.4.1982	Scotland*	1–1	Belfast
25.6.1982	Spain (sub.)‡	1–0	Valencia
1.7.1982	Austria‡	2–2	Madrid

Kieran O'Regan (Rep. of Ireland) – 4 games

Date	Opponents		Venue
16.11.1983	Malta§	8–0	Dublin
23.5.1984	Poland	0–0	Dublin
8.8.1984	Mexico	0–0	Dublin
26.5.1985	Spain (sub.)	0–0	Cork

Gary Howlett (Rep. of Ireland) – 1 game

Date	Opponents		Venue
3.6.1984	China (sub.)	1–0	Sapporo

Steve Penney (N. Ireland) – 17 games

Date	Opponents		Venue
16.10.1984	Israel	3–0	Belfast
11.9.1985	Turkey†	0–0	Izmir
16.10.1985	Romania†	1–0	Bucharest
13.11.1985	England†	0–0	Wembley
26.2.1986	France	0–0	Paris
26.3.1986	Denmark	1–1	Belfast
23.4.1986	Morocco	2–1	Belfast
3.6.1986	Algeria‡	1–1	Guadalajara
7.6.1986	Spain‡	1–2	Guadalajara
15.10.1986	England§	0–3	Wembley
12.11.1986	Turkey§	0–0	Izmir
18.2.1987	Israel (1 g)	1–1	Tel Aviv
23.3.1988	Poland	1–1	Belfast
27.4.1988	France	0–0	Belfast
21.5.1988	Malta† (1 g)	3–0	Belfast
14.9.1988	Rep. of Ireland†	0–0	Belfast
21.12.1988	Spain†	0–4	Seville

Dean Saunders (Wales) – 5 games

Date	Opponents		Venue
26.3.1986	Rep. of Ireland (sub.)	1–0	Dublin
10.5.1986	Canada	0–2	Toronto
20.5.1986	Canada (2 g)	3–0	Vancouver
10.9.1986	Finland	1–1	Helsinki
18.2.1987	U.S.S.R.	0–0	Swansea

Danny Wilson (Northern Ireland) – 3 games

Date	Opponents		Venue
12.12.1986	Turkey§	0–0	Izmir
18.2.1987	Israel	1–1	Tel Aviv
1.4.1987	England (sub.)§	0–2	Belfast

John Byrne (Rep. of Ireland) – 1 game

Date	Opponents		Venue
6.2.1991	Wales (1 g)	3–0	Wrexham

'B' international appearances

Date	Opponents		Venue	Date	Opponents		Venue
Jimmy Langley (England) – 3 games				**Peter Ward (England) – 1 game**			
23.3.1955	West Germany	1–1	Sheffield	14.10.1980	U.S.A. (sub.)	1–0	Manchester
19.10.1955	Yugoslavia	5–1	Manchester				
29.2.1956	Scotland	2–2	Dundee				

Under-23 international appearances

Date	Opponents		Venue	Date	Opponents		Venue	Date	Opponents		Venue
Freddie Jones (Wales) – 1 game				**John Napier (Northern Ireland) – 1 game**				**Peter O'Sullivan (Wales) – 6 games**			
25.11.1959	Scotland	1–1	Wrexham	20.3.1968	Wales	1–0	Cardiff	13.1.1971	Scotland (sub.)	1–0	Swansea
Dave Hollins (Wales) – 2 games								5.1.1972	England	0–2	Swindon
25.11.1959	Scotland	1–1	Wrexham					26.1.1972	Scotland	0–2	Aberdeen
8.2.1961	England	0–2	Everton					29.11.1972	England	0–3	Wrexham
								14.3.1973	Scotland	1–2	Swansea
								4.2.1976	Scotland	2–3	Wrexham

Under-21 international appearances

§ European Championship qualifier   g goal scored

Date	Opponents		Venue	Date	Opponents		Venue	Date	Opponents		Venue
Peter Ward (England) – 2 games				**Gary Howlett (Rep. of Ireland) – 4 games**				**Paul McCarthy (Rep. of Ireland) – 9 games**			
6.9.1977	Norway§ (3 g)	6–0	Hove	5.6.1983	France (1 g)	1–1	Toulon	30.5.1990	Malta (sub.)	1–1	Valetta
23.4.1980	East Germany§	0–1	Jena	7.6.1983	Argentina	0–1	Hyeres	13.11.1990	England§	0–3	Cork
Steve Foster (England) – 1 game				9.6.1983	U.S.S.R.	0–1	Toulon	26.3.1991	England (sub.)§	0–3	Brentford
23.4.1980	East Germany	0–1	Jena	11.6.1983	China	5–1	Six-Fours	30.4.1991	Poland§	1–2	Dundalk
	(sub.)§			**Gerry Ryan (Rep. of Ireland) – 1 game**				24.3.1992	Switzerland	1–1	Dublin
Andy Ritchie (England) – 1 game				25.3.1985	England	2–3	Portsmouth	25.5.1992	Albania§	3–1	Dublin
7.4.1982	Poland§	2–2	West Ham	**Terry Connor (England) – 1 game**				17.11.1992	Spain§ (1 g)	1–2	Jerez
Gary Stevens (England) – 1 game				11.11.1986	Yugoslavia§ (1 g)	1–1	Peterborough	27.4.1993	Denmark§	0–2	Dublin
26.4.1983	Hungary§	1–0	Newcastle	**Derek McGrath (Rep. of Ireland) – 3 games**				26.5.1993	Albania§	1–1	Tirana
Kieran O'Regan (Rep. of Ireland) – 5 games				30.5.1990	Malta	1–1	Valletta	**John Robinson (Wales) – 1 game**			
5.6.1983	France	1–1	Toulon	26.3.1991	England§	0–3	Brentford	19.5.1992	Romania§	3–2	Bucharest
7.6.1983	Argentina	0–1	Hyeres	30.4.1991	Poland§	1–2	Dundalk				
9.6.1983	U.S.S.R.	0–1	Toulon								
11.6.1983	China	5–1	Six-Fours								
25.3.1985	England	2–3	Portsmouth								

Youth internationals

Player	Country	Years
Keith Watkins	Wales	1969
Mark Fleet	Rep. of Ireland	1980–82
Martin Lambert	England	1983
Kevin Russell	England	1984
Jack Dineen	Rep. of Ireland	1987–88
Paul McCarthy	Rep. of Ireland	1988–90
Derek McGrath	Rep. of Ireland	1988–89
Brian McKenna	Rep. of Ireland	1989–90
Greg O'Dowd	Rep. of Ireland	1989
Jamie Williams	Wales	1991
David Wood	Scotland	1992

England international trialists

g goal scored

Date	Match	Score	Venue
Fred Blackman			
23.1.1911	Stripes v. Whites	1–4	Tottenham
Billy Booth			
25.11.1912	The South v. England XI	2–1	Tottenham
20.1.1913	England XI v. The North	0–5	Manchester
Tommy Cook			
19.1.1925	The South v. The North	3–1	Chelsea
9.2.1925	England XI v. The Rest (1 g)	2–2	Manchester

321

League representative appearances

Players representing Albion first-team leagues only. g goal scored.

Date	Opponents		Venue	Date	Opponents		Venue	Date	Opponents		Venue
Fred Blackman (Southern Lge) – 2 games				**Charlie Webb (Southern League) – 1 game**				**Bill Jones (Southern League) – 1 game**			
11.4.1910	Football League	2–2	Chelsea	30.9.1912	Football League (1 g)	1–2	Manchester	12.10.1914	Scottish League	1–1	Millwall
14.11.1910	Football League	3–2	Tottenham	**Charlie Webb (Southern Alliance) – 1 game**				**Jimmy Langley (Football League) – 1 game**			
Billy Booth (Southern League) – 7 games				8.10.1913	Croydon Common	2–1	Selhurst	31.10.1956	Irish League	3–2	Newcastle
24.10.1910	Scottish League	1–0	Millwall	**Joe Leeming (Southern Alliance) – 1 game**							
14.11.1910	Football League	3–2	Tottenham	8.10.1913	Croydon Common	2–1	Selhurst				
20.3.1911	Irish League	4–0	West Ham	**Gunner Higham (Southern League) – 2 games**							
30.9.1911	Irish League	2–1	Belfast	11.10.1913	Irish League	4–1	Dublin				
2.10.1911	Scottish League	2–3	Clyde	13.10.1913	Scottish League	0–5	Glasgow				
15.3.1913	Irish League	1–1	Millwall								
9.2.1914	Football League	1–3	Millwall								

Football League Division 3 (South) representatives

All matches v. Division 3 (North). g goal scored.

Date	Score	Venue	Date	Score	Venue
Jimmy Langley			**Peter Harburn**		
16.3.1955	2–0	Reading	18.3.1958	(1 g) 1–0	Carlisle
8.10.1956	2–1	Coventry	**Dave Sexton**		
Glen Wilson			18.3.1958	1–0	Carlisle
16.3.1955	(sub.) 2–0	Reading	**Frankie Howard**		
2.4.1957	1–2	Stockport	18.3.1958	(sub.) 1–0	Carlisle
20.10.1957	2–2	Selhurst Pk.			

Other miscellaneous representative appearances

g goal scored

Date	Match	Score	Venue	Date	Match	Score	Venue
Joe Leeming				**Peter O'Sullivan**			
1910	F.A. summer tour		South Africa	26.4.1976	Wales XI v. London XI (1 g)	1–0	Highbury
Jack Woodhouse				**Tony Grealish**			
1920	F.A. summer tour		South Africa	1.6.1982	R. of Ireland XI v. A.S.L. XI	3–1	Port of Spain
Denis Foreman				**Gerry Ryan**			
27.11.1952	F.A. XI v. Cambridge University	8–0	Cambridge	1.6.1982	R. of Ireland XI v. A.S.L. XI (1 g)	3–1	Port of Spain
12.3.1956	Springboks XI v. Scotland XI	1–2	Glasgow	**Steve Foster**			
Jimmy Langley				9.2.1982	England XI v. Manchester City	2–1	Manchester
3.11.1954	F.A. XI v. The Army	1–1	Sheffield	23.3.1982	England XI v. Athletic Bilbao	1–1	Bilbao
1955	F.A. summer tour		West Indies	18.5.1982	England XI v. Aston Villa (1 g)	2–3	Birmingham
12.10.1955	F.A. XI v. R.A.F.	9–0	Bristol	**John Byrne**			
1956	F.A. summer tour		South Africa	11.8.1991	R. of Ireland XI v. Man. Utd (sub.)	1–1	Manchester
10.10.1956	F.A. XI v. R.A.F.	2–1	Sheffield				
7.11.1956	F.A. XI v. The Army	7–3	Manchester				

Albion beneficiaries

The following players, ex-players and other employees have enjoyed benefit games or collections (for long service except where indicated).
Note that in earlier years it was the custom to grant the proceeds of a scheduled league game to the beneficiary.

Beneficiary	Date	Match	Type of match	Score	Attendance	Proceeds
John Jackson	25.4.1905	Albion v. Tottenham Hotspur	Testimonial	3–3		

Albion's former manager was awarded a testimonial match on Easter Tuesday which was played for the 'Jackson Souvenir Cup'. At a post-match social gathering, it was announced that the trophy was to be offered for competition annually between schoolboy teams representing Brighton and Tottenham.

Ben Garfield						

After moving to Tunbridge Wells Rangers in 1905, the former winger had to retire because of injury. Albion launched an appeal on his behalf in September 1905.

Arthur Hulme	27.11.1907	Albion v. Southampton	Western League	3–0	1,500	
Ralph Routledge	30.4.1913	Albion v. Millwall	Southern Alliance	2–2	1,000	£51 9s. 9d.

Ralph was forced into retirement by a knee injury received in the Southern League match with Coventry City in September 1912. A fund was set up for his benefit to which the receipts from the above fixture were donated. Routledge subsequently made a comeback in 1914–15.

Bert Longstaff	16.4.1913	Albion v. Portsmouth	Southern Alliance	3–0	2,000	£135 3s.
	5.5.1923	Albion v. Merthyr Town	Football League	0–0	5,000	

The Merthyr Town game was a joint benefit with Bill Miller.

Billy Booth	14.3.1914	Albion v. Exeter City	Southern League	2–1	3,000	
Joe Leeming	13.4.1914	Reserves v. Southampton	South Eastern League	3–2	3,500	£118

Club captain Joe stepped down to play for the Lambs in his benefit match on Easter Monday.

Bob Whiting	21.10.1914	Albion v. Chelsea	Testimonial			

Bob's benefit match against his former club was postponed indefinitely owing to the poor wartime attendances. Whiting unfortunately lost his life during the conflict and his benefit was therefore never realised.

Fred Bates	21.11.1914	Albion v. Croydon Common	Southern League	4–1	3,000	£3 2s. 9d.

Albion's groundsman was killed in the early days of the war while serving with the Royal Scots Fusiliers, and a collection was made on behalf of his widow at the above match.

Gunner Higham	24.4.1920	Albion v. Newport County	Southern League	3–1	10,500	£605 3s.
Charlie Webb	23.4.1921	Albion v. Watford	Football League	0–3	10,000	£495 15s. 11d.
	28.9.1949	Portsmouth v. Arsenal	Testimonial	2–1	13,000	

The two First Division sides met at the Goldstone in a splendid tribute to the man who was associated with the Albion as player and manager from 1908 until 1947.

Jack Bollington	30.11.1921	Albion v. Cardiff City	Testimonial	0–3	4,500	

Jack retired after breaking a leg in the F.A. Cup tie with Cardiff City at the Goldstone in January 1921, and the two clubs met the following November for his benefit.

Jack Woodhouse	22.4.1922	Albion v. Gillingham	Football League	0–1	6,000	
George Coomber	7.4.1923	Albion v. Reading	Football League	3–1	7,703	£480
Bill Miller	5.5.1923	Albion v. Merthyr Town	Football League	0–0	5,000	

A joint testimonial with Bert Longstaff.

Reg Phillips	2.4.1924	Reserves v. Southampton	Southern League	2–1		£125

Reg died at the age of 23 in March 1924 and the receipts from the above match were donated to his family.

Wally Little	28.3.1925	Albion v. Queen's Park Rangers	Football League	5–0	6,500	
Jack Thompson	3.3.1926	Albion v. Portsmouth	Testimonial	4–4	1,124	
Tommy Cook	5.3.1927	Albion v. Gillingham	Football League	3–2	9,447	£437 15s. 1d.
Jack Nightingale	2.4.1927	Albion v. Charlton Athletic	Football League	3–2	7,823	£338
Ernie Wilson	10.3.1928	Albion v. Gillingham	Football League	0–0	7,860	£326 15s. 2d.
	4.5.1933	Albion v. Birmingham	Testimonial	2–1	4,700	£323 6s. 9d.
Jack Jenkins	24.3.1928	Albion v. Merthyr Town	Football League	5–0	7,663	
Ernie Ison, Reg Smith and						
Reg Wilkinson	18.4.1930	Albion v. Coventry City	Football League	1–1	9,100	
	19.4.1930	Albion v. Queen's Park Rangers	Football League	2–3	6,411	
	21.4.1930	Reserves v. Coventry City	London Combination	3–1		

These three long-serving players were unfortunate that their benefit season coincided with a financial crisis at the Goldstone, which meant that they were not granted a game. Collections were made on their behalf at the above Eastertide matches.

Paul Mooney and Stan Webb	14.3.1931	Albion v. Notts County	Football League	1–3	14,037	

Mooney and Webb had to make do with the proceeds of a collection at the above fixture, attended by the biggest crowd of the season.

Jack Williams	27.4.1932	Albion v. Portsmouth	Testimonial	0–2	3,804	

Jack was forced to retire through injury.

Bobby Farrell	1.5.1935	Albion v. Portsmouth	Testimonial	2–3	3,200	

Bobby was due a benefit in 1934 but it was held over for a year because of the financial situation.

Potter Smith	29.4.1936	Albion v. Brentford	Testimonial	1–2	3,354	
Dave Walker	28.4.1937	Albion v. Southampton	Testimonial	1–1	2,617	
Albert Underwood	30.10.1937	Reserves v. Arsenal	London Combination	3–3	3,935	

Albion's long-serving secretary died in January 1937 and the gate receipts from the above match were donated to his widow.

Ernie King	4.5.1938	Albion v. Bolton Wanderers	Testimonial	1–5	3,022	
Ted Martin	19.4.1939	Albion v. West Ham United	Testimonial	2–0	794	
Dickie Meades	3.5.1939	Albion v. Brentford	Testimonial	0–1	752	

Dickie retired after nineteen years as Albion's trainer and was rewarded with a testimonial match.

Jack Carruthers	20.12.1947	Albion v. Hartlepools United	F.A. Cup	2–1	15,000	

Jack died in November 1947 at the age of 45 and a collection was made on behalf of his family at the above match.

Len Darling, Ernie Marriott,						
Stan Risdon and Bert Stephens	26.4.1948	Notts County	Testimonial	1–7	6,068	
	27.9.1948	Albion v. Wolverhampton Wanderers	Testimonial	1–4	5,128	
	25.4.1949	Albion v. Charlton Athletic	Testimonial	1–3	3,618	

All three games were joint testimonials with Joe Wilson.

Albion beneficiaries (cont.)

The following players, ex-players and other employees have enjoyed benefit games or collections (for long service except where indicated).
Note that in earlier years it was the custom to grant the proceeds of a scheduled league game to the beneficiary.

Beneficiary	Date	Match	Type of match	Score	Attendance	Proceeds
Joe Wilson	26.4.1948	Albion v. Notts County	Testimonial	1–7	6,068	
	27.9.1948	Albion v. Wolverhampton Wanderers	Testimonial	1–4	5,128	
	25.4.1949	Albion v. Charlton Athletic	Testimonial	1–3	3,618	
The above three games were joint testimonial matches with Len Darling, Ernie Marriott, Stan Risdon and Bert Stephens.						
	14.11.1961	Albion v. G. Gunn International XI	Testimonial	0–5	12,600	£1,530
	3.5.1974	Albion v. All-Star XI	Testimonial	2–2	4,464	c. £2,000
Reg Hipkin	14.1.1950	Albion v. Newport County	Football League	5–0	11,502	
A collection was made at the above match for Reg who had to give up the game because of a knee injury sustained at Bristol Rovers in November 1948.						
Harry Baldwin and Jack Ball	28.9.1950	Albion v. All-Star XI	Testimonial	4–3	7,965	
	30.4.1951	Albion v. Liverpool	Testimonial	1–1	11,254	
The Liverpool game was a joint testimonial with Jack Dugnolle.						
Jack Dugnolle	10.2.1951	'A' team v. Dagenham	Metropolitan League	0–3	1,065	
	30.4.1951	Albion v. Liverpool	Testimonial	1–1	11,254	
	5.5.1951	'A' team v. Southwick	Testimonial	5–4		
Jack first came to the Goldstone in 1933 and spent five years with the club. He returned in 1946 and two years later became coach of the newly formed 'A' team. The Liverpool game was a joint testimonial with Harry Baldwin and Jack Ball.						
Jess Willard	17.4.1952	Reserves v. Chichester Invitation XI	Testimonial	4–2	1,200	Over £50
Played at Priory Park, Chichester.						
	2.5.1952	Albion v. Nottingham Forest	Testimonial	5–4	6,000	
Alex Wilson	29.9.1952	Arsenal v. All-Star XI	Testimonial	2–4	9,350	
When Alex decided to give up his job as Albion's trainer, his former club Arsenal brought their team to the Goldstone to play an All-Star team including many international players.						
Des Tennant	1.5.1954	Des Tennant's XI v. Brentford	Testimonial	6–1	3,500	
Tennant's XI consisted mainly of Albion and ex-Albion players.						
Albion Players' Benefit Fund	3.5.1957	Albion v. Liverpool	Testimonial	0–2	2,678	
	14.4.1959	Albion v. Kilmarnock	Testimonial	3–1	4,430	
	1.5.1959	Albion v. Newcastle United	Testimonial	1–1	6,682	
	30.3.1960	Albion v. Djurgarden (Sweden)	Testimonial	0–0	5,500	
In the late 1950s a general fund was set up for those long-serving players who were due a benefit. Eric Gill, Dennis Gordon, Roy Jennings, Don Bates and Tommy Bisset were among those to receive monies from the fund.						
Frankie Howard	12.11.1962	Albion v. G. Gunn International XI	Testimonial	5–5	5,827	
	3.3.1975	Albion v. Queen's Park Rangers	Testimonial	2–1	7,210	
Albion's groundsman enjoyed a third testimonial season in 1988–89 but did not have a benefit match.						
Steve Burtenshaw	11.11.1963	Albion v. G. Gunn International XI	Testimonial	3–7	5,500	£670
The match was abandoned after 85 minutes when the crowd invaded the pitch thinking the final whistle had been blown.						
Jack Bertolini and Cyril Hodges	13.11.1967	Albion v. All-Star XI	Testimonial	5–6	15,768	£3,500
Jack was forced to give up the game in 1965 after suffering a serious knee-ligament injury. Cyril first came to Hove in October 1946 but soon retired because of injury. He returned in 1957 as assistant trainer and remained at the Goldstone for eleven years.						
Norman Gall and Brian Powney	11.5.1971	Albion v. Wolverhampton Wanderers	Testimonial	0–2	6,385	£1,888
	16.5.1971	Albion v. International Club	Testimonial	?–?		
The above match was played at the greyhound stadium, Hove.						
	5.5.1972	Albion v. Chelsea	Testimonial	2–3	14,230	
Geoff Sidebottom	11.5.1972	Albion v. Birmingham City	Testimonial	2–2	8,886	
Geoff was forced into retirement because of serious head injuries.						
Joe Kinnear	23.3.1976	Albion v. Tottenham Hotspur	Testimonial	1–6	7,124	c. £4,000
Joe spent ten years as a professional at White Hart Lane before coming to the Goldstone.						
Chris Cattlin	9.8.1977	Albion v. Coventry City	Testimonial	3–1	8,918	
Chris had eight years with Coventry City prior to joining the Albion.						
Peter Grummitt	2.5.1978	Albion v. Alan Mullery's All-Star XI	Testimonial	8–7	5,615	
Peter had to give up the game because of chronic injuries to his knee and hip.						
Peter O'Sullivan	22.4.1980	Albion v. Southampton	Testimonial	1–3	6,881	c. £10,000
Gary Williams	14.5.1984	Albion v. Ex-Albion XI	Testimonial	3–3	2,600	
Gary spent five years at the Goldstone before moving to Crystal Palace where he received the injury that cut short his League career. He was playing for Whitehawk when he was granted this testimonial match.						
Gerry Ryan	8.8.1986	Albion v. Tottenham Hotspur	Testimonial	0–4	10,759	c. £20,000
Gerry had to hang up his boots after suffering a severely broken leg at Crystal Palace in April 1985.						
Graham Moseley	3.4.1990	Albion 1983 v. Tottenham Hotspur	Testimonial	0–3	6,410	c. £18,000
Graham left the Goldstone for Cardiff City after almost nine years, but was forced into early retirement owing to injuries incurred in a car crash. The Albion 1983 side contained nine of the players who represented the club in the 1983 F.A. Cup final and replay.						
Steve Gatting	17.8.1990	Albion v. Arsenal	Testimonial	2–2	5,517	
	12.11.90	Albion v. Eastbourne Select XI	Testimonial	6–0	1,300	
Above match played at Priory Lane, Langney Sports F.C.						
Perry Digweed						
The long-serving goalkeeper had a testimonial season in 1991–92 but did not have a benefit match.						
Gary Chivers	7.8.1992	Albion v. Crystal Palace	Testimonial	0–1	3,273	
Albion's captain received a testimonial after just over four years at the club and fourteen as a professional.						

NOTES ON SOME OPPONENTS AND COMPETITIONS

Aberdare Athletic: originally formed as Aberdare Town 1893 and competed in Southern League Division Two for five seasons prior to First World War. Reformed as Aberdare Athletic 1920, playing at Athletic Ground, Ynis. Members of Football League 1921–27 but failed re-election. Amalgamated with Aberaman Athletic as Aberdare & Aberaman Athletic and returned to Southern League for 1927–28. Club folded 1928 because of lack of support, but an Aberaman club continued to play in Welsh League and a new Aberdare Town was formed in the early 1930s.

Aldershot Town: founded 1926, became known simply as **Aldershot** around 1930. Members of Football League 1932–1992. Club folded March 1992 because of financial problems but new Aldershot Town arose from ashes same year to compete in Diadora Isthmian League.

Amateur Football Association: formed 1907 by number of amateur clubs unhappy with the Football Association. The Amateur F.A. recognised the authority of the F.A. in 1914 and in 1934 became the Amateur Football Alliance (A.F.A.). Still controls number of amateur leagues for old boys, banks, civil servants, etc.

A.P.V. Athletic: works team based in Crawley. Members of Sussex County League 1954–1972 and 1985–88.

Ashford United: formed by the amalgamation of two works sides. Founder members of Kent League 1894–1906. Not connected with present Ashford Town.

Barry Town: original Barry club formed 1891. Re-formed 1923 as Barry Town and changed name to Barri 1992. Will return home in 1993 to play in League of Wales after exile in Worcester.

Bedford Queen's: works team from the Queen's electrical engineering company.

Bedford Town: founded 1908. Contested Southern League from 1945 onwards but folded 1982 after losing ground. New club formed 1989 now in South Midlands League.

Bedminster: formed 1887 as Southville, becoming Bedminster 1893. Absorbed by Bristol City 1900 when latter club took over Bedminster's Ashton Gate ground.

Bexleyheath & Welling: changed name to Bexley United in 1963 but disbanded 1976.

Birmingham: became **Birmingham City** 1945.

Borough Polytechnic: still compete in A.F.A.'s Southern Amateur League as South Bank Polytechnic.

Boscombe: became **Bournemouth & Boscombe Athletic** 1923 upon joining Football League, and **AFC Bournemouth** 1971.

Bradford (Park Avenue): formed 1907 by Bradford rugby league club. Rather curiously contested Southern League 1907–08 before entering Football League. Failed re-election 1970 and folded 1974. Played at Park Avenue cricket ground. Re-formed 1988 and contest North West Counties League at Bramley RLFC ground, Leeds.

Brighton Athletic: combined with Brighton Hornets 1902 to form short-lived **Brighton Amateurs**.

Brighton Challenge Shield: inaugurated 1886 as Brighton Challenge Cup, but replaced 1896 by the Shield which was donated by Frank Allen, later a Brighton United director and founding member of Albion's club committee. Still competed for by local clubs.

Burgess Hill: became **Burgess Hill Town** at unknown date.

Burton Wanderers: members of Football League 1894–97. Combined with Burton Swifts 1901 to form Burton United. No connection with current Burton Albion.

CADM & TC: military side based in the Eastbourne area during Second World War.

Callenders Athletic: works team of Callender cable-manufacturing company, Erith, Kent. Contested London League 1925–29, Spartan League 1930–39 and Metropolitan League 1949–53.

Chatham: formed 1882. Changed name to **Chatham Town** by 1920 then Medway 1974, but reverted to former name 1979. Members of Kent League.

Chesham Generals: formed 1887. Combined with **Chesham Town** (formed 1879) 1917 to form Chesham United, now members of Diadora Isthmian League.

Chester: became **Chester City** 1983.

Chingford Town: appear to have folded around 1987 but re-formed as Chingford Town Wanderers, playing in Spartan League.

Chipperfield: amalgamated with Tudor Corinthians 1987 and contest Herts Senior County League as Chipperfield Corinthians.

Clapton: formed 1878 and have contested every Diadora Isthmian League season at the Spotted Dog Ground, Forest Gate, London E7. The first English club to visit the Continent (Antwerp 1890). No connection with Clapton Orient club.

Clapton Orient: changed name to **Leyton Orient** 1946, to **Orient** 1966, and back to Leyton Orient 1987. (Not to be confused with Clapton or Leyton.)

Corinthians: formed 1882 to improve teamwork in the England international side. Most famous amateur club before Second World War with gentlemen amateurs invited to join. Amalgamated with Casuals 1939 as Corinthian-Casuals. Now compete (still as amateurs) in Spartan League with ground at Tolworth, Surrey.

Cowes: folded 1899 and withdrew from Southern League. Re-formed as amateur club and have contested Hampshire League ever since, now as Cowes Sports.

Crouch End Vampires: uniquely named club still contests A.F.A.'s Southern Amateur League at their north London home.

Croydon Common: formed 1897. Turned professional 1907 and played in Southern League at The Nest, Selhurst (now site of railway depot). One season in wartime London Combination. Folded 1917.

Croydon Rovers: professional club with brief existence at Mitcham Stadium. May or may not be connected with the present Croydon club which was founded 1953 as Croydon Amateurs.

Dagenham: founded 1949 and initiated Metropolitan League same year as had no other competition to enter. Combined with Redbridge Forest 1992 to form Dagenham & Redbridge in GM Vauxhall Conference, playing at Dagenham.

Dartford: formed 1888. Folded as senior club 1992 in wake of Maidstone United's crash (they shared ground in Dartford which was sold) but survive as youth team.

Dickinson (Apsley): works team from Apsley near Hemel Hempstead.

Dolphins: invitational side for gentlemen amateurs based in Sussex, a sort of 'local Corinthians' playing mostly in charity matches.

Dunstable Town: founded 1895. Became Dunstable 1976 and play in Beazer Homes Southern League.

Eastbourne: formed 1881. Became **Eastbourne Town** 1976. Compete in Sussex County League.

Eastbourne Old Town: played at Larkin's Field and Upwick Farm. Disbanded in December 1905, their second season in South Eastern League, following F.A. censure for mismanagement; Eastbourne F.C. took over their fixtures.

Eastbourne Swifts: founder members of East Sussex Senior League 1896. Played at The Saffrons with Eastbourne F.C. but folded January 1899. Re-formed following season but appear to have folded again 1903.

Folkestone: formed 1884. Became Folkestone Town at unknown date and then Folkestone & Shepway 1974. Reverted to Folkestone Town 1980 but folded late 1990 owing to financial problems. Kent County League side **Folkestone Invicta** (formed 1946) took over lease on ground and gained membership of Kent League in 1991. (Albion played in Invicta's inaugural game on the ground.)

Football Combination: the continuation, from 1946 onwards, of the London Combination (q.v.) which was founded in 1915.

Glengall Rovers: members of the Brighton F.A. Rovers played in Preston Park and had their headquarters at the Marquess of Exeter pub in Upper Hamilton Road.

Gravesend: became Gravesend United and combined with Northfleet Utd 1946 as **Gravesend & Northfleet**. Play in Beazer Homes Southern League at Northfleet.

Grays United: became **Grays Thurrock United** and continued to at least 1932 but not connected with present Grays Athletic club (formed 1890).

Guildford United: formed 1921. Became **Guildford City** 1927 but hit hard times 1974 and combined with Dorking as Guildford & Dorking United. Folded 1976 and present Dorking club was formed 1977.

Hartlepools United: became simply **Hartlepool** 1968 but changed name again 1977 to **Hartlepool United**.

Hastings & St Leonards: formed 1895. Combined with professional St Leonards United 1906 (having been found guilty by F.A. of paying players) to form **Hastings & St Leonards United**. Wound up 1910 and re-formed same year as amateur club, dropping 'United' suffix. Known as **Hastings Town** since 1976 and competed in Beazer Homes Southern League since Hastings United's collapse.

Hastings United: professional club founded 1948 which competed in Southern League until it folded in 1985.

Haywards Heath: became Haywards Heath Town 1988.

Headington United: formed 1893 as Headington, adding 'United' a year later. Became **Oxford United** 1960.

Hillingdon Borough: formed 1872 as Yiewsley Town, becoming Hillingdon Borough 1964. Combined with Burnham 1985 as Burnham & Hillingdon, but dropped '& Hillingdon' 1987. Compete in Beazer Homes Southern League at Burnham, near Slough. A new Hillingdon Borough club was formed 1990 and plays in Spartan League.

Hitchin Town: formed 1865 but disbanded 1913. Present Diadora Isthmian League club formed 1928.

Hove: formed 1884. Played at Goldstone Ground 1901–04. Disbanded 1914 and re-formed as short-lived Brighton & Hove Amateurs 1919 which subsequently folded 1922. Another Hove club was formed same year and contested Sussex County League until 1949. There followed two years in the Metropolitan League and change of name to **Hove United** 1950, but club sold Rowan Avenue ground 1952 and again disbanded. From ashes came Hove White Rovers, members of County League 1952–59 playing at Wish Park, Aldrington. Changed name to Hove Town 1956 before folding April 1959.

Ilford: founded 1881. Combined with Leytonstone 1979 amid ground problems as Leytonstone-Ilford, which changed name to Redbridge Forest 1989 upon amalgamation with Walthamstow Avenue. A 1992 merger with Dagenham formed Dagenham & Redbridge, members of Vauxhall Conference playing at Dagenham.

Leeds City: formed 1904 upon demise of Hunslet F.C., but disbanded in October 1919 after being expelled from Football League for illegal payments and other financial irregularities. The present **Leeds United** was formed the following year.

Leicester Fosse: became **Leicester City** 1919.

Leyton: original club formed 1868 but disbanded 1880. Re-formed as Matlock Swifts 1889, becoming Leyton 1893. Adopted professionalism in period 1905–1912 in Southern League. Playing at Brisbane Road (Leyton Orient's current ground), club reverted to amateur status and combined with Wingate 1975 to form Leyton-Wingate, members of the Diadora Isthmian League. Known simply as Leyton again since 1992. No connection with Leyton Orient.

London Combination: founded 1915 as a competition for clubs in the capital during the break in normal fare caused by war. When normal competitions resumed in 1919, London Combination continued as reserve league. (A second, non-reserve division was run 1930–33.) Another break occurred 1939–44, but two years later the League dropped 'London' prefix to continue as 'Football Combination'.

London Midweek League: formed late 1940s as competition for third or 'A' teams of Football League clubs and continued into the 1950s. Resurrected in late '60s as reserve league for those clubs in the South-East which were not members of Football Combination. 'London' prefix dropped 1971 and Midweek League continued until disbanded 1984 with just seven clubs in membership.

London Welsh: formed 1885. Better known for their rugby union team but maintain a football side in A.F.A.'s Southern Olympian League.

Maidenhead: formed 1869. Amalgamated with Maidenhead Norfolkians 1921 to become Maidenhead United, currently competing in Diadora Isthmian League.

Maidstone United: played football in Maidstone from 1897 until 1988 when the ground was sold. Club moved to Dartford and won a place in Football League in 1989. A professional club in 1897–1939 and since 1971, United folded 1992 because of its ground difficulties.

Merthyr Town: founded 1909 and joined Southern League. Members of Football League 1920–30. Re-formed 1945 as Merthyr Tydfil, now members of GM Vauxhall Conference.

Metropolitan & District League: formed 1949 by newly founded Dagenham F.C. who had no competition to play in. Comprised 'A' teams of Football League clubs, reserves of Southern League sides and number of amateur teams from large area of south-east England and south Midlands. Second division 1963-64, but combined 1971 with Greater London League as Metropolitan-London League which itself amalgamated with Spartan League 1975 to form London-Spartan League, an alliance which continues today under the old Spartan League title.

Metropolitan Police: founded 1919 and play in Diadora Isthmian League at Imber Court, East Molesey, Surrey.

Mid Rhondda: a professional club which competed in Southern League and Welsh National League in the period 1912–28.

Midweek League: see London Midweek League.

Millwall: F.A. records suggest any 'Athletic' suffix was officially dropped before 1898.

New Brompton: became **Gillingham** in 1913.

Newport County: formed 1912. Lost Football League status 1988 and folded April 1989 while in Vauxhall Conference. Newport AFC was formed shortly after but play across the English border at Gloucester in Beazer Homes Southern League.

Northfleet United: amalgamated with Gravesend United 1946 to form **Gravesend & Northfleet**, members of Beazer Homes Southern League playing at Northfleet.

Nuneaton Town: not connected with present Nuneaton Borough (formed 1937).

Orient: see Clapton Orient.

Peterborough City: combined with Fletton United 1923 to form **Peterborough & Fletton United**. This club was suspended by the F.A. in 1932–33 and disbanded. The present **Peterborough United** was formed 1934.

Poole: formed 1880. Became Poole Town c. 1946. In Beazer Homes Southern Lge.

R.A. Portsmouth (Royal Artillery): Southern League club ejected from Amateur Cup for professional practices in 1899 and folded shortly after. No connection with the present **Portsmouth** club which was formed as a professional outfit in April 1898.

Richmond Association: founder members of Southern Amateur League 1907–14.

Romford: formed 1876 and re-formed 1929. Professional from 1959 but folded 1978 when ground was sold. Re-formed 1992 and play in Essex Senior League.

Rushden: formed 1889 and re-formed after First World War as Rushden Town. Merged with Irthlingborough Diamonds 1992 as Rushden & Diamonds, playing in Beazer Homes Southern League at Irthlingborough.

Ryde: formed 1888. Now known as Ryde Sports and playing in Wessex League.

St Albans Amateurs: together with St Albans F.C., this club was an indirect predecessor of the current St Albans City club which was formed in 1908 and plays in the Diadora Isthmian League.

St Neots & District: became **St Neots Town** 1961 but folded 1988.

Salisbury City: competed in Southern, Western and Hampshire Leagues 1902–39. Present Salisbury club (formed 1947) plays in Beazer Homes Southern League.

Shepherd's Bush: formed as Old St Stephen's and changed name in 1898, competing in Southern League 1894–1902. Appear to have folded about 1911, although a Shepherd's Bush club did contest London League 1932–33.

Sheppey United: founded as Sheppey Athletic 1890, playing in Sheerness. Now members of Kent League and play at Faversham Town's ground.

Skyways: works team from Dunsfold Aerodrome, Surrey, which won Brighton League 1950 and contested Sussex Senior Cup final same year.

South Eastern League: formed 1901 by a number of amateur teams in Home Counties and reserve sides of Southern League and Football League clubs in the capital. It proved a popular competition, expanding its boundaries northwards and westwards, and two divisions were run for five season 1905–10. After the Great War, attempts to revive the South Eastern League were not a great success and it disbanded 1921.

South Liverpool: formed 1934 but folded 1991. Played in Garston area of city.

Southern Alliance: a very short-lived competition formed in 1912 at the instigation of Albion chairman Peter Vey.

Southern Counties Combination: a Saturday league founded in 1971.

Southern League: formed 1894, the first professional league in the South flourishing alongside Football League until 1920 when First Division clubs were absorbed into latter competition. Thereafter continued with reserve sides of Football League clubs and smaller professional teams. Continues as Beazer Homes League, a feeder league to the GM Vauxhall Conference.

Southern Professional Charity Cup: competed for by many of the professional clubs in London and the South-East from 1901 until 1915.

Southern United: a short-lived professional club operating in 1904–06 at Brown's Field in the Nunhead area of south London.

Southern Youth League: formed 1975 and comprised mainly Sussex and Kent clubs until 1981. Re-formed 1982 by clubs from Surrey.

Southwick: original club formed 1882 but folded April 1899 after being fined £5 for fielding a professional (Jimmy Paige of Brighton United). Present Sussex County League club formed 1906 following Southwick Swifts (1899–1902), Southwick Alliance (1902–03) and Southwick St Michael's (1905–06).

Stoke: became **Stoke City** 1925.

Sussex Sunday League: one of the largest Sunday leagues in the country, formed 1960 by, among others, Ron Pavey, now Albion chief executive.

Swansea Town: became **Swansea City** February 1970.

Swaythling Athletic: formed 1946. Dropped 'Athletic' 1973. Moved from Southampton to Eastleigh 1975, changing name to Eastleigh 1980. Play in Wessex League.

Thames Ironworks: wound up June 1900 and relaunched a month later as **West Ham United**.

Thames: a short-lived professional club which played at the West Ham Greyhound Stadium, Prince Regent Lane. It lasted only four seasons, 1928–30 in Southern League and 1930–32 in Football League, before folding through lack of support.

Thames & Medway Combination: a league formed 1896 and competed for until 1930, largely as a complement to Kent League; many clubs competed in both. Re-formed 1954 and lasted until 1966 when superseded by Kent Premier League.

Thorneycrofts: works team of a shipbuilding company in Woolston area of Southampton. Played as Thornycrofts Athletic at least 1972.

Tunbridge Wells Rangers: formed originally 1886 as Tunbridge Wells, adding 'Rangers' around 1900. Folded at start of Second World War. Re-formed as **Tunbridge Wells United** 1951. Changed name back to Tunbridge Wells Rangers 1963 but subsequently disbanded 1967. The present Tunbridge Wells club, members of Kent League, was formed same year.

Twickenham: formed 1943. Founder members of Corinthian League 1945. Subsequently in Metropolitan and Parthenon Leagues, but appear to have folded around 1959.

United League: formed 1896 to supplement the fixture lists of its member clubs, most of which competed in Southern League. Most Southern League clubs withdrew 1899 to leave a rump of teams in Northamptonshire. Folded 1902 but re-formed 1905 and continued until 1909.

Vernon-Wentworth Challenge Cup: a Brighton, Hove and Worthing competition played for since 1895 when given by Bruce Vernon-Wentworth, M.P. for Brighton.

Vickers: works team which became (British Aircraft Corporation) BAC Weybridge 1964 and then (British Aerospace) BAe Weybridge. Changed name to Weybridge Town 1989 in Combined Counties League but appear to have folded in 1990.

Walthamstow Avenue: formed 1900 but, after losing their ground, merged with Leytonstone-Ilford 1989 as Redbridge Forest. Subsequently combined with Dagenham 1992 to form Dagenham & Redbridge, playing at Dagenham in Vauxhall Conference.

War Office Sports Club: spent one season in South Eastern League. Now coming under the Ministry of Defence, the club still competes in A.F.A.'s Civil Service League under its original name.

Warmley: Bristol-based club formed 1882. Turned professional 1897 but left Southern League January 1899. Had brief spell in Western League until 1904.

West Hampstead: played in London League 1897–1910.

West Norwood: competed in Isthmian and Surrey Senior Leagues until 1939.

Western League: formed 1892 by clubs in Bristol region. From 1897 a number of Southern League sides also competed in Western League but there was a mass withdrawal in 1909 because of the travelling costs involved. Continues as Great Mills Western League, a feeder league to the Beazer Homes Southern League.

Whitehawk & Manor Farm Old Boys: became **Whitehawk** in 1958. Members of Sussex County League.

Willesden Town: competed in London League at various times 1898–1921. No connection with post-Second World War clubs in Willesden.

Woolwich Arsenal: became **Arsenal** 1913 when club moved from Plumstead area of Woolwich to Highbury.

Woolwich Polytechnic: now play in Kent County League as Thames Polytechnic.

Worthing & District League: a Saturday league formed in 1921.

Yeovil & Petters United: formed 1895. Became Yeovil Town 1946. Currently members of GM Vauxhall Conference.

INDEX

Principal entries in **bold** type, illustrations and 'snippets' in *italics*. Players and opponents not generally indexed.

admission charges   **296**, 34, 42, *125*, 209, 213, 217, 222, 239, 243
age records   **318**
air-raids   118–119, *123*
Aitken, George (joint acting manager)   202, 220, 223, 231, 238
'Albion' (the name)   **26–27**
Albion Shield   *71*
Albion Week (Supporters' Club)   *137, 139*
'And Smith Must Score' (fanzine)   *245*
appearances
    player-by-player   **300–313**
    records   **314**
Arsenal FC   *104*, 105–106, *109*, 119, *119*, *140*, 213
'A' team   **275–277**, 136, 139, *142*, 143, *145*, 161, *165*
attendances   **294–296**, 98, 102, *108*, 131, 137, 138, 141, *142*, 147, 161, 163, 167, *179*, 180, *205*, 216, *220*, *252*
Avenell, William (Brighton & Hove Rangers chairman)   16, 20, 21, 24, 25, 26
badges   *201*
Bailey, Mike (manager)   220, 221, 222, 223, 233
Baldwin Cup   **284**
Bamber, Mike (chairman)   193, 194, 196, *196, 196*, 197, 199, 202, 206, 207, *213*, 215, 217, *218*, 220, 223, 229, 231, 232, 233, 234, 243, 247, 253, 255
Bedson, Bryan (chairman)   *213*, 231, 233, 234, 238, 240, 241
benefit matches   **262–265, 323–324**
Berks & Bucks Hospital Charity Cup   **266**, *84*
BISA (Brighton Independent Supporters Association)   **255**, *255*
board of directors   34, 36, 38, 39, 42–43, 67, 94, 110, 112, 117, *131*, 134, 145, 175, 187, 200, 205, 220, 238, 240, 246, 247, 255, 256
    chairmen   **299**
    personnel (directors)   **299**, 34, 36, 39, 40, 118, *125, 127*, 193, 194, 255, 256
    takeover bids   164, 167, 168, 231, 234
    see also limited company
Bott, Daniel (chairman)   25, 26
bribery allegations   **159**
Brighton Athletic FC   11, *12*, 23, 31, 325
Brighton Boys   22, *82, 89*, 94, *153*
Brighton Challenge Shield/Cup   12, 20, 21, 23, 325
Brighton Charity Cup   **283**, 23
Brighton Council   *212*, 253
    arms   *201*
Brighton Hockey Club   29
Brighton & Hove Albion Women's FC   *248*
Brighton & Hove FC
    (1915–19)   **68**
    see also formation of Albion
Brighton & Hove Rangers FC   **20–25**, *18*, 26, 27, *199*
Brighton & Hove Sports and Leisure Ltd (parent company)   **205**, 206
Brighton & Hove United FC
    see formation of Albion
Brighton United FC (first professional club)   **12–20**, 25, 26, 27, 28
British Caledonian Airways (sponsors)   216, 227

Broadbridge, George (chairman)   *36*, 34, 38, 39, 40, 136
Brown, Charles (chairman)   *40*, 40, 85, *96*
Butt-Thompson, Edward (Brighton United chairman)   *13*, 13
Callaghan, Harry (chairman)   33
Campbell, Carlo (chairman)   118, *125, 127*, 146–147, 158
captains   **319**
Cattlin, Chris (player & manager)   202, 213, 231, 232, 233, 234, 236, 238
chairmen   **299**
championships   31, 33, 51, 53, 54, *57*, 65, 73, 87, *96*, 158, *161*, 174, 268, 278
charity cups   **266, 282–283**
Clark, John (Goldstone landlord)   13, 25, 29, *30*, 31, 36, *42*, 49, 53, *58*, 68, 70, 85
Clark, Noah (director)   *40, 96*, 25, 26, 32, 34, 36, 39, *45, 53*
Clough, Brian (manager)   159, *159*, 194, 195, 196, *196*, 197, 201, 210, 215, *215*, 217, 243
Coleman-Cohen, Reggie (takeover bid)   164
colours   **297**, 28, 37, *109*, 137, 143, *155*, 173, 187, 189, 197, 199, 236, 241, 251, 253
Community Scheme   247, *248, 249*
competitive record   **285**
Cook, Tommy (player & manager)   68, 75, 82, *84*, 85, 91, 98, 134
Corinthians FC   76–77, *77*, 91, 325
County Ground (Hove)   *12*, 12, 13, 15, 20, 21, 22, 24, 25, 27, 28, 34
Courtney-King, Eric (chairman)   168, 175, 180
Cowan, Sam (trainer)   113, 129, *132*, 136, 275
crowd behaviour   22, *210*
    celebrations etc.   31, 32, 47, 53, 55, *58*, 93, 129, 158, 174, 203, 211, 242, 250
    enthusiasm etc.   78, 92, 157, 230, *242, 243*, 252
    demonstrations etc.   58, 134, 168, 182, 194, 231, 232, 238, 240, 246, 247, 255, *255*
    hooliganism etc.   22–23, *38*, 47, *73*, 83, 146–147, 172, 173, 175–176, 179, 180, 183, 184, 187, 191, 193, 197, 200, 205, 207, 208–209, 210, 213, 224, 231, *231*, 240, 241, *242*
Crystal Palace FC   114, 197, 199–200, *201*, 202, *204*, 205, 211, 215, *218*, 244
Curtis, George (manager)   121,166,168,169,171
defeats, records   **293**
directors   *see* board of directors
'Dolphins' (nickname)   **201**, *196*
doubles (home & away), records   **292**
Dyke Road Field   27, 28
Eastbourne Charity Cup   **283**
English Cup   *see*
    Football Association Challenge Cup
Everest, Edgar (founder, Brighton United FC)   *11*, 12, 13, 17, 20, *22*, 31, *51*, *139*
finances   28, 31–32, 34, 38, 39, 40, 45, 49, 51, 54, 65, 68, 70, 75, 78, 80, 89, 91, 92, 96, 98, 117–118, 150, 156, 175, 181, 193, 194, 199, 205, 206, 219, 222, 230, 231, 234, *236*, 238, 240, 245, 246, 250, 252–253, 255, 256, 258
    see also limited company – share issues
floodlights   **166**, *144, 160*, 163

Football Association (F.A.)   **11**, 21, 24, *27*, 40, 47–48, 247, 256
    disciplinary trouble with   38–39, 42, 73, 125, 176, 184, 201, 207, 210–211, 227, 231
Football Association Challenge Cup (F.A. Cup, also known as the English Cup)   11, 13, *63*, 83–84, 117, 129, *131, 142*, 255
    run to final   **224–230**
Football Association Charity Shield   **54–56**, *22, 57, 96*
Football Association County Youth Cup   *145*
Football Association Youth Cup   **279–280**, 147
Football Combination and Cup   **268, 272–273**, *325*, 131, 167
    see also London Combination
Footballers' Battalion (First World War)   **67**
Football League   11, 13–14, 38, 40, 70, 115, 117, 119, 123, *125*, 220
Football League Cup   *166*
Football League War Cup   *117*
foreign opposition at home   37, *143, 154*, 163, *166*
foreign tours   **260**, *21, 37, 147*, 166, 187, *187*, 211, 220, 231, 259, 261
formation of Albion   **24–27**, *199*
Freeman-Thomas Charity Shield (Hastings)   **283**
friendly matches   **261, 262–265**
fund-raising   45, 68, 168, *181*, 187–188, *188*, 193, 205, *205*, 211, 234, *244*, 256
    lotteries etc.   87, 168, *171, 174, 194*, 199, *205*, 238, 239, 241, 251
    sponsorship   *175*, 216, 227, *233*, 238, 253
    see also limited company – share issues; records (musical)
giant-killing   **297**
goalscoring records
    team   **293**
    players   **315–317**
Goldstone (rock in Hove Park)   29, *29, 30*
Goldstone Farm   29, *30*, 31, *94*
Goldstone Ground   **29–31**, *30*, 36, *43, 52, 53*, 68, 85, *94*, 118, *123*, 148, 211, 213, 215, 240, 245, 247, 253, 256
    capacities   36, 161, 179, 207, 216, 243, 245, 252
    east side   31, *52, 79*, 81, 85, *108*, 207, 209, 216, 231, 241, 243
        'Chicken Run'   *97, 108*, 138
        improvements   36, 54, 70, 81, 94, 97, 138, 139, 148, 205, 243
        plans   85, 208, 211-212, 216, 222, 243, 245, 247
        'Spion Kop'   *97*
    fences and pens   205, 207, 209, 220–221, 243, 253
        see also Goldstone Ground – east side – 'Chicken Run'
    floodlights   *166, 160*, 163
    north side   43, 85, 216, 231, 232
        improvements   54, 94
        North Stand (first)   81, 85, 94, *94, 123*, 156, 175, 207, 216
        North Stand (second)   234, 241
        plans   216, 222
    other events   67, *96*, 220, 245
    representative matches   53, 89, *137, 155*, 162, *164, 168*, 207, 247, 253, 255

Goldstone Ground (continued)
  south side
    improvements   139, *143*
    plans   212
    South Stand (first)   *30*, 36, *43*, *53*, 139, *141*, 150
    South Stand (second)   150, 215–216, *216*, 241
  west side   *30*, 31, 36, *43*, 241
    improvements   101, 138, 216, 220–221
    'Lego' Stand   213, *214*, 236
    plans   85, 111, *153*, 156, 208, 212, 245
    West Stand (first)   29, *30*, 31, 43, *58*, 70, 94, *94*, *123*, *131*, 139, 158
    West Stand (second)   156, 159, *160*, 161, 191
Goldstone House   29, *30*, 31, *52*, *152*
Goodwin, Freddie (manager)   184, 185, 187
Goodwin, William (chairman)   **40**, 40, 55, 98, 118, 138
Grand Stand
    see Goldstone Ground – west side –
      West Stand (second)
Greater London Minor Combination   **278**, 277
Greenwood, Ron (director)   231, 233
greyhound stadium (Nevill Road)   118, 143, 148, 168, *181*
    possible move to   111, 118, *200*, 240
ground   see County Ground, Dyke Road Field, Goldstone Ground, greyhound stadium, Rowan Avenue
    possible new grounds   36, *53*, 111, 118, *200*, 212, *218*, 240, 247, 253, 255 256
'Gulls Eye' (fanzine)   *245*, 255
Hampshire Youth League and Cup   **278**
Hastings Charity Cup   **283**
Helsinki (pub, Ship Street)   see Seven Stars
Hillman, Albert (chairman)   **117**, 117–118
Home Farm (Brighton & Hove Rangers FC at Withdean)   **21**, 21, **22**, **22**
honours   **259**
Hove Council   94, *157*, 211, *212*, , 230, 247, 255, 256
    arms   *201*
Hove FC   **325**, 11, 26, 27, 29–30, 31, 34, 36, *58*, 68
Imperial Hotel (Queen's Road)   12, 14, 17
international appearances   **320–322**
Jackson, John (founder & manager)   13, 21, 24, *24*, 25, 26, 28, 31, 32, *38*, 38–39, 97
Jones, Bill 'Bullet' (player & assistant trainer)   51, *52*, *58*, 59, 63, 70, 107, 118, *123*
juniors (wartime)   **284**, 118, 121, 125, 131, 136
    see also youth team
Junior Seagulls   236, 238
Lambs (nickname for reserves)   **96**
Lane, Billy (manager)   92, 121, 140, 142, 143, 148, 156, 157, 158, 159, *160*, 166, *166*
Leitch, Archibald (architect)   *53*, *77*
Lifeline   **239**
limited company   **34–36**, *96*, 178, 205
    dividends   78, 80, 82
    share issues etc.   **34–36**, 68, 85, 87, *141*, 168, 199
    see also Brighton & Hove Sports and Leisure Ltd
Liverpool FC
    wartime guests   119, 121, 123, 125, 127
Lloyd, Barry (manager)   238, 240, 241, 243, 245, 246, 247, 248, 249, 253, 254, 255, 256, 257, 258
local competitions   **280–284**, 277–278
London Combination and Cup   **268**, **271**, **326**, 87, 113, 117, 131
    see also Football Combination
London Invitation Youth Cup   **278**
London Midweek League   see Midweek League
London War League and Cup   **121**
Macaulay, Archie (manager)   169, 171, 173, 175, 177, 178, 180, 182, 183–184
managers   **298**
Meaden, Charles (Brighton United chairman)   12, 13, 16, 17

Melia, Jimmy (manager)   162, 220, 223, 224, 225, 226, 227, 229, 231, 232
membership scheme   **241**, 243, 252, 253
Metropolitan League, Cup and Professional Cup   **275–277**, **326**, 143, 161, *166*
Midweek League and Cup   **268**, **274–275**, **326**, 139, 187
Miles, Henry (chairman)   40, 68, 118
miscellaneous first-team matches   **260**, **266**
mini-tournaments   **260**
Miss Albion (Supporters' Club)   **149**
Mullery, Alan (manager)   202, *204*, 205, 206, 207, *208*, 208, 210, 211, 213, 215, 217, 220, 238, 239, 240
Nelmes, Alf (acting manager)   67
Newham, Billy (treasurer & cricketer)   **27**, 13, 24, 25, 26
Newtown Road   *30*, 31, *94*, *179*
nicknames   **201**
Nobo (sponsor)   238
North End Rangers FC   **20–21**, 11, *18*
Olympic Games (at Goldstone)   *137*, *162*
opponents, record against   **286–291**, **292**
Paling, Gerald (chairman)   164, 166, 168
'Pep Group' (takeover bid)   167, 168
Petchey, George (acting manager)   238
Phoenix Brewery Company (sponsor)   *233*
Players of the Season   *184*, **318**
players
    appearances and goals   **300–311**
      wartime   **312–313**
    records etc   **314–324**
pond (at Goldstone)   **31**, *30*
'Pools War'   **108**
practice matches   **37**, 145, 161, 166
presidents   **299**
Preston Park   11, 12, *12*, 21, 23, 36, *53*
promotion   31, 150, 158, 174, 191, 203, 211, 242
radio broadcasts   119, *134*, 176
records (musical)   221, 229
re-election   34, 44, 134, 136
relegation   166, 169–171, 192, 224, 240, 255
reserves (also known as 'Lambs')   **267–275**, 31, 34, 36, 37, *37*, 44, 54, 62, 73, 78, 82, 87, *91*, 93, *96*, 113, 117, 131, 136, *140*, 143, *144*, 147, 150, 161, 163, 167, 171, *179*, 181, *205*, 220, 240, 243, 245, 255
    see also local competitions
Richards Hospital Cup (East Grinstead)   **283**
Robey, George (comedian)   31
Robson, Jack (manager)   48, 49, 51, 67
Rowan Avenue ground (Hove)   *142*, 143, 275
Roy Haydon Memorial Trophy   **281**
St Agnes's Church (Newtown Road)   92, *94*, *215*
Saward, Pat (manager)   187, 188, 189, *189*, *189*, 190, 191, 192, 193, 194
Scott-Walford, Frank (manager)   38, 39, 40, 42, 47, 48, 56
Seagull Line   **209**
'Seagulls' (nickname)   **201**, 202, 243
'Seagull News' (magazine)   **249**
season tickets   33, *83*, *140*, 167, 205, 213, 217, 222
seasonal records   **292**
selection committee   **184**
sequence records   **291**
Seven Stars (pub, Ship Street, now Helsinki)   **26**, 25, 27, 31
'Shrimps' (alleged nickname)   *201*
Sizen, Dudley (chairman)   193, 220, 223, 234, 241, 255
Southampton FC   12, *14*, 17, 20, *47*
South East Counties League and Cup   **278**, 277
South Eastern League   **267**, **269**, **326**, 31, 34, 37, 44
Southern Alliance   60, *63*, **326**
Southern Counties Combination and Cup   **278**, 326
Southern Junior Floodlit Cup   **278**
Southern League   **13–14**, **326**
    first team   **13–14**, 12, 13, 23, 24, 31, 33, *37*, 38, 54, 56, 70
    reserves   **267–268**, **270**, 37, 73, 93, *96*, 113

Southern Professional Charity Cup   49, 54, *57*, 62, 326
Southern Section Cup (Division 3(South) Cup)   102, *102*
Southern Youth League   **278**, **326**, *210*
sports day   *45*
Stanley, Greg (chairman)   240, 255, 256
Stringer, Len (joint chairman)   168, 193, 194
substitutes   177, *183*
Sunday football   *196*, 225, 233, 239, 249, 251
    see also Sussex Sunday League
Supporters' Club   60, *62*, 75, *84*, 85, 87, 94, 97, 107, 136, *137*, *139*, *143*, *149*, 161, 168, 197, 201, 205, 222, *240*, *248*
Sussex County Cricket Club   12, 13, 15, 17, 24, 25, 26, *27*, 40, 68, 75, 98, 208, *220*
    see also County Ground
Sussex County League   **284**, 118, 131
Sussex County Football Association   **11**, *11*, 12, 13, 22, 23, *51*
Sussex County Youth team   *145*
Sussex Floodlight Challenge Cup   **282**
Sussex Professional Challenge Cup   **280**, 167, 186
Sussex (R.U.R.) Charity Cup   **282**, 21, 68, 118
Sussex Senior Challenge Cup   **281**, 11, 12, 21, 22–23, *27*, 29–30, 243, 245, 255
Sussex Sunday League and Minor Cup   **278**, 326
Sussex Wartime Cup   **284**, 118
Tamplins Brewery   13, 17, 26, 27, 36, *233*
Tarbuck, Jimmy (comedian)   *165*
Taylor, Peter (manager)   194, 196, *196*, 197, 201, 202, 210, *215*
Taylor Report (Hillsborough disaster)   **245**, *247*
television and videos   *160*, *190*, 191, 195, 202, 230, 233, *237*, *250*
Thames & Medway Combination   **326**, 17
Toad's Hole (Hove)   253, 255, 256
tour matches   **261**, *147*
trains   14, 47, 54, 58, *58*, 93, 96, 179, 201, 205, *210*, 211, 216
transfer records   **319**
TSB (sponsors)   238, 253
Ullman Cup   **278**
Underwood, Albert (secretary)   68, 98, 111
unions (players)   *27*, *52*, 132, *166*
United League   **326**, 14, 17, 40
Vernon-Wentworth Cup   13, 278
Vey, Peter (chairman)   40, 60
victories, records   **293**
wages   *27*, *38*, *45*, *52*, 67, 117, 132, 145, *166*, 171, 219, 222, 231, 253
Wakeling, Charles (chairman)   118, 119, 121, *125*, *127*, 136
Waterhall (Patcham)   247, 253
Webb, Charles (player & manager)   49, *51*, 54, 55, 66, 68, *72*, 77, 78, 80, 91, 97, 102, 105, 112, 117, 119, 134, 139, 194
Welsh, Don (manager)   121, 134, *136*, 137, 138, 142, 143
Wembley Stadium   226, 227–230, 250–253
Western League   **326**, 36, 49, 51, 60
Whitcher, Alec (chairman)   125, *125*, *127*, 159, 161, 164
Whiting, Tom (chairman)   168, 180, 193
Wilson, Glen (player, trainer & acting manager)   139, 145, 147, 150, 159, *159*, 161, 163, 180, 189, 194, 238
Wilson, Joe (player, trainer & acting manager)   109, 119, 133, 136, 145, 167, 169, 233
Wisdom, Norman (director)   173, 193
Withdean (Brighton & Hove Rangers FC ground)
    see Home Farm
Worthing Benevolent Fund Cup   278
Worthing (Crowshaw) Cup   278
Worthing & District Junior Charity Cup   278
Worthing & District League   **278**, 326
youth team   **277–280**, 147, 181, *210*
    as junior A team   **277**, 139